COMMUNITIES OF THE PAST

COMMUNITIES OF THE PAST

Edited by

Jane Gray
University of Oregon, Eugene

A. J. Boucot
Oregon State University, Corvallis

William B. N. Berry
University of California, Berkeley

Hutchinson Ross Publishing Company
Stroudsburg, Pennsylvania

Library of Congress Catalog Card Number: 81–4069
ISBN: 0-87933-362-6

83 82 81 1 2 3 4 5
Manufactured in the United States of America

LIBRARY OF CONGRESS CATALOGING IN PUBLICATION DATA

Main entry under title:
Communities of the past.
Papers solicited for the 2nd North American Paleontology Convention, held in Lawrence Kan., Aug. 10, 1977.
Includes index.
1. Animal communities—Congresses. 2. Paleoecology—Congresses.
I. Gray, Jane, 1931– II. Boucot, A. J. (Arthur James), 1924–
III. Berry, William B. N. IV–North-American Paleontology Convention (2nd : 1977 : Lawrence, Kan.)
QE720.C65 560′.45 81–4069
ISBN 0–87933–362–6 AACR2

Distributed world wide by Academic Press,
a subsidiary of Harcourt Brace Jovanovich,
Publishers.

Contents

Preface

At the time that the program for the Second North American Paleontology Convention was being developed, one of us (W.B.N. Berry) suggested to the others that some consideration of fossil communities ought to be included on the program. The others agreed and arrangements were made for inclusion of a session on fossil communities.

The three of us then solicited papers, some of which were given orally in the session on communities in the fossil record at the Second North American Paleontology Convention at Lawrence, Kansas, August 10, 1977. All solicited papers, those presented orally and all others, are included in this symposium volume.

The editors believe strongly that community analyses of fossil floras and faunas are essential to an increased awareness of precision in stratigraphic correlations by geologists and in patterns in evolutionary process among biologists. For the geologist, comprehension and use of fossil community analyses will enhance precision in correlations and lead to reconstructions of basin and shelf-margin history. For the biologist, community analyses may mean a greater appreciation for the constraints imposed on evolutionary development by community changes through time.

To achieve these goals, ancient communities need to be recognized and described, time interval by time interval from the Precambrian onward to the present. Community analyses of fossil floras and faunas are still in their infancy and still essentially descriptive. Community studies are, therefore, still at an early stage of development. This volume incorporates a sample of the kinds of community studies that are needed to provide the basic data for examining community evolution and its significance in single-organism evolution and the uses of ancient communities in precisely weaving the history of the earth. Many, many more such compilations are needed before patterns in community evolution may be discerned. It is the intent of the editors, therefore, to indicate through this volume something of the data basic to understanding community development through time. Present analyses of community evolution are inappropriate and , of necessity, incomplete for the data needed for them are not yet adequate. Only through disciplined collection of data, that is, through studies similar to those herein, can the body of data requisite for syntheses of community evolution be assembled.

It should be noted that each author who has contributed to this volume is individually responsible for the contents of his or her contribution. The editors have not wanted to nor have they imposed their own views on any of the authors. We all, editors and contributors, are grateful to the editorial personnel provided by Hutchinson Ross Publishing Company who labored to make the individual contributions editorially acceptable in format, layout, and style.

Jane Gray
A. J. Boucot
William B. N. Berry

List of Contributors

Stephen F. Barrett
Department of Geophysical Sciences, University of Chicago, Chicago, Illinois 60637

Anna K. Behrensmeyer
Department of Anthropology, Yale University, New Haven, Connecticut 06520

Gale A. Bishop
Department of Geology, Georgia Southern College, Statesboro, Georgia 30458

A. J. Boucot
Department of Geology, Oregon State University, Corvallis, Oregon 97331

H. Paul Buchheim
Paleobiology and Geology Research Group, Loma Linda University, Loma Linda, California 92350

Gerald Glenn Forney
Amerada Hess Corporation, Denver, Colorado 80202

Norman O. Frederiksen
U.S. Geological Survey, 970 National Center, Reston, Virginia 22092

J. M. Hurst
The Geological Survey of Greenland, Øster Voldgade 10, DK-1350 Copenhagen K, Denmark

Peter E. Isaacson
Department of Geology, University of Idaho, Moscow, Idaho 83843

Erle G. Kauffman
Department of Geological Sciences, University of Colorado, Boulder, Colorado 80309

Douglas A. Lawson
Paleoecological Research Institute and Museum, 6613 Cervantes Avenue, Fort Worth, Texas 76133

Donald G. Mikulic
Illinois State Geological Survey, Urbana, Illinois 61801

Michael J. Novacek
San Diego State University, San Diego, California 92182

Ellis F. Owen
Department of Palaeontology, British Museum (Natural History), Cromwell Road, London SW7 5BD, England

David G. Perry
Deceased
William C. Rember
Department of Geology, University of Idaho, Moscow, Idaho 83843
Greg J. Retallack
Department of Biology, Indiana University, Bloomington, Indiana 47405
D. M. Rohr
Department of Geological Sciences, University of Washington, Seattle, Washinton 98195
June R. P. Ross
Western Washington University, Bellingham, Washington 98225
Charles J. Smiley
Department of Geology, University of Idaho, Moscow, Idaho 83843
Calvin H. Stevens
Department of Geology, San Jose State University, San Jose, California 95192
Ronald R. Surdam
Department of Geology, University of Wyoming, Laramie, Wyoming 82071
Donald Francis Toomey
Cities Service Company, Midland, Texas 79702
Robert James Wallace
Department of Geology, Brooklyn College, City University of New York, Brooklyn, New York 11210
Rodney Watkins
P.O. Box 469, Bella Vista, California 96008
Thomas Henry Wolosz
Department of Earth and Space Sciences, State University of New York at Stony Brook, Stony Brook, New York 11794
Thomas E. Yancey
Department of Geology. Texas A & M University , College Station, Texas 77843

COMMUNITIES OF THE PAST

1

Ordovician Environmental Heterogeneity and Community Organization

June R. P. Ross

ABSTRACT

The organization of Chazyan (lower Middle Ordovician) marine benthic communities from Vermont and New York State shows that local species abundance was influenced spatially by environmental heterogeneity and temporally by environmental fluctuations. In the shallow-shelf environments, different types of communities reflect patterns that resulted from different amounts of interaction of physical factors, such as substrate, sedimentation, wave force, topography of the shelf, and biological factors, such as food resources, settlement, colonization, feeding mechanisms of organisms. Chazyan communities had few trophic categories so that community organization of filter feeders (ectoprocts, stromatoporoids, sponges, brachiopods, and echinoderms) reflects the success of certain guilds to become established and to maintain themselves in predominantly unpredictable environmental conditions. Most filter-feeder guilds had one dominant species. Where conditions remained predictable, this dominance was maintained. As organic buildups and bioherms became increasingly widespread, they created topographic and environmental variability that resulted in a greater number of habitats and greater species diversity. In contrast, where rates of sedimentation became high and topographic relief was greatly reduced, relatively few species formed geographically large and uniform communities. The greatest species abundance appears to occur where physical and biological factors caused intermediate levels of disturbance.

INTRODUCTION

Attempts to analyze and clarify the organization within extant biological communities have led to the formulation of many elaborate models of community relationships. Such relationships are difficult to analyze because extant communities are the products of a long and progressive development of complex interspecific and intraspecific relationships through much of Cenozoic time and perhaps longer. These relations are a result of the gradual accumulation of strongly modified interactions, evolutionary adaptations, extinctions, dispersals, and ecologic replacements. An approach to analyzing community organization that may be informative is to locate in the geologic record those communities that were in their early stages of development. Such communities have few trophic levels and, therefore, may have less complex interactions. The role of species that were progressively assimilated into such communities might be assessed. From such sets of fossil communities, additional information may be acquired about the processes involved in the establishment and maintenance of communities.

The early Middle Ordovician Chazyan sequences and faunas of northeastern New York State and Vermont provide the framework to examine the organizational development of such a rudimentary, evolving set of carbonate shelf communities. This carbonate sequence contains an early, well-preserved and well-studied set of fossil communities. Early Middle Ordovician faunas at or about this stratigraphic position include the first appearance of several important families, orders, classes, and even subphyla. Although Cambrian and Early Ordovician faunas had developed a gradually increasing number of types of communities based on the use of a series of trophic resource levels, the beginning of the Middle Ordovician appears to mark a drastic change in these early community relationships. During Middle Ordovician time, new community associations developed and new levels of trophic resources gradually formed. These new community associations were maintained apparently by ecologic replacement and evolutionary change through much of the remainder of the Paleozoic.

COMMUNITY ORGANIZATION

Examination of many local assemblages of organisms in various parts of the biosphere had led ecologists to attempt to establish broad and general models of community organization that will permit comparison of the internal organization of different communities. This comparison must be capable of spanning a wide range of marine and terrestrial environments over a broad geographic scale. Most proposed models of community organization seek to elucidate the dynamic relations that are commonly shared features of communities such as spatial heterogeneity, patterns of distribution, boundaries, diversity, trophic relations, size, abundance, stage of succession, and degree of maturity. The term "community" is used in the sense of Menge (1976) and Menge and Sutherland (1976) for a collection of organisms of all trophic positions that interact directly and indirectly and that occur in a particular habitat. The community includes all species in a habitat ranging from primary producers to top predators. Community organization can also be viewed as an expression of the amount or level of organization in particular ecosystems (Margalef, 1968).

Models of community organization for present-day communities have considered predation, food interrelationships, competition, and level of environmental disturbance as major factors in the establishment and maintenance of communities. Paine (1966, 1971) suggested that selective predation through time on dominant competitors can maintain a relatively high species diversity by preventing the dominant competitors from monopolizing a major resource such as food or space. If predation keeps species of lower trophic levels below their optimum population densities, other species, both predator and prey, can invade and be assimilated into the community organization. This is possibly an important means of increasing species diversity within communities. Stanley (1973) suggested that severe predation may actually cause a genetic discontinuity between parts of a population that, if continued long enough, could eventually lead to speciation. Potentially, this is another means of increasing species diversity within communities.

Turpaeva (1959) concluded that particular species and groups of species are adapted to partitioning food resources, and within each food partition, organisms having the same range of types of feeding requirements could be expected to form a predictable portion of the composition of communities. If a number of diverse species dominate a community, the food for these dominant organisms would come from different food-resource partitions and, as a result, such community organization represents the fullest use of the available food by the dominant species. Less numerous species in the community would be nourished by residual food.

The dominant group of species in a community could be established by at least two means (Turpaeva, 1959). If colonizers consist of several species with very similar food needs, the competition for food would result in the species that was better adapted to the environmental conditions becoming dominant. If colonizers consist of several species with different food needs, competition for food would not play an important role in the community organization, and a variety of species having different feeding types would become established. More species could coexist abundantly.

Predictability of the environment is a factor in community establishment and maintenance. Margalef (1968) noted that where little environmental disruption exists over extended periods of time, the communities are able to progress to established and mature stages. Such communities tend to become more diverse and the trophic levels become complex. In such community organization, competition among species using a specific type of resource from a particular food-resource partition may arise. Root (1967) introduced the term "guild" to identify as a group all those species in a community that use a specific type of resource, for example, the filter feeders of a benthic marine community. Increased competition between species for the same resource generally reduces the breadth of habitats that any particular species attempts to occupy and this leads to increased specialization that serves to reduce the intensity of competition. Turpaeva (1959) showed that active filter feeders may be divided into those groups of animals that filter the fine, extreme bottom layer of water and those that filter the higher bottom layer of water. Passive filter feeders termed "awaiters" by Turpaeva (1959) trapped food particles from water currents and fed in the same water layer as the active filter feeders in the higher bottom water layer. Turpaeva's findings are corroborated in studies by Jackson (1972), Jackson and Buss (1975), and Menge (1976). The primary structuring factor in those communities having simple trophic levels is guild competition. Disruptive and environmental factors are effective in interacting with guild competition to maintain a simple trophic system with few levels.

Certain kinds of communities do not experience strong environmental disturbance and exist in a predictable environment. These communities tend to have many trophic levels because predation at higher trophic levels is effective in reducing lower trophic level prey. This leads to maintenance of larger populations of primary producers as a result of less predatory stresses. Margalef (1968) pointed out that predictability of and fluctuations in the ecosystem can greatly modify community organization. Margalef (1968) stated, "the process of self-organization of a community will stop when fluctuations in the ecosystem are unpredictable or insurmountable." Within an ecosystem, some patches of different community maturity may be distributed in a honeycomb pattern, rather than in a mosiac pattern, with precisely delimited discontinuous areas of lower density enclosed in a honeycomb of higher diversity. Where fluctuations in the ecosystem occur, the usual changes in succession and progression to maturity of the community may be disturbed. Levin and Paine (1974) proposed a model in which disturbance in space and time may lead to the accumulation of greater species abundance through the renewal of limited resources that can be used by species that are not dominant competitors.

CHAZYAN COMMUNITIES

The benthic community assemblages of the Chazyan are principally epifauna and epiflora. Only casts, molds, tracts, burrows, and tubules provide evidence of the infauna. However, as the epifauna commonly includes about 80 percent of the benthic animals at a particular site in the present-day benthic communities, this represents a large part of the closely interacting species groups. The Chazyan communities are mostly dominated by filter feeders, of which some sought food by actively filtering the water, and others more passively awaited food that drifted by. Most of the filter feeders were positioned several centimeters or more above the general level of the substrate and included ectoprocts, sponges, stromatoporoids, brachiopods, tabulate corals, and pelmatozoans. Some sponges may have encrusted the substrate at the water-substrate interface. Detritus feeders included at least four groups: trilobites, echinoderms, ostracodes, and cephalopods. Gastropods were the dominant grazers, but some of these may also have been detritus feeders. The cephalopods, echinoderms, and trilobites were the scavengers in the communities. Little evidence remains of symbionts. However, some algae had apparently a symbiotic association with stromatoporoids, and borings of tube-producing organisms in stromatoporoids also suggest symbiotic or parasitic relationships. Benthic calcareous algae provide some data about sessile photosynthesizers. Acritarchs were present as phytoplankton, but other photosynthesizers are not recorded. Bacteria and fungi are part of the community association that has been lost from the record. This is a reminder that in the geological record, sedimentary sequences and fossil communities provide an incomplete history of past events, relationships, and spatial patterns. The stages of colonization, the stages of succession of the community, the amount of disruption of the community, and the maturity of the community are not readily assessed from a fossil community. The mechanical redistribution and resorting of preserved parts of the communities may, at times, distort interpretations of community organization. In some instances, this incomplete record suggests abrupt boundaries and discontinuities in the fossil record. Such artefacts of the record have led to incorrect assumptions that catastrophes are a consistent feature of phyletic evolution. The Chazyan communities illustrate that they are natural benthic communities and that even with the limitations of the process of fossilization, particular patterns of community association consistently occur. Filter feeders in the Chazyan formed distinct guilds of particular species associations. Filter feeders appear to have dominated early Middle Ordovician benthic communities in many parts of the world.

CHAZYAN STRATIGRAPHY AND FAUNA

Since the mapping and description of the "Chazy Formation" by Brainerd and Seely (1888, 1896) and Cushing (1905) and the extensive faunal analysis by Raymond (1906), various aspects of the Chazyan faunal assemblages have been studied in greater detail. My interpretation of species and community relationships draws on the reports by Oxley (1951), Flower (1955), Oxley and Kay (1959), Ross (1963a, b, c, d, e; 1964a, b; 1972), Pitcher (1964), Finks and Toomey (1968), Shaw (1968), Kapp (1974, 1975), and Kapp and Stearn (1975).

The early Middle Ordovician clastic and carbonate rocks of the Chazyan sequence were deposited on a shallow shelf that had sufficient topography to offer considerable environmental heterogeneity (Figures 1-1 and 1-2). These sediments, exposed in the Champlain Valley of northeastern New York State and western Vermont and in southern Quebec, consist of sandstones, siltstones, limestones, and shaly limestones, many of which are extensively dolomitized. They are exposed in a narrow belt between the Precambrian Adirondack Dome, which was a low-lying land area during Middle Ordovician times, and the Champlain thrust belt to the east, which was a deepwater trough at that time. Post-Middle Ordovician faulting and Pleistocene erosion and sediments obscure some of the geologic relations of the Chazyan stratigraphic sequence and facies relations.

In this analysis of species community associations, faunas from the northern belt of exposures of Chazyan sediments are used. This belt extends from near Chazy, New York, southeastward to the southern parts of Isle La Motte, Vermont (Figure 1-1). The Chazyan Stage is represented by three formations: Day Point; Crown Point; and Valcour in ascending succession (Figure 1-3). Further division of these formations was established by Oxley and Kay (1959). The lower part of the Day Point Formation, the Head Member, appears to be a transgressive sandy unit, probably unconformable on the Canadian Bridport dolostone. Higher in the Day Point Formation, the sandy facies (the Wait Member, 5 m thick) may represent a regression of the Chazyan seas. The Day Point Formation is about 40-45 m thick near Chazy. The Scott Member (about 14 m thick), which overlies the Head Member, and the Fleury Member (about 20 m thick), which overlies the Wait Member, are well-developed

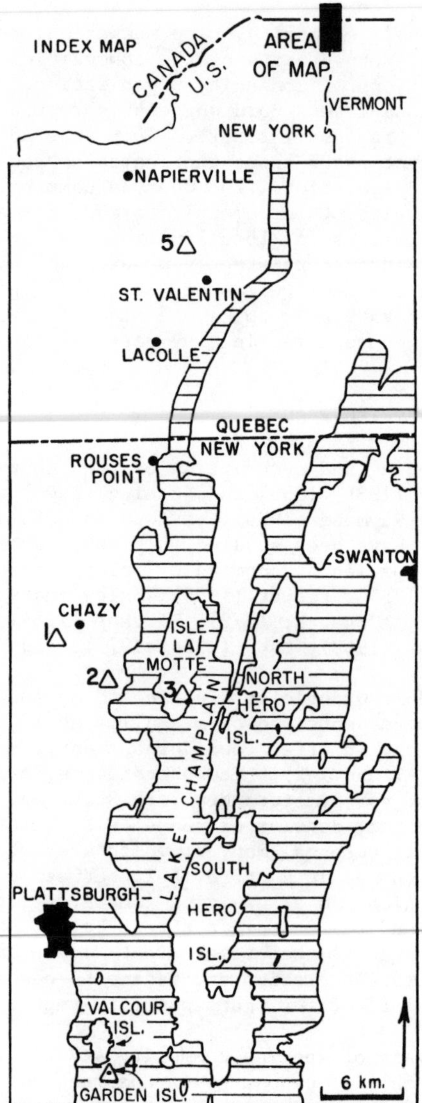

Figure 1-1
Locality map of parts of New York State, Vermont, and Quebec showing five localities of exposures of Chazyan rocks. 1. Type area, Chazy. 2. Sheldon Lane. 3. Isle La Motte. 4. Garden Island. 5. Near St. Valentin.

identifiable units on the eastern part of the shelf on Isle La Motte where they form extensive carbonate deposits characterized by biohermal buildups. However, these two members are more difficult to identify on the western part of the shelf near Chazy where both members are predominantly calcarenites.

The overlying Crown Point Formation is principally calcarenite

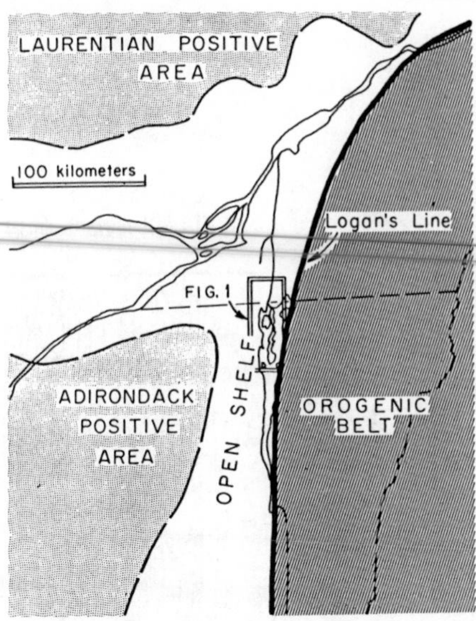

Figure 1-2
Structural and depositional setting of the Chazy Group for the region shown in Figure 1-1. The orogenic belt was thrust against the eastern edge of the open shelf in post-Chazyan time.

and calcilutite (about 55 m thick) on the western margin with numerous bioherms punctuating the remainder of the shelf. An informal division into lower, middle, and upper Crown Point Formation is commonly used in association with the extensive biohermal exposures on Isle La Motte.

The Valcour Formation overlies the Crown Point Formation and is divided into two units, the Hero and Beech members, in the southern belt of exposures. However, in the northern belt, the sequence is mainly a continuation of the depositional pattern in the Crown Point Formation. In the west near Chazy, the Valcour Formation (about 32 m thick) is dolomitic calcarenite, calcisiltite, and calcilutite; and in the east, it has biohermal buildups and shoal and channel deposits.

DAY POINT COMMUNITIES

WESTERN SHELF

Communities on the western shelf developed on carbonate sand flats that were dissected in places by quartz pebble channels. Except for occasional undisturbed patches, this substrate was continuously disrupted, and an incomplete history of the total community association is recorded on this part of the shelf. Its topographic and sedimentary features were similar to marine sand flats in the present-day ecosystem, and its sediments and biota are similar to early Middle Ordovician counterparts in the Holston Formation of the central and southern Appalachian region. Chazyan

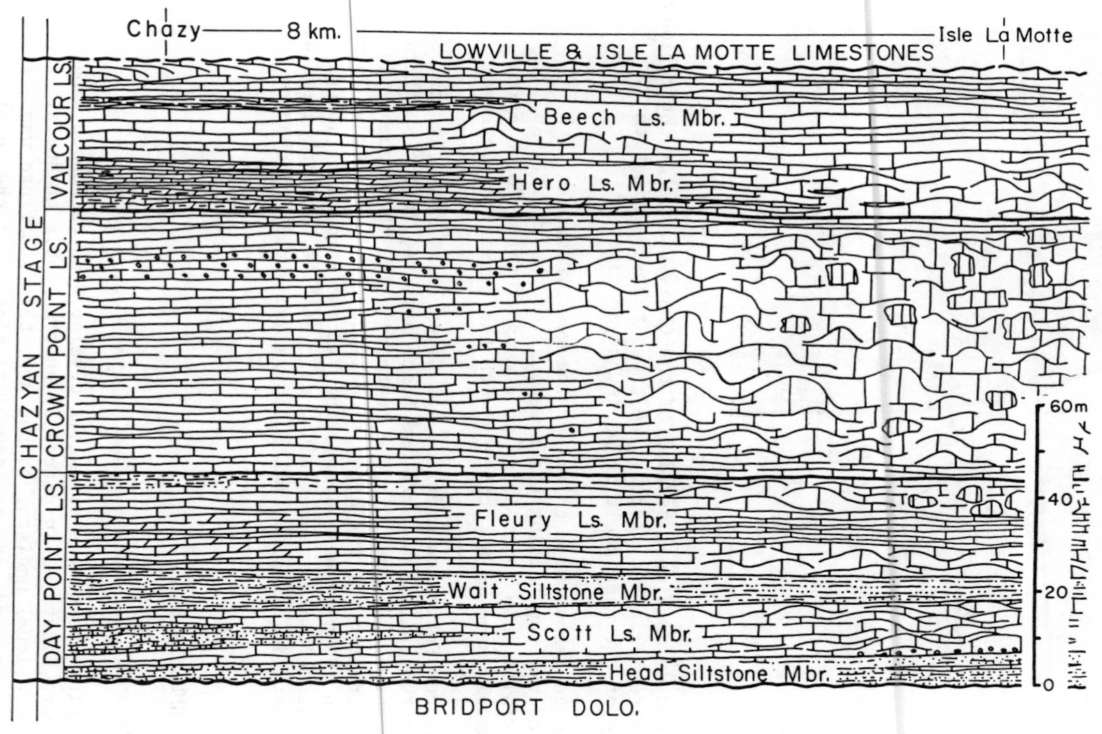

Figure 1-3
Generalized cross section of the Chazy Group based on data from localities 1, 2, and 3 of Figure 1-1.

ectoproct communities colonized the shifting, sand substrates, but were not maintained because of physical disruption by wave action and currents. The cross-bedded, calcareous, sandy sediments have abundant ectoproct, algal, and echinodermal fragments. The algal and echinodermal fragments are mostly unidentifiable to a specific taxon, and the fragments of ectoproct colonies are of several types such as abundant, short, ramose colonies of the trepostome *Champlainopora chazyensis*, rare reticulate colonies of the cryptostome *Phylloporina* sp., and rare bifoliate blades of the cryptostome *Chazydictya chazyensis*. Algae, one of the principal photosynthesizers, apparently provided food for the ectoprocts and pelmatozoan echinoderms, both of which filtered the higher bottom layer of water. Algal mats developed on the tidal flats. In this unpredictable nearshore environment, the colonization and establishment by a particular ectoproct or echinoderm species was a chance event that depended on the availability of a suitable substrate rather than on competition or predation.

Slightly higher sediments in the lower part of the Day Point Formation are dolomitic biosparites that are dominated by brachiopod communities with *Orthambonites? exfoliatus*. These brachiopod-rich sediments pass laterally into black oolitic lenses. Brachiopods were consistent colonizers in a number of vertically successive communities and apparently so dominated stable substrate space that they excluded most other organisms. Usually only an occasional ectoproct is present in these strata, principally the cryptostome *Chazydictya chazyensis*, the trepostome *Champlainopora chazyensis*, and a new arrival, *Nicholsonella* sp., a ramose trepostome possibly having an aragonitic instead of calcitic skeleton.

The sedimentary sequence in the upper part of the Day Point Formation suggests more predictable environmental conditions on the nearshore shelf that permitted the establishment of brachiopod-echinoderm-trilobite communities. These communities were accompanied by a marked influx of additional organisms. The presence of trilobites, vagrant detritus feeders, suggests a buildup of trophic categories and a maturing of the established communities. In algal biosparites an increasing diversity of ectoproct species is recorded. The cryptostome *Chazydictya chazyensis*, the stick-shaped bifoliate cryptostome *Stictopora fenestrata*, and two species of the trepostome *Champlainopora* are common, and rare fragments of the cryptostome *Phylloporina* sp. are also present. The two species of *Champlainopora* suggest that competition or habitat division took place between these species. This increasing complexity of trophic levels also suggests greater abundance of food resources and possible competition for this food. Isolated patches of trilobite communities are present. One community has abundant *Bumastoides aplatus*, rare *Hibbertia* sp., *Pliomerops canadensis*, and *Sphaerexochus parvus*; and another has common *Basiliella whittingtoni* and rare *H. valcourensis* and *Remopleurides canadensis*. Archeogastropods *Raphistoma stamineum* and *Lophospira rectistriata* form additional local patch communities. Identifiable algae include *Girvanella* and *Solenopora*.

SHELDON LANE

A short distance of 3.2 km southeastward across the Chazyan shelf from Chazy village at Sheldon Lane, the sediments exposed are mostly cross-laminated calcarenites that are extensively reworked. Little information on the Day Point communities at this site is available because most shelf material here has been severely abraded and poorly preserved.

EASTERN SHELF

The almost barren sandy clastics of the Head Member (Figure 1-3) have only rare inarticulate brachiopods and a few trilobites such as *Remopleurides canadensis* and *Bumastoides aplatus*. The overlying Scott Member has a rich accumulation of carbonate sediments. Colonizers were small guilds of ectoprocts, pelmatozoan echinoderms, and brachiopods. Trilobites, ostracodes, and cephalopods, all sparsely distributed in the bioherms, apparently fed on detritus in the fine calcareous muds that were trapped and bound by the ectoprocts. Fragments of these organisms along with trepostomes and cryptostomes are also found in channels between bioherms and interbiohermal sediments (Figure 1-4). Shaw (1968) recorded a few specimens of each of four trilobite species, *Bumastoides gardensis*, *B. aplatus*, *Hibbertia* sp., and *Isotelus harrisi*, ranging from low in the Day Point Formation to the lower part of the Fleury Member. Algal mats are lacking. Low biohermal mounds, 1.5 to 2 m in diameter, are dominated by the trepostome *Batostoma chazyensis*. The broad encrusting colonies of this trepostome helped bind sediments and ultimately established a stable and fixed substrate upon which other organisms could become established. The cystoporate *Cheiloporella* sp. commonly encrusted the laminate sheets of *B. chazyensis* and also formed sheets that acted as sediment traps. At one site, hemispherical colonies of *Cheiloporella* formed mounds. Farther to the south, a greater number of ectoprocts, brachiopods, and trilobites became established in micritic bioherms (Figure 1-4). Occasionally, colonies of the trepostome *Champlainopora*, the reteporid cryptostome *Phylloporina*, and the cryptostome *Eopachydictya gregaria* became established and apparently represent opportunistic transient species that from time to time became established in the mound communities. They also colonized parts of the channel areas; the most successful of these species was the trepostome *Champlainopora chazyensis* (Figure 1-5).

As noted by Pitcher (1964), bioherms in the lower part of the Scott Member established a trend of elongation N10°E that is repeated in higher units in the Fleury Member. In the Scott Member, the communities were probably space limited because of the lack of available fixed substrate on which organisms could colonize. Channels with cross-bedded, sand-size, calcareous skeletal fragments indicate considerable current action; however, the lack of marked erosion on the biohermal flanks suggests a nondisrupted environment. Under these conditions, predation was limited and the biohermal communities tended toward a homogenous association of the dominant trepostome *Batostoma chazyensis*.

Biohermal accumulations in the Scott Member are abruptly

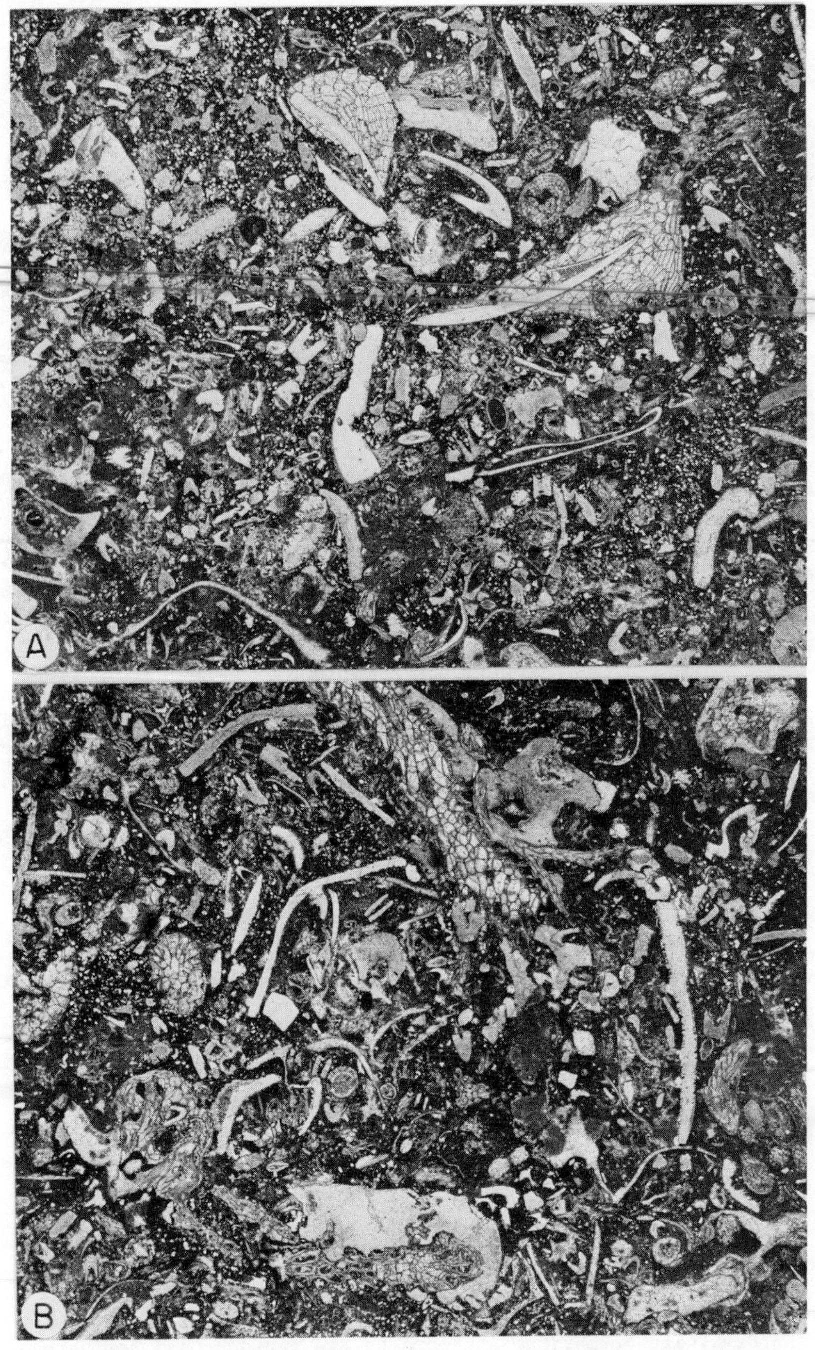

Figure 1-4
Scott Member, Day Point Formation; biohermal rock; X7; Garden Island.
A. Micrite filled with fragments of pelmatozoan echinoderms, trilobites, algae, and trepostomes. B. Micrite filled with fragments of trilobites, algae, brachiopods, trepostomes, and cryptostome.

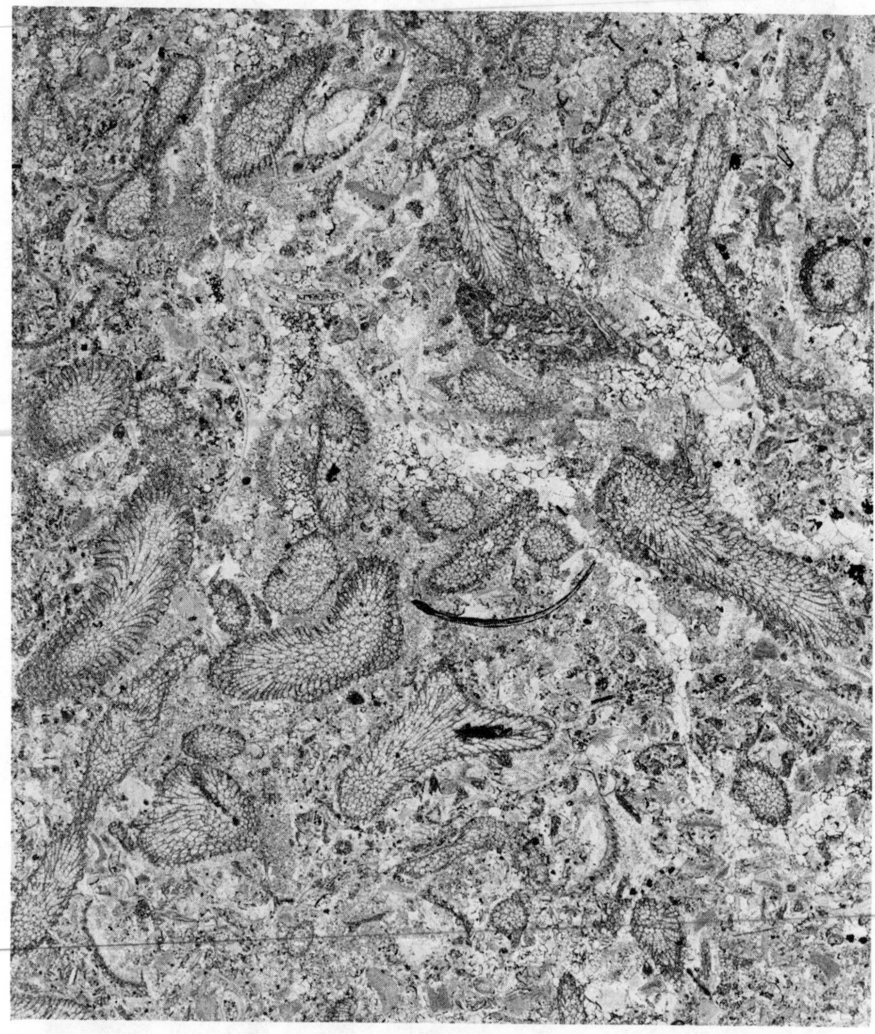

Figure 1-5
Scott Member, Day Point Formation; interbiohermal rock; X3.2; Garden Island. *Champlainopora chazyensis* in biosparite with brachiopod, reteporid cryptostome, trilobite, and echinodermal fragments.

succeeded by a thin wedge of quartz sandstone and siltstone about 1 to 4 m thick. These sediments are succeeded by calcarenites and bioherms that form the middle and upper parts of the Fleury Member of the Day Point Formation. Ectoprocts are abundant and dominate many of the communities (Figures 1-6, 1-7, and 1-8). Many additional species, not present in the underlying Scott Member, include ectoprocts, brachiopods, a tabulate coral, and a nautiloid. Algae are rare. Patchiness in the distribution of species has increased in comparison to the Scott Member. The trepostome *Batostoma chazyensis*

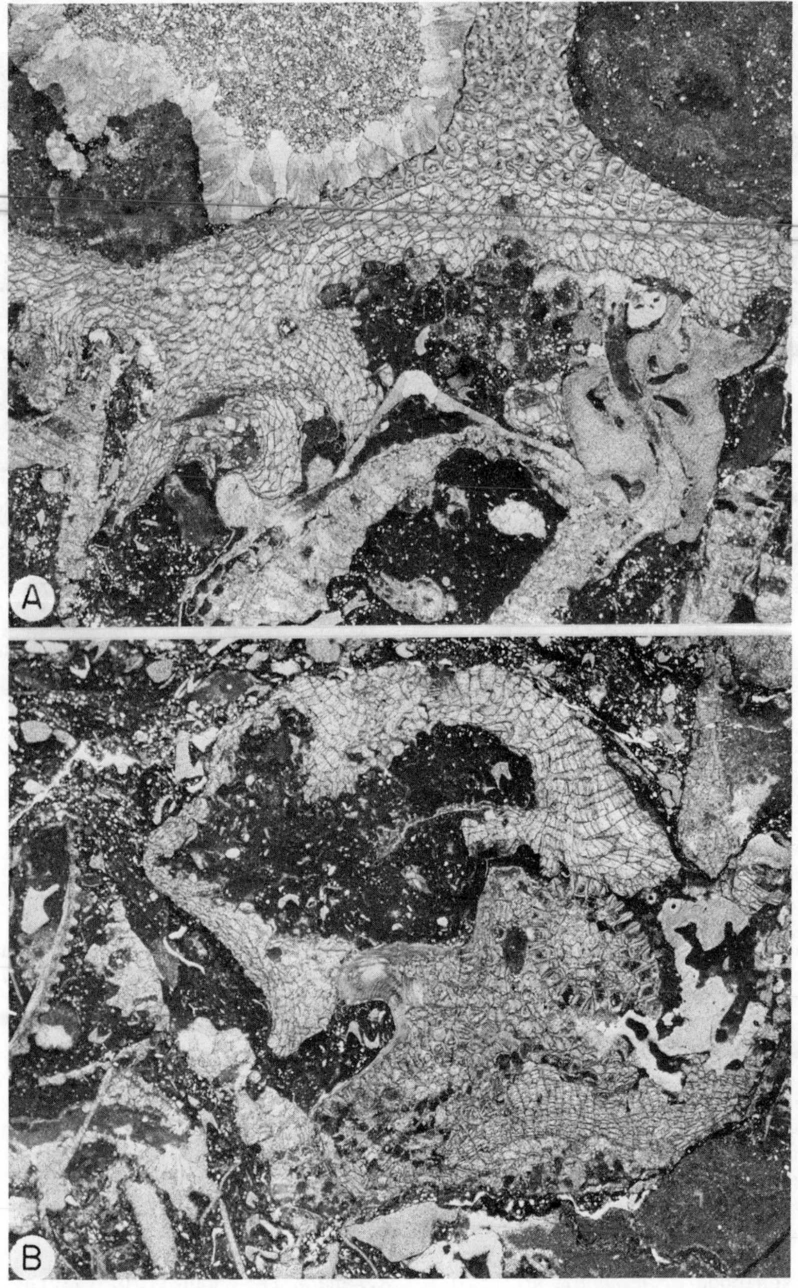

Figure 1-6
Fleury Member, Day Point Formation; biohermal rock; X7.6; Isle La Motte. A. *Champlainopora chazyensis* and *Stromatactis* binding micritic sediments. B. Trepostomes *Batostoma* and *Champlainopora* in micrite.

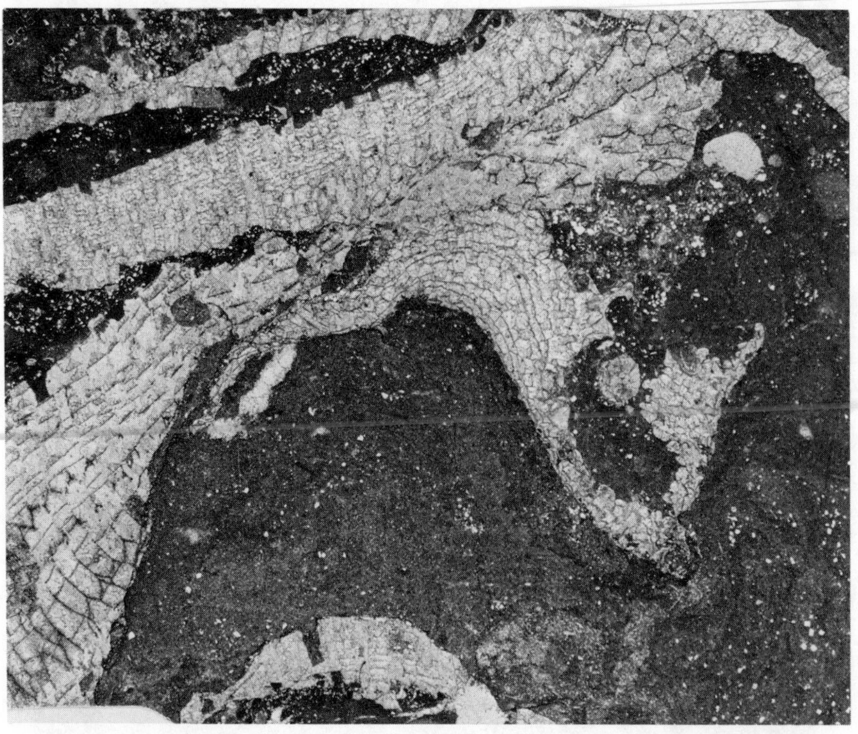

Figure 1-7
Fleury Member, Day Point Formation; biohermal rock; X6.4; Isle La Motte. *Batostoma* and tabulate coral binding micrite.

not only bound and trapped sediments (Figures 1-7 and 1-8), but in some bioherms, it also encrusted the tabulate coral *Lichenaria heroensis* (Figure 1-7), one of the earliest tabulate corals. Pitcher (1964) interpreted these colonies of *L. heroensis* as boulders that had been transported, abraded, and encrusted by the trepostome. Such an interpretation suggests an environmental setting similar to many modern reef flats where large brain corals are torn from the substrate by battering waves and winds and carried up or across the reef flat. The cystoporate *Cheiloporella* sp. maintained its position in the bioherms and encrusted *B. chazyensis* as it did in bioherms in the lower Scott Member. The trepostome *Champlainopora chazyensis* is present in both bioherms and interbiohermal sediments. Some biohermal patches contain the lithistid sponge *Zittelella*, another filter feeder. Locally, colonies of *Zittelella* are surrounded by the ramose trepostome *Champlainopora chazyensis* that forms thickets about 2 m in diameter and in height. On the flanks of these bioherms are abundant fragments of *Champlainopora*, the brachiopod *Orthambonites? exfoliatus*, and a rare nautiloid (vagrant predator). In some patches about 1 km to 2.5 km northeast of the well-exposed *Batostoma chazyensis* bioherms on The Head, Isle La Motte, typical ramose colonies of this trepostome form thickets with the reteporid cryptostome *Phylloporina* that extends as horizontal growths among the *Batostoma* branches. The encrusting mode of growth of *Batostoma* is lacking in these thickets. Echinodermal fragments are common in parts of the bioherms and interbiohermal sediments; however, as noted previously, fragmentation is so extensive that specific distributional patterns are not determinable.

In higher parts of the Fleury Member, additional ectroproct species appear, possibly reflecting extended maintenance of the ectoproct guilds in which competition was an increasingly important factor in community organization. In some of the interbiohermal patches, the trepostome *Jordanopora heroensis* is as abundant as *Champlainopora chazyensis*, and they occur with rare colonies of *Phylloporina* and *Chazydictya*. The cryptostome *Eopachydictya gregaria* is more common than in lower strata and the cryptostome *Helopora?*, a new guild member, is also present.

In calcarenites associated with bioherms, trilobite species include *Pliomerops canadensis*, *Hibbertia* sp., *Bumastoides gardensis*, *B. aplatus*, *Sphaerexochus parvus*, and *Amphilichas minganensis*. All these species are sparse. In the upper part of the Fleury Member, a greater profusion of trilobite species are present among these detritus feeders. At one site on central Isle La Motte the trilobite association has abundant *Bumastoides aplatus* and *Sphaerexochus parvus* and sparse *Encrinuroides insularis*, *Platillaenus limbatus*, *Hibbertia* sp., *A. minganensis*, *P. canadensis*, *Kawina? chaziensis*, *Vogdesia? obtusus*, *Isotelus harrisi?*, *Remopleurides canadensis?*, and *Ceraurinella latipyga* (Shaw, 1968).

CROWN POINT COMMUNITIES

WESTERN SHELF

Sedimentary patterns in the Crown Point Formation show a continuation of the nearshore depositional history of the Day Point Formation. This part of the shelf tract developed low carbonate mounds (Figure 1-9) and shoal and lagoonal deposits. The sedimentary units are more massively bedded than those in the Day Point Formation. The alga *Girvanella* and the archeogastropod *Maclurites* occur in patches with rare occurrences of the cephalopods *Proteoceras perkinsi* and *Nybyoceras cryptum*. Isolated thickets of the trepostome *Champlainopora chazyensis* and small patches with a few colonies of the cryptostomes *Phylloporina* sp., *Chazydictya chazyensis*, and *Stictopora fenestrata* are also found. Several ectoproct community assemblages have *S. fenestrata* dominant; *Phylloporina* sp. A and *Chazydictya chazyensis* common; and *Phylloporina* sp., *Jordanopora heroensis*, and *Nicholsonella* sp. A rare. However, depending on which set of species was able to colonize the substrate, the percentage mix of species in the ectoproct communities varies considerably. In the middle part of the Crown Point Formation, the trepostome *Batostoma* is an important new addition to the community assemblage and is able to maintain itself in these communities. Algae are the other most common group of organisms in these ectoproct communities.

Shaw (1968) likewise found few trilobites except at local sites. An assemblage with a great number of species, such as *Apianurus narrawayi*, *Eobronteus* sp., *Bumastoides aplatus*, *Thaleops longispina*,

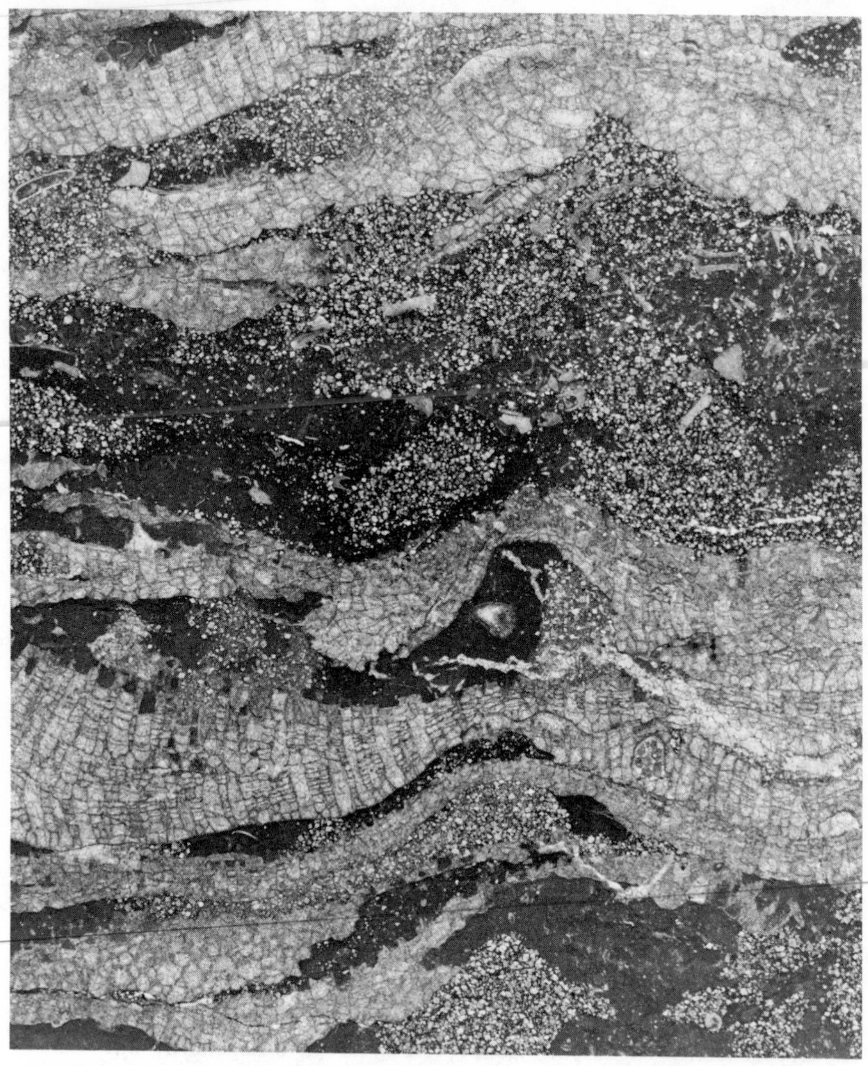

Figure 1-8
Fleury Member, Day Point Formation; biohermal rock; X6.4; Isle La Motte. Sheets of the encrusting trepostome *Batostoma chazyensis* forming layers in fine micritic sediment with patches of dolomite rhombs.

Sphaerocoryphe goodnovi, *Dimeropyge clintonensis*, *Amphilichas minganensis*, *Basiella whittingtoni*, *Remopleurides canadensis*, *Pliomerops canadensis*, *Heliomeroides akocephala*, *Ceraurinella latipyga*, and *Calyptaulax annulata*, suggests complex trophic relations to maintain such an association. Small unidentified articulate brachiopods are locally abundant in some patches. Occasional, large colonies of the stromatoporoid *Pseudostylodictyon* are abundant in other patches.

SHELDON LANE

On this part of the Chazyan shelf, the sediments in the lower part of the formation are calcisiltites with colonies of the stromatoporoid *Pseudostylodictyon lamottense*. The community associations are difficult to determine because of limited exposure. The upper part of the Crown Point Formation shows marked accumulation of organisms having several community assemblages, each of which is distinguished by the dominance of only one or two species in highly diverse community associations of at least ten to twelve species. Interbiohermal deposits have a limited number of species of ectoprocts, algae, and echinoderms, some of which presumably were transported and are not *in situ*.

The topography of this eastern portion of the shelf was much more variable than portions closer to the shoreline to the west, and the biohermal and interbiohermal sediments were more strongly eroded than the nearshore shoal and lagoonal environment because of stronger wave action in the eastern portion. The sediment thickness (about 20 m) is considerably less than that at Chazy. The bioherms at Sheldon Lane reach .6 to 3 m in height and extend lateral distances of 50 to 150 m. They have a northerly alignment and presumably paralleled the shoreline. *Pseudostylodictyon* colonies form a large part of the biomass of the individual bioherms; the colonies are about 2 to 3 m in length. Closely associated with the stromatoporoids, but forming a distinctly smaller proportion of the bioherms, are several species of ectoprocts, the gastropod *Maclurites*, and orthocone nautiloid cephalopods. The cryptostome *Pachydictya sheldonensis* consistently dominates the ectoproct filter-feeding guild, but occasionally the cryptostome *Chazydictya chazyensis* dominates. The trepostome *Batostoma sheldonensis* or *B. lanensis* is common in some of the guilds. In bioherms where *P. sheldonensis* is dominant, four or five other ectoproct species occur in far fewer numbers to form guilds. One guild with *P. sheldonensis* includes rare colonies of the cryptostomes *C. chazyensis* and *S. fenestrata* and rare colonies of the trepostome *Lamottopora duncanae;* another guild includes common colonies of the reteporid cryptostome *Phylloporina* sp. A and rare colonies of the trepostomes *Jordanopora heroensis* and *Nicholsonella* sp. B. and the cystoporate *Ceramoporella?* sp. Still another guild includes abundant *C. chazyensis*, common *B. lanensis*, and rare *Phylloporina* sp. A and *S. fenestrata*. In another more highly diverse assemblage, the cryptostome *Pachydictya sheldonensis* dominates a filter-feeder guild which has more trophic categories that includes trilobites, the gastropod *Maclurites*, and an orthocone cephalopod. The only other ectoproct species present is the trepostome *Batostoma sheldonensis*, which is common. A separation of resources apparently permitted these two species to coexist; however, no other ectoproct species became established in this guild.

Oxley (1951) recorded an assemblage with abundant colonies of the sponge *Zittelella varians*, the tabulate coral *Billingsaria parva*, and fragments of several trilobite species, including *Bumastus globosus* and *Isotelus harrisi*, from calcilutite and fine calcisiltite that enclose the stromatoporoid- and ectoproct-rich bioherms. Brachiopods are not abundant in these bioherms although occasional species, such as *Leptaena incrassata*, are common locally. Cephalopods commonly occur in patches among the bioherms. Pelmatozoan echinoderms are present and were apparently abundant in many biohermal communities, but their particular pattern of distribution in different types of bioherms is uncertain. The gastropod *Maclurites magnus*, found in calcarenite deposited over and around the bioherms, was apparently a persistent grazer in and adjacent to the bioherms. Stressed physical environmental conditions and an increase in vagrant detritus feeders and predators suggest that some of the species in these bioherms were of necessity opportunistic and became established where chance conditions and predation permitted their existence.

Higher, near the top of the Crown Point Formation, the abundance of trilobites increases and patches with various trilobite species associations are found. For example, *Glaphurus pustulatus* is common; and *Sphaerexochus parvus*, *Hibbertia valcourensis*, and *Glaphurina lamottensis* are rare. At this stage in growth of the bioherms, *Pseudostylodicton?*, *Billingsaria*, and *Leptaena* are still part of the biohermal species association even though the trilobites now dominate the communities.

EASTERN SHELF

The lower part of the Crown Point Formation is calcarenitic. Small patches have abundant shells of the gastropod *Maclurites*. The stromatoporoid *Pseudostylodictyon lamottense* encrusts substrate formed from eroded bioherms of the underlying Day Point Formation and in places forms extensive colonies 1 m high over cleanly sorted oolites (Pitcher, 1964). Overlying calcarenites with either a sparry calcite or micritic mud matrix have an abundance of the nodular alga *Solenopora* and oncolites. The oncolites are skeletal grains covered by the alga *Girvanella* that is coated by lime mud. *Solenopora* and oncolites are common throughout most of the Crown Point Formation in sediments adjacent to bioherms. Sponges are more common than in the Day Point Formation.

Higher in the sequence and extending to the top of the Crown Point Formation are extensive bioherms that are 8 to 9 m thick, 10 to 11 m wide, and 30 to 90 m long. The bioherms have a number of community associations that developed contemporaneously in patches on the eastern portion of the shelf. Many of the bioherms are dominated by a particular species of stromatoporoid including *Labechia (L. eatoni*, *L. prima*, and *Labechia* cf. *L. pustulosa)* and *Pachystylostroma (P. vallum* and *P. goodsellense)* that formed sheet-like colonies. The stromatoporoids present a sudden influx of organisms that successfully colonized this portion of the shelf area. As biohermal builders, they appear to have colonized patches that lower in the Crown Point Formation had been settled by ectoprocts. In some of the stromatoporoid bioherms, other organisms, such as the gastropod *Maclurites*, brachiopods, ostracodes, and the cryptostomes *Chazydictya chazyensis* and *Pachydictya sheldonensis?* are present. Some of the stromatoporoid bioherms are crowded with tube-like borers that form extensive networks through the stromatoporoids and overlying calcareous mud (Kapp, 1975). In other bioherms, stromatoporoids, such as *Pachystylostroma*, and the alga

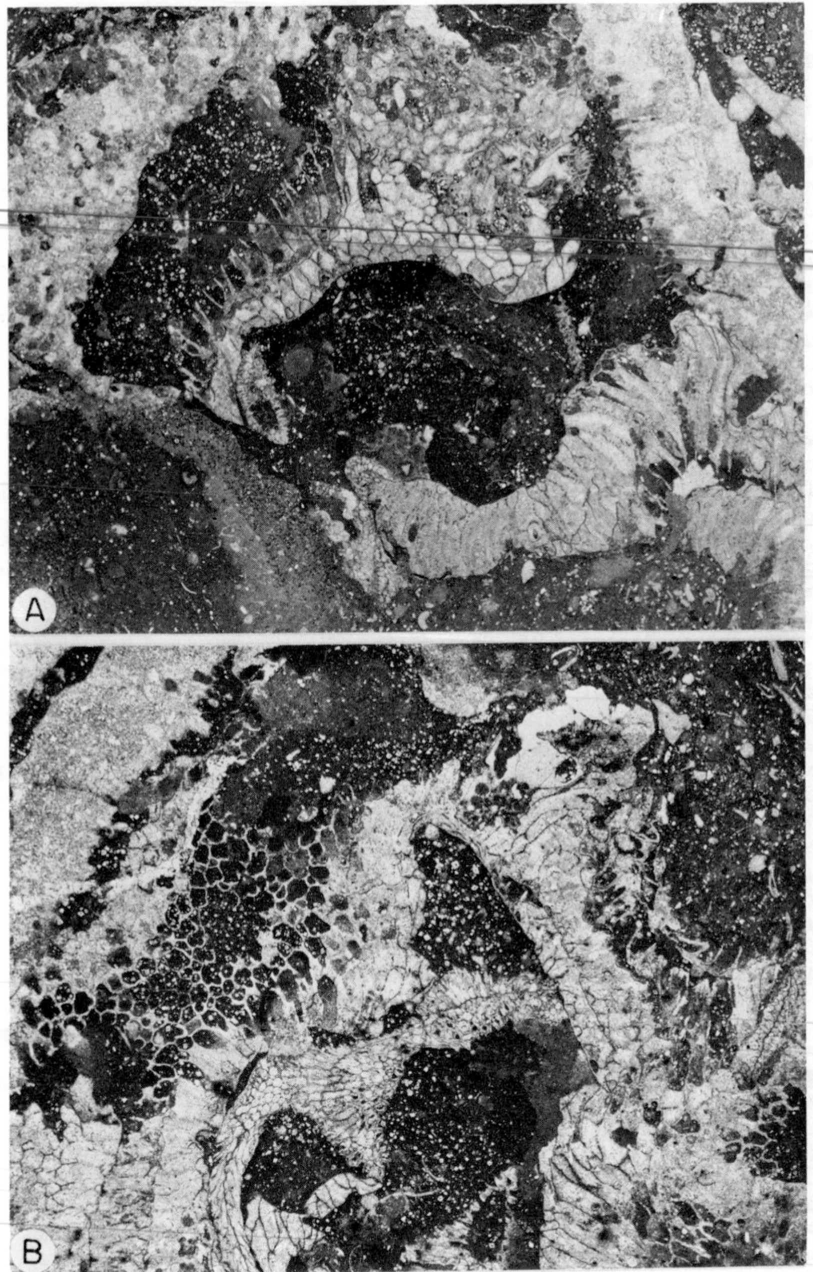

Figure 1-9
Crown Point Formation; biohermal rock; X6.3; 3.3 km northwest of St. Valentin, Quebec, Canada. A. Sponge, tabulate coral, cystoporate *Cheiloporella*, and small cryptostome fragments in micrite. B. Cystoporate *Cheiloporella*, tabulate coral, and sponge fragments in micrite.

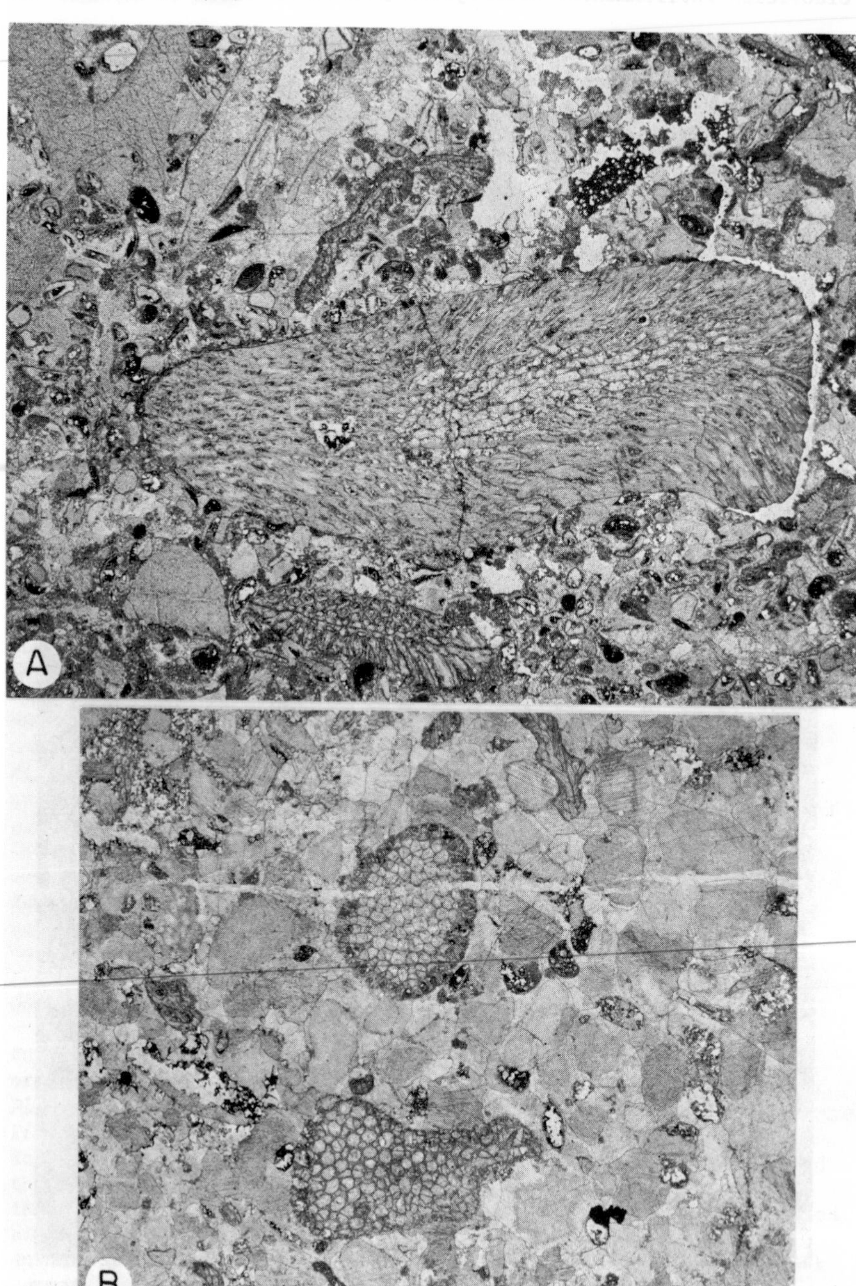

Figure 1-11
Crown Point Formation; Channel rock; X6.4; 3.3 km northwest of St. Valentin, Quebec, Canada. A. Cryptostome *Chazydictya* in pelmatozoan debris; B. Trepostome and reteporid cryptostome in pelmatozoan biosparite.

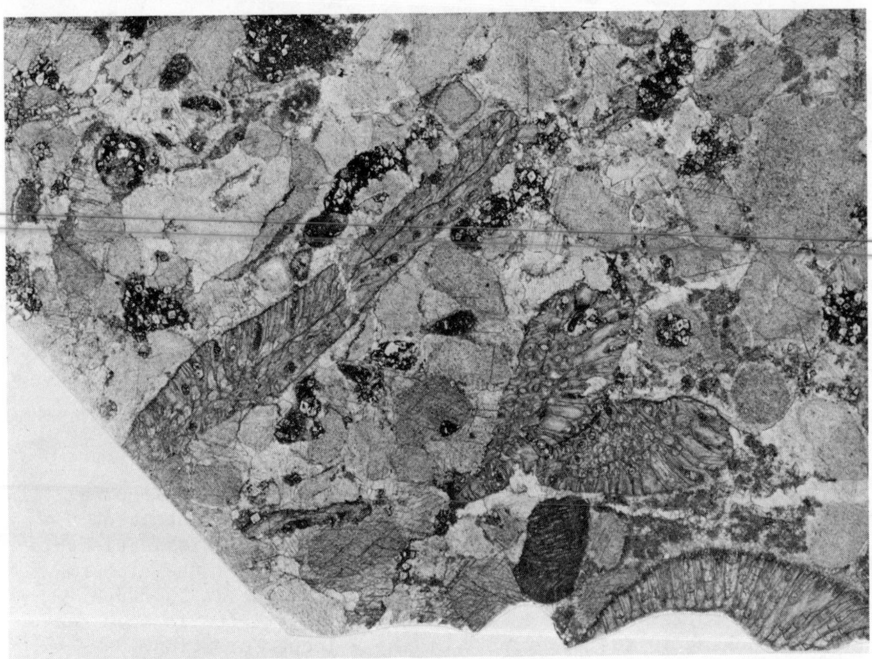

Figure 1-12
Crown Point Formation; channel rock; X8.8; 3.3 km northwest of St. Valentin, Quebec, Canada. Pelmatozoan fragments and the cryptostome *Chazydictya* in biosparite with dolomite rhombs.

VALCOUR COMMUNITIES

WESTERN SHELF

Massive layers of dolomitic calcilutite and calcisiltite have local assemblages of abundant gastropod shells of *Lophospira rectistriata*. Most of these gastropod shells are encrusted and enclosed by thick lamellae of the alga *Girvanella* sp. Other patches are calcarenites with numerous brachiopods, *Rostricellula plena* and *Mimella vulgaris*, and abundant ramose colonies of an unidentified trepostome. Local ectoproct assemblages have the trepostome *Batostoma chazyensis*, the most common species, and rare fragments of the cryptostomes *Stictopora fenestrata* and *Chazydictya chazyensis?*. At this time on the nearshore portion of the shelf, only limited and isolated areas were colonized by organisms.

SHELDON LANE

The bioherms typical of the Crown Point Formation continue upwards so that the separation of Crown Point and Valcour formations is uncertain because of closely similar sedimentary and biotic characteristics of the two units. The community associations are similar to those described for the upper part of the Crown Point Formation. The stromatoporoid-ectoproct bioherms contain the stromatoporoid *Pachystylostroma goodsellense* that is found also in bioherms of the Crown Point Formation on Isle La Motte (Kapp and Stearn, 1975). This stromatoporoid appears to replace *P. champlainense* that colonized bioherms in the underlying Crown Point Formation.

It appears that predation, possibly combined with a change in environmental conditions, brought an end to these biohermal communities because the succeeding horizons have much reduced numbers of species. An influx of the brachiopod *Rostricellula plena*, that formed extensive communities across the seafloor to the exclusion of almost any other species, was able to use the void created by the elimination of the biohermal communities.

EASTERN SHELF

As at Sheldon Lane to the west, biohermal and interbiohermal accumulations continue from the Crown Point Formation into the Valcour Formation and these two units appear to be indistinguishable for the most part. Ectoprocts again dominate many of the bioherms and the community associations are similar to those in the upper Crown Point Formation. Stromatoporoids are restricted in occurrence and are lacking in the upper part of the Valcour Formation. Brachiopods are common in some bioherms with echinoderms, trilobites, and ectoprocts (Figures 1-13, 1-14, and 1-15). Other bioherms have an ectoproct-algal association of the trepostome *Batostoma* and the alga *Solenopora*. In an ectoproct-sponge *(Zittelella)* bioherm on central Isle La Motte, eight species of ectoprocts comprise the ectoproct guild. The cryptostome *Chazydictya chazyensis* and the trepostome *Lamottopora duncanae* are abundant, the cryptostomes *Eopachydictya gregaria* and *Pachydictya sheldonensis* and the trepostomes *Bastostoma lanensis* and *Jordanopora heroensis* are common, and two species of the cryptostome *Phylloporina* are sparse. The trilobites and cephalopods also have similar species association to those in the upper part of the Crown Point Formation.

Shaw (1968) recorded that certain trilobites in the Crown Point and Valcour formations occur in particular habitats; for example, *Glaphurus pustulatus* was in the bioherms, *Glaphurina lamottensis* was in the bioherms and calcarenites surrounding the bioherms, and *Bumastoides* sp. was also in calcarenites surrounding the bioherms. Other trilobites, such as *Remopleurides canadensis*, *Isotelus harrisi*, *Sphaerexochus parvus*, *Pliomerops canadensis*, *Amphilichas minganensis*, and *Bumastus globosus*, were present in both biohermal and interbiohermal areas and apparently did not inhabit specific niches. Some trilobites, including *Isotelus harrisi* and *Bumastus globosus*, attained considerably larger size and were far more abundant in the bioherms than elsewhere in the shelf habitats.

The upper part of the Valcour Formation reflects the reworking of the calcareous deposits on the shelf. Calcilutite and thin argillite deposits are interspersed with calcarenites and biostromes of brachiopods, ectoprocts, and trilobites (Figures 1-13, 1-14, and 1-15). Massive colonies of the trepostome *Anolotichia*, found also in the lower part of the Valcour Formation, are locally abundant on

Figure 1-13
Valcour Formation; X3.2; Rockwell Bay. Fragments of trilobites, trepostome *Batostoma*, cryptostomes, gastropods, echinoderms, and brachiopods in micrite.

the eastern portion of the shelf. The guild with the brachiopods *Rostricellula* and *Mimella* and the ramose trepostome *Batostoma* is well established. The overlying sediments of post-Chazyan age, where preserved, are calcilutite with wormborings of *Phytopsis* sp.

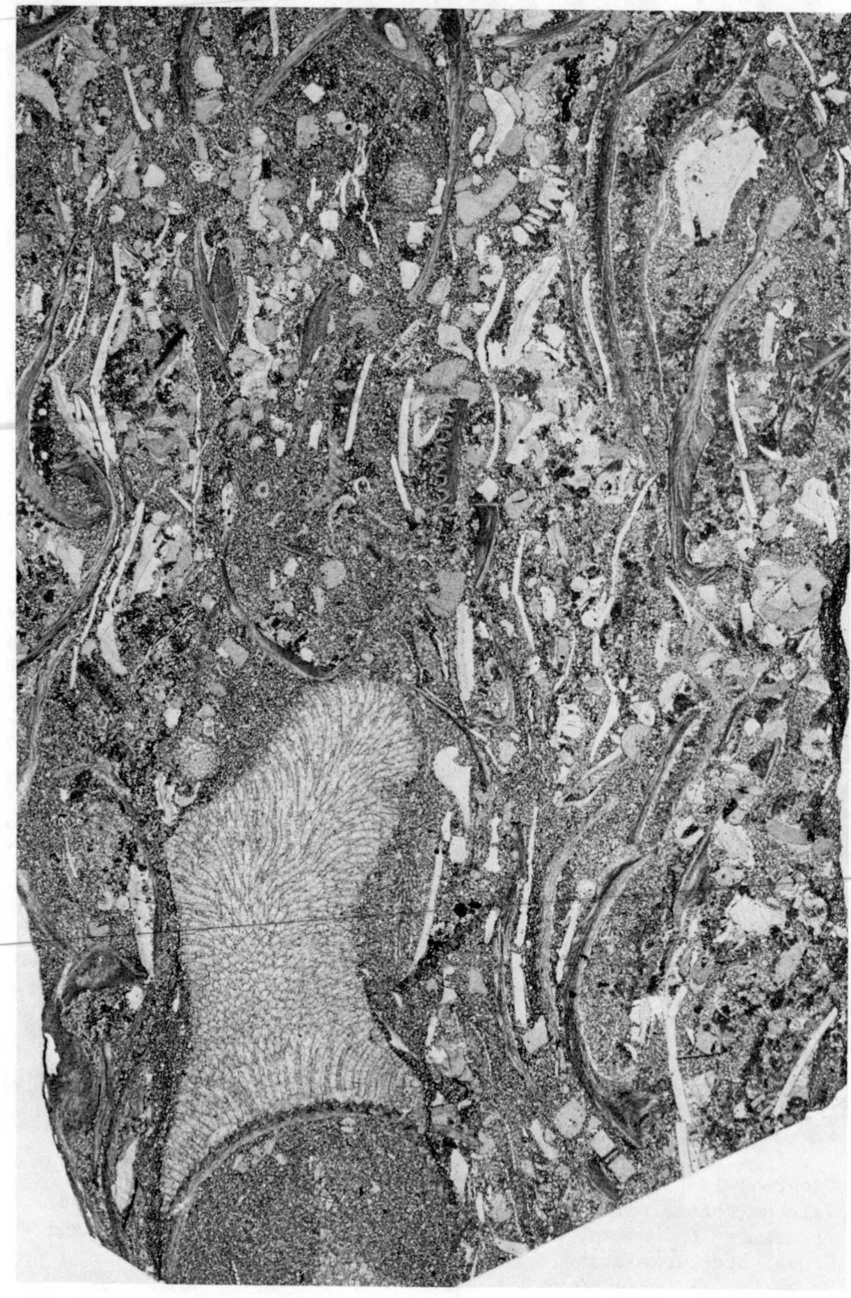

Figure 1-14
Valcour Formation; biohermal rock; X3.2; Rockwell Bay. Biosparite with lower and upper layer of brachiopod, trilobite, and echinodermal fragments and a middle layer of finer-grained fragments that are predominantly brachiopods and trepostomes.

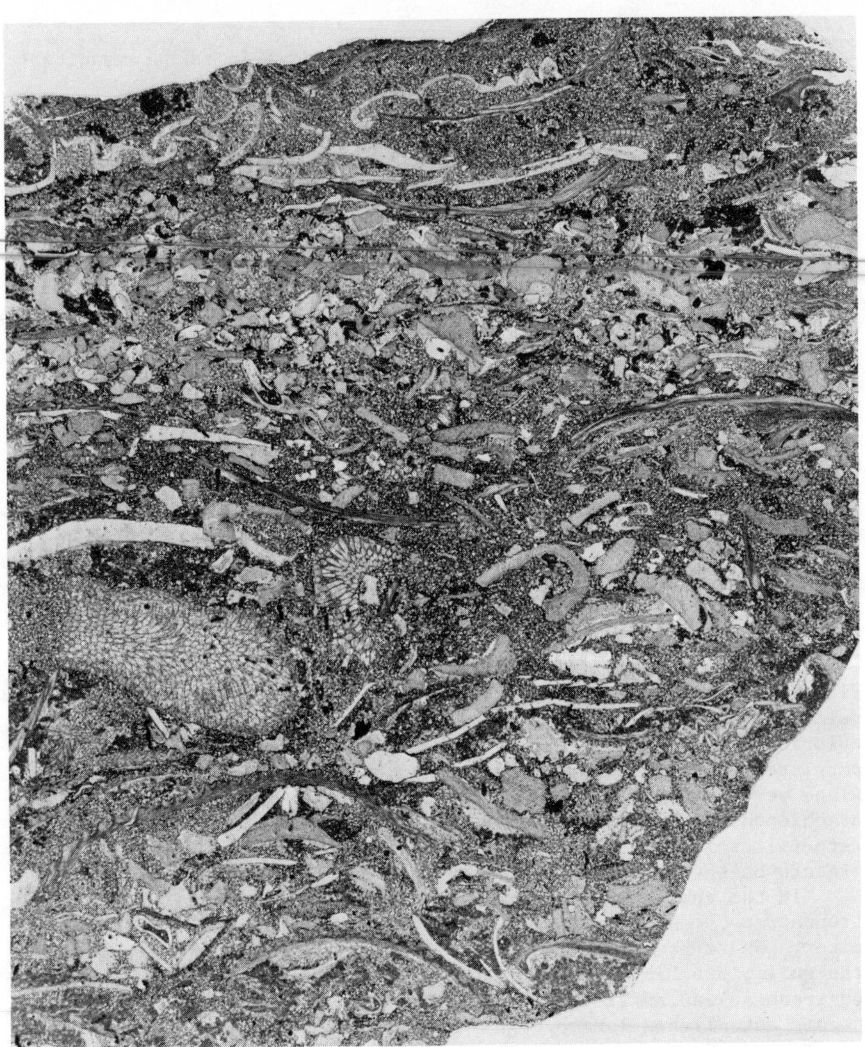

Figure 1-15
Valcour Formation; biohermal rock; X3.2; Rockwell Bay. Alternating layers of fine- and coarse-grained skeletal carbonate fragments. Brachiopods and echinodermal fragments predominate in coarse layers. Trepostomes are also present with brachiopods in fine layer in lower part of photograph and cryptostomes and trilobites are present with brachiopods in fine, upper layer.

COMMUNITY ORGANIZATION

The following biological and physical environmental characteristics of Chazyan benthic communities have been examined to reconstruct the community associations:

1. Estimates of relative abundance of organisms in each community.
2. Species diversity.
3. Postulated method of feeding of each type of organism.
4. Relative species abundance in guilds.
5. Position of the organism with respect to substrate, for example, distance above substrate or location on substrate.
6. General physical environmental parameters (for example, sediment type, mineral composition) of communities.
7. Distribution of patchiness within a habitat.
8. Sequential changes of organisms and communities through time.
9. Lateral variations across the shelf relative to different environmental conditions.

Reconstruction of Chazyan community organization can only be based on preserved organisms and trace fossils. It is important to bear in mind with respect to Chazyan communities that at least one group of organisms, the echinoderms, which were abundant in some Chazyan communities, have been so fragmented that information about their relative species abundance and even the classes of echinoderms that were present may only be inferred.

During deposition of the lower part of the Day Point Formation, communities on the western, nearshore portion of the shelf had few distinctive characteristics. Only a few major taxa representing two or three trophic categories were present. Species numbers were low (five filter feeders in addition to algae and echinoderms). Filter feeders represented by ectoprocts and echinoderms (possibly pelmatozoans) were the dominant consumer groups that successfully colonized and recolonized the substrate after successive and persistent physical disruptions of the substrate by wave action. Algae were apparently one of the principal primary producers. Brachiopods and gastropods were far less abundant. The brachiopods were filter feeders above the substrate and the gastropods, probably grazers on the substrate.

In the guild that filtered the higher bottom layers, the ramose trepostome *Champlainopora chazyensis* was the most successful colonizer. Where brachiopods and ectoprocts were present together in the guild, brachiopods usually dominated the guild. However, the environment was sufficiently unpredictable that ectoprocts could become established long enough to outcompete the brachiopods. Under these conditions, the cryptostome *Chazydictya chazyensis* was the most successful species to gain dominance.

During the deposition of the upper part of the Day Point Formation on the western portion of the shelf, a greater number of taxa became established and population density increased. Patchiness also was more pronounced. Communities with filter feeders, either ectoprocts, brachiopods, or echinoderms or a combination of these taxa, existed in a more predictable environment. In addition to filter feeders, a number of species of trilobites, detritus feeders, became established in the communities.

On the eastern portion of the shelf at the time of deposition of the Head Member, the biota consisted of an inarticulate brachiopod and two species of trilobites. This biota was much sparser than that on the western shelf. The overlying Scott Member has a marked accumulation of carbonate sediments that relates to a rapid colonization by filter feeders of ectoprocts and echinoderms.

Where these two groups were in great abundance, brachiopods, cephalopods, trilobites, and ostracodes were far less numerous. Sheet-like colonies of the cystoporate *Cheiloporella* encrusted many colonies of *Batostoma* and were abundant in these bioherms. In addition, at least three opportunistic ectoproct species are found in some of the bioherms. Another ectoproct guild, which was commonly dominated by the trepostome *Champlainopora chazyensis*, colonized interbiohermal and channel areas. The growth of bioherms and their limited occurrence on the eastern shelf appear to have been the result of restricted areas of firm and fixed substrate suitable for settlement by larvae.

Changes in environmental conditions led to deposition of quartz sands and silts (Wait Member, Day Point Formation). These sediments, barren of nutrients, were unsuitable for filter feeders or detritus feeders.

With the deposition of calcarenites at the beginning of the Fleury Member, suitable conditions existed for establishment of filter-feeder guilds that were dominated by ectoprocts. The two ectoprocts, *Batostoma* and *Cheiloporella* reappeared and maintained their dominance in the bioherms. A greater diversity of species was shown with the appearance of sponges, a tabulate coral, and three or four species of ectoprocts. The ectoproct *Batostoma* also invaded the interbiohermal areas where it grew as ramose colonies, and its sheet-like form of the bioherms is lacking. Locally, trilobites, represented by as many as twelve species, are found in calcarenites associated with the bioherms. These detrital feeders, represented by abundant *Bumastoides aplatus* and *Sphaerexochus parvus*, may have preyed on other biota in the bioherms, and their abundance may relate to fluctuation and reductions in the numbers of ectoprocts. On both the western and eastern portions of the shelf, an increase in abundance and in number of species of trilobites occurred.

During the deposition of the Crown Point Formation on the western portion of the shelf, low carbonate mounds, shoals, and lagoons were colonized by various organisms, and their distribution was variable and patchy. Local populations included algae, gastropods, cephalopods, trilobites, brachiopods, stromatoporoids, and ectoprocts. Ectoprocts generally formed small guilds of four to six species. Trilobites had an association of 13 species.

Farther to the east at Sheldon Lane, stromatoporoids, although sparse, became established in the lower part of the Crown Point Formation. In the upper part of the Crown Point Formation, several community associations were restricted to the bioherms. Large colonies of the stromatoporoid *Pseudostylodictyon* dominated the bioherms, which also may have had several ectoproct species, a gastropod, a cephalopod, a sponge, a tabulate coral, several trilobite species, and echinoderms. The cryptostome *Pachydictya sheldonensis* most commonly dominated the ectoproct guild. Variations in the guild structure at times permitted *Chazydictya chazyensis* to be dominant. The great variability in species composition of bioherms suggests unpredictable environmental conditions, that, combined with predation, led to marked fluctuations in colonization and maintenance of communities in the bioherms. Some species in the bioherms were transient opportunists established under random chance conditions. Trilobites increased markedly in abundance in the upper part of the Crown Point Formation on both the western and eastern portions of the shelf.

On the eastern portion of the shelf, the community organization in bioherms and interbiohermal areas was similar to that at Sheldon Lane. However, species diversity was considerably greater on the eastern part of the shelf. The stromatoporoid *Pseudostylodictyon* encrusted eroded bioherms of the Day Point Formation and was the distinctive filter feeder when the lower part of the Crown Point Formation was being deposited. The alga *Solenopora* and oncolites consistently recurred at this time, and sponges became more abundant than in the Day Point Formation.

In the middle and upper parts of the Crown Point Formation, a great increase in species diversification occurred. One of possibly five or more stromatoporoid species dominated many of the bioherms. These species were sheet-like encrusting colonies and did not have the massive form of *Pseudostylodictyon*. The biohermal communities also had gastropods, brachiopods, ostracodes, sponges, algae, trilobites, and tabulate corals. Several community associations in which one or two filter feeders were dominant appeared in the bioherms.

Stromatoporoids decreased and ectoprocts increased in the upper part of the Crown Point Formation and they formed several guilds. Echinoderms were abundant on the flanks of the bioherms. Trilobites and cephalopods increased in abundance. Stromatolites, interpreted as algal mats, covered many of the bioherms, and cephalopods found in these deposits may be transported skeletons that became caught in the algal mats.

On the western portion of the shelf, the Valcour Formation contains patches of small gastropods in calcilutite. These animals appear to have been grazers that inhabited muddy lagoons. Calcareous algae coated the gastropod skeletons. Other patches of calcarenite had numerous brachipods represented by two species and abundant colonies of an ectoproct. Still other patches of calcarenite had small assemblages of ectoprocts. Species diversity in all these communities was low.

The community associations in the bioherms of the upper part of the Crown Point Formation also were found in the Valcour Formation at Sheldon Lane. Higher in the Valcour Formation, local abundances of trilobites (possibly predators in the bioherms) and reduction in height of the bioherms resulted in reduced species diversity. Certain trilobites inhabited a variety of sites, but some were restricted to the bioherms. Increased sedimentation on the shelf filled much of the topographic relief. As topographic relief became appreciably reduced, brachiopods established communities similar to those on the western portion of the shelf.

On the eastern portion of the shelf, as at Sheldon Lane, the community associations of the upper part of the Crown Point Formation persisted. Ectoprocts still dominated most bioherms and brachiopods were common in some of the bioherms. Particular ectoproct species may have had specific associations with other filter feeders such as sponges. Trilobites also increased in abundance, paralleling the changes in community associations at Sheldon Lane. Likewise, during deposition of the upper part of the Valcour Formation, brachiopods and ectoprocts, represented by low species diversity, maintained communities on a shelf that had little topographic relief. Biohermal growth had ceased, and environmental conditions across the shelf from the eastern to the western portions were far more uniform than before.

SUMMARY

Several kinds of community organizations occur in the Chazyan bioherms. The earliest community organization in bioherms of the Day Point Formation demonstrates that one or two species of ectoprocts of the filter-feeder guild were able to stabilize an otherwise shifting substrate. Once the substrate was stabilized, the bioherms gradually grew to heights that gave topographic relief to the shelf. Minor differences in the heights of bioherms and other physical factors apparently influenced the subsequent colonization by additional organisms. At this stage of growth, stromatoporoids were able to colonize and to form bioherms in competition with ectoprocts, sponges, and corals. Bioherms become larger and more massive from the upper part of the Day Point Formation into the upper part of the Crown Point Formation. Domal stromatoporoid colonies in the lower part of the Crown Point Formation are replaced by sheet-like stromatoporoid colonies in the upper part. This stage of growth of bioherms is shown in the Crown Point Formation at Sheldon Lane and on the eastern portion of the shelf. Species diversity and community organization increase markedly in these complex bioherms. In the upper part of the Crown Point Formation and the lower part of the Valcour Formation, an influx of calcareous muds appears to have restricted growth of stromatoporoids, and this gave an opportunity for ectoprocts to recolonize broad areas. Trilobites were abundant in these later Crown Point communities.

In the lower part of the Valcour Formation on the eastern portion of the shelf, the bioherms are small patches that are dominated by ectoprocts. Locally, brachiopods are common. An infilling of the topographic relief appears to have taken place, and conditions apparently became more uniform across the shelf. The upper part of the Valcour Formation has extensive areas colonized by brachiopods and ectoprocts in well-stratified beds. Trilobites are abundant.

In contrast to the eastern portion of the shelf, the western portion has more sand-flat communities in the lower part of the succession. An almost complete lack of biohermal communities in the middle part of the succession contrasts with communities to the east. Communities in the upper part of the succession are locally dominated by small gastropods, brachiopods, or a few species of ectoprocts.

This study shows that in comparing species diversity in fossil communities from strata of the same age but different localities, it is necessary to compare information from closely similar communities. Different communities of the same age only a few tens of meters apart may have strongly contrasting faunas and species diversities.

ACKNOWLEDGMENTS

I am greatly indebted to Dr. D. Toomey, Cities Service Oil Company for making available Figures 1-4 through 1-15.

REFERENCES

Brainerd, E., and H. M. Seely. 1888. The original Chazy rocks. *Am. Geologist* 2:323-330.

Brainerd, E., and H. M. Seely. 1896. The Chazy of Lake Champlain. *Am. Mus. Nat. History Bull.* 8:305-315.

Cushing, H. P. 1905. Geology of the northern Adirondack region. *New York State Mus. Bull.* 95:271-453.

Finks, R. M., and D. F. Toomey. 1968. The paleoecology of Chazyan (Lower Middle Ordovician) "reefs" or "mounds." *Guidebook to Field Excursions*, pp. 93-120. New York State University, Plattsburgh, New York. *New York State Geol. Assoc.*

Flower, R. H. 1955. New Chazyan orthocones. *Jour. Paleontology* 29: 806-830.

Jackson, J. B. C. 1972. The ecology of molluscs of *Thalassia* communities, Jamaica, West Indies. II. Molluscan population variability along an environmental stress gradient. *Mar. Biology* 14:304-337.

Jackson, J. B. C., and L. Buss. 1975. Allelopathy and spatial competition among coral reef invertebrates. *Natl. Acad. Sci. Proc.* 72:5160-5163.

Kapp, U. S. 1974. Mode of growth of Middle Ordovician (Chazyan) stromatoporoids, Vermont. *Jour. Paleontology* 48:1235-1240.

Kapp, U. S. 1975. Paleoecology of Middle Ordovician stromatoporoid mounds in Vermont. *Lethaia* 8:195-207.

Kapp, U. S., and C. W. Stearn. 1975. Stromatopotoids of the Chazy Group (Middle Ordovician), Lake Champlain, Vermont and New York. *Jour. Paleontology* 49:163-186.

Levin, S. A., and R. T. Paine. 1974. Disturbance, patch formation, and community structure. *Natl. Acad. Sci. Proc.* 71:2744-2747.

Margalef, R. 1968. *Perspectives in Ecological Theory*. Chicago: The University of Chicago Press, 111 p.

Menge, B. A. 1976. Organization of the New England rocky intertidal community: role of predation, competition, and environmental heterogeneity. *Ecol. Mon.* 46:355-393.

Menge, B. A., and J. P. Sutherland. 1976. Species diversity gradients: synthesis of the roles of predation, competition, and temporal heterogeneity. *Am. Naturalist* 110:351-369.

Oxley, P. 1951. Chazyan reef facies relationships in the northern Champlain Valley. *Denison Univ. Sci. Lab. Jour.* 42:92-106.

Oxley, P., and M. Kay. 1959. Ordovician Chazyan Series of Champlain Valley, New York and Vermont, and its reefs. *Am. Assoc. Petroleum Geologists Bull.* 43:817-853.

Paine, R. T. 1966. Food web complexity and species diversity. *Am. Naturalist* 100:65-75.

Paine, R. T. 1971. A short-term experimental investigation of resource partitioning in a New Zealand rocky intertidal habitat. *Ecology* 52:1096-1106.

Pitcher, M. 1964. Evolution of Chazyan (Ordovician) reefs of eastern United States and Canada. *Canadian Petroleum Geology Bull.* 12:632-691.

Raymond, P. E. 1906. The Chazy formation and its fauna. *Carnegie Mus. Annals* 3:498-598.

Root, R. B. 1967. The niche exploitation pattern of the blue-gray gnatcatcher. *Ecol. Mon.* 37:317-350.

Ross, J. R. P. 1963a. *Constellaria* from the Chazyan (Ordovician), Isle La Motte, Vermont. *Jour. Paleontology* 37:51-56.

Ross, J. R. P. 1963b. New Ordovician species of Chazyan trepostome and cryptostome Bryozoa. *Jour. Paleontology* 37:57-63.

Ross, J. R. P. 1963c. Chazyan (Ordovician) leptotrypellid and atactotoechid Bryozoa. *Palaeontology* 5:727-739.

Ross, J. R. P. 1963d. The bryozoan trepostome *Batostoma* in Chazyan (Ordovician) strata. *Jour. Paleontology* 37:857-867.

Ross, J. R. P. 1963e. Ordovician cryptostome Bryozoa, standard Chazyan Series, New York and Vermont. *Geol. Soc. America Bull.* 74:577-608.

Ross, J. R. P. 1964a. Champlainian cryptostome Bryozoa from New York state. *Jour. Paleontology* 38:1-32.

Ross, J. R. P. 1964b. Morphology and phylogeny of early Ectoprocta (Bryozoa). *Geol. Soc. America Bull.* 75:927-948.

Ross, J. R. P. 1972. Paleoecology of middle Ordovician ectoproct assemblages. *24th Internat. Geol. Congress Proc.* 7:96-102.

Shaw, F. C. 1968. *Early Middle Ordovician Chazy trilobites of New York. New York State Mus. Sci. Serv. Mem.* 17:1-163.

Stanley, S. 1973. An ecological theory for the sudden origin of multicellular life in the late Precambrian. *Natl. Acad. Sci. Proc.* 70:1486-1489.

Turpaeva, E. P. 1959. Food interrelationships of dominant species in marine biocoenoses. Washington, D.C.: American Institute of Biological Sciences, pp. 137-147. (Translation of article in Russian in B. N. Nikitin, edit. 1957. Marine Biology, U.S.S.R. Trans. Inst. Oceanology 20:171-185).

2

Organic-Buildup Constructional Capability in Lower Ordovician and Late Paleozoic Mounds

Donald Francis Toomey

ABSTRACT

Evolution of the organic-buildup community has gone on since Precambrian time. During this long time span various groups of organisms have risen to prominance and later been supplanted by other biotic groups. Seemingly, this change in organic-buildup communities exemplifies organism adaptive response to a changing and challenging set of physical conditions imposed by the paleo-environment, state of evolution of a particular organic group, paleo-geography, and tectonic setting. Algal-sponge mounds of the Lower Ordovician, as shown by the buildups of the McKelligon Canyon Formation (El Paso Group) of West Texas and the Kindblade Formation (Arbuckle Group) of southern Oklahoma, demonstrate these changes. These are relatively small buildups dominated by simple biotic forms consisting of stromatolitic algae and *problematica,* lithistid sponges, and a questionable colonial laminated coelenterate. Vertical biological zonation is only developed on those structures that demonstrate rapid upward growth into shallow water with ultimate subaerial exposure. Microfacies indicate that depositional environments ranged from the subtidal to the intertidal zones. These buildups appear to be most common along the Lower Ordovician cratonic margin. Their biotic simplicity appears to be due primarily to the state of development of a biota possessing rather limited constructional capabilities. Conversely, Late Paleozoic buildups are dominated by leafey or phylloid algae. These small erect plants with their rapid reproductive ability and potential to dominate the seafloor selectively molded and constructed organic buildups of variable size. These structures appear to have been initiated in relatively shallow water and to have grown upward into very shallow water. The microfacies patterns associated with selected examples of phylloid algal buildups of Middle and Late Pennsylvanian ages from the southwestern United States demonstrate distinctive and recurring rock and biotic microfacies relationships. Most phylloid algal buildups of Late Paleozoic age appear to have developed best in tectonic settings along basin margins and associated with active basin-shelf structure related to overall cratonic fragmentation.

INTRODUCTION

I define a mound as an organic carbonate buildup, commonly of relatively small size, devoid of obvious bedding, and containing a biota different from the usually bedded surrounding sediments. Used in this sense, this definition accurately describes most Lower Ordovician and Late Paleozoic organic buildups of the southwestern United States. These organic buildups are believed to have been centers of organic activity whose contained fossil skeletons are in growth positions and whose biotic activities influenced and modified the resulting surrounding sedimentational and biotic patterns we now see. The resultant microfacies pattern developed because of the relative relief of the organic buildups in relationship to the surrounding seafloor.

These particular organic buildups are not "reefs" in the sense we commonly use this word primarily because the biotic potential necessary to build and perpetuate a massive resistant organic structure did not exist this early in geologic time. The development of the scleractinian corals with their significant corallite edge-zone potential did not evolve until Middle Triassic time. Accordingly, I restrict the term "reef" to those post-Middle Triassic organic buildups whose climax community is dominated by massive hermatypic scleractinian corals that are to some degree welded together with coralline crustose algae. This interplay of massive corals and coralline algae, combining together to build a structure able to withstand a high degree of wave-buffetting action, is a distinctive post-Middle Triassic phenomenon, and one that is not apparent in pre-Middle Triassic organic buildups.

In this contribution, I describe algal-sponge buildups of Early Paleozoic (Lower Ordovician) age and contrast their organic constructional capability with that of Late Paleozoic (Middle and Upper Pennsylvanian) phylloid algal structures. Specifically, I describe the various organic communities and attempt to define their constructional role in the formation of mound structures and the resultant distinctive microfacies patterns associated with these centers of organic growth.

LOWER ORDOVICIAN ALGAL-SPONGE MOUNDS

LOCATION AND FACIES BELTS

The Lower Ordovician organic buildups described herein have been found in two major outcrop areas in the southwestern United States. These are in the West Texas-southern New Mexico region and in southern Oklahoma. The organic buildups are of Canadian (Arenig) age and occur in the McKelligon Canyon Formation of the El Paso Group in West Texas and southern New Mexico and in the Kindblade Formation of the Arbuckle Group in southern Oklahoma. The mound-bearing interval in the West Texas region is 70 m thick, and the same sequence is approximately 170 m thick in the Oklahoma outcrops.

Figure 2-1 shows the outlines of Texas and Oklahoma and the positions of the two major facies belts involving strata of Early Ordovician age in this region. A sinuous line marks the approximate northwestern edge of the Quachita Facies that consists mostly of black

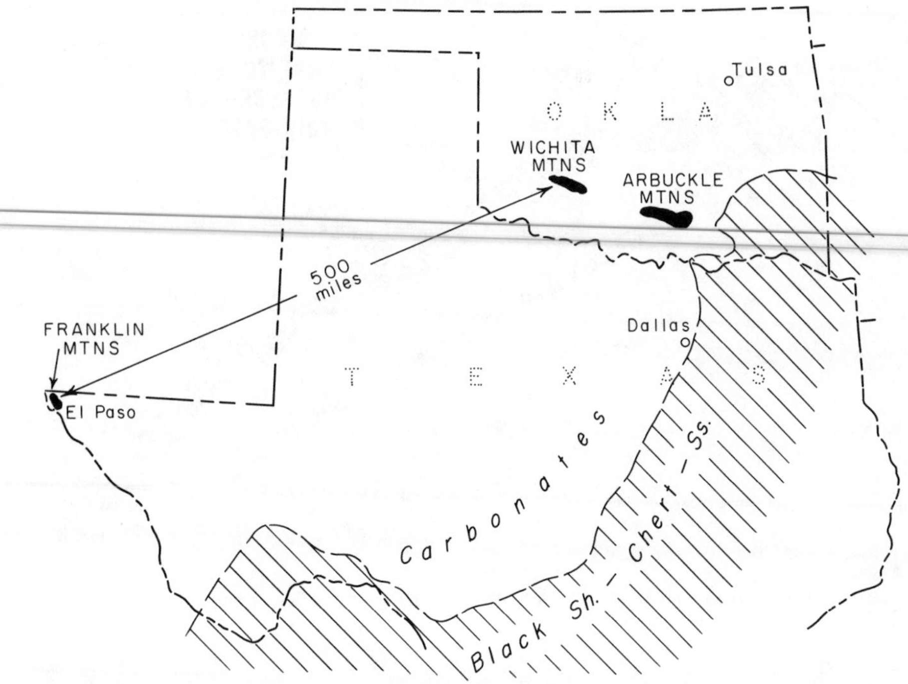

Figure 2-1
Generalized diagram showing Lower Ordovician facies belts in the southwestern United States in relation to the outcrop areas of the Arbuckle and Wichita mountains of southern Oklahoma and to the Franklin Mountains of West Texas.

shale and sandstone and some chert. Above this is a broad belt of carbonate rocks at least 800 kms wide and extending over 3,000 kms northeastward into Newfoundland, Canada. These carbonate rocks were deposited in the shallow waters of a broad, elongate, carbonate platform (Toomey, 1970).

WEST TEXAS LOWER ORDOVICIAN ORGANIC BUILDUPS

One of the best areas of Lower Ordovician mound exposures occurs along the east-facing scarp of the southern Franklin Mountains in the West Texas-Mexico border area. At this location, 530 m of Lower Ordovician strata is well exposed (Figure 2-2).

Typical organic buildups of the Lower Ordovician McKelligon Canyon Formation are massive nonbedded structures that are enclosed by thin, well-bedded, marine limestones without accompanying flank beds. The largest organic buildup present in the West Texas region is Lechuguilla Mound, which attains a height of 6 m and a width of 15 m (Figure 2-3A and 2-4). However, most of the Lower Ordovician organic buildups exposed in this area are smaller than the Lechuguilla Mound and are closely spaced forming a mound complex.

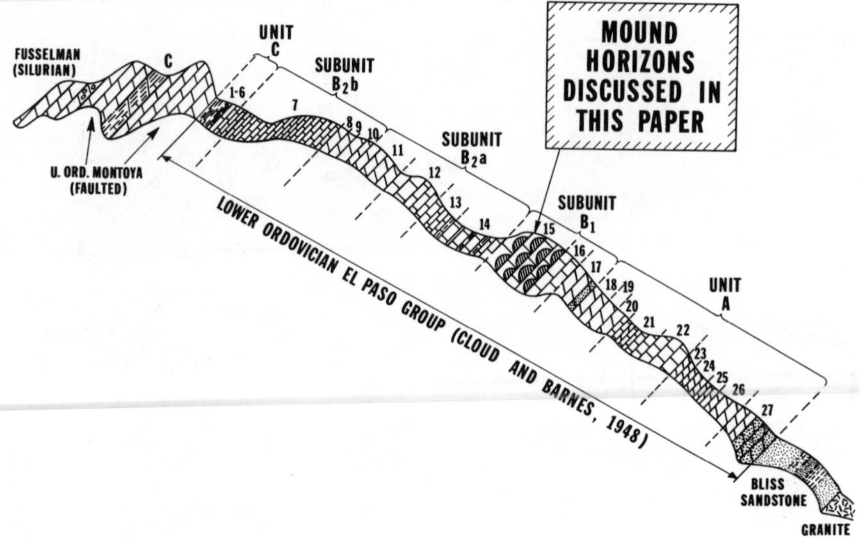

Figure 2-2
Generalized Lower Ordovician stratigraphic sequence present at southern end of Franklin Mountains, West Texas.

The McKelligon Canyon buildups are usually surrounded with grainstones and packstones containing abundant silicified cephalopod siphuncles (Figure 2-3B) intermixed with appreciable mound-shed debris of which intraclasts are a dominant component. The mounds are crowded with three principal organisms. These include lithistid sponges (Figure 2-5A) (principally *Archaeoscyphia annulata* Cullison), receptaculitid algae (*Calathium*) (Figure 2-5C), and a laminated spinose organism (*Pulchrilamina spinosa*) of probable coelenterate affinity (Figure 2-3C and 2-3D) described by Toomey and Ham (1967). Accessory biotic components include algae and *problematica*, pelmatozoans, orthid brachiopods, gastropods, cephalopods, trilobites, and conodonts.

It is important to note that the three primary mound-building groups show a vertical zonation on some McKelligon Canyon buildups. Principally, close to the tops of many buildups, there are conspicuous accumulations of *Pulchrilamina spinosa* (Figure 2-3C) that for all

Figure 2-3 (at right)
A. Lechuguilla Mound as exposed in the Lower Ordovician McKelligon Canyon Formation at the southern end of the Franklin Mountains, West Texas. The mound is approximately 6.3 m high and 15 m wide and is cut by dark-colored calcarenite-filled channels. B. Close-up of a small McKelligon Canyon organic buildup showing sharp contact of light-colored mound rock with darker-colored channel rock containing abundant silicified cephalopod siphuncles. Lamellar colonies on left side of photograph are *Pulchrilamina spinosa* Toomey and Ham. Length of hammer 38.4 cm. C. Close-up of colony of *Pulchrilamina*. Diameter of tape 15 cm. D. Thin-section photomicrograph of the *Pulchrilamina spinosa* Toomey and Ham showing two laminae with well-preserved spines on the upper surface, and mud infill between the laminae, X24.

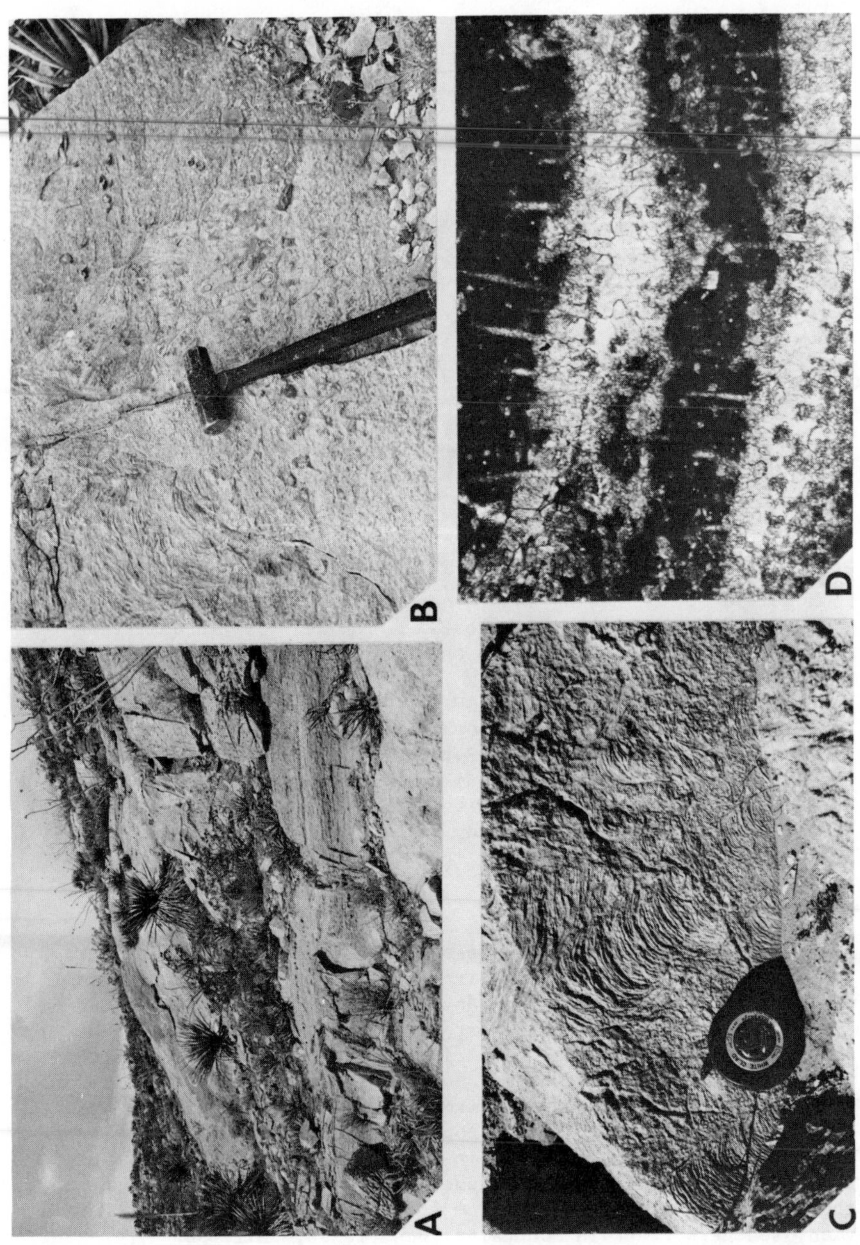

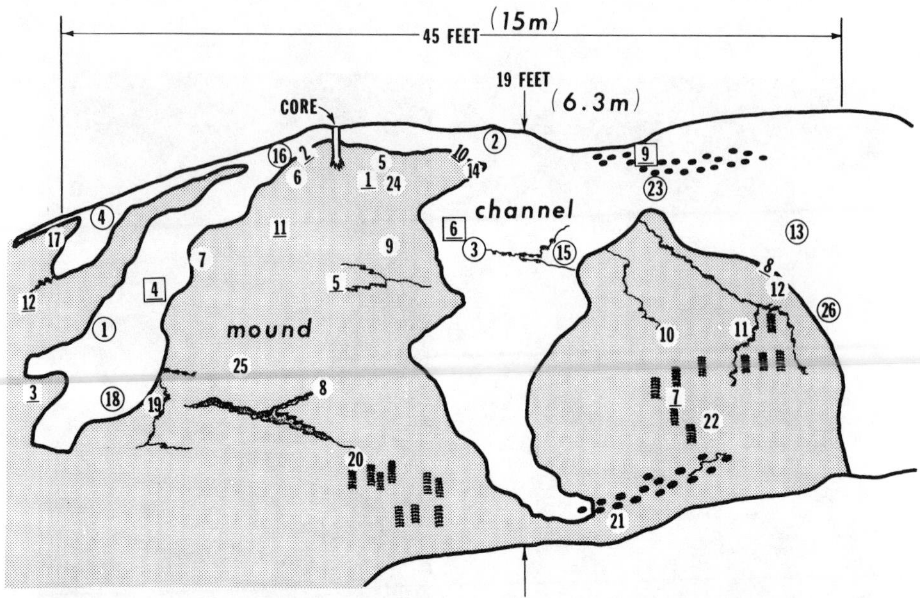

Figure 2-4
Lechuguilla Mound showing sample control (circles) and location of grid control (squares). Stippled area = mound rock, blank areas = channels, blacked-in ellipses = chert nodules, and stacked layers = digitate stromatolite colonies.

practical purposes exclude the other two organic groups. This is regarded as the dominant climax biotic component in the evolution of these Early Paleozoic organic buildups. Superficially, without thin-section examination, the resemblance between *Pulchrilamina* and algal stromatolites is striking. Study of many thin-sections has clearly

Figure 2-5 (at right)
A. Thin-section photomicrograph of an exceptionally well-preserved lithistid sponge and fragments from mound rock (burrowed skeletal wackestone) of the McKelligon Canyon Formation at McKelligon Canyon, southern Franklin Mountains, West Texas, X2.4. B. Thin-section photomicrograph of channel rock (intraclastic skeletal grainstone) with large, abraded, lithistid sponge surrounded by intraclasts and echinodermal debris embedded within a sparry calcite matrix, McKelligon Canyon Formation, McKelligon Canyon, southern Franklin Mountains, West Texas, X3.2. C. Thin-section photomicrograph of mound rock (burrowed skeletal wackestone) with a conspicuous fragment of the receptaculitid alga *Calathium* from the McKelligon Canyon Formation, southern Franklin Mountains, West Texas, X3.2. D. Thin-section photomicrograph of channel rock (intraclastic skeletal packstone-wackestone) showing well-rounded intraclasts and echinodermal ossicles from the McKelligon Canyon Formation, southern Franklin Mountains, West Texas, X6.4.

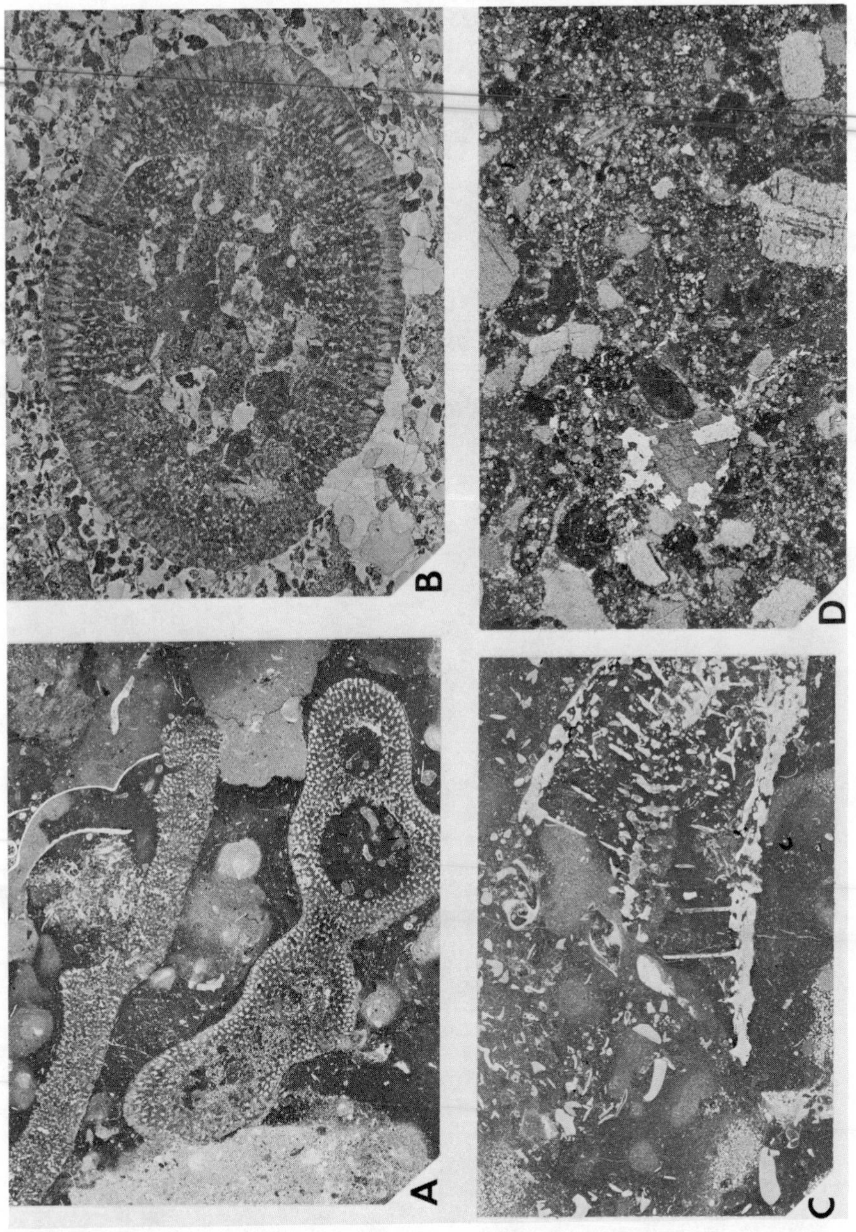
A
B
C
D

demonstrated that alternating, curved, spiny layers of mosaic calcite represent recrystallized calcium carbonate that had originally been secreted by a colonial organism. A thin-section photomicrograph of *Pulchrilamina spinosa* Toomey and Ham, with its characteristic spinose upper surface, is shown in Figure 2-3D.

One distinctive feature of these Lower Ordovician organic buildups is that they appear to grow on a highly burrowed dolomite surface.

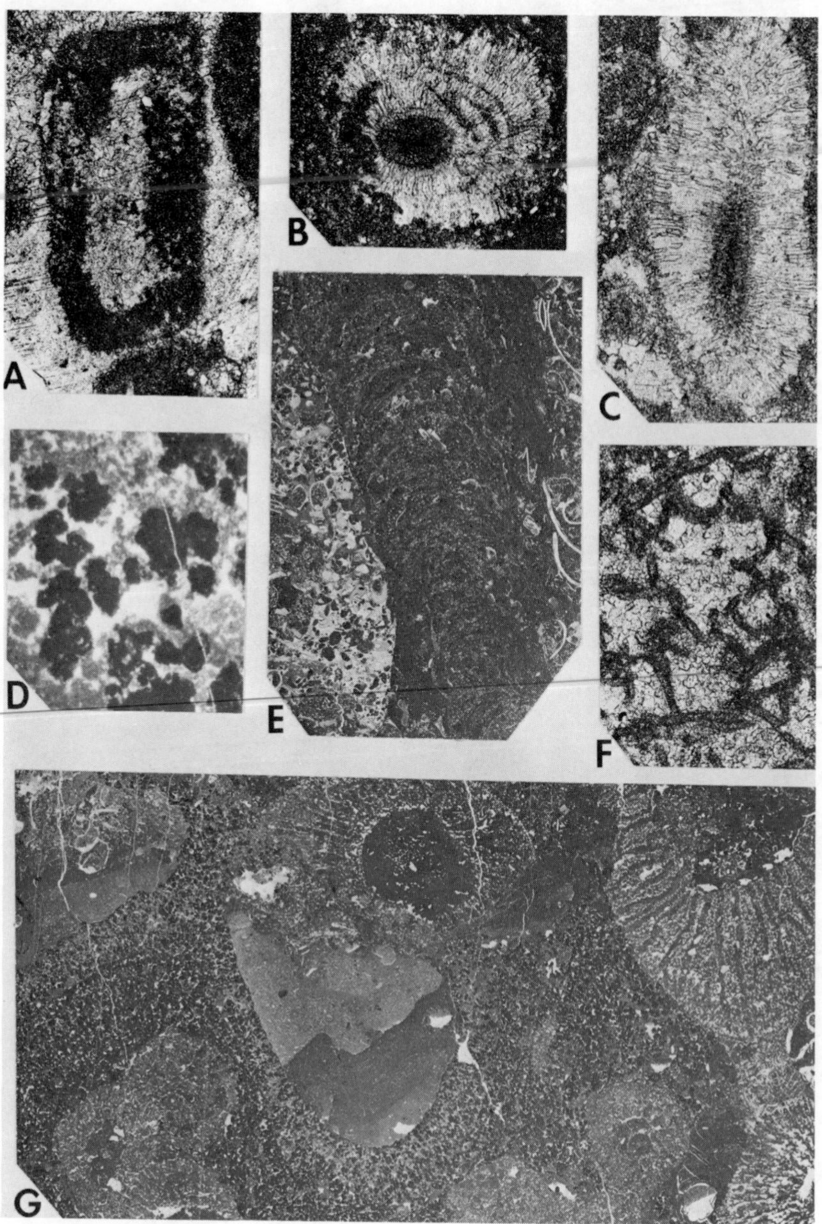

This is shown in Figure 2-3B. Usually overlying this foundational rock unit is mound rock containing abundant clusters of rather small digitate algal stromatolites (Figure 2-4). Another important feature that is conspicuous, especially on the larger mounds, is the presence of well-developed channels cutting into the mound surface. The channels are mostly less than 1 m in width although some reach a depth of almost 4 m. The channels are darker than the surrounding light-colored mound rock and may contain up to 15 percent dolomite. They are filled in with coarse packstone-grainstone debris of which broken and abraded sponges, silicified brachiopods, echinodermal debris, and cephalopod siphuncles are the most common constituents (Figure 2-5B and 2-5D). Some of the better-developed channels show conspicuous cross-bedded sedimentary structures.

Petrologically, typical mound rock can be described as a burrowed, intraclastic, skeletal wackestone. Where well-developed swirls of stromatolitic algae have enmeshed skeletal debris and *Pulchrilamina* colonies have encrusted and bound sediment, the mound rock is a true boundstone. Conversely, the channel rock is most commonly an intraclastic, skeletal packstone-grainstone in which echinodermal debris and intraclasts are the dominant components.

The exuberant growth of the principal mound-building organisms (*Calathium*, *Archaeoscyphia*, and *Pulchrilamina*) characterize these Early Paleozoic organic buildups. However, it should be emphasized that algae and various *problematica* are also common and aid in both binding the organisms and sediment and, perhaps more importantly, in the overall diminution and destruction of grains to micrite (Figure 2-6A). This algal-*problematica* assemblage consists of laminated algal stromatolites, *Girvanella*, and *Nuia*. Representative examples of this assemblage are shown in Figure 2-6.

Figure 2-6 (at left)
A. Photomicrograph of an echinoderm ossicle with circumscribed micrite envelope showing pronounced effect of algal boring and corrosion on skeletal grain. Channel rock from McKelligon Canyon Formation organic buildup, southern Franklin Mountains, West Texas, X64. B and C. Photomicrographs of problematical microorganism *Nuia*. Note effect of algal boring in B. Mound rock from McKelligon Canyon Formation, southern Franklin Mountains, West Texas, X64. D and G. Photomicrographs of growths of problematical forms *Renalcis* and *Epiphyton*. D. Close-up of colony present in mound rock from the Kindblade lower-mound interval at the Kindblade Ranch Section, Wichita Mountains, southwestern Oklahoma, X13.6. G. Dense growths of *Renalcis-Epiphyton* associated and encrusting specimens of the lithistid sponge *Archaeoscyphia annulata* Cullison and intraclasts, Kindblade lower mound interval, Southern Tishomingo Anticline section, Arbuckle Mountains, southern Oklahoma, X2.4. E. Photomicrograph of a digitate stromatolite colony from mound rock of the Kindblade upper-mound interval, Highway 77 section, Arbuckle Mountains, southern Oklahoma, X1.6. Dark material along sides of colony contains abundant threads of *Girvanella*, and tiny white flecks delineating stromatolitic laminae are entrapped silt-size quartz grains. F. Photomicrograph of *Girvanella* threads from McKelligon Canyon Formation mound rock, southern Franklin Mountains, West Texas, X64.

EVOLUTION OF McKELLIGON CANYON MOUND GROWTH

The organic buildups of the McKelligon Canyon Formation are unique in that some of them show a particularly well-developed vertical biotic zonation that allows interpretation of the depositional sequence of mound growth, exposure, and eventual burial. The process appears to have taken place repeatedly during this time interval. I believe that at least six stages occurred during the depositional history of the Lower Ordovician organic buildups of West Texas. This is shown schematically in Figure 2-7.

Within a shallow-water subtidal zone, a pioneer colony was initiated on a foundational substrate of burrowed mud. This is regarded as Stage I (Figure 2-7) and is characterized by scattered clumps of rooted echinoderms, sponges, simple orthid brachiopods, and sparse trilobites. The pioneer colony perpetuated itself by clustering with similar surrounding assemblages. As a center of organic growth, the mound grew upward keeping pace with sedimentation. The pioneer colony evolved into a more biotically diverse community regarded as Stage II. During this interval, varied algae, more abundant sponges, orthid brachiopods, small turbinate gastropods, coiled and straight nautiloids, and trilobites enriched the community assemblage. Stage III appears to represent the development of the climax community in the growth history of the McKelligon Canyon organic buildups. This stage is characterized by the occurrence and rise to dominance of the laminated colonial growth *Pulchrilamina*.

During these first three stages, skeletal debris was concurrently shed within and around the buildup' and as the mound was growing, relief at any one time was not particularly great. In essence, these organic structures were rather low dome-shaped features.

Growing within the subtidal zone, the mounds were undoubtedly affected by sea level changes. A postulated drop in sea level, shown as Stage IV (Figure 2-7), would result in subaerial mound exposure that would immediately terminate upward mound growth. Surrounding skeletal debris was also exposed at this time. Continued subaerial exposure during Stage V, coupled with intertidal erosion of the mound surfaces, would result in the development of an anastomizing pattern of erosional channels. Stage VI is the culminating event in mound growth. This occurred with a postulated rise in sea level and resubmergence of the eroded organic buildup. Deposition of skeletal debris, primarily derived from eroded mound rock and from sediments immediately adjacent to the buildups, filled in the erosion-induced irregularities on and around the buildup. This sequence of events imparted to the organic buildups a characteristic "halo-like" effect composed of fairly well-sorted packstones and grainstones containing much skeletal debris and intraclasts.

Because the channel filling contains fossils identical to those found within the organic buildups, although much abraded and broken, and because such channeled buildups occur at more than one stratigraphic horizon, I assume that this entire sequence of events took place rapidly and repeatedly during this time interval. The biotic subdivisions seen on these Early Paleozoic organic buildups reflecting pioneer, mature, and climax communities probably are a simple series of organic responses to ecological requirements within increasingly shallower depositional environments of the subtidal-intertidal regime.

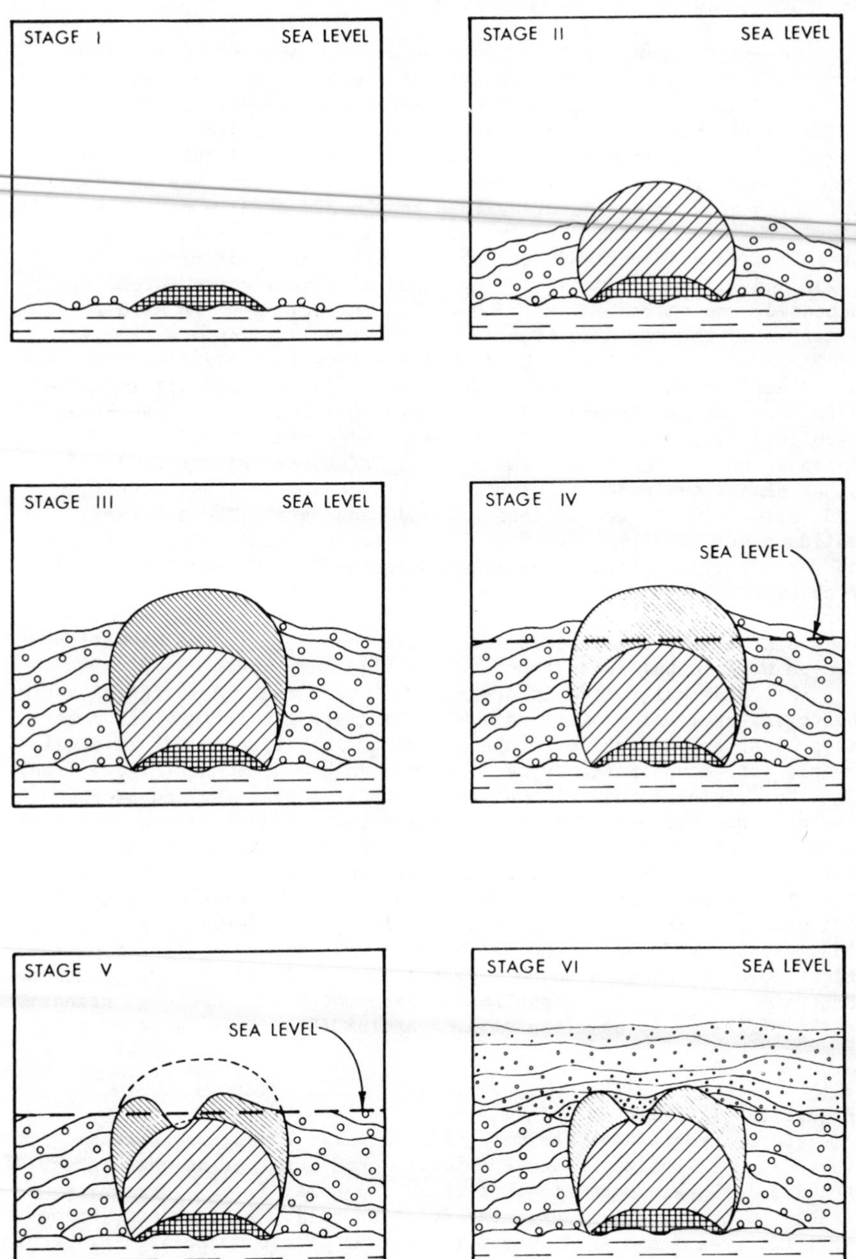

Figure 2-7
Diagramatic sequence of growth stages and burial of typical organic buildups of the McKelligon Canyon Formation.

OKLAHOMA LOWER ORDOVICIAN ORGANIC BUILDUPS

As noted above, similar Lower Ordovician organic buildups outcrop in both the Arbuckle Mountains of southern Oklahoma and the Wichita Mountains of southwestern Oklahoma (Figure 2-1). The organic buildups in these mountain ranges occur within two distinctive stratigraphic intervals within the lower 167 m of the Kindblade Formation (Toomey and Nitecki, 1979). The lower mound interval has an average thickness of 22 m and occurs within the lowermost 33 m of the formation. The organic buildups are usually less than 3 m in height and up to 5 m in diameter and are composed principally of stromatolitic algae and lithistid sponges. The mound rock is light colored, massive, unbedded, and characterized by high concentrations of *in situ* fossil organisms. The dominant organism is the lithistid sponge *Archaeoscyphia annulata* Cullison. Laminated stromatolitic algal colonies are abundant, and much included organic debris is entwined within stromatolitic swirls (Figure 2-8A). Other organisms include the receptaculitid alga *Calathium* and various *problematica*, especially the colonial encrusting forms *Renalcis* and *Epiphyton* (Figure 2-6D and G), other algae, echinoderms, orthid brachiopods, gastropods, straight and coiled nautiloids, trilobites, and conodonts. These organic buildups are usually encased in dark-colored, thin-bedded sediments of various types although pelletal mudstone is a common intermound rock type. The boundary of the buildup is a sharply defined line marking the contact between light colored, massive, unbedded mound rock and darker, thin-bedded, non-mound rock. As in the McKelligon Canyon organic buildups, there are no flanking beds.

Petrologically, the lower-interval mound rock is an intraclastic, burrowed, skeletal wackestone. When much stromatolitic algal material is present and indigenous skeletal debris is caught-up within algal swirls, the mound rock may be described as a boundstone (Figure 2-8A).

No erosional channels cut the surface of these buildups, and there is no evidence of subaerial exposure. In addition, no vertical biotic zonation is apparent. Accordingly, I think that these organic buildups developed entirely within the shallow-marine subtidal zone.

The upper-mound interval has an average thickness of 13 m and all mound occurrences begin at a stratigraphic interval approximately 133 m above the base of the Kindblade Formation. The mound rock is light colored, massive, unbedded, and distinguished by clustered concentrations of *in situ* organisms. These mounds are composed principally of the receptaculitid alga *Calathium* (Figure 2-8C), stromato-

Figure 2-8 (at right)
A. Photomicrograph of stromatolitic, algally bound, mound rock (boundstone) from the Kindblade lower-mound interval at the Highway 77 section, Arbuckle Mountains, southern Oklahoma, X2.4. Note white flecks of quartz grains delineating stromatolite laminae and various skeletal grains enmeshed within the stromatolitic material. B. Photomicrograph of channel rock (intraclastic skeletal grainstone) from the Kindblade upper-mound interval at the Unap Mountain section, Wichita Mountains, southwestern Oklahoma, X2.4. C. Photomicrograph of mound rock (burrowed skeletal wackestone) showing abundant remains of the double-walled receptaculitid alga *Calathium* from the Kindblade upper-mound interval at the Mill Creek section, Arbuckle Mountains, southern Oklahoma, X2.4.

litic algae, the lithistid sponge *Archaeoscyphia annulata* Cullison, and the lamellar colonial organism *Pulchrilamina spinosa* Toomey and Ham. The dominant biotic component is *Calathium*. Accessory organisms include algae and *problematica* (especially the encrusting and binding forms *Renalcis* and *Epiphyton*), bryozoans, pelmatozoans, orthid brachiopods, gastropods, chitons, cephalopods (both straight and coiled

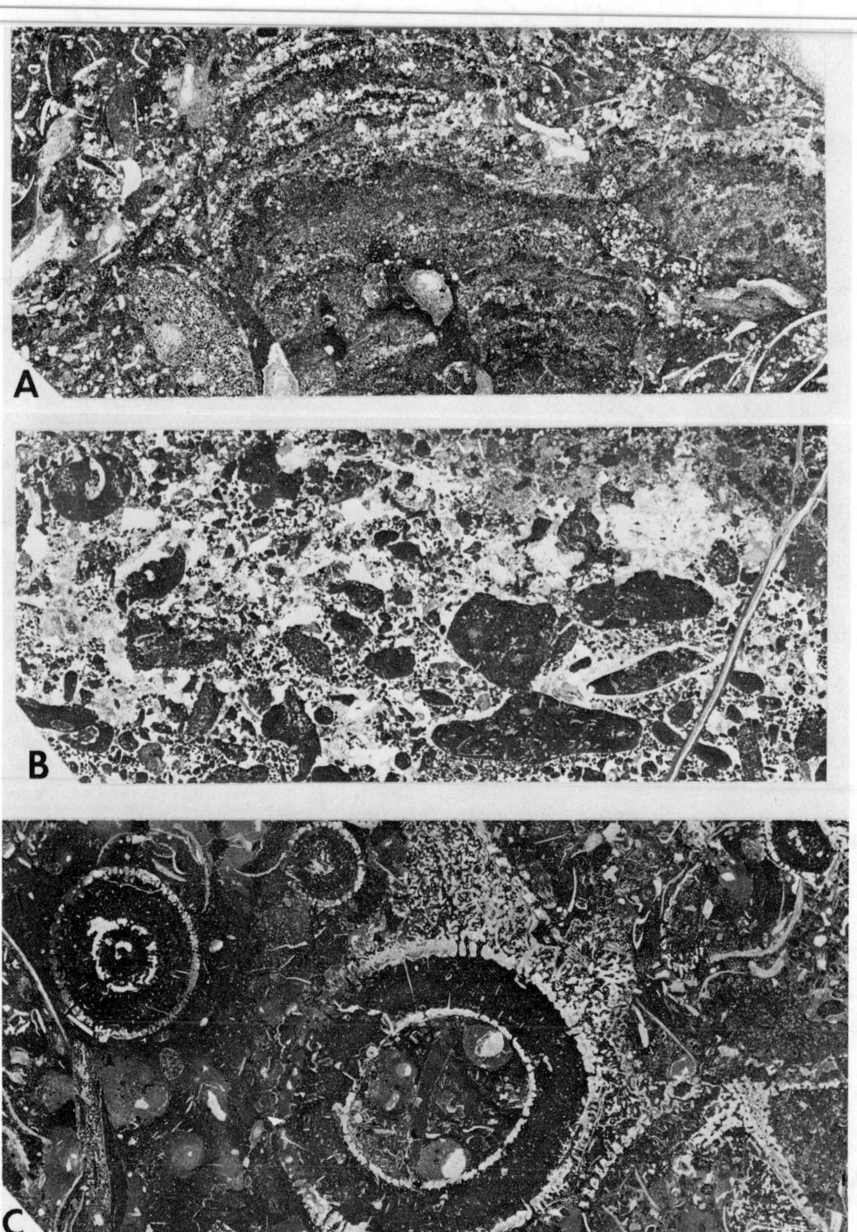

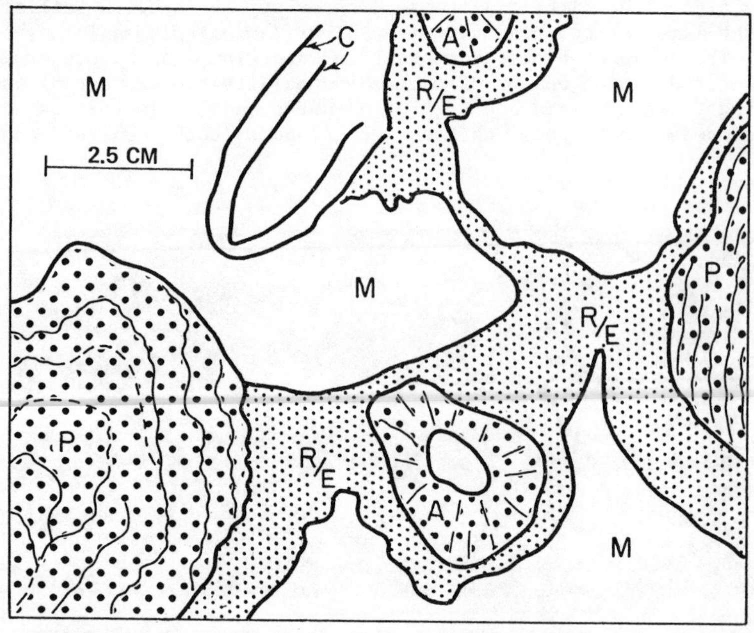

Figure 2-9
Overlay of a polished slab of mound rock from the Unap Mountain section, Wichita Mountains, southwestern Oklahoma. This diagram shows the relative amounts of the major mound-framework contributors and mud infilled areas. *Pulchrilamina* (P), *Archaeoscyphia* (A), and *Calathium* (C) denote major contributors: M = mud infill, R/E = appreciable *Renalcis-Epiphyton* contribution. Note the association of *Renalcis-Epiphyton* with the major framework contributors.

forms), trilobites, and conodonts. Individual buildups are less than 3 m in height with a diameter of up to 5 m although the largest Kindblade buildup occurs within this interval and measures 21 m in height and 58 m in length. The boundary between light colored, massive, unbedded mound rock and darker thin-bedded non-mound and intermound rock is abrupt and is conspicuous by the lack of mound-derived talus or flanking beds. The mound rock is a burrowed, intraclastic, skeletal wackestone. When much stromatolitic material and *Pulchrilamina* occur, either separately or with *Renalcis* and *Epiphyton* encrusting or binding other skeletal grains, the mound rock is a boundstone (Figure 2-9).

Erosional channels up to a meter in width separate many of the organic buildups present in the upper-mound interval, and the channels form a characteristic anastomozing pattern around the buildups. The channel rock is a packstone-grainstone made up of well-rounded intraclasts associated with broken and abraded, mound skeletal debris (Figure 2-8B).

No evidence of subaerial exposure or a vertical biotic zonation has been observed on these organic buildups, and it is thought that they grew in shallow, well-agitated subtidal water. At any one time, these structures stood no more than 1 to 3 m above the surrounding seafloor. In essence, I think they were low-relief domical features colonized by a clustered biota deominated by algae and sponges.

SUMMARY

On the basis of a detailed study of Lower Ordovician organic buildups outcropping in southern Oklahoma and West Texas, some generalizations can be made. Firstly, these Early Paleozoic organic structures are biotically relatively simple; that is, their organic assemblages are limited to a few characteristic biotic components. These are stromatolitic algae, lithistid sponges (principally *Archaeoscyphia annulata* Cullison) receptaculitid algae (*Calathium*), a colonial lamellar organism of probable coelenterate affinity (*Pulchrilamina spinosa* Toomey and Ham), and questionable algae and various *problematica* (*Girvanella*, *Nuia*, *Renalcis*, and *Epiphyton*). Accessory organisms are consistently made up of pelmatozoans, simple orthid brachiopods, various gastropods (mainly high-spired and turbinate types), straight and coiled nautiloids, trilobites, and simple distocodid conodonts. Vertical ecological zonation within an organic buildup occurs only on those buildups that appear to have grown upward into increasingly shallower depositional environments with resultant ecologic response to changing physical conditions. When this is carried to completion, as in the West Texas McKelligon Canyon organic buildups, we see the development of a distinctive organic climax community dominated by *Pulchrilamina*. Conversely, when the depositional setting of the mound interval remains only within the subtidal zone, there is no development of a vertical organic zonation, for example, the Kindblade organic buildups of southern and southwestern Oklahoma. However, we still find evidence of shallow-water depositional environments in the presence of erosional channels surrounding many of these organic buildups.

Secondly, most Lower Ordovician organic buildups are relatively small-scale features. At many localities, the average size is 2 to 3 m in height and from 3 to 5 m in diameter. Larger buildups do occur, but they are decidedly exceptional.

Thirdly, we can say that all Lower Ordovician mound rock is light colored, massive, unbedded, and contains significant concentrations of *in situ* organisms. Petrologically, mound rock is burrowed, intraclastic, skeletal wackestone. Where stromatolitic material or *Pulchrilamina* dominates, sediment is bound, and skeletal debris is entwined within algal laminations, the mound rock is a true boundstone. In contrast, the channel and intermound rock is generally dark-colored, thin-bedded, and varies from either intraclastic skeletal packstone-grainstone to burrowed mudstone.

Lastly, a feature that seems to be common to all Lower Ordovician organic buildups is the complete absence of flank and draping beds adjacent to the organic buildup. Even the occurrence of significant amounts of mound-shed debris at this contact is uncommon.

In general terms, the relative simplicity of Lower Ordovician organic buildups can be explained to some extent by the stage of development of the contributing mound biota. Precursors to the Lower Ordovician organic buildups can be traced from a beginning in the Lower Cambrian with the first true organic structures, the archaeocyathid buildups. These were biotically simple, small-scaled structures dominated by double-walled, goblet-shaped, sponge-like organisms associated, and to some extent bound and encrusted, with various *problematica* or algae such as *Renalcis* (Brasier, 1976), *Epiphyton*, and stromatolites (hill, 1972). Accessory organisms included primitive echinoderms, simple brachiopods, trilobites, hyolithids, and various *problematica*. The organic buildups formed by the archaeocyathid assemblages were vertically insignificant. Most archaeocyathid buildups only attained a height of a little more than 1 m and an average base diameter of approximately 12 m. In reality, these were biostromal units that reflect intensive lateral organic clustering, the obvious result of organisms possessing limited constructional and binding capability.

By the end of Lower Cambrian time, archaeocyathid buildups had disappeared, and this organic niche was not to be successfully exploited until Lower Ordovician time. At that point in earth history, lithistid sponges combined with stromatolitic algae and various *problematica* to again initiate organic mound growth. There is a total absence in the rock record of organism-dominated organic buildups anywhere in the world during the vast span of time from late Lower Cambrian to Lower Ordovician in spite of the fact that algal-constructed mounds existed and flourished in some regions, especially in Upper Cambrian time (Ahr, 1971; Chafetz, 1973).

UPPER PALEOZOIC PHYLLOID ALGAL BUILDUPS

PROLOGUE

We now move from the Lower Paleozoic of 500 million years ago to Upper Carboniferous time approximately 300 million years ago and two examples of Late Paleozoic organic buildups in which phylloid algae are the dominant, controlling biotic components. However, before we examine these two examples, I believe it is necessary to discuss phylloid algae and briefly describe their potential organic constructional capability.

The phylloid, or leafy, algae are represented in the southwestern United States by two forms commonly grouped under the calcareous green algae (Codiaceae); these are *Ivanovia* and *Eugonophyllum*. Carbonate rocks composed primarily of phylloid algal remains are widely distributed in the western United States in rocks of Pennsylvanian and Lower Permian ages (Wray, 1968, Text-figure 2). They also occur worldwide, and as Wray (1977:84) has noted, "may be the dominant skeletal constituents in mounds and other carbonate facies of Late Carboniferous and Early Permian age."

The growth habit of these plants is not precisely known, but there is some evidence that suggests that they grew as upright plants. The outer portion of the "leaves" were carbonate encrusted, and the plant probably consisted of a limited number of relatively broad "leaves." These "Leaves" could not have withstood a high degree of wave turbulance. Entire plants may have reached a height of 12 cm or more and probably grew in thickets or "gardens." A reconstruction of a phylloid algal community of late Paleozoic time (Toomey, 1976) is given in Figure 2-10. Still, the important point to keep in mind in attempting to reconstruct phylloid algal communities is their probable ability for rapid growth expansion and seabottom domination. As noted by Wray (1977:144-146), studies on Recent algal forms, such as *Rhipocephalus*, *Udotea*, and *Halimeda*, indicate that some forms have a rapid growth rate allowing them to produce up to nine crops per year and

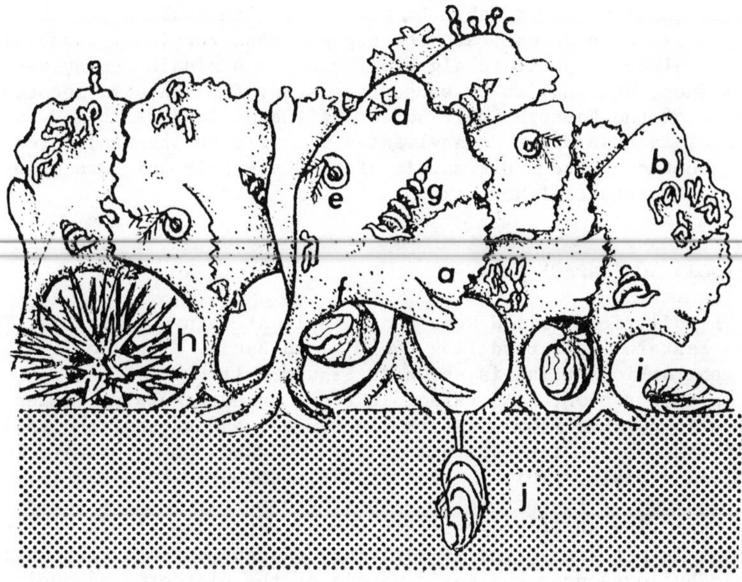

Figure 2-10
A reconstruction of the phylloid algal community based on a Lower Permian example from the Franklin Mountains of West Texas. The phylloid algae (a) dominate the seabottom. Encrusting organisms such as the foraminifers *Tolypammina* (b), *Tuberitina* (c), *Tetrataxis* (d), and the polychaete worm *Spirorbis* (e) cover the algal "leaves." The pedunculate brachiopod *Composita subtilita* (Hall) (f) attaches itself to the upright phylloid algae, thus placing itself in a more favorable feeding position, while various snails (g) and an echinoid (h) graze the algal meadow. A few pelecypods such as the epifaunal *Myalina* (i) and the infaunal *Bakevellia* (j) round out and balance this unique community.

yielding a corresponding mud contribution to the seabottom of 90 gm per square meter, a truly phenomenal growth rate and mud production capability. I believe that the Late Paleozoic phylloid algae also possessed a comparable reproductive capability that allowed them to form dense seabottom growths. Most importantly, these plants with their rapid growth rate and ability to create dense plant "gardens" were able to impose strict limitations on organic exploitation of available ecologic niches within the plant community. Accordingly, this tended to exclude many "normally expected" shallow-water organisms so that a unique plant-dominated community evolved. Thus, the phylloid algae possessed the capability to selectively mold the potential biotic composition of the community by favoring those organisms that could live on, live within, or live under the protective plant umbrella. The consequence is a unique, though monotonous, and relatively undiversified biotic assemblage of obligatory epiphytes and epizoans. Significantly, these plants possessed the capability of baffling and trapping suspended sediment. This, coupled with their rapid growth rate and seabottom domination, allowed them to construct organic buildups of appreciable dimensions, especially in areas where tectonic conditions were able to keep pace with buildup growth.

Two examples demonstrate the organic constructional capability of Paleozoic phylloid algae. These are a Middle Pennsylvanian (Des Moines, Westphalian-C) subsurface study from an area located on the edge of the Eastern Shelf bordering the Midland Basin and called Nena Lucia and an Upper Pennsylvanian (Virgil, Stephanian) outcrop study located on the shelf margin of the Late Paleozoic Oro Grande Basin in southcentral New Mexico.

NENA LUCIA SUBSURFACE STUDY

The oil field called Nena Lucia is located in northcentral Texas on the Eastern Shelf bordering the Midland Basin. The location and paleogeographic setting is shown in Figure 2-11.

In this region, Late Paleozoic rocks undergo complex facies changes in passing from platform limestones, sandstones, and shales on the Eastern Shelf to basinal shales and sandstones westward into the Midland Basin. This is schematically shown in Figure 2-12. This rock sequence is transgressive with progressively younger basinal sediments overlying shelf sediments in an eastward direction. Of especial interest is a series of north-striking, elongate-shaped, carbonate organic buildups near the basin margin of the platform and positioned in an *en echelon* trend as shown in the inset of Figure 2-12. These phylloid algal buildups are encased in dark-gray to black shales. Nena Lucia is one of these subsurface organic buildups located close to the northern limits of an interrupted chain that extends for approximately 200 km.

Nena Lucia produces from a porous phylloid algal buildup 30 m thick. The field has produced approximately thirty million barrels of petroleum. The shape of the field and the line of cross section

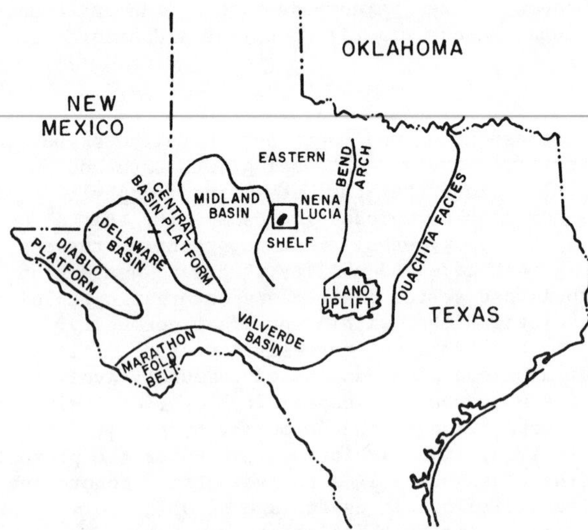

Figure 2-11
Index map showing location and paleogeographic setting of the Nena Lucia Field in Texas.

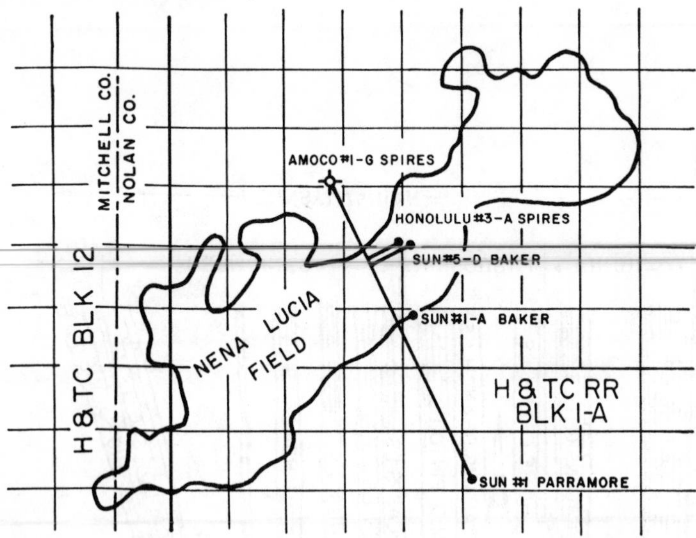

Figure 2-13
Configuration of the subsurface Nena Lucia Field and location of cored wells used in study, Nolan County, Texas.

from which five cores were studied in detail (Toomey and Winland, 1973) are shown in Figure 2-13. Dimensions of Nena Lucia are 18 km in length and up to 5 km in width. The cross section through the field showing identified facies is given in Figure 2-14. A number of litho-biofacies were recognized and plotted. The most significant facies from top to bottom, as shown in the cross section, are crinoidal, pelletal-foraminiferal, algal-plate, and algal-intraclastic. In addition, lagoon-type shales and shaly sandstones have been identified behind the organic buildup. Photomicrographs of some typical Nena Lucia facies are shown in Figure 2-15.

The microfacies associations and sequential patterns seen at Nena Lucia are commonly found in Late Paleozoic phylloid algal sequences. Most of the petroleum found in these sequences is from the phylloid algal facies where good porosity development is usually found with evidence to demonstrate that the growing organic buildup underwent subaerial exposure. Evidence of subaerial exposure usually manifests itself in irregular zones of red staining (iron oxide zones) and phylloid algal remains that show *in situ* collapse brecciation (Figure 2-15B). This brecciation is thought to represent a "drying out" of the algal-plate organic framework concurrently with subaerial exposure. Channels for porosity development were greatly enlarged during these times.

The phylloid algal facies is present in two of the studied wells (Figure 2-13) and appears as sinuous bands of "leaves" packed horizontally much like piles of debris. An example of this algal-plate stacking" is shown in a partially acid-etched specimen of silicified hylloid algae from the Lower Permian Hueco Formation of the Franklin untains, West Texas (Figure 2-16).

Of all the facies studied in Nena Lucia, the phylloid algal facies s the lowest taxonomic diversity of all. On the buildup, the phyl-id algae grew in such profusion and occupied and dominated the sea-

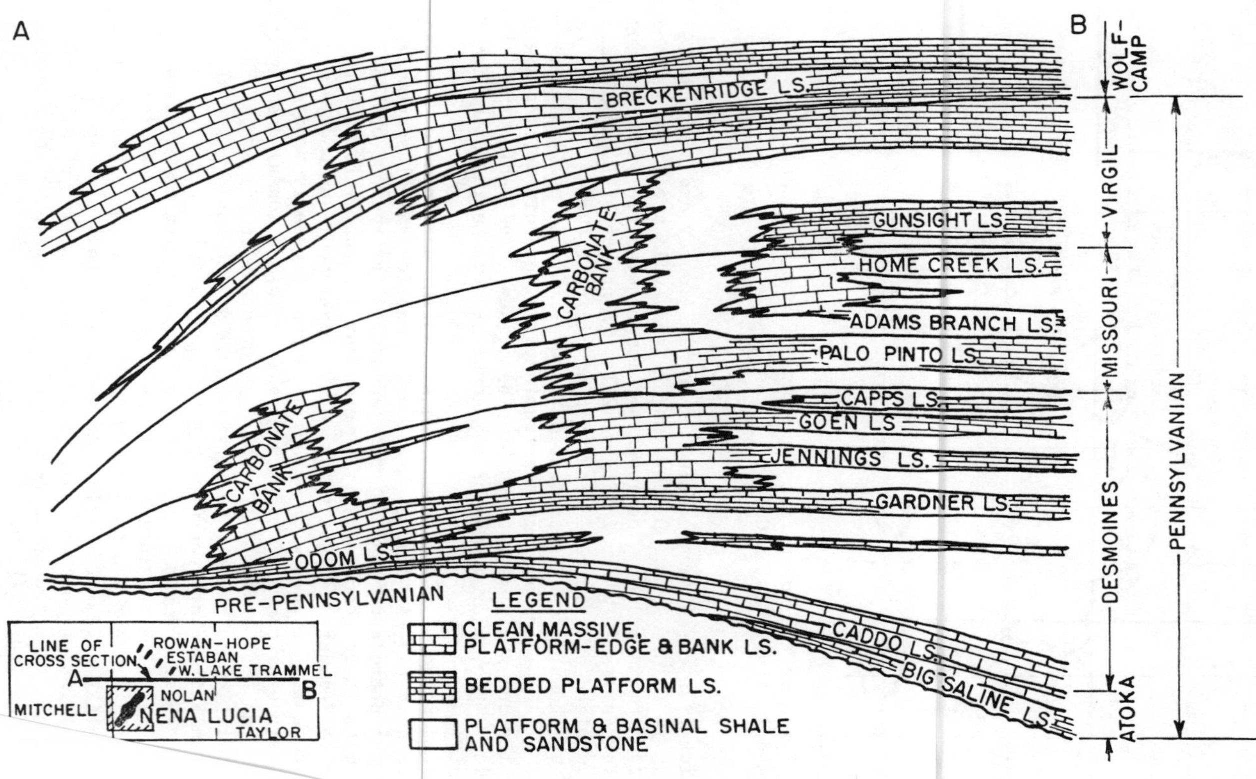

... Paleozoic sediments from the Eastern Shelf to the

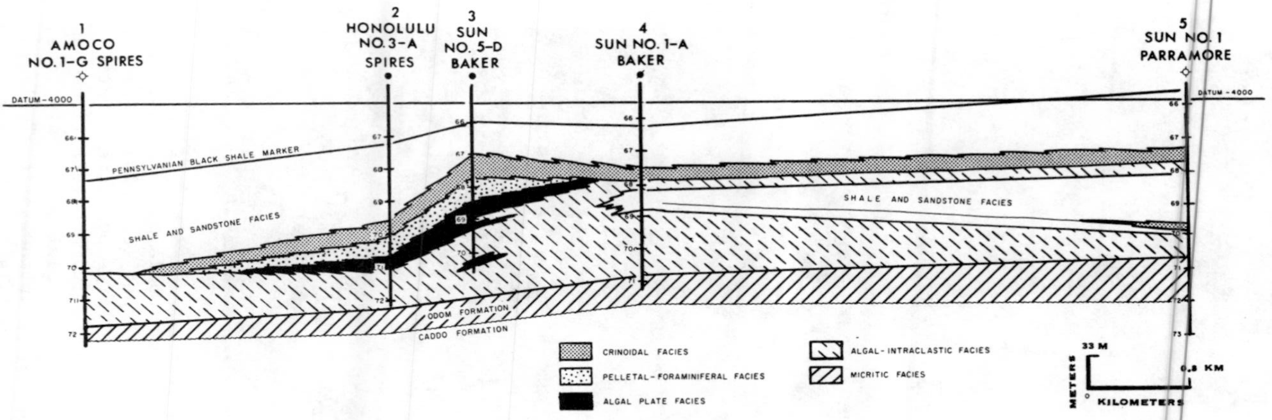

Figure 2-14
Northwest-southeast cross section across Nena Lucia Field showing delineated facies relations. Line of cross section is shown in Figure 2-13.

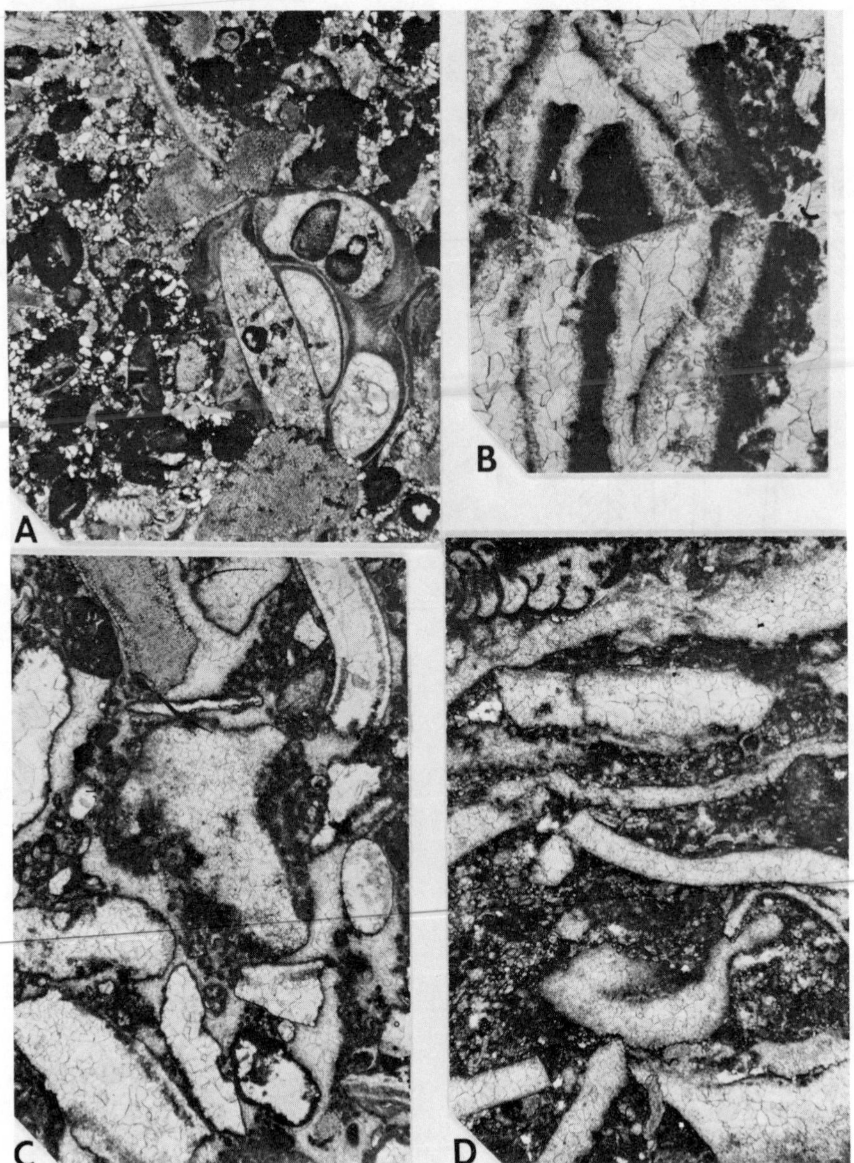

Figure 2-15
Thin-section photomicrographs of typical Nena Lucia microfacies, all X15.6. A. Silty-pelletoidal, crinoidal packstone (crinoidal facies), Honolulu No. 3A Spires, depth 2,323 m. Note large polychaete worm tube (*Spirorbis*) encrusting skeletal fragment. B. Recrystallized and broken algal plates due to *in situ* collapse brecciation (algal-plate facies), Sun No. 5D Baker, depth 2,288 m. C. Intraclastic algal-plate packstone with broken plates of *Eugonophyllum* (algal-intraclast facies), Sun No. 5D Baker, depth 2,335 m. D. Algal-plate packstone-wackestone (algal-plate facies), Sun No. 5D Baker, depth 2,297 m.

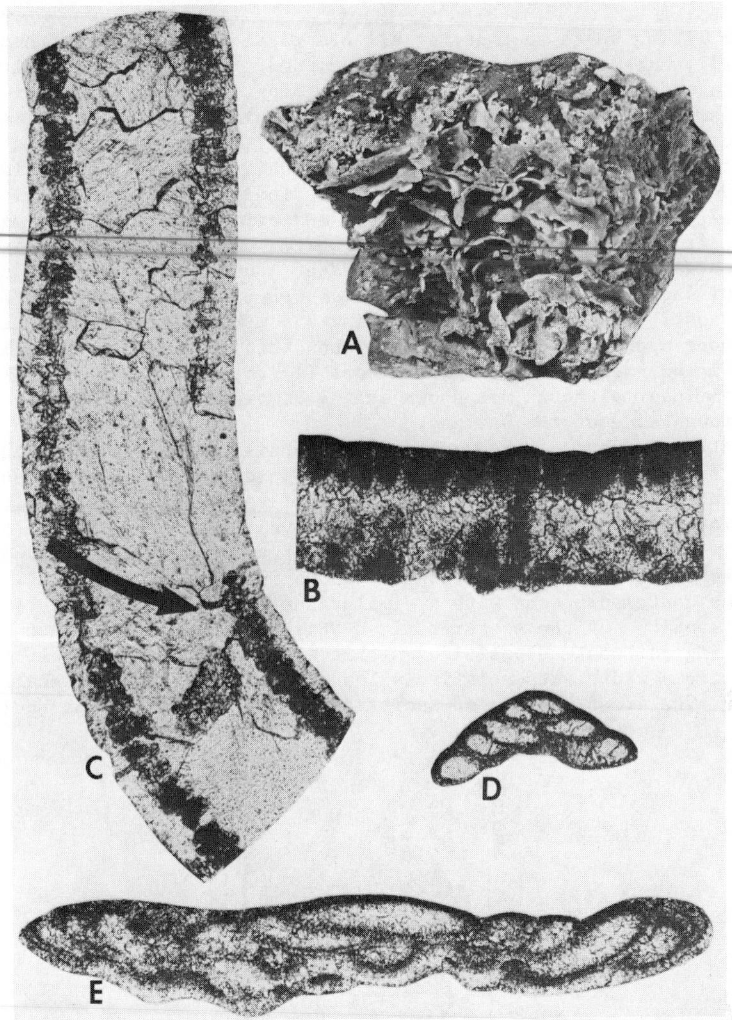

Figure 2-16
A. Partially acid-etched sample of silicified algal plates (*Eugonophyllum*) from the Lower Permian (Wolfcamp) Hueco Formation, northern Franklin Mountains, West Texas, showing a typical piled accumulation of algal "leaves," X.67. B. Thin-section photomicrograph of codiacean alga *Ivanovia* (note position of utricles along plate edge), algal-plate facies, Nena Lucia Field, Sun No. 1 Parramore, depth 2,259 m, X53.6. C. Thin-section photomicrograph of the codiacean alga *Eugonophyllum* (arrow points to characteristic utricles), algal-intraclast facies, Nena Lucia Field, Sun No. 5D Baker, depth 2,335 m, X53.6. D. Thin-section photomicrograph of calcareous, encrusting foraminifer *Tetrataxis*, pelletal-foraminiferal facies, Nena Lucia Field, Honolulu No. 3A Spires, depth 2,347 m, X53.6. E. Thin-section photomicrograph of a large *Tetrataxis* morphologically adapted for encrusting algal plates, algal-intraclast facies, Nena Lucia Field, Honolulu No. 3A Spires, depth 2,384 m, X53.6.

bottom living space so that for all practical purposes most other "normally expected" organisms were excluded. The only biotic elements able to offer what might be considered competition were epiphytic organisms. In this instance, the ecologic niche was filled primarily by encrusting types of foraminifers (Figure 2-16D and 2-16E) and encrusting bryozoans. The biota present in the phylloid algal facies is shown in Figure 2-17. Paleontological changes indicate that algal calcispheres, minor red algae, fusulinids, and crinoids are more common on the "ocean fronting" side of the buildup whereas minor blue-green algae, rugose corals, and brachiopods show greater abundance on the back side of the buildup. Phylloid algae (both *Eugonophyllum* and *Ivanovia*), Figure 2-16B and 2-16C, calcareous encrusting and mobile foraminifers, and bryozoans are present in comparable abundance throughout the buildup. In addition, agglutinated foraminifers (*Tolypammina*, *Ammovertella*, and *Hyperammina*), although not shown on the diagram, are restricted to the back-mound side of the buildup.

After formation, the phylloid algal buildup was buried by the silty crinoidal facies and later encased in deeper-water black shales and minor thin sandstones containing pyritized cephalopods.

The associated facies seen at Nena Lucia were deposited on a shallow-marine shelf that covered broad areas of central Texas. This shelf extended northward through Oklahoma into the Midcontinent region and was contemporaneous with a similar shelf or platform that covered large sections of the western United States. The main elements influencing carbonate deposition on this widespread shallow shelf were its extreme width, its relatively low regional dip, and its shallow water. The gross pattern of facies distribution in the Nena Lucia

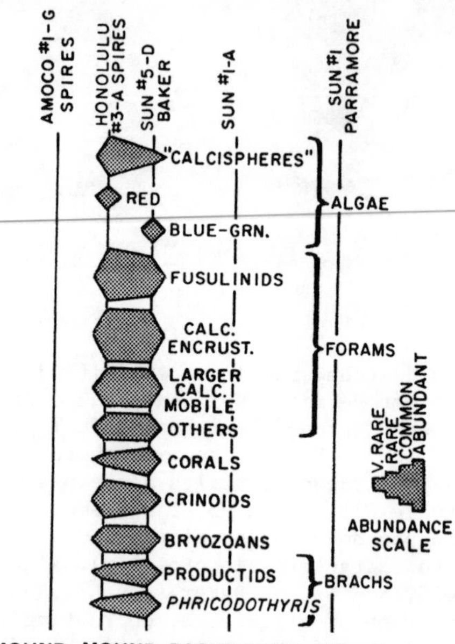

Figure 2-17
Distribution of significant fossils present in the phylloid algal facies, Nena Lucia Field, Nolan County, Texas.

Field suggest a decrease in hydraulic-energy levels from northwest to southeast from the relatively deep margin of the Midland Basin onto the shallower Eastern Shelf. All the facies present at Nena Lucia reflect shallow-water environments probably no deeper than 33 m. Lateral variation in one or more of the parameters affecting deposition or organic growth would produce unlike environments in which discrete sedimentologic and biotic patterns could develop in juxtaposition--in essence, facies. The present superposition of these facies is interpreted as a result of migration of environments through time. It should be noted that phylloid algal buildups commonly occur along basinal edges adjacent to shallow-marine platform areas; this is clearly shown in Wilson (1975:186).

YUCCA MOUND COMPLEX

Another example of a phylloid-algal, shelf-margin buildup is the Yucca Mound complex exposed in the Sacramento Mountains of south-central New Mexico (Figure 2-18). The age of this phylloid algal-mound complex is Late Pennsylvanian (Virgil-Stephanian) although it should be noted that phylloid algal buildups are also relatively common in younger rocks (Lower Permian) of many of the mountain ranges of the southwestern United States.

Outcrops of phylloid algal buildups in this area show relief of only 30 m or so, but locally, depositional slopes as much as 35° exist on the buildup margins. These organic buildups usually rim basins and appear to be intimately related to persistent cyclical sedimentation associated with and directly responsive to tectonic impulses of nearby active land masses (Wilson, 1969, 1977).

Examination of numerous Late Pennsylvanian phylloid algal buildups in the Sacramento Mountains shows that they are associated with two distinctive rock units repeated many times within the sequence. These are a series of massive unbedded lime-mud cores containing much phylloid algal material and a variety of thin-bedded intermound and flanking beds consisting of wackestones, packstones, and grainstones composed of the organic debris shed from mound crests into flanking positions surrounding the phylloid algal cores. Typical outcrop examples of phylloid algal buildups exposed in the Sacramento Mountains are shown in Figure 2-19.

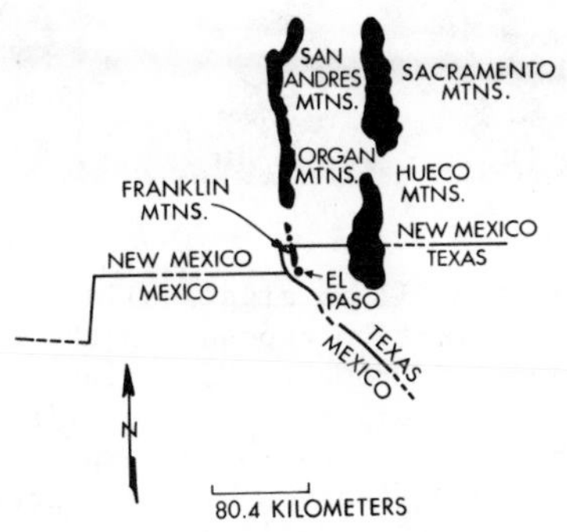

Figure 2-18
Index map showing location of Sacramento Mountains of New Mexico.

Figure 2-19
A. Outcrop photograph of phylloid algal buildups in the Late Pennsylvanian (Virgil) Holder Formation exposed on the western end of the north wall of Dry Canyon, Sacramento Mountains, southcentral New Mexico. Greatest vertical height of buildups is approximately 25 m. B. Outcrop photograph of the Yucca Mound complex looking in a southwestward direction toward Dry Canyon with the Lower Mound (LM), Flank Beds (FB), and Upper Mound (UM) delineated on the photograph.

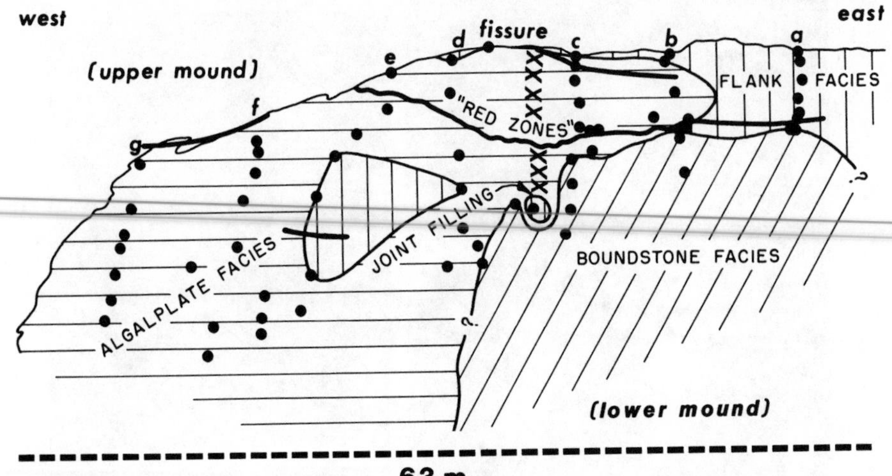

Figure 2-20
Yucca Mound complex showing facies distribution, extent of "red zones," and locations of measured sections (letters) with sample collection points (dots) indicated.

In a recent study, Toomey et al (1977) found that within the mound "cores" there are three recognizable growth stages for a so-called "simple" normal sequence. These are termed as follows:

1. Foundational phase, usually a lime mud with numerous clusters of rostrospiracid brachiopods (*Composita*), which on weathered outcrop looks deceivingly porous due to the concentrations of hollowed-out shell interiors.
2. A baffle-type constructional phase dominated by *in situ* accumulations of phylloid algae (*Eugonophyllum* and *Ivanovia*).
3. A climax boundstone phase in which encrusting plumose colonies of algae and foraminifers, associated with abundant dasyclad algae and algally bound molluscs, mark the termination of phylloid algal growth into extremely shallow water.

Detailed study of the Yucca Mound complex illustrates, to some extent, this particular sequence, and this is shown in Figure 2-20. On outcrop, we find that the oldest beds exposed in the complex are plumose masses of algal-foraminiferal boundstone. Accordingly, this is the climax boundstone phase, and this microfacies formed within wavebase on the crest of an earlier phylloid algal buildup. The crest of this older buildup was subaerially exposed while a thick accumulation of lime mud with abundant phylloid algae started forming against its western (seaward) flank. It should be emphasized that on this flanking position, in what is regarded as the initial mound growth stage, abundant clusters of brachiopods (*Composita*) are present, representing the mound foundational growth phase. As sea level rose and submerged the crest of the earlier buildup, the accumulation of phylloid algae, with its rapid growth rate, kept pace with sea level rise and onlapped the older mound in spite of a few brief interrup-

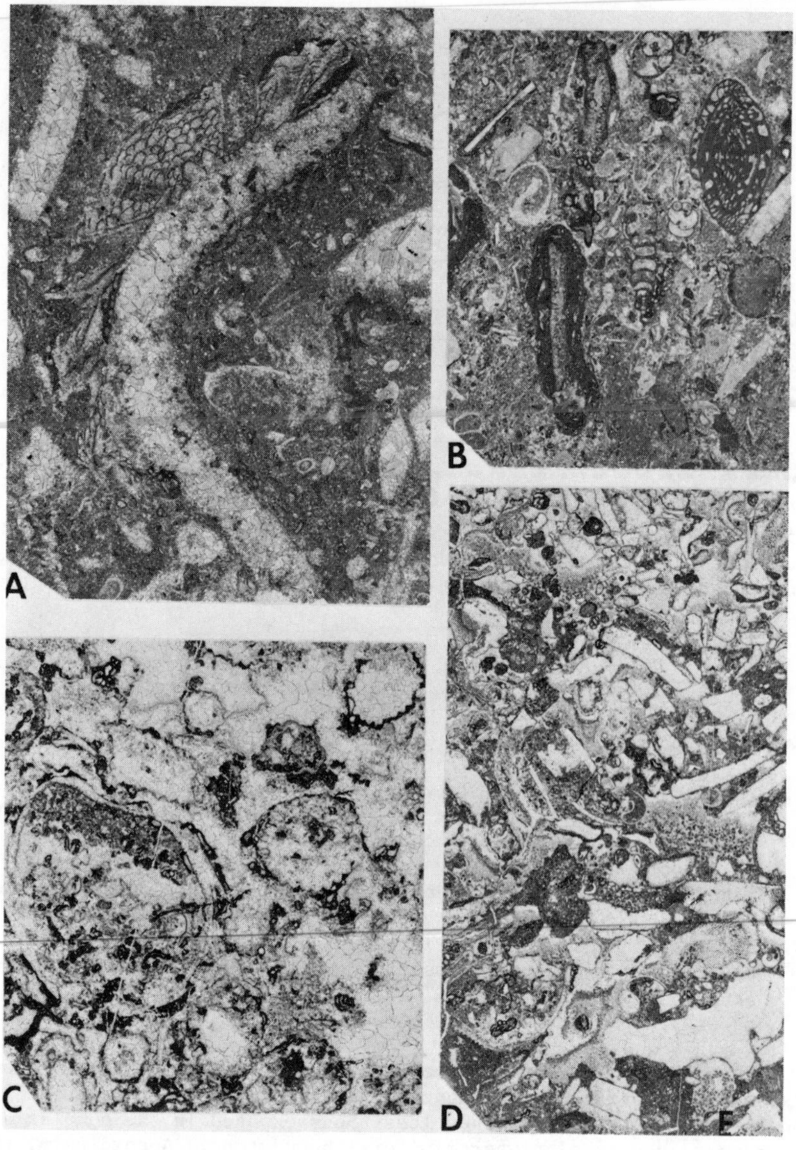

A B C D E

Figure 2-21
Thin-section photomicrographs of typical Yucca Mound microfacies. A. Recrystallized algal-plate wackestone with bryozoans and foraminifers encrusting algal plate, algal-plate facies, C-5, X15. B. Oncolitic-skeletal wackestone with conspicuous foraminifers and algally coated grains, flank facies, A-9, X6. C. Recrystallized algal-foraminifer boundstone with abundant dasyclad algae (*Macroporella*) and pelecypod fragment coated with dark-colored algal-foraminifer material, boundstone facies, B-10, X6. D. Intraclastic, skeletal packstone-wackestone from the flank facies, B-1, X6. Note abundance of broken skeletal debris derived from mound crest and swept into flank position.

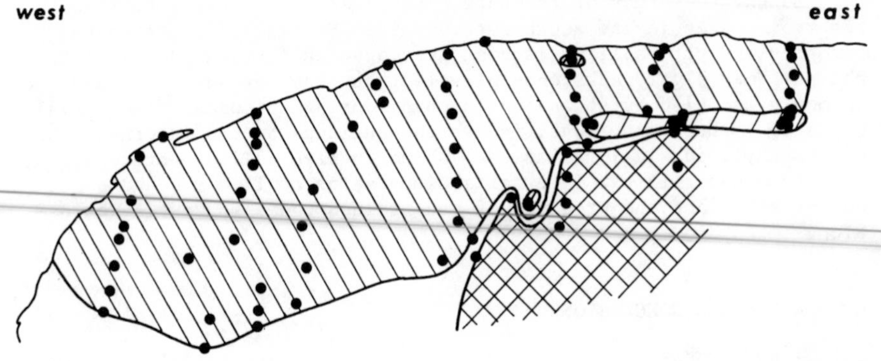

LEGEND

\\\\\\\\\\\\\\ PHYLLOID ALGA (C.F. IVANOVIA)

XXXXXX MACROPORELLA - PLUMOSE ALGAL - FORAMINIFERAL COLONIES

/////// "COATED - GRAINS," GIRVANELLA, EPIMASTOPORA

Figure 2-22
Distribution of algal components as seen in the Yucca Mound complex.

tions. When the phylloid algal community built into wave base and attained its climax stage of evolution, a typical shallow-water microfacies developed. This characteristic rock type, preserved on the rounded mound crest, contains abundant encrusting and mobile foraminifers, fish remains, and conodonts. Concurrently, a bedded flank facies composed of broken and abraded phylloid-algal plates, concentrated remains of foraminifers, fish remains, and conodonts was being formed on the shelfward side of the complex. Abundant, algally coated grains (oncolites) also characterize the flank facies. Figure 2-21 shows some of the distinctive microfacies seen on the Yucca Mound complex, and Figure 2-22 shows the distribution of distinctive algal components on the complex.

When sea level dropped, Yucca Mound complex growth ceased, and smaller boundstone accumulations were formed down the offshore flank of the main mound complex.

Detailed measurements of sections and tracing and mapping of key beds in this region indicate that mound cores and their related flanking beds are a progression of offlapping growth stages down the western flank of the La Luz Anticline, one of a series of north-trending anticlines that may be traced along the front of the Sacramento Mountains. This is significant because it shows the influence of an actively growing tectonic structure on the genesis of organic buildups and the direction of submarine slope during Virgil time. Thus, during the process of seaward growth off the La Luz Anticline, a northward-trending organic complex approximately 4.8 km long from southeast to northwest was constructed. When supplemented by subsequent strong uplifting of the La Luz Anticline to the east, this organic-built platform formed a broad shoal area that had a direct bearing on the later cyclic sedimentation in the area.

Subsurface study of the Late Pennsylvanian and Early Permian reservoir rocks in the southwestern United States indicates that porosity and permeability is best developed in fabrics identical to the phylloid algal packstones prevalent on these organic buildups and commonly modified by secondary leaching during episodes of subaerial exposure. These are identified on the buildups by the internal fabric of the phylloid algal facies that shows *in situ* collapse brecciation, calcite druse filling, internal sedimentation of lime mud and some quartz silt, and the presence of red-stained zones suggesting oxidation.

COMPARISON AND CONCLUSIONS

I have briefly examined representative organic buildups of two widely separated Paleozoic time periods: the Lower Ordovician of 500 million years ago and the Late Carboniferous of approximately 300 million years ago. We noted that the organic constructional capability of these two time-separated examples is decidedly different but that in some instances both examples show vertical organic zonations controlled primarily by differing physical events within contrasting paleoenvironmental settings.

In the Lower Ordovician, organic buildups are of very limited size mainly because of the limited constructional capability of the primitive algae-*problematica* and sponges. The paleoenvironmental setting for these Early Paleozoic organic buildups is on the margin of the craton where depositional environments range the shallow-water regime of the subtidal and intertidal zones. However, in some instances (such as the McKelligon Canyon Formation buildups of West Texas), I was able to delineate a rather simple vertical progression of organic zonation reflecting an evolution of pioneer to mature to climax biotic communities. This organic zonation appears to have developed in response to changing organic requirements within increasingly shallower depositional paleoenvironments. Most importantly, I see good evidence this early in geological time of definitive animal-plant clustering coupled with sediment-organism binding to form distinctive organic structures, a significant event that had basically remained dormant since the end of Lower Cambrian time.

In the Upper Paleozoic examples, I examined somewhat larger, more widespread, distinctive organic buildups constructed primarily through the baffling and trapping action of erect phylloid algae. These plant-controlled communities, with their rapid reproductive growth cycles and their ability to dominate the seafloor, appear to have most successfully developed on shelf margins adjacent to basinal areas. These shelf-margin organic buildups are apt to be best developed in those areas undergoing concurrent spasmodic tectonic activity associated with cratonic fragmentation. Again, I recognized a vertical biotic zonation that also appears to reflect organic response to increasingly shallow-water depositional environments. Subaerial exposure appears to be a common phenomenon associated with the evolution of these phylloid algal buildups and definitely assisted in developing potential porosity that aided in creating future significant petroleum reservoirs in these structures.

The changes we see in the biotic composition that we have discussed in the above examples are only one small portion of the overall evolution of organic-buildup communities that has taken place for more than one billion years (Newell, 1972). This is schematically shown in Figure 2-23.

One point that needs to be emphasized, and one that is clearly shown on this diagram, is that the long evolutionary development of organic buildups has not been a continuous episode throughout earth history. Instead, there are periods of geologic time in which no representative organic-buildup community existed anywhere on our planet. It appears that there have been favorable geologic-time spans in which certain areas were able to develop particular organic groups that constructed significant buildups, that is archaeocyathids in the Lower Cambrian and rudistids in the Cretaceous. In most cases, the time span was finite and then, for some cryptic reason(s), the buildup community became extinct or retreated into insignificance. This process has occurred a number of times since the Precambrian. In some examples, the changes in dominance of a specific organism within a buildup association has been coupled with increased biotic capability lending itself to the construction of massive and biotically mature structures, for example the change from rather simple algal-sponge buildups in the Lower Ordovician to the more complex coral-stromotoporoid-bryozoan-sponge buildups of the Middle Ordovician (Pitcher, 1964). Although there have been significant exceptions to this general progression, in particular the extinction of abundant large-scale Devonian coral-stromotoporoid buildups in Late Devonian time and the total absence of comparable organic buildups for a long period of time until the appearance on a worldwide scale of the enigmatic Lower Carboniferous mud mounds--structures of a very different and limited constructional capability. The geologic-time span necessary to recoup the organic constructional capability, so well developed in the Devonian, did not reappear until at least Middle Triassic time and, then, not on a comparable scale.

However, the time span from the Late Carboniferous to Middle Triassic is marked by a series of attempts at dominance by various organisms such as the small buildups constructed by red phylloid algae in the Lower Pennsylvanian and problematical chaetitids in the Middle Pennsylvanian to the somewhat larger buildups of codiacean phylloid algae from the Upper Pennsylvanian through the Lower Permian culminating in the more substantial reef-like structures of the Middle and Late Permian dominated by various algae, calcareous sponges, encrusting bryozoans, and attached brachiopods. This "trial and error" buildup community evolvement was made possible by the demise of the stromotoporoids and the continued decline and final extinction of the rugose and tabulate corals with resultant opportunistic organisms, in particular the calcareous and siliceous sponges, moving into weakly held or recently vacated buildup niches. From the Middle Triassic, with the advent of the scleractinian corals, the corals began a slow ascendance towards ultimate organic-buildup dominance. Coral ascendance was interrupted to some extent during the Jurassic by the deep-water lithistid sponge buildups of central Europe and during the Cretaceous by the rudistids, which largely supplanted the corals for approximately sixty million years. It was not until the close of the Paleocene Epoch, ten million years after the extinction of the rudistids, that the scleractinian corals and lithothammnid-coralline algae (a group that appeared during the Cretaceous) formed dominant organic buildups. During late Eocene through Oligocene time, there was a continued increase of climatic seasonality with resultant lowering of mean temperature in all the ocean basins (Newell, 1972:65).

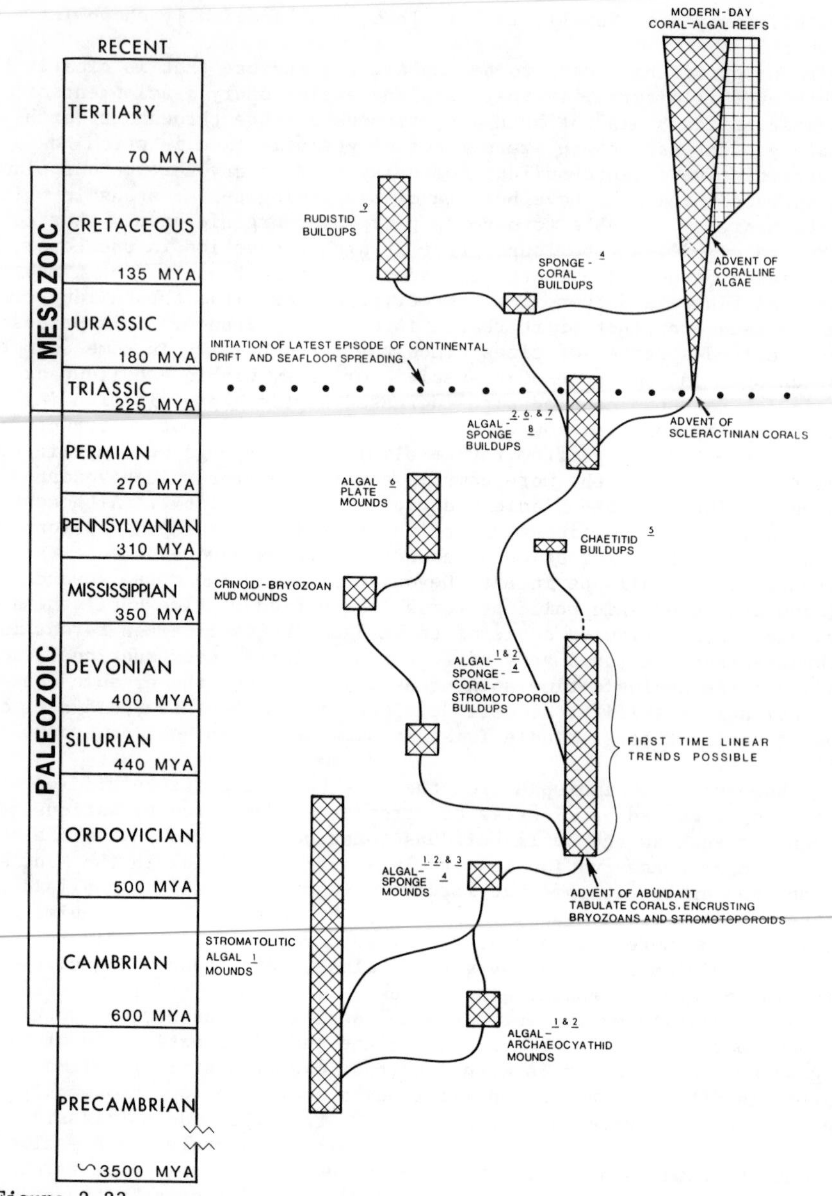

Figure 2-23
Schematic diagram showing postulated evolution of organic buildups through geologic time and indicating dominance of certain organic groups during this progression. Various biotic components are organic-sedimentary structures formed by the trapping and binding action of blue-green algae (1), blue-green and red? algae and *problematica* (2), receptaculitid algae (3), siliceous lithistid sponges (4), chaetitids (organisms of uncertain affinity) (5), phylloid algae (green) (6), dasyclad algae (green) (7), calcareous sponges (sphinctozoans) (8), and aberrant molluscs (pelecypods) (9).

Still, organic buildups dominated by scleractinian corals and coralline algae built extensive massive structures in the Caribbean, in southern Europe, and in southeast Asia. Continued seafloor spreading, reactivated as early as Middle and Late Triassic time and associated with deepening of the major ocean basins, effectively contributed to isolating an earlier pantropical organic-buildup community into two distinctive enclaves: an Indo-Pacific region and an Atlantic region. This is the present situation we find today that defines the reef-building community to a global distribution generally S35°N and N32°S.

The evolution of the organic-buildup community has been a long process in which various organic groups have risen to predominance only to be supplanted by other organic groups seemingly more adaptive to a unique set of physical conditions imposed by the environment, paleogeography, and tectonic setting.

ACKNOWLEDGMENTS

It is with pleasure that I acknowledge the help given to me in the field by a number of individuals. Foremost of these is the late Dr. William E. Ham of the Oklahoma Geological Survey who spent much time with me examining numerous Lower Ordovician outcrops in the Arbuckle and Wichita mountains of southern Oklahoma and who gave most generously of his great knowledge of Oklahoma geology. I was most privileged to work with Dr. Richard Rezak of Texas A&M University under the leadership of Dr. James Lee Wilson of Rice University on the Yucca Mound complex as an integral part of a larger study concentrating on Late Paleozoic cyclic sedimentation in the Sacramento Mountains of southcentral New Mexico. Dr. Dale H. Winland of the Amoco Research Laboratory, Tulsa, Oklahoma, worked long and most capably with me on the subsurface study of the Nena Lucia buildup. To all of the above, I am most grateful. I am also grateful to Alisanne Toomey for assistance in preparing the illustrations.

REFERENCES

Ahr, W. M. 1971. Paleoenvironment, algal structures, and fossil algae in the Upper Cambrian of central Texas. *Jour. Sed. Petrology,* 41:205-216.

Brasier, M. D. 1976. Early Cambrian intergrowths of archaeocyathids, *Renalcis*, and pseudostromatolites from South Australia. *Palaeontology*, 19:223-245.

Chafetz, H. S. 1973. Morphological evolution of Cambrian algal mounds in response to a change in depositional environment. *Jour. Sed. Petrology*, 43:435-446.

Cloud, P. E., Jr., and V. E. Barnes. 1948. The Ellenburger Group of central Texas. *Texas Univ. Bur. Econ. Geology Publ.*, 4621, 473 p.

Hill, D. 1972. Archaeocyatha, in Moore, R. C., ed., *Treatise on Invertebrate Paleontology*. Lawrence, Kansas: Univ. Kansas Press and Geol. Soc. America, 158 p.

Newell, N. D. 1972. The evolution of reefs. *Sci. American*, 226:54-65.

Pitcher, M. 1964. Evolution of Chazyan (Ordovician) reefs of eastern United States and Canada. *Canadian Petrol. Geol. Bull.*, 12:632-691.

Toomey, D. F. 1970. An unhurried look at a Lower Ordovician mound horizon, southern Franklin Mountains, West Texas. *Jour. Sed. Petrology*, 40:1318-1334.

Toomey, D. F. 1976. Paleosynecology of a Permian plant dominated marine community. *N. Jb. Palaont. Abh.*, 152:1-18.

Toomey, D. F., and W. E. Ham. 1967. *Pulchrilamina*, a new mound-building organism from Lower Ordovician rocks of West Texas and southern Oklahoma. *Jour. Paleontology*, 41:981-987.

Toomey, D. F., and M. H. Nitecki. 1979. Organic buildups in the Lower Ordovician (Canadian) of Texas and Oklahoma. *Chicago Field Mus. Nat. Hist. Publ.* 1299, 181 p.

Toomey, D. F., and H. D. Winland. 1973. Rock and biotic facies associated with Middle Pennsylvanian (Desmoinesian) algal buildup, Nena Lucia Field, Nolan County, Texas. *Am. Assoc. Petroleum Geologists Bull.*, 57:1053-1074.

Toomey, D. F., J. L. Wilson, and R. Rezak. 1977. Evolution of Yucca Mound complex, Late Pennsylvanian phylloid algal buildup, Sacramento Mountains, New Mexico. *Am. Assoc. Petroleum Geologists Bull.*, 61:2115-2133.

Wilson, J. L. 1969. Cycles of Late Pennsylvanian beds of the Sacramento Mountains, Otero County, New Mexico, in Elam, J. G., and S. Chuber, eds., *Cyclic Sedimentation in the Permian Basin, A Symposium*. West Texas Geol. Soc. Publ. 69-56:100-114.

Wilson, J. L. 1975. *Carbonate Facies in Geologic History*. New York: Springer-Verlag, 471 p.

Wilson, J. L. 1977. Regional distribution of phylloid algal mounds in Late Pennsylvanian and Wolfcamp strata of southern New Mexico, in Butler, J., ed., *Geology of the Sacramento Mountains, Otero County, New Mexico, Fieldtrip Guidebook*. West Texas Geol. Soc. Publ. 77-68:1-7.

Wray, J. L. 1968. Late Paleozoic phylloid algal limestones in the United States. *23rd Internat. Geol. Congress Proc.*, Prague, 8:113-119.

Wray, J. L. 1977. *Calcareous Algae*. Amsterdam: Elsevier Scientific Publishing Co., 185 p.

3

Lower Paleozoic Clastic, Level-Bottom Community Organization and Evolution Based on Caradoc and Ludlow Comparisons

J. M. Hurst and R. Watkins

Upper Caradoc and Ludlow sediments are very similar and are directly analogous and genetically related to some modern shelf sediments. Upper Caradoc sediments represent a transgression from proximal to distal shelf environments, whilst Ludlow sediments record a regression from distal to proximal shelf environments.

Along the Caradoc and Ludlow environmental gradients faunal associations in three facies, Sands and Silts, Bioturbated Silts, and Bioturbated Mud are similar in diversity, density, relative abundance patterns and morphologic expression of the constituent species. Similar species morphologies are repetitively produced in comparable environments, during evolutionary diversitication of various stocks. Nearshore communities in the Sands and Silts Facies are numerically dominated by large pedically attached enteletacean and free-lying concavo-convex strophomenid brachiopods. The Bioturbated Silts Facies are characterized by diverse and numerous strophomenid brachiopods and bryozoan faunas. The offshore Bioturbated Mud Facies are numerically dominated by small suspension-feeding brachiopods but characterized by deposit-feeding paleotaxodont bivalves.

Substrate and sedimentation processes were important facets of the physical environment determining community organization. In both the Caradoc and Ludlow species diversity increases into more distal shelf environments. As far as can be ascertained from sedimentary information, this correlates with decreasing environmentally related stress. Diversity decreases occur in offshore environments in the vacinity of the Laminated Shale Facies. Generally, the trilobite contribution to diversity in the Caradoc appears to have been taken over by bivalves in the Ludlow.

The faunal diversity of the Caradoc Bioturbated Mud Facies is significantly lower than in the Ludlow, and is tentatively attributed to the Ordovician to Silurian brachiopod adaptive radiations. Community evolution in terms of morphologic turn-over rate appears to affect offshore communities most. A low rate of generic continuity exists between Caradoc and Ludlow communities.

INTRODUCTION

The purpose of our study was to investigate and interpret common organizational patterns in upper Caradoc (Ordovician) and Ludlow (Silurian) faunal communities. In this report we cast the overwhelming amount of Caradoc and Ludlow data collected by us into a number of models that should be tested and subsequently modified or rejected by reference to other parts of the Paleozoic stratigraphic column.

The basis of this current work is twofold. First, a report on the ecology and sedimentology of the Ludlow shelf deposits in Wales and the Welsh Borderland (Figure 3-1) has recently been published by Watkins (1979). Second, the ecology and sedimentology of type Caradoc sediments of the Welsh Borderland (Figure 3-1) have been investigated by Hurst (1979a,b,c). The work in both the Caradoc and Ludlow was intimately coordinated and much of it was completed together; consequently, although Watkins concentrated on the Ludlow his understanding of Caradoc environments is equal to Hurst's and visa versa. The obvious advantages of such a situation are that we fully appreciate the extent and limitations of our comparisons and are fully familiar with the successions under discussion.

Two points must be mentioned here. First, there was a long period of time between the Caradoc and the Ludlow. During this period, many faunal turnovers may have occurred. Certainly, at least one major faunal reorganization took place in the Ashgill (Late Ordovician) due to glaciation (Sheehan, 1975). Consequently, an apparently simple directly comparable, community-structure pattern between the Caradoc and the Ludlow may actually be an artifact of limited stratigraphic sampling. Second, areas covered by this study are limited geographically, and were in the past. Thus, the applicability of the developed models can only be determined by extensive testing in other geographic provinces and for different times.

METHODS

Many of the methods used in this study have been outlined in detail elsewhere (Hurst and Hewitt, 1977; Hurst, 1979a,b,c; Watkins, 1979) and require only limited mention here.

STRATIGRAPHIC SECTIONS

Figure 3-1 shows the geographic setting of the type Caradoc and Ludlow rocks in the Welsh Borderland where stratigraphic sections were measured. Because of limited outcrop, sections were combined to obtain a composite record of succession.

FAUNAL SAMPLING

In each section, bulk rock and not individual fossils was collected. Generally, samples were taken as near as possible to 1 m apart stratigraphically although closer sampling grids were occasionally used in obviously complicated situations (Hurst and Hewitt, 1977; Hurst, 1979a,b; Watkins, 1979). Such sampling techniques did

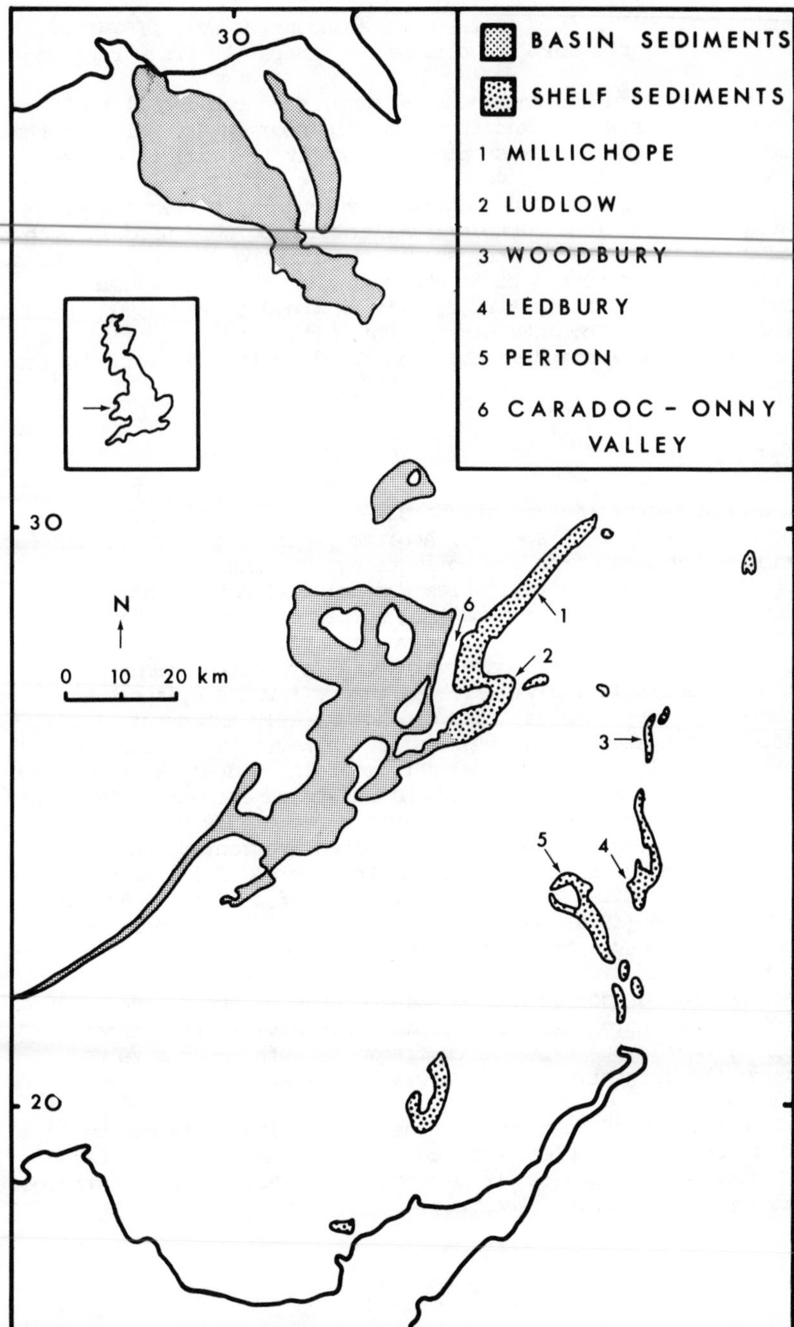

Figure 3-1
Ludlow sediment outcrop of Wales and the Welsh Borderland, showing the location of study areas including the Caradoc.

not bias the collections in favor of abundant or well preserved fossils and ore probably the nearest we can get to truly representative samples.

The stratigraphic thickness of samples ranged from 1 to 20 cm, and many samples were taken from a single sedimentary unit. In the laboratory, all bulk-rock samples were split to small chip size, and all observed macrofossils were counted.

Such methods produced quantitative faunal profiles for each stratigraphic section. Further, similar methods were used in both Caradoc and Ludlow sediments, so the results are directly comparable. All collections referred to in the text and tables have been deposited along with locality details in the British Museum (Natural History, London). Complete data on which this study is based are deposited in the British Museum, and supplementary data can be found in Hurst (1979a,b,c) and Watkins (1979).

QUANTIFICATION

Sample comparison and standardization are based on relative abundance of component species. Arbitrary criteria were defined for scoring individuals from the collections. The number of individuals of brachiopod and bivalve species was calculated by adding the articulated shells with the maximum number of either pedicle or brachial valves (right or left valves for bivalves) plus half the number of single indeterminate valves. A cephalopod fragment was counted as a single individual; as two or fewer specimens were encounted in most samples, this did not greatly exaggerate their abundance. Isolated septal impressions, however, were counted together as only one individual. Bryozoan individuals were defined as the number of separate pieces. Globular and encrusting bryozoans are more often than not preserved intact, so "individuals" are direct counts of colonies. Ramose forms are often fragmented, so their relative abundance is an artifact of the degree of fragmentation. Ecdysis of trilobites represented somewhat of a problem. In the Ludlow, Watkins (1979) took the number of pygidia as representing individuals. Because trilobites are sufficiently rare, he concluded that this method did not exaggerate their abundance. However, such a method in the Caradoc is not tenable because of the common occurrence of trilobites. Hurst (1979a,b) arbitrarily divided the largest number of homologous exoskeleton fragments into rough size classes; the largest number in a class indicating the species abundance.

The purpose of such methods was to establish consistency in quantification of samples. With consistent quantification, Caradoc and Ludlow collections can be directly compared. Except for trilobite abundances, taxa equate precisely.

STRATIGRAPHY

CARADOC STRATIGRAPHY

Figure 3-2 shows the classification of stratigraphic units present in Caradoc measured sections. Bancroft (1933) errected a

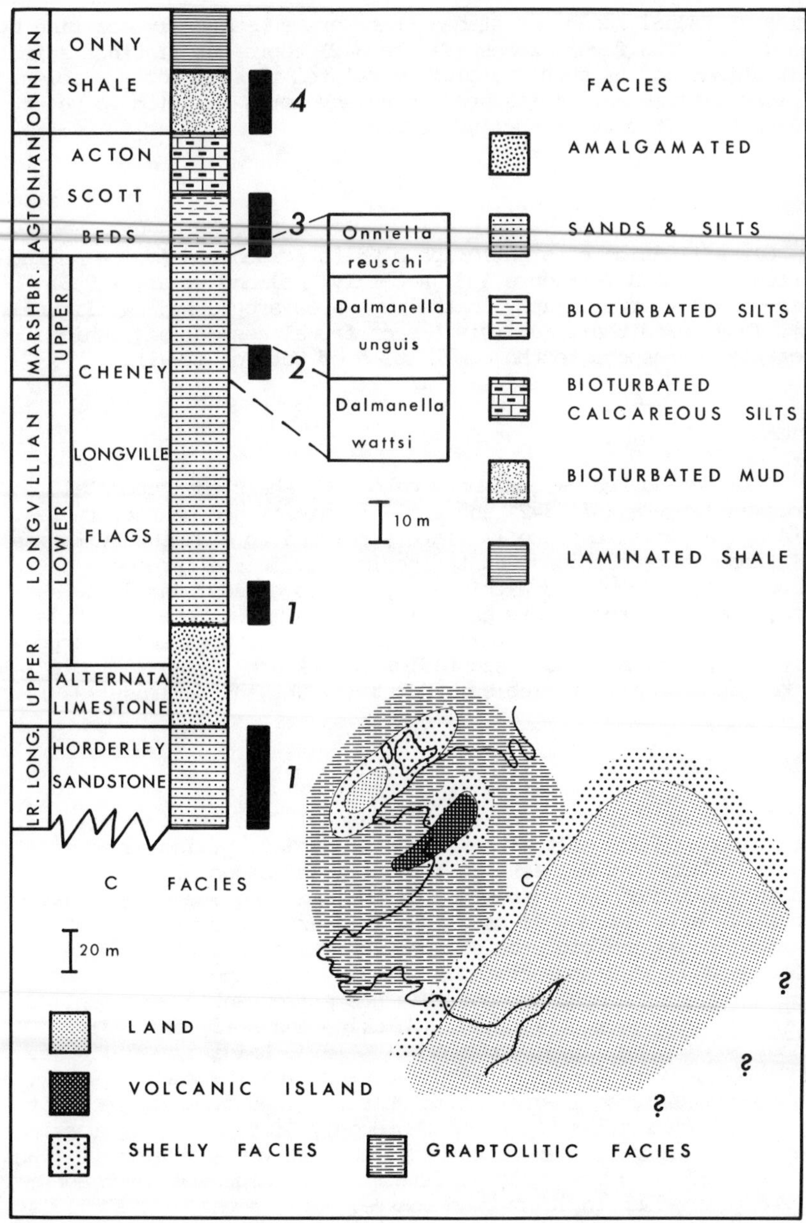

Figure 3-2
Caradoc paleogeography (from Williams, 1969) and stratigraphy and facies of the upper Caradoc rocks (C). The small column indicates the faunal zones of the upper Cheney Longville Flags. The numbered black column indicates the stratigraphic range of the facies that correlate with the Ludlow Whitcliffe Beds (1), Lower Leintwardine Beds (2), Lower Bringewood Beds (3), and Elton Beds (4). Caradoc stratigraphy is being revised by Hurst (1979c).

series of faunal zones and stages that were subsequently modified by Dean (1958). The faunal zones (Figure 3-2) represent distinct animal associations and as such are closely related to sedimentary facies. The fossil zones and facies are convenient terms in which to refer to a particular part of the succession.

LUDLOW STRATIGRAPHY

Classification of stratigraphic units present in Ludlow measured sections is shown in Figure 3-3. Recently, Holland et al. (1963) revised Ludlow stratigraphy in the type area around Ludlow (Figure 3-1). They based their subdivisions on faunal assemblages, which generally correspond to the communities of Watkins (1979).

SEDIMENTOLOGY

Caradoc and Ludlow sediments belong to shelf environmental complexes (Figure 3-1, 3-2) and are a mosaic of sedimentary facies. As faunal associations are intimately related to sedimentary facies it is important to understand the sediments. In the Caradoc and Ludlow Hurst (1979b) and Watkins (1979) recognized 7 and 5 facies respectively. As the facies are relatively simple there is little need to describe them in detail. The salient features and interpretation of the main Caradoc and Ludlow facies are listed in Table 3-1. Further details are available in Hurst (1979b) and Watkins (1979).

SEDIMENTATION MODEL

In the Mediterranean and North Sea shelf sediments consist of bioturbated mud and silt with interbedded sheets of laminated sand and silt (Gadow and Reineck 1969; Reineck and Singh, 1972, 1973). With increasing distance from shore the laminated sheets decrease in thickness, have infrequent basal shell layers along nearly flat erosional bases and bioturbated upper surfaces (Howard and Reineck, 1972). A model of storm-related shelf sedimentation was proposed to account for such a sequence and this has subsequently been applied to many modern and ancient settings (Goldring and Bridges, 1973; Brenner and Davies, 1973; Bowen et al., 1974; Bridges, 1975; Kumar and Sanders, 1976: Anderton, 1976; Watkins, 1979; Hurst, 1979a,b).

Normal shelf sedimentation is characterized by suspended silt and clay which settles to become thoroughly bioturbated. Retreating wave and ebb currents generated by periodically passing storms transport sediment onto the shelf. Sediment in the southern North Sea may be re-deposited up to 50 km from source. Emplacement of a shell layer and minor erosion of the shelf surface may preceed the rapid settling of sand or silt as tabular laminated sheets. This in turn may be followed by rapid mud settling.

Examination of Figures 3-2 and 3-3 together with Table 3-1 indicates that Caradoc and Ludlow sediments are directly analogous and genetically related to some modern shelf sediments. There is a transgression from proximal to distal shelf environments in the upper Caradoc, whilst Ludlow sediments record a regression from distal to proximal shelf environments. The Laminated Shale Facies

Table 3-1
Scheme of main facies in the upper Caradoc and Ludlow (Hurst 1979a,b; Watkins 1979).

Facies	Grain sizes	Main structures	Interpretation
Sands & Silts	Medium fine sand to sandy silt.	Sand: parallel lamination, grading. Ripple cross lamination. Basal coquinas; bioturbation.	Proximal to distal storm layers. Finer silts settled out from suspension.
Bioturbated Silts	Silt.	Rare ripple lamination. All transitions to total burrow mottling. Swell lags.	Swell lags, distal storm swell passage. Silts settled from suspension.
Bioturbated Mud	Clay to mud.	Total burrow mottling.	Deposition from suspension in low energy environment.

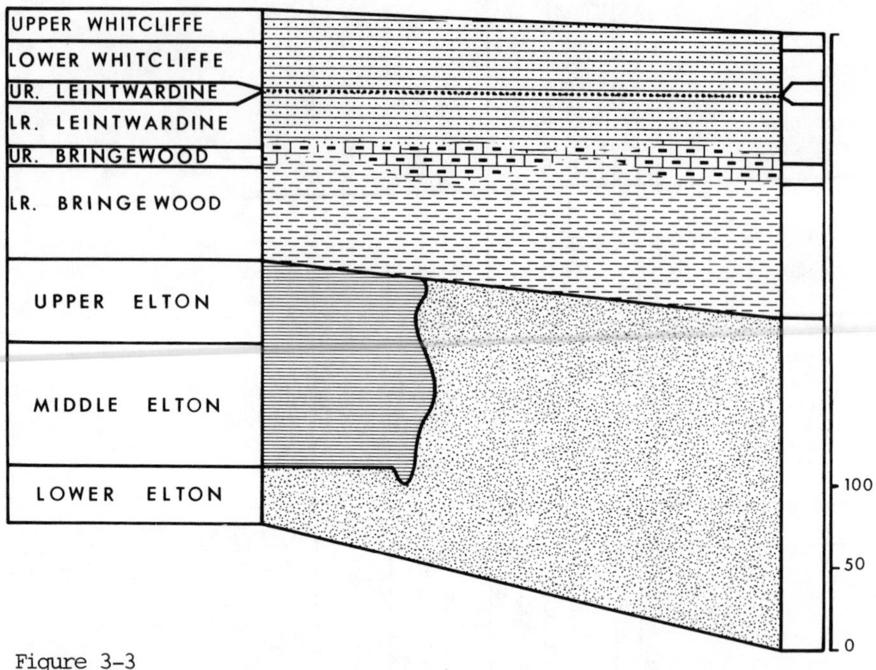

Figure 3-3
Generalised cross section showing the stratigraphic relationship of Ludlow sedimentary facies. Facies symbols explained in Figure 3-2.

indicates anoxic conditions (Emery and Hülsemann, 1962; Calvert, 1964; Rhoads and Morse, 1971).

SHELL OCCURRENCE

In the Bioturbated Mud and Bioturbated Silts Facies, shells are scattered evenly throughout the sediment in many orientations and represent disturbed neighborhood assemblages (Scott, 1974) that have been produced by intensive bioturbation. In the Sands and Silts Facies, scattered, variably orientated shells in the bioturbated horizons represent disturbed neighborhood assemblages whereas transported assemblages of concentrated shell layers occur in the interbedded laminated siltstone.

There is little evidence of faunal mixing of both epifauna and infauna as community replacements coincide with facies changes (Hurst, 1979b; Watkins, 1979). This suggests that transported faunas in coquinas or swell lags have only been displaced over small distances. As coquina faunas compare closely with disturbed neighborhood assemblages in the same facies and faunal association, transportation of faunas appears restricted to within facies and communities. Such a pattern probably applies to other Lower Paleozoic sequences, although occasionally there are exceptions (Hurst, 1979a,b).

FAUNAL ORGANIZATION

In developing the parallel-community model for present-day faunas, Thorson (1957) significantly extended the marine community concept. Basically, his thesis, (Thorson 1966: 147) is: "the same type of sediment substratum at the same depth, whether in cold, temperate or warmer regions, would be inhabited by a series of macro-fauna communities, in which the quantitatively predominating animals will belong to the same genera but to different species."

Within the context of the Thorson model, it should be possible to analyze and compare Caradoc and Ludlow communities. Examination of Figures 3-4 and 3-5 shows that faunal consistency exists on a broad scale between Caradoc and Ludlow sediments. This is especially true of brachiopods, which are the dominant faunal element. Thus, on a finer scale, might there be similar faunal assemblages in similar sedimentary facies in the Caradoc and Ludlow? Of course, one cannot expect congeneric species, but do similar functional groupings of various animals occur in similar environments? This in itself represents a further type of faunal parallelism, which is closely allied to the parallel community concept, but is not precisely synonymous with it. However, if such patterns could be shown, it would add a new dimension (temporal persistence) to the already established spatial patterns for the present and past as regard Silurian faunas (Watkins et al., 1973; Watkins, 1974). Boucot (1975) also demonstrated some common patterns within Silurian and between Silurian-Devonian communities. Recognition of similar functional groupings is an important aspect in gaining insight into community organization and evolution.

Because of many local inconsistencies, sedimentary facies in the Ludlow and Caradoc will not be compared one for one. This is misleading and impracticable. For example, the *Shaleria ornatella* association of Watkins (1979) is apparently a unique event, so no parallel can be expected to exist in other Ludlow sequences or in Caradoc ones. Also, both Caradoc and Ludlow Bioturbated Calcareous Silts Facies are apparently the result of basin restriction caused by various sorts of barrier formation. However, they are not directly comparable because of differences in geographic setting, and thus, they are largely ignored in this report. Other, local events also occur in the Sands and Silts Facies of the Caradoc succession that have no direct parallel in the Ludlow.

Thus, for the sake of clarity and space, only the following distinct and in-common facies and environments will be discussed in detail: (1) the Bioturbated Mud Facies of the Onny Shale and Elton Beds; (2) the Bioturbated Silts Facies of the lower Acton Scott Beds and the Bringewood Beds; (3) the Sands and Silts Facies of the *Dalmanella wattsi* zone of the Cheney Longville Flags and Lower Leintwardine Beds; (4) the Sands and Silts Facies of the uppermost Horderley Sandstone, lowest Cheney Longville Flags, and the Whitcliffe Beds. In effect, these four facies types represent the transgressive and regressive sequences of the Caradoc and Ludlow.

COMPARISON OF SANDS AND SILTS FACIES: (1)

The comparison concerns the Ludlow Whitcliffe Beds and the uppermost Horderley Sandstone and lowest Cheney Longville Flags of the

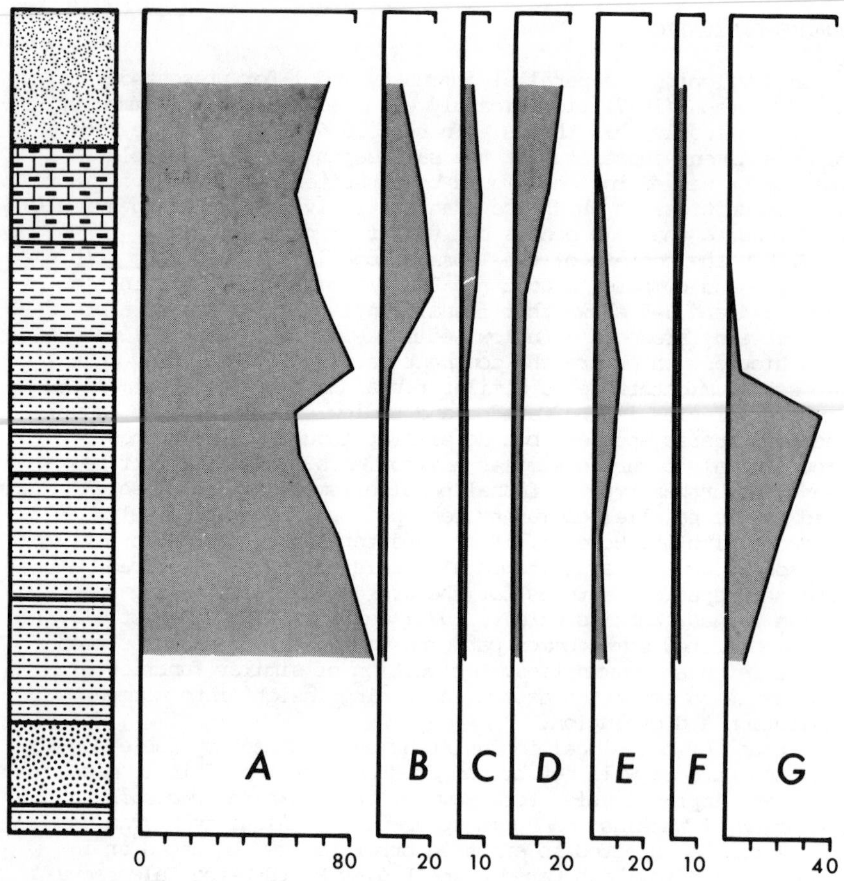

Figure 3-4
Relative abundance of the major Caradoc taxa along the environmental gradient. Brachiopods (A), bivalves (B), gastropods (C), trilobites (D), bryozoans (E), cephalopods (F), *Tentaculites* (G) Facies explained in Figure 3-2.

Caradoc (Figure 3-2).

Brachiopods comprise a high percentage of both Caradoc and Ludlow taxa, approximately 88 percent and 85 percent respectively (Figures 3-4, 3-5). However, close examination of Figures 3-6 and 3-7 reveals some important differences. Brachiopod abundances in the Caradoc are dominated by plectambonitacean, enteletacean, and strophomenacean brachiopods; inarticulate or orthacean brachiopods occur only rarely. Taxonomically the Ludlow equivalents appear vastly different. Chonetacean, rhynchonellid, and enteletacean groups dominate but subordinant numbers of strophomenacean, spiriferacean and athyroid/atrypoid brachiopods occur. More agreement exists, however, at the functional-morphologic level. The Caradoc plectambonitacean *Sowerbyella sericea*, which is a free-lying concavo-convex form, is a direct analogue of the Ludlow chonetacen *Protochonetes ludloviensis*, and the Ludlow pedically attached enteletaceans *Salopina lunata* and *Isorthis clivosa* are analogues of the Caradoc *Bancroftina*

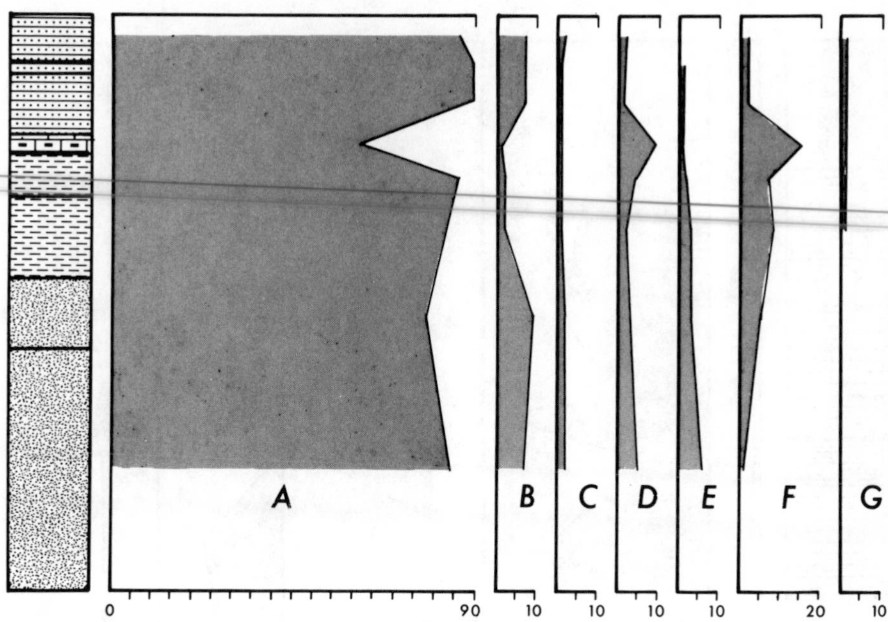

Figure 3-5
Relative abundance of the major Ludlow taxa along the environmental gradient. Brachiopods (A), bivalves (B), cephalopods (C), gastropods (D), trilobites (E), bryozoans (F), *Tentaculites* (G). Facies explained in Figure 3-2.

typa and *Dalmanella multiplicata prima*. Further parallels are the burrowing inarticulates *Palaeoglossa* sp. in the Caradoc and *Lingula lewisii* in the Ludlow. However, the large plano-convex to concavo-convex strophomenacean *Kjaerina bipartita* in the Caradoc and the Ludlow development of the rhynchonellid and spiriferacean faunas dominated by *"Camarotoechia" nucula* and *Howellella elegans* have no corresponding analogues.

Among the bivalves, cephalopods, and gastropods, there are no parallels; and among the bryozoans, there are contradictions. Ramose morphotypes predominate in the Ludlow and prasoporid types, in the Caradoc. The Caradoc *Tentaculites anglicus* and the Ludlow *Cornulites serpularius* are direct morphologic analogues and possibly functional ones as well.

In addition to the brachiopods the only other group to display some morphologic parallels is the trilobites. The homalonotids *Brongniartella bisulcata* of the Caradoc and *Homolonotus knightii* of the Ludlow compare closely, and the Caradoc *Kloucekia (Phacopidina) apiculata* compares with the Ludlow *Acastella spinosa*. The Caradoc trinucleid *Broeggerolithus longiceps* and the Ludlow *Encrinurus stubblefieldi* do not have analogues.

In both the Caradoc and the Ludlow, there are three dominant brachiopod species, and each may form as much as 80 percent of the fauna of single samples. Eleven other species have been recorded from the Ludlow and six from the Caradoc but these are rare and only

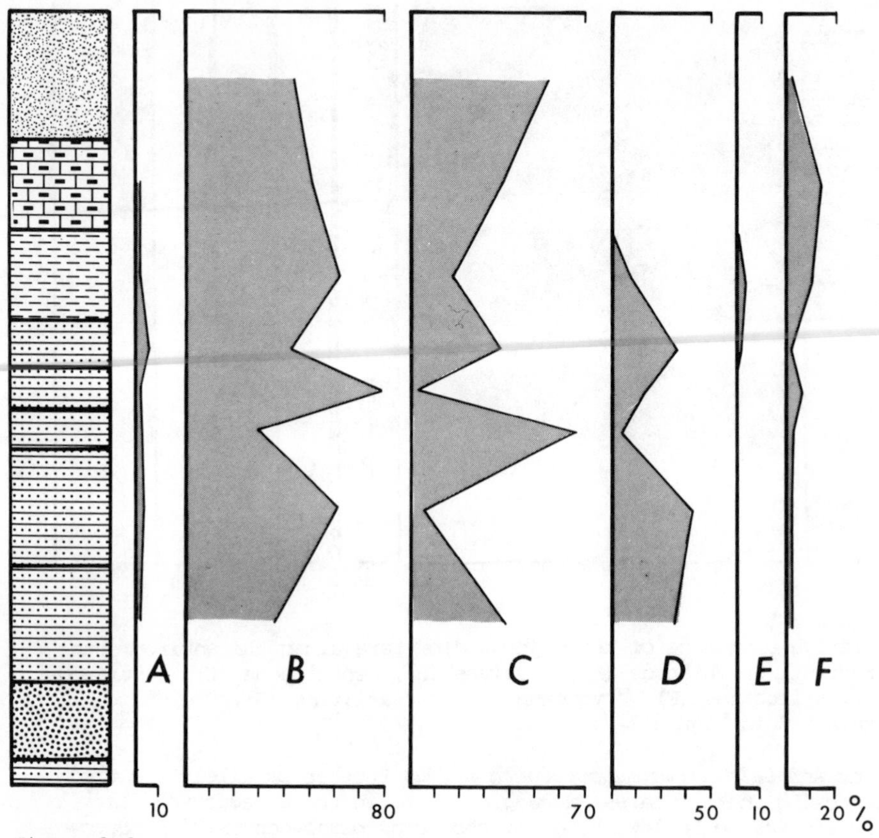

Figure 3-6
Relative abundance of major brachiopod groups along the Caradoc environmental gradient. Orthaceans (A), enteletaceans (B), plectambonitaceans (C), strophomenaceans (D), athyrids and atrypids (E), inarticulates (F). Facies explained in Figure 3-2.

appear sporadically in stratigraphic profiles. In both sequences, the dominant species show extreme small scale fluctuations in abundance in stratigraphic sections (Figure 3-8). Bivalves are far more abundant in the Ludlow (compare Figures 3-4 and 3-5) and may locally reach 30 percent of the fauna. They are dominated by the endobyssate *Sedwickia amygdalina*, which comprises 42 percent of the individuals. Other common species include *Goniophora cymbaeformis*, *Pterinea tenuistriata*, *Pteronitella retroflexa* (all endobyssate forms), and the free burrowing *Nuculites antiqua*. Bryozoan and gastropod abundances are similar. As might be expected, Caradoc trilobite abundances are greater and their occurrence less sporadic than in the Ludlow.

Rarefaction data show that faunal diversity varies between 3 and 17 for the Ludlow samples and between 3 and 12 in Caradoc samples. The mean is approximately 8 in both cases. However, of all the fauna recovered from both successions, only the trilobites, as a group, are

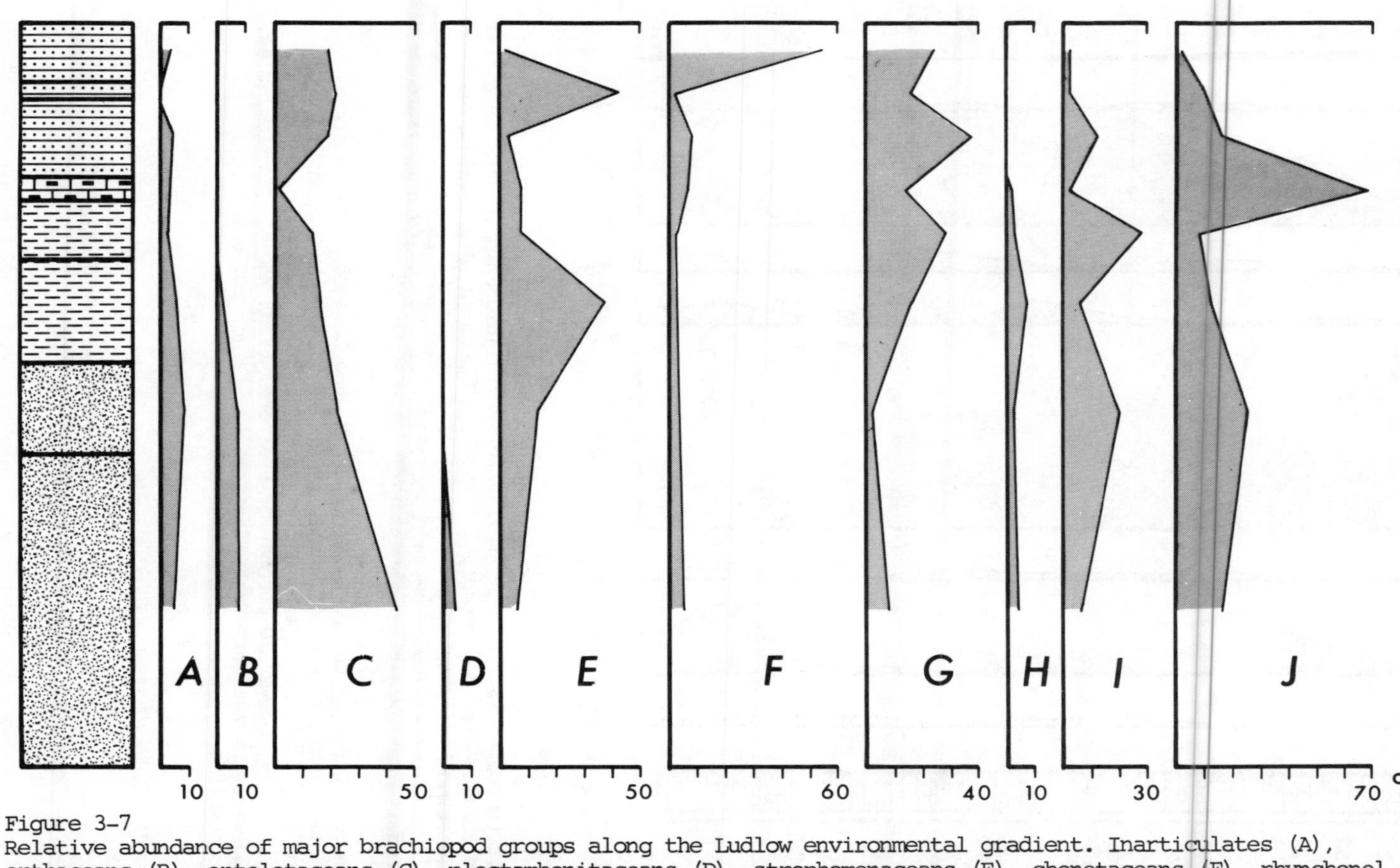

Figure 3-7
Relative abundance of major brachiopod groups along the Ludlow environmental gradient. Inarticulates (A), orthaceans (B), enteletaceans (C), plectambonitaceans (D), strophomenaceans (E), chonetaceans (F), rhynchonellids (G), pentamerids (H), spiriferaceans (I), athyrids and atrypids (J). Facies explained in Figure 3-2.

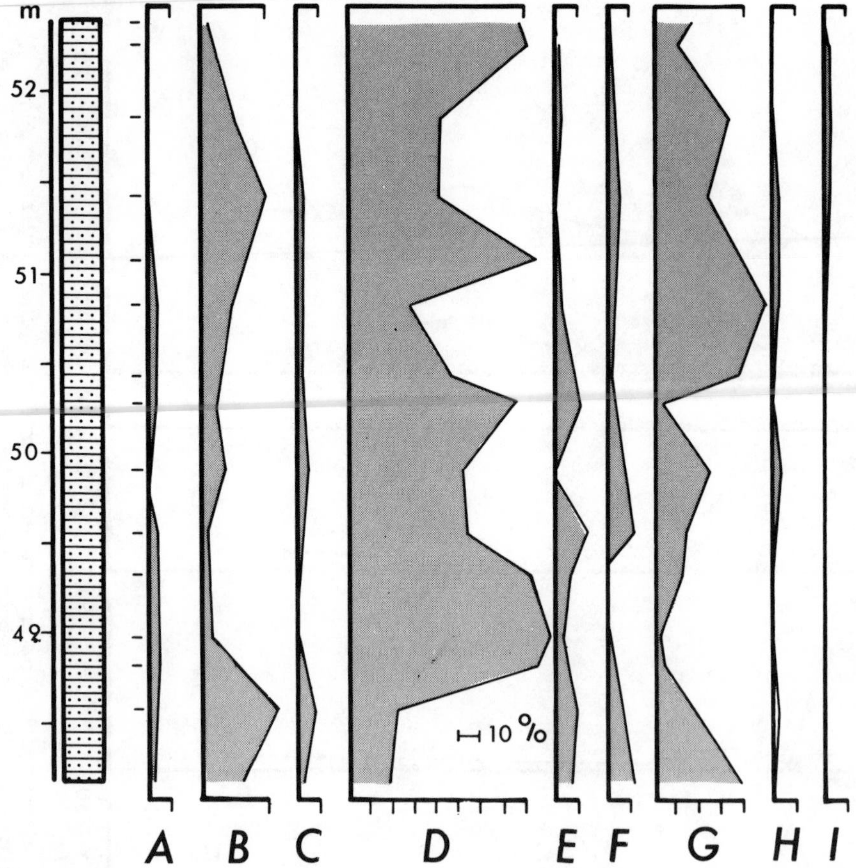

Figure 3-8
Patterns of occurrence of various brachiopods (A), bivalves (B), gastropods (C), *Protochonetes ludloviensis* (D), *Salopina lunata* (E), bryozoans (F), *"Camarotoechia" nucula* (G), *Cornulites serpularius* (H), and *Dayia navicula* (I) in the Sands and Silts Facies (*Protochonetes ludloviensis* Association) of the Ludlow Whitcliffe Beds.

more diverse in the Caradoc. In short, the Caradoc contains the smaller number of co-occurring taxa. The greater Ludlow diversity is reflected in the heterogeneity of the samples; that is ten samples will only recover 70 percent of the total fauna known from the facies. However, overall diversity differences are not reflected in significant differences among samples.

COMPARISON OF SANDS AND SILTS FACIES: (2)

The comparison concerns the Ludlow Lower Leintwardine Beds and the Caradoc *Dalmanella wattsi* Zone of the Cheney Longville Flags (Figure 3-2).

Brachiopods predominantly enteletaceans and plectambonitaceans comprise 60 percent of the total fauna in the Caradoc (Figure 3-4). Conversely, brachiopods in the Ludlow constitute approximately 90 percent of the total fauna and consist of a wide range of morphologic types (Figure 3-5). At the taxonomic level, there are basic differences between the Caradoc and Ludlow, yet there is agreement at the functional level. This is exemplified by the free-lying concavo-convex *Sowerbyella sericea* (plectambonitacean) and *Protochonetes ludloviensis* (chonetacean) analogue. The large size and internal morphologic characteristics of *Bancroftina hewitti* compare closely with the Ludlow *Isorthis orbicularis* (Hurst, 1978; Hurst and Watkins, 1978). Also, *Dalmanella multiplicata multiplicata* and *Salopina lunata* are direct morphologic analogues shown particularly by the nature of their cardinalia.

A number of rarely occurring brachiopod species, for example, *Paracraniops doyleae/Craniops implicata, Palaeoglossa lockleyi/ Lingula lewisii* and *Dolerorthis virgata/Dolerorthis* sp. also indicate close similarity between Caradoc and Ludlow community organization. In both the Caradoc and Ludlow plano-convex to weakly concavo-convex, generally free-lying large strophomenaceans are not common, but nevertheless, form a significant contribution to the faunal composition. These include *Leptostrophia filosa* and *Shaleria ornatella* in the Ludlow and *Strophomena grandis* in the Caradoc. Finally, the ventrally geniculate strophomenacean *Kjerulfina trigonalis* has an analogue in the Ludlow dorsally geniculate *Leptaena depressa* and *Lepidoleptaena* sp. Conversely, the presence of the Ludlow spire bearers, *Atrypa reticularis, Dayia navicula, Howellella elegans*, and *Hyattidina canalis*, is unparalleled in the Caradoc.

Comparisons of molluscs are, again, limited, mainly because they are scarce in the Caradoc (Figures 3-4, 3-5). However, some parallels do exist, notably, the rare occurrences of *Modiolopsis* sp/*Modiolopsis complanata* and *Nuculites planulatus/Nuculites antiqua* (in the Caradoc/ Ludlow, respectively). Prasoparid bryozoan morphotypes still predominate in the Caradoc, and ramose forms in the Ludlow. The Caradoc *Tentaculites anglicus* is paralleled by the Ludlow *Tentaculites tenuis* although the latter is not as common. Trilobites are rare in the Ludlow, but the few that do occur morphologically mirror some Caradoc forms. Close comparisons include *Flexicalymene caractaci/Calymene* sp. and *Kloucekia (Phacopidina) apiculata* with *Acastella spinosa*. The Ludlow *Proetus obconicus* and the other Caradoc species have no obvious parallels.

In the Ludlow, any one of eight brachiopod species *Salopina lunata, Isorthis orbicularis, Protochonetes ludloviensis, Shaleria ornatella, Sphaerirhynchia wilsoni, "Camarotoechia" nucula, Hyattidina canalis*, or *Howellella elegans*, may comprise over 70 percent of the fauna in single samples. Bivalves reach local abundances of 20 percent of the fauna and are dominated by *"Paracyclas" insueta, Nuculites antiqua, Pteronitella retroflexa*, and *Sedgwickia amygdalina*. Trilobites and gastropods have a more sporadic stratigraphic occurrence. In the Caradoc, two species of brachiopod, *Dalmanella multiplicata multiplicata* and *Sowerbyella serices*, and *Tentaculites anglicus* dominate individual samples up to about 70 percent. All molluscs in the Caradoc have a sporadic stratigraphic occurrence, but most trilobite species are consistently present, albeit in low numbers. In both successions, the overall dominant species occur in fluctuating patterns (Watkins, 1979).

Faunal diversity for the Ludlow samples varies between 7 and 19 and for the Caradoc, 8 and 16; the mean in both cases is approximately 10 per sample. As in the previous comparison only the trilobites, as a group, were more diverse in the Caradoc. Again, bivalves are significantly less diverse in the Caradoc than in the Ludlow; four species are recorded in the Caradoc as opposed to fifteen in the Ludlow. Similarly, ten species of brachiopod are known from the Caradoc and nineteen from the Ludlow.

Patterns of larger total diversity of Ludlow fauna but similar sample diversities appears to be a characteristic throughout the Caradoc and Ludlow Sands and Silts Facies. As mentioned earlier, there appears to be a smaller number of co-occurring taxa in the Caradoc. The total fauna is overwhelmingly dominated by brachiopods, but the individual sample diversity is often dominated by trilobites in the Caradoc and by bivalves in the Ludlow.

COMPARISON OF BIOTURBATED SILTS FACIES

Communities in these sediments are the most diverse and are dominated by bryozoans and brachiopods in the Ludlow (Figure 3-5) and by brachiopods, molluscs, and bryozoa in the Caradoc (Figure 3-5). Strophomenids are the dominant brachiopods except in the Caradoc (compare Figures 3-6 and 3-7). Twelve species have been recorded from the Ludlow and five from the Caradoc; they are the most diverse strophomenid fauna along any part of the environmental gradient in both Series. Such diversification is associated with a variety of functional adaptations, many of which are in common. These include the small (2 to 12 mm wide), free-lying, strongly concavo-convex forms *Mesopholidostrophia laevigata* (stropheodontid), *Protochonetes minimus* and *P. ludloviensis* (chonetids) in the Ludlow and *Chonetoidea radiatula*, *Sowerbyella sericea* and *Leptestiina oepiki* (plectambonitaceans) in the Caradoc. Larger (up to 50 mm wide) forms are also common, including gently concavo-convex/geniculate forms, the stropheodontid *Strophomena euglupha* (Ludlow), and the rafinesquinid *Hedstroemina fragilis* (Caradoc). These two species are close morphologic analogues except for the denticulate hinge of the former and the occasional presence of a pedicle tube in adults of the latter. Strongly dorsally geniculate/resupinate forms are represented by *Amphistrophia funiculata*, *Leptaena depressa*, and *Lepidoleptaena* sp. in the Ludlow, but only by *Leptaena salopiensis* in the Caradoc. The rare dorsally reclining, free-lying productorthid *Nicolella actoniae* of the Caradoc is a peculiar strophomenid analogue. Further, the resupinate, pedically attached, Ludlow strophomenid *"Schuchertella"* sp. is paralleled by the Caradoc harknessellid orthid *Reuschella bilobata*. The flat free-lying stropheodontid *Leptostrophia filosa* does not have a direct Caradoc parallel. However, populations of *Hedstroemina fragilis* are variable, often spanning the variation range between *Leptostrophia filosa* and *Strophonella euglypha*.

Generally, the small, free-lying forms tend to dominate, and in fact this can be narrowed down to one species in each case, *Mesopholidostrophia laevigata* in the Ludlow and *Chonetoidea radiatula* in the Caradoc. Most of the remaining species have a patchy distribution and are concomitantly less abundant.

Taxonomic and functional consistencies also exist among the remaining brachiopod groups. Among the pedically attached orthids, *Skenidioides* cf. *costata* in the Caradoc is replaced by *S. lewisii* in the Ludlow. Similarly, the enteletacean *Onniella reuschi* is replaced by *Isorthis clivosa.* The striking morphological similarity between these two orthides in many similar and varied environments, has recently been demonstrated by Hurst (1978). However, *Onniella reuschi* is generally far more abundant than *Isorthis clivosa* and often dominates samples. A greater diversity of inarticulates is known from the Caradoc but the only obvious morphologic and abundance analogues are the burrowing *Palaeoglossa lockleyi/Lingula lewisii* and *Paracraniops doyleae/Craniops implicata* in the Caradoc/Ludlow, respectively.

In all, a great many more brachiopod species have been recorded from the Ludlow. This is partly because of the greater diversity of strophomenids, but mainly because of the presence of pentamerids *(Gypidula lata)*. rhynchonellids *(Sphaerirhynchia wilsoni)*, and most importantly spiriferids *(Atrypa reticularis* and *Eospirifer radiatus)*. Accordingly, the Ludlow facies is not continuously dominated through extensive stratigraphic intervals by any single brachiopod species, although any one of several species, usually strophomenid, may predominate in single samples. Conversely, in the Caradoc four or five species of strophomenid and orthid tend to dominate. Large scale species population fluctuations, reminiscent of those in the Sands and Silts Facies do not occur in the Ludlow but are known very occasionally in the Caradoc. Generally, most species abundance patterns change only gradually and through continuous sections.

In both the Caradoc and the Ludlow, bryozoans are an important constituent of the animal communities associated with this facies. Owen (in Holland et al. 1963) listed twenty-one species of bryozoa from the Lower Bringewood Beds of the Ludlow area, which indicates their high diversity. Species diversity is unknown in the Caradoc because the fossil is usually an internal mold but if morphotype variation can be used as a yardstick, it appears to be high. A great variety of morphotypes are present; this facies is the acme. The morphotype diversity is also great in individual samples.

Bivalves comprise 19 percent of total individuals in the Caradoc, but only 2 percent in the Ludlow (Figures 3-4, 3-5). Conversely, Ludlow bivalves are represented by at least twenty-two species, but Caradoc, by only 10. Patterns of occurrence are very similar as most species occur in small numbers at widely separated, stratigraphic intervals. Only *Similodonta* sp. and *Nuculites planulatus* in the Caradoc and *Cypricardinia subplanulata* and *Actinopteria sowerbyi* in the Ludlow show a fairly consistent pattern of occurrence. Here the similarity ends because Caradoc bivalve faunas are dominated by infaunal deposit feeding nuculoids *Similodonta* sp., *Nuculites planulatis, Praeleda* sp., *Praenucula* sp. and *Palaeoneilo* sp., whereas the Ludlow fauna is more varied. Deposit feeders *Nuculites antiqua* and the endobyssate form *Goniophora cymbaeformis* are common.

Gastropods are also more common in the Caradoc (Figures 3-4, 3-5) but the diversity is similar; at least ten species are recorded from the Caradoc and Ludlow. Species occur in a similar fashion to the bivalves, that is small numbers at scattered intervals. There is some degree of morphologic parallelism, for example, *Liospira* sp./ *Leptozone striatissima, Lophospira* sp./*Bembexia lloydi,* and indeterminate trochiform gastropods/*Oriostoma* sp. in the Caradoc/

Ludlow, respectively. However, it appears that Caradoc and Ludlow gastropod faunas are quite different morphologically.

Trilobites are still fairly minor members of both Caradoc and Ludlow faunas (Figures 3-4, 3-5). Seven species are known from the Ludlow and nine from the Caradoc, and they occur continuously throughout stratigraphic profiles. Many of the Caradoc species have morphologic analogues in the Ludlow, for example *Onnicalymene laticeps*/*Calymene* sp., *Chasmops extensa*/*Dalmanites myops*, *Platylichas laxtus*/*Hemiarges* sp., and *Otarion* sp./*Otarion megalops*.

With regard to the minor faunal groups, cephalopod abundance is similar but their diversity is greater in the Ludlow. *Tentaculites* is now very rare.

Faunal diversity for the Ludlow samples varies between 11 and 24 and for the Caradoc 10 and 24: the mean in both cases is approximately 16. Table 3-2 shows the diversity of both Caradoc and Ludlow Bioturbated Silt Facies faunas in terms of the Shannon Index and indicates there to be no significant differences. However, a point of interest is that a greater range of variation exists in the Ludlow than in the Caradoc. Again, there is a larger total diversity in the Ludlow, but sample diversities are similar. Brachiopods still overwhelmingly dominate the fauna, and sample diversity, which in the Caradoc is constituted by trilobites, appears to be taken over by the bivalves in the Ludlow.

COMPARISON OF BIOTURBATED MUD FACIES

The Ludlow community is dominated by brachiopods and molluscs whereas the Caradoc is dominated by brachiopods and trilobites. (Figures 3-4, 3-5).

The most abundant brachiopod occurring in the Ludlow is the plectambonitacean *Aegeri grayii*. However, Watkins (1977) considered this species to have possessed an epiplanktic mode of life; thus, we disregard it here as it is not directly related to the bottom fauna. Similarly, in the Caradoc, the plectambonitacean *Sericoidea homolensis* is the most abundant species (Figure 3-6), but it is considered a benthic species. Bergström (1968) and Havlíček (1967) have shown that some species of *Sericoidea* and the closely related *Chonetoidea* probably had an epiplanktic mode of life. This does not mean however that all *Sericoidea* and *Chonetoidea* species were epiplanktic, nor indeed, that all populations of the species were. The case for *Aegeria grayi* being epiplanktic is its ubiquitous occurrence, its association with a wholly pelagic fauna of graptolites, small orthoconic nautiloids, and praecardiacean bivalves and the fact that it reaches local densities of 18,000 shells per square meter. In contrast, *Sericoidea homolensis* and *Chonetoidea radiatula* from the Bioturbated Silts Facies, are facies restricted and do not reach such local high abundances. Normally, *Sericoidea homolensis* occur in densities of around 200 to 300 shells per square meter, the highest density is 1000 per square meter.

Sericoidea homolensis is a small concavo-convex strophomenid (2 to 4 mm wide). The only obvious analogue to this in the Ludlow is the chonetacean strophomenid *Protochonetes minimus* and the stropheodontid *Mesopholidostrophia laevigata*. However, *P. minimus* and *M. laevigata* are only minor constituents of the Ludlow community, whereas *S. homolensis* overwhelmingly dominates in the

Table 3-2
Shannon indices of diversity for offshore Caradoc and Ludlow facies. N = number of individual sample diversities, $\bar{n}$ = mean diversity.

Facies	N	$\bar{n}$	range	+95% C.I.	-95% C.I.
Bioturbated Silts					
1) Caradoc	19	1.9180	1.5107–2.3328	2.0036	1.8324
2) Ludlow	34	1.9600	0.8400–2.7800	2.1200	1.8000
Bioturbated Mud					
1) Caradoc	14	1.8170	1.5835–2.1902	1.8316	1.8024
2) Ludlow	15	2.0995	1.5928–2.4567	2.2530	1.9470

Caradoc. Strophomenids, in general, have a low diversity in both the Caradoc and Ludlow; and the only other form of note is the Ludlow leptaenid *Ludfordina pixis*, which is not paralleled morphologically in the Caradoc.

Striking morphologic similarity exists in the orthids between *Onniella broeggeri* and the Ludlow *Isorthis clivosa* (Hurst, 1978). Both species are very common, occur throughout the samples, and often dominate them. There are a number of other Ludlow orthid species none of which are common except *Skenidoides lewisii*, and they do not have Caradoc analogues. Inarticulate brachiopods characteristically occur in small numbers at widely spaced stratigraphic intervals, but there are no apparent morphological parallels between the Caradoc and Ludlow species.

The most important difference between Caradoc and Ludlow faunas is the increased diversity of pentamerids *(Parastrophinella* sp. and *Gypidula lata)*, rhynchonellids *(Plagiorhynchia* sp.*)*, and spiriferids *(Glassia obovata* and *Howellella elegans)* in the Ludlow. Fifty percent of the brachiopod species in the Ludlow are more common members of other communities and may be considered at the extremes of their tolerance ranges in this facies. Four of the five Caradoc species are facies restricted and *Obolus salopiensis* is known only from two facies. Two types of brachiopod occurrence are seen in the Ludlow. First, a variety of species and adaptive types occur in fairly equal numbers and with continuous and relatively constant shell densities in the vertical profiles. As seen from Figure 3-7 such an occurrence pattern is unknown in the Caradoc. Rather *Onniella broeggeri* and *Sericoidea homolensis* greatly predominate over other brachiopods and comprise the most individuals in the association. This pattern is the second type of occurrence in the Ludlow, but the predominant brachiopods are *Isorthis clivosa* and *Glassia obovata* instead of *Onniella broeggeri* and *Sericoidea homolensis* (Figure 3-9).

Bivalves are more diverse in the Ludlow; eighteen species are recorded as opposed to five in the Caradoc. By far the most important group in both successions is the deposit-feeding, free-burrowing nuculoids. These include *Similodonta* sp., *Nuculites planulatus*, and *Praenucula* sp. in the Caradoc and *Nuculites pseudodeltoideus*, *N. woolphopensis*, *Praenucula* sp., and *Praectenodonta ludensis* in the Ludlow. Species are commonly found together in samples, but only *Praenucula* sp. in the Ludlow and *Nuculites planulatus* in the Caradoc are persistently present. Occasionally in the Ludlow, *Nuculites* spp. and *Praenucula* sp. become the dominant members of the fauna (Figure 3-9). The remaining bivalves show a sporadic pattern of occurrence and are seldom represented by more than one or two individuals per sample. Most remaining Ludlow species show adaptation for an endobyssate mode of life, but epibyssate and free-burrowing forms are present as well. The epifaunal suspension feeders *Modiolopsis* sp. B in the Caradoc and *Modiolopsis consors* and *M. solenoides* in the Ludlow are the only other morphologic forms in common.

Sixteen species of gastropod have been recorded from the Ludlow. They are present throughout the stratigraphic profiles, but are seldom represented by more than a few individuals. Conversely, only five species are known from the Caradoc and they are scattered, rarely occurring together, but often in fairly large numbers. Taxonomic/morphologic comparison between the Caradoc and Ludlow are limited to *Cymbularia* sp/*C.* cf. *fastigata* and *Temnodiscus* sp./*T. salopiensis*.

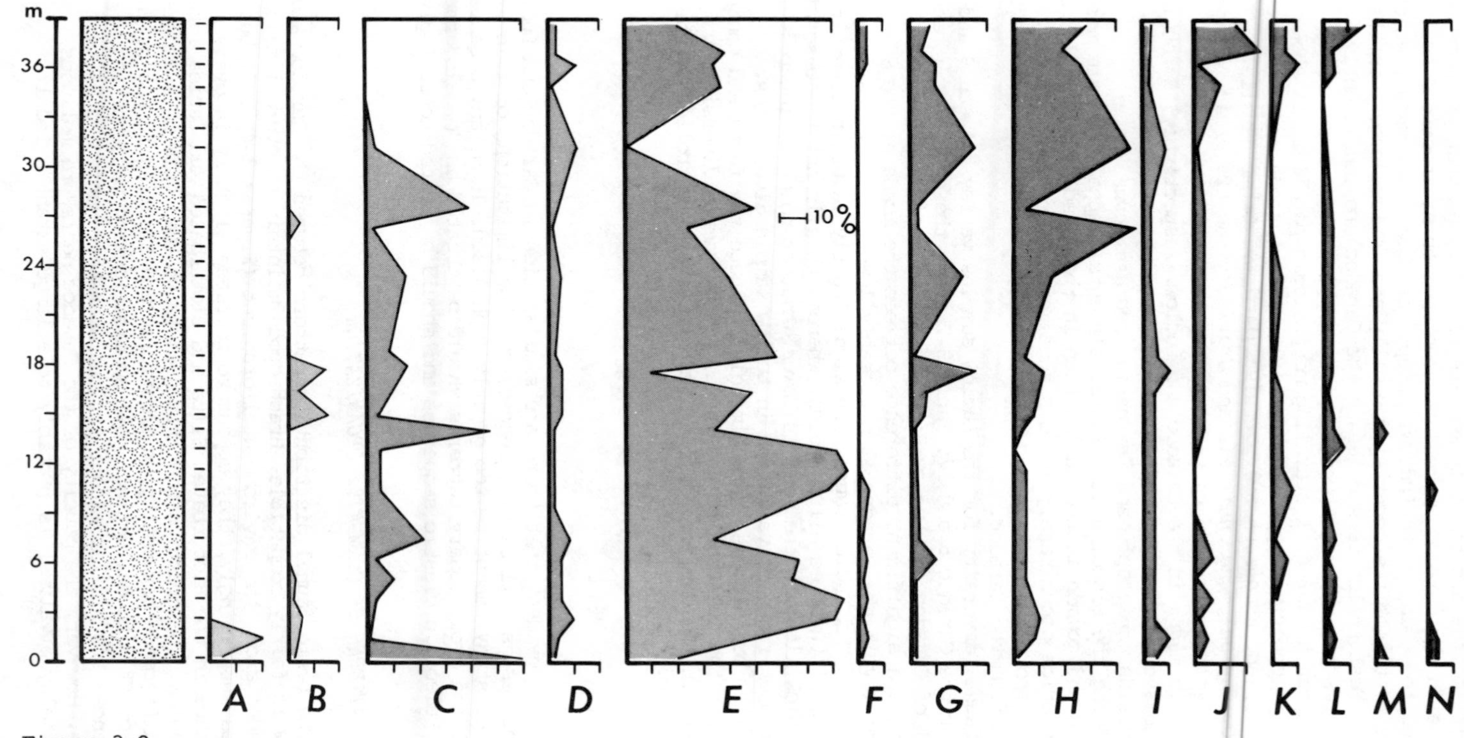

Figure 3-9
Patterns of occurrence of *Ludfordina pixis* (A), *Parastrophinella* sp. (B), *Glassia obovata* (C), *Protozeuga* sp. (D), *Isorthis clivosa* (E) *Hyolithes forbesi* (F), gastropods (G), bivalves (H), trilobites (I), *Protochonetes minimus* (J), *Skenidioides lewisii* (K), *Howellella elegans* (L), solitary corals (M), and stropheodontids (N) in the Bioturbated Mud Facies (*Glassia obovata* Association) of the Ludlow Elton Beds.

Trilobites are the only members of the fauna that are more diverse in the Caradoc where seventeen species are recorded as opposed to seven in the Ludlow. Except for *Dalmanites myops*, which is abundant, trilobites occur sporadically and in low numbers in the Ludlow. Most trilobite species in the Caradoc are consistently present; some are very abundant, for example, *Onnia* spp. and *Lonchodomas pennatus*. A startling morphologic parallel, is shown by the rhaphiophorids *Ampyxella edgelli* and *Lonchodomas pennatus* (Caradoc) and *Rhaphiophorus parvulus* (Ludlow). Other parallels include *Onnicalymene onniensis* and *Gravicalymene* cf. *praecox/Calymene* sp., *Calyptaulax actoniensis/Phacops* sp., and *Chasmops extensa/ Dalmanites myops* in the Caradoc and Ludlow, respectively. No obvious analogues exist for the Ludlow *Proetus astringens* and the Caradoc trinculeids *Onnia* spp. and *Tretaspis ceroides favus*.

Among the miscellaneous faunal elements, cephalopods are more diverse and common in the Ludlow than in the Caradoc. Hyolithids and phyllocarids occur rarely in both successions. Bryozoa, solitary corals, and tentaculitids occur very rarely in the Ludlow, and are absent from the Caradoc.

Faunal diversity for the Ludlow samples varies between 9 and 33 and for the Caradoc 6 and 17. Table 3-2 shows the diversity (Shannon index) of Caradoc and Ludlow Bioturbated Mud Facies faunas and indicates a significant difference between the means at the 95 percent level; the Caradoc is noticeably lower. Further, Caradoc Bioturbated Mud Facies faunas are significantly lower in diversity than the Bioturbated Silts Facies, whereas this is not the case with the Ludlow although the mean is lower. Another point of interest is the greater range of variation in Ludlow sample diversities. Generally, brachiopods overwhelmingly dominate the fauna and contribute with the mulluscs to the large, Ludlow sample diversities. However, in the Caradoc, sample diversities are controlled by the trilobites.

DISCUSSION

It is evident that there are similarities in Caradoc and Ludlow communities as well as differences, but the limitations of this selected study cannot be too greatly emphasized. Thus, any organizational and evolutionary patterns should be treated as "models" for Lower Paleozoic clastic sequences and should be tested accordingly.

MAJOR PATTERNS OF COMMUNITY ORGANIZATION

The basic faunal distribution pattern between the Caradoc and Ludlow is fairly compatible. Brachiopods maintain an overall majority abundance along the environmental gradient (Figures 3-4, 3-5) but perhaps surprisingly, they appear to increase slightly in overall abundance in the Bioturbated Silts and Bioturbated Mud Facies into the Ludlow. The question now arises as to whether this is a consistent difference between Upper Ordovician and Silurian faunas or an artifact of data collecting. Mollusc distribution patterns and abundances are similar except for the nearshore Sands and Silts Facies. However, the paucity of the Caradoc nearshore molluscs (especially bivalves) is probably to a large extent a local phenomenon (cf. Bretsky, 1969, 1970). As might be expected, trilobites are far more abundant in the Caradoc.

These changes in abundance patterns of the major taxonomic group should be viewed from the historical aspect. Generally, trilobites decline in abundance throughout the upper-Lower Paleozoic into the Upper Paleozoic whereas brachiopods (see Williams et al., 1965), and most especially molluscs increase (cf. Thayer, 1974). Conversely, pre-Caradoc Paleozoic faunas are often dominated by trilobites (cf. Fortey, 1975). Thus, the evolutionary state of the group involved primarily controls the difference in Caradoc and Ludlow comparative abundances and diversities.

As expected there is little taxonomic continuity between Caradoc and Ludlow communities. However, there is a great deal of morphologic parallelism between communities in similar facies. Hurst (1979b) envisaged three community groupings, along the environmental gradient in the Caradoc, based on the prevailing adaptive modes of the species present. These included:

1. a nearshore group of large epifaunal suspension-feeding brachiopods, bryozoans and *Tentaculites anglicus*, restricted to the Sands and Silts Facies.
2. a mid-shelf group of small epifaunal suspension-feeding brachiopods, epifaunal bivalves and gastropods, typically found in the Bioturbated Silts Facies.
3. a distal shelf group of small epifaunal suspension-feeding brachiopods, infaunal deposit-feeding bivalves and epifaunal (and possibly infaunal) deposit and filter-feeding trilobites, typically found in the Bioturbated Mud Facies.

Ludlow communities (Watkins, 1979) follow very similar patterns. The major differences concern communities in the distal shelf Bioturbated Mud Facies, where the diversity contribution of trilobites in the Caradoc is taken over by molluscs, particularly bivalves, in the Ludlow. In general molluscs tend to be more abundant and diverse in the Ludlow, apparently at the expense of trilobites. Further, there is morphologic correspondence between many individual species in similar Caradoc and Ludlow communities and the overall diversity, density and numerical abundance patterns closely compare. The distribution of opportunistic and characteristic species (Johnson, 1972) along the environmental gradient is also similar.

SPECIES DIVERSITY PATTERNS

Diversity of individual collections from any facies presumably reflects some diagenetic and other post-depositional control. It is unknown how reliable raw diversity data are, as well as numerical abundance of species, and no amount of standardized collecting alone can circumvent the problem. Comparison of diversity patterns along similar environmental gradients in temporally and spatially separated successions provides a way of testing the validity of raw diversity data.

In Caradoc and Ludlow communities, diversity patterns are similar along the environmental gradients (Hurst, 1979, Watkins, 1979), and diversities within many facies closely compare. The most striking similarity is the diversity increase, of the very same order, from the Sands and Silts Facies into the Bioturbated Silts Facies. It is thought unlikely that similar patterns would develop in stratigraphically separated sequences if the diversity patterns did not largely reflect original patterns. Further testing of such patterns along similar environmental gradients may shed more light onto the problem.

The Caradoc and Ludlow shelf facies probably represent gradients of increasing environmental stress on bottom faunas. The proximal-shelf environment probably represents the high stress end of the gradient; this can be deduced from the frequent erosion surfaces, storm-deposited sands and silts and lack of bioturbation. These suggest an environment of fluctuating deposition patterns and high local rates of sedimentation. Conversely, sedimentary conditions were most stable in the Bioturbated Silts Facies as indicated by uniform sediments and extreme rarity of current-deposited or storm beds. The Caradoc Bioturbated Mud Facies was probably subject to slightly more variable physical stress and sedimentation as evidenced by patchily distributed, interbedded Laminated Shale Facies, indicating oxygen deficient sediments (Hurst, 1979). In the Ludlow, Laminated Shale Facies is not as intimately related with the Bioturbated Mud Facies. The plethora of factors involved in determining biologically directed stress remain almost totally unknown, but sediment type and sedimentation rate appear to show a decreasing gradient, from the nearshore Sand and Silts Facies through the Bioturbated Silts Facies, probably followed by an increase into the Bioturbated Mud Facies, in the Caradoc.

The increase in species diversity from proximal to distal shelf environments and the decrease in the Caradoc Bioturbated Mud Facies follows the predictions of the stability time hypothesis (Sanders, 1968), and it is tempting to relate increased diversity to decreased sediment-produced environmental stress. The diversity drop into the Caradoc Bioturbated Mud Facies is also possibly related to increased environmental stress related to oxygen deficiency (Hurst, 1979b). Conversely, the diversity of the Ludlow Bioturbated Mud Facies is similar to the Bioturbated Silts Facies. Ludlow Bioturbated Mud Facies are not as intimately associated with laminated shales as in the Caradoc.

Underlying the general diversity trends are many independent patterns that are worthy of consideration; many bear on the problem of whether the communities are physically controlled or biologically accommodated at all.

Sanders (1968, 1969) predicted that physically controlled communities would be characterized by small numbers of eurytopic species primarily adapted to the environment, whereas biologically accommodated communities would be composed of large numbers of stenotopic species in stable complex associations developed through a history of biologic accommodation in physical conditions uniform and constant through time. Along an environmental gradient, physically controlled communities in areas of physiologic stress will grade into biologically accommodated communities.

Shannon indices of species diversity for Caradoc and Ludlow Bioturbated Silts and Bioturbated Mud Facies are shown in Table 3-2. There is no significant difference between the Caradoc and Ludlow Bioturbated Silts Facies. However, the Ludlow Bioturbated Mud Facies is significantly more diverse than the Caradoc equivalent. This diversity increase may be a historical result of species interactions: biologic accommodation, a consequence of niche partitioning and more efficient utilization of resources in a low stress environment (cf. Sanders, 1968, 1969; Poulsen and Culver, 1969; Levinton, 1970). Again, it cannot be ruled out that the differences are artifacts of local conditions, perhaps a result of physical instability of reworked muds, (caused by deposit feeders) that inhibit or exclude suspension feeders (Rhoads and Young, 1970; Levinton and Bambach, 1970). If this was the case, however, it is difficult to see why only Caradoc faunas are apparently so adversely affected. Thus, we need to rigorously test diversity differences in offshore facies between the Caradoc and the Ludlow.

In this context, Watkins (1979) examined Silurian data and found no evidence of diversity increases. To reconcile such opposed results, we propose the following hypothesis: Diversity increases in low stress environments are not necessarily constant and in this case are rapid (episodic). They are related to a major evolutionary event and are followed by a period of relatively stable diversities. Caradoc and Ludlow diversity differences can be related primarily to the great number of pentamerid, rhynchonellid, and spiriferid species. These major brachiopod groups, in particular the spiriferids, undergo major adaptive radiation events in the Late Ordovician-Early Silurian (Boucot, 1975; Williams and Hurst, 1977). Thus, we suggest that the increase in diversity from the Caradoc to the Ludlow (if real) is primarily a consequence of this evolutionary process.

Recently, a searching analysis by Bambach (1977) indicates that in open-marine environments (correlating with offshore of this report), there is an increase in the median number of species between what he terms the Lower Paleozoic (Cambrian and Ordovician) and the middle Paleozoic (Silurian and Devonian). Such evidence strongly supports our limited conclusions. On the other hand, Raup (1976a,b) has shown that the major taxonomic turnover in the Paleozoic occurs in the Ordovician with the replacement of trilobite-dominated faunas by a wider variety of taxa. Raup indicates that little change occurs between the Ordovician and the Silurian where, in fact, the increase in diversity occurs. This led Bambach (1977) to conclude that increase in species richness is not correlateable with faunal replacements. Direct faunal replacements may not account for increased species richness, but adaptive radiation events (without direct replacement) may.

Finally, it should be borne in mind that benthic life did not proceed merrily from the Caradoc to the Ludlow. For instance, the terminal Ashgill (Ordovician) glaciation probably reduced the area of the shelf seas, contributing greatly to faunal changes (cf. Schopf, 1974; Simberloff, 1974), particularly as regards species area effects (Simberloff, 1972, 1976).

Implicit in the above arguments is that the Ludlow community in the Bioturbated Mud Facies should be composed of stenotopic narrow-niched species. With regard to one limiting resource, food, Levinton (1972) argued that suspension feeders generally rely on phytoplankton as their food source, which is not predictable due to seasonal successions and other variables. Consequently, he predicted that unlike some deposit feeding system, suspension feeders would not be expected to separate trophically; they would develop a series of contiguous nonoverlapping niches. At face value, such an argument mitigates against Caradoc-Ludlow biologic accommodation of suspension feeding brachiopods. Of course food may not be a limiting resource, but if so, is it a coincidence that diversity increases derive from the brachiopods that develop the most complex lophophores (Williams, 1956; Fürsich and Hurst, 1974) and thus may perhaps specialise trophically? Recent experimental work by McCammon and Reynolds (1976) shows that brachiopods are capable of feeding by direct nutrient assimilation, which presumably is a predictable food source.

Related to the above argument is the fact that the stratigraphic mode of occurrence of some of the brachiopods of the Caradoc Bioturbated Mud Facies is very occasionally opportunistic in nature; very few of the Ludlow species are (Levinton, 1970; Hallam, 1972; Watkins, 1979). Levinton (1970) argued that opportunistic species are not resource limited whereas equilibrium species are, thus lending support to the suggestion of biologic accommodation between the Caradoc and the Ludlow.

In the higher stress environment of the Sands and Silts Facies both the Caradoc and the Ludlow communities conform to the patterns predicted for physically controlled communities (Sanders, 1968; Bretsky and Lorenz, 1970). However, there is a major difference between Caradoc and Ludlow communities concerned with diversities. Although within a sample, diversities are very similar, the number of recorded species in the Ludlow is far greater than in the Caradoc. Superficially, this may be a consequence of greater environmental heterogeneity in the Ludlow. Alternatively, because the pool of species in the Ludlow is greater but sample diversities are comparable, species in the physically controlled communities are, in fact, subject to some limiting resources reflecting some inherent biologic interaction.

On the basis of the Levinton (1970) and Hallam (1972) stratigraphic models for the recognition of opportunistic species, a few brachiopods in the Sands and Silts Facies are opportunistic, suddenly appearing in great abundance but disappearing stratigraphically a few centimetres later. Conversely, the patterns of occurrence of the trilobites in the Caradoc and the molluscs in the Ludlow generally conform to that of equilibrium species; it is these species that are responsible for the diversity of individual Ludlow and Caradoc samples.

Caradoc and Ludlow nearshore communities thus appear to be a mixture of nonresource-limited opportunistic species that tend to be suspension feeding brachiopods (Levinton, 1970, 1972) and constitute the bulk of the relative abundances. Diversities are controlled by the equilibrium species (resource limited?) of trilobites in the Caradoc and molluscs in the Ludlow. However, there is still no obvious reason why sample diversities should equate, other than the suggestion that the whole community is to some extent resource limited and thus by inference, not purely physically controlled. The fact that the brachiopods are the opportunists reflects that they are the generalists; this must be a factor in their overall dominance of the community spectrum, not just the nearshore as predicted by Bretsky and Lorenz (1970).

COMMUNITY EVOLUTION

Probably the first attempt at moulding spatial community patterns into an evolutionary model was that of Bretsky (1969). He claimed that the Lower Paleozoic rocks contain three broad community types, ranging from onshore to offshore: linguloid-molluscan, strophomenid-trilobite, and atrypid-bryozoan. The Caradoc and Ludlow communities do not fit into these categories because there is a great deal of overlap. For instance, the Bioturbated Silts Facies is the point for the greatest diversity and dominance of the strophomenides, but not for the trilobites, which is instead in the Bioturbated Mud Facies. Further, in the Caradoc, bryozoans do not occur in most offshore facies, and they are rare in the Ludlow. In short, the Bretsky (1969) model is not applicable to the Ordovician and Silurian of the Welsh Borderland

Bretsky and Lorenz (1970) projected community evolution in terms of environmental stability and concluded that in unstable environments (most commonly onshore), there should be low rates of evolution and, hence, persistence of stable community structures. Conversely, in more stable environments (most commonly offshore), there should be high rates of evolution and, hence, frequent faunal reorganizations and changes in community structure. These predictions can be investigated in the Caradoc and Ludlow by reference to change or persistence in the morphologic and taxonomic variety of groups. Watkins and Boucot (1975) summarized community changes in four categories, namely, continuity, morphologic replacement, morphologic disappearance, and morphologic appearance.

A high rate of trilobite morphologic replacement occurs between the Caradoc and the Ludlow with no apparent bias in favor of the offshore or onshore communities. However, complete morphologic disappearance is an important aspect of this group and mainly affects the offshore communities. This maybe a reflection of the higher diversity of trilobites in these facies and thus the higher probability of loss.

Morphologic replacement of brachiopods, mainly confined to the orthids and strophomenids occurs commonly in both the nearshore and offshore facies. Such replacements are orthid for orthid and strophomenid for strophomenid. Perhaps the most striking replacement is the plectambonitiid, and strophomenacean faunas of the Caradoc Bioturbated Silts Facies by the Ludlow stropheodontid faunas. Such strophomenid dominance and subsequent replacements appear to carry into the Devonian (De Keyser, 1977). The evolutionary radiation of the pentamerids, rhynchonellids, and spiriferids manifests itself in the great rate of morphologic appearance in the Ludlow offshore communities, which directly relates to the increased diversity in the Bioturbated Mud Facies. Eldredge (1974) related speciation patterns to stability diversity patterns and remarked that if speciation proceeded in offshore environments, there should be some partitioning of niche space. Relating this to offshore spiriferids may provide an ideal opportunity to test the niche variation hypothesis in relation to speciation events.

Examples of generic continuity between the Caradoc and the Ludlow are rare and limited to the orthid *Skenidioides* which is restricted to offshore facies and *Dolerorthis* in predominantly nearshore facies. Brachiopod morphologic disappearances are rare apart from those that affect the inarticulates across the whole environmental spectrum.

Mollusc diversities increase enormously between the Caradoc and the Ludlow, and concordantly, there is a great morphologic appearance of gastropods and bivalves in offshore communities. The environmental tolerance of the palaeotaxodont bivalve *Nuculites* is continuous between the Caradoc and the Ludlow.

On the basis of Caradoc-Ludlow community comparisons (cf. Thayer, 1974), community evolution in terms of morphologic continuity and turn-over rates appears more pronounced in the offshore facies, as predicted by Bretsky and Lorenz (1970). However this is a generalization. In further detail, the highest rate of morphologic replacement affects trilobites and orthid and strophomenid brachiopods whereas the remaining brachiopods and the molluscs are characterized by a high rate of morphologic appearance, predominantly in offshore communities. This is reflected in the increased diversity in the Ludlow Bioturbated Mud Facies.

CONCLUSIONS

The following conclusions are tentative and require rigorous testing both spatially and temporally in other Lower Paleozoic sequences. We feel that as there is much continuity between Caradoc and Ludlow communities and their distribution and relation to facies, many of the patterns can be justifiably used to relate to other sequences.

1. In the Caradoc to Ludlow, a series of equivalent onshore to offshore facies represent gradients of decreasing environmental stress (owing to sedimentary factors), along which community diversity increases, but not at a constant rate. In the Caradoc community diversity decreases into the offshore Bioturbated Mud Facies, whereas in the Ludlow it is the same. The decreased diversity in the Caradoc relates directly to the Laminated Shale Facies. Similar trends are seen in the Ludlow Laminated Shale Facies, but the facies is not interbedded with the Bioturbated Mud Facies as in the Caradoc (Watkins, 1979). In short diversity increases correlate with decreasing environmental stress as deduced from sedimentary factors.

2. There is morphologic parallelism between communities in similar Caradoc and Ludlow facies. Similar species morphologies are repetitively produced during evolutionary diversification of various stocks.

3. Opportunistic species are mainly found in nearshore facies and communities and are mainly represented by brachiopods. Opportunistic species decrease and equilibrium species increase in number into Caradoc and Ludlow offshore facies and communities. Nearshore Caradoc and Ludlow communities are a mixture of opportunistic species that are mainly suspension feeding brachiopods and equilibrium species of trilobites in the Caradoc and molluscs in the Ludlow.

4. Nearshore communities in the Sand and Silt Facies are numerically dominated by pedically attached enteletacean and free-lying concavo-convex strophomenid brachiopods. The diversity contribution of trilobites in the Caradoc is taken over by molluscs in the Ludlow.

5. The Bioturbated Silts Facies are characterized by a diverse strophomenid brachiopod and bryozoan fauna.

6. Bioturbated Mud Facies, although numerically dominated by small suspension feeding brachiopods, are characterized by deposit feeding palaeotaxodont bivalves. Bivalve diversity is greater in the Ludlow and appears to have taken over from trilobites in the Caradoc.

7. As communities are numerically dominated by brachiopods the trophic structure of Caradoc and Ludlow communities is dominated by epifaunal suspension feeders. Only in more offshore communities of

the Bioturbated Silt and Bioturbated Mud Facies is there any obvious trophic structuring with the appearance of infaunal bivalves and epifaunal or infaunal gastropods and trilobites.

8. Community evolution in terms of morphologic turn-over rates affects offshore communities most, as predicted by the Bretsky and Lorenz (1970) model. A low rate of generic continuity exists between Caradoc and Ludlow communities.

9. The faunal diversity of the Caradoc offshore Bioturbated Mud Facies is significantly lower than the Ludlow. The difference is tentatively attributed to the Late Ordovician and Early Silurian pentamerid, rhynchonellid and especially spiriferid adaptive radiations. It supports the stability-time hypothesis of Sanders (1968, 1969; Slobodkin and Sanders, 1969). Recently, Hoffman (1977) has presented a thorough reappraisal of the problems involved with this hypothesis.

ACKNOWLEDGEMENTS

For help and discussion of the many problems aired in this paper, we would like to thank the following persons: A. J. Boucot, P. W. Bretsky, M. G. Lockley, W. S. McKerrow, J. S. Peel and A. Williams. J. M. Hurst's work was supported by a National Environment Research Council postdoctoral fellowship; he publishes with the permission of The Director of the Geological Survey of Greenland.

REFERENCES

Anderton, R. 1976. Tidal-shelf sedimentation: an example from the Scottish Dalradian. *Sedimentology* 23:429-458.

Bambach, R. K. 1977. Species richness in marine benthic habitats through the Phanerozoic. *Paleobiology* 3:152-167.

Bancroft, B. B. 1933. *Correlation Tables of the Stages Costonian-Onnian in England and Wales*. Blakeney, Glos., 4p, (Printed privately).

Bergström, J. 1968. Some Ordovician and Silurian brachiopod assemblages. *Lethaia* 1:230-237.

Boucot, A. J. 1975. Evolution and Extinction Rate Controls. Amsterdam: Elsevier Scientific Publishing Co., 427p.

Bowen, Z. P., D. C. Rhoads, and A. McAlester 1974. Marine benthic communities in the Upper Devonian of New York. *Lethaia* 7:93-120.

Brenner, R. L. and D. K. Davies 1973. Storm-generated coquinoid sandstone: genesis of high-energy marine sediments from the Upper Jurassic of Wyoming and Montana. *Geol. Soc. Am. Bull.* 84:1685-1698.

Bretsky, P. W. 1969. Evolution of Paleozoic benthic marine invertebrate communities. *Palaeogeography, Palaeoclimatology, Palaeoecology* 6:45-60.

Bretsky, P. W. 1970. Upper Ordovician ecology of the central Appalachians. *Peabody Mus. Bull.* 34:1-150.

Bretsky, P. W. and D. M. Lorenz 1970. Adaptive response to environmental stability: a unifying concept in Paleoecology. *North Am. Paleont. Convention Proc.*, E:522-550.

Bridges, P. H. 1975. The transgression of a hard substrate shelf: the Llandovery (Lower Silurian) of the Welsh Borderland. *Jour. Sed. Petrology* 45:79-94.

Calvert, S. E. 1964. Factors affecting distribution of laminated diatomaceous sediments in Gulf of California, in van Andel, T. H., and G. G. Shor, eds., *Marine Geology of the Gulf of California*. Am. Assoc. Petroleum Geologists, Tulsa: pp. 311-330.

Dean, W. T. 1958. The faunal succession in the Caradoc Series of South Shropshire. *Brit. Mus. (Nat. History) Bull., Geology* 3: 191-231.

Eldredge, N. 1974. Stability, diversity, and speciation in Paleozoic epeiric seas. *Jour. Paleontology* 48:540-548.

Emery, K. O., and J. Hülsemann 1962. The relationships of sediments, life, and water in a marine basin. *Deep-Sea Research* 8:165-180.

Fortey, R. 1975. Early Ordovician trilobite communities. *Fossils and Strata* 4:331-352.

Fürsich, F. T., and J. M. Hurst 1974. Environmental factors determining the distribution of brachiopods. *Palaeontology* 17:879-900.

Gadow, S., and H. E. Reineck 1969. Ablandiger sandtransport bei sturmfluten. *Senkenberg. Marit.* 1:63-78.

Goldring, R., and P. Bridges 1973. Sublittoral sheet sandstones. *Jour. Sed. Petrology* 43:736-747.

Hallam, A. 1972. Models involving population dynamics, in Schopf, T. J. M., ed., *Models in Paleobiology*. Freeman, Cooper and Co., San Francisco: pp. 62-80.

Havlíček, V. 1967. Brachiopoda of the suborder Strophomenidina in Czechoslovakia. *Rozpravy. Ustred. Ust. Geol.* 33,235 p.

Hoffman, A. 1977. Synecology of macrobenthic assemblages of the Korytnica Clays (Middle Miocene, Holy Cross Mountains, Poland). *Acta Geol. Polonica* 27:227-280.

Holland, C. H., J. D. Lawson, and V. G. Walmsley 1963. The Silurian rocks of the Ludlow district, Shropshire. *Brit. Mus. (Nat. History) Bull., Geology* 8:95-171.

Howard, J. D., and H. E. Reineck 1972. Georgia coastal region, Sapelo Island, USA. Sedimentology and biology. IV. Physical and biogenic structures of the nearshore shelf. *Senkenberg. Marit.* 4: 81-123.

Hurst, J. M. 1978. A phenetic strategy model for dalmanellid brachiopods. *Palaeontology* 21:535-554.

Hurst, J. M. 1979a. The environment of deposition of the Caradoc *Alternata* Limestone and contiguous deposits of Salop. *Geological Jour.* 14:15-40.

Hurst, J. M. 1979b. Evolution, succession and replacement in the type upper Caradoc (Ordovician) benthic faunas of England. *Palaeogeography, Palaeoclimatology, Palaeoecology* 27:189-246.

Hurst, J. M. 1979c. The stratigraphy and brachiopods of the upper part of the type Caradoc of south Salop. *Brit. Mus. (Nat. History) Bull., Geology* 32:183-304.

Hurst, J. M., and R. A. Hewitt 1977. On Tubular Problematica from the type Caradoc (Ordovician) of England. *Neus Jahrb. Geologie u. Paläontologie Abh.* 153:147-169.

Hurst, J. M., and R. Watkins 1978. Evolutionary patterns in a Silurian orthide brachiopod. *Geologica et Palaeontologica.* 12:73-100.

Johnson, J. G. 1972. Conceptual models of benthic marine communities. in Schopf, T. J. M., ed., *Models in Paleobiology*, San Francisco: Freeman, Cooper and Co., pp. 148-159.

De Keyser, T. L. 1977. Late Devonian (Frasnian) brachiopod community patterns in western Canada and Iowa. *Jour. Paleontology* 51:181-196.

Kumar, N., and J. E. Sanders 1976. Characteristics of shoreface storm deposits: modern and ancient examples. *Jour. Sed. Petrology* 46: 145-162.

Levinton, J. S. 1970. The paleoecological significance of opportunistic species. *Lethaia* 3:69-78.

Levinton, J. S. 1972. Stability and trophic structure in deposit-feeding and suspension-feeding communities. *Am. Naturalist* 106: 472-486.

Levinton, J. S., and R. K. Bambach 1970. Some ecological aspects of bivalve mortality patterns. *Am. Jour. Sci.* 268:97-112.

McCammon, H. M., and W. A. Reynolds 1976. Experimental evidence for direct nutrient assimilation by the lophophore of articulate brachiopods. *Marine Biology* 34:41-51.

Poulson, T. L., and D. C. Culver 1969. Diversity in terrestrial cave communities. *Ecology* 50:153-158.

Raup, D. M. 1976a. Species diversity in the Phanerozoic: a tabulation. *Paleobiology* 3:279-288.

Raup, D. M. 1976b. Species diversity in the Phanerozoic: an interpretation. *Paleobiology* 3:289-297.

Reineck, H. E., and I. B. Singh 1972. Genesis of laminated sand and graded rhythmites in storm-sand layers of shelf mud. *Sedimentology* 18:123-128.

Reineck, H. E., and I. B. Singh 1973. Depositional Sedimentary Environments. Berlin: Springer-Verlag, 439 p.

Rhoads, D. C., and J. W. Morse 1971. Evolutionary and ecologic significance of oxygendeficient marine basins. *Lethaia* 4:413-428.

Rhoads, D. C., and D. K. Young 1970. The influence of deposit-feeding organisms on sediment stability and community trophic structures. *Jour. Marine Research* 28:150-178.

Sanders, H. L. 1968. Marine benthic diversity: a comparative study. *Am. Naturalist* 102:243-282.

Sanders, H. L. 1969. Benthic marine diversity and the stability-time hypothesis. in Woodwell, G. M., and H. H. Smith, eds. *Diversity and Stability in Ecological Systems*. Brookhaven Symp. in Biology 22:71-81.

Schopf, T. J. M. 1974. Permo-Triassic extinctions: relation to sea-floor spreading. *Jour. Geology* 82:129-143.

Scott, R. W. 1974. Bay and shoreface benthic communities in the Lower Cretaceous. *Lethaia* 7:315-330.

Sheehan, P. M. 1975. Brachiopod synecology in a time of crisis (Late Ordovician-Early Silurian). *Paleobiology* 1:205-212.

Simberloff, D. 1972. Models in biogeography. in Schopf, T. J. M., ed., *Models in Paleobiology*, San Francisco: Freeman, Cooper and Co., pp. 160-191.

Simberloff, D. 1974. Permo-Triassic extinctions: effects of area on biotic equilibrium. *Jour. Geology* 82:267-274.

Simberloff, D. 1976. Experimental zoogeography of islands: effects of island size. *Ecology* 57:629-648.

Slobodkin, L. B., and H. L. Sanders 1969. On the contribution of environmental predictability to species diversity. in Woodwell, G. M., and H. H. Smith, eds. *Diversity and Stability in Ecological Systems*. Brookhaven Symp. in Biol. 22:82-95.

Thorson, G. 1967. *Bottom Communities (Sublittoral or Shallow Shelf)*. Geol. Soc. Am. Mem. 67:461-534.

Thorson, G. 1966. Some factors influencing the recruitment and establishment of marine benthic communities. *Netherlands Jour. Sea Research* 3:267-293.

Thayer, C. W. 1974. Marine paleoecology in the Upper Devonian of New York. *Lethaia* 7:121-155.

Watkins, R. 1979. Benthic community organisation in the Ludlow Series of the Welsh Borderland. *Brit. Mus. (Nat. History) Bull. Geology* 31:175-280.

Watkins, R., W. B. N. Berry, and A. J. Boucot 1973. Why "Communities"? *Geology* 1:55-58.

Watkins, R., and A. J. Boucot 1975. Evolution of Silurian brachiopod communities along the southeastern coast of Acadia. *Geol. Soc. Am. Bull.* 86:243-254.

Williams, A. 1956. The calcareous shell of the Brachiopoda and its importance to their classification. *Biol. Rev.* 31:243-287.

Williams, A. 1969. Ordovician faunal provinces with reference to brachiopod distributions. in Wood, A. ed., *The Pre-Cambrian and Lower Palaeozoic Rocks of Wales*. Cardiff: University of Wales Press, pp. 117-154.

Williams, A., and J. M. Hurst 1977. Brachiopod Evolution. in Hallam, A., ed., *Patterns of Evolution*. Amsterdam: Elsevier Scientific Publishing Co., pp. 79-121.

Williams, et al. 1965. Brachiopoda. in Moore, R. C., ed., Treatise on Invertebrate Paleontology, H. Lawrence: University of Kansas Press., pp. 927.

4

Trilobite Ecology in the Ludlow Series of the Welsh Borderland

Donald G. Mikulic and Rodney Watkins

ABSTRACT

Stratigraphic sections of the Ludlow Series in the Welsh Borderland represent an environmental gradient from deep-shelf muds to shallow-shelf, storm-deposited silts. Trilobites show an increase in species diversity and abundance relative to other invertebrates from the shallow to deep ends of the shelf gradient, apparently controlled in distribution by bottom-type and sedimentation conditions. Interrelations of bottom type and trilobite feeding methods may have been a major factor in this environmental zonation. Although the trilobite assemblages are part of an essentially *in situ* fauna in bioturbated sediment, disparate ratios of various parts of the exoskeleton were found, and hypostomata and free cheeks are notably uncommon.

INTRODUCTION

This chapter is the partial outcome of a trilobite ecology study in the Upper Silurian Ludlow Series of the Welsh Borderland. Sediments and benthic communities in this area were described by Watkins (1978, 1979). The stratigraphic succession of communities and sedimentary facies is shown in Figure 4-1. This succession is summarized as a gradient of shelf environments in Figure 4-2. The gradient represents a transect of a shelf dominated by active terrigenous deposition. It begins with quiet-water, deep-shelf mudstones and culminates with siltstones and shell beds deposited under higher-energy conditions on shallow portions of the shelf. Trilobites are characteristic members of benthic communities across all portions of this gradient (Figures 4-1, 4-2).

MATERIAL AND METHODS

Ludlow trilobites of the Welsh Borderland are generally well preserved and readily identifiable to genus and species. In this study, most specimens were decalcified with dilute hydrochloric because fine details of the exoskeleton are most apparent on molds.

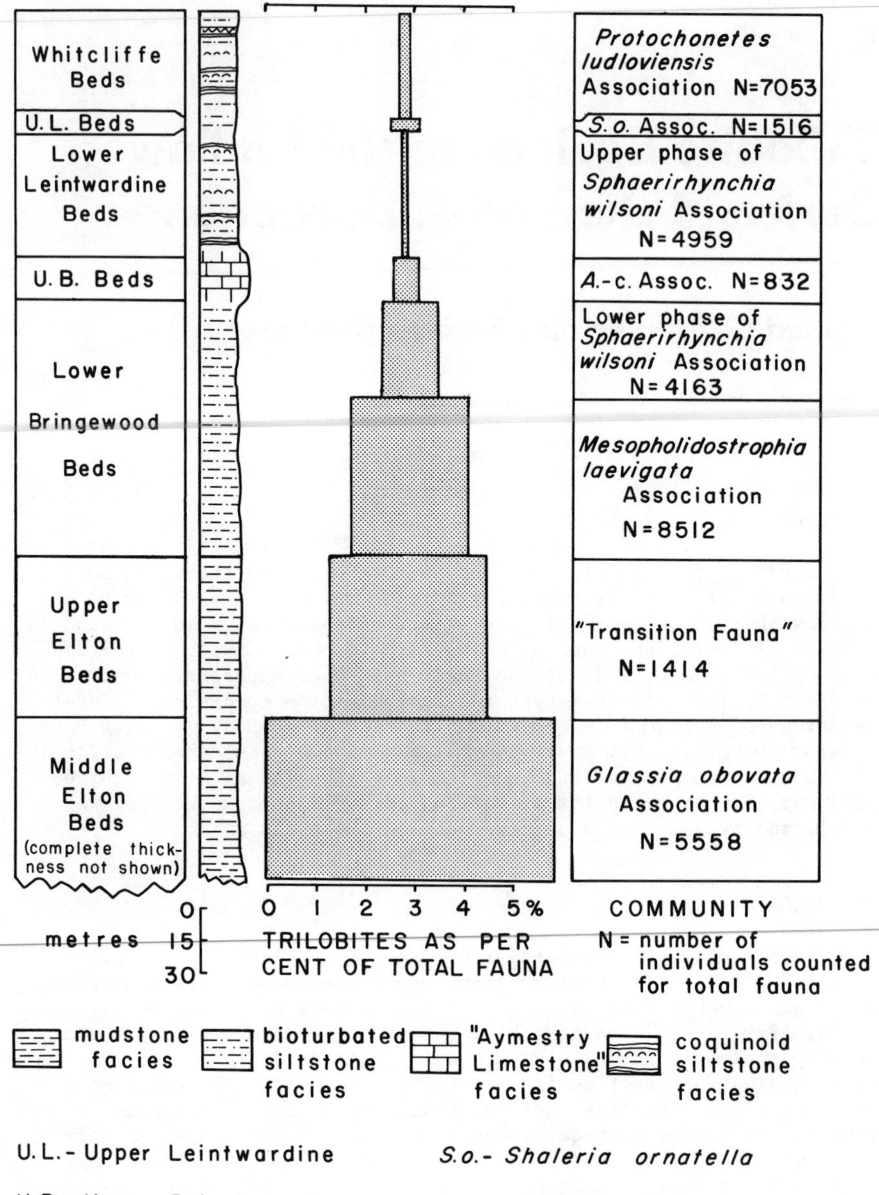

Figure 4-1
Stratigraphy, sedimentary facies, and benthic communities of the Ludlow Series, based on sections measured by Watkins (1979) at Perton, Ledbury, and Woodbury Quarry (see Figure 4-3).

Specimens have been deposited in the University of California Museum of Paleontology, Berkeley, with the exception of encrinurids, which are housed in the British Museum (Natural History), London.

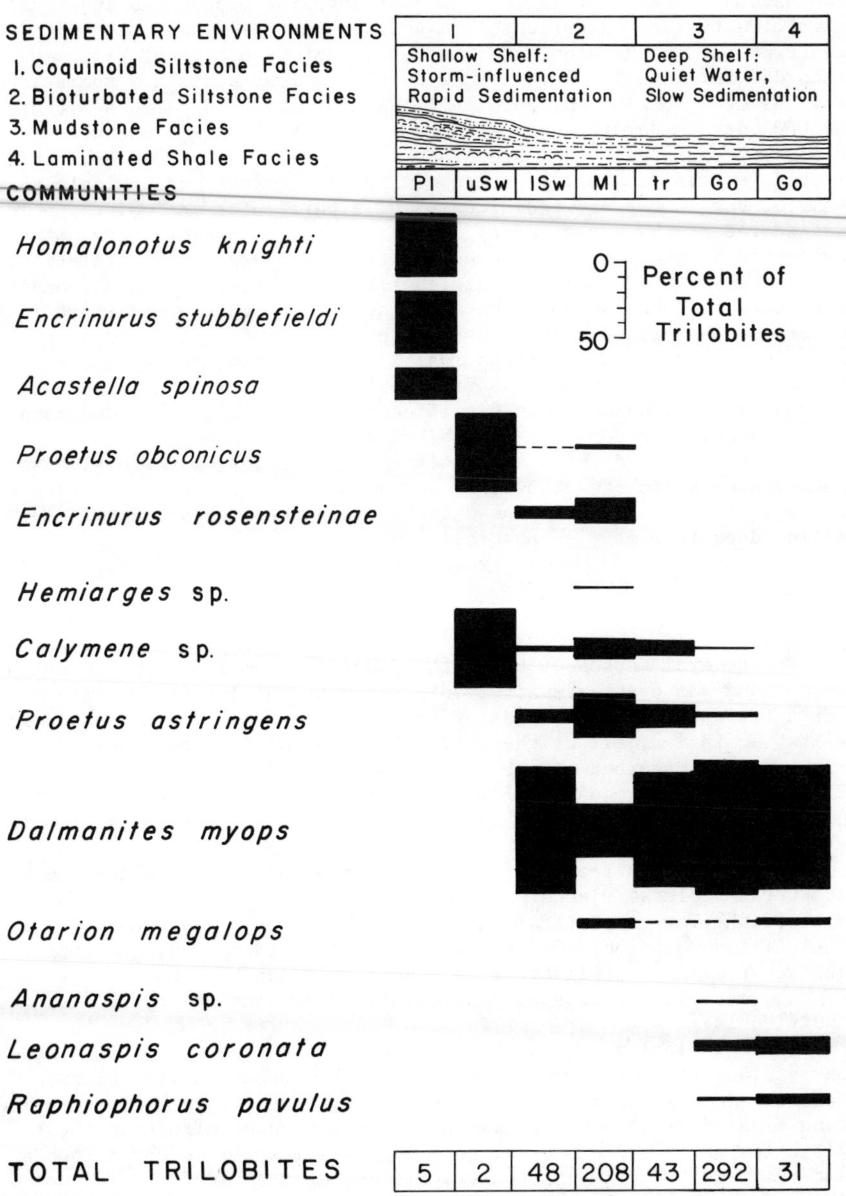

Figure 4-2
Reconstruction of the stratigraphic column on Figure 4-1 as an environmental gradient, showing distribution and abundance of the Ludlow trilobite species. The "Aymestry Limestone" facies is omitted from this gradient for reasons discussed by Watkins (1979).

Collections of Ludlow trilobites were obtained during a broad ecologic study in which 417 samples of bulk rock were taken along measured sections in five areas of the Welsh Borderland (Figure 4-3;

see Watkins, 1979, for full details of sampling procedures and localities). With rare exceptions, trilobites occur as dissociated elements of the exoskeleton, and the numbers of each type of part were recorded for each sample. Counts of the various parts are summarized for selected species in Table 4-1. Watkins (1979) used an arbitrary method for standardizing these data so that trilobite abundance could be consistently compared to that of other invertebrates. This method is retained here in spite of certain limitations. Within each sample, the number of "individuals" of a particular trilobite species was scored as the number of pygidia present. If pygidia were not represented in the sample but other parts were present, the trilobite species was scored as one "individual." This method obviously underestimates the abundance of those trilobites in which pygidia are less numerous than cranidia and other skeletal elements. This bias mainly affects species of *Raphiophorus, Leonaspis,* and *Ananaspis* (Table 4-1). These trilobites are sufficiently rare that any alternate method of counting does not significantly alter their recorded abundance relative to dominant trilobites and total fauna.

Figures 4-4 and 4-5 are stratigraphic examples of the basic data gathered on trilobite occurrence and abundance. The general pattern of trilobite distribution shown in Figure 4-2 was obtained by compiling data from many such stratigraphic logs.

TAPHONOMY

The general taphonomy of Ludlow fossils assemblages in the Welsh Borderland has been extensively discussed by Watkins (1979). Except for a few specimens from beds of transported shells in the coquinoid siltstone facies, all of the trilobite material discussed here derives from "disturbed neighborhood assemblages" (cf. Scott, 1974). These assemblages consist of mud-supported, scattered shells within highly bioturbated sediment and occur within the approximate area in which they lived.

The trilobites are generally represented by disarticulated and scattered skeletal elements that do not show any significant wear. None of the few complete or partially complete specimens were found in a living position. On the basis of this evidence and the moulting characteristics of trilobites in general, it can be assumed that most of this material represents disarticulated exuviae as opposed to dead individuals.

Disarticulation of trilobite exuviae can be the result of a number of factors, but current activity and bioturbation are primary causes. Because of the low density of light-weight trilobite exuviae, even minor current activity may have had a greater effect on their disarticulation and dispersal than on heavier shells of brachiopods and molluscs. The associated brachiopods show an increase in numbers of articulated specimens from the shallow coquinoid siltstone facies to the deeper mudstone facies (Watkins, 1979). The trilobites appear to show a similar pattern of articulation. However, because of the small number of total trilobite remains in the shallow facies and the small number of complete specimens in the deeper-shelf facies, the real trend is uncertain.

As an attempt was made to save every trilobite part in each sample, it is possible to determine if all skeletal elements had an equal chance to be preserved. No trilobites under 3 mm were disco-

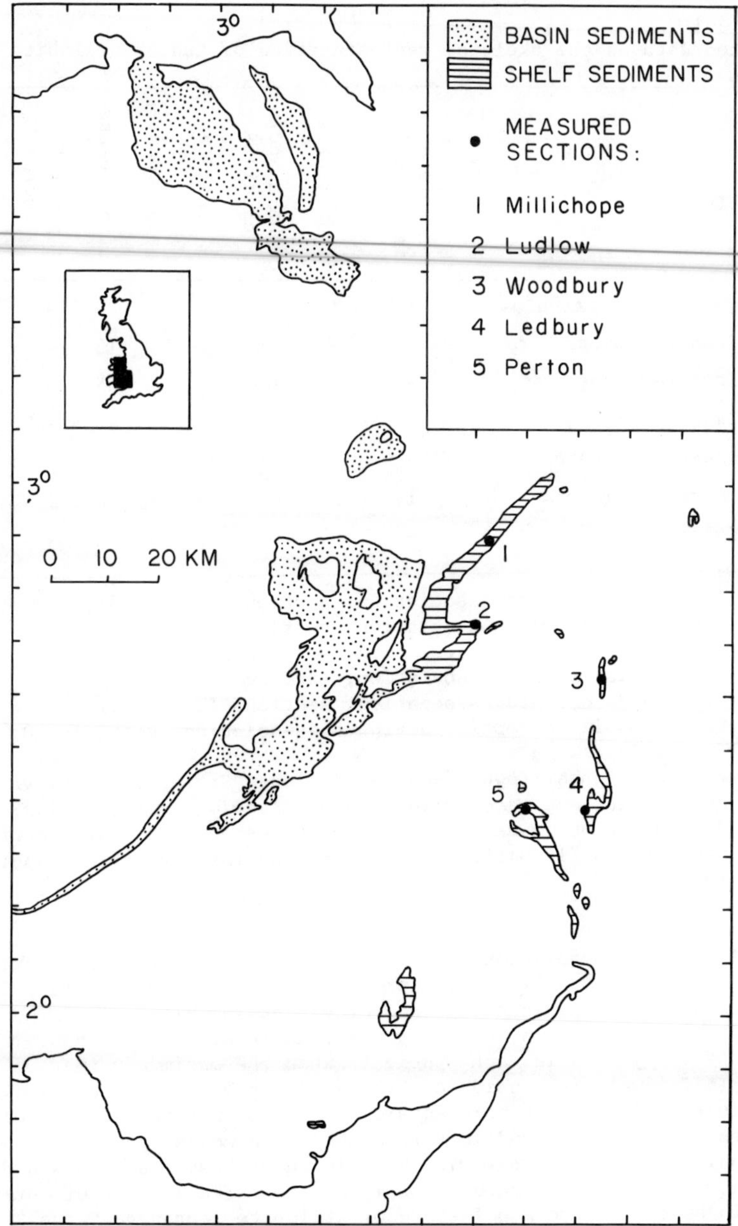

Figure 4-3
Ludlow outcrop of Wales and the Welsh Borderland, showing the location of study areas (after Watkins, 1979, Figure 1).

vered. This might reflect only the difficulties of thoroughly examining large volumes of the particular matrix involved. Trilobites such as *Raphiophorus* are probably under-represented in collections because of their small size, but this is not thought to greatly affect the

Table 4-1
Selected data on the skeletal representation of Ludlow trilobite species

Trilobite	complete individual	partial individuals	cephala and/or cranidia	cranidia	hypostomata	free cheeks	partial thorax	pygidia
1. *Raphiophorus parvulus*	1	2	11	-	-	-	-	-
2. *Dalmanites myops*	-	-	16	-	2	13	-	22
3. *Dalmanites myops*	-	-	109	-	5	55	-	131
4. *Dalmanites myops*	-	-	57	-	1	42	-	98
5. *Leonaspis coronata*	-	-	-	15	1	8	-	9
6. *Proetus astringens*	1	3	-	15	-	26	1	34
7. *Calymene* sp.	-	-	-	15	-	1	-	18

Note: 1.=*Glassia obovata* Association, sections 1E, 2J, 5I;
2.=*Glassia obovata* Association, section 2J
3.=*Glassia obovata* Association, section 1E
4.=*Glassia obovata* Association, section 5I
5.=*Glassia obovata* Association, sections 1E, 2J, 5I
6.=*Mesopholidostrophia laevigata* Association, sections 1D, 2F, 3A, 4B
7.=Upper *Sphaerirhynchia wilsoni*, lower *Sphaerirhynchia wilsoni* Association, *Mesopholidostrophia laevigata* Association, transition fauna, *Glassia obovata* Association, all sections.
See Watkins (1979) for location of the various stratigraphic sections.

overall faunal composition. It is also apparent that certain skeletal parts are significantly under-represented in most samples (Table 4-1). Hypostomata are conspicuously rare or absent for all taxa. Free cheeks are not uncommon, but they occur in fewer numbers than either cranidia or pygidia in each species. When the maximum number of possible individuals is considered by dividing the free cheeks by two, the discrepancy is even more apparent. No attempt was made to differentiate between right and left free cheek. A comparison of the number of cranidia and/or cephala with pygidia in each species shows a discrepancy that is independent of sample size. The absence or rarity of certain parts is a common feature of trilobites throughout the Paleozoic.

The reason for these discrepancies in number of parts is unclear. Size of specimens may be a factor in the rarity of hypostomata of *Raphiophorus* and *Leonaspis*, but in *Dalmanites* the hypostoma is as large as the cranidia or pygidia of many of the associated trilobites and is, therefore, unlikely to have been missed. Sorting and transportation of parts is unlikely because the missing parts have not been found in other areas. Biological or chemical destruction resulting from differing rates of burial or slight differences in chemical

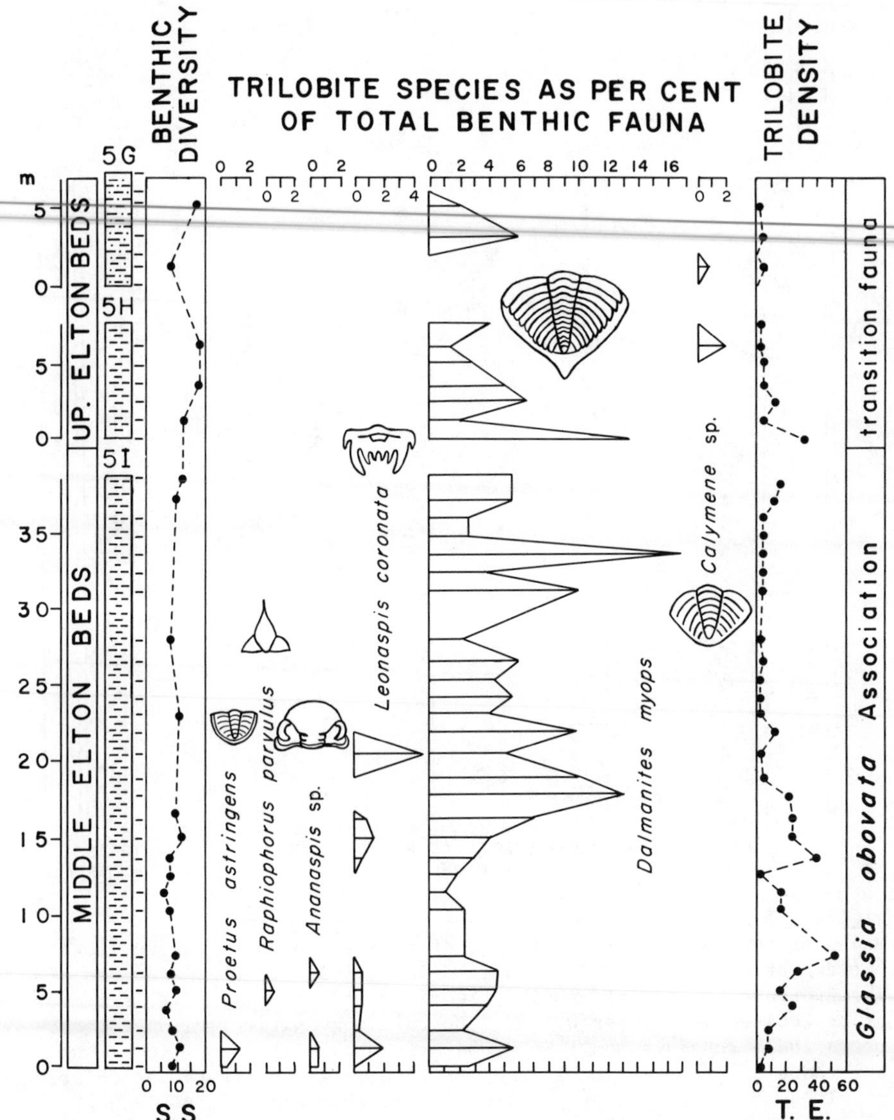

Figure 4-4
Measured sections and trilobite occurrences near Perton (located between grid references SO 59233918 and SO 59253950). S.S. = number of invertebrate species at sample size of 50 individuals. T.E. = number of trilobite exuviae per 0.1 m^2. See Figure 4-1 for explanation of lithologic symbols.

composition of individual skeletal elements may be factors to consider, but these considerations cannot be tested with the specimens under study. It is possible that some of the absence of parts may be due to random variations of occurrence in each sample, but the signi-

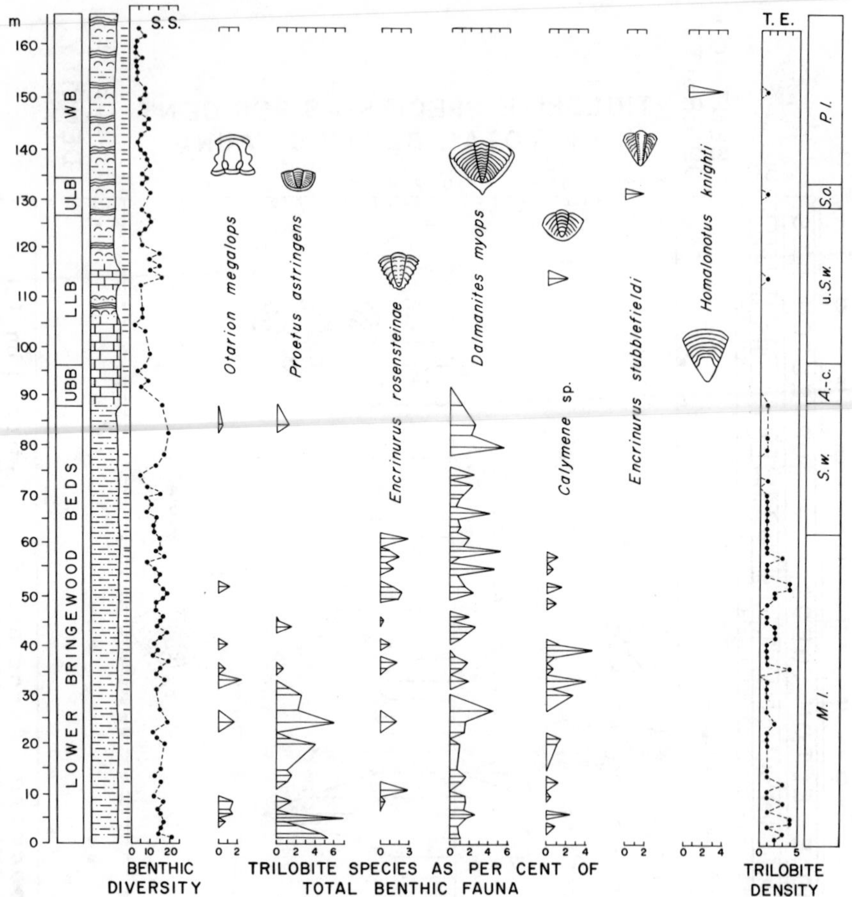

Figure 4-5
Measured section and trilobite occurrences at Woodbury Quarry (located between grid reference SO 744637 and SO 74256363). S.S. = number of invertebrate species at sample size of 50 individuals. T.E. = number of trilobite exuviae per 0.1 m^2. Benthic communities: Pl = *Protochonetes ludloviensis* Assoc.; So = *Shaleria ornatella* Assoc.; uSw = upper phase of *Sphaerirhynchia wilsoni* Assoc.; A-c = *Atrypa reticularis*-coral Assoc.; lSw = lower phase of *Sphaerirhynchia wilsoni* Assoc.; Ml = *Mesopholidostrophia laevigata* Assoc. See Figure 4-1 for explanation of lithologic symbols.

ficant variety of hypostomata and free cheeks is not easily explained.

SIZE RELATIONS OF THE TRILOBITES

No apparent trends in increase or decrease of trilobite size exist across the Ludlow shelf gradient. Most of the species in mid- and outer-shelf sediments are of small size, but they are overshadowed by large specimens of the more abundant *Dalmanites myops* (Table

Table 4-2
Mean size in millimeters for width of pygidium (P) and length of glabella (G) of Ludlow trilobite species. Figures in parentheses give the number of measured specimens.

Trilobite	Coquinoid siltstone facies	Bioturbated siltstone facies	Mudstone facies and laminated shale facies
P *Homalonotus knighti* (König)	18.5(2)	--	--
G *Acastella spinosa* (Salter)	5.0(1)	--	--
P *Encrinurus stubblefieldi* Tripp	8.9(4)	--	--
P *Proetus obconicus* (Dalman)	6.6(2)	--	--
P *Calymene* sp.	--	15.2(8)	12.2(5)
P *Encrinurus rosensteinae* Tripp, Temple & Gass	--	7.2(16)	--
P *Hemiarges* sp.	--	4.0(1)	--
P *Proetus astringens* Owens	--	5.9(30)	8.0(7)
G *Otarion megalops* (M'Coy)	--	3.0(6)	--
P *Leonaspis coronata* (Salter)	--	--	9.0(8)
G *Raphiophorus parvulus* (Forbes)	--	--	2.1(9)
G *Ananaspis* sp.	--	--	6.5(5)
P *Dalmanites myops* (König)	--	16.1(19)	16.8(135)

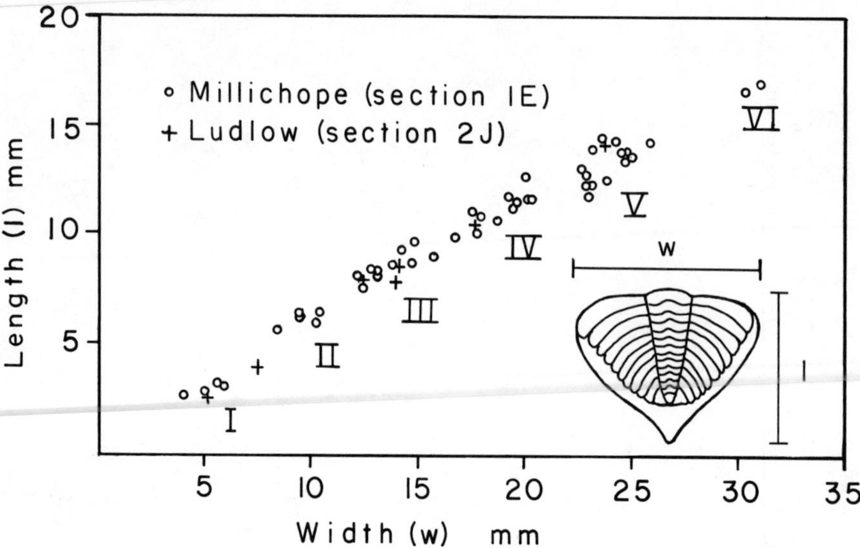

Figure 4-6
Pygidium dimensions of *Dalmanites myops* from the *Glassia obovata* Assoc. These data suggest that individuals with pygidia larger than about 4 mm went through 6 molt stages.

4-2). One notable feature shown in Table 4-2 is the heterogeneity of trilobite size in the offshore facies. This may reflect feeding specialization based on the ability to manipulate and swallow particulate matter of different sizes.

Pygidium measurements for two of the common Ludlow trilobite species appear to indicate the presence of several distinct molt stages. A scatter diagram of pygidium dimensions for *Dalmanites myops* is shown in Figure 4-6. These data suggest six molt stages in the holaspid period. A similar scatter diagram for the pygidia of *Proetus astringens* suggests five molt stages (Figure 4-7). On the basis of these results, we suggest that large, unbiased collections of trilobite material from bulk rock samples offer a reliable method for defining the number and relative abundance of molt stages among trilobite species.

GENERAL PATTERN OF ABUNDANCE AND DIVERSITY

Ludlow trilobites of the Welsh Borderland show maximum abundance in deep-shelf sediments of the laminated shale facies and mudstone facies and decline in abundance in sediments deposited under shallower-shelf conditions. This is a gradual and continuous trend as shown in Figure 4-1. In communities of the outer-shelf mudstone facies, trilobites comprise 5.8 to 3.1 percent of the benthic fauna. In communities of the bioturbated siltstone facies, trilobites comprise 2.4 to 1.2 percent of fauna; and in the coquinoid siltstone facies of the shallow shelf, they form 0.7 to 0.1 percent of fauna. These figures are based on methods of faunal counting used by Watkins (1979). Point-

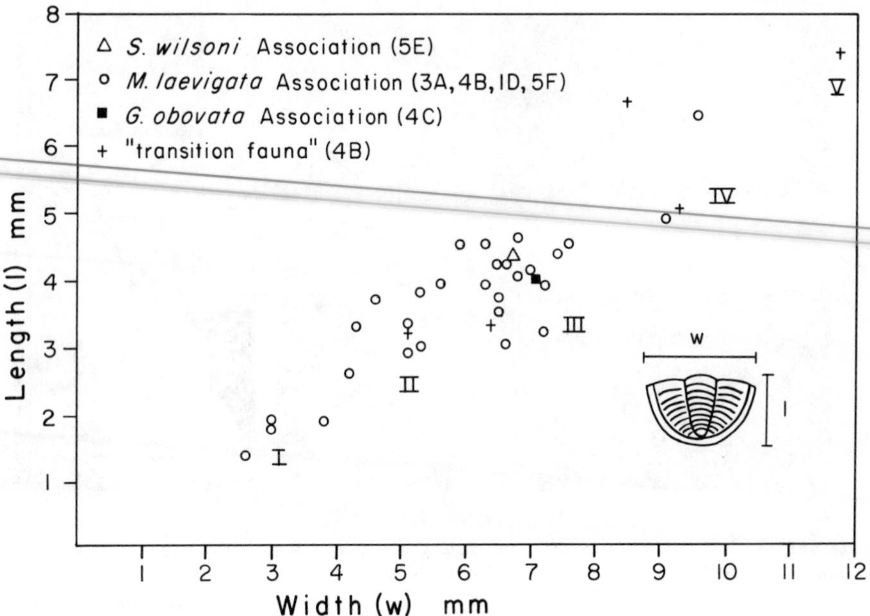

Figure 4-7
Pygidium dimensions of *Proetus astringens*. These data suggest that individuals with pygidia larger than 2 mm went through 5 molt stages.

count data from polished sections show the same trend in trilobite abundance. In the outer shelf mudstone facies, trilobites may comprise as much as 25 percent of skeletal material in single samples. The maximum abundance of trilobites recorded in samples from the bioturbated siltstone facies and coquinoid siltstone facies is 5 percent of skeletal material. The point-count data are given in Watkins and Hurst (1977, Figure 7).

This trend in abundance is paralleled by an apparent decline in trilobite diversity from deep- to shallower-shelf environments. Maxima of seven trilobite species have been recorded in communities of the mudstone facies and bioturbated siltstone facies whereas communities of the coquinoid siltstone facies have yielded only two or three trilobite species (Figure 4-2). Although we feel that the numbers of recorded species shown in Figure 4-2 reflect a real trend, it must be noted that trilobite sample sizes from the shallow-shelf sediments are extremely small.

ASSEMBLAGES OF TRILOBITES ACROSS THE SHELF GRADIENT

The environmental plot of trilobite species in Figure 4-2 shows that each species can be characterized by a particular environmental range and some area of optimum occurrence. The overlaps of these ranges define characteristic assemblages of trilobites along various parts of the shelf gradient. The general pattern of the environmental zonation differs in no essential way from that of bivalves or brachiopods in the same sediments (Watkins, 1978, 1979).

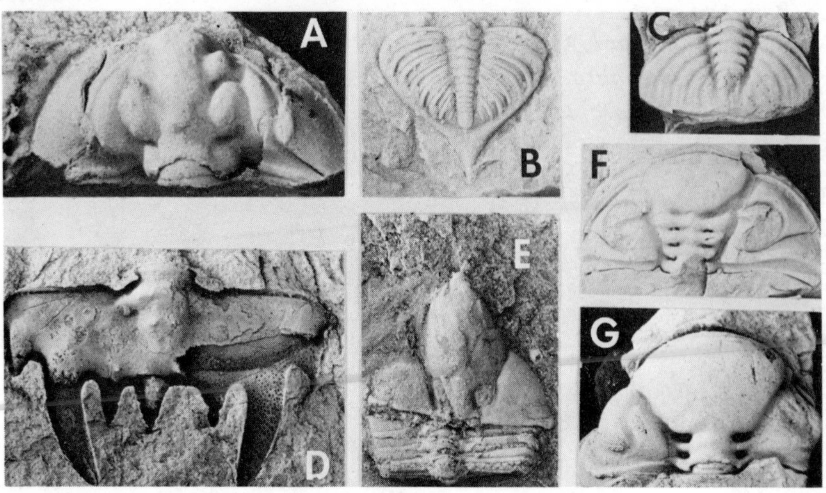

Figure 4-8
Outer shelf trilobites of the mudstone facies and laminated shale facies. All specimens from the Middle Elton Beds. A. *Leonaspis coronata*, cephalon, x4, Ludlow district, UCMP 14635; B. *Dalmanites myops*, pygidium, x1, Millichope, UCMP 14636; C. *Calymene* sp., pygidium, x1.3, Millichope, UCMP 14637; D. *L. coronata*, pathologic pygidium showing reduction in number of spines, x3.2, Millichope, UCMP 14638; E. *Raphiophorus parvulus*, complete individual, x5.1, Ludlow district, UCMP 14639; F. *D. myops*, cephalon, x1.3, Perton, UCMP 14640; G. *Ananaspis* sp., cephalon, x2.6, Millichope, UCMP 14641.

MUDSTONE FACIES AND LAMINATED SHALE FACIES

The mudstone facies is a clay-rich, nonbedded sediment in which over 99 percent of primary sedimentary structures have been destroyed by bioturbation. The laminated shale facies is a textural and compositional equivalent with very little bioturbation probably because of very low oxygen content of bottom waters. These sediments contain communities described as the *Glassia obovata* Association and "transition fauna" by Watkins (1979). *Dalmanites myops* greatly predominates among trilobites in these facies (Figure 4-2). In sections of the mudstone facies, *D. myops* shows a continuous stratigraphic occurrence and peaks of abundance in which it comprises as much as 17 percent of all benthic shells (Figure 4-4). Associated trilobites, in rank order, include *Leonaspis coronata*, *Proetus astringens*, *Calymene* sp., *Raphiophorus parvulus*, *Ananaspis* sp., and *Otarion megalops*. These species are present only in sporadic samples along stratigraphic sections and always show very low abundance relative to other invertebrates. Trilobites of the mudstone facies and laminated shale facies are illustrated in Figure 4-8.

BIOTURBATED SILTSTONE FACIES

This is a facies that accumulated along the middle part of the shelf gradient and in which 96 percent of primary sedimentary struc-

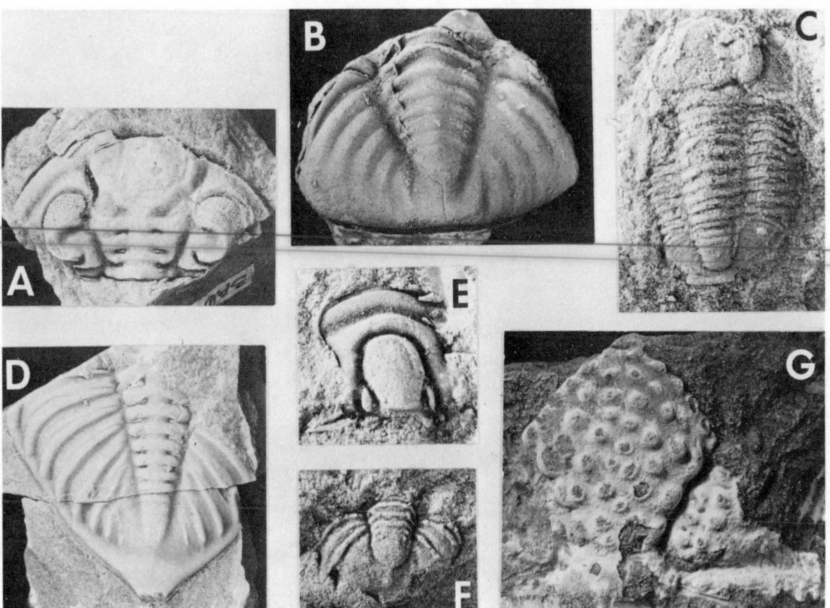

Figure 4-9
Mid-shelf trilobites of the bioturbated siltstone facies. All specimens from the Lower Bringewood Beds. A. *Dalmanites myops*, cephalon, x1.4, Woodbury Quarry, UCMP 14642; B. *Calymene* sp., pygidium, x2.1, UCMP 14643; C. *Proetus astringens*, complete individual, x4.4, Millichope, UCMP 14644; D. *D. myops*, pygidium, x1, Woodbury Quarry, UCMP 14645; E. *Otarion megalops*, cranidium, x4.8, Woodbury Quarry, UCMP 14646; F. *Hemiarges* sp., pygidium, x4.8, Ludlow district, UCMP 14647; G. *Encrinurus rosensteinae*, cranidium, x4, Ludlow district, UCMP 14648.

tures have been destroyed by bioturbation. It contains communities described as the *Mesopholidostrophia laevigata* Association and lower phase of the *Sphaerirhynchia wilsoni* Association by Watkins (1979). In rank order, the predominant trilobites are *Dalmanites myops*, *Proetus astringens*, *Encrinurus rosensteinae*, and *Calymene* sp. These species show generally high frequencies of occurrence through closely samples along stratigraphic sections. Although they commonly co-occur, they often alternate stratigraphically in dominance of the trilobite fauna as shown in Figure 4-5. Less common species include *Otarion megalops*, *Proetus obconicus*, and *Hemiarges* sp. Trilobites of the bioturbated siltstone facies are illustrated in Figure 4-9.

COQUINOID SILTSTONE FACIES

This facies represents the shallowest phase of Ludlow deposition, with active, storm-related pulses of sedimentation. Twenty-five percent of primary sedimentary structures have escaped destruction by bioturbation due to the thickness and probable rapid deposition of storm-emplaced sheets of siltstone. Trilobites are generally uncom-

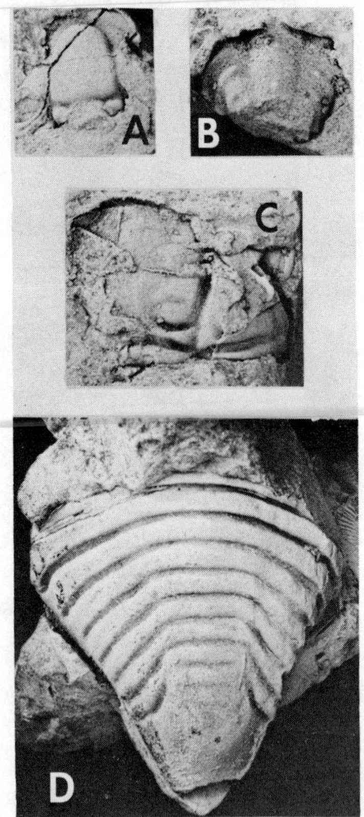

Figure 4-10
Shallow shelf trilobites of the coquinoid siltstone facies. A. *Proetus obconicus*, cranidium, x1.1, Upper Leintwardine Beds, Ledbury area, UCMP 14649; B. *Encrinurus stubblefieldi*, pygidium, x3.8, Lower Whitcliffe Beds, Ludlow, UCMP 14650; C. *Acastella* sp., incomplete cephalon, x4.2, Upper Leintwardine Beds, Ledbury area, UCMP 14651; D. *Homalonotus knighti*, pygidium, x2.1, Whitcliffe Beds, Woodbury Quarry, UCMP 14652.

mon in this facies and our sample is too small to accurately measure relative abundance within the trilobite fauna (Figure 4-2). In the upper phase of the *Sphaerirhynchia wilsoni* Association of the Lower Leintwardine Beds, we have recorded *Proetus obconicus* and *Calymene* sp. In the *Protochonetes ludloviensis* Association of the Whitcliffe Beds, we have recorded *Homalonotus knighti*, *Acastella spinosa*, and *Encrinurus stubblefieldi*. These species are illustrated in Figure 4-10.

OTHER TRILOBITE ASSEMBLAGES

The *Shaleria ornatella* Association of the Upper Leintwardine Beds and the *Atrypa reticularis*-coral Association of the Upper Bringewood Beds have been omitted from the gradient of shelf environments reconstructed in Figure 4-2. These communities were short-lived anomolies related more to brief changes in hydrographic patterns than to the overall succession of major shelf environments (Watkins, 1979). The *Atrypa reticularis*-coral Association is a low-diversity "relict" community derived from the fauna of the bioturbated siltstone facies. It has yielded only rare specimens of *Dalmanites myops*. The *Shaleria ornatella* Association occupies a thin stratigraphic interval of the coquinoid siltstone facies and contains more common trilobites than are normally found in this facies (Figure 4-1). We have recorded *Proetus obconicus*, *Encrinurus stubblefieldi*, and *Calymene neointermedia* from this association.

DISCUSSION

Watkins (1979) summarized the major trends in environmental conditions from the deep to shallow ends of the Ludlow shelf gradient. Toward the shallow shelf, these trends involve decrease in clay content of sediment, increase in grain size of silt and sand, decrease in amount of sediment bioturbation, increase in general sedimentation rate, and increased frequency and intensity of storm-sedimentation events. These trends are associated with decreased trilobite abundance, decrease in trilobite diversity, and progressive changes in the species content of trilobite assemblages. This correlation suggests that trilobites, like other Ludlow benthos, were highly sensitive to sedimentation conditions on the shelf. Water depth, as such, should not be considered as an important factor controlling the trilobite distribution.

Modes of trilobite feeding may account for many of the distributional relational relations of Ludlow trilobites to sedimentary facies. They are thought to have been mainly deposit feeders and filter feeders (Bergström, 1969). Trilobites could have functioned as deposit feeders in two manners. One method would be direct ingestion of organic-rich sediment; alternatively, some trilobites may have picked up particulate matter with their appendages and transferred it to the mouth. As filter feeders, trilobites may have created currents beneath the body in the manner of many modern decapods, stirring up organic matter from the bottom by movement of their appendages.

These considerations suggest that trilobites were mainly dependent on organic material concentrated at or near the sediment surface. In this regard, it is significant that Ludlow trilobites are most abundant and diverse in highly bioturbated muds and silts of the mid- to outer-shelf region. Such sediments would probably have afforded them higher concentrations of organic material than the cleaner silts and sandy silts of the shallower-shelf sediments. It is also significant that the mudstone facies contains the greatest abundance of deformative bioturbation and nucloid bivalves in the Ludlow, indicating that deposit feeding was an important activity in outer-shelf environments (Watkins, 1979).

Although the decrease in trilobite abundance and diversity correlates with increased rates of sedimentation toward the shallow shelf, high sedimentation rate as such was probably not lethal to the Ludlow trilobites. High sedimentation rates would tend to dilute the organic material in sediments and secondarily limit the potential for trilobite feeding on a large scale. These considerations are not meant to imply that all Ludlow trilobites fed in the modes suggested above. Some species may have been scavengers or occasional predators on small organisms, and others may have been filter feeders utilizing organic material directly from the water column.

Explanations for the restricted facies distribution of the individual trilobite species pose a more difficult problem. Most trilobites were probably vagrant benthos with some swimming and burrowing capabilities. Clarkson (1969) suggested that *Leonaspis* could function both as a filter feeder and a deposit feeder by changing the orientation of its cephalon relative to the sediment surface. Whereas *Leonaspis* may have had some swimming capability, it probably spent most of its time on the bottom. Its spinosity indicates that it was not a significant burrower. Clarkson's (1966) study of *Eophacops* applies to the functional behavior of the closely related *Ananaspis* of the Ludlow. Both are characterized by an anterior arch of the cephalon. In life orientation, this arch would raise the hypostome off the substrate, which suggests a filter-feeding mode of life (Clarkson, 1966). Alternatively, Eldredge (1970) suggested that the anterior arch in trilobites was a burrowing adaptation. Even if used in burrowing, however, the anterior arch could still have been primarily a feature of feeding behavior in trilobites.

Little can be said concerning the functional morphology of other trilobites encountered in this study. *Raphiophorus* and *Encrinurus* were probably not burrowers because of their spinosity and tuberculation. *Homalonotus* has been considered as a burrower by Bergström (1973). In the Welsh Borderland, it occurs in a shallow water and presumably well-lit environment, and its small eyes are in accord with a burrowing mode of life. Life habits of the other Ludlow trilobites are uncertain.

In summary, our data show that the occurrence of Ludlow trilobite species in the Welsh Borderland is closely tied to the distribution of sedimentary facies along a shallow- to deep-shelf gradient. Although we cannot explain the environmental relations of Ludlow trilobites on a species-by-species basis, their general pattern is typical of both ancient and modern shelf invertebrates. Work in progress by Mikulic suggests that the environmentally controlled assemblages of Ludlow trilobites have taxonomic and morphologic parallels in other areas of Silurian terrigenous rocks.

ACKNOWLEDGMENTS

Many of the ideas presented in this paper were discussed with Joanne Mikulic, who also typed the manuscript and drafted the figures. Part of this research was supported by National Science Foundation grant EAR74-22051, A03 to A. J. Boucot, Oregon State University, Corvallis.

REFERENCES

Bergström, J. 1969. Remarks on the appendages of trilobites. *Lethaia* 2:395-414.

Bergström, J. 1973. Organization, life, and systematics of trilobites. *Fossils and Strata 2*, 69 p.

Clarkson, E. N. K. 1966. The life attitude of the Silurian trilobite *Phacops musheni* Salter 1864. *Scottish Jour. Geol.* 2:76-83.

Clarkson, E. N. K. 1969. A functional study of the Silurian odontopleurid trilobite *Leonaspis deflexa* (Lake). *Lethaia* 2:329-344.

Eldredge, N. 1970. Observations on burrowing behavior in *Limulus polyphemus* (Chelicerata, Merostomata), with implications on the functional anatomy of trilobites. *Am. Mus. Novitates* 2436, 17 p.

Scott, R. W. 1974. Bay and shoreface benthic communities in the Lower Cretaceous. *Lethaia* 7:315-330.

Watkins, R. 1978. Bivalve ecology in a Silurian shelf environment. *Lethaia* 11:41-56.

Watkins, R. 1979. Benthic community organization in the Ludlow Series of the Welsh Borderland. *Brit. Mus. (Nat. History) Bull., Geology* 31:178-277.

Watkins, R., and J. M. Hurst. 1977. Community relations of Silurian crinoids at Dudley, England. *Paleobiology* 3:207-217.

5

Silurian and Lower Devonian Zoogeography of Selected Molluscan Genera

Gerald Glenn Forney, A. J. Boucot, and D. M. Rohr

ABSTRACT

Several Lower Devonian level-bottom molluscan genera have a biogeographic distribution in agreement with patterns previously noted in brachiopod studies. *Oriostoma* and *Poleumita* are two closely related, possibly congeneric, gastropods with a cosmopolitan, North Silurian Real distribution in the Silurian. *Oriostoma* is restricted to the Old World Realm of the Lower Devonian in Alaska, Australia, Austria, Czechoslovakia, France, Turkey, and the Soviet Union. The gastropod *Boiotremus* and its probable ancestor *Tremanotus* are widely distributed in the Silurian, but *Boiotremus* is known only from the Old World Lower Devonian of Alaska, Austria, Arctic Canada, Czechoslovakia, and Australia. *Euomphalopterus* has a similarly widespread Silurian distribution that contrasts with an Old World Realm Devonian distribution. The pelecypod *Hercynella* is a widely distributed Old World Realm Lower Devonian element that has been reported from Alaska, California, Michigan, Austria, Bulgaria, Czechoslovakia, France, Germany, Turkey, Morocco, Australia, and the Soviet Union. *Hercynella* was described from Pridoli strata in New York, but is otherwise unknown from the Silurian.

The stratigraphic ranges of *Oriostoma*, *Boiotremus*, and *Hercynella* suggest that the Lower Division on Kasaan Island, Alaska, is Early rather than Middle Devonian in age.

We conclude that the biogeography of these selected molluscan genera is in agreement with the brachiopod-based biogeography of the Lower Devonian for which a high level of cosmopolitanism is indicated in the Silurian followed by provincialism in the Lower Devonian.

INTRODUCTION

Boucot et al. (1969) and Boucot (1975) established and modified three Early Devonian animal realms (*sic*, provinces) based on the global distribution of numerous brachiopod genera. Silurian brachiopod faunas tend to be cosmopolitan whereas the more limited marine deposits of the Lower Devonian contain endemic faunas. The Old World Realm is characterized by a high percentage of brachiopods that are Silurian relicts whereas the Eastern Americas and the Malvinokaffric realms are characterized by newly evolved forms.

Boucot et al. (1969) and Boucot (1975) noted in passing that other faunal elements besides brachiopods have similar distributional patterns. Poleumitid gastropods are cited as Silurian holdovers characteristic of the Old World Realm Lower Devonian. The Lower Devonian molluscs of Victoria, Australia, include relict Silurian forms, including *Tremanotus*, *Phanerotrema*, *Valatotheca*, and *Cyclonema* until the lower Emsian. One of the newly evolved forms noted as characteristic of the Lower Devonian Old World Realm is the bivalve *Hercynella*.

The Bohemian gastropod fauna of Siegenian and Emsian ages is very similar to contemporaneous faunas in Austria and France. Two gastropod genera, *Phanerotrema* and *Plectonotus*, are widespread in Lower Devonian strata and do not respect provincial boundaries.

The widespread, level-bottom, gastropod genera selected to illustrate the above distributional patterns are *Oriostoma* and *Poleumita* in the family Oriostomatidae, *Tremanotus* and *Boiotremus* in the family Sinuitidae, and *Euomphalopterus* in the family Euomphalopteridae. The pelecypod *Hercynella* in the family Antipleuridae is also included.

The above genera will be reviewed and their worldwide distribution will be examined to determine any biogeographic patterns during the Silurian and Lower Devonian.

ORIOSTOMA AND *POLEUMITA*

The genus *Oriostoma* was erected by Munier-Chalmas (1876:103), and *O. barrandei* was its sole species from the Lower Devonian. Knight (1941:219) did not select a neotype because several species of *Oriostoma* occur at the type locality. Knight (1941:218) also pointed out that Fischer's (1885:813-814) emendation of *Oriostoma* to *Horiostoma* was incorrect.

J. Sowerby (1814:113) described *Euomphalus discors* from the Silurian Wenlock limestone at Coalbrookdale, Shropshire. De Koninck (1881:107) realized that *E. discors* was not congeneric with other euomphalids, so he based a new genus, *Polytropis*, on it. Lindström (1884:156) felt that *Polytropis* was a junior synonym of *Oriostoma* even though his specimens from Gotland were not operculate. Fischer (1887:813) also felt that they were a single genus. However, Koken (1889:427, 477) disagreed and described *Polytropis* and *Oriostoma* as two distinct genera.

Clarke and Ruedemann (1903:60) realized that the grounds for distinguishing *Oriostoma* from *Polytropis* were flimsy. "Our impulse is to array the species from the Guelph which we are about to discuss under Munier-Chalmas genus." They resisted that impulse and instead introduced the name *Poleumita* to replace *Polytropis*, but based the generic characters on *P. Scamnata*. Bassler (1915:1017) also listed *P. Scamnata* as type species. However, Knight (1941:263) pointed out that a change in type species was not proper so that *Poleumita* must be based on *Euomphalus discors*.

Donald (1905:575) also realized that *Polytropis* was preoccupied, but because of the confusion about the type species for *Poleumita* she introduced *Polytropina*, junior objective synonym of *Poleumita* (Knight, 1941:263).

Knight et al. (1960:1245) place *Oriostoma* in the family Oriostomatidae of the superfamily Oriostomatacea. They place *Poleumita* in the family Euomphalidae of the Euomphalacea. They state that *Poleumita* differs "from *Oriostoma* with which it has long been confused, in closure of abandoned whorls by septae, in lacking a nacreous inner layer, and in having no calcareous operculum" (Knight et al., 1960:I192).

The presence or absence of an operculum and of an outer calcitic shell may be an artifact of preservation, and the indications of septae are confusing. Boucot and Yochelson (1966:A13) placed *Poleumita* in the family Oriostomatidae rather than the Euomphalidae. However, they state that "the evidence for neither emplacement is strong" (Boucot and Yochelson, 1966:A13).

We feel that *Poleumita* is a junior subjective synonym of *Oriostoma* and have included occurrences of the two together. However, all our citations are original-author usage; the genus to which an author referred his specimens is obvious. Formal reassignment will have to await a revision of the two genera.

Oriostoma and *Poleumita* have a stratigraphic range from the Lower? or Upper Llandovery to the Emsian (Table 5-1). There are three reports of *Oriostoma* from the Middle Devonian, but these are ambiguous. *Polytropis subcostata* Perner, 1907 (:182-183, Plate 63, Figures 18-20) is based on a single specimen that may be from the Eifelian Suchomasty Limestone at Menany or between Manany and Koneprusy. Vostakova (1961:30, Plate 7, Figure 4) figured *O.* aff. *barrandei* Munier-Chalmas 1876 from Eifelian strata on the South Island of Novaya Zemlya. This identification is questionable.

Table 5-1
Stratigraphic range and occurrences of *Oriostoma* and *Poleumita*. A question mark indicates taxonomic or stratigraphic uncertainty. Probably misidentified specimens from Maryland, Missouri, and Georgia are omitted.

	ALASKA	WISCONSIN	ILLINOIS	INDIANA	KENTUCKY	OHIO	NEW YORK	MAINE	ONTARIO	QUEBEC	NEW BRUNSWICK	IRELAND	GREAT BRITAIN	FRANCE	NORWAY	SWEDEN	CZECHOSLOVAKIA	AUSTRIA	ITALY	PODOLIA	LATVIA	TURKEY	ASIAN USSR	MALAYSIA	VIETNAM	CHINA
EIFELIAN																	?		?				?			
EMSIAN	X													X				X								
SIEGENIAN-EMSIAN																	X					X				
SIEGENIAN																										
GEDINNIAN																				?						
PRIDOLI								X									X			X			X			
LUDLOW-PRIDOLI				X				X		X							X									
LUDLOW				X			X		X	X			X		X	X	X			X				X		
WENLOCK-LUDLOW		X	X	X	X	X		X	X	X		X				X										?
WENLOCK													X		X	X	X			X			X			
LLANDOVERY-WENLOCK									X	X																
UPPER LLANDOVERY								X	X		X		X													

Gortani (1911:209-210) described *Horiostoma venetum* from Middle Devonian strata at Monumenz in the Carnic Alps. These are the only reports we know that include *Oriostoma* in strata younger than Emsian. Neither *Oriostoma* nor *Poleumita* have been reported from the Malvinokaffric Realm (Figure 5-1 and 5-2).

Poleumitid gastropods, and *Poleumita* and *Oriostoma* in particular, are among the most widespread and abundant of the Silurian gastropods of the North Silurian Realm. They are also widespread in the Old World Realm of the Early Devonian. In these realms, they occur in more than one high-diversity, low-dominance, shelly association commonly found in the Benthic Assemblage 3, shallow-subtidal, photic-zone position. The calcareous shales of the Mense Group on Gotland, for example, have yielded many specimens. Deep-water, offshore Benthic Assemblage 4 and 5 communities yield fewer poleumitids than Benthic Assemblage 3 communities. *Poleumita* are very rare in the high and low intertidal Benthic assemblages 1 and 2, the latter interpreted as high and low intertidal, respectively. Opercula of poleumitids are rarely found *in situ*, which is evidence of moderate current activity. Concentrations of poleumitids are found in molluscan-rich associations adjacent to some late Silurian and Early Devonian reefs. These concentrations may represent somewhat different, possibly more turbulent conditions.

Oriostoma is one of several gastropod genera from the Ordovician to the Middle Devonian that are known to have opercula (Figure 5-3). Other genera may have had opercula of conchiolin, but only those composed of calcium carbonate were likely to be preserved. Gastropod opercula may be divided into three groups based on the method in which the gastropod forms its operculum: concentric, planispiral, and multispiral. A good discussion of these types is provided in Yochelson and Linsley (1972). The following genera have been observed with the operculum in place:

Oriostoma coronatum Lindström, 1884. Multispiral operculum. Lindström, G., 1884. On the Silurian Gastropoda and Pteropoda of Gotland. *Kongl. Svenska Vetenskaps-Akademiens Handlingar* Bd. 19, Plate 17, Figure 11.

Straparollus (Euomphalus) northi (Etheridge, 1890). Multispiral operculum. Yochelson, E. L., and R. M. Linsley, 1972. Opercula of two gastropods from the Lilydale Limestone (Early Devonian) of Victoria Australia. *Natl. Mus. Victoria Mem.* 33:1014. (This species was originally assigned to *Oriostoma*.)

"*Cyclonema*" *lilydalensis* Etheridge, 1891. Paucispiral operculum. Yochelson, E. L., and R. M. Linsley, 1972. Opercula of two gastropods from the Lilydale Limestone (Early Devonian) of Victoria, Australia. *Natl. Mus. Victoria Mem.* 33: 1014. (This species was originally assigned to *Oriostoma*.

Loxoplocus (Lophospira) conradi (Teller, 1910). Paucispiral operculum. Teller, E. E., 1910. An operculated gastropod from the Niagara Formation of Wisconsin. *Wisconsin Acad. Sci., Arts and Letters Trans.* 16:1286-1288. (This species was originally assigned to *Murchisonia*.)

Omphalocirrus manitobensis (Whiteaves, 1880). Multispiral operculum. Whiteaves, J. F., 1890. Descriptions of some new or previously unrecorded species of fossils from the Devonian rocks of Manitoba. *Royal Soc. Canada Trans.* 7:93-110.

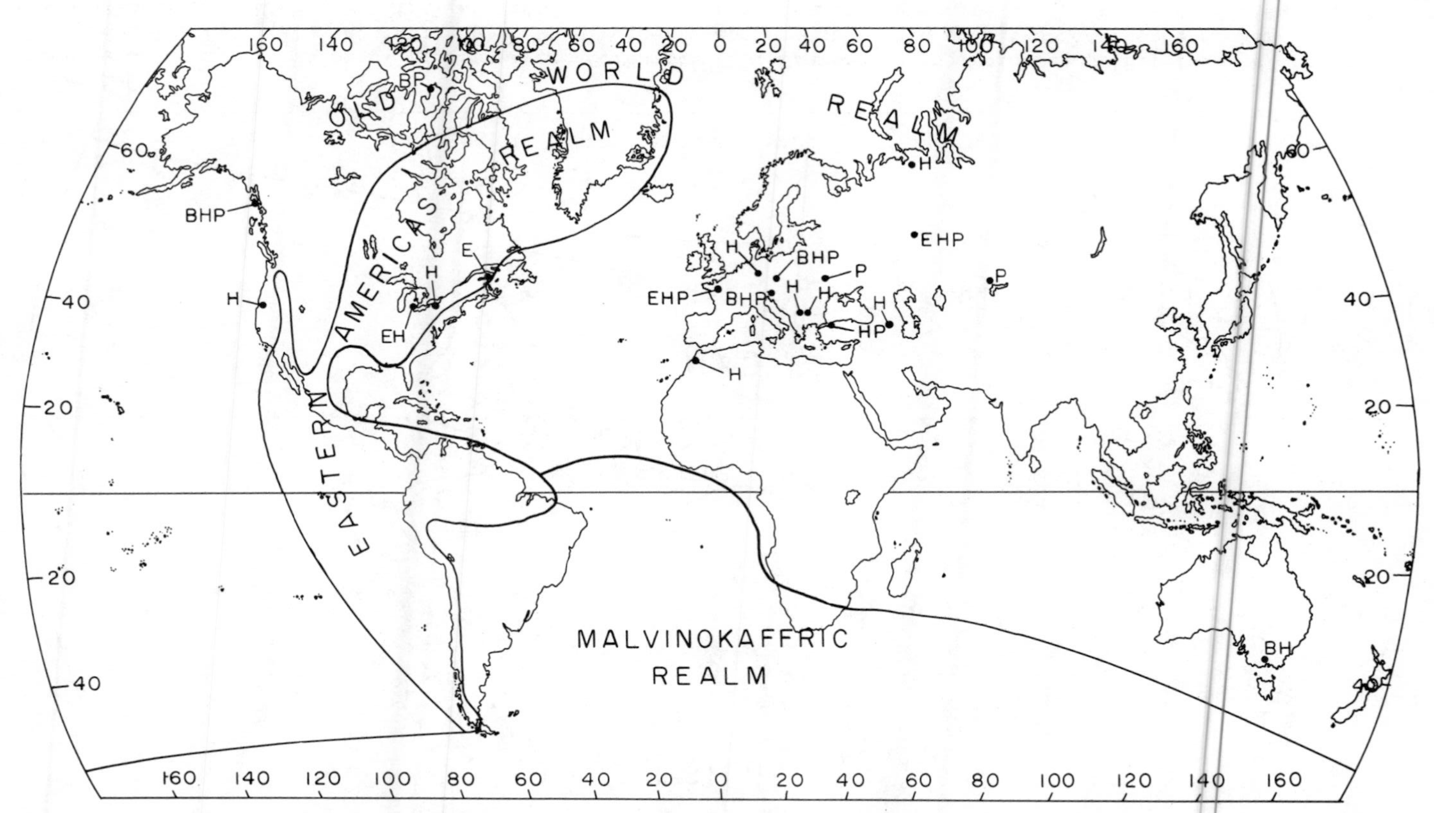

Figure 5-1
Silurian distribution of *Oriostoma* and *Poleumita* (P), *Tremanotus* and *Boiotremus* (B), *Euomphalopterus* (E), and *Hercynella* (H). Italics indicate questionable generic assignment. References for data points in appendix.

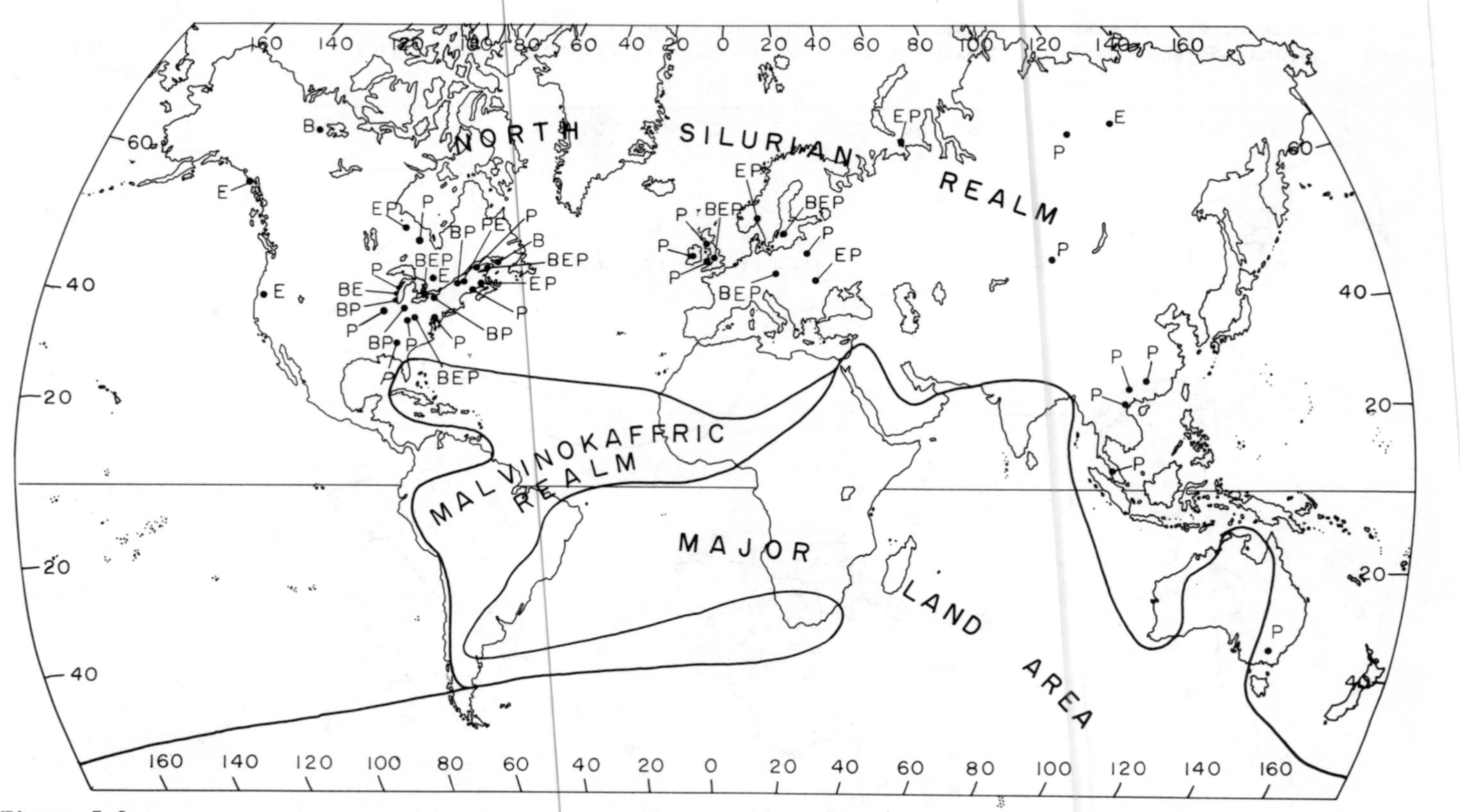

Figure 5-2
Lower Devonian distribution of *Oriostoma* and *Poleumita* (P), *Tremanotus* and *Boiotremus* (B), *Euomphalopterus* (E), and *Hercynella* (H). Italics indicate doubtful generic assignment. Note that the occurrence of *Hercynella* and *Euomphalopterus* in Michigan (Eifelian) represent a later time when the limits of the Eastern Americas Realm were somewhat more restricted, and of *Hercynella* in New York represent Pridoli, latest Silurian time, whereas the Gaspe occurrence of *Euomphalopterus* is interpreted as a boundary-mixing phenomenon in beds of Gedinnian age.

Ceratopea unguis (Yochelson and Bridge, 1957). Horn-like, paucispiral operculum. Yochelson, E. L., and A. O. Wise, 1972. A life association of shell and operculum in the Early Ordovician gastropod *Ceratopea unguis*. *Jour. Paleontology* 46:681-684.

Maclurites sp. Paucispiral operculum. Yochelson (pers. comm.) Other gastropods have been described as having opercula. The opercula, however, have not been observed in place, or the gastropods are known only from their operculum.

Helicotoma. Paucispiral operculum. Yochelson, E. L., 1966. An operculum associated with the Ordovician gastropod *Helicotoma*. *Jour. Paleontology* 40:748-749.

Cyclospongia discus (Miller, 1891). A Silurian-Devonian gastropod known only from its concentric operculum. Solem, A., and M. H. Nitecki, 1968. *Cyclospongia discus* Miller, 1891: gastropod operculum, not a sponge. *Jour. Paleontology* 42:1007-1013.

Turbinilopsis anacarina (Tyler, 1965). Concentric operculum. Tyler, J. H., 1965. Gastropods from the middle devonian four mile limestone (Hamilton) of Michigan. *Jour. Paleontology* 39:341-349. (Yochelson and Linsley, 1972, suggest that *Turbinilopsis anacarina* be transferred to *Cyclospongia*.)

Palliseria. Concentric operculum. Yochelson, E. L. (pers. comm.)

Teiichispira. An elongate horn-shaped operculum having a fiberous texture when weathered. Yochelson, E. L., and C. R. Jones. 1968. *Teiichispira*, a new Early Ordovician gastropod genus. *U.S. Geol. Survey Prof. Paper* 613B: B1-B13.

In addition to the preceding taxa, a variety of presumed oriostomatid opercula were illustrated by Lindström (1884) from the Silurian of Gotland. These opercula range from the typical disc-shaped opercula of *Oriostoma* to bullet-shaped forms (multispiral) of unknown affinities. Rohr (1977) illustrated a variety of paucispiral opercula from the Middle Ordovician of northern California that are presumed to belong to a species of *Maclurites*.

TREMANOTUS and *BOIOTREMUS*

Hall (1865:347) based *Tremanotus* on *T. alpheus* from the Upper Silurian at Bridgeport, Illinois. Knight (1941:353) discussed the date of Hall's publication and is the authority for the 1865 date. He also pointed out that Fischer's (1885:854) emendation of *Tremanotus* to *Trematanotus* was incorrect.

Knight (1941:353) declared *Gyrotrema* Lindström 1884 a stillborn objective synonym of *Tremanotus*. Knight et al. (1960:I180) placed *Tremagyrus* Perner, 1903, in the synonymy of *Tremanotus*. However Horny (1963:125-126) denied that *Tremagyrus* had the requisite orofices (tremata) and decided that it was a form of *Bellerophon (Bellerophon)*.

In 1962, he erected the genus *Boiotremus* and *Tremanotus* with tremata throughout its life history. *Tremanotus* has five to seven

A

B

Figure 5-3
Oriostoma sp. Apical (A), umbilical (B), and side views (C, D) of a silicified specimen with operculum in place. Bouleaux Formation (Late Silurian), Pointe Bouleaux, Quebec x2.5.

C

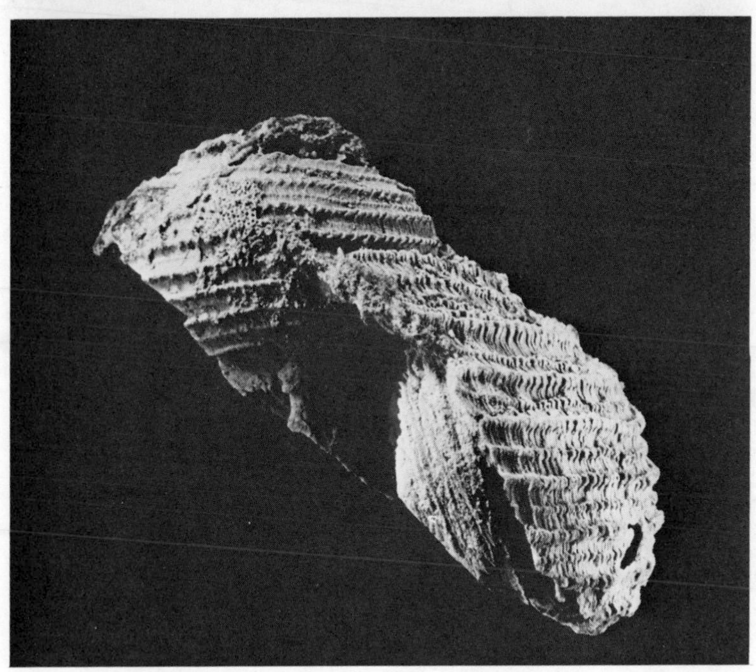

D

tremata whereas *Boiotremus* may have several times that number.

Knight et al. (1960:I180) assigned *Tremanotus* and *Salpingostoma* to the tribe Salpingostomatides of the family Bellerophontidae. Horny (1962:474) emphasized the unique aspect of this tribe and elevated it to familial status as the Salpingostomatidae and included *Boiotremus* in it. Peel (1972:412) studied muscle scars in these and other Bellerophontaceans and proposed the abandonment of the Salpingostomatidae. Instead, he created the Tremanotinae, a subfamily of the Sinuitidae for *Tremanotus* and *Boiotremus* and placed *Salpingostoma* in the subfamily Bucaniinae of the Bellerophontidae.

Horny (1963:64) gave the stratigraphic range of *Tremanotus* as Middle Ordovician to Upper Silurian. However, the Bohemian species occurs only in Llandovery and Wenlock strata. *Boiotremus* ranges from the Lower Silurian to the Lower Devonian, but is present only in Ludlow to Emsian rocks in Czechoslovakia (Figures 5-1 and 5-2).

We found only one possible occurrence of *Tremanotus* in the Ordovician. Lindström (1884:86) reported a single specimen from Ordovician strata on Oland. We have not been able to re-examine the specimen, but it could be a misidentification or a case of mislabeling. *Tremanotus* probably evolved from *Salpingostoma*, a Middle and Upper Ordovician gastropod, about the Middle Llandovery or near the Silurian-Ordovician boundary. *Tremanotus* and *Boiotremus* seem to form an evolutionary lineage. We found only one certain *Tremanotus* (Rohr and Smith, 1978:1233) above the Wenlock and no definite *Boiotremus* below the Ludlow (Table 5-2). A revision of these genera might demonstrate some stratigraphic significance, but their useful-

Table 5-2
Stratigraphic range and occurrences of *Tremanotus* and *Boiotremus*. A question mark indicates taxonomic uncertainty. Occurrences from the Yukon described only as "Silurian" are omitted.

	ALASKA	WISCONSIN	ILLINOIS	INDIANA	OHIO	NEW YORK	ONTARIO	QUEBEC	GREAT BRITAIN	SWEDEN	CZECHOSLOVAKIA	AUSTRIA	AUSTRALIA
EMSIAN	X											X	X
SIEGENIAN-EMSIAN											X		
SIEGENIAN													
GEDINNIAN													
PRIDOLI								X					
LUDLOW-PRIDOLI				X				X		X			
LUDLOW				X		X	X	X	X	X	X		
WENLOCK-LUDLOW		X	X	X	X			X					
WENLOCK									X	X	X		
UPPER LLANDOVERY										X			
MIDDLE LLANDOVERY								X	X				
LOWER LLANDOVERY													
LATE ORDOVICIAN										?			

ness would be minimal because of their rarity.

Tremanotids occur under circumstances almost identical to those characteristic of the poleumitids with the important exception that tremanotids are far rarer than poleumitids. Euomphalids, and *Euomphalus* in particular, are commonly associated in moderate abundance with level-bottom communities yielding both poleumitids and tremanotids. Commonly, however, platyceratid gastropods are more abundant in many of the Silurian-Lower Devonian level-bottom communities than euomphalids, poleumitids, or tremanotids. The abundance of the platyceratids may correlate with a corresponding abundance of pelmatozoan debris, which in turn suggests widespread occurrence of crinoid thickets as their organic substrate.

EUOMPHALOPTERUS

Roemer (1876) based *Euomphalopterus* on *Turbinites alatus* Wahlenberg, 1821, from the Silurian of Gotland. Knight (1941:51) made clear that he considered Kirk's genus *Bathmopterus* a synonym of *Euomphalopterus*. Knight's 1941 position was reiterated in Knight et al. (1960:212).

Euomphalopterus is an almost purely Silurian genus restricted to the North Silurian Realm (Figure 5-1). Except for a few forms known from the western portion of the Old World Realm in the Lower Devonian (Figure 5-2) the Ordovician form assigned to the genus by Longstaff (1924) is rejected on the basis of its radically different ornamentation. *Euomphalopterus* occurrences of Eifelian age in Michigan are considered to represent Old World Realm boundary phenomena.

Euomphalopterus commonly occurs in the same communities and is similarly widely distributed as the poleumitids and tremanotids. In terms of abundance, *Euomphalopterus* and euomphalids are less abundant than the poleumitids, but tend to be more abundant than the tremanotids. It should be emphasized that none of these gastropods is commonly abundant at any one locality despite their wide geographic and stratigraphic distributions. Their absence from the Malvinokaffric Realm of the Silurian and Devonian indicates a warm-water environment in the shallow parts of the subtidal. During this time interval, the most abundant gastropods in the intertidal region were the plectonotids.

HERCYNELLA

Kayser (1878:103) based *Hercynella* on specimens from the Lower Devonian of the Harz Mountains in Germany. In 1895, Cossmann (1895: 142) designated *H. beyrichi* Kayser the type species. Two objective synonyms attributed by courtesy to Barrande Manuscripts are *Pilidium* Kayser, 1878, and *Pilidion* Perner, 1911.

Tschernyschew described *Hercynella bohemica* from the Urals in 1885, more than a quarter century before Perner's publication of Barrande's manuscript. Unfortunately, the Russian and Czech material may not be conspecific (Pribyl and Spasov, 1960:105). Therefore, we use the incorrect, but widely accepted, citation of *H. bohemica* "Barrande." We eliminated all other such courtesy citations and refer only to the actual authors. The matter of priority of this specific name and common usage should be resolved in systematic revision of *Hercynella*.

For more than a century after its discovery by Barrande, *Hercynella* was thought to be a gastropod. Perner (1911:273) realized that some specimens of *Hercynella* bore a strong resemblance to the Silurian pelecypod *Silurina*, but, nevertheless, he considered it a pulmonate. O'Connell (1914) agreed and argued that the presence of the pulmonate *Hercynella* and eurypterids supported the theory that the Bertie Waterlime was formed under brackish-marine conditions. Chapman (1917:126) pointed out that the deep-water fauna associated with *Hercynella* in Victoria, Australia, precluded the possibility that it originated in freshwater and was washed into the ocean.

Knight (1941:147) considered *Hercynella* a problematic gastropod. Gill (1950) described several species of *Hercynella* from Australia. He considered it a gastropod, but rejected the possibility that it was a pulmonate.

H. Termier and G. Termier (1950a, b) studied newly discovered examples of *Hercynella* from Gedinnian strata in Morocco and reconsidered the systematic position of the genus. They felt that although shell morphology of *Hercynella* converged with several patelliform gastropods, the snails were of a much younger geologic age, and a phyletic relationship was unlikely. Instead, they decided that *Hercynella* was a pelecypod and placed it in the family Antipleuridae with the Ludlow lamellibranch, *Silurina* and *Dualina*.

Prantl (1958:162) re-examined Barrande's types and agreed with the Termiers' conclusion that *Hercynella* was a specialized *Silurina*. Knight et al. (1960:I324) included it in a list of Paleozoic genera incorrectly considered gastropods. Chernov (1959, 1961a) clarified the systematic position of *Hercynella* when he described numerous bivalved examples in life position from the Polar Urals. Cox et al. (1969:N247) also placed *Hercynella* in the family Antipleuridae of the suborder Praecardioda.

Hercynella occurs primarily in strata of Gedinnian, Siegenian, and Emsian age (Table 5-3). It might be of stratigraphic importance if an evolutionary lineage could be developed. Prantl (1960:150) accepted Barrande's stratigraphy and indicated *Hercynella* ranged from the Ludlowvian to the Eifelian. Our re-examination of Barrande's types indicates that in Czechoslovakia *Hercynella* is present only in the Late Gedinnian and Emsian.

Although *Hercynella* occurs only in the Devonian of the Barrandian (Figure 5-2), there are two possible Silurian occurrences reported elsewhere (Figure 5-1) by Kayser (1878) and O'Connell (1914). These are at least Upper Pridoli or younger and are quite close to the Silurian-Devonian boundary. More stratigraphic work should be done to check the authenticity of these reports, and the specimens discussed by O'Connell (1914) should be re-examined to check the generic determination.

The only possible Middle Devonian occurrence in the Barrandian is *Hercynella fastigiata* Perner, 1911 (:284-285, Plate 1, Figure 1-2; Plate 41, Figure 23?, 24-26; Plate 123, Figure 9-21). This species is very similar to *H. bohemica*, and it may have been collected from the lower Eifelian Trebotov Limestone at Hlubocepy near Praha. Another possible Middle Devonian occurrence of *Hercynella* is *Hercynella* sp. (Perner, 1911:288, Plate 105, Figure 36-37) from "g-1 Branik." This is probably from the Dvorce-Prokop Limestone of Siegenian-Lower Emsian age at Branik. The only other possible occurrence of *Hercynella* in the Middle Devonian is the Kasaan Island specimen discussed below.

Table 5-3
Stratigraphic range and occurrences of *Hercynella*. A question mark indicates taxonomic uncertainty.

	ALASKA	CALIFORNIA	MICHIGAN	NEW YORK	MOROCCO	FRANCE	GERMANY	CZECHOSLOVAKIA	AUSTRIA	YUGOSLOVIA	BULGARIA	TURKEY	URALS	AUSTRALIA
EMS	X													
SIEGEN-EMS			X			X			X					
SIEGEN								X				X	X	
GEDINNE-SIEGEN								X						X
GEDINNE		X			X									
PRIDOLI-GEDINNE							X							
PRIDOLI				?										

KASAAN ISLAND HERCYNELLA

Kasaan Island in southeastern Alaska is a fault block emplaced during the Tertiary, and it is, therefore, in an anomalous position with respect to the surrounding rock (Sainsbury, 1961:299). Kindle (1907) proposed a Middle Devonian age for a fauna collected on Kasaan Island. Chapin and Kirk (1929:100) re-examined the collection and suggested that it could be of Lower or Middle Devonian age. Oliver (1964:D150) studied the corals and agreed that they are Lower or Middle Devonian. He felt that a Middle Devonian age is more likely because of the presence of the stromatoporoid genus *Amphipora*. Merriam (1972:19) suggested that the *Amphipora* might indicate a Silurian age for the Lower Division formation on Kasaan Island. However, neither *Amphipora* nor well-described *Hercynella* have been reported from definite Silurian strata.

We feel that the presence of *Hercynella* cf. *bohemica* "Barrande," *Boiotremus* cf. *Tremanotus fortis* Frech, 1894, and *Oriostoma* sp. aff. *O. princeps* Oehlert, 1877, from Kasaan Island suggests Lower rather than Middle Devonian age. *Boiotremus* is unknown above the Emsian. The several possible occurrences of *Hercynella* and *Oriostoma* in the Middle Devonian are based on a few poorly known specimens.

Finally, Savage (pers. comm.) has recovered Lower Devonian concodonts from the Kasaan Island Devonian at localities identical to those from which the older macrofossil collections were obtained.

In contrast to the gastropods being considered, the bivalve genus *Hercynella* is far less common. However, there is a definite tendency for *Hercynella* to occur as a highly dominant genus when it does occur. *Hercynella* is known from several localities as masses of shells forming the dominant species: a situation unusual for Silurian and Early Devonian gastropods.

BIOGEOGRAPHY DISCUSSION

Silurian occurrences of *Oriostoma*, *Poleumita*, *Tremanotus*, and *Boiotremus* are plotted on the map in Figure 5-1. The sources of the data points are listed in the appendix. These genera are relatively cosmopolitan and are present in North America, Europe, Asia, and Australia. The boundaries of the major Lower Devonian brachiopod realms (Boucot, 1975) and the occurrences of *Oriostoma*, *Boiotremus*, and *Hercynella* are shown in Figure 5-2. These genera are widely distributed in the Old World Realm, but they are conspicuously absent in the Eastern Americas and Malvinokaffric realms.

Stratigraphic ranges and occurrences given by Knight et al. (1960) suggest that the Eastern Americas Realm of the Lower Devonian in North America includes *Elasmonema*, *Isonema*, *Trochonema* (*Trochonemopsis*), and *Palaeotrochus* as endemic genera. The record for these gastropods is fragmentary but except for *Elasmonema* and *Palaeotrochus*, they are from strata of Eifelian age. The other genera could be endemic Lower Devonian genera.

Gastropod genera described from the well-studied Siegenian and Emsian of Bohemia include *Agniesella*, *Aulacostrepsis*, *Katoptychia*, *Leptozone*, *Meandrella*, *Semitubina*, *Sinistracirsa*, and *Stylonema*. These genera may be Old World Realm endemics because Jhaveri (1969) also reported *Aulacostrepsis*, *Katoptychia*, *Meandrella*, and *Stylonema* in the Emsian of the Carnic Alps. The Oriostomatacean genus *Tubina* is well known from Bohemia, from the Carnic Alps of Austria, and from the Lower Devonian at Erbray, France (*T. ligeri* Barrois, 1889:210, Plate 15, Figure 2). Restudy and redescription of the French Lower Devonian snails would probably demonstrate other links with the Czech and Carnic faunas.

One possible endemic gastropod of the Lower Devonian Rhenish facies is *Aspidotheca* Teichert, 1935, from the Oberste Siegener Schichten at Unkelmuhle bei Eitorf, Germany. Jhaveri (1969:147) considered the Lower Devonian gastropods of the Carnic Alps dissimilar to the contemporaneous faunas of the Rheinisches Schiefergebirge and Podolia, but similar to faunas from Bohemia, Northern France, and New York State.

The Malvinokaffric Realm of the Lower Devonian is characterized by a near-total absence of bryozoans and corals and a few gastropods except for *Plectonotus* (Boucot, 1975). *Plectonotus* is commonly associated with the trilobite *Homalonotus* and is cosmopolitan during the Lower Devonian and the Silurian (Boucot, 1975).

In summary, the biogeography of these selected molluscs agree with the brachiopod-based biogeography in which a high level of cosmopolitanism is indicated in the Silurian followed by provincialism in the Lower Devonian.

ACKNOWLEDGMENTS

The cited occurrences of *Oriostoma*, *Poleumita*, *Tremanotus*, *Boiotremus*, *Euomphalopterus*, and *Hercynella* (Figures 5-1, 5-2; Tables 5-1, 5-2, and 5-3) are primarily from old literature. With the help of many specialists, we have attempted to bring the old stratigraphy and locality names into conformity with modern usage.

R. Horny and R. J. Prokop (Narodni Muzeum, Praha) and I. Chlupac and J. Kriz (Ustredni Ustav Geologicky, Praha) pointed out localities in Bulgaria and Yugoslavia and revised strata and place names for the Barrandian. Forney spent August of 1970 as their guest examining Barrande types in the Narodni Muzeum.

G. Henningsmoen of the Paleontologisk Museum, Oslo, provided catalog numbers and localities for Kiaer's (1908) specimens.

A. Martinsson, Department of Palaeobiology, Uppsala Universitet, revised the Gotland stratigraphy and localities.

J. A. Talent, Macquarie University, Sydney, and E. D. Gill, National Museum of Victoria, Melbourne, gave information on Australian occurrences.

B. S. Norford searched the collections of the Geological Survey of Canada and let us use unpublished information. W. A. Oliver and J. Pojeta, U.S. Geological Survey, Washington, helped with the Alaskan locality. H. R. Kramer, Emory University, and T. M. Chowns, University of Georgia, provided localities and specimens from Georgia. E. S. Richardson, Field Museum of Natural History, Chicago, loaned the M. E. Wing collection of gastropods from the Silurian of Illinois. Unfortunately, the specific names in Wing (1923, 1925) were never published with descriptions and are *nomina nuda*. In our listing, those names are numbered rather than repeated.

R. L. Batten, American Museum of Natural History, New York City, let us examine the Hall Collection in that institution. J. A. Fagerstrom, University of Nebraska, and H. B. Rollins, University of Pittsburgh, pointed out occurrences in Michigan and Ohio. R. H. Shaver, Indiana Geological Survey, Bloomington, let us consult two unpublished manuscripts revising fossil localities in Northern Indiana.

We are especially grateful to E. L. Yochelson, U.S. Geological Survey, Washington, for providing Russian literature on Silurian snails and for helping our search of the collections of the U.S. National Museum. R. M. Linsley, Colgate University, New York, let us consult E. M. Kindle's unpublished bibliography of Devonian gastropods in North America, which he is maintaining for the Geological Survey of Canada. The manuscript benefitted from suggestions by T. J. M. Schopf and A. M. Ziegler of the University of Chicago.

Forney's work was supported in part by a grant from the Student Aid Fund administered by H. G. Richards of the Department of Geology of the Academy of Natural Sciences, Philadelphia. Boucot's work was supported by National Science Foundation Grant EAR 74 22051 A03.

APPENDIX

In this appendix a listing with only a page number indicates a faunal list, and unless noted we have not re-examined the material. A plate number means that we have examined the illustration and are satisfied with the generic identification.

ORIOSTOMA AND POLEUMITA IN THE SILURIAN

North America

CANADA

New Brunswick

1. *Oriostoma* cf. *O. globosum* (Schlotheim, 1820). Boucot et al., 1966:39-40, Plate 16, Figures 15-23. Upper Llandovery strata, Back Bay.

Ontario

1. *Cyclonema sulcata* Hall, 1852:347-348, Plate 84, Figures 1a, b, d. Guelph Dolomite (Ludlow), Galt.
2. *Polytropis sulcatus* (Hall, 1852). Whiteaves, 1895:89-90, Plate 13, Figure 9. Guelph Dolomite (Ludlow), Hespeler, Durham, Elora, and Bellwood.
3. *Euomphalus macrolineatus* Whitfield, 1882. Whiteaves, 1884:20, Plate 3, Figure 6, Guelph Dolomite (Ludlow), Elora and Durham. Assigned to *Polytropis* by Whiteaves, 1895:91.
4. *Straparollus crenulatus* Whiteaves, 1884:21, Plate 3, Figure 8. Guelph Dolomite (Ludlow), Durham. Assigned to *Polytropis* by Whiteaves, 1895:91.
5. *Polytropis durhamensis* Whiteaves, 1895:91-92, Plate 14, Figures 1-2. Guelph Dolomite (Ludlow), Edge Mills near Durham.
6. *Polytropis parvulus* Whiteaves, 1895:92-93, Plate 13, Figure 10. Guelph Dolomite (Ludlow), Durham.
7. *Poleumita* sp. Bolton, 1957, Tables 11 and 12. Wiarton Member of the Amabel Formation (Late Wenlock-Ludlow) near Colpoy Bay Village, Adamsville and Ferndale. Guelph Formation (Ludlow) near Chatsworth.
8. *Poleumita durhamensis* (Whiteaves, 1884). Bolton, 1957, Tables 11 and 12. Wiarton Member of the Amabel Formation (Late Wenlock-Ludlow), Wiarton, and near Colpoy Bay Village, Hope Bay and Edenhurst. Guelph Formation (Ludlow) near Ferndale.
9. *Poleumita* cf. *crenulata* (Whiteaves, 1884). Bolton, 1957, Table 11. Wiarton Member of the Amabel Formation (Late Wenlock-Ludlow) near Rockford Station, Colpoy Bay Village and Edenhurst.
10. *Poleumita parvula* (Whiteaves, 1895). Bolton, 1957, Table 11. Wiarton Member of the Amabel Formation (Late Wenlock-Ludlow), Wiarton and near Colpoy Bay Village.
11. *Poleumita* cf. *scamnata* Clarke and Ruedemann, 1903. Bolton, 1957, Table 11. Wiarton Member of the Amabel Formation (Late Wenlock-Ludlow) near Owen Sound, Colpoy Bay Village and Hope Bay.
12. *Poleumita hudsonica* Parks, Tyrell, 1913:194, Parks, 1915:67, Plate 4, Figures 1-2. Llandovery-Wenlock strata, Limestone

Rapids of the Severn River, District of Patricia. The specimen is too poorly figured to be definitely included in *Poleumita*.

13. *Oriostoma* sp. Parks, 1915:71. Llandovery-Wenlock strata, Limestone Rapids of the Severn River, District of Patricia. Three multispiral opercula from two species possibly referable to *Oriostoma*.
14. *Oriostoma* sp. B. S. Norford (pers. comm.) Ekwan River Formation (Upper Llandovery) at Geological Survey of Canada Locality 380611 (Field #514NE&F) from 5.5 m of beds on the west side of the Severn River at 55°37'N., 99°04½'W. An operculum referable to *Oriostoma*.
15. *Poleumita* sp. B. S. Norford (pers. comm.) Attawapiskat Formation (C_6-Wenlock) at Geological Survey of Canada Locality 80568 from 7.5 m of beds at 52°53½'N., 83°31'W. on the Attawapiskat River.
16. *Poleumita* sp. B. S. Norford (pers. comm.) Attawapiskat Formation (C_6-Wenlock) at Geological Survey of Canada Locality 80572 from 2.4 m of beds at 52°56½'N., 83°04'W. on the Attawapiskat River.

Quebec

1. *Poleumita chaleurensis* Northrop, 1939:213, Plate 22, Figure 1; Plate 23, Figure 3. La Vieille Formation (C_6-Wenlock) near Marcils and at Black Cape. Bouleaux Formation (Ludlow) near Gascons and at Pointe L'Enfer near Port Daniel Est. Ayrton (1967) includes the outcrops at Pointe L'Enfer in the West Point Formation (Ludlow-Pridoli).
2. *Poleumita discors* (Sowerby, 1814). Northrop, 1939:213-214, Plate 21, Figure 7. La Vielle Formation (C_6-Wenlock), Black Cape.
3. *Poleumita (Pleurotomaria princessa* (Billings, 1874:59, Figure 29); Tolman, 1936:15; Clark, 1942:32. Cranbourne Formation (Pridoli), Cranbourne, Eastern Townships.
4. *Poleumita* aff. *transversalis* Prouty, in Swartz and Prouty, 1923; Crickmay, 1932:374. Val Brillant Formation (C_6-Early Wenlock), 1.2 km north of Val Brillant on the south shore of Lake Matapedia.
5. *Poleumita* sp. Crickmay, 1932:374-375. At the type locality of the Sayabec Formation (Wenlock-Ludlow), a quarry on the south shore of Lake Matapedia 4.8 km east of Sayabec.

UNITED STATES

Georgia

1. *Gyronema* cf. *Poleumita transversa* Prouty, in Swartz and Prouty, 1923. Butts and Gildersleeve, 1948:37. Upper Division (C_3-C_5) of the Red Mountain Formation. Possibly not *Poleumita*.
2. *Poleumita* sp. Chowns and Howard, 1972:97. Red Mountain Formation (Llandovery), Ringgold Gap on I-75. We have examined this specimen and reject it from *Poleumita*.

Illinois

1. *Poleumita* cf. *crenulata* (Whiteaves, 1884). Wing, 1923:75-76, Plate 7, Figure 8-9. Racine Dolomite (Late Wenlock-Ludlow), Thornton near Chicago.

2. *Poleumita?* sp. 1. Wing, 1923:74-75, Plate 8, Figure 6. Racine Dolomite (Late Wenlock-Ludlow), Thornton, Hawthorne, and McCook near Chicago.
3. *Poleumita* sp. 2. Wing, 1923:76-77, Plate 7, Figures 15, 18. Racine Dolomite (Late Wenlock-Ludlow), Thornton near Chicago.
4. *Poleumita* sp. 3. Wing, 1923:77-78, Plate 7, Figure 14, 17. Racine Dolomite (Late Wenlock-Ludlow), Thornton near Chicago.
5. *Poleumita* sp. 4. Wing, 1923:79, Plate 7, Figure 7. Racine Dolomite (Late Wenlock-Ludlow), Thornton near Chicago.
6. *Poleumita* sp. Wing, 1923:79-80, Plate 8, Figure 16. Racine Dolomite (Late Wenlock-Ludlow), Thornton near Chicago.

Indiana

1. *Poleumita crenulata* (Whiteaves, 1884). Cumings and Shrock, 1928: 81 and R. H. Shaver (pers. comm.). Mississinewa Shale Member (Ludlow) of the Wabash Formation, Markle, Huntington County.
2. *Oriostoma huntingtonensis* Kindle and Breger, 1904, in Kindle, 1904:465, Plate 14, Figures 14-15; Cumings and Shrock, 1928:99; and R. H. Shaver (pers. comm.) Salamonie Dolomite (Wenlock) at Fairview, Randolph County. Liston Creek Limestone Member (Ludlow) of the Wabash Formation, Little Wabash River, Huntington County.
3. *Oriostoma huntingtonensis alternatum* Kindle and Breger, 1904:465, Plate 14, Figure 9; and R. H. Shaver (pers. comm.). Liston Creek Limestone Member (Ludlow) of the Wabash Formation, Huntington, Huntington County.
4. *Poleumita scamnata* Clarke and Ruedemann, 1903. Cumings and Shrock, 1928:81, 99; R. H. Shaver (pers. comm.). Salamonie Dolomite (Wenlock) New Corydon, Adams County, and Ridgeville, Randolph County. Mississinewa Shale Member (Ludlow) of the Wabash Formation, Markle and Lancaster, Huntington County.
5. *Poleumita* sp. Cumings and Shrock, 1928:99; R. H. Shaver (pers. comm.). Salamonie Dolomite (Wenlock), New Corydon, Adams County. Liston Creek Limestone Member (Ludlow-Pridoli) of the Wabash Formation, Huntington, Huntington County; Monon, White County; Delphi, Carroll County; Georgetown, Cass County; and Lapel, Madison County.

Kentucky

1. *Euomphalus (Cyclonema) rugaelineata* Hall and Whitfield, 1872:186, figured in Hall and Whitfield, 1875, Plate 13, Figure 2, and in Nettleroth, 1889:187, Plate 33, Figure 21. Louisville Limestone (Late Wenlock-Ludlow), several quarries east of Louisville.

Maine (Northern)

1. *Oriostoma* sp. Boucot and Yochelson, 1966:A13, Plate 2, Figure 18, 22. Hornfels of Late Llandovery age, Limestone Hill, Stratton Quadrangle, Somerset County.
2. *Oriostoma* sp. Boucot and Yochelson, 1966:A13, Plate 2, Figure 23. Oriostomatid operculum from the Hardwood Mountain Formation (Pridoli), 3.2 km north-northeast of Baker Pond, Spencer Quadrangle, Somerset County.
3. *Poleumita* sp. Boucot and Yochelson, 1966:A13, Plate 2, Figure 18, 22. Hornfels of Late Llandovery age at Limestone Hill, Stratton

Quadrangle, Somerset County. Boucot and Yochelson, 1966:A13, Plate 2, Figures 18, 19. Hardwood Mountain Formation, Spencer Quadrangle, Somerset County.

4. *Oriostoma?* sp. Hall 1970:50. Spider Lake Formation (Ludlow-Pridoli), intersection of the main Great Northern Paper Company Road with the branch road to Cliff Lake. From U.S. National Museum (USNM) locality 11363, identified by Boucot.

Maine (Southern)

1. *Oriostoma* sp. Boucot and Yochelson, 1955:A13, note that the collections of the U.S. National Museum contain specimens from Whiting Bay and Field Point, Edmunds Township, Washington County.
2. *Oriostoma* sp. Boucot and Yochelson, 1955:A13, note that the collections of the U.S. National Museum contain oriostomatid opercula from Whiting Bay and Burnt Cove in Edmunds Township, Washington County.
3. *Oriostoma* sp. Collected by Olcott Gates in 1967 from USNM locality 17087 from the Edmunds Formation (Wenlock-Ludlow) from the west side of Mahar Point opposite Little Dram Island at the end of Leighton Neck, Eastport Quadrangle, Washington County.

Maryland

1. *Poleumita transversa* Prouty, in Swartz and Prouty, 1923:487, Plate 29, Figure 27-28. Rochester Formation (Wenlock), Rose Hill. This is probably not *Poleumita*.
2. *Poleumita mckenzica* Prouty, in Swartz and Prouty, 1923:487, Plate 29, Figure 26. McKenzie Formation (Wenlock-Ludlow) near Cedar Cliff. This is probably not *Poleumita*.

Missouri

1. *Poleumita bellasculptalis* Savage, 1913:101, Plate 6, Figure 3; reprinted in Savage, 1917:143, Plate 8, Figure 3. Edgewood Dolomite (Early Llandovery), Pike County. The figured specimen may be *Cyclonema*.

New York

1. *Poleumita crenulate* (Whiteaves, 1884). Clarke and Ruedemann, 1903:64-65, Plate 9, Figure 9-11, 16-24. Guelph Limestone (Ludlow), Shelby.
2. *Poleumita scamnata* Clarke and Ruedemann, 1903:60-62, Plate 9, Figure 1-8; Plate 10, Figure 12-15. Guelph Limestone (Ludlow), Rochester and Shelby.
3. *Poleumita? sulcata* (Hall, 1852). Clarke and Ruedemann, 1903:62-63, Plate 10, Figure 1-4. Probably not *Poleumita*.
4. *Poleumita vernonensis* Fisher, 1957:26, Plate 2, Figure 3-6. Vernon Shale (Ludlow) near Vernon. Probably not *Poleumita*; material is poorly preserved.

Ohio

1. *Oriostoma* sp. H. B. Rollins (pers. comm.), Peebles Formation (Late Wenlock-Ludlow), Plum Run Stone Company Quarry, Peebles.

2. *Poleumita prosseri* Foerste,1919:383-384, Plate 17, Figure 8. Lilley Member of the West Union Formation (Wenlock), Zink Quarry, eastern part of Hillsboro. The holotype is USM 87029.
3. *Poleumita pavayi* Foerste, 1919:384, Plate 17, Figure 9. Lilley Member of the West Union Formation (Wenlock), Zink Quarry, eastern part of Hillsboro. The holotype is USM 87030. This is not *Poleumita*.

Wisconsin

1. *Euomphalus macrolineatus* Whitfield, 1882:294, Plate 18, Figure 5-6. Racine Dolomite (Late Wenlock-Ludlow), Kunz's Quarry, Manitowoc Rapids.

Europe

CZECHOSLOVAKIA

1. *Polytropis actaeon* Perner, 1907:174-175, Plate 107, Figure 1-2. Lower Budnanian (Ludlow), probably Kopanina Formation at Tachlovice.
2. *Polytropis aspirans* Perner, 1907:178, Plate 78, Figure 25-26. Budnanian (Ludlow or Pridoli Formation at Dvorce Quarry, Praha, Podoli.
3. *Polytropis assidua* Perner, 1907:171, Plate 79, Figure 14-16. Upper Budnanian (Pridoli) Pridoli Formation at Dvorce Quarry, Praha, Podoli.
4. *Polytropis compar* Perner, 1907:180-181, Plate 68, Figure 6-8. Wenlockian Liten Formation at Lodenice.
5. *Polytropis confertissima* Perner, 1907:173-174, Plate 79, Figure 11-13, Plate 254, Figure 22-28. Upper Budnanian (Pridoli) Pridoli Formation at Dvorce Quarry, Praha, Podoli.
6. *Polytropis conjugata* Perner, 1907:180, Plate 77, Figure 28-31. Wenlockian, Upper Liten Beds at Bubovice.
7. *Polytropis corniculum* Perner, 1907:183-184, Plate 80, Figure 17-18, Text-figure 190. Wenlockian. Liten Beds at Barrande's diggings on the road Lodenice-Bubovice.
8. *Polytropis costata* Perner, 1907:184-185, Plate 72, Figure 33-38; Plate 80, Figure 29-30. Wenlockian, Liten Beds at Barrande's diggings on the road Lodenice-Bubovice.
9. *Polytropis delicata* Perner, 1907:180, Plate 79, Figure 22-25. Lower Budnanian (Ludlow) Kopanina Formation at Butovice.
10. *Polytropis discors* (Sowerby, 1814). Perner, 1907:187-188, Text-figure 191. Wenlockian, Liten Formation at Bubovice.
11. *Polytropis dives* Perner, 1907:169-170, Plate 80, Figure 37-39; Plate 243, Figure 1-27; Plate 244, Figure 8-10, 15-21; Plate 245, Figure 1-8. Upper Budnanian (Pridoli) Pridoli Formation at Dvorce Quarry, Praha, Podoli, and lower Budnanian (Ludlow) probably Kopanina Formation at Zadni Kopanina.
12. *Polytropis dives* var. *conferta* Perner, 1907:171, Plate 80, Figure 37-39; Plate 245, Figure 18-21. Lower Budnanian (Ludlow) probably Kopanina Formation at Zadni Kopanina and at Karlstejn.
13. *Polytropis dulcis* Perner, 1907:176-178, Plate 72, Figure 39-47; Plate 77, Figure 32-36; Plate 80, Figure 33-34; Plate 235, Figure 5-8; Plate 246, Figure 29-33. Wenlockian, high Liten Formation at Bubovice, Wenlockian or Lower Budnanian (Ludlow)

Liten or Kopanina Formation at Lodenice and probably Upper Budnanian (Pridoli) Pridoli Formation at Dvorce Quarry, Praha, Podoli.

14. *Polytropis ingenua* Perner, 1907:175-176, Plate 78, Figure 4-7. Wenlockian, high Liten Formation at Listice near Beroun.
15. *Polytropis oblita* Perner, 1907:178, Plate 80, Figure 23-24. Budnanian (Ludlow or Pridoli) Kopanina or Pridoli Formation at Kosor.
16. *Polytropis ornatula* Perner, 1907:178-179, Plate 76, Figure 19; Plate 79, Figure 1-5; Plate 207, Figure 15-19. Probably Upper Budnanian (Pridoli) Pridoli Formation at Kosor and Lochkov.
17. *Polytropis parens* Perner, 1907:171, Plate 78, Figure 23-24. Probably Upper Budnanian (Pridoli) Pridoli Formation at Dvorce Quarry, Praha, Podoli. This specimen was not relocated during August of 1970.
18. *Polytropis persculpta* Perner, 1907:171-172, Plate 246, Figure 1-10. Probably Upper Budnanian (Pridoli) Pridoli Formation at Dvorce Quarry, Praha, Podoli.
19. *Polytropis potens* Perner, 1907:172, Plate 80, Figure 31-32; Plate 244, Figure 22-28, Plate 246, Figure 24-28. Upper Budnanian (Pridoli) Pridoli Formation at Dvorce Quarry, Praha, Podoli. The locality Karlstejn was hand corrected in the author's copy on the plate explanations for Plate 246, Figures 24-28, but that specimen could not be relocated in August of 1970.
20. *Polytropis pulchra* Perner, 1907:172-173, Plate 79, Figure 17-21; Plate 244, Figure 11-14; Plate 245, Figure 9-17; Plate 246, Figure 10-13. Upper Budnanian (Pridoli) Pridoli Formation at Dvorce Quarry, Praha, Podoli.
21. *Polytropis recedens* Perner, 1907:181-182, Plate 70, Figure 6-7; Plate 71, Figure 48-50; Plate 78, Figure 11-13; Text-figure 189. Lower Budnanian (Ludlow) Kopanina Formation at Kozel and probably Kopanina Formation at Zadni Kopanina.
22. *Polytropis robusta* Perner, 1907:176, Plate 80, Figure 35-36. Upper Budnanian (Pridoli) Pridoli Formation at Dvorce Quarry, Praha, Podoli, and Wenlockian, Liten Formation at Bubovice near Lodenice. These specimens are probably not conspecific.
23. *Polytropis sequens* Perner, 1907:179, Plate 79, Figure 28-31. Wenlockian, Upper Liten Formation at Bubovice.
24. *Polytropis tegulata* Perner, 1907:175, Plate 79, Figure 26-27. Lower Budnanian (Ludlow) Kopanina Formation at Dlouha hora near Beroun.
25. *Polytropis tenera* Perner, 1907:175, Plate 78, Figure 8-10. Lower Budnanian (Ludlow) Kopanina Formation at Dlouha hora near Beroun.
26. *Polytropis ventricosa* Perner, 1907:174, Plate 73, Figure 35-38, Plate 244, Figure 1-7. Upper Budnanian (Pridoli) Pridoli Formation at Dvorce Quarry, Praha, Podoli.

GREAT BRITAIN

1. *Euophalus funatus* Sowerby, 1825:71, Plate 450, Figure 1-2. Sowerby, 1839:616, Plate 12, Figure 20, Bringewood Beds ("Amestry Limestone") (Middle Ludlow) at Walls Grave Quarry, Aymestry, Herefordshire, and Usk, Monmouthshire. Sowerby, 1839: 616, Plate 12, Figure 20. Lower Ludlow Formation (Lower Ludlow

or Eltonian) at Myddleton Hall (Middleton Hall), Caermarthenshire and Abberley, Worchestershire. Sowerby, 1839:626, Plate 12, Figure 20, Wenlock Limestone (Upper Wenlock) at Wenlock, Shropshire; Dudley, Staffordshire; Abberley, Worcestershire; Walsall, Staffordshire; and Benthall Edge, Shropshire. Sowerby, 1839:631, Plate 12, Figure 20, Wenlock Shale (Wenlock) at Woolhope, Herefordshire.

2. *Euomphalus carinatus* Sowerby, in Murchison, 1839:616, Plate 6, Figure 10. Bringewood Beds ("Aymestry Limestone") (Middle Ludlow) at Aymestry, Herefordshire and the "Wenlock Formation" (Wenlock) at Delves Green, Walsall, Staffordshire.
3. *Euomphalus discors* Sowerby, 1814, v. 1, p. 113, Plate 53, Figure 1. Sowerby, in Murchison, 1839:626, Plate 12, Figure 18. Wenlock Limestone (Upper Wenlock) at Wenlock, Shropshire and Dudley, Staffordshire.
4. *Euomphalus rugosus* Sowerby, 1814, v. 1, p. 113, Plate 52, Figure 2. Sowerby, in Murchison, 1839:626, Plate 12, Figure 19. Wenlock Limestone (Upper Wenlock) at Wenlock, Shropshire, and Dudley, Staffordshire.
5. *Euomphalus sculptus* Sowerby, in Murchison, 1839:626, Plate 12, Figure 17. Wenlock Limestone (Upper Wenlock) at Ledbury, Herefordshire and Eastnor Park, Herefordshire.
6. *Polytropina globosa* (Schlotheim, 1820). Donald, 1905:576-577, Plate 37, Figure 16. Wenlock strata at Llangadock, Caermarthenshire.
7. *Polytropina conferta* Lamont, 1946:640-641, Plate 2, Figure 6. Camregan Limestone ("Upper Pentamerus Limestone") (Early Upper Llandovery) on Penwhapple Burn, near Penkill Castle, Girvan, Ayrshire, Scotland.

EIRE

1. *Horiostoma discors* (Sowerby, 1814). Gardiner and Reynolds, 1902:234. Calcareous flagstone with coralline limestone of Wenlock or Ludlow age near the Stone Cross and Penitential Station in the Clougher Head District, County Kerry.
2. *Horiostoma globosum* (Schlotheim, 1820). Gardiner and Reynolds, 1902:234-235. Calcareous flagstones interbedded with limestone of Wenlock age near Carrigcam and Owen and of Wenlock or Ludlow age near the Stone Cross and Penitential Station in the Clougher Head District, County Kerry.

NORWAY

1. *Oriostoma* sp. with operculum. Paleontologisk Museum Oslo 50583. Stage 9d (Ludlow) in the northern part of Langøya, Holmestrand.
2. *Poleumita* sp. Paleontologisk Museum Oslo 50585. Stage 9d (Ludlow) on Langøya, Holmestrand.
3. *Poleumita* sp. Paleontologisk Museum Oslo 50528. Stage 9d (Ludlow) on the northwestern point of Langøya, Holmestrand.
4. *Poleumita* sp. Paleontologisk Museum Oslo 49839, 49840, 49842, 49843, 49844, 49845. Silurian strata on the northeastern side of Langøya, Holmestrand.
5. *Poleumita* sp. Paleontologisk Museum Oslo 50464. Stage 9d (Ludlow) on the western side of Langøya, Holmestrand.
6. *Poleumita* sp. Paleontologisk Museum Oslo 49824, 49825, 49827,

49828, 49831, 49832, 49833, 49835. Stage 9b (Wenlock) at Wankel's Old Quarry in the northeastern part of Langøya, Holmestrand.

7. *Poleumita* sp. Paleontologisk Museum Oslo 50034, 50034. Stage 9a (Wenlock), 1-1.5 m below 9b on Langøya, Holmestrand.
8. *Poleumita* sp. Paleontologisk Museum Oslo 49610-49614. Stage 9 (Wenlock-Ludlow) on Langøya, Holmestrand.
9. *Poleumita* sp. Paleontologisk Museum Oslo 44431, 44432. Stage 8c (Wenlock) at the top of Malmøya near Oslo.

SWEDEN

1. *Oriostoma acutum* Lindstrom, 1884:166-167, Plate 17, Figure 37-40. Slite Beds (Middle Wenlock) of Gotland at Lannaberg, Slite and Slite, slite.
2. *Oriostoma alatum* Lindstrom, 1884:171, Plate 16, Figure 14-19. Hogklint Beds (Lower Wenlock) of Gotland at Kyrkberget, Visby Beds at Visby, Visby.
3. *Oriostoma anguilifer* Lindstrom, 1884:168, Plate 20, Figure 17-21. Hemse Beds (Upper Ludlow) of Gotland near Herrvik, Ostergarn.
4. *Oriostoma angulatum* (Wahlenberg, 1818). Lindstrom, 1884:171-172, Plate 20, Figure 34-41. This is the type of *Euomphalopterus* Roemer, 1876, and is not assigned to *Oriostoma*.
5. *Oriostoma contrarium* Lindstrom, 1884:160, Plate 20, Figure 8-15. Hogklint Beds (Lower Wenlock) of Gotland at Visby and Kyrkberget in Visby and Vastos, Hall. Slite Beds (Middle Wenlock) at Lansa and Louterhorn in Faro; Vialmsudd, Fleringe; Samsugns, Othem. Hamra-Sundre Beds (Ludlow) at Hoburgen, Sundre.
6. *Oriostoma coronatum* Lindstrom, 1884:164-166, Plate 17, Figure 11-16, 18-22. Hemse Beds (Early Ludlow) of Gotland at Ostergarn, Ostergarn; Ardre, Ardre; Lau, Lau; and Lindeklint, Linde.
7. *Oriostoma discors* (Sowerby, 1814). Lindstrom, 1884: 157-159, Plate 16, Figure 20-36, Plate 17, Figure 1-5. Hogklint Beds (Lower Wenlock) of Gotland at Kyrkberget and Visby in Visby; Vastos, Hall. Hogklint Beds or Upper Visby Beds (Lower Wenlock) at Kristklint in Kappellshamm, Hangvar. Slite Beds (Middle Wenlock) at Vialmsudd, Fleringe; Vastergarn, Vastergarn; Lansa and Lauterhorn in Faro; Alnase, Faro; Samsugns, Othem; Follingbo, Follingbo; Bara Backe, Horane; Martebo, Martebo; and Vallve Ref, Eskelhem. Halla Beds (Upper Wenlock) at Horsne, Horsne. Klinteburg Beds (Early Ludlow) at Klinteberg, Klint.
8. *Oriostoma discors rugosum* (Sowerby, 1814). Lindstrom, 1884:159-160, Plate 17, Figure 5-10. Hogklint Beds (Lower Wenlock) at Faro, Faro; Vialmsudd, Fleringe; Samsugns, Othem; Lannaberg, slite; Moiner, Boge; Stora Vede, Follingbo; Martebo, Martebo; Bara Backe, Slite. Klinteberg Beds (Early Ludlow) at Klinteberg, Klint. Hemse Beds (Early Ludlow) at Ostergarn, Ostergarn; Ardre, Ardre; Linde, Linde.
9. *Oriostoma dispar* Lindstrom, 1884:173, Plate 21, Figure 11-14. Slite Beds (Middle Wenlock) of Gotland at Follingbo, Follingbo.
10. *Oriostoma globosum* (Schlotheim, 1820:162). Lindstrom, 1884:160-162, Plate 17, Figure 24-25, 29-31, Plate 18, Figure 24, Plate 20, Figure 16. Hogklint Beds (Lower Wenlock) at Visby, Visby and Hall, Hall. Slite Beds (Middle Wenlock) at Vastergarn, Vastergarn; Slite, Slite; Lansa and Lauterhorn, Faro; Rute,

Rute; Vialmsudd, Fleringe; Samsugns, Othem; Martebo, Slite. Mulde Beds (Upper Wenlock) at Frojel, Frojel. Halla Beds (Upper Wenlock) at Horsne, Horsne. Klinteberg Beds (Early Ludlow) at Hammar, Kraklingbo; Gothemshammar, Gothem; Ganthem, Ganthem; Klinteberg, Klint. Hemse Beds (Early Ludlow) at Petesvik, Hablingbo; Burge, Fardhem; Visne Myr, Fardhem; Eimunds A, Fardhem; Sandarve Kulle, Fardhem.

11. *Oriostoma helicinum* Lindstrom, 1884:170-171, Plate 3, Figure 27-31, Plate 20, Figure 30-33. Hogklint Beds (Lower Wenlock) of Gotland at Vastos, Hall. Hogklint Beds or Upper Visby Beds (Lower Wenlock) at Halls Huk, Hallshuk. Slite Beds (Middle Wenlock) at Samsugn, Othem; and Vialmsudd, Fleringe.
12. *Oriostoma lineatum* Lindstrom, 1884:173, Plate 20, Figure 42-44. Mulde Beds (Upper Wenlock) of Gotland at Frojel, Frojel. Klinteberg Beds (Lower Early Ludlow) at Klinteberg, Klint.
13. *Oriostoma nitidissumum* Lindstrom, 1884:173, Plate 21, Figure 4-10. Hemse Beds (Early Ludlow) at Sandarve Kulle, Fardnem; Linde, Linde. Probably in Slite Beds (Middle Wenlock) at Stora Vede, Follingbo.
14. *Oriostoma roemeri* Lindstrom, 1884:168-169, Plate 18, Figure 22-29. Upper Visby Beds (Lower Wenlock) of Gotland at Gnisvard, Tofta. Hogklint Beds (Lower Wenlock) at Visby, Visby. Hogklint or Visby Beds at Halls Huk, Hallshuk. Slite Beds (Middle Wenlock) at Vastergarn, Vastergarn.

USSR

Podolia and Moldavia

1. *Oriostoma discors* (Sowerby, 1814). Malvinovetski Formation (Ludlow) at Braga (Wieniukow, 1899:180-181), between Braga and Zwaniec (48-50), at Khutor Muksha (61), at Kamieniec Podolski (55-60), at Laskorum (66-68), at Malinowiecka Sloboda (46-47), at Muksza (180-181), at Orynin (63-64), at Pudlowce (62), at Sokol (45-46), at Uscie (44-45) and at Zwaniec (180-181). Skala Formation (Pridoli) at Zawale (53).
2. *Horiostoma discors* (Sowerby, 1814). Siemiradzki, 1906:231. Malinovetsky Formation (Ludlow) at Braga, at Kamieniec Podolski, at Laskorun, at Malinowiecka Sloboda, at Muksza, at Orynin, at Pudlowce, at Sokol, at Uscie, and at Zwaniec. Skala Formation (Pridoli) at Zawale).
3. *Poleumita discors* (Sowerby, 1814). Vascautanu, 1932. Mukshinsky Formation (Wenlock) at Gruseva and the Mouth of the Sost (503-505) and at Nagureni (458). Malvinovetsky Formation (Ludlow) at Camauca and Hotin (507-510).
4. *Oriostoma discors* var. *rugosum* (Sowerby, 1814). Wieniukow, 1899. Malinovetsky Formation (Ludlow) at Kamieniec Podolski (55-60) and at Orynin (63-64).
5. *Horiostoma discors* var. *rugosum* (Sowerby, 1814). Siemiradzki, 1906:321. Malinovetsky Formation (Ludlow) at Kamieniec Podolski and Orynin.
6. *Oriostoma globosum* (Schlotheim, 1820). Wieniukow, 1899. Malinovetski Formation (Ludlow) at Braga (182-183), between Braga and Zwaniec (48-50) at Khutor Muksha (61), at Kamieniec Podolski (55-60), between Karmelitka and Zwanchik (5-52), at Laskorun (66-68), at Malinowiecka Sloboda (46-47), at Orynin (63-64), at

Podzamcze (182-183), at Sokol (45-46), and at Zwaniec (182-183).

7. *Horiostoma globosum* (Schlotheim, 1820). Siemiradzki, 1906:231. Malinovetski Formation (Ludlow) at Braga, Kamieniec Podolski, Laskorun, Malinowiecka Sloboda, Orynin, Podzamzce, Satanowka, Sokol, and Zwaniec. Skala Formation (Pridoli) at Dzwinograd, Kozina, Skala and Zawale.
8. *Oriostoma globosum* (Schlotheim, 1820) var. *sculptum* (Sowerby, 1839. Wieniukow, 1899. Malinovetski Formation (Ludlow) at Braga (183-184), between Braga and Zwaniec (48-50), at Kamieniec Podolski (55-60), between Karmelitka and Zwanchik (50-52), at Malinowiecka Sloboda (46-47) and at Zwaniec (183-184). Skala Formation (Pridoli) at Zawale (183-184).
9. *Oriostoma globosum* (Schlotheim, 1820) var. *sculptum* (Sowerby, 1839). Siemiradzki, 1906:231. Malinovetski Formation (Ludlow) at Braga, Kamieniec Podolski, Malinowiecka Sloboda, Zwaniec.
10. *Horiostoma globosum sculptum* (Sowerby, 1839). Vascautanu, 1932. Malinovetsky Formation (Ludlow) at Conovca and Voronovita (460-461) and at the mouth of the Sost (457-458). Skala Formation (Pridoli) at Percauti, Rascov, the mouth of the Sost, and Vornovita (517-520).
11. *Oriostoma Heliciforme* Wieniukow, 1899:37-39, 184-185, Plate 6, Figure 3. Kitaygorod Formation (Wenlock) at Studenica.
12. *Oriostoma* cf. *heliciforme* Wieniukow, 1899. Siemiradzki, 1906: 232. Kitaygorod Formation (Wenlock) at Studenica. Skala Formation (Pridoli) at Skala.
13. *Oriostoma* cf. *heliforme* Wieniukow, 1899. Vascautanu, 1932:526. Skala Formation (Pridoli) at Ruhotin.
14. *Oriostoma simplex* Wieniukow, 1899:185, Plate 6, Figure 7. Malinovetski Formation (Ludlow) at Braga (185) and between Braga and Zwaniec (48-50).
15. *Horiostoma simplex* Wieniukow, 1899. Siemiradzki, 1906:232. Malinovetski Formation (Ludlow) at Braga and Skala Formation (Pridoli) at Dzwinograd.

Latvia

1. *Oriostoma virbalica* Saladzhius, 1966:43-44, Plate 7, Figure 8-10. Late Silurian ("Ludlow") Ooraskie Formation at Taurage, Vyarkneskie Formation at Virbalis, Latvia.

Asia

CHINA

1. *Poleumita? changyiensis* Grabau, 1926:64-65, Plate 4, Figure 14-15. Horizon C of Section 7b of the Miaokao Group of Upper Silurian age at Sehwaying, Chagyi Distruct, Yunnan. Probably not *Poleumita*.
2. *Poleumita* sp. Chiang, 1958:38. Silurian Wenghsiang Shale in the District of Lushan in southeast Kueichou about 150 km east of Kueiyang.

MALAYSIA

1. *Poleumita* sp. cf. *discors* (Sowerby, 1814). Gobbett, 1964:77. Kuala Lumpur Limestone (Ludlow) near Kuala Lumpur.

2. *Poleumita scamnata* Clarke and Ruedemann 1903. Gobbett, 1964:77. Kuala Lumpur Limestone (Ludlow) near Kuala Lumpur.

USSR

1. *Poleumita* cf. *globosum* (Schlotheim, 1820). Nikiforova and Obut, 1965:337. Wenlock age strata, Tuva, southeast of the Sayan Mountains.
2. *Poleumita discors* (Sowerby, 1814). Vostakova, 1962:24, Plate 5, Figure 4. Wenlock age strata along the Omnutakh River in the Siberian Platform region. The figured specimen seems too high spired to be *Poleumita*.
3. *Poleumita globosa* (Schlotheim, 1820). Vostakova, 1961:31-32, Plate 8, Figure 1. Graben Horizon (Pridoli) on Vaigatch Island.

VIETNAM

1. *Poleumita asiatica* Mansuy, 1913:11, Plate 1, Figure 15, Plate 2, Figure 1a-d. Silurian "Schistes a *Spirifer crispus*" between Langchiet and Ban-pap, Tonkin.

ORIOSTOMA AND POLEUMITA IN THE LOWER DEVONIAN

Australia

1. *Oriostoma* n. sp. Tassell, 1977:242, Plate 1, Figure 3. Late Siegenian Deep Creek Limestone, Victoria.

North America

CANADA

1. *Oriostoma* sp. Rohr and Smith, 1978:1239, Plate 1, Figure 15-16, Peel Sound Formation (Lochkovian). Prince of Wales Island, Canada.

UNITED STATES

Alaska

1. *Oriostoma* sp. *O. princeps* var. Oehlert, 1877. Kindle, 1907:327. Chapin and Kirk, in Buddington and Chapin, 1929:99-100. Lower Devonian strata on Kasaan Island (Long Island), Kassaan Bay, Prince of Wales Island, southeastern Alaska. Forney has examined this specimen labelled "Field No. 818" in the U.S. National Museum. It is probably *Oriostoma*.

Europe

AUSTRIA

1. *Polytropis guilleri* (Barrois, 1889). Frech, 1894:464-465, Plate 35, Figure 1. Emsian "Grauen riffkalk zum theil dem Schwarzen gastropoden-kalk," Wolayer Thorl in the Carnic Alps.
2. *Horiostoma tubiger* Frech, 1894:475, Plate 34, Figure 5. Emsian

Riffkalk, Wolayer Thorl. This is probably not *Oriostoma*.

3. *Polytropis involuta* (Barrois, 1889). Spitz, 1907:140, Plate 13, Figure 15-16. Emsian Hellen Kalk, Wolayer See and Judenkopf, in the Carnic Alps.
4. *Cyclonema persimile* Spitz, 1907:141-142, Plate 13, Figure 21. Emsian Hellen and Dunklen Kalk, Wolayer See, Wolayer Thorl, Valentintorl and Judenkopf in the Carnic Alps.
5. *Polytropis? barroisi* Spitz, 1907:141, Plate 14, Figure 9. Emsian Hellen Kalk Judenkopf in the Carnic Alps.
6. *Oriostoma barroisi* (Spitz, 1907). Jhaveri, 1969:151. Emsian Liegende Graue Kalke, Westwande, Seewarte, Carnic Alps.
7. *Oriostoma involuta* (Barrois, 1889). Jhaveri, 1969:151. Emsian Liegende Graue Kalke, Westwande, Seewarte, Carnic Alps.

FRANCE

1. *Oriostoma barrandei* Munier-Chalmas, 1876:103. Lower Devonian, Rennes. Genotype of *Oriostoma*.
2. *Oriostoma echinatum* Oehlert, 1877:588-589, Plate 10, Figure 4. Lower Devonian, LaBaconniere, Mayenne.
3. *Oriostoma gerbaulti* Oehlert, 1877:589-590, Plate 10, Figure 2. Lower Devonian, LaBaconniere and St. Germaine, Mayenne.
4. *Oriostoma konincki* Oehlert, 1877:588, Plate 10, Figure 1. Lower Devonian, LaBaconniere and St. Jean, Mayenne.
5. *Oriostoma multistriatum* Oehlert, 1877:590, Plate 10, Figure 2. Lower Devonian, LaBaconniere, Mayenne.
6. *Oriostoma princeps* Oehlert, 1877:589, Plate 10, Figure 5. Lower Devonian, LaBaconniere, Mayenne.
7. *Cyclonema guilleri* Barrois, 1889:220, Plate 15, Figure 12. Emsian, Erbray, Loire Inferieure.
8. *Horiostoma disjunctum* Barrois, 1889:220, Plate 15, Figure 10. Emsian, Erbray, Loire Inferieure.
9. *Horiostoma involutum* Barrois, 1889:218-219, Plate 15, Figure 8. Emsian, Loire Inferieure.
10. *Horiostoma polygonum* Barrois, 1889:219-220, Plate 15, Figure 9. Emsian, Erbray, Loire Inferieure.

CZECHOSLOVAKIA

1. *Polytropis approximans* Perner, 1907:182, Plate 71, Figure 40-42. Pragian (Siegenian-Emsian) Koneprusy Limestone, Koneprusy.
2. *Polytropis involuta* (Barrois, 1889). Perner, 1907:185-187, Plate 72, Figure 23-32, Plate 80, Figure 12-16. Pragian (Siegenian-Emsian) Koneprusy Limestone, Koneprusy. Probably not *Poleumita*.
3. *Polytropis laudabilis* Perner, 1907:188, Plate 70, Figures 38-40, Plate 80, Figure 19. Pragian (Siegenian-Emsian) Koneprusy Limestone, Koneprusy.
4. *Polytropis selecta* Perner, 1907:183, Plate 70, Figure 38-40, Plate 80, Figure 19. Pragian (Siegenian-Emsian) Koneprusy Limestone, Koneprusy.
5. *Polytropis subcostata* Perner, 1907:182-183, Plate 63, Figure 18-20. Although the legend of "f2 Menany" indicates Lower Devonian, the matrix suggests Middle Devonian, Eifelian, Suchomasty Limestone, Menany or between Menany and Koneprusy.

USSR

1. *Oriostoma princeps* Oehlert, 1877. Tschernyschew, 1885:21, Plate 4, Figure 41. Lower Devonian, west flank of the Urals. Questionable identification.
2. *Horiostoma heliciforme* Wieniukow, 1899. Siemiradzki, 1906:232. Borsczczow Formation (Lower Gedinnian) at Borsczczow, Chudykowce and Chudykowce-Olhowce, Podolia.

Asia

USSR

1. *Poleumita* sp. Rohr, Boucot, and Ushatinskaya 1979:987, Text-figure 3C, F. Pribalkhash horizon, Kazakhstan.

TURKEY

1. *Oriostoma princeps* Oehlert, 1877. Leidhold, 1918:316. Lower Devonian, Siegenian-Emsian, Yakadjik on the Bithynian Peninsula, Sea of Marmara region.

TREMANOTUS AND BOIOTREMUS IN THE SILURIAN

North America

CANADA

Ontario

1. *Tremanotus alpheus* Hall, 1865. Williams, 1963:235. Guelph Dolomite (Ludlow), Wiarton. Whiteaves, 1884:34-35. Guelph Dolomite (Ludlow) Guelph, Elora, and Durham.
2. *Bucania angustata* Hall, 1852:349, Plate 84, Figures 6a, b. Guelph Dolomite (Ludlow), Galt. Clarke and Ruedemann, 1903:57 consider *Tremanotus angustata* a synonym for *T. Alpheus*, but Peel, 1972:420 considered them to be two distinct species and assigned *T. angustata* to *Boiotremus*.
3. *Tremanotus alpheus* Hall, 1865. Bolton, 1957, Table 12. Guelph Formation (Ludlow), Albemarle Township.

Quebec

1. *Tremanotus angustatus* (Hall, 1852). Whiteaves, 1895:71. Division 2 (Llandovery) of the Anticosti Group, Cape Sand Bay, Anticosti.
2. *Tremanotus longitudinalis* Lindstrom, 1884. Northrop, 1939:207-208, Plate 21, Figure 6. Bouleaux Formation (Ludlow), Gascons near Port Daniel. Peel, 1972:420 recognized this species of *Boiotremus* in the Gascons Formation (Early Ludlow) at Port Daniel.
3. *Tremanotus minutus* Northrop, 1939:208, Plate 21, Figure 1-4. West Point Formation (Ludlow-Pridoli), West Point Lighthouse, Port Daniel Bay. Peel, 1972:420 assigned it to the tremanotids, but the plates are inadequate for generic determination.

4. *Tremanotus profundus* (Hall, 1859). Tolman, 1936:15, and Clark, 1942:31-32. Cranbourne Formation (Pridoli), Rante St. Thomas, St. Joseph Seignory near its boundary with Range IV, Cranbourne Township. Hall, 1859:341, Plate 68, Figure 1-3, described this species from the "Upper Pentamerus Limestone" at Schoharie and Carlisle, Schoharie County, New York. Hall's specimens of *Bucania profunda* (AMNH 2588-1&2) are now in the collections of the American Museum of Natural History (AMNH). The species is based on two composite molds that show no signs of tremata or a flaring aperture, but the general shape suggests *Bucania* rather than *Tremanotus*. We have not reexamined the material that Clarke described, but did not illustrate. However, Boucot did collect a single specimen of *Tremanotus* near Cranbourne.

Northwest Territories

1. *Tremanotus* cf. *angustatus* (Hall, 1852). Williams, 1963:234. Mount Kindle Formation (Silurian), Franklin Mountains about 20.8 km northeast of Fort Wrigley.

UNITED STATES

Indiana

1. *Tremanotus alpheus* Hall, 1865. Cumings and Shrock, 1928:99 and R. H. Shaver (pers. comm.). Salamonie Dolomite (Wenlock), Ridgeville, Randolph County. Louisville Limestone (Wenlock-Ludlow), Linn Grove, Adams County. Mississinewa Shale Member (Ludlow) of the Wabash Formation, Bluffton, Wells County.
2. *Tremanotus chicagoensis* (McChesney, 1860). Cumings and Shrock, 1928:81, 99 and R. H. Shaver (pers. comm.). Louisville Limestone (Wenlock-Ludlow), Linn Grove, Adams County. Mississinewa Shale Member (Ludlow) of the Wabash Formation, Bluffton, Wells County and Markle, Huntington County. Liston Creek Limestone Member (Ludlow) of the Wabash Formation, Huntington, Huntington County and Liston Creek Limestone Member (Ludlow-Pridoli), Delphi, Carroll County.

Illinois

1. *Tremanotus alpheus* Hall, 1865. Wing, 1923:12-15, Plate 1, Figure 1-2. Racine Dolomite (Late Wenlock-Ludlow), Hawthorne, Thornton, Bridgeport, Stony Island, Chicago area.
2. *Tremanotus chicagoensis* (McChesney, 1860:69, 1865:Plate 8, Figure 4-5). Wing, 1923:15-16, Plate 1, Figure 3-4. Racine Dolomite (Late Wenlock-Ludlow), Hawthorne, Thornton and Stony Island, Chicago area.
3. *Tremanotus* sp. 1 Wing, 1923:18-19, Plate 2, Figure 9. Racine Dolomite (Late Wenlock-Ludlow), Thornton. Peel, 1972:420 tentatively places this species in the synonymy of *T. chicagoensis*.
4. *Tremanotus crasseolaris* (McChesney, 1861:91). Wing, 1923:17-18, Plate 1, Figure 5-6. Racine Dolomite (Late Wenlock-Ludlow), Thornton, Stony Island and Hawthorne, Chicago area.

New York

1. *Tremanotus alpheus* Hall, 1865. Clark and Ruedemann, 1903:54-59,

Plate 5, Figure 20-23, Plate 6, Figure 1-9. Guelph Formation, Upper and Lower Shelby (Ludlow), Rochester.

Ohio

1. *Tremanotus alpheus* Hall, 1865. Hall and Whitfield, 1875:145, Plate 8, Figure 1. Cedarville Dolomite (Wenlock-Ludlow), Genoa and Springfield.
2. *Tremanotus* sp. H. B. Rollins (pers. comm.). Peebles Formation (late Wenlock-Ludlow), Plum Run Stone Company Quarry, Peebles.

Wisconsin

1. *Tremanotus* sp., UC22004 in the Van Horne Collection of the Walker Museum now housed in the Field Museum of Natural History. Racine Dolomite (Late Wenlock-Ludlow), Wauwatosa.
2. *Tremanotus alpheus* Hall, 1865. UC21791 in the Van Horne Collection of the Walker Museum now housed in the Field Museum of Natural History. Racine Dolomite (Late Wenlock-Ludlow), Racine.

Europe

CZECHOSLOVAKIA

1. *Boiotremus caelatus* (Perner, 1903). Horny, 1963:101-102, Plate 20, Figure 4-5. Lower Budnanian (Ludlow), Kopanina Beds, upper parts, probably from Jinonice (Butovice) near Praha.
2. *Boiotremus incipiens* (Perner, 1903). Horny, 1963:102-103, Plate 23, Figure 2; Plate 24, Figure 1-3. Lower Budnanian (Ludlow), basal layers of Kopanina Beds at Jinonice (Butovice) near Praha.
3. *Boiotremus beraunensis* (Perner, 1903). Horny, 1963:103-105, Plate 21, Figure 4-7; Plate 24, Figure 1-3. Lower Budnanian (Ludlow), Kopanina Beds at Dlouha hora near Beroun.
4. *Boiotremus kosovensis* Horny, 1963:105-106, Plate 21, Figure 1-3. Lower Budnanian (Ludlow), Kopanina Beds at Dlouha hora (Kosov) near Beroun.
5. *Tremanotus tuboides* (Perner, 1903). Horny, 1963:98-99, Plate 18, Figure 1-5. Wenlockian, Liten Beds at Barrande's diggings on the road Lodenice-Bubovice near Praha.
6. *Tremanotus civis* (Perner, 1903). Horny, 1963:99-100, Plate 19, Figure 1-6; Plate 20, Figure 1. Wenlockian, Liten Beds at Barrande's diggings on the road Lodenice-Bubovice near Praha.
7. *Tremanotus? inopinatus* (perner, 1903). Horny, 1963:100-101, Plate 20, Figure 2-3. Lower Budnanian (Ludlow), Kopanina Beds at Jinonice (Butovice) near Praha.

GREAT BRITAIN

1. *Bellerophon aymestriensis* Sowerby, in Murchison 1839:616, Plate 6, Figure 12, from the Bringewood Beds ("Aymestry Limestone") (Middle Ludlow), Aymestry, Herefordshire.
2. *Bellerophon dilatatus* Sowerby, in Murchison, 1839:627, Plate 12, Figure 23-24, from the Wenlock Limestone (Upper Wenlock), Burrington, near Ludlow, Shropshire.
3. *Trematonotus aymestriensis* Sowerby, 1839). Reed, 1921:79-80, Plate 12, Figure 7-8, from the Bringewood Beds ("Aymestry Lime-

stone") (Middle Ludlow), Aymestry and Leintwardine in Herefordshire and from the Eltonian (Lower Ludlow), Mary Knoll, Ludlow, Shropshire.

4. *Trematonotus dilatatus* (Sowerby, 1839). Reed, 1921:80-83, Plate 13, Figure 1, from the Wenlock Limestone (Upper Wenlock), Burrington near Ludlow, shropshire, from the Wenlock Shale (Wenlock), Dudley, Staffordshire, from the "Lower Ludlow?," Kingsland, Herefordshire, and from the Woolhope Beds (Basal Wenlock), along the Worcester Railway near Malvery, Herefordshire.
5. *Trematonotus britannicus* Newton, 1892:339-341, Plate 9, Figure 1-4, from the Wenlock Limestone (Upper Wenlock), near Dudley, Staffordshire. Reed, 1921:81, included this species in the synonymy of *Trematonotus dilatatus*.
6. *Trematonotus* sp. Pitcher, 1939:122-123, Plate 7, Figure 17. From the Venusbank Formation ("Arenaceous Purple Shales") (Middle Llandovery) of the Bog Mine Outliers, Shelve, Shropshire.

SWEDEN

1. *Trematonotus longitudinalis* Lindstrom, 1884:87-88, Plate 4, Figure 8-12. Hogklint Beds (Lower Wenlock) of Gotland at Vastos, Hall; Lauterhorn, Faro; Kalens Kvarn and Visby, Visby. Hogklint Bess or Visby Beds (Lower Wenlock) at Halls Huk, Hallshuk. Slite Beds (Middle Wenlock) at Martebo, Martebo; Slite, Slite; Vialmsudd, Fleringe. Mulde Beds (Upper Wenlock) at Djupvik, Eksta. Klinteberg Beds (Early Ludlow) at Frojelklint, Frojel; Stjarnatve, Eksta. Hemse Beds (Early Ludlow) at Petesvik, Hablingbo; Lau, Lau; Visne Myr, Fradhem. Burgsvik-Hamra Beds (Upper Ludlow) at Burgsvik, Oja. Horny, 1963:101 called this species "one of the typical representatives of the genus *Boiotremus*."
2. *Tremanotus compressus* Lindstrom, 1884:87-88, Plate 4, Figure 8-12. Klinteberg Beds (Early Ludlow) at Hammar, Kraklingbo. Hemse Beds (Early Ludlow) at Ostergarn, Ostergarn.

BOIOTREMUS IN THE LOWER DEVONIAN

Australia

1. *Tremanotus pritchardi* Cresswell, 1893. Tassell, 1976:5, Plate 1, Figure 17. Lilydale Limestone, Early Devonian. Victoria, Australia.

North America

CANADA

Prince of Wales Island

1. *Tremanotus* cf. *T. alpheus* Hall, 1865. Rohr and Smith, 1978:1233, Plate 1, Figure 17-19. Peel Sound Formation (Lochkovian), Prince of Wales Island, Canada.

UNITED STATES

Alaska

1. *Tremanotus* cf. *fortis* (Frech, 1894). Kindle, 1907:327; Chapin and Kirk, in Buddington and Chapin, 1929:99-100. Lower Devonian strata on Kasaan Island (Long Island), Kasaan Bay, Prince of Wales Island, southeastern Alaska. Forney has examined this specimen labelled "Field No. 817" in the U.S. National Museum. It is probably *Boiotremus*.

Europe

AUSTRIA

1. *Tremanotus fortis* Frech, 1894:461-462, Plate 33, Figure 2. Emsian "Schwarzen gastropoden-kalke des Wolayer Thorls" and the "Riffkalk" in the Carnic Alps.
2. *Tremanotus fortis* Frech, 1894. Spitz, 1907:123-124, Plate 11, Figure 15-17. Emsian Dunkler Kalk, Wolayer Thorl, Valentinthorl and south of Wolayer See in the Carnic Alps.
3. *Boiotremus fortis* (Frech, 1894). Jhaveri, 1969:154. Lower Emsian Liegender Grauer Kalk, Sudliches Valentintorl, Wolayer See.
4. *Tremanotus insectus* Frech, 1894:462-463, Plate 33, Figure 1. Emsian "Grauen riffkalk des Wolayer Thorls," Carnic Alps. Horny, 1963:109, assigned this species to *Boiotremus*.
5. *Boiotremus insectus* (Frech, 1894). Jhaveri, 1969:154. Lower Emsian, Liegender Graue Kalke and Seewarte-Kalke, Sudliches Valentintorl, Wolayer See.
6. *Tremanotus involutus* Frech, 1894:462, Plate 33, Figure 3. Emsian "Crinoidenbreccie des kleinen Pasterfelsens bei Seeland Karawanken."
7. *Tremanotus parvus* Spitz, 1907:122-123, Plate 11, Figure 10. Emsian Heller Kalk, Wolayer Torl.
8. *Boiotremus parvus* (Spitz, 1907). Jhaveri, 1969:154-155, Plate 20, Figure 11-13. Lower Emsian Liegender Grauer Kalk, Wolayer See, Karnische Alpen, and Westwand der Seewarte.

CZECHOSLOVAKIA

1. *Boiotremus fortis* (Frech, 1894). Horny, 1963:106-108, Plate 26, Figure 1-3; Plate 27, Figure 1-5. Pragian (Siegenian-Emsian) Upper Koneprusy Limestone, Koneprusy. A lectotype of Frech, 1894, from this locality is the type for *Boiotremus* Horny, 1962.
2. *Boiotremus insectus* (Frech, 1894). Horny, 1963:108-110, Plate 25, Figure 1-6; Plate 26, Figure 4. Pragian (Siegenian-Emsian) Upper Koneprusy Limestone, Koneprusy.

Australia

VICTORIA

1. *Tremanotus pritchardi* Cresswell, 1893:42, Plate 8, Figure 1. Lower Devonian (Emsian) Lilydale Limestone, Cave Hill Quarry, Lilydale.
2. *Tremanotus pritchardi* Chapman, 1916:79. Lower Devonian, Thomson River, Gippsland, 3½ miles northwest of Mount Lookout.
3. *Tremanotus cyclocostatus* Talent and Philip, 1956:61-62, Plate 6,

Figure 11, 15; Plate 7, Figure 16-17, Text-figure 4. Lower Devonian (Emsian) limestones, Lower Quarry at Marble Creek, Thomson River.

EUOMPHALOPTERUS IN THE SILURIAN

North America

CANADA

New Brunswick

1. *Euomphalopterus* sp. Boucot and others, 1966:40, Plate 17, Figure 2-3. Unnamed beds of map unit 4 (Late Llandovery C_4-C_5), St. George may area (1094A), beach south of the village of Back Bay, 0.5 mile northwest of the west end of Douglas Island.

Ontario

1. *Euomphalopterus valeria* (Billinas, 1865). Bolton, 1957, Tables 11 and 12. Guelph Formation (Ludlow) on Highway 6, Albemarle Township.
2. *Euomphalopterus elora* (Billings, 1865). Bolton, 1957, Tables 11 and 12. Wiarton Member of the Amabel Formation (Late Wenlock-Ludlow) at Wiarton, near Purple Valley, near Colpoy Bay Village, and near Hope Bay. Guelph Formation (Ludlow) near Chatsworth. This species does not belong in *Euomphalopterus*.
3. *Euomphalopterus halei* (Hall, 1861). Bolton, 1957, Tables 11 and 12. Wiarton Member of the Amabel Formation (Late Wenlock-Ludlow) at Wiarton, near Colpoy Bay Village, at Adamsville, and near Edenhurst. Guelph Formation (Ludlow) near Chatsworth.
4. *Pleurotomaria valeria* Billings. Whiteaves, 1884:23, Plate 4, Figure 1, 1a. Durham, Guelph Formation (Ludlow).
5. *Pleurotomaria valeris* Whiteaves, 1895, 72-73, Plate 11, Figure 4, 4a. Guelph Formation (Ludlow), Elora.
6. *Pleurotomaria* (or *Euomphalopterus*) sp. indet. Whiteaves, 1906: 257. Silurian, Ekwan River.
7. *Pleurotomaria valeria* (Billings, 1865). Guelph Formation (Ludlow), Galt.
8. *Euomphalopterus valeria* (Billings, 1865). Parks, in Tyrell, 1913:196, and Parks, 1915:64-65. Llandovery-Wenlock strata at the Limestone Rapids of the Severn River.
9. *Euomphalopterus tyrelli* Parks, in Tyrell, 1913:194, and Parks, 1915:63-64, Plate 3, Figure 15-16. Llandovery-Wenlock strata at the Limestone Rapids of the Severn River.

Quebec

1. *Euomphalopterus* sp. Northrop, 1939:212-213, Plate 22, Figure 5. Bouleaux Formation (Ludlow), near Gascons.
2. *Euomphalopterus aequilaterus* (Wahlenberg, 1818). Northrop, 1939: 211. La Vieille Formation (C_6-Wenlock) at Port Daniel East, on Little Port Daniel River and on Bonaventure River.
3. *Euomphalopterus valeria* (Billings, 1865). Northrop, 1939:211. La Vieille Formation (C_6-Wenlock) near Anse Cascon, and at Port

Daniel East.

4. *Euomphalopterus halei* (Hall, 1861). Northrop, 1939:211-212. West Point Formation (Ludlow-Pridoli) near Gascons, and at West Point, Port Daniel Region.
5. *Euomphalopterus gasconensis* Northrop, 1939:212, Plate 22, Figure 3-4. Gascons Formation (Ludlow) at Anse-aux-Gascons, Port Daniel Region.
6. *Euomphalopterus alatus* (Wahlenberg, 1818). Northrop, 1939:210-211. La Vieille Formation (C_6-Wenlock) at Port Daniel East, on Little Port Daniel River, and at Black Cape.
7. *Euomphalopterus* sp. Bolton, T. E., and M. J. Copeland, 1972:14. Thornlow Formation, Upper Silurian, Lake Timiskaming Region, Canada.

UNITED STATES

Alaska

1. *Bathmopterus liratus* Kirk, 1928:2-4, Plate 1, Figure 1-5. Tidal Formation (Ludlow-Pridoli) on Willoughby Island, Glacier Bay, southeastern Alaska.

California

1. *Euomphalopterus* sp. Rohr, 1977:197, Plate 12, Figure 15-17. Roundstone polymictic conglomerate member of the Lovers Leap Formation (Late Silurian). Klamath Mountains, California.

Indiana

1. *Euomphalopterus alatus* var. Kindle and Breger, 1904, in Kindle 1904:461, Georgetown, "Niagaran" (Ludlow).
2. *Euomphalopterus alatus* var. *americanus* Kindle and Breger, 1904, in Kindle, 1904:459-461, Plate 13, Figure 6, Little Deer Creek, Carroll County, "Niagaran" (Probably Kenneth Limestone Member of Pridoli age; Shaver (pers. comm.).
3. *Euomphalopterus alatus obsoletus* Ulrich, in Ulrich and Scofield, 1897:934, Text-figures 5g-i. "Niagaran" (Wenlock-Ludlow) at Waldron.

Maine

1. *Euomphalopterus* sp. Boucot and Yochelson, 1966:A10, Plate 1, Figure 18. Hornfels of Late Llandovery age at Limestone Hill, Stratten Quadrangle, Somerset County.

Wisconsin

1. *Pleurotomaria halei* Hall, 1861, in Hall, 1861:344, Racine Formation (Wenlock-Ludlow), Racine.

Europe

GREAT BRITAIN

1. *Euomphalopterus apedalensis* Pitcher, 1939:98-99, Plate 4, Figure

1-3. Venusbank Formation ("Arenaceous Purple Shales") (Middle Llandovery) of Harley Brook, about a half mile to the south of Harley.

NORWAY

1. *Euomphalopterus* sp. indet., identified by John Peel, PMO 54754. Uppermost stage 7a (Middle Llandovery), Bjerkøya, Holmestrand. Collected by Kiaer in 1904.
2. *Euomphalopterus* sp. indet., identified by John Peel, PMO 51208. Stage 7c (Upper Llandovery), quarry south of tileworks, Brattsberg, Skien. Collected by Kiaer in 1904.
3. *Euomphalopterus* sp. indet., Identified by John Peel, PMO 51111. Stage 7, above "Klammern," south of Skien. Collected by Kiaer in 1904; see Kiaer, 1908, Figure 62, for locality.
4. *Euomphalopterus* sp. indet., identified by John Peel, PMO 21291, 21292. "Stage 6," Malmøykalven. Possibly collected by Kjerulf in the nineteenth century. Possibly identified by Kiaer as *Pleurotomaria* sp. Peel concluded that the stage 6 assignment may be in error as the lithology is similar to material adjacent to the 6/7 boundary, and probably lowermost stage 7.
5. *Euomphalopterus alatus*, identified by John Peel, PMO 54563, 54564, 54565, 54566, 54567. Uppermost 6 m of stage 6 (Lower Llandovery, southern tip of Bjørkøya. Collected by Kiaer in 1902.
6. *Euomphalopterus* sp. indet., Identified by John Peel, PMO 54595, 54596. Uppermost 6 m of stage 6 (Lower Llandovery), southern tip of Bjørkøya, Holmestrand. Collected by Kiaer in 1902.
7. *Euomphalopterus* sp. ident., identified by John Peel, PMO 39945. Uppermost stage 6 (Lower Llandovery), Mjøndalen, near Drammen; see Kiaer, 1908:436-437. Collected by Kiaer in 1902.

SWEDEN

1. *Pleurotomaria cirrhoa* Lindstrom, 1884:121-122, Plate 11, Figure 27-29; Plate 12, Figure 1-3. Hemse Beds (Early Ludlow) Ostergarn in Ostergarn and Linde in Linde.
2. *Pleurotomaria marklini* Lindstrom, 1884:121, Plate 11, Figure 24-26. Klinteberg Beds (Early Ludlow) at Klinteberg in Klint.
3. *Pleurotomaria undulans* Lindstrom, 1884:120-121, Plate 11, Figure 15-23. Upper Visby Beds (Upper Llandovery), Gnisvard, Tofta. Hogklint Beds (Lower Wenlock), Visby, Visby.
4. *Pleurotomaria frenata* Lindstrom, 1884:120, Plate 11, Figure 14. Hogklint Beds (Lower Wenlock), Visby, Visby.
5. *Pleurotomaria togata* Lindstrom, 1884:119-120, Plate 11, Figure 8-13. Hogklint Beds (Lower Wenlock), Visby, Visby. Hemse Beds (Early Ludlow), Petesviken, Hablingbo.
6. *Pleurotomaria alata opposita* Lindstrom, 1884:119, Plate 10, Figure 38-40. Hemse Beds (Early Ludlow), Petesviken, Hablingbo.
7. *Pleurotomaria praetexta* Lindstrom, 1884:119, Plate 11, Figure 1-7. Hogklint Beds (Lower Wenlock), Visby, Visby.
8. *Pleurotomaria alata subcarinata* Lindstrom, 1884:118-119, Plate 10, Figure 33-37. Slite Beds (Middle Wenlock), Vastergarn, Vastergarn; Faro, Faro. Mulde Beds (Upper Wenlock), Djupviks Fisklage, Eksta. Eke Beds (Middle Ludlow), Lingsarve, Nas. Burgsvik-Hamra Beds (Upper Ludlow), Burgsvik, Oja.
9. *Pleurotomaria replicata* Lindstrom, 1884:115-116, Plate 13, Figure

39-44. Hogklint Beds (Lower Wenlock), Visby, Visby.

10. *Pleurotomaria alata* (Wahlenberg, 1818). Lindstrom, 1884:116-118, Plate 10, Figure 18-32. Lerberg Marlstone (Wenlock), Stora Karlso. Hogklint Beds (Lower Wenlock), Visby, Visby; Lauterhorn, Faro; Vastos, Gall; Kalens Kvarn, Visby. Slite Beds (Middle Wenlock), Vastergarn, Vastergarn; Slite, Slite; Lansa, Faro; Samsugns, Othem; Kyllei, Hallvi; Atlingbo, Atlingbo. Klinteberg Beds (Early Ludlow), Klinteberg, Klint.

CZECHOSLOVAKIA

1. *Euomphalopterus aliger* Barrande, in Perner, 1907. Perner, 1907: 151-152, Plate 65, Figure 14-18; Plate 78, Figure 14-17, Text-figure 186. Probably Kopanina Formation (Ludlow) at Dlouha hora near Beroun. Probably Kopanina Formation (Ludlow) near Svaty Jan Pod Skalou. Kopanina Formation (Ludlow), Lochkov. Pridoli Formation (Pridoli) and highest Kopanina Formation (Ludlow), Kosor.
2. *Pleuromphalis seductor* Barrande, in Perner, 1907:153, Plate 77, Figure 16-19. Pridoli Formation (Pridoli) and highest Kopanina Formation (Ludlow), Kosor. Probably not *Euomphalopterus*.

USSR

1. *Pleurotomaria alata* (Wahlenberg, 1818). Wieniukow, 1899. Malinovetski Formation (Ludlow), Kamieiiec Podolski (55-60), Karmelitka and Zwanchik (50-52), Malinowiecka Sloboda (46-47), Orynin (63-64), and Zwaniec (186-187).
2. *Pleurotomaria alata* (Wahlenberg, 1818). Siemiradzki, 1906. Malinovetski Formation (Ludlow), Kamieniec Podolski (233), Malinowiecka Sloboda (233), Orynin (233), and Zwaniec (233).
3. *Pleurotomaria alata* (Wahlenberg, 1818). Vascautanu, 1932. Malinovetski Formation (Ludlow), Camauca (507-510), Hotkin (507-510), Percauti (507-510), and Voronovita (460-461). Skala formation (Pridoli), Conovca (517-520), Percauti (517-520), the mouth of the Sost (517-520) and Voronovita (517-520).
4. *Euomphalopterus alatus subcarinata* (Lindstrom, 1884). Vostokova, 1961:15-16, Plate 2, Figure 1-3; Plate 3, Figure 8-11. (Ludlow), Talata Karskaya River, Vaigatch.
5. *Euomphalopterus alatus subcarinata* (Lindstrom, 1884). Vostokova, 1962:14-15, Plate 3, Figure 1. Llandovery of Voiero River, Siberian Platform. Generic determination questionable.

EUOMPHALOPTERUS IN THE LOWER DEVONIAN

North America

CANADA

Quebec

1. *Euomphalopterus* sp. Bourque's locality 76F-235-1B, Helderberg portion of the West Point Formation, Caleur Bay region.

UNITED STATES

Michigan

1. *Euomphalopterus valeria* (Billings, 1865). Grabau and Sherzer, 1910:191-192, Plate 28, Figure 1-3. Lucas Dolomite (Eifelian), Salt Shaft, Detroit.

Europe

FRANCE

1. *Pleurotomaria (Euomphalopterus) subalata* (Verneuil, 1850). Barrois, 1889:212-214, Plate 15, Figure 6a-b (not 6c-d). Emsian, Erbray, Loire Inferieure.

USSR

1. *Euomphalus subalatus* Verneuil. Tschernychew, 1885:21, Plate 4, Figure 36. Lower Devonian, Tirliansk Works, west slope of the central Urals.

HERCYNELLA IN THE LOWER DEVONIAN

North America

UNITED STATES

Alaska

1. *Hercynella bohemica* Barrande. Kindle, 1907:326. Early Devonian limestone at Kasaan Island (Long Island), Kasaan Bay, Prince of Wales Island, southeastern Alaska. Boucot has examined the specimens at the U.S. National Museum and agrees that they are *Hercynella*.
2. *Hercynella nobilis* Barrande. Kindle, 1907:326. Early Devonian limestone at Kasaan Island (Long Island), Kasaan Bay, Prince of Wales Island, southeastern Alaska. Boucot has examined the specimens at the U.S. National Museum and agrees that they are *Hercynella*.

California

1. *Hercynella* sp. Merriam, 1961:189. Silurian and Lower Devonian Gazelle Formation at Gregg Ranch, east of Parker Rock in the Klamath Mountains. Although the author is unsure of the age, the material is probably Helderberg Lower Devonian or Ludlow-Gedinne age.

Michigan

1. *Hercynella canadensis* Grabau, in Sherzer and Grabau, 1909:549; Grabau, in Grabau and Sherzer, 1910:195-196, Plate 25, Figure 5-6. Amherstburg Dolomite (Eifelian), Detroit River region.

New York

1. *Hercynella buffaloensis* O'Connell, 1914:96-97, Plate 1, Figure 1-3. Bertie Waterlime (Pridoli), North Buffalo.
2. *Hercynella patelliformis* O'Connell, 1914:97-99, Plate 1, Figure 4-6. Bertie Waterlime (Pridoli), North Buffalo.

Europe

AUSTRIA

1. *Hercynella bohemica* Barrande. Spitz, 1907:167, Plate 16, Figure 9. Dunkler and Hellen Kalke (Emsian), Wolayer See, Wolayer Thorl, south from Wolayer See in the Carnic Alps.
2. *Hercynella bohemica* Barrande *plana* Spitz, 1907:167, Plate 16, Figure 10. Dunkler Kalke (Emsian), Wolayer See in the Carnic Alps.
3. *Hercynella carnica* Spitz, 1907:16, Figure 2-3. Dunkler Kalke (Emsian), south from Wolayer See and at Wolayer See in the Carnic Alps.

BULGARIA

1. *Hercynella* cf. *bohemica* Barrande. Pribyl and Spasov, 1960:105-106, Plate 1, Figure 1. Gradistke Beds of Lochkov (Gedinnian-Early Siegenian) age northwest of Sofia on the northern slope of Gradistke Hill near the village of Krestina (formerly known as Suma). This specimen is Akc. Kat. BR308 R.1961 in the Narodni Muzeum in Praha.
2. *Hercynella* sp. aff. *nobilis* Barrande. Pribyl and Spacov, 1960: 106-107, Plate 2, Figure 2. Gradistke Beds of Lochkov (Gedinnian-Early Siegenian) age northwest of Sofia on the northern slope of Gradistke Hill near the village of Krestina (formerly known as Suma). This specimen is Akc. Kat. BR307 R.1961 and an unillustrated example is BR330 in the Narodni Muzeum in Praha.

CZECHOSLOVAKIA

1. *Hercynella acuminans* Perner, 1911:278, Plate 118, Figure 1-2; Plate 123, Figure 7-8. Lochkovian (Gedinnian-Early Siegenian) Lochkov Formation, Lochkov.
2. *Hercynella bohemica* Perner, 1911:274-276, Plate 1, Figure 3; Plate 39, Figure 23-25; Plate 44, Figure 6-22; Plate 45, Figure 1-19; Plate 50, Figure 18-20, 24-29; Plate 121, Figure 5-10; Text-figure 316. Lochkovian (Gedinnian-Early Siegenian) Lochkov Formation (Kotys and Radotin Facies), Lochkov, Trebotov near Radotin and probably near Beroun. The example from Beroun in Plate 45, Figure 14-15, could possibly be of Pragian (Siegenian-Early Emsian) age.
3. *Hercynella insolita* Perner, 1911:286-287, Plate 122, Figure 4-5. Lochovian (Gedinnian-Early Siegenian) Lochkov Formation, Velka Chuchle.
4. *Hercynella minor* Perner, 1911:285-286, Plate 2, Figure 32-34; Plate 48, Figure 12-13. Pragian (Siegenian-Lower Emsian) Slivenec Limestone, Praha, Zlichov and in the Koneprusy Limestone of the same age as Koneprusy.
5. *Hercynella nobilis* Perner, 1911:276-278, Plate 46, Figure 1-16;

Plate 47, Figure 4-18; Plate 49, Figure 27-30, 32-35; Plate 122, Figure 9-19. Lochkovian (Gedinnian-Early Siegenian) Lochkov Limestone, Lochkov and Velka Chuchle. The specimen illustrated in Plate 46, Figure 7-8, is most probably from the lowest Pragian (Siegenian) Slivenec Limestone at Praha, Podoli, Dvorce Quarry.

6. *Hercynella paraturgencens* Perner, 1911:280-281, Plate 39, Figure 20-22; Plate 45, Figure 20-21; Plate 123, Figure 3. Lochkovian (Gedinnian-Early Siegenian) Lochkov Limestone, Lochkov and Lochkov Limestone (Radotin Facies), Kosor (Cerna Rokle) near Radotin.
7. *Hercynella peckai* Perner, 1911:281, Text-figure 318. Pragian (Siegenian-Lower Emsian) Dvorce-Prokop Limestone, Kosor (Cerna Rokle?) near Radotin.
8. *Hercynella praecursor* Perner, 1911:282-283, Plate 121, Figure 1-4; Text-figure 319. Lochkovian (Gedinnian-Early Siegenian) Lochov Limestone, Lochkov.
9. *Hercynella radians* Perner, 1911:280, Plate 43, Figure 20-21; Plate 48, Figure 16-24; Plate 121, Figure 15-18. Lochkovian (Gedinnian-Early Siegenian) Lochkov Limestone, Lochkov, except the specimen illustrated in Plate 48, Figure 20-21, which is Lochkov Limestone (Radotin Facies), Kosor (Cerna Rokle) near Radotin.
10. *Hercynella rigescens* Perner, 1911:278-279, Text-figure 317. Pragian (Siegenian-Lower Emsian), Dvorce-Prokop Limestone, Tetin near Beroun.
11. *Hercynella ruderalis* Perner, 1911:278-279, Text-figure 317. Pragian (Siegenian-Lower Emsian), Dvorce-Prokop Limestone, Damil near Beroun.
12. *Hercynella transiens* Perner, 1911:283, Plate 2, Figure 30-31. Pragian (Siegenian-Lower Emsian) Slivenec Limestones or Zlichovian (Upper Emsian) Zlichov Limestones, Praha, Zlichov.
13. *Hercynella turgescens* Perner, 1911:280, Plate 105, Figure 34-35; Plate 123, Figure 1-2. Lochkovian (Gedinnian-Lower Siegenian) Lochkov Limestone, Lochkov.

FRANCE

1. *Hercynella bohemica* Barrande. Peneau, 1929:193. Lower Devonian "Grauwacke des fourneaux d'Angers," southwestern part of the Armorican Massif.
2. *Hercynella(?) dubia* Barrois, 1889:182-183, Plate 12, Figure 3. Lower Devonian (Emsian), Erbray, Loire Inferieure. Pribyl and Spasov, 1960:103, accept this as *Hercynella*.
3. *Hercynella(?) incerta* Barrois, 1889:183-184, Plate 12, Figure 4. Lower Devonian (Emsian, Erbray, Loire Inferieure. Pribyl and Spasov, 1960:103, accept this as *Hercynella*.

GERMANY

1. *Hercynella beyrichi* Kayser, 1878:103, Plate 17, Figure 10. Silurian-Lower Devonian (Pridoli-Gedinnian), Harzgeroder Ziegle-hutte, Harz Mountains. Genotype of *Hercynella*.
2. *Hercynella hauchecorni* Kayser, 1878:103, Plate 17, Figure 9. Silurian-Lower Devonian (Pridoli-Gedinnian), Harzgeroder Ziegelhutte, Harz Mountains.

USSR

1. *Hercynella bohemica* Barrande. Tschernyschew, 1885:12-13, Plate

3, Figure 24-25. Lower Devonian, Huttenwerk Tirliansk, west flanks Ural Mountains. Pribyl and Spasov, 1960:105, do not agree with this specific determination.
2. *Hercynella* sp. Tschernyschew, 1885:12-13, Plate 5, Figure 40. Lower Devonian, Huttenwerk Tirliansk, west flank, Ural Mountains.
3. *Hercynella polaris* Chernov, 1961:1107, Figure 1a-c, e. Lower Devonian (Siegenian-Emsian), Lek-Elats River, western slope of Polar Urals.

YUGOSLAVIA

1. *Hercynella(?)* sp. Boucek, Kriz and Stojanovish-Kuzenko, 1968:32. Lochkov (Gedinnian-Lower Siegenian) slates, Mount Bistra, West Macedonia.

USSR

Caucasus

1. *Hercynella bohemica* Barrande, 1885. Yanishevski, 1917:57, Plate 2, Figure 17. Unnamed unit, Caucasus, Late Silurian or Early Devonian.

<u>Asia</u>

TURKEY

1. *Hercynella elevata* Leidhold, 1918:318, 345, Plate 12, Figure 1. Lower Devonian, Yakadjik, Bithynian Peninsula, Sea of Marmara region.

<u>Africa</u>

MOROCCO

1. *Hercynella bohemica* Barrande. Termier and Termier, 1950a:222, 175, Figure 18-19. Gedinnian strata, southeast of Rsiffa.
2. *Hercynella radians* Barrande. Termier and Termier, 1950a:222, Plate 175, Figure 1-3. Gedinnian strata, Oued Akrech.
3. *Hercynella* cf. *radians* Barrande. Termier and Termier, 1950a:222, Plate 175, Figure 23-24. Gedinnian strata, southeast of Rsiffa.
4. *Hercynella turgescens* Barrande. Termier and Termier, 1950a:222, Plate 175, Figure 16-17. Gedinnian strata, Ain Kareima, east of Tizi <u>n</u> Draa (Tizi <u>n</u> Tafilelt).

<u>Australia</u>

1. *Hercynella victoriae* Chapman, 1916:99-100, Plate 5, Figure 47-48. Yeringian (Upper Siegenian) Lilydale Limestone, Cave Hill, Victoria.
2. *Hercynella victoriae* Chapman. Gill, 1950:88-89, Plate 7, Figure 4. Yeringian (Upper Siegenian), Syme's Quarry, Killara, Victoria.
3. *Hercynella petasoida* Gill, 1950:89-90, Plate 7, Figure 1-2. Yeringian (Upper Siegenian), Syme's Tunnel, Killara, Victoria.
4. *Hercynella killarensis* Gill, 1950:90-91, Plate 7, Figure 3. Yeringian (Upper Siegenian), Syme's Tunnel, Killara, Victoria.

5. *Hercynella* sp. Gill, 1950:91, Yeringian (Upper Siegenian), Ruddock's Quarry near Lilydale, Victoria.

REFERENCES

Ayrton, W. G. 1967. Chandler-Port-Daniel area, Bonaventure and Gaspe-South Counties. *Quebec Dept. Nat. Resources, Geol. Rept.* 120:1-91.

Barrois, C. 1889. Faune du calcaire d'Erbray (Loire Inferieure) *Mem. Soc. geol. du Nord, Lille* 3:1-348.

Bassler, R. S. 1915. Bibliographic index of American Ordovician and Silurian fossils. *U.S. Nat. Mus. Bull. 92*, 1521 p.

Berry, W. B. N., and A. J. Boucot. 1970. Correlation of the North American Silurian rocks. *Geol. Soc. America Spec. Paper* 102, 289 p.

Billings, E. 1865. Palaeozoic Fossils, v. I, Containing descriptions and figures of new or little known species of organic remains from the Silurian rocks. *Canada Geol. Survey*, 426 p.

Billings, E. 1874. Palaeozoic Fossils, v. II, Description of fossils from the Silurian and Devonian rocks of Gaspe. *Canada Geol. Survey*, 1-64.

Bolton, T. E. 1957. *Silurian Stratigraphy and Palaeontology of the Niagara Escarpment in Ontario. Canada Geol. Survey Mem.* 289:1-145.

Bolton, T. E., and M. J. Copeland. 1972. Paleozoic formations and Silurian biostratigraphy, Lake Timiskaming Region, Ontario and Quebec. *Canada Geol. Survey Paper 72-15*, 48 p.

Boucek, B., J. Kriz, and A. Stojanovish-Kuzenko. 1968. O fosilonosum lochkovienu u zapadnoj Makedonii: Geoloskiot Zavod na socialisticka Republika Makedonija, Trudova 1967-68, 13:31-38.

Boucot, A. J. 1975. *Evolution and Extinction Rate Controls.* Amsterdam: Elsevier Scientific Publishing Co., 427 p.

Boucot, A. J., J. G. Johnson, C. Harper, and V. G. Walmsley. 1966. Silurian brachiopods and gastropods of southern New Brunswick. *Canada Geol. Survey Bull.* 140:1-45.

Boucot, A. J., J. G. Johnson, and J. A. Talen. 1969. Early Devonian brachiopod zoogeography. *Geol. Soc. America Spec. Paper 119,* 113 p.

Boucot, A. J., and E. L. Yochelson. 1966. Paleozoic Gastropods from the Moose River Synclinorium, Northern Maine. *U.S. Geol. Survey Prof. Paper 503-A*, 20 p.

Butts, C., and B. Gildersleeve. 1948. Geology and mineral resources of the Paleozoic area in northwest Georgia. *Georgia Geol. Survey Bull.* 54:1-176.

Chapin, T., and E. Kirk. 1929. In E. F. Buddington and T. Chapin, Geology and mineral deposits of southeastern Alaska. *U.S. Geol. Survey Bull.* 800:1-398.

Chapman, F. 1916. New or little-known Victorian fossils in the National Museum. Part 19. The Yeringian gastropod fauna. *Royal Soc. Victoria Proc.* 29:75-103.

Chapman, F. 1917. On the probable environment of the Palaeozoic genus *Hercynella* in Victoria. *Royal Soc. Victoria Proc.* 29:123-126.

Chernov, G. A. 1959. O Niznedevonskom Mollyuski *Hercynella* Na Zapadnom Sklone. *Acad. Sci. USSR, Earth Sci. Sec.*, Amer. Geol. Inst., 127:806-809.

Chernov, G. A. 1961a. Devonskie *Hercynella* Polyarnogo Urala. *Paleont. Zhur.* 2:20-27.

Chernov, G. A. 1961b. New data on stratigraphy of Lower and Middle Devonian deposits of the Polar Urals. *Acad. Sci. USSR, Earth Sci. Sec.*, Amer. Geol. Inst., 135:1234-1236.

Chiang, R. J. 1958. On the Palaeozoic stratigraphy of the District of Lushan. *Acta Geologica Sinica* 38:449-461. English summary in *Science Abstracts of China, Earth Sciences* 2:21-23 (1959).

Chowns, T. M., and J. H. Howard. 1972. Section of Ordovician and Silurian strata exposed in road cuts on I-75 at Ringgold Gap, Georgia. In T. M. Chowns, ed., *Sedimentary Environments in the Palaeozoic Rocks of Northwest Georgia. Georgia Geol. Survey Guidebook* 11:97-100.

Clark, T. H. 1942. Helderberg faunas from the eastern townships of Quebec. *Royal Soc. Canada Trans.* 36:11-36.

Clarke, J. M., and R. Ruedemann. 1903. *Guelph Fauna in the State of New York. New York State Mus. Mem.* 5:1-195.

Cossman, M. 1895. Essais de paleoconchologie comparee, v. 1: Paris.

Cox, L. R., N. D. Newell, D. W. Boyd, and others. 1969. Systematic descriptions. In R. C. Moore, ed., *Treatise on Invertebrate Paleontology, Part N Mollusca 6*. Lawrence, Kansas: Univ. Kansas Press and Geol. Soc. America 1:N225-N489.

Cresswell, A. W. 1893. Notes on the Lilydale Limestone. *Royal Soc. Victoria Proc.* 5:38-44.

Crickman, G. W. 1932. Evidence of Taconic orogeny in Matapedia Valley, Quebec. *Am. Jour. Sci.* 24:368-386.

Cumings, E. R., and R. R. Shrock. 1928. Geology of the Silurian rocks of northern Indiana. *Indiana Geol. Survey Pub.* 75:1-226.

Donald, J. 1905. On some Gastropods from the Silurian rocks of Llangadock (Caermarthenshire). *Geol. Soc. London Quart. Jour.* 61:567-577.

Fischer, P. 1885. *Manuel de conchyliologie et de paleontologie conchyliologique, ou histoire naturelle des mollusques vivants et fossiles, Pt. 9*, 785-896, Paris.

Fisher, D. W. 1957. Lithology, Paleoecology, and Paleontology of the Vernon Shale (Late Silurian) in the type area. *New York State Mus. and Sci. Service Bull.* 364:1-31.

Foerste, A. F. 1919. Silurian fossils from Ohio with notes on related species from other horizons. *Ohio Jour. Sci.* 19:367-408.

Frech, F. 1894. Ueber das Devon des Ostalpen. III. Die fauna des unterdevonischen riffkalkes. *Deutsche Geol. Gesell. Zeitschr.* 46:446-479.

Gardiner, C. I., and S. H. Reynolds. 1902. Fossiliferous Silurian beds and associated igneous rocks of the Clougher Head District (County Kerry). *Quart. Jour. Geol. Soc. London* 58:226-266.

Gardiner, C. I., and R. P. Whitfield. 1872. Descriptions of new species of fossils from the vicinity of Louisville, Kentucky and the Falls of the Ohio. *New York State Mus. Ann. Rept.* 24:181-200.

Gardiner, C. I., and R. P. Whitfield. 1875. Descriptions of new species of fossils from the vicinity of Louisville, Kentucky and the Falls of the Ohio. *New York State Mus. Ann. Rept.* 27:9-13.

Gill, E. D. 1950. A study of the Palaeozoic genus *Hercynella*, with description of three species from the Yeringian (Lower Devonian) of Victoria. *Royal Soc. Victoria Proc.* 59:80-92.

Gobbett, D. J. 1964. Lower Palaeozoic rocks of Kuala Lumpur, Malaysia. *Federation Mus. Malaysia Jour.* 9:67-79.

Gortani, M. 1911. La fauna mesodevonico di Monumenz. Part 4 of Contribuzioni all studio del paleozoico Carnico. *Paleontographica Italica* 17:141-228.

Grabau, A. W. 1909. New Upper Siluric fauna from southern Michigan. *Geol. Soc. America Bull.* 19:540-553.

Grabau, A. W. 1910. The Monroe Formation of southern Michigan and adjoining regions. *Michigan Geol. Survey Pub.* 2:1-248.

Grabau, A. W. 1926. Silurian faunas of eastern Yunnan. *Paleontologica sinica* 3:1-101.

Hall, B. A. 1970. Stratigraphy of the southern end of the Musungun Anticlinorium, Maine. *Maine Geol. Survey Bull.* 22:1-63.

Hall, J. 1852. *Paleontology of New York, Vol. 2. Containing Descriptions of the Organic Remains of the Lower Middle Division of the New York System.* C. van Benthuysen, Albany, 362 p.

Hall, J. 1859. *Paleontology of New York, Vol. 3. Descriptions and Figures of the Organic Remains of the Lower Helderberg Group and the Oriskany Sandstone*, 1855-1859. C. van Benthuysen, Albany, 532 p.

Hall, J. 1861. Descriptions of new species of fossils from the investigations of the Survey. *Geol. Survey of Wisconsin Report*, pp. 9-52.

Hall, J. 1864 (1865). Account of some new or little known species of fossils from rocks of the age of the Niagara Group. *18th Report New York State Cabinet*, 47 p.

Horny, R. J. 1962. New genera of Bohemian Lower Paleozoic Bellerophontina. *Ustred. Ustavu Geol., Vestnik* 37:473-476.

Horny, R. J. 1963. Lower Paleozoic Bellerophontina (Gastropoda) of Bohemia. *Geol. Paleont. Sbornik*, Ser. P, 2:57-164.

Jhaveri, R. B. 1969. Unterdevonische gastropoden aus den Karnischen Alpen. *Palaeontographica* 133(A):146-176.

Kayser, F. H. E. 1978. Die fauna der altesten Devon-Ablagerungen des Harzes. *Geol. Specialkarte Preussen, Thuringischen Staaten, Abhandl.* 2:1-296.

Kiaer, J. 1908. Das Obersilur im Kristianiagebiete (Ein Stratigraphische-Faunistische Untersuchung). *Videnskabets-Selskabets Skrifter I, Mat.-Naturv. Klasse* 2:1-596.

Kindle, E. M. 1904. The stratigraphy and paleontology of the Niagara of northern Indiana. *Indiana Dept. Geol. Nat. Resources Ann. Rept.* 28:286-397.

Kindle, E. M. 1907. Notes on the Paleozoic faunas and stratigraphy of southeastern Alaska. *Jour. Geology* 15:314-337.

Kirk, E. 1928. *Bathmopterus*, a new fossil gastropod genus from the Silurian of Alaska. *U.S. Nat. Mus. Proc.* 74:1-4.

Knight, J. B. 1941. Paleozoic gastropod genotypes. *Geol. Soc. America Spec. Paper 32*, 510 p.

Knight, J. B., R. L. Batten, and E. L. Yochelson. 1960. Descriptions of Paleozoic Gastropoda. In R. C. Moore, ed., *Treatise on Invertebrate Paleontology, Part 1, Mollusca 1.* Lawrence, Kansas: Univ. Kansas Press and Geol. Soc. America, 350 p.

Koken, E. 1889. Ueber die Entwickelung der Gastropoden vom cambrium bis zur Trias. *Neues Jahrb. Geologie u. Palaontolgie Abh.* 6:305-484.

Koninck, L. G. 1881. Faune du calcaire carbonifere de la Belgique. 3e Partie: Gasteropodes. *Mus. Royal Hist. Nat. Belgique, Ann., Ser. Paleont.* 6:1-210.

Lamont, A. 1946. Some Ashgillian and Llandovery gastropods from the Girvan District, Scotland. *Quarry Manager's Jour.* 29:635-644.

Leidhold, C. 1918. Devon-Fossilen von der Bithynischen Halbinsel (Kleinasien). *Deutsch. Geol. Gessell. Zeitschr.* 69:308-347.
Lindstrom, G. 1884. On the Silurian Gastropoda and Pteropoda of Gotland. *Kongl. Svenska Vetensk.-Akad., Handl.* 19:1-250.
Longstaff, J. 1924. Descriptions of Gasteropoda, chiefly in Mrs. Robert Gray's Collection from the Orodovician and Lower Silurian of Girvan. *Geol. Soc. London Quart. Jour.* 80:408-446.
Mansuy, H. 1913. Contribution a l'etude des faunes paleozoiques et triasiques du Tonkin. *Service Geol. de L'Indochine Mem. 2*, 5:1-40.
McChesney, J. H. 1860. Descriptions of new species of fossils from the Paleozoic rocks of the western states. *Chicago Acad. Sci. Trans.* 1:1-76.
McChesney, J. H. 1861. Descriptions of new fossils from the Paleozoic rocks of the western states. *Chicago Acad. Sci. Trans.* 2:77-95.
McChesney, J. H. 1865. Descriptions of fossils from the Paleozoic rocks of the western states, with illustrations. *Chicago Acad. Sci. Trans.* 1:1-57.
Merriam, C. W. 1961. Silurian and Devonian rocks of the Klamath Mountains, California. *U.S. Geol. Survey Prof. Paper 424C*:C188-C190.
Merriam, C. W. 1972. Silurian rugose corals of the Klamath Mountains Region, California. *U.S. Geol. Survey Prof. Paper 738*, 50 p.
Munier-Chalmas, E. 1876. Mollusques nouveaux des terrains paleozoiques des environs de Rennes. *Jour. Conchyologie* 16:102-109.
Nettleroth, H. 1889. Kentucky fossil shells: a monograph of the fossil shells of the Silurian and Devonian rocks of Kentucky. E. Polk Johnson, Frankfort, pp. 1-245.
Newton, R. B. 1892. On the American Palaeozoic gasterpod *Trematonotus* (Hall emend. P. Fischer), and its identification in Britain with description of a new species. *Geol. Mag.* 9:337-341.
Nikiforova, O. I., and A. M. Obut. 1965. Siluriiskaia Systema, Stratigrafia SSSR, v. 10: Moscow:Izdatelstvo"Nedra," 529 p.
Northrop, S. A. 1939. Paleontology and stratigraphy of the Silurian rocks of the Port Daniel-Black Cape region, Gaspe. *Geol. Soc. America Spec. Paper* 21, 302 p.
O'Connell, M. 1914. Descriptions of some new Siluric gastropods. *Buffalo Soc. Nat. Hist. Bull.* 11:93-101.
Oehlert, M. D. 1877. Sur les fossiles devoniens du department de la Mayenne. *Soc. Geol. France Bull.* 5:578-603.
Oliver, W. A. 1964. New occurrences of the rugose coral *Rhizophyllum* in North America. *U.S. Geol. Survey Paper 475-D*:D149-D158.
Parks, W. A. 1913. In J. B. Tyrell, ed., *Hudson Bay exploring expedition, 1912.* Ontario Bur. Mines Ann. Rept. 22:161-209.
Parks, W. A. 1915. Paleozoic fossils from a region southwest of Hudson Bay. *Royal Canadian Inst. Sci. Trans.* 11:3-95.
Peel, J. S. 1972. Observations on some Lower Palaeozoic tremanotiform Bellerophonracea (Gastropoda) from North America. *Palaeontology* 15:412-422.
Peneau, J. 1929. Etudes stratigraphique et paleontologique dans le sud-est du massif Armoricain (Synclinal de Saint-Julien-de-Vouvantes). *Soc. Sci. de l'Ouest de la France, Nantes, Bull., Ser. 4*, 8:1-300.
Perner, J. 1903, 1907, 1911. Gasteropodes, in Barrande, J., Systeme Silurien du centre de la Boheme, Primiere Partie: Recherches Paleontologiques, v. 4, t. 1, 164 p.; t. 2, 380 p.; t. 3, 390 p.

Pitcher, B. L. 1939. Upper Valentian gastropod fauna of Shropshire. *Ann. and Mag Nat. Hist.*, Ser. 11, 4:82-132.

Prantl, F. O. 1958. O systematiken postaveni rodu *Hercynella* Kayser. *Narodni mus. Odd. Prirodoved., Casopis* 127:159-162.

Prantl, F. O. 1960. Die systematischen stellung der Gattung *Hercynella* Kayser (Pelecypoda). *Palaont. Zeitschr.* 34:150-153.

Pribyl, A., and C. Spasov. 1960. Neue Faunas des Bulgarischen Obersilurs (Ober-Ludlow). *Akad. Nauk. Bulgaria, Geol. Inst. Trans., Ser. Paleont.* 2:101-141.

Prouty, W. F. 1923. In C. K. Swartz and W. F. Prouty, *Systematic Paleontology of Silurian deposits.* Maryland Geol. Survey, Silurian, 1-794.

Reed, F. R. C. 1921. A monograph of the British Ordovician and Silurian Bellerophontacea. *Paleontograph. Soc. Monogr.* 72:1-48; 73:49-92.

Roemer, C. F. 1876. Lethea geognostica oder Beschreibung und Abbildung der fur die Gebirgs Formationen bezeichnendsten Versteinerungen, Vol. 1, *Lethea Palaeozoica*, E. Schweizerbart'sche Verlaghandlung, Stuttgart, 323 p.

Rohr, D. M. 1977. *Structure, Stratigraphy, and Paleozoic Gastropoda of the Callahan, California Area.* Ph.D. thesis, Oregon State University, Corvallis, 318 p.

Rohr, D. M., A. J. Boucot, and G. T. Ushatinskaya, in press, Early Devonian gastropods from the North Pribalkhash region, central Kazakhstan, U.S.S.R. *Jour. Paleontology.*

Rohr, D. M., and R. E. Smith. 1978. Lower Devonian Gastropods from the Canadian Arctic Islands. *Canadian Jour. Earth Sci.* 15:1228-1241.

Sainsbury, C. L. 1961. Geology of a part of the Craig C-2 Quadrangle and adjoining areas, Prince of Wales Island, southeastern Alaska. *U.S. Geol. Survey Bull.* 1058H:299-362.

Saladzhius, V. Yu. 1966. Fauna Molluskov Siluriskikh Otlozhenii Oozhnoi Pribaltiki. Paleontologiya i Stratigrafiya Pribaltiki i Belorussii. *Izdatelstvo "Mintis" Vilnoos, Sbornik* 1:31-73.

Savage, T. E. 1913. Stratigraphy and paleontology of the Alexandri Alexandrian Series in Illinois and Missouri. *Illinois Geol. Survey Bull.* 23:67-160.

Schlotheim, E. F. 1820. *Die Petrefactenkunde auf Ihrem jetzigen standpunkte durch die Beschreibung.* Gotha, Becker'shen, 437 p.

Siemiradzki, J. 1906. Die Palaozoischen Gebilde Podoliens. *Beitr. Palaont. Geol. Osterreich-Ungarns* 19:173-286.

Sowerby, J. de C. 1814. *Numbers IX and X in the Mineral Conchology of Great Britain*, Vol. 1. London: Benjamin Meredith, 244 p.

Sowerby, J. de C. 1825. *Mineral Conchology of Great Britain*, Vol. 5. London: Taylor, 171 p.

Sowerby, J. de C. 1839. In R. I. Murchison, *The Silurian System.* London: John Murray, 768 p.

Spitz, A. 1907. Die gastropoden des Karnischen Unterdevon. *Beitr. Palaont. Geol. Osterreich-Ungarns* 20:115-190.

Talent, J. A., and G. M. Philip. 1956. Siluro-Devonian Mollusca from Marble Creek, Thomson River, Victoria. *Royal Soc. Victoria Proc.* 68:73-84.

Tassell, C. B. 1976. A revision of the gastropod fauna of the Lilydale Limestone (Early Devonian) of Victoria. *Victoria Natl. Mus. Mem.* 37:1-22.

Tassell, C. B. 1977. Gastropods from some Early Devonian limestones of the Walhalla Synclinorium, Central Victoria. *Victoria Natl. Mus. Mem.* 38:231-245.

Teichert, T. 1935. Ueber *Pterotheca* Salter und verwandte Bellerophontacean. *Palaont. Zeitschr.* 17:167-177.

Termier, G., and H. Termier. 1950a. Paleontolgie Marocaine, Pt. II: Invertebres de L'Ere Primaire, v. 3, Mollusques: *Service Geol. Maroc, Notes et Mem.* 78:1-246.

Termier, G., and H. Termier. 1950b. On the systematic position of the genus *Hercynella*, Kayser. *Malacol. Soc. London Proc.* 28:156-162.

Tolman, C. 1936. Lake Etchemin map-area, Quebec. *Geol. Survey of Canada Mem.* 199:1-20.

Tschernyschew, T. 1885. Die fauna des Unteren Devon am West-Abhange des Urals. St. Petersbourg: *Kommissioneriyi Geol. Koimmitata*, 221 p.

Ulrich, E. O., and W. H. Scofield. 1897. The Lower Silurian Gastropoda of Minnesota. *Minnesota Geol. Nat. Hist. Survey Final Rept.* 3:813-1081.

Vascautanu, T. 1932. Formatiunile silurienne din malul Romanesc al Nistrului. *Inst. Geol. Romaniei Anuarul* 15:425-663.

Verneuil, E. 1850. Classification des terrains paleozoiques due department de la sarthe, avec une liste des foggiles. *Soc. Geol. France Bull.* 7:769-784.

Vostakova, V. A. 1961. Paleozoiiskii gastropodi Novoi Zemli i Ostrova Vaigatch. *Naunchna-Issled. Inst. Geol. Arktiki Minist. Geol. i Okrani Nedr SSR. Sbornik statei Po Paleont. i Biostrat. vipusk* 25:5-43.

Vostakova, V. A. 1962. Ordovikskie i Siluriiskie gasteropodi Sibirskoi Platformi. *Vsesounogo Nauchno-Issled., Geol. Inst. (Vsegei), Trudy, New Ser.* 75:1-46.

Wahlenberg, G. 1818-1821. Petrificata telluris Svecanae examinata. *Soc. Reg. Sci. Upsala, Nova Acta* 8:1-116, 293-296.

Whiteaves, J. F. 1884. On some new, inperfectly characterized or previously unrecorded species of fossils from the Guelph Formation of Ontario. *Canada Geol. Nat. Hist. Survey Palaeozoic Fossils* 3:1-43.

Whiteaves, J. F. 1895. Revision of the fauna of the Guelph Formation of Ontario with descriptions of a few new species. *Canada Geol. Nat. Hist. Survey Palaeozoic Fossils* 3:45-109.

Whiteaves, J. F. 1906. The Fossils of the Silurian (Upper Silurian) rocks of Keewatin, Manitoba, the northeastern shore of Lake Winnipegosis, and the lower Sasketchewan River. *Canada Geol. Nat. Hist. Survey Palaeozoic Fossils* 3:243-352.

Whitfield, R. P. 1882. Geology of Wisconsin: Description of fossils. *Wisconsin Geol. Survey* 4:161-363.

Wieniukow, P. N. 1899. Fauna Siluriskikh Otlozhenii Gubernii. *St. Petersborg. Materiiay dlya Geologii Rossii* 19:1-266.

Williams, M. Y. 1963. The age of the Mount Kindle Formation of the Franklin Mountains. *Canadian Petroleum Geologists Bull.* 2:228-237.

Wing, M. E. 1923. Silurian Gastropoda of northeastern Illinois. Ph.D. dissertation, University of Chicago, 111 p.

Wing, M. E. 1925. Silurian Gastropoda of northeastern Illinois (abstract): *Chicago Univ., Abstr. of Theses, Sci. Ser.*, 1:311-317.

Yanishevsky, M. 1917. On some representatives of the Upper Silurian fauna of the Caucasus. *Ezhegodnik, Rissakago Paleontologicheskago* 1:48-63.

6

Faunal Assemblages Developed in a Coarse Clastic Sequence

Stephen F. Barrett and Peter E. Isaacson

ABSTRACT

In the past, the large-shelled fauna, massive beds, and monotonous lithology of the Early Devonian Oriskany Sandstone have suggested near-shore, possibly littoral, deposition in the Appalachian Basin. Data from three stratigraphic sections from the easternmost outcrops of Oriskany Sandstone in western Maryland and West Virginia indicate that wave and current agitation may not have been as significant in disrupting faunal assemblages as had been thought. Faunas consist principally of brachiopods and some platyceratid gastropods, crinoids, shell borers, sediment burrowers, and others. Analyses of size frequency, valve orientation, ratios of valves preserved, articulation ratios, and condition of fossil brachiopods suggest oscillatory rather than strong unidirectional currents. In our stratigraphic sections, brachiopod assemblages show a vertical replacement of communities containing abundant *Rensselaeria* or *Costispirifer* by communities with abundant *Acrospirifer,* which apparently correlated with a slight increase in water depth. This is accompanied by increased overall faunal diversity. Rather than invoke a complex series of transgressions and regressions to account for faunal diversity and community changes, we propose that the east-central portion of the Oriskany Sandstone represents an east to west progradational sequence in a transgressive sea. This accounts for a shallowing midway through the stratigraphic section. An increase in water depth is the last event visible in the upper, fossiliferous parts of the section; a final regression is not recorded. Post-Oriskany subaerial exposure created a distinct disconformity and attendant erosion of regressive beds in the region studied.

INTRODUCTION

Determining depositional paleoenvironments in clastic sequences can be difficult; at times, detailed study of faunal assemblages is required. The Oriskany Sandstone of the Appalachian Basin (called the Ridgeley Formation of the Oriskany Group by Woodward, 1943) offers a challenge to the paleoecologist because its lithologic character does not vary greatly and only minor fluctuations in lithology occur in any particular sequence (Hall, 1859; Clarke, 1908; Schuchert et al., 1913; Woodward, 1943; Cloos, 1951). The unit has thick, poorly defined bedding, and primary sedimentary structures, such as cross-bedding, are absent in the part of the eastern outcrop belt of the Appalachian Basin (from Berkeley Springs, West Virginia, to Needmore, Pennsylvania) that we examined in the field. Trace fossils, although present in the unit elsewhere, are similarly rare. The Oriskany Sandstone is unusually widespread (Woodward, 1943), lithologically consistent, generally coarse grained, and well sorted. The formation contains varying amounts of calcareous cement. In the western outcrop belt (extending north-northeast and south-southwest from Cumberland, Maryland), the formation is usually more calcareous than elsewhere.

The lack of sedimentary structures makes paleoenvironmental analysis difficult. Fortunately, the well-preserved and abundant fauna provide information about the environment, both postmortem, as sedimentary particles (valve orientation and condition of fossils), and premorten, from functional morphology and community structure.

The Oriskany Sandstone contains large-shelled brachiopods, large platyceratid gastropods, and articulated pelmatozoans (Hall, 1859). Few previous workers attempted to document faunal-assemblage change-overs through the formation although some (Schuchert et al., 1913; Woodward, 1943) described a two-part occurrence of the brachiopods. The lower Oriskany contains an abundance of *Acrospirifer murchisoni* whereas abundant *Costispirifer arenosus* occur in the upper Oriskany (Woodward, 1943). However, our data show that *Acrospirifer* becomes more abundant in the upper portion of the sections and thereby suggests attendant transgression. Faunal diversities in the upper portion, moreover, are higher than those of the lower portion, indicating less turbulent conditions.

Our work generally supports the environmental conclusions of others (Clarke, 1980; Woodward, 1943): the Oriskany Sandstone was deposited under shallow, nearshore, possibly littoral, marine conditions. Our faunal data support the general notion that the Oriskany Sandstone is a time-transgressive or diachronous unit (Dennison and Head, 1975). Subtleties in faunal patterns through the stratigraphic sections suggest that either a brief regressive phase occurred during Oriskany deposition or the east-central portion of the Oriskany represents a slow clastic progradation from the east during transgression. The former case suggests a sequence of transgressive, regressive, transgressive, and finally regressive (represented by post-Oriskany erosion) events. The latter case, which requires a simpler model, is supported by Dennison and Head (1975) who suggested that the clastic materials of the Oriskany were contributed chiefly from eastern and southern source areas and that the detritus was distributed throughout the basin by the shallow sea.

The paleogeographic setting of the Oriskany Sandstone is a shallow sea occupying the Appalachian Basin (Head, 1974; Dennison and Head, 1975). The basin was elliptical in plan, extending from Alabama to New York and beyond, and the northeast-trending depositional axis ran through southwestern Pennsylvania. The basin was bordered to the northwest by lowlands and to the southeast by the source rocks for much of the clastic sediments filling the basin.

STRATIGRAPHIC SETTING

Dennison and Head (1975) showed the extent of Oriskany Sandstone in outcrop and in the subsurface. The unit is found in the southern half of New York, western two-thirds of Pennsylvania, eastern quarter of Ohio, western part of Maryland, most of West Virginia, and northern Tennessee. The thickest portions of the Oriskany Sandstone (approximately 80 m, Woodward, 1943) lie along the eastern outcrop belt from south-central Pennsylvania through eastern West Virginia. Our data are from the thick portion of the unit in western Maryland and the eastern panhandle of West Virginia. For our study we used stratigraphic sections at the following locations: one of the Pennsylvania Glass Sand Company quarries at Berkeley Springs, West Virginia; a railroad cut at Woodmont, Maryland; and a roadcut at the intersection of Sandy Mile Road with U. S. 40, Maryland (Figure 6-1). Each section is at least sparsely fossiliferous throughout, but only the upper beds are highly fossiliferous. Bulk samples for faunal analysis were taken from these upper beds. Figure 6-2 shows the general Early Devonian stratigraphy of the central Appalachian Basin.

In general, the Oriskany Sandstone is a well-sorted, medium grained quartzarenite, which frequently contains carbonate cement. Most grains are well rounded and some show frosting. These aspects, plus the presence of well-rounded heavy minerals (Woodward, 1943), suggest a reworked sandstone. Much postdepositional reworking may have been done by burrowing infaunas, so little evidence of original bedding thickness remains. In the central Appalachians, the Oriskany Sandstone coarsens upward from a fine- to medium-grained sandstone at the base to a granule or pebble conglomerate at the top. In some areas, a basal conglomerate has been noted (Clarke, 1908; Woodward, 1943) and the Connelly Conglomerate in New York (Chadwick, 1908) underlies the calcareous equivalent of the Oriskany (the Glenerie Formation) in the Hudson Valley and to the east in the Green Pond Outlier. In eastern West Virginia near Cherry Run, the entire Oriskany Sandstone is possibly represented by a conglomerate 1 to 2 m thick. Correlation within the Oriskany is difficult because of the variation in thickness and because some upper beds of the "Helderbergian" Licking Creek Limestone (Little Cove Member) may actually be carbonate-facies equivalents of the lower Oriskany Sandstone (Head, 1974; Lockett, 1977). The amount of carbonate cement remaining in the Oriskany is variable (Seilacher, 1968), but it is generally assumed that most of the unit throughout the Appalachian Basin had carbonate cement at one time. In the central Appalachians, carbonate cement increases to the west, near the deep portions of the Appalachian Basin (Dennison and Head, 1975).

PALEONTOLOGY

The general faunal composition of the Oriskany at our study localities is shown in Table 6-1. Table 6-2 lists abundance of brachiopods from the same localities. Brachiopods dominate the fauna; crinoids at the opposite extreme represent less than one percent of the fossils collected. Fossils in our collection are entirely represented by molds and casts. Articulation ratios and percentages of brachial and pedicle valves of brachiopods are discussed on the following pages.

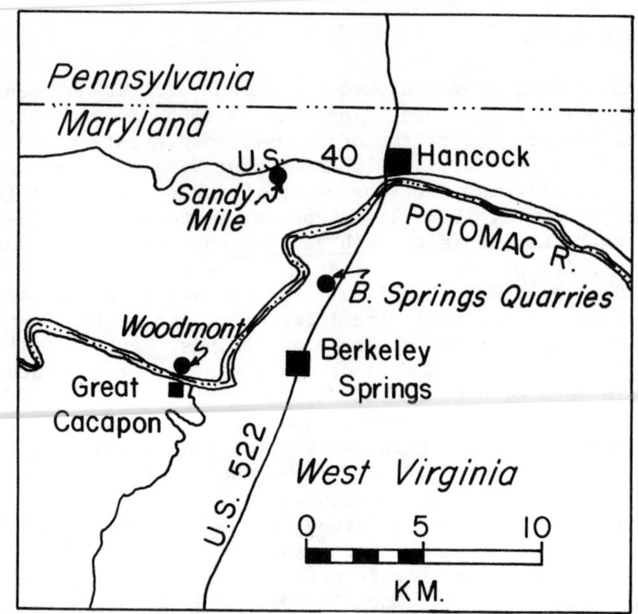

Figure 6-1
Locations of measured sections in West Virginia and Maryland. Sections are indicated by circles: Woodmont, Sandy Mile, and the Berkeley Springs quarries.

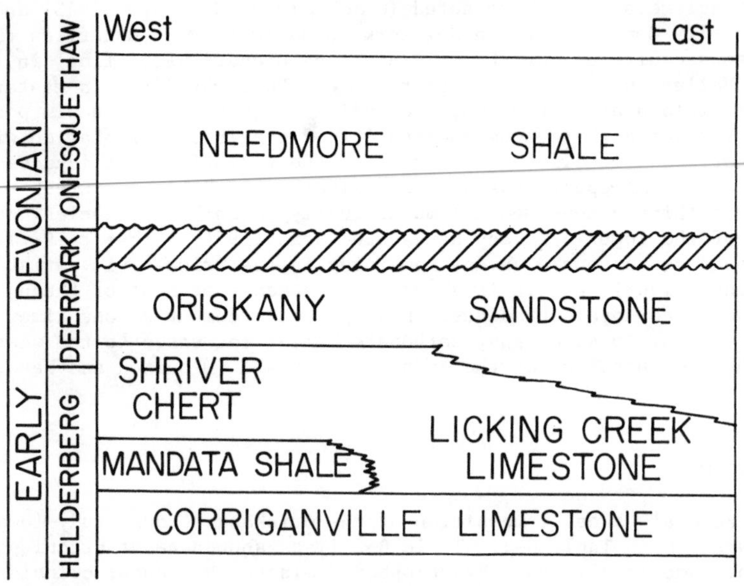

Figure 6-2
Early Devonian stratigraphy of the central Appalachian Basin, (after Head 1974).

Table 6-1
Constituents of the fossil faunas: Upper Oriskany Sandstone, Hancock, Maryland vicinity. Sample size (n) = 1300 individuals.

Brachiopods	94%
Gastropods	3
Unidentified borers	3
Crinoids (fragments)	less than 1

Preservation of the fossils is generally quite good. Seilacher (1968) suggested that at least this part of the Oriskany was subjected to freshwater solution, which removed any traces of originally aragonitic remains while the sediment was still soft.

Some crinoids are exceptionally well preserved; complete calices, arms, and pinnulae are found intact. Many crinoids, however, are quite thoroughly disarticulated, possibly by postdepositional compaction or bioturbation, since the fragments have not been scattered. The good preservation of entire crinoids indicates a narrow range of conditions during burial: rapid deposition; weak, possibly unidirectional currents.

The crinoids and gastropods present show a symbiotic relationship; for example, coprophagous platyceratid gastropods are found on crinoid calices (Yochelson and Kriz, 1974). Borings, mostly in brachiopod shells, were produced by polychaete worms (Cameron, 1969) and clinoid sponges (Yochelson and Kriz, 1974). Most of the borings observed by us do not penetrate to the interior of the shells. They average 1 mm in diameter and can be several centimeters in length, occurring as irregularly sinuous burrow casts within the void formerly occupied by the shell. Measured diameters fall into two size groups: 0.3 to 0.6 mm and 0.7 to 1.5 mm. The larger borings are comparable to Devonian borings ascribed to a *Polydora*-like polychaete (Camerson, 1969), and the smaller borings may have been produced by clionid sponges as suggested by Yochelson and Kriz (1974) for borings in Oriskany Sandstone gastropods from the Cumberland, Maryland, area.

Burrowing organisms were also present in the Oriskany Sandstone, but many of their traces have become obscured. Infrequent *Ophiomorpha*-like burrows (*sensu* Weimer and Hoyt, 1964) and burrow casts are found throughout our measured sections.

BRACHIOPOD ASSEMBLAGES

In the paleoecological approach to faunal assemblages, it is important to determine if each assemblage is representative of the original community, a life assemblage (biocoenosis, *sensu* Schafer, 1972), or if it is a random mixture of communities or a community altered beyond recognition, a death assemblage (thanatocoenosis, *sensu* Schafer, 1972). As used here, the term *community* means a recurring association of species that presumably lived closely together and formed a natural ecologic unit.

Brachiopods of the Oriskany Sandstone from our stratigraphic sections in the Hancock, Maryland, vicinity are shown in Table 6-2. The following criteria are used in assessing the Oriskany Sandstone faunal assemblages: size-frequency distributions, valve orientation, ratios of valves preserved, articulation ratios, and fossil conditions (judged by abrasion and breakage).

Table 6-2
Brachiopods and gastropods of the Oriskany Sandstone, Hancock, Maryland, vicinity (as percent of total individuals in each collection). Stratigraphic location of collections is shown in Figures 6-7 and 6-8.

collection no.	% *Acrospirifer*	% *Costispirifer*	% *Rensselaeria*	% *Costellirostra*	% *Plethorhyncha*	% *Merista*	% *Beachia* + *Prionothyris*	% *Cryptonella*	% *Centronella*	% *Discomyorthis*	% *Hipparionyx*	% strophomenids	% gastropods	% unidentifiable	total number of individuals
2	3	38	12	--	11	--	15	4	--	1	--	--	9	6	76
3	7	51	6	16	3	--	--	4	2	--	--	--	4	6	94
4 + 4A	6	30	16	25	8	--	--	2	2	--	--	--	3	9	109
5	53	10	7	2	9	5	--	1	--	4	4	--	4	2	136
6	44	15	--	7	6	--	--	--	--	12	2	2	10	--	68
11	5	51	18	6	10	4	3	1	1	1	--	--	1	1	155
14	12	46	17	--	2	--	--	2	--	--	--	3	7	3	41
15	4	32	47	--	--	--	3	5	--	--	--	--	5	4	106
17	8	41	40	--	--	--	1	5	--	--	--	--	--	1	84
18	6	24	54	--	--	1	3	3	--	--	--	--	3	1	106
20	--	72	28	--	--	--	--	--	--	--	--	--	--	--	46
23	3	32	8	10	5	29	1	--	5	1	--	--	5	1	157
24	--	92	5	--	--	--	--	2	--	--	--	--	--	--	100
all collections	10	36	18	6	5	5	2	2	1	1	1	1	3	2	1278

SIZE-FREQUENCY

Figure 6-3 shows frequency and size distributions for the most abundant brachiopod genera from six collections. The polymodalities and wide size ranges suggest that these collections reflect original community structures. All members of the population may have been preserved even if they underwent some transportation.

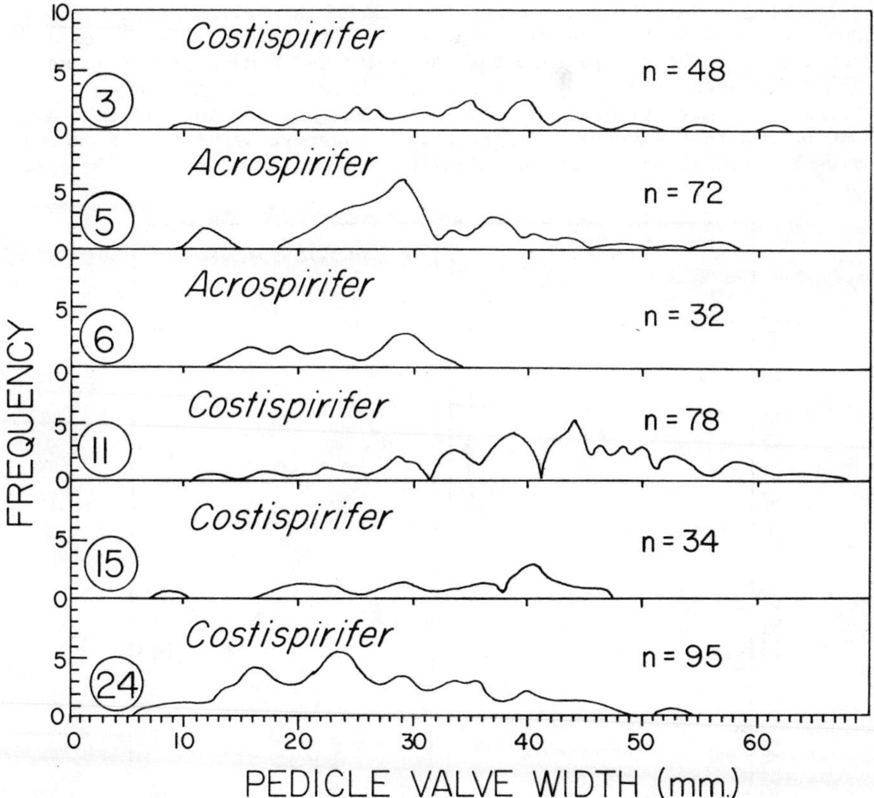

Figure 6-3
Size-frequency distributions of some Oriskany Sandstone brachiopods. Moving average at interval of 3 mm of measurement in increments of 1 mm. Circled numbers refer to collections: 3 = Berkeley Springs quarries; 5, 6, 11, 15 = Sandy Mile; 24 = Woodmont; *n* is number of individuals of each genus in that collections.

VALVE ORIENTATION

Of all disarticulated shells observed for orientation, 60 percent are concave-down in the rocks. For the sample size involved (482 shells), this is a significant difference from the expected 50 percent at the

95 percent confidence level. A concave-down position is slightly favored; such a position can be produced by currents or agitation of the water (Schafer, 1972). The apparent preferred stability of concave-down valves indicates at least some current or water movement.

RATIOS OF VALVES PRESERVED

Figures 6-4 and 6-5 show that pedicle valve percentages (relative to brachial valves present in any collection) for *Rensselaeria* and *Costispirifer* vary from 0 percent (only brachial valves present) to 100 percent (only pedicle valves present) but that pedicle valves predominate. These data show that some damage to many specimens has occurred. Such damage may have occurred because both genera are strongly inequivalved (their brachial valves are lighter and thus more susceptible to breakage). Differential transport of valves, produced by weak currents operating on slight hydrodynamic differences in valve

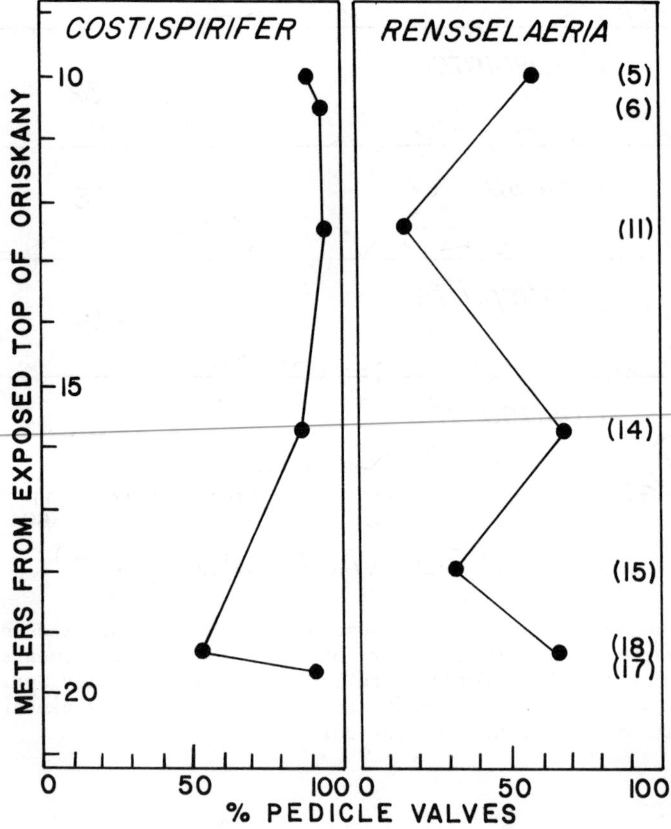

Figure 6-4
Ratios of valves preserved, expressed as number of pedicle valves divided by number of pedicle plus brachial valves, all X 100. Values for brachiopods from the Sandy Mile locality.

morphology, may also explain the data. However, as Figure 6-3 shows, small valves were not transported, and breakage, perhaps aided by boring organisms, seems a more likely explanation for the preponderance of pedicle valves.

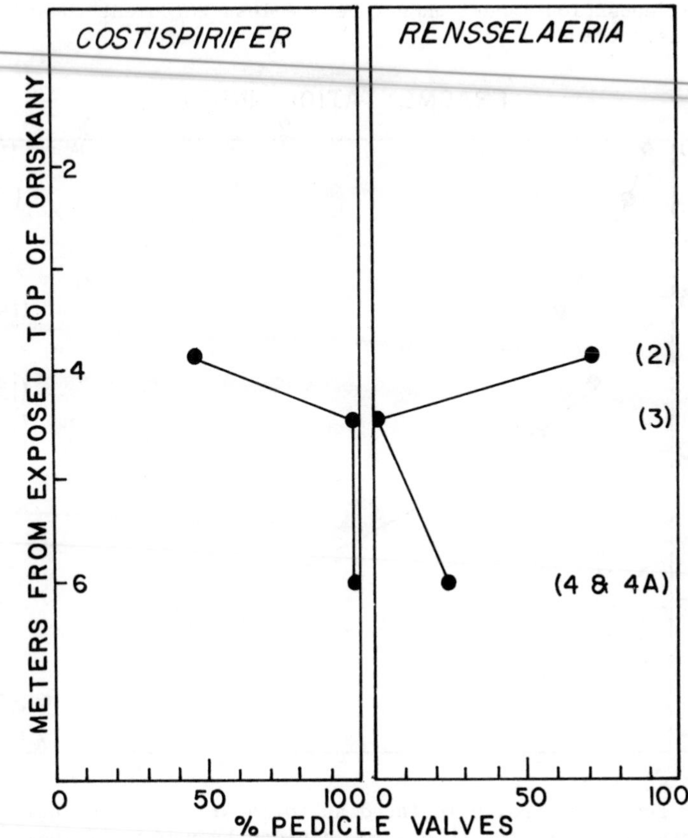

Figure 6-5
Ratios of valves preserved, expressed as number of pedicle valves divided by number of pedicle plus brachial valves, all X 100. Values for brachiopods from the Berkeley Springs quarries section.

ARTICULATION RATIOS

Most individuals are disarticulated; articulation ratios, therefore, approach zero in all cases. This parameter suggests that death or burial took place in a turbulent environment.

FOSSIL CONDITION

Except for a few heavily abraded fossils, most brachiopods are well preserved. As a quantitative indicator of the degree of fragmentation for each collection, an arbitrary fragmentation index was devised (Figure 6-6). The index is the ratio of fragments to individuals, counting only fragments greater than 1 cm long. This index permits exclusion of heavily mixed and fragmented collections in community assessment, for example, the lowest two collections from the Sandy Mile stratigraphic section. In addition, the index indicates that the depositional environment became less turbulent toward the top of the section.

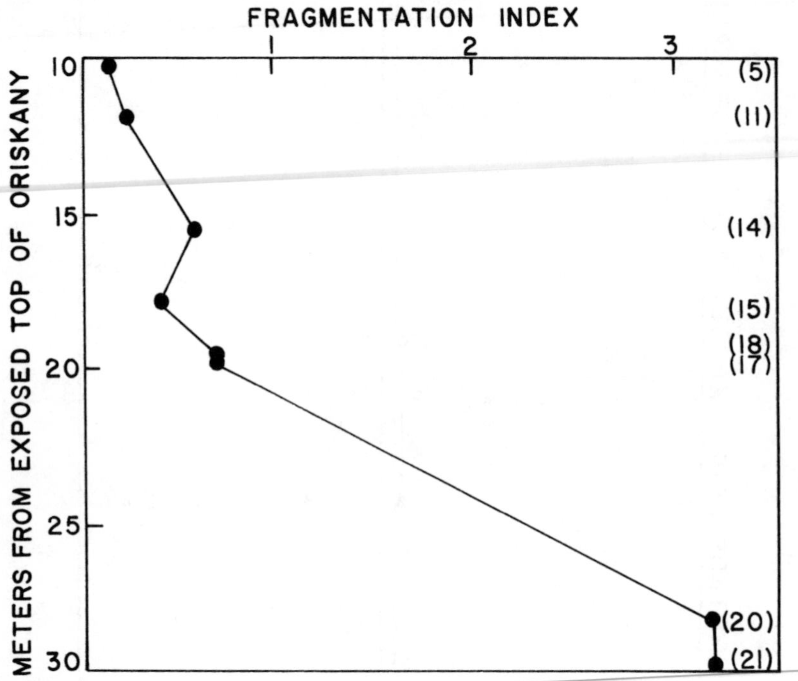

Figure 6-6
Index of fragmentation, calculated as follows: number of unidentifiable fragments greater than 1 mm, divided by number of individuals present for that collection. Values for the Sandy Mile section.

To summarize the data used in assemblage assessment, some indicators suggest postmortem transport or agitation of the original biocoenoses. The size-frequency curves suggest, however, that the community structure is not greatly changed and that long distance transport was quite minimal. A possible explanation of the apparent conflict in environmental indicators is that postmortem movement may not have been unidirectional. We suggest that the bottom currents were dominantly oscillatory, as might be expected in the nearshore environment. This is partially in accord with the environmental conclusions of Seilacher (1968) for the Oriskany. He cited both long distance transportation and moderate *in situ* agitation of fossils. Seilacher involked severe, effective current action in some collections because of articulated, stemless crinoid calices. Our collections show good preservation of columnals even though many crinoid calices are disarticulated. We feel that the invocation of strong currents is unjustified. Boucot (1975) summarized the transportation problem and demonstrated that postmortem transport is probably insufficient to completely destroy original community structure and thoroughly mix adjacent communities. Shells would be largely destroyed before that could happen. Our data support Boucot's (1975) conclusions.

We will treat our brachiopod assemblages as communities in the paleoecological sense. The large, durable brachiopods are good indicators of community structure, because they apparently were least affected by bottom currents. Fortunately, 80 percent of all individuals described from the Oriskany Sandstone belong to genera that had large shells, apparently well adapted for the moderately agitated environments during Oriskany time.

VERTICAL COMMUNITY SUCCESSION

Figures 6-7 and 6-8 show the change in brachiopod faunal composition through the stratigraphic section, and Figures 6-9 and 6-10 show the change in faunal diversity through the section. The following conclusions can be drawn from these data:

1. When *Costispirifer* is abundant in a collection, *Acrospirifer* occurs as a minor element. The latter replaces the former in abundance toward the top of the section.
2. *Rensselaeria,* abundant in collections from lower portions of the sections, becomes less abundant upsection. It is replaced initially by *Costispirifer* and later by *Acrospirifer.*
3. Due to some small sample sizes, species diversity (S) is not a valid measure of diversity for all collections. A small collection will not contain all numerically rare species. The Simpson Diversity Index (D_S) is more effective for small sample sizes because it is a diversity index weighted against rare taxa present. Both D_S and S are shown in Figures 6-9 and 6-10. Regardless of the index used, overall brachiopod diversity increases slightly toward the top of the stratigraphic sections.

DISCUSSION

The appearance of spiriferids accompanied by a general increase in brachiopod diversity indicates an environmental changeover, possibly from an intertidal to a shallow-subtidal environment. Boucot (1975) showed a *Hipparionyx* community as representing the Oriskany faunal assemblages. This community contains *Acrospirifer, Costispirifer, Rensselaeria,* and others. We feel that this community can be subdivided; a *Rensselaeria-Costispirifer* subcommunity is vertically replaced by an *Acrospirifer* subcommunity. Both of these subcommunities have shells adapted for "rough water" conditions. Eighty percent of the individuals belong to large-shelled genera, and the dominant genera (*Rensselaeria* and the spiriferids) have stabilizing, secondary calcite deposits in the ventral (pedicle) valve. The major difference between the two subcommunities is that the one dominated by *Acrospirifer* has slightly higher diversity and contains those genera found in a variety of Devonian environments: for example, *Discomyorthis* and *Meristella.*

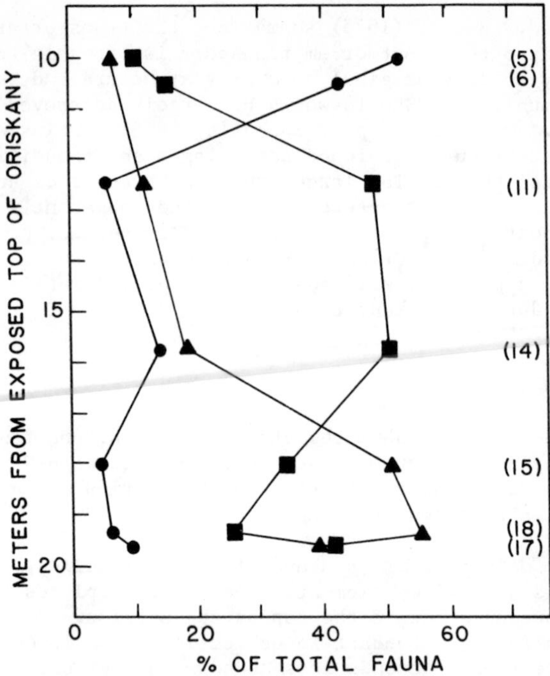

Figure 6-7
Faunal composition (percentage of total fauna) for Sandy Mile section. ● = *Acrospirifer* ■ = *Costispirifer* ▲ = *Rensselaeria*. Numbers in parentheses refer to collection.

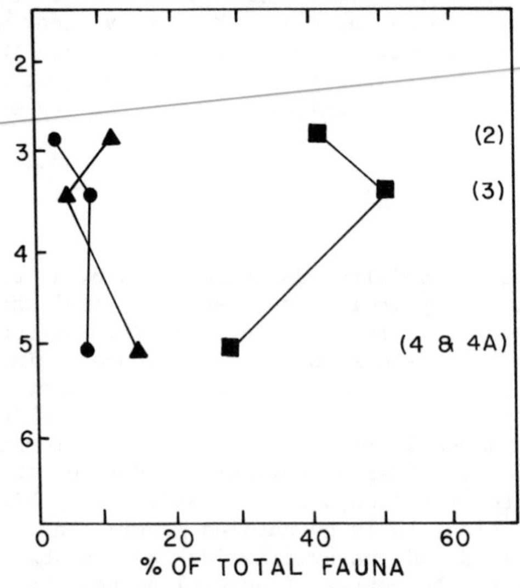

Figure 6-8
Faunal composition (percentage of total fauna) for Berkeley Springs quarries section. ● = *Acrospirifer* ■ = *Costispirifer* ▲ = *Rensselaeria*. Numbers in parentheses refer to collections.

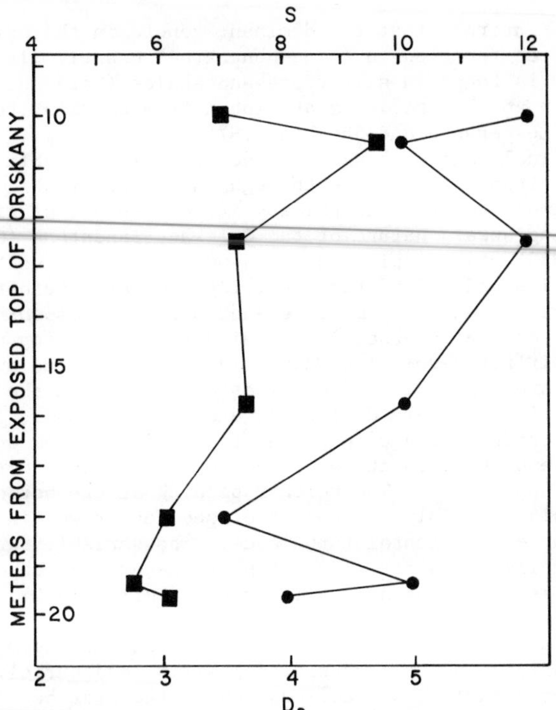

Figure 6-9
Number of species (S) and Simpson Diversity Index ($D_s = 1/(P_i)^2$, where P_i is proportion of each taxon, for Sandy Mile brachiopods. ■ = D_s, ● = S.

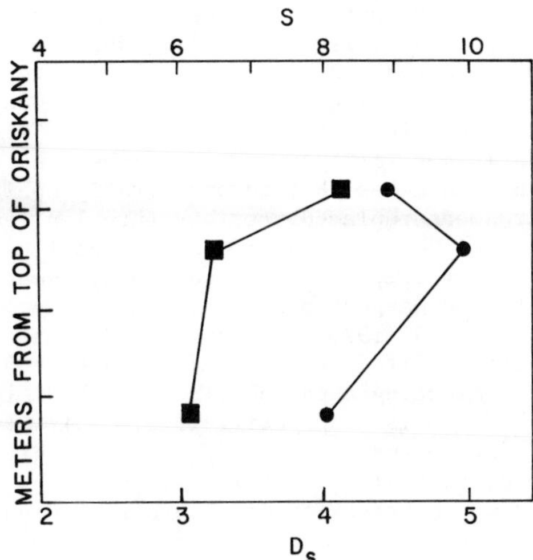

Figure 6-10
Number of species (S) and Simpson Diversity Index ($D_s = 1/(P_i)^2$, where P_i is proportion of each taxon, for brachiopods in Berkeley Springs quarries section. ■ = D_s, ● = S.

It is of interest that the dominant genera in the Oriskany Sandstone have been reported in (fine-noncoarse) clastic lithologies. *Acrospirifer* is found in siltstones and shales (Morales, 1965); *Costispirifer* and *Rensselaeria* are known from calcilutites and calcisiltites (Lesperance and Sheehan, 1975).

The vertical faunal changes may be the only reliable clue to indicate an environmental change through the stratigraphic sections because sediment texture and primary structures are of little help. The coarsening-upward nature of the Oriskany Sandstone (Clarke, 1908; Woodward, 1943) might imply that this portion of the unit is regressive. Coarse clastics and spiriferid assemblages occur together. Bedding, however, that is generally massive and contains *Costispirifer*- and *Rensselaeria*-dominated assemblages thins toward the top of the section where the spiriferid-dominated assemblages occur. The uppermost bedding planes are traceable for hundreds of meters (in the Berkeley Springs quarries) and are defined by a shell pavement. The change in bedding indicates a change in style of deposition from an apparently constant rate of sedimentation in the lower beds to a more variable rate in the upper beds. The thicker bedding at the bottom of the section is also possibly the result of sediment reworking by both burrowers and environmental turbulence. The variable rate of sedimentation implies episodic (perhaps storm-generated) deposition such as found in shallow-subtidal environments (Swift, 1969).

The following evidence also supports our environmental conclusions: Well-articulated crinoid specimens, which occur at the middle of the sequence, indicate a rapid rate of deposition and burial. Their fragile arms, pinnulae, and calices would otherwise be disarticulated as they are in other parts of the sections. Morphological differences suggest that the three major brachiopod genera *(Costispirifer, Rensselaeria,* and *Acrospirifer)* were adapted for slightly different environments. *Rensselaeria* has a high length to width ratio, and *Costispirifer* and *Acrospirifer* have wide hinge lines. The elongated nature of *Rensselaeria* suggests that individuals of the genus tended to clump together for support. The same adaptation was observed in populations of *Pentamerus* (Ziegler et al., 1966). In addition, Gauri and Boucot (1970) reported that thickened shell material in the posterior serves as a stabilizing factor for brachiopods. The three genera show this adaptation. Shell thickening in *Costispirifer* is much greater than in *Acrospirifer*. Furthermore, the fragmentation index (Figure 6-6) indicates that in one stratigraphic section a quiet-water environment replaced previous turbulent environments.

The appearance of *Acrospirifer* may also signal a return to less turbulent and probably deeper-water conditions. Near Cumberland, Maryland, close to the deepest part of the Early Devonian Appalachian Basin (Dennison and Head, 1975), assemblages dominated by *Acrospirifer* contain brachiopods in life position in conjunction with primary bedding structures, indicating a paleoenvironment "far less turbulent than to the east" (Yochelson and Kriz, 1974: 475). In addition, comparison of *Acrospirifer* and *Costispirifer* morphologies, specifically the less-developed, ventral valve thickenings in the former, suggests that *Acrospirifer* was adapted for less-turbulent conditions than *Costispirifer*.

Using faunal assemblage successions to show changing environments is not a new concept (Ziegler, 1965). Using brachiopod assemblages, Isaacson (1975) delineated a transgressive-regressive event in Devonian clastic rocks of Bolivia. Boucot (1975) also outlined environmental habitats occupied by several Silurian and Devonian brachiopod assemblages. It is reasonable, therefore, to assume that our Lower Devonian assemblages (*Rensselaeria-Costipirifer-*, and *Acrospirifer*-dominated) represents at least slightly different environments. A vertical change in assemblages in any section then implies an environmental change.

THE MODEL

Figure 6-11 shows our concept of the best fit for the data cited above. We postulate a progradational sequence of coarse clastics from east to west. This sequence, in the area studied, includes mainly the upper, fossiliferous portions of the Oriskany Sandstone. However, the sequence probably extends down stratigraphically to include the regression noted by Head (1974) in the carbonates (Licking Creek Limestone) and siliceous siltstones (Shriver Chert) below the Oriskany. In the lower part of this sequence, deposition took place below wave base, but with continued shallowing, the paleoenvironment made a transition from below wave base to above wave base. Organisms such as *Costispirifer* and *Rensselaeria* were well adapted for such an environment. As sedimentation contined, depositional environments became slightly shallower. Progradation then apparently stopped, but transgression continued because the upper brachiopod assemblages indicate a slightly deeper and quieter marine environment. We are not certain whether these changes in water depth might be correlative along the eastern margin of the Appalachian Basin. Variations in basin topography and bathymetry may complicate the succession near the margins. Post-Oriskany erosion has removed the Oriskany Sandstone throughout the basin to varying degrees; any regressive beds may no longer be present in the eastern outcrop belt of the central Appalachians.

Of course, other scenarios could produce the observed faunal and sedimentary changes. However, the preponderance of available evidence (the coarse-grained, well-sorted nature of the sediment, the massive beds without fine-grained interbeds, the large shells and their morphologies) suggests a shallow, turbulent, marine environment. Within this larger environmental framework, the fossil data provide paleoenvironmental refinement.

CONCLUSIONS

1. We need more data from the western outcrop belt (where the Oriskany is more calcareous and shows more primary-bedding features than in the east) to check for model accuracy. Because the western outcrop belt was near the center of the depositional basin (Head, 1975; Dennison and Head, 1975), the Oriskany environments there were probably indicative of a more offshore, deeper-water environment than further east.
2. We feel that our study is a case where sediment textures and depositional structures alone cannot provide adequate paleoenvironmental data; analysis of the faunal assemblages is necessary.

PARAMETERS	West		East
BRACHIOPOD ASSEMBLAGES	*ACROSPIRIFER*	*COSTISPIRIFER*	*RENSSELAERIA*
TOPOGRAPHY	mean sea level 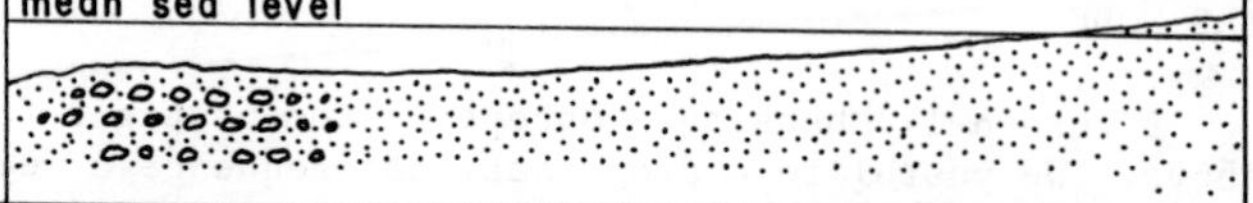		
LITHOLOGY	CONGLOMERATE TO COARSE-GRAINED SS.		COARSE-TO MEDIUM-GRAINED SS.
BEDDING	THIN, DEFINED BY FOSSILS		THICK, POORLY DEFINED
FAUNAL DIVERSITY	"HIGH" (S = 12)		"MODERATE" (S = 8)
BURROWING	LITTLE BIOTURBATION		EXTENSIVE BIOTURBATION
ENVIRONMENT	SHALLOW SUBTIDAL		SHALLOW SUBTIDAL TO LOWER INTERTIDAL
DEPOSITIONAL RATE	INTERMITTENT		RAPID, CONSTANT

Figure 6-11
Conceptual model of depositional environments of the Oriskany Sandstone, eastern outcrop belt of the Central Appalachians. *Costispirifer* and *Rensselaeria* are abundant in the lower portion of the sequence and are replaced by abundant *Acrospirifer* in the upper part, indicating an environmental change. Sedimentological and faunal patterns for the respective communities are shown. The shallowest environment (*Acrospirifer*-dominated communities) does not imply presence of a shoreline.

3. The progradational and transgressive nature of the early Oriskany beds will be better understood with more work on the relationship between the Oriskany Sandstone and the underlying Licking Creek Limestone.
4. Community structure is still recognizable in many Oriskany Sandstone brachiopod assemblages, despite an apparently turbulent and rigorous environment.
5. Low-diversity, large-shelled brachiopod assemblages are replaced by high-diversity assemblages up the stratigraphic sections, indicating a deeper, quieter environment up-section. Water depth was apparently only slightly deeper.

ACKNOWLEDGMENTS

Financial assistance was provided, in part, by a Sigma Xi Grant-in-Aid-Of-Research. Assistance in the field was provided by the Early Devonian Research Group (a field cooperative) and in the laboratory by S. C. Soloyanis. Officials of the Pennsylvania Glass Sand Corporation kindly provided access to their quarries on several occasions. The Department of Geology and Geography, University of Massachusetts, supplied vehicles without the use of which this project would have been impossible. This work represents a portion of an M. S. project undertaken by S. F. Barrett at the University of Massachusetts.

NOTE ADDED IN PROOF

Additional field work, including an extensive reconnaissance of the Oriskany outcrop belt from New York through Virginia, affirms our suggestion that the Oriskany paleoenvironments inferred in this paper are restricted to the east-central portion of the unit in the central Appalachians. Further west, the sediments indicate a more offshore, less turbulent environment because of finer-grained lithologies, a higher overall faunal diversity, and more common and varied trace fossils. In the Hancock, Maryland area, the lower third of the Oriskany Sandstone (generally unfossiliferous) has yielded monospecific assemblages of articulated brachiopods: *Costispirifer arenosus*, *Rensselaeria marylandica*, *Leptocoelia flabellites*, and *Meristella lata*. This supports our argument that deposition of the lower Oriskany Sandstone was characterized by high sedimentation rates, as opposed to the more intermittent sedimentation at the top.

REFERENCES

Boucot, A. J. 1975. *Evolution and Extinction Rate Controls.* Amsterdam: Elsevier Scientific Publishing Co., 427 p.

Cameron, B. 1969. New name for *Paleosabella prisca* (McCoy), a Devonian worm-boring, and its preserved probable borer. *Jour. Paleontology* 43:189-192.

Chadwick, G. H. 1908. Revision of the New York series. *Science* 28: 346-348.

Clarke, J. M. 1908. *Early Devonic History of New York and Eastern North America.* New York State Mus. and Sci. Service Mem. 9, 250 p.

Cloos, E. 1951. Stratigraphy of sedimentary rocks of Washington County, *The Physical Features of Washington County.* Maryland Geol. Survey, 333 p.

Dennison, J. M., and J. W. Head. 1975. Sealevel variations interpreted from the Appalachian Basin Silurian and Devonian. *Am. Jour. Sci.* 275:1089-1120.

Gauri, K. L., and A. J. Boucot. 1970. *Cryptothyrella* (Brachiopoda) from the Brassfield Limestone (Lower Silurian) of Ohio and Kentucky. *Jour. Paleontology* 44:125-132.

Hall, J. 1859. *Paleontology Vol. 3.* New York Geol. Survey, 532 p.

Head, J. W. 1974. Correlation and Paleogeography of upper part of Helderberg Group (Lower Devonian) of central Appalachians. *Am. Assoc. Petroleum Geologists Bull.* 58:247-259.

Isaacson, P. E. 1975. Faunal evidence for a Devonian transgression-regression in Bolivia. *Prim. Cong. Argentino Paleont. y Bioestrat. Actas, Tucuman,* 1:255-273.

Lesperance, P. J., and P. M. Sheehan. 1975. Middle Gaspe Limestone Communities on the Forillon Peninsula, Quebec, Canada, (Siegenian, Lower Devonian). *Paleogeography, Paleoclimatology, Paleoecology* 17:309-325.

Lockett, L. 1977. *The Paleoecology and Sedimentology of the Licking Creek Limestone (Lower Devonian) of the Central Appalachian Basin.* A.B. honors thesis, Smith College, Northampton, Mass. 125 p.

Morales, A. P. 1965. A contribution to the knowledge of the Devonian faunas of Colombia. *Univ. Indus. de Santander, Colombia, Bol. de Geologia* 19:51-111.

Schafer, W. 1972. *Ecology and Paleoecology of Marine Environments.* Chicago: The University of Chicago Press, 568 p.

Schuchert, C., C. K. Swartz, T. P. Maynard, and R. B. Rowe. 1913. *The Lower Devonian Deposits of Maryland.* Maryland Geol. Survey, 560 p.

Seilacher, A. 1968. Origin and diagenesis of the Oriskany Sandstone (Lower Devonian, Appalachians) as reflected in its shell fossils, in Muller, G., and G. M. Friedman, eds., *Recent Developments in Carbonate Sedimentology in Central Europe.* Berlin: Springer-Verlag, pp. 175-185.

Swift, D. J. P. 1969. Inner shelf sedimentation: processes and products, in Stanley, D. J., ed., *The NEW Concepts of Continental Margin Sedimentation.* Am. Geol. Inst. Short Course Lecture Notes, pp. DS-4-1 - DS-4-46.

Weimer, R. J., and J. H. Hoyt. 1964. Burrows of *Callianassa major* Say, geological indicators of littoral and shallow neritic environments. *Jour. Paleontology* 38:761-767.

Woodward, H. P. 1943. Devonian System of West Virginia. *West Virginia Geol. Survey* 15, 655 p.

Yochelson, E. L., and J. Kriz. 1974. Platyceratid gastropods from the Oriskany Sandstone (Lower Devonian) near Cumberland, Maryland: synonymies, preservation, and color markings. *Jour. Paleontology* 48:474-483.

Ziegler, A. M. 1965. Silurian marine communities and their environmental significance. *Nature* 207:270-272.

Ziegler, A. M., A. J. Boucot, and R. P. Sheldon. 1966. Silurian pentameroid brachiopods preserved in position of growth. *Jour. Paleontology* 40:1032-1036.

7

Lower Devonian Brachiopod Dominated Communities of the Cordilleran Region

A. J. Boucot and David G. Perry

ABSTRACT

A review and consideration of the level-bottom, brachiopod-dominated Early Devonian communities of the Cordilleran Region, including faunas from the Great Basin of the United States, northern British Columbia, Yukon, and mainland Northwest Territories, and the Arctic Islands of Canada, indicates that their shoreline and depth relations can be worked out in a manner similar to faunas from other biogeographic units. Notable is the absence, or at least nonrecognition to date, of shoreline faunas belonging to Benthic Assemblages 1 and 2 and brackish, estuarine, and nonmarine faunas in Nevada and their rarity in northern and arctic Canada. The common absence of shoreline material probably reflects a combination of post-Early Devonian, largely pre-Middle Devonian erosion and dolomitization that preferentially affected the shoreline position. The community groups characteristic of the Silurian-Early Devonian elsewhere are easily recognized in the Cordilleran Region although distinct species-level communities characteristic of the Cordilleran Region predominate.

INTRODUCTION

As coauthors with Gabrielse (Perry, et al., in press), we described the stratigraphic position, structural situation, and brachiopods from the late Early Devonian of the Mount Lloyd George area, northern British Columbia. In the course of our work, we considered the paleoecologic data provided by the Mount Lloyd George fossils. The Mount Lloyd George fauna does little to clarify the Early Devonian brachiopod community picture. This is a result of the allochthonous nature of parts of the fauna, the lack of stratigraphic data available to place the collection in a known stratigraphic section in the area, and the complexity of the community problem. The rocks yielding the fauna comprise a suite of loose blocks derived from a stratigraphic interval of approximately 3 m. The blocks show considerable lithologic variation: sandy dolostone matrix with rounded intraclasts of dolomitic sandstone, dolostone, and limestone. Some 60 to 80 percent of the material is represented by acid-insoluble residues.

The thirty-four brachiopod genera present in the Mount Lloyd George collection are a considerably higher diversity than usually encountered elsewhere in unmixed collections of similar age and type except for those described by Lenz (1977a, b). The large number of taxa present in the collection is probably the result of telescoping of communities by bottom transport and possibly due to parts of the fauna being derived from clasts as well as matrix. The dolomitic clasts may be older than the associated matrix from which most of the fauna was derived. Although we are unable to say much about the paleoecology of the Mount Lloyd George material, we feel that the information we integrated in the course of the work is of interest for specialists in the Devonian.

BENTHIC ASSEMBLAGE CONCEPT

The benthic assemblage (B. A.) concept (Boucot, 1975) is a useful tool whereby Silurian and Devonian brachiopod faunas have been interpreted in a depth *cum* shoreline-proximity scheme composed of six benthic assemblages ranging from high and low intertidal (B. A. 1-2) to the shelf-margin, subphotic depth zones (B. A. 6). B. A. 3 is concluded to represent inner-shelf, photic zone conditions whereas B. A. 4 and 5 represent outer-shelf to shelf-margin conditions.

The brachiopod communities proposed by Boucot (1975) are based on examples familiar to him from experience with Paleozoic brachiopods. The communities are not rigorously defined in a quantitative manner, and some of the communities may be difficult to understand for the worker unfamiliar with the examples. No quantitative ground rules were proposed for naming medium- or high-diversity communities. The level at which the communities have been defined is controlled by how frequently a particular community recurs and whether it appears useful in discussing faunal associations. No formal statistical tests have been employed, and the interpretations are more subjective for high- than for low-diversity communities. It is not unusual to have a data matrix of 20 genera times 50 percent variation compounded by such factors as local environmental fluctuations, selective sorting and preservation, and the original patchy distribution of the benthos. To set precise quantitative limits on individual taxa from high-diversity communities is difficult because of ecoclinal as opposed to ecotonal variation among communities and is probably not biologically meaningful. The shallow-water, B. A. 1-2 communities contain fewer taxa and commonly show more clear-cut ecotonal boundaries, which makes community definition easier.

The benthic assemblage concept evolved from the work of Ziegler (1965) who defined a series of five depth-related, shoreline-proximity, Silurian brachiopod "communities" based on faunal succession in the British Isles. Ziegler's "communities" served the same purpose as benthic assemblages. The benthic assemblage terminology eliminates the problem of assigning beds of a particular region to a Ziegler "community" where the name bearer of the "community" is absent. Additionally, Ziegler's "communities" bear little correspondence conceptually to those employed by most marine ecologists today.

SAMPLING PROBLEMS

The major problem in defining brachiopod communities from the Cordilleran Region, Early Devonian, high-diversity, B. A. 4-5 position is that the available sample of localities and fauna is small. Nowhere is the collecting systematic (statistically speaking) in terms of the problems presented by community analysis although it is entirely adequate for normal biostratigraphic purposes. The comparison of faunal content and percentage data from collections preserved in different ways poses problems. In calcareous crack-out collections, the larger shells are more readily obtained, and their percentages are correspondingly biased. Many small elements are commonly missed altogether. Silicified collections probably provide the best estimate of true faunal abundance. Selective silicification of brachiopod shells does occur and sometimes strophomenids, chonetids, and some pentamerids (commonly thin-shelled groups) are partially destroyed during etching. The third common mode of preservation is the noncalcareous matrix shales, siltstones, and sandstones whose casts and molds are studied by exposing shell-bearing surfaces with a rock splitter and acid dissolution of the calcareous shell material. This type of preservation gives a good representation of all shells, large and small, as long as enough surfaces are inspected to reveal all elements present.

CORDILLERAN REGION COMMUNITY DEFINITION QUESTIONS

An attempt was made to establish a series of Lower Devonian brachiopod communities based on data available in Johnson (1974a, b; 1977), Johnson and Niebuhr (1976), Johnson and Kendall (1976), Johnson, et al. (1978), Niebuhr (1974, 1977) from central Nevada and in Lenz (1976; 1977a, b), and Perry (1974) from the Canadian north. It must be recalled that Nevada was represented by an enclave of the Eastern Americas Realm during the Pragian whereas the rest of western North America belonged to the Old World Realm throughout the Lower Devonian (Boucot et al., 1969; Boucot, 1975; Savage et al., 1978).

Comparison of Nevada and northwestern Canada early- to mid-Lochkovian faunas of comparable B. A. 4-5 positions shows no obvious correlation in percentage or presence-absence data (Table 7-1; Johnson, 1974a: 811). In Early Lochkovian samples Nevada faunas are numerically dominated by orthids with few rhynchonellids present whereas the Canadian Mackenzie Mountain faunas are dominated by rhynchonellids with much smaller numbers of orthids and pentamerids present (Tables 7-2, 7-3). Comparison on the ordinal level of younger Lower Devonian faunal percentages from Nevada and Sekwi Mountain map-area, Northwest Territories, (Tables 7-2, 7-3) shows no obvious correlation. This is to be expected considering the biogeographic differences and the shallow-water nearer shore position of some of the Nevada faunas. Brachiopod faunas from the Royal Creek area, Yukon, and sections from the Sekwi Mountain map-area probably belong to a B. A. 4-5 position throughout the Lower Devonian. Comparison of ordinal percentages for the whole Royal Creek and Mount Sekwi Lower Devonian are comparable. Both areas show a high percentage of atrypids and spiriferids. Fürsich and Hurst (1974) studying Silurian brachiopods from Wales and the Welsh Borderland, concluded that the distribution of brachiopods on the paleoslope (transect) was deter-

Table 7-1
Percentages of Various Brachiopod Taxa from Sekwi Mountain and Glacier Lake Map-areas, Northwest Territories, in Strata of Early Lochkovian Age

	A1760	A1765T	A1770-90	A1785	OLDA1730T
Skenidioides variabilis	0.5	-	1.0	-	6.2
Protocortezorthis aff. *fornicatimcurvata*	1.7	-	-	-	0.7
Dalejina sp.	1.0	-	2.0	-	-
Schizophoria spp.	8.0	1.8	1.0	55.7	8.3
Schizophoria paraprima	-	-	-	-	-
Salopina submurifer	0.9	?0.2	-	1.3	4.3
Muriferella masurskyi	-	-	-	-	0.4
Grayina cf. *magnifica*	0.2	-	-	-	-
Gypidula sp.	1.7	-	-	-	4.0
Gypidula sp. 4	-	-	-	-	0.4
Leptagonia sp.	-	-	-	1.3	0.4
Eoschuchertella sp.	-	-	-	-	0.7
Aesopomum variastriatus	0.4	0.2	-	-	-
Mesodouvillina sp.	-	-	-	-	-
Machaeraria sp.	28.3	-	16.7	-	11.2
Ancillotoechia sp. 1	-	0.2	-	-	-
Ancillotoechia sp. 2	0.5	92.7	31.4	2.5	-
Decoropugnax? sp.	1.1	-	-	-	-
Linguopugnoides sp.	-	-	-	-	0.4
Atrypa spp.	0.7	0.3	41.2	-	-
Atrypa sp. 1	10.5	-	-	11.4	15.9
Atrypa nieczlawiensis	-	-	-	-	-
Desquamatia sp.	15.8	-	-	-	-
Ogilviella cf. *prolifica*	13.8	-	-	-	5.8
Reticulatrypa cf. *neutra*	-	-	-	-	-
Spirigerina sp. 1	5.7	-	2.0?	-	2.2
Spirigerina marginaliformis	-	-	-	2.5	-
Toquimaella kayi	-	-	-	-	14.1
Sibirispira? sp.	-	-	-	-	-
Notoparmella gilli	-	-	-	-	-
Cryptatrypa sp.	1.0	-	-	-	-
Protathyris sp.	-	-	-	-	6.5
Nucleospira sp.	2.1	0.2	3.9	5.1	1.4
Rhynchospira sp.	-	0.2	-	1.3?	-
Howellella sp.	-	0.3?	-	-	-
Warrenella sp.	?0.1	1.1	-	?5.1	?1.4
Ambocoelia sp.	2.0	1.8	-	6.3	1.8
Cyrtina sp.	4.0	0.8	-	7.6	13.8
Total Number of Valves in Each Collection	810	896	102	79	276

Source: Data from Perry, 1974.

OLDA1765	B805	B810	B815-870	B835	B1105	B1130	GSC69059	Average Percent
0.9	-	-	-	-	-	-	-	0.7
-	-	-	-	-	-	-	-	0.2
-	-	-	-	-	-	-	-	0.2
0.9	23.2	33.3	24.5	79.2	9.8	-	18.3	20.3
-	-	-	-	-	-	29.5	-	2.3
-	-	-	-	-	3.1	2.3?	-	0.9
-	-	-	-	3.1	-	-	-	0.3
-	-	-	-	-	-	-	-	0.0
-	-	-	-	-	1.9	2.3	-	0.8
-	-	-	-	-	-	-	-	0.0
-	-	-	-	?0.2	-	-	1.7	0.3
-	-	2.2	-	1.3	0.7	2.3	-	0.6
0.9?	3.0?	-	1.9?	0.9	-	2.3	3.3	1.0
-	?2.0	-	-	?0.4	1.2	-	-	0.3
2.8	-	-	-	-	-	-	-	4.5
-	-	?0.9	-	-	-	-	-	0.1
87.9	-	-	-	-	-	-	-	16.5
-	-	-	-	-	-	-	-	0.1
-	-	-	-	-	-	-	-	0.0
-	-	-	-	-	-	-	-	3.2
-	-	-	-	0.9	-	-	-	3.0
-	-	-	-	-	-	-	3.3	0.3
-	-	-	-	-	-	-	-	1.2
-	-	-	-	-	-	-	-	1.5
-	-	-	-	-	31.0	38.6	35.9	8.1
-	-	-	-	-	-	-	-	0.8
-	-	-	-	-	-	-	-	0.2
-	-	-	-	-	-	-	-	1.1
-	-	-	-	-	-	-	5.8	0.5
-	-	-	-	0.2	-	-	-	0.0
-	-	-	17.0	?2.0	-	-	-	1.5
3.7	29.6	21.9	?45.2	-	-	-	-	8.2
-	-	-	-	-	-	-	21.7	2.6
-	1.0	0.4	-	?0.4	-	-	-	0.3
-	-	-	-	-	47.1	13.6	?1.7	4.8
-	?0.5	-	5.7?	1.4	-	-	-	1.2
0.9	1.5	?1.3	-	0.7	-	-	8.3	1.9
1.9	39.4	39.5	5.7	9.4	5.2	9.1	-	10.5
107	203	228	53	554	420	44	60	3832

Note in Tables 7-1, 7-5, 7-6, 7-7: Sample numbers A----, OLDA----, are from 63°18'18"N, 128°34'W; B---- is from 63°19'24"N, 128°36'W; GSC 69059 is from 62°33'N, 127°45'W; S4---- from 63°16'45"N, 128°32'40"W; Blusson -- from 63°06'16"N, 128°41'W. Sample numbers indicate stratigraphic distance in feet from the top of Delorme Formation; a double thickness line separating percentage figures indicates samples from a different measured section. A question mark preceding a percentage figure indicates fragmentary material or material or material unknown internally that it questionably assigned to the particular genus, a question mark following the percentage figure indicates a questionable specific assignment. The "Average Percent Column" has no particular significance other than to give some idea of average abundance in collections listed. Tables 7-1 through 7-7 are in terms of the Lower Devonian brachiopod intervals of Johnson et al. (1978). Early Lochkovian=Intervals 1, 2; Late Lochkovian=Intervals 3, 4; Early Pragian=Intervals 5, 7; Emsian=Intervals 8-14.

mined by their ability to collect food, and the ability to collect food was closely related to the surface area of the lophophore. In theory, this seems reasonable, but how is the complexity of the lophophore estimated in extinct shells where we have few, if any, indications of soft-part morphology? Fürsich and Hurst suggest that orthids, strophomenids, and rhynchonellids predominated in shallow water because of a simple lophophore and that spiriferids and pentamerids predominated in deeper water because of a more-complex lophophore. Fürsich and Hurst also noted that orthids, strophomenids, and rhynchonellids decreased in size from shallow to deep water. Spiriferids and pentamerids were noted to increase in size in deeper water.

Table 7-2
Ordinal Composition of Faunas from Nevada

Order	Early Lochkovian	Late Lochkovian	Early Pragian	Emsian
Orthida	54.6%	45.3%	24.6%	13.7%
Strophomenida	1.8	5.2	7.0	41.0
Pentamerida	13.0	8.2	0.3	0.6
Rhynchonellida	1.6	1.5	1.1	0.6
Spiriferida	7.8	12.1	25.5	15.9
Atrypidina	17.0	25.2	25.3	19.8
Athyrididina	4.2	2.5	15.0	8.0
Terebratulida	0.0	0.0	1.2	0.3

Source: Data from Johnson, 1974a, b; Niebuhr, 1974; Johnson et al., 1978. Data for Emsian column from Niebuhr, 1974; Johnson, 1974a: 816; Johnson and Kendall, 1976:1115.

Table 7-3
Ordinal Composition of Faunas from the Mackenzie Mountains

Order	Early Lochkovian	Late Lochkovian	Early Pragian	Emsian
Orthida	23.6%	7.7%	26.9%	41.6%
Strophomenida	1.4	0.6	10.6	28.3
Pentamerida	1.0	3.6	3.9	0.4
Rhynchonellida	32.8	11.5	5.4	0.9
Spiriferida	16.5	12.4	23.4	12.3
Atrypidina	18.8	45.6	25.7	12.4
Athyrididina	6.2	18.5	4.1	4.0
Terebratulida	0.0	0.0	0.0	0.01

Source: Data from Perry, 1974.

These observations fit the Silurian of Wales although the evidence is not compelling enough to make it an acceptable model for different areas and times. It is of concern here that the data presented in Tables 7-2, 7-3, and 7-4 do not support Fürsich and Hurst's (1974) proposal that rhynchonellid brachiopods in this time interval are most abundant in the shallowest-water faunas; note that during the Early Pragian interval shown in Tables 7-2, 7-3, and 7-4, rhynchonellids form only a small percentage of the total brachiopod fauna for shallow-water locales. Large *Cortezorthis* and *Schizophoria* (both orthids) occur commonly in deeper-water, more offshore areas in the

Table 7-5
Percentages of Brachiopod Taxa from Sekwi Mountain Map-area, Northwest Territories in Strata of Late Lochkovian Age

	A1530	A1545	A1560	A1590	A1600	A1620	A1688	A1690–1695	A1705	A1735	OLDA1370
New Genus Hesperorthid	–	–	–	–	–	–	–	–	–	–	–
"*Dolerorthis*" sp.	0.3	1.2	0.6	0.2	0.1	0.6	–	–	–	–	–
Skenidioides sp.	–	0.1	0.6	–	–	–	–	–	–	–	–
Cortezorthis cf. *windmillensis*	–	0.7	–	–	0.2?	–	–	–	–	–	–
Protocortezorthis sp.	–	–	–	0.6	–	1.2	0.4	1.6	2.8	2.4	4.0
Dalejina sp.	0.3	–	–	–	0.1	1.2	0.7	–	–	0.4	–
Resserella elegantuloides	–	–	–	–	–	–	–	–	–	–	–
Schizophoria sp.	12.0	5.5	–	2.8	2.9	6.1	2.2	2.7	2.6	2.8	3.2
Salopina submurifer	–	–	–	–	0.1	–	–	–	0.4?	0.6	–
Muriferella masurskyi	–	–	4.5	–	–	–	–	–	–	–	?1.6
Grayina cf. *magnifica*	–	–	–	–	–	–	–	–	–	0.1	–
Gypidula spp.	1.4	–	–	0.6	0.9	–	0.7	3.5	1.4	–	–
Gypidula sp. 4	–	2.8?	3.2?	0.6	1.0	0.9	–	–	–	1.6?	–
Gypidula sp. 5	5.2	2.7	–	–	–	–	–	–	–	–	–
Sieberella sp.	0.7	0.4	–	–	–	–	–	–	–	0.1	–
Carinagypa sp.	–	–	–	–	–	–	–	–	–	–	1.2
Clorinda sp.	–	–	–	–	–	1.2	0.7	2.4	2.1	1.1	–
Eoschuchertella sp.	–	–	–	–	–	–	0.1	–	0.2	0.2	–
Aesopomum varistriatus	0.3?	0.2	1.3?	–	0.2	?0.3	–	–	0.9?	0.3?	0.8
Mesodouvillina sp.	–	–	–	–	–	–	–	–	–	0.1	–
Megastrophia sp.	–	–	–	–	–	–	–	–	–	–	–
Phragmostrophia sp.	–	–	–	–	?0.1	–	–	–	–	–	–
Strophochonetes sp.	–	–	–	–	–	–	–	–	–	–	–
Stegerhynchus sp.	–	–	–	–	–	–	–	–	–	–	–
Machaeraria sp.	–	–	–	–	–	–	–	24.3	25.2	19.2	24.2
"*Franklinella*" *pedderi*	12.4	2.5	–	–	–	–	–	–	–	–	–
"*Franklinella*" *kerri* n. subsp.	–	–	–	–	–	–	–	1.6	0.7	1.5	4.0
Nymphorhynchia sp.	–	–	–	–	–	–	–	–	–	–	–
Isopoma sp.	–	2.1	3.2	3.5	1.8	0.6	–	–	–	?0.1	–
Linguopugnoides cf. *carens*	–	0.1	–	?0.3	–	–	–	?1.6	–	–	–
Phoenicitoechia? sp.	–	–	–	–	–	–	–	–	–	–	–
Atrypa sp. 1	17.9	22.7	13.4	14.2?	–	13.5	7.5	10.6	7.2	6.5	12.3
Desquamatia sp.	–	–	–	–	–	–	–	–	–	11.9	7.5
Reticulatrypa sp.	–	–	–	–	–	–	–	–	–	–	–
Ogilviella cf. *prolifica*	–	–	15.3	–	–	1.2?	4.1?	–	18.9	20.5	16.3
Atrypina simpsoni	–	–	0.6	–	–	–	–	–	–	–	–
Spirigerina supramarginalis	6.9	1.6	0.6?	?0.1	–	0.6	–	8.6	3.5	2.3	7.9
Toquimaella kayi	14.8	9.1	–	54.6	64.1	45.7	31.0	5.1	7.0	–	–
Cryptatrypa sp.	?3.8	0.5	–	5.9	4.9	11.3	–	?18.8	10.2	?0.3	–
Meristella cf. *robertsensis*	0.3?	0.1	–	–	–	–	–	–	–	–	–
Protathyris sp.	?12.0	24.7	40.8	–	?1.9	–	48.5	16.1	?1.6	?13.7	4.0
Nucleospira sp.	?4.8	4.7	–	15.5	20.6	1.8	3.0	0.4	5.3	4.8	5.6
Rhynchospirina sp.	–	–	–	–	–	–	–	–	0.4	–	–
Howellella sp.	–	–	–	–	–	–	–	–	–	–	–
Warrenella sp.	0.3	0.5	1.3	0.1	0.1	1.8	–	–	0.7	0.8	–
Ambocoelia sp.	4.5	7.6	7.6	0.2	0.1	0.6	0.7	–	–	0.4	–
Plicoplasia acutiplicata	–	1.0	–	–	–	–	–	–	–	–	–
Cyrtinella cf. *causa*	–	2.2	–	–	–	–	–	–	–	–	–
Cyrtina sp.	2.1	7.0	7.0	1.0	0.9	11.0	0.4	2.7	8.9	8.4	4.4
Indet. Spiriferid	–	–	–	–	–	–	–	–	0.2	–	–
Total Number of Valves in Each Collection	291	1467	157	1158	1402	326	268	255	571	2168	252

Source: Data from Perry, 1974.

OLDA1560T	OLDA1580T	OLDA1615	OLDA1620T	OLDA1690T	B545	B545–600	B595–600	B725	B740	Average Percent
0.7	1.1	–	–	–	–	–	–	–	–	0.1
–	–	–	0.3	–	–	1.9	0.4	–	–	0.3
–	–	–	0.8	–	5.0	0.3	0.2	–	3.9	0.5
0.7?	2.1	–	–	–	–	2.4	–	–	–	0.3
–	–	1.7	0.5	–	–	–	–	1.3	5.5	1.0
–	–	–	0.3	–	–	–	–	–	–	0.1
–	–	–	–	–	–	–	–	–	1.7	0.1
5.1	6.3	0.8	11.8	1.8	–	22.3	6.0	3.5	6.0	5.1
–	–	0.4?	–	–	–	–	–	–	12.0	0.6
–	–	–	–	–	–	1.1	–	0.8?	–	0.4
–	–	–	–	–	–	–	–	–	0.5	0.0
3.6	4.2	1.7	0.8	2.7	–	1.3	–	–	–	1.1
–	–	–	1.1	–	–	2.7	–	2.2	–	0.8
–	–	–	–	–	–	–	–	–	7.0	0.7
–	–	–	–	–	–	–	1.5	–	–	0.1
–	–	–	–	–	–	–	–	–	–	0.1
–	3.2	2.5	5.0	0.9	–	1.3	–	0.3	–	1.0
0.7	–	–	?0.8	–	–	–	?0.2	–	–	0.1
1.4	–	–	1.1	–	0.8	0.5	1.0	–	0.5	0.5
–	–	–	–	–	–	–	–	–	–	0.0
–	–	–	0.5	–	–	–	1.2	–	–	0.1
5.1	–	–	0.8	–	–	–	–	–	–	0.3
–	–	–	0.3	–	–	–	–	–	–	0.0
–	–	–	–	–	–	–	–	0.9	–	0.0
2.9	69.5	8.7	0.8	41.6	–	–	–	17.8	2.9	11.3
–	–	–	–	–	0.8?	–	–	0.9	–	0.8
–	–	–	–	3.5	–	–	–	4.4	–	0.7
–	–	–	–	–	–	–	–	0.2	–	0.0
–	?2.1	–	2.4	–	–	1.3	1.9	?0.2	–	0.9
11.6	–	–	–	–	13.4	–	–	–	–	1.3
10.9	–	–	–	–	–	–	–	–	–	0.5
29.7	9.5?	19.4	25.0	7.1	5.9	15.4	4.4	10.4	–	12.0
–	–	–	–	–	–	–	–	–	–	0.9
–	–	–	–	–	–	–	–	–	5.0	0.3
–	–	6.6	1.1	17.7	–	–	–	16.9	1.0	5.7
–	–	–	–	–	–	–	–	–	–	0.0
1.4	–	7.9	0.5	3.5	–	1.1	0.4?	1.1	–	2.3
11.6	–	17.8	17.9	?8.0	?1.7	15.2	6.5	?6.9	–	15.1
–	–	–	–	–	37.0	0.5	1.9	1.5	?7.0	4.9
–	–	–	–	–	?1.7	–	?2.1	–	–	0.2
–	1.1	26.9	21.1	1.8	–	–	–	?16.6	–	11.0
5.1	–	3.7	1.3	7.1	4.2	2.4	6.5	5.1	0.2	4.9
–	–	–	–	–	–	–	–	–	–	0.0
–	–	–	–	–	?0.8	?0.3	–	–	–	0.1
2.9	–	–	–	–	3.4	2.1	4.0	0.2	0.2	0.9
–	1.1	0.8	1.1	–	11.8	6.9	11.0	1.1	4.6	2.9
–	–	–	–	–	–	–	–	–	–	0.0
–	–	–	–	–	–	–	–	–	–	0.1
6.5	–	1.2	5.0	4.4	13.4	20.2	50.8	7.3	41.0	9.7
–	–	–	–	–	–	0.3	–	–	–	0.0
138	95	242	380	113	119	376	520	916	415	11629

Table 7-6
Percentages of Brachiopod Taxa from Sekwi Mountain Map-area, Northwest Territories in Strata of Early Pragian Age

	A585-95	A690-765	A765-820	A895	A900	A915-25	A1045	A1055	A1075	A1085	A1110
"*Dolerorthis*" sp.	-	-	-	-	-	-	1.3	-	-	-	-
Skenidioides sp.	-	-	-	-	-	-	-	-	7.6	0.8	1.6
Cortezorthis maclareni	-	?1.5	5.8?	6.3?	-	-	-	-	-	-	-
Cortezorthis sp. 2	-	-	-	-	5.6?	12.3?	13.8	13.0	-	3.3?	-
Cortezorthis sp. 3	-	-	-	-	-	-	-	-	-	-	-
Protocortezorthis sp.	-	-	-	-	-	-	-	-	-	-	0.5
Dalejina sp.	-	-	-	-	-	?2.5	?1.3	-	-	4.1	1.0
Schizophoria sp.	-	-	-	-	8.9	2.5	-	6.5	13.9	5.8	7.3
Salopina submurifer	-	-	-	-	-	-	-	-	1.3?	-	2.1
Muriferella masurskyi	-	-	-	-	3.3	-	-	-	-	-	-
Grayina cf. *magnifica*	-	-	-	-	-	-	-	-	-	-	-
Gypidula spp.	-	3.1	2.5	39.3	13.3	12.3	-	6.5	12.6	10.7	3.1
Sieberella sp.	-	-	-	-	-	-	3.8	-	-	3.3	-
Clorindina sp.	-	-	-	-	-	-	-	-	-	-	-
Indet. Gypidulid	-	-	-	-	-	-	-	-	-	-	-
Leptaenisca cf. *concava*	-	-	-	-	-	-	-	-	-	-	-
Leptagonia sp.	-	-	-	-	-	-	-	-	-	-	-
Eoschuchertella sp.	-	-	-	-	-	3.7	-	6.5	-	9.9	1.6
Iridostrophia? sp.	-	-	-	-	-	-	-	-	-	-	-
Aesopomum sp.	-	-	-	-	-	1.2	1.3	4.3	-	-	5.7
"*Brachyprion*" sp.	-	-	-	-	-	2.5	-	-	-	-	-
Strophonella sp.	-	-	-	-	-	-	-	-	-	0.8	-
Mesodouvillina sp.	-	-	-	-	-	-	-	-	-	-	-
Cymostrophia sp.	-	-	-	-	-	-	-	-	-	0.8	-
Megastrophia sp.	-	-	?3.3	-	?3.3	-	-	-	?5.1	-	8.3
Megastrophia cf. *transitans*	-	-	-	-	-	-	-	-	-	-	-
Stropheodonta sp.	-	-	-	-	-	-	-	-	-	-	-
Leptostrophia sp.	-	-	-	-	-	-	-	-	-	-	-
Phragmostrophia merriami	-	1.5	-	-	-	-	-	-	-	-	-
Phragmostrophia sp.	-	-	-	-	-	-	-	10.9	-	6.6	-
"*Strophochonetes*" sp.	-	-	-	-	-	-	-	-	-	-	-
Thliborhynchia julli	-	-	?2.5	1.3?	4.4	2.5	13.8	2.2?	-	3.3	-
"*Franklinella*" sp.	-	-	-	-	-	1.2	-	-	1.3	-	-
Ancillotoechia sp.	-	-	-	-	-	-	-	-	-	-	6.7
Nymphorhynchia cf. *nympha*	-	-	-	-	-	-	-	-	-	-	-
Linguopugnoides? sp.	-	-	-	-	-	-	-	-	-	-	-
Athyrhynchus sp.	-	55.4	0.8	6.3	-	-	-	-	-	-	-
Werneckeella hartensis	-	-	-	-	-	?2.5	-	-	?1.3	-	-
Atrypa cf. *nevadana*	-	9.2	23.1?	-	18.9	-	-	-	-	-	-
Atrypa sp. 1	-	-	-	-	-	-	-	-	-	-	-
Atrypa spp.	-	-	-	17.7	-	12.3	22.5	-	-	-	-
Desquamatia sp.	-	-	-	-	-	7.4	-	-	5.1	?3.3	4.2
Spinatrypa spp.	-	-	4.1	-	-	-	11.3	8.7	?10.1	9.9	-
Atrypina simpsoni	-	-	-	2.5	2.2	2.5?	-	-	-	3.3	1.0
Spirigerina supramarginalis?	-	-	-	-	-	-	-	-	-	-	-
Vagrania cf. *intermediafera*	-	-	-	7.6?	-	-	6.3?	?28.3	-	5.8	31.3
Vagrania sp. 3	98.2	15.4	-	-	-	-	-	-	-	-	-
Davidsoniatrypa johnsoni	-	-	-	-	-	-	-	-	-	-	-
Sibirispira? sp.	-	-	-	-	-	-	-	-	-	-	-
Notoparmella sp.	-	-	-	-	-	-	-	-	-	-	-
Cryptatrypa sp.	-	-	-	-	-	-	-	-	-	-	-
Meristella sp.	-	-	-	1.3	-	-	-	2.2	1.3	5.0	-
Protathyris sp.	-	-	-	-	-	-	-	-	-	-	-
Nucleospira sp.	-	-	5.8	3.8	4.4	3.7	5.0	-	-	-	2.1
Rhynchospirina sp.	-	-	-	-	-	-	-	-	-	-	-
Howellella cycloptera?	-	-	-	5.1	-	-	5.0	-	-	-	-
Howellella sp.	-	-	?0.8	-	-	-	-	-	-	-	-
Plicocyrtina sinuplicata	-	-	-	3.8	26.7	2.5	-	4.3	-	1.7	3.1
"*Plicocyrtina*" sp.	-	3.1	-	-	-	-	-	-	-	-	-
Spinella? sp.	-	-	-	-	-	-	-	-	-	-	-
Warrenella sekwensis	1.8	10.8	49.6	-	-	-	-	-	-	-	-
Warrenella sp. 1	-	-	-	2.5	-	-	2.5?	-	3.8	2.5	0.5?
Ambocoelia sp.	-	-	-	-	4.4	-	-	-	3.8	2.5	-
Cyrtinaella sp.	-	-	-	-	-	-	-	-	-	-	-
Cyrtina sp.	-	-	2.5	2.5	4.4	28.4	12.5	6.5	32.9	16.5	19.8
Total Number of Valves in Each Collection	112	65	121	79	90	81	80	46	79	121	192

Source: Data from Perry, 1974.

A1125	A1135	A1180	A1230	A1265	A1280	A1300	A1345	A1432	A1450	A1470	OLDA915	OLDA1005	OLDA1105	OLDA1130	OLDA1160
-	-	-	-	-	-	-	-	-	-	-	-	-	0.6	-	-
-	-	-	1.2	-	-	1.1	9.3	0.3	0.4	-	-	-	2.2	2.6	-
-	-	-	-	-	-	-	-	-	-	-	6.1?	-	-	-	-
5.2?	-	-	4.8?	4.8?	-	-	11.6	3.0	10.7	20.4	-	4.9?	-	-	-
-	-	-	-	-	-	-	-	-	-	-	-	-	1.1	1.7?	-
-	6.0	-	-	-	-	2.3	-	0.3	-	-	-	-	?1.1	-	-
-	-	-	4.8	-	1.6	5.7	4.7	2.2	1.1	-	-	4.9	1.7	6.0	19.1
-	16.7	7.1	16.7	9.0	21.0	5.7	9.3	8.1	18.3	11.7	-	17.1	7.2	5.1	1.5
-	-	-	-	0.6?	-	-	-	-	-	-	-	-	?0.8	-	-
-	3.6?	-	-	-	-	5.7	-	3.0	1.2	1.2	-	-	-	-	-
-	-	-	-	-	-	-	-	-	-	1.2	-	-	-	-	-
14.3	4.8	7.2	1.2	1.2	?1.6	8.0	2.3	-	1.8	1.9	40.2	-	7.5	-	5.8
-	-	-	-	-	-	-	-	-	-	-	-	?2.4	-	-	-
-	-	-	-	-	-	-	-	-	-	-	-	-	-	-	-
-	-	-	-	-	-	-	-	-	-	-	-	-	-	-	-
-	-	-	-	-	-	-	-	-	-	-	-	-	-	-	-
1.3	-	-	1.2	-	-	-	-	-	0.2	-	-	2.4	0.6	1.7	-
1.3	-	-	-	0.6	-	-	2.3	-	0.9	-	-	-	0.8	-	-
-	-	-	-	-	-	-	-	-	-	-	-	-	-	-	-
-	7.1	-	1.2	3.0	1.6	-	-	-	-	-	-	2.4	3.6	7.7	4.4
-	-	-	-	-	-	-	-	-	-	-	-	-	-	-	-
-	1.2	-	-	-	-	-	-	-	-	-	-	-	0.8	-	-
-	-	-	-	-	-	-	?4.7	0.3	-	-	-	-	-	-	-
-	-	-	-	-	-	-	-	-	-	-	-	-	-	-	-
5.2	-	-	-	-	-	-	-	-	-	-	-	-	-	-	-
-	-	-	-	-	-	-	-	10.8	1.7	-	-	-	-	-	-
-	-	-	-	-	-	-	-	-	0.5	?4.9	-	-	-	-	-
-	-	-	-	-	-	-	?2.3	-	-	-	1.2	-	-	-	-
-	-	-	-	-	-	-	-	-	-	-	-	-	-	-	-
-	16.7?	-	3.6?	0.6	-	?2.3	-	24.9	21.8	17.3	-	-	7.2	17.1	19.1
-	-	-	-	-	-	-	-	-	-	-	-	-	-	-	-
-	-	4.8	1.2	2.4	9.7	-	-	-	-	-	-	4.9	-	-	-
-	-	-	-	0.6	-	-	-	-	-	1.9	-	-	-	-	-
-	6.0	?7.1	7.1	10.8	12.9	10.2	-	-	-	-	-	-	0.6	0.9	-
-	-	-	-	-	-	-	-	-	-	-	-	12.2?	-	-	14.7
-	-	-	-	-	-	-	-	-	-	-	-	-	1.1	-	-
-	-	-	-	-	-	-	-	-	-	-	-	-	-	-	-
-	-	-	-	-	-	-	-	?0.8	-	-	-	-	-	-	-
-	-	-	-	-	-	-	-	-	-	-	20.7	-	-	-	-
-	-	-	-	-	-	-	-	-	16.1	16.0	-	-	-	-	-
-	4.8	7.1	1.2	6.6	14.1	9.1	25.6	3.0	-	-	-	-	-	-	-
-	-	-	-	-	-	4.5	-	-	-	-	-	-	-	-	-
26.0	-	-	-	-	-	-	-	?5.4	-	0.6	6.1	?9.8	12.4	6.8	4.4
-	-	-	2.4	-	-	-	-	-	-	-	-	-	1.7	-	-
-	-	-	-	-	-	-	-	-	-	-	-	-	-	-	-
33.8	8.3	26.2	33.3	44.3	21.0	33.0	-	-	-	-	-	29.3	20.7	26.5	8.8
-	-	-	-	-	-	-	-	-	-	-	-	-	-	-	-
-	?2.4	-	?2.4	5.4	-	-	-	-	-	-	-	-	1.9	-	-
-	-	-	-	-	-	-	-	-	-	-	-	-	-	-	-
-	-	-	-	-	-	-	-	-	-	-	-	-	-	-	-
-	-	?14.3	-	-	?6.5	-	?4.7	?0.5	-	-	2.4	-	-	-	-
-	-	-	-	-	-	-	-	-	0.1	-	-	-	0.6	-	-
-	-	-	-	-	-	-	-	-	?0.2	-	-	-	-	-	-
9.1	4.8	-	-	-	1.6	-	2.3	2.7	5.4	7.4	3.7	7.3	0.8	3.4	7.4
-	-	-	-	-	-	-	-	-	-	-	-	-	-	-	-
-	-	-	-	-	-	-	-	-	-	-	3.7	-	-	-	-
-	-	-	-	-	-	-	-	-	-	-	-	-	-	-	-
2.6	1.2	14.3	-	1.8	3.2	-	-	-	-	-	8.5	-	6.9	-	2.9
-	-	-	-	-	-	-	-	-	-	-	-	-	-	-	-
-	-	-	-	-	-	-	-	-	-	-	-	-	-	-	-
-	-	-	-	-	-	-	-	-	-	-	-	-	-	-	-
-	2.4?	-	-	0.6?	1.6?	8.0	2.3	0.3	1.5	1.2	2.4?	-	1.7	-	-
-	-	11.9	-	-	-	-	?4.7	0.8	1.3	-	-	-	-	1.7	-
-	-	-	-	-	-	-	-	-	-	-	2.4	-	-	-	-
1.3	14.3	-	17.9	7.8	6.5	4.5	14.0	33.6	16.6	14.2	2.4	2.4	16.8	18.8	11.8
77	84	42	84	167	62	88	43	370	815	162	82	41	363	117	68

Table 7-7
Percentages of Brachiopod Taxa from Sekwi Mountain Map-area, Northwest Territories in Strata of Emsian Age

	S4-50-75	S4-120	S4-175-180	S4-210-215	S4-265	S4-310	S4-330	S4-390	S4-405-410	S4-470	S4-530-40
Skenidioides spp.	-	-	0.8	2.3	0.3	-	-	-	-	1.0	2.1
Cortezorthis maclareni	-	24.1	14.8	8.6	5.7	22.2	10.1	2.9	4.5	29.1	0.9
Protocortezorthis? sp.	-	-	-	-	-	-	-	-	-	0.8	-
Dalejina sp.	-	-	5.9	7.3	1.0	3.7	-	6.8	-	0.9	40.4
Didymoparcium costata	-	4.6	-	-	-	-	-	-	-	0.1	-
Schizophoria cf. *nevadaensis*	-	36.8	49.1	5.2	0.3	1.9?	-	14.6	16.9?	37.2	1.8?
Salopina submurifer	-	-	-	-	-	-	-	-	-	-	-
Muriferella masurskyi	-	-	2.4	1.0	-	1.9	-	-	-	2.0	2.4
Prokopia sp.	-	-	-	-	-	-	-	-	-	-	-
"*Phragmophora*" sp.	-	-	-	-	-	-	-	-	-	-	-
Mystrophora arctica	-	-	0.1	0.8	1.7	-	15.2	-	1.1	0.5	0.2
Kayserella costatula	-	-	-	-	-	-	-	-	-	0.0	-
Gypidula spp.	-	-	-	0.0	-	1.9	-	-	-	-	0.1
Sieberella spp.	-	-	-	-	-	-	2.5	-	4.5	-	-
Carinagypa loweryi?	-	-	-	-	-	-	-	-	-	-	-
Carinagypa praeloweryi	-	-	-	-	-	-	-	-	-	-	-
Leptagonia sp.	-	-	-	0.1	-	-	1.3	-	-	0.0	0.1
Eoschuchertella sp.	-	-	-	0.4	0.3	-	-	-	-	0.0	-
Aesopomum sp.	-	-	-	-	-	-	-	-	-	-	-
"*Brachyprion*" sp.	-	-	-	-	-	-	-	-	-	-	0.1
Strophonella sp.	-	-	-	0.0	-	-	-	-	-	-	-
Mesodouvillina sp.	-	-	-	0.4	-	-	-	-	-	-	0.4
Malearnites cf. *invasor*	-	-	-	-	-	-	-	-	-	-	-
Megastrophia iddingsi	-	-	4.8	16.2	58.9	-	2.5?	-	-	3.6	2.3
Stropheodonta sp.	-	-	-	-	-	-	-	-	-	0.1	-
Leptostrophia sp.	-	10.3	0.9	5.3	5.7	-	27.8	1.9	1.1	5.7	3.3
Phragmostrophia merriami	-	18.4	14.0	21.5	24.6	5.6?	6.3?	6.8?	-	4.9	9.3
Parapholidostrophia sp.	-	-	-	-	-	-	-	-	-	-	-
"*Strophochonetes*" *filistriata*	100.0	1.1	1.0	16.6	0.7	-	3.8	-	-	1.4	2.1
Parachonetes macrostriatus	-	-	-	0.4	-	-	-	1.0?	-	-	-
New Genus Chonetid	-	-	-	-	-	-	-	-	-	-	-
Chattertonia sp.	-	-	-	-	-	-	-	-	-	-	0.2
Thliborhynchia sp.	-	-	?0.1	-	-	?1.9	-	-	1.1	-	-
Trigonirhynchia cf. *occidens*	-	-	-	0.1	-	-	?3.8	-	?5.6	0.2	2.0
Pleiopleurina? sp.	-	-	-	-	-	-	-	-	-	-	-
Linguopugnoides sp.	-	-	-	?0.1	-	-	-	-	-	-	-
Athyrhynchus susanae	-	-	?0.2	0.1	-	-	-	-	-	-	0.3
Atrypa cf. *nevadana*	-	-	1.4	1.6	-	46.3	25.3	17.4	51.6	5.4	12.7
Atrypa spp.	-	-	-	1.2	-	-	-	-	1.1	-	-
Desquamatia sp.	-	-	-	-	-	-	-	-	-	-	-
Spinatrypina asymmetrica?	-	-	-	1.2	-	-	-	-	-	-	-
Atrypina sp.	-	-	-	-	-	-	-	-	-	-	-
Vagrania sp.	-	-	-	-	-	-	-	-	-	-	-
Carinatina sp.	-	-	-	0.0	-	-	-	-	-	-	-
Biconostrophia sp.	-	1.1	-	-	-	-	-	-	-	-	-
Sibirispira? bisulcata	-	-	0.2	0.7	-	-	-	-	-	2.1	0.4
Lissatrypa? sp.	-	-	-	-	-	-	-	-	-	-	0.6
Cryptatrypa sp.	-	-	-	-	-	3.7	-	3.9	2.2	-	-
Coelospira? sp.	-	-	-	-	-	-	-	-	1.1	-	-
Protathyris sp.	-	-	-	-	-	-	-	-	-	-	8.0
Nucleospira sp.	-	1.1	1.4	5.9	-	1.9	-	2.9	1.1	1.9	3.8
Howellella cf. *textilis*	-	-	-	-	-	-	-	-	-	-	0.1
"*Hysterolites*" sp.	-	-	-	-	-	-	-	-	-	-	-
Howittia sp.	-	-	-	-	-	-	-	-	-	-	-
Warrenella sekwensis	-	1.1?	2.2	1.0	-	1.9	?1.3	39.8	3.3	0.9	2.1
Ambocoelia sp.	-	1.1	0.6	1.0	0.7	-	-	-	1.1	1.7	4.0
Cyrtina sp.	-	-	-	1.0	-	7.4	-	1.9	3.3	0.5	-
indet. Terebratulid	-	-	-	-	-	-	-	-	-	-	-
Total Number of Valves in Each Collection	91	87	995	4295	297	54	79	103	89	2831	817

Source: Data from Perry, 1974.

S4-580	S4-605	S4-715	S4-845	S4-900	S4-1475	S4-1530	S4-1560	S4-1615	S4-1650-65	S4-1685-90	S4-1705	S4-1840-80	A25-35	A205-225	Average Percent
8.4	2.9	-	-	-	0.8	0.6	1.8	1.1	0.9	-	-	-	-	3.4	1.0
3.2	5.1	5.3	6.3	6.8	17.4	36.9	10.3	12.1	5.9	12.9	10.6	18.0	6.0	1.2	10.8
-	-	-	-	-	-	-	-	-	-	-	-	-	-	-	0.0
3.2	6.6	1.6	-	-	0.4	33.8	10.3	11.4	6.6	1.2	0.5	-	-	20.4	6.2
-	-	-	-	-	0.2	-	-	-	3.8	-	-	-	-	-	0.3
0.4	-	4.2?	18.8	6.8?	20.2	1.1	13.3	19.9	7.4	13.3	7.4	1.4	-	2.7	10.8
-	-	-	-	-	-	-	-	-	-	-	-	0.2	-	-	0.0
-	-	-	-	-	-	0.2	-	1.8	0.1	1.2	-	-	-	0.7	0.5
-	-	-	-	-	-	-	-	-	-	-	-	-	-	3.5	0.1
-	-	-	-	-	-	-	-	-	-	-	-	-	-	0.6	0.0
0.4	-	-	-	-	0.4	1.3	1.2	-	0.1	-	-	-	-	-	0.9
-	-	-	-	-	-	-	-	-	-	-	-	-	-	-	0.0
-	0.7	1.6	-	-	-	-	-	-	-	-	-	0.4	-	0.6	0.2
-	-	-	-	-	-	-	-	-	-	-	-	-	-	-	0.3
-	-	-	-	-	0.4	0.1	-	-	-	-	-	-	-	-	0.0
-	-	-	-	-	-	-	-	-	-	-	-	0.8	-	0.7	0.1
-	-	-	-	-	-	0.1	-	0.2	0.4	-	-	-	-	2.4	0.2
0.4	-	-	-	-	-	0.1	-	0.2	0.1	-	0.5	-	-	1.6	0.1
0.4	-	-	-	-	-	-	-	-	-	-	-	-	-	-	0.0
-	-	-	-	-	-	-	-	-	0.1	-	-	-	-	-	0.0
-	-	-	-	-	-	-	-	-	-	-	-	-	-	-	0.0
-	-	-	-	-	-	-	-	0.4	-	-	-	-	-	0.8	0.1
-	-	-	-	-	-	-	-	0.4	-	-	-	-	-	-	0.0
3.2	3.6	28.0	20.7	4.1	9.0	8.1	1.2	1.8	3.8	-	-	-	-	1.2	6.7
-	-	-	-	-	-	-	-	-	-	-	-	0.1	-	-	0.0
3.2	-	-	15.4	-	3.1	0.7	2.4	4.5	1.6	-	-	-	-	0.1	3.6
0.4	2.2?	2.1	22.1	-	18.8	0.1	-	20.1	2.1?	-	-	5.8	8.0	2.0	7.5
14.4	-	-	-	-	-	-	-	-	2.4	15.7	30.2	-	-	-	2.4
27.6	10.9	-	3.4	-	1.0	-	1.2	4.0	1.2	21.5	19.6	-	-	0.1	8.4
-	-	-	1.9	-	-	-	-	1.4	0.3	-	-	-	-	-	0.2
-	-	-	-	-	-	-	-	-	-	-	-	-	-	0.2	0.0
-	-	-	-	-	-	-	-	0.4	0.1	-	-	-	-	0.1	0.0
-	-	-	-	-	-	-	-	-	-	-	-	-	-	-	0.1
-	0.7?	-	-	?2.7	?0.8	-	-	0.7	0.8	-	?0.2	?0.1	8.0	0.2	1.0
-	-	-	-	-	-	-	-	-	-	-	0.2	-	-	-	0.0
-	-	-	-	-	-	-	-	-	-	-	-	-	-	1.0	0.0
2.4	-	1.6	-	-	-	-	-	-	-	-	-	-	-	2.0?	0.3
12.4	32.1	53.5	8.7	79.5	13.5	6.6	32.7	4.0	6.5	27.1	19.9	4.0	72.0	6.4	20.8
?1.6	-	-	-	-	4.3	-	-	4.2	6.1	-	-	-	-	-	0.7
-	-	-	-	-	-	-	-	-	-	-	-	2.7	-	-	0.1
0.8	-	-	-	-	-	-	-	-	1.2	-	-	-	-	-	0.1
-	-	-	-	-	-	-	-	-	-	-	-	-	-	4.2	0.2
-	-	-	-	-	2.3	-	-	-	-	-	-	2.0	-	-	0.2
-	-	-	-	-	-	-	-	-	-	-	-	-	-	-	0.0
-	-	-	-	-	3.3	-	-	?2.0	-	-	-	-	-	-	0.2
-	2.2	-	-	-	-	0.1	9.1	0.4	25.1	-	4.1	-	-	4.2	1.9
-	-	-	-	-	-	-	-	-	-	-	-	-	-	-	0.0
?1.2	8.8	?1.1	-	-	-	-	-	-	?1.8	0.8	0.9	0.2	-	?2.2	1.0
-	-	-	-	-	-	-	-	-	-	-	-	-	-	-	0.0
-	-	-	-	-	-	-	-	-	?1.8	-	-	-	-	-	0.4
7.0	10.9	-	-	-	0.2	1.6	3.6	5.8	4.5	-	0.2	2.0	-	6.7	2.2
1.2	-	-	-	-	-	0.1?	-	-	-	-	-	?0.1	-	-	0.1
-	-	-	-	-	-	-	-	-	-	-	-	-	-	9.3	0.4
0.8	-	-	-	-	-	-	-	-	-	-	-	0.2	2.0	-	0.1
8.0	8.8	1.1	1.0	-	1.6	8.2	7.3	1.8	6.6	3.1	3.4	62.1	4.0?	4.3	6.7
4.0	3.6	-	1.4	-	2.3	0.4	2.4	1.3	7.9	2.4	2.3	-	-	8.2	1.8
-	0.7	-	0.5	-	-	-	3.0	-	0.9	0.8	-	0.6	-	8.7	1.1
0.4	-	-	-	-	-	-	-	-	-	-	-	-	-	-	0.0
250	137	189	208	73	511	1794	165	553	758	255	443	1029	50	2838	18989

late Lower Devonian of western North America. Many large and small rhynchonellids are abundant in B. A. 4-5 of western North America, although the spire-bearing spiriferids do commonly predominate in more offshore strata.

Table 7-4
Ordinal Composition of Faunas from Royal Creek, Yukon Territory

Order	Early Lochkovian	Late Lochkovian	Early Pragian	Emsian
Orthida	50.3%	21.8%	15.9%	14.8%
Strophomenida	7.9	11.1	14.5	42.3
Pentamerida	1.1	4.8	2.7	0.1
Rhynchonellida	11.8	8.2	9.7	7.2
Spiriferida	14.1	14.4	33.1	18.9
Atrypidina	9.4	36.9	23.8	15.8
Athyrididina	5.3	2.8	0.3	0.0
Terebratulida	0.0	0.0	0.0	0.0

Source: Data from Lenz, 1977a, b.

Johnson's (1974a:811) Table 1 shows the large variation in percentages of taxa and the difficulties in separating and naming communities from these high-diversity faunas. Without some sort of ground rules for defining communities, we are approaching the problem in much the same way as MacArthur (1971:189-190), the well-known ornithologist and biogeographer, who substantiated his definition of the term community by the following quotation from *Alice in Wonderland*: Humpty Dumpty told Alice, "When I use a word, it means just what I choose it to mean--neither more nor less." Irrespective of how other people use the term "community"--and there are almost as many uses as there are ecologists--I use it here to mean any set of organisms currently living near each other and about which it is interesting to talk."

The problem of naming communities is further complicated when tables of taxic abundances from Lower Devonian beds of Sekwi Mountain map-area (Tables 7-1, 7-5, 7-6, 7-7) are compared with taxic abundances from central Nevada (Johnson, 1974a, Tables 1-4). In Nevada and the Sekwi Mountain map-area, a few diagnostic elements establish the age correlation; however, the relative abundances and associated taxa are very different. The problem in trying to formulate a unified community picture is complicated by biogeographic differences between the areas and ecoclines. Individual patches of fossil brachiopod communities may have a very limited geographic distribution, and their occurrences are strongly controlled by local environmental factors. At present, there are insufficient data to set out rigorous guidelines for naming communities although absence of ground rules leads to the potential absurdity of each collection of each worker belonging to a different community. On the other hand, simply lumping all collections together and making a benthic-assemblage-type assignment obscures real faunal differences. Community names must be proposed at a level useful to the worker involved although not all names useful in one area will have application in another. This is shown in the discussion of some of the communities that follows.

The community group concept developed by Boucot (1975) established both an environmental and temporal hierarchy of related communities. Boucot (1975:232) defined a community group as a sequence of communities commonly containing a large number of taxa with common antecedents and descendants that recur together under similar environmental conditions through time. Members of a community group are regarded as homologous if the constituent elements are taxonomically related although the environmental constraints need not be precisely the same. An analogous community is defined as a community occupying a similar environmental position, but with few, if any, taxa having a common phylogenetic origin.

Furthermore, Boucot (1975) proposed that community-framework diagrams (of the type employed here as Figures 7-3 through 7-7) be used. The purpose of these diagrams is to provide a conceptual device for the comparison of contemporaneous and noncontemporaneous communities. The use of such diagrams makes it possible to readily compare and contrast the environmental parameters thought to correlate with the presence and absence of varied communities during a single time interval and through time. The common practice of describing communities, commenting at length on the environmental parameters possibly responsible for their presence and absence, is necessary. Inevitably, it becomes difficult in the course of commonly lengthy, involved descriptions and discussions for one to keep all of the relevant comparative information in mind for all of the community units. The community-framework diagrams were proposed as a simple graphical device that would help to obviate this problem. The problem is particularly difficult when dealing with community units from outside one's own immediate sphere of experience. One seldom has difficulty keeping in mind the myriad details pertinent to an understanding of the community units in one's own sector after some years experience in handling the data. In considering community-framework diagrams, it must be kept in mind that assignment to a benthic assemblage is an appropriate undertaking. We seldom have enough localities and measured sections (that is, adequate statistics) to be really certain of the upper and lower depth or shoreline proximity limits. The placement of community boundaries to commonly coincide with benthic assemblage boundaries should make it clear that a certain element of arbitrariness enters into the drafting. However, as our sample becomes larger, we should be able to gradually refine the benthic assemblage assignments and determine which communities occur in limited portions of a benthic assemblage. Our general approach has been to indicate the greatest possible benthic-assemblage range for a particular community with full knowledge that some ranges will ultimately turn out to have been overly generous.

Western and Arctic North American Lower Devonian brachiopod faunas are known only from a few widely separated geographic localities, and even smaller numbers from sections collected in detail, which makes any attempt to formulate an integrated community picture somewhat speculative until more data and more exact biogeographic correlation are available. The development of a truly comprehensive Devonian brachiopod community framework for the Cordilleran Region B. A. 4-5 must await collection of more data to corroborate it and the formulation of necessary guidelines to make it usable by all workers.

Johnson (1974a) tackled the problem in a less-detailed manner and proposed two brachiopod biofacies for the Lower Devonian of western North America. His brachiopod biofacies are somewhat analogous to Boucot's benthic assemblages as they are defined as major groupings of benthic marine genera that occur extensively in the same relative positions with respect to ancient shorelines. He defined a *Gypidula-Atrypa-Schizophoria* (G-A-S) Biofacies that occupies the outer shelf adjacent to the pelagic facies and an Acrosporoferid-Leptocoeliid Biofacies that occupies the inner, shallow-water shelf between the G-A-S Biofacies and the tidal-flat areas. Johnson's model has the following two problems: First, his Acrospiriferid-Leptocoeliid Biofacies is clearly recognizable because of its affinity with the Appalachian faunas, which makes it distinct from contemporaneous Pragian Old World Cordilleran and Arctic faunas. This biogeographic effect is greater than the community-depth, shoreline-proximity effect (see Savage et al., 1979, for a statistical analysis; also Boucot, 1975; Johnson et al., 1978). Second, the name elements of Johnson's G-A-S Biofacies are present in nearly every large brachiopod collection of Old World affinity in western or Arctic North America whether from the inner or outer shelf (B. A. 3 or B. A. 4-5). The total absence of the Acrospiriferid-Leptocoeliid Biofacies in other regions of western and Arctic North America, no matter what rock facies or paleogeographic position, and its faunal affinity to the Eastern Americas Realm suggests that this biofacies has strong biogeographic control and cannot be interpreted purely as the result of ecological-community, depth-shoreline effects alone (see also Lenz, 1976, for a similar opinion).

The reason(s) for the presence of a major biogeographic boundary (Old World Realm against Eastern Americas Realm) in Pragian time in the Cordilleran Region at the boundary between benthic assemblages 3 and 4 is unknown. On the eastern side of the Eastern Americas Realm in the central and northern Appalachians from Gaspe through Virginia and West Virginia plus Tennessee, there are many localities where B. A. 3, 4, and 5 communities belonging to the Eastern Americas Realm are well known (Boucot, 1975, Figure 7). Possibly the Cordilleran anomaly represents a boundary between two water masses possessing physical properties sufficiently unique to have separated larvae belonging to the two realms whereas such a distinction was lacking on the eastern side of the Eastern Americas Realm in the Appalachians from Gaspe southwest into the Virginias.

Watkins and Boucot (1975) proposed a series of fossil brachiopod communities for the Silurian of the Atlantic seaboard. Their sampling of the brachiopod fauna is from several geographic localities; none was sampled in bed by bed detail and the communities encountered are of low to medium diversity. They concluded (:245) that the content of collections from brachiopod coquinas does not differ significantly from collections derived from beds of low shell density. This disagrees with data from high-diversity faunas derived from silicified carbonates where beds of low shell density yield only small numbers of genera and are mostly the cosmopolitan elements. Watkins and Boucot presented a series of rarefaction graphs that show the relationship between sample size (number of specimens) versus number of species. The purpose of these curves is to indicate adequate sample size; that is, the sample size is adequate at the value where the curve levels out (additional collections do not increase the number of species). If the curve does not level out, it has little predictive value as there is no way of knowing where the point of inflection will fall. This type of curve for paleontological data may be misleading because each sample is from a different locality and, therefore, probably not exactly the same age. It is possible that local environmental conditions may not have remained totally stable over the time interval involved in the correlation. Rarefaction curves constructed for the Late Lochkovian and Emsian strata of the Delorme Formation, Sekwi Mountain map-area plot total numbers of brachiopod genera against cumulative total numbers of specimens (Figures 7-1, 7-2). The curves fail to flatten out with samples of more than 11,000 and 18,000 shells, respectively, for each time interval. The curves

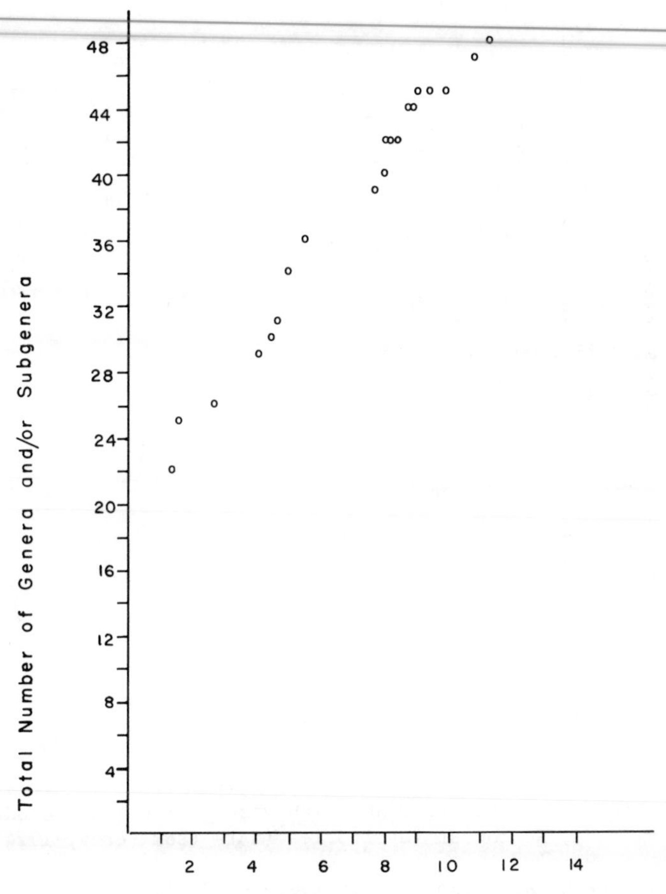

Figure 7-1
Rarefaction curve for Late Lochkovian (*Spirigerina* Unit-*Quadrithyris* Zone) brachiopods from Delorme Formation, Northwest Territories (data from Perry, 1974).

imply that present sampling is inadequate. What is really needed is a series of samples from the same locality (bed) to test the diversity-sampling relationships. Unfortunately, such samples do not exist.

The following are comments on some of the community units established by Boucot (1975) and others (particularly Johnson, 1977; Lenz,

1976, 1977a, b; Niebuhr, 1977) as applied to known Lower Devonian brachiopod faunas of western and northern North America. The faunas discussed from Sekwi Mountain map-area, Northwest Territories, and

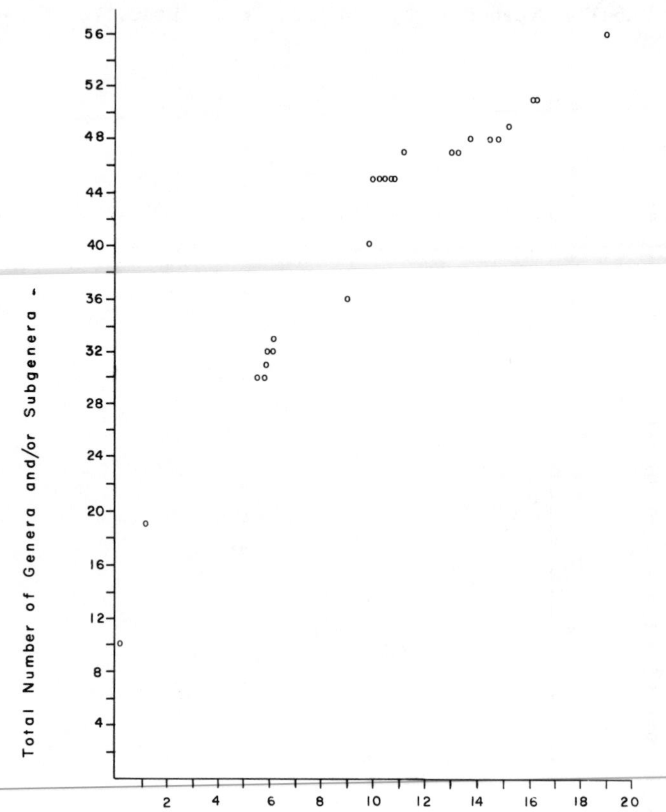

Figure 7-2
Rarefaction curve for Late Pragian-Zlichovian Emsian brachiopods from Delorme Formation, Northwest Territories (data from Perry, 1974).

Royal Creek, Yukon, are almost exclusively of B. A. 4-5 position. The naming and separation of communities are difficult because dominance is the exception rather than the rule in these deeper water faunas. The Cordilleran Region communities discussed above are shown in their relative shoreline and depth positions in Figures 7-3 through 7-7.

ALPHABETICAL LISTING OF CORDILLERAN REGION LOWER DEVONIAN COMMUNITY UNITS

The following descriptive material is a summary of currently available published data regarding Cordilleran Region, largely brachiopod dominated level bottom communities. We have also added ma-

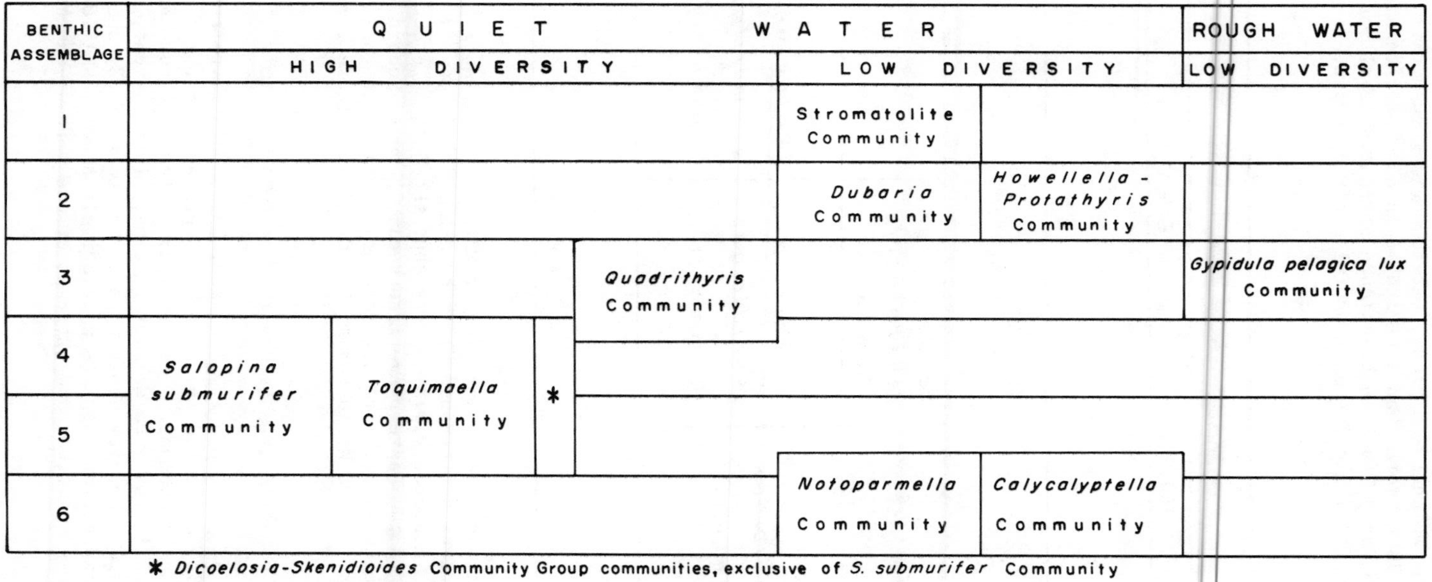

BENTHIC ASSEMBLAGE	QUIET WATER — HIGH DIVERSITY	QUIET WATER — LOW DIVERSITY	ROUGH WATER — LOW DIVERSITY
1		Stromatolite Community	
2		*Dubaria* Community; *Howellella - Protathyris* Community	
3	*Quadrithyris* Community		*Gypidula pelagica lux* Community
4	*Salopina submurifer* Community; *Toquimaella* Community; *		
5	*Salopina submurifer* Community; *Toquimaella* Community; *		
6		*Notoparmella* Community; *Calycalyptella* Community	

* *Dicoelosia-Skenidioides* Community Group communities, exclusive of *S. submurifer* Community

Figure 7-3
Lochkovian, level-bottom, benthic communities from the Cordilleran Region (Johnson's 1977, intervals 1 through 4). The community framework concept is explained in Boucot (1975).

terial available to us which is in press. It is obvious that this descriptive material is no more than a beginning in our understanding of Cordilleran Region Early Devonian brachiopod dominated level bottom communities. We hope it will serve as a useful outline for future investigations.

<table>
<tr><th rowspan="2">BENTHIC ASSEMBLAGE</th><th colspan="3">QUIET WATER</th></tr>
<tr><th colspan="3">HIGH DIVERSITY</th></tr>
<tr><td>1</td><td colspan="3"></td></tr>
<tr><td>2</td><td colspan="3"></td></tr>
<tr><td>3</td><td>Spinoplasia Community</td><td>Acrospirifer-Rensselaeria Community</td><td></td></tr>
<tr><td>4</td><td rowspan="2">Dicoelosia-Skenidioides Community Group</td><td rowspan="2">Vagrania-Skenidioides Community</td><td rowspan="2">Salopina submurifer Community</td></tr>
<tr><td>5</td></tr>
<tr><td>6</td><td colspan="3"></td></tr>
</table>

Figure 7-4
Pragian, level-bottom, benthic communities from the Cordilleran Region (Johnson's, 1977, intervals 5 through 7). The community framework concept is explained in Boucot (1975). Note that the Benthic Assemblage 3 units belong to the Eastern Americas Realm, Nevadan Subprovince, whereas the deeper water, more offshore units belong to the Cordilleran Region of the Old World Realm (Boucot, 1975. Figure 25).

ACROSPIRIFER-ATRYPA COMMUNITY (Figure 7-5)

The *Acrospirifer-Atrypa* Community (Johnson, 1977) belongs to the *Striispirifer* Community Group and may have been derived from the *Acrospirifer-Rensselaeria* Community (Figure 7-4) of the same community group that occurred in the area earlier in time. In any event, the *Acrospirifer-Atrypa* Community appears to belong to B. A. 3, and its high-diversity composition suggests a relatively normal, shallow, subtidal-marine environment free from extremes of one sort or another.

BENTHIC ASSEMBLAGE	QUIET WATER — HIGH DIVERSITY			
1				
2				
3	*Strophochonetes-Proreticularia*-receptaculitid Community	*Nymphorhynchia-Athyrhynchus* Community	*Acrospirifer-Atrypa* Community	*Anoplia klapperi* Community
4	*Dicoelosia-Skenidioides* Community Group			
5				
6				

Figure 7-5
Late Pragian, level-bottom, benthic communities from the Cordilleran Region (Johnson's, 1977, intervals 8 and 9). The community framework concept is explained in Boucot (1975). Note that the Benthic Assemblage 3 units belong to the Eastern Americas Realm, Nevadan Subprovince, whereas the deeper water, more offshore units belong to the Cordilleran Region of the Old World (Boucot, 1975, Figure 25).

ACROSPIRIFER-RENSSELAERIA COMMUNITY (Figure 7-4)

The *Acrospirifer-Rensselaeria* Community (Johnson, 1977) belongs to the *Striispirifer* Community Group (Boucot, 1975:235-236). See discussion of *Spinoplasia* Community. Both the *Acrospirifer-Rensselaeria* and *Spinoplasia* Communities belong to the Nevadan Subprovince and are unknown outside of a small sector of the Cordilleran region during a part of Early Devonian time. Both presumably grade laterally into Old World Realm units of the Cordilleran Region. They are currently known only in Nevada although one would predict that they will eventually be found in parts of southern California (the *Acrospirifer-Atrypa* Community has been so recognized) and in the Caborca region of northern Sonora.

ALATIFORMIA COMMUNITY (Figure 7-7)

See *Elythyna* Community.

AMBOCOELIID COMMUNITY

Boucot (1975) assigned this community to a deeper water B. A. 4-5 position and stated that it consists of abundant (well over 50 percent) individuals of any one ambocoeliid genus. The presence of ambocoeliids in the *Dicoelosia-Skenidioides* Community of the Silurian

BENTHIC ASSEMBLAGE	QUIET WATER								ROUGH WATER	
	HIGH DIVERSITY			MEDIUM DIVERSITY		possibly reduced O_2	LOW DIVERSITY		MEDIUM DIVERSITY	LOW DIVERSITY
1										
2									*Eurekaspirifer - Atrypa* Community	
3	*Carinagypa - Atrypa* Community	*Strophochonetes - Proreticularia* receptaculitid Community	*Nymphorhychia - Athyrhynchus* Community	*Brachyspirifer - Atrypa* Community	*Pacificocoelia* Community high diversity	*Pacificocoelia* Community low diversity				*Atrypa nevadana* Community
4	*Dicoelosia - Skenidioides* Community Group	*Cortezorthis - Warrenella* Community		*Bifida - Muriferella* Community			*Vagrania* Community	"*Strophochonetes*" *filistriata* Community		
5										
6										

Figure 7-6
Emsian, level-bottom, benthic communities from the Cordilleran Region (Johnson's, 1977, intervals 10 through 12). The community framework concept is explained in Boucot (1975).

BENTHIC ASSEMBLAGE	QUIET WATER			ROUGH WATER
	HIGH DIVERSITY		MEDIUM DIVERSITY possibly reduced oxygen	MEDIUM DIVERSITY
1				
2				
3			* *Elythyna* Community	*Alatiformia* Community
4	*Dicoelosia-Skenidioides* Community Group		*Bifida-Muriferella* Community	
5				
6				

* Atrypacean reef associated communities

Figure 7-7
Late Emsian, level-bottom, benthic communities from the Cordilleran Region (Johnson's, 1977, intervals 13 and 14). The community framework concept is explained in Boucot (1975). Source: Data from Perry, 1974. (See supplementary note)

Roberts Mountains Formation is evidence of a deep-water origin for the ambocoeliids. In the Cordilleran Region, ambocoeliids are commonly present in low abundance (less than 5 percent) in Lochkovian through Emsian faunas of B. A. 4-5; although locally in early Pragian beds of Sekwi Mountain map-area and Royal Creek they represent more than 20 percent of the fauna. In central Nevada, ambocoeliids are common, but in low abundance in all except the early Pragian beds. Thus, we lack this community in the Cordilleran Region Lower Devonian.

ANOPLIA KLAPPERI COMMUNITY (Figure 7-5)

The *A. klapperi* Community (Johnson, 1977) is a relatively high-diversity, although high dominance, B. A. 3 association that probably has strong environmental ties to the *Acrospirifer-Atrypa* Community of the same horizon. The reasons for the high dominance of *A. klapperi* are not well understood.

ATRYPA COMMUNITY

Boucot (1975) defined the *Atrypa* Community for faunas with a high-dominance (over 90 percent) *Atrypa sensu lato* that occupied a B. A. 3-5, quiet-water environment. A good example of the high-dominance *Atrypa* Community is the Frasnian interreef, gray mudstone and shale beds of the Job Pass area, southwestern Alberta (McLaren, 1955:53).

Here, articulated *Atrypa* spp. represent well over 90 percent of a fauna composed of not more than five to six genera in any one bed (Perry, pers. observ.). In the high-diversity B. A. 4-5 beds of northwestern Canada from the Lochkovian-Emsian interval and from the central Nevada Early Lochkovian, *Atrypa* commonly comprises 15 to 25 percent of the fauna. A few small collections from Sekwi Mountain map-area show relatively high dominance (greater than 50 percent) although this is partially biased due to small sample size (less than 100 individuals). Lenz (pers. comm.) has seen dominant *Atrypa* communities in the Delorme Formation of the central Mackenzie Mountains. Niebuhr (1974) documented the widespread occurrences of the *Atrypa nevadana* Community in the Emsian *Eurekaspirifer pinyonensis* Zone. Niebuhr's *A. nevadana* Community is approximately 35 to 60 percent *A. nevadana* and contains six or seven less abundant associated taxa. He placed the *A. nevadana* Community seaward of the nearshore *E. pinyonensis* Community and shoreward of the G-A-S "Community" (Biofacies of Johnson, 1974a). Considerable revision of this community model and biostratigraphic scheme is available in Johnson and Niebuhr (1976). Niebuhr (1977) renamed his *Atrypa nevadana* Community the *Carinagypa-Atrypa* Community. The latter name is appropriate for occurrences in which *A. nevadana* makes up substantially less than 50 percent of the specimens. Both the *Atrypa nevadana* and *Carinagypa-Atrypa* communities are thought to belong to the *Striispirifer* Community Group (Boucot , 1975:229, 235-236).

In northern Canada, *Atrypa* spp. *sensu lato* occurs commonly in the 15 to 40 percent abundance range in high-diversity faunas throughout the Lower Devonian. The absence of *Atrypa* from the central Nevada *Spinoplasia* and *Trematospira* Zones and very low abundance in the *Acrospirifer kobehana* Zone, all shallow-water, nearshore biofacies of Johnson (1974a), is noteworthy. Thus, this community is uncommon in the Cordilleran Region Lower Devonian.

ATRYPACEAN REEF ASSOCIATED COMMUNITIES (Figure 7-7)

In the Cordilleran Region, atrypacean brachiopods dominate biohermal associations and quiet-water coral-thicket communities. These types of communities are only recognized with certainty in Emsian and younger Middle and Upper Devonian units, perhaps because the reef record is not well documented in the older Lower Devonian. Lenz (1973) reported Gedinnian bioherms from Bathurst Island, Arctic Archipelago, that contained some atrypaceans associated with massive stromatoporoids. Emsian bioherm communities of northwestern and Arctic Canada are of moderate diversity and show dominance by atrypaceans such as *Atrypa*, *Biconostrophia*, *Carinatina*, *Spinatrypa*, *Vagrania*, *Variatypa*, *Crypatrypa* (Johnson, 1975; Perry, in press). These faunas are known from relatively few collections but they commonly contain a moderately diverse brachiopod fauna (ten to twenty taxa) associated with an abundance of massive stromatoporoids and tabulate and rugose corals. At the present time, data are too few to comment on the similarity or difference of these atrypacean reef associations. Watkins (1975) reported a brachiopod fauna dominated by the smooth-shelled atrypacean *Lissatrypa* in association with stromatoporoid bioherms from the Ludlovian of Gotland. It would not be surprising if the atrypacean-reef-associated community appears in the Cordilleran Region after poorly studied Silurian reefal carbonates of northern Canada are sampled in more detail. Copper (1966) reported the widespread association of atrypaceans with a variety of reef-related environments. His massive stromatoporoid biotope contained an association of *Mimatrypa*, *Carinatina*, *Glassia*, *Punctatrypa*, *Dubaria*, *Cryptatrypa*, *Karpinskia*, and *Vagrania*. However, Copper noted that other brachiopod orders such as the rhynchonellids and terebratulids were often dominant over the atrypaceans in reef-related associations in the Middle Devonian of western Europe.

Copper (1966) and Johnson and Flory (1972) recognized a Middle Devonian Rasenriff fauna that is a low-diversity *Thamnopora-Spinatrypa* coral-thicket community of shallow-water, low-energy environments in western Europe and central Nevada. To date, this association has not been recognized in the Lower Devonian of the Cordilleran Region.

ATRYPA NEVADANA COMMUNITY

See *Atrypa* Community.

BIFIDA-MURIFERELLA COMMUNITY (Figures 7-6, 7-7)

See *Dicoelosia-Skenidioides* Community Group.

BRACHYSPIRIFER-ATRYPA COMMUNITY (Figure 7-6)

The *Brachyspirifer-Atrypa* Community (Johnson, 1977; Niebuhr, 1977) is a medium- to high-diversity community in B. A. 3. The absence of genera characteristic of the B. A. 4-5 *Dicoelosia-Skenidioides* Community Group makes the B. A. 3 assignment reasonable as does the lateral relation with the B. A. 2 to nearshore 3 *Eurekaspirifer-Atrypa* Community (Niebuhr, 1977, Figure 10). It is possible that the *Brachyspirifer-Atrypa* Community belongs to the *Striispirifer* Community Group in the broad sense. The community presumably represents normal marine conditions as suggested by its diversity.

CALYCALYPTELLA COMMUNITY (Figure 7-3)

See *Notoparmella* Community.

CARINAGYPA-ATRYPA COMMUNITY (Figure 7-6)

The *Carinagypa-Atrypa* Community (Johnson, 1977; Niebuhr, 1977) is a B. A. 3, high-diversity unit, possibly belonging to the *Striispirifer* Community Group as evidenced by the absence of elements of the more offshore, deeper-water B. A. 4-5 *Dicoelosia-Skenidioides* Community Group. The environmental factor(s) responsible for separating this unit from the other co-occurring B. A. 3 units in the Cordilleran Region of Nevada, the *Pacificocoelia* High- and Low-Diversity Communities and the *Carinagypa-Atrypa* Community, are uncertain (see discussion under those communities).

CORTEZORTHIS-WARRENELLA COMMUNITY (Figure 7-6)

See *Dicoelosia-Skenidioides* Community Group.

CYRTINA COMMUNITY

Boucot (1975) named the type example of the high-diversity *Cyrtina* Community from the Coeymans Limestone of the northern Appalachians, which is interpreted to be of shallow-water B. A. 3 position and is characterized by the association of the terebratulids *Nanothyris* and *Podolella* and by the absence of deeper shelf elements such as *Skenidium* and dicoelosiids. The genus *Cyrtina* alone has a wide range of benthic-assemblage occurrence (B. A. 2-5). The *Cyrtina* Community is absent in northwestern Canada although the genus itself commonly represented 5 to 10 percent of the faunas from Lochkovian and Pragian age beds. Locally at Royal Creek, Yukon, *Cyrtina* is a markedly dominant genus. In Emsian strata of northwestern Canada and throughout the Lower Devonian of Nevada, it is a common constituent of the faunas, but of low abundance.

DICOELOSIA-SKENIDIOIDES COMMUNITY GROUP (Figures 7-3 through 7-7)

The *Dicoelosia-Skenidioides* Community Group was proposed for the Ashgill-Ems interval (Boucot, 1975:229). The community group is present in early Lochkovian beds of the Roberts Mountains Formation, Nevada (Johnson, 1974a:811) and in Early Lochkovian strata of the Road River Formation, Royal Creek, Yukon (Lenz and Pedder, 1972:21). *Skenidioides* is present, but is commonly of low abundance in both areas. *Salopina submurifer* is a characteristic element. Because of its high abundance (commonly greater than 25 percent) in Nevada (Figure 7-3), a *Salopina submurifer* Community (Johnson, 1977) is designated as part of the *Dicoelosia-Skenidioides* Community Group. Several good examples of the *Salopina submurifer* Community are available from Johnson (1974a, Table 1, collections UCR 5444, 5462; Johnson, 1977; Johnson et al., 1978).

The ecologic niche distinction between *Salopina sensu stricto* and *Salopina submurifer* is important. Typical large *Salopina* of the Silurian occur in B. A. 2 communities. *S. submurifer* is a morphologically distinct end member of the genus closely allied with the septate descendant genus *Muriferella*. Some populations of Pridolian and Lochkovian *S. submurifer* developed a progressively higher dorsal myophragm in progressively younger beds until it reached septal stature in the Late Lochkovian (*Muriferella*). Both *S. submurifer* and *Muriferella* are characteristically found in B. A. 4-5 in the Lower Devonian of northwestern Canada.

In Nevada, there is a stratigraphic gap between the Lochkovian occurrences of *S. submurifer* of B. A. 4-5 (Figures 7-3, 7-4) and *Muriferella masurskyi* of the *Bifida-Muriferella* Community (Johnson, 1977; Figures 7-6, 7-7) from the Emsian *Eurekaspirifer pinyonensis* Zone. This stratigraphic gap is attributed to both the Eastern Americas Realm influences and the nearer shore nature of the intervening Pragian faunas in Nevada (*Spinoplasia* through *Trematospira* Zones). It is of interest to note that the Nevada *M. masurskyi* is known only from offshore communities of *E. pinyonensis* Zone in the Cortez Range

(Johnson, 1970:38) and elsewhere (Johnson, 1977).

Salopina crassiformis From the Pridolian Skala Formation and early Gedinnian Borszczow Formation of Podolia also bears a long, low, dorsal myophragm with bead-like cross section; and it too occurs in probable B. A. 4-5 position judging from the diverse, small-size, associated fauna (Kozlowski, 1929:5-8; Boucot and Pankiwskyj, 1962:108-109).

In the Sekwi Mountain map-area, *Dicoelosia* has not been found in early Lochkovian beds although other constituents of the fauna show close affinity with the *Dicoelosia-Skenidioides* Community Group. *Salopina submurifer* is never as abundant in available Early Lochkovian collections from northwestern Canada as it is in Nevada. This is interpreted as an example of an ecocline. As noted by Johnson (1974a), a few large shells of *Atrypa, Gypidula, Schizophoria* are present and are sometimes common in Early Lochkovian collections; they show no evidence of transport.

In northwestern Canada, the dicoelosiid genus *Didymoparcium* occurs commonly, but is of low dominance in Emsian age strata. These Emsian beds of the *Dicoelosia-Skenidioides* Community Group also yield small numbers of *Skenidioides*. Other common small shells (less than 6 mm diameter) in this fauna include *Sibirispira?, Ambocoelia, Protathyris?, Cryptatrypa?, Biconostrophia,* and *Muriferella*. These same beds also contain abundant large shells (greater than 25 mm diameter) that include *Cortezorthis, Schizophoria, Megastrophia, Phragmostrophia, Atrypa,* and *Warrenella*. The presence of *Warrenella* provides additional support for Savage and Boucot's (1978) conclusion that the *Warrenella kirki* Community of the Cordilleran Eifelian is a B. A. 4-5 community. This unique faunal association is here designated the *Cortezorthis-Warrenella* Community (Figure 7-6).

In connection with the *Warrenella kirki* Community, it is worth pointing out in review that Johnson (1971) noted the low species diversity and dominance of *Warrenella* and *Leiorhynchus* in the upper fauna of the *W. kirki* Zone of Nevada and referred to it as the "*Warrenella* Community." Noble and Ferguson (1971) recognized a similar "*Warrenella*-Rhynchonellid Community" from the shale-limestone transition in the Headless/Nahanni Formation of the southwestern District of Mackenzie. These authors placed this community seaward from communities dominated by tabulate corals and stromatoporoids and landward from the Pelagic Community. The "*Warrenella* Biotope" of the Upper Devonian Genesee Group of New York was assigned an outer-neritic life zone landward of the pelagic biotope (Harrington, 1970). Ludvigsen and Perry (1975) reported the *Warrenella* Community from beds of Early to Late Devonian age in northern Canada where it persistently occupies a soft-substrate habitat in a low-energy, moderately deep-water environment.

Late Lochkovian and early Pragian beds of northwestern Canada contain small numbers of *Skenidioides, Salopina, Muriferella,* and *Atrypina*. These beds may reprsent a shallower water community of B. A. 4 or 3-4 boundary region position. Details of the percentage abundances of taxa in collections from Sekwi Mountain map-area are shown in Tables 7-1, 7-4, 7-5, and 7-6.

DUBARIA COMMUNITY (Figure 7-3)

The term *Dubaria* Community (Boucot, 1975) covers low-diversity units with high dominance of *Dubaria*. These units occur in a B. A. 2, quiet-water environment as evidenced by the commonly articulated nature of the brachiopods. Johnson et al. (1978) discuss an occurrence of this community in the Lochkovian of Nevada. It is of some interest that this relatively shallow-water community occurs in Nevada well to the west of deeper water faunas and lithofacies, indicating the presence of a shallow region well to the west of the main North American platform. Matti and McKee (1977) discussed the physical aspects of this phenomenon.

ELYTHYNA COMMUNITY (Figure 7-7) Source: Data from Perry, 1974. (See supplementary note)

The *Elythyna* Community (Johnson, 1977; Johnson and Kendall, 1976) is a B. A. 3 medium- to low-diversity unit. Its relations to the co-occurring *Alatiformia* Community (Figure 7-7) are gradational. Both communities occur in thinly laminated beds, which is consistent with poorly aerated, somewhat anaerobic conditions, and relative low-diversity of shelly fauna. The commonly disarticulated nature of the shells militates, however, against quiet-water, stagnant conditions. A community group assignment is difficult, but possibly the *Elythyna* Community might be viewed as a somewhat anaerobic unit belonging to the *Striispirifer* Community Group and closely related to the *Pacificocoelia* Community-Low Diversity (Figure 7-6), which contains another species of *Elythyna* in similarly, finely laminated beds.

EUREKASPIRIFER-ATRYPA COMMUNITY (Figure 7-6)

Typical examples of the *Eurekaspirifer-Atrypa* Community occur in the McColley Canyon Formation of the Sulfur Springs Range, central Nevada (Johnson, 1977; Niebuhr, 1977). *E. pinyonensis* is dominant (commonly more than 70 percent of the fauna) with smaller numbers of *Atrypa nevadana* and a low representation of five to six additional taxa (see Boucot, 1970:570, for abundance count of one collection). Niebuhr (1974, 1977) suggested that this community lived in a shallow-water, moderately rough-water environment as indicated by the commonly disarticulated condition of most bivalved shells, shell abrasion, and the presence of pellets and coarse bioclasts. The *A. nevadana* shells within the *E.-A.* Community have been observed by Niebuhr to have thicker shells than those *A. nevadana* living in deeper-water, less-agitated environments. Shell thickening is a characteristic commonly associated with rough-water environments as it is a means by which shells can stabilize themselves (Seilacher, 1968). Niebuhr (1974) assigned the *E.-A.* Community a shallow, nearshore B. A. 3 or possible B. A. 2 position. Other possible shallow-water B. A. 2 Emsian faunas may be present in beds located shoreward of the Lowther Island reefs, Arctic Canada. In many areas, B. A. 2 brachiopod shells may be absent because of dolomitization strandward or removal by post-Emsian erosion.

GYPIDULA COMMUNITY GROUP

The *Gypidula* Community Group was defined by Boucot (1975) as communities of any one of several gypidulinid genera occurring in abundance (greater than 90 percent) and commonly by itself. In none of the available collections from central Nevada or northwestern Canada do gypidulinids become so abundant. Some Early Lochkovian beds from the Birch Creek area of Nevada (Johnson, 1974a:811; 1977) contain nearly 60 percent *Gypidula pelagica lux* (*Gypidula pelagica lux* Community). Beds of similar age from Prince of Wales and Baillie-Hamilton islands contain commonly up to 40 percent *Gypidula pelagica*. These collections are from a probable B. A. 3, rough-water position.

GYPIDULA PELAGICA LUX COMMUNITY (Figure 7-3)

See *Gypidula* Community Group.

HOWELLELLA-PROTATHYRIS COMMUNITY (Figure 7-3)

Lenz (1976) reports a B. A. 2, quiet-water, low-diversity fauna from the Lower Lochkovian of the Delorme Formation platform facies. The shells are largely articulated. Lenz's description includes both physical features (absence of sand-sized material and oolites) and biological features (seldom more than four or five species and high dominance of one or two species) consistent with a shallow-water, intertidal environment. Lenz's *Howellella-Protathyris* Community of his Lower Lochkovian beds is clearly similar to Boucot's (1975) Ludlow and Pridoli *Protathyris* Community.

NOTOPARMELLA COMMUNITY (Figure 7-3)

Johnson's (1977) *Notoparmella* Community is one of two Cordilleran Region outer B. A. 5 and B. A. 6 notanoplid communities; the other being the *Callicalyptella* Community; both are of Lochkovian age. A Notanoplid Community Group is necessary to include the various endemic community units dominated by notanopliid genera in the Tasman Region (*Notanoplia, Boucotia*), in the northern Appalachians (Bourque, 1977), in Europe (Havlíček, 1973; Langenstrassen, 1972), and in eastern Asia (Xu Hankui, 1977). The Notanoplid Community Group was earlier discussed merely in terms of the Tasman genera plus *Callicalyptella* (Boucot, 1975:254), but enough material is now known from about the B. A. 5-6 position to make it clear that a community group designation is warranted for all of the notanoplid genera when they dominate.

NYMPHORHYNCHIA-ATHYRHYNCHUS COMMUNITY (Figures 7-5, 7-6)

Lenz (1976) reported the brachiopod genera present in the high-diversity *Nymphorhynchia-Athyrhynchus* Community. The Old World Realm brachiopod genera present in his B. A. 3 unit, associated in one area with the Lowther Island reefs, contrast markedly with the Eastern Americas Realm genera present in the Late Pragian (Figure 7-5) in Nevada, but not nearly as much with the Emsian units in Nevada

(Figure 7-6) that occur as well in B. A. 3. The *Nymphorhynchia-Athyrhynchus* Community belongs to the *Striispirifer* Community Group.

ORBICULOID-LINGULOID COMMUNITY

Boucot (1975) established the Orbiculoid-Linguloid Community for B. A. 1-2 position faunas dominated by orbiculoids and linguloids. This community, with dominant inarticulate brachiopods, is not known from the Cordilleran Region. Collections of probable B. A. 4-5 with abundant fish plates, conularids, and silicified brachiopods also yield abundant orbiculoids and linguloids in the Sekwi Mountain map-area Mid-Lochkovian (Table 7-1:B805, B810, B835, B815-870). The host strata are finely laminated, nonbioturbated, argillaceous limestones or dolostones that also contain abundant *Schizophoria*, *Protathyris*, and *Cyrtina*. Silicified, articulated brachiopods from these beds greatly outnumber fish and inarticulates although direct comparisons of abundances is strongly biased by the mode of preservation and amount of material dissolved in different acids for various elements. These beds are well removed from nearshore deposits and document the wide depth distribution of orbiculoids and linguloids as noted by Boucot (1975).

PACIFICOCOELIA COMMUNITY-HIGH DIVERSITY (Figure 7-6)

The *Pacificocoelia* Community-High Diversity (Johnson's, 1977, "*Leptocoelia* Diverse Community", Niebuhr, 1977) is possibly another *Striispirifer* Community Group unit. The lack of genera characteristic of the *Dicoelosia-Skenidioides* Community Group rules out an assignment to it. Niebuhr (1977, Figure 9) suggested that the *Pacificocoelia* Community-High Diversity occurred farther offshore than does the co-occurring B. A. 3, *Striispirifer* Community Group and *Carinagypa-Atrypa* Community Group. Because of this more offshore interpretation, Niebuhr concluded that a deeper water environment was present. However, it is alternatively possible that factors other than depth may be controlling the occurrences of these two community units; for example, the lower taxic diversity of the *Pacificocoelia* Community-High Diversity as contrasted with the *Carinagypa-Atrypa* Community is consistent with a more restrictive environment. The name change for the community is occasioned by the reassignment of "*Leptocoelia*" *infrequens* to *Pacificocoelia* (Boucot, 1975); *Leptocoelia sensu strictu* has not been recognized outside of the Appohimchi Subprovince of the Eastern Americas Realm (Boucot, 1975; Boucot and Rehmer, 1977).

PACIFICOCOELIA COMMUNITY-LOW DIVERSITY (Figure 7-6)

This community (Johnson, 1977, his "*Leptocoelia* Non-diverse Community", Niebuhr, 1977) has low diversity. Niebuhr (1977, Figure 9) suggested a more offshore, deeper-water position than the co-occurring *Pacificocoelia* Community-High Diversity unit. However, the lower diversity can also reflect more restrictive environmental conditions that could correlate with both the low taxic diversity and the absence of any elements of the B. A. 4-5 *Dicoelosia-Skenidioides*

Community Group. The laminated nature of the strata enclosing the fauna of this community is consistent, for example, with a more anaerobic environment than is characteristic of the more diverse *Pacificocoelia* Community. Possibly the low-diversity *Pacificocoelia* unit reflects some complex of oceanographic conditions that were conducive to low oxygen supply. The assignment of " *L.*" *infrequens* to *Pacificocoelia* (Boucot, 1975)[1] occasioned the name change in this unit.

PELAGIC COMMUNITY

Boucot (1975) cited the Road River Formation (Cambrian-Lower Devonian) of northwestern Canada as his typical example of the Pelagic Community and a group of typical faunal contents for the community (at present ammonoids and radiolaria have not yet been published from the Road River Formation). Another good example of the Lower Paleozoic Pelagic Community is the Cape Phillips Formation of Arctic Canada with its abundant graptolite and radiolarian faunas. In the Mount Sekwi map-area, Northwest Territories, and Royal Creek, Yukon, dacryoconarid tentaculitids and graptolites are locally interbedded with shelly faunas at several levels within the Lower Devonian section. Ammonoids, which are quite rare in Emsian beds have been recovered from one locality each in the Delorme and Michelle Formations. The close proximity of basinal shales containing these pelagic elements and local interbedding of pelagic elements with shelly faunas shows the near shelf-edge position of the Mount Sekwi and Royal Creek areas in the Lower Devonian.

PELECYPOD COMMUNITIES

Boucot (1975) noted the abundance of infaunal pelecypod communities in B. A. 1-2. Pelecypods are very uncommon in the Lower Devonian Royal Creek and Mount Sekwi areas and in Nevada. *Conocardium*, a genus known from reef beds (Formosa Reef of southern Ontario) to graptolitic shales, is the only commonly recurring pelecypod. It should be pointed out that Pojeta et al. (1972) considered *Conocardium* distinct from the main line of pelecypods because of

---

[1] Johnson erected the genus *Leptocoelina* to include only the type species and assigned a number of other Devonian leptocoelids to *Leptocoelia*. Boucot (1975) erected the genus *Pacificocoelia* to include the bulk of the Devonian species that Johnson (1970) had left in *Leptocoelia*. Johnson (pers. comm.) has recently considered, however, that most of the leptocoelids having convex brachial valves, which he earlier had left in *Leptocoelia*, might be best assigned to *Leptocoelina*. Such a procedure would result in placing *Pacificocoelia* in synonymy and necessitate using the term *Leptocoelina* Community rather than *Pacificocoelia* Community. Before taking this step, however, the morphology of all the species involved must be carefully reviewed.

their inflexible hinge; perhaps their environmental tolerances are also different. Pelecypods account for less than 0.1 percent of the total 60,000 brachiopod shells from the Lower Devonian in the Royal Creek and Sekwi Mountain areas. However, numerous Lochkovian collections (R. E. Smith) of probable B. A. 3 position from Prince of Wales and Baillie-Hamilton islands, Arctic Archipelago, yield considerably higher numbers of pelecypods.

PLICOPLASIA COMMUNITY

The genus *Plicoplasia* is present in Late Lochkovian and Early Pragian beds of northwestern Canada in high-diversity B. A. 4-5 faunas, but the typical B. A. 3 *Plicoplasia* Community with abundant *Plicoplasia* is not known outside the Appohimchi Subprovince.

PROTATHYRIS COMMUNITY

Boucot (1975) defined this community as a single taxon community in the Wenlock-Pridoli interval of the North Atlantic Region. Abundant shells of *Protathyris* and/or *Cryptathyris* (difficult to distinguish because of small, articulated, quartz-filled shells) commonly comprise 15 to 20 percent of Lochkovian collections and commonly less than 5 percent of Pragian collections in northwestern Canada (Delorme Formation; Broad and Lenz, 1972:461). Nowhere in the western North American Devonian is *Protathyris* known as a single taxon community.

QUADRITHYRIS COMMUNITY (Figure 7-3)

The type example of the *Quadrithyris* Community is from the Mandagery Park Formation, New South Wales (Savage, 1974). The Late Lochkovian of central Nevada is also represented by the *Quadrithyris* Community (Johnson, 1977) of probable B. A. 3 or 4 position. The genus *Quadrithyris* is unknown in northwestern Canada although correlation of beds is certain by the presence of other distinctive elements that occur in both areas, such as *Toquimella kayi*, *Spirigerina supramarginalis*, *Cortezorthis windmillensis*, and *Aesopomum varistriatus*.

SALOPINA SUBMURIFER COMMUNITY (Figures 7-3, 7-4)

See *Dicoelosia-Skenidioides* Community Group.

"*STROPHOCHONETES*" *FILISTRIATA* COMMUNITY (Figure 7-6)

See *Vagrania-Skenidioides* Community.

SPINOPLASIA COMMUNITY (Figure 7-4)

The *Spinoplasia* Community (Johnson, 1977; Johnson et al., 1978) of the Eastern Americas Realm Nevadan Subprovince is a parallel community of the *Striispirifer* Community Group (Boucot, 1975:235-236). It belongs in B. A. 3 and occurs in moderately quiet water, aerobic conditions. The relatively high diversity of the *Spinoplasia* Community is consistent with its having occupied a relatively normal environment reflecting no extremes. It is fairly similar to the *Acrospirifer-Rensselaeria* Community (Figure 7-4) of the same Nevadan Subprovince. The factor(s) that resulted in the differences between these two communities are not presently well understood. Johnson et al. (1978) concluded that the *Spinoplasia* Community in their sections occurs seaward of the *Acrospirifer-Rensselaeria* Community, which could indicate correlation with depth or with a non-depth factor that happens to occur farther out.

STROMATOLITE COMMUNITY (Figure 7-3)

Lenz (1976) reported birdseye limestones associated with stromatolites from very shallow-water situations that correspond to Boucot's (1975) high intertidal Stromatolite Community.

STROPHOCHONETES-PRORETICULARIA-RECEPTACULITID COMMUNITY (Figures 7-5, 7-6)

Lenz's (1976) *Strophochonetes-Proreticularia*-receptaculitid is closely enough associated with reefy facies and algae to make certain that it belongs in the photic zone (B. A. 3). However, the presence of *Warrenella* also suggests that it may be in the deeper part of the benthic assemblage. The high-diversity fauna presumably represents fairly normal marine level-bottom conditions. It has some features taxonomically in common with the *Carinagypa-Atrypa* Community and may have had ecoclinal relations. It belongs to the *Striispirifer* Community Group.

TOQUIMAELLA COMMUNITY (Figure 7-3)

See *Vagrania-Skenidioides* Community.

VAGRANIA COMMUNITY (Figure 7-6)

Vagrania occurs as a high-dominance, commonly single-taxon community in Late Emsian beds of the Ogilvie Formation, northwestern Yukon (Perry et al., 1974:1094), Middle Pragian and/or Early Emsian beds of the Delorme Formation (Table 7-5:A585-595) Sekwi Mountain map-area, and in Eifelian beds at Lone Mountain, Nevada (Johnson, 1968). The *Vagrania* Community is regarded as analogous to the *Atrypa* Community; it commonly contains a large number of articulated shells and is assigned a quiet-water, B. A. 3-5 position.

VAGRANIA-SKENIDIOIDES COMMUNITY (Figure 7-4)

The *Vagrania-Skenidioides* Community was proposed by Boucot (1975) for a high-diversity, Benthic Assemblage 4-5 community of Pragian-Emsian age in northwestern Canada belonging to the *Dicoelosia-Skenidioides* Community Group. *Skenidioides* is not an abundant element in these faunas, but is one of the characteristic small elements. A Late Lochkovian community, here named the *Toquimaella* Community (Figure 7-3), of similar benthic assemblage and closely related in taxonomic constituents to the *Vagrania-Skenidioides* Community is present in this same geographic area. *Toquimaella*, the obvious ancestor to *Vagrania*, is the most common element in the community. Atrypaceans, including *Spirigerina*, *Ogilviella*, *Atrypa*, and *Atrypina* also occur. Atrypaceans are by far the most dominant group of shells in the Late Lochkovian interval in northwestern Canada (Tables 7-3, 7-5). The rhynchonellids represented in the Pragian *Vagrania-Skenidioides* Community have counterparts in these older faunas. The Sekwi Mountain map-area Late Lochkovian faunas, however, have a lower percentage of orthids and higher percentage of atrypids and athyrids than the Pragian and Emsian faunas (Table 7-3).

Another example of possible ecoclinal variation is evident between *Toquimaella* and *Spirigerina* in some beds of the *Spirigerina* Unit (=*Quadrithyris* Zone) in the Royal Creek area where *Spirigerina* is dominant over *Toquimaella*. These beds with abundant *Spirigerina* have a similar B. A. 4-5 position to the *Toquimaella* Community. Perhaps when adequate data are available, these occurrences should be named *Spirigerina* Community of the *Dicoelosia-Skenidioides* Community Group. An apparent enigma develops when similar-age beds of the Stuart Bay Formation, Bathurst Island, are considered. Lenz (1973) illustrated a typical *Spirigerina* Unit fauna from beds interpreted to be of shallow water off-reef origin (faunas collected within 61 m of pinnacle reefs 6 to 15 m high and 9 to 12 m wide). These beds yield a high-diversity (twenty-two genera) fauna that apparently belong to B. A. 4-5 although Lenz (1973:1405) interpreted this fauna, based primarily on geographic proximity to the reefs proper, as follows: "...if the Bathurst Island fauna represents a community association with its concomitant depth limitations, it is reasonable that the *Quadrithyris-Spirigerina* faunas represent a fairly shallow, subtidal community." An alternative explanation that is well within the data limitations and more in agreement with the brachiopod B. A. 4-5 depth assignment is that these off-reef beds were deposited a considerable distance below the surface; that is, the reef tops were well below mean low water or the off-reef depth gradient was steep.

In the younger Pragian-Emsian faunas of Sekwi Mountain map-area, *Vagrania* is no longer common. Overall abundance of small elements such as *Skenidioides*, *Muriferella*, *Sibirispira*? and the dicoelosid *Didymoparcium* increases. The larger elements such as *Cortezorthis*, *Warrenella* (referred to as *Reticulariopsis* by some workers), *Megastrophia*, *Parapholidostrophia* and *Leptostrophia* also increase. The suggestion of Boucot (1975) that the *Vagrania-Skenidioides* Community was the source of the Middle Devonian *Warrenella*-Rhynchonellid Community (Noble and Ferguson, 1971) seems reasonable judging from the increased abundance of *Warrenella* and decrease of *Vagrania* in the Mount Sekwi map-area Emsian beds. This B. A. 4-5 community of Emsian age with common large and small elements is the earlier named *Cortezorthis-Warrenella* Community (Figure 7-6) of the *Dicoelosia-*

Skenidioides Community Group. Examples are shown in Table 7-7 (S4-1475, S4-1840-80).

The "*Strophochonetes*" *filistriata* Community (Figure 7-6) is named for faunas dominated by high percentages of "*S.*" *filistriata*. "*S.*" *filistriata* commonly occurs in the same Mount Sekwi map-area strata as the *Cortezorthis-Warrenella* Community although occasionally it is represented by a very high-dominance community in argillaceous, platy limestones of high insoluble residue (greater than 80 percent). The community is probably B. A. 5 position (Table 7-7:S4-50-75).

ACKNOWLEDGMENTS

We are grateful to Dr. J. G. Johnson, Oregon State University, and Dr. Alfred C. Lenz, University of Western Ontario, for reviewing and commenting on the manuscript during various stages of its writing.

REFERENCES

Boucot, A. J. 1970. Practical taxonomy, zoogeography, paleoecology, paleogeography and stratigraphy for Silurian and Devonian brachiopods. *North Am. Paleontol. Convention Proc.* F:566-611.

Boucot, A. J. 1975. *Evolution and Extinction Rate Controls*. Amsterdam: Elsevier Scientific Publishing Co., 427 pp.

Boucot, A. J., J. G. Johnson, and J. A. Talent. 1969. Early Devonian brachiopod zoogeography. *Geol. Soc. America Spec. Paper* 119, 113 p.

Boucot, A. J., and V. A. Pankiwskyj. 1962. Llandoverian to Gedinnian fossil localities of Podolia and adjacent Moldavia. Pasadena, California: Published privately, 128 pp.

Boucot, A. J., and J. Rehmer. 1977. *Pacificocoelia acutiplicata* (Conrad, 1841)(Brachiopoda) from the Esopus Shale (Lower Devonian) of eastern New York. *Jour. Paleontology* 51:1123-1132.

Bourque, P.-A. 1977. Le Silurien et le Devonien basal du nord-est de la Gaspesie. *Serv. Explor. Geol.* ES-29, 232 pp.

Broad, D. S., and A. C. Lenz. 1972. A new Upper Silurian species of *Vernonaspis* (Heterostraci) from the Yukon Territory, Canada. *Jour. Paleontology* 46:415-420.

Copper, P. 1966. Ecological distribution of Devonian atrypid brachiopods. *Palaeogeography, Palaeoclimatology, Palaeoecology* 2:245-266.

Fürsich, F. T., and J. M. Hurst. 1974. Environmental factors determining the distribution of brachiopods. *Palaeontology* 17:879-900.

Harrington, J. W. 1970. Benthic communities of the Genesee Group (Upper Devonian). *Field Trip Guidebook, New York State Geological Association* 42:A1-A15.

Havlicek, V. 1973. New brachiopod genera in the Devonian of Bohemia. *Vest. Ustred. ustav. geol.* 48:337-340.

Johnson, J. G. 1968. A new species of *Vagrania* (Devonian, Brachiopoda) from Nevada. *Jour. Paleontology* 42:1200-1204.

Johnson, J. G. 1970. *Great Basin Lower Devonian Brachiopoda*. Geol. Soc. America Mem. 121, 421 pp.

Johnson, J. G. 1971. Lower Givetian brachiopods from central Nevada. *Jour. Paleontology* 45:301-326.

Johnson, J. G. 1974a. Early Devonian brachiopod biofacies of western and Arctic North America. *Jour. Paleontology* 48:809-819.

Johnson, J. G. 1974b. *Oriskania* (terebratulid brachiopod) in the Lower Devonian of central Nevada. *Jour. Paleontology* 48:1207-1212.

Johnson, J. G. 1975. Late Early Devonian brachiopods from the Disappointment Bay Formation, Lowther Island, Arctic Canada. *Jour. Paleontology* 49:947-978.

Johnson, J. G. 1977. Lower and Middle Devonian faunal intervals in central Nevada based on brachiopods. In Murphy, M. A., W. B. N. Berry, and C. A. Sandberg, eds., *Western North America: Devonian.* Univ. California-Riverside Campus Mus. Contrib. 4:16-32.

Johnson, J. G., and R. A. Flory. 1972. A Rassenriff fauna from the Middle Devonian of Nevada. *Jour. Paleontology* 46:892-899.

Johnson, J. G., and G. W. Kendall. 1976. Late Early Devonian brachiopods and biofacies from central Nevada. *Jour. Paleontology* 50: 1113-1128.

Johnson, J. G., and W. W. Niebuhr II. 1976. Anatomy of an assemblage zone. *Geol. Soc. America Bull.* 87:1693-1703.

Johnson, J. G., N. L. Penrose, and M. T. Wise. 1978. Biostratigraphy, biotopes and biogeography in the Lower Devonian (Upper Lochkovian, Lower Pragian) of Nevada. *Jour. Paleontology* 52:793-806.

Kozlowski, R. 1929. Les Brachiopodes Gothlandiens de la Podolie Polonaise. *Palaeontologica Polonica* 1:1-254.

Langenstrassen, F. 1972. Fazies und Stratigraphie der Eifel-Stufe in ostlichen Sauerland. *Gott. Arb. Geol. Palaont.* 12, 106 pp.

Lenz, A. C. 1973. *Quadrithyris* Zone (Lower Devonian) near-reef brachiopods from Bathurst Island, Arctic Canada; with a description of a new rhynchonellid brachiopod *Franklinella*. *Canadian Jour. Earth Sci.* 10:1403-1409.

Lenz, A. C. 1976. Lower Devonian brachiopod communities of the northern Canadian Cordillera. *Lethaia* 9:19-27.

Lenz, A. C. 1977a. Upper Silurian and Lower Devonian brachiopods of Royal Creek, Yukon, Canada. *Palaeontographica* A159:37-109.

Lenz, A. C. 1977b. Upper Silurian and Lower Devonian brachiopods of Royal Creek, Yukon, Canada. *Palaeontographica* A159:111-138.

Lenz, A. C., and A. E. H. Pedder. 1972. Lower and Middle Paleozoic sediments and paleontology of Royal Creek and Peel River, Yukon, and Powell Creek, Northwest Territories. *24th Internat. Geol. Congress Guidebook* A14, 43 p.

Ludvigsen, R., and D. G. Perry. 1975. The brachiopod *Warrenella* in the Lower and Middle Devonian formations of northwestern Canada. *Canada Geol. Survey Bull.* 235:59-107.

MacArthur, R. 1971. Patterns of terrestrial bird communities. In Farner, D. S., J. R. King, and K. C. Parks, eds., *Avian Biology.* New York: Academic Press, pp. 189-221.

Matti, J. C., and E. H. McKee. 1977. Silurian and Lower Devonian paleogeography of the outer continental shelf of the Cordilleran miogeocline, central Nevada. In Stewart, J. H., C. H. Stevens, and A. E. Fritsche, eds., *Paleozoic Paleogeography of the Western United States.* S.E.P.M. Pac. Sec., Pacific Coast Paleogeography Symposium 1:181-215.

McLaren, D. J. 1955. Devonian formations in the Alberta Rocky Mountains between Bow and Athabasca rivers. *Canada Geol. Survey Bull.* 35, 59 pp.

Niebuhr, W. W., II. 1974. Paleoecology of the *Eurekaspirifer pinyonensis* Zone, Eureka County, Nevada. M.S. thesis, Oregon State University, Corvallis, Oregon.

Niebuhr, W. W., II. 1977. Brachiopod communities of the *Eurekaspirifer pinyonensis* Zone (Devonian), Eureka County, Nevada. In Murphy, M. A., W. B. N. Berry, and C. A. Sandberg, eds., *Western North America: Devonian*. Univ. California-Riverside Campus Mus. Contrib. 4:232-248.

Noble, J. P. A., and Ferguson, R. D. 1971. Facies and faunal relations at edge of Early Mid-Devonian carbonate shelf South Nahanni River area, N. W. T. *Can. Petrol. Geol. Bull.* 19:570-588.

Perry, D. G. 1974. Paleontology and biostratigraphy of Delorme Formation (Siluro-Devonian), Northwest Territories, Ph.D. thesis, University Western Ontario, London, Ontario.

Perry, D. G. in press. Late Early Devonian reef associated brachiopods of the Prongs Creek Formation, northern Yukon. *Jour. Paleontology.*

Perry, D. G., A. J. Boucot, and H. Gabrielse. in press. Late Early Devonian brachiopods from Mount Lloyd George area, northern British Columbia. *Canada Geol. Survey Bull.*

Perry, D. G., G. Klapper, and A. C. Lenz. 1974. Age of the Ogilvie Formation (Devonian), northern Yukon: based primarily on the occurrence of brachiopods and conodonts. *Canadian Jour. Earth Sci.* 11:1055-1097.

Pojeta, J., Jr., B. Runnegar, N. J. Morris, and N. D. Newell. 1972. *Rostroconchia*: a new class of bivalve molluscs. *Science* 177:264-267.

Savage, N. M. 1974. The brachiopods of the Lower Devonian Maradana Shale, New South Wales. *Palaeontographica* A146:1-51.

Savage, N. M., and A. J. Boucot. 1978. Middle Devonian brachiopods from the Kennett Formation, Northern California. *Jour. Paleontology* 52:807-811.

Savage, N. M., D. G. Perry, and A. J. Boucot. 1979. A quantitative analysis of Lower Devonian brachiopod distribution. In Gray, J., and A. J. Boucot, eds., *Historical Biogeography, Plate Tectonics, and the Changing Environment.* Corvallis, Oregon: Oregon State University Press.

Seilacher, A. 1968. Origin and diagenesis of the Oriskany Sandstone (Lower Devonian, Appalachians) as reflected in its shelly record. In Muller, G., and G. M. Friedman, eds., *Recent Developments in Carbonate Sedimentology in Central Europe.* New York: Springer-Verlag, pp. 175-185.

Watkins, R. 1975. Silurian brachiopods in a stromatoporoid bioherm. *Lethaia* 8:53-61.

Watkins, R., and A. J. Boucot. 1975. Evolution of Silurian brachiopod communities along the southeastern coast of Acadia. *Geol. Soc. America Bull.* 86:243-254.

Xu Hankui. 1977. Early Middle Devonian plicanoplids from Nandan of Guangxi. *Acta Palaeontologica Sinica* 16:59-70.

Ziegler, A. M. 1965. Silurian marine communities and their environmental significance. *Nature, Physical Science* 207:270-272.

SUPPLEMENTARY NOTE

Subsequent to the completion of this paper, Robert Blodgett, Oregon State University, pointed out to Boucot that the *Elythyna* Community in the Ogilvie Formation of east-central Alaska and adjacent Yukon Territory (Blodgett, R. B., 1978, Biostratigraphy of the Ogilvie

Formation and Limestone and Shale Member of the McCann Hill Chert [Devonian], east-central Alaska and adjacent Yukon Territory, M.S. thesis, University of Alaska, Fairbanks, pp. 30, 33, 35, 115, Figs. 4, 5) occurs in thin-bedded limestone above massive, Benthic Assemblage 3-type reef limestone, and is associated with such genera as *Leptathyris*, *Bifida*, and *Phragmostrophia*. The occurrence of abundant *Carinagypa* in the same sections suggests that a position for the *Elythyna* Community near the Benthic Assemblage 3-4 boundary or well into 4 is indicated, as well as a high enough diversity fauna to indicate relatively normal conditions. The co-occurrence in Nevada of *Carinagypa* and *Elythyna* (Johnson and Kendall, 1976, p. 115) is consistent with a Benthic Assemblage 3 assignment, but the Lowther Island (Johnson, 1975, p. 950) occurrences of *Elythyna* are above and below a reef-type occurrence, and the associated shells such as *Bifida* and *Crurithyris* are more consistent with a Benthic Assemblage 4 assignment than with 3. Therefore, it appears most consistent to consider the *Elythyna* Community as spanning the Benthic Assemblage 3 to 4 interval.

8

Coral Population Variations in a Colonizing Community (Devonian)

Thomas Henry Wolosz and Robert James Wallace

ABSTRACT

In many modern communities, the relative proportion of colonizing populations may vary considerably within the same region. Studies of succession in ancient communities have not documented similar population variations. A roadcut along Interstate 80 near Stroudsburg, Pennsylvania, has exposed a section through the Centerfield coral horizon of the Devonian Hamilton Group (Mahantango Formation) that allows this documentation. The unit is a black siltstone within which are a variety of coral assemblages that occur in two large biostromes. These biostromes probably represent coral populations that comprise the colonizing phase of patch-reef development.

Four coral assemblages have been recognized: the Solitary Rugose Assemblage, a mixture of many coral species; the *Striatopora* Assemblage; the *Eridophyllum* Assemblage; and the *Syringopora* Assemblage. Each is dominated by its respective genus.

With the exception of the *Striatopora* Assemblage, all of them could act as colonizers of the barren substrate. Although the Solitary Rugose Assemblage dominates the final stages of the biostromes, this is not necessarily indicative of greater competitive ability because the successional sequences among the assemblages are highly varied and are attributed to the control of some environmental parameter (possibly sedimentation rate). Autogenic control of the community development appears to have been of minimal importance. As a result, patterns of succession are highly varied and cannot be predicted from one place to another. It is only in settings where environmental conditions were more optimal for the corals that any generalizations regarding succession patterns may be made.

INTRODUCTION

In the past few decades, the principle of ecologic succession has been an important aspect of the study of modern communities (Odum, 1971). This principle describes communities as constantly evolving toward some goal or climax stage. Each stage of the community succession either alters the environment in some way, preparing it for the stage that will follow, or the component species change in proportion through time as a result of competitive interactions and growth rates.

Walker and Alberstadt (1975) presented an overview of the principle of community succession as it has been applied to both reef and shallow-bottom communities of the fossil record and defined four stages of succession that are evident in all such studies: stabilisation, colonization, diversification, and dominance. They also proposed a theoretical model for changes in such parameters as production, growth rate, and niche complexity as a community progresses from the early stabilization stage to the final dominance stage.

In modern examples, succession may be controlled by either biotic interaction (autogenic control) or by inorganic environmental parameters (allogenic control). The interplay of autogenic and allogenic controls is often subtle and almost impossible to separate according to importance. Evidence for the truly allogenic control of a succession consists of cases in which the succession has become arrested (stalled at some predomination stage) or in which the succession has become cyclical (Bretsky and Bretsky, 1975; Walker and Alberstadt, 1975). Even in such well-defined cases, the actual causitive factor may be either difficult or impossible to discern.

Many workers have tried to apply the concept of community succession to the fossil record: reef communities, Nicol (1962), Finks and Toomey (1969), Kaufman (1974), Alberstadt and Walker (1973), Alberstadt et al. (1974), Walker and Alberstadt (1975), Wallace and Chamberlain (1975) and shallow-bottom communities, Johnson (1972), Bretsky and Bretsky (1975), Walker and Alberstadt (1975). They studied the community to discern the successional sequence and describe the roles played by the species present with respect to their overall position in the framework of community succession.

With few exceptions, there has been a tendency to emphasize the successional sequence, usually a description of the species present in each stage. As a result, the concept of succession in ancient communities has been well documented. Details of the individual stages have not been emphasized. When this has been done, the focus is on the later stages of the community development, which are usually the best preserved and show maximum development of faunal organization.

In this study, we have investigated the interactions among coral populations within the colonization stage of reef succession. This has been preserved in the Middle Devonian Centerfield biostromal deposits of northeastern Pennsylvania.

LOCATION

The site of this study is an exposure of the Middle Devonian Centerfield Horizon (Mahantango Formation) that crops out along the southwest side of Interstate 80 approximately 1.6 km southeast of the Bartonsville exit in the extreme northwest corner of the Stroudsburg 7.5' Quadrangle, Monroe County, Pennsylvania (Figure 8-1).

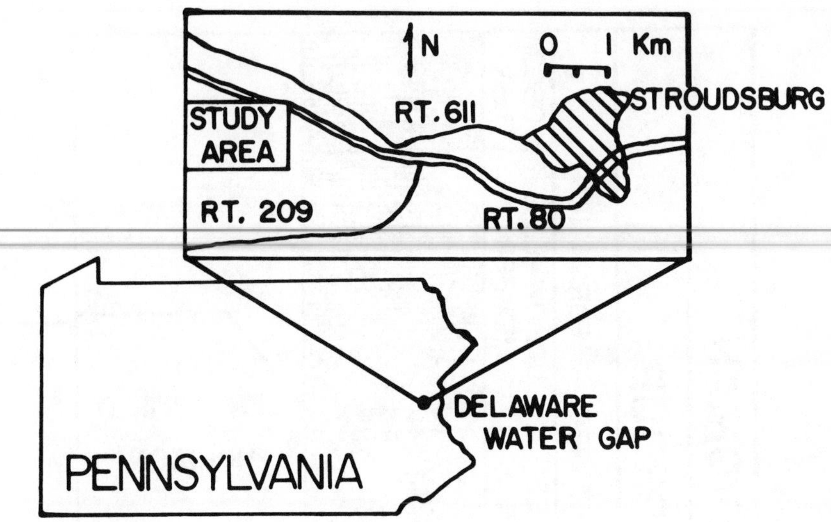

Figure 8-1
Location map.

PREVIOUS WORK

The Centerfield Horizon has been known for almost 100 years; it was first described by I. C. White (1882). The earliest studies concentrated on its stratigraphic position within the Hamilton Group in both New York and Pennsylvania (Prosser, 1894; Cooper, 1930; Willard and Cleaves, 1933; Willard, 1936; Ellison, 1965).

The first ecological studies of the Centerfield were carried out by Beerbower (1957) and Beerbower and McDowell (1960) who used a statistical approach to define the communities in the biostrome. Caramanica (1968) studied six exposures of the Centerfield in northeastern Pennsylvania and dealt with the systematic paleontology of the biostromes and the paleoecology in terms of the coral-sediment relationships and overall species correlations. Wallace and Chamberlain (1975) and Wallace et al. (1975) centered their attention on the Brodhead Creek outcrop and described the deposits there as the early pioneer stage of patch-reef development.

STRATIGRAPHY

The Middle Devonian Centerfield Limestone of New York and the Centerfield Horizon of Pennsylvania are Tioughiogan in age (Oliver et al., 1967). In Pennsylvania, this horizon is an arenaceous, gray to brown, massive-bedded calcareous siltstone that occurs at the base of the Ludlowville Member of the Mahantango Formation, Hamilton Group (Cooper, 1930; Willard and Cleaves, 1933; Willard, 1936; Epstein, 1973; Ellison, 1965; Figure 8-2).

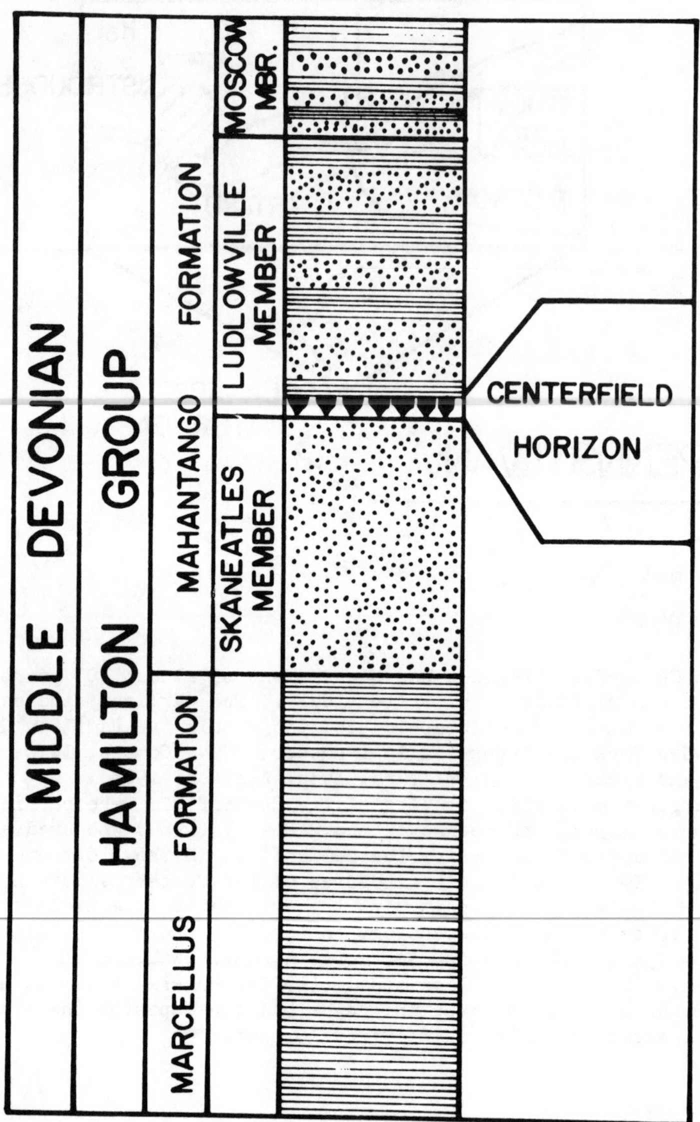

Figure 8-2
Stratigraphy of the Mahantango and Marcellus formations (data from Willard and Cleaves, 1933).

FIELD METHODS

Data were collected at the outcrop by marking out a series of fifteen vertical transect lines (Figure 8-3) each separated by a distance of 10.7 m. The sample areas along each transect were all 1 m wide; the height depended on the thickness of the fossil zones encountered. For example, for a fossil zone 15 cm high, the sample comprised an area of 100 cm by 15 cm. All genera within each sample

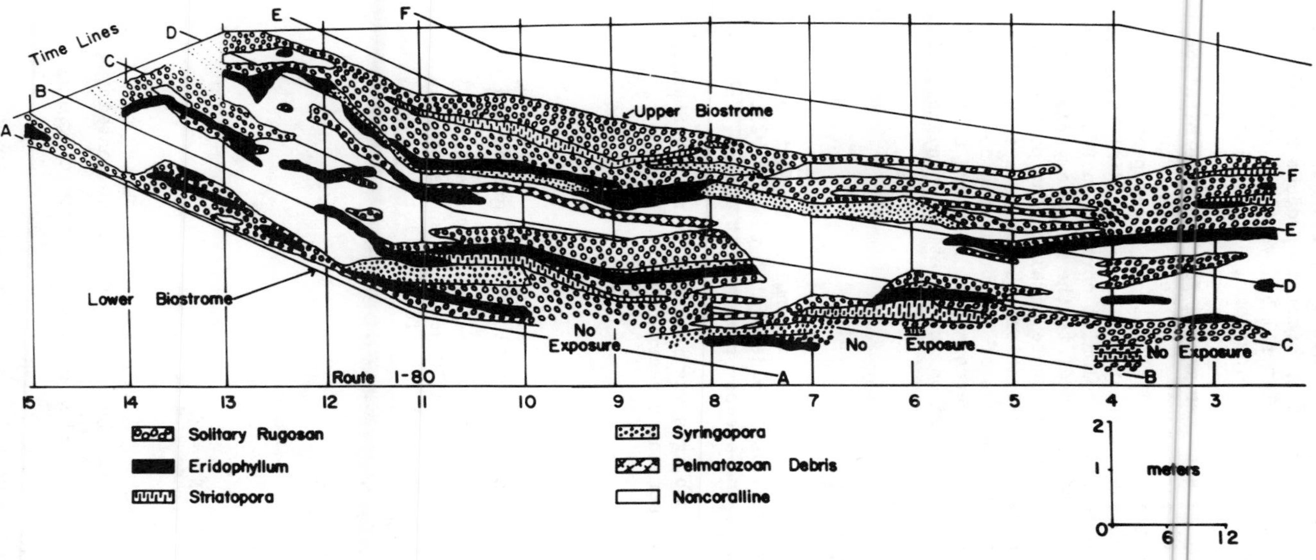

Figure 8-3
Facies map of the biostromes. The base line is Interstate 80. The vertical lines (numbered) indicate transect locations. The lettered lines are arbitrarily drawn time lines.

area were counted.

After point counting was completed, assemblages, based on the abundance of the fossil genera, were defined. The boundaries between these assemblages were then walked out in order to produce a cross section of the biostromes showing the lateral and vertical extent of component assemblages, position in the biostrome, and spacial relations (Figure 8-3).

Although biovolume may be a better method for the determination of the relative abundance of coral genera (Walker, 1972), the lithology of the outcrop is such that it is difficult to free specimens from the matrix to make such a determination. A second difficulty is the comparison of the open-lattice colonial corals, such as *Syringopora*, *Eridophyllum*, or *Striatopora*, to the massive varieties, such as *Favosites*, or to the solitary rugose corals. The point-count was used for its relative ease of application; however, these data tend to increase the relative abundances of the branching corals versus the massive varieties. It is necessary to be aware of this bias when making interpretations based on the relative abundances of the various genera.

STATISTICAL TREATMENT OF THE DATA

Three statistical measures were used to analyze the data collected in the field. These were used to determine the diversity of the assemblages, the presence and absence of dominant genera, and the covariance of the genera.

The diversity of the assemblages was measured using the Shannon-Weiner Diversity Measure (Wilson and Bossert, 1971):

$$H_s = -\sum_{i=1}^{n} p_i \ln p_i$$

where H_s equals the total diversity, i equals the ith genus, and p_i the probability of the ith genus occuring in the assemblage.

To determine if any mutually exclusive relationships existed among the dominant genera, the Jaccard test for similarity (Cheetham and Hazel, 1969) was employed:

$$J = \frac{C}{N_1 + N_2 - C},$$

where

$$N_1 = E_1 + C, \quad N_2 = E_2 + C,$$

J equals the Jaccard Coefficient of Similarity, C the number of samples containing both genera, E_1 the number of samples containing only the first genus, and E_2 the number of samples containing only the second genus.

Finally, to determine the covariance of the genera present, both a Pearson Correlation and a Partial Correlation program were run using the Statistical Package for the Social Sciences program package (Nie et al., 1975). The Pearson Correlation program results in a data matrix showing the correlation coefficients and statistical confidence limits for each pair of genera, whereas the Partial Correlation program allows the user to hold various parameters constant in order to check for spurious relationships in the Pearson results (for example, one parameter correlating to another because both correlate to a third parameter). These programs used normalized data from each coral-dominance assemblage.

THE INTERSTATE 80 OUTCROP

The outcrop along the southwestern side of Interstate 80 measures approximately 235 m in length (Figure 8-4). Beginning at the western end of the outcrop, the exposed fossil zone extends approximately 168 m to the east. This zone is separated into two distinct biostromes, an upper and a lower, that are laterally continuous. The biostromes are separated by a generally nonfossiliferous zone that contains five small, distinct coral zones isolated from both the upper and the lower biostromes; two other zones that are separate from both the overlying and underlying biostromes where they are exposed, which may merge with either one or both of the biostromes; and a thin bed of pelmatozoan debris (Figure 8-3).

At this locality, where both the top and the base of the entire Centerfield Horizon are exposed, it measures approximately 4.4 m thick.

The lower biostrome measures at least 2.3 m at its maximum thickness and reaches a minimum of 0.1 m near its eastern extremity. The upper biostrome ranges in thickness from 1.8 to 0.8 m. The isolated coral zones are generally thin (averaging 0.1 m), but reach a considerable thickness at both the western (0.5 m) and the eastern (0.8 m) extremities of the exposure. The barren zone that separates the two biostromes ranges from 2.5 to 0.6 m in thickness. The thin (0.1 m) bed of pelmatozoan debris is present near the top of the barren zone, but does not contact the upper biostrome.

For the purposes of this study, the two biostromes and the isolated coral zones have been subdivided into coral-dominance assemblages, based on both the numerical and visual dominance of an area by one genus or coral type. In this way, four assemblages have been recognized: the Solitary Rugose Assemblage, the *Syringopora* (a reptant tabulate coral) Assemblage, the *Eridophyllum* (a phaceloid rugose coral) Assemblage, and the *Striatopora* (a dendroid tabulate coral) Assemblage. These assemblages vary greatly in both thickness and lateral extent.

THE SOLITARY RUGOSE ASSEMBLAGE

The Solitary Rugose Assemblage is the most common of the four assemblages comprising approximately 64 percent of the exposed area. These assemblages tend to be relatively thick. Those in the upper biostrome range from 6 to 50 cm whereas those in the lower biostrome range from 7 to 52 cm, and both average 23 cm. In places, this assemblage can be traced continuously across both biostromes.

These assemblages are characterized by the relatively high pro-

Figure 8-4
The Interstate 80 Outcrop.

portion of solitary rugose corals, predominantly *Heliophyllum* and *Heterophrentis*, although they do not dominate the assemblage numerically (Figure 8-5). Other coral genera are common within this assemblage as evidenced by the high Jaccard similarity coefficient between the large solitary rugosans and *Syringopora* (0.86), *Eridophyllum* (0.82), and *Striatopora* (0.72). In addition, these assemblages have the highest diversity indices of all the assemblages (average diversity, 1.50; 1.63 for the upper biostrome, 1.33 for the lower biostrome; Figure 8-6).

Fossil densities (number of specimens exposed per square meter) vary from 38 to 2,049, averaging 838, in the lower biostrome and 108 to 3,067, averaging 969, in the upper biostrome. The interbiostromal masses have lower densities, 166-337, averaging 246.

THE *STRIATOPORA* ASSEMBLAGE

The *Striatopora* Assemblage comprises 8 percent of the total area of the two biostromes. They are thin, ranging from 10 to 43 cm thick (average 19 cm) in the lower biostrome (Figure 8-7). Only two of these assemblages were recognized in the upper biostrome (5 and 9 cm in thickness). The assemblages in the lower biostrome range from 21 to 30 m in lateral extent. The only well-exposed assemblage in the upper biostrome was approximately 36 m long (Figure 8-3).

Figure 8-5
Solitary rugose assemblage. Bedding is horizontal in the photograph. The scale is 1 m long.

The diversity of the *Striatopora* Assemblages is high (1.01), second only to the Solitary Rugose Assemblage. The upper biostrome has a diversity of 0.73, the lower, 1.07. This is the greatest diversity difference between similar assemblages found in both biostromes. This difference is due to the higher density of *Striatopora* in the upper biostrome (average 3,562 specimens per square meter) versus that of the lower (average 1,540). *Striatopora* is the dominant genus in this assemblage. There are very low Jaccard similarity coefficients between *Striatopora* and each of the other coral genera. The lowest is with *Eridophyllum* (0.38).

THE *ERIDOPHYLLUM* ASSEMBLAGE

Approximately 13.5 percent of the vertical area of the two biostromal masses is made up of the *Eridophyllum* Assemblage (Figures 8-3, 8-6, 8-8). The thickness of the assemblages in both the biostromes average 13.5 cm (the upper ranges from 5 to 34 cm, the lower, from 7 to 17 cm). In lateral extent, the assemblages in the upper biostrome range from 25 to 36 m, the lower from 4.5 to 36 m.

The assemblages have a very low diversity. The average is 0.50 (upper, 0.69; lower, 0.46). *Eridophyllum* is the dominant genus in the assemblage and has a negative correlation with both *Syringopora* and *Striatopora* and low Jaccard similarity coefficients (0.52 with *Syringopora* and 0.38 with *Striatopora*). Only the solitary rugosans

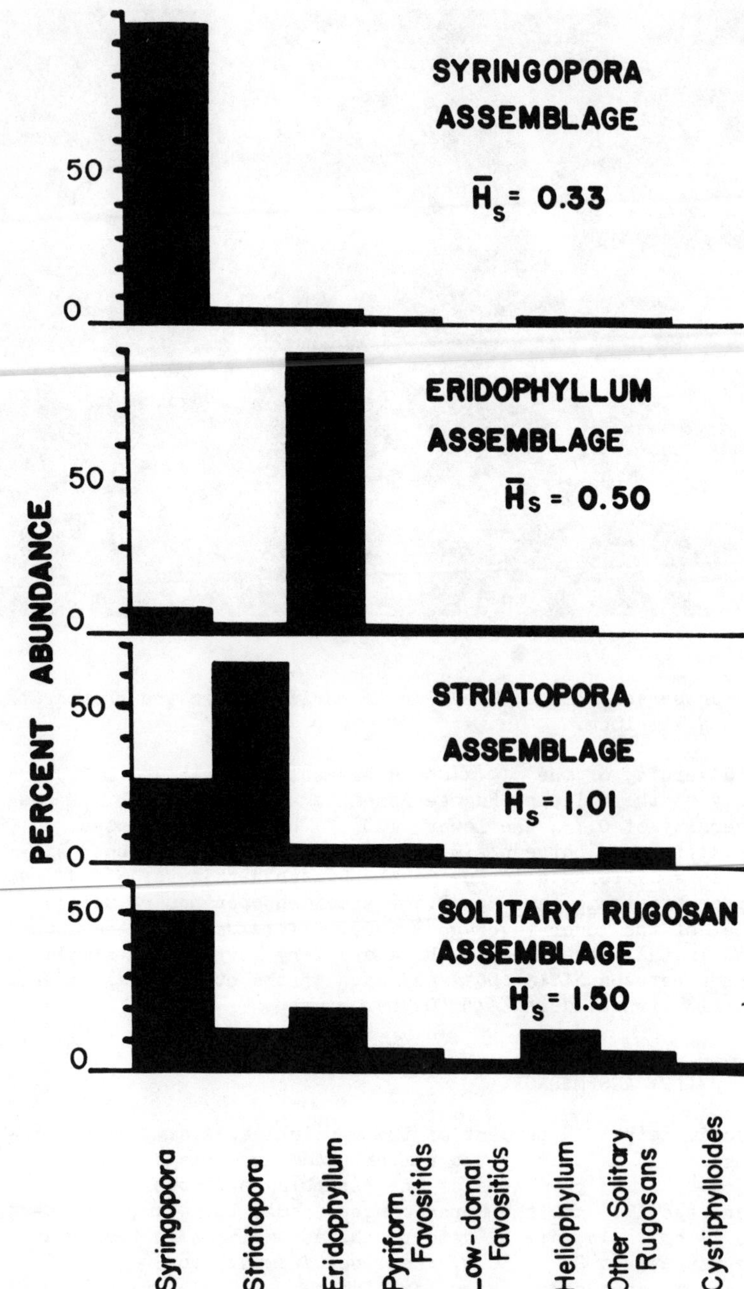

Figure 8-6
Percent abundance of various coral genera in each assemblage.

display a positive correlation as well as a relatively high Jaccard coefficient (0.82).

Fossil density for these assemblages is quite high with a range of 842 to 3,377, averaging 1,996, in the lower biostrome and 870 to 3,550, averaging 1,656, in the upper biostrome. The interbiostrome assemblages average 1,635.

The distribution of *Eridophyllum* assemblages along time lines (Figure 8-3) indicates that in some places the biostrome was dominated by this genus whereas in nearby regions it was only a minor component.

THE *SYRINGOPORA* ASSEMBLAGE

The *Syringopora* Assemblage comprises approximately 14.3 percent of the total, vertical, biostromal area. In the lower biostrome, these assemblages range in thickness from 8 to 41 cm, averaging 21cm. In lateral extent, they range from 6 to 21 m. In the upper biostrome these assemblages range from 5 to 50 cm in thickness (average 24 cm). The lateral extent of the *Syringopora* Assemblage in the upper biostrome ranges from 3 to 40 m.

These assemblages are characterized by the presence of large numbers of *Syringopora* coralla (Figure 8-6, 8-9). They have the lowest diversity of the four coral-dominance assemblages (average 0.33). Only *Eridophyllum* appears to have a major negative correlation with *Syringopora*; the Jaccard similarity coefficient is 0.52.

As a result of the extreme density of *Syringopora* coralla, these assemblages have the highest overall fossil density. In the lower biostrome, densities range from 2,331 to 5,266, averaging 4,017. The upper biostrome ranges from 1,938 to 11,020, averaging 4,703.

NONCORALLINE FOSSILS

Noncoralline fossils do not appear to be common in the biostromes. This may be due to the mode of preservation, which for the brachiopods, bryozoans, trilobites, pelecypods, gastropods, and cephalopods in the deposits below the biostromes most commonly takes the form of internal and external molds in the siltstone. In the fairly fresh blast-face of the Interstate 80 outcrop, such fossils do not stand out in contrast to the rock as do the corals, which are recrystallized calcite. Thus, they would be difficult to observe. Extensive sampling from the talus at the base of the outcrop has failed to result in any meaningful numbers of such fossils. Pelmatozoan debris is preserved as calcite, similar to the corals, but these have only been found in thin beds between the biostromes and in a small cap at the top of the lower biostrome.

DISCUSSION

GENERAL ENVIRONMENT

The silt and clay present in the formation suggest that the environment within which the corals were living was turbid. Such

Figure 8-7
Striatopora Assemblage. Bedding is horizontal.

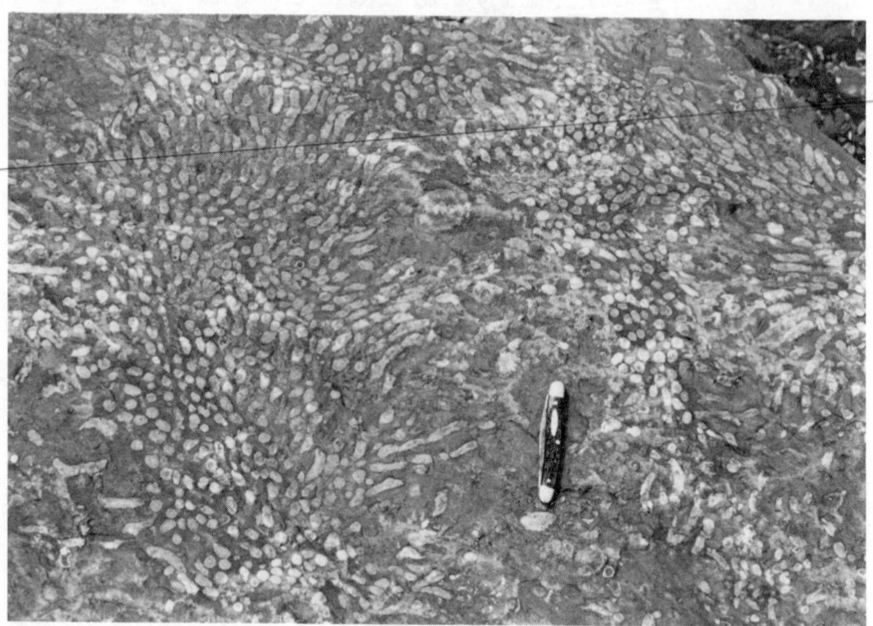

Figure 8-8
Eridophyllum Assemblage. Bedding-plane view showing the radiating growth form of the coral *Eridophyllum*.

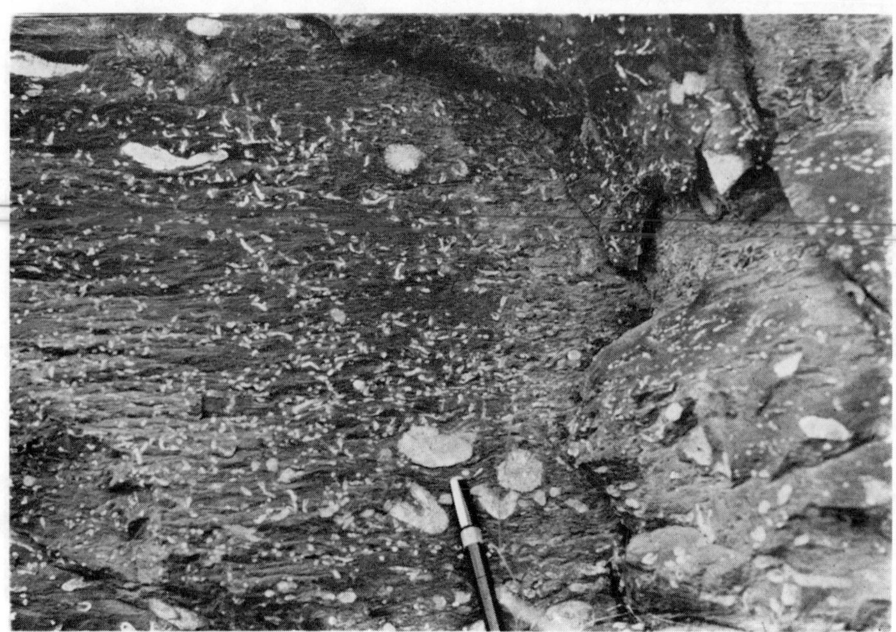

Figure 8-9
Syringopora Assemblage. Bedding is horizontal.

conditions are commonly detrimental to corals today (Endean, 1976; Hubbard and Pocock, 1972; Frost, 1977). It is likely that the environment was marginal for coral growth. The absence of corals from the Hamilton Group in general suggests that the environment was normally prohibitive to coral development. It seems likely that the Centerfield Horizon represents a time when conditions improved slightly to enable corals to colonize this region for some brief period of time (Wallace and Chamberlain, 1975; Wallace et al., 1975).

The corals are in a variety of orientations, but most suggest that they have been preserved in approximate positions of growth. The massive corals and *Eridophyllum* colonies have been the least disturbed and are in life orientations. The more delicate corals such as *Syringopora* and *Striatopora* are broken and form layered masses of coral debris. The lack of abrasion and roundness suggests that they have collapsed, perhaps due to the effects of burials rather than transport. The solitary rugose corals and some of the pyriform colonial corals show elbowing that suggests that they fell over during life and continued to grow, reorienting themselves toward the vertical.

There are minor variations in the grain-size proportions in the sediment, ranging from silt to clay, that suggest that the depositional rate of the sediment must have fluctuated. However, unlike some other Centerfield biostromes (Wallace et al., 1975), no correlation between sediment grain size and changes in the biota have been recognized. There is abundant indirect evidence that fluctuating sediment deposition affected the development of the corals. First, the abundance of massive corals is very low. In modern reefs, this has

Figure 8-10
Complex growth form in *Favosites* thought to be caused by a variable sedimentation rate. Colony thickness is approximately 45 cm.

ben associated with sediment influx (Wallace and Schafersman, 1977; Lang, 1970, 1973; Hubbard and Pocock, 1972; Frost, 1977; Endean, 1976). In addition, the shapes of the few massive corals include all of the varieties that have been recognized by Philcox (1971) as due to fluctuating sedimentation rate (Figure 8-10). The elbowed rugose corals suggest times when sediment influx was very low, considerably less than the growth rate of the corals (Bookman, 1977; Wallace and Chamberlain, 1975). Patterns of these various coral morphologies have not been determined for the Centerfield, so it is not possible to demonstrate the relative importance of sediment-deposition fluctuations on these populations. However, it is likely that it was a major factor.

Another feature of this deposit that could be explained by fluctuating environmental parameters is the irregular boundary of the various biostromes and the component fossil assemblages. These complicated and irregular boundaries are the result of changes in the size and distribution of the various coral assemblages. These changes can be due to either biotic or abiotic control. Biotic controls, such as competition, aggressive exclusion, or any other adaptive advantage of one group over another, usually result in succession that leads to a dominance by a particular assemblage. The organization (zonation) of the community also tends to increase. In modern coral reefs, for example, massive corals often become the more prominent members of the community, and the diversity tends to increase toward a maximum, although it sometimes decreases again in more mature phases. In assemblages dominated by abiotic controls, the patterns may be more complex. Species that can colonize an area rapidly are favored. The distributions tend to be a function of settling and reproductive rate (Hutchinson, 1953) as well as the nature of the limiting environmental parameter. Succession may begin as biotic interactions increase. However, these may be restarted due to a change in the limiting environmental parameter (Grassle, 1973). Complicated and varied successions are common in these biostromes.

In the lower biostrome, the dominant colonizer is the Solitary Rugose Assemblage. However, in the upper biostrome, colonization has been affected by the *Eridophyllum*, *Syringopora*, and the Solitary Rugose Assemblages. The trend through time has varied. In places, *Eridophyllum* is followed by *Syringopora* and then solitary rugosans (Figure 8-3, 9-D). In other areas, *Syringopora* is the colonizer followed by *Eridophyllum* then solitary rugosans (Figure 8-3, 10-D). Elsewhere, it may be solitary rugosans followed by *Eridophyllum* and then *Syringopora* (Figure 8-3, 11-A-B). There is a slight tendency for the successions to become dominated by the Solitary Rugose Assemblage, which would be consistent with successive progression toward an assemblage with increasing diversity. However, no organization of this assemblage has been recognized, so it is unlikely that biotic interactions had become the dominant factor during this stage. The only assemblage that does not occur at the base of the biostromes is that of *Striatopora*. This could mean that *Striatopora* was not as good at colonization in this region as were the other groups. However, it has been described at the base of the Centerfield biostromes in other parts of Pennsylvania (Wallace et al., 1975). *Eridophyllum* and *Syringopora* appear to be the best colonizers because they are the most common at the base of the large biostromes and are the dominant colonizers of the interbiostromal areas. These two groups have been described from other reefs and seem to function as the colonizers there as well (Oliver, 1951; Caramanica, 1968; Hasson and Dennison, 1974; Williams, 1977; Lowenstam, 1957).

CONCLUSIONS

The base of the lower biostrome appears to mark a point of significant change in the environmental conditions of the Centerfield sea. The change allowed the survival of large numbers of coral planulae and resulted in the haphazard colonization of the substrate by many coral genera that formed an undifferentiated coral biostrome (Solitary Rugose Assemblage). Fluctuating conditions resulted in the quick demise of parts of the biostrome at the same time that the patchy development of *Eridophyllum* thickets was taking place. In a more hospitable environment, development would be expected to continue and the thickets coalesce to form a basal zone similar to that described by Williams (1977) at Thompson's Lake reef. Elsewhere, other rapidly reproducing coral, for example, *Syringopora*, were also establishing thickets. Fluctuating environmental conditions caused the alternate demise or expansion of these corals and resulted in complex distribution patterns of assemblages as seen in the outcrop. In earlier stages, fluctions in size among the *Eridophyllum*, *Syringopora*, and Solitary Rugose Assemblages were common. In later stages, these fluctuations in size were between *Striatopora* and the Solitary Rugose Assemblage. The lower biostrome eventually divided into a number of small solitary rugose coral thickets before the final demise of the patch.

Recolonization of the seafloor by *Eridophyllum*, solitary rugosa, and in one case, by pelmatozoans, formed the interbiostromal thickets. These did not become well established.

The upper biostrome displays evidence of a more widely varying gradient of environmental conditions than the lower biostrome because it was colonized by a wider variety of thickets of *Eridophyllum* and *Syringopora* within the dominant Solitary Rugose Assemblage. Ultimately, the thickets of *Striatopora* appeared. The reappearance of extensive barren areas, the demise of the *Striatopora* thickets, and the return to the less-dense Solitary Rugose assemblages suggest a degradation of the environmental conditions ultimately leading to the final demise of the upper biostrome.

SUMMARY

1. The coral assemblages of the Centerfield represent a colonizing community in an environment that was detrimental to the growth of corals.

2. As is typical in colonizing communities, the controls on the population development were primarily allogenic rather than autogenic. This resulted in a wide variety of colonization patterns reflecting patchy colonizing populations followed by a variety of apparent successional patterns caused by the gradual increase in biotic interactions and the restarting of succession due to environmental fluctuation.

3. All of the common genera, with the exception of *Striatopora*, were able to colonize the barren seafloor. This stage of colonization is characterized by the Solitary Rugose Assemblage. The development of the assemblages of *Eridophyllum*, *Syringopora*, and *Striatopora* reflect their probable rapid reproduction rate and their ability to exclude many of the other genera, perhaps by the nature of their growth form and/or by some aggressive advantage they might have had over other corals.

4. In the early stages of colonization, no predictable successional pattern developed in marginal environments. It is only in optimal settings that patterns of succession tend to be more uniform and predictable.

ACKNOWLEDGMENTS

We thank John A. Chamberlain, Jr., for his suggestions pertaining to the functional morphology of the genera observed in the outcrop and Nicholas E. Pingitore, Jr., for his suggestions concerning the statistical treatment of the data. Thanks also to Enrico Pomella, who was always willing to help with laboratory materials, and to Marcia G. Bookman for help as field assistant to the senior author and for typing early drafts of this manuscript. This work is based on a thesis by the senior author that served as partial fulfillment of the requirements for the Master of Arts degree in geology at Brooklyn College of the City University of New York.

The final preparation of this study was supported, in part, by National Science Foundation Grant #EAR7812490.

REFERENCES

Alberstadt, L. P., and K. R. Walker. 1973. Stages of ecological succession in Lower Paleozoic reefs of North America. *Geol. Soc. America Abs. with Programs*. 5:530-532.

Alberstadt, L. P., K. R. Walker, and R. P. Zurawski. 1974. Patch reefs in the Carters Limestone (Middle Ordovician) in Tennessee, and vertical zonation in Ordovician reefs. *Geol. Soc. America Bull.* 85:1171-1182.

Beerbower, J. R. 1957. Paleoecology of the Centerfield Coral Zone, East Stroudsburg locality, Monroe County, Pennsylvania. *Pennsylvania Acad. Sci. Proc.* 31:91-97.

Beerbower, J. R., and F. W. McDowell. 1960. The Centerfield biostrome, an approach to a paleoecologic problem. *Pennsylvania Acad. Sci. Proc.* 34:84-91.

Bretsky, P. W., and S. S. Bretsky. 1975. Succession and repitition of Late Ordovician fossil assemblages from the Nicolet River Valley, Quebec. *Paleobiology* 1:225-237.

Bookman, M. 1977. Solitary rugose coral stability: effects of critical current velocity and sedimentology. M.A. honors project, Brooklyn College, New York, 20 p.

Caramanica, F. P. 1968. Coral paleontology and paleoecology of the "Centerfield" Biostromes of Northeastern Pennsylvania. M.A. thesis, State University of New York at Binghamton, 223 p.

Cheetham, A. H., and J. E. Hazel. 1969. Binary (presence-absence) similarity coefficients. *Jour. Paleontology* 43:1130-1136.

Cooper, G. A. 1930. Stratigraphy of the Hamilton Group of New York. *Am. Jour. Sci.* 19:116-123, 214-236.

Ellison, R. L. 1965. Stratigraphy and paleontology of the Mahantango Formation in South-central Pennsylvania. *Pennsylvania Geol. Survey Bull.* G48, 298 p.

Endean, R. 1976. Destruction and recovery of coral reef communities, in, Jones, O. A., and R. Endean, eds., *Biology and Geology of Coral Reefs*, New York: Academic Press, 3:215-255.

Epstein, J. B. 1973. Geologic Map of the Stroudsburg Quadrangle, Pennsylvania-New Jersey. *U. S. Geologic Survey Geol. Quad. Map* GQ-1047.

Finks, R. M., and D. F. Toomey. 1969. The paleoecology of lower Middle Ordovician "reefs" and "mounds". *New York State Geol. Assoc. Ann. Meeting Field Trip Guidebook* 41:93-102.

Frost, S. H. 1977. Ecologic controls of Caribbean and Mediterranean Oligocene reef coral communities. *Internatl. Coral Reef Symposium* 3:367-373.

Grassle, J. F. 1973. Variety in coral reef communities, in, Jones, O. A., and R. Endean, eds., *Biology and Geology of Coral Reefs*. New York: Academic Press, 2:247-270.

Hasson, R. O., and J. M. Dennison. 1974. The Pokejoy Member, a new subdivision of the Mahantango Formation (Middle Devonian) in West Virginia, Maryland, and Pennsylvania. *West Virginia Acad. Sci. Proc.* 46:78-86.

Hubbard, J. A. E. B., and Y. P. Pocock. 1972. Sediment rejection by recent scleractinian corals: a key to paleoenvironmental reconstruction. *Geol. Rundschau.* 61:598-626.

Hutchinson, G. E. 1953. The concept of pattern in ecology. *Acad. Nat. Sci. Philadelphia Proc.* 105:1-12.

Johnson, R. G. 1972. Conceptual models of benthic marine communities, in, Schopf, T. J. M., ed., *Models in Paleobiology.* San Francisco: Freeman, Cooper and Co., pp. 148-159.

Kauffman, E. G. 1974. Structure, succession, and evolution of Antillean Cretaceous "reefs": rudistid frameworks, in, Ziegler, A. M., ed., *Principles of Benthic Marine Community Analysis.* University of Miami, Sedimenta. 4:12.14-12.27.

Lang, J. C. 1970. Inter-specific aggression within the scleractinian reef corals. Ph.D dissertation, Yale University, 177 p.

Lang, J. C. 1973. Interspecific aggression by scleractinian corals 2, Why the race is not only to the swift. *Marine Sci. Bull.* 23:260-279.

Lowenstam, H. A. 1957. Niagaran reefs in the Great Lakes area, in, Hedgpeth, H. A., ed., *Treatise on Marine Ecology and Paleoecology* Geol. Soc. America Mem. 67:215-248.

Nicol, D. 1962. The biotic development of some Niagaran reefs - an example of an ecological succession or sere. *Jour. Paleontology* 36:172-176.

Nie, N. H., C. H. Hull, J. G. Jenkins, K. Steinbrenner, and D. H. Bent. 1975. *Statistical Package for the Social Sciences.* New York:McGraw-Hill, 675 p.

Odum, E. P. 1971. *Funda entals of Ecology.* Philadelphia: W. B. Saunders Co., 574 p.

Oliver, W. A., Jr. 1951. Middle Devonian Coral Beds of Central New York. *Am. Jour. Sci.* 249:705-728.

Oliver, W.A., Jr., W. DeWitt, Jr., J. M. Dennison, D. M. Hoskins, and J. W. Huddle. 1967. Devonian of the Appalachian Basin, United States, in, Oswald, D. H., ed., *International Sy posium on the Devonian System.* Calgary, Alberta: Alberta Society of Petroleum Geologists 1:1001-1040.

Philcox, M. E. 1971. Growth forms and role of colonial coelenterates in reefs of the Gower Formation (Silurian), Iowa. *Jour. Paleontology* 45:338-346.

Prosser, C. W. 1894. Devonian System of eastern Pennsylvania and New York. *U. S. Geol. Survey* 120:3-81.

Walker, K. R. 1972. Trophic analysis: a method for studying the function of ancient communities. *Jour. Paleontology* 46:82-93.

Walker, K. R., and L. P. Alberstadt. 1975. Ecological succession as an aspect of structure in fossil communities. *Paleobiology* 1:238-257.

Wallace, R. J., and J. A. Chamberlain, Jr. 1975. Paleoecology and community structure of a Devonian patch reef. *Geol. Soc. America Abs. with Programs* 7:129-130.

Wallace, R. J., J. A. Chamberlain, Jr., and T. H. Wolosz. 1975. Succession in a Devonian patch reef in a presumed turbid environment. *Geol. Soc. America Abs. with Programs* 7:1311.

Wallace, R. J., and S. D. Schafersman. 1977. Patch-reef ecology and sedimentology of Glovers Reef Atoll, Belize, in, Frost, S., and M. Weiss, eds., *Reefs and Related Carbonates - Ecology and Sedimentology.* Tulsa: American Association of Petroleum Geologists Studies in Geology 4:37-52.

White, I. C. 1881. The Geology of Pike and Monroe Counties. *Pennsylvania Geol. Survey 2nd Ser. Rept.* G-6, 407 p.

Willard, B. 1936. A Hamilton coral reef in Pennsylvania. *Pennsylvania Acad. Sci. Proc.* 10:30-36.

Willard, B., and A. B. Cleaves. 1933. The Hamilton Group of eastern Pennsylvania. *Geol. Soc. America Bull.* 44:757-782.

Williams, L. A. 1977. Successional patterns in a Middle Devonian Patch Reef. *Geol. Soc. America Abs. with Programs* 9:330-331.

Wilson, E. O., and W. H. Bossert. 1971. *A Primer of Population Biology.* Stamford, Connecticut: Sinauer Associates, Inc., 192 p.

9

Early Permian Fossil Communities in Northeastern Nevada and Northwestern Utah

Thomas E. Yancey and Calvin H. Stevens

ABSTRACT

In Early Permian strata deposited in an interior seaway located near the western continental margin, three groups of commonly occurring communities are present: nearshore, mollusc-dominated; open-shelf, non molluscan; and deeper water, offshore mollusc-dominated. Both shallow and deep waters are dominated by molluscan biotas. Along some portions of the eastern margin of the seaway, both normal-marine and hypersaline waters were present, and a community sequence developed along the salinity gradient. Another community sequence was developed along the depth gradient into the axis of the seaway.

The nearshore group includes the *Meekospira*, Euphemitid, and *Astartella* communities, listed in order of increasing numbers of stenotopic taxa. They occupied restricted-to-open bays and sounds and shoreline areas within wave base. Clustering of component species results in considerable variation within the Euphemitid Community, and the previously described Nuculanid Community is included within the redescribed Euphemitid Community. Species diversity is high (up to 70 species) in the *Astartella* Community.

The open-shelf group includes the Dictyoclostid-*Composita*, Colonial Tetracoral, Fusulinid, and Palaeotextulariid Communities, which generally occurred in this sequence across the shelf from the shoreline seaward. The Dictyoclostid-*Composita* Community occupied a variety of nearshore and shallow-shelf environments, and the others are believed to have occupied zones of increasing water depths. Fusulinids occur commonly in both Fusulinid and Palaeotextulariid communities, and available evidence suggests that they occupied depths from about 10 m to at least 35 m. The more offshore mollusc-dominated *Anthraconeilo* Community occurs in sediment that is partly pelagic in origin. It may have lived in depths up to 200 m.

INTRODUCTION

Early Permian strata in northeastern Nevada and northwestern Utah were deposited in environments ranging from continental, non-aquatic to deep-basinal marine, and contain fossil biotic communities of all depositional environments except the nonaquatic ones. The depositional area was located near the outer edge of the Permian continental shelf (Stevens, 1977) and was the site of a long-lived interior seaway occupying a topographic low just east of the uplifted continental margin. The seaway generally was shallow with widely fluctuating shorelines, but ocean waters were always present in a deep-marine trough that lay close to the western side of the seaway. The average bathymetric gradient on the west side of the trough was at least twice as steep as that on the east side where the distance from the trough axis to shoreline commonly was 100-150 km compared to an average of 50 km for the west side of the trough.

The sediment fill of this seaway is a mixed siliclastic and carbonate sequence, with carbonates most abundant on the open-shelf areas distant from shorelines. Siliclastic sediment is dominant in both the deep-trough area and in marginal-marine areas, and small amounts of evaporites occur in some of the marginal-marine deposits, especially on the eastern margin of the seaway. Siliclastic sediment typically is of coarser grain size (silts, sands, and pebble conglomerates) on the west margin of the seaway than on the east margin (clays, silts, and sands) and contains notable quantities of chert-pebble clasts not present in sediments on the east margin of the seaway. Siliclastic sediment in the deeper trough is of clay and silt size and is not turbiditic.

Nearly continuous deposition occurred throughout the area, and the trough and seaway persisted throughout most of the Early Permian. However, by Late Leonardian, the trough was either infilled or uplifted, and the bathymetric gradient changed. At the end of the Leonardian, uniform, shallow-water limestones of the Kaibab Formation were deposited over most of the eastern half of the seaway, and the western half of the area was probably everywhere uplifted above sea-level. Our study is based on Early Permian strata deposited within the seaway from the Wolfcampian through the Middle Leonardian interval (Riepe Spring through Loray formations and equivalents), but does not include the latest Leonardian strata deposited after the disappearance of the central trough when the seaway was greatly altered. Zonation of the Early Permian deposits based on fusulinids and corals permits correlation of stratigraphic units averaging about 100 m thick throughout the area (Stevens, 1979) and demonstrates the age equivalence of deposits of contrasting depositional environments.

Depositional environments follow the shorelines and bathymetric trends within the seaway. They are generally arranged in north-south directions and are partly symmetrical to the basin axis. Environments represented by fossil communities include hypersaline marine, marginal marine, marine open shelf, and deep marine. Deep-basinal marine deposits are restricted to the axial part of the trough in the western part of the area. Marginal-marine and open-shelf deposits, resulting from continually fluctuating shorelines over the region, are very common throughout the area although in some parts of the western area marginal-marine communities are almost absent at the margin of the seaway. Marginal-marine sequences include a complex of sediments deposited in shoreline, bay, and nonaquatic environments. Deposits of hypersaline environments occur predominantly to the east and include thick evaporite beds in some areas. Deposits of nonaquatic environments include redbeds and dunal sands and occur predominantly in the eastern part of the area. Definite brackish-water or freshwater deposits have not been recognized, and coaly, carbonaceous sediments apparently are not present in the Permian strata of this area. The occurrence of hypersaline-water deposits and redbeds and lack of brackish-water or freshwater deposits strongly indicates that dry climatic conditions prevailed along the margins of the seaway.

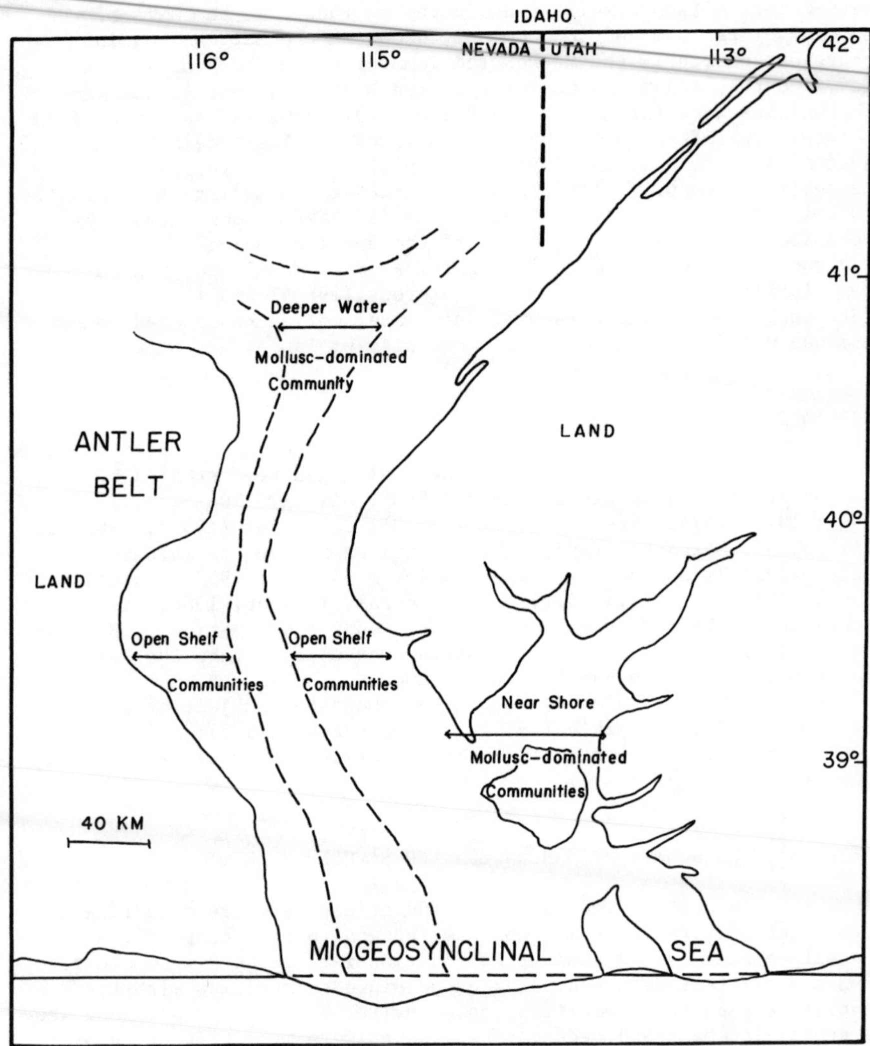

Figure 9-1
Positions of community groups within a generalized reconstruction of the Early Permian miogeosynclinal seaway in northeastern Nevada and northwestern Utah. Shoreline positions are stylized (they fluctuated widely during this time) and show possible shoreline configurations in different areas.

The numerous biotic communities of this interior seaway can be arranged in three main groups corresponding to major depositional environments. From the shore zone seaward (Figure 9-1), there is a group of mollusc-dominated communities associated with marginal-marine and nearshore environments followed by a group of nonmolluscan communities associated with open-shelf environments followed by a deep-water, offshore mollusc-dominated community in the axis of the seaway. Three communities commonly occur in the marginal-marine nearshore cluster: the *Meekospira* Community, the Euphemitid Community, and the *Astartella* Community. The *Meekospira* and *Astartella* communities were first named by Yancey (1971) whereas the Euphemitid Community was first named by Stevens (1965b). The Nuculanid and *Heteralosia* communities of Stevens (1966) are here grouped into the Euphemitid Community although the *Heteralosia* Community as originally envisioned is partly equivalent to the *Astartella* Community. The open-shelf, nonmolluscan cluster of communities includes the Dictyoclostid-*Composita*, Colonial Tetracoral, Fusulinid, and Palaeotextulariid communities, named by Stevens (1965b) and later modified (Stevens, 1966). The offshore, deep-water mollusc-dominated community was named the *Anthraconeilo* Community by Yancey and Stevens (1977).

PREVIOUS WORK

The Permian stratigraphy of the region has been studied by many geologists including Steele (1959, 1960), Bissell (1962z, b; 1964; 1967; 1970; 1974), Stevens (1965a, 1979), Collinson (1968), Zabriskie (1970), and Marcantel (1975). Correlations in the region have been made primarily on the basis of fusulinids (Steele, 1959; Bissell, 1962b; Stevens et al., 1979), and on corals (Easton, 1960; Wilson and Langenheim, 1962; Stevens, 1967). The fusulinid zonation of Stevens et al. (1979), supplemented by corals, was used to make the correlations that are the bases of this study.

Environmental interpretations have been the subject of work by Stevens (1966), Zabriskie (1970), and Marcantel (1975); and fossil communities have been studied by Stevens (1966), Yancey (1971), and Yancey and Stevens (1977).

METHODS OF COMMUNITY DETERMINATION AND SAMPLE COLLECTION

The communities identified and described here are recurring assemblages of fossils having the same general biotic composition. Fossil samples having similar composition were grouped into clusters, and the clusters were evaluated as possible communities with the available data on composition, paleoenvironment, recurrence, and geographic placement and necessary revisions were made. Grouping of samples into clusters was done by comparing their biotic composition and the relative abundances of taxa within each sample because samples with a small number of individuals may not contain a representative selection of species nor have reliable relative abundances. This method of community description is similar to methods used by other workers (see Scott and West, 1976, for summaries); although as Parker (1975) notes, there are as many methods of community determination as there are workers in the field. In the same study, Parker goes on to show that different methods will usually produce compatible results of community recognition.

Only those assemblages that have a distinctive composition and were available in multiple samples are described as communities, so it is possible that some rarely occurring communities have not been described. There are some samples that suggest the occurrence of a bryozoan-dominated community and another high-salinity community, but these are not describable without additional samples. However, any undescribed communities are of minor occurrence within the seaway. We are defining communities primarily for their practical value in recognizing Early Permian paleoenvironments, which Stanton (1976) shows is the most reliable aspect of paleocommunity studies.

All of the communities have gradational boundaries to other communities, and many transitional samples were collected. Even with hundreds of samples available, there is a significant proportion of samples that can not, or can only with difficulty, be assigned to a community. Stanton (1976:113) notes the same characteristic in modern faunas of southern California where approximately one-fifth of the samples did not fall into the defined groups after grouping them on the basis of sample composition. The Permian communities are segments of a compositional continuum, but are the most characteristic portions of the continuum. They appear to have biological unity because most of them are common, and some are very similar to upper Carboniferous communities (Stevens, 1965b; Watkins, 1973).

The communities described here tend to be more inclusive, containing a higher diversity of taxa, and allow for greater variability among the dominant taxa than communities described by some other workers. All communities have many taxa in the trophic nucleus, and in only a few cases does a single taxon account for more than 25 percent of a biota. No single taxon is consistently dominant in any of the mollusc-dominated communities. A broad approach to communities has been used because of the unsatisfactory results obtained from defining communities on a more restricted basis among our samples, and the realization that within modern level-bottom communities proportions among dominant taxa can vary significantly over small areas (Stanton and Evans, 1972; Peterson, 1976). Patchiness is believed to be the cause for much variation in our samples of nearshore molluscan communities. Applying a more limited approach to community determination, such as used by Boucot (1975) and Fursich (1977), would no doubt increase the number of describable units, especially in the nearshore environments, but it would not produce a more useful group of communities. Choosing broad versus narrow limits for a community is probably a function of the species diversity available in the samples, and most of our samples have a high species diversity (up to seventy recoverable species in some samples). Mixing due to transport of dead shells may increase the diversity in some samples, but it will not mask the dominant taxa in a community and is not considered to be a problem.

Species counts to determine abundances in the fossil assemblages has been done in several ways because of the different manner of preservation of fossils in different lithologies. In several cases where the same community was collected from both siltstone and limestone (with silicified fossils), no major discrepancies in community composition were determined. Macrofossils contained in noncalcareous rocks were counted on rock surfaces and bedding planes in the field and on slabs collected for later study. Fossils contained in limestone often were silicified. These samples were etched in acid, and all of the fossils were sorted and counted. Acid etching of silicified fossils provides a much better recovery of small and juvenile individuals, but does not add much to the total biovolume of the assemblage as determined by other means. Most samples of the Colonial Tetracoral, Fusulinid, and Palaeotextulariid communities were studied in thin sections of the fossil-bearing rocks, and fossils were counted in the same manner as on rock surfaces or bedding planes to determine abundances.

Several hundred samples were available for this study and were collected in the course of regional work on Early Permian strata. Sampling intensity is approximately equal for all depositional environments. Sample numbers with a D prefix (D-5557, and so forth) are localities recorded in the files of the Museum of Paleontology, University of California, Berkeley, and sample numbers beginning with a number prefix (3 N 22, and so forth) or sample numbers without prefix are those of C. H. Stevens, Department of Geology, San Jose State University, San Jose, California.

NEARSHORE MOLLUSC-DOMINATED COMMUNITIES

MEEKOSPIRA COMMUNITY

The *Meekospira* Community consists of about six taxa that consistently occur together in abundance, and about ten taxa that are occasional components of the biota (Table 9-1). The taxa are almost entirely molluscan, with the bivalves *Schizodus* and *Bakevellia* and the gastropods *Meekospira*, *Yunnania*, and *Goniasma* being most characteristic. Ostracodes are the only nonmolluscan taxa consistently found in the community, and the annelid *Spirorbis* occasionally is present. The community has very limited biotic diversity, and none

Table 9-1
Abundances of taxa in randomly selected samples of the *Meekospira* Community. Counts show numbers of individuals in each sample. Ostracodes are present in all samples, but are not counted.

	Localities							
	D-5520	D-5533	D-5551	D-5552	D-5558	D-5559	D-5560	D-5561
Molluscs								
Nuculavus	1	–	–	–	–	–	1	2
Schizodus	3	2	5	40	20	10	–	50
Bakevellia	30	20	160	40	–	1	2	50
Permophorus	–	–	–	–	5	1	10	–
Bellerophon	–	–	–	–	–	–	–	1
Leptomphalus	–	–	–	15	–	–	5	6
Yunnania	–	22	–	–	–	200	200	–
Platyworthenia	24	–	5	70	–	–	–	–
Goniasma	–	2	–	1	50	400	50	400
Naticopsis	–	–	4	–	–	10	5	2
Meekospira	10	10	25	20	15	75	50	200
Prodentalium	1	–	–	–	3	–	–	30
Annelids								
Spirorbis	–	–	10	–	–	–	–	–

of the taxa are restricted to this community.

The rocks containing this community are calcareous siltstones, mudstones, argillaceous wackestones, and packstones. Coarse-grained material comprises only a few percent of the sediment and generally consists of shells that are seldom broken or abraded. Bedding in the sediments is of thin clay and silt layers and shell bands, and large-scale sedimentary structures are normally lacking. Some beds have mud cracks, and one shows possible salt-crystal casts.

The fine-grain size of the sediment indicates lack of waves and infrequent currents, and the mud cracks indicate exposure to air. The occurrence of the *Meekospira* Community in sediments containing some evaporite minerals suggests hypersaline water. All of the species in the community are eurytopic, indicating variable salinity. The depositional environment indicated by these factors is one of restricted bays or lagoons or mud flats in the intertidal to supratidal zone.

EUPHEMITID COMMUNITY

The Euphemitid Community is the most commonly occurring nearshore community. About twenty-five species occur consistently in the community of which generally only ten are abundant in any one sample. A large number of species occur in small numbers and in relatively few samples (Table 9-2). Most of these taxa and all of the dominant ones are molluscs. The most characteristic taxa are the gastropods *Euphemitopsis subpapillosa* (White, 1876) and *Leptomphalus arcturus* Yancey (1969), the bivalves *Polidevcia obesa* (White, 1879) and *Nuculavus levatiformis* (Walcott, 1874), and the scaphopod *Prodentalium canna* (White, 1874). *E. subpapillosa* is so abundant in the upper Arcturus Group that early workers referred to these strata as the "*Bellerophon* beds". Oyster-like patches of *Pseudomonotis* are present in places, and patches of the phylloid calcareous algae *Ivanovia* and *Eugonophyllum* are also present. Several species of micromolluscs are known only from this community. Ophiuroid starfish, collected by us and by Mayou (1967), also occur in the community, and pentacrinoids are often present. In addition, annelids (*Spirorbis*) and ostracodes are uncommon to common.

Samples of the Euphemitid Community usually have three to five very common taxa that account for a majority of the sample, but these three to five taxa vary among about ten different species, so a species dominant in one sample may be uncommon in another. This probably is due to the combined effects of clustering of species in one area within the community limits and to limited transport after death. The oyster-like clusters of *Pseudomonotis* are an example of this clustering. Grouping the clusters together leads to a broadly defined community, but it does not seem useful to describe as communities assemblages of fossils that are most readily interpreted as clusters of species occurring in the same general environment. Stanton and Evans (1972) and Peterson (1976) have discussed the problem of sampling when clustering is present and show that clustering occurs commonly in modern communities.

For this reason, the Euphemitid Community is defined broadly enough to include the Nuculanid Community and to partly include the *Heteralosia* Community of Stevens (1966). These assemblages have the same general range of composition and differ primarily in dominance

Table 9-2
Abundances of taxa in randomly selected samples of the Euphemitid Community. Counts show numbers of individuals in each sample.

	Localities								
	D-5516	D-5526	D-5544	D-5554	D-5557	D-5590	D-5591	D-5602	D-5613
Algae									
Ivanovia	–	–	–	1	20	–	–	1	–
Eugonophyllum	–	–	–	–	–	100	–	–	–
Sponges	–	–	1	–	–	–	–	–	–
Bryozoa									
encrusting forms	–	1	16	1	–	–	–	–	–
Brachiopods									
Lingula	–	–	–	–	–	–	10	–	–
Costellarina	10	–	–	–	–	–	–	–	–
Molluscs									
Polidevcia	300	170	1	40	50	–	3	50	30
Nuculavus	70	23	8	2000	5000	55	750	25	30
Promytilus	–	–	–	–	1	–	–	–	–
Myalina	–	–	–	1	–	–	–	–	–
Dunbarella	–	–	–	–	–	–	–	1	–
Pseudomonotis	1	–	–	45	250	2	1	2	–
Schizodus	100	70	2	70	40	–	200	10	5
Bakevellia	7	3	4	–	–	–	1	–	–
Parallelodon	–	–	–	–	4	–	–	–	–
Permophorus	–	1	1	100	250	–	–	1	2
Allorisma	–	–	–	–	1	–	–	–	–
Aviculopinna	–	–	–	–	–	–	–	1	–
Sanguinolites	–	–	–	–	–	–	1	–	–
Bellerophon	9	2	–	8	1	–	–	10	10
Euphemites	–	–	–	2	1	–	1	–	–
Euphemitopsis	150	65	20	1500	400	4	200	40	50
Leptomphalus	70	10	2	1000	500	120	500	30	30
Glabrocingulum	–	–	–	–	–	–	–	40	25
Ananias	–	–	–	12	1	–	–	–	–
Goniasma	–	5	3	350	750	90	30	50	20
Naticopsis	4	2	1	11	3	9	20	–	–
Strianematina	–	–	–	20	100	–	–	–	–
Meekospira	65	40	–	8	1	1	75	20	5
Soleniscus	–	–	–	8	–	–	–	–	–
Subulites	–	–	–	–	180	10	–	–	–
Prodentalium	50	15	10	100	20	–	30	30	15
Pseudorthoceras	–	5	1	2	–	–	–	–	–
Metacoceras	1	1	–	–	–	–	–	–	–
Annelids									
Spirorbis	1	1	75	60	100	13	30	–	–
Ostracodes	100	50	1	3	–	–	500	400	500
Echinoderms									
pentacrinoids	–	–	–	20	10	6	1	10	2
ophiuroids	–	–	10	–	–	–	–	–	–

of the common species. The species and enclosing rocks indicate deposition in the same environmental setting. The free-living productoid *Costellarina* (=*Heteralosia* of the *Heteralosia* Community) is particularly prone to clustering, as are most other free-living productoids, and clusters of this genus occur in at least three other nearshore communities. As originally envisioned, the *Heteralosia* assemblage was a more open-marine environment than the Euphemitid Community, but it is not easily definable as a community.

The rocks containing this community are calcareous mudstones and siltstones and wackestones with a high proportion of clay and noncalcareous silt. Occasionally the community occurs in coarser-grained muddy sandstone or packstone. The sediment generally is thin bedded and occasionally laminated. Clay layers produce many partings, so the rocks tend to weather into thin slabs. Shells commonly are concentrated into layers, but they show little evidence of breakage or wear. Bivalves commonly occur with both valves attached and spread into a butterfly position. Very low-angle cross-laminae and small-scale scour structures are present.

The occurrence of pentacrinoids [but not ophiuroids, which may be salinity tolerant (Parker, 1960)] suggests that water salinity was near normal or normal marine most of the time, but the overall scarcity of salinity-sensitive groups such as brachiopods and echinoderms indicates that the water salinity was variable. The pentacrinoids occur in most samples of the community and are often complete, suggesting that they were adapted to the environment and not transported into the community by chance. This is further supported by their relative scarcity in other communities. The high content of clay and noncalcareous silt in the sediment implies rapid sedimentation of land-derived muds, and the sedimentary structures indicate low-energy conditions with persistent tidal currents but little influence of waves. These factors suggest the development of this community in conditions of rapid sediment deposition in the subtidal to lower-intertidal zone of large bays or sounds. The community was subject to tidal currents, and variable, but near normal salinity conditions.

ASTARTELLA COMMUNITY

The *Astartella* Community is recognized by its high diversity of molluscan species and by the abundance of the characteristic genera *Nuculavus*, *Astartella*, *Bellerophon*, and *Glyptospira* (Table 9-3). Most species in the community are small (several mm to 1 cm), and of the seventy species recovered, fifty are molluscan. This is the highest diversity of molluscs present in any of the communities.

Among the molluscan species, bivalves are nearly as abundant as gastropods. Dominant genera include the bivalves *Nuculavus*, *Streblochondria*, *Acanthopecten*, *Bakevellia*, and *Astartella*; the gastropods *Bellerophon*, *Anomphalus*, *Platyworthenia*, *Yunnania*, *Apachella*, *Glyptospira*, and *Goniasma*; and scaphopod *Prodentalium*. The productoid brachiopod *Costellarina* is occasionally one of the dominants. Apart from molluscs, there are sponges, bryozoans, brachiopods, ostracodes, trilobites, and echinoderms present. Brachiopods are taxonomically varied, but usually uncommon.

The enclosing rock consists of wackestone or packstone that was a sediment of mud or muddy sand containing a small to moderate amount of clay and noncalcareous silt. Commonly, the limestone beds are separated by thin, clayey shale partings and are interbedded with noncarbonate strata. The coarse component of the sediment consists

Table 9-3
Abundances of taxa in randomly selected samples of the *Astartella* Community. Counts show numbers of individuals in each sample.

	Localities							
	D-5539	D-5546	D-5550	D-5555	D-5586	D-5621	D-5626	D-5627
Foraminifera								
Pseudoreichelina	75	–	–	–	–	--	–	–
Sponges								
demosponge	1	2	–	–	–	–	1	–
Dactyletes	–	–	–	–	–	–	2	–
Bryozoa								
encrusting forms	5	4	–	–	–	–	–	–
ramose forms	1	–	–	–	–	25	10	10
fenestellid forms	15	10	4	1	1	2	1	–
Brachiopods								
Costellarina	75	14	12	5	5	–	–	–
Squamaria	–	–	1	–	1	–	8	15
Composita	7	2	1	–	–	3	3	2
Cleiothyridina	–	3	–	–	–	–	5	–
Wilberrya	–	2	–	2	–	–	–	–
Rhipidomella	–	–	5	–	–	–	–	–
Molluscs								
Polidevcia	9	3	1	–	–	–	–	20
Nuculavus	200	100	30	20	2	13	–	4
Myalina	–	–	–	–	–	–	3	–
Limipecten	2	–	–	2	–	5	–	–
Streblochondria	70	15	8	2	1	4	–	–
Acanthopecten	50	20	10	5	4	5	4	–
Pseudomonotis	2	2	1	–	1	13	1	1
Schizodus	4	1	–	–	–	–	–	10
Astartella	100	85	15	30	25	1	8	–
Parallelodon	40	45	16	15	3	–	15	–
Bakevellia	105	45	7	4	7	35	6	–
Permophorus	20	15	4	5	–	1	1	3
Aviculopinna	1	–	–	–	–	–	–	–
Sanguinolites	3	–	–	–	–	–	–	–
Bellerophon	100	50	20	13	3	2	–	20
Amphiscapha	50	15	4	1	1	2	–	–
Anomphalus	150	140	30	21	22	–	–	–
Glabrocingulum	80	65	25	8	2	–	–	–
Platyworthenia	250	175	60	30	9	–	–	–
Yunnania	150	45	25	15	17	–	–	10
Apachella	155	200	12	15	2	–	4	–
Glyptospira	300	400	100	90	125	–	–	–
Lamellispira	4	–	–	–	–	–	–	–
Worthenia	1	–	–	–	–	–	–	–
Goniasma	500	400	100	100	2	7	2	–
Trachydomia	1	–	–	–	–	–	–	–
Naticopsis	8	7	2	3	–	–	2	–
Paleostylus	65	55	15	4	–	–	–	–
Meekospira	20	–	2	1	–	–	–	–
Soleniscus	12	13	–	6	–	1	2	–
Oncochilus	2	1	–	–	–	–	–	–
undetermined	420	325	115	70	–	–	–	–

Table 9-3 (cont.)
Abundances of taxa in randomly selected sample of the *Astartella* Community. Counts show numbers of individuals in each sample.

	Localities							
	D-5539	D-5546	D-5550	D-5555	D-5586	D-5621	D-5626	D-5627
Molluscs (cont.)								
Prodentalium	175	150	20	15	12	6	3	5
Pseudorthoceras	3	3	-	-	1	-	-	-
Metacoceras	1	-	1	-	2	-	-	1
Helminthochiton	2	-	-	-	-	-	-	-
Annelids								
Spirorbis	3	-	-	-	-	2	6	-
Arthropods								
Bekena	1	1	-	-	-	-	-	-
Knightina	-	-	-	-	-	-	1	-
Anisopyge	15	12	2	-	1	1	-	-
Echinoderms								
crinoids	2	-	-	1	2	-	-	2
echinoids	2	1	1	1	6	-	-	-

of shell material, some of which is broken and abraded. In some samples, abraded, well-rounded shell fragments are present, which strongly suggests that wave action was important. Rounding of shell material requires oscillatory water movement such as that supplied by waves. The high diversity of taxa in the community and the presence of brachiopods and echinoderms indicates fully normal salinity. The *Astartella* Community is believed to have inhabited the intertidal zone and the shallow-subtidal zone within wave base in areas of extensive sandflats or mixed sand and mudflats.

COMPARISON OF THE NEARSHORE COMMUNITIES

The nearshore communities differ in their dominant genera and show an increase in diversity, proportion of nonmolluscan taxa, and numbers of stenohaline taxa from the *Meekospira* to Euphemitid to *Astartella* communities (Table 9-4, Figure 9-2). In addition, individuals of the *Meekospira* Community are never as abundant as those of the Euphemitid or *Astartella* communities, which occur in the hundreds in typical samples.

All of the taxa found in the *Meekospira* Community are eurytopic, and are found in other communities in both normal-marine and hypersaline environments. The genera *Schizodus* and *Meekospira* are especially common in the *Meekospira* Community and seem to be preferentially adapted for high-salinity or highly variable environments. The Euphemitid Community has two dominant genera rarely found outside that community: *Euphemitopsis* and *Leptomphalus*. They are reliable indicators of the community. *Polidevcia* is much more abundant in this community than any other, but is not a reliable indicator whereas the other common taxa in the community are found frequently in several communities. Phylloid calcareous algae and pentacrinoids occur preferentially in this community, and the pentacrinoids, with their easily recognized star-shaped columnals, are very characteristic. These crinoids are often complete, suggesting that they were

Table 9-4
Comparison of components of the *Meekospira*, Euphemitid, and *Astartella* communities; taxa arranged in order of dominance in each community. Dominance is judged subjectively as a function of abundance and size of individuals. Nonmolluscan taxa are marked with an asterisk (*).

Meekospira Community	Euphemitid Community	*Astartella* Community
Meekospira	*Euphemitopsis*	*Glyptospira*
Bakevellia	*Leptomphalus*	*Goniasma*
Schizodus	*Polidevcia*	*Prodentalium*
Goniasma	*Nuculavus*	*Bellerophon*
Yunnania	*Schizodus*	*Platyworthenia*
Leptomphalus	*Prodentalium*	*Nuculavus*
Naticopsis	*Goniasma*	*Astartella*
Permophorus	*Meekospira*	*Apachella*
Platyworthenia	*Pseudomonotis*	*Bakevellia*
	Bellerophon	*Parallelodon*
	Permophorus	*Streblochondria*
	pentacrinoid*	*Acanthopecten*
	*Bekena**	*Anomphalus*
	Naticopsis	*Yunnania*
	Bakevellia	ramose bryozoa*
	Pseudorthoceras	fenestellids*
	Metacoceras	*Squamaria**
	*Ivanovia**	*Pseudorthoceras*
	*Eugonophyllum**	echinoids*
	*Spirorbis**	*Permophorus*
		Amphiscapha
		Glabrocingulum
		Paleostylus
		*Composita**
		crinoids*
		Pseudomonotis
		*Anisopyge**
		Metacoceras
		*Cleiothyridina**
		encrusting bryozoa*
		Polidevcia
		Meekospira
		Soleniscus
		*Rhipidomella**
		*Wilberrya**

adapted to the environment. The *Astartella* Community has about ten very abundant taxa of which *Glyptospira* and *Astartella* are especially characteristic but not restricted to the community. *Bellerophon*, *Apachella*, and *Prodentalium* are also most common in this community, but are more wide ranging than *Glyptospira* and *Astartella*. A variety of stenotopic brachiopods and echinoderms occur in this community and are always present.

Molluscan Community	Diversity	Stenotopic Taxa	Overlapping Genera	Distinctive Features
<u>Meekospira</u>	low (6)	none	<u>Meekospira</u> <u>Bakevellia</u>	mudcracks low diversity
Euphemitid	moderate (25)	few	<u>Polidevcia</u>	euphemitids <u>Leptomphalus</u>
<u>Astartella</u>	high (50)	many	<u>Bakevellia</u>	high diversity
NON-MOLLUSCAN SHELF COMMUNITIES				
<u>Anthraconeilo</u>	moderate (15)	moderate	<u>Meekospira</u> <u>Polidevcia</u>	ammonites calc. mud
				Offshore ↓

Figure 9-2
Comparison of selected characteristics of Early Permian molluscan communities.

OPEN-SHELF COMMUNITIES

DICTYOCLOSTID-COMPOSITA COMMUNITY

This is a moderately diverse community, rather variable in composition, and characterized by common free-living productoid brachiopods. Taxa that occur consistently in the community are a variety of encrusting, branching, and fenestellid bryozoans, which are occasionally abundant enough to be dominants; the dictyoclostid productoid *Squamaria* (or *Costellarina*); the spiriferoid brachiopod *Composita*; crinoid and echinoid echinoderms; and the encrusting annelid worm tube *Spirorbis* (Table 9-5). Pelmatozoan echinoderms and echinoids are never as abundant as either the brachiopods or bryozoans, but seem to be an integral part of the community. Bivalve and gastropod molluscs occur uncommonly and are mostly small. The species present in different samples are seldom the same, so there is a moderate diversity of accessory molluscan species in the community. Encrusting organisms, including sponges, bryozoans, and *Spirorbis*, are common in many samples, especially as encrustations on brachiopod and echinoid spines. Ostracodes and fusulinids seldom occur in the community.

Significant variations in the composition of the Dictyoclostid-*Composita* Community occur in the dominance of brachiopods versus bryozoans, in the species of productoid brachiopods present, and in the proportion of molluscan taxa. Free-living productoid brachiopods

Table 9-5
Abundances of taxa in randomly selected samples of the Dictyoclostid-*Composita* Community. Counts show numbers of individuals in each sample.

	Localities				
	D-5614	D-5615	D-5617	D-5575	D-5540
Sponges					
Dactyletes	1	–	2	–	–
Corals					
solitary rugose	–	–	–	–	14
Syringopora	–	–	–	–	4
Pleurodictyum	1	–	–	–	–
Bryozoa					
encrusting forms	–	–	–	1	20
ramose forms	2	15	20	–	30
fenestellid forms	2	–	5	–	25
Brachiopods					
Meekella	–	–	–	–	6
Squamaria	6	3	10	–	15
Costellarina	–	–	–	100	–
Composita	7	6	8	–	75
Cleiothyridina	–	1	–	–	–
Dielasma	–	–	1	–	–
Wellerella	–	–	5	–	4
Molluscs					
Nuculavus	–	–	–	–	1
Aviculopecten	–	1	–	–	–
Limipecten	–	1	–	1	4
Acanthopecten	–	–	2	–	1
Pseudomonotis	1	4	7	–	1
Bakevellia	–	–	–	3	–
Astartella	2	2	–	–	–
Aviculopinna	1	–	–	–	1
Bellerophon	8	–	–	–	–
Omphalotrochus	–	–	–	–	1
Platyworthenia	–	–	–	–	1
Yunnania	2	–	–	–	–
Lamellispira	–	–	–	4	–
Goniasma	1	2	–	–	–
Naticopsis	1	–	–	–	–
Prodentalium	–	–	1	–	–
Annelids					
Spirorbis	–	5	8	20	–
Ostracodes	–	–	1	1	–
Echinoderms					
crinoids	1	–	1	–	15
echinoids	–	–	–	–	5
ophiuroids	–	–	–	–	1

and erect bryozoans commonly occur together. Productoids are usually dominant in our samples although bryozoan-dominated assemblages occur uncommonly in the northern part of the seaway. In places outside the study area, bryozoan-dominated assemblages appear to be part of a community distinct from the Dictyoclostid-*Composita* Community.

In the Dictyoclostid-*Composita* Community, either *Squamaria* or *Costellarina* may occur as the dominant productoid, but *Squamaria* is far more common than *Costellarina*. *Costellarina* occurs more commonly in mollusc-dominated nearshore communities. Although common in some samples, molluscs are not an essential part of the Dictyoclostid-*Composita* Community, and higher molluscan abundances indicate transition to mollusc-dominated communities.

The enclosing rocks of the community have a wide range of grain size and sediment type: from fine-grained mudstone or siltstone to coarse sandstone, and from wackestone to packstone. Occurrences on the west side of the seaway tend to be in limestones and sandstones and occasionally in coarse pebble-bearing sediment, whereas occurrences on the east side of the seaway tend to be in finer-grained sediments with large clasts consisting entirely of shell material. There seldom are any sedimentary structures preserved in the sediment due to bioturbation, and even small-scale bedding is rare. The productoids seldom show breakage and commonly are preserved in life position, indicating predominantly low-energy conditions (although their occurrence in coarser sediments suggests a tolerance for higher-energy conditions as well). The relatively large size of the productoids, as well as their semiburied life habits, would enable them to survive occasional high-energy conditions of a variable-energy environment.

The consistent occurrence of brachiopods and echinoderms indicates normal-salinity waters, and the scarcity of corals and fusulinids is probably due to the sediment intolerance of those groups. These characteristics indicate an environment of low energy or variable energy in the subtidal zone without sustained wave action (but not excluding tidal currents), and waters of normal-marine salinity. The community occurs adjacent to mollusc-dominated nearshore communities of the shore zone, and it was the most nearshore of the open-shelf communities. All of the groups present in the community were probably moderately tolerant of shifting or depositing sediment, but not as tolerant as members of the mollusc-dominated nearshore communities.

COLONIAL TETRACORAL COMMUNITY

This community is characterized by the presence of large colonial tetracorals, which occur as separate coral heads and not as intergrown masses. The corals of this community are fasciculate with widely spaced corallites, and the other fossil remains occur in direct association with the coral heads (Table 9-6). Pelmatozoan echinoderms are the second most common group after the corals and occur in roughly one-half of the samples. Foraminifera are the next most common: endothyraceans occur in about one-half of the samples (Palaeotextulariids are rare), *Tuberitina* occurs in small numbers in about one-quarter of the samples, and fusulinids occur rarely in less than one-quarter of the samples. The alga (?) *Tubiphytes* occurs encrusting corals in more than one-third of the samples, and phylloid calcareous algae are rare. Bryozoans, productoid brachiopods, and echinoids are uncommon; and molluscs and ostracodes are rare. The large gastropod *Omphalotrochus* occurs in association with corals in a few samples and is a distinctive, but uncommon, component of the community.

Table 9-6
Abundances of accessory taxa occurring with fasciculate tetracorals in randomly selected samples of the Colonial Tetracoral Community. Corals are the dominant group in each sample although not tabulated separately. Numbers refer to scale of abundance: (1) rare, (2) few, (3) uncommon, (4) common, and (5) abundant.

	Localities									
	502	523	535	545	562	575	591	597	616	634
Tubiphytes	2	–	2	–	2	2	–	–	–	2
endothyraceans	4	–	–	1	–	1	–	1	4	–
Tuberitina	–	1	–	–	–	–	1	1	–	–
fusulinids	–	1	–	–	–	–	–	–	3	–
nodosariids	–	–	–	1	–	–	–	–	–	–
bryozoa	–	–	–	–	–	–	–	–	–	1
productoid brachiopods	–	–	–	1	–	–	–	–	–	3
molluscs	–	–	–	–	–	–	–	–	–	3
ostracodes	–	–	–	–	–	–	–	–	–	3
pelmatozoan columnals	4	3	5	–	–	1	5	4	–	–

The enclosing rock almost always consists of packstone or grainstone, and packstone is slightly more common than grainstone. At some localities the coral heads are overturned, and at other localities coral fragments are aligned parallel to one another. These characters suggest periodic high-energy conditions. The presence of common corals and echinoderms indicates normal-marine salinity.

The description of the coral community given here is based on thin section study of sediment containing the corals, commonly in the interspaces between the corallites of the coral head. Some of the differences between this description and that of Stevens (1966) is probably because the majority of the corals reported in the earlier study had cerioid form rather than the fasciculate form encountered in the present study, and perhaps adapted to slightly different environmental conditions. However, both coral types are part of the same coral community.

FUSULINID COMMUNITY

The Fusulinid Community is characterized by an abundance of fusulinids and a moderate to low diversity of other fossils (Table 9-7). In thin sections from thirty-four samples of this community, fusulinids occur in numbers ranging from 7 to $18/cm^2$ and average $9.5/cm^2$. Miscellaneous endothyraceans occur in two-thirds of the samples, but average less than $1.5/cm^2$. Palaeotextulariid foraminifers occur in two-thirds of the samples, but these average less than $1/cm^2$. The foraminifer *Tuberitina* occurs in about one-third of the samples and ranges in abundance from rare to as many as $11/cm^2$. All samples contain pelmatozoan columnals, which average about $5/cm^2$. About half of the samples contain portions (mostly spines) of productoid brachiopods, but in thin section these occur in densities of only about $1/cm^2$. Bryozoans and echinoids occur in about one-third of the samples, but are rare.

Table 9-8
Abundances of taxa in randomly selected samples of the Palaeotextulariid Community. Counts show average numbers of individuals per square centimeter in thin-section slices.

	Localities									
	3N7	3N11	1P18	1R1	1R16	1R18-1	1R18-2	1R24	1R26	1U12
endothyraceans	5	-	11	4	4	-	-	4	1	½
Tuberitina	-	-	-	11	4	-	-	8	-	-
palaeotextulariids	4	5	6	4	6	5	4	4	4	4
fusulinids	12	1	2½	6	1	6	5	4	5	5
bryozoa	½	½	-	-	-	-	1	-	-	-
productoid brachiopods	-	-	-	-	½	-	-	-	5	-
pelmatozoan columnals	12	4	5	2	7	21	16	10	13	1
echinoids	½	-	-	-	½	-	-	-	-	-

COMPARISON OF THE FUSULINID AND PALAEOTEXTULARIID COMMUNITIES

The biotic composition of the Fusulinid and Palaeotextulariid communities differs considerably. The Fusulinid Community contains larger numbers of fusulinids, bryozoans, productoid brachiopods, and echinoids and far fewer foraminiferans than the Palaeotextulariid Community (Table 9-9). However, the differences are those of proportion, and the two communities contain the same basic groups of fossils.

Table 9-9
Comparison of the Fusulinid and Palaeotextulariid Communities (measured in average numbers of individuals per square centimeter in thin sections).

	Fusulinid Community	Palaeotextulariid Community
endothyraceans	1.5	4
Tuberitina	½	2
palaeotextulariids	½	5
fusulinids	9.5	3
bryozoa	uncommon	rare
productoid brachiopods	1	rare
pelmatozoan columnals	5	10
echinoids	uncommon	rare

In a study of 159 thin-section samples containing fusulinids and/or palaeotextulariids from the Early Permian calcareous rocks in eastern Nevada and western Utah, after excluding 27 samples that showed evidence of transport, only 30 percent of the remaining 132 samples could be definitely placed in one of the two communities. Of the 159 samples containing one or more fusulinids, 87 also contained one or more palaeotextulariids, and all of the samples with palaeotextulariids also contained fusulinids. Bias in favor of collecting samples with the more conspicuous fusulinids is possible, but is probably a minor factor. The degree of overlap between the two assemblages and the difficulty of placing many foraminiferal samples into either of the two communities suggests that the limits proposed by Stevens (1966) are too strict, but until a natural break is discovered, we will continue to employ these definitions of the communities.

ANTHRACONEILO COMMUNITY

This community occupied the deepest part of the seaway and is dominated by molluscs (Table 9-10). Characteristic taxa in the community are the bivalves *Nuculopsis girtyi* Schenck (1934), *Quadratonucula stella* Yancey (1978), *Polidevcia bellistriata* (Stevens, 1858), *Girtyana stellara* Yancey (1978), *Anthraconeilo mcchesneyana* (Girty, 1910) (all nuculoids), *Streblochondria montpelierensis*

Table 9-10
Abundances of taxa in randomly selected samples of the *Anthraconeilo* Community. Counts show numbers of individuals in each sample. Most microfossil groups are not included in this tabulation.

	Localities					
	1J2	1J6	1K5	1K8	1X8	D-5644
Foraminifera						
palaeotextulariids	–	–	–	–	–	20
nodosariids	–	–	–	–	50	–
Brachiopods						
Rhipidomella	–	–	–	–	2	–
Lissochonetes	–	–	–	–	–	1
Echinauris	–	–	–	–	–	2
Composita	–	–	–	–	–	4
unidentifieds	–	6	–	–	3	–
Molluscs						
Clinopistha	1	–	–	–	–	–
Nuculopsis	5	4	1	1	2	15
Quadratonucula	18	–	–	–	–	–
Anthraconeilo	–	1	3	5	20	8
Polidevcia	1	8	1	5	3	7
Girtyana	8	–	–	–	–	–
Streblochondria	10	5	–	2	5	1
Limipecten	1	–	–	–	–	–
Schizodus	–	4	–	1	–	–
"*Edmondia*"	10	4	–	22	1	–
Prothyris	1	–	–	–	–	–
Oriocrassatella	–	–	–	–	1	–
Worthenia	4	1	–	4	–	–
Euconospira	2	4	–	–	–	–
Meekospira	–	–	11	–	–	–
Calstevenus	25	2	–	5	1	–
Medlicottia	15	–	–	–	–	9
Pterochiton	1	–	–	–	–	–
Ostracodes	–	–	–	25	–	–

(Girty, 1910), and "*Edmondia*"; the gastropods *Worthenia* and *Meekospira*; the siphonodentaliid scaphopod *Calstevenus arcturus* Yancey (1973); and the ammonoid *Medlicottia*. Brachiopods are uncommon and include *Lingula*, *Orbiculoidea*, several chonetoids, and unidentified smooth types. Nodosariid foraminiferans, radiolaria, siliceous sponge spicules, and ostracodes are uncommon to common, and conodonts are also common(D. Clark, pers. comm.). These fossils are virtually restricted in distribution to rocks containing the *Anthraconeilo* Community. Although there are some genera that also occur in shallow-water communities (*Polidevcia*, *Streblochondria*, *Meekospira*), there are no species in common between the shallow-water and deep-water molluscan communities.

The rocks containing this community are light-colored (yellowish brown to medium brown), fine-grained, argillaceous and silty limestones (with insoluble residues of 20 to 40 percent) or calcareous siltstones. Sand-size grains rarely exceed a few percent of the sediment. The rock is quite uniform in character and shows little bedding except for roughly aligned shell material. Many of the species have thin shells, and shell material is sometimes broken, but not abraded or rounded. Many samples show sediment compaction, indicating high clay content in the sediment.

This community and its containing sediments have several indicators of deep-water deposition, especially among the biota. The total taxonomic difference from shallow-water species, the presence of radiolaria, siliceous sponge spicules, conodonts, ammonoids, and siphonodentaliid scaphopods all imply deep, quiet-water deposition. The presence of planktic radiolaria and nektic ammonoids is especially good evidence because these groups normally occur in deep-water areas of open oceans. The thin-shelled character of many species, such as *Streblochondria* and "*Edmondia*", is another indicator. The uniform fine-grain size of the sediment also suggests deposition in quiet waters typical of deep-water areas. It is probable that deposition was within 200 m of sea level. The uniform light coloration of the sediments indicates that the sediments and the overlying water masses were well oxygenated.

ENVIRONMENTAL CONTROLS ON THE COMMUNITIES

The most important controls on the communities were salinity and energy levels of the waters, and different series of communities developed along the salinity gradient and the energy-level gradient (Figure 9-3). Another factor that appears to have been important is the sediment tolerance of the species, which in general relates to the turbidity of the waters and the clay content of the sediment. This was a major factor in the development of the Dictyoclostid-*Composita* Community, which probably had a moderate sediment tolerance. Other factors were not significant and either developed in response to the primary controls, such as sediment grain size controlled by energy level, or were masked by them.

Marginal-marine communities developed primarily along a salinity gradient, corresponding to increasingly open-marine conditions from restricted bay to open-ocean. This was also a variability gradient as well. The low taxonomic diversity of the *Meekospira* Community and lack of stenotopic taxa suggest that salinity and temperature were highly variable and that this community occupied the most restricted

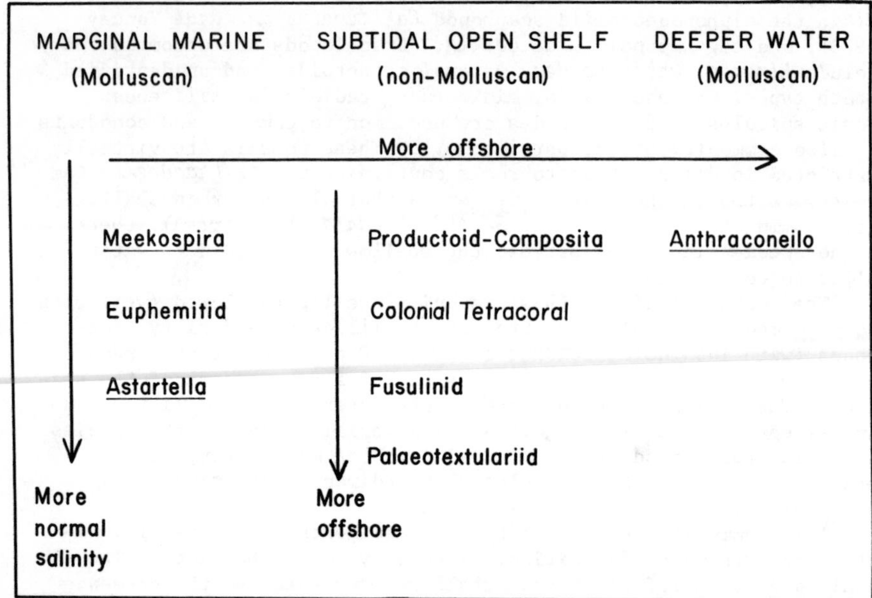

Figure 9-3
Environmental relationships of Early Permian communities.

and most-variable salinity conditions. The occurrence of the community in strata containing desiccation cracks and association with strata containing molds of evaporite minerals in a few cases suggests that at least some occurrences were in hypersaline environments. These conditions would include a range of occurrences from the high intertidal zone, and possibly supratidal zone, down into the subtidal portions of restricted lagoons and bays. This is the only described community that could have inhabited the high intertidal or supratidal zone.

The Euphemitid Community contains a moderate diversity of organisms including some that may be partly stenotopic: the productoid *Costellarina*, ophiuroids, and pentacrinoids. Modern ophiuroids can occur in lagoonal environments with waters of variable salinity (Parker, 1960) and are not always stenotopic; *Costellarina* is an uncommon component of the community and appears to have been unusually tolerant of marginal-marine conditions for an articulate brachiopod. The pentacrinoid, with its easily recognizable star-shaped columnals, is a common member of the community and is the most stenotopic taxon present. Although it may have been washed in, its consistent occurrence there and its scarcity in other communities suggests that it was adapted to the environment of the community. These indicators suggest that the Euphemitid Community lived in an environment of near-normal salinity, but probably experienced common variations in salinity. The sediments containing the community have indicators of current action, but not of wave action, and are predominantly fine grained with some coarse-grained material. The biota and sediments suggest an environment of semiprotected shallow bays, sounds, or straits occurring in the mid-intertidal to subtidal depths.

Table 9-7
Abundances of taxa in randomly selected samples of the Fusulinid Community. Counts show average numbers of individuals per square centimeter in thin section slices.

	Localities									
	3I1	1N17	3N22	307	1P8	1P29	1R17	1R27	1U13	2Z2
endothyraceans	1	1	-	7	3	3	2	½	½	-
Tuberitina	-	-	-	½	-	-	-	-	-	-
palaeotextulariids	-	½	1	1	1	1	1	½	½	2
fusulinids	7	9	7	7	10	8	9	16	7	7
bryozoa	-	-	-	½	½	-	-	1	-	1
productoid brachiopods	-	2	-	1	4	-	-	1	-	1
ostracodes	½	-	-	-	-	-	-	-	-	-
pelmatozoan columnals	2	3	5	12	4	½	2	5	½	½
echinoids	-	-	1	1	½	½	-	-	-	1

The enclosing rock consists of packstone and sandy packstone, grainstone, calcareous sandstone, and siltstone, and occasionally consists of micrite. Many sediments contain a significant component of sand grains suggesting that fusulinids preferred a granular substratum similar to the preference of modern large foraminiferans for firm substrates. This indicates a moderate-energy environment.

Ross (1963) and Ozawa (1970) conclude that as a group, fusulinids occupied a wide range of environments, and the test morphology of fusulinids roughly corresponds with major environments. Nearly all of the fusulinids in the study area have the same subventricose shape and occur in nearly the same environmental setting. This leads to the conclusion that they lived in a single community and therefore, in only a portion of the environmental range occupied by fusulinids in other regions.

PALAEOTEXTULARIID COMMUNITY

The Palaeotextulariid Community is characterized by large numbers of palaeotextulariid and other foraminiferans, common pelmatozoan columnals, and low abundances of other fossils (Table 9-8). Palaeotextulariid abundances average about 5/cm^2, and fusulinids are almost always present in abundances averaging about 3/cm^2. The small foraminiferan *Tuberitina* is present in large numbers in some samples and averages 2/cm^2, whereas miscellaneous other endothyraceans average 4/cm^2. Pelmatozoan columnals generally are abundant, almost always occurring in greater numbers than the palaeotextulariids, but not in sufficient volume to be the major rock constituent. Bryozoans, productoid brachiopods, and echinoids occur in small numbers in some samples.

The rock containing this community consists of wackestone, packstone or grainstone, and less commonly, calcareous siltstone. In some of the grainstones, the palaeotextulariid foraminiferans are associated with algal-coated grains and are believed to have been transported. The sediment is generally fine grained, indicating a low-energy environment.

The *Astartella* Community has high taxonomic diversity and a moderate number of stenotopic taxa in it. These indicate an environment of essentially normal salinity. The presence of broken and rounded shell fragments indicates some occurrences within the wave zone and a position within the mid-intertidal to shallow-subtidal zone. This is a higher-energy environment than that of the Euphemitid Community, but in a more open-marine, less-variable area. It is sedimentologically and biotically similar to the lower-intertidal zone environment described by Thompson (1968) for the head of the Gulf of California (pers. observ.), which is typical of areas with moderate to high rates of sedimentation. Although the salinity conditions and open-ocean character of the *Astartella* Community differ from that of the Euphemitid Community, it may have occupied the same depth zone.

The open-shelf communities generally occur in a sequence of Dictyoclostid-*Composita*, Colonial Tetracoral, Fusulinid, and Palaeotextulariid communities from nearshore to offshore, and all of them contain many stenohaline taxa and must have lived in fully normal-marine salinity. The Dictyoclostid-*Composita* Community lived in close association with the marginal-marine communities and, in part, occupied nearshore or shoreline environments. The community lived in a considerable range of conditions from low-energy environments with muddy substrates to moderately high-energy environments with sandy substrates. Occurrences of echinoid spines completely overgrown with bryozoans in the community in the Ely area on the east side of the seaway and of common productoids in pebble-bearing sandstone in the Diamond Mountains on the west side of the seaway indicate at least periodic high-energy conditions. It occurs in close association with some marginal-marine communities and appears to have inhabited similar substrates and energy conditions, but in part, occupied deeper waters than the marginal-marine communities.

The rarity of very stenotopic corals and fusulinids in this community and abundance of equally stenohaline groups like brachiopods and echinoderms is probably related to sediment tolerance of these groups. The dominant groups are moderately sediment tolerant, much more so than the corals and fusulinids. This places the Dictyoclostid-*Composita* Community on the middle of a sediment-tolerance gradient. The marginal-marine communities were highly sediment tolerant, and the other open-shelf communities were sediment intolerant. The placement of the Dictyoclostid-*Composita* Community is probably determined as much by the rate of sedimentation in an area as by the energy regime and substrate. It may occur in shoreline environments in some areas and in offshore, deeper environments in other areas.

The Colonial Tetracoral, Fusulinid, and Palaeotextulariid communities occupied a gradient of increasing depth and decreasing energy conditions, with the Colonial Tetracoral Community located in the shallowest waters. Other environmental factors (salinity, sedimentation, and so forth) appear to have been similar for these communities. The Colonial Tetracoral Community lived in a moderately high-energy environment, commonly with a sandy (grainstone) substrate. In some occurrences, corallites of fasciculate corals were broken apart and the pieces aligned by currents; and in some cases, both fasciculate- and cerioid-coral heads are tipped over on the substrate. This indicates periodic strong currents or wave action in relatively shallow water.

The Fusulinid Community occurs commonly in granular sediments (sandy packstones and grainstones) and less commonly in fine-grained sediments; it probably occurred in lower-energy environments than the Colonial Tetracoral Community. Most of the fusulinids have a subventricose shape, which usually correlates with moderate- to low-energy levels (Ross, 1963; Ozawa, 1970). The scarcity of globose and subcylindrical fusulinids, indicative of low-energy and high-energy environments respectively, suggests that the fusulinids inhabited only one general environment of the seaway. The occurrence of productoid brachiopods in some samples suggests energy conditions similar to those of the Dictyoclostid-*Composita* Community.

The Palaeotextulariid Community occurs in fine-grained sediments and inhabited the lowest-energy environment of any of the open-shelf communities. It differs from the Fusulinid Community mostly in containing a greater abundance of small foraminiferans, and it probably inhabited deeper water well below wave base.

The *Anthraconeilo* Community occurs in the center of the basin, seaward of the carbonate shelves that border the eastern and western margins of the seaway. It occupied a low-energy environment that is inferred to be deep water because of the presence of planktic and nektic fossils, presumed moderately deep-water trace fossils (Clark, 1974), and because of its occurrence in uniformly fine-grained sediments typical of deep-basinal environments. The light color of the sediments indicates fully oxygenated conditions at the sediment surface.

BATHYMETRY

The bathymetric sequence of communities is best seen in the distribution of the major groups of communities, which occupy regular bathymetric zones. The nearshore, mollusc-dominated group of communities occupied the littoral and very-shallow neritic zone, the non-molluscan group of communities occupied open-shelf areas in the neritic zone, and a mollusc-dominated community occupied the deepest water in the center of the seaway (Figure 9-1). These bathymetrically controlled groups are similar to, but more inclusive than, the benthic assemblages of Boucot (1975).

The marginal-marine communities occupy similar depth ranges. The *Meekospira* Community occupied the intertidal zone and may have occupied some of the shallow-subtidal and supratidal zone as well. It is the only described community that could have inhabited the high intertidal and supratidal zone, but its normal bathymetric position was probably in the intertidal zone. The Euphemitid and *Astartella* communities occupied the mid-intertidal to subtidal zone and probably had very similar bathymetric ranges. They occupied environments that differed primarily in energy level and salinity. The *Astartella* Community lived within the wave zone in shallow water.

The open-shelf communities often occur in a regular sequence supporting the conclusion of Stevens (1966) that from the shore seaward across the shelf, the community sequence is Dictyoclostid-*Composita*, Colonial Tetracoral, Fusulinid, and Palaeotextulariid. In general, this is a depth-controlled sequence with the Dictyoclostid-*Composita* Community occurring in shallow waters and the succeeding communities occurring in progressively deeper waters. However, it is still not certain if the Palaeotextulariid Community is primarily a deeper-water community than the Fusulinid Community or is simply a lower-energy environment community that commonly occurs in deeper water than the Fusulinid Community. The normal sequence of communities is modified in cases where a carbonate buildup formed at the outer edge of the shelf, which occurred during the Early Permian in northeastern Nevada, when the Colonial Tetracoral Community reappeared seaward of the Fusulinid and Palaeotextulariid communities.

The Dictyoclostid-*Composita* and Colonial Tetracoral communities both inhabited shallow waters, probably with the low intertidal as an upper limit, and ranged well down into the subtidal zone. The high-energy conditions inferred for some occurrences of these communities suggest predominantly shallow-water depths. Relatively shallow-water depths for the Colonial Tetracoral Community are suggested by comparison with the preferred distribution of modern colonial corals.

The depth range of the Fusulinid Community apparently overlaps that of the Colonial Tetracoral Community although absolute depths are difficult to determine. Stevens (1969) was able to show that the upper depth limit for this community in the Middle Pennsylvanian of Colorado was about 13 m, and we believe that this is a reasonable figure for the Permian fusulinids in Nevada. In the Moorman Ranch section on the outer part of the eastern shelf, fusulinid-bearing limestone occurs in very large crossbeds of which one set is 22 m thick. This crossbed set is overlain and underlain by fusulinid-bearing limestones. Assuming that the overlying limestones were deposited in water at least 13 m deep, the depth of water on which the fusulinids in the lower limestone lived is a least 35 m deep.

The Palaeotextulariid Community is similar in faunal composition to the Fusulinid Community, but occupied lower-energy environments. These could have overlapped the depth range of the Fusulinid Community extensively, but probably extended into deeper water as well.

The *Anthraconeilo* Community is considered to occur in deeper water than the shelf communities because of the dominance of fine-grained sediment, the geographic occurrence beyond the carbonate shelves that fringe both the eastern and western shores of the seaway (and presumably below the carbonate-producing depth range), occurrence of presumed moderately deep-water trace fossils (Clark, 1974), and presence of nektic ammonoids and planktic radiolaria, which are essentially restricted to this community. The water depth was at least 35 m on the outer shelf, and this is an approximate minimum water depth for the *Anthraconeilo* Community. Because of the lack of turbidites in the sequence, the slope into the central trough is presumed to have been shallow. If the slope were 0.5°, the depth of water in the center of the trough would have been about 120 m; if the slope were 1°, the depth would have been about 210 m.

SIGNIFICANCE OF THE ANTHRACONEILO COMMUNITY

The *Anthraconeilo* Community has the distinction of being possibly the oldest, deep-water, mollusc-dominated community described. During the Early Permian, mollusc-dominated communities occupied very-shallow and relatively deep-water environments and flanked typical nonmolluscan communities of the open-shelf areas. Benthic molluscs in these environments were not greatly different from Early Triassic molluscs and did not suffer the major extinctions seen in other groups at the end of the Permian. Major extinctions occurred primarily among stenotopic groups (fusulinids, corals, brachiopods) occupying the shallow-shelf environments. It seems likely that with the elimination of these groups at the end of the Permian, molluscs were able to spread immediately onto the shallow shelves where previously they had been at an adaptive disadvantage.

Both the shallow and deep-water environments could serve as reservoirs for repopulating the depleted shelf environments, and because the reservoir populations were largely molluscan, the subsequent post-Permian shelf communities were mollusc dominated. Molluscs were well placed for this expansion made possible by the disappearance of the other groups because they were already taxonomically diverse, ecologically diverse (benthic infaunal, benthic epifaunal, nektic) and included many species that were quite sediment tolerant. Their sediment tolerance appears to be a major factor in their establishing dominance in so many Permian communities, and it probably was a major advantage at the end of the Permian in helping them to survive into the Triassic without major extinctions. When major radiations of organisms occurred again in the Late Triassic, molluscs had already spread into all major environments and continued as the dominant benthic group thereafter.

REFERENCES

Bissell, H. J. 1962a. Pennsylvanian and Permian rocks of cordilleran area, in Branson, C. C., ed., *Pennsylvanian System in the United States - A Symposium*. Am. Assoc. Petroleum Geologists, pp. 188-263.

Bissell, H. J. 1962b. Permian rocks of parts of Nevada, Utah, and Idaho. *Geol. Soc. America Bull.* 73:1083-1110.

Bissell, H. J. 1964. Ely, Arcturus, and Park City groups (Pennsylvanian-Permian) in eastern Nevada and western Utah. *Am. Assoc. Petroleum Geologists Bull.* 48:565-636.

Bissell, H. J. 1967. Pennsylvanian and Permian basins in northwestern Utah, northeastern Nevada, and south-central Idaho: Discussion. *Am. Assoc. Petroleum Geologists Bull.* 51:791-802.

Bissell, H. J. 1970. Realms of Permian tectonism and sedimentation in western Utah and eastern Nevada. *Am. Assoc. Petroleum Geologists Bull.* 54:285-312.

Bissell, H. J. 1974. Tectonic control of Late Paleozoic and Early Mesozoic sedimentation near the hinge line of the Cordilleran Miogeosyncline belt. *Soc. Econ. Paleontologists & Mineralogists Spec. Pub.* 22:83-97.

Boucot, A. J. 1975. *Evolution and Extinction Rate Controls*. Amsterdam: Elsevier Scientific Publishing Co., 427 p.

Clark, D. L. 1974. Factors of Early Permian conodont paleoecology in Nevada. *Jour. Paleontology* 48:710-720.

Collinson, J. W. 1968. Permian and Triassic biostratigraphy of the Medicine Range, northeastern Nevada. *Wyoming Geol. Assoc. Earth Sci. Bull.* 1:25-44.

Easton, W. H. 1960. Permian corals from Nevada and California. *Jour. Paleontology* 34:570-583.

Fursich, F. T. 1977. Corallian (Upper Jurassic) marine benthic associations from England and Normandy. *Palaeontology* 20:337-385.

Marcantel, J. B. 1975. Late Pennsylvanian and Early Permian sedimentation in northeast Nevada. *Am. Assoc. Petroleum Geologists Bull.* 59:2079-2098.

Mayou, T. V. 1967. Paleontology of the Permian Loray Formation in White Pine County, Nevada. *Brigham Young Univ. Geology Studies* 14:101-122.

Ozawa, T. 1970. Notes on the phylogeny and classification of the superfamily Verbeekinoidea. *Kyushu Univ. Fac. Sci. Mem., Ser. D, Geology* 20:17-58.

Parker, R. H. 1960. Ecology and distributional patterns of marine macro-invertebrates, northern Gulf of Mexico, in Shepard, F. P., F. B. Phleger, and T. H. van Andel, eds. *Recent Sediments, Northwest Gulf of Mexico.* Tulsa: Am. Assoc. Petroleum Geologists, pp. 302-337.

Parker, R. H. 1975. *The Study of Benthic Communities; A Model and a Review.* Amsterdam: Elsevier Scientific Publishing Co., 279 p.

Peterson, C. J. 1976. Relative abundances of living and dead molluscs in two Californian lagoons. *Lethaia* 9:137-148.

Ross, C. A. 1963. *Standard Wolfcampian Series (Permian), Glass Mountains, Texas.* Geol. Soc. America Mem. 88, 205 p.

Scott, R. W., and R. R. West. 1976. *Structure and Classification of Paleocommunities.* Stroudsburg, Pa.: Dowden, Hutchinson & Ross, 291 p.

Stanton, R. J., Jr. 1976. Relationship of fossil communities to original communities of living organisms, in Scott, R. W., and R. R. West, eds. Stroudsburg, Pa.: Dowden, Hutchinson & Ross, pp. 107-142.

Stanton, R. J., Jr., and I. Evans. 1972. Community structure and sampling requirements in Paleoecology. *Jour. Paleontology* 46:845-858.

Steele, G. 1959. *Stratigraphic Interpretation of the Pennsylvanian-Permian Systems of the eastern Great Basin.* Ph.D. dissertation, University of Washington, 294 p.

Steele, G. 1960. Pennsylvanian-Permian stratigraphy of east-central Nevada and adjacent Utah, in *Geology of East-Central Nevada.* Intermtn. Assoc. Petroleum Geologists Field Conf. Guidebook, 11:91-113.

Stevens, C. H. 1965a. Pre-Kaibab Permian stratigraphy and history of the Butte Basin, Nevada and Utah. *Am. Assoc. Petroleum Geologists Bull.* 49:139-156.

Stevens, C. H. 1965b. Faunal trends in near-shore Pennsylvanian deposits near McCoy, Colorado. *Mtn. Geologist* 2:71-77.

Stevens, C. H. 1966. Paleoecologic implications of Early Permian fossil communities in eastern Nevada and western Utah. *Geol. Soc. America Bull.* 77:1121-1130.

Stevens, C. H. 1967. Leonardian (Permian) compound corals of Nevada. *Jour. Paleontology* 41:423-431.

Stevens, C. H. 1969. Water depth control of fusulinid distribution. *Lethaia* 2:121-132.

Stevens, C. H. 1977. Permian depositional provinces and tectonics, western United States, in Steward, J. H., C. H. Stevens, and A. E. Fritsche, eds., *Paleozoic Paleogeography of the Western United States.* Soc. Econ. Paleontologists & Mineralogists, pp. 113-135.

Stevens, C. H. 1979. Lower Permian of the central Cordilleran Miogeosyncline. *Geol. Soc. America Bull.*, Part II, 90:381-455.

Stevens, C. H., D. B. Wagner, and R. S. Sumsion.1979. Permian fusulinid biostratigraphy, central Cordilleran Miogeosyncline. *Jour. Paleontology* 53:29-36.

Thompson, R. W. 1968. *Tidal Flat Sedimentation on the Colorado River Delta, Northwestern Gulf of California.* Geol. Soc. America Mem. 107, 133 p.

Watkins, R. 1973. Carboniferous faunal associations and stratigraphy, Shasta County, Northern California. *Am. Assoc. Petroleum Geologists Bull.* 57:1743-1764.

Wilson, E. C., and R. L. Langenheim, Jr. 1962. Rugose and tabulate corals from Permian rocks in the Ely Quadrangle, White Pine County, Nevada. *Jour. Paleontology* 36:495-520.

Yancey, T. E. 1971. Biostratigraphy, paleoecology and paleontology of the Arcturus Group. Ph.D. Dissertation, University of California, Berkeley, 154 p.

Yancey, T. E., and C. H. Stevens 1977. Lower Permian communities in the western North American Miogeosyncline. *Jour. Paleontology* 51(supp.):33.

Zabriskie, W. E. 1970. Petrology and petrography of Permian carbonate rocks, Arcturus Basin, Nevada and Utah. *Brigham Young Univ. Geology Studies* 17:83-160.

10

Two New Approaches for Reconstructing Fossil Vegetation with Examples from the Triassic of Eastern Australia

Greg J. Retallack

ABSTRACT

A system of classification used by modern phytosociologists can be readily applied to fossil plant associations. A distinctive association name is formed from the name of a characteristic plant in its reference collection. The three-dimensional shape of this fossil plant association can be mapped in rocks, and its range in time, its preferred sedimentary environments, soil types, and likely habit are then open to interpretation. Also, paleosols may be classified using modern soil mapping units. Reconstruction of paleosols often gives a detailed idea of the local physico-chemical environment and the phytogeography of fossil plant associations and some indication of basin topography, tectonics, and paleoclimate. As an example of these new approaches, I reconstruct the environment of the Triassic rocks exposed in the sea cliffs north of Sydney, Australia. Here, Voltziopsetum coniferous forest on grey-brown podzolic (ferrod) soils was succeeded by Dicroidietum zuberi swamp woodland on humic gley (fibrist) soils with a relative rise in water table, which also formed large coastal lagoons. These were reclaimed by lobate deltas, fringed with Pleuromeietum meadows around inter-distributary bays, and supporting a Dicroidietum zuberi heath on gleyed podzolic (aquod and ochrept) and alluvial (aquent) soils. Higher within the sequence, grey clay (fluvent) soils of levees in the river floodplain supported a scrubby Taeniopteretum lentriculiformis. No paleosols have been found in the overlying sandstones deposited by braided streams, where the fossil flora is a moderately xerophytic Dicroidietum zuberi xylopterosum.

INTRODUCTION

A multidisciplinary approach is needed for the reconstruction of fossil vegetation. Such studies should consider sedimentary petrography and environments, paleocurrents, paleontology, palynology, and fossil soils as well as the mode of preservation, accumulation, associations, and systematic paleobotany of the fossil plant material. Two of these approaches, previously neglected, are of great value in giving a clear picture of ancient vegetation. These are ecostratigraphy and paleopedology. My preferred classification schemes for these relatively new stratigraphic categories are contrasted with those for other stratigraphic categories in Table 10-1.

ECOSTRATIGRAPHY

There are many approaches for classifying modern vegetation, for example, according to its physical structure, growth type, habitat, community ecology, internal layering or floristic composition (Whittaker, 1973). Of these approaches the classical system of Braun-Blanquet (1932) is still widely applied and most easily adapted for classifying fossil vegetation. According to this system, vegetation is classified into named associations, defined by their floristic composition.

Two schools of thought have run counter to the idea of recognizing and classifying associations. Some workers (such as Curtis and MacIntosh, 1951) observed that association boundaries may be so indistinct that they are impossible to map, and vegetation grades in a continuum from one type to another. Others (such as Johnson, 1972) maintained that "associations" are merely the accidental overlapping of various independent species ranges limited by different and complexly related parameters. Thus, each synecological situation is different and "associations" from different areas cannot be compared as if they were "quasi-organisms."

These objections have done little to undermine continued association analysis of modern vegetation. Fossil associations (Zeigler, et al., 1968) and paleobiogeographic provinces (Whittington and Hughes, 1972; Jell, 1974) have also been widely recognized. As a first order approximation of regional patterns, association analysis of fossil assemblages is most useful. Detailed ordination studies may show a different picture, but such studies are not always practical, particularly with megafossil plants. I believe that the naming, definition, classification, and interpretation of fossil associations should continue, although on a more standardized basis.

The naming system of phytosociologists can be used to derive unique and distinctive names for fossil associations and paleobiogeographic provinces. Association names are formed from the Latin name of a prominent species by addition of the suffix "-etum" to the stem of the genus name and, if more detailed distinction is necessary, by also adding the specific epithet in the genitive case (Braun-Blanquet, 1932). For example, the Dicroidietum odontopteroidium (unitalicized) is a fossil plant association characterized by *Dicroidium odontopteroides*. Associations can be subdivided into smaller units (synusiae) or classified within a hierarchy of larger units (alliances, orders, classes). The alliance (suffix "-ion") could be useful for naming paleobiogeographic provinces.

Fossil plant associations should be based on a type collection. Without such an objective basis, there can be no stability in association nomenclature. Thus, the fossil plant association is theoretically just such, rather than a reconstruction of past communities. It has the same relationship to a modern plant association as a fossil species to a living one or a paleosol to a soil. To express the concept of reconstructed ancient vegetation, I

Table 10.1
Units of various stratigraphic categories (partly after Hedberg, 1975).

Ecostratigraphy	Lithostratigraphy	Paleopedology
alliance	supergroup	association
association	group	series
synusia	subgroup	paleosol
	formation	variant/stage
	member	
	bed	

Geochronology	Chronostratigraphy	Biostratigraphy
eon	eonothem	biozones
era	erathem	e.g.
period	system	assemblage,
epoch	series	range, acme,
age	stage	& interval
chron	chronozone	zones.

have found it convenient to use the fossil association name, some indication of its likely habit, and the past tense. Such theoretically-loose usage is widespread in paleontology, but may prove unacceptable to some workers.

To facilitate further identification of the fossil association, the type collection should be as large and well preserved as possible. It should also be from a narrowly-defined locality, both geographically and stratigraphically.

Quantitative assessment of ecological parameters in fossil plant material is often impractical. Most sampling is non-statistical both in numbers and methodology, given the usual limitations of what can be recognized by the collector, losses during deposition and preservation and the restricted nature of many outcrops. For the purposes of regional ecostratigraphic work, the assessment of associations and their diagnostic species will probably remain largely a judgement of the collector.

Taphonomy is the study of the information lost in a fossil assemblage compared to the former living community from which it was derived. Krassilov (1975) coined a complex nomenclature for the various taphonomic modifications of fossil plant associations. All such interpretive studies should be independent of the naming and definition of fossil associations. Evidence from taphonomy, functional morphology, sedimentary environment, and paleosols are all critical to the interpretation of fossil plant associations. The distinctive differences between associations can often be explained in terms of environmental parameters. From my own studies of fossil plant associations (Retallack, 1977b, d), such parameters as water stress, proximity to the sea, and paleosol type seem to have been important for Triassic fossil plant associations of eastern Australasia.

Synusiae (subunits of associations) are difficult to interpret. In many Triassic plant localities, the abundant remains of pteridophytes, including filicaleans and equisetaleans, may outnumber those of the more constant seed plants. The fossil record of pteridophytes is probably exaggerated because, as in the modern world, they were more abundant near moist depositional environments. In this case, they are better regarded as synusiae of the seed plant association. Nevertheless, distinctive pteridophytic associations also exist, for example, the Pleuromeietum (discussed later).

PALEOPEDOLOGY

The study of fossil soils (paleosols) can give a detailed impression of the ancient biological, geochemical, and hydrologic microenvironment as well as clues to regional paleotopography, paleoclimate, and tectonics of sedimentary basins. Paleosols are often as distinct from each other as the plant associations that helped to form them. The combined study of paleosols and fossil plant associations can give a precise idea of the terrestrial paleoecology of an area. One of the more exciting aspects of additional interpretative paleosol studies is the prospect of documenting the evolution of world soils from abiotic, Precambrian weathered surfaces to the great array of modern soils. This promises to furnish new information on important events in the history of the earth's land surfaces: the evolution of atmosphere, the appearance of vascular land plants, the development of forests, the expansion of grasslands, and the impact of man.

Most modern classifications of soils (Stace et al., 1968; Buol et al., 1973) are highly interpretive. An objective naming system is needed for paleosols. For this purpose, the soil mapping units of the United States Department of Agriculture (Soil Survey Staff, 1951, 1962) are best for several reasons. The names are not interpretive and not dependent on modern soil classification whose criteria cannot always be applied to paleosols or be unequivocally distinguished from diagenetic modifications. A separate name can be given to any particular paleosol. The paleosols can be interpreted at several conceptual levels within the hierarchy of the classification. Finally, the units of classification are already defined and accepted by soil scientists.

By this system, a name is coined from a locality name and a textural term derived by point-counting the grain-size distribution in thin sections of the A horizon, for example, the Avalon silt loam (discussed later). Variants and stages can also be named if a more distinctive name is required. Individual paleosols can also be grouped into series and these into associations, both named after localities.

Because geologists usually do not have training in soil science, the greatest initial problem for paleopedology may be the recognition of paleosols and their relationship to enclosing sedimentary rocks. The most obvious and diagnostic feature of paleosols is evidence of fossil roots in place. There may also be leached or reddened, massive-looking, clay-rich layers; prismatic or blocky jointing; coaly layers; trace fossils; mottles; nodules; or concretions.

The following terms and concepts are useful in understanding the relationships of paleosols in sedimentary sequences. Relict features of a given paleosol are those not believed to have been caused by processes active in the formation of that particular paleosol. Pedorelicts are features formed by erosion and deposition of older paleosols or formed by preservation of parts of older paleosols within the profiles of younger ones. Sedimentary relicts are structures formed during the deposition of the parent material, and not obliterated during formation of the paleosol (Brewer, 1964). These are commonly ripple-drift cross-laminations and bedding. A pedolith is a bed of transported and deposited paleosol material showing sedimentary organization, but pedological mineralogy and clast microstructure (Gerasimov, 1971). Books by Brewer (1964) and Buol et al. (1973) are excellent guides to other, more usual, soil concepts and nomenclature.

The interpretation of paleosols is not easy. The micromorphological nomenclature of Brewer (1964), detailed field observations, point-counting of thin sections for grain-size distribution and X-ray diffraction studies are all helpful. The biggest problem is assessing pH, Eh, and cation exchange capacity of the former soil, data essential to parts of some modern soil classifications. These can only be inferred from soil structures commonly associated with particular geochemical environments or established by the tortuous process of establishing evidence (usually field or thin-section structures) for the original (non diagenetic) mineralogies. The former geochemistry can then be assessed from the mineral-stability fields provided by Krumbein and Garrels (1952) and Baas-Becking et al. (1960).

AN EXAMPLE FROM THE SYDNEY BASIN

As an example of these approaches to reconstructing ancient vegetation, consider this account of Triassic rocks in the sea cliffs between Long Reef and Palm Beach, 15 km north of Sydney, Australia (Figure 10-1).

STRATIGRAPHY

The Triassic rocks exposed in these sea cliffs are an almost flat-lying sequence with local dips of less than 1° to the west and north (Figure 10-2A). These are local anomalies to the regional dip of the Sydney Basin of which they are part. The outcrop pattern in the Pittwater area (Figure 10-1) is best understood as due to extensive erosion of a plateau capped by Hawkesbury Sandstone. Here, I only briefly characterize the formations and give their maximum exposed thicknesses for the Pittwater area. A more detailed treatment is given by Retallack (1973).

The Bulgo Sandstone (uppermost 1 m only exposed at Long Reef, 3 km south of the area mapped in Figure 10-1) is a grey-green volcanogenic sandstone. The Bald Hill Claystone (18 m) consists largely of red, kaolinitic claystone with minor grey-green lithic sandstone. The Garie Formation (7.6 m) is best mapped on the presence of grey-green volcanogenic sandstone, but also contains grey-green, kaolinitic claystone, and claystone breccia with minor, red-claystone intercalations. The Newport Formation (49 m) is a varied unit of polymictic pebble conglomerate, quartz-lithic sandstone, siltstone, and grey kaolinitic-illitic shale. The Hawkesbury Sandstone (255 m) is a glistening, quartz-lithic sandstone with relatively few shale interbeds. The base of the Hawkesbury Sandstone is best placed at the erosional base of the lowest sandstone channel deposit, which has some of the following features: oligomictic quartz-granule conglomerate, cross-sets 1.2

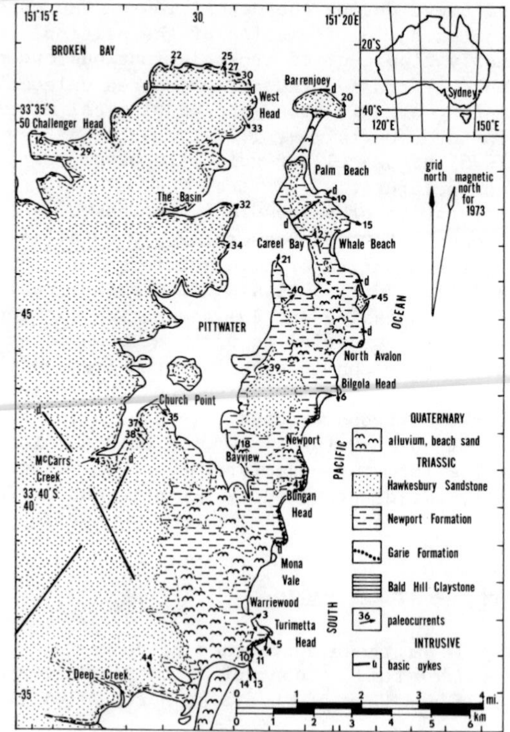

Figure 10-1
A geological interpretation map of the area around Pittwater, New South Wales. Grid after the 1:63,360 "Broken Bay" map sheet.

to 3.6 m thick, and extensive convolution of the top-and bottom-sets.

SEDIMENTARY ENVIRONMENTS

The Bald Hill Claystone consists largely of paleosols. However, in the southeast wall of Long Reef (3 km south of the area mapped in Figure 10-1), there are thin sandstone beds and an epsilon cross-set. Similar cross-sets are also seen in plan in the uppermost Bulgo Sandstone in the rock platform at Long Reef as arcuate deposits of interbedded red claystone and grey-green lithic sandstone. Such structures, better exposed and understood in the Newport Formation (Figure 10-3), were probably levees of meandering streams.

Some channel sandstones are found within the Garie Formation at Turimetta Head and north of Mona Vale. Little internal cross-bedding has been preserved by the soft lithic grains. These sandstones are usually asymmetrically lenticular in cross section. The steeper side is probably the cut bank of the original stream, often associated with growth faults of minor displacement (for example, the channel in unit B at Turimetta Head, Figure 10-3). These features suggest that they were deposited by small meandering creeks. Some extensive beds of claystone breccia are also found in the Garie Formation at Turimetta Head. Like the distinctive, normally graded,

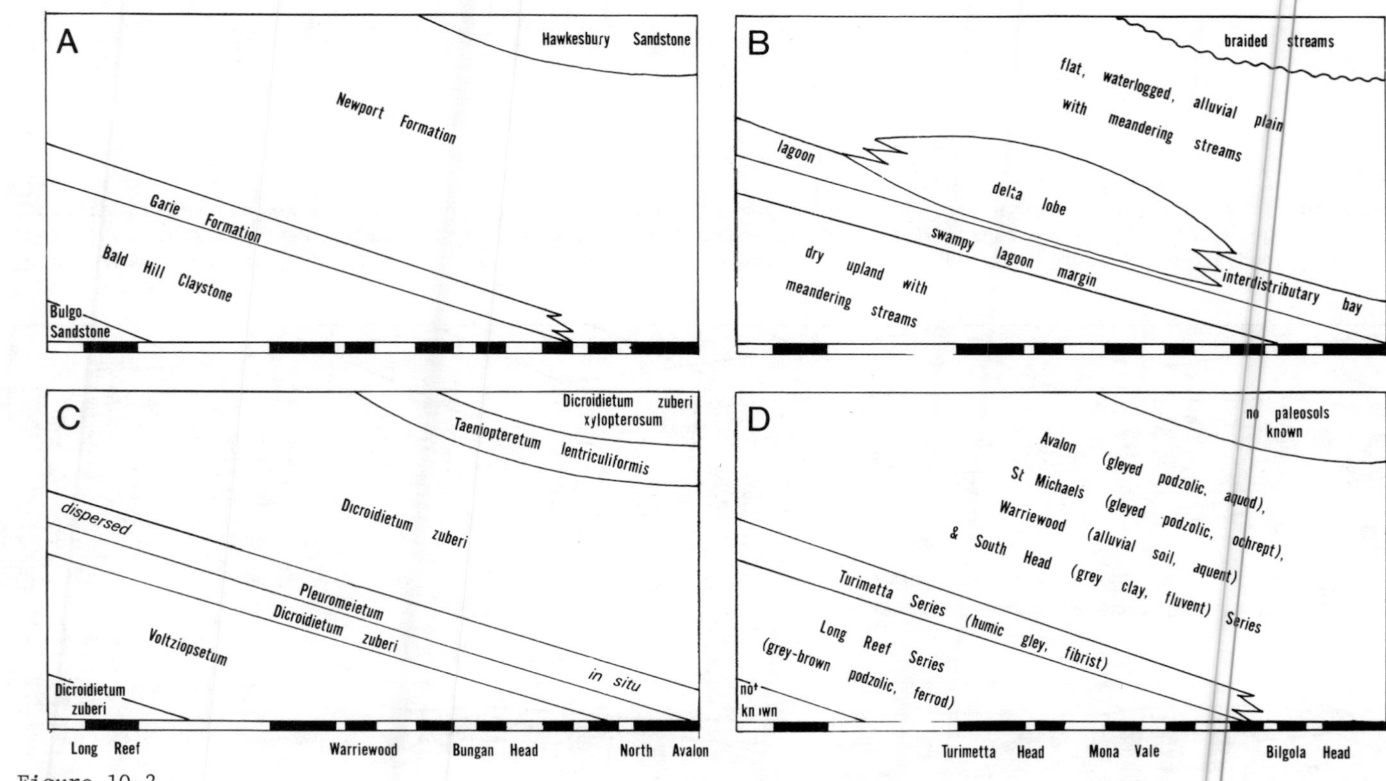

Figure 10-2
Stratigraphy (A), interpreted sedimentary environments (B), fossil plant associations (C), and paleosols (D) on a schematic geological cross section of the sea cliffs from Long Reef (3 km south of the area mapped in Figure 10-1) to Palm Beach. The shaded bar represents the length of the various sea-cliff exposures in this part of the coast.

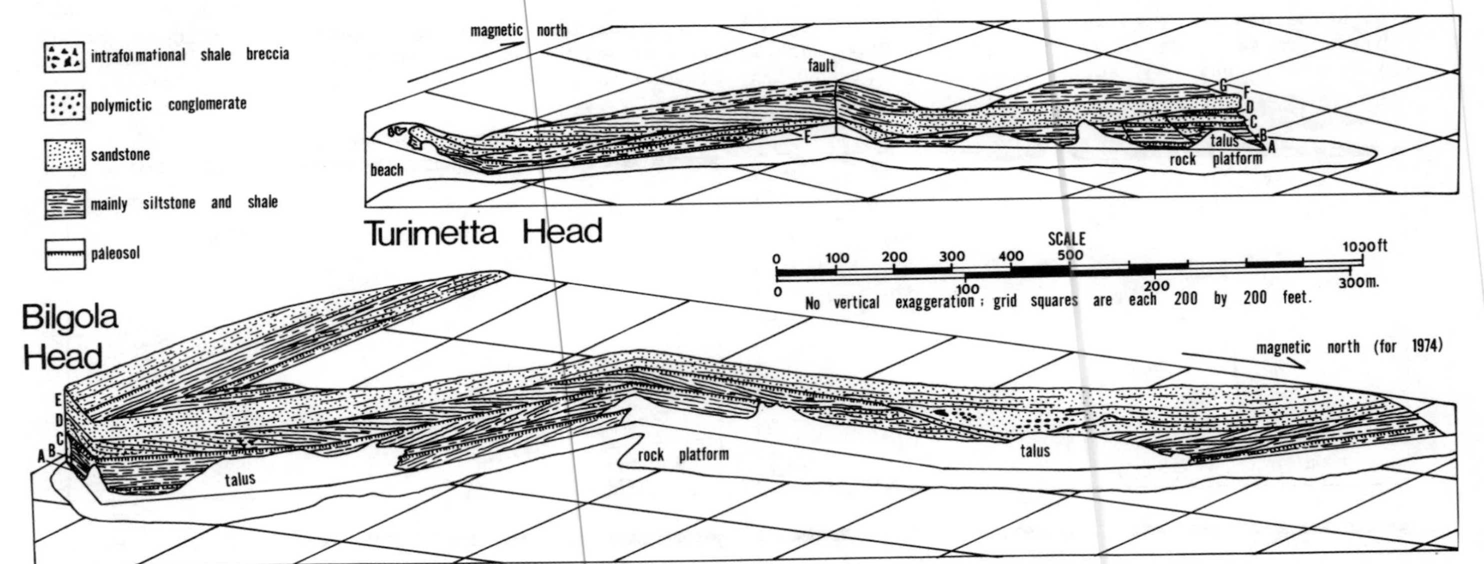

Figure 10-3
Three-dimensional geological sketch of the sea-cliff exposures at Turimetta Head (above) and Bilgola Head (below) showing the lateral transition from levee deposits (large epsilon cross-sets) into sandstone channel deposits (Turimetta Head unit F and Bilgola Head unit D) and into floodplain shale deposits (Bilgola Head unit C).

pelletal claystones of the Garie Formation on the south coast of New South Wales (Bunny and Herbert, 1971), these are interpreted as formed by pedolith beaches on a lagoonal shoreface.

The lower Newport Formation shows considerable variation from north to south (Figure 10-2B). At Turimetta Head (Figure 10-3), the outcrop is dominated by channel sandstones that become larger upsection. The shales associated with these channel sandstones contain a diverse *Dicroidium*-dominated flora. However, immediately above the redbeds (unit A at Turimetta Head, Figure 10-3) there is a distinctive unit (B) of evenly bedded, ripple-drift cross-laminated siltstone and shale that contains few plant fossils other than *Cylostrobus* cones (Figure 10-4E) and fragments of *Sigillariophyllum* leaves. Farther north, around Avalon, there are no channel sandstones at a similar stratigraphic horizon, but there is a succession of siltstone and shale interpreted as crevasse splay and floodplain deposits. Most of these contain a *Dicroidium*-dominated flora, but near the base of the section is a thin, poorly-differentiated paleosol overlain by a coaly band formed of abundant, in-place remains of *Pleuromeia longicaulis* (Figure 10-4F). As I have argued in more detail elsewhere (Retallack, 1975), *Pleuromeia-Cyclostrobus* lycopod fossils characterize a large lagoonal deposit formerly bounded to the north by interdistributary bays fringed with thickets of *Pleuromeia*, which scattered its supposed cones (*Cylostrobus*) and leaves (*Sigillariophyllum*) over a large area of the lagoon to the south. This lagoon was infilled by a delta (now exposed at Turimetta Head) similar to modern deltas of the Gippsland Lakes (Bird, 1962). Some authors (Bunny and Herbert, 1971) have argued that this Triassic lagoon was brackish or marine, but the balance of evidence (Retallack, 1975: 5) supports freshwater. This Triassic delta and lagoon have been loosely labelled the Gosford Delta and Narrabeen Lake (Conolly, 1969).

All of the fluvial depositional environments described by McDonnell (1974) from the partly stratigraphically equivalent Gosford Formation north of Broken Bay can also be recognized in the upper Newport Formation. Large outcrops of the Newport Formation (Figure 10-3) show a variety of structures mostly deposited by meandering streams. In-channel deposits consist largely of thick, trough cross-bedded sandstone units with basal lenses of polymictic, pebble conglomerate. Some channel sandstones have steep cut banks eroded into older sediments and associated intraformational shale breccia (Figure 10-3, Turimetta Head unit F, Bilgola Head unit E). Channel sandstones can also be traced laterally into complex units of finely interbedded sandstone, siltstone, and shale (Figure 10-3, Turimetta Head unit F, Bilgola Head unit D). These mixed units can be traced laterally into flat-lying floodplain shale capped by increasingly thick and differentiated paleosols toward the floodplain deposits (Figure 10-3, Bilgola Head unit C). The mixed units consist of interbedded sandstone, siltstone, and shale up to 10 m thick and cross-bedded at angles of 5 to 15° with the toe-sets bending to concordance with the base of the set. In plan, on the rock platform at Bilgola Head, these units appear to be composed of very large, intersecting trough cross-sets. Individual cross-strata may display linguoid or straight-crested, asymmetric ripple marks and occasionally pebbles or intraformational shale clasts. This structure is similar to that widely identified as epsilon cross-bedding (of Allen, 1963) by many authors (Allen and Friend, 1968;

Dodson, 1971; Leeder, 1973). In the Newport Formation, at least, they appear to be largely levee deposits formed of scroll bars (as discussed by Reineck and Singh, 1973), chutes (as defined by McGowan and Garner, 1970), flood-spillover deposits and crevasse splays (like those figured by Hatch et al., 1971). Other horizontally bedded shales and siltstones of the Newport Formation were probably deposited in distal crevasse splays, lakes, ponded floodwaters, and billabongs (oxbow lakes). These floodplain deposits can be differentiated by the various criteria discussed by McDonnell (1974).

From my own observations of the Hawkesbury Sandstone in the Pittwater area, I agree with the interpretation of its depositional environment presented by Conaghan and Jones (1975). From a consideration of flood cycles within the sandstone, these authors envisaged

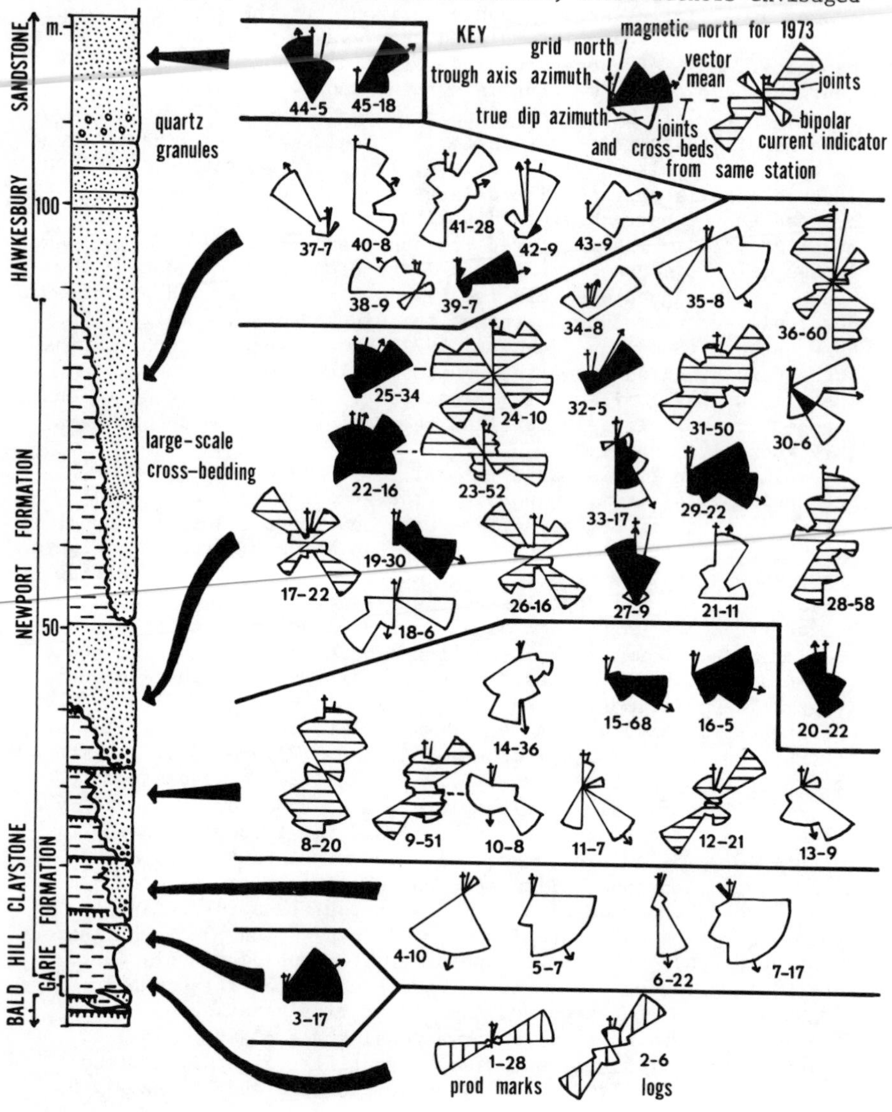

deposition by a periodically flooding, braided stream of a size and stream power comparable to the modern Brahmaputra River of India.

PALEOCURRENTS AND PALEOTOPOGRAPHY

No paleocurrents could be obtained from the Garie Formation, Bald Hill Claystone, or Bulgo Sandstone in the Pittwater area. However, from the paleocurrents (Ward, 1972) and petrography (Culey, 1938) of these units on the coast south of Sydney, they were evidently derived from a volcanic ridge to the east. These volcanics were petrologically similar to the Permian Gerringong Volcanics on the south coast of New South Wales (Raam, 1969). Magnetic mapping (Ringis et al., 1970; Mayne et al., 1974) of the narrow continental shelf east of Sydney revealed a volcanic basement of considerable topographic relief. This is possibly a twenty-million-year-old buried Triassic landscape in the Permian volcanics (Retallack, 1977b). The present low position of these volcanics in the continental shelf, with respect to their presumed Triassic outwash in the coastal cliffs, may be explained by meridional faulting of the classic rift-margin type.

Trough cross-bedding is widespread in the Newport Formation and Hawkesbury Sandstone. Great care was taken to ensure that all measurements (Figure 10-5) were taken from a single sandstone channel. Direct measurement of the trough axes exposed in plan gave the most reliable paleocurrent readings, but this could also be approximated

Figure 10-4 (at left)
Common plant megafossils of the Pittwater area. A. *Dicroidium zuberi* var. *feistmantelii* (Johnston) Retallack (1977d); a relatively small frond for this species; x1/2; Geology Department, University of New England, Armidale, UNEF13955; from North Avalon (locality UNEL1383). B. Cuticle of *Dicroidium zuberi* var. *papillatum* (Townrow) Retallack 1977d; x75; after Townrow (1957, Figure 11A); from near Derby, Western Australia. C. "*Pterorrachis*" *barrealensis* Frenguelli, 1942, a pair of sporangial heads of the likely microsporophyll of *Dicroidium zuberi*; UNEF13903 from North Avalon (UNEL1385). A similar paired structure was observed by Townrow (1962) in the closely related species, *Pteruchus dubius*. D. *Umkomasia* sp.; dehisced cupules of the likely megasporophyll of *Dicroidium zuberi*; Mining Museum, Geological Survey of New South Wales, MMF17905; from the Newport Formation north of Sydney. E. *Cylostrobus sydneyensis* (Walkom) Helby and Martin 1965; x1; its microspore *Aratrisporites* (X125) and megaspore *Banksisporites* (X19); reconstruction drawn from Retallack (1975). F. *Pleuromeia longicaulis* (Burges) Retallack 1975; size in bar scale; reconstruction drawn from Retallack (1975). G. *Xylopteris elongata* var. *rigida* (Dun) Stipanicic and Bonetti (in Stipanicic, 1957); x12; Australian Museum, AMF18581; from Brookvale. H. Cuticle of *Xylopteris tripinnata* (Jones and de Jersey) Frenguelli, 1943; X75; AMF18590; from Brookvale. I. *Taeniopteris lentriculiformis* (Etheridge) Walkom 1917; X1/2; after Etheridge (1894); from Gosford. J. *Lepidopteris madagascariensis* Carpentier 1935; x1/2; UNEF13853; from Bungan Head (UNEL1417). K. Cuticle of *L. madagascariensis*; X75; UNEF13961; from Mona Vale (UNEL1418). L. *Voltziopsis angusta* (Walkom) Townrow, 1967; X1; after Townrow (1967); from Turimetta Head.

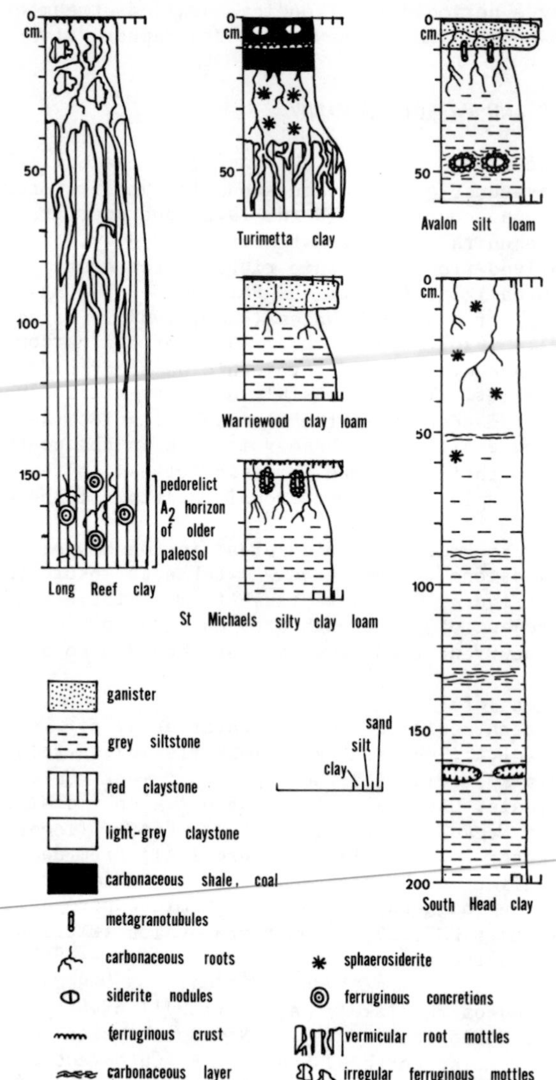

Figure 10-5
Paleocurrents from Triassic rocks in the Pittwater area. Current roses are plotted by 30° class intervals and labelled with a station number that is plotted in Figure 10-1. The number following the hyphen is the number of readings at each station. Lithological key as for Figure 10-3. Further details are given by Retallack (1973). The current rose for station 19 is replotted from that of Ward (1972).

by calculating the true dip of cross-strata from their apparent dip in two intersecting near-vertical faces exposing the same cross-set. I had hoped that the orientation of joints in the sandstones would show some relationship to the elongate axis of channel sandstone and thus to paleocurrent. However, there was no consistent relation

(Figure 10-5). Jointing is probably related to compaction also involving overlying sediments of different geometry.

Paleocurrents of the Newport Formation are largely from the northwest. There is considerable variation in the central deltaic portion of the formation. In some cases (Figure 10-5, stations 22, 25, 27 versus 30, 33 at West Head; stations 4, 5, 6, 7 versus 3 at Turimetta Head), these divergences may be due to distributary branching similar to the Head of Passes in the modern Mississippi Delta. These paleocurrents are in general agreement with findings from studies of pebbles and heavy mineral composition (Culey, 1938; Ward, 1972), indicating that the Newport Formation was derived from hilly terrain of varied geology to the north and west.

My paleocurrent measurements for the Hawkesbury Sandstone are similar to those of Standard (1969) who found a relatively consistent basin-wide direction towards the northeast. The channel sandstone marking the base of the Hawkesbury Sandstone in the Pittwater area forms a major erosional feature trending in the same direction. This channel feature is topographically lowest at Deep Creek and west of Barrenjoey and highest at Bungan and Challenger Heads. This evidence from paleocurrents and paleochannels is also supported by the heavy mineral composition of the sandstone (Standard, 1969), which indicates it was derived from a mixed granitic, metamorphic, and sedimentary sourceland of moderate relief to the southwest.

PALEOPEDOLOGY

The following discussion is a summary of the more interesting conclusions of my detailed studies on Pittwater paleosols (Retallack, 1977a, b, c). The type sections of the various paleosol series are shown in Figure 10-6 and their stratigraphic distribution in Figure 10-2D.

No paleosols can be seen in the small amount of Bulgo Sandstone exposed at Long Reef, but there are several well-preserved profiles at the base of the Bald Hill Claystone there. These Long Reef Series paleosols have a thin, surficial ferruginous layer, commonly with a polygonal cracking (A_1) horizon, overling about 30 cm of grey clay (A_{2cn}). This contains diffuse yellow and orange staining, slickensided lenticular soil peds, and ferric mottles and concretions. The grey clay passes down through a zone of vermicular grey mottles in red claystone (after plant roots, B_{1ir}) into completely red clay-sandstone (B_{2ir}). The sandstone grains are so soft, coated with clay and heavily oxidized that this may appear more like claystone than sandstone in hand specimen. These paleosols were probably grey-brown podzolic soils in the Australian classification (Stace et al., 1968), ferrods in the North American classification (Buol et al., 1973), and Uf2 in the Northcote (1974) Key. Modern soils of this type are usually well drained and forested. The erosion and redeposition of such paleosols in the upper Bald Hill Claystone appears to have been complex. However, the paleosols show a similar breakdown pattern of upper horizons after immersion in tapwater (slaking as discussed by Emerson, 1954) to that found in modern soils. From the weathering profile at Long Reef, as many as eight superimposed paleosols may form the Bald Hill Claystone there.

Within the Garie Formation, lowermost Newport Formation, and uppermost Bald Hill Claystone, two or three superimposed paleosols

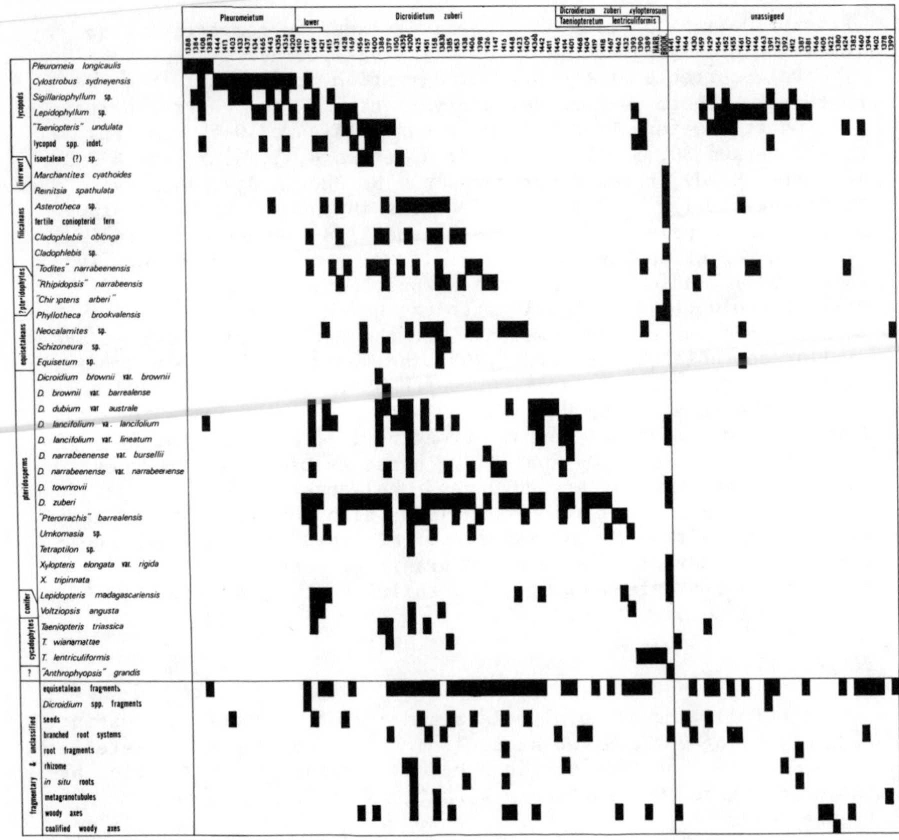

Figure 10-6
Type profiles of paleosols from the Pittwater area (adapted from Retallack, 1977b).

of the Turimetta Series crop out in most of the sea cliffs between Bilgola Head and Long Reef. These have a thick (about 20 cm) organic horizon of clay and fibrous fossil plant material (some of it identifiable) overlying about 15 cm of leached grey claystone (A_{2g}) which in turn overlies about 10 cm of red claystone ($B\&A_{gir}$) with a vermicular mottled contact. Each vermicular mottle is a reduced halo around a fossil plant root that is often preserved in the center. Other plant remains found within the profile include in-place stem bases of the equisetalean *Neocalamites* penetrating the uppermost grey clay and fragments of *Dicroidium zuberi* seeds and large logs in the organic horizon. Burrows, some remarkably like those of modern earthworms, are common in the grey A_2 horizon. Siderite crystals around burrow margins and within fossil roots in the A_2 horizon and siderite nodules in the organic horizon appear to have formed shortly after covering of the paleosol with overlying sediment. These paleosols are identified as humic gleys or fibrists and are of a type not yet subdivided in the Northcote Key. Modern soils of this type form in poorly drained swamplands.

A variety of paleosols are found in the Newport Formation. Most characteristic are the Avalon Series paleosols. These consist of a thin, carbonaceous shale (0) underlain by about 10 cm of ganister (A_2) containing abundant metagranotubules and carbonaceous roots that also penetrate the underlying, leached, grey clay. This clay (B_{2t}) becomes progressively darker and more clearly bedded with depth until a horizon of siderite nodules (B_{3hirg}) at a depth of about 40 cm. Ganister is a strongly outcropping, silicified, fine sandstone. From the evidence of microscopic texture, associated paleosols, plant fossils, and comparison with modern soils, it is likely that the ganisters of the Pittwater area were cleaned as acid, sandy, eluvial horizons of soils and diagnetically silicified by the in-place remobilization of abundant opal phytoliths from the *Dicroidium*-dominated vegetation originally growing in them. Metagranotubules (vertical burrows filled with ganister) were probably excavated by cicada-like insects. They are quite distinct from root casts that contain abundant carbonaceous lamellae and a concertina-like outline due to differential compaction of the tap-root around lateral roots. The best evidence that the siderite nodules are in place and formed at the same time as the paleosol is the rare occurrence of metagranotubules sidling closely around their edges. Geochemically, siderite indicates reducing, relatively alkaline or neutral conditions. The concentration of siderite nodules in layers probably marks a zone of slight humus illuviation and of water table oscillation. The Avalon Series paleosols were probably gleyed podzolics (aquods, Dg3.41). Modern soils of this type form in low-lying sites, intermittently waterlogged. They commonly support heath and coniferous forest, but also some broad-leaf vegetation.

Warriewood Series paleosols consist of ganister (A_2) penetrated by carbonaceous roots, sometimes also metagranotubules, and over-lying moderately leached shale (B_t). These immature soils were probably alluvial soils (aquents, Uc2.21). Given time, and perhaps less waterlogging in some cases, these might have developed into soils similar to paleosols of the Avalon Series.

The St. Michaels Series paleosols are similar to those of the Avalon Series, but the St. Michaels Series paleosols have several features indicating drier conditions at the time of formation: ferruginized surface crust and burrows, some ferric mottling through-out the profile, and a lack of siderite nodules. These were most likely gleyed podzolic soils (ochrepts, Dy3.41). These immature paleosols may indicate that yellow podzolic soils or ultisols were formed in the Triassic hinterland to the north and west. Yellow podzolic soils also form on Newport Formation exposures in the Pittwater area today.

Capping many of the large epsilon cross-sets in the middle and upper Newport Formation are the South Head Series paleosols. These consist of leached, pink-weathering, sphaerosideritic claystone, often with a blocky ped structure in the uppermost 40 cm (A_2), over-lying layered claystone (AC) with a deep-seated zone of weak iron accumulation at depths of one to two meters. The South Head Series paleosols may originally have been grey clays (fluvents, Uf4.2). In modern river systems, such soils are common on clayey levees.

No paleosols and few overbank shales have been preserved in the Hawkesbury Sandstone in the Pittwater area. Presumably, this is due to exceedingly low subsidence rates during deposition leading to continuous reworking of the floodplain fines by laterally migrating channels.

The various soil series fall within two associations based on the type of parent material. The Long Reef Association, including the Long Reef and Turimetta Series, are paleosols with red B horizons formed on volcanogenic, kaolinitic materials derived from the east. The Avalon Association, consisting of Avalon, Warriewood, St Michaels, and South Head Series, formed on quartz-lithic, kaolinitic-illitic materials from the north and west.

Taking 2,000 years as a reasonable time estimate for developing a mature soil profile (Buol et al., 1973), the Bald Hill Claystone probably contains an accumulated depositional hiatus of at least 16,000 years, and the alluvial plain that formed the Newport Formation probably subsided at a rate of less than a meter every 2,000 years.

No firm paleoclimatic conclusions can be drawn from the study of these paleosols. The dominance of podzolic paleosols is compatible with the evidence of paleolatitude (Smith et al., 1973), growth rings in fossil wood (Burges, 1935), and the moderate diversity of the fossil flora and indicates that the climate was cool temperate.

ECOSTRATIGRAPHY

The Braun-Blanquet phytosociology chart (Figure 10-7) does not show the fossil plant associations organized into fields as clearly as is often the case in studies of modern vegetation. This is because of taphonomic modifications of the original plant associations and the uneven quality of the collections. Some localities were so poor that collections from them could not be assigned to a defined fossil plant association. Nevertheless, the diagram is a convenient summary of otherwise unwieldy data. All these fossil plant associations are defined by Retallack (1977d), so only a short explanation and additional comments are offered here. The stratigraphic distribution of the associations in the Pittwater area is shown in Figure 10-2C. Some of the common plant fossils are illustrated in Figure 10-4.

No megafossils have been found in the highly oxidized Bald Hill Claystone except for burrows and plant roots. However, fossil pollen and spores recovered from the Bald Hill Claystone by Helby (1973) suggest that it was vegetated by conifers rather than pteridosperms. The conifer pollen are similar to those from palynological assemblages found at lower stratigraphic levels in the Sydney Basin. These little known Early Triassic coniferophytic associations are grouped together as the Voltziopsetum. They evidently formed forests because of the type, thickness, maturity and root mottling of the paleosols they produced and the large logs found with remains of this association in underlying formations (described by Baker, 1931; Burges, 1935).

The Pleuromeietum in the Pittwater area is a monodominant association of *Pleuromeia longicaulis* (Figure 10-4F) and its supposed cones (*Cylostrobus sydneyensis*, Figure 10-4E) and leaves (*Sigillariophyllum*). The association shows a differential distribution of plant parts from north to south. To the north at North Avalon where the plants appear to have grown in

Figure 10-7
Braun-Blanquet phytosociology chart for fossil plant collections from the Pittwater area. Numbered localities are registered with the Geology Department, University of New England, Armidale, New South Wales, and discussed by Retallack (1973). The flora of the Newport Formation and also of Harbord (HARB.) and Brookvale (BROOK.) localities are discussed by Retallack (1977d, microfiche frames G6, G9, G10).

interdistributary bays, *Pleuromeia* is found in a thin coaly layer containing rhizophores, stems, and leafy apices. A little farther south, north of Newport, cones, leaves, bark fragments, and sterile apices are scattered in lagoonal shales. Similar shales, cropping out in most of the cliffs south as far as Long Reef, contain cones and leaves. No rhizophores, stems, bark fragments, or sterile apices are found south of Newport. Presumably these changes are due to the differential distribution of plant parts into the lagoon to the south from stands at North Avalon.

For several localities (Figure 10-7) where the collections were derived from mixed boulders in littoral talus that contained remains of both the Pleuromeietum and Dicroidietum zuberi (localities 1383, 1435, 1436, 1420), I separated the associations on the basis of matrix. However, *Cylostrobus* does occur mixed with pteridosperms and conifers in the lowermost Newport Formation at Bungan Head (locality 1417). Other lycopod remains also occur in several collections of the Dicroidietum zuberi and some unassigned collections. Perhaps these belong to an additional lycopod association. Definition of this association will have to await description of better preserved and more abundant new lycopod material such as that from similar stratigraphic levels north of Broken Bay and in Tasmania (Ash, 1979).

The Dicroidietum zuberi is the most common and widespread association of the Pittwater area. It is a diverse broadleaf pteridosperm association that commonly includes filicalean and equisetalean remains and rarely, lycopods. Within the Newport Formation there are several lines of evidence indicating it was a heath vegetation (Retallack, 1977b). It is intimately associated with paleosols of the Avalon Series, a soil type today commonly supporting heath. Cradle knolls, egg-cup podzols and radiating root impressions found in the ganisters of these paleosols are all small and probably produced by vegetation less than 2 m high. *Dicroidium zuberi* (Figure 10-4A, B) leaves from the Newport Formation have a very thick leaf substance and cuticle (veins are seldom seen in impressions) compared with the same species associated with the same reproductive structures (Figure 10-4C, D) 100 km west of Sydney at Mt. Piddington. Finally, no large fossil logs have been found in the Newport Formation above the basal lagoonal shales.

Figure 10-7 is artifically arranged to show the proportions of localities for the Dicroidietum zuberi that contain equisetaleans, filicaleans, and lycopods. These pteridophytes probably formed synusiae as an understory to the pteridosperms, or perhaps stream or lakeside thickets marginal to the Dicroidietum zuberi.

The Dicroidietum zuberi associated with the Turrimetta Series paleosols is not particularly distinct floristically from the association elsewhere, but is interpreted as quite a different type of vegetation. Large logs have been found lying in the organic horizon of these paleosols indicating that here the association was a swamp woodland. There is also a greater abundance of the conifer *Voltziopsis angusta* (Figure 10-4L) and the pteridosperm, *Lepidopteris madagascariensis* (Figure 10-4J, K) in collections from this stratigraphic level (Figure 10-7, localities 1410, 1417, 1449, 1421). The *Neocalamites* stem bases observed in the uppermost A_2 horizon of Turimetta Series paleosols may have been a successional stage in a hydrosere towards swamp-woodland climax.

No megafossils have been found below the Bald Hill Claystone in the Pittwater area, but the Dicroidietum zuberi occurs in that stratigraphic position north of Garie Beach on the coast south of Sydney and in the north wall of the Skillion, Terrigal, north of Broken Bay (Retallack, in press).

The Taeniopteretum lentriculiformis is characterized by a remarkable abundance of the nominate species (Figure 10-4I). Considering the abundant, slender, branching twigs found in this association, these plants may have had a bushy habit. The association occurs with South Head Series paleosols in the uppermost Newport Formation at North Avalon and was probably a levee vegetation. The Taeniopteretum lentriculiformis has also been found at Gosford north of Broken Bay and at Harbord 5 km south of the mapped area (Retallack, in press).

The Dicroidietum zuberi xylopterosum is known best in the Sydney region from a single locality near Brookvale 4 km south of the mapped area (Figure 10-1). *Xylopteris* and several other narrow-leaved species form relatively xerophytic elements in an association otherwise similar to the Dicroidietum zuberi. These xerophytic elements may have been adapted to drier, sandier, soils low in nutrients. Such modern soils on the Hawkesbury Sandstone, support dry sclerophyll vegetation.

BIOSTRATIGRAPHY AND CHRONOSTRATIGRAPHY

The entire Triassic sequence exposed in the Pittwater area was deposited during the *Dicroidium zuberi* Oppel-zone (of Retallack, 1977d). The Bald Hill Claystone, Newport Formation, and Hawkesbury Sandstone have yielded, respectively, the *Protohaploxypinus samoilovichii*, the upper zonule of the *Aratrisporites tenuispinosus*, and lower zonule of the *A. parvispinosus* palynological assemblages (Helby, 1973). These plant remains are correlated with the late Scythian to early Anisian Stages of the European Triassic largely on the basis of *Pleuromeia* and *Aratrisporites* (Retallack, 1975). *Taeniopteris lentriculiformis* is also abundant within a restricted interval of Anisian marine rocks in the Murihiku Supergroup, New Zealand (Retallack, 1977d).

SYNTHESIS

In describing the likely panorama and processes in the Pittwater area during the Triassic (Figure 10-8), I have paraphrased my earlier work (Retallack, 1977b: 31) with little modification.

From a position high in the sky west of Sydney, the extensive waters of Narrabeen Lake can be seen to be the freshwater northern portion of a large lagoonal system intermittently open to the sea in the south. To the east, low rolling hills rise gradually to scattered plugs of the twenty-million-year-old Gerringong Volcanic Ridge, which separates the lake from the glistening waters of the Eopacific Ocean in the far distance. Sluggish streams drain down to the lake from the crest of the ridge. Their meandering and branching is marked by deep linear shadows through the Voltziopsetum coniferous forest of the low hills and the Dicroidietum zuberi swamp woodland of the lake margins.

These streams are floored by unaltered, grey-green, volcanogenic sandstones. When exposed, these sandstones weather quickly to form the predominantly red, kaolinitic claystone soils of the Long Reef Association. In better drained areas, the clay is strongly oxidized to grey-brown podzolic soils (ferrods) of the Long Reef Series formed under Voltziopsetum coniferous forest. Well-drained conditions prevailed for at least 16,000 years, with very slow subsidence, to form the Bald Hill Claystone.

In lowland areas around the lake, the soft lithic sandstones form clayey gley soils accumulating small thicknesses of peat under Dicroidietum zuberi swamp woodland. Local thickets of *Neocalamites* are trapping sediment as an early stage in the hydrosere toward a woodland climax. The mature soils are humic gleys (fibrists) of the Turimetta Series. With the slow relative rise of the Narrabeen Lake,

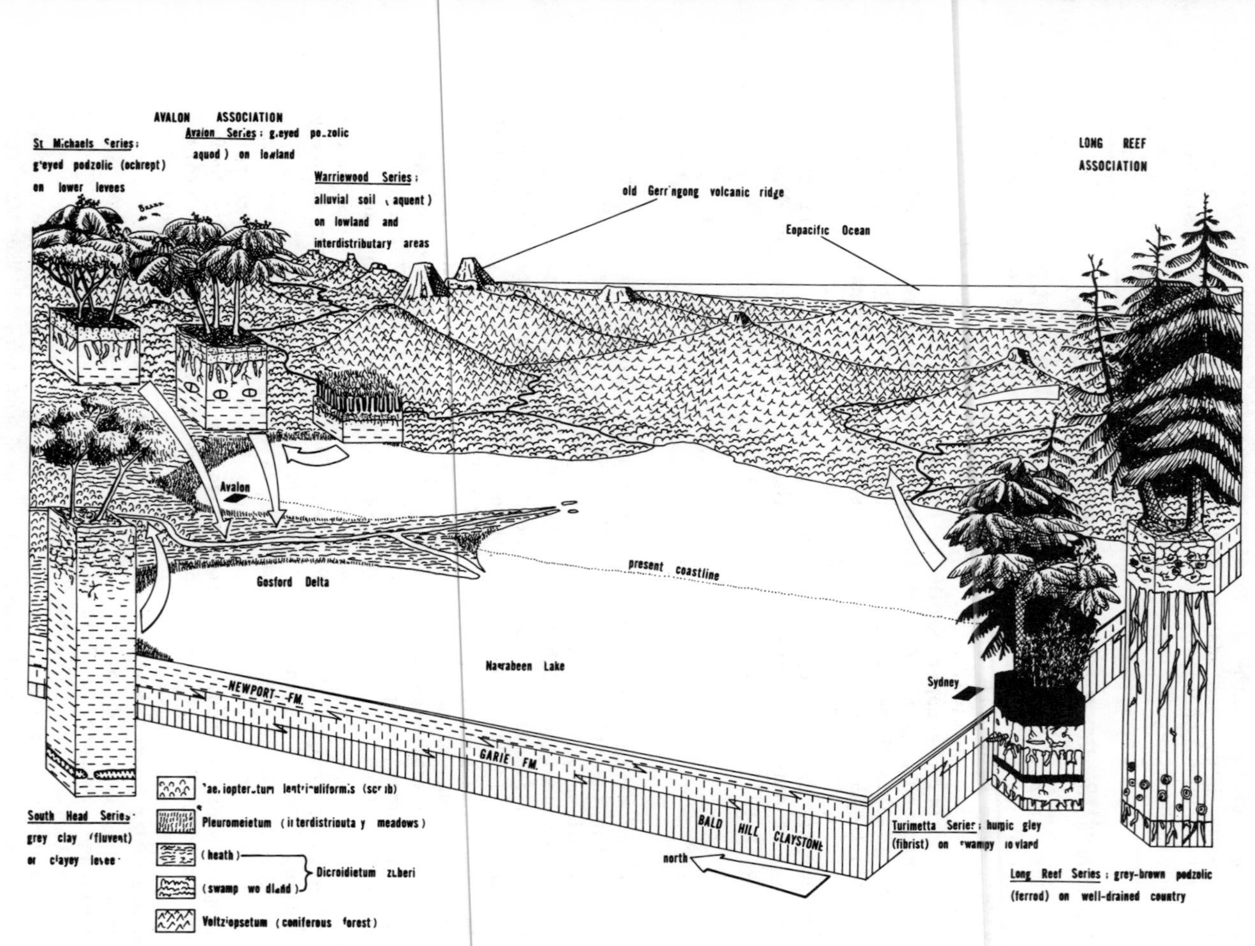

Figure 10-8
Reconstructed environment of the Pittwater area during the latest Early and earliest Middle Triassic (from Retallack, 1977b:30, with permission).

drab clayey sediments and soils of this type came to continuously overlie the Bald Hill Claystone forming the Garie Formation.

At the northern margin of the lake, the Gosford Delta is imperceptibly building southwards concomitant with the slow relative rise of lake level. The delta channels drain a broad river plain extending far to the north. A few hundred kilometers to the north and west hilly country is barely visible on the horizon. This large and geologically varied source terrain supplies quartzose sand and silt and kaolinitic-illitic clay to the delta.

From the air, the Gosford Delta is an interesting patchwork of dark Pleuromeietum meadows in marshy interdistributary bays; light drab-green Dicroidietum zuberi heath on sandy-surfaced soils and bright-green islands of pteridophytes around small lakes and billabongs; all dissected by sinuous ribbons of shining water in clean sandy channels. Beneath the still waters, the lakefloor is predominantly grey clay littered with comminuted plant fragments, but there are lighter-colored sand bars around distributary mouths.

Within the low-lying and sedimentologically active delta, only gleyed and immature soils are formed. Alluvial soils (aquents) of the Warriewood Series are formed under Dicroidietum zuberi heath in lowlands recently covered by flood deposits and under partly submerged Pleuromeietum meadows in interdistributary bays. On older lowlands Dicroidietum zuberi heath grows on more differentiated gleyed podzolic soils (aquods). These have a dry, acid surface, but the water table is almost permanently within a meter of the surface. On slightly more elevated ground also vegetated by Dicroidietum zuberi heath, there are more oxidized gleyed podzolic soils (ochrepts) of the St. Michaels Series. These are immature, but indicate that yellow podzolic soils (ultisols) may have developed on similar parent materials in more inland and better-drained sites.

The southward growth of the Gosford Delta lobes and bay shorelines eventually filled much of the Narrabeen Lake to form the Newport Formation. Slow but steady subsidence of less than a meter every 2,000 years prevailed during the progradation of the Gosford Delta and the final covering of the Gerringong Volcanic Ridge. After a time, subsidence proceeded even more slowly. As a result, the sandy river channels more frequently reworked the shaly floodplain by lateral meandering, so only immature grey clays (fluvents) of the South Head Series supporting Taeniopteretum lentriculiformis scrub on clayey levees are preserved in the geological record.

Subsidence was extremely slow when the Hawkesbury Sandstone was deposited by powerful braided streams from the southwest. These eroded deeply into older sediments and reworked the floodplain to such an extent that few shaly sediments and no paleosols have been preserved. Local billabongs and lakes still supported a lush growth of ferns and equisetaleans, but the sandy, drier, low-nutrient substrate supported a relatively more xerophytic vegetation. This Dicroidietum zuberi xylopterosum is a diverse broadleaf association including several narrow-leaved pteridosperms such as *Xylopteris*.

As in many other regions of prolonged geological study, the broad outlines of this reconstruction had been established by previous research on sedimentary petrography and environments, paleocurrents, paleobotany, palynology and paleozoology. However, most details of this new reconstruction are due primarily to new approaches in studying fossil soils and associations of fossil plants. I hope this brief illustration of the potentials of these approaches will stimulate additional research into their methodology and application elsewhere.

ACKNOWLEDGMENTS

I thank Dr. J. Gray for encouragement to speak at the Second North American Paleontological Convention and to contribute to this volume. Thanks are also due to Dr. P. N. Webb for employment at Northern Illinois University during the preparation of this manuscript and to my typist there, Brenda Mathesius. Much of this work was done under Commonwealth Postgraduate Awards held at the Geology Department, University of New England, Armidale, New South Wales, Australia. I am also indebted to Marcia King of the Biology Department, Indiana University, Bloomington, for typing the final copy for replication.

REFERENCES

Allen, J. R. L. 1963. The classification of cross-stratified units, with notes on their origin. *Sedimentology* 2:93-114.

Allen, J. R. L., and P. R. Friend. 1968. Deposition of the Catskill facies, Appalachian region, with notes on some other Old Red Sandstone basins, in G. de V. Klein, ed., *Late Paleozoic and Mesozoic Continental Sedimentation, Northeastern North America. Geol. Soc. America Spec. Paper* 106:21-74.

Ash, S. R. 1979. *Skilliostrobus* gen. nov., a new lycopsid cone from the Early Triassic of Australia. *Alcheringa* 3:73-89.

Baas-Becking, L. G. M., I. R. Kaplan, and D. Moore. 1960. Limits of the natural environment in terms of pH and oxidation-reduction potentials. *Jour Geology* 68:64-87.

Baker, R. T. 1931. On a specimen of fossil timber from the Sydney Harbour Colliery. *Royal Soc. New South Wales Jour. and Proc.* 65:96-111.

Bird, E. C. F. 1962. The river deltas of the Gippsland Lakes. *Royal Soc. Victoria Proc.* 75:65-74.

Braun-Blanquet, J. 1932. *Plant Sociology: The Study of Plant Communities*, G. S. Fuller and H. S. Conard, eds. and trans. New York: McGraw-Hill, 439 p.

Brewer, R. 1964. *Fabric and Mineral Analysis of Soils.* New York: John Wiley and Sons, 470 p.

Bunny, M. R., and C. Herbert. 1971. The Lower Triassic Newport Formation, Narrabeen Group, southern Sydney Basin. *Geol. Survey New South Wales Rec.* 13:61-81.

Buol, S. W., F. D. Hole, and R. J. McCracken. 1973. *Soil Genesis and Classification.* Ames: Iowa State University Press, 360 p.

Burges, N. A. 1935. Additions to our knowledge of the flora of the Narrabeen Stage of the Hawkesbury Series in New South Wales. *Linnaean Soc. New South Wales Proc.* 60:257-264.

Carpentier, A. 1935. Études paléobotaniques sur le groupe de la Sakoa et de la Sakamena (Madagascar). *Annales Géol. Service Mines Madagascar* 5:7-32.

Conaghan, P. J., and J. G. Jones. 1975. The Hawkesbury Sandstone and the Brahmaputra: a depositional model for continental sheet sandstones. *Geol. Soc. Australia Jour.* 22:275-283.

Conolly, J. R. 1969. Models for Triassic deposition in the Sydney Basin. *Geol. Soc. Australia Spec. Pub.* 2:209-223.

Culey, A. G. 1938. The heavy mineral assemblages of the Upper Coal Measures and Upper Marine Series of the Kamilaroi System, N.S.W. *Royal Soc. New South Wales Jour. and Proc.* 72:75-105.

Curtis, J. T., and R. P. MacIntosh. 1951. An upland forest continuum in the prairies forest border region of Wisconsin. *Ecology* 32:476-496.

Dodson, P. 1971. Sedimentology and taphonomy of the Oldham Formation (Campanian), Dinosaur Provincial Park, Alberta (Canada). *Palaeogeography, Palaeoclimatology, Palaeoecology* 10:21-74.

Emerson, W. W. 1954. The determination of the stability of soil crumbs. *Jour. Soil Sci.* 5:233-250.

Etheridge, R. 1894. The occurrence of *Oleandridium* in the Hawkesbury Sandstone Series. *Geol. Survey New South Wales Rec.* 4:49-51.

Frenguelli, J. 1942. Contribuciones al conocimiento de la flora del Gondwana Superior en la Argentina. VI. *Pterorrachis* n. gen. *Notas Mus. La Plata 7 Paleont.* 47:297-302.

Frenguelli, J. 1943. Reseña critica de los géneros atribuídos a la "Serie de *Thinnfeldia*" *Revta Mus. La Plata 2 Paleont.* 12:225-236.

Gerasimov, I. P. 1971. Nature and originality of paleosols, in D. H. Yaalon, *Paleopedology.* Jerusalem: Israel University Press, pp. 15-28.

Hatch, F. H., R. H. Rastall, and J. T. Greensmith. 1971. *Petrology of the Sedimentary Rocks.* London: Murby, 502 p.

Hedberg, H. D. 1975. *International Stratigraphic Guide.* New York: John Wiley and Sons, 200 p.

Helby, R. J. 1973. Review of late Permian and Triassic palynology of New South Wales. *Geol. Soc. Australia Spec. Pub.* 4:141-155.

Helby, R. J., and A. R. H. Martin. 1965. *Cylostrobus* gen. nov., cones of lycopsidean plants from the Narrabeen Group (Triassic), New South Wales. *Australian Jour. Botany* 13:389-404.

Jell, P. A. 1974. Faunal provinces and possible planetary reconstruction of the Middle Cambrian. *Jour. Geology* 82:319-350.

Johnson, R. G. 1972. Conceptual models of benthic marine communities, in T. J. M. Schopf, *Models in Paleobiology.* San Francisco: Freeman, Cooper and Co., pp. 148-159.

Krassilov, V. A. 1975. *Paleoecology of Terrestrial Plants: Basic Principles and Techniques*, H. Hardin, trans. New York: John Wiley and Sons, 283 p.

Krumbein, W. C., and R. M. Garrels. 1952. Origin and classification of chemical sediments in terms of pH and oxidation-reduction potential. *Jour. Geology* 60:1-33.

Leeder, M. R. 1973. Sedimentology and palaeogeography of the Upper Old Red Sandstone in the Scottish Border Basin. *Scottish Jour. Geology* 9:117-144.

McDonnell, K. L. 1974. Depositional environments of the Triassic Gosford Formation, Sydney Basin. *Geol. Soc. Australia Jour.* 21:107-132.

McGowen, J. H., and L. E. Garner. 1970. Physiographic features and stratification types of coarse-grained point bars: modern and ancient examples. *Sedimentology* 14:77-111.

Mayne, S. J., E. Nicholas, A. L. Bigg-Wither, J. S. Rasidi, and M. J. Raine. 1974. Geology of the Sydney Basin--a review. *Bull. Bur.*

Miner. Resour. Geol. Geophys. Aust. 149:1-229.

Northcote, K. H. 1974. *A Factual Key for the Recognition of Australian Soils.* Glenside, South Australia: Rellim Technical Publications, 123 p.

Raam, A. 1969. Gerringong Volcanics, in *The Geology of New South Wales*, G. H. Packham, ed. *Geol. Soc. Australia Jour.* 16:366-369.

Reineck, H. E., and I. B. Singh. 1973. *Depositional Sedimentary Environments.* Berlin: Springer-Verlag, 439 p.

Retallack, G. J. 1973. Stratigraphy, palaeobotany and environmental analysis of an area around Pittwater, N.S.W. B.S. Honours thesis, University of New England, Armidale, New South Wales, Australia.

Retallack, G. J. 1975. The life and times of a Triassic lycopod. *Alcheringa* 1:3-29.

Retallack, G. J. 1977a. Triassic palaeosols in the upper Narrabeen Group of New South Wales. Part I. Features of the palaeosols. *Geol. Soc. Australia Jour.* 23:383-399.

Retallack, G. J. 1977b. Triassic palaeosols in the upper Narrabeen Group of New South Wales. Part II. Classification and reconstruction. *Geol. Soc. Australia Jour.* 24:19-34.

Retallack, G. J. 1977c. Triassic palaeosols in the upper Narrabeen Group of New South Wales: descriptions of type profiles. Open File, Geology Department, University of New England, Armidale, New South Wales 2351, Australia.

Retallack, G. J. 1977d. Reconstructing Triassic vegetation of eastern Australasia: a new approach for the biostratigraphy of Gondwanaland. *Alcheringa* 1:247-277 *Alcheringa-fiche* 1:G1-J17.

Retallack, G. J. In Press. Late Carboniferous to Middle Triassic megafossil floras from the Sydney Basin, in C. Herbert and R. J. Helby, eds., *A Guide to the Sydney Basin*, Geological Survey of New South Wales, Sydney.

Ringis, J., L. V. Hawkins, and K. Seedsman. 1970. Offshore seismic and magnetic anomalies of the southern coalfields off Stanwell Park. *Australasian Inst. Min. and Metall. Proc.* 234:7-16.

Smith, A. J., J. C. Briden and G. E. Drewry. 1973. Phanerozoic world maps, in N. F. Hughes, ed., *Organisms and Continents Through Time. Palaeontology Spec. Pub.* 12:1-42.

Soil Survey Staff. 1951. Soil Survey manual survey manual. *U.S. Dept. Agriculture Handb.* 18, 503 p.

Soil Survey Staff. 1962. *Supplement to U.S.D.A. Handbook* 18, *Soil Survey Manual.* Washington, D.C.: U.S. Govt. Printing Office, pp. 173-188.

Stace, H. C. T., G. D. Hubble, R. Brewer, K. H. Northcote, J. R. Sleeman, M. J. Mulcahy, and E. D. Hallsworth. 1968. *A Handbook of Australian Soils.* Glenside, South Australia: Relim Technical Publications, 435 p.

Standard, J. C. 1969. Hawkesbury Sandstone, in G. H. Packham, ed., *The Geology of New South Wales, Geol. Soc. Australia Jour.* 16: 407-417.

Stipanicic, P. N. 1957. El sistema Triásico en la Argentina. *Internatl. Geol. Congress Mexico Sec. 2 Proc.* 21:73-112.

Townrow, J. A. 1957. On *Dicroidium*, probably a pteridospermous leaf and other leaves now removed from this genus. *S. Afr. Geol. Soc. Trans.* 60:21-60.

Townrow, J. A. 1962. On *Pteruchus*, the microsporophyll of the Corystospermaceae. *British Mus. (Nat. Hist.) Bull., Geol.* 6:285-316.

Townrow, J. A. 1967. On *Voltziopsis*, a southern conifer of lower Triassic age. *Royal Soc. Tasmania Proc.* 101:73-188.

Walkom, A. B. 1917. Mesozoic floras of Queensland, the flora of the Ipswich and Walloon series. *Geol. Survey Queensland Pub. 257*, 46 p.

Ward, C. R. 1972. Sedimentation in the Narrabeen Group, southern Sydney Basin, N.S.W. *Australia Geol. Soc. Jour.* 19:393-409.

Whittaker, R. H. 1973. *Ordination and Classification of Communities. Handbook of Vegetation Science 5.* Hague: Junk, 737 p.

Whittington, H. B., and C. P. Hughes. 1972. Ordovician geography and faunal provinces deduced from trilobite distribution. *Royal Soc. London Philos. Trans.* B263:235-278.

Ziegler, A. M., L. R. T. Cocks, and R. K. Bambach. 1968. The composition and structure of lower Silurian marine communities. *Lethaia* 1:1-27.

11

Distribution of Some Mesozoic Brachiopods in North America

Ellis F. Owen

ABSTRACT

This is a review of the work carried out on isolated Mesozoic brachiopod faunas on the continent of North America since the latter part of the last century. It deals exclusively with articulate genera and species and concentrates mainly on records from Cretaceous localities. It includes systematic descriptions of two species from the Lower Cretaceous of Mexico, one of which is a dallinid formerly assigned to a European Lower Jurassic genus and described here as *Colinella* gen. nov. The other is a rhynchonellid formerly described as "*Rhynchonella*" *miquihuanensis* Imlay and now described as *Proteorhynchia* gen. nov.

INTRODUCTION

Although never common, Mesozoic brachiopods are distributed fairly widely in North America from Mexico in the south to Alaska in the north. A few species have been recorded from eastern Exposures, but the main occurrences follow the outcrops of Jurassic and Cretaceous rocks along the western seaboard from California to Vancouver. The chief inland records are from deposits of Lower and Upper Cretaceous sediments in Mexico, Arizona, and Texas.

Schuchert (1897) listed eighty-two Mesozoic species from the continent of America as a whole. From this total, eleven Triassic and thirty-nine Jurassic species were recorded. Of these, the North American Jurassic species are restricted chiefly to the midwestern states and California. Since Schuchert's records, very few Triassic and Jurassic species have been added and most of the interest in Mesozoic brachiopods of recent years appears to have been concentrated on Cretaceous species.

TRIASSIC

Six of the recognizable Triassic species from Canada and the United States are terebratulids and rhynchonellids. They are the terebratulids "*Terebratula*" *semisimplex* White, described from the sandy facies of southeastern Idaho; "*Terebratula*" *humboldtensis* Gabb from Nicola Lake, Canada; "*Zeilleria*" *liardensis* (Whiteaves) from the basal arenaceous beds in the Liard facies of the Liard River, Canada; and the rhynchonellids "*Rhynchonella*" *halli* Gabb from Bath County, Virginia, and "*R.*" *aequiplicata* Gabb, which is similar to *Misolia noetlingi* (Bittner). "*R.*" *aequiplicata* Gabb and "*R.*" *lingulata* occur in Triassic sandstones of Humboldt County, Nevada. The remaining five species have been assigned to the genus *Spiriferina* and are not discussed here.

Few of these species have been further investigated although Ager and Westermann (1963), in a description of some new brachiopod species from the Mesozoic of Western Canada, listed and recorded several European and North Pacific species from both Triassic and Jurassic localities in the area. Their records extend the geological range of the European genera *Furcirhynchia*, *Rimirhynchia*, *Tetrarhynchia*, and *Piarhorhynchia* to include the North American continent.

JURASSIC

Records of Jurassic brachiopods from the United States are almost exclusively from California and South Dakota where three species have been described from the Sundance Formation of the Upper Jurassic. *Lingula brevirostris* Meek and Hayden, "*Rhynchonella*" *gnathophora* Meek, and "*R.*" *myrinia* Hall and Whitfield are representatives of this sparse fauna.

Ager (1968:63) described a new rhynchonellid genus, *Anarhynchia* The type species is *A. gabbi* from the Upper Jurassic, probably Callovian, of Bedford Canyon, Santa Ana Mountains, southern California. Examples of this species had formerly been referred to the Triassic genus *Halorella*.

Crickmay (1933), in an attempt to zone the North American Jurassic by using brachiopod species as horizon markers, selected Jurassic specimens from three main areas: California and the Rocky Mountains of Alberta and British Columbia. In doing so, he assigned many American species to European genera that needed further investigation, including the use of transverse serial sectioning for confirmation. In the same work, Crickmay (1933:877) described a new rhynchonellid genus as *Ptilorhynchia* and named *P. plumasensis*, a new form from the Callovian of Mount Jura, California, as type species. More recent work (Owen, 1972) suggests that the genus had a more extensive vertical range, appearing in the uppermost Portlandian and Upper Tithonian stages of British Columbia. Dagys (1968), in a description of Jurassic and early Cretaceous rhynchonellidae from Siberia, had already assigned species from both Upper Jurassic and Lower Cretaceous to *Ptilorhynchia*. Previous records of American Upper Jurassic rhynchonellidae also include *Rhynchonella schucherti* Stanton, now considered referrable to *Lacunosella*, which was originally described from the Knoxville beds of Paskenta, California.

Further north, in the Canadian Mesozoic, Jurassic brachiopods seem as rare as in other areas of the North American continent. It is possible that some of the species of rhynchonellidae previously recorded as Cretaceous age may be Jurassic. Crickmay (1933) suggests that *Rhynchonella obesula* Whiteaves, *R. orthioides*, and *Terabratula skidegatensis* Whiteaves are Upper Jurassic whereas *Rhynchonella maudensis* Whiteaves is from the Lower Jurassic.

CRETACEOUS

The Cretaceous, especially the Upper Cretaceous, is probably the most widely exposed sedimentary system on the North American continent. Though much of it is marine in origin, brachiopods are rare, particularly by contrast with the rich brachiopod faunas of similar age in Europe.

The Lower Cretaceous is well exposed along the Atlantic coast and the marine Upper Cretaceous rests unconformably upon it. The best known deposits in this area are in New Jersey where there is a complete sequence from Cretaceous to Tertiary containing a fauna of brachiopods. A conspicuous species from this sequence is *Choristothyris plicata* (Say) from the Upper Cretaceous. Although the very strong costae and almost circular outline are different externally, the internal structures of this species closely resemble those of *Ruegenella* from the Maastrichtian of Rügen, North Germany (Owen, 1977). The similarities of cardinalia and brachial loop are not, however, sufficiently close to suggest that the two forms are congeneric.

A large part of the Western Interior of North America shows Upper Cretaceous at the surface but only a few small areas of Lower Cretaceous. In the Rocky Mountains, very extensive outcrops occur, but they are somewhat deformed and not covered by later deposits. The distribution of invertebrate faunas as a whole is very patchy, and the most extensive outcrops have few brachiopods. The same is true of the midwestern states of Colorado, eastern Utah, and Arizona where the Upper Cretaceous is more prominent.

Further east in middle Texas, especially in the areas of Fort Worth and Waco, the Lower and Upper Cretaceous are both fairly well developed and brachiopods exist, though somewhat rarely, in many exposed beds. One of the more commonly quoted species is *Waconella* (formerly *Kingena*) *wacoensis* (Roemer), which is well represented by *W. choctawensis* and *W. leonensis* in beds of the Comanchean Series in Texas and also occurs in beds of a similar age in Mexico (Owen, 1970).

Ager et al. (1963:375) described a new rhynchonellid from the Bluff Limestone (Lower Cretaceous) of the Indio Mountains, Trans-Pecos, Texas, as *Lamellaerhynchia indi*. One of the points of distinction raised by Ager in his discussion of the species was in the form and orientation of the distal ends of the hinge plates that give rise to the typical radulifer crura. Ager's transverse serial sections of the species (Ager et al., 1963, Figures 3, 4) have recently been compared with those of the type species of *Cyclothyris*, *C. latissima* (J. de C. Sowerby) (Owen, 1962:46), and while admitting that *Lamellaerhynchia* and *Cyclothyris* have much in common, the shape and orientation of the hinge plates shown in Ager's serial sections of *L. indi* suggest that the species would be better assigned to the genus *Cyclothyris*.

In the Upper Cretaceous beds of the same area in Texas, the brachiopods are less frequent and are represented mainly by species of *Terebratulina*. Here again, the species show an affinity with those of a similar age in Mexico. The Gulfian species *Terebratulina filosa* Conrad, *T. floridana* (Morton), and *T. guadalupae* (Roemer) occur sporadically. Adkins (1929:211), in a description of *Terebratulina brewsterensis* from the Taylor Formation near Terlingua, Texas, remarked that Roemer's *Terebratula guadalupae*, originally described from the Austin Chalk, was probably congeneric with *T. brewsterensis*. This is quite likely, but the two forms are not typical of *Terebratulina* and probably belong to an undescribed genus. A species that is probably a synonym of *T. guadalupae* Roemer was described by Stephenson (1941:70) as *Terebratulina noakensis* from the Navarro Group, Kemp Clay, Texas. It differs from *T. guadalupae* in its larger dimensions and slightly more produced umbo, but the shell ornament and general outline are similar.

As in Texas, there was a clear and unusually deep epicontinental sea over much of Mexico during the Cretaceous. This resulted in widespread deposits of pure limestone. Perhaps the maximum northward extension of this dea took place during the late-Early Cretaceous (Washita) when marine waters reached as far as Nebraska.

Prior to this, however, much of the sea covering the same area in the Mexico sector must have provided similar ecological conditions to those that existed at the same time in parts of southwestern France and Morocco; many of the brachiopods described by Imlay (1937, 1940) from the Lower Cretaceous of Tamaulipas, northern Mexico, can be readily referred to European and North African genera. For example, Imlay (1937) described a fauna including terebratulids and rhynchonellids from beds considered to be of Lower Cretaceous, possibly Upper Valanginian, age. The transverse serial sections that accompany the description of "*Terebratula*" *sillimani* (Imlay, 1937:572) are unmistakably referable to *Cyrtothyris*, a genus originally described by Middlemiss (1959) from the Upper Aptian of Upware, England. Likewise, a species later described as "*Terebratula*" *coahuilensis* (Imlay, 1940: 140) from beds of Lower Hauterivian age can be referred to *Sellithyris*, also described by Middlemiss (1959) from the Upper Aptian of England. Externally, both species bear a strong resemblance to European forms although it is not suggested that Imlay's species are conspecific with the English ones. It is interesting to note, since their original description from the Upper Aptian, representative species of both *Sellithyris* and *Cyrtothyris* have been recorded from north German and British localities of Valanginian to Hauterivian age (Middlemiss, 1976).

Imlay (1937:568) also described two species of a dallinid brachiopod from Tamaulipas that he somewhat dubiously assigned to the Jurassic genus *Antiptychina* Zittel, 1880, a zeilleriid terebratellacean from Europe. Transverse serial sections have been made of a duplicate specimen of Imlay's *Antiptychina? mullerriedi* from the type locality, and these have been compared with a series of sections of a similar dallinid species from the Lower Hauterivian of Safi, Morocco. The sections, which are figured here (Figures 11-1, 11-2) as *Colinella* gen. nov., are remarkably close, suggesting a direct relationship between the Mexican and Moroccan species. They also illustrate a strong affinity with the dallinid *Waconella* that was described from the Comanchean of Fort Worth, Texas (Owen, 1970:74) to which *Colinella* may prove ancestral.

Anderson (1902), in a description of the Cretaceous deposits of the Pacific Coast of North America, described two rhynchonellid species as *Rhynchonella densleonis* and *R. whiteana* from the Middle Cretaceous, Horsetown Group, Shasta County, California. Anderson (1958:86) considered these beds to be younger than Lower Cenomanian. Both these species were recently assigned (Owen, 1976) to the genus *Cyclothyris* after examination of transverse serial sections of a specimen from the type locality. Previous records of the occurrence of this genus in the North American Cretaceous were those of Cooper (1955) who described a rhynchonellid from the Mural Limestone,

Middle Albian, of Arizona as *Cyclothyris americana* and Imlay (1937: 571) who assigned a rhynchonellid from the Lower Cretaceous of Tamaulipas, Mexico, tentatively to *Cyclothyris? subtrigonalis*. Serial sections of this species (Imlay, 1937, Figure 7) and those of a specimen described as "*Rhynchonella*" *miquihuanensis* from the same horizon and locality (Imlay, 1937:570) were figured. The series of sections have a great deal in common, but do not support Imlay's assignment of *C.? subtrigonalis* to *Cyclothyris*. Both "*Rhynchonella*" *miquihuanensis* and *Cyclothyris? subtrigonalis* are assigned here to *Proteorhynchia* gen. nov.

Anderson (1938:93) also recorded a species of rhynchonellid that has recently received attention from European palaeontologists. This is Gabb's species *Rhynchonella whitneyi*, originally thought to have come from beds of Miocene age and found in "the sandy shales of both east and west of localities in California and Oregon." The typical form, which has now been assigned to the European genus *Peregrinella*, is found in tough, fine-grained limestone in the West Coast Cretaceous of Paskenta age. The occurrence in California of this strictly tethyan form was noted by Ager (1967:141) who, in a paper published in the following year (Ager, 1968:65), gave a series of transverse serial sections through a specimen of *P. whitneyi* from Wilbur Springs Resort, Calusa County, California.

Anderson (1938) also described several new brachiopod species as Terebratulida. One of these, *Terebratula averilli*, was listed (1938: 65) and described in the explanation of Plate 9 (1938:254). The figures (Anderson, 1938, Figures 10-13), shown of this specimen collected from the Lower Horsetown Group (Lower Aptian, Barr Zone), Mitchell Creek, California, bear a strong resemblance to examples of *Cyclothyris deluci* (Pictet) from the Upper Aptian Sainte Croix district, Switzerland. *Terebratula averilli* Anderson is, therefore, tentatively referred to the genus *Cyclothyris*.

Other species described by Anderson (1938:95) are *Terebratula durelli* from the Lower Horsetown, which was figured (Plate 9, Figure 16) as a subcircular terebratulid and *Terebratula hannana* (1938:95), which Anderson described as a smooth shell, "almost without ornament." He figured, however (Plate 9, Figures 14, 15), a specimen clearly showing the longitudinal radiating striae and the raised, concentric growth lines of a reticulate shell ornament. Also included was a terebratellid brachiopod described as *Terebratella ovula* from the Upper Horsetown (Middle Albian) of Hullen Creek, Shasta County. Once again, the figured specimen is poor; it may belong to a zeilleriid genus. The specimen is said (Anderson, 1938:94) to have a faint median sinus in the dorsal valve and thus may be related to a similar zeillerii species sometimes associated with large *Cyclothyris* spp. collected from the Albian of the Narbonne district in southwestern France. An example of this terebratellid is shown here (Figure 11-3 [4]) for comparison.

A terebratellid species figured by Whiteaves (1903, Plate 51, figures 5, 6) and described (1903:403) as *Terebratella harveyi* from the extension mine, Nanaimo, Texada Island, closely resembles *Gemmarcula crassicosta* (Leymerie) from the Lower Cretaceous of the French Pyrenees. *T. harveyi* also bears a striking resemblance to specimens described and figured by Cooper (1955) as *Gemmarcula arizonensis* from the Mural Limestone of Arizona. It differs from this species, however, in having fewer and stronger radiating costae that have less tendency to marginal bifurcation than is seen in other

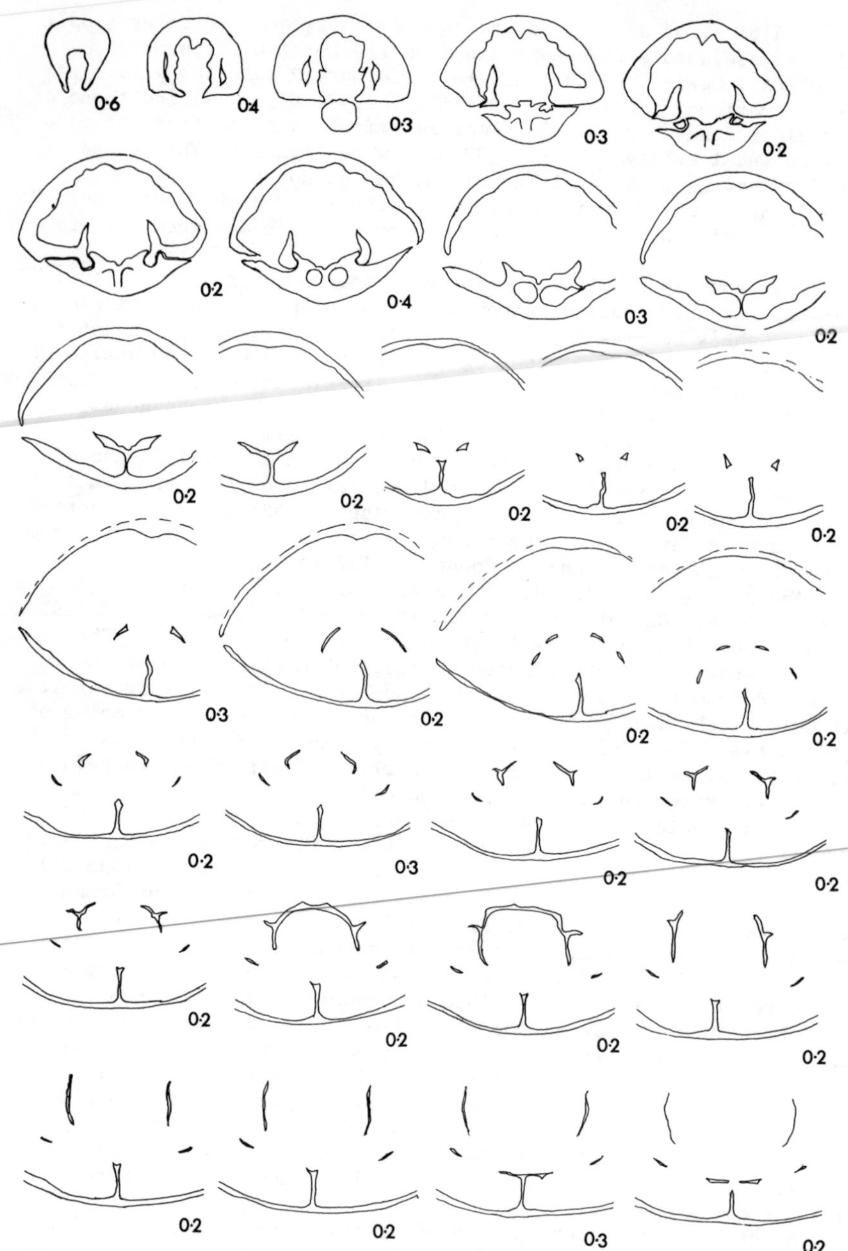

Figure 11-1
Thirty transverse serial sections through a specimen of *Colinella mullerriedi* (Imlay) showing the extensive triangular hinge plates with strong supporting median septum in the brachial valve and the development of the broad laqueiniform hood. Late attachment of the descending branches of the loop to the median septum is seen in the last three sections.

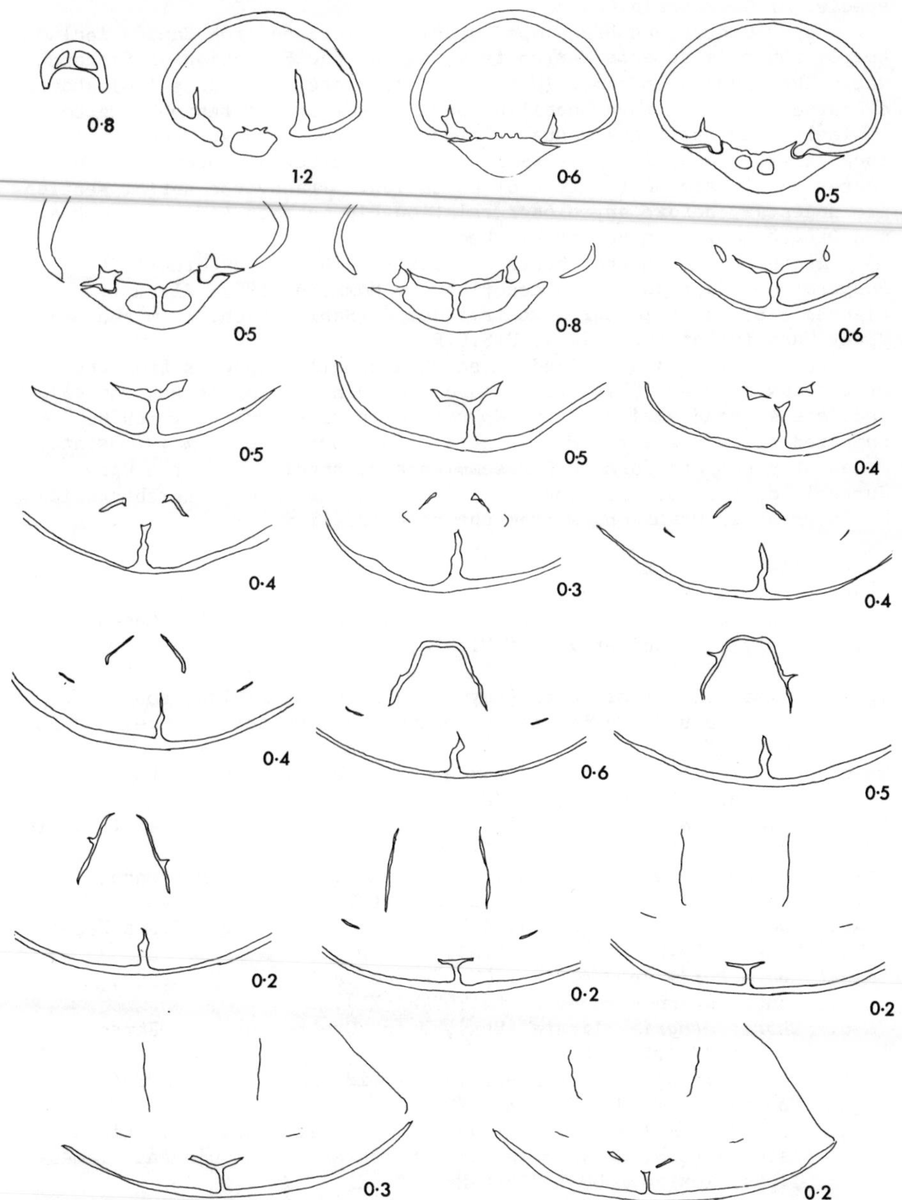

Figure 11-2
A series of twenty-one transverse sections through a dallinid here referred to *Colinella* sp. (BM BB 76527), from the Lower Hauterivian of Sidi Bon Zid, near Safi, Morocco. It illustrates the extensive triangular hinge plates, laqueiniform hood with lateral spines, and late attachment of the descending branches of the brachial loop and can be compared to the serial sections of *C. mullerriedi* shown in Figure 11-1.

species of *Gemmarcula*.

Upper Cretaceous brachiopod species described from Canada include *Hesperorhynchia superba* Warren from the Bearpaw Formation of Saskatchewan. The figured specimen (Warren, 1937, Plate 1, Figures 1-6) shows a coarsely costate rhynchonellid that bears a strong resemblance to typical examples of the genus *Orbirhynchia* from British Upper Chalk localities. Such similarities are based on external appearances and center mainly around the type of costation. Transverse serial sections are necessary before any closer relationship between *Hesperorhynchia* and *Orbirhynchia* can be established.

Another species that bears a close resemblance externally to *Hesperorhynchia superba* was described by Moskvin (1959: Plate 1, Figures 6-8) as *Cyclothyris ventriplanata* (Schloenbach) from the Upper Turonian of the Crimea, U.S.S.R.

Burwash (1914) described three rhynchonellid species from the Cretaceous of Queen Charlotte Island, western Canada, as *Rhynchonella undulata* a broad striate form; *Rhynchonella non-sinuata*, which he compared to J. Sowerby's *R. plicatilis* and *Rhynchonella magnicostata*, a coarsely costate form that resembles some species from the Upper Jurassic of Europe. Burwash (1914:86) also described a terebratulid as *Terebratula grahamensis* from the same locality.

Figure 11-3 (at right)
Standard views: a = dorsal; b = lateral; c = anterior. BM denotes British Museum (Natural History) collection and UM denotes Museum of Paleontology, The University of Michigan.

1a-c. *Gemmarcula crassicosta* (Leymerie) from the Albian, southeast of Chateau de Castellas, Narbonne, southwestern France. BM BB 76528 (X1).

2a-c. *Gemmarcula crassicosta* (Leymerie), Albian, Vieuport Fox, France. BM B 6685 (X1 1/2).

3a-c. *Gemmarcula arizonensis* Cooper, Mural Limestone, Bisbee Triangle, Arizona. BM BB76541 (X1 1/2).

4a-c. ?*Psilothyris* sp., Albian, Chateau de Castellas, Narbonne, Southwestern France. BM BB 76529 (X1).

5a-c. *Cyclothyris indi* (Ager), Albian, Indio Mountains, Trans Pecos, Texas. BM BB 76540 (X1 1/2).

6a-c. *Cyclothyris* sp., Albian, Chateau de Castellas, Narbonne, Southwestern France. BM BB 76542 (X1).

7a-c. *Choristothyris plicata* (Say), Upper Cretaceous, New Jersey. BM B 10838 (X1 1/2).

8a-c. *Colinella* sp., Lower Hauterivian, Sidi Ban Zid, near Safi, Morocco. BM BB 76527 (X1 1/2).

9a-c. *Colinella mullerriedi* (Imlay), Lower Cretaceous, Valanginian, Asteria Zone, above reservoir, northeastern Miquihuana, Tamaulipas, Mexico. UM 18754 PARATYPE (X1 1/2).

10a-c. *Cyrtothyris tamaulipana* (Imlay), Valanginian, 1.6 km east of center of Miquihuana, Tamaulipas, Mexico. UM 18743 HOLOTYPE (X1).

11a-c. *Cyrtothyris sillimani* (Imlay), Valanginian, 1.6 km east of center Miquihuana, Tamaulipas, Mexico. Mexico. UM 18751 HOLOTYPE (X1).

12a-c. *Proteorhynchia subtrigonalis* (Imlay) gen. nov., Valanginian, northeast limit of Miquihuana, Tamaulipas, Mexico. UM 18748 HOLOTYPE (X1 1/2).

13a-c. *Cyclothyris densleonis* (Anderson), Horsetown Group, Shasta County, California. BM BB 76201 (X1 1/2).

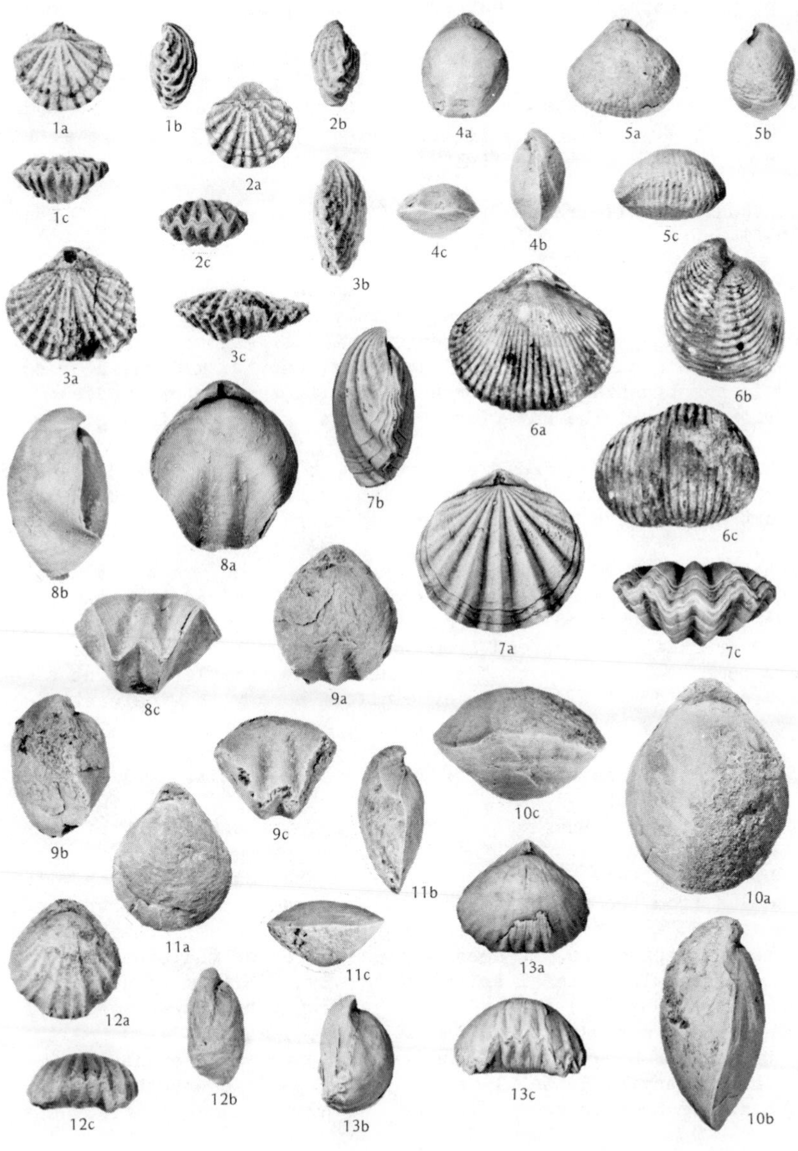
1a
1b
2b
4a
5a
5b
2a
1c
2c
3b
4c
4b
5c
3c
3a
6b
6a
7b
8a
8b
6c
7a
7c
8c
9a
10c
9c
9b
11b
10a
11a
11c
13a
12a
12b
13c
12c
13b
10b

SYSTEMATIC DESCRIPTIONS

Superfamily TEREBRATELLACEA King, 1850
Family LAQUEIDAE Thomson, 1927
Subfamily LAQUEINAE Thomson, 1927

Genus *COLINELLA* gen. nov.

Type species: *Antiptychina*? *mullerriedi* Imlay, 1937

DIAGNOSIS. Subpentagonal to broadly oval, intraplicate, biconvex dallinid. Umbo massive, truncated; foramen medium, beak ridges sharp, permesothyridid. Test smooth. Brachial loop laqueiniform.

GEOLOGICAL RANGE. Lower Cretaceous, Valanginian to Hauterivian.

Colinella mullerriedi (Imlay)
Figure 11-3(9a-c); Figure 11-1

Antiptychina? *mullerriedi* Imlay 1937:568, Plate 82, Figures 9-24; Text-figure 4.

DESCRIPTION. Biconvex with acute inflation of brachial umbo. The narrow median sulcus of the pedicle valve is bordered by strong lateral carinae that extend anteriorly to correspond with the shallow sulci in the brachial valve. The strong, narrow, median-anterior fold in the brachial valve corresponds with the deeper, pedicle-anterior sulcus. The anterior commissure is acutely intraplicate.

INTERNAL CHARACTERS. *Pedicle valve*. Test thick. Transverse outline semicircular. Short, thickened, slightly convergent, dental lamellae support subquadrate, inwardly inclined hinge teeth.

Brachial valve. No cardinal process is developed. A broad, shallow, hinge trough widens anteriorly, giving rise to elongate-triangular hinge plates supported by low median septum. The descending branches of the brachial loop extend from the distal ends of the hinge plates and appear to connect with the median septum anteriorly. The ascending branches develop a broad laqueiniform hood with wide central aperture and lateral spines.

Type specimens: The holotype of Imlay's *Antiptychina*? *mullerriedi*, UM 18752 and paratypes UM 18745, 18754, 18742, 18733 are in the collections of the Museum of Paleontology, The University of Michigan.

DISCUSSION. Although *Colinella* gen. nov. has much in common with *Waconella* from the Comanchean of Texas, it differs from that genus in having a later or more anteriorly placed point of attachment on the median septum for the descending branches of the brachial loop and in possessing lateral spines on the laqueiniform hood.

Imlay (1937:569) gave a series of transverse serial sections through species as *Antiptychina*? *mullerriedi* and *A.*? *lata*. Although the triangular hinge plates, low median septum with connecting band, and the converging dental lamellae in the pedicle are shown, no laqueiniform hood is seen. In 1940, Imlay (:141) again figured a series of serial sections through a third species as *A.? formosa*. This series, though more complete than the previous series, shows only part of a poorly developed laqueiniform hood.

Superfamily Rhynchoellacea Gray, 1848
Family Rhynchonellidae Gray, 1848
Subfamily UNCERTAIN

Genus *PROTEORHYNCHIA* gen. nov.

Type species: "*Rhynchonella*" *miquihuanensis* Imlay, 1937

DIAGNOSIS. Broadly oval to subtrigonal rhynchonellid; brachial fold well defined, pedicle sulcus shallow. Linguiform extension trapezoidal. Umbo slightly incurved, beak ridges rounded, interarea poorly defined. Subparallel dental lamellae support elongate, deeply inserted hinge teeth. Dorsal septum high, supporting marked, deep septalium. Concave distal ends of hinge plates developing calcarifer crura.

Proteorhynchia miquihuanensis (Imlay)
Figure 11-4

"*Rhynchonella*" *miquihuanensis* Imlay, 1937:570, Plate 83, Figures 14-21, Text-figure 6.

This species has been adequately described by Imlay in his original description (Imlay, 1937:570) and needs no further comment except I here refer it to the genus *Proteorhynchia* gen. nov.

Type specimens: The holotype of the species UM 18738 and three paratypes, UM 18734, 18746, and 18784, are in the collections of the Museum of Paleontology, The University of Michigan.

Proteorhynchia subtrigonalis (Imlay)
Figure 11-3(12a-c)

Cyclothyris? subtrigonalis Imlay, 1937:571, Plate 83, Figures 12, 13, 22-27; Text-figure 7.

As in the case of *P. miquihuanensis*, the original description is adequate for the species. Likewise, the species formerly known as Cyclothyris? subtrigonalis Imlay is here referred to the genus *Proteorhynchia* gen. nov.

Type specimen: The holotype (Figure 11-3[12a-c]) UM 18748, and three paratypes, UM 17948, 18747, 18749, are in the collections of the Museum of Paleontology, The University of Michigan.

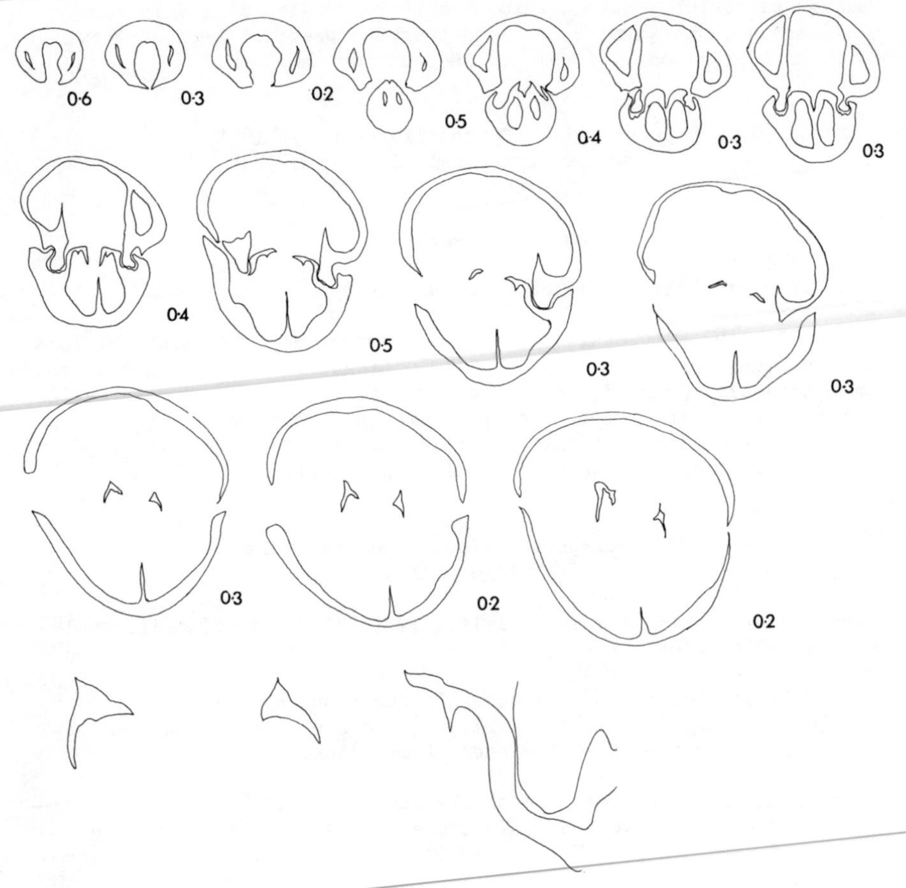

Figure 11-4
Fourteen transverse serial sections through a specimen (UM 18734) of *Proteorhynchia miquihuanensis* (Imlay) from the Lower Cretaceous, Miquihuana, Tamaulipas, Mexico, showing the deep septalium, concave ends of the hinge plates, and the calcarifer crura.

REFERENCES

Adkins, W. S. 1929. Some Upper Cretaceous Taylor Ammonites from Texas. *Univ. Texas Bull.* 2901:203-222.

Ager, D. V. 1967. Some mesozoic brachiopods in the Tethys region. *Systematics Assoc. Pub.* 7:135-151.

Ager, D. V. 1968. The supposedly ubiquitous Tethyan brachiopod *Halorella* and its relations. *Jour. Palaeont. Soc.* India 5-9 (1960-1964):54-70.

Ager, D. V., and G. E. G. Westerman. 1963. New Mesozoic brachiopods from Canada. *Jour. Paleontology* 37:595-610.

Ager, D. V., J. R. Underwood, and R. K. Ford. 1963. New Cretaceous brachiopod from Trans-Pecos Texas. *Jour. Paleontology* 37:371-378.

Anderson, F. M. 1902. Cretaceous deposits of the Pacific Coast.

California Acad. Sci. Proc. 3(2):1-129.

Anderson, F. M. 1938. Lower Cretaceous deposits in California and Oregon. *Geol. Soc. America Spec. Paper 16*, 339 p.

Anderson, F. M. 1958. Upper Cretaceous of the Pacific Coast. *Geol. Soc. America Mem. 71*, 378 p.

Burwash, E. M. 1914. On some new species of marine invertebrates from the Cretaceous of the Queen Charlotte Islands. *Royal Soc. Canada Trans.* 7:77-89.

Cooper, G. A. 1955. New Cretaceous Brachiopoda from Arizona. *Smithsonian Misc. Colln.* 131:1-18.

Crickmay, C. H. 1933. Attempt to Zone the North American Jurassic on the basis of its brachiopods. *Geol. Soc. America Bull.* 44: 871-894.

Dagys, A. S. 1968. Jurassic and early Cretaceous brachiopods of northern Siberia. *Trudy. Inst. Geol. Geofiz. sib. Otd.* 41:1-167.

Imlay, R. W. 1937. Lower Neocomian Fossils from the Miquihuanana region, Mexico. *Jour. Paleontology* 11:552-574.

Imlay, R. V. 1940. Neocomian faunas of northern Mexico. *Geol. Soc. America Bull.* 51:117-190.

Middlemiss, F. A. 1959. English Aptian Terebratulidae. *Palaeontology* 2:94-142.

Middlemiss, F. A. 1976. Lower Cretaceous Terebratulidina of Northern England and Germany and their geological background. *Geol. Jahrb.* 30:21-104.

Moskvin, M. M. 1959. Atlas of the Upper Cretaceous fauna of the Northern Caucasus and Crimea. Chief Administration Central Scientific Gas Industry of the Soviet Ministry. *All Union Scient. Res. Inst. Natural Gas* 1959:1-500.

Owen, E. F. 1962. The brachiopod genus *Cyclothyris*. *Bull. British Museum (Natural History) Geology* 7:37-63.

Owen, E. F. 1970. A revision of the subfamily Kingeninae Elliott. *Bull. British Museum (Natural History) Geology* 19:27-83.

Owen, E. F. 1972. A new rhynchonellid brachiopod from the Upper Jurassic rocks of British Columbia. *Canada Geol. Survey Paper 72-26*, pp. 1-8.

Owen, E. F. 1976. *Cyclothyris* (Cretaceous Brachiopoda) from California. *Bull. British Museum (Natural History) Geology* 27:301-304.

Owen, E. F. 1977. Evolutionary trends in some Mesozoic Terebratellacea. *Bull. British Museum (Natural History) Geology* 28:205-253.

Roemer, F. A. 1852. *Die Kreidebildungen von Texas*, pp. 1-100, Bonn.

Schuchert, C. 1897. American fossil brachiopoda. *U.S. Geol. Survey Bull. 87*, 464 p.

Stephenson, L. W. 1941. The larger invertebrate fossils of the Navarro Group of Texas. *Univ. Texas Pub. 4101*, 641 p.

Warren, P. S. 1937. A rhynchonellid brachiopod from the Bearpaw Formation of Saskatchewan. *Royal Soc. Canada Trans.* 31:1-3.

Whiteaves, J. E. 1903. Mesozoic Fossils. *Canada Geol. Survey 1*, 415 p.

12

Ecological Reappraisal of the German Posidonienschiefer (Toarcian) and the Stagnant Basin Model

Erle G. Kauffman

ABSTRACT

The Toarcian Posidonienschiefer of Germany has long been regarded as a classic example of a dysaerobic to anoxic, stagnant epicontinental silled basin. Supportive evidence includes: High organic carbon and pyrite content; very thin-bedded, evenly-laminated, generally non-bioturbated shales; exceptional preservation of fossils, including articulated skeletons and soft parts, representing diverse marine organisms; and biotas dominated by pelagic and planktonic organisms, and normally benthic forms which could have had a pseudoplanktonic life habit. Detailed stratigraphic, paleoenvironmental, and paleoecological observations on two of the most complete sequences of the Posidonienschiefer in southwestern Germany provide diverse evidence which contradicts this hypothesis. Nearly continuous benthic circulation, in some cases involving strong currents, is suggested by current stable, moderately to strongly aligned dead shells and vertebrate skeletons, by current shadows and shell stringers, by zones of bioclastic debris, and by ammonite conchs with the living chamber selectively filled by bioclastic material on otherwise barren mud surfaces. The numbers of normally benthic invertebrates, especially bivalves, far exceed the number of observed potential pseudoplanktonic "host" surfaces; they probably lived benthically for the most part. Encrusted logs and ammonite shells, the proposed pseudoplanktonic "hosts" for normally benthic invertebrates, are relatively rare; for the most part they show benthic encrustation patterns, not pseudoplanktonic patterns. *In situ* benthic bivalves and sparse burrows were observed at numerous intervals throughout the Posidonienschiefer. *"Posidonia"* (=*Bositra*) itself, described as a planktonic bivalve, primarily has characteristics and facies distribution patterns of a free-living to weakly byssate benthic form. Paleocommunities in the Posidonienschiefer predominantly suggest fluctuating weakly to moderately oxygenated benthic environments, and only episodic, short term anoxic events. Ammonite encrustation patterns and decay patterns among vertebrates strongly suggest an oxygenated water column but largely anoxic sediment-water interface zone, not an anoxic basin, during deposition of most of the Posidonienschiefer.

INTRODUCTION

Black, organic-rich, finely laminated shale, in many cases yielding exceptionally well-preserved fossils, is a recurrent facies throughout the Phanerozoic. This facies is further characterized by little or no bioturbation, abundant pyrite and phosphate, and biotas composed of pelagic and supposedly allochthonous benthonic organisms. The Middle Cambrian Burgess Shale, Ordovician-Silurian "graptolite facies," Devonian Chattanooga and Cleveland (Ohio) shales, the Upper Mississippian "Fayetteville Black Kerogen Shale" (Zangerl et al., 1969), the Pennsylvanian Mecca and Logan Quarry shales of Indiana (Zangerl and Richardson, 1963), and the Upper Cretaceous Sharon Springs Member, Pierre Shale in the Western Interior are typical North American marine examples. Enrichment of similar facies by pelagic carbonate produces light-colored counterparts (limestones, calcareous shales, and shaley chalks) that otherwise have the same physical, chemical, and biological characteristics (Seilacher and Westphal, 1971). The Upper Jurassic Solnhofen lithographic limestone of Germany, the Cenomanian "Plattenkalke" of Lebanon, and parts of the Upper Cretaceous Smoky Hill Member, Niobrara Formation of Kansas are marine examples, whereas the "Mahogany Zone" oil shale of the Lower Eocene Green River Formation in northwestern Colorado is a similar lacustrine deposit.

Seilacher (1970) and Seilacher and Westphal (1971) classified this type of deposit as "Fossil-Lagerstätten": sediment bodies yielding an unusual amount of paleontological information because of exceptional preservation. Such preservation is thought to occur under the following conditions: 1. The lower part of the water column and all of the benthic sediment is severely oxygen depleted or anaerobic and water circulation is limited (Type A, Stagnation Fossil-Lagerstätten of Seilacher, 1970). Hydrogen sulfide levels are commonly high; sedimentation is normally slow. Most of the above-mentioned deposits fall into this category as currently interpreted. 2. Organisms are rapidly buried in anaerobic to oxygen-depleted, hydrogen sulfide-enriched sediments (Type C, Verschüttungs or Obrutions-Lagerstätten of Seilacher, 1970) usually as a result of mud or debris flows or turbidites. Most of the organisms buried are allochthonous and transported from shallower, oxygenated environments (for example, the Burgess Shale biota). A stagnant water column is not necessarily implied.

In either case, exceptional preservation of entire individuals, articulated skeletons, and even soft parts is thought to result from great restriction of predation, scavenging, sediment recycling, and aerobic bacterial decay because of low oxygen or anaerobic conditions in the sediment and overlying water column, hydrogen sulfide poisoning, and (in Obrutions-Lagerstätten) rapid burial.

The most famous black shale unit representing "Stagnation Fossil-Lagerstätten" (Figures 12-1 through 12-4) is the Jurassic (Toarcian) Posidonienschiefer of southwestern Germany (Lias Epsilon, "*Posidonia*" Shales, Holzmaden Shales of literature), especially as exposed in large quarries in the Dotternhausen and Holzmaden areas (Figure 12-1). The Posidonienschiefer is composed of up to 12 m of

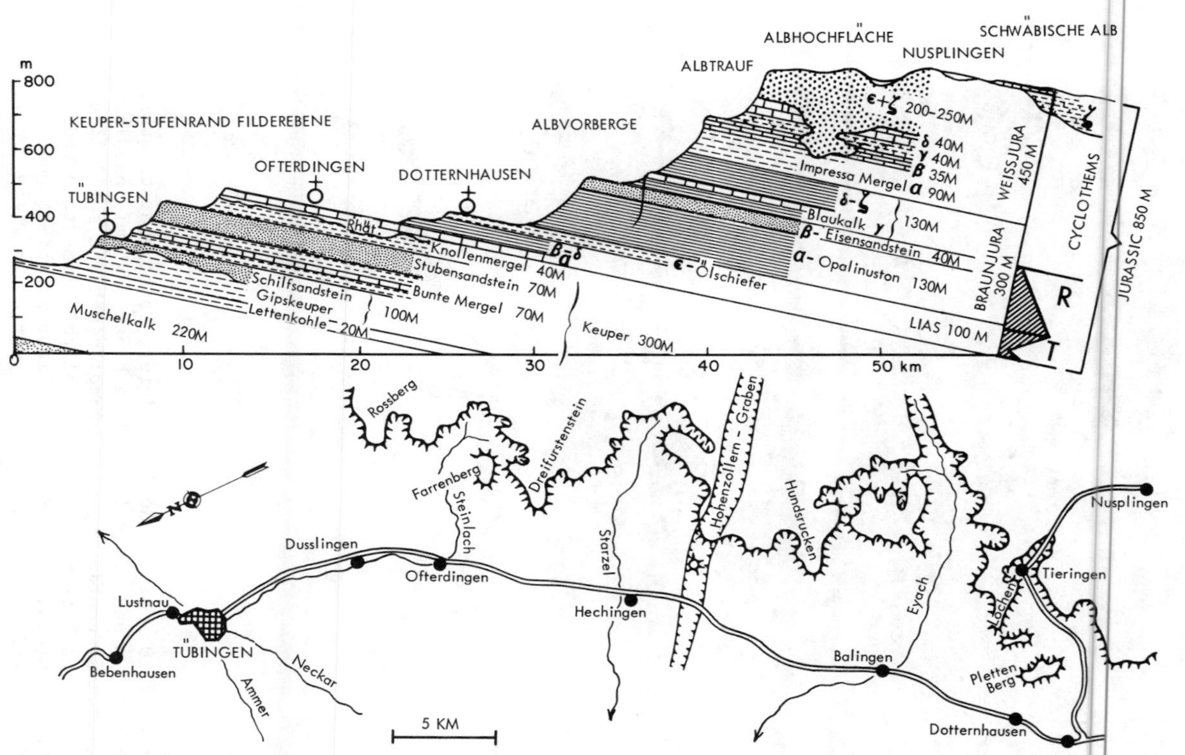

Figure 12-1
Generalized stratigraphic section through Triassic and Jurassic rocks of southern Germany (top) and areas of principal outcrops (from Seilacher and Westphal, 1971, Figure 3): quarries at Dotternhausen (lower right) constituted the primary study site for the Posidonienschiefer (Lias Epsilon, Ölschiefer on diagram).

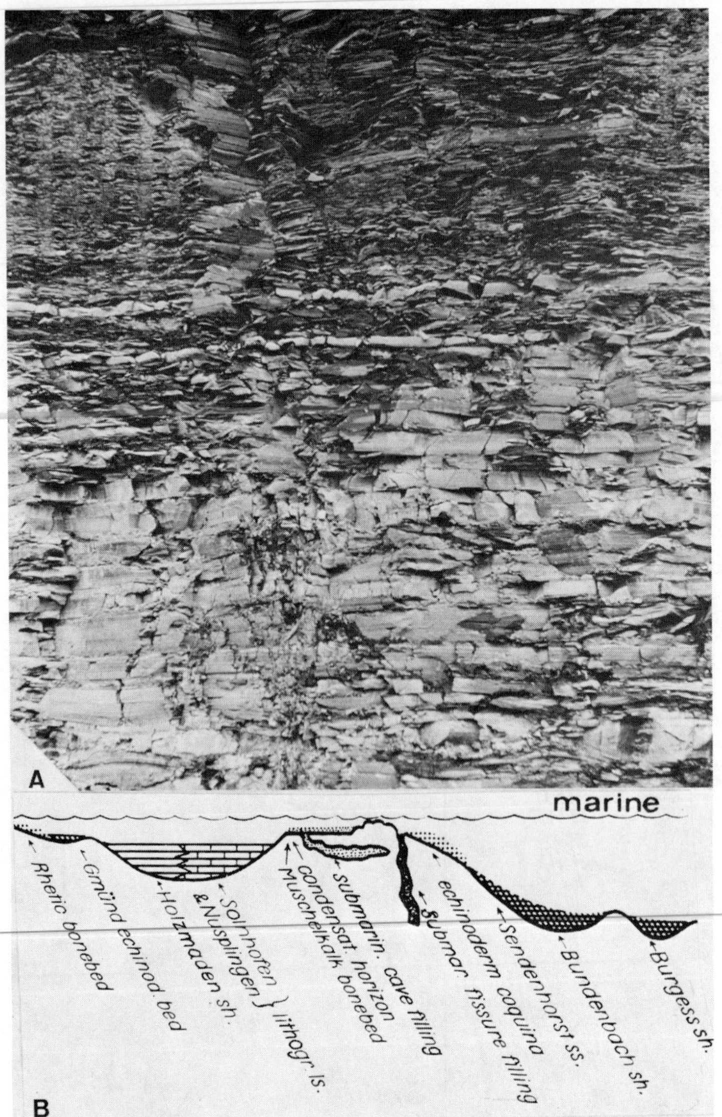

Figure 12-2
A. Outcrop of 10 m of Posidonienschiefer, Dotternhausen quarry, lacking basal 2 m and upper 1 m. Note blocky rythmic bedding (small-scale cyclothems; continuity of laminae; pinch and swell limestone bed near base (Laibstein); paired coccolithic limestone beds near middle (Oberer Stein, Gelbe Platte); thin upper limestones (Schlacken), and thinner bedding of upper shale where *"Posidonia"* (=*Bositra*) is abundant. B. Seilacher and Westphal's (1971) interpretation of the depositional environment of the Posidonienschiefer (=Holzmaden Shale): a stagnant, largely anaerobic, silled, marine epicontinental basin with only the upper part of the water column sufficiently oxygenated to support a diverse biota.

black to dark-gray, finely and evenly laminated, generally nonbioturbated, pyritic bituminous shale (Figure 12-2A). Thin limestone beds in the middle Posidonienschiefer and very thin carbonate laminae and pellets throughout the shale reflect pelagic (coccolithophorid) carbonate enrichment of the facies. Exceptional fossils occur abundantly at many levels within the Posidonienschiefer. These include entire articulated vertebrate skeletons, some of which preserve soft parts and stomach contents, and exquisite whole specimens representing a vast array of marine invertebrates (Figures 12-3, 12-4). These world famous fossils are highly prized as exhibit specimens by museums and have been extensively researched.

Exceptional preservation of fossils, diverse geochemical data, and characteristic bedding features in the Posidonienschiefer have led the great majority of workers to interpret this formation as the deposit of a stagnant, anaerobic to severely oxygen-restricted, epicontinental marine basin (Pompeckj, 1901; Hauff, 1921; Hauff, Jr., 1960; Seilacher, 1970; Seilacher and Westphal, 1971). Many mechanisms have been described to explain the development of oxygen-depleted epicontinental basins, including both regional controls (for example, intersection of oceanic oxygen-minimum zone or stagnant zones with areas covered by epicontinental seas during eustatic rise and transgression) and localized causes (for example, silled- or constricted-basin apertures or deep tectonically generated basins in otherwise shallow seas). Of these, Seilacher and Westphal (1971, Figure 1) have applied the silled-basin model (Figure 12-2) to explain stagnation of the Toarcian seaway during deposition of the Posidonienschiefer, a situation perhaps comparable structurally to the Baffin Bay Basin (Richards, 1957, Figure 9) with oxygen depletion approaching that of the Black Sea today (Weyl, 1970:471-476). This sill has not yet been clearly demonstrated in the field, and other interpretations are possible.

CONFLICTING ENVIRONMENTAL MODELS

A large amount of evidence has been carefully assembled in support of the stagnant-basin hypothesis for the Posidonienschiefer. Special emphasis has been placed on exceptionally preserved fossils and on geochemistry and sedimentology. The Posidonienschiefer has been more extensively studied than any Mesozoic deposit thought to represent a largely anaerobic epicontinental marine basin, and the supportive fossil evidence is more spectacular than for most Phanerozoic counterparts. Consequently, the physical, chemical, and biological characteristics of the Posidonienschiefer have become an international standard, an actualistic model, for comparison of other deposits thought to be formed under euxinic conditions. So convincing have been the published arguments in support of the anaerobic-basin model that paleoceanographers interested in eustatic and related oxygen fluctuations during the Jurassic have cited the Posidonienschiefer as strong evidence for widespread stagnation of world oceans and deep epicontinental basins, especially during eustatic rise of sealevel and global transgression (Hallam, 1978:3,4; Fisher and Arthur, 1977).

Principal arguments developed in support of the stagnant, anaerobic-basin model are as follows:

1. The Posidonienschiefer is a low- to moderage-grade oil shale, and

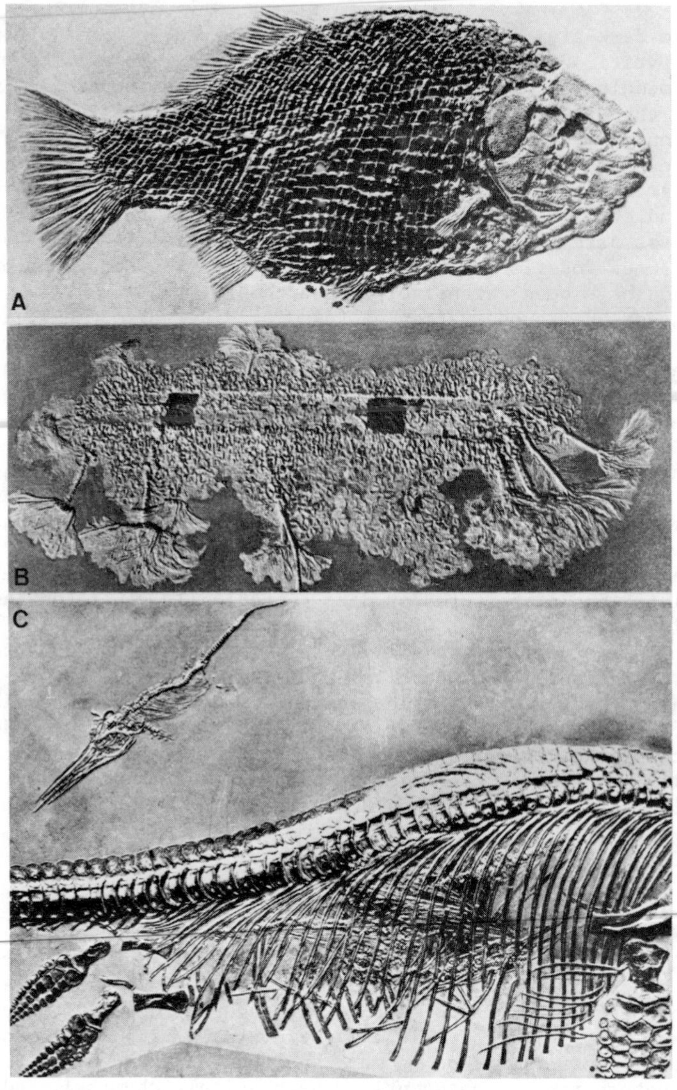

Figure 12-3
Exceptional fossil preservation in the Posidonienschiefer (from Hauff, Jr., 1960, Pls. 17, 49, 65, with permission). All specimens prepared from lower side. A. *Dapedius punctatus* Aggasiz, bed II6, Holzmaden; length 40 cm; Museum Hauff. Note loose scales derived from decay of upper surface. B. Log with attached crinoids and "*Inoceramus*" (Length, 175 cm; Lias epsilon II3C, Ohmden). Note sparser inoceramid growth on bottom of log; preferential orientation of epibionts. C. Articulated skeleton of *Stenopterygius disinteger antecedens* (Lias Epsilon II9; Ohmden, Museum Hauff) note unborn and newly born young (60 cm long) within and beside parent; broken backbone; opposed *en echelon* arrangement of vertebrae, upper rib fragments under complete lower ribs, rotation of upper paddle outside of lower paddle.

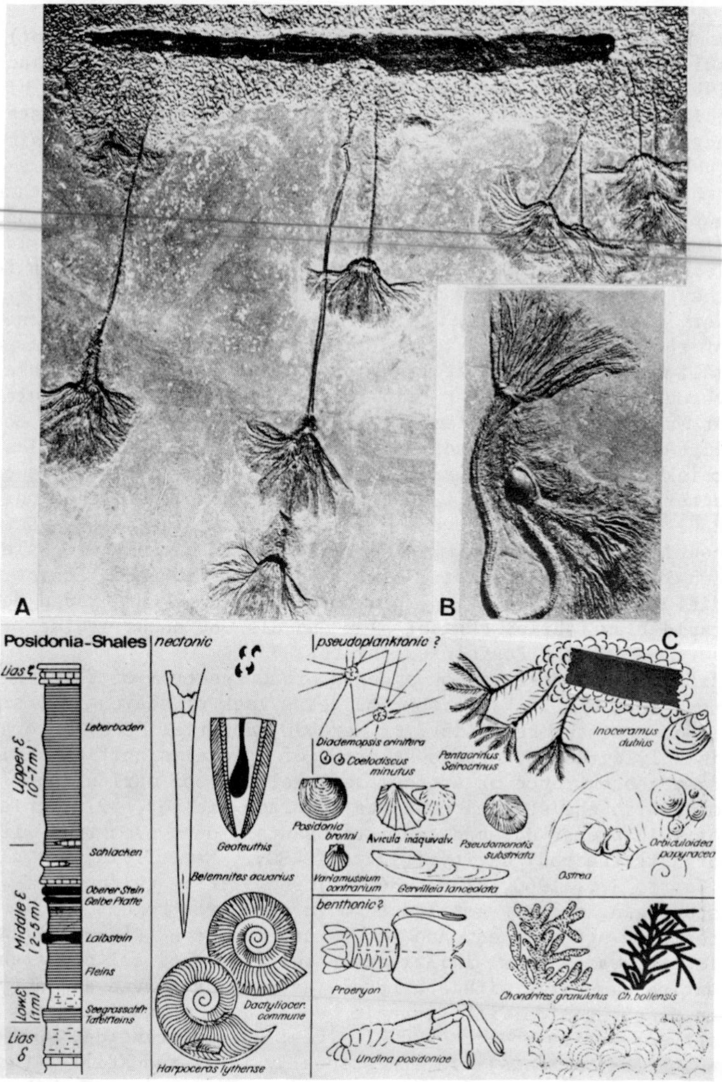

Figure 12-4
A. Large log, prepared from underside, showing lack of epibionts under log, encrustation by inoceramid bivalves on sides and probably upper surface, and large *Seirocrinus* current-aligned to one side (Hauff, Jr., 1960, Plate 64). Encrustation pattern suggests attachment to sunken log on bottom, not to driftwood (C, below) (zone II_3, Holzmaden; length 250 cm.). B. Two isolated "*Pentacrinus subangularis* Miller" (Hauff, 1960, Plate 68a, p. 49; Lias Epsilon II_3, Holzmaden; height 18 cm), one with oyster attached to stem, phototropically oriented toward crown, suggesting crinoid grew upright. C. Generalized stratigraphic section of the Posidonienschiefer (left), and interpretation of life habits of biota by Seilacher and Westphal (1971, Figure 4) as predominantly pelagic and pseudoplanktonic.

contains high percentages of organic carbon (to 15 percent) and sulfur compared to normal marine shale (Einsele and Mosebach, 1955). Original hydrogen sulfide levels were presumably high. This strongly suggests deposition in a reducing, oxygen-starved environment where bacterial decay and scavenging were minimal (Hallam, 1967). Veizer (1977) reported iron and manganese concentrations in the Posidonienschiefer as somewhat lower than, but close to, the predicted level for euxinic basins. Abundant disseminated and nodular pyrite occurs throughout the Posidonienschiefer (Einsele and Mosebach; 1955; Figure 1). This further suggests reducing primary environments.

2. Very thin, continuous, undisturbed lamination characterizes most of the Posidonienschiefer (Figure 12-2A). Bioturbation is normally rare to absent at levels above the basal Seegrasschiefer, though exceptions exist (Einsele and Mosebach, 1955, Figure 1). At many levels, fine laminations alternate between light coccolith-enriched and organic-rich dark-clay layers 1 mm or less in thickness suggesting marine "varves." These features are characteristic of anaerobic benthic environments where the anoxic zone extends to or above the sediment-water interface. Lateral continuity of very thin, planar laminae in bituminous shales are considered characteristic of low current flow and stagnant conditions (Hallam, 1967). Thin laminae and lack of graded beds or rapid-flow fabrics suggest slow and discontinuous sedimentation for most of the Posidonienschiefer.

3. Exceptional preservation among a broad spectrum of fossils (Figures 12-3 and 12-4) further suggests lack of scavenging, predation, sediment recycling, or aerobic bacterial decay of organisms lying dead on the seafloor. Of special significance is the common occurrence of articulated skeletons of marine reptiles, many with the stomach contents in place (Keller, 1976), pieces of skin preserved, and (in icthyosaurs) young preserved within or near the body cavity (Figure 12-3C). Rare flying reptiles (Hauff, Jr., 1960, Plates 34, 35) show little evidence of scavenging as they settled through the water column. Fish are commonly articulated, and scales are in place (Figure 12-3A). Invertebrates show similar examples of exceptional preservation: entire ammonites with apertural features preserved and aptychi in place; squids with tentacle hooks *in situ* and ink sacks preserved; entire co-attached bivalves; entire crinoids, some of which (*Seirocrinus*) are exceptionally large and still attached to logs (Figures 12-3B, 12-4A), and entire arthropod skeletons (Hauff, 1960, Plates 60-77). Most paleontological research on the Posidonienschiefer has concentrated on these exceptionally preserved fossils. Small, rare, and unspectacular fossils, and broken or disarticulated specimens have received disproportionately little attention since the basic documentation of the biota by Hauff (1921). The mode of preservation of shelled invertebrates, especially molluscs, is that of an anaerobic environment. Aragonite layers are missing in virtually all bivalves and gastropods. Seilacher et al. (1976) reported widespread early diagenetic dissolution of aragonite without replacement in ammonite shells, but retention of the organic periostracum, aptychi, and calcitic conellae.

4. Published interpretations of Posidonienschiefer paleoecology (Figure 12-4C) suggest mainly pelagic, planktonic or pseudo-

planktonic habitats in the upper water column. Taxa with benthonic life modes are reported to be rare or absent at most levels. There are no published reports of benthonic organisms (except sparse burrows) preserved *in situ*; benthic foraminifera are sparse, widely scattered, and show an inverse relationship between occurrence and organic content of the sediment (that is, oxygen depletion) (Hoffman and Martin, 1960; Franke, 1936). Pelagic fishes and reptiles comprise most of the vertebrate assemblage. Ammonites, whose weakly ornamented discoid shells suggest an active pelagic life habit, are one of the most common invertebrate elements. Byssate and cemented bivalves and inarticulate brachiopods are also common. These represent groups that are normally epibenthic in habitat, but have been widely interpreted as pseudoplanktonic, attached to floating wood, seaweed, and living or floating-dead ammonite shells during deposition of the Posidonienschiefer (Figure 12-4C). Large ammonites are commonly encrusted with epibionts. "*Posidonia*" (=*Bositra*), which is extremely abundant in the lower and upper parts of the Posidonienschiefer, has been interpreted as a nektoplanktonic bivalve (Jefferies and Minton, 1965). Small gastropods and diademoid echinoids, less common than bivalves, are viewed as having been mobile epibenthos on seaweed and floating logs, respectively. The great majority of crinoids belong to a genus (*Seirocrinus*) that Seilacher et al. (1968) interpreted as functionally adapted to hanging pendant from floating logs; clusters of *Seirocrinus* are commonly found attached to large logs associated with byssate inoceramid bivalves (Figures 12-3B, 12-4A,C).

5. Among both infaunal and epifaunal organisms that have been interpreted as partially or wholly benthonic under normal conditions, diversity is always low and one to two generation population structure is most characteristic. The assemblage is characterized by rare individuals or sparse populations of infaunal taxa, benthic fish, Crustacea, echinoids, and benthic foraminifera. Also present are small localized populations of cemented and byssate bivalves and inarticulate brachiopods, and very large populations of inoceramid bivalves. These occurrences are characteristic of short-lived, physically controlled, pioneer communities.

This is the support for the stagnant-basin model. On the other hand, several aspects of the Posidonienschiefer and its biota raise questions about its interpretation. These questions prompted the current investigation, which produced the following contradictory lines of evidence, subsequently discussed and illustrated (Figures 12-5 through 12-19):

1. Organisms that could only have had a partial or wholly benthic habitat are known from the Posidonienschiefer. These include rare bottom-feeding (shell-crushing) fish; sparse but widely distributed, adult uncinid and eryonid lobsters (Hauff, Jr., 1960, Plate 60-62); infaunal scaphopods; and rare, but complete, infaunal bivalves such as *Goniomya*; Solenomyidae, (Riegraf, 1977), *Solemya*, *Unicardium* (Hauff, 1921) and others found in this study. Burrows of infaunal worms and thalassinoid shrimp are usually very sparse, but occur at many levels (Einsele and Mosebach, 1955, Figure 1). Locally, *Chondrites*

burrows are abundant within narrow intervals (Einsele and Mosebach, 1955). Tests and spines of diademoid and cidarid echinoids are rare, but widely distributed through the black shale units. Small numbers of agglutinated benthonic foraminifera are known from the Posidonienschiefer (Herm, pers. comm.). Among the crinoids, short-stalked *"Pentacrinus"* with dense crowns and cirri along the stalks (for example, *"P." briareus* Mill.) suggest a benthic "rooted" life mode. Although most *Seirocrinus subangularis* recovered from the Posidonienschiefer are long stalked and associated with logs, some specimens have short stems with cirral "roots" at the base and, rarely, epibiont oysters on the stem that are phototropically orientated toward the crown (Figure 12-4B) suggesting a benthic life mode with the crown facing upwards. Further, the pseudoplanktonic habitat of long stalked *Seirocrinus* on logs (Figures 12-3B, 12-4A,C; Seilacher et al., 1968) has been seriously challenged by Rasmussen (1977) and by evidence subsequently presented in this paper.

Apparently obligate benthic species cannot be regarded as allochthonous, rapidly introduced into the depositional site of the Posidonienschiefer by storm events, mud, or debris flows; no sedimentary structures characteristic of rapid transport have been identified in rocks associated with well-preserved fossils. Analogy to the Cambrian Burgess Shale environment, where microturbidites are clearly preserved, is not warranted.

2. Byssate and cemented, normally benthic bivalves (for example, *"Inoceramus," Ostrea, Plicatula*, Pectinidae, Pteriacea, and *Pseudomonotis* are extremely abundant, occurring mainly in densely packed, laterally persistent beds or clusters throughout the Posidonienschiefer (Hauff, 1921); yet pieces of wood, cited as the principal "hosts" for these bivalves in a pseudoplanktonic habit, are relatively uncommon and scattered. Fossils interpretable as floating "seaweed" are virtually unknown. Large ammonites with dense byssate and cemented bivalve encrustation are not common; the great majority of ammonites have little or no epibiont encrustation (Hauff, Jr., 1960, Plates 73-76). Byssate and cemented bivalves are much more abundant and occur densely at more levels than can be accounted for by their proposed pseudoplanktonic "hosts" in the same sections. Floating driftwood today is a poor substrate for bivalves other than Teredinidae, and drifting seaweed, alive or dead, is even worse (Kauffman, 1975). Most epifaunal bivalves may have actually lived as benthos in the Posidonienschiefer sea.

3. *"Posidonia"* (=*Bositra*) and related Paleozoic and Mesozoic Posidoniidae have many features of functional morphology and facies distribution that preclude a swimming or floating habitat. Most have shells that are too large and thick to permanently maintain a pelagic habitat. Musculature known from representatives of the Posidoniidae is *not* similar to either pelagic molluscs (for example, pteropods to which Jefferies and Minton compared *"Posidonia"*) or to benthic bivalves with short-term swimming ability (for example, Pectinacea or Limidae) but resembles many epibenthic bivalves. *"Posidonia"* (=*Bositra*) was probably a free-living or very weakly byssate epibenthic bivalve as suggested by Beurlen (1925), Craig (1954), and others. It does not occur associated with logs or large ammonite shells,

possible pseudoplanktonic hosts. It is facies-restricted, occurring as adults almost totally in the basal and topmost 1-2 m of the Posidonienschiefer, where it seems to have occupied a specific benthic habitat in facies between well-oxygenated and oxygen-depleted benthic environments.

4. Broken and disarticulated fossils are common in the Posidonienschiefer. Yet the published paleobiological and ecological record of the unit is heavily weighted toward well-preserved vertebrates (Figure 12-3A,C); Fraas, 1891; Hauff, 1921), exceptional invertebrate occurrences (Figures 12-3B, 12-4A; Seilacher et al., 1968), ammonites and their preservation (Seilacher, et al, 1976), and *"Posidonia"* (Jefferies and Minton, 1965). Because of exceptional fossil preservation, certain stratigraphic levels have been emphasized and others poorly studied. Most of what we know about the fossil record is further influenced by preparation of the fossils: virtually all large specimens (especially vertebrates) are prepared from the underside because they are better preserved on that surface. Except for documentation by Quenstedt (1856) and Hauff (1921), the *normal* aspect of the Posidonienschiefer biota and its preservation has not received equal attention.

5. Geochemical and sedimentologic data led Einsele and Mosebach (1955) to support a gyttja model for the benthic zone of the Posidonienschiefer sea (oxygenated, nutrient-rich waters overlying anaerobic sediment) instead of a sapropel model of sedimentation (anaerobic to oxygen-depleted water overlying soft anaerobic sediment). The occurrence of benthic arthropods, bivalves, gastropods, crinoids, and scaphopods provides supportive evidence, as do certain geochemical characteristics (Veizer, 1977). Einsele and Mosebach's data (1955) also suggest that fluctuations in the occurrence of pyrite documented for ten sections is correlative with fluctuations in the occurrence of burrows, undisputed evidence of benthic oxygenation. The reverse would be expected in a euxinic-basin model. Finally, the stagnant-basin model requires greatly restricted current circulation, yet initial research on the orientation of fossils within the Posidonienschiefer (Brenner, 1976b) shows well-defined orientation of belemnites (the heaviest of invertebrate remains) and ammonites. My study, which analyzed current orientation throughout the Posidonienschiefer (Figure 12-7), found evidence for weak to moderate currents at nearly all levels; this strongly suggests almost continuous oxygenation of the lower part of the water column during deposition of the Posidonienschiefer.

6. Many detailed studies have been done on modern euxinic epicontinental and shelf basins viewed as possible analogues to the Posidonienschiefer. Foremost among the modern analogues are the Black Sea, the Baltic Sea, the Baffin Basin, the California borderland basins, and deep basins within the Gulf of California. Rhoads and Morse (1971) recently summarized the biologic, chemical, and physical aspects of oxygen-deficient marine basins: 1. Below 0.1 ml/1 oxygen, the benthic zone is azoic. 2. Between 0.1 and 1.0 ml/1 oxygen a low diversity, small-bodied infauna, mainly composed of procaryotes, protists, fungi, Platyhelminthes, and Aschelminthes is characteristic; more complex worms and sparse thin-shelled molluscs and arthropods are

found in the upper part of the oxygen range. 3. Above 1.0 ml/l oxygen, a diverse calcareous fauna predominates (in addition to soft-bodied infauna and epifauna) and includes many epibenthic taxa. The Posidonienschiefer fauna, dominated by ammonites and epibenthic bivalves but poor in infauna, does not fit any of these models; it is closest to 3 but has lower diversity among shelled benthos and rare infauna. This indicates an oxygenated water column. The lack of infauna might result from a largely anoxic, hydrogen sulfide-enriched sediment column; the lower than predicted benthic diversity could result from some oxygen depletion in the lower water column or the predominance of pioneer communities.

Sufficient questions concerning established paleoenvironmental interpretations are raised by these facts to merit a detailed re-investigation of the paleobiology, ecology, and sediments of the Posidonienschiefer in southwestern Germany. This work is especially important because of the eminance of the Posidonienschiefer as a popular model for Phanerozoic euxinic basins elsewhere. The contradictory lines of evidence suggest that emphasis in new research should be placed on normal aspects of the stratigraphy and paleontology by a thorough, systematic approach to collecting data. Ultimately, this investigation should provide a rigorous test of the hypothesis that the Posidonienschiefer represents an anaerobic to oxygen-depleted, stagnant, epicontinental basin in which favorable life conditions were restricted to the upper part of the marine water column.

The Toarcian seaway was extensive (Hauff, Jr., 1960, Fig. 1), and the Posidonienschiefer bituminous shale facies widespread, grading laterally to nearshore facies. Therefore, a comprehensive interpretation of paleoenvironments and paleoecology for the entire Posidonienschiefer cannot be made from the geographically restricted data of this study. Instead, I view this study as an exhaustive test of the hypothesis that the Posidonienschiefer of southwestern Germany represents part of a stagnant silled-basin system (Figure 12-2B); most of the evidence leading to this interpretation has come from the same areas sampled in the present study. This study is also designed to produce a new actualistic model based on detailed analyses of representative stratigraphic sequences, rock types and fossils, depositional history and ecological response throughout one of the classic examples of "Stagnation Fossil Lagerstätten" (Seilacher, 1970).

SAMPLING PROCEDURE

Two complete, fresh, quarry sections were systematically sampled during the study: the main quarries near Dotternhausen (principal study site) and in the Holzmaden-Bolle area. Available time permitted no more. Numerous marker beds allowed precise correlation of different parts of each quarry system. In each site, a 0.5 by 0.5 m area was defined on the surface at the top of the Posidonienschiefer and the entire section down to the Seegrasschiefer was excavated in 1 to 2 cm thick intervals to provide uniform, closely spaced samples throughout the bituminous shale facies. All samples were orientated as to top and bottom. Small, 3 to 25 cm thick, depositional cycles of the middle Posidonienschiefer (Figure 12-2A) were each collected as a unit, broken down, and studied in 1 to 2 cm intervals to test for ecological and environmental patterns within the cycle. After systematic sampling and analysis, many individual units were traced laterally within and between quarries and sampled at irregular intervals to check results. Great lateral continuity of even the smallest stratigraphic units or marker beds seems typical of the Posidonienschiefer. Museum collections and random collecting in additional quarries provided supplemental data.

On each 0.5 by 0.5 by 0.01 to 0.02 meter sample, the following observations were made: taxa present, their general size range and relative abundance; condition of preservation; orientation and distribution patterns (biofabric); abundance and morphology of associated pyrite; bedding and sedimentary structures (including thin sections); and all biogenic structures. Where present, the interrelationship of body or trace fossils in point contact was noted and special sedimentary or biologic features were recorded. The interpretations and ecologic relationships discussed in this chapter were founded on these detailed observations.

STRATIGRAPHIC AND SEDIMENTOLOGIC INTERPRETATIONS

THE TOARCIAN CYCLOTHEM

In southwestern Germany, the Posidonienschiefer lies in the middle of a subsymmetrical marine cyclothem (Figure 12-1) that begins in the Early Sinemurian (Upper Angulatensandstein; Gryphaeenkalke), reaches a transgressive peak in the Early to early-Middle Toarcian (middle Posidonienschiefer), and peak regression in the Middle Aalenian (sandstones at top of Opalinustone, and overlying Eisensandstein). The cyclothem is the major pulse in a more general transgression (representing eustatic rise) that may begin as early as the Late Hettangian (middle Angulatensandstein); with smaller regressive pulses in the Early Sinemurian and Early Pleinsbachian before peaking in the Toarcian. Hallam (1978) cited this as the second major eustatic rise in the Jurassic with regional expression in western Europe.

Similar, but not identical, transgressive and regressive facies sequences are developed in reverse order on either side of the transgressive peak (Figures 12-1, 12-5). Thus, during transgression nearshore sandstones (Angulatensandstein; Late Hettangian; earliest Sinemurian) are succeeded by shallow-water calcareous and argillaceous sands and sandy carbonates (Gryphaeenkalke; Early Sinemurian); offshore clay shales formed under normal marine conditions (Schwarzjuraton, Lias Beta, and lower Lias Delta on either side of a possible Lower Pleinsbachian regressive pulse); more offshore normal marine marls, calcareous shales, and argillaceous limestones (upper part of the upper Schwarzjuraton, upper Lias Delta), and near-maximum transgressive, dark clay shales and marls of the lower Posidonienschiefer (Figure 12-5; lower Lias Epsilon, Early Toarcian). Maximum transgression and water depth is probably marked by interbedded, black bituminous shale and coccolithic limestones (Laibstein, Oberer Stein, Schlacken) of the middle Posidonienschiefer (Figures 12-1A, 12-5). The regressive facies sequence is reversed (Figures 12-1, 12-5). Black organic-rich shales (upper Posidonienschiefer) are successively overlain by the following sequence of deposits. Offshore marls and argillaceous limestones interbedded with calcareous shales (Upper Schwarzjuramergel; Upper Toarcian); dark, normal marine shales becoming silty at the top (lower Opalinuston; Early Aalenian), and nearshore calcareous and argillaceous quartz sandstones at maximum regression (Middle Aalenian sandstones of the upper Opalinuston and the Eisensandstein) (Figure 12-1).

Kauffman (1969, 1973, 1977, 1979) described such symmetrical cyclothems as typical of tectonically subsiding cratonic basins where subsidence exceeds depositional rates during transgression, and the basin fills during regression. Einsele and Mosebach (1955) described the sedimentary structures, petrology, and biofabric of the Posidonienschiefer in detail and interpreted many sedimentary environments.

MAJOR SMALL-SCALE FACIES

Small-scale facies are variable and remarkably symmetrical within the main body of the Posidonienschiefer (Figure 12-5). The following major facies are recognized in the late transgressive-early regressive sequence (Figure 12-5):

1. *Chondrites*-bioturbated mudstone, thin-bedded shale, and bedded to nodular argillaceous limestone representing offshore, quiet-water, normal-marine benthic conditions. This facies occurs at the base (Seegrasschiefer, lower Lias Epsilon, 0.5 m) and top of the Posidonienschiefer (uppermost Lias Epsilon limestone and overlying limestones at the base of the upper Schwarzjuramergel, Lias Zeta). Crustose algae associated with Lias Zeta suggest photic depths (less than 100 m).
2. *"Posidonia"* (=*Bositra*) shell beds (Fleins) in a matrix of thinly and subevenly laminated clay shale and platy calcareous and calcisiltic shale. This facies occupies less than a meter near the base and 1 to 3 meters at the top of the Posidonienschiefer in the studied sections (Figure 12-5; Hauff, Jr., 1960, diagram in pocket). Moderately quiet-water benthic environments and slow, interrupted sedimentation rates are inferred. Dense *"Posidonia"* populations containing adult specimens are almost entirely restricted to these zones at the margins of the bituminous facies (transgressive peak); *"Posidonia"* is rare in the main body of the Posidonienschiefer, contrary to the assumption of Jefferies and Minton (1965) that *"Posidonia"* is characteristic of Jurassic "euxinic" black shale facies.
3. Black to dark-gray bituminous shale, thinly and evenly laminated, nonbioturbated, commonly "varved" (alternating coccolith-rich and clay-rich bands), and arranged in blocky units 3 to 25 cm thick representing small-scale depositional cycles (Figure 12-2A). This facies forms the main bulk of the Posidonienschiefer below and above facies 4 and is characterized by abundant ammonite and inoceramid bivalve accumulations. Deep quiet-water conditions and a toxic, but rarely lethal, substrate are inferred.
4. Beds and lenticular concretionary zones of blocky, gray, coccolithic, argillaceous limestone interbedded with dark shales as in facies 3. These preserve fine continuous laminae, lack much bioturbation, and show maximum surface-dissolution effects.

From base to top of the cyclothem these facies are arranged in the following order: 1-2-3-4-3-2-1 (Figure 12-5). Implications of the depositional cycles are important. The environment of the Posidonienschiefer was not uniform in terms of both broad facies progressions and details of small-scale depositional cycles within the shales. Most examples of exceptional preservation suggesting oxygen restriction come from the middle part of the Posidonienschiefer associated with peak transgression, especially shales of facies 3 and 4 (Hauff, Jr., 1960, diagram in pocket); and the *"Posidonia"*-rich beds lie only between facies that show evidence of normal-marine benthic conditions (facies 1) and those suspected of representing anaerobic benthic conditions or severe oxygen depletion (facies 3, 4). This infers that *"Posidonia"* favored moderately oxygenated benthic environments.

MICROFACIES

Within the major facies divisions, several distinct microfacies characterize the main body of the Posidonienschiefer; Einsele and Mosebach (1955) provide extensive data and interpretation of many facies types.

1. Uniform, thinly and evenly laminated, bituminous shale is the principal matrix (Figure 12-2A); but at many levels, dark clay bands several millimeters thick alternate with light-gray coccolith-enriched bands less than 1 millimeter thick; these may represent marine varves or climatic-productivity cycles. This microfacies is especially well developed in the lower and middle part of the formation (Fleins and above·(Figure 12-5). Most layers are sparsely fossiliferous, but dense shell accumulations (ammonite-rich beds, mass-mortality zones, *"Inoceramus"* biostromes, *"Posidonia"*-dominated beds) occur at numerous levels. The "varving" and the frequent appearance and disappearance of shell beds suggest abundant short-term fluctuations in the environment of the Posidonienschiefer seaway.
2. Shale microfacies of lithology 1 are grouped in generally repetitive successions within distinct, blocky, persistent bedding units 3 to 25 centimeters thick (Figures 12-2A and 12-6) representing small-scale sedimentary rhythms. The origin of these rhythms probably involves alternating periods of oxygenation (allowing benthic habitation and development of *"Inoceramus"* biostromes) and moderate to severe oxygen depletion (allowing little or no benthic biota). A rapid environmental transition between these environments is commonly marked by a dense ammonite bed (mass-mortality zone?; Figure 12-6). These small cyclothems occur in the middle Posidonienschiefer.
3. Thin-bedded to platy calcisilts and fine-grained argillaceous calcarenites a few millimeters to a centimeter thick occur at many levels within the main body of the Posidonienschiefer and are commonly associated with *"Posidonia"*-rich beds at the base and top of the formation. Thin sections reveal no graded bedding. This facies is characterized by extensive breakage and wear on bioclastic materials (mainly bivalve shell fragments and fine fish debris) and, in the thicker beds, sparse to (rarely) abundant burrows (*Chondrites; "Planolites,"* locally *Thalassinoides*). These probably represent finely winnowed and extensively reworked, shell-bone, lag deposits formed during periods of low sediment rates or bypass.

4. Thin-bedded to platy and slabby, fine- to coarse-grained, shelly calcarenite beds contain abundant fish and belemnite debris (Schlacken, Figure 12-5). These commonly have irregular contacts, coquinoid zones, and lensing bodies of clay that Seilacher et al. (1976) interpreted as fillings of dissolved ammonite body chambers, but which in some cases, may represent compressed burrow fillings. Current orientation is weakly to moderately well defined with belemnites (Brenner, 1976a). Brenner called on "current events," and others have called on debris flows to ac-

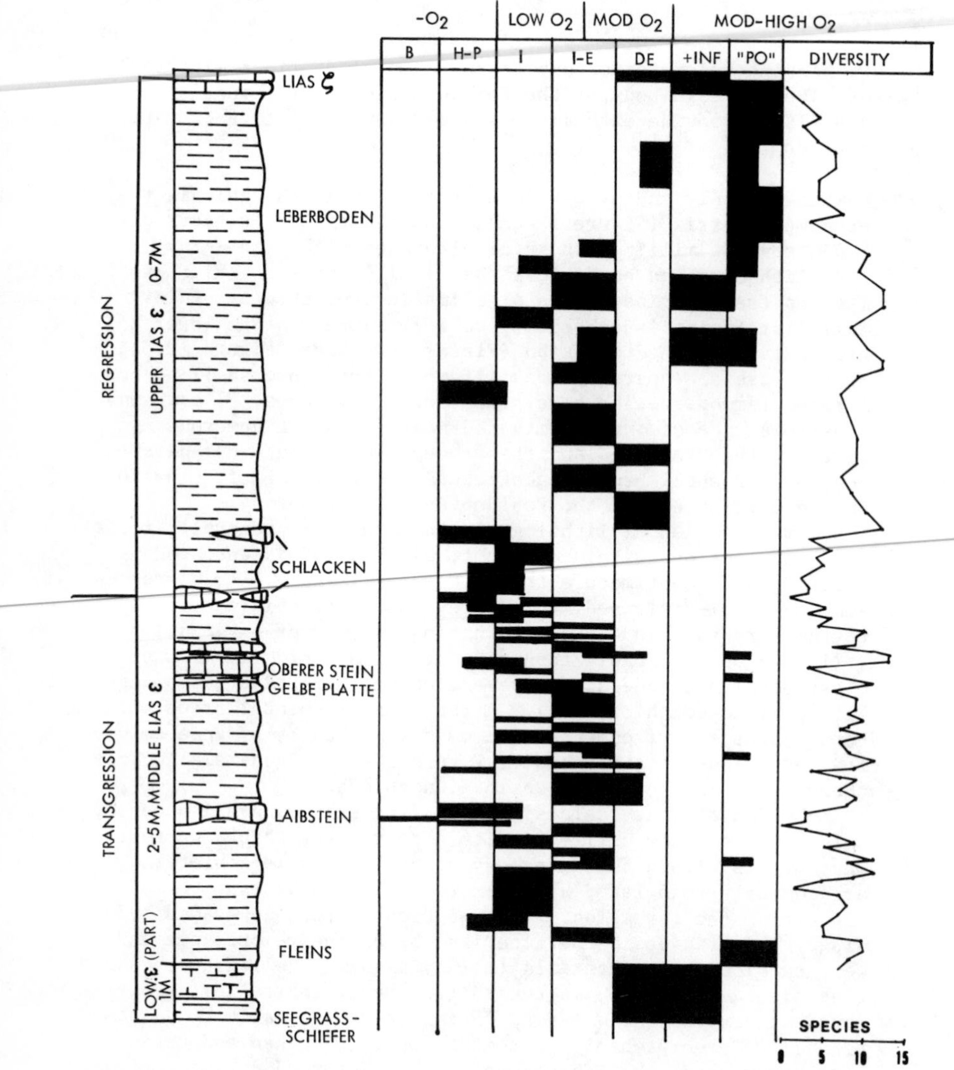

count for these beds. However, no graded bedding, sole marks, or escape burrows were observed during the present study. These beds are interpreted as lag deposits and *in situ* shell concentrates formed in a moderate current regime during periods of very slow clay sedimentation or sediment bypass.

5. Bituminous and coccolith-rich limestone beds occur at several levels in the middle Posidonienschiefer (Figures 12-2A, 12-10); the beds are blocky to lenticular and extend over broad areas. Several microfacies exist. Most beds are fine to medium-fine grained, contain disseminated and locally concentrated fish and bivalve shell debris (mainly fragmental *"Inoceramus"*), and many show high levels of dissolution among ammonites (some prior to burial). Evidence for early diagenetic cementation is cited by Seilacher et al. (1976) for one of these (Laibstein bank). Some microfacies lack obvious internal bedding, others have very fine laminae well preserved within the limestones, and others have beds and lenses of calcarenite. Bioturbation and shelly benthic biota are relatively rare in these limestones, inferring deposition in quiet water and toxic (reducing) benthic conditions.

These microfacies depict diverse environmental situations during deposition of the Posidonienschiefer, including short-term changes in sedimentation rate and type, periodically heavy coccolith rains (high productivity?), low to moderate current activity becoming strong for at least short periods of time, and fluctuation of oxygen levels in the benthic zone. This stands in contrast to the substable stagnant-basin model so widely accepted for the deposit.

Figure 12-5 (at left)
Summary of paleocommunity distribution, diversity, and inferred oxygen content of the benthic zone during deposition of the Posidonienschiefer. Generalized stratigraphy at left after Seilacher and Westphal (1971, Figure 4). Oxygen tolerance of each community or combination of communities based on both living analogues and paleontologic data; normal marine oxygenation not implied for any community. Key: B = Barren zones; H-P = *Harpoceras-Phylloceras* ammonite community with or without sparse benthic inoceramid bivalves; I = *"Inoceramus"*-dominated community with diverse ammonites (mainly *Dactylioceras*), but rarely other benthos; I - E = *"Inoceramus"* biostrome community with moderately diverse epibionts (mainly bivalves, serpulid worms, inarticulate brachiopods) on inoceramid shells; DE = Diverse epibiont community on dead ammonite shells and *"Inoceramus"* shell beds; epibionts in simple succession include boring and serpulid worms, many byssate and cemented bivalve groups, inarticulate brachiopods, echinoids, and small gastropods; +INF = the preceding three communities with sparse infaunal bivalves, serpulid worms, burrows, and rare scaphopods; "PO" = *Posidonia"* (=*Bositra*)-dominated community associated with *Dactylioceras*, rare inoceramids, and inarticulate brachiopods. Data from more than 1,000 samples. Species diversity (right) drops markedly in more oxygen-depleted environments, mainly associated with deposition of coccolithic limestones.

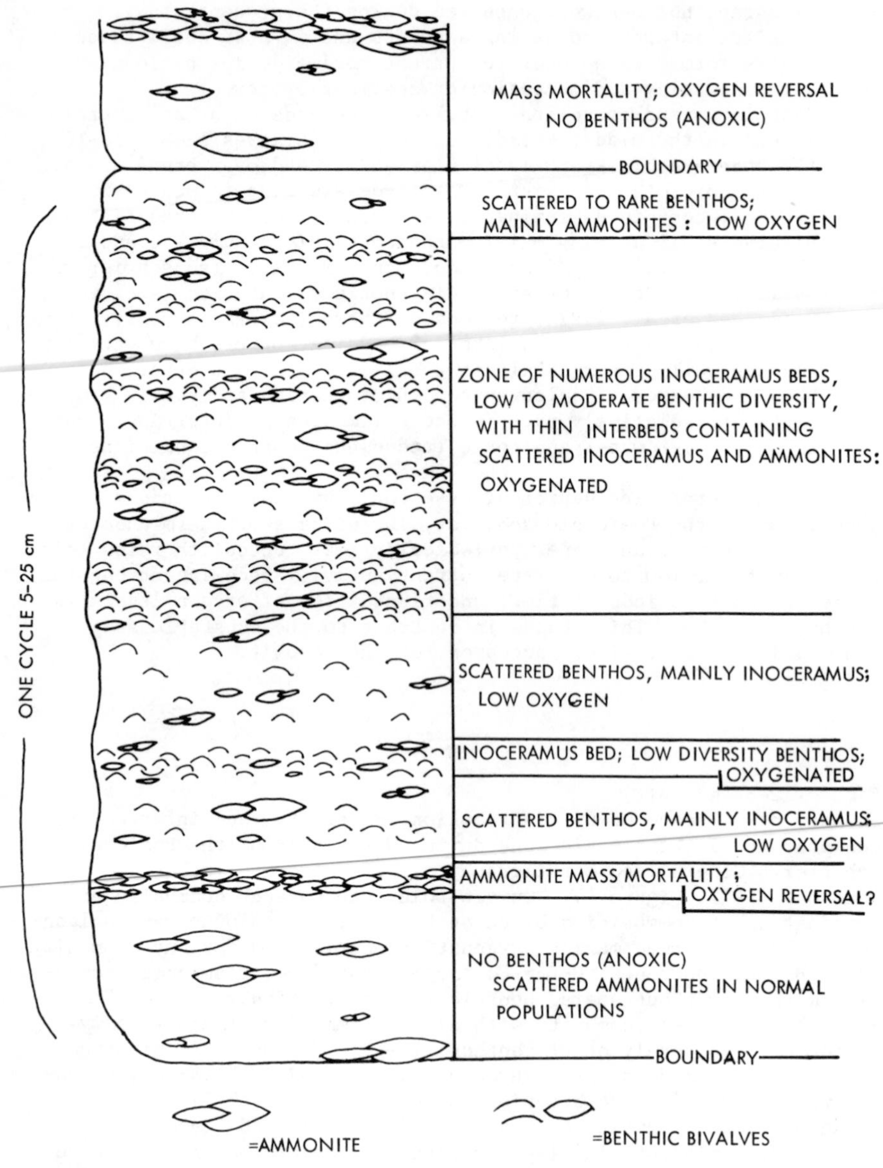

Figure 12-6
Detailed graphic representation and interpretation of a typical shale cyclothem from the middle of the Posidonienschiefer, below the Schlacken, at Dotternhausen quarry. Note that most of environmental history, as defined by biota, involves low to moderate oxygenation of the benthic zone and colonization by mainly inoceramid bivalves. Onset of anaerobic conditions in bottom waters begins a new cycle. History suggests delicately balanced anaerobic boundary near sediment-water interface.

BIOFABRIC ANALYSES

Biofabric is defined as the orientation, density, packing, and breakage patterns of organic constituents in the rock; it takes into account both the life and death history of fossils. Detailed biofabric analyses, in particular tests for organisms in possible life position, current orientations, current transport and reworking, and analysis of final depositional history were made on all 1 to 2 centimeter thick slabs recovered during systematic sampling of the Posidonienschiefer. The principal biofabric observations that relate to paleoenvironmental and ecological interpretations of the Posidonienschiefer are as follows:

1. Throughout both sections, numerically dominant molluscan shells are mainly preserved whole or nearly so (discounting compaction fracturing and dissolution), suggesting little reworking by currents. Exceptions are 0.5 mm to 5 cm thick beds composed mainly of fragmented fish and bivalve (especially *"Inoceramus"*) shell debris (Figure 12-7C) associated, in some cases, with current-oriented belemnites (Figure 12-7D; Brenner, 1976a). These thin bioclastic beds comprise argillaceous calcisilt, calcarenite, and coquinoid calcarenite microfacies that are common in the lower and uppermost Posidonienschiefer and are interbedded with shale and coccolithic limestone beds in the middle part of the formation. They are scattered elsewhere. The absence of sole marks, escape burrows, and graded bedding suggest that these microfacies are not rapidly deposited debris flows, turbidites, or storm dumps. The finely comminuted and worn biogenic elements of calcisilt and fine-grained calcarenite and the broken nature of large thick shells in these facies suggest long-term reworking by at least moderate currents accompanied by decrease or virtual cessation of clay sedimentation.
2. Sparse to very abundant bivalves occur at almost every level sampled in the Posidonienschiefer *"Posidonia" radiata* Goldfuss strongly dominates the biota near the base and top of the formation (Figure 12-5) and *"Inoceramus" (Pseudomytiloides?) dubius* Sowerby is common throughout the intervening beds, being totally absent only from scattered, thin stratigraphic intervals (Figures 12-5 and 12-6). The great majority of specimens from all levels are single valves (Figure 12-7C), and in most cases, they are not obviously in point contact or close proximity to the counterpart valve. This suggests at least weak currents acting to disperse valves of the epibenthic species after death, but more importantly, it suggests aerobic bacterial decay over relatively long periods of time at the sediment surface to break down both the muscles and (especially) the ligament that holds the valves together. Even if these shells had dropped off floating driftwood into the benthic zone (Seilacher and Westphal, 1971), their settling velocity would be great enough to prohibit ligament decay prior to deposition. Following deposition in deep-water facies like the Posidonienschiefer, even aerobic decay would be slow, involving years perhaps (Jannasch and Wirsen, 1973; Degens and Mopper, 1975), and organic breakdown would be virtually nonexistent in deoxygenated waters or hydrogen sulfide-enriched environments. Abiotic breakdown of chemically inert ligament in these environments is improbable.

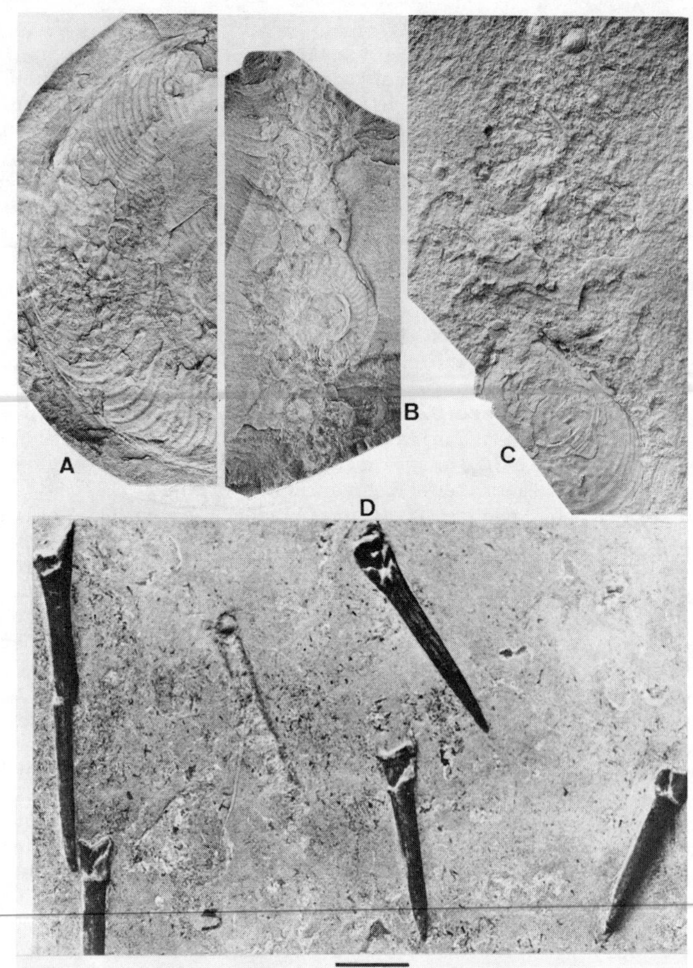

Figure 12-7
Indicators of current activity during deposition of the middle Posidonienschiefer, a sequence previously considered to represent the most anaerobic environments. A. Living chamber of *Harpoceras* selectively filled with shell debris; surrounding matrix lacks debris. B. Single, starved ripple made of shell debris, mainly immature *Harpoceras* conchs; note predominant current orientation of preserved apertural margins to left depicting currents from right. C. Current shadow of shell debris behind an "*Inoceramus*" shell; current from bottom of picture. Note triangular shape of shadow with apex at top; current stable orientation of bivalves; upper surface shown. Height of slabs: A = 4.6 cm; B = 9.2 cm; C = 10.5 cm; USNM 243003 to 243005, respectively. D. Current-orientated *Belemnites* (Hauff, Jr., 1960, Plate 72e) in shales containing abundant fish and shell debris; Lias Epsilon II_{11}, Holzmaden; Museum Hauff. Currents from bottom. Bar is 5 cm. Similar current indicators occur throughout the Posidonienschiefer.

The ligament was thin and probably weak in *"Posidonia"* (Jefferies and Minton, 1965) and possibly could have been fractured by current action; but the multivincular ligament of *"Inoceramus" dubius* was large and strong, well anchored in ligamental pits along the hinge line, and difficult to break or remove (allowing individual valve dispersal) except through bacterial decay, very strong currents, or scavenging activity. There is little evidence for scavenging and continuous strong-current activity. The primary mode of preservation of dominant bivalves throughout the Posidonienschiefer thus supports extensive aerobic bacterial decay at or near the sediment-water interface during most of its depositional history.

3. In every 1 to 2 cm thick sample except one in this study, most single valves of Bivalvia were found to have current-stable orientation, convex surface upward (Figure 12-7C; Hauff, Jr., 1960, Plate 77 show typical slabs). Significant percentages of bivalves with concave-up orientation were mainly found associated with the upper parts of bivalve shell beds where they were probably trapped in this orientation by the uneven topography of the shell-bed surface. The concave-up orientation of *"Posidonia"* valves cited by Jefferies and Minton (1965) is atypical. Because current-stable bivalves were found on most bedding planes, commonly dominating in numbers, at least moderate currents are indicated at the sediment-water interface during most of the depositional history of the Posidonienschiefer. A near-constant current flow is hypothesized.
4. Orientation studies on bivalves (beak direction), ammonites (orientation of preserved apertural margin; Brenner, 1976a, Figures 2-3, 2-4), belemnites (apex of guard; Figure 12-7; Brenner, 1976a, Figure 2-5), and marine reptiles (snout direction from quarry maps, Hauff, 1921; work in progress by Brenner) showed weak to moderately strong preferential orientation of shells and skeletons throughout the Posidonienschiefer. Figure 12-8 shows typical data selected from over thirty mollusc shell analyses completed to date on slabs from the two measured sections. Brenner (1976a) provides additional data. As would be expected, orientation is strongest among shells forming a single layer on the substrate, weakest on the irregular surfaces of dense shell beds. These data further suggest that weak to moderate current flow, with episodic strong current flow, may have characterized the benthic depositional history of the formation.
5. Other indicators of moderate current activity are common at all levels. They include well-defined, subtriangular current shadows of small ammonites, bivalves, and fish-mollusc debris behind large ammonites and isolated inoceramid shells (Figure 12-7C); living chambers of medium to large ammonites filled with small molluscs and bone-shell debris whereas surrounding substrate surfaces are nearly barren (Figure 12-7A); current-orientated epibionts, cemented and byssate, on or at the margins of ammonite shells lying on the substrate; and large crinoids *(Seirocrinus)* and *"Inoceramus" dubius* clusters attached to logs that commonly show preferential growth and post-mortem current orientation on one side of the log (Figures 12-3B, 12-4A). This orientation is especially significant as evidence for bottom currents if *Seirocrinus* is interpreted as a benthic, upward-growing crinoid (Rasmussen, 1977; subsequent discussion)

rather than having a pseudoplanktonic habit, hanging pendant from large logs (Seilacher et al., 1968). Inoceramid bivalves densely overgrow both flanks of logs, but their shells are more extensively distributed on the lee side (Figure 12-4A). Sections through two small logs, one with associated inoceramids the other with oysters, show the sides and tops overgrown by bivalves (reflecting benthic habitation), and single valves in current-stable position comprise much of the shell material

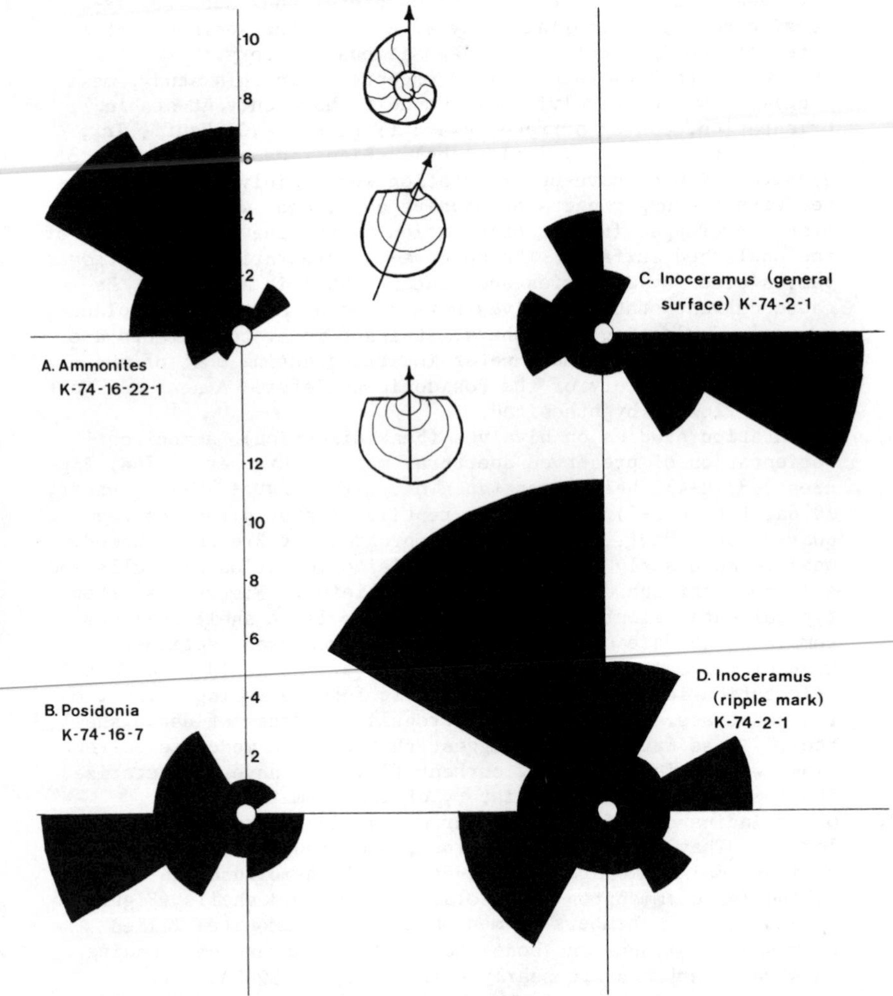

Figure 12-8
Rose diagrams of typical ammonite- and bivalve-rich slabs from the lower (*"Posidonia"* data) and middle Posidonienschiefer (ammonite, inoceramid data). Slabs not orientated to north; field numbers and scale given on each. Note strong preferential orientation of beak direction of bivalves and of apertural margin in ammonites.

found on the "lee side" of the log. The differential distribution of bivalves on these logs mainly reflects development of large current shadows of dead shells. This, in turn, supports an hypothesis that *Seirocrinus* specimens attached to these logs were benthos and are current-orientated at death.

6. Dark shales between the Schlacken and upper *"Posidonia"* beds (Figure 12-5) contain long "stringers" of small shells (Figure 12-7B) 1 to 5 cm wide and 1 m or more long. These are mainly composed of small ammonites (mixed taxa) and, less commonly, of inoceramid bivalves and light-colored fecal pellets. Where more than one stringer occurs on a bedding plane, they are subparallel and spaced 25 to 100 cm apart. Shells within these stringers are strongly orientated with long axes parallel to the axis of the stringer, but subequally in both directions; thus, the stringers do not form from current flow along the axis or unimodal flow fabrics would result. Shells between the stringers show weak to moderate orientation at high angles (50 to 90°) to the axes of shell stringers, suggesting current flow across the shell stringers (compare Figure 12-8 *"Inoceramus"* diagrams). The characteristics of the stringers infer that they are starved ripple marks composed of the only coarse sediment available. In a few cases, radiating clusters of bivalved adult *"Inoceramus" dubius* (a strongly byssate species) are preserved on the crests of the ripples suggesting byssal attachment to them as a raised, firm substrate. The stringers infer moderate strength, long-term currents, a firm substrate at the time of their formation, and oxygenated benthic environments only a short distance above the sediment-water interface.

7. Detailed sampling revealed rare burrows at many levels in the Posidonienschiefer (Figure 12-9; "Fucoiden" of Einsele and Mosebach, 1955, Figure 1), but no persistent zones of bioturbation above the Seegrasschiefer and below the uppermost limestones where one or two species of *Chondrites* dominate (Figure 12-9E). Seilacher and Westphal (1971, Figure 4) recorded three types of burrows in the lower Lias Epsilon. Hauff, Jr., (1960; diagram in pocket) reported scattered *"Fucoides"* (=*Chondrites*) *granulatus* in the middle Posidonienschiefer (Gelbe Platte and adjacent shales), presumably the most anoxic part of the sequence. Thus, burrows of worms and arthropods are more abundant and widespread than generally recognized in the Posidonienschiefer, but they are still uncommon. Most sediment is generally nonbioturbated. Superficially, this seems to support the stagnant basin model with oxygen levels around or below 0.1 ml/1 (Rhoads and Morse, 1970), but these burrows have unusual distribution patterns within the Posidonienschiefer. For example, rare occurrences of dense *Chondrites* networks are limited to mud fillings of living chambers in ammonites (Figure 12-9C). Also, small, single-generation populations of *Chondrites* commonly occur in mud laid on top of, but not below, vertebrate carcasses (Figure 12-9D). Isolated *Planolites* and *Chondrites* burrows occur sparsely, but at many levels, in microfacies containing small to moderate amounts of finely disseminated fish and shell debris (Figure 12-9F). *Thalassinoides* burrows are restricted to coarser calcisilt and calcarenite beds; a slab of this facies on the wall of the Museum für Geologie und Paläontologie at the Universität Tübingen shows several indivi-

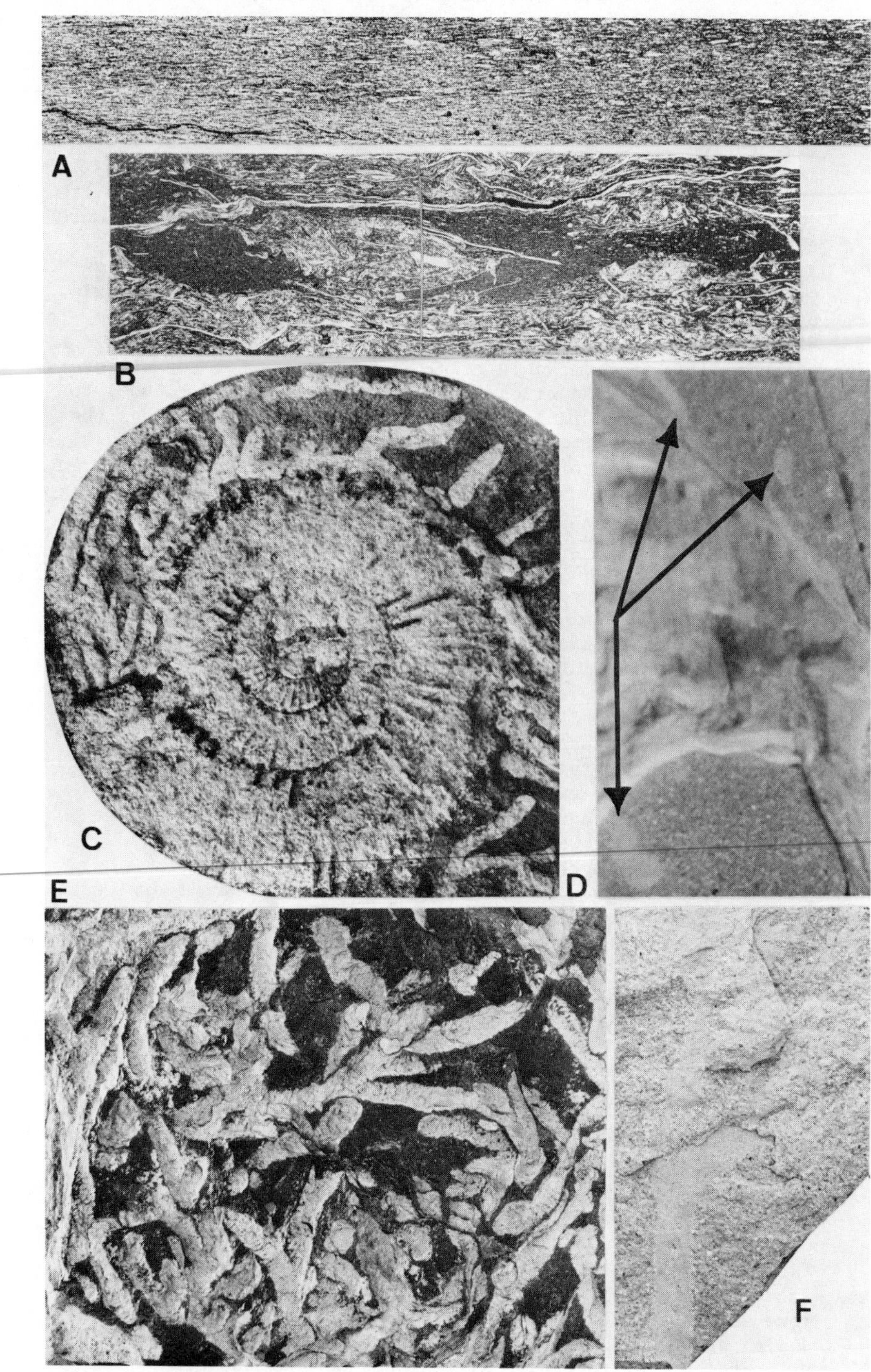
A
B
C
D
E
F

dual burrows arranged in an open network on one surface. Unfortunately, the precise stratigraphic level of the slab is unknown. These observations suggest a delicate balance between anoxic and partially oxygenated, benthic, sedimentary environments. Addition of calcisilt and bioclastic fragments apparently increased permeability and led to oxygenation of the upper substrate for sufficient time to allow establishment of simple populations of burrowing worms and callianassid shrimp. Clay muds were apparently toxic (low oxygen and high hydrogen sulfide), but exceptions were newly deposited muds separated from the main substrate by an impermeable object such as a fresh reptile carcass or an ammonite-shell wall. These observations strongly suggest that the substrate, not the overlying water column, was anaerobic during much of the depositional history of the Posidonienschiefer, and the aerobic-anaerobic boundary normally fluctuated from a position just above the sediment-water interface, to several centimeters below it.

8. Burrow boundaries are sharply defined (Figure 12-9F), and rare ammonite and belemnite shells that are orientated at high angles to the bedding plane do not show deep penetration into underlying muds. Both observations suggest moderately firm substrates without high levels of water saturation rather than soft inhospitable substrates overlain by a thick layer of suspended sediment: the latter conditions might allow significant elevation of the anaerobic-aerobic interface into the water column and prohibit benthic colonization by most invertebrates. Widespread current dispersal and orientation of shells, the presence of probable starved ripple marks, and numerous laterally extensive beds of normally benthic, byssate bivalves (subsequently discussed) support this contention.

Figure 12-9 (at left)
Bedding characteristics and burrows in the Posidonienscifer of southern Germany; burrows indicate sporadic oxygenation of the substrate. A. Normal bedding fabric of the shale showing lack of bioturbation (X18). White blebs are probably fecal pellets with concentrated coccoliths (copepod pellets?). B. Bivalve-shell coquina with clay parting, possibly containing shell-filled burrows (X9) similar to those of callianassid shrimps (middle Schlacken, Holzmaden Quarry). C. Partially dissolved conch (X2) of *Dactylioceras commune* Sowerby showing dense *Chondrites* burrows within it; no burrows noted outside of conch in shale (middle Posidonienschiefer, Holzmaden, University of Tübingen collections). D. Part of eye socket of an icthyosaur (X1/2) prepared from underside, showing single generation of small *Chondrites* burrows (light gray; arrows) in shales immediately overlying skeleton; no burrows noted in shale beyond perimeter of skeleton (Uppsala Museum, Sweden). E. *Chondrites bollensis* Schlotheim (X1.8) from the Seegrasschiefer, Holzmaden quarries, showing dense burrow networks characteristic of the oxygenated benthic zone just prior to deposition of the middle (bituminous) Posidonienschiefer (USNM 243007). F. Large, simply branching burrow (*Chondrites* or *Planolites?*) and small *Chondrites* (upper right) network (X0.9) in float from the lower part of the Posidonienschiefer between the Laibstein and Gelbe Platte (USNM 243008). Light color of shale due to abundant fine fish and shell debris.

9. Preburial dissolution features in ammonite tests (perforated or caved, sediment-filled tops), aptychi concentrations, and the greatest concentrations of disarticulated fish debris mainly occur in and adjacent to coccolith-rich limestone units of the middle Posidonienschiefer (especially Oberer Stein and lower Schlacken, Figure 12-5). This is also the level where diversity is consistently the lowest (Figure 12-5), and evidence for an anaerobic benthic zone is best developed. This interval probably marks peak transgression, the greatest water depth, lowest level of water circulation, and seemingly, the most severe oxygen reduction and hydrogen sulfide enrichment during the depositional history of the Posidonienschiefer, yet scattered *Chondrites granulatus* burrows (Hauff, Jr., 1960) and abundant adult byssate "*Inoceramus*" with probable benthic life modes even occur at these levels.

Biofabric data conclusively demonstrate the presence of gentle to moderate bottom currents throughout most of the depositional history of the Posidonienschiefer. Currents were episodically strong, and evidence for nearly complete lack of currents, producing true stagnation, is rare and mainly associated with deposition of coccolithic limestone units and associated shales in the middle of the formation. This evidence supports the hypothesis of an oxygenated water column and seriously challenges the stagnant, anaerobic-basin model in which oxygen depletion extended up into the water column for a significant distance. Biological data, subsequently discussed, also support this contention and the persistence of a largely anaerobic sediment column with the aerobic-anaerobic boundary delicately situated at or near the sediment-water interface and frequently fluctuating.

PALEOECOLOGICAL INTERPRETATIONS

Much of the evidence that has led to development and widespread acceptance of the stagnant-basin model for the German Posidonienschiefer has come from imaginative paleoecological analysis of exceptionally preserved fossils including "*Posidonia*." Of particular importance has been interpretation of the exquisitely preserved vertebrate assemblage as predominantly composed of pelagic fish and marine reptiles (Figure 12-3A,C) deposited without significant scavenging, predation, or decay in an anaerobic benthic zone (Fraas, 1891; Hauff, 1921; Hauff, Jr., 1960); interpretation of "*Posidonia*" as a nektoplanktonic bivalve and the assumption that this bivalve characterizes the entire Posidonienschiefer (Jefferies and Minton, 1965); and interpretation of the crinoids, especially *Seirocrinus*, as pseudoplanktonic, hanging pendant from floating driftwood (Seilacher et al., 1968) (Figures 12-3B, 12-4A). From this has come the parallel interpretation that virtually all byssate bivalves (especially "*Inoceramus*" *dubius*) found attached to the same logs as *Seirocrinus*, and byssate or cemented bivalves and cranioid brachiopods commonly found attached to large ammonite shells also had a pseudoplanktonic habitat. This mode of life is called on to account for the presence of normally benthic invertebrates in the Posidonienschiefer (Seilacher and Westphal, 1971).

It is, therefore, of particular interest that the most devastating arguments against the stagnant-basin model come from the paleoecological and paleobiological analyses of the normal, less spectacular, invertebrate elements of the Posidonienschiefer biota and from their distribution patterns. Of particular relevance are the small bivalves that strongly dominate most assemblages in numbers and, in many cases, diversity. Interpretation of the biology and ecology of these small, normally benthic invertebrates is greatly enhanced by modern analogues whose ecology is well known and strongly reflected in functional morphology.

The current study based initial paleoenvironmental and paleoecological interpretations on the mass of evidence collected during bed-by-bed sampling in the Dotternhausen and Holzmaden sections, and secondarily considered data and interpretations made from less common examples of exceptional preservation and rare elements of the biota. All previous paleoecological interpretations were subjected to rigorous re-examination based on the original specimens wherever possible. With the exception of specimens found associated with calcarenite and calcisilt microfacies and those obviously of pelagic origin (most ammonites, reptiles, fishes, coccolithophorids), taphonomic analysis of the Posidonienschiefer biota strongly suggests that most of the biota was preserved at or near to its place of habitation ("in place" or "disturbed neighborhood" assemblages of Scott, 1970). In the analysis of normally benthic organisms recovered during detailed sampling, two levels of paleoecological interpretation could be made: Interpretation based on the functional morphology and, in some cases, preserved life position of individual taxa; and interpretation based on repetitive faunal associations (Paleocommunities; Figure 12-5), the preserved parts of marine benthic communities. At each level, analogy to living taxa allow assignment of probable paleoenvironmental factors such as sediment character, sedimentation rate, water and sediment chemistry (including oxygen and hydrogen sulfide levels), environmental stability measured by age and maturity of populations and paleocommunities, and so forth. The generalized results of the analyses are shown in Figure 12-5. Of nearly 1,000 available samples collected from the two studied sections, more than 300, spread evenly through the section, have been analyzed in great detail to date; the rest are predominantly repetitious but have been carefully surveyed for this study. My paleoecological and paleoenvironmental interpretations are made from this data base.

PALEOBIOLOGY AND ECOLOGY OF THE INVERTEBRATES

BIVALVIA

Nearly all sampled bedding planes in the Posidonienschiefer are fossiliferous; bivalves are the most consistently occurring and commonly the dominant fossil group; bivalves are wholly absent from only a few thin intervals (1 to 5 cm) in the middle Lias Epsilon (Hauff, Jr., 1960, diagram in pocket; Figure 12-5). *"Posidonia"* (=*Bositra*) *radiata magna* Quenstedt is scattered through the lower Lias Epsilon and strongly dominates in the overlying Fleins (Figure 12-5). Less than a meter of *"Posidonia"* shell beds occur at the base of the black bituminous shale facies. *"Posidonia"*(=*Bositra*) *radiata parva* Quenstedt similarly dominates the assemblage of the upper 1 to 3 m of the formation (uppermost Lias Epsilon), but contrary to the claims of Jefferies and Minton (1965) that these bivalves characterize the Posidonienschiefer and similar "euxinic" black shale facies, *"Posidonia"* is almost wholly absent from the main body of the formation where systematically sampled in this study. It is represented only by rare, small, adult individuals and a few bedding planes containing clusters of spat with individuals less than 2 mm in size (Figure 12-5). Hauff (1921), and Hauff, Jr., (1960) noted similar distribution. *"Inoceramus"* (*Pseudomytiloides;* fide Cox, 1969:N320) *dubius* Sowerby occurs sparsely in *"Posidonia"*-rich beds, but strongly dominates the bivalve fauna and (with ammonites) most paleocommunities in intervening strata of the Posidonienschiefer (Figure 12-5; Hauff, Jr., 1960, diagram in pocket). Thus, *"Posidonia"* and *"Inoceramus"* seem to have occupied distinct, mutually exclusive habitats during deposition of the southwest German Posidonienschiefer.

A small species of *"Ostrea"* (s.l., probably *Liostrea*) is the third most common bivalve; it occurs throughout the formation. *Pseudomonotis, Plicatula,* and *Placunopsis?* and other cemented forms are less common. In addition, a diverse assemblage of byssate bivalves that includes *"Monotis?," Hypoxytoma* (=*"Avicula"*), *Oxytoma,* three species of Pectinidae, two Arcidae, and forms seemingly referable to *Meleagrinella, Pseudavicula, Arctotis,* and *Gervillia* are scattered through the Posidonienschiefer. Hauff, Jr., (1960, diagram in pocket) provides additional data on distribution, and museum collections contain other taxa from other localities. Surprisingly, rare specimens of semi-infaunal bivalves (the modiolid *Geukensia,* cf. *Limopsis,* cf. *Cosmetodon,* and *Nemodon*) and well-preserved infaunal bivalves (*Solemya,* a small lucinid, *Goniomya,* possible Solenomyidae; Riegraf, 1977; this study) are found at scattered levels in the middle and upper Posidonienschiefer. These diverse, normally benthic bivalves, no matter how sparse, cannot be considered rare or unique occurrences because all were found in just two sampled quarry sections in slabs only 0.5 by 0.5 meters in size; for any one level, therefore, the sample size is very small. Statistically, with increasing sample size, one would expect a considerable expansion of the known biota and more common occurrences of taxa that appear rare in the two studied sections (Koch, 1978).

"Posidonia" was considered a nektoplanktonic bivalve by Jefferies and Minton (1965); all other members of this moderately diverse bivalve assemblage belong to groups that are normally benthic in habit, both in the fossil record and among living representatives. Seilacher and Westphal (1971) view the byssate and cemented forms as pseudoplanktonic on driftwood, floating ammonite conchs, and possibly seaweed (Figure 12-4C). Riegraf (1977), following Brenner (1976b), called on sporadic "current events" (storms and turbidites?) to account for the introduction of allochthonous benthic forms, especially infaunal taxa. In these imaginative ways, various authors have attempted to explain the dominant occurrence of normally benthic organisms in the Posidonienschiefer while still retaining the stagnant-basin model for the deposit. In search of a more simplistic hypothesis, I have re-examined all of these interpretations.

The ecological interpretation of *"Posidonia"* (=*Bositra*) *radiata* Goldfuss as a nektoplanktonic, passively swimming bivalve similar in habit to living pteropods such as *Spiratella, Creseis,* and *Cavolinia* (Jefferies and Minton, 1965:179-179) is perplexing. Except for small bivalve larvae, no living analogues to nektoplanktonic *"Posidonia"* exist among Bivalvia. There are major dissimilarities between *"Posidonia"* and cited pteropods in shell morphology and thickness (subsequent discussion), muscle attachment, and relative size and role of the soft parts in swimming. Pteropods swim by "flapping" greatly expanded, wing-like, mantle lobes that extend well beyond the small shell; the soft parts are weakly attached to the shell interior mainly by a small dorsally inserted adductor muscle. None of these characteristics can be attributed to adult bivalves, including *"Posidonia."* Jefferies and Minton (1965) reasoned that swimming was possible for *"Posidonia" radiata* because of its small thin shell (as preserved, 50 μ cited), round shell form without evidence of byssal attachment at any stage in life, a probable posterior commissural gape, and the apparent ability of the animal to open the shell at a wide angle (60° or more) during life (as evidenced by fully gaped, co-attached dead valves). They reported an internal resilifer and narrow, external, ligament-attachment areas, as in some Pectinacea, and speculated that long mantle tentacles might have aided in swimming. Finally, they cited the facies distribution of this and other Posidoniidae, widespread in bituminous shales associated with ammonites and a sparse benthos, as characteristic of pelagic or planktonic organisms.

Re-examination of the morphology and facies distribution of *"P." radiata* in the Holzmaden and Dotternhausen areas failed to confirm many of these observations. Detailed morphologic study of other Paleozoic and Mesozoic Posidoniidae casts further doubt on the nektoplanktonic interpretation. The great majority of German specimens examined do not preserve original shell, but a coarsely crystalline gypsum or calcitic replacement and, in some cases, relict prismatic structure. The inner shell layer, which in most Pectinacea is nacre, crossed-lamellar aragonite or foliated calcite and is thicker than the outer prismatic layer, is not preserved in *"Posidonia"* from the study area (also the source of Jefferies and Minton's material). This is seemingly confirmed from observations of other Jurassic Posidoniidae. Further, in larger Jurassic species, the prismatic outer layer may reach 0.1 mm thickness, as compared to 50 μ for *"P." radiata*. The complete shell of *"P." radiata* may have been significantly thicker and heavier than proposed by Jefferies and Minton (1965) and thus not comparable to pteropod shells. If the inner shell layer was aragonite, its absence in the Posidonienschiefer would be easily explained by early diagenetic dissolution as in associated ammonites (Seilacher et al., 1976).

The small shell size cited by Jefferies and Minton (1965) for *"P." radiata* probably reflects relative ecological success and age not a genetically controlled adult feature. In my sampling, specimens of *"P." radiata* up to 5 cm long were collected at several levels, and museum specimens occur to 8 cm in height. This takes the species (at this stage of growth at least) out of the mechanical range for nektoplanktonic life when the total shell thickness is considered.

Musculature is not known for *"P." radiata* except for pallial-muscle traces, but complete musculature has been observed on several Paleozoic representatives of the family (for example, Carboniferous *"P." becheri*), on Cretaceous *Didymotis* and *Sergipia*, and on other Jurassic species of *Bositra* and *"Posidonia."* Small differences exist between genera and species, but the basic muscle plan is similar for all: a single elongate-ovate to arcuate, moderate-size, posterior, adductor insertion area situated near the posterventral margin; a pitted pallial line throughout at the terminus of radial pallial-muscle tracks; and, in rare Paleozoic and Cretaceous representatives of the family, small accessory dorsoanterior muscles that might be interpreted as weak pedalbyssal retractors. The size and placement of the adductor and the pitted pallial line do not resemble musculature of any swimming bivalve among the Pectinacea or Limidae or even of occasional swimmers. This musculature mechanically precludes a nektobenthonic habitat for the Posidoniidae, but is typical of many benthic bivalves within the Pteriacea.

No posterior "swimming gape" was observed with certainty on any Posidoniidae studied in this project. Jefferies and Minton (1965) suggested the wide death gape of bivalved *"Posidonia"* indicates its ability to gape widely in life and thus to swim like Pectinacea. Studies of swimming scallops and Limidae (Waller, pers. comm.) indicate that wide gapes between the valves are not prerequisite to swimming in these groups and rarely exceed 30°. Wide death gapes are also not characteristic of dead and gaping scallops and limids (Waller, pers. comm.; pers. observ.). Death gapes among bivalves lying on the substrate seem to be more related to ligament type and size and to dentition than to life habit. The widest gapes I have observed in natural environments are among weakly dentate to edentulous, weakly ligamented bivalves (many Pteriacea) and some arcids; *"Posidonia"* falls into the first group. Jefferies and Minton's (1965) observations of fully gaping, co-attached, concave-up *"Posidonia"* valves probably reflect a wide death gape owing to weak ligamenture, burial, and subsequent compression. The concave-up position is atypical of *"Posidonia"* in sampled beds.

The ligamenture of *Bositra buchi* (Römer), as interpreted from a single poorly preserved cardinal area (BM LL1744; Jefferies and Minton, 1965, Text-figure 1) consists of a large triangular internal resilium and thin, external lateral bands not unlike some swimming Pectinacea. No ligament attachment areas are known from *"P." radiata*, but a partially preserved ligamental area on the morphologically similar but larger *"P." somaliensis* Cox from the Middle Kimmeridgian of Somalia (BM 163688) shows only a very small central depression (not a true resilifer) and, externally, a weakly defined series of broad, very shallow, apically inclined pits separated by narrow ridges posterior to the beaks. This is clearly not the ligament of swimming bivalves like the Pectinacea and Limidae.

Jefferies and Minton (1965) precluded an epibenthic habitat for *"Posidonia" radiata* because the rounded anterior margin showed no trace of a byssal notch at the commissure or indentation in the growth-line trace through ontogeny; yet some Paleozoic Posidoniidae (*"P." becheri*; some specimens of *"P." opalina* or *"P." ornati?* from the English Jurassic; BM L17550) commonly have an anterior flattening or inward bend in the growth-line trace and possible weak pedalbyssal musculature. Byssal adult attachment is thus known in the family. *"Posidonia" radiata* and similar forms could have been byssate, attached by a single row of byssal threads linearly arranged along the plane of the commissure, without requiring a well-defined gape or indentation in the anterior margin. Morphologically similar modern analogues among the Mytilidae support this postulate, for example, *Musculus discors* Linne and several species of *Crenella* (especially *C. glandula* from the western Atlantic and *C. adamsiana* from the Red Sea). These bivalves have a well-rounded anterior margin; they are identical in shape to *Bositra buchi* as illustrated by Jefferies and Minton (1965, Text-figure 6). The Limopsidae are another weakly byssate group with rounded anterior margins. The rounded anterior margin of *"Posidonia"* or *Bositra* is, therefore, not a valid criterion for excluding possible byssal attachment to a benthic substrate, or even a free-living life habit.

Finally, Jefferies and Minton (1965) called on the widespread "pelagic" facies distribution of *"Posidonia"* in bituminous shales like the Posidonienschiefer to support their contention of a nektobenthonic life mode; yet in detailed sampling of sections from the Dotternhausen and Holzmaden areas, adult *"P." radiata* were found to be almost wholly restricted to the lower part and top of the Posidonienschiefer in beds that are transitional to marls, shales, and limestones yielding a normal-marine benthonic fauna (Figure 12-5). *"Posidonia" radiata* is replaced by *"Inoceramus" (Pseudomytiloides?) dubius* as the dominant bivalve in the main body of the formation. This distribution clearly suggests near ecological exclusion of *"Posidonia"* and *"Inoceramus"* in distinct benthic environments. The distribution of *"Posidonia"* in these beds suggests that it was an opportunistic benthic species, living free or weakly attached to substrates in subnormal (low to moderate) oxygen regimes, whereas *"Inoceramus"* was opportunistic in even lower oxygen regimes, as developed at the sediment-water interface during deposition of the middle Posidonienschiefer.

"Inoceramus" (Pseudomytiloides?) dubius Sowerby (Figure 12-10) is the most abundant and consistently occurring bivalve in the Posidonienschiefer. It occurs sparsely in beds yielding masses of *"Posidonia"* at the base and top of the formation, but predominates in intervening beds except within scattered intervals a few centimeters thick (Figure 12-5). Characteristically, *"I." (P?) dubius* shells are moderately to highly crowded along specific bedding planes. In some cases, they form coquinoid marker beds 1 to 3 cm thick with wide lateral extent. Between these surfaces, inoceramids are more scattered, but occur in virtually all beds though rarely in point contact. Single valves in current-stable position are most common (Figure 12-7C). Hauff (1921), Hauff, Jr., (1960), and Seilacher and Westphal (1971) all noted large clusters of *"I." (P?) dubius* associated with logs, many of which have long-stalked *Seirocrinus* specimens attached to them (Figures 12-3B, 12-4A). Inoceramids are also sparse to moderately abundant on and around large ammonite conchs (subsequently discussed), inferring byssate attachment to them. Seilacher and Westphal (1971), as many authors before them, considered that the majority of *"I." (P?) dubius* and other byssate and cemented bivalves lived as pseudoplankton on floating logs, on living and floating-dead ammonite conchs, and on seaweed and dropped to the bottom of the stagnant Toarcian seaway mainly as dead shells where they were well preserved in an anaerobic environment.

Several lines of evidence suggest that the interpretation of *"I." (P?) dubius* as a pseudoplanktonic bivalve in the Posidonienschiefer is incorrect although the possibility that a few lived that way cannot be discounted. There is little doubt that the species was strongly byssate during life; well-preserved, uncompressed specimens from other formations show a narrow, but distinct, anterior byssal slit and musculature that consists of a pitted pallial line, a ventroposterior arcuate posterior adductor, and one or more well-defined pedalbyssal retractors usually inserted in the

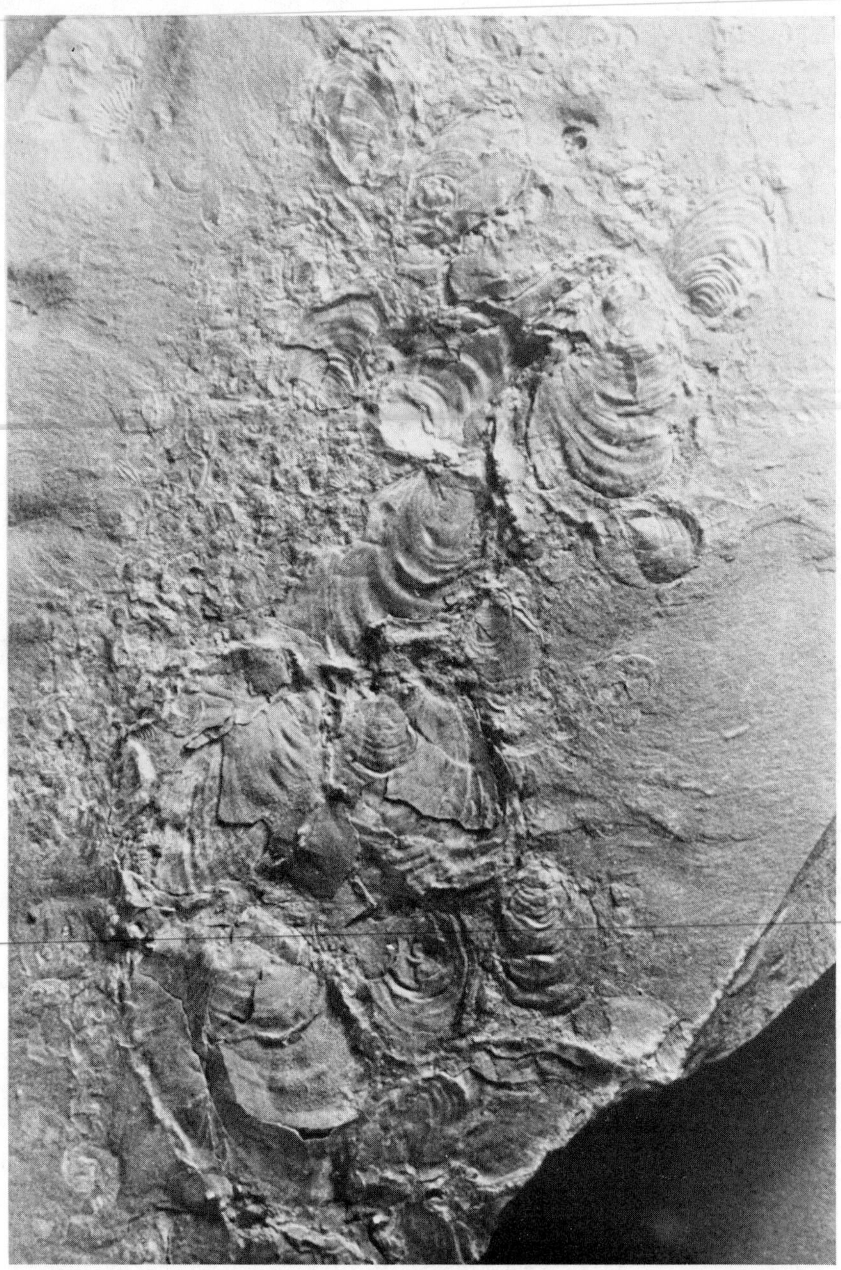

Figure 12-10
Starved ripple (X1.5) in Posidonienschiefer trending from lower left to upper right, mainly composed of small immature *Harpoceras* and *Dactylioceras* tests, overgrown *in situ* by byssally attached radiating clusters of bivalved *"Inoceramus" (Pseudomytiloides?) dubius*. USNM 243006, from the lower part of the upper Posidonienschiefer 2 to 3 m above the Schlacken beds.

anterodorsal quadrant of the shell. The truncated anterior shell margin suggests close attachment to hard substrates such as shell surfaces. Obvious byssal clusters of bivalved *"Inoceramus,"* such as those on logs and shell stringers, have been observed. The main question is where these bivalves were byssally attached during life.

The principal argument against a pseudoplanktonic origin for *"Inoceramus"* in the Posidonienschiefer is the sheer abundance and mode of occurrence of these bivalves (Figures 12-5 and 12-6). In the same sections where many thousands of complete inoceramid valves were recovered, only six small wood fragments were found. Two of the wood fragments are overgrown on the upper surface (benthic encrustation pattern), one by oysters and the other by a few inoceramids. Similarly, although large ammonite conchs are common throughout the sampled sections, less than 5 percent are moderately to densely encrusted with bivalves (rarely more than a few associated inoceramids per conch). All *"Inoceramus"*-encrusted ammonites recovered in this study are overgrown only on the upper surface and (on the largest ones) around the venter, indicating benthic attachment to dead shells. The numbers of well-preserved inoceramids outnumber their potential pseudoplanktonic hosts found in the same sections by hundreds of orders of magnitude. The alternative idea that beds of inoceramid shells accumulated during turbidity, storm, or "current" events (Brenner, 1976b; Riegraf, 1977) is not confirmed by sedimentary structures found in the studied sections. Instead, biofabric analysis suggests long-term current reworking during formation of the beds.

The simplest explanation for the occurrence of abundant byssate inoceramids, especially in persistent beds, is that they lived as gregarious benthos, byssally attached to shell fragments (Figure 12-10), ammonite conchs, sunken wood (Figures 12-3B, 12-4A), and to each other at or near the sediment-water interface. Encrustation patterns on small pieces of wood and ammonite conchs recovered in this study support this contention. Further, re-examination of the large logs that are densely overgrown by *"I." (P?) dubius* and *Seirocrinus* (Figures 12-3B, 12-4A) and are the focal point of the pseudoplanktonic life-mode hypothesis (Seilacher et al., 1968; Seilacher and Westphal, 1971) revealed a consistent pattern of inoceramid overgrowth. As pointed out by Seilacher et al. (1968:276), these specimens were prepared from the underside of the logs to take advantage of the better preservation that characterizes that surface. Considering this and assuming that fossils were not removed from the log during preparation (confirmed by contemporary preparators), it is obvious from these specimens that *"Inoceramus" dubius* is absent or much more sparsely represented on the undersides of these logs than on their lateral flanks (Figures 12-3B, 12-4A). A cut section through a small specimen revealed dense bivalve encrustation on top of the log; lateral accumulations of redeposited single valves mainly occur on one side, forming a current shadow, and overlie the flanks of the log. This encrustation pattern is that expected of epibionts on a sunken log and not of floating wood where the densest bivalve overgrowths would be expected on the underside. Kauffman's (1975) detailed literature survey and personal observations on floating driftwood and seaweed as possible hosts for pseudoplanktonic bivalves confirms these findings. Both are poor substrates for bivalve epibionts when floating and are rarely encrusted (excepting for *Gaimardia* in the specific *Sargassum* community) because of the physical and chemical nature of the decaying vegetal surface. Wood, however, is commonly overgrown after it becomes waterlogged and sinks to the bottom, and the surface chemistry is altered.

Finally, in addition to overgrowths on large logs, *in situ* byssal clusters of bivalved inoceramids, with individuals radiating from the central point of byssal attachment (Figure 12-10), have been found in the Holzmaden section attached to probable starved, current ripple marks consisting of ammonite shells (ammonite "stringers"). *"Inoceramus"* clusters were also found on top of dead ammonite shells, radially arranged around the umbilicus, on top of one small piece of wood, and associated with *"Inoceramus"* shell-bed surfaces mainly composed of single valves. These are all clearly *in situ* benthic life assemblages formed in at least partially oxygenated environments on available hard substrates near the sediment-water interface. The evidence is overwhelming that this is the principal life mode of *"I." (P.?) dubius* in the Posidonienschiefer.

Just how *"Inoceramus"* extensively colonized oxygen deficient and hydrogen sulfide-enriched benthic habitats is still open to question, but a biogeographic dispersal and facies survey of Mesozoic Inoceramidae around the world (Kauffman, 1975) reveals that they were commonly the first, and in some cases the only, benthic bivalves to colonize such substrates through time. This suggests that Inoceramidae were highly tolerant of low oxygen (but not anaerobic) and high hydrogen sulfide benthic conditions and were opportunistic pioneers of simple, physically controlled, benthonic communities established in such environments (Kauffman, 1979). Where the sediment-water interface was highly toxic and anaerobic and prevented settlement of spat, inoceramids seem to have colonized any firm substrate elevated only slightly above this interface, as in parts of the Posidonienschiefer, and for short periods of time, in the Solnhofen and Nusplingen lithographic limestone facies (Kauffman, 1978). The demise of such pioneer colonies would presumably signal rise of the anaerobic or toxic hydrogen sulfide boundary up into the water column (Kauffman, 1978). Establishment of extensive *"Inoceramus"* biostromes directly on the substrate would, conversely, signal a major change in the benthic environment of the sediment-water interface involving oxygenation of the sediment, at least surficially. This happened frequently during deposition of the Posidonienschiefer as evidenced by numerous *"Inoceramus"* shell beds; the occurrence of these beds is generally patterned within small-scale (3 to 25 cm thick) sedimentary rhythms in black shales in the middle part of the formation (Figure 12-6).

Cemented bivalves in the Posidonienschiefer include moderate numbers of small (to 3 cm high) ovate species of *"Ostrea"* s.l. (=*Liostrea?*) and rare specimens of *Placunopsis?*, *Plicatula spinosa* Sowerby, and *Pseudomonotis substriata* Ziet (Figure 12-4C). Like the byssate bivalves in the fauna, these have been interpreted as pseudoplankton on swimming or floating ammonite conchs, wood and its epibionts, or possibly seaweed (Figure 12-4C). Most occurrences of these taxa have been noted in association with ammonite tests (Figure 12-11). Seilacher (1960) defined criteria for recognizing life associations of ammonites and their shell epibionts. He used preferred orientations of epibionts relative to light and slope (gravity) and produced evidence that ostreid bivalves did grow on the venter and subequally on both flanks of some swimming ammonites *(Buchiceras)*, gravity- or phototropically-orientated with their feeding margins facing upward (Seilacher, 1960, Text-figure 3). I used Seilacher's model to analyze cemented epibionts on ammonite shells in the Posidonienschiefer.

"Ostrea" occurs in small clusters or as solitary individuals, mainly on ammonite shell surfaces (Figure 12-11C), throughout the entire Posidonienschiefer (Hauff, Jr., 1960, diagram in pocket). Attachment to ammonites is evidenced by xenormorphism (Figure 12-11C), where the ammonite shell has been dissolved. In most cases, size-frequency studies indicate a single generation; but up to three generations have been found in oyster populations on the flanks of large ammonites, indicating long-term favorable environments on the conch surface. The encrusting patterns of oysters do not support the hypothesis that they lived primarily as pseudoplankton. In the sampled sections, all occurrences of oysters encrusting ammonite shells and the one occurrence of oysters on a piece of wood were restricted to the upper shell surface, indicating attachment after deposition of the ammonite. The orientation and extent of ostreid encrustation on ammonites supports this view. They are absent or rare on small ammonites (less than 5 cm diameter; Figure 12-11A). On ammonites 5 to 10 cm in diameter, ostreids preferentially settled in the umbilicus of the upper surface and grew in a more or less radial pattern outward and up the umbilical wall, that is, upslope and toward the light if the ammonite test is assumed to be lying on its side (Figure 12-11C). Assuming the same control on these oysters in their orientation as on those used by Seilacher (1960) to demonstrate a life association, this is clearly the pattern of benthic encrustation on a dead shell rather than a symbiosis. Large ammonites (Figure 12-12A,B), are more heavily encrusted by oysters (up to four generations) than are small ammonites, and the patterns of orientation are more varied (Figure 12-12). Oysters attached to the venter in these samples mainly face outward into the water (Figure 12-12A). Only the largest ammonites observed in museum collections (above 30 cm diameter) are encrusted by oysters on both sides and suggest a possible pelagic life association. On all of the examined specimens, however, oysters are much sparser on the under surface of the ammonite. They are mainly concentrated around the venter and in the umbilicus (areas raised above the substrate when the ammonite lay prone on semifirm substrates) and strongly orientated radially toward the venter, the main light source for this semicryptic habitat. Again, these encrustation patterns are those predictable for benthic habitation of oysters on dead ammonite shells. By calculating the width of ammonites in the Posidonienschiefer from well-preserved examples found elsewhere and noting the extent of epibiont encrustation on ammonites at any one stratigraphic level, the depth of burial of the ammonite and the height of the aerobic-anaerobic boundary above the substrate can be determined. Large ammonites apparently provided "islands" of suitable, oxygenated substrate for epibionts on the otherwise inhospitable Toarcian seafloor.

Other cemented bivalves are less common, but support the existence of the oxygenated benthic zone during their life span. All three specimens of *Plicatula spinosa* recovered in this study show attachment to small shell fragments and were found isolated in the shale away from ammonite conchs and other hard substrates; they probably lived free, propped up by the nodes and spines, in the benthic zone. Some *Plicatula* are reported on ammonite shells. Rare *Placunopsis* were cemented to the up-facing flank of ammonite conchs.

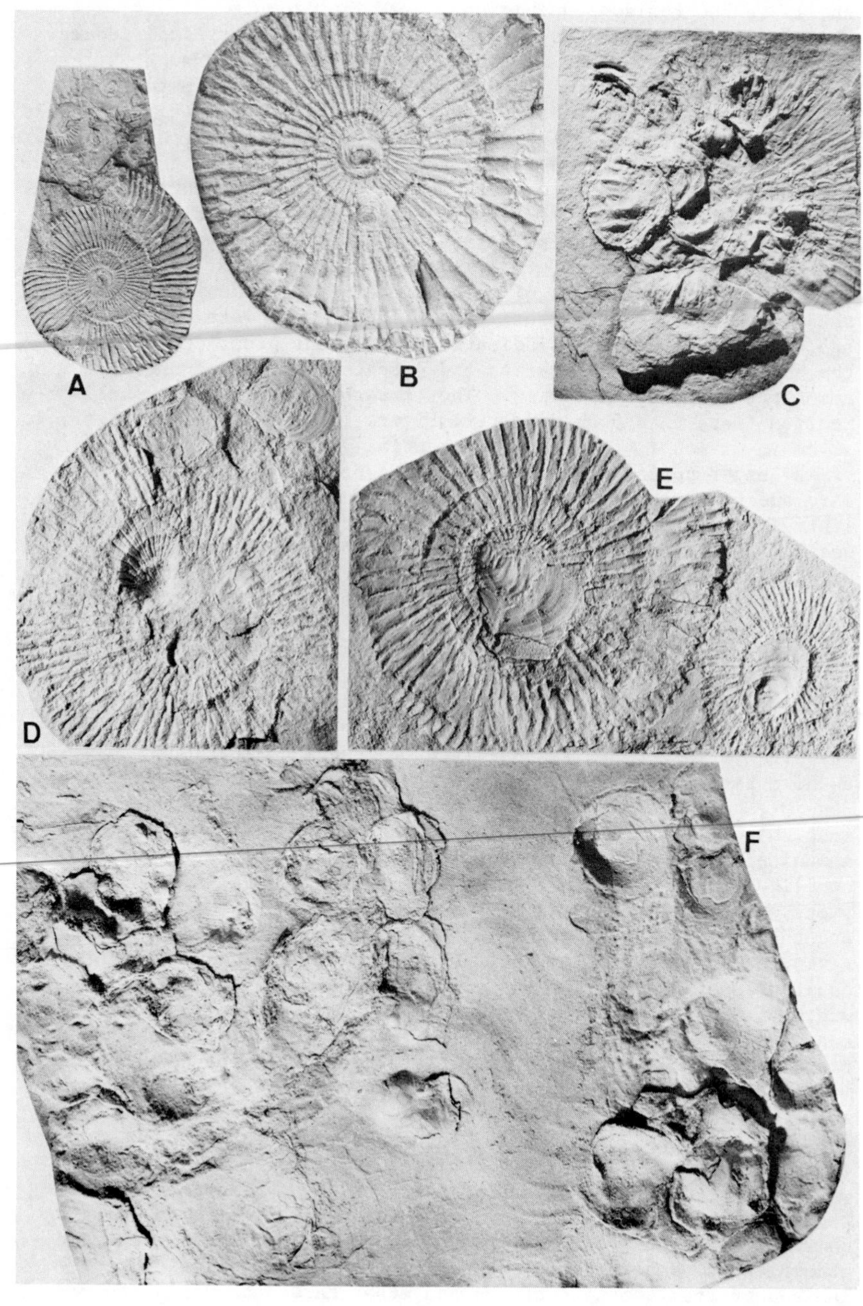
A
B
C
D
E
F

Pseudomonotis was cemented as an adult, byssate as a young organism. A few isolated upper valves were found in the shale, but all attached valves and whole shells are associated with ammonite conchs (Figure 12-11F) and large bivalve shell surfaces (mainly "*Inoceramus*," but also some large "*Posidonia*"). In both sampled sections and in museum collections, specimens of *Pseudomonotis* are attached only to the upper surface of ammonites, mainly in the umbilicus, the spiral suture, and along the venter with the feeding margin extending into the water column. On large ammonites, single generations of *Pseudomonotis* are predominantly orientated with their long axes radiating outward and ventral margins facing the venter of the ammonite (Figure 12-11F). This does not represent progressive colonization during growth of the ammonite (Seilacher, 1960), nor slope (gravity) control because some *Pseudomonotis* are inclined upward and others downward. This orientation may reflect growth response to currents or to a genetic programming that directs growth in the direction most likely to extend the ventral feeding margin of the *Pseudomonotis* shell beyond the margin of the substrate of attachment. In this orientation, the feeding margin is free for feeding in the water column.

The less common byssate bivalves (Pectinacea, *Gervillia*, various Oxytomidae) show similar encrustation patterns on ammonites and large inoceramid and posidoniid bivalves. No preferred orientation was noted except for *Gervillia*, which most commonly occurs in small clusters loosely attached to the venter of large ammonites (apertural side). Individuals were freely pendant in the water column and apparently aligned in the direction of current flow (Figure 12-12A). These data support the idea that byssal attachment was to dead ammonite conchs on the bottom. The Oxytomidae seem to be epibionts that

Figure 12-11 (at left)
Encrustation patterns on ammonites associated with the diverse epibiont-shell surface community in the Posidonienschiefer. A. Small ammonites (X1.6) below 5 cm diameter, nonencrusted to very rarely encrusted in umbilicus of upfacing surface; *Dactylioceras* (ribbed) and small *Lytoceras* or *Harpoceras* form current shadow, apertures facing away from current (USNM 243009). B. Upper surface of *Dactylioceras raristriatum* Quenstedt (X1.6) with a small *"I." (Pseudomytiloides?) dubius* Sowerby near growth position (valves slightly separated) in umbilicus (USNM 243010). C. Upper surface of a partially dissolved *Dactylioceras* (X0.8) with umbilicus heavily encrusted by *"Ostrea"* sp.; some show xenomorphism (USNM 243012). D. Upper surface of a *Dactylioceras* sp. (X0.8) with a small "*Ostrea*" and ornate *"Avicula"* (=*Oxytoma?*) in growth position attached to umbilicus. A pair of *"Inoceramus" (Pseudomytiloides?) dubius* valves nearby were once attached to the upper shell surface. E. Upper surfaces of two *Dactylioceras* conches (X0.8) with *"Inoceramus" (Pseudomytiloides?) dubius* shells in growth position on the umbilicus (USNM 243013). F. Upper surface of a large *Harpoceras* conch (X0.8) showing diverse epibiont bivalves in umbilical area *("Ostrea," "Inoceramus," "Pseudomonotis")* in diverse orientation, and monotid bivalves on ventrolateral slopes orientated toward venter. Note aptychus in place in body cavity (right) (USNM 243014). All specimens from middle Posidonienschiefer at Dotternhausen Quarry.

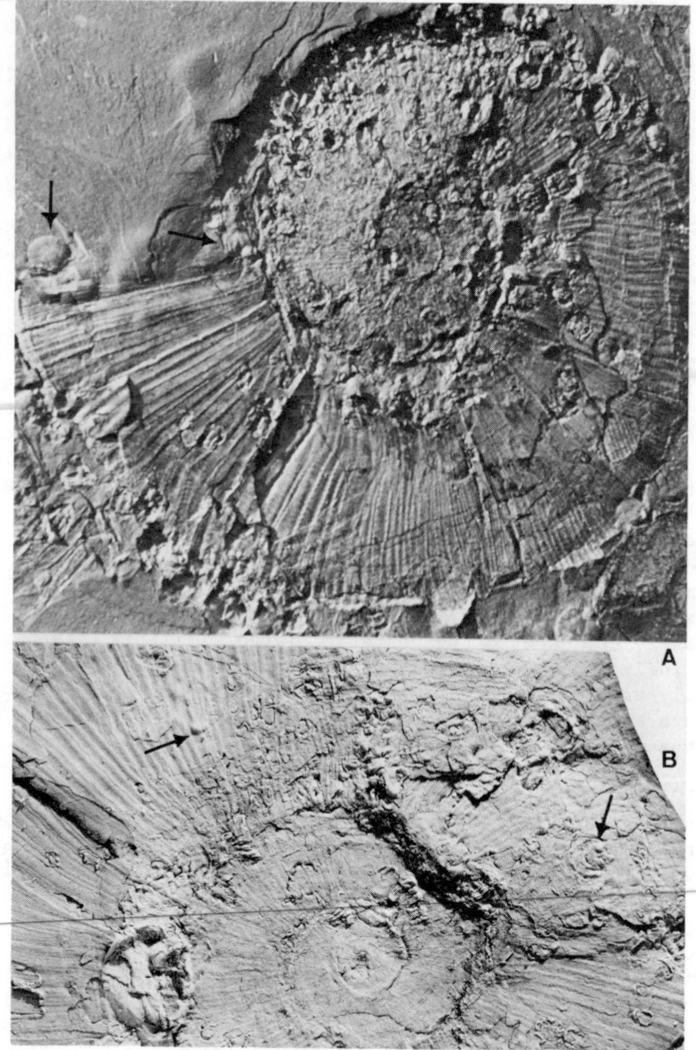

Figure 12-12
Encrustation patterns on large ammonites from the middle Posidonienschiefer. A. Diverse epibiont community on upper surface of a large *Lytoceras* (X1/4). Note extent of encrustation of upper surface, size variation representing several generations (mainly oysters), encrustation of venter by *"Ostrea,"* byssate *Gervillia* (lower left), and encrustation of aperture of living chamber (arrows) by monotids (left) and *"Ostrea"* (on venter of preceding whorl) (Universität Tübingen collection; from Holzmaden). B. Upper surface of a large *Lytoceras* (X0.8) showing three generations of *"Ostrea"* encrustation on flanks and in umbilicus plus scattered impressions of oysters encrusting opposite side (arrows) more sparsely (USNM 243014)

appeared later in the succession on top of other ammonite encrusters or on the upper surfaces of *"Inoceramus"* and *"Posidonia"* biostromes. They are scattered; populations are small and usually a single generation is represented. Pectinacea, numbering three to four species and mostly represented by small individuals, are moderately rare. All species recovered retain an adult byssal notch and thus were probably capable of attachment. In sampled sections and among museum specimens, Pectinacea predominantly occur as single valves associated with open, mud bottoms rather than on shell or wood substrates; this might imply that they lived predominantly free, as do their modern counterparts, actually attaching by the byssus only when in proximity of a "hard" substrate or when environmental factors required stability. The Toarcian evidence, however, is inconclusive.

The few infaunal and semi-infaunal bivalves that were recovered during the course of this study and were previously reported (Hauff, Jr., 1960; Riegraf, 1977) are of particular interest because they may reflect periods of oxygenation of the upper substrate in the main part of the Posidonienschiefer. Hauff, Jr., (1960, diagram in pocket) recorded *Unicardium bollense* Quenstedt (a shallow infaunal burrower) and deep infaunal *Solemya bollense* (Quenstedt) in his faunal lists, but did not note their precise stratigraphic distribution in the Posidonienschiefer. Riegraf (1977, Figures 1-3) reported a bivalved specimen of *Goniomya rhombifera* (Goldfuss) from a few centimeters above the Laibstein (Figure 12-5) and refigured Quenstedt's specimen of *"Anodonta" (=Solemya) bollense* (1858, Plate 37, Figure 13) from the same level.

Infaunal and possible semi-infaunal bivalves were discovered at six levels (1 to 2 valves per level; Figure 12-5) from sampled sections of Posidonienschiefer in the Holzmaden and Dotternhausen areas, suggesting they are not as rare as originally inferred (Koch, 1978). These include the normally semi-infaunal modiolid *Geukensia?* sp. (single valves) bivalved specimens of the epibenthic or semi-infaunal byssate arcids *Nemodon* and *Cosmetodon*, a single valve of a small infaunal Lucinidae (gen. indet.), bivalved specimens of *Solemya?* in the transition zone between *"Inoceramus"*-rich and *"Posidonia"*-rich shales of upper Lias Epsilon, and a single valve of shallow infaunal *Limopsis?* sp. from the same zone.

The unbroken and commonly bivalved nature of these shells and their association with beds showing no evidence of rapid deposition or allocthonous shell accumulations suggests that they were not introduced into the site by strong "current events" (Riegraf, 1977), but lived in the immediate area. Some bivalved specimens gape concave upward in current-unstable position, suggesting that they died, gaped, and were buried at the sediment-water interface without transport. They may have been driven out of the sediment to the surface by deoxygenation or hydrogen sulfide poisoning. All specimens, except the small lucinoid, are normal adults. Sparse populations of a few semi-infaunal and infaunal bivalve taxa were established in the upper layers of the sediment column during periods of oxygenation on the Toarcian seafloor. Of the taxa present, *Solemya*, the Arcidae, *Goniomya*, and Lucinidae have living analogues that are common elements of low diversity, mid-shelf to bathyal, organic-rich mud communities often characterized by subnormal oxygen levels. Most of these semi-infaunal and infaunal bivalves are ecologically compatible with the hypothesis that low to moderate oxygen levels characterized the lower water column and periodically the upper part of the substrate during deposition of the Posidonienschiefer.

SCAPHOPODS

Two small, nearly complete scaphopods (*Laevidentalium?* sp.), the first reported from the Posidonienschiefer, were collected in the shales of upper Lias Epsilon below and in beds with abundant *"Posidonia."* These are normally infaunal suspension feeders and, like the infaunal bivalves, are today normal parts of dark mud communities and capable of inhabiting environments with somewhat lower than normal oxygen levels. They cannot be explained as pseudoplankton because they lack attachment mechanisms and do not occur with sediments bearing evidence of debris flow and rapid deposition.

GASTROPODS

The tiny gastropod *Coelodiscus*, which rarely exceeds 3 mm in diameter, is reported by Hauff, Jr. (1960, diagram in pocket) to co-occur with the rare gastropod taxa "*Natica pelops* d'Orbigny" and "*Turbo sedgwicki* Munster" exclusively in the Unterer Stein (Figure 12-5) level of the middle Posidonienschiefer. The last two species are clearly related to normal benthic gastropods; the *"Natica"* possibly represents a predator on benthic (especially infaunal) bivalves. *Coelodiscus* is reported to be abundant at this and other levels; it is "ubiquitous" according to Einsele and Mosebach (1955) and Jefferies and Minton (1965). They argued that *Coelodiscus*, because of its small size, thin shell, and broad distribution, was probably a pelagic gastropod like the pteropod *Spiratella*. This may be possible, but because all *Coelodiscus* I have observed from the Posidonienschiefer are preserved only as recrystallized internal molds with no shell, I cannot confirm the thin-shelled nature of the species. *Coeleodiscus minuta* could just as easily represent a small opportunistic benthic species adaptive to subnormal oxygen levels and feeding primarily on benthic detritus. Evidence for either interpretation is inconclusive.

BRACHIOPODS

Hauff, Jr. (1960, diagram in pocket) reported articulate brachiopods (*Spiriferina villosa* Quenstedt, *Rhynchonella amalthei* Quenstedt) from the lower Lias Epsilon, in the Tafelfleins, Seegrasschiefer, and lower Aschgraue Mergel: all levels whose biota reflect oxygenated benthic environments including upper levels of the substrate. No articulates have been reported in typical, black, bituminous shale facies of the Posidonienschiefer, but the inarticulate *"Discina"* (=*Orbiculoidea*) *papyracea* Munster is known from the middle Posidonienschiefer (Hauff, Jr., 1960). Seilacher and Westphal (1971, Figure 4) noted its local occurrence on ammonite shells and interpreted it as pseudoplankton on living or floating dead ammonites; yet living analogues among discinacean brachiopods attach firmly to hard substrates by a strong, short pedicle and are wholly benthic in habitat. The existing literature gives the impression that *Orbiculoidea* is uncommon. Detailed sampling in the two 0.5 by 0.5 m sequences used in this study revealed *Orbiculoidea* at thirteen levels through the formation; there is a tendency for the brachiopod to be more common in the upper Lias Epsilon, above the Schlacken, than elsewhere (Figure 12-5). One to several individuals occur at each level in my collections, and all occur as complete brachial valves (probably with smaller pedicle valves below them) resting (attached?) on the upper surfaces of horizontally orientated ammonite conchs and current-stable single valves (rarely bivalved specimens) of *"Inoceramus" (Pseudomytiloides?) dubius*. The occurrence of *Orbiculoidea papyracea* strongly suggests that these specimens are in normal life position and thus attached, like their living counterparts (Discinacea), to dead shell surfaces in the benthic zone. In well-lighted waters, living inarticulate counterparts tend to be photonegative, but in deeper and darker environments, like that postulated for the bituminous shales of the Posidonienschiefer, up-facing hard surfaces are most commonly colonized (G. A. Cooper, pers. comm.). No living discinid brachiopods are known to be pseudoplanktonic on floating logs, seaweed, or the shells of nektonic invertebrates.

SERPULID WORMS

Two forms of serpulids were recovered from the Posidonienschiefer in the detailed sampling. The most common forms are attached to flanks of ammonite conchs and the upward-facing surfaces of single, current-stable *"Inoceramus"* valves, but rare specimens of sediment-dwelling serpulids with semistraight, thin calcareous tubes also are known. Attached serpulids mainly occur in the middle and upper Lias Epsilon; two tubes of sediment dwellers were found in bituminous shales of the middle Posidonienschiefer at different levels. The latter are clearly benthic types, and because they are nearly complete tubes associated with sediments showing no evidence of rapid deposition, the worms are presumed to have lived near to their place of burial. Shell-attached serpulids appear to have been pioneer colonizers of dead ammonite and inoceramid shell surfaces. Where they co-occur with oysters, the latter commonly overgrow them. Like living serpulids, the Toarcian forms seem to have settled in photonegative or protected niches (in the umbilicus or spiral suture, just under the venter, and within the living chamber of ammonites) and grown photopositively toward the light. Also like modern analogues, they seem to have had a high tolerance for subnormal oxygen and possibly increased hydrogen sulfide levels; thus, with or without oysters, they form simple associations on the undersurface of large ammonites that are diversely encrusted by bivalves and brachiopods on the upper surface. Both the settlement patterns and orientations of shell-encrusting serpulids recovered from the Posidonienschiefer suggest that they lived as benthos on dead ammonite and bivalve shells. No serpulids have been found on logs or observed on ammonites in the symbiotic orientation described by Seilacher (1960), precluding a predominantly pseudoplanktonic habitat.

ECHINOIDS

Two types of echinoids are represented by scattered spines from the middle Posidonienschiefer (cidarids, diademoids) and by a single crushed test of the long-spined *Diademopsis* sp. (Hauff, Jr., 1960; this study). Echinoid (mainly diademoid) spines are abundant in *"Posidonia"*-rich beds at the base and top of the formation. Echinoids were apparently an important component of the *"Posidonia"* community. Seilacher and Westphal (1971, Figure 4) have questionably assigned *Diademopsis* to a pseudoplanktonic mode of life on floating logs to account for its occurrence in the Posidonienschiefer. Living representatives of both the cidarids and diademoids are strictly benthonic and have not yet been found attached to floating logs (P. M. Kier, pers. comm.). They are not adapted to such a life mode and would not find adequate food in this environment.

Whereas modern cidarids and diademoids primarily inhabit rocky, sandy, and heavily vegetated surfaces in shallow water, they also occur in abundance grazing on open sediment surfaces in quiet or deep water. Living representatives are rare to absent on clay-mud substrates such as the main body of the Posidonienschiefer. The great abundance, however, of complete tests with spines and skeletal debris of *Diademopsis crinifera* in the black, finely laminated, bituminous shales, and silty shales of Lias Alpha, and the rarity of this species in coarser clastic facies of the same sequence would seem to indicate that mud substrates were its preferred habitat. Firm mud surfaces are implied by the long delicate spines of *Diademopsis*, which seem poorly adapted to mobility on fluid or viscous muds. The *"Posidonia"* shell beds in the Posidonienschiefer apparently were such substrates whereas much of the black shale in the middle of the formation was not. A vegetal food source would be necessary to support large populations: abundant grasses and algae, plant detritus, or broad algal-fungal mats. Comparison with living representatives and their ecology and with the occurrence of *Diademopsis crinifera* in black bituminous shales elsewhere in the Lias of southwestern Germany suggests that a benthic mode of life is far more likely for these echinoids than a pseudoplanktonic mode on floating logs.

CRINOIDS

The most spectacular invertebrate fossils in the Posidonienschiefer are the long-stalked *Seirocrinus subangularis* (Miller) attached to large logs and commonly associated with byssally attached mats of *"Inoceramus" (Pseudomytiloides?) dubius* (Figures 12-3B, 12-4A). Complete calyces and stalks showing the finest detail are preserved. Shorter-stalked *S. subangularis* and *"Pentacrinus" briareus* Miller are equally well preserved (Figure 12-4B) in the bituminous shale facies; in some cases, they are also attached to logs (Hauff, Jr., 1960, Plates 63-68). Seilacher et al. (1968) interpreted the life habit of these crinoids as pseudoplanktonic, attached to floating logs and hanging downward (also Seilacher and Westphal, 1971, Figure 4): This life mode is compatible with the stagnant-basin model for the Posidonienschiefer and with the exquisite preservation of articulated crinoids. Seilacher et al. (1968) reported the following supportive evidence for this life mode:

1. Stalk attachment to logs.
2. Great length of the stem (to 15 m); consequently, viewed as incapable of rigid upright growth to support crowns that reach 80 cm in length.
3. Weight and flexibility of the stalk, as measured by columnal size and internodal length, grades away from the calyx. According to these authors, this indicates greater flexibility at the stem base than at the base of the crown. This was viewed

as the inverse relationship to that expected of rooted, upward-growing crinoids.

4. Preservation of some crinoids with the arms underlying the calyces and stalks, indicating that the crown settled onto the substrate first.
5. Association with a biota that was regarded by Seilacher et al. (1968) and Seilacher and Westphal (1971) as almost wholly pelagic, nektoplanktonic, and pseudoplanktonic.

The idea that most normally benthic, attached invertebrates in the Posidonienschiefer biota lived as pseudoplankton is largely based on these outstanding crinoid examples.

Several lines of evidence seriously challenge the concept of a pseudoplanktonic mode of life for these taxa, especially in association with floating logs. There are no known examples of living pseudoplanktonic crinoids and there are no consistent morphologic differences between the stalks of Jurassic *Seirocrinus* and "*Pentacrinus*," and many modern examples of the long-stalked (to 2 m) Isocrinidae that live attached to benthic substrates and grow upward (Rasmussen, 1977). Decreasing internodal length and increasing columnal size near the crown, as found in *S. subangularis*, was noted in several living, benthic species.

Meyer (1971) noted that collagen fibers or ligaments strung through the skeletal elements of crinoids are probably responsible for articulating and providing rigidity to cirri, arms, pinnules, and stalks as opposed to the idea that the size, shape, and spacing of skeletal elements is the main control on rigidity. Meyer made comparisons to the collagen ligaments at the base of echinoid spines that control rigidity by extension and contraction. A similar system in living crinoids allows the arms to maintain a feeding posture (spread fan-like in even strong currents), the cirri to grip the substrate, and stalks of even considerable length to maintain rigidity sufficient to keep the crown elevated. Meyer further observed that living long-stalked crinoids stand erect and rigid in the face of strong currents without great movement even when bumped by a diver, yet they have the ability to flex rapidly with extension of collagen ligaments or to droop like wilted flowers when the current slows considerably or when the crinoid is sich and dying (pers. comm.). If collagen ligament controls rigidity of the skeletal parts in stalked crinoids, the arguments of Seilacher et al. (1968) relative to size and arrangement of columnals in the stalk are of secondary importance. Short-stalked "*Pentacrinus*" and *Seirocrinus* are within the size range of living crinoids with a benthic habitat and rigid erect stalks, but through the action of collagen ligament, perhaps even the long-stalked *Seirocrinus* stood erect, gaining mutual support from adjacent crinoids. Intertwining of *Seirocrinus* specimens is known (Seilacher et al., 1968).

Rasmussen (1977) presented another challenge to the pseudoplanktonic interpretation of *Seirocrinus*. He reasoned, as did Kirk (1911), that if large *Seirocrinus* lived as pseudoplankton on floating logs, they would have had to settle on the wood as larvae and retain attachment by the juvenile stalk for many years; most attached *Seirocrinus* are large, old adults. These authors considered it impossible for detached individuals to swim upward, stalk first, and attach to floating wood at a later growth stage; no known living crinoids have this ability. Kauffman (1975) showed that driftwood is, today, a poor substrate for settling of epibionts, especially as larvae, probably because of decay at the vegetal surface; he also noted that most wood sinks in less than a year because it becomes waterlogged. Thus, the Posidonienschiefer *Seirocrinus* are too large and too old to have been on driftwood all of their lives because of the improbability that the wood would have floated for an adequate amount of time. All *Seirocrinus* observed by Rasmussen (1977) on logs in the Posidonienschiefer are secondarily attached by adult portions of the stalk; they had shed the long, distal, weak juvenile part. This is compelling evidence that these pentacrinids attached to sunken logs as adults after breaking loose from the juvenile attachment and drifting across the bottom, and thus, they were not pseudoplanktonic in habit.

This study strongly supports Rasmussen's observations and reveals that crinoid-stalk bases were not usually attached to the undersides of logs (Figures 12-3B, 12-4A) as would be expected for a pseudoplanktonic life mode, but were attached to the sides and, presumably, the top of the logs as would be expected of a benthic life mode. The best examples of the *Seirocrinus*-log association (Figures 12-3B, 12-4A) do not show the articulated stalks directly underlying the log (specimens prepared from underside; Seilacher et al., 1968). Further, although short-stalked specimens of *Seirocrinus* and *Pentacrinus* are associated with wood in some cases, many complete specimens are not and still retain the cirral "roots" at the base of the stem; presumably, these were rooted directly in the substrate. The co-occurrence of oysters on the stems of two short-stalked specimens of *"Pentacrinus" (Seirocrinus)* (Figure 12-4B), phototropically orientated with feeding margins facing the crown, probably indicates that the host crinoids lived erect in the benthic zone. Seilacher (1960) used similar orientations in oysters to determine symbioses with ammonites and bivalves and life orientations of the host.

These observations collectively indicate that short-stalked and probably most long-stalked crinoids in the Posidonienschiefer lived as benthos, rooted directly in the sediment or strongly attached to sunken logs by cirri. The effectiveness of the rooted or grasping cirri and the rigidity of the upright stem were mainly controlled by collagen ligament and muscle fibers such as those that bind skeletal elements together in modern Isocrinidae. The crinoids apparently died rapidly, possibly as a result of overturn of anoxic bottom waters, and fell to the substrate coming to rest mainly on their sides (Figures 12-3B, 12-4A; Rasmussen, 1977) in a thin, benthic, anaerobic zone that other evidence suggests was at or slightly above the sediment-water interface. Here they were protected from scavenging and decay. In cases where the arms and pinnules underlie the crown and stem (Seilacher et al., 1968), death may have been slow so that the crown drooped beside the still attached stem before coming in contact with the bottom; the stem eventually collapsed on top of it.

ARTHROPODS

Large crustaceans are sparse, but commonly well preserved in the Posidonienschiefer (Hauff, Jr., 1960, Plates 60-62). Two types of lobsters are most common: *Proeryon* and *Uncina*. Their presence has worried workers who otherwise have interpreted the Posidonienschiefer as the deposit of a stagnant basin (for example, Seilacher and

Westphal, 1971) because both have modern analogues with a benthic life mode during the adult stage and neither can be interpreted as pseudoplankton. Jefferies and Minton (1965) attempted to explain their presence by noting that juveniles of living representatives have midwater swimming stages (Bouvier, 1917); others have suggested that the specimens were carried alive into the stagnant part of the Posidonienschiefer basin by turbidity currents. Neither interpretation is supported by the evidence. I noted no structure indicating rapid deposition in samples containing well-preserved arthropods, and virtually all specimens are large, full adults. Like their modern counterparts the Nephropidae and Polychelidae (Firth and Pequegnat, 1971, Gulf of Mexico data), these large Jurassic lobsters were probably benthic burrowers in mud substrates, fed as vagrant benthos, and were killed and completely preserved by episodic, short-term deoxygenation of the lower part of the water column.

PALEOCOMMUNITY ANALYSIS

Interpretations of functional morphology, ecology, mode of occurrence, and taphonomic history of the Posidonienschiefer biota have produced two distinct models for Toarcian marine paleoenvironments in southwestern Germany. On the one hand, the Posidonienschiefer is viewed as the deposit of a stagnant, largely anaerobic basin with a diverse biota restricted in life to the upper part of the water column as nekton, nektoplankton, plankton, and pseudoplankton (Figures 12-2B, 12-4C). Exceptional preservation of fossils, geochemistry, sedimentary lamination, ammonite functional morphology, and vertebrate paleoecology strongly support this hypothesis. On the other hand, diverse evidence from the functional morphology, ecology, and mode of occurrence of invertebrate fossils other than ammonites strongly supports an hypothesis of a largely oxygenated, well-circulated water column in which the aerobic-anaerobic interface fluctuated from a few centimeters within the sediment to a few centimeters above the sediment-water interface. Surficial sedimentary structures support the latter viewpoint.

Documentation of paleocommunities within the Posidonienschiefer is critical to the resolution of this problem because two entirely different temporal and spatial patterns of organism distribution on the seafloor would be expected from the two models. In the stagnant-basin model, where virtually all organisms deposited in the benthic zone would be derived from the overlying water column, a basically uniform fossil biota with broad facies distribution would be expected; the biota might be expected to change gradually toward the margins of the basin and through time as different environmental regimes developed. This is the distribution pattern envisioned by Jefferies and Minton (1965) in their nektoplanktonic interpretation for *"Posidonia"* and *Bositra*. In the alternative model, where the anaerobic-aerobic interface was delicately balanced near the sediment-water interface and large areas of the seafloor were periodically habitable for benthic organisms, a patchy distribution of discrete paleocommunities in space (reflecting distinct microenvironments) and time (reflecting short-term fluctuations of environmental parameters) would be expected; frequent recurrence of individual paleocommunities should occur.

In an attempt to test these hypotheses, all biotic elements (except microflora) on each 1 to 2 cm slab in the two measured sections through the main bituminous shale facies of the Posidonienschiefer were identified and counted, their relative abundance calculated, and the data plotted stratigraphically. Figure 12-5 is a summary of these data and shows the distribution of bio-associations interpreted from the taxa plots. At all levels of resolution, this analysis clearly supports the hypothesis that the bituminous shale facies of the Posidonienschiefer was deposited in a largely oxygenated, current-circulated, marine basin with an anaerobic-aerobic boundary near the sediment-water interface. The marls and low-bitumin shales of Lower Epsilon (lowest Posidonienschiefer) contain a normal-marine benthic biota and were not included in this detailed analysis.

MAJOR PALEOCOMMUNITIES

Taxonomic co-occurrence data for the Posidonienschiefer, including lower Epsilon strata, clearly cluster into six discrete paleocommunities (Figure 12-5). These are generally arranged in a repetitive sequence reflecting cyclic benthic environments during transgressive and regressive phases of the Toarcian cyclothem. Within any major facies characterized by one of these paleocommunities, other bio-associations commonly occur, reflecting small-scale environmental fluctuations. The best examples of these short-term biological-environmental fluctuations are in the 3 to 25 cm thick sedimentary rhythms in the middle part of the formation (Figures 12-2A, 12-6).

The Plicatula-Liostrea-Belemnite Paleocommunity

This assemblage characterizes marls and dark calcareous shales of the lower Lias Epsilon (Blaugraue Mergel, Aschgraue Mergel of Hauff, Jr., 1960, diagram in pocket) and marls of the upper Schwarzjuramergel that immediately overlie the Posidonienschiefer. These three taxa strongly and subequally dominate the community in numbers. *Harpoceras* is the principal associated ammonite; "*Posidonia*," small Pectinidae, and rhynchonellid brachiopods are secondary but consistently occurring elements on mud substrates. *Plicatula* and solitary or small clusters of oysters are found attached directly to the sediment surface or to small shell fragments. Belemnites are more common and diverse in this community than elsewhere in the Posidonienschiefer, and some authors have suggested that they were largely nektobenthic. Oysters also are attached to large shell surfaces. Small *Chondrites* and *Planolites* burrows are scattered through the well-bedded marl and shale; they comprise the only known infauna. This is clearly a marine fauna with an abundant benthos largely preserved *in situ*. It reflects normal oxygenation of the water column and sediment surface, but subnormal oxygenation of the upper part of the substrate. This community bounds the bituminous shale facies of the Posidonienschiefer.

The Chondrites Paleocommunity

This benthic community (Figure 12-9E) is strongly dominated by two different size species of *Chondrites* (*C. granulatus* Schlotheim and *C. bollensis* Schlotheim). The larger *C. granulatus* appears to have fed on detritus at lower levels in the substrate than the smaller species, possibly reflecting niche partitioning of food resources. Sparse planolitid burrows are associated with both species, and uncommon dwelling burrows of *Thalassinoides* were noted at a still lower level than *C. granulatus*. Deep oxygenation of the substrate is implied. This community, where fully developed (Seegrasschiefer), rarely contains abundant shelled invertebrates. Scattered *"Posidonia," Plicatula, "Pentacrinus,"* and *Harpoceras* and moderately abundant belemnites are principal associates. The reduction in epifaunal bivalves and crinoids probably reflects high turbidity levels produced by extensive burrowing at the sediment-water interface. In addition to the Seegrasschiefer, which is a series of highly bioturbated shales up to 25 cm thick in the lower Posidonienschiefer, the *Chondrites* paleocommunity occurs in thin units interbedded with the *"Ostrea"-Plicatula*-Belemnite Paleocommunity of the lower Lias Epsilon, locally in a thin zone of the Unterer Schiefer or Ölflöz (Hauff, Jr., 1960), and mixed with abundant *"Posidonia"* in the uppermost part of the upper Posidonienschiefer limestone (Schlacken) bed (Figure 12-5). With the exception of the Seegrasschiefer, the *Chondrites* Paleocommunity contains representatives of the *"Ostrea"-Plicatula*-Belemnite Paleocommunity and appears to be gradational into it. The stratigraphic positioning of this assemblage in beds transitional between marls with *"Ostrea"-Plicatula*-Belemnite Paleocommunity and bituminous shales with the *"Posidonia"* Paleocommunity suggests that subnormal oxygen levels may have been a factor in restricting epibenthic organisms.

The *"Posidonia"* Paleocommunity

This community (Figures 12-5, 12-13) occupies a unique position at the margins of the main bituminous shale facies in the Posidonienschiefer in the Fleins beds near the base of middle Lias Epsilon and sporadically below them, and in the upper 1 to 3 m of the formation (Wilder Schiefer, lower part of overlying Schlacken; Hauff, Jr., 1960, diagram in pocket). In the latter case, *"Posidonia"*-rich beds alternate at many levels with sparsely fossiliferous units containing scattered *"Posidonia"* and more numerous ammonites, suggesting small-scale environmental fluctuations at the niche limits of *"Posidonia."* Presumably, this distribution pattern infers a benthic habitat for *"Posidonia,"* and its disappearance in ammonite-rich beds may reflect severe oxygen depletion at the sediment-water interface. Within the typical *"Posidonia"* Paleocommunity, this bivalve completely dominates the assemblage in numbers and biomass; it forms extensive shell beds of mostly disarticulated valves. Other typical elements of the *"Posidonia"* Paleocommunity are the ammonite *Dactylioceras*, inarticulate brachiopods *(Orbiculoidea)*, belemnites, and sparse shell epibionts like *"Inoceramus," Pseudomonotis, "Ostrea,"* and serpulid worms. *Seirocrinus subangularis*, considered a benthic crinoid in this study, is relatively more abundant in the Fleins and below it than elsewhere in the Posidonienschiefer (Hauff, Jr., 1960) and was probably an important component of the *"Posidonia"* Paleocommunity. Burrows (indet.) are sparse and only locally recorded from *"Posidonia"*-rich beds. The restricted stratigraphic occurrence of abundant *"Posidonia"* (1 to 3 generations), the great dominance of this bivalve within the community, and the paucity of other benthic taxa suggest that this genus was an opportunistic colonizer of benthic substrates that were inhospitable to most other

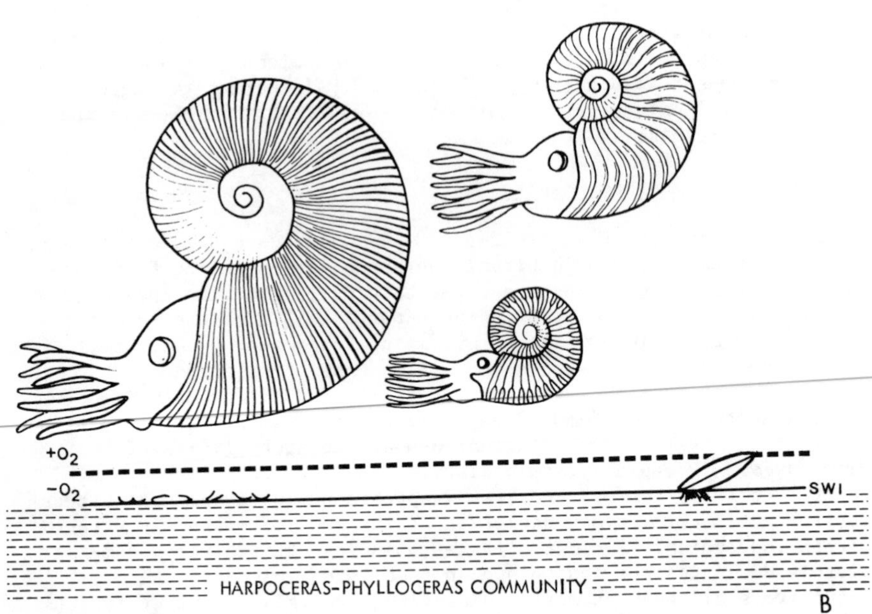

Figure 12-13
A. Diagrammatic representation of *"Posidonia"* (=*Bositra*) Paleo-community with commonly associated *Dactylioceras* (epibenthic feeding ammonite?) and sparse *"Inoceramus"*, inarticulate brachiopods, and *Thalassinoides* burrows. Typical musculature of Posidoniidae (upper left) indicates a non-swimming, benthic, free living or weakly byssate lifestyle. Position of aerobic-anaerobic boundary indicated at lower right. B. Midwater *Harpoceras-Phylloceras* Paleocumminity associated in death with rare inoceramids and *Dactylioceras*, characteristic of severely oxygen-depleted benthic environments. Dashed line indicates aerobic-anaerobic interface.

organisms due to oxygen reduction and hydrogen sulfide enrichment; here, it covered vast surfaces for short periods of time. The bivalve apparently lived free or weakly attached by an anterior string of small byssal threads.

Colonization of relatively inhospitable substrates by *"Posidonia"* initiated a simple two-stage succession by providing extensive shell mats elevated a few millimeters to more than a centimeter above the sediment. These were subsequently colonized at approximately the same time by scattered epibiont brachiopods and bivalves *(Pseudomonotis, "Ostrea," "Inoceramus")* and served as a firm substrate for cirral rooting of pentacrinids. The strong dominance of *Dactylioceras* over other ammonites in these *"Posidonia"* and *"Inoceramus"* shell beds suggests it may have primarily lived as a nektobenthic feeder and thus was a part of the *"Posidonia"* Paleocommunity. Belemnites have a similar distribution in shelly facies of the Posidonienschiefer. *"Posidonia"* thus appears to have been the base for a simple, physically controlled, benthic community that was able to exist on chemically somewhat deleterious substrates gradational between those able to support a normal benthos and those that were so oxygen depleted and hydrogen sulfide enriched at the interface that only the most tolerant of benthic taxa *("Inoceramus")* could colonize it. The stratigraphic position of the *"Posidonia"* Paleocommunity strongly supports this conclusion. The sparse occurrence of *"Posidonia"* in the main bituminous shale facies of the Posidonienschiefer, where it occurs mainly as small clusters of immature spat that were killed off soon after settling, also supports this conclusion.

The *"Inoceramus"* Biostrome Paleocommunity

This is the most common bioassociation of the middle Lias Epsilon (Figures 12-5, 12-14), the bituminous shale facies thought to represent anaerobic benthic environments by most workers. Just as in the *"Posidonia"* Paleocommunity, this association is strongly dominated, in numbers and biomass, by a single species, *"Inoceramus" (Pseudomytiloides?) dubius*, that forms thin shell-covered mats and coquinoid biostromes up to 3 cm thick at more than fifty levels in the middle Posidonienschiefer, and at more scattered intervals in beds above and below this where it alternates with the *"Posidonia"* Paleocommunity. These strongly byssate inoceramids far exceed in numbers possible pseudoplanktonic hosts in studied sections; further, *in situ* clusters of bivalved specimens have been noted around hard substrates (Figure 12-10). All evidence suggests that inoceramids were predominantly sessile benthos in the Posidonienschiefer sea. Infaunal organisms, including burrows, are rare and scattered in the middle Posidonienschiefer, and benthic foraminifera are virtually absent. This implies that *"Inoceramus" dubius* was an opportunistic colonizer of substrates that were inhospitable for many other organisms: there were probably substrates characterized by low oxygen and high hydrogen sulfide levels at the sediment-water interface and in anaerobic sediment below. This interpretation fits the global distribution of Mesozoic Inoceramidae, which inhabited virtually all marine facies including flysche and bituminous shales of deep-water environments that supported little other benthic life.

"Inoceramus" dubius formed the base of a low-diversity, physically controlled, benthic paleocommunity throughout most of the depositional history of the middle Posidonienschiefer. Massive

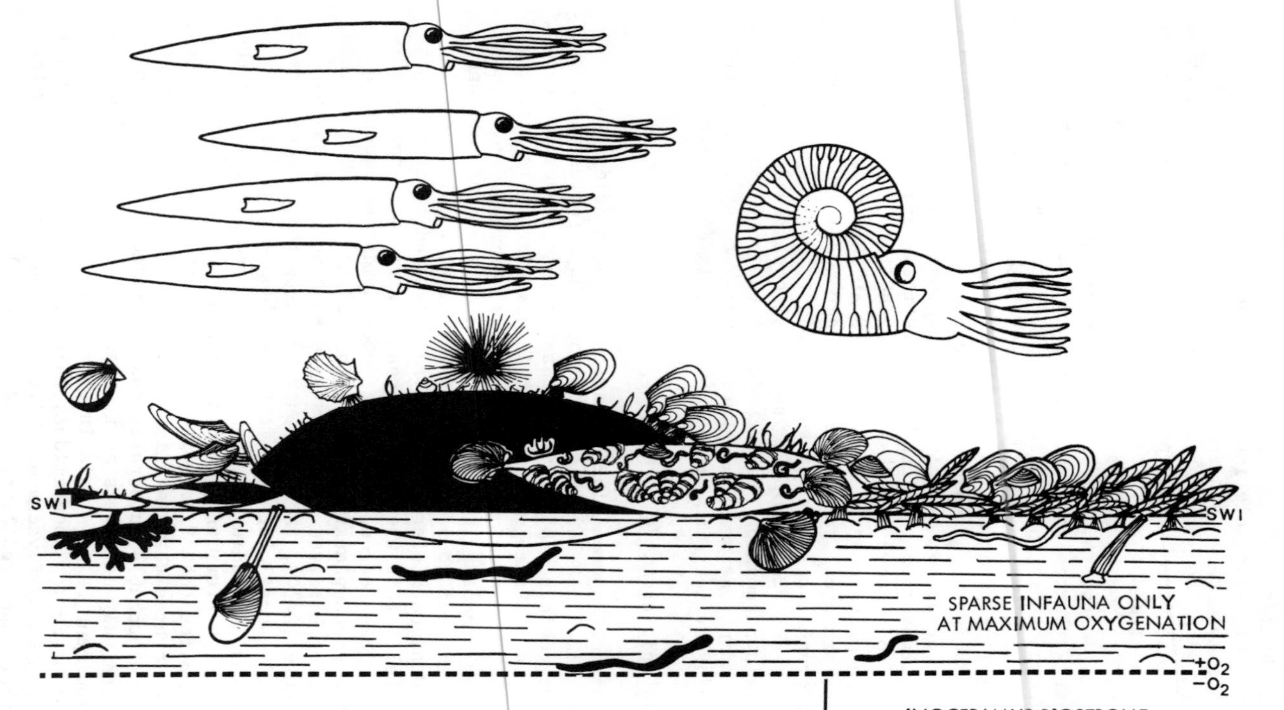

Figure 12-14
Diagrammatic representation of the "*Inoceramus*" biostrome Paleocommunity containing moderately diverse epibiont molluscs, brachiopods, and rare infaunal elements (right); and (left) the diverse epibiont community on ammonite and inoceramid shell surfaces associated with rare infaunal elements at maximum levels of oxygenation. Belemnites and *Dactylioceras* are the most common associated cephalopods with both paleocommunities.

colonization of surfaces that could not be inhabited by other epibionts took place whether or not the underlying sediment was partially oxygenated. This suggests that inoceramid opportunism was a response mainly to chemistry and physical parameters of the sediment-water interface. Thin inoceramid shell layers, representing one or two generations, have few associated organisms other than *Dactylioceras* (nektobenthic?), belemnites, and diverse nektonic ammonites and vertebrates. Thicker inoceramid biostromes have a moderately diverse benthic fauna associated with their upper surfaces. This fauna generally shows a three-stage succession: "*Inoceramus*" colonization; scattered *Clione* sponge borings associated with overgrowth by second generation inoceramids, serpulid worms, and small oysters; and attachment of byssate Oxytomidae, Pectinidae, cemented *Pseudomonotis*, and pediculate *Orbiculoidea*. These relationships are tenuous, however, because only a few specimens show overgrowth patterns between component taxa. There is a tendency in fully developed successions on "*Inoceramus*" biostromes for the third stage colonizers, elevated the greatest distance (a few millimeters to 1 cm) above the substrate, to represent groups that, today, are less tolerant of low oxygen and high hydrogen sulfide conditions than those that were early colonizers.

The Ammonite-Shell Surface Paleocommunity

This paleocommunity (Figures 12-5, 12-11, 12-12, 12-14, 12-15) comprises one of the most interesting and useful associations for paleoecological interpretation of the Posidonienschiefer. Whereas Seilacher and Westphal (1971) envisioned large swimming or dead, floating ammonite shells as hosts for pseudoplanktonic organisms, all specimens systematically collected in the current study and the great majority of museum specimens examined were not encrusted (about 90 percent), were encrusted only on the upper surface (ammonite lying in plane of bedding, about 9 percent), or were differentially encrusted on both sides with sparse epibionts on the underside (less than 1 percent). Rare specimens show encrustation patterns indicating a life symbiosis between the ammonite and its epibionts (as per Seilacher, 1960). Further, for any bedding plane or narrow stratigraphic interval, a clear relationship exists between the size of the ammonite (measured as maximum diameter) and the amount and pattern of epibiont encrustation (Figures 12-11, 12-12, 12-15, 12-16), suggesting a close correlation between size and extent of habitable substrate. Two aspects of size are important here: surface area and width of the ammonite, which reflects elevation of the colonizing surface above the substrate. Width had to be estimated from diameter of well-preserved material because Posidonienschiefer ammonites are laterally compressed. In general, ammonites below 5 cm diameter are not encrusted (Figures 12-11A, 12-16A); those between 5 and 10 cm diameter are sparsely encrusted around the umbilicus and mid-flank area of the up-facing surface (Figures 12-11B-E, 12-16A); and those from 10 to 20 cm diameter are broadly encrusted over most of the upper surface (Figures 12-11F, 12-12, 12-16B). Large ammonites may show encrustation as well on the underside, especially around the umbilicus and venter (Figures 12-15, 12-16B). In some layers, representing more toxic environments, even the largest specimens are not overgrown. Large dead ammonites thus acted as islands of habitable substrate on the Posidonienschiefer seafloor, elevated above zones of

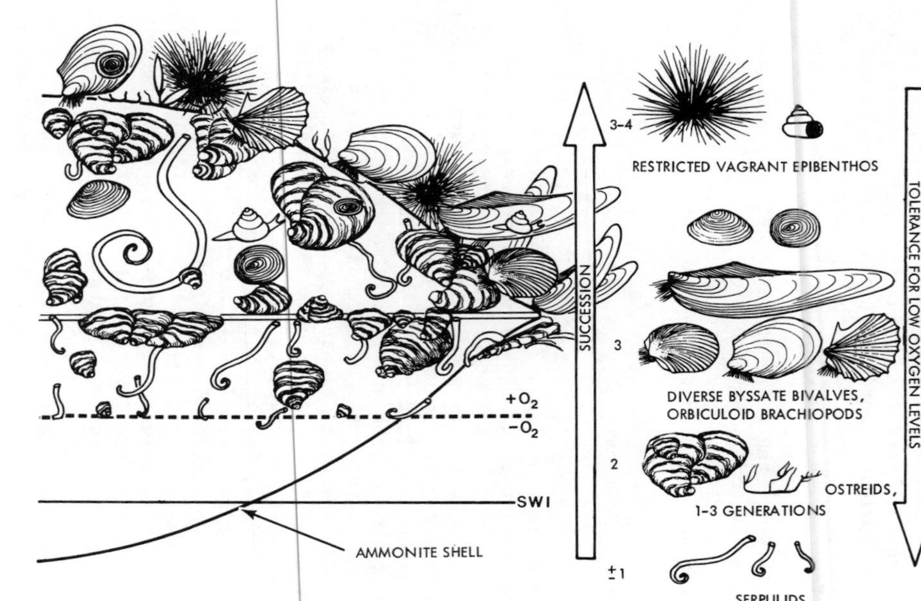

Figure 12-15
Encrustation patterns and ecological succession on largest ammonite conchs from the middle Posidonienschiefer (diverse Ammonite Shell Surface Paleocommunity). Note uneven encrustation of upper and lower surfaces, phototropic orientation and low diversity of epibionts on underside of ammonite conch; aerobic-anaerobic boundary (+O_2,-O_2) defines lower limit of encrustation at or slightly above the sediment-water interface (SWI). Note also, taxa that are today more tolerant of low oxygen (serpulid worms, oysters) exclusively occupy lower part of conch while those with less tolerance occur progressively higher on the conch, defining a narrow oxygen gradient near the interface. Encrustation and successional patterns based on observed growth superposition on several specimens; maximum development shown. Encrustation patterns define height of anaerobic boundary and oxygen gradient above sediment-water interface.

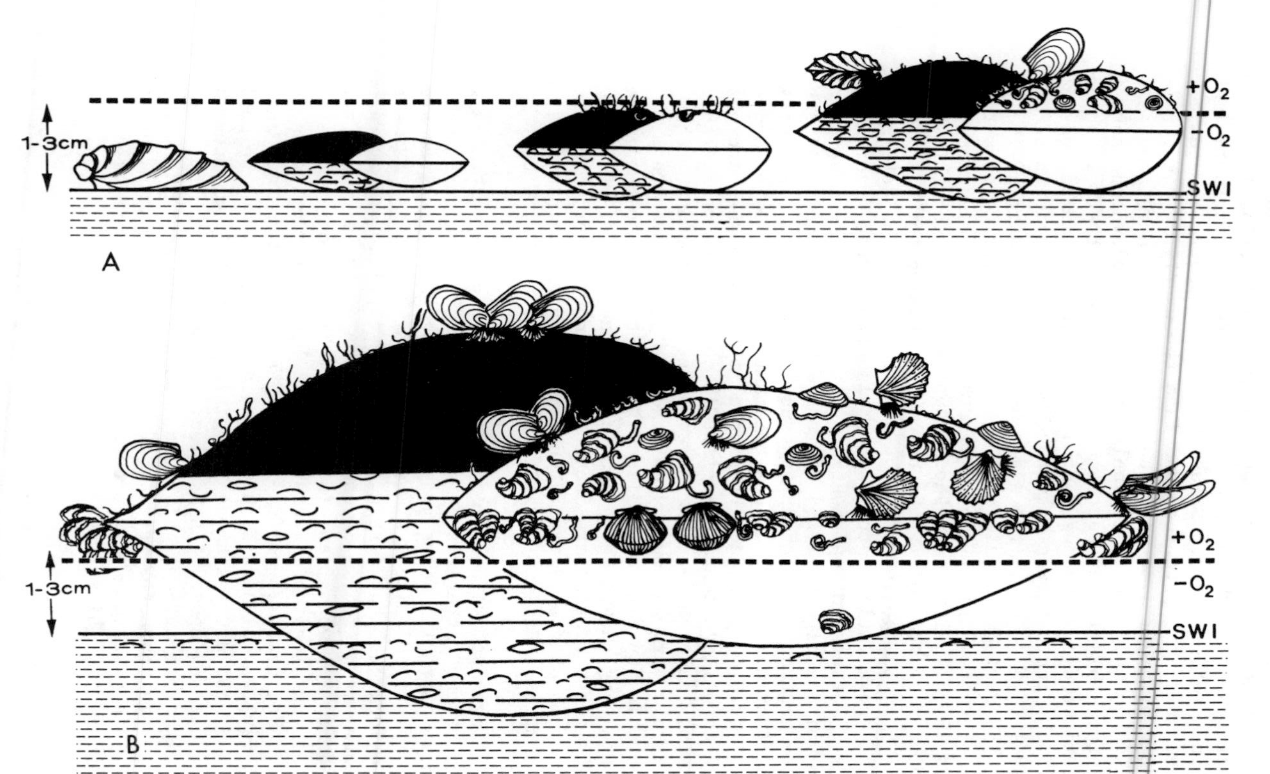

Figure 12-16
Summary diagram of observed relationships between dead ammonite-shell size, elevation of upper flank above substrate (SWI), encrustation patterns, and position of aerobic-anaerobic boundary (dashed line). Encrustation patterns suggest the oxygen boundary normally lay from 0-3 cm above the substrate. Average observed relationship shown.

oxygen depletion and hydrogen sulfide enrichment. These ammonite-epibiont associations comprise a measuring stick for plotting the position of toxic benthic environments relative to the sediment-water interface (Figure 12-16). If the ammonite shell was lying prone on habitable substrates, epibionts should encrust all surfaces that are not in direct contact with the sediment; differential encrustation patterns mainly reflect light variations. If, however, the toxic zone extended above the interface and into the overlying water column, ammonites of small size might not be encrusted, and larger ones would be differentially encrusted only on surfaces elevated above the toxic boundary. This latter pattern predominates in the Posidonienschiefer where studied. Reconstructed widths for the ammonites relative to epibiont encrustation patterns indicate the toxic interface normally lay 1 to 5 cm above the sediment surface (Figure 12-16). In parts of the Posidonienschiefer where the biota indicates more widespread oxygen depletion (the *Harpoceras-Phylloceras* Paleocommunity; Figures 12-5, 12-13B) even the largest ammonites show little or no evidence of encrustation in the sequences studied for this report.

Not only can the position of the anoxic boundary be determined from ammonite encrustation patterns but also the oxygen gradient near the boundary. Patterns of epibiont encrustation are the most complex on large ammonites (Figure 12-15) and suggest that those organisms living on the highest surfaces and encrusting latest in the succession represent groups that are less tolerant today of low oxygen levels (Pectinidae, Oxytomidae, Pteriacea) than those that encrust lower on the ammonite conch and earlier in the succession (serpulid worms, oysters, inoceramids, and inarticulate brachiopods). This pattern depicts a very narrow oxygen gradient just above the aerobic-anaerobic boundary and raises the question as to the mechanism for maintaining such a sharp boundary in the face of at least weak currents a few centimeters above the sediment-water interface. Development of an extensive algal-fungal mat above the interface, as in the Santa Barbara Basin off California, seems to be the best hypothesis.

A four-stage succession of epibionts on top of ammonite "islands" is indicated by the "stratigraphy" and overgrowth relationships of the epibionts. Serpulid worms and byssate inoceramid bivalves are commonly the first colonizers; *"Ostrea"* or small *Liostrea* may also be initial colonizers, but settle later than serpulids and overgrow them when both are present. Second generation oyster growths, rare boring polydorid (?) worms, and inarticulate brachiopods represent a third wave of encrustation; diverse byssate bivalves (Oxytomidae, Pectinidae, Monotidae?, *Gervillia)* and cemented *Pseudomonotis* encrust surfaces of earlier colonizers as well as unoccupied ammonite-shell surfaces. The most diverse ammonite-epibiont associations occur in the upper-middle and upper Lias Epsilon. In some cases, they are associated with rare infaunal bivalves, scaphopods, serpulid worms, and burrows; this indicates retreat of the anoxic interface into the substrate. This paleocommunity occurs patchily in strata also yielding *"Inoceramus"* biostromes.

The Harpoceras-Phylloceras Paleocommunity

These two streamlined nektonic ammonite genera predominate in this paleocommunity, which probably represents the most oxygen-depleted phase in the history of the Posidonienschiefer. Common associates are ecologically similar *Hildoceras* and *Dactylioceras* (possibly nektobenthic, see previous discussion), scattered belemnites, and isolated single valves of *"Inoceramus" dubius*. No infauna is known with this association. Ammonite-packed surfaces, probably representing mass mortalities caused by rapid oxygen overturn, are a common feature and show population structure for all taxa with extremely high juvenile mortality. Normal populations characterize other occurrences of the community. Except for small sparse inoceramids, no benthic organisms were recovered in this paleocommunity during the sampling program; most large ammonites are only sparsely encrusted on the upper surface or not overgrown by epibionts. This community reflects predominantly anaerobic conditions at, and for at least several centimeters above, the sediment-water interface; thus, it represents the environment commonly envisioned for the entire Posidonienschiefer. Even here, fluctuations in the benthic environment allowed brief colonization of the sediment by small, scattered *"Inoceramus"* populations. This community occurs at thin intervals throughout the middle Posidonienschiefer, alternating with *"Inoceramus"* Biostrome and Ammonite-Shell Surface paleocommunities, but it predominates only through thin sequences that also contain coccolithic limestone units having the same association (Schlacken, Unterer Stein).

In summary, diverse paleocommunities characterize the Posidonienschiefer; all but one indicate low to moderate levels of oxygenation at or near the sediment-water interface and, in some cases, in the upper sediment layers. Intervals indicating anaerobic conditions in the benthic zone that exclude all benthos are short term and of secondary importance (Figure 12-6). The aerobic-anaerobic interface and lethal hydrogen sulfide boundary apparently fluctuated from a position a few centimeters above the sediment-water interface to a position a few centimeters within the sediment. These data clearly support an alternative hypothesis (aerobic water column) for the origin of the bituminous shales of the Posidonienschiefer. Relatively frequent and rapid fluctuations of the benthic environment owing to migration of the oxygen boundary are indicated by interbedded paleocommunities (Figure 12-6) reflecting different oxygen regimes in the benthic zone; for example, the *Plicatula-"Ostrea"*-Belemnite Paleocommunity or the *Inoceramus* Biostrome Paleocommunity alternates with the *Harpoceras-Phylloceras* Paleocommunity. A detailed look at short-term fluctuations between oxygenated and anoxic benthic environments reveals some important clues to the cause for these oscillations.

SEDIMENTARY AND PALEOCOMMUNITY RHYTHMS

The middle part of the Posidonienschiefer (middle Lias Epsilon) is characterized by small-scale sedimentary cycles that weather to blocky-shale units 3 to 25 cm thick (Figures 12-2A, 12-6). Two communities alternate extensively through these sequences: the *Harpoceras-Phylloceras* Paleocommunity and the *"Inoceramus"* Biostrome Paleocommunity. Patches ("islands") representing the Ammonite-Shell

Surface Paleocommunity occur with the latter. This alternation reflects frequent migrations of the anaerobic-aerobic boundary up and down through the lower few centimeters of the water column and into the sediment. Three of these small cyclothems have been dissected at 1 cm intervals, and all three have similar, though not precise, patterns within them. Figure 12-6 models the general pattern and is taken from an actual unit situated between the Unterer Stein and the Oberer Stein (Figure 12-5).

In these small cycles, a *Harpoceras-Phylloceras* Paleocommunity with normal population structure occurs at the base with rare isolated adult inoceramids or no benthos. Anaerobic benthic conditions predominated, and the lethal oxygen-hydrogen sulfide interface was elevated at least several centimeters above the sediment-water interface. A mass mortality followed leaving a densely packed, thin, ammonite-shell bed in which populations of all taxa show high juvenile mortality. A rapid overturn of deep anoxic waters is the suggested cause of the mass mortality, and thus, possibly the Toarcian sea occupied a stratified basin. Many modern examples are known in which mass mortalities of fish result (for example, from seasonal overturn of anaerobic waters in the Arabian Sea and Bay of Bengal; Banse, 1959, 1968). Colonization by benthic bivalves of the "*Inoceramus*" Biostrome Paleocommunity followed the mass mortality, and early settlers probably attached in small groups to the top of the ammonite-shell bed. Benthic waters were partially oxygenated as a result of the overturn, and the anaerobic boundary was trapped in the sediment below the ammonite mass-mortality bed.

Increasingly dense populations of "*Inoceramus*" occur upsection in the cycle, and addition of more bivalve-shell debris further changed the nature of the sediment surface. It lowered the lethal hydrogen sulfide-oxygen boundary into the substrate until dense "*Inoceramus*" biostromes developed over wide areas and became secondarily colonized on top by a simple assemblage of other epibionts (serpulid worms, other bivalves, brachiopods); belemnites and possibly *Dactylioceras* may have been nektobenthic and fed on such surfaces. Small fluctuations in oxygen levels near the sediment-water interface produced numerous alternations of dense biostromes and more sparsely colonized mats of "*Inoceramus*" associated with ammonites of the *Harpoceras-Phylloceras* Paleocommunity. "*Inoceramus*" biostromes become less abundant and benthic bivalves more scattered at the top of the rhythm (Figure 12-6). This and a commensurate increase in the number of pelagic ammonites reflects gradual lowering of oxygen (and hydrogen sulfide increase?) near the interface. The anaerobic-lethal hydrogen sulfide interface rose from within the sediment up into the water column. The anaerobic waters eventually killed the benthos, and another cycle began.

Long-term fluctuations in current intensity and circulation patterns may account for this pattern. Of particular importance is the frequent fluctuation in oxygen levels and paleocommunities near the sediment-water interface suggested by these cycles (Figure 12-6). The predominance of paleocommunities indicates at least a partially oxygenated benthic zone. More rhythms need to be tested to determine how uniform this pattern is and to establish the periodicity of anaerobic conditions. These rhythms do indicate a delicately balanced anoxic boundary near the sediment-water interface rather than an extensive anoxic water column.

VERTEBRATE FOSSILS

The vertebrate fossil record of the Posidonienschiefer poses a major problem for the environmental hypothesis widely suggested by the invertebrates; that is, the benthic zone of the Toarcian seaway in southern Germany was swept by gentle currents and partially oxygenated during most of the depositional history of the bituminous shale facies. The vertebrate fossils are not uncommon and are exceptionally well preserved for the most part: skeletons are articulated, or nearly so, scales and skin are intact, and stomach contents, fecal material, and even unborn young (in ichthyosaurs) are retained inside the body cavity or around the skeletons. Because of their size and generally excellent preservation without extensive evidence for scavenging, predation, bacterial decay, or physical reworking prior to burial, the Posidonienschiefer vertebrates have stood as *prima-facie* evidence for the stagnant anaerobic-basin model of Seilacher and Westphal (1971) and others. Several facets of the vertebrate record must be reconciled before an alternative environmental hypothesis can be considered viable.

The first problem is one of vertebrate ecology. Most authors have indicated that there is little or no representation among the Posidonienschiefer vertebrates of benthic-feeding taxa, for example, shell-crushing fish or reptiles with pavement teeth. Most of the taxa were probably first or second order carnivores that fed on active prey. Stomach contents of icthyosaurs, for example, yield squid hooks, fish bones, and occasionally belemnite skeletons (Keller, 1976). Less is known of fish diets, but most fish appear to have been large to moderate size, open-water taxa that fed on smaller vertebrates and invertebrates. It has been assumed that, like modern analogues with the same trophic style, the fish and reptiles of the Toarcian seaway were predominantly nektonic carnivores and scavengers inhabiting the middle and upper (photic) zones of the marine water column. Even though rare pavement teeth of shell-crushing (benthic) fish from the Posidonienschiefer were discovered in museum collections during the course of this study, the apparent paucity of benthic vertebrates, but abundance of benthic invertebrates (especially bivalves, a potential food source) is a contradiction.

Two factors, at least in part, explain this apparent ecological discrepancy. The oxygenated-basin model for the Posidonienschiefer, so strongly supported by invertebrate evidence, calls for low to moderate, but still subnormal, levels of oxygen in the lower water column and at the seafloor: there was enough oxygen to support short-lived, largely low-diversity, pioneer communities at frequent intervals, but not enough oxygen to allow normal marine, diverse, "climax" communities to develop in the benthic zone. Whereas many invertebrates can tolerate low oxygen levels for long periods of time, and some prefer them, most lower vertebrates cannot because of their high metabolic levels and more complex biochemistry. For example, most fish of marine shelf-depth environments avoid dysaerobic waters and have low lethal thresholds for oxygen depletion. Some deep basinal fishes are more tolerant, but these groups are not yet known from the Posidonienschiefer. In stratified basins, oxygen overturns produce mass mortalities among fish, but rarely have the same effect on coexisting benthic molluscs or other invertebrates. It may be that oxygen levels were low enough near the Posidonienschiefer seafloor to exclude most marine shallow-water fish while still supporting abundant oxygen-tolerant invertebrates. The main invertebrate elements of the Posidonienschiefer biota belong to groups whose geologic distribution and modern analogues suggest great tolerance for low oxygen conditions; the ammonites are a major exception and seem to have been widely killed by oxygen depletion events or overturns in the Posidonienschiefer. The contention that Jurassic Posidonienschiefer fish were intolerant of low oxygen levels gains support by the common occurrence of thin beds crowded with fish debris that probably represent mass mortalities due to oxygen overturn in the bituminous shale facies of the Posidonienschiefer.

It should further be noted that the ecology of Jurassic fishes is not well known. Workers have erroneously used the presence or absence of shell-crushing forms with pavement teeth to determine whether or not a benthic fish assemblage was present. Many "normal" looking teleosts today are actually nektobenthonic feeders and mainly reside in the lower few meters of the water column; the Posidonienschiefer fish should be investigated for this possibility.

But what of the reptiles, air breathers that should not have been as sensitive to reduced oxygen levels within their depth range? Why are there no obvious benthic-feeding reptiles in the Posidonienschiefer? Again, possible explanations exist for the pelagic nature of the reptilian fauna. First, benthic feeding by convergent evolution of pavement teeth in marine reptiles was a newly evolving adaptive strategy during the Mesozoic and never reached significant proportions. The Placodontia is the principal group involved, but it became extinct at the end of the Triassic. *Globidens* and related mosasaurs are Cretaceous analogues, but obvious benthic-feeding reptiles are unknown in Jurassic deposits. Second the jaw structures of the more normal pelagic marine Jurassic reptiles (pleiosaurs, icthyosaurs, mystriosaurs) were poorly developed for crushing, in contrast to some later Cretaceous mosasaurs. Instead, they were mainly adapted for catching, grasping, tearing, and positioning live prey that was then probably swallowed whole. It would have been unlikely that Jurassic marine reptiles with more normal dentition would have developed active benthic-feeding life styles where shell or carapace crushing would have been largely necessary. Third, the major food resources (fish and squids) of the Jurassic marine reptiles were themselves sensitive to low oxygen levels and experienced (as today) mass mortalities because of oxygen overturn or immersion in poorly oxygenated waters. Like living Black Sea Cetaceans that are relatively insensitive to dissolved oxygen levels in deep waters, the marine reptiles lived mainly in the epipelagic zone because oxygen-sensitive prey were concentrated there. In summary, Jurassic marine reptiles did not evolve structures or behavior patterns that would permit them to use food resources of the benthic life zone. They would not be expected to be a significant component of benthic communities under the best of conditions.

A second major question concerning the vertebrates in the Posidonienschiefer is related to an apparent lack of scavenging on the carcasses. Icthyosaurs, plesiosaurs, mystriosaurs, many fish, and even flying reptiles died and commonly sank through the water column without becoming disarticulated (Figure 12-3A,C). Naturally, the pelagic reptiles themselves would have been effective scavengers on dead carcasses, as would a variety of fishes and larger arthropods. Several factors should be considered. First, complete skeletons are emphasized in research and reporting on the Posidonienschiefer reptiles; many colleagues tell me that disarticulated and broken reptilian bone fragments are equally common, but rarely noted. This may represent a certain level of scavenging and decay prior to burial. Furthermore, although fish are also preserved as articulated specimens, commonly with the scales in place (Figure 12-3A), this type of preservation is rare and stratigraphically localized. Fish fossils are more commonly represented by extensively broken debris (scales and bone fragments) that mainly occurs in very thin (1 mm to 1 cm) beds and in the coccolithic limestone units; in many cases, these may represent mass mortalities followed by decay and scavenging of the carcasses. Similar modern deposits result from large fish kills caused by oxygen overturns such as those reported by Banse (1959, 1968) in the Arabian Sea.

Still another factor that might have prevented widespread scavenging and decay of dead vertebrate skeletons in the water column is the potential rate of settling of the carcasses. Dead vertebrates today commonly bloat with gases during early decay and float near the surface or in midwater zones of marine environments. Highly decomposed carcasses are typical, representing bacterial decay and scavenging in the upper water column prior to sinking. But the Posidonienschiefer reptiles and many fish do not show high levels of decay. This suggests that either the vertebrates lived near the margins of an expanded anoxic zone and floated or sank slowly into anoxic waters just after death, or that the vertebrate carcasses sank quickly through the lower water column after death preventing exposure to decay or scavenging and came to rest on substrate in oxygen-depleted bottom waters. The latter explanation seems most tenable for the following reasons.

1. Evidence for a partially oxygenated, current-swept benthic zone during deposition of the black shale facies predominates among invertebrates and sedimentary structures.
2. The marine reptiles clearly show preferred orientation indicating deposition of articulated specimens in current-swept, probably oxygenated environments (Brenner, 1976b).
3. The association of newly born young icthyosaurs next to the mother still containing unborn young (Figure 12-3C), clearly indicates abrupt death and rapid sinking of at least some specimens.
4. The lower part of the water column in the Posidonienschiefer basin was probably not inhabited by healthy marine reptiles, the principal scavengers, because their main food resources were oxygen-sensitive epipelagic fish and squids. Dead and dying carcasses sinking even slowly through this zone would not be commonly encountered by healthy reptiles as long as oxygen levels were subnormal and oxygen-sensitive fish and squids were largely excluded. The Posidonienschiefer biota yields no demonstrable benthic scavengers other than rare lobsters; these are less common than articulated vertebrates.

These factors, in part, explain lack of scavenging on vertebrate carcasses, especially the large reptiles, while still allowing partial oxygenation of the benthic zone sufficient to support a restricted benthos.

A final question to be answered concerns the apparent lack of aerobic bacterial decay that led to exquisite preservation of vertebrates and invertebrates in the Posidonienschiefer. This, above all, seems to contradict the oxygenated basin model. Modern studies of bacterial decay in deep marine environments and re-examination of vertebrate fossils from the Posidonienschiefer in the Museum Hauff and the Universität Tübingen resolved this problem and yielded some surprising results.

Much work has recently been done on aerobic bacterial decay in marine benthic environments, especially in offshore, deep-water sites equivalent to that of the Posidonienschiefer paleoenvironment. Degens and Mopper (1975) and Jannasch and Wirsen (1973), among others, found that rates of bacterial decay on exposed or sediment-bound nutrients are remarkably slow in the presence of normal oxygen and abundant bacteria and almost negligible in subnormally oxygenated environments; the latter environments also tend to exclude many benthic scavengers (Rhoads and Morse, 1971). Even in well-oxygenated waters, bacterial decay rates are surprisingly minute over the course of a year. A large carcass may take many years to decay in these environments if no scavenging occurs and may be covered with sediment, or partially so, before the effects of decay are obvious. If covering or underlying sediments were largely anoxic and hydrogen sulfide-enriched, as proposed for the Posidonienschiefer and typical of many basins with subnormal oxygen levels, effective decay would cease on contact with the sediment thus preventing breakdown and ultimate disarticulation of carcasses. In part, the preservation of large reptile carcasses in the Posidonienschiefer may reflect these processes and is not incompatible with the relatively deep, subnormally oxygenated, benthic environments suggested by invertebrate evidence.

An even more important factor, discovered upon re-examination of many vertebrate specimens, is that the skeletons are predominantly better preserved on one side than the other. This has been known for many years by collectors who have consistently prepared vertebrate skeletons from the underside because of superior preservation on that surface. This is also the surface that was in contact with the sediment-water interface or partially embedded in the sediment from the time of initial deposition of the carcass until its burial. All other evidence accumulated in this study suggests that this interface and underlying sediments were hydrogen sulfide-enriched and anaerobic during much of the depositional history of the Posidonienschiefer. If scavenging and bacterial decay did not break down vertebrate carcasses before deposition, there was little chance that the underside of these carcasses would ever be decayed; this adequately explains the excellent preservation of this surface in many specimens.

Whereas it seems natural to view the whole lower part of the water column as anaerobic because of the beautiful preservation of the vertebrates, neither differential preservation of upper and lower surfaces of vertebrate carcasses nor the invertebrate evidence supports this contention. The occurrence of sparse *Chondrites* burrows in oxygenated sediment overlying the carcasses (Figure 12-9), but not below them, seems to suggest that oxygenated waters came in contact with the upper surface of these carcasses. Ammonite epibiont studies (Figures 12-15, 12-16) suggest that the water might have been sufficiently oxygenated to support diverse invertebrates only a

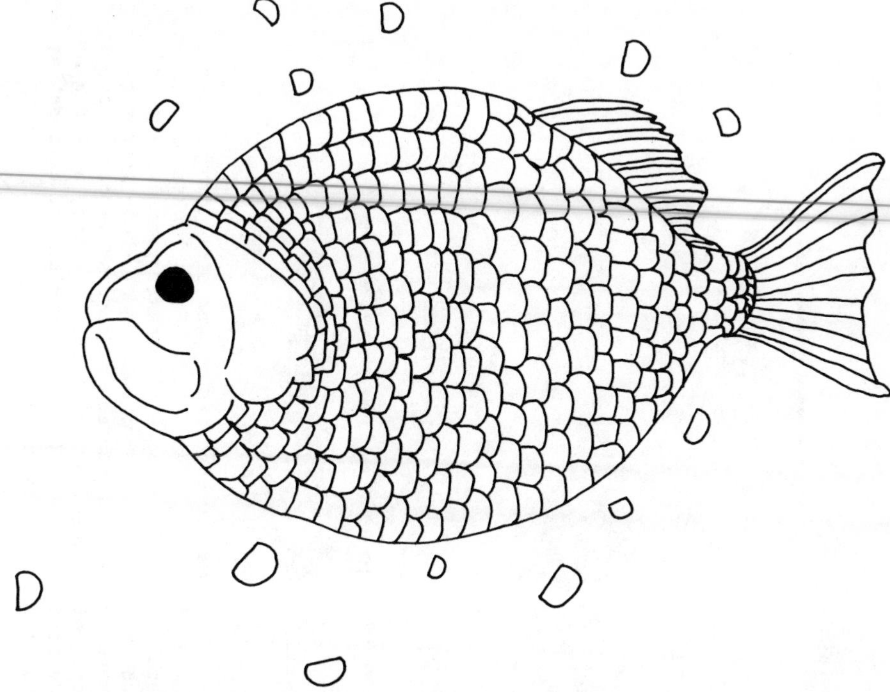

Figure 12-17
Generalized diagram of fish *(Dapedius*; Figure 12-3A) showing common occurrence of loose scales around specimen that is completely preserved on lower side; scales probably derived from aerobic bacterial decay of upper part of carcass (University of Tübingen specimen).

few centimeters above the anoxic sediment-water interface. If this were the case, evidence of decay on the upper portions of vertebrate carcasses would be expected and, if found, would strongly support the oxygenated-basin model over the stagnant-basin model for the Posidonienschiefer. Examination of numerous articulated vertebrate skeletons reveals evidence for bacterial decay and even some scavenging on the upper surface of many carcasses.

Fish debris characterizes the entire Posidonienschiefer; whole fish are less common and at least some of these (Hauff, Jr., 1960, Plates 36-40, 54) show disarticulation of small skeletal elements on the upper surface prior to burial. Scavenging of carcasses in the upper water column and widespread benthic decay in low current regimes is inferred. Other fish (Figures 12-3A, 12-17) are perfectly preserved on the lower side, but show loose scales around the skeleton that have been derived from the upper side presumably during early phases of decay. Still other specimens show no evidence of decay (Hauff, Jr., 1960, Plates 42-53, 55-59) and presumably were completely immersed in an anaerobic benthic zone shortly after death. This would be possible for most fish if the anaerobic boundary were only a few centimeters above the sediment-water interface.

Reptile skeletons, especially certain icthyosaurs (Figure 12-18), show the same relationships more dramatically. In many cases,

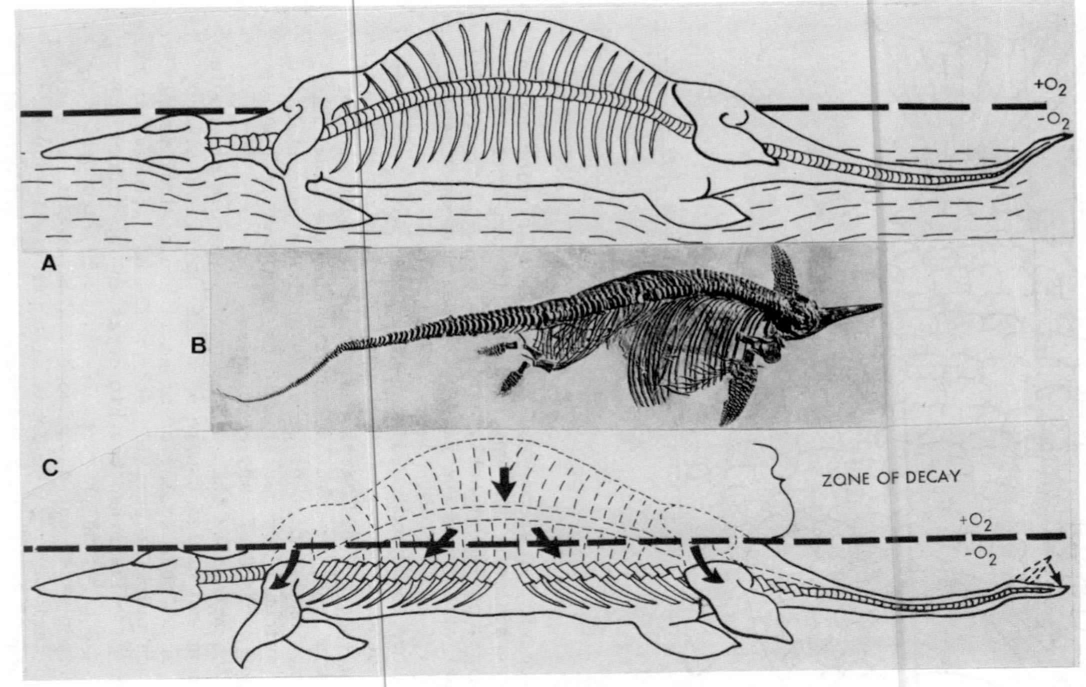

Figure 12-18
Interpretation of common preservation patterns of marine reptiles, as prepared from lower side; exemplified by B, the icthyosaur *Stenopterygius crassicostatus* von Huene (from Hauff, 1960, Plate 14b). Note: broken backbone in middle with vertebrae arranged *en echelon* in different directions on either side of break; opposed curvature of ribs on either side of break; displaced upper ribs; position of upper paddles on outside of those representing lower surface. Interpretation: A. Bacterial decay and scavenging of upper surface of carcass exposed above the aerobic-anaerobic interface causes. C. Collapse of upper part of carcass, breaking the backbone, splaying of ribs and vertebrae, and shifting of upper paddles to outside position; lower (exhibit) surface of carcass lay within anaerobic zone from time of deposition of reptile and remained well preserved.

the backbone is broken and vertebrae aligned *en echelon* in opposite directions on either side of the break, the ribs are splayed in different directions from mid-carcass, and the upper limbs of the skeleton (orientated parallel to the sediment surface) are rotated to positions outside of the lower limbs (Figure 12-18). Ribs and limb bones of the upper side are sometimes disarticulated whereas those of the lower side are preserved in place. Such a pattern of preservation is best explained by collapse of the carcass from the upper side after exposure in oxygenated waters long enough to initiate decay (Figure 12-18A) while keeping the lower side intact in anaerobic or oxygen-depleted benthic environments at and just above the sediment-water interface. This is the precise interpretation of dominant paleoenvironments in the Posidonienschiefer concluded from independent lines of evidence presented in this study; it is certainly compatible with the occurrence of sparse burrows on top of some carcasses (Figure 12-9) but not below them. Not all skeletons show this collapse pattern and some obviously decayed little, if at all, before burial; but this would be possible if the aerobic-anaerobic boundary was only one to a few meters above the substrate during burial of the carcass, if the carcass sank deeply into soft anaerobic substrate, or if aerobic decay was very slow because of subnormal oxygen levels (Degens and Mopper, 1975). A stagnant, anaerobic water mass of considerable depth is not prerequisite to exceptional preservation.

In summary, cumulative evidence from vertebrates, in particular their inferred ecology and preservational features, does not contradict an environmental reconstruction for the Posidonienschiefer sea based on the moderately oxygenated, current-circulated basin model as much as has been suggested by past workers. The paucity of benthic vertebrates was in part due to ecological factors (the apparent sensitivity of fishes and cephalopods to subnormal oxygen levels because of gill breathing and physiological factors) and consequent restriction of principal predators (marine reptiles) to epipelagic habitats despite their ability as air breathers to tolerate deep-water habitats with subnormal oxygen. In part, the lack of benthic vertebrates is an evolutionary feature. Among reptiles, no shell-crushing benthic forms with pavement teeth evolved during the Jurassic, and those with normal jaw structure had not reached evolutionary grade where shell crushing was possible. Jurassic marine reptiles were not widely adapted for benthic habitation.

Exceptional preservation among Posidonienschiefer vertebrates has been overemphasized. An overwhelming number of fish fossils occur as disarticulated debris, and disarticulated reptile material is more common than reported. In both cases, bacterial decay and scavenging prior to burial are implied. Finally, differential preservation of the tops and bottoms of some articulated reptile and fish skeletons, disarticulation and collapse of carcass tops, and the occurrence of burrows in mud on top of but not below large skeletons suggest low levels of scavenging and extensive bacterial decay on their upper surfaces in an oxygenated environment. The oxygenated zone would have been situated a few centimeters to more than a meter above the sediment-water interface. This is compatible with invertebrate evidence that also suggests low to moderate oxygen levels at or just above the interface during most of the depositonal history of the Posidonienschiefer.

CONCLUSIONS

The great majority of evidence obtained from detailed study of two complete sections through the middle and upper Lias Epsilon, the bituminous shale facies of the Posidonienschiefer, does not support the hypothesis that this deposit was formed in a largely stagnant, severely oxygen-depleted to anaerobic basin. Surficial sedimentary structures and biofabric analyses depict almost continuous, low to moderately intense current activity with periodically stronger levels; however, no "current events" such as debris flows, storm surges, or turbidity currents are indicated by sedimentary structures in these sections. Whereas this does not rule out the possibility that such currents periodically affected the basin locally, it suggests that they were not the primary mode of depositon and cannot account for most current features or the abundance of normally benthonic invertebrate taxa in the Posidonienschiefer. Instead, the extensive evidence for bottom currents throughout much of the depositional history of the bituminous shale facies suggests a mechanism for almost continuous oxygenation of the lower water column.

Systematic collecting and analysis of the Posidonienschiefer biota, using a standard sample size of 0.5 by 0.5 by 0.01 to 0.02 m throughout each section and taking into account all fossils (the "normal" aspect of the biota), yielded thousands of complete, well-preserved specimens and abundant fragmental material of invertebrates and vertebrates (mainly small fish); but no examples of exceptional preservation, for which the deposit is so famous, were encountered. That is, no complete vertebrate skeletons; only rare large fragments of large fish and reptiles; and no arthropods, crinoids, squids (other than belemnites), or exceptionally large complete ammonites were recovered. Of special significance was the scarcity of wood in the sections; no large logs, such as those illustrated in Figures 12-3B and 12-4A that are densely encrusted with *"Inoceramus" (Pseudomytiloides?) dubius*, long-stalked complete *Seirocrinus*, and shorter *"Pentacrinus,"* were found in the sampling program or in general collecting through both areas. These specimens are the basis for Seilacher, Drozdzewski, and Haude's hypothesis (1968) that floating driftwood was a primary host for pseudoplanktonic crinoids and normally benthic, byssate bivalves. Large swimming or dead, floating ammonite conchs were also considered hosts (Seilacher and Westphal, 1971). Of six, small, wood fragments found, only two were overgrown by bivalves, both on the upper surface as would be expected in benthic encrustation. Tens of thousands of small byssate bivalves were recovered in the same sequences. Of several hundred, complete, adult ammonites collected, less than 10 percent were encrusted with epibionts, almost all of them only on the upper surface as they lay parallel to the substrate after deposition (a benthic habitation pattern). Floating wood, ammonites, and seaweed could not have been "pseudoplanktonic hosts" for a significant number of normally benthic invertebrates that characterize most of the Posidonienschiefer.

Studies in the functional morphology, ecology, population structure, and mode of occurrence of these small invertebrates conclusively demonstrate that most bivalves, brachiopods, serpulid worms, scaphopods, echinoids, and probably large gastropods and short-stalked crinoids lived as benthos on the Toarcian seafloor. This indicates oxygenation at or near the sediment-water interface during most of the depositional history of the Posidonienschiefer. Whereas most cephalopods in the biota seem functionally adapted for an active nektonic lifestyle, the relatively high abundance of belemnites and more ornate *Dactylioceras* in association with dense biostromes of benthic bivalves suggests that these taxa may have been saltating nektobenthos that fed on the bottom. It is significant that many normally benthic invertebrates considered as rare and as having a restricted stratigraphic distribution are represented by several individuals spread through numerous stratigraphic levels in the two sampled sections. Statistical projection of their occurrence to a larger sample size indicates that they probably represent common elements of the benthos characterized by small population sizes.

Systematic sampling of these two sections at closely spaced intervals also produced several taxa never before reported from the Posidonienschiefer; all were normally benthic in habitat. Small epifaunal byssate bivalves, new infaunal bivalves, scaphopods, and sparse but widely dispersed burrows (*Chondrites, Planolites, Thalassinoides)* comprise important new discoveries. Again, statistical projection to a larger sample size suggests that these are potentially common elements of the biota. Some of these are evidence for a periodically oxygenated, upper sediment column in the benthic life zone.

The discovery that the bituminous shale facies of the Posidonienschiefer in southwestern Germany is heavily dominated by benthic invertebrates whose numbers and distribution cannot be accounted for by pseudoplanktonic life habits has required re-examination of the evidence originally presented for this hypothesis and for the nektoplanktonic habitat of the common bivalves *"Posidonia"* and *Bositra* (Jefferies and Minton, 1965). Neither hypothesis is supported by the current investigation. Rasmussen's (1977) observations that *Seirocrinus subangularis* (Miller) and other pentacrinids are attached to logs by adult stem bases, are older than the projected floatation life of the log, and thus must have attached to these logs as benthos seriously challenges the interpretation of Seilacher et al. (1968) that they lived throughout life as pendant pseudoplankton on floating logs. Meyer's contention that collagen ligaments (not columnal morphology) are mainly responsible for keeping arms, pinnules, cirri, and probably stems of crinoids stiff and erect in the face of currents provides a mechanism for upright growth from the seafloor of long-stalked *Seirocrinus*. Re-examination of some German specimens of *Seirocrinus* associated with logs reveals no stem attachment to the undersides of the logs as would be expected in a pseudoplanktonic life mode, but to the sides and possibly tops of the logs. Benthic attachment and upright growth of *Seirocrinus* and *Pentacrinus* in the Posidonienschiefer is supported by the majority of the evidence.

The discovery of musulature in several Posidoniidae, which functionally precludes a nektobenthonic swimming habit, and of large adult shells of species studied by Jefferies and Minton (1965) challenges their interpretation. Further, because the inner shell layer is apparently missing in specimens from the Posidonienschiefer, the shell was thicker and heavier than that of pelagic molluscs today. Facies distribution of *"Posidonia"* in the Posidonienschiefer is restricted and more like that of a benthic bivalve. *"Posidonia"* probably lived weakly attached by byssal threads or free on moderately oxygenated substrates in the Toarcian seaway of southwestern Germany; it probably occupied a niche between fully oxygenated substrates supporting normal marine communities and oxygen-depleted (but not anoxic) substrates preferred by simple pioneer communities dominated by *"Inoceramus."*

Paleocommunity analysis (Figure 12-5) further supports a model of an oxygenated seaway and environmentally diverse substrates with widespread benthic habitation rather than a model of a stagnant anaerobic basin supporting a more uniform, predominantly nektonic, planktonic and pseudoplanktonic biota. Six distinct paleocommunities, five of them dominated by benthic invertebrates, occur in the Posidonienschiefer; the pelagic ammonite-dominated community characterizes only a small percent of the sequence. More than one benthic community may occur at a single level in patchy distribution, and paleocommunities alternate frequently within short time periods (Figure 12-6). This indicates fluctuating environments mainly controlled by delicately balanced oxygen and hydrogen-sulfide levels and movement of the anaerobic-aerobic interface back and forth a few centimeters above or below the sediment-water interface (Figure 12-19).

An overwhelming amount of evidence gathered in this study thus supports an interpretation of oxygenated benthic environments (but at subnormal levels) during most of the depositional history of the Posidonienschiefer. Oxygenation of the upper sediment column was sporadic and short-lived. The anaerobic or lethal-hydrogen sulfide boundary seems to have been at or a few centimeters above the sediment-water interface most of the time. This prohibited colonization of the substrate by all except the most tolerant of opportunistic species, in this case *"Inoceramus" (Pseudomytiloides?) dubius*, but allowed diverse encrustation of dead ammonite and bivalve shell surfaces elevated only slightly above the aerobic-anaerobic boundary. Because evidence also indicates near-continuous current flow during deposition of the bituminous shale, a mechanism must be sought to account for maintenance of an anaerobic zone above the sediment-water interface in current-circulated waters. I consider the model that proposes an extensive algal-fungal mat situated a few centimeters above the interface, entrapping anaerobic waters below it even in the face of currents, to be the most probable of several possible hypotheses. The Santa Barbara Basin off the Coast of California is a good modern analogue; an extensive vegetal mat covers much of the bottom and is coherent even in the face of moderately strong currents. The aerobic-anaerobic boundary lies below this mat in more gently circulating waters a few centimeters above the sediment-water interface. Sedimentation can take place through the mat, and laminated bituminous muds underlie it.

Finally, the exceptional preservation of articulated skeletons of large vertebrates and of diverse invertebrates in the Posidonienschiefer has been thought to indicate lack of predation, scavenging, and aerobic bacterial decay. Systematic sampling, however, revealed a predominance of disarticulated fish material instead of whole skeletons and more abundant reptile fragments than previously reported; both occurrences suggest widespread decay and perhaps limited scavenging. Unequal preservation of articulated vertebrate skeletons, in which the bottom side in contact with the anaerobic sediment-water interface is very well preserved, but the upper side commonly is caved in and contains disarticulated bones and scales, indicates decay in aerobic environments within a few centimeters to a meter or so of the substrate. Considering modern rates of aerobic bacterial decay in deep marine basins, this implies long-term

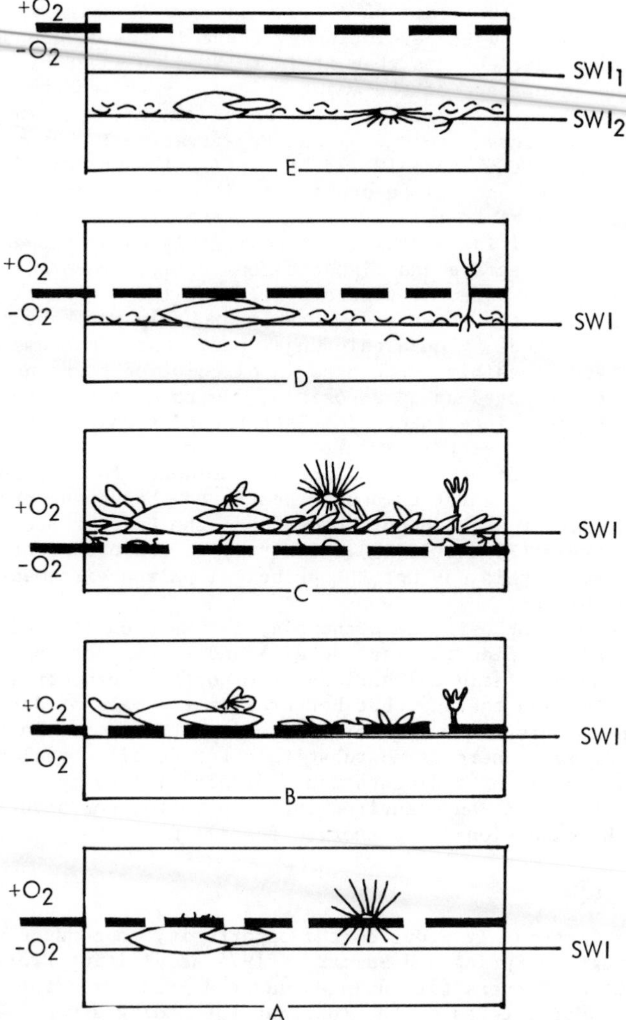

Figure 12-19
Summary diagram of benthic environments interpreted for most of the depositional history of the Posidonienschiefer in southern Germany. Aerobic-anaerobic boundary (dashed line) was delicately balanced and shifted frequently between a position just above (A,D) the sediment-water interface (SWI), allowing partial surface colonization of largest dead ammonite shells; to a position at the interface (B); within the sediment (C), allowing extensive epibionts and some infauna, or rarely to a position well up into the water column (E), excluding all benthos. A and D possibly represent times when an algal-fungal mat was widely established a few centimeters above the interface.

exposure of vertebrate carcasses to oxygenated waters. These features support an hypothesis of benthic oxygenation, at least at subnormal levels, for the Posidonienschiefer. The lack of obvious benthic reptiles and paucity of bottom-feeding fish in the Posidonienschiefer is more an artifact of ecological relationships within the marine food chain and the evolutionary stage in the development of benthic-feeding vertebrates than it is related to anaerobic conditions in the lower part of the water column. Most aspects of the vertebrate fauna are compatible with the oxygenated-basin hypothesis.

Thus, the diverse ecological and preservational phenomena that characterize both the "normal" and "exceptional" aspects of the Posidonienschiefer can all be explained with a model of benthic environments (Figure 12-19) in which the aerobic-anaerobic or lethal-hydrogen sulfide boundary was delicately balanced near the sediment-water interface and migrated constantly across this boundary from (rarely) a few centimeters below to (predominantly) a few centimeters above the interface where it probably was kept in place for extended periods by an algal-fungal mat. Under extreme conditions generated possibly by changes in circulation patterns, the lethal interface moved up to a position one to several meters above the sediment-water interface. The latter condition potentially led to frequent oxygen overturn events and mass mortalities of pelagic organisms, mainly fish and cephalopods. Evidence for widespread anoxia in the lower water column is scattered throughout the Posidonienschiefer and concentrated around the Unterer Stein and Schlacken levels (Figure 12-15). Contrary to the prevalent hypothesis, however, this was not the principal paleoenvironment of the Posidonienschiefer.

This new hypothesis, like the old, is based on limited data (two sequences sampled in great detail) and re-evaluation of museum and miscellaneous field collections from southwestern Germany. It requires extensive testing, but better fits the mass of data. Its derivation in this study reinforces one important point in the study of paleoecology: there is no substitute for detailed evaluation of the normal aspects of sedimentation and paleobiology in the interpretation of ancient paleoenvironments, no matter how beautiful and exciting the exceptionally preserved fossils might be.

ACKNOWEDGMENTS

I was fortunately provided the opportunity to conduct this study during the Spring and Summer of 1974 as Visiting Professor of Geology at the Universität Tübingen under a grant from the German Government administered by the Institut für Geologie und Paläontologie within the Sondersforschungbereich 53 (Palökologie) program. This is publication No. 94 of the Fossil-Vergesellschaftungen research program. I am greatly indebted to these organizations for their support and extend special thanks to my hosts A. Seilacher, J. Wiedmann, D. Herm, and G. Einsele for inviting me to come to Tübingen; for their warm hospitality; and especially for the many stimulating discussions and good advice during the course of this study. Dr. Seilacher kindly permitted republication of some of his diagrams. Special thanks are due Mr. David Govoni, Mrs. Barbara D. Heffernan, and Ms. Dana Geary for their immense assistance in processing the data and making illustrations for this project, and to Mrs. Paulina Franz for typing assistance. Special thanks are offered to Dr. Bernard Hauff, Director of the Hauff Museum, Germany, who allowed me free access to his magnificent collection of Posidonienschiefer fossils and kindly permitted me to use several illustrations in this paper from his *Das Holzmadenbuch*.

REFERENCES

Banse, K. 1959. On upwelling and bottom trawling off the southwest coast of India. *Marine Biol. Assoc. India Jour.* 1:33-49.

Banse, K. 1968. Hydrography of the Arabian Sea shelf of India and Pakistan and effects on demersal fishes. *Deep-Sea Research*. 15:45-79.

Beurlen, K. 1925. Finige Bemerkungen zur Sedimentation in dem Posidonienschiefer Holzmadens. *Jber. oberrhein Geol. Ver.*, 14:298-302.

Bouvier, E. L. 1917. *Crustacês dêcapodes (Macroures marcheurs) provenant des Campagnes des yachts Hirondelle et Princesse-Alice. Result.* Campagnes Scient. accomplies sur son yacht par Albert 1er; Monaco, Fasc. L, pp. 1-140.

Brenner, K. 1976a. Ammonitengehäuse als Anzeiger von Paleo-Strömungen: *Neues Jahrb. Geologie u. Palaeontologie Abh.* 151:101-118.

Brenner, K. 1976b, 2. Schwarzschiefer. Biostratinomische, Untersuchungen im Posidonienschiefer (Lias Epsilon, Unteres Toarcium) von Holzmaden (Wurttemberg, Sud-Deutschland), in Sondersforschungsbereich 53, Palökologie, Arbeitsbericht, 1970-1975, *Zbl. f. Geol. u. Paläont.* II, S. 223-226.

Craig, G. Y. 1954. The palaeoecology of the Top Hosie Shale (Lower Carboniferous) at a locality near Kilsyth. *Geol. Soc. London Quart. Jour.* 110:103-119.

Cox, L. R. 1969. Family Inoceramidae Giebel, 1852. in Moore, R. C., ed., *Treatise on Invertebrate Paleontology, Bivalvia.* Univ. Kansas Press and Geol. Soc. America, 6:N314-N321.

Degens, E. T., and K. Mopper. 1975. Early diagenesis of organic matter in marine soils. *Soil Sci.* 119:65-72.

Einsele, G., and R. Mosebach. 1955. Zur petrographie, fossilerhaltung und entstehung des Posidonienschiefers im Schwabischen Jura: *N. Jb. Geol. Palaont., Abh.* 101:319-430.

Firth, R., and W. Pequegnat. 1971. Deep sea lobsters of the Families Polychelidae and Nephropidae (Crustacea, Decapoda) in the Gulf of Mexico and Caribbean Sea. Texas A and M Dept. Oceanography Pub., pp. 1-103.

Fischer, A. G., and M. A. Arthur. 1977. Secular variations in the pelagic realm. in Cook, H. E., and P. Enos, eds., *Deep Water Carbonate Environments.* Soc. Econ. Paleont. Mineral. Spec. Pub. 25:19-50.

Franke, A. 1936. Die Foraminiferen des Deutschen Lias. *Abh. Preuss. Geol. Landes., N. Folg.*, 169:6-138.

Fraas, E., 1891, *Die Icthyosaurier der süddeutschen Trias- und Juraablagerungen:* Tübingen, Laupp, p. 1-81.

Hallam, A., 1967, The depth significance of shales with bituminous laminae. *Marine Geology*. 5:481-493.

Hallam, A., 1978. Eustatic cycles in the Jurassic. *Palaeogeography, Palaeoclimatology, Palaeoecology*. 23:1-32.

Hauff, B. 1921. Untersuchung der Fossilfundstätten von Holzmaden im Posidonienschiefer des Oberen Lias Wurttembergs. *Paläontographica* 64:1-42.

Hauff, B., Jr. 1960. *Daz Holzmadenbuch*. Ohringen, F. Rau, p. 1-54.

Hoffman, K., and G. P. R. Martin. 1960. Die Zone des *Dactylioceras tenuicostatum* (Toarcien, Lias) in NW- und SW-Deutschland. *Paläont. Zietschr*. 34:103-149.

Jannasch, H. W., and C. O. Wirsen. 1973. Deep-sea microorganisms: in situ response to nutrient enrichment. *Science* 180:641-643.

Jefferies, R.P.S., and P. Minton. 1965. The mode of life of two Jurassic species of "*Posidonia*" (Bivalvia). *Palaeontology* 8:156-185.

Kauffman, E. G. 1969. Cretaceous marine cycles of the Western Interior. *Mt. Geologist*. 6:227-245.

Kauffman, E. G. 1973. Stratigraphic evidence for Cretaceous eustatic changes. *Geol. Soc. America Abs. with Programs*, p. 687.

Kauffman, E. G. 1975. Dispersal and biostratigraphic potential of Cretaceous benthonic Bivalvia in the Western Interior, in Caldwell, W. G. E., ed., *The Cretaceous System in the Western Interior of North America*. Geol. Assoc. Canada Spec. Paper 13:163-194.

Kauffman, E. G. 1978. Short-lived benthic communities in the Solnhofen and Nusplingen Limestones. *N. Jb. Geol. Paläeont. Mh.*, 2:717-714.

Kauffman, E. G. 1979. Cretaceous. in Robison, R. A., and C. Teichert, eds., *Treatise on Invertebrate Paleontology, Part A. Introduction*. Univ. Kansas Press and Geol. Soc. America A418-A487.

Keller, T. 1976. Magen - und Darminhalte von Ichthyosauriern des Süddeutschen Posidonienschiefers. *Neues Jahrb. Geologie u. Paläontologie Monatsh*. 5:266-283.

Kirk, E. 1911. The structure and relationships of certain eleutherozoic Pelmatozoa. *U. S. Natl. Mus. Proc.* 41:1-137.

Koch, C. F. 1978. Bias in the published fossil record. *Paleobiology* 4:367-372.

Meyer, D. L. 1971. The collagenous nature of problematical ligaments in crinoids (Echinodermata). *Marine Biology*. 9:235-241.

Pompeckj, J. F. 1901. Die Juraablagerungen zwischen Regensburg und Regenstauf. *Geogn. Jh.* 14:139-220.

Quenstedt, F. A. 1856, *Der Jura:* Tübingen, p. 1 - 368.

Rasmussen, H. W. 1977. Function and attachment of the stem of Isocrinidae and Pentacrinitidae: review and interpretation. *Lethaia* 10:51-57.

Rhoads, D. C., and J. W. Morse. 1971. Evolutionary and ecologic significance of oxygen-deficient marine basins. *Lethaia* 4:413-428.

Richards, F. A. 1957. Oxygen in the Ocean, in Hedgpeth, J. W., ed., *Treatise on marine ecology and paleoecology, Ecology*. Geol. Soc. America Mem. 67:185-238.

Riegraf, W. 1977. *Goniomya rhombifera* (Goldfuss) in the Posidonia Shales (Lias Epsilon). *N. Jb. Geol. Paläont. Mh.* 7:446-448.

Scott, R. W. 1970. Paleoecology and paleontology of the Lower Cretaceous Kiowa Formation, Kansas. *Kansas Univ. Paleont. Contr.* 52:1-94.

Seilacher, A. 1960. Epizoans as a key to ammonoid ecology. *Jour. Paleontology* 34:189-193.

Seilacher, A. 1970. Begriff und Bedeutung der Fossil-Lagerstätten. *Neues Jahrb. Geologie u. Paläontologie Monatsh.* 1:34-39.

Seilacher, A., F. Andalib, G. Dietl, and H. Gocht. 1976. Preservational history of compressed Jurassic ammonites from southern Germany. *Neues Jahrb. Geologie u. Paläontologie Abh.* 152-307-356.

Seilacher, A., Drozdzewski, G., and R. Haude. 1968. Form and function of the stem in a pseudoplanktonic crinoid *(Seirocrinus)*. *Palaeontology* 11:275-282.

Seilacher, A. and F. Westphal. 1971. "Fossil-Lagerstätten." in *Sedimentology of Parts of Central Europe; Guidebook.* Internatl. Sediment. Congress 8:327-335.

Veizer, J. 1977. Geochemistry of lithographic limestones and dark marls from the Jurassic of southern Germany. *Neues Jahrb. Geologie u. Paläontologie Abh.* 153:129-146.

Weyl, P. K. 1970. *Oceanography: An Introduction to the Marine Environment*. New York. John Wiley and Sons, Inc., pp. 1-535.

Zangerl, R., and E. S. Richardson, Jr., 1963. The Paleoecological history of two Pennsylvanian black shales. *Fieldiana-Geological Mem.* 4:1-158.

Zangerl, R., B. G. Woodland, E. S. Richardson, Jr., and D. L. Zachry, Jr., 1969. Early diagenetic phenomena in the Fayetteville black shale (Mississippian) of Arkansas. *Sed. Geology.* 3:87-119.

13

Occurrence and Fossilization of the *Dakoticancer* Assemblage, Upper Cretaceous Pierre Shale, South Dakota

Gale A. Bishop

ABSTRACT

Five thousand decapods were collected from six localities in the Upper Cretaceous Pierre Shale of South Dakota. The decapods and associated fossils are preserved enclosed in apatite concretions. The concretions are distributed through 3 to 7m of shale and are laterally persistent over areas of 15 to 15,000 km.

The decapods may have been buried as corpses or molts. A few molts are preserved in "Salter's position." After or during burial the thin membranes between segments were destroyed and the decomposing crustaceans were partly or completely filled with sediment. The sediment in and around the hard parts was ingested by deposit-feeding organisms and extruded as fecal pellets. Compression due to the weight of overburden then flattened, broke, and rearranged the parts of the decapods. The concentration of phosphates in the fecal material and the micro-environment of enclosed spaces within the skeletons of the animals caused the formation of the concretions.

The uniformity of distribution, faunal composition, and mode of preservation of the faunas suggest that they are parts of a recurrent community dominated by the decapod *Dakoticancer overanus* Rathbun, baculitid cephalopods, and inoceramids. Less-common taxa are the decapods *Homolopsis punctata* Rathbun, *Necrocarcinus pierrensis* Rathbun, *Raninella oaheensis* Bishop, *Sodakus tatankayotankaensis* Bishop, *Palaeonephrops browni* Whitfield, *Callianassa* sp., and *Homolopsis* n. sp.; the bivalves *Nucula* and *Ostrea s. l.*; cephalopods other than baculitids; bony fish; sharks; and reptiles. The abundance of several types of fecal pellets suggests that soft-bodied organisms were common.

The consistency of the *Dakoticancer* Assemblage repeated at numerous localities stands in marked contrast to the preservation of other fossil decapods from the Pierre Shale that occur as isolated, single specimens.

INTRODUCTION

Marine shales, deposited in a shallow epeiric sea, should contain numerous animals common to continental shelves. Among these animals should be many decapods. The apparent rarity of fossil decapod crustaceans in the Upper Cretaceous Pierre Shale has been a puzzle. I believe the apparent absence of fossil crabs is due primarily to lack of adequate conditions for preservation and secondarily to inadequate collecting techniques. The presence of numerous crab fossils in a few laterally persistent and vertically restricted intervals of the Pierre Shale and the mode of preservation of these fossils indicate that crabs were either present at many times in great numbers, but were only preserved periodically in areas of exceptional conditions, or they existed periodically in large populations at several different times and perhaps initiated conditions that led to their preservation.

The geologic history of the Western Interior Basin was summarized by Reeside (1957) and by Kauffman (1977), and the geologic history of the Pierre Shale was summarized by Gill and Cobban (1966, 1973). The basin occupied a north-south trough through the Western United States and Canada from the Tethys Seaway in Texas northward to the Arctic Ocean (Figure 13-1). The seaway was 4,800 km long and averaged 1,600 km wide. The size, shape, and physical conditions of the seaway varied greatly with eustatic and tectonic fluctuations. These fluctuations caused variation in sedimentation patterns that we today interpret as cyclothems (Kauffman 1967, 1977). Each major transgressive-regressive pulse contained small-scale fluctuations that gave rise to small cyclothems superimposed on major ones. The basin has been divided into the following tectonic zones (Kauffman, 1977:84):

1. A tectonically active western margin characterized by rapid subsidence and thick, coarse, progradational clastic wedges.
2. A west-central zone of rapid subsidence and thick sediments.
3. A hinge zone where sediments thin, become finer (and begin picking up numerous disconformities), and
4. An eastern, stable platform characterized by numerous disconformities within a relatively thin sedimentary package.

Occurrences of the *Dakoticancer* Assemblage are all confined to the Pierre Shale deposited during Late Cretaceous (Campanian and Maastrichtian ages) on the stable eastern shelf.

THE PIERRE SHALE

Rocks deposited on the stable eastern shelf during Coniacian through Maastrichtian time in South Dakota include (from older to younger) the Niobrara Chalk, the Pierre Shale, the Fox Hills Formation, and the Hell Creek Formation (Figure 13-2), a marine to continental sequence deposited during the final withdrawal of the sea from the Western Interior.

The Pierre Shale is a body of fine clastic sediments up to 2,400 m thick found throughout the eastern half of the Western Interior. In western South Dakota the upper part of the Pierre Shale consists of noncalcareous gray shale, calcareous gray shale, and silty shale. Thin bentonite beds and layers of concretions, commonly fossiliferous, occur throughout the Pierre Shale. These fine clastics appear to be water and wind transported sediment and volcanic ash derived from the tectonically active western shore. The Pierre Shale, particularly the concretions, contain abundant, beautifully preserved fossils.

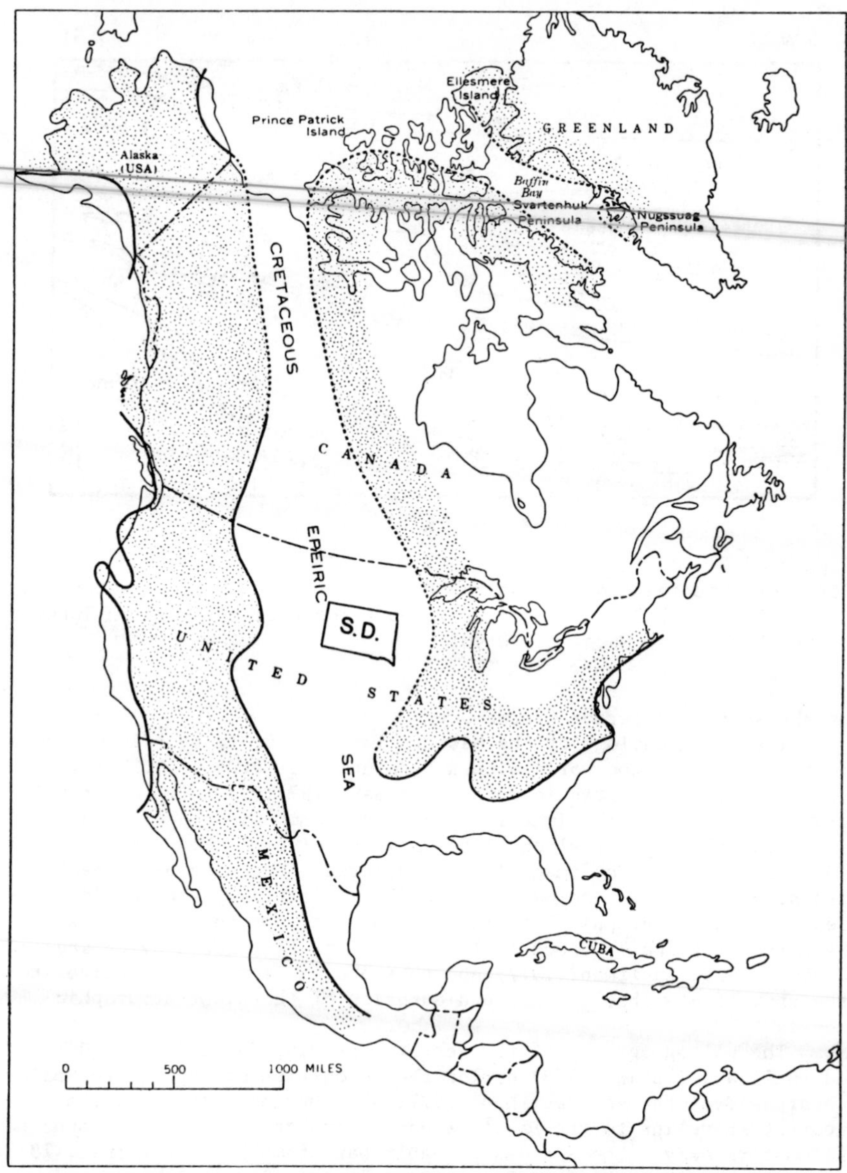

Figure 13-1
Late Cretaceous paleogeography of North America (after Gill and Cobban, 1966:A44).

The marine faunas of the Pierre Shale have been known and studied for many years. Many authors (Sohl, 1967, 1969; Kauffman, 1967, 1977; Scott, 1970) have commented on the depauperate nature of the faunas because of the rarity of such marine organisms as sponges, corals, bryozoans, brachiopods, some molluscs, and echinoderms. We should add decapods to this list as they remain poorly represented in most

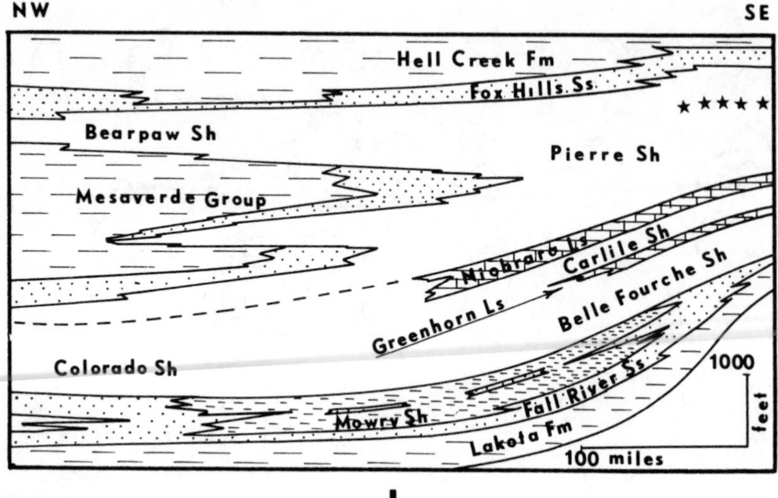

Figure 13-2
Stratigraphic relationship of the *Dakoticancer* Assemblage (asterisks) to the Pierre Shale and other Cretaceous rocks of the Western Interior (after Dunbar and Waage, 1970:383).

of the Western Interior Cretaceous.

The geochronology of the Western Interior Cretaceous is one of the most detailed in the world with a resolution of 0.25 to 0.33 million years per biostratigraphic zone (Kauffman, 1977:97). The biostratigraphic net is based primarily on abundant ammonoid cephalopods (particularly baculites) and inoceramid bivalves (Cobban et al., 1966, 1973, 1975, 1977; Kauffman, 1977). Numerous bentonite beds, each an isochronous surface and many regionally correlative, provide independent time-stratigraphic correlation. Many of the bentonite beds have been radiometrically dated (Gill and Cobban, 1966; Obradovich and Cobban, 1975; Kauffman, 1977) and thus provide a method to calculate the approximate absolute age and duration of the biostratigraphic zones.

The paleogeography of the Western Interior Basin is well documented (Gill and Cobban, 1973) during the deposition of the Pierre Shale (Bearpaw Cyclothem of Kauffman, 1977:89). During this time, the nearest shoreline to the *Dakoticancer* assemblages was several hundred kilometers away. The sea was probably warm-temperate (Kauffman, 1977; Tourtelot and Rye, 1969; Sohl, 1967; Jeletzky, 1969) about 100 m or less deep (Gill and Cobban, 1966:938; Mello, 1969:35; Asquith, 1970: 1219; Kauffman, 1977:84), and of normal to brackish salinity. The salinity may have varied vertically (Kauffman, 1977) and changed through time with variable conditions. Local flooding on the basin margins may have had considerable effect on the salinity of parts of the basin. Circulation patterns for the Western Interior Sea have been postulated and usually include a northward-flowing warm current originating in the Tethys. This influx of warm Tethyan waters pushed biogeographic boundaries far to the north and provided the source for and means of transportation of Tethyan faunas, which periodically mixed with the boreal faunas to the north in a broad boundary separating two general Western Interior biologic subprovinces, Northern and Southern (Kauffman, 1977:96).

In each subprovince, fossil assemblages have been described by many authors (Kauffman, 1967, 1977; Sohl, 1967, 1969; Scott, 1973, 1977; Waage, 1968; Kauffman et al., 1977). Kauffman (1977:96) grouped these and other citations of "Paleocommunities" into the following types:

1. Low diversity assemblages dominated by and nearly restricted to one or a few taxa.
2. High diversity assemblages containing up to fifty or more taxa.

PREVIOUS INVESTIGATIONS

The literature on stratigraphy, sedimentation, mineralogy, and paleontology of the Pierre Shale is extensive (bibliographies in Searight, 1937; Reeside, 1957; Robinson et al., 1959; Weimer, 1960; Gill and Cobban, 1966; Kauffman, 1977). The literature on fossil decapods from the Western Interior is limited although many authors mention the presence of fossil decapods in concretions near Mobridge, South Dakota. Fossil decapods were first collected in 1914 and 1915 by W. H. Over, and those specimens were described as *Dakoticancer overana*, *Homolopsis punctata*, and *Campylostoma pierrense* by M. J. Rathbun in 1917. Rathbun (1930) described an additional species, *Callianassa cheyennensis*, from the Pierre Shale from specimens collected by W. L. Russell. Subsequent authors (Russell, 1930; Searight, 1937; Gries, 1939, 1942; Rothrock, 1947; Crandell, 1958) were interested in the fossil decapods of the Pierre Shale as stratigraphic markers. Roberts recognized a new species of *Raninella* from the Red Bird Reference Section (Gill and Cobban, 1966:A26) in Wyoming. Bishop studied the crabs and lobsters from these rocks (Bishop, 1972a, 1972b, 1973, 1974, 1975, 1976, and 1977; Feldmann et al., 1977).

COLLECTION LOCALITIES

Six collections of decapods were made from the *Dakoticancer* Assemblage in the Pierre Shale in western South Dakota (Figure 13-3, Table 13-1). Three of these consist of several hundred specimens and were used for this study. The other three collections were much smaller and are not described here.

The largest collection was made in the Mobridge area, north-central South Dakota. Specimens were collected at three sites. Because the three sites are at the same stratigraphic and biostratigraphic level, they are treated as a single collection. The Mobridge collection is composed of collections from the Sitting Bull locality (GAB 4), the Promise Locality (GAB 9), and the U.S. Coast and Geodetic Survey (U.S.C.G.S.) BM J304 locality (GAB 10). This collection of 2,400 numbered and about 2,000 unnumbered specimens is from the zone of *Baculites grandis* (Table 13-1). The interval of shale containing the fossil decapods is laterally continuous over at least 1,500 km^2.

The second largest collection was made 24 km southeast of Rapid City around Thomson Butte (GAB 1). About 1,100 specimens were

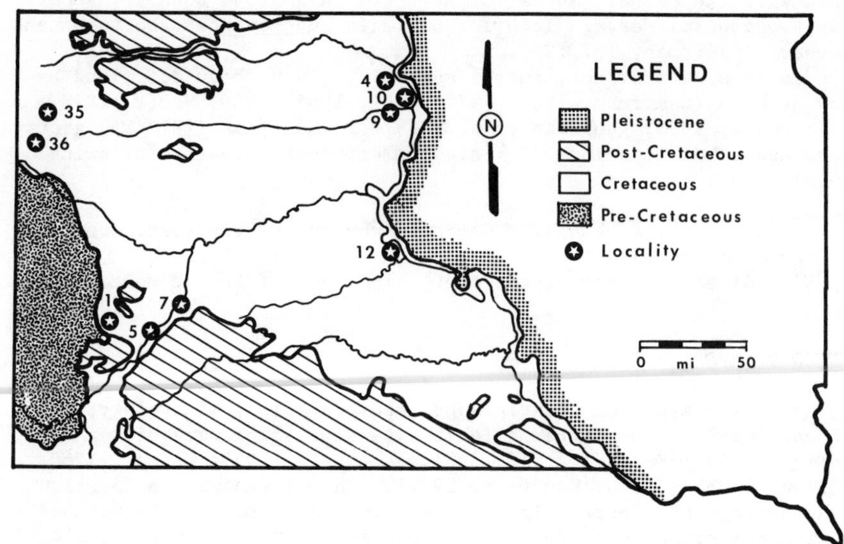

Figure 13-3
Selected decapod collection localities in South Dakota.

collected in an area of 15 km^2. The crabs were found associated with *Baculites rugosus* Cobban, which ranges through the zones of *Exiteloceras jenneyi* and *Didymoceras cheyennense* (Table 13-1).

The third collection is from outcrops near the town of Creston (GAB 5, 6). The fossil decapods were traced over an area of 330 km^2. This collection consists of about 500 specimens from the zone of *Didymoceras cheyennense* (Table 13-1).

Small collections were made at Wasta (GAB 7), north of Pierre (GAB 12), and north of Belle Fourche (GAB 35). They are from the zones of *Baculites compressus*, *Baculites grandis*, *Exiteloceras jenneyi*, respectively (Table 13-1).

The following decapod taxa were found in these collections (Figure 13-4 A-H): *Dakoticancer overanus* Rathbun, *Homolopsis punctata* Rathbun, *Homolopsis* n. sp., *Necrocarcinus pierrensis* Rathbun, *Raninella oaheensis* Bishop, *Sodakus tatankayotankaensis* Bishop, *Callianassa sp.*, and *Palaeonephrops browni* (Whitfield).

SUMMARY OF THE DATA

DISTRIBUTION

The fossil decapods occur in thin, continuous intervals of rock that are laterally persistent over hundreds of square kilometers and vertically restricted to intervals a few meters thick.

The Creston locality (Figure 13-5) covers 330 km^2, and the limits have been accurately delineated on three sides. The interval containing *Dakoticancer* extends from 15 to 20 m above the base of the section. Eighty-one single claws of *Callianassa* (Figure 13-4D) were collected in an interval from near the top of the *Dakoticancer* zone to 29 m

Table 13-1
Summary of distribution of localities with *Dakoticancer* Assemblage.

Locality	Distribution Area (sq km)	Thickness (m)	No. Specimens	Absolute Age mybp	Biostratigraphic Zone
					Baculites clinolobatus
Mobridge (GAB 4,9,10)	1500	3	3400		
				68.5	*Baculites grandis*
Peoria Bottom (GAB 12)	?	3	19		
					Baculites baculus
MAASTRICHTIAN STAGE					
CAMPANIAN STAGE					
					Baculites eliasi
					Baculites jenseni
					Baculites reesidei
					Baculites cuneatus
Wasta (GAB 7)	?	?	51	71.5	*Baculites compressus*
Creston (GAB 5,6)	337	7.6	500		*Didymoceras cheyennense*
				71.75	
Thomson Butte (GAB 1,2)	15.5	1.5	1100		*Exiteloceras jenneyi*
					Didymoceras stevensoni
				72	*Didymoceras nebrascense*
Baresch (GAB 35)	?	?	9		*Baculites scotti*
(earliest known *Dakoticancer* from Western Interior)					

above the base of the section. The measured section was the only locality where *Callianassa* was found in great concentrations; therefore, this occurrence is judged atypical.

Fossils, preserved both in the shale and in concretions, are common throughout this interval of the Pierre Shale (Table 13-1). The ammonites *Didymoceras cheyennense* (Meek and Hayden) and *Baculites rugosus* Cobban were found at nearly all collecting sites in the Creston area. These two taxa place the mapped interval in the zone of *Didymoceras cheyennense*.

The collections from the Thomson Butte locality (Figure 13-7) are from an interval of Pierre Shale that was intensively weathered and eroded before the Early Oligocene Chadron Formation was deposited. This erosion and weathering formed a surface of rolling topography and a weathered interval of variable thickness. The weathered interval was called the "Interior Formation" by Ward (1922) and recognized as a soil zone by Wanless (1923:197). This interpretation has been generally accepted (Clark et al., 1967:9), and the soil zone is called the "Interior Paleosol."

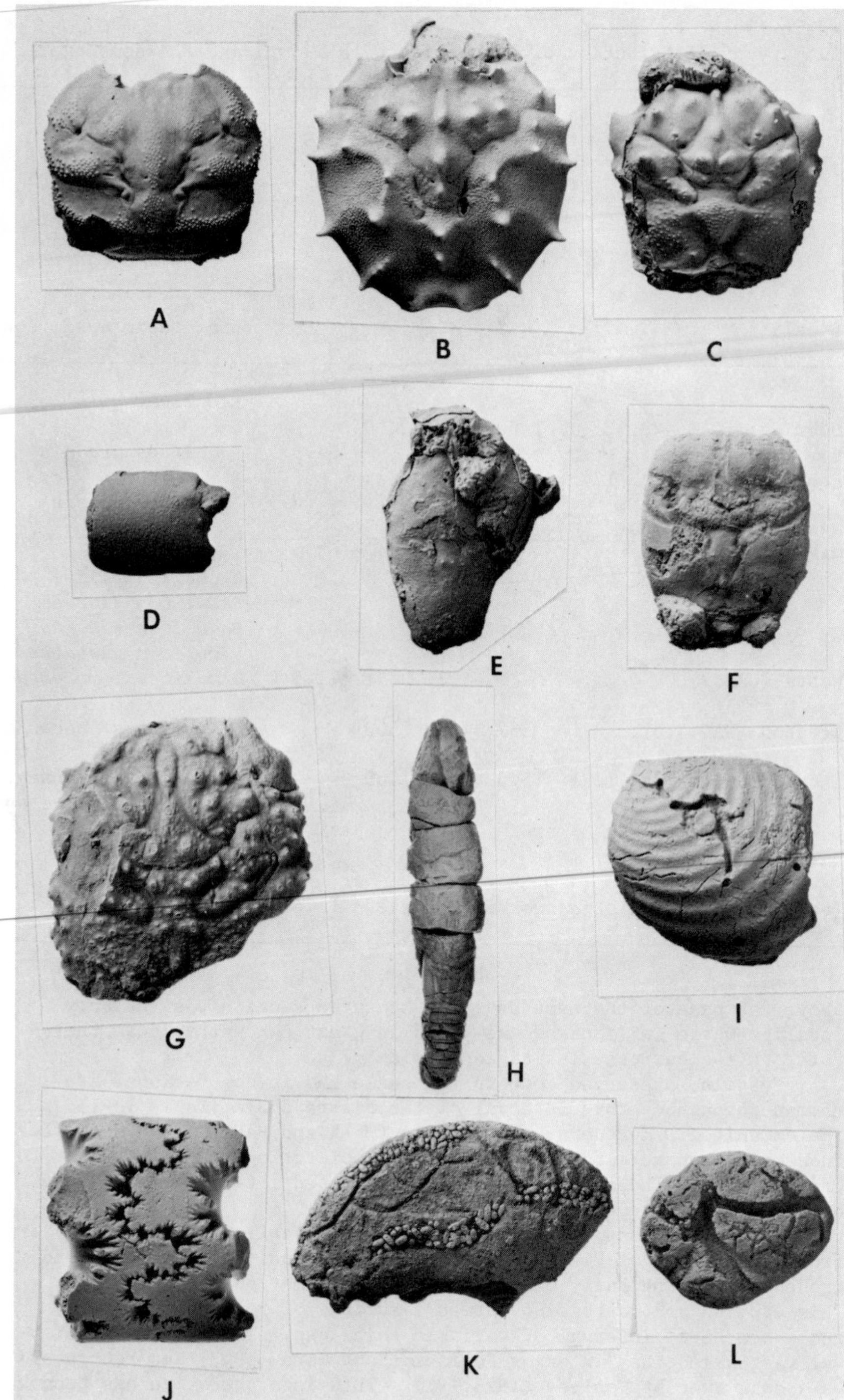
A
B
C
D
E
F
G
H
I
J
K
L

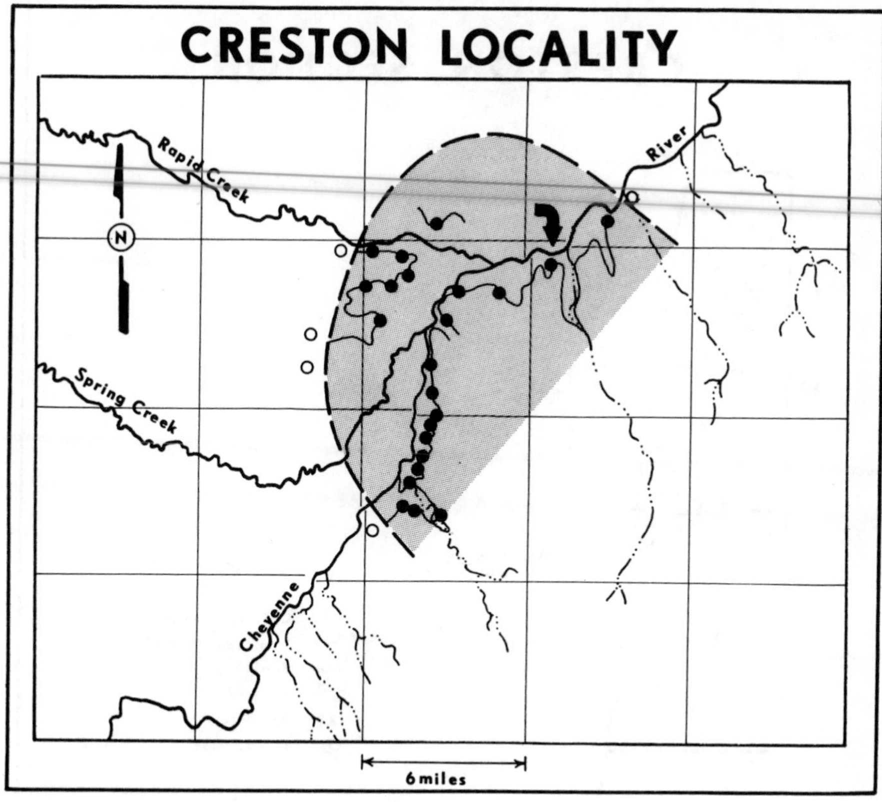

Figure 13-5
The Creston locality showing the collection sites yielding crabs (solid circles) and those not yielding crabs (open circles) and the inferred distribution of the *Dakoticancer* Assemblage (shaded).

Figure 13-4 (at left)
Decapod crustaceans of the *Dakoticancer* Assemblage. A. *Dakoticancer overanus* Rathbun, GAB 4-2006 (USNM 173529) X1.5. B. *Necrocarcinus pierrensis* Rathbun), GAB 4-509, X1.5. C. *Homolopsis punctata* Rathbun, GAB 2-2, X1.5. D. *Callianassa* sp., GAB 14-33, X1.5. E. *Raninella oaheensis* Bishop, lying within a partial carapace of *D. overanus*, GAB 4-1967, X1.5. F. *Sodakus tatankayotankaensis* Bishop, GAB 4-2036, X1.5. G. *Homolopsis* n. sp., anterior of carapace only, GAB 4-2192, X1.5. H. *Palaeonephrops browni* (Whitfield), cheliped enclosed in concretion from rostrum to end of concretion, GAB 11-26 (USNM 239936) X0.3. Common noncrustacean elements of *Dakoticancer* Assemblage. I. *Inoceramus* sp., steinkern with two sizes of trails, GAB 4-1998, X1. J. *Baculites grandis* Hall and Meek, steinkern of air chambers, GAB 4-198, X1. K. *Hoploscaphites* sp., steinkern with open trails and fecal pellet filled trails, GAB 4-1989, X1. L. *Inoceramus* sp., steinkern with two sizes of open trails, the larger preserving an impression of the segmented burrower, GAB 4-1991, X1.

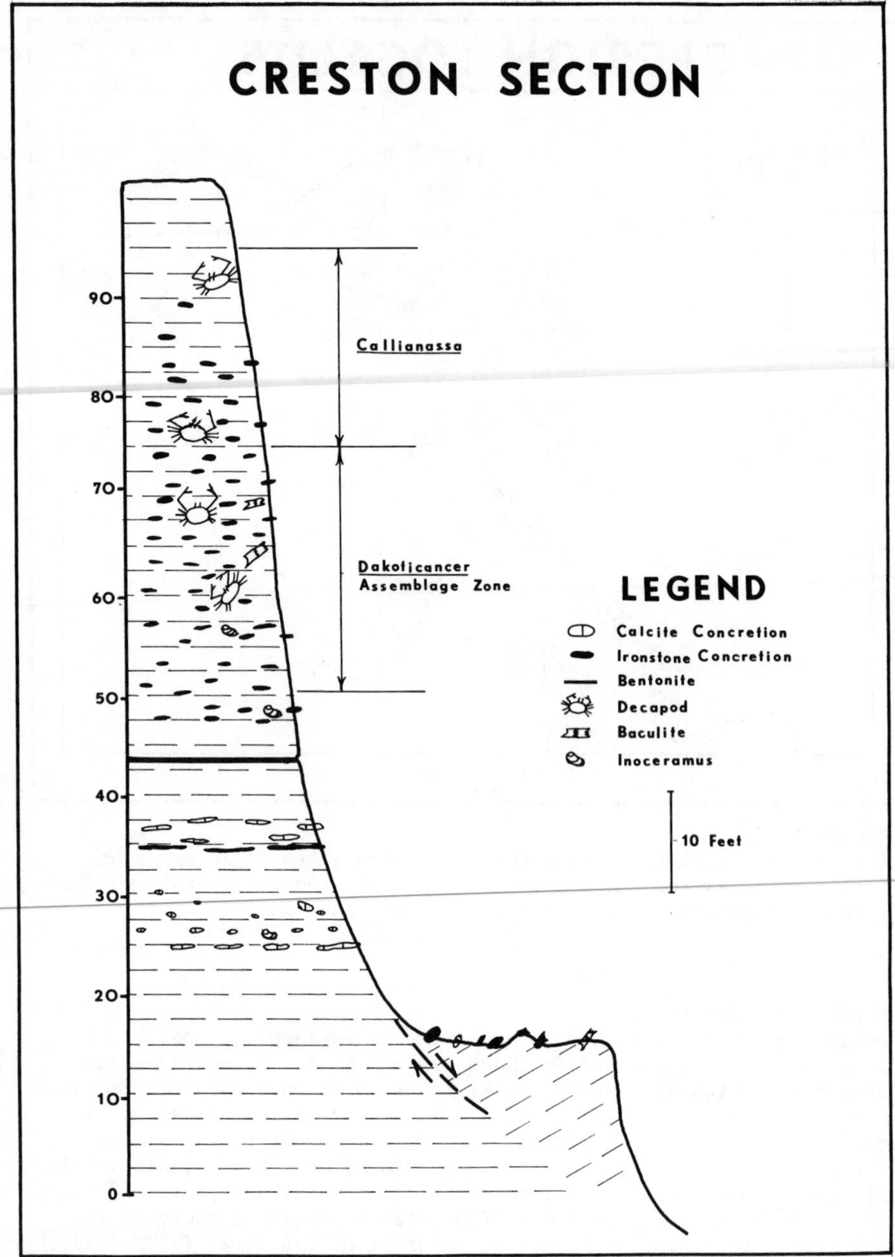

Figure 13-6
Measured section, Creston locality (at arrow on Figure 13-5).

Small apatite concretions (Figure 13-9A, D, P-S) and steinkerns occur within the weathered zone (Figure 13-8). Their exact strati-

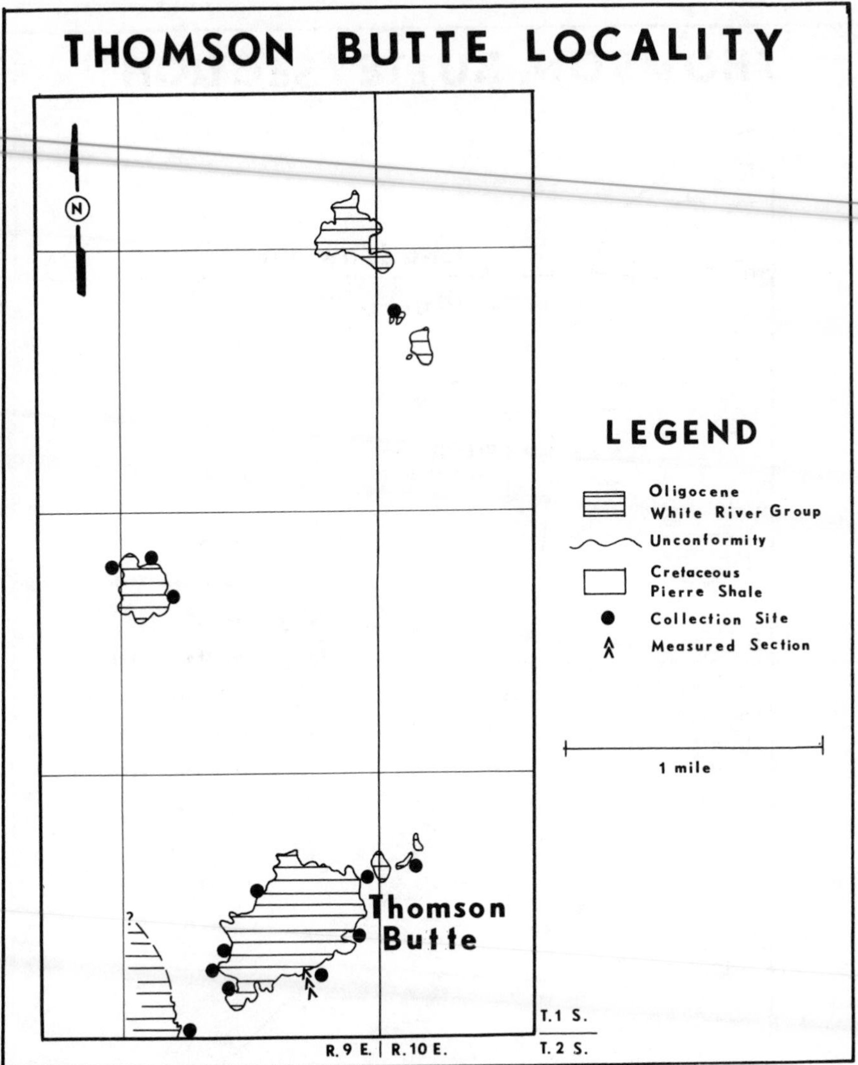

Figure 13-7
The Thomson Butte locality.

graphic range is uncertain as only one apatite concretion was found at the measured section, and it was float. Exposures are poor where concretions containing decapods are concentrated in saddles and on gentle slopes. I believe the decapod concretions occur above the large oxidized concretions in the position indicated on the measured section (Figure 13-8). The crab interval is sometimes cut out by the disconformity.

The biostratigraphic position of the Thomson Butte locality is not known precisely because no index ammonites were found. The few poorly

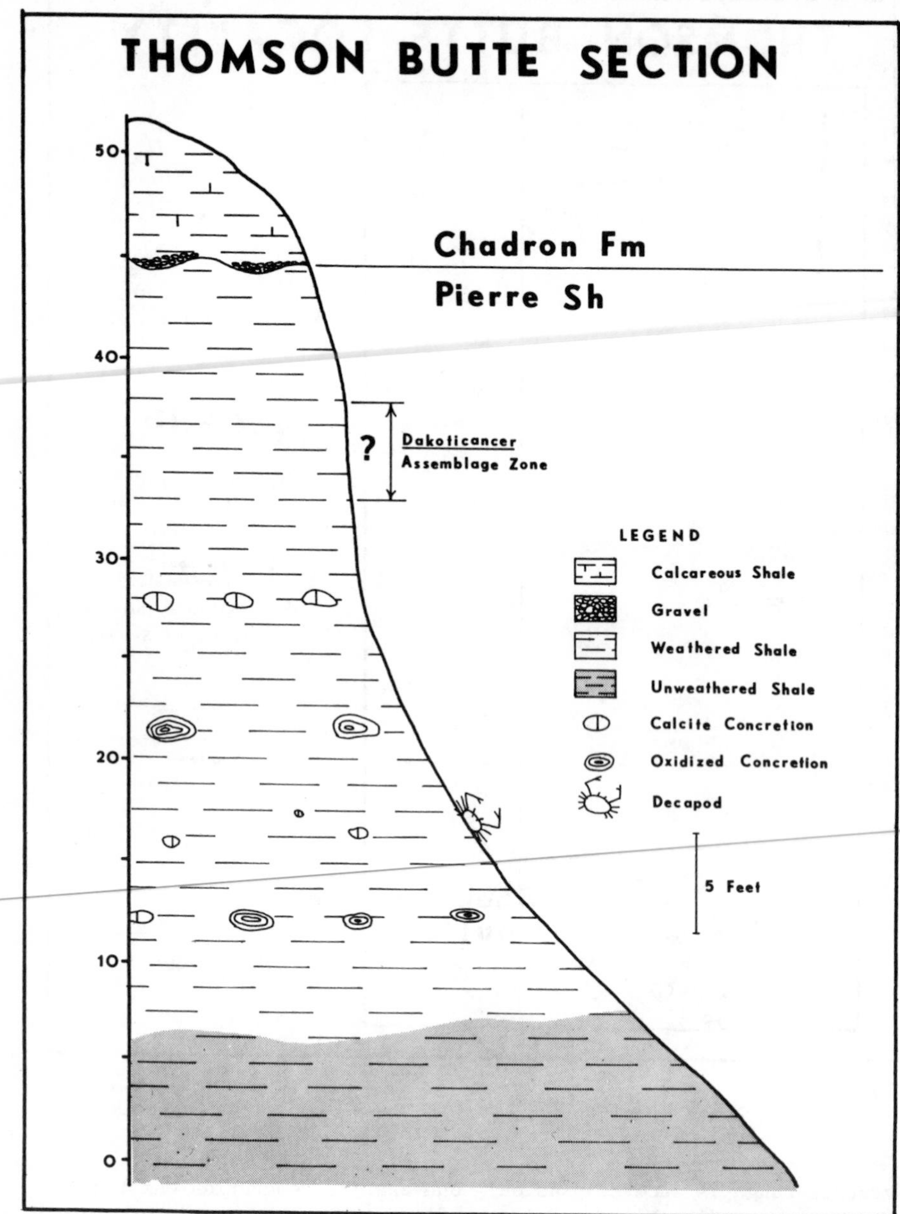

Figure 13-8
Measured section, Thomson Butte locality.

preserved ammonites that were found were submitted to Dr. W. A. Cobban in 1969 for comment. He replied:

> The badly weathered ammonites from Thomson Butte suggest the zone of *Didymoceras cheyennense*. Many of the baculites have well-ribbed venters and narrow cross sections suggesting *Baculites rugosus* Cobban. This species is best developed in the zone of *Exiteloceras jenneyi*, but it persists into the younger zone of *D. cheyennense*. The two scaphites, which can be assigned to *Scaphites (Hoploscaphites) nodosus* Owen s. l., are best matched by specimens from the *D. cheyennense* beds. The *Placenticeras* is *P. intercalare* Meek.

The locality may be slightly younger or the same age as the Creston locality. The fauna is presented in Table 13-2.

Fossil decapods from the Mobridge localities are persistent over 1,500 km^2 in north-central South Dakota. Three collections were made in this area: at the Sitting Bull Burial Site across from Mobridge, at Promise, and north of the Moreau River (Figure 13-10). Sections were measured at Mobridge (Figure 13-11) and Promise.

Rothrock (1947) mapped the crab zone at Mobridge. Fossil crabs occur at the same biostratigraphic position in Potter County (Russell, 1930) and near Pierre (GAB 12) (Crandall, 1958). I suspect that the distribution is continuous. If this is so, the distribution would cover about 3,000 km^2.

The Sitting Bull locality is on the west bank of the Missouri River (Oahe Reservoir) opposite the town of Mobridge, South Dakota. Specimens were collected from 3 m of gray, slightly calcareous to noncalcareous, bentonic shale interbedded with at least four, thin bentonite beds. Concretions that contain fossil decapods and steinkerns of molluscs (Figure 13-4A, B, F, G, I-L; Figure 13-9B, C. E, F, H-K, M, N, T) including *Baculites grandis* Hall and Meek (Figure 13-4I) are found throughout the interval.

The Promise locality is located near the community of Promise where a section was measured and collected at the type locality of the Virgin Creek Member of the Pierre Shale. Decapods were found in 1.5 m of gray, calcareous, bentonitic shale interbedded with thin bentonite beds near the top of the section. Steinkerns of *Baculites grandis* Hall and Meek are present throughout the interval of the bentonite beds.

The U.S.C.G.S. BM J 304 locality is situated on the bluffs on the north side of the Moreau River. This locality lies between the Mobridge and Promise localities. Numerous steinkerns of *B. grandis* were collected with the decapods.

LITHOLOGY

The fossil crabs at all three localities were collected as float. The fossils, preserved in apatite concretions, weather out of the shale and are concentrated as a lag deposit on the surface.

The shale at the Creston locality varies from a blocky claystone to a semifissile shale. Fresh exposures at the locality show that local concentrations of very fossiliferous shale contain many fragments of inoceramid pelecypods. Ironstone concretions are common throughout the interval that yielded the crab fauna.

The unweathered Pierre Shale at the Thomson Butte locality is olive gray, noncalcareous, fissle, and contains concretions of two types: large, 30 to 60 cm, spheroidal, calcareous concretions; and

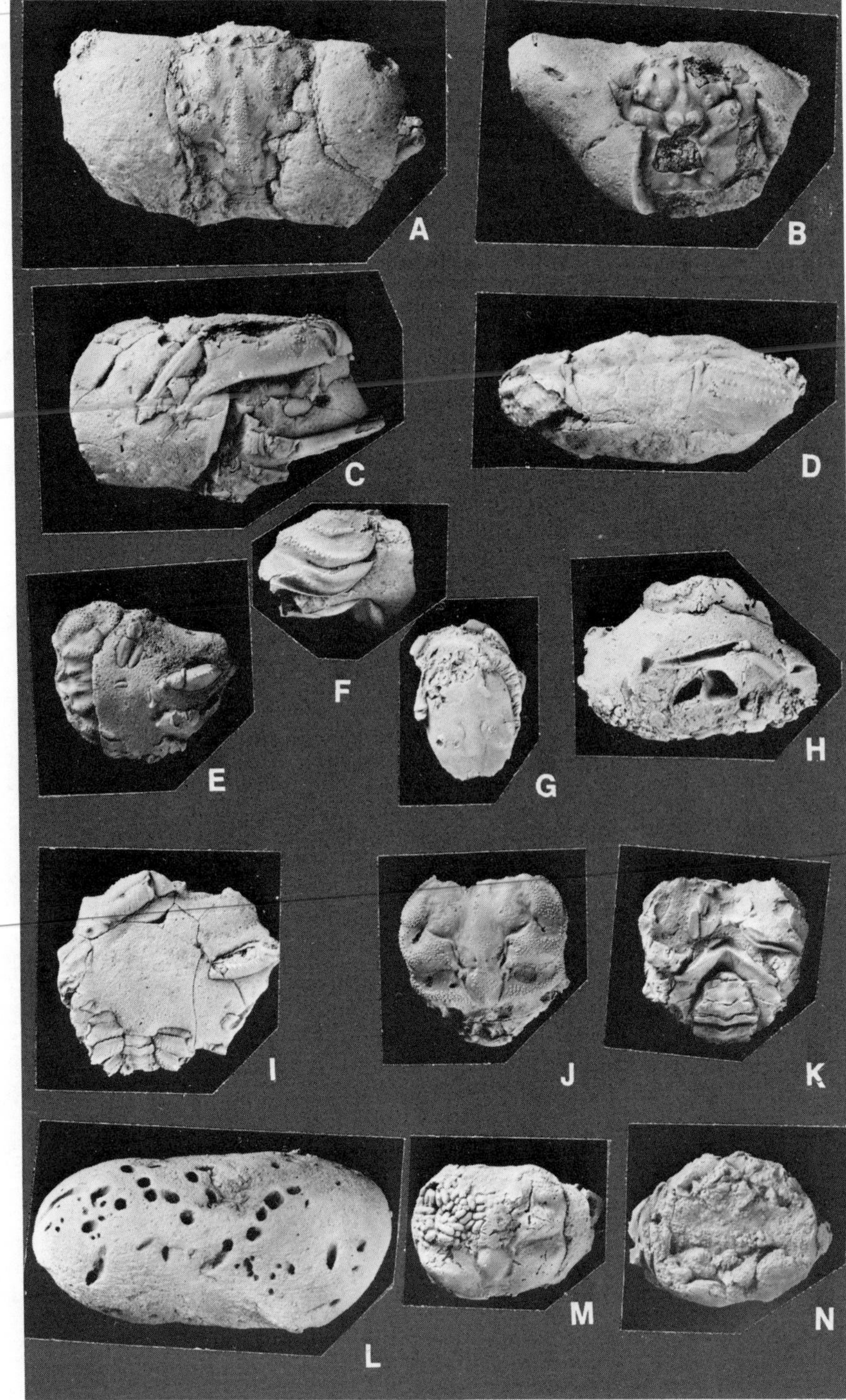
A
B
C
D
E
F
G
H
I
J
K
L
M
N

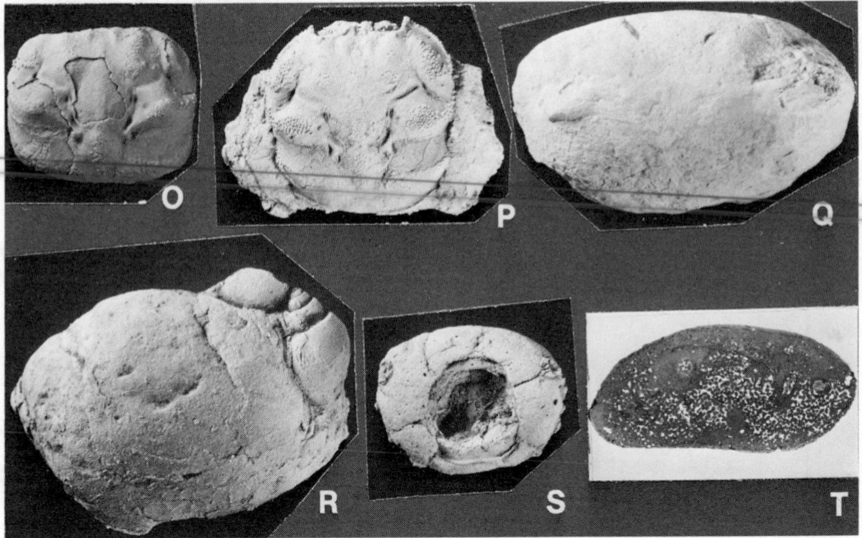

Figure 13-9
Death of the crabs. A. *Dakoticancer overanus* in relaxed position with walking legs extended in normal position and enclosed proximally by concretion, GAB 1-239, X1. B. *Homolopsis punctata* in relaxed position with walking legs extended in normal position and enclosed proximally by concretion, GAB 1-138, X1. C. Venter of *D. overanus* showing walking legs in normal position and left claw tucked beneath front of carapace, GAB 4-383, X1. D. Anterior of *H. punctata* with claws folded in front of carapace (enclosed in concretion) and forming part of concretion boundary, GAB 3-400, X1. E. Molt of *D. overanus* preserved in "Salter's Position" with carapace flipped over and rotated above the sternum, GAB 4-1039, X1. F. *Dakoticancer overanus* showing split along pleural suture on right anterior, GAB 4-1531, X1. G. Carapace of *Raninella oaheensis* exhibiting bite marks, GAB 12-3, X1. H. *Dakoticancer overanus* disarticulated by predation, GAB 4-1206, X1. I. Alignment of chelipeds of *D. overanus*, GAB 4-33, X1. J-K. Dorsum and venter of *D. overanus* showing minor effects of early compaction, GAB 4-661, X1.

Preservation of the fauna. L. Ovoid concretion devoid of megafossils preserving open burrows, GAB 4-1999, X1. M. Steinkern of *D. overanus* partly filled by large fecal pellets, GAB 4-1935, X1. N. Partly filled carapace of *D. overanus* forming right-side-up geopetal, GAB 6-52, X1. O. *Dakoticancer overanus* preserved by concretion formed along exterior of exfoliating exoskeleton, GAB 6-50, X1. P. *Dakoticancer overanus* preserved by concretion formed along exterior of carapace exoskeleton and enclosing the proximal part of legs, GAB 1-498, X1. Q. *Dakoticancer overanus* in concretion enclosing carapace and sternum and extending to the distal part of thoracopods and along the exoskeleton of the claws, GAB 1-358, X1. R. *Dakoticancer overanus* preserved in concretion enclosing carapace, sternum, most of the legs and extending into nearby gastropods, GAB 1-233, X1. S. *Dakoticancer overanus* enclosed in concretion and crushed in over carapace by late compaction, GAB 1-443, X1. T. Transverse thin section of *D. overanus* showing ubiquitous fecal pellets filling and surrounding the telescoped carapace, GAB 9-436, X1.

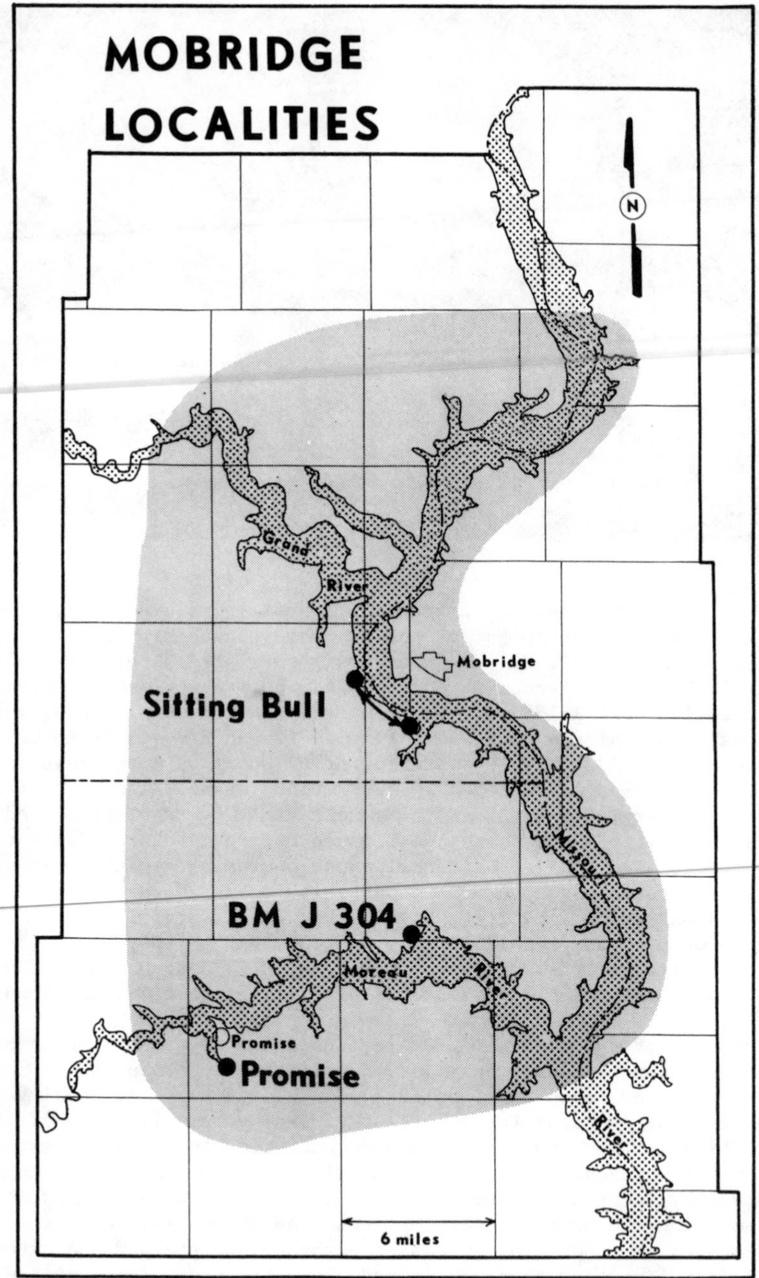

Figure 13-10
The Mobridge localities and the distribution of the *Dakoticancer* Assemblage as mapped by Rothrock, 1947.

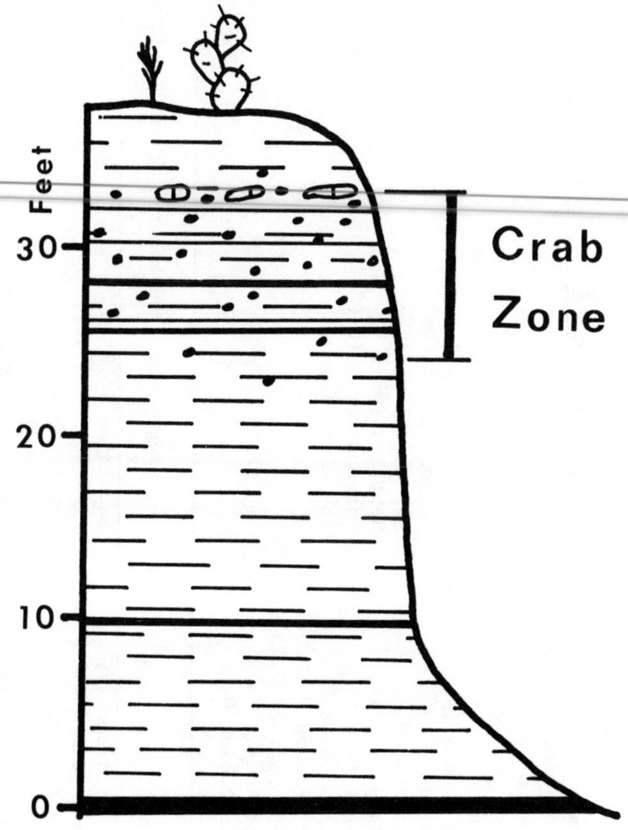

Figure 13-11
Measured sections at the Sitting Bull locality.

small, apatite concretions measuring a few centimeters. The weathered Pierre Shale, or Interior Paleosol, is light olive gray with fractures stained grayish orange. Large concretions in this interval are intensely oxidized, dark brown, and banded. The banding parallels the outside of the concretion and fractures within it. The crab zone at Mobridge is an interval of gray, fissile shale interbedded with a series of thin bentonite beds. The apatite concretions that contain the crabs are found through an interval of 3 m of shale. Bentonite beds are generally thin with a sharp lower boundary and a gradational upper boundary. The bentonites are commonly graded, coarse at the bottom, and much of the coarse fraction is composed of euhedral crystals of dark mica, probably biotite. These beds are usually some shade of yellow or green. The bentonites are devoid of body fossils. However, one bentonite in the crab interval at Mobridge contained a few burrows that were filled with gray mud.

Table 13-2
Fauna collected at each of the three localities with estimates of their relative abundance.

Infauna	Semi-infauna	Epifauna	Plankton and Nekton
MOBRIDGE LOCALITIES			Zone of *Baculites grandis* Hall and Meek
Fecal Pellets	*Inoceramus* (0.8)	**Dakoticancer* (75)	*Baculites* (20)
**Callianassa* (0.5)	*Dentalium* (0.04)	Foraminifera	Foraminifera
Nuculana (0.2)	*Drepanochilus* (0.08)	*Ostrea s. l.* (1.5)	Bony fish (2.8)
	Turitella (0.04)	**Necrocarcinus* (7.6)	(scales in coprolites)
	**Raninella* (0.3)	**Homolopsis* (0.8)	*Scaphites* (0.6)
n = 3,380		**Sodakus* (0.04)	(*Hoploscaphites*)
		*Lobsters (0.4)	*Belemnitella* (1.7)
		Chlamys (0.04)	Reptiles (0.3)
		Pteria (0.08)	*Eutrephoceras* (0.08)
		Acmaea (0.08)	Sharks (0.17)
		Hercorhyncus? (0.04)	
		Cryptorhytis (0.13)	
		Ostracods	
		Micrabacia (0.04)	
CRESTON LOCALITY			Zone of *Didymoceras cheyennense* (Meek and Hayden)
Fecal Pellets	*Inoceramus* (1.2)	**Dakoticancer* (79)	*Baculites* (4.2)
**Callianassa* (1.0)	*Durania?* (0.1)	*Homolopsis* (0.1)	*Didymoceras* (3.6)
Nuculana (0.1)	*Graphidula?* (0.1)	*Lobsters (3.1)	*Scaphites* (1.2)
Thetis? (0.5)		*Acmaea* (0.5)	(*Hoploscaphites*)
Breviarca (0.1)		*Syncyclonema* (0.3)	*Placenticeras* (0.3)
		Ostrea s. l.	*Osybeloceras* (0.3)
n = 650		Bryozoa (0.1)	*Eutrephoceras* (0.3)
		Worms (0.3)	Wood Fragments
		(Calcareous tube)	
		Necrocarcinus (0.1)	

THOMSON BUTTE			Zone of *Baculites rugosus* Cobban
Fecal Pellets	*Inoceramus* (0.6)	**Dakoticancer* (90)	*Baculites* (5.8)
**Callianassa* (1.6)	*Vanikoropsis?* (2.0) (or *Euspira*)	**Homolopsis* (2.4)	*Scaphites* (0.3) (*Hoploscaphites*)
Nuculana (1.8)		**Necrocarcinus* (0.1)	*Placenticeras* (0.2)
Burrow fillings		*Lobsters (1.1)	*Eutrephoceras* (0.3)
"Indiana Bead (2.5)			Fish (0.3)
"Ophiomorpha" (1.0)			Reptiles (0.1)
n = 1,200			Vertebrate (bone) (0.3)

Note: The collections were not made for statistical analysis and are biased. Estimates of relative abundance were made from data on hand and are reported in percentages. Infauna = animals that spend most of their lives in the substrate. Semi-infauna = animals partly buried in the substrate. Epifauna = animals that live on the bottom. Plankton = floating animals. Nekton = swimming animals. Asterisks indicate decapods. n = number of specimens.

CONCRETIONS

The majority of the crab specimens are preserved in small light-brown to gray concretions. Only organisms with mineralized tissues composed of apatite or calcite are commonly preserved outside the concretions. Crabs preserved in concretions are in excellent condition, but those not preserved in concretions are commonly crushed almost beyond recognition.

Concretions, in the sense used here, are patches of mineral cement that bind the shale together in coherent masses. The concretions preserving the specimens described in this chapter differ from concretions usually found in the Pierre Shale in the following ways: composed of apatite instead of calcite or siderite, small and measured in centimeters rather than decimeters, and their shape closely conforms to the shape of a single enclosed animal rather than a spherical or discoidal shape independent of enclosed fossils. Concretions from the three localities are remarkably similar to one another. They are all composed of apatite, they are all small, and most of them have their shape determined by enclosed remains. The following generalities can be made about these concretions:

1. The concretions are cemented by apatite.
2. Concretions with no obvious organic remains tend to be spherical, discoidal, or irregular (Figure 13-9L).
3. Concretions that enclose large pieces of organic remains, such as lobsters or vertebrate bones, have a size and shape that closely conforms to that of the enclosed fossil (Figure 13-4H).
4. Small animals are filled with concretionary material. Steinkerns of molluscs are common. Occasionally the shell of the mollusc is preserved. Crabs are commonly preserved as steinkerns (Figure 13-9M) or with their exoskeleton present and forming the boundary of the concretion (Figure 13-9O). The concretionary material may extend beyond the exoskeleton and partly enclose the animal (Figure 13-9P).
5. Very small molluscs are preserved in concretions that formed around nearby larger animals (Figure 13-9R).
6. There are two types of burrow fills. An *Ophiomorpha* type was found in small numbers only at Thomson Butte. Cylindrical burrows with a concentric layering (Indian Beads or *Serpula? wallencensis*) were found at Mobridge and Thomson Butte.
7. Coprolites (Bishop, 1977) are included as concretions because they have the same mineralogic composition. Half-cylinders (which contain concentric layers of fish scales), spiral coprolites, and fecal pellets are present.

FAUNAL ASSOCIATIONS

The taxa collected at the three localities are remarkably similar (Table 13-1 and Figure 13-4). The consistency of the composition of the fossil assemblages suggests that they are community fractions killed and preserved by similar processes. *Dakoticancer overanus* Rathbun is dominant at each locality and comprises the major portion of each collection. Many other taxa are present in relatively insignificant quantities (Table 13-1). The stratigraphic and geographic proximity of the Creston and Thomson Butte localities is reflected in similarities in faunal assemblages. Also, the temporal and geographic separation of the Mobridge locality from these two is reflected by significant differences.

SYNTHESIS OF THE DATA

The faunal assemblages found in the Pierre Shale are interpreted as community fractions because of their similarity in distribution, faunal composition, and mode of preservation. Characterization of the community fraction according to trophic levels, consistent associations, and mode of life was attempted. The arrangement of the taxa according to their probably mode of life was most productive (Table 13-2). This arrangement resembles "Assemblage R" described by Kauffman (1967:126) from the Western Interior Cretaceous.

THE DAKOTICANCER ASSEMBLAGE

"Assemblage R" is interpreted as a "diverse, moderately deep water, middle and outer shelf assemblage" composed of the following elements (Kauffman, 1967:126):

1. Oysters reduced to small, flat, thin-shelled encrusting types.
2. A few, large, ornate ammonites.
3. Consistently occurring scaphites and smooth, involute ammonites such as *Placenticeras*.
4. Common *Baculties* and small, finely ornate ammonites.
5. *Lucina*; *Nucula*; *Nuculana*; *Pteria*; *Tellina*; *Syncyclonema*; subequivalved, thin-shelled inoceramids like *Mytiloides*; and large, flat, thin-shelled inoceramids.
6. The gastropods *Certithiella*, *Lispodesthes*, *Acmaea*, *Bellifusus*, and *Euspira* may be present.

This assemblage is postulated to have inhabited the seabottom at a depth of 92 to 150 m.

Kauffman's "Assemblage R" and the *Dakoticancer* assemblages are very similar and differ principally by the addition of the decapods to the molluscan assemblage.

Waage (1964, 1968:160) also described assemblages from the Upper Cretaceous of South Dakota. The assemblages are from the Maastrichtian Fox Hills Formation and have the following characteristics:

1. A great abundance of specimens and one or two species numerically dominant.
2. Excellent preservation of most specimens in which the bivalves commonly are preserved with unseparated valves.
3. Random orientation and lack of size sorting of specimens in individual concretions, but a tendency for dominant bivalve species to occur in size-group aggregations.
4. Distribution over a limited area beyond which the horizon is unfossiliferous.
5. Dominance of one particular faunal association in a settlement with patterned distribution of subdominant associations relative to it.
6. Aggregation of individual species in clusters.

The *Dakoticancer* assemblage resembles Waage's assemblages, but differs from them because the *Dakoticancer* assemblage was a community composed of a large proportion of vagrant benthos whereas Waage's molluscan assemblages were sessile benthos.

The *Dakoticancer* assemblage has the following characteristics:

1. Infauna: Restricted, consisted of soft-bodied organisms, a few burrowing crustaceans (*Callinassa*, burrow fills), and bivalves *Lucina*, *Nucula*, *Thetis?*, and *Breviarca*.
2. Semi-infauna: Numerous subequivalve, convex, thin-shelled inoceramids; gastropods *Turritella*, *Vanikoropsis*, and *Drepanochilus*; decapods *Raninella*, and lobsters.
3. Epifauna: Dominated by decapods, especially *Dakoticancer*; gastropods *Hercorheyncus*, *Cryptorhytis*, and *Acmaea*. The bivalves *Syncyclonema*, *Pecten*, *Pteria*, and *Ostrea s. l.* are present in small numbers. A few scaphopods and benthonic foraminifer are also present. The rest of the epifauna is composed of the decapods *Homolopsis*, *Necrocarcinus*, and *Sodakus*.
4. Plankton: Dominated by planktonic foraminifer, the bulk of the plankton probably was not preserved.
5. Nekton: Dominated by *Baculites*; other cephalopods, *Scaphites*, *Placenticeras*, *Didymoceras*, *Oxybeloceras*, *Eutrephoceras*, and *Belemnitella*; bony fish; sharks; and reptiles.

In the *Dakoticancer* assemblages, it is likely that the worms or small, soft-bodied defactors and crabs lived at the same time in the same area.

These assemblages resemble Holocene communities in their consistent faunal composition and the numerical dominance of one or two species in each assemblage (Thorson, 1957:519). Decapod communities have been described only from warm seas, which are therefore somewhat characterized by their presence. Miyadi (1941) described the *Pinnixa rathbuni* Community from Ise Wan and Mikawa Wan, Japan. The community, reaching a density of 3,000 mature crabs per square meter was found in water depths of 7 to 37 m on gravel, sand, and muddy-sand substrates. Thorson (1957:518) described the *Xenophthalamus pinnotheroides* Community in the Persian Gulf. The crab *Xenophthalamus pinnotheroides* reaches densities of 1,500 mature crabs per square meter in 20 m of water on a loose-sand substrate. Other taxonomic members of these communities are quantitatively insignificant. Thorson interpreted both communities as enormous populations that could exist only in warm, shallow, turbulent water where they fed on highly productive plankton. Although these communities are not completely analogous to the *Dakoticancer* Assemblage, parallels are extremely suggestive of the *Dakoticancer* community that we see preserved in the Pierre Shale.

DEATH OF THE CRABS

The crab specimens preserved in the *Dakoticancer* Assemblage often have considerable portions of their appendages preserved. These crabs are usually preserved with claws loosely drawn in front of the carapace and the walking legs extended in a normal manner away from their body (Figure 13-9A-D). Because none were found in an escape position (Schäfer, 1972:138) with appendages raised and claws open, I assume the crabs were dead when buried. They, therefore, must be buried corpses or molts. Criteria are available to distinguish corpses from molts only if the crab is preserved with the carapace flipped upward and forward on the sternum (Salter's Position) as the body decomposes and currents or scavengers move the carapace. Molts are split along the plural suture whereas corpses are separated from the sternum with the pleural suture intace (Schäfer, 1972:139). Bishop (1972b) described molts from the *Dakoticancer* Assemblage and concluded that about 0.5 percent of the specimens from the Mobridge localities are definitely molts (Figure 13-9E). The rest of the specimens (99.5 percent) do not present clear evidence of their condition at time of burial. The specimens of *Dakoticancer* are usually split along the pleural suture (Figure 13-9F) and the carapace is pushed down with the edges of the pleural suture overlapping (Figure 13-9T). One specimen of the 5,000 examined crabs shows evidence of predation (Bishop, 1972a) tooth marks (Figure 13-9G). The jumbled condition of a few others (Bishop, 1975:277) may also be evidence for predation, scavenging, or postecdysis ingestion (to recover the nutrients by the molter). Only one specimen (Figure 13-9I) shows any evidence of appendage alignment reminiscent of movement of the exoskeleton by scavengers or currents. The preservation of the vast majority of crabs of all sizes (that is, all ages) combined with the lack of evidence of scavenging seems to point toward the conclusion that the crabs were killed in catastrophic mass-killing events. The occurrence of crab fossils interbedded with several bentonite beds (isochronous surfaces) necessarily means that the *Dakoticancer* Assemblage did not accumulate at one time. I, thus, suggest that *Dakoticancer* communities occasionally inhabited parts of the stable eastern shelf and existed in an unstable environment that fluctuated between conditions favorable to the decapod community and those that repeatedly killed large parts of the community. This hypothesis is confounded by limited quarry data that indicates the crabs are not concentrated along bedding planes as one might expect in a mass killing. However, because this data is limited to one quarry between two bentonites at the Sitting Bull locality, the hypothesized repeated mass killings seems to be the best hypothesis now available.

Brongersma-Sanders (1957) presents a comprehensive discussion of mass mortalities. She divides them into the following categories:

- *1. Vulcanism
- *2. Salinity changes
- *3. Temperature changes
- *4. Noxious waterbloom
- *5. Oxygen depletion or poisonous gases
- 6. Sea or earthquake
- 7. Spawning
- 8. Stranding
- 9. Storms
- 10. Vertical currents

Any combination of the first five categories (starred) seems posible (or probable) in the faunas collected from the Pierre Shale. As mentioned previously, transport of sediment by fresh surface currents would allow large amounts of fine sediment to be transported great distances. This would allow local conditions in one part of the basin to affect other parts by transfer of large quantities of water and sediment. It, also, would locally change salinity, temperature, and nutrient levels. Local flooding due to terrestrial rains could cause these drastic changes.

Waage (1964:541) concluded that the assemblages described from the Fox Hills are the result of mass killings of recurrent benthonic communities by "conditions of excessive turbidity and lowered salinity, possibly brought about by repeated influx of sediment-charged fresh water from rivers in flood."

BURIAL

The decapods were probably buried by a rapid rain of fine-grained sediment. The lack of alignment of skeletal elements and the discrete thin beds of bentonite indicate the bottom was unaffected by currents strong enough to move the volcanic ash or the dead animals. Possibly the mud was transported by low-salinity surface currents and flocculated at the contact with more saline, deep waters. This mechanism would allow for rapid changes in temperature, salinity, and turbidity and could affect levels of gas in the water and the growth of phytoplankton. Any combination of these factors could have exceeded the tolerance limits of the biota and caused mass deaths.

Shortly after burial, the soft parts of the decapods and other animals began decaying. The thin articulating membranes of the decapods probably decomposed fairly rapidly. Mud began filling the inside of the shells and exoskeletons. The sediment was reworked by several kinds of soft-bodied organisms as the remains filled (Bishop, 1977). The organisms included segmented worms as evidenced by impressions (Figure 13-4L). The organisms moved through the sediment ingesting it and extruding it as feces (Figures 13-4I, K, L; Figure 13-9L, M. T). The intensity of burrowing in the sediment filled decapods and molluscs indicates that great numbers of burrowers were present shortly after burial. The amount of time before burial and concretion formation was relatively short because the decapods are still articulated (Zangerl, 1971:1207). The infaunal burrowers were probably not affected by mass mortalities of the epibiota.

Some of the crabs were only partly filled with sediment. These specimens usually collapsed during diagenesis (Figure 13-9S). Fragments of the crushed carapace are preserved on the sediment surface inside the cephalothorax. The effects of compaction due to the weight of overburden slightly disarranged skeletal elements of most specimens (Figure 13-9J, K). The carapace and ventral side are commonly crushed together, which results in the ventral side sliding backward (Figure 13-9K). Other compaction effects are a split carapace along lines of weakness (Figure 13-9F, T); a disarrangement of abdomen somites, either as a crushing against the sternum or a twisting of the somites out of their relative positions (Figure 13-9K); and a crushing of appendages where exposed at the surface of concretions (Figure 13-9D).

Thin sections of Mobridge concretions often show that the exoskeleton has been removed by dissolution and the void space squeezed shut with no fracturing of the concretion (Figure 13-9T); on some specimens the exoskeleton is completely missing.

CONCRETION FORMATION

The formation of concretions is, at least in part, directly related to organic remains. A progressive tendency in the degree of concretion growth is present at the three localities; concretions from the Creston locality are body fillings (Figure 13-9O), those from Mobridge commonly extend beyond the exoskeleton (Figure 13-9A-C), and those from Thomson Butte often completely enclose the decapods except for the distal ends of the appendages (Figure 13-9D, P-S).

Apparently, the inside of decapods and molluscs were especially susceptible to concretion formation. The interior of decapods and molluscs have the following characteristics in common:

1. They are relatively closed spaces.
2. They were once living and contained decaying organic matter.
3. The sediment filling the spaces has been burrowed and pelleted.

Some concretions grew only until they filled the interior of the shells or exoskeletons, as at the Creston locality. Others continued to grow outside the skeletons of the animals, as at Mobridge and Thomson Butte. The size and shape of the concretions were strongly influenced by the type of organic remains they grew in or around. The factor controlling shape of the concretions seems to be the relative thickness of the concretionary material compared to the size of the enclosed fossil. The factors that controlled the amount of material precipitated are unknown. They undoubtedly include physical-chemical conditions and available time.

The processes of preservation can be summarized in a model from the time of embedding to discovery (Figure 13-12; Table 13-3).

Table 13-3
Evidence and summary of events in the preservation of the *Dakoticancer* assemblages.

OBSERVATION	DEDUCTION
1. The specimens that have appendages show them to be in a "normal" position, not raised above the carapace in the escape position.	1. Most crabs were not buried alive.
2. One-half of one percent of the Mobridge specimens are preserved in "Salter's position" and several of them have the carapace split along the pleural sutures with the lower part of the carapace sitting on the sternum.	2. Some specimens are molts.
3. Crabs of all sizes (=ages) are present in the collections.	3. The decapods were probably involved in a series of mass

Table 13-3 (continued)

OBSERVATION	DEDUCTION
There is little evidence that scavengers survived to prey on the dead animals. The decapods are found interspersed among several bentonites at Mobridge indicating a series of events must have happened.	killings.
4. Only one specimen was seen that showed any alignment of appendages. Geopetal structures inside the crabs are right-side-up.	4. The dead animals were rapidly buried by a process that did not involve currents of sufficient strength to rearrange appendages.
5. The carapaces on some specimens are crushed onto the flat sediment surface that was inside the crabs. Some specimens are partly filled and not crushed.	5. The specimens were filled with sediment. Some were partially filled.
6. Nearly all decapods and molluscs have been intensely burrowed and pelleted.	6. Soft-bodied organisms moved through the sediment ingesting it and extruding it as fecal pellets.
7. In most specimens, the abdomen and sternum are crushed into the carapace. The carapace of most specimens has broken along the pleural sutures.	7. There was some compaction of the specimens before concretion formation.
8. Many specimens from the Mobridge localities have the carapace dissolved away in some areas and the resulting void closed without fracturing the overlying concretionary material.	8. Early diagenesis involved dissolution of the carapace of some specimens.
9. Parts of decapods extending beyond the concretions are crushed. Specimens from Thomson Butte have concretionary material brecciated and pushed down into the crabs' interiors.	9. There was some crushing of the specimens after the concretions formed.
10. Thomson Butte specimens that were not completely filled with sediment have the void spaces filled with euhedral barite crystals. Weathering rinds are present on nearly all specimens.	10. Late diagenesis involved filling void spaces with barite and weathering effects.

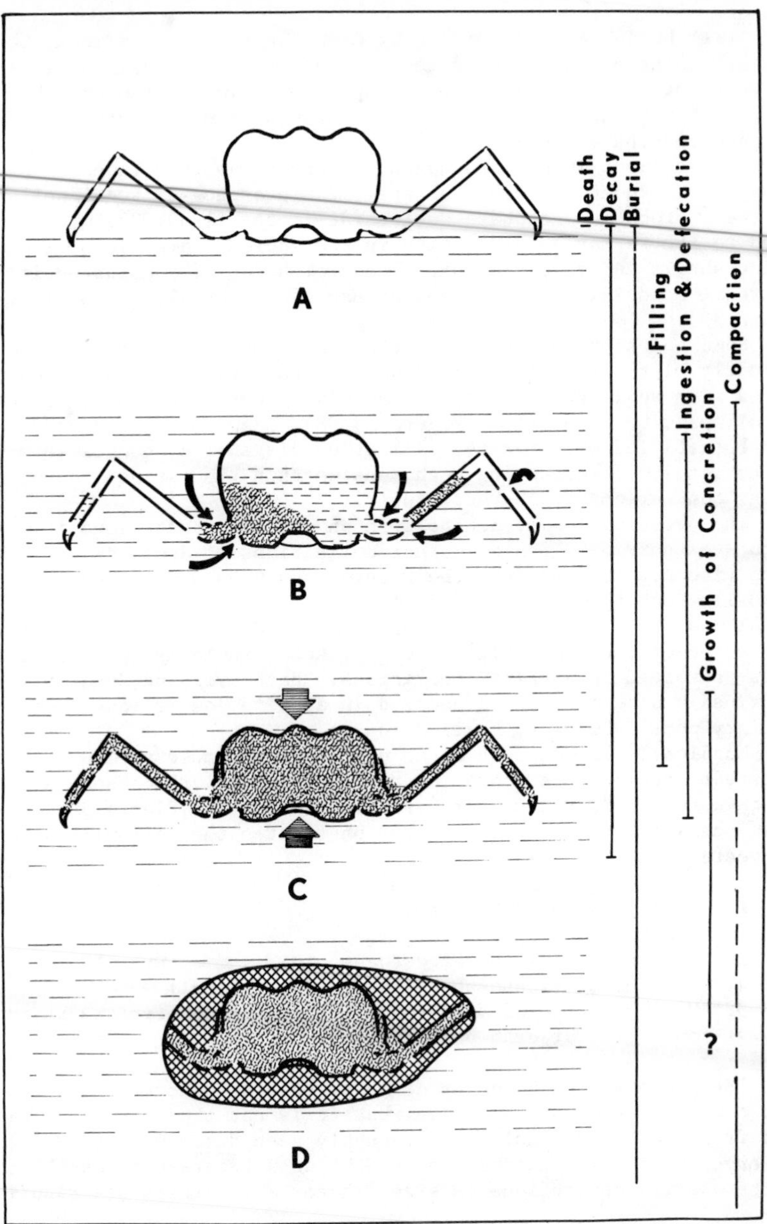

Figure 13-12
Fossilization of specimens from the *Dakoticancer* Assemblage. Transverse cross section of dead decapod lying on the bottom (A) and decapod after articulating membranes have broken down (B). Mud begins to fill the interior and be ingested and extruded as fecal pellets (mottled). Completely filled burrowed, and pelleted decapod undergoing preconcretion compaction (C). Specimen enclosed in apatite concretion with portions extending beyond concretion destroyed by Diagenesis (D).

After burial of the remains by a gentle rain of sediment, the thin articulating membranes were destroyed allowing sediment to enter the interior of the decomposing decapods. Sediment also probably entered through the buccal frame and through openings between the carapace and the sternum.

The sediment in and around the decapods was then ingested by worms and extruded as fecal pellets. The presence of fecal pellets and their probable phosphate enrichment (Moore, 1939:522) may be related to the formation of apatite in the enclosed organic environments inside shells and exoskeletons. The prominence of phosphates in fossil fecal material is emphasized by Hantzschel et al. (1968, Text-Figure 35).

Some solution of the exoskeletons of some specimens occurred concurrently with concretion formation. If the crabs were not completely filled with sediment, the growing partially hardened concretion could be collapsed by compaction (Figure 13-9S). Remaining void spaces were then filled with barite. All other diagenetic changes seem to be the result of weathering phenomena; a thin rind around the outside of the concretions is characteristic.

The preservation of decapods in phosphatic concretions is not unique to the Pierre Shale. Other collections of decapods preserved in apatite concretions from the Pierre have been made at Wasta (GAB 7), Belle Fourche (GAB 36), and Fort Pierre (GAB 12), South Dakota; and Albion, Montana. A collection from the Carlile Formation (Turonian) north of the Black Hills, South Dakota, includes numerous lobsters preserved in apatite concretions. Bachmayer and Mundlos (1968) described a decapod fauna preserved in apatite concretions from the Tertiary near Helmstedt, Lower Saxony.

Mundlos (1975) described the processes of preservation of the Helmstedt specimens as a process remarkably similar to those envisioned for the *Dakoticancer* assemblages from the Pierre Shale. The basic scenario presented by Mundlos postulates the following sequence of events:

1. Burial in the substrate.
2. Death.
3. Sediment infilling of corpses.
4. Enrichment by phosphate matrix due to small worms.
5. Precipitation of four types of apatite concretions based on degree of crab preservation.

The preservation of decapods in phosphatic concretions seems to be a common mode of preservation, but it is not the only one. Decapods from the Pierre Shale have recently been discovered (GAB 35) preserved in calcite concretions that bear a remarkable resemblance to the apatite concretions in size, shape, and perhaps distribution.

DISCUSSION

The hypothesized accumulation as corpses is challenged (Richards, 1975:1855) on the basis that most of the specimens collected are probably molts and not corpses. The common occurrence of carapaces split along pleural sutures and the lack of preserved internal skeletons support this possibility. I currently interpret these phenomena to be the result of differential decomposition exhibited first by thin membranes and zones of weak mineralization. Research currently underway should develop criteria useful in distinguishing molts from corpses when not preserved in "Salter's Position" and at advanced stages of decomposition.

Should the specimens prove to be molts, the hypothesis presented here will have to be modified somewhat. The reality of the *Dakoticancer* Assemblage and the hypothesized preservation will remain unchanged. The hypothesized, repeated mass killings would have to be rejected in favor of acculations of molts in great numbers and without evidence of postmolting ingestion of the exuviae that is so common in the behavior of the decapods.

ACKNOWLEDGMENTS

Many persons and organizations helped make this study possible. To all of them I extend my thanks. Especially helpful was field support from the South Dakota Geological Survey; a grant from the Geological Society of America; laboratory, office, and library facilities of the Departments of Geology at South Dakota School of Mines, The University of Texas at Austin, and Georgia Southern College; and financial support provided by the Geology Foundation of The University of Texas, the Faculty Research Committee at Georgia Southern College, and the National Geographic Society.

The manuscript was typed by Mrs. Rebecca Shinta at Georgia Southern College and Miss Beth Tippins.

REFERENCES

Asquith, D. O. 1970. Depositional topography and major marine environments, Late Cretaceous, Wyoming. *Am. Assoc. Petroleum Geologists Bull.* 54:1184-1224.

Bachmayer, F., and R. Mundlos. 1968. Die Tertiaren Krebse von Helmstedt bei Braunschweig, *Deutchland. Ann. Naturhistor. Mus. Wien* 72:649-692.

Bishop, G. A. 1972a. Crab bitten by a fish from the Upper Cretaceous Pierre Shale of South Dakota. *Geol. Soc. America Bull.* 83:3823-3826.

Bishop, G. A. 1972b. Moults of *Dakoticancer overanus*, an Upper Cretaceous crab from the Pierre Shale of South Dakota. *Paleontology* 15:631-636.

Bishop, G. A. 1973. *Homolopsis Dawsonensis:* a new crab (Crustacea, Decapods) from the Pierre Shale (Upper Cretaceous, Maastrichtian) of Cedar Creek Anticline, Eastern Montana. *Jour. Paleontology* 47:19-20.

Bishop, G. A. 1974. A sexually aberrant crab *(Dakoticancer overanus* Rathbun, 1917) from the Upper Cretaceous Pierre Shale of South Dakota. *Crustaceana* 26:212-218.

Bishop, G. A. 1976. *Ekalakia lamberti* N. Gen., N. sp. (Crustacean, Decapoda from the Upper Cretaceous Pierre Shale of Eastern Montana. *Jour. Paleontology* 50:398-401.

Bishop, G. A. 1977. Pierre feces: a scatological study of the *Dakoticancer* Assemblage, Pierre Shale (Upper Cretaceous) of South Dakota. *Jour. Sed. Petrology* 47:130-136.

Brongersma-Sanders, M. 1957. Mass mortality in the sea, in J. W.

Hedgpeth, ed., *Treatise on Marine Ecology and Paleoecology. Geol. Soc. Am. Mem.* 67:941-1010.

Clark, J., J. R. Beerbower, and K. K. Kieke. 1967. Oligocene sedimentation, stratigraphy, paleoecology, and paleoclimatology in the Big Badlands of South Dakota. *Fieldiana-Geology* 5:1-158.

Crandell, D. R. 1958. Geology of the Pierre area, South Dakota. *U.S. Geol. Survey Prof. Paper* 307:1-83.

Feldman, R. M., G. A. Bishop, and T. W. Kammer. 1977. Macrurous decapods from the Bearpaw Shale (Cretaceous: Campanian) of northeastern Montana. *Jour. Paleontology* 51:1161-1180.

Gill, J. R., and W. A. Cobban. 1966. The Red Bird Section of the Upper Cretaceous Pierre Shale in Wyoming. *U.S. Geol. Survey Prof. Paper* 393-A:1-73.

Gill, J. R., and W. A. Cobban. 1973. Stratigraphy and geologic history of the Montana Group and equivalent rocks, Montana, Wyoming, and North and South Dakota. *U.S.Geol. Survey Prof. Paper* 776: 1-37.

Gries, J. P. 1939. A structural survey of part of the Upper Missouri Valley in South Dakota. *South Dakota Geol. Survey Rept. Inv.* 31:1-38.

Gries, J. P. 1942. Economic possibilities of the Pierre Shale. *South Dakota Geol. Survey Rept. Inv.* 43:1-79.

Häntzschel, W. F., El-Baz, and G. C. Amstutz. 1968. *Coprolites: An Annotated Bibliography. Geol. Soc. Am. Mem.* 108:1-132.

Jeletzky, J. A. 1969. Marine Cretaceous biotic provinces of Western and Arctic Canada. *North Am. Paleont. Conv. Proc.* L:1638-1659.

Kauffman, E. G. 1967. Coloradoan macroinvertebrate assemblages, Central Western Interior, in *Symposium on Paleoenvironments of the Cretaceous Seaway in the Western Interior.* Colorado School of Mines.

Kauffman, E. G. 1977. Geological and biological overview: Western Interior Cretaceous Basin. *Geologist* 14:75-99.

Kauffman, E. G., D. E. Hattin, and J. D. Powell. 1977. *Stratigraphic Paleontologic, and Paleoenvironmental Analysis of the Upper Cretaceous Rocks of Cinnarron County, Northwestern Oklahoma. Geol. Soc. Am. Mem. 143.*

Mello, J. F. 1969. Foraminifera and stratigraphy of the upper part of the Pierre Shale and lower part of the Fox Hills Sandstone (Cretaceous) north-central South Dakota. *U.S. Geol. Survey Prof. Paper* 611:1-121.

Miyadi, D. 1941. Marine benthic communities of the Ise-wan and the Mikawa-wan. *Mem. Imp. Marine Obs.* 7:502-524.

Moore, H. B. 1939. Faecal pellets in relation to marine deposits, in P. D. Trask, ed., *Recent Marine Sediments.* Tulsa: Am. Assoc. Petrological Geology, pp. 516-524.

Obradovich, J. D., and W. A. Cobban. 1975. A time scale for the Late Cretaceous of the Western Interior of North America, in W. G. E. Caldwell, ed., *The Cretaceous System in the Western Interior of the North America. Geol. Soc. Canada Spec. Paper* 13:31-54.

Rathbun, M. J. 1917. New species of South Dakota Cretaceous crabs. *U.S. Natl. Mus. Proc.* 2182: 52:385-391.

Rathbun, M. J. 1930. A new *Callianassa* from the Cretaceous of South Dakota. *Wash. Acad. Sci. Jour.* 20:1-3.

Reeside, J. B., Jr. 1957. Paleoecology of the Cretaceous seas of the Western Interior of the United States, in H. S. Ladd, ed., *Treatise on Marine Ecology and Paleoecology. Geol. Soc. Am. Mem.* 67:505-542.

Richards, B. C. 1975. *Longusorbis cuniculosus:* a new genus and species of Upper Cretaceous Crab; with comments on Spray Formation at Shelter Point, Vancouver Island, British Columbia. *Canadian Jour. Earth Sci.* 11:1850-1863.

Robinson, C. S., W. J. Mapel, and W. A. Cobban. 1959. Pierre Shale along western and northern flanks of Black Hills, Wyoming and Montana. *Am. Assoc. Petroleum Geologists Bull.* 43:101-123.

Rothrock, E. P. 1947. Geology of the Missouri Valley and vicinity near Mobridge. *South Dakota Geol. Survey Rept. Inv.* 58:1-29.

Russell, W. 1930. The possibilities of oil and gas in western Potter County. *South Dakota Geol. Survey Rept. Inv.* 7:1-13.

Schäfer, Wilhelm. 1972. *Ecology and Palaeoecology of Marine Environments.* Chicago: University of Chicago Press, 568 p.

Scott, R. W. 1970. Paleoecology and paleontology of the Lower Cretaceous Kiowa Formation, Kansas. *Univ. Kansas Paleont. Contrib., Art. 52*, 94 p.

Sohl, N. F. 1967. Upper Cretaceous gastropod assemblages of the Western Interior of the United States, in E. G. Kauffman and H. C. Kent, eds., *Paleoenvironments of the Cretaceous Seaway: A Symposium.* Colo. School Mines Spec. Pub., pp. 1-37.

Sohl, N. F. 1969. North American Cretaceous Biotic provinces delineated by gastropods. *North American Paleont. Conv. Proc.* L:1610-1638.

Thorson, Gunnar. 1957. Bottom Communities (Sublittoral or shallow shelf), in H. S. Ladd, ed., *Treatise on Marine Ecology and Paleoecology. Geol. Soc. Am. Mem.* 67:461-534.

Tourtlot, H. A., and R. O. Rye. 1969. Distribution of oxygen and carbon isotopes in fossils of Late Cretaceous age, Western Interior region of North America. *Geol. Soc. America Bull.* 80:1903-1922.

Waage, K. M. 1964. Origin of repeated fossiliferous concretion layers in the Fox Hills Formation. *Kansas Geol. Survey Bull.* 169:541-563.

Waage, K. M. 1968. The type of Fox Hills Formation, Cretaceous (Maestrichtian) South Dakota: Part 1: Stratigraphy and Paleoenvironments. *Peabody Mus. Nat. History (Yale Univ.) Bull.* 27:1-175.

Wanless, H. R. 1923. The stratigraphy of the White River beds of South Dakota. *Am. Philos. Soc. Proc.* 62:190-269.

Weimer, R. J. 1960. Upper Cretaceous stratigraphy, Rocky Mountain area. *Am. Assoc. Petrological Geology* 44:1-20.

Zangerl, Rainer. 1971. On the Geologic significance of perfectly preserved fossils. *North Am. Paleont. Conv. Proc.* I:1207-1222.

14

Paleoenvironments and Fossil Fishes of the Laney Member, Green River Formation, Wyoming

H. Paul Buchheim and Ronald R. Surdam

ABSTRACT

Although much has been written about the taxonomic aspects of the fossil fishes of the Green River Formation, little attention has been given to the paleoecologic aspects. This work attempts to fill this gap by a study of the relationship of the fossil fishes to other fossils, sedimentology, stratigraphy, and mineralogy of the lacustrine Laney Member of Green River Formation. These relationships are considered in making interpretations concerning paleoenvironments and paleocommunities.

Two major paleoenvironments and paleocommunities are recognized in the Laney Member: the littoral (near-shore), and the limnetic (open-water). The littoral paleocommunity is characterized by an association of juvenile *Knightia*, fish fry, *Equisetum*, *Typha*, and abundant ostracodes. Littoral paleoenvironments are dominated by coarse-grained sediments, including siltstones, sandstones, mudstones, flat-pebble conglomerate, alternating aragonite and clay laminae, ostracode-rich laminae, strand-line deposits of ostracodes, oolites, pisolites, fish bones, and algal stromatolites.

The limnetic paleocommunity is represented by an association of adult *Knightia*, *Phareodus*, *Erismatopterus*, *Priscacara*, *Astephus*, and *Asineops*. The limnetic paleoenvironment is characterized by fine-grained laminated carbonates, and the conspicuous absence of sandstones, siltstones, mudstones, stromatolites, oolites, and pisolites.

Evidence suggests that the paleoenvironments and paleocommunities were significantly altered by cyclic changes in climate, and that the Laney Member was deposited in a shallow lake with oscillating levels in a closed hydrographic basin with a low topographic gradient.

INTRODUCTION

PREVIOUS STUDIES

The Eocene Green River Formation of Wyoming has become famous for its oil shale, unusual minerals, sedimentological features, and above all, for its well-preserved fossil fishes.

Since Leidy (1856) recorded the first discovery of a fossil fish from the Green River Formation, many workers have studied the Green River Formation and its fish fauna. The abundance of fossil fish became noteworthy in the 1860's when important discoveries were made during Union Pacific railroad construction near the town of Green River. Hayden (1871) referred to these excavations as the "Petrified Fish Cut" and the name has persisted. The cut exposes basal beds of the Laney Member of the Green River Formation. Edward Drinker Cope described these fishes in Hayden's (1871) report. In the 1870's, fish were collected from the famous Fossil Butte about 16 km west of Kemmerer, Wyoming. Cope (1877) probably collected from this area as he described a locality "nearer the mainline of Wasatch Mountains," where Fossil Butte is located. Peale (1879) was the first worker to mention fish quarrying at Fossil Butte.

Cope (1884a, b) published two large volumes on the Tertiary vertebrates of the west. In these, he gave good descriptions of most of the now known species of Green River fishes.

Since those early days no comprehensive works involving the Green River fishes have appeared. Eastman (1917) figured several Green River fishes and described several new species. Thorpe (1938) provided a key to aid in identifying many of the fishes and described a new species.

In more recent years, Bradley (1948, 1963, 1964) extensively studied the geology of the Green River Formation. He noted the presence of fossil fish in many of his stratigraphic sections and proposed a model for the death and preservation of the fishes (Bradley, 1948). Schaeffer and Mangus (1965) gave an overview of the Green River Formation fishes and a geologic history of the Green River Formation.

Most recently, Baer (1969), Lundberg and Case (1970), Perkins (1970), Lundberg (1975), McGrew (1975), McGrew and Casilliano (1975), and Buchheim and Surdam (1977) contributed to our knowledge of fishes from the Green River Formation.

Despite this large amount of literature, knowledge of the stratigraphic and paleogeographic distribution and paleoecology of the fossil fishes is minimal. Baer (1969) discussed the paleoecology of the fishes, but his study was restricted to one locality in the Uinta Basin, Utah. McGrew (1975), and McGrew and Casilliano (1975) gave insights into the taphonomy and paleoecology of fossil fishes in Fossil Basin, Wyoming.

PURPOSE OF STUDY

The purpose of this study is to define and describe the paleoenvironments of the Laney Member of the Green River Formation and to interpret the paleoecology of the fossil fish. This study is restricted to the Laney Member because the Laney contains an abundant and varied fish fauna, it displays most of the depositional environments characteristic of the Green River Formation, and it is well exposed.

The study involved an area of 43,000 km^2. The Laney Member was examined at eighty localities, and twenty-four stratigraphic sections were measured. Time has not permitted a detailed analysis and species identification of all the fossil organisms encountered. However, we have noted occurrences of all fossils including fish, ostracodes, insects, plants, molluscs, and stromatolites; and their presence has been considered when drawing paleoenvironmental conclusions. Also, sedimentological, mineralogical, geochemical, and stratigraphic data have been used in making conclusions.

Because this is a reconnaissance study, we will define paleoenvironments and the relationship of the fossil fishes to them, but not define specific paleoecologic associations.

ORIENTATION

Throughout the chapter, reference will be made to study areas in Figure 14-1, which shows the distribution of the Laney Member, locations of measured stratigraphic sections, and major study areas (A through J). Each study area is characterized by certain geologic and paleontologic features that differ from adjacent areas.

Abbreviations will be used to refer to stratigraphic sections, for example, BSR for Big Sandy River section. Table 14-1 is a key to these abbreviations, and their respective locality numbers. Figure 14-1 indicates the geographic areas in which these sections are located. Space does not permit every section to be figured; however, a few representative sections will be illustrated. Reference will be made to lithologic units (for example, BSR-14) from particular sections using the section abbreviation (BSR) and unit number (14). The unit number refers to a particular lithologic unit studied or measured.

Table 14-1
Abbreviations for sections and key to locations in Figure 14-1

Locality no.	Locality area	Abbreviation	Stratigraphic Section
1	B	BSR	Big Sandy River
2	C	LSC	Little Sandy Creek
3	D	BRE	Bush Rim East
4	D	SM	Steamboat Mountain
5	D	WMN	White Mountain North
6	E	FMR	Fourteen Mile Reservoir
7	E	SC	Scotts Canyon
8	F	GCSB	Greens Canyon South-B
9	F	WMR	White Mountain Road
10	F	BR	Blue Rim
11	F	WB	Whalen Butte
12	F	FG	Flaming Gorge
13	F	FGS	Flaming Gorge South
14	F	CC	Currant Creek
15	F	LC	Lowe Canyon
16	G	MMC	Middle Marsh Creek
17	G	AW	Anvil Wash
18	A	FD	Fontenelle Dam
19	H	TR	Tipton Road
20	I	LR	Lyclede Rim
21	I	AC	Antelope Creek
22	I	TD	Trail Dugway
23	J	SCR	Shell Creek
24	J	LM	Lookout Mountain

Exact locality data are not given due to possible commercial exploitation and subsequent destruction or loss of scientifically valu-

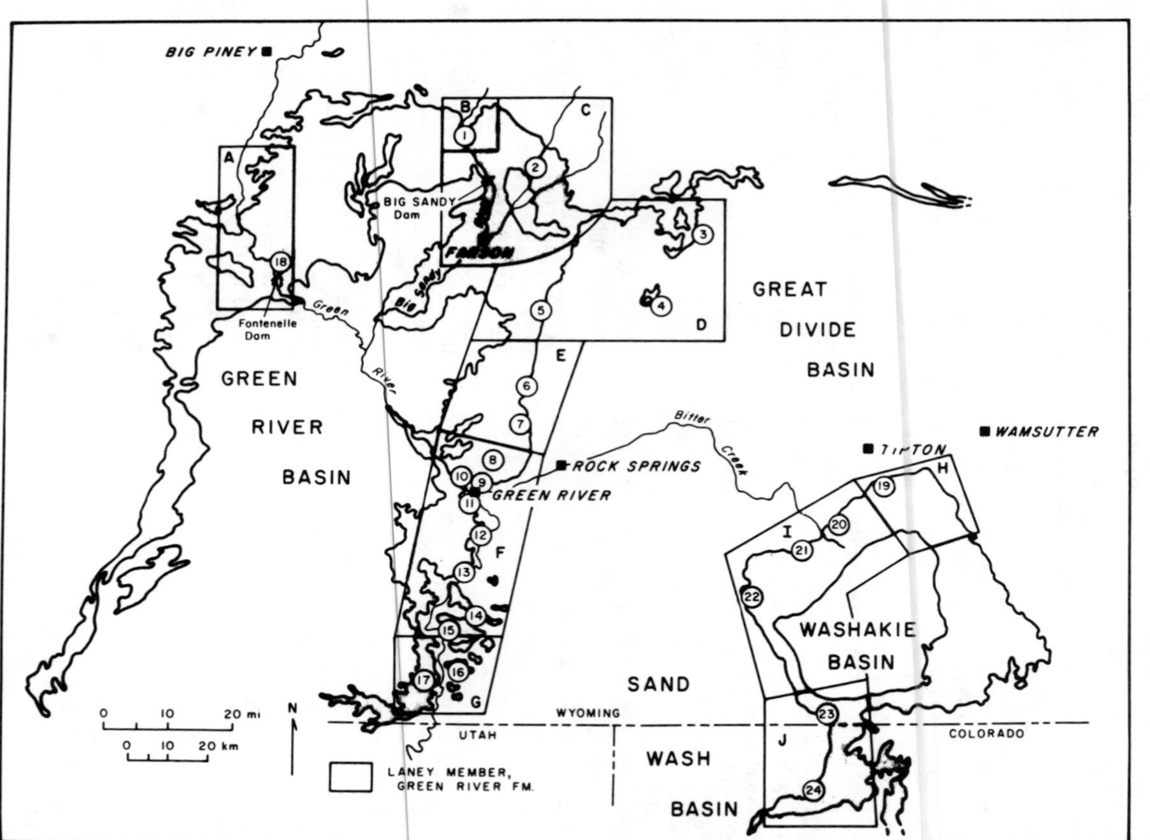

Figure 14-1
Distribution of the Laney Member of the Green River Formation showing locations of measured stratigraphic sections and major study areas.

able fossil deposits. Qualified workers may contact the authors or the University of Wyoming Geology Museum for more detailed locality information.

Rock lithologies are classified according to mineralogy and sedimentary structure. This is to emphasize the geochemical environment and processes operating during deposition.

The fossils symbolized adjacent to the Flaming Gorge Section (Figure 14-18, locality 12) represent a composite of fossils found in correlative units throughout areas E and F. The section illustrated by Figure 14-18 is at locality 12, but is very similar to other sections measured throughout areas E and F.

PALEOECOLOGICAL TERMS

The use of the terms paleocommunity, assemblage, and association will be consistant with definitions given by Kauffman and Scott (1976).

The community may be defined as a unique group of interacting organisms adapted to and restricted by physical, chemical, and biological factors operating within a distinct space. The paleocommunity is a community that existed in geologic history and is represented by the remains of organisms that made up that community. Here, the term is applied to groups of organisms peculiar to the littoral and limnetic paleoenvironments of ancient Lake Gosiute.

Assemblage is defined as, and will be used to describe, a group of fossil organisms derived from more than one community.

Association will be applied to a group of organisms characteristic of a single paleocommunity such as the littoral paleocommunity.

GEOLOGIC SETTING

The lacustrine strata of the Green River Formation were deposited in Lake Gosiute, which occupied a large intermontane basin in southwestern Wyoming (Figure 14-2).

The original depositional basin has been modified into four, major structural units. Collectively, these are known as the Greater Green River Basin. The four units include the Green River (or Bridger), Washakie, and Great Divide basins, and the Rock Springs Uplift (Figure 14-2). The first two structures are large, shallow, synclinal basins. The Great Divide Basin is a northern extension of the Washakie Basin, but is separated from it by the low east-west trending Wamsutter Arch. The Rock Springs Uplift is an anticline trending north-south that separates the Green River and Washakie basins. The uplift exposes Upper Cretaceous shales and sandstones.

The Green River Formation in Wyoming has undergone little tectonic disruption. Beds are essentially flat lying except immediately adjacent to the mountain fronts where they dip more steeply (Bradley, 1964).

The formation is well exposed, and some mappable units in the Green River and Washakie basins are traceable for as much as 80 km. This facilitates detailed stratigraphic and paleoenvironmental studies. Outcrops are particularly extensive in the vicinity of Green River, Wyoming, and along the Laney and Kinney rims in the Washakie Basin. Less-spectacular exposures are found in the White Mountain scarp (eastern edge of Green River Basin), from Steamboat Mountain to Oregon Buttes (western margin of Great Divide Basin), along the Big

Figure 14-2
LANDSAT mosaic of Wyoming. The Green River Formation in Wyoming was deposited in the basin formed by the uplift of the Thrust Belt on the West, the Wind River Range and Sweetwater Arch on the north, the Rawlins Uplift and Sierra Madre on the East, and the Uinta Mountains on the south. (LANDSAT mosaic produced by Western Ariel Photography Laboratory, USDA, ASCS.)

Sandy River (northern part of the Green River Basin), and from Fontenelle Reservoir northward along the Green River (northwest corner of the Green River Basin).

The Green River Formation forms a large lens of fine-grained rocks within the fluvial mudstones, siltstones, and sandstones of the Wasatch and Bridger formations (Figure 14-3). The Wasatch and Bridger underlie and overlie the Green River Formation, respectively, and interfinger with it.

The major members of the Green River Formation are the Tipton, Wilkins Peak, and Laney. The Tipton and Laney members were deposited during high levels of ancient Lake Gosiute whereas the Wilkins Peak Member was deposited during a low stand. Large quantities of saline minerals (trona and halite) characterize the Wilkins Peak Member. The lake deposits in the Laney Member are exposed over an area of about 43,000 km^2 (Figure 14-1). The Laney and the Tipton contain abundant fish fauna whereas the Wilkins Peak is not known to contain any fish fossils.

The members vary lithologically, but all are dominated by fine-

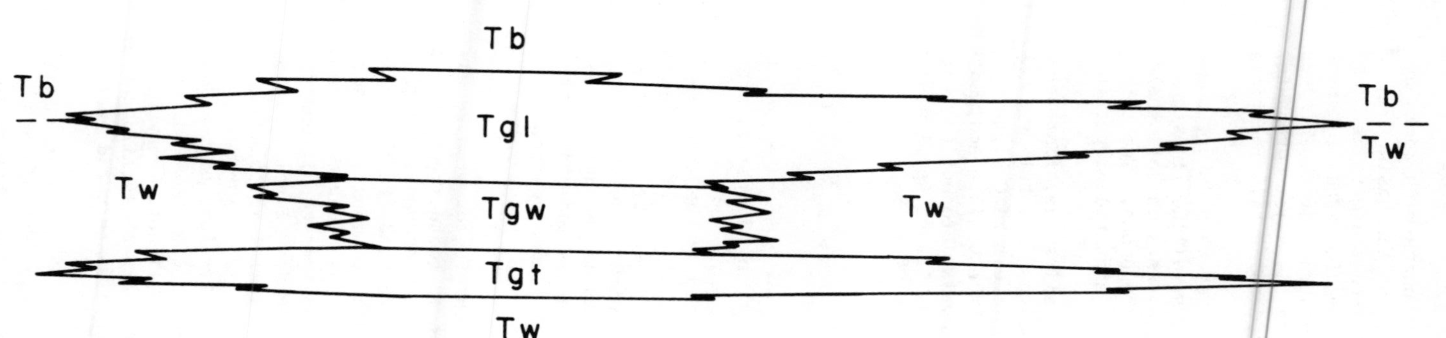

Figure 14-3
In the Green River Basin, the Green River Formation forms a lens of sediments within the fluvial Wasatch and Bridger formations. Tb, Bridger Formation; Tgl, Laney Member of the Green River Formation; Tgw, Wilkins Peak Member of the Green River Formation; Tgt, Tipton Member of the Green River Formation; Tw, Wasatch Formation. (After Bradley, 1964).

grained carbonate rocks. The dilution of the carbonate-rich rocks by siliclastic detritus is ubiquitous at the margins of the basin. Grain size of all mineral fractions increases toward the margins. Lacustrine carbonate rocks of the Green River Formation grade laterally into fluvial mudstones, siltstones, and sandstones of the Bridger and Wasatch formations. Calcite and dolomite are the major carbonate minerals. Aragonite is common, but is restricted to certain locations or units.

The fine-grained lacustrine rocks are laminated carbonates, mudstones, and claystones, or less commonly, hard crystalline limestone. The kerogenous carbonates described by previous workers as "oil shale" are in varying degrees laminated, fissile, and kerogenous. The term "oil shale" comes from the kerogenous nature of a significant portion of these rocks.

Other common lithologies include sandstone, siltstone, flat-pebble conglomerate, tuff, oolites, algal stromatolites, and tufa.

Twelve genera of fossil fish are known from the Lake Gosiute sediments. Other fossils commonly occurring in Lake Gosiute sediments and the interfingering fluvial sediments are mammals, crocodiles, turtles, birds, a variety of molluscs, insects, wood, leaves, pollen, and stromatolites.

PALEOENVIRONMENTS

DEFINITIONS

The two major zones of modern lakes, littoral and limnetic, are recorded in the sediments of Eocene Lake Gosiute.

The littoral zone of a lake is usually defined as the zone extending from the shoreline to the limit of rooted plants in the lake (Reid, 1961). It is characterized by the greatest variety of species because of the variety and number of ecological niches available.

The littoral paleoenvironment is here defined as the paleoenvironment dominated by near-shore sedimentary processes and characterized by littoral communities. This definition includes nearshore sediments, such as beach and delta deposits, whether or not rooted plants are present.

The limnetic zone of a lake is defined as the region of open water, and the boundary is delineated by the zone of rooted vegetation. The limnetic zone is divided vertically into the trophogenic and tropholytic zones. The upper, trophogenic zone corresponds to the lighted zone and is inhabited by a light-dependent community of microscopic plants and animals classified collectively as plankton. The lower, tropholytic zone is characterized by low-oxygen conditions and by abundant bacteria and animals adapted to low-oxygen levels. This zone may not be present in shallow lakes or in clear lakes where light penetrates to the bottom.

Obviously, the organisms inhabiting the subdivisions of the limnetic zone would be preserved as fossils in the same bottom sediments. Because of this, facies containing these fossils (limnetic communities) and sediments characteristic of open water are classified as the limnetic paleoenvironment. This includes all sediments not directly affected or produced by nearshore processes.

The epilittoral zone is that zone fringing the lake, but entirely above the water level and uninfluenced by the spray (Hutchinson, 1967:240). The epilittoral paleoenvironment is defined here as the fringing dolomitic mudflats wetted by occasional floods, but subject to intense desiccation most of the time (Surdam and Wolfbauer, 1975). Mud chips, ripped from the mud-cracked flats, and dolomitic sediments were washed into the lake during the floods (Surdam and Wolfbauer, 1975; Surdam and Stanley, 1979). During arid times, the paleoenvironment occupied large areas around the lake. It is likely that streams reached the outer borders of the mudflats, but died out before reaching the lake. Remnant marshes or ponds fed by springs or streams also may have existed on the outer edge of these flats (Surdam and Stanley, 1979). Discussion of this environment will be limited, as fish remains are not known from epilittoral sediments.

These paleoenvironments show various modifications related to paleogeographic location. Regressions and transgressions of the lake and inflow of sediment-laden rivers and streams produced minor modifications. Small changes in lake depth resulted in major fluctuations of shoreline due to the closed hydrographic nature and low topographic gradient of the lake basin (Surdam and Wolfbauer, 1975; Surdam and Stanley, 1979). Therefore, stratigraphic sections that are intermediate between the paleogeographic center and the margin of the ancient lake basin record alternating littoral and limnetic paleoenvironments. Sections near the town of Green River, at the paleogeographic center of Lake Gosiute, record limnetic paleoenvironments and communities through time. Sections near the basin's margin (Big Sandy River section, 80 km north of Farson, Wyoming) record littoral paleoenvironments and communities through time.

THE LITTORAL PALEOENVIRONMENT

Bradley (1926, 1964) described a number of biological criteria for recognizing shore phases. They include calcareous algal stromatolites, oolites, pisolites, ostracodes, carbonate-encrusted logs, larval cases of trichopterous insects, plant remains such as *Equisetum* and leaves of higher plants, and "beach" lag deposits characterized by a mixture of terrestrial vertebrates and fish bones.

Bradley also presents sedimentological evidence for shore phases including increase in sediment grain size as a unit is traced shoreward and increase in fluvial units in a given section (interfingering of fluvial and lacustrine rocks). Stream channel deposits become finer grained lakeward, and cross-bedded sandstone is replaced in the same direction by regular bedding. Away from shore, sands become thinner, finer grained, and finally grade lakeward into finely laminated carbonates. A lakeward increase of lime content characterizes sandstones.

The Big Sandy River section (Figures 14-1, 14-4, locality 1; 14-5A) displays many of the littoral criteria. Calcareous sandstones show ripple lamination or plane bedding. Several miles north, the basal sandstone is trough cross-bedded. This sandstone probably originated at or near the mouth of a river. Subsequent increase in lake depth resulted in a transgression of lake waters, which in turn resulted in the deposition of fine-grained, laminated, siliceous shales just above the sandstone unit. This did not persist, however, as the upper part of the section is composed primarily of calcareous mudstones, siltstones, and sandstones. The increase in coarse-grained sediment and the high percentage of silicate minerals (quartz, feldspar, and clays) relative to carbonate minerals (calcite, dolomite, aragonite) suggest a nearshore littoral environment. Silicate min-

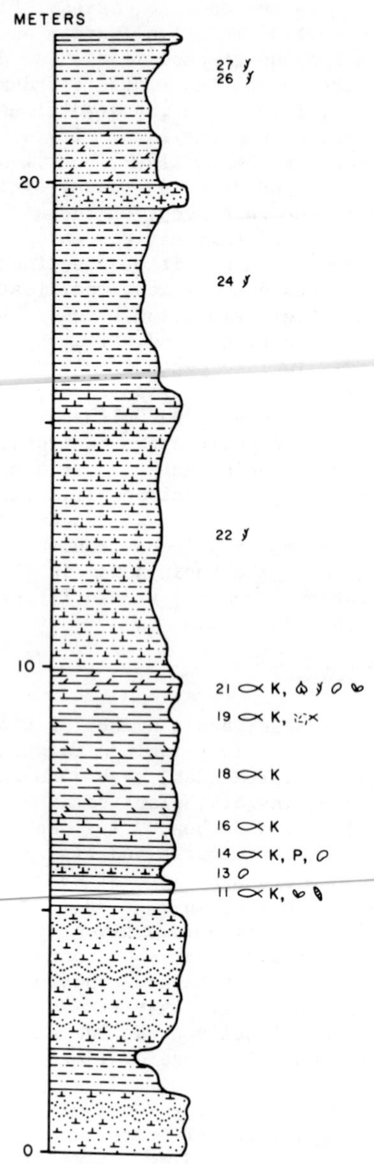

Figure 14-4
Big Sandy River stratigraphic section, locality 1.

erals compose about 70 percent of the mineral content of the sediments in this section.

Deposits representing the littoral paleoenvironment yield a well-preserved assemblage of fish fry (Figure 14-6D, F), juvenile fish (Figures 14-7D, 14-8B), scouring rushes (*Equisetum*, Figure 14-7A), cattail leaf fragments (*Typha*, Figure 14-6B), leaves of higher plants (Figure 14-7D), insects (Figure 14-6B), and ostracodes.

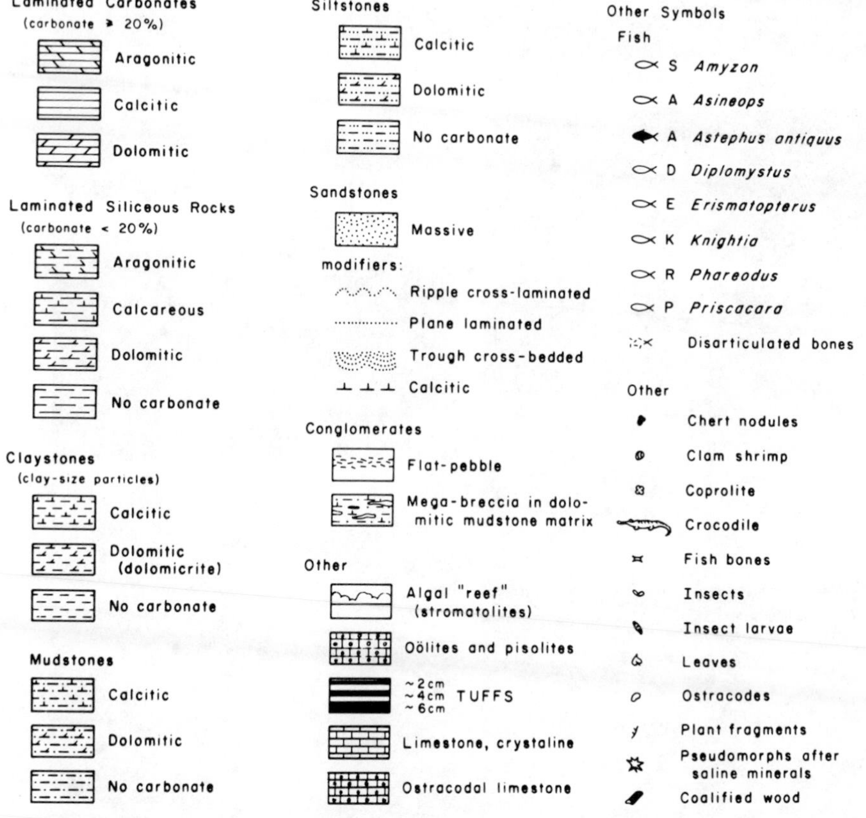

Explanation of lithologic and stratigraphic symbols used in stratigraphic columns.

The fish fry and juvenile *Knightia* probably were seeking the protection of the shallows and aquatic vegetation characteristic of the littoral environment. Also, an adjacent marsh or fluvial environment might have harbored these organisms. The apparent absence of root structures disturbing the sediments and the presence of terrestrial insects suggests that some of the fossils are allochthonous. This may be true particularly of the *Equisetum* (horsetails) and

Figure 14-5
A. Big Sandy River section, BSR, locality 1; B. Antelope Creek section, AC, locality 21; C. Flaming Gorge section, FG, locality 12; D. Shell Creek section, SC, locality 23; E. Bush Rim East section, BRE, locality 3; F. Anvil Wash section, AE, locality 17.

leaves. *Equisetum* typically grows along stream borders, meadow areas, thickets, or woods (Palmer and Fowler, 1975). It is also known as a widespread emergent aquatic plant (Hutchinson, 1967:31). Cattails (*Typha*) are common today in shallow waters or marshlands (Palmer and Fowler, 1975).

Ostracodes are extremely abundant, especially in certain units of the littoral deposits (BSR-14). Bradley (1926) felt that ostracodes are indicative of shallow areas characteristic of shore phases. Reid (1961) stated that ostracodes are not typically found in open waters of lakes (limnetic zone), but are common in the littoral zone. They thrive in areas where dead plants and animals have passed stages of active decay and where decay is continuing slowly (Palmer and Fowler, 1975). Abundant vegetable and animal detritus is common in the littoral zone. Ostracodes may have provided a food supply for the abundant juvenile *Knightia*, as they are known to make excellent food for the earlier stages of fish (Palmer and Fowler, 1975).

Presence of sunfish (*Priscacara*) in BSR-14 is compatible with the littoral zone interpretation. The littoral zone is commonly used as a breeding and nesting area by sunfishes (Reid, 1961). However, *Priscacara* is found also in areas interpreted as the limnetic paleoenvironment.

BSR-18, a papery siliceous shale, consists of alternating white, chalky, aragonitic laminae and gray-green, clay-quartz mineral laminae. Reeves (1968) pointed out that lacustrine aragonite laminae may indicate freshwater flooding of a saline lake that has a high concentration of magnesium ion. Berner (1975) found that magnesium ion inhibits the crystal growth of calcite by adsorbing onto the surface and incorporating into the crystal structure of calcite, which causes the resulting magnesium calcite to be much more soluble than pure calcite. He also concludes that dissolved magnesium ion is not readily adsorbed onto the surface of aragonite or incorporated into its crystal structure, and as a result, aragonite is unaffected by the presence of magnesium ion. Berner (1975) cites a number of workers who show that the presence of magnesium ion favors the precipitation of calcium carbonate as aragonite.

The presence of pseudomorphs after saline minerals (sodium carbonate) rather than sulfate minerals indicates a saline-alkaline lake during portions of Laney time. Surdam and Stanley (1979) and Surdam and Sheppard (1978) interpret Lake Gosiute as saline and alkaline during most of Laney deposition. Bradley and Eugster (1969) also provide abundant evidence of Lake Gosiute's saline-alkaline nature during deposition of the Wilkins Peak Member.

We conclude that the presence of aragonitic siliceous shales at Big Sandy River and at other littoral sections (Table 14-1:TR, AC, LM, LS) and in parts of limnetic sections in areas E and F (Figure 14-1, Table 14-1) suggests that these rocks were deposited when calcium-rich river waters entered the lake. The littoral zone would receive the greatest amount of aragonitic sediment as mixing would occur there first. These papery, aragonitic siliceous shales at the Big Sandy River section and elsewhere contain occasional adult forms of *Knightia* (Figure 14-8C). It is possible that *Knightia* inadvertently entered the lake during periods of freshwater flooding and succumbed as a result of subsequent mixing of saline-alkaline lakewater with the fresher inflow water. Most of the time, however, the fish were restricted to rivers, marshes, and ponds that terminated on or bordered the expansive carbonate mudflat that fringed the lake.

Throughout rocks deposited in area C (Figure 14-1, Table 14-1), the littoral paleoenvironment is dominated by fluvial features. Nearly a quarter mile below the face of Big Sandy Reservoir Dam along the Big Sandy River an outcrop of the Laney Member consists completely of sandstone exhibiting large-scale cross-stratification. Farther east, a section along Little Sandy Creek (Figure 14-1, locality 2) is composed of 36 m of sandstones, mudstones, and siltstones. No fine-grained laminated rocks occur here. A resistant fine-grained siltstone unit capping this section contains numerous fish. According to Lance Grande of the University of Minnesota (pers. comm.), they include many *Knightia* and less common *Asineops* (pirate perch, Figure 14-9F), *Astephus* (catfish similar to a bullhead, Figure 14-10A), *Diplomystus* (a predaceous herring, Figure 14-9E), *Hypsidoris* (a catfish), juvenile catfish (Figure 14-6E), and very rare *Lepisosteus* (gar, Figure 14-9D) and *Amia* (bowfin, Figure 14-9C). These fish are preserved in a thickly and irregularly laminated feldspathic-quartz siltstone (Figure 14-8E). This unit also contains algal stromatolites and upright silicified tree trunks (Figure 14-8A). Ostracodes and plant remains are common also. McGrew and Berman (1955) reported abundant crocodile remains, fragments of turtles, gar scales, and mammalian remains in Laney exposures in this same area. These criteria are highly suggestive of a nearshore, littoral paleoenvironment.

In area D (Figure 14-1, Table 14-1), sections studied at locations 3 (Steamboat Mountain) and 4 (Bush Rim, Figure 14-5E) are composed primarily of alternating sandstones, siltstones, and mudstones. Some of the sandstones are trough cross-laminated. Using stratification sequences and sedimentary structures, Surdam and Stanley (1979) interpreted these rocks as a prograding shoreline. Leaves, *Equisetum*, and fragments of palms occur at location 3. The unit containing *Equisetum* occurs about 20 m above the base of the Laney and appears to be filled with small rootlets (Figure 14-7F). The *Equisetum* are in an upright position (Figure 14-7E). The lower 4 m of this section consist of papery-laminated carbonates containing abundant *Knightia* and ostracodes. This unit, and the rest of the section, is interpreted as a littoral paleoenvironment. The lower, kerogenous, laminated carbonates appear to be correlative with the lower 10 m of kerogenous, laminated carbonates in areas E and F (Figure 14-1, Table 14-1). If the correlation is valid, it is important to note that ostracodes are generally lacking in this unit throughout areas E and F. The unit in those areas is interpreted as a limnetic paleoenvironment.

From area D, the shroeline appears to have curved southeast. A section measured at location 19 in area H (Tipton Road section, Figure 14-11) contains stromatolites, abundant ostracodes, aragonitic-siliceous shales, and coarse-grained sediments.

TR-9 (Figure 14-8F) is typical of the ostracode-rich laminated carbonates in the littoral paleoenvironments of areas H and I. Disarticulated fish bones and complete *Knightia* occur in these ostra-

---

Figure 14-6
A. Conchostracans (clam shrimp) from AW, locality 17; B. Hymenopteran (ant) from BSR, locality 1; C. Dipteran (probably a robber fly, family Asilidae from BR, locality 10; D. Fish fry (probably *Knightia*) from BSR, locality 1; E. Juvenile catfish, from LSC, locality 2 (Photo courtesy of Lance Grande, University of Minnesota); F. Fish fry and juvenile fish (probably *Knightia*) from BSR, locality 1.

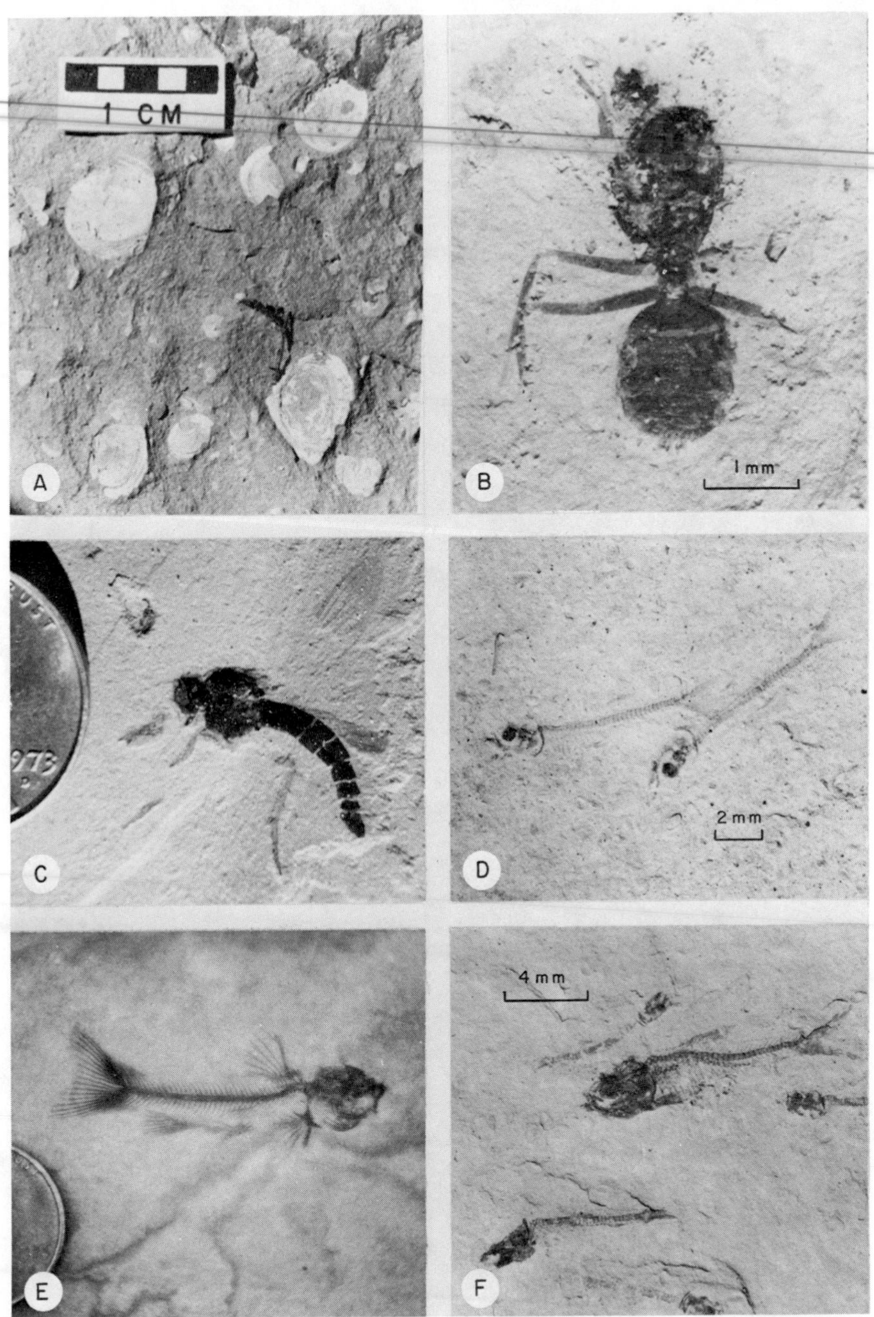
1 CM
A
B
1 mm
C
D
2 mm
E
F
4 mm

A
B
2 CM
C
D
E
Top
BRE
F

code-rich rocks.

TR-14, a massive unit, is interpreted as a shore strandline deposit because it contains flat-pebble conglomerate, abundant ostracodes, disarticulated fish bones and plant fragments. Flat-pebble conglomerates were probably transported into the lake from fringing mudflats (Surdam and Stanley, 1979). The activity of wave-zone waters, necessary for the accumulation of the coarse-grained debris, would also result in disarticulation of fish carcasses in a short period of time. Ostracodes, abundant in the littoral waters, would accumulate in the lag deposits. In areas H, I, and J, stromatolites are associated with strandline deposits of ostracodes (Figure 14-8D), flat-pebble conglomerate, fish bones, and oolites or pisolites. This stromatolite association is indicative of active, shallow waters in the littoral zone; the best known stromatolites occur in shore zones (Eardley, 1938; Logan et al., 1974).

The section measured at locality 21 (Antelope Creek section, Figures 14-5B, 14-12) is characteristic of sections in area I. It contains numerous littoral and epilittoral deposits (Figure 14-13A). Gradual lateral changes in shoreline litholigies can be traced perpendicular to the ancient shoreline for as much as 40 km parallel to time lines defined by tuff beds. The parallel-time relationship of these units implies a very low topographic gradient (Surdam and Stanley, 1979). The Antelope Creek section is in an intermediate paleogeographic position between the highest and lowest stands of the lake and reflects many fluctuations in lake depth. Toward the east, the rocks display increasing epilittoral characteristics.

For the most part, however, the Antelope Creek section is dominated by littoral characteristics: ostracodal limestones, pisolites, stromatolites, flat-pebble conglomerates, mudstones, siltstones, sandstones, disarticulated fish bones in strandline deposits, laminated carbonates rich in ostracodes, and some aragonitic-siliceous shales. Other sections measured within area I are similar to the Antelope Creek section.

Sections studied in area J (Figure 14-5) are similar to those in area I, having alternating laminated carbonates, strandline deposits and epilittoral dolomitic mudstones. However, this is only true for the lower third of the Shell Creek section (locality 23) and the lower half of Lookout Mountain section (locality 24). The upper two-thirds of the Shell Creek section is dominated by siliciclastic mudstones containing abundant ostracodes and disarticulated catfish bones (Figure 14-14B). The Lookout Mountain section shows the same trend except that the upper half consists of coarse-grained strandline deposits composed of ostracodes, catfish bones, and gastropod and pelecypod coquinas (Kornegay, 1976). About 80 percent of the sediment in the upper part of the Shell Creek section consists of quartz and clay minerals, suggesting proximity to a large fluvial system. These

---

Figure 14-7
A. *Equisetum* (horsetail) from BSR, locality 1; B. *Typha* (cattail) from BSR, locality 1; C. Water lily from GCSB, locality 8, found in stratigraphic equivalent of unit FG-29; D. Leaf with juvenile *Knightia* from BSR, locality 1; E. Mudstone with vertical *Equisetum* from BRE, locality 3 (note rootlets in circular pattern extending from stem); F. Mudstone with roots of *Equisetum* from BRE, locality 3 (an *Equisetum* stem extends vertically through the rock (not seen in photo)).

lithologies and fossil organisms indicate a littoral paleoenvironment.

Along the Uinta Mountain front in the Green River Basin, one finds littoral deposits similar to those in area I, but not many well-developed strandline deposits such as stromatolites, ostracodal limestones, or epilittoral dolomitic mudflat deposits. The large influx of siliciclastics from the nearby Uinta Mountains and the probable ponding of the lake against the Uinta front prevented widespread and cyclic transgressions and regressions in this area. However, a few stromatolitic units and dolomitic mudstones reflect some arid times when a high influx of siliciclastics was at a minimum.

Locality 17 (Anvil Wash section, Figure 14-5F, 14-15) is an interesting section that contains an assemblage of fossils similar to that found at the Big Sandy River section: insects, juvenile *Knightia*, and plant fragments. In addition, abundant conchostracans (clam shrimp, Figure 14-6A) occur throughout the section. They live today in the littoral zones of lakes, ponds, and temporary pools; a few live in muddy water or alkaline pools (Klots, 1966). Tasch (1973:562) notes, "successive generations of conchostracans in a thin slab of calcareous argillite denote seasonal wetting and drying cycles." In the upper part of the section, conchostracans occur in a cyclic fashion between pulses of quartz-rich sediment. Perhaps these pulses represent flooding followed by drying cycles.

Sediments, fossils, and the paleogeographic position at the edge of the basin close to the Uinta Mountains indicate that a littoral paleoenvironment existed at locality 17.

In the western part of the Green River Basin, particularly in the south, Laney sediments are poorly exposed. Bradley (1964) measured a section consisting primarily of mudstones and muddy sandstones in the extreme southwestern part of the basin (T. 14 N., R. 117 W.). He reported no fish remains.

In area A, lacustrine rocks consist of thick, ripple cross-laminated sandstones; some interbedded laminated carbonates; mudstones; and several stromatolite units. The thick sands, some with large-scale trough-stratification, contain masses of compressed fossil logs. These features suggest significant fluvial influence during deposition.

At least one of the fine-grained, well-laminated units (locality 18) contains an assemblage of reed stems (probably *Typha*, juvenile *Knightia*, and a few leaves of higher plants. *Astephus* is also present in shales in this area. Lance Grande (pers. comm.) also found the above species in the area as well as remains of *Equisetum*, uncommon *Asineops*, *Diplomystus*, and *Amyzon* (sucker). These fossils and sediments suggest a littoral paleoenvironment for area A.

Figure 14-8
A. Silicified tree in vertical position from LSC, locality 2; B. Juvenile *Knightia* from BSR, locality 1; C. Shale with alternating aragonite, clay laminae (note *Knightia*) from LM, locality 24; D. Algal stromatolite from ostracodal strandline deposit (note ostracodes in depressions) from TR, locality 19; E. Algal stromatolites protruding through a feldspathic-quartz siltstone. Silicified tree trunks are also associated with this unit; F. Laminated carbonate composed primarily of ostracodes (note disarticulated fish bones) from TR, locality 19.

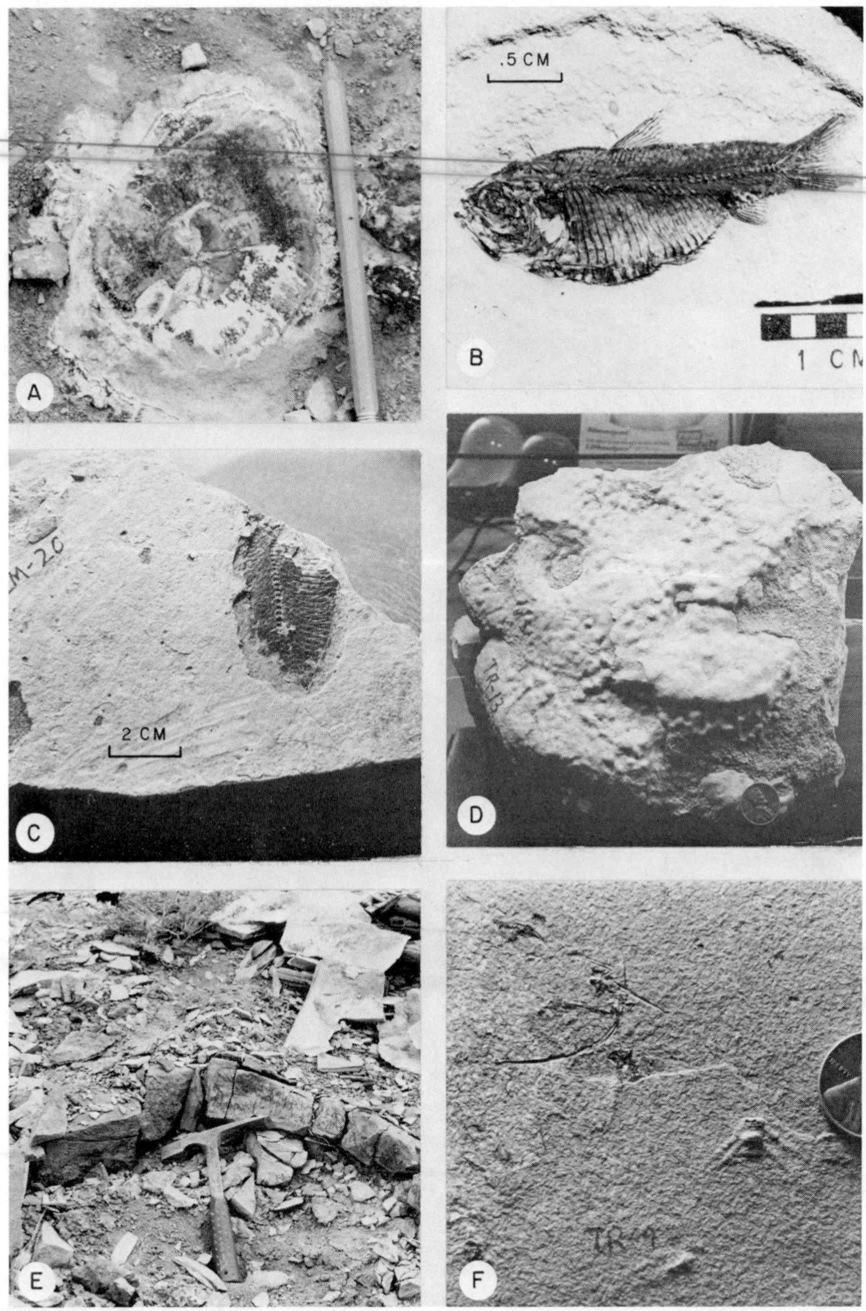
.5 CM
B
1 CM
A
M-20
2 CM
C
TR-13
D
E
TR-9
F

A
8 CM
B
3 CM
C
10 CM
D
20 CM
E
5 CM
F

THE LITTORAL PALEOCOMMUNITY

The littoral paleocommunity of ancient Lake Gosiute (Figures 14-14, 14-17) is characterized by an association of juvenile *Knightia*, ostracodes, *Equisetum*, *Typha*, and fish fry. These fossil organisms and terrestrial insects may be considered an assemblage characteristic of the littoral paleocommunity. Variations of the association include the occasional addition of catfish (*Astephus* and *Hypsidoris*), juvenile catfish, *Lepisosteus*, *Amia*, and crocodile. The association of ostracodes and stromatolites characterize the littoral paleocommunity during arid stages.

THE LIMNETIC PALEOENVIRONMENT

Fine-grained carbonate sediments typically occupy the central limnetic areas of lakes (Twenhofel, 1932). The Flaming Gorge section (Figures 14-18, 14-5C) is typical of sections studied in areas E and F. It represents a central position in Lake Gosiute and is characterized by well-laminated, fine-grained, carbonate-rich rocks (Figure 14-14D). Coarse-grained rocks such as sandstones, siltstones, and mudstones and littoral features including stromatolites, oolites, pisolites, and ostracodal limestones are conspicuously absent.

Carbonate content averages over 60 percent (X-ray diffraction data) and organic content about 8 percent (weight), particularly in the lower 10 m of the Laney Member. Laminated rocks in areas interpreted as littoral usually contain less than 40 percent carbonate minerals and less than 5 percent organic carbon. This relationship is probably due to the siliciclastics being filtered out in the littoral zone by vegetation and/or settling out before reaching the open waters of the limnetic environment.

An association of fishes well adapted to open waters of the limnetic zone is abundantly represented in areas E and F. Numerous *Knightia* (as many as 25/m^2) occur in particular laminae within units (Figure 14-10D), especially in the lower 10 m. Like their modern relatives the herring-type fishes, *Knightia* probably swam about in schools foraging on the abundant phytoplankton. Their schooling and feeding habits necessitate open water of the limnetic environment.

Predatory fishes include *Phareodus* (Figure 14-9A) and *Priscacara*; these occur uncommonly in comparison to the large numbers of *Knightia*. Predators, however, are higher order consumers than *Knightia* and are usually less abundant in modern ecosystems as well.

Scavenging *Astephus* (catfish, Figure 14-10A, B) and *Amyzon* (sucker) could have been attracted by mass mortalities of *Knightia* and other fishes. Both the catfish and the suckers probably occupied the lower trophogenic zone because they are bottom feeders. Catfish are adapted to low oxygen, turbid waters (Sigler and Miller, 1963).

Erismatopterus (pirate perch, Figure 14-10F) occur abundantly in

---

Figure 14-9
A. *Phareodus* (University of Wyoming collection); B. *Priscacara* (bass-like fish, University of Wyoming collection); C. *Diplomystus* with smaller *Priscacara* (University of Wyoming collection); D. *Amia* (bowfin), from LSC, locality 2 (Photo courtesy of Lance Grande, University of Minnesota); E. *Lepisosteus* (gar, University of Wyoming collection); F. *Asineops* (pirate perch) from GCSB, locality 8.

several rich oil shales. They probably filled the niche of *Knightia* when lake conditions were extremely eutrophic.

THE LIMNETIC PALEOCOMMUNITY

The limnetic paleocommunity of ancient Lake Gosiute (Figures 14-16, 14-17) is characterized by an association of adult *Knightia*, *Phareodus*, *Priscacara*, *Astephus*, *Asineops*, and *Erismatopterus*. Large schools of adult *Knightia* are most characteristic of the limnetic paleocommunity. Abundant phytoplankton served as the primary producers. Invertebrate organisms such as molluscs were absent, perhaps due to intolerable salinities. Hanley (1974, 1976) pointed out that molluscs found in the Green River Formation are intolerant of saline waters. It is doubtful that the absence of molluscs is due to anaerobic conditions because the presence of abundant bottom-dwelling *Astephus* suggests aerobic conditions. Abundant coprolites associated with the catfish (Figure 14-14E) show that the catfish were a resident population. Buchheim and Surdam (1977) showed that aerobic conditions existed in the hypolimnia of ancient Lake Gosiute, at least for intervals of time.

MODIFICATIONS OF PALEOENVIRONMENTS BY CLIMATIC CYCLES

Some of the rocks studied in areas E and F contain fossils characteristic of the littoral paleoenvironment. For example, FG-29 contains an assemblage of plant remains (pond lily, Figure 14-7C), insects (Figures 14-6C, 14-14C), ostracodes, and uncommon to rare *Knightia*. It also contains significant amounts of aragonite. These features appear anomalous until the entire context of the rocks is considered. Unit FG-29 grades upward into a poorly laminated, dolomitic carbonate that stands out as a conspicuous marker when observed from a distance (Figure 14-18). This bed will be referred to as the "Orange Marker" and is correlative with the Buff Marker in the Washakie Basin (Surdam and Stanley, 1979). The Orange Marker is irregularly laminated and is dolomitic. It contains common, erratic sediment chips and calcite pseudomorphs after saline minerals, probably trona (Figures 14-13B, 14-14F). It also contains 10 to 20 percent more silicate minerals than the lower 10 m of calcareous carbonates.

Farther north, at location 7 (Scotts Canyon section), the Orange Marker contains ripple cross laminations, lenticular laminae, and small scour and fill structures, and rip-up clasts (Figure 14-13E, F). These characteristics, particularly the pseudomorphs after saline minerals, and the dolomite suggest that the lake was highly saline and alkaline (Surdam and Stanley, 1979) during deposition of the Orange Marker. The Orange Marker, therefore, represents an arid period when the lake regressed to a very low level.

Figure 14-10
A. *Astephus antiquus* from GCSB, locality 8 (note coprolites); B. *Astephus antiquus* in thin laminae of brown clay on top of a thickly laminated dolomite, from LC, locality 15; C. *Knightia* (herring) from GCSB, locality 8; D. Mass mortality of *Knightia* from GCSB, locality 8; E. *Amyzon* (sucker) from GCSB, locality 8 (Photo courtesy of Lance Grande, University of Minnesota); F. *Erismatopterus* (pirate perch) from GCSB, locality 8.

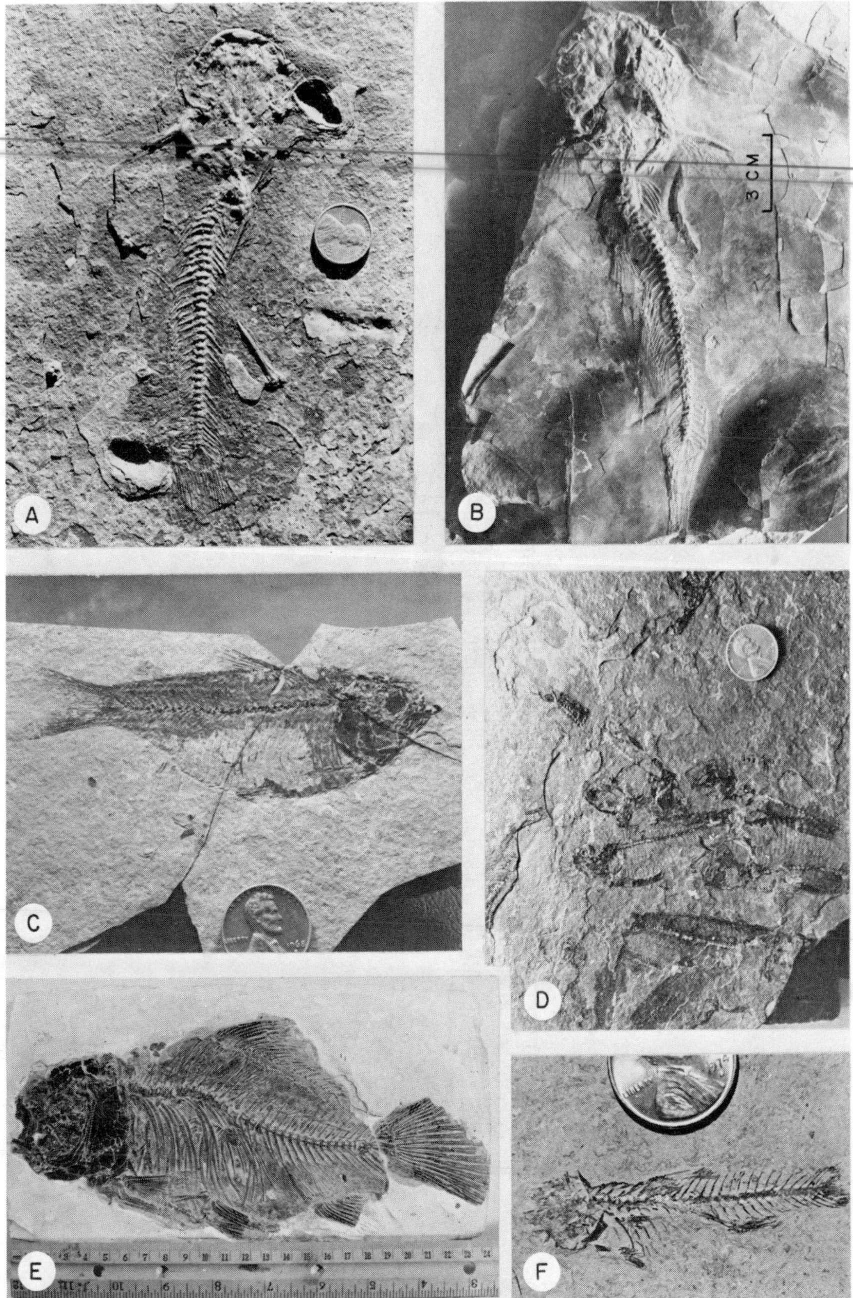
A
B
3 CM
C
D
E
F

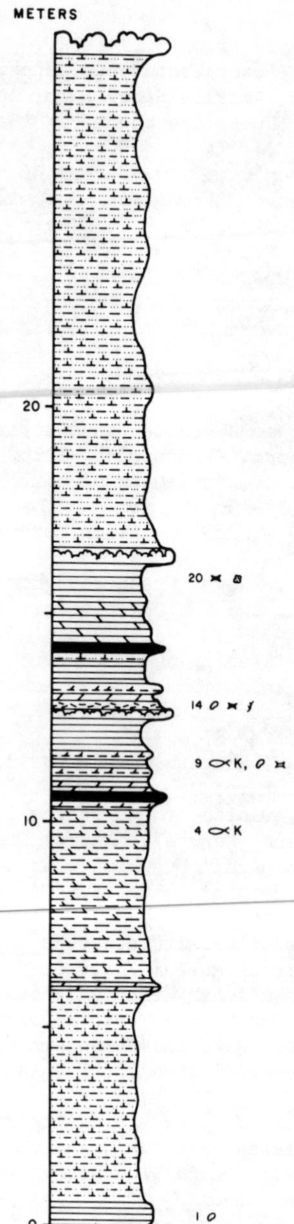

Figure 14-11
Tipton Road stratigraphic section, locality 19.

South of the Flaming Gorge section, the Orange Marker is dominated by siltstone and contains stromatolites. Recent stromatolites that are morphologically similar to those in the Green River Formation form today in the highly saline waters of Hamelin Pool (Sharks Bay), Australia (Logan et al., 1974). The sedimentary structures at the

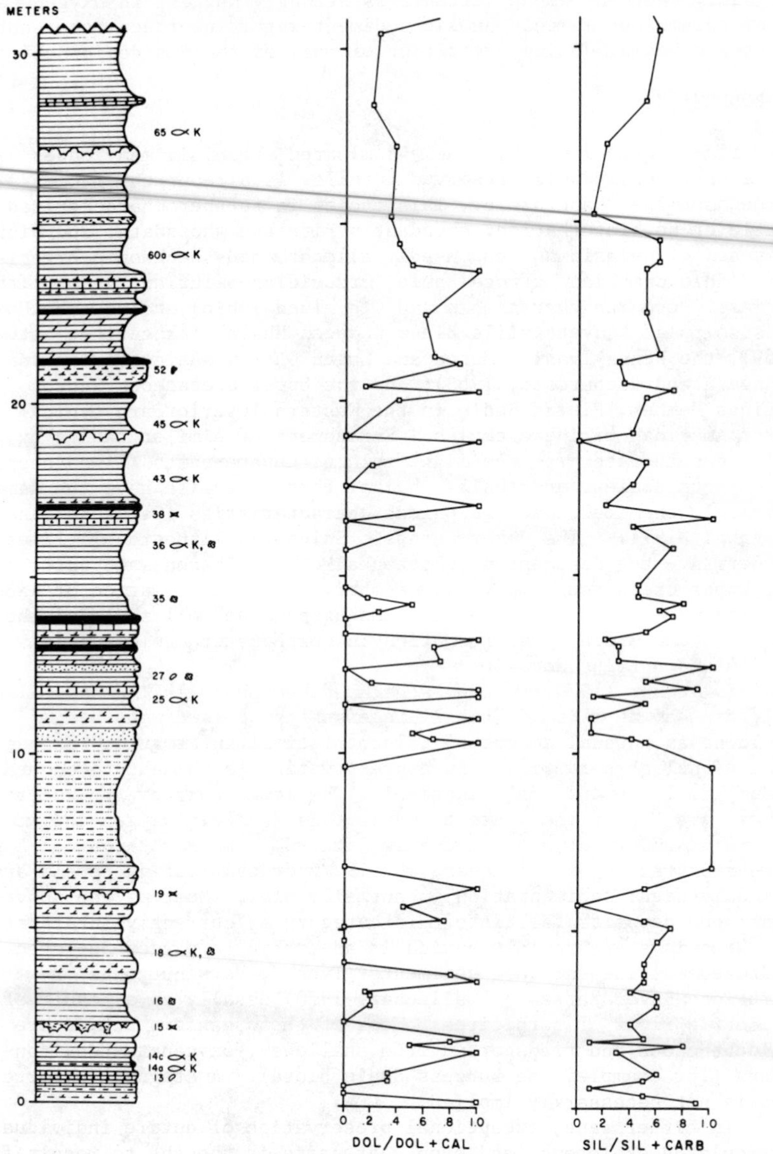

Figure 14-12
Antelope Creek stratigraphic section, locality 21.

Scotts Canyon section suggest that a mudflat affected by sheet wash was present there.

These features help to explain the apparently anomalous littoral characteristics in FG-29. This unit probably represents a transition period between a wet an an arid cycle when the waters were still fresh enough to support life in and around a restricted lake perhaps a meter or two deep. The entire lake was basically a littoral paleoenviron-

2 CM
A
B
2 CM
C
D
1 CM
E
1 CM
F

ment. Its restricted, shallow nature allowed life adapted to a littoral environment to invade the site of a former limnetic environment; skulls of two crocodiles in FG-56 also indicate such an invasion. Expansive mudflats surrounding the lake and lack of precipitation prevented coarse sediments from reaching the lake margins. During deposition of the dolomite-rich carbonates of the Orange Marker, the lake was too saline and alkaline to support much life except insects.

The Orange Marker was the first major arid cycle during Laney deposition. Note that the Flaming Gorge section (Figures 14-5C, 14-18) is dominated by dolomitic sediments and is interrupted occasionally by relatively thin units of calcitic rocks that contain rich fossils. Even the lower 10 m of calcareous carbonates contain significant peaks (Figure 14-18) of dolomite, indicating intermediate stands of the lake. These regressions of the lake were dramatically reflected in the littoral environments that were left high and dry. This is indicated by much thinner sequences observed at the Antelope Creek section (Figures 14-5B, 14-12, 14-13D) and other marginal sections throughout areas H, I, and J. These cyclic fluctuations in lake size and salinity must have had a decided effect on the fish and other organisms. Needham and Lloyd (1916) suggest that in closed-basin lakes continually alternating between high and low stands, organisms must be able to withstand euryhaline conditions to survive. This may explain the occurence of *Knightia* and other fossil fishes in mass-mortality layers and the lack of fish fossils between these units. Fishes such as *Knightia* entered the lake during fresh, high stands only to succumb to change in salinity, alkalinity, oxygen, temperature, pH, or a combination of these during a regressive stage. The present evidence suggests that changing salinities were most responsible for the fish mortalities. The fact that *Knightia* are far more abundant than other fishes may be due to the ability of herring-type fishes to adjust easily to euryhaline conditions. The nearly complete absence of fishes in highly dolomitic rocks, such as the Orange Marker, reflects the high-saline conditions that existed during deposition of dolomitic rocks.

During major regressive stages of the lake and perhaps during intermediate stages, fish retreated to fringing lakes, lagoons,

---

Figure 14-13

A. *Astephus antiquus* from GCSB, locality 8. This specimen was found just above the Orange Marker. Note that even the soft parts are preserved as a dark organic film. B. Lower 20 m at Greens Canyon South-B section, locality 8. Note the pockets or holes in the upper light-colored sediments (Orange Marker). These are weathered-out molds of calcite pseudomorphs after saline minerals, probably trona, a sodium carbonate. Many have not been weathered out and cannot be seen in this photo. C. *Astephus antiquus* in a clay lamina on top of a thickly laminated dolomite, from LC, locality 15. D. Sedimentary cycles at Antelope Creek section, locality 21. Note stromatolitic layer near base and massive dolomicrite in center (AC-52). E. Laminated dolomicrite from the Orange Marker SC-52 at Scotts Canyon, locality 7. Ferroan-dolomite, high Mg calcite, calcite, and other silicate mineral grains are concentrated in the lenticular laminae. A tuffaceous ripple cross-laminated sandstone has scoured the top of the dolomicrite and incorporated dolomitic clasts and peloids within it. F. Laminated dolomicrite from SC, locality 7.

ponds, and rivers. Remnant populations survived in these marginal areas. Evidence supporting this hypothesis is the presence of fish remains in the fluvial Cathedral Bluffs tongue of the Wasatch Formation (McGrew, 1975) and in the fluvial Bridger Formation (McGrew and Sullivan, 1970). The Cathedral Bluffs tongue is correlative with the Wilkins Peak Member, which contains abundant saline minerals and is interpreted as a highly saline lake (Eugster and Hardie, 1975). Also, disarticulated fish remains in strandline deposits and rare fish in laminated dolomites suggest the occasional entrance of fish into the lake during arid times. Perhaps they entered with occasional floods over the fringing mudflats. Most of the time, however, rivers terminated on the mudflats or in fringing swamps, lagoons, and marshes before reaching the lake (Surdam and Stanley, 1979). The presence of *Astephus* in quartz and clay-rich laminae underlain by a thickly laminated dolomite (Figures 14-10B, 14-13C) is additional evidence that fish entered the lake during floods of fresh inflow waters. This situation occurs at the Lowe Canyon section, locality 15. The quartz and clay suggest that an ephemeral river reached the lake for a short time, transporting siliciclastics into the lake. The catfish apparently entered the lake during this event.

A similar situation exists today at Great Salt Lake, Utah. The Bear River terminates in a series of marshes (Bear River Migratory Bird Refuge) fringing the mudflat. These marshes contain numerous carp that were observed attempting to escape upstream into the Bear River during the spring of 1977. The marshes were rapidly drying up and many of the carp had already died. Hundreds of carp skulls, vertebrae, and other bones lay half buried in the mud; and complete carp were observed washed up on an oolite beach of Great Salt Lake at Promontory Point. As fish are not known to inhabit the highly saline lake, they had to enter it from fringing marshes and rivers, probably during spring flooding of the flats. If the carp originated from the Bear River area, they would have had to travel some 25 km over temporarily flooded mudflats. It is also possible that they entered from another tributary area such as the Weber River or the marshes of Farmington Bay. In any case, temporarily flooded mudflats must have allowed access to the lake.

The wet and arid stages and their accompanying paleocommunities are illustrated in Figures 14-16 and 14-17.

FINAL FILLING OF LAKE GOSIUTE

Surdam and Stanley (1979) showed that Lake Gosiute was filled primarily from the north by prograding siliciclastic beaches and mudflats. This becomes apparent when one observes the relative stratigraphic position of the siliciclastics in sections selected along a

---

Figure 14-14
A. Strandline deposit of carp bones from marsh area at the Bear River Migratory Bird Refuge, Great Salt Lake, Utah; B. Mudstone with masses of disarticulated catfish bones from SC, locality 23; C. *Typha* with Coleoptera (probably a ground beetle, family Carabidae) and Diptera (fly) from BSR, locality 1; D. Thin section of finely laminated kerogenous carbonate with catfish bone (*Astephus*) from GCSB, locality 8; E. Fossil coprolites from GCSB, locality 8; F. Calcite pseudomorphs after saline minerals, probably trona, from GCSB, locality 8.

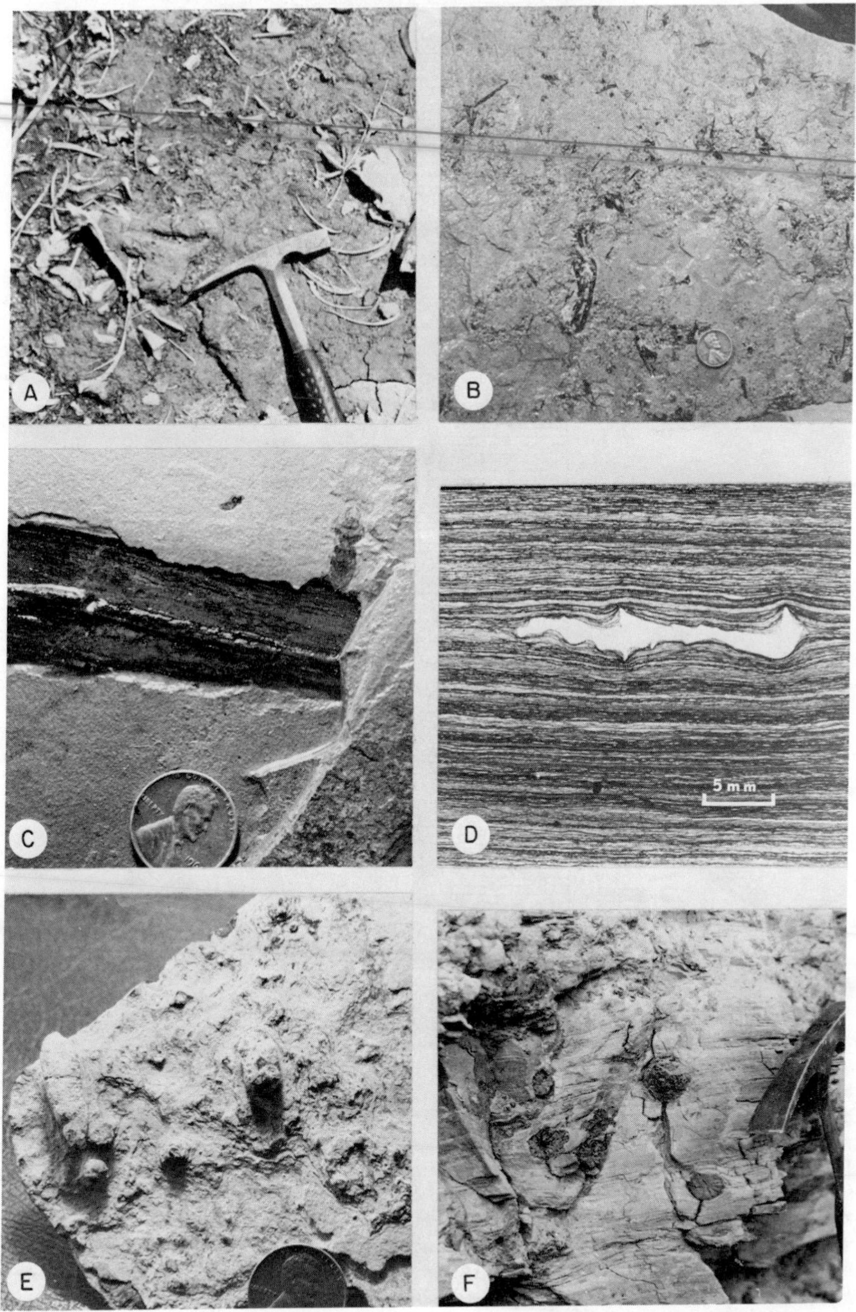
A
B
C
D
5 mm
E
F

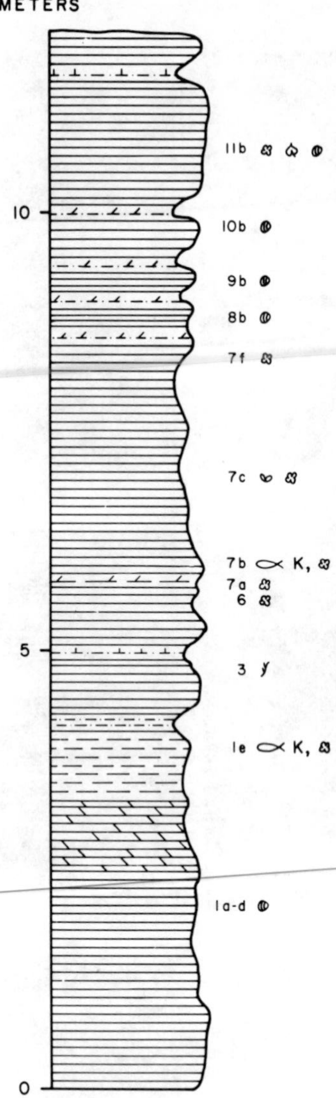

Figure 14-15
Anvil Wash stratigraphic section, locality 17.

north-south traverse. Lacustrine sediments are much thicker towards the south, indicating that the lake existed there longer. Kornegay (1976) also recognized this in the Sand Wash Basin, which was the southern extremity of Lake Gosiute. He shows that during later stages the lake was no longer closed, but overflowed to the south and existed as a shallow freshwater littoral paleoenvironment. This is indicated by stratigraphic relationships and the common occurrence of molluscs that require freshwater (Hanley, 1974, 1976). A prograding siliciclastic wedge finally filled the remnant lake, ending Lake

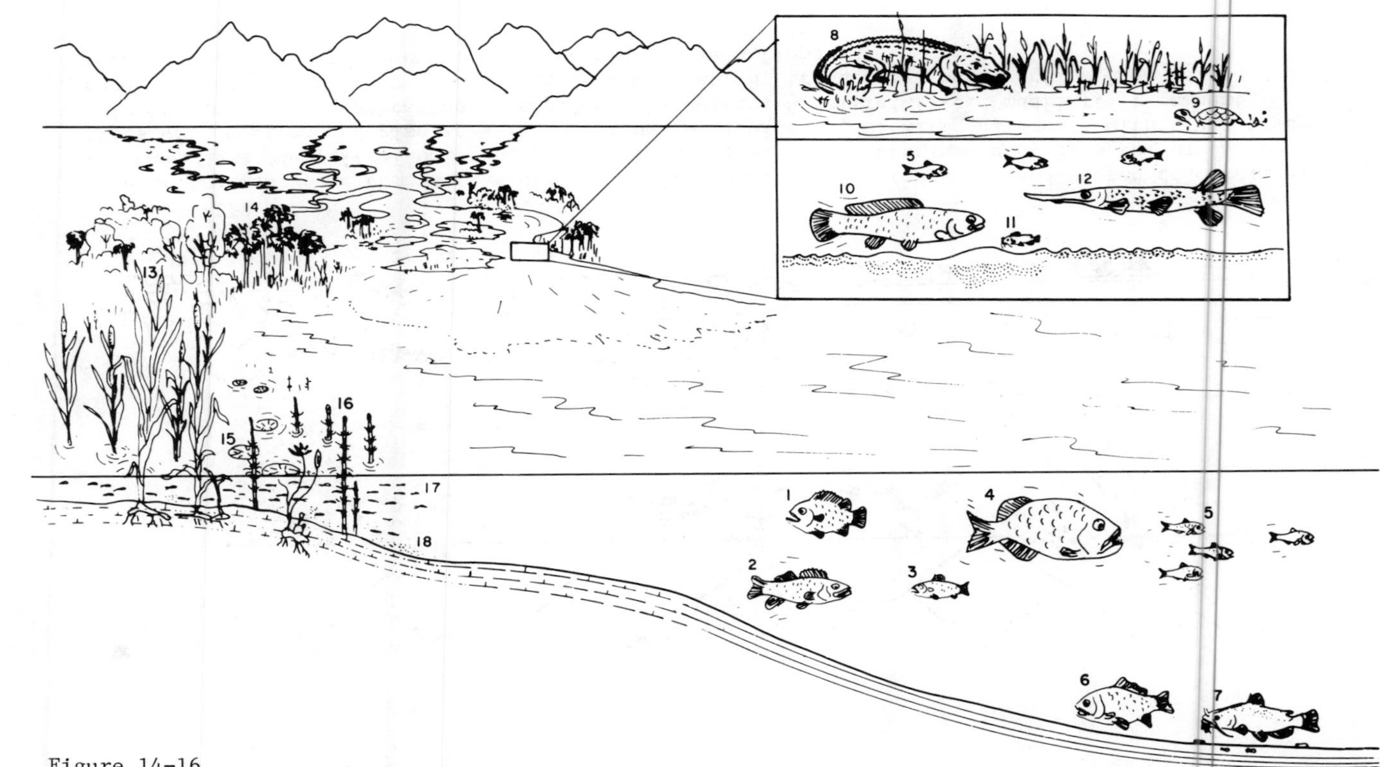

Figure 14-16
Paleoenvironments and communities of Lake Gosiute during humid stage: 1. *Priscacara*, 2. *Asineops*, 3. *Erismatopterus*, 4. *Phareodus*, 5. school of adult *Knightia*, 6. *Amyzon*, 7. *Astephus*, 8. crocodile, 9. *Knightia*, 10. *Amia*, 11. juvenile catfish, 12. *Lepisosteus*, 13. *Typha*, 14. palms, 15. pond lilies, 16. *Equisetum*, 17. fish fry, 18. ostracodes.

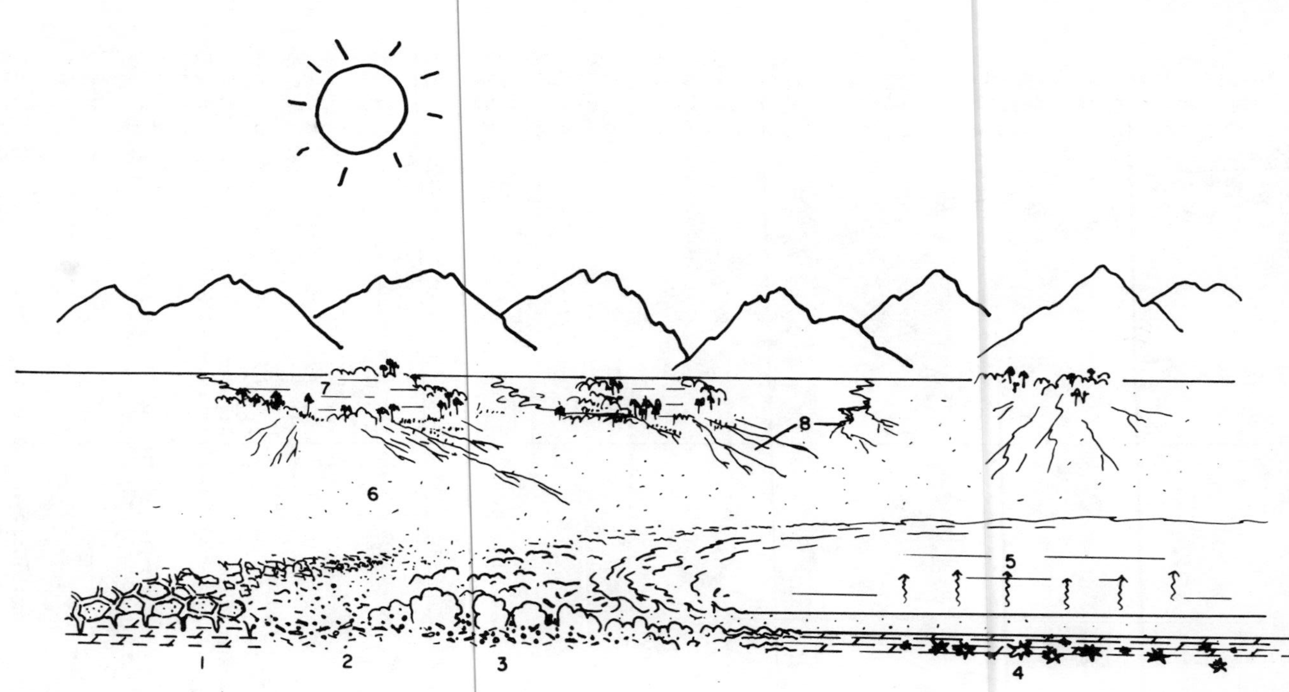

Figure 14-17
Paleoenvironments and communities of Lake Gosiute during arid stage: 1. Mudcracked dolomicrite, 2. strandline deposit of oolites, pisolites, and flat-pebble conglomerate, 3. algal stromatolites with oolites and pisolites in wave zone, 4. laminated dolomitic carbonate with trona crystals, 5. intensive evaporation of shallow lake waters, 6. siliciclastic mudflat, 7. remnant ponds, lakes, and marshes on outer edge of mudflat, 8. tributaries and overflow from marshes terminate on mudflat, except during occasional flash floods.

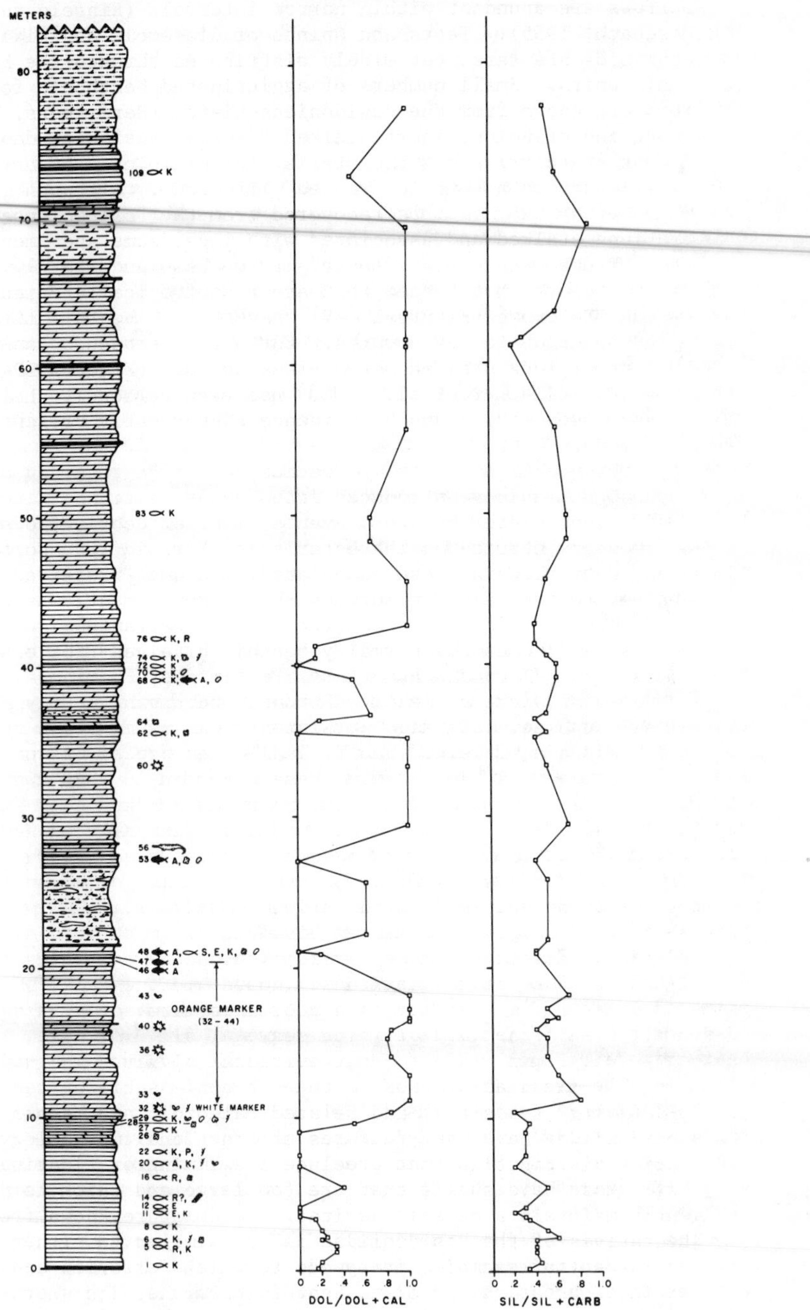

Figure 14-18
Flaming Gorge stratigraphic section, locality 12.

Gosiute's existence and bringing to a close deposition of Laney sediments.

SYNOPSIS

Two major paleoenvironments and paleocommunities, littoral and limnetic, can be recognized in the sediments of ancient Lake Gosiute. Each is characterized by a combination of organic and physical characteristics.

The characteristics of these environments and communities during high stands of the lake are summarized in Figure 14-16. The littoral zone was inhabited by numerous fish fry, juvenile *Knightia* (herring), less common *Priscacara* (sun fish), and *Astephus* and *Hypsidoris* (catfishes). Turtles and crocodiles entered the lake occasionally, but were primarily inhabitants of the fluvial environment. Insects were common inhabitants of the shore zones. Ostracodes thrived in such numbers at times that their remains contributed greatly to the sediments. The shallows were heavily vegetated by *Equisetum* (horsetails), *Typha* (cattails), and other emergent vegetation. Palms and other trees flourished along the rivers and in the moist lowlands surrounding the lake. Coarse-grained sediments entering the lake were deposited as calcareous sandstones, siltstones, and mudstones.

The limnetic environment and community was characterized by large schools of adult *Knightia*, and predaceous fishes such as *Phareodus* and *Priscacara*. *Astephus* and *Amyzon* scavenged in the turbid low-oxygen waters of the trophogenic zone.

During arid times (Figure 14-17) when the lake was greatly restricted and surrounded by expansive carbonate mudflats, most of the fish found sanctuary in small lakes, ponds, marshes, lagoons and rivers that existed on the margins of the mudflats. Most tributaries terminated on the mudflats, but during periods of heavy precipitation, they reached the lake as sheet wash or flash floods. Fish entered the lake during the floods, but died when the fresh flood waters mixed with the highly saline-alkaline lake waters. Their remains became preserved in aragonitic-siliceous shales and clay laminae or as disarticulated bones in strandline deposits.

Calcareous deposits such as stromatolites, oolites, pisolites, and ostracodal limestones formed in the littoral zones. Mud-cracked sediments surrounding the lake were ripped up during sheet-wash floods and deposited as flat-pebble conglomerates in the lake. Sodium carbonate minerals, such as trona, precipitated as radial crystals in the dolomitic lake sediments.

Ancient Lake Gosiute was filled primarily from the north by a prograding siliciclastic wedge of sediments. In its waning stages, it existed as a shallow freshwater lake with an outflow. However, it was eventually filled by siliciclastic sediments (Surdam and Stanley, 1979).

The relationship of the fossil fishes and their associated organisms to the sediments of the Laney Member of the Green River Formation supports the concept of a shallow lake with oscillating levels in a hydrographically closed basin with a low topographic gradient.

ACKNOWLEDGMENTS

We are especially indebted to Carole Buchheim for the excellent drafting and many hours spent in typing preliminary drafts of this paper.

Others we would like to acknowledge for their support are: Ray Kablanow for his assistance in the field through three field seasons; Venus Clausen for typing of the final manuscript as it appears in this volume; Dr. Ken Stanley of Ohio State University for his suggestions; Dr. Paul McGrew and Dr. George Baxter of the University of Wyoming for their suggestions; and to Dr. Jack Murphy for chemical analysis of rock samples.

Financial support from the National Geographic Society, the National Science Foundation (EAR 77-08636), Marathon Oil Company, the Geological Society of America (two Penrose grants), and from the National Sigma Xi and University of Wyoming Chapter of Sigma Xi is gratefully acknowledged.

This work formed part of a Ph.D. dissertation completed in 1978 at the University of Wyoming.

REFERENCES

Baer, J. L. 1969. Paleoecology of cyclic sediments of the Lower Green River Formation, Central Utah. *Brigham Young Univ. Geology Studies* 16:3-95.

Berner, R. A. 1975. The role of magnesium in the crystal growth of calcite and aragonite from sea water. *Geochim. et Cosmochim. Acta* 39:489-504.

Bradley, W. H. 1926. Shore phases of the Green River Formation in northern Sweetwater County, Wyoming. *U.S. Geol. Survey Prof. Paper* 140D:121-131.

Bradley, W. H. 1948. Limnology and the Eocene Lakes of the Rocky Mountain Region. *Geol. Soc. American Bull.* 59:635-648.

Bradley, W. H. 1963. Paleolimnology. In D. G. Frey, ed., *Limnology in North America.* Madison: The University of Wisconsin Press, pp. 621-648.

Bradley, W. H. 1964. Geology of the Green River Formation and associated Eocene rocks in southwestern Wyoming and adjacent parts of Colorado and Utah. *U.S. Geol. Survey Prof. Paper* 496-A, 86 p.

Bradley, W. H., and H. P. Eugster. 1969. Geochemistry and paleolimnology of the trona deposits and associated authigenic minerals of the Green River Formation of Wyoming. *U.S. Geol. Survey Prof. Paper* 496-B, 71 p.

Buchheim, H. P., and R. C. Surdam. 1977. Fossil catfish and the depositional environment of the Green River Formation, Wyoming. *Geology* 5:196-198.

Cope, E. D. 1877. A contribution to the knowledge of the icthyological fauna of the Green River Shales. *U.S. Geol. Geog. Survey Territories Bull.* 3:807-819.

Cope, E. D. 1884a. The Vertebrata of the Tertiary Formations of the West, Book 1 (text). *Geol. Survey of the Territories Rept.* Washington, D.C.: U.S. Government Printing Office, 3:1-1009.

Cope, E. D. 1884b. The Vertebrata of the Tertiary Formations of the West, Book 2 (plates). *Geol. Survey of the Territories Rept.* Washington, D.C.: U.S. Government Printing Office, 3:50 plates.

Eardley, A. J. 1938. Sediments of Great Salt Lake, Utah. *Am. Assoc. Petroleum Geologists Bull.* 22:1305-1411.

Eastman, C. R. 1917. Fossil fishes in the collection of the United States Museum. *U.S. Natl. Mus. Proc.* 39:235-304.

Eugster, H. P., and L. A. Hardie. 1975. Sedimentation in an ancient playa-lake complex: the Wilkins Peak Member of the Green River Formation of Wyoming. *Geol. Soc. American Bull.* 86:319-334.

Hanley, J. H. 1974. *Systematics, Paleoecology, and Biostratigraphy of Nonmarine Mollusca from the Green River and Wasatch Formations (Eocene) Southwestern Wyoming and Northwestern Colorado.* Ph.D. dissertation, University of Wyoming, 285 p.

Hanley, J. H. 1976. Paleosynecology of nonmarine Mollusca from the Green River and Wasatch formations (Eocene), southwestern Wyoming and northwestern Colorado. In R. W. Scott and R. R. West, eds., *Structure and Classification of Paleocommunities.* Stroudsburg, Pa.: Dowden, Hutchinson & Ross, pp. 235-261.

Hayden, F. V. 1871. Preliminary report of the U.S. Geological Survey of Wyoming and portions of contiguous territories, 511 p.

Hutchinson, G. E. 1967. *A Treatise on Limnology: Introduction to Lake Biology and the Limnoplankton.* New York: John Wiley and Sons, 1115 p.

Kauffman, E. G., and R. W. Scott. 1976. Basic concepts of community ecology and paleoecology. In R. W. Scott and R. R. West, eds., *Structure and Classification of Paleocommunities*. Stroudsburg, Pa.: Dowden, Hutchinson & Ross, pp. 1-28.

Klots, E. B. 1966. *The New Field Book of Freshwater Life*. New York: G. P. Putnam's Sons, 398 p.

Kornegay, G. L. 1976. *Lithologic Mineralogic and Paleontologic Variations in the Laney Member, Green River Formation, Sand Wash Basin and Southernmost Washakie Basin, Colorado and Wyoming*. M.S. thesis, University of Wyoming, 72 p.

Leidy, J. 1856. Notice of some remains of fishes discovered by Dr. John E. Evans. *Acad. Nat. Sci. Philadelphia Proc.* 8:256-257.

Logan, B. W., J. F. Reed, G. M. Hagan, P. Hoffman, R. G. Brown, P. J. Woods, and C. D. Gebelein. 1974. *Evolution and Diagenesis of Quaternary Carbonate Sequences, Sharks Bay, Western Australia*. Am. Assoc. Petroleum Geologists Mem. 22, 358 p.

Lundberg, J. G. 1975. The fossil catfishes of North America. *The Univ. of Michigan Papers on Paleontology* 11, 51 p.

Lundberg, J. G., and G. R. Case. 1970. A new catfish from the Eocene Green River Formation, Wyoming. *Jour. Paleontology* 44: 451-457.

McGrew, P. O. 1975. Taphonomy of Eocene fish from Fossil Basin, Wyoming. *Fieldiana-Geology* 33:257-270.

McGrew, P. O., and J. E. Burman. 1955. Geology of the Tabernacle Butte area, Sublette County, Wyoming. In *Wyoming Geol. Assoc. Field Conf. Guidebook* 10:108-111.

McGrew, P. O., and M. Casilliano. 1975. The geological history of Fossil Butte National Monument and Fossil Basin. *Nat. Park Service Occasional Paper* 3, 37 p.

McGrew, P. O., and R. Sullivan. 1970. The stratigraphy and paleontology of Bridger. *Wyoming Univ. Contr. Geology* 9:66-85.

Needham, J. G., and J. T. Lloyd. 1916. *The Life of Inland Waters*. Ithaca, New York: Comstock, 438 p.

Palmer, L. E., and H. S. Fowler. 1975. *Fieldbook of Natural History*, 2nd ed. New York: McGraw-Hill, 779 p.

Peale, A. C. 1879. Report on the geology of the Green River district. In F. V. Hayden, ed., *11th Annual Report U.S. Geol. Survey of the Territories*, pp. 509-646.

Perkins, P. L. 1970. Equitability and trophic levels in an Eocene fish population. *Lethaia* 3:301-310.

Reeves, C. C., Jr. 1968. *Introduction to Paleolimnology, Developments in Sedimentology 11*. Amsterdam: Elsevier Scientific Publishing Co., 228 p.

Reid, G. K. 1961. *Ecology of Inland Waters and Estuaries*. New York: Reinhold, 375 p.

Schaeffer, B., and M. Mangus. 1965. Fossil lakes from the Eocene. *Am. Mus. Nat. History Bull.* 74:11-21.

Sigler, W. F., and R. R. Miller. 1963. Fishes of Utah. Salt Lake City: Utah Dept. Fish and Game, 203 p.

Surdam, R. C., and R. A. Sheppard. 1978. Zeolites in saline, alkaline-lake deposits. In L. Sand and F. Mumpton, eds., *Natural Zeolites*. New York: Pergamon Press, pp. 145-174.

Surdam, R. C., and K. O. Stanley. 1979. Lacustrine sedimentation during the culminating phase of Eocene Lake Gosiute, Wyoming (Green River Formation). *Geol. Soc. America Bull.* 90:93-110.

Surdam, R. C., and C. A. Wolfbauer. 1975. The Green River Formation--a playa-lake complex. *Geol. Soc. America Bull.* 86:335-345.

Tasch, P. 1973. *Paleobiology of the Invertebrates.* New York: John Wiley and Sons, 946 p.

Thorpe, M. R. 1938. Wyoming Eocene fishes in the Marsh collection. *Am. Jour. Sci.* 36:279-295.

Twenhofel, W. H. 1932. *Treatise on Sedimentation,* 2nd ed. Baltimore: Williams and Wilkins, 926 p.

15

Structure and Change in Three Eocene Invertebrate Communities from Nearshore-Marine Environments

Douglas A. Lawson and Michael J. Novacek

ABSTRACT

A modified principal-components analysis, applied to recent and ancient benthic communities, is especially suitable when the initial data matrix is large and consists of many samples of disparate size, as is characteristic of community data. Application of this technique to the study of the fauna of a southern California lagoon facilitated the recognition of four biotopes: proximal flood-tidal delta, distal flood-tidal delta, subtidal eelgrass, and intertidal. The relationships of the biotopes and communities accurately reflect the environmental gradients of sediment texture and geography of the lagoon. From a survey of feeding types, highly recurrent associations containing different trophic levels were identified as subunits within the invertebrate communities.

The analysis of a collection of middle Eocene invertebrates from San Diego, California, reveals the presence of three distinct communities associated with the Delmar, Ardath, and Scripps formations representing estuarine, offshore, and foreshore depositional environments, respectively. Significant variation through time in the structure (measured by a diversity index) of these Eocene communities was strongly correlated with fluctuations in trophic level, species, and predator dominance. Therefore, the possibility that these nearshore marine communities were highly integrated and capable of structural change in the absence of gross fluctuations in their physical environment remains to be falsified.

INTRODUCTION

The recognition and characterization of biotic communities is most refined in studies of living organisms, but only the fossil record can provide direct evidence of community change over long periods of time. Accordingly, paleoecological research can be responsible for major contributions to community studies of all categories.

In this study we wish to consider the recognition and characterization of ancient and living communities by means of the same quantitative technique, the patterns of community change over a significant period of time (greater than two million years), and the relationship of these patterns to ecological generalizations.

TECHNIQUES

The arsenal of multivariate techniques presently at the disposal of paleoecologists has stimulated an increased use of quantitative criteria in the recognition of communities (Anderson, 1971; Gevirtz et al., 1971; Parker, 1975; Stanton and Dodd, 1970; Valentine and Peddicord, 1967; Warme, 1971). The application of a modified version of principal-components analysis, designated here as community-components analysis, is demonstrated in studies of a modern lagoon and middle Eocene invertebrate (mainly molluscan) communities from nearshore-marine environments.

COMMUNITY-COMPONENTS ANALYSIS

The mathematical technique employed here to delineate both biogeographic and taxonomic associations is a modified, principal-components analysis. This multivariate statistical method attempts to reduce the originally observed variables to a smaller number of uncorrelated variates that are each composed of a set of highly correlated variables. Principal components may be given a geometrical interpretation that can be conveyed with a two-variate hypothetical example. The given variates X_1 and X_2 (Figure 15-1) have a high positive correlation as indicated by the linear cloud of sample points passing through the origin Z of the X_1 - X_2 coordinate system.

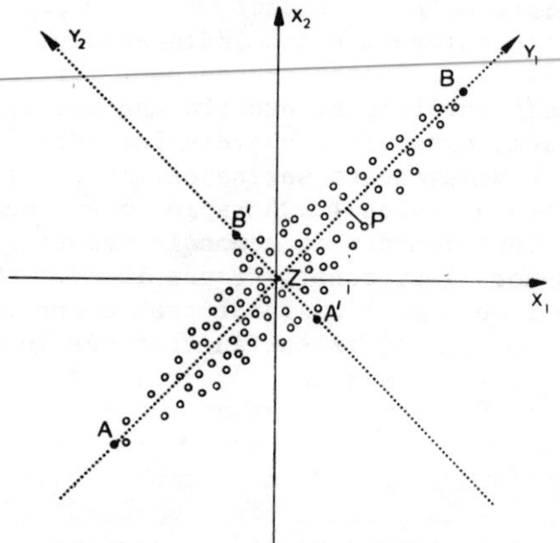

Figure 15-1
Geometric interpretation of principal components. X_1 and X_2 are the axes that represent two original variables whereas Y_1 and Y_2 represent the first and second principal components, respectively. The distance between points A and B represents the eigenvalue of Y_1. The distance between points A' and B' represents the eigenvalue of Y_2.

If Y_1 is made to pass through the mean point of this cloud, its orientation is defined by the cosine of the angles separating it from the original axes. The second principal component Y_2 is oriented at 90° to the first and has its orientation defined by two direction cosines. The first component passes through the cloud such that the projections of the sample points (such as P) display the maximum dispersion along the component. The dispersion or variance along each component is its eigenvalue (λ) and the set of cosines that defines its orientation is its eigenvector (a').

In the biogeographic mode of analysis (mode-1), each principal component represents a set of correlated taxa. This new coordinate system, composed of axes defined by groups of taxa, is used to position the localities in a new principal components space and to evaluate the similarity of taxonomic composition of such localities. In the taxonomic mode (mode-2), the roles of samples and the taxa are reversed.

More generally, the principal components of the universe of N p-dimensional observations are the new variates specified by the axes of a rigid rotation of the original variable coordinate system into an orientation corresponding to the directions of maximum variance. The direction cosines ($a_{11}, \ldots, a_{p1}$) of the new axes are the normalized eigenvectors corresponding to the sequentially smaller eigenvalues of the variable correlation matrix. If

$$Y_1 = a_{11}x_{11} + a_{21}x_{21} + \cdots + a_{p1}x_{p1}$$

where the eigenvector for this component is

$$a_1' = (a_{11}, a_{21}, \cdots, a_{p1})$$

with a_{ij} being the coefficients of the linear equation relating x_{ij} to Y_i, the standard variance of the projections of the samples to the Y_i axis is

$$\begin{aligned} \frac{s^2_{yi}}{\sigma_i\sigma_j} &= \frac{1}{\sigma_i\sigma_j} \cdot \frac{1}{N-1} \sum_{i=1}^{N} y_i^2 \\ &= \frac{1}{\sigma_i\sigma_j} \cdot \frac{1}{N-1} \sum_{i=1}^{N} (a_{j1}(x_{ij} - \bar{x}_j))^2 \\ &= \frac{1}{\sigma_i\sigma_j} \cdot \frac{1}{N-1} \sum_{i=1}^{N} ((x_i - \bar{x})a_1)^2 \\ &= a_1' C a_1 \end{aligned}$$

where $\sigma_i\sigma_j$ is the product of the standard deviations of the ith and the jth variables, s^2_y is the variance of Y_i, $\bar{x}_j$ is the mean of the jth variable, and C is the correlation matrix. Because we wish to pass this principal component through the direction of standardized maximum variance of all the sample points in the N-dimensional space, its eigenvector will be associated with the largest eigenvalue. The constraint on this maximization is

$$1 = \sum_{i=1}^{p} a_{i1} = a_1' a_1$$

which is the sum of the squares of all the cosines of the angles defining the position of the new first axis which equals one. This provides that the maximum variance is normalized. Subsequent eigenvectors, r, will not only have this constraint but will also have the constraint of being perpendicular to the preceding r-1 vectors:

$$a_r' a_r = 1$$

$$a_{r-1}' a_r = 0.$$

To maximize the function $g(a,\lambda)$ for the standard variance

$$a_1' C a_1$$

subject to the constraint $a_1' a_1 = 1$ on the values of a, the form of this new function is

$$g(a,\lambda) = a_1' C a_1 + (1 - a_1' a).$$

For the value of this new function to remain constant, its change with respect to a must equal zero. Therefore, the partial derivative of this new equation is a system of linear equations

$$(C - \lambda I)a = 0$$

defining the eigenvectors where C is the correlation matrix of the variables and I is the unit matrix (defined as a matrix in which all of the elements are equal to zero except those along the diagonal that are equal to one). The eigenvector matrix A is then post-multiplied by the initial matrix X to complete the rotational transformation to the principal-components coordinate system:

$$P = [A]\,[X]\ .$$

The position of the samples in the first and second principal-components space is usually plotted for visual inspection. Higher components are generally neglected because they have progressively lower eigenvalues.

The formulation of community-components analysis is based on two concepts fundamental to all qualitative assessments of communities. The first is the Continuum Theory, a spatial extension of Liebig's and Shelford's laws (Odum, 1959: 254). Because many physical regimes are congruent, the gradients at coincident boundaries are similar and the geographic variation in the abundance of individuals of taxa with similar tolerances are coincident and commensurate. Therefore, a community may be characterized as the region that contains the localities with the same taxonomic composition in relative proportions of individuals for like species. The second principal, the Trophic Theory (Odum, 1959: 49), states that a food web exists through which an energy flow is sustained from the primary producer to final consumer, and the energy entering each trophic level is less than that available to the preceding level. Therefore, a dynamically stable pyramid of numbers of individuals of distinct populations exists from abundant primary producers at the base to the scarce consumers at the top. A community may consequentially be characterized as a set of taxa maintaining a statistical constancy of proportional abundance of individuals within a given physical regime. The modifications that bring principal-components analysis into harmony with these basic ecological concepts are discussed below.

An initial matrix in which the rows are the samples (L_i), the columns are the taxa (S_j), and the elements of the matrix are the members of individuals for each taxon in the sample (x_{ij}) may be represented by

$$\begin{array}{cc} & S_j, S_{j+1}, \ldots\ldots S_n \\ \begin{array}{c} L_i \\ L_{i+1} \\ \cdot \\ \cdot \\ \cdot \\ L_m \end{array} & \left[\begin{array}{cccccc} x_{ij} & \cdots & \cdots & \cdots & \cdots & x_{in} \\ \cdot & \cdot & & & & \cdot \\ \cdot & & \cdot & & & \cdot \\ \cdot & & & \cdot & & \cdot \\ \cdot & & & & \cdot & \cdot \\ x_{mj} & \cdots & \cdots & \cdots & \cdots & x_{mn} \end{array}\right] \end{array}$$

One problem affecting community data arranged in such a matrix is that samples are often disparate in size. Such variation can give rise to artifacts of enhanced correlation among taxa. To alleviate this problem, one might calculate the percent contribution of each taxon to the total number of individuals from a locality. These percentage values could then substitute for the elements of the initial matrix. This approach, however, eliminates the actual numbers of individuals found at a locality. Moreover, any information on the degree to which a sample effectively represents a set of taxa in an optimal environment is lost. A preferable alternative is to divide the standard deviation for each sample (s_{1i}) into the appropriate row composed of elements that are the difference between the value of the initial element (x_{ij}) and the mean number of individuals in the sample. This produces a standard normal form for each row or a matrix of Z values

$$\begin{array}{cc} & S_j, S_{j+1}, \ldots\ldots S_n \\ \begin{array}{c} L_i \\ L_{i+1} \\ \cdot \\ \cdot \\ \cdot \\ L_m \end{array} & \left[\begin{array}{cccccc} z_{ij} & \cdots & \cdots & \cdots & \cdots & z_{in} \\ \cdot & \cdot & & & & \cdot \\ \cdot & & \cdot & & & \cdot \\ \cdot & & & \cdot & & \cdot \\ \cdot & & & & \cdot & \cdot \\ z_{mj} & \cdots & \cdots & \cdots & \cdots & z_{mn} \end{array}\right] \end{array}$$

where

$$z_{ij} = \frac{x_{ij} - \bar{x}_{\cdot j}}{s_{\cdot j}}$$

and $s_{\cdot j}$ is the standard deviation of the jth sample. In this way, each sample retains a reflection of the number of individuals observed and the problem of enhanced correlation due to marked disparity in sample size is alleviated. This produces a matrix that is a useful derivative of the initial matrix because the number of individuals of taxa that inhabit similar environments will deviate in the same manner from the mean number of individuals in samples taken from similar environments. Those from samples taken from different environments will deviate in different ways from one another.

A sum of squares cross-product correlation matrix C is then generated and the eigenvectors are calculated. From the above discussion, it can be understood why a high eigenvalue represents a set of taxa (for mode-1, biogeographic mode) composed of identically large numbers of individuals in their optimal environment and zero individuals outside of such an environment or a set of samples (for mode-2, taxonomic mode) in which some taxa contain many individuals and others are represented by no individuals. These sets can be discovered by examining the elements of the eigenvectors. The sum of the cosines of the angles defining the position of an eigenvector relative to an orthogonal coordinate system must equal one, and these new eigenvectors are themselves orthogonal. Conversely, the smaller the angle of separation between the eigenvector and the original coordinate, the closer is the element representing the cosine to one and the other elements to zero. However, many elements of the eigenvector matrix A will have values between zero and one, making interpretation of the sets of variables difficult. To aid in the interpretation of the eigenvectors, McCammon (1970) introduced a minimum entropy criterion for rotation of the small number of resulting eigenvectors within the degenerate matrix space. The rotated vectors approach more closely the original variables forming the set predominantly responsible for the eigenvector's position. The minimum entropy criterion is incorporated into this analysis.

In community-components analysis, a large number of eigenvalues are necessary to describe a major portion of the total variance of the original variables and each eigenvector generally includes only a small set of variables. Therefore, visual examination of the scatter of cases (samples in mode-1, taxa in mode-2) in a graph of any two principal components resulting from the matrix multiplication

$$P = [A]\,[B]$$

where B is the rotated matrix is virtually useless. Because of this problem and the desirability of describing communities on the basis of the Trophic Theory (dynamic stability of relative proportions of individuals or populations at different trophic levels), cases are correlated with one another in the principal-components space. For mode-1, the samples with the greatest similarity in proportions of individuals in the various sets (vectors) of taxa have the highest correlation coefficient. For mode-2, the taxa with the greatest similarity in proportions of individuals in the

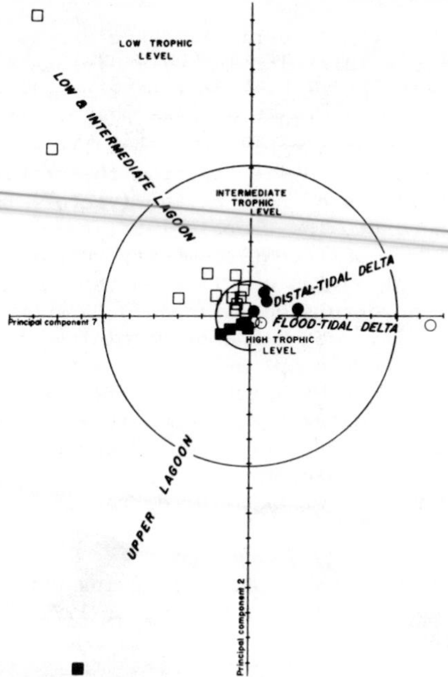

Figure 15-2
Graphic relation of cases and principal components. Community interpretation of Mugu Lagoon invertebrate distribution from mode-2. The position of component seven is controlled by the tidal delta localities (variables). The position of component two is controlled by upper lagoon localities (variables).

various sets of samples (vectors) have the highest correlation coefficient.

In community-components analysis, a search is made through this correlation matrix of cases to find the most highly correlated pair of cases that are closely spaced in a two-dimensional network. The procedure of single-linkage is continued until all the cases have been placed in the diagram at their point of highest correlation. The resulting plot is, therefore, derived from the product-moment correlation matrix of cases based on their constancy of proportional relation in the multidimensional space defined by the principal components, the latter being highly correlated sets of variables. The two-dimensional diagram is referred to here as an anagram if the array is composed primarily of acronyms and an ananum if composed primarily of numbers. The path through the anagram or ananum that connects the greatest number of cases is the major chain. Of course, within any highly correlated group in the network, the major chain passes through the cases with the highest correlation coefficients.

The relation between the biogeographic and taxonomic associations can be determined by plotting the cases on the principal-components coordinate system for those components whose orientation was shown to be controlled by particular variables. However, the bi- and trivariate plot must be interpreted in a special way, unlike that of a morphometric analysis where clusters of points are sought (Figure 15-2). Because the rotated eigenvector matrix B is premultiplied by the initial matrix X, the clusters of cases associated by their correlated distribution of individuals among variables expand along the component or explode from the origin of the bi- or trivariate graph due to the trophic-level distribution of taxa. For mode-2, taxa of the lowest trophic level usually contain the greatest number of individuals and lie far from the origin. Therefore, taxa of a community lie on or near a line (vector) that passes through the most abundant, low trophic-level taxa and the origin of the coordinate system. Different community vectors radiate out of the origin at different angles and lie closest to the component that describes the maximum correlated variance. By knowing the component closest to the community vector and by examining the multiplier-rotated eigenvector, the biotope associated with a particular group of taxa in a community can be determined. The same procedure may be employed to determine the taxonomic communities influencing the biotope pattern. Species habitat preferences and tolerances determine the nature of the biotope vector.

A program, COMMU, was written in Fortran IV to include the following items:

1. A principal-components analysis using Hottelling's accelerated iterative solution (Tatsuoka, 1971: 269).
2. An entropy criterion (developed by McCammon, 1970) for analytical rotation of eigenvectors.
3. A correlation matrix for cases in principal-components space.
4. An anagram or ananum for cases.
5. The Shannon-Weaver information index for each case.

Mode-1 of the program treats the localities as cases and the taxa as variables whereas mode-2 of the program treats the taxa as cases and the localities as variables. The former procedure is useful for recognizing biotopes or biogeographic zones through the association of localities according to their taxonomic composition; the latter is useful for recognizing communities based on taxon associations according to their individuals' distributions and abundance through the localities.

TEST OF COMMUNITY-COMPONENTS ANALYSIS

The effectiveness of community-components analysis can be demonstrated by considering data from a Recent California lagoon Warme (1971) collected approximately 45,000 tests of living and dead individuals representing 66 species of invertebrates (primarily molluscs and some echinoderms, crustaceans, and annelids) from fifty-five localities. Only the dead individuals are considered in this analysis because the numbers of living individuals of many taxa are small (often less than twenty) and dead assemblages approach closely fossil assemblages not far removed from their original habitats (Warme, 1971).

Figure 15-3 shows the mode-1 ananum for 42,179 tests of dead individuals representing sixty species taken from fifty-five localities in Mugu Lagoon. Locality numbers in Figure 15-3 correspond to the computer designations for the localities given in Warme's initial data matrix (Warme, 1971, Plate 1). The ananum may be

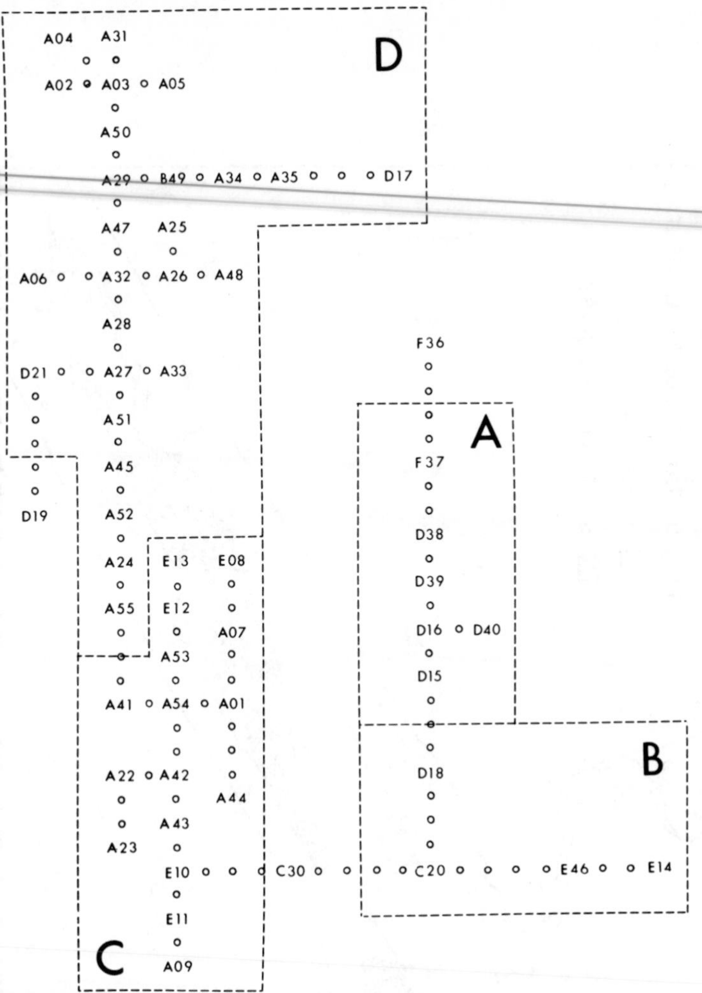

Figure 15-3
Mugu Lagoon Community ananum: mode-1. A = proximal flood-tidal delta biotope; B = distal flood-tidal delta biotope; C = intertidal biotope; D = subtidal-eelgrass biotope. The degree of correlation of the cases is indicated by the number of circles lying between them: one circle for $0.9 \leq r \leq 1.0$, two circles for $0.8 \leq r < 0.9$, three circles for $0.7 \leq r < 0.8$, and so forth. For alpha equal to 0.01 the critical r value is 0.641.

divided into two groups, A-B and C-D, that are separated by the lowest correlation along the major chain (r=0.6063) between localities 20 and 30. The loosely associated group A-B can be divided at the lowest correlation along the major chain within the group (r=0.7315) between localities 18 and 15. The more tightly associated group C-D may be divided at the lowest correlation of the major chain within the group (r=0.7539) between 41 and 55. These four divisions of the localities are mapped in Figure 15.4.

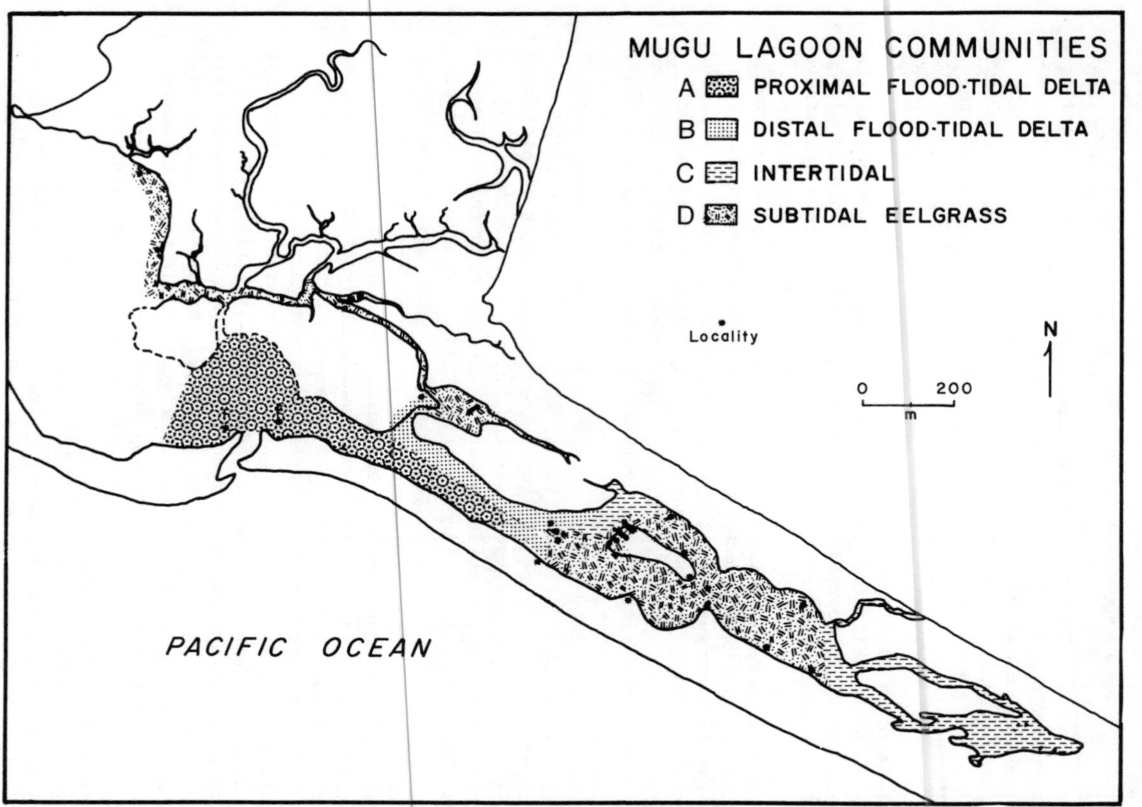

Figure 15-4
Biogeographic map of Mugu Lagoon based on mode-1 of community components analysis of dead invertebrates. (Base map modified from Warme, 1971).

The biotopes interpreted from the ananum form a continuous series of environments that extend from the flood-tidal delta to the uppermost lagoon following gradients in flow regime and sediment texture outlined by Warme (1971). The localities in group A of Figures 15-3 and 15-4 are interpreted as part of the proximal flood-tidal delta biotope because they lie in or near the tidal channel inlet that passes through the barrier island and then proceeds southeastward. Group B is a loosely defined set of four localities that include the subtidal shoals adjacent to the flood-tidal delta channel. Warme (1971) called these the barren zones at the distal end of the flood-tidal delta. The upper lagoon may be divided into a subtidal and intertidal portion. The subtidal portion extends through the entire lagoon along the backshore and into the reaches of channels dissecting the marshes of the greater lagoon where eelgrass is common. The intertidal portion lies at the back of the lagoon extending to the distal end of the flood-tidal delta under the protection of the small island in the lower lagoon. An intertidal zone is also present in the northern portion of the lagoon where eelgrass is rare. Localities at or near the boundaries between the ananum biotopes (Figure 15-3) are not necessarily adjacent geographically in the lagoon. It appears that local fluctuations of a community under the given environmental regime do not precipitate local changes in the state of a community in an adjacent regime.

Warme (1971) collected four pairs, or couplets, of geographically close samples from very similar environments in Mugu Lagoon to test the reproducibility of the cluster analysis he employed. These couplets may be used for the same purpose of testing community-components analysis. The couplets 42-43 (intertidal part of the lagoon), 38-39 (proximal flood-tidal delta), 25-26 (subtidal part of the lagoon), and 47-48 (subtidal part of the lagoon) show expected high correlation and proximity in the ananum, yielding values of 0.9747, 0.9926, 0.9236, and 0.8893, respectively (Figure 15-3). All four of these couplets are geographically (and presumably physiographically) removed from the boundaries of their biotopes and, therefore, lie well within their group in the ananum. A more detailed comparison of these results with those of Warme's would be of little value because Warme (1971) concentrated on the living populations whereas this study deals with the dead populations.

The communities interpreted from the anagram of COMMU mode-2 are displayed in Figure 15-5 and their species composition is tabulated in Table 15-7. As in mode-1 ananum for Mugu Lagoon, communities in extreme environments lie at opposite ends of the major chain of the anagram. The results show reasonable groupings of species of common or interdependent habitats. Community A of the flood-tidal delta is composed of littoral and sublittoral suspension feeders (Table 15-1 and Figure 15-5) found on sand beaches and in tidal channels. _Nuttallia nuttalli_ is found in tidal channels of bays along the California coast (Pohlo, 1972). _Donax gouldi_ and _Tivela stultorum_ commonly are beach-foreshore inhabitants (Pohlo, 1967) but they have been found living in tidal channels (MacGinitie, 1935). The distal flood-tidal delta community (B) is a loosely connected (low correlation) group of suspension feeders including _Dendraster excentricus_ and _Cryptomya californica_, which are found in abundance in tidal channels of bays along the coast (Merrill and Hobson, 1969; MacGinitie, 1935) and in the barren zones at the distal reaches of the tidal delta. Warme (1971) pointed out that individuals of

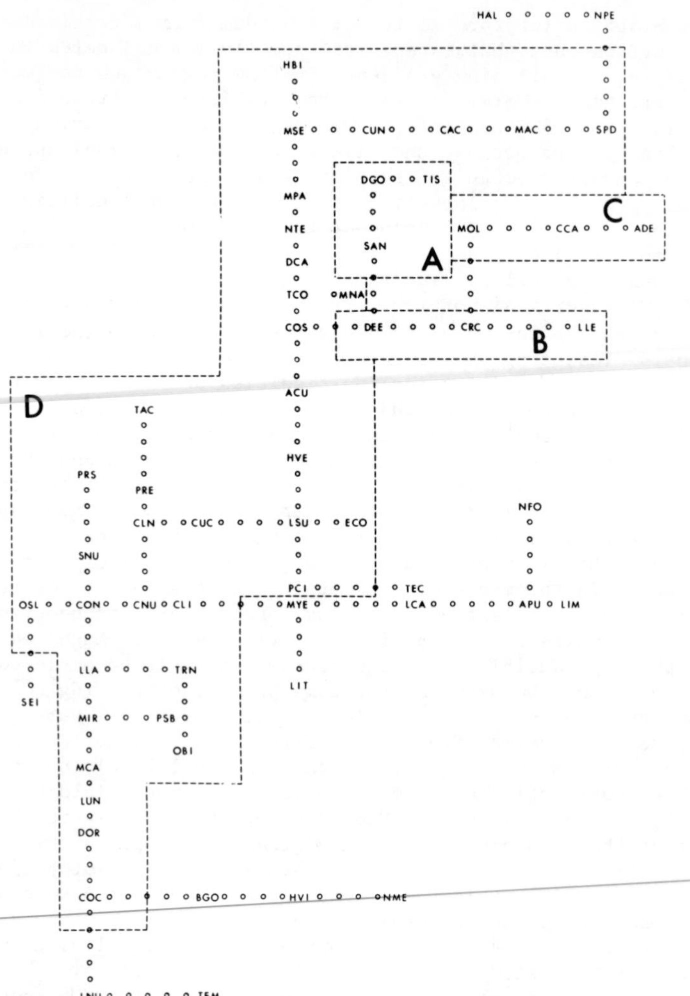

Figure 15-5
Mugu Lagoon Community anagram: mode-2. A = proximal flood-tidal delta community; B = distal flood-tidal delta community; C = intertidal community; D = subtidal-eelgrass community. Acronyms stand for species listed in Table 15-1. See Figure 15-3 for explanation.

Cryptomya californica and Callianassa presently living in the lagoon do not go beyond the tidal channels into the muddly lower lagoon. However, dead individuals of Cryptomya californica are found in the upper reaches of the tidal channels where Callianassa presently is not, indicating the crustacean's past distribution.

Beyond the distal flood-tidal delta community, the anagram bifurcates toward the upper intertidal lagoon community C and the subtidal lagoon community D. The latter is composed of the following three groups (according to their position along the major chain):

1. the subtidal middle lagoon.

2, the intertidal lower lagoon.

3. the subtidal lower lagoon.

Table 15-1
Molluscan benthic communities from Mugu Lagoon recognized by community-components analysis. Acronyms following species names correspond to acronyms in Figure 15-5.

PROXIMAL FLOOD-TIDAL DELTA COMMUNITY	
Tivela stultorum (TIS)	Donax gouldi (DGO)
Nuttallia nuttalli (SAN)	
DISTAL FLOOD-TIDAL DELTA COMMUNITY	
Dendraster excentricus (DEE)	Cryptomya californica (CRC)
Lunantia lewisi (LLE)	
INTERTIDAL UPPER-LAGOON COMMUNITY	
Melampus olivaceus (MOL)	Cerithidea californicus (CCA)
Acmaea depicta (ADE)	
SUBTIDAL MIDDLE-LAGOON COMMUNITY	
Mactra californica (MAC)	Chione californiensis (CAC)
Chione undatella (CUN)	Heterodonax bimaculata (HBI)
Macoma secta (MSE)	Margarites parcipictus (MPA)
Nassarius tegulus (NTE)	Donax californica (DCA)
Tricolia compta (TCO)	Macoma nasuta (MNA)
Cooperella subdiaphana (COS)	Acteon culcitella (ACU)
Haminoea vescula (HVE)	Laevicardium substriatum (LSU)
Epitonium cooperi (ECO)	Pecten circularis (PCI)
Cumingia californica (CUC)	Clinocardium nuttalli (CLN)
Polinices reclusiana (PRE)	
INTERTIDAL LOWER-LAGOON COMMUNITY	
Crepipatella lingulata (CLI)	Crepidula nummaria (CNU)
Crepidula onyx (CON)	Saxidomus nuttali (SNU)
Ostrea lurida (OSL)	
SUBTIDAL LOWER-LAGOON COMMUNITY	
Leptopecten latiauratus (LLA)	Macoma irus (MIR)
Psammotreta biangulata (PSB)	Lacuna unifasciata (LUN)
Mitrella carinata (MCA)	Diplodonta orbella (DOR)
Conus californicus (COC)	

The subtidal middle-lagoon group includes the suspension feeders Cooperella subdiaphana (69 shells) and Donax californica (129), the selective deposit-feeder Macoma nasuta (9297), the browsing herbivorous gastropods Tricolia compta (682) and Margarites parcipictus (26), and the scavenger Nassarius tegulus (10). The intertidal lower-lagoon group consists of the suspension feeders Ostrea lurida (144) and Saxidomus nutalli (842) and the algae-detritus feeders Crepipatella lingulata (27), Crepidula nummaria (40), and Crepidula onyx (122), which trap organically rich deposits thrown into suspension (Purchon, 1968: 33; Johnson, 1972: 32). This latter assemblage is closely associated with the subtidal lower-lagoon group that includes the suspension feeders Diplodonta orbella (22) and Leptopecten latiauratus (1969); the deposit feeder Macoma irus (86); two algae feeders, Nitidella (=Mitrella) carinata (218) (Abbott, 1968: 130) and Lacuna unifasciata (69), commonly a browser on eelgrass (Morton, 1958: 90); and a predaceous gastropod Conus californicus (10). The fourth community from the lagoon (C) is a loosely knit group (low correlation) of molluscs including Melampus, a pulmonate that is generally a browsing herbivore and Cerithidea californica and Acmaea depicta, which inhabit intertidal mudflats and brackish marshes of Zostera.

Table 15-1 shows that each of the communities distinguished in mode-2 analysis is represented by a number of different feeding types. Particularly interesting are the close associations (high correlation) of some of the molluscs in lagoonal community D. The constancy of the relative proportional abundance of the shells in these groups suggests a trophic interaction among their members.

MIDDLE EOCENE BENTHIC COMMUNITIES

To apply the community-components analysis, we used the La Jolla group of southern California and constructed a three-dimensional framework. We were concerned with the fidelity of ancient communities to particular depositional environments and community change over a geologically short period.

LA JOLLA GROUP OF SOUTHERN CALIFORNIA

Stratigraphy and sedimentology

The La Jolla Group possesses some of the most structurally uncomplicated exposures of shallow-shelf and nearshore Eocene fossil-bearing strata in southern California. As a consequence, it has been studied many times since early interpretations of the geology of the San Diego area. Up to the present, the geologic interpretation of western San Diego County, particularly the stratigraphy, has been described by Ellis (1919), Clark (1926), Hanna (1926,1927), Kennedy and Moore (1971), and Boyer and Warme (1975).

Clark (1926) and Hanna (1926) provided the initial stratigraphic interpretations. Hanna (1926) established, from oldest to youngest, the Delmar Sand, the Torrey Sand, and the Rose Cañon Shale. These lower members of the La Jolla Formation were earlier referred to the Tejon Stage (Clark, 1926). The fourth and highest member was designated the Poway Conglomerate by Hanna (1926). Later, Kennedy and Moore (1971) elevated the Delmar and the Torrey to formational status and divided the Rose Cañon Shale into three formations: the Ardath, Scripps, and Friars in ascending stratigraphic order. The general stratigraphic relationship among the facies of the La Jolla Group is shown in a schematic geologic cross section (Figure 15-6).

Delmar Formation

The Delmar Formation consists of medium to very thin beds and laminae of medium-gray shale to medium-grained, olive-gray sandstone (Figure 15-7). Hanna (1926) estimated the thickness of the Delmar as 60m. Locally, the formation consists of well-indurated beds or lenses of oysters or other molluscs, thin lignite beds, and

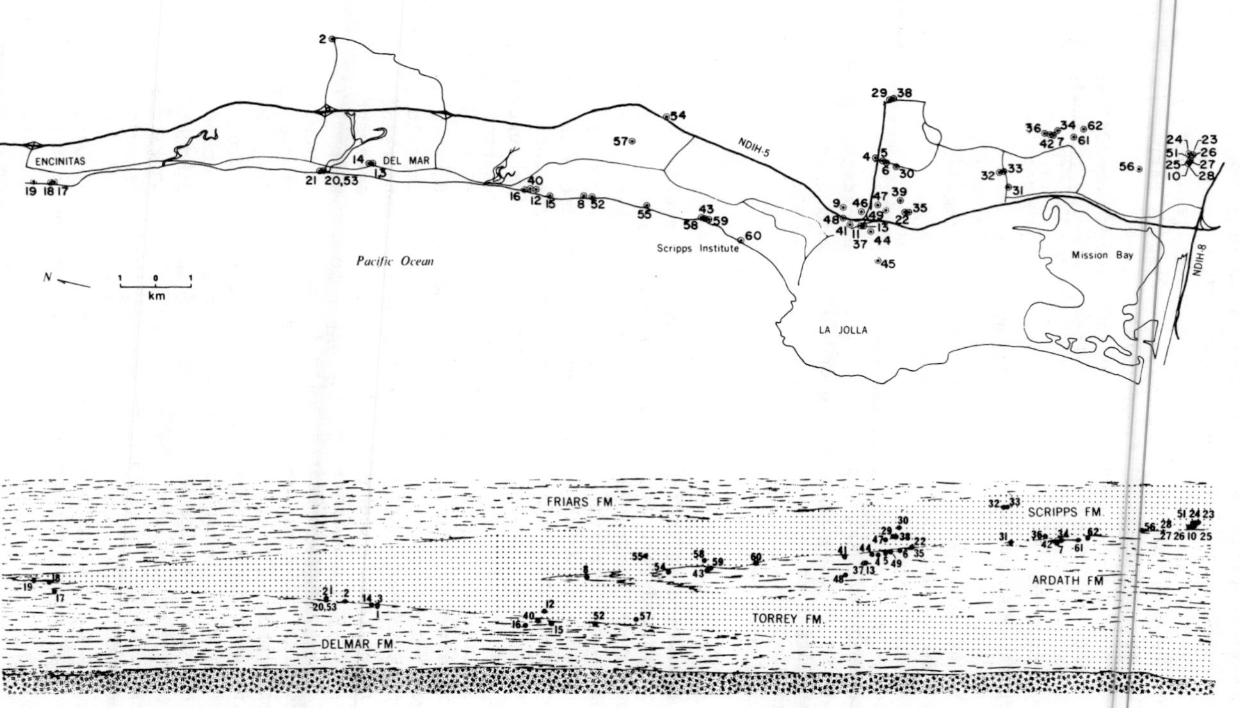

Figure 15-6
Map and schematic geologic cross section (modified from Kennedy and Moore, 1971) showing the distribution of the marine invertebrate localities from the middle Eocene La Jolla Group of southern California. Numbers correspond to those of samples shown in Figure 15-10.

pebble-sized blebs of amber. Generally, the medium-gray shale and siltstone give way upward to medium to fine-grained sandstone with root tubes and burrows or shell lag at the base. These may be overlain by medium- to fine-grained brown or hematite-cemented sandstone, lignite, and oyster beds. As Boyer and Warme (1975) asserted, the lower 9m of the Delmar Formation consists of sediment laid down initially in the quieter portions of a tidal flat or lagoon followed by backshore marsh or oyster banks and flood-tidal deltas.

Boyer and Warme (1975) divided the upper portion of the Delmar, which grades into the overlying Torrey Formation, into the following three facies:

1. Oyster beds, resting on shale or muddy sandstone
2. Flaser beds, consisting of flaser, wavey, or lenticular bedding, micrograded beds, and abundant plant material, interpreted as tidal flat deposits
3. Fining-upward sequences of sand and siltstone exhibiting a variety of primary sedimentary structures along with clay clasts and plant material indicative of tidal channels.

Torrey Formation

The Torrey Formation consists of fine-grained to conglomeratic, white to light-brown sandstone with local lenses of thin- to medium-bedded, muddy sandstone (Figure 15-7). The Torrey is particularly conglomeratic where it interdigitates with the Scripps Formation. In this zone, it is clean, white to light-yellow sandstone with conglomerate at the base containing pebbles and cobbles. The basal part of the Torrey generally has a sharp contact with the underlying Delmar Formation and is thickly bedded containing a large number of large-scale, trough, cross-bed sets. This gives way upward to low-angle, cross-bedded, and parallel, laminated sandstone. Boyer and Warme (1975) divided the Torrey into two depositional facies: large-scale, trough, cross-bedded sandstone with coarse to light-granular, muddy sandstone deposited in subaqueous dunes and tidal deltas of a barrier; and large channels up to 80 m wide and 2 to 6 m deep filled with slightly granular, muddy sandstone with lag deposits of coarse sediment and clay clasts. Boyer and Warme (1975) said that the barrier was subaqueous because they found no aeolian, berm, or backshore deposits in the Torrey. Such deposits, however, would be destroyed by wave action as the barrier island retrograded. Moreover, large channels generally develop where rivers frequently debouch into the estuary causing a hydraulic disequilibrium between esturine and marine bodies of water. Also, the marked difference between the faunas of the Ardath and Delmar (see below) seems to indicate the former existence of a significant physiographic barrier between such as the subaerial to subaqueous sand bar represented by the Torrey Formaton.

Ardath Formation

The Ardath Formation consists of green and blue-gray sandy shale and silty-fine sandstone (Figure 15-8). Kennedy and Moore

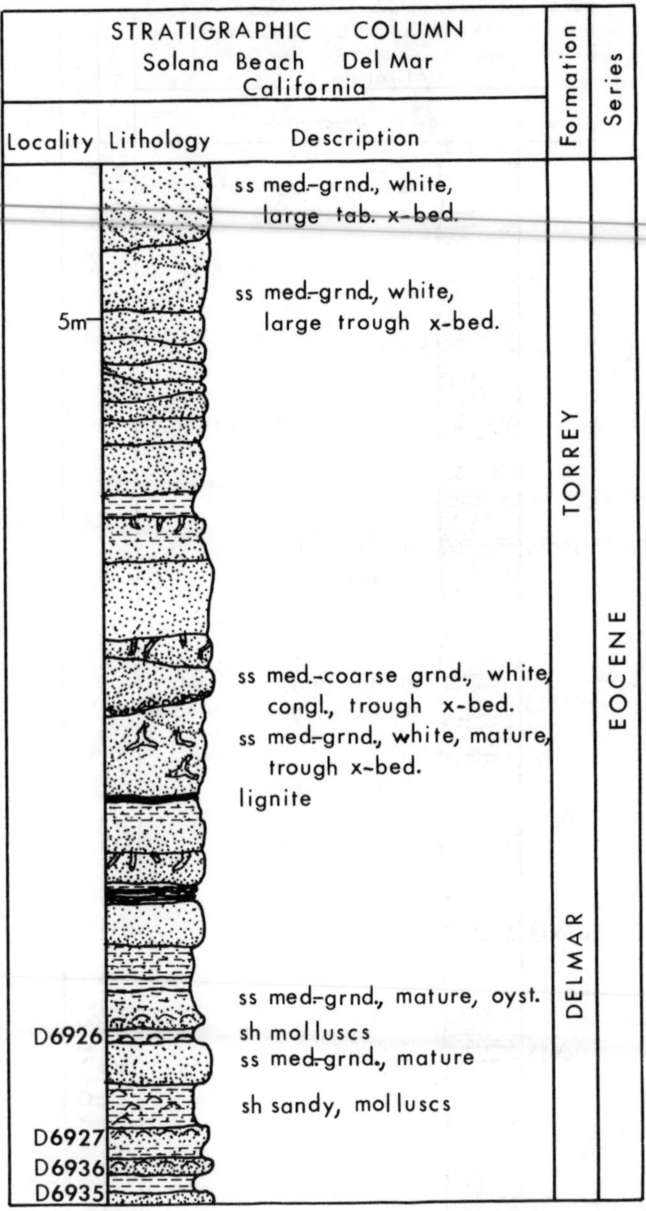

Figure 15-7
Stratigraphic column of the Delmar and Torrey formations measured at Solana Beach near the town of Delmar at the mouth of San Dieguito Valley, Del Mar, California.

(1971) estimated the Ardath Formation to be 70 m thick, but it thins northward and intertongues with the Scripps and Torrey. The upper few meters contain broad, lenticular, fine- to medium-grained sandstone beds approximately 30 m wide and 1 to 2 m thick. Below these

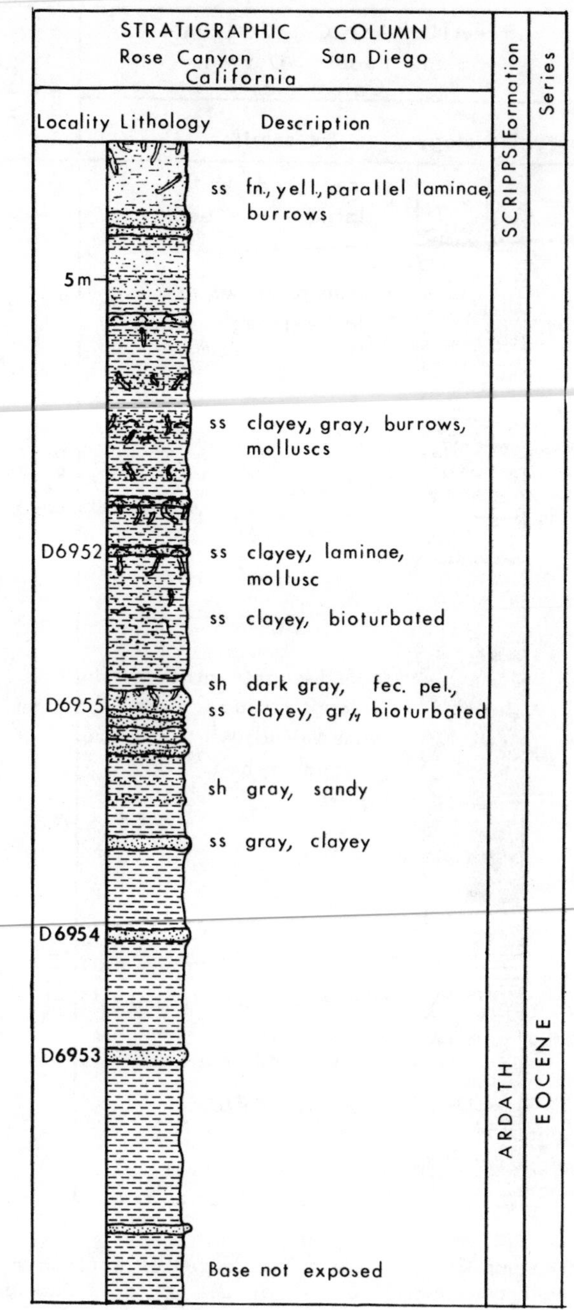

Figure 15-8
Stratigraphic column of the Ardath Formation at the junction of San Clemente and Rose canyons, San Diego, California.

beds are thinner, concretionary, sandy shale and shaley sandstone beds that contain abundant fossils including rare wood fragments. Northward over the study area, the Ardath becomes more thinly bedded and increasingly sandier. In the east-central portion of the study area, it is composed of light olive-brown shale and yellow to light-brown sandstone. The shale and sandy shale beds are commonly less than 50 cm thick and interbedded with thinner sandstone lenses. Scattered gypsum and sulfur laminae are also present. Except for gypsum and sulfur laminae, the Ardath Formation is the same in the west-central part of the study area. The Ardath deposited under deep nearshore conditions consists of medium-gray sandy shale that is thickly bedded and exhibits ripple marks and small-scale laminae. The interbedded siltstones have loaded into the underlying shale beds producing contortions in the shale. Molluscs are distributed sporadically with large, low-density, trough cross-bedded, sandy lenses. Where deposited in shallow water, some of the lenses contain scattered burrows with sulfur and limonite layers surrounding them. Where the Ardath Formation thins northward between the Scripps and the Torrey, it grades laterally into a sandier, light-brown facies that is more thinly bedded than to the south.

The Ardath was deposited in bathyal to sublittoral environments. The water shallowed northward into an embayment that lay south of the main lobe of a fan delta that sloped into the sea from the northwest in the center of the study area. All of the Ardath fossil localities in this study are in the upper half of the formation, but outside of the thinly laminated sandstone and shale containing sulfur laminae.

Scripps Formation

The Scripps Formation is composed of fine- to coarse-grained, white to light-brown sandstone that locally contains granule- or cobble-size conglomerate and gray silty sandstone (Figure 15-9). Kennedy and Moore (1971) measured a maximum thickness of 67 m for the Scripps. The Scripps commonly consists of parallel beds from 7 to 100 cm thick in the basal part. Most of these beds are thinly laminated with some irregular wavey laminations. Above these beds are about 20 m of clayey sandstone that is fairly massive, but contains some parallel laminations or low-angle cross-bedding and very thin beds of light-gray silty sandstone that are highly burrowed. Near the top of this interval, the formation contains blebs of shale indicating that the original bedding has been almost completely disrupted. The shales are generally green and micaceous, locally form continuous shale beds without silt or sand, and exhibit conchoidal fracture. In the southern part of the study area, this shaley interval is represented by only a few centimeters of shale containing scattered clusters of oysters. To the north, the interval consists of thin beds of carbonaceous shale. Above this is another sequence of silty sandstone beds with a few concretionary sandstone layers and widely scattered one-pebble thick conglomerate lenses that are laterally extensive. Locally, the pebbles have numerous specimens of *Calyptraea* attached indicating that these pebble layers are beach-wave lag deposits colonized by a rocky-shore gastropod. Near the central portion of the study area, the Scripps Formation is highly conglomeratic containing abundant pebble lenses 1 to 5 m thick that

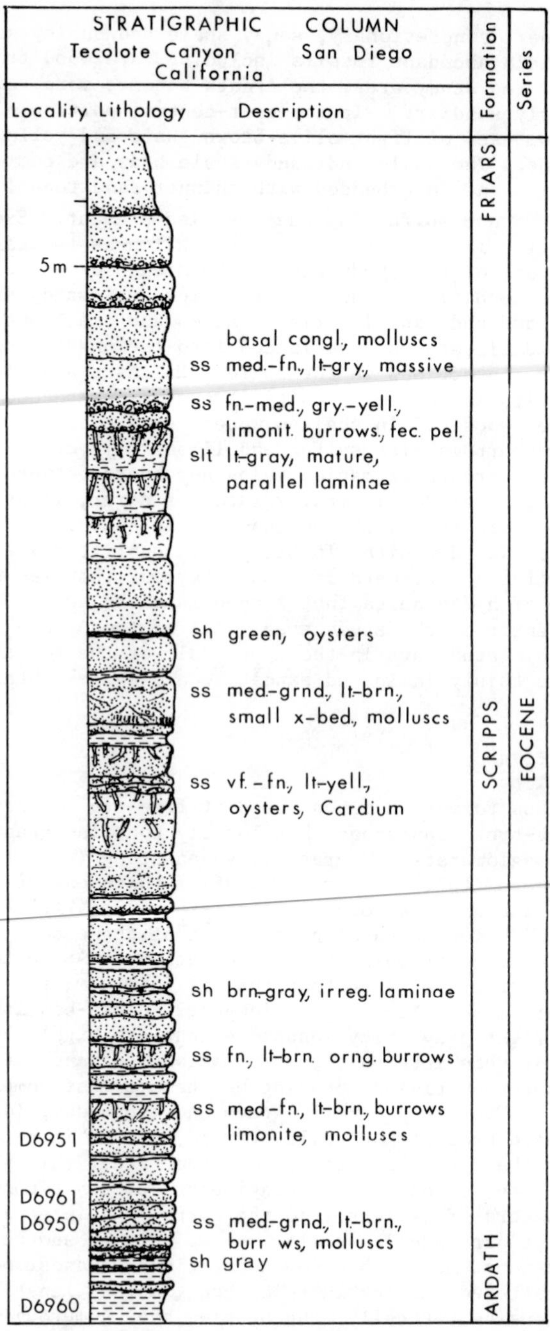

Figure 15-9
Stratigraphic column of the Scripps Formation at the northern end of Tecolote Canyon, San Diego, California.

contain rare cobbles of Ardath Shale.

The Scripps Formation was probably deposited by a fan delta fed by a high-gradient stream. Evidence in favor of such an interpretation includes the local conglomeratic nature of the formation, lack of significant shale deposits in the upper part of the formation, lack of widespread interdistributary fine-grained sediment, and the laterally extensive stratigraphically uniform contact between the Ardath and the Scripps formations. It appears that the major channel that brought the sediment to the fan delta passed through the central portion of the study area where the Ardath Shale is drag folded and contorted directly under the intraformational conglomeratic sandstone of the Scripps Formation.

Community-Components Analysis

Sixty-two localities containing over 35,000 shells representing 109 species (Figure 15-10) were analyzed. Thirty-eight samples of approximately equal bulk (30 to 50 kg) were collected during the winter of 1975 and the summer of 1976. These samples were broken down mechanically or by soaking in kerosene and washed so the greatest variety and number of specimens were obtained. Only complete shells or fragments that consisted of more than 50 percent of the average adult-size shell and samples collected by Hanna (1927) that approached the bulk of the recent samples were used in the study. All the material used in this study is preserved at the University of California Museum of Paleontology.

In the mode-1 ananum (Figure 15-11), three distinct biotopes can be distinguished. Examination of the major chain of the ananum shows that biotope A is separated from B by the lowest correlation of 0.6908 between localities A06 and T21. Biotope B is separated from biotope C by the low correlation of 0.6053 between D14 and S52. Biotope A is composed predominantly of localities from the Ardath Formation; Biotope B is equivalent to the Delmar Formation. Biotope C is primarily composed of localities from the Scripps Formation. However, the subset of the Scripps biotope that lies closest to the Delmar biotope in the ananum is composed of localities from the Delmar and Torrey formations as well as the Scripps. The localities in this subset are from the tidal channel deposits of the Delmar and Torrey and the lag gravel and shaley sandstone beds of the Scripps.

Mode-1 analysis of the La Jolla Group material produced a number of poorly correlated samples scattered about the periphery of the ananum. Most of these were collected by Hanna. There appear to be two reasons for this scattering. First, Hanna was primarily interested in describing the invertebrate fossils from the Eocene of San Diego. We suspect that some of the original material collected was disposed of in favor of rare taxa. Second, many of Hanna's samples came from the deep deposits of the Ardath exposed along the seacliff. These samples may represent a distinctive deep-water fauna that we did not adequately sample.

Mode-2 of community-components analysis delineates three groups (Figure 15-12) with low correlations (inferred break points) along the major chain between *Clabornites diegoensis* (CLD) and *Vitrinella monta* (TEM), *Ancilla gabbi* (ANG) and *Flabellum sandiegoense* (FLS; Table 15-2). Community D includes the lagoonal fauna of the Delmar Formation. In the Delmar community, there are few carnivorous spe-

Locality	1 Balanophyllia imbulata	2 Dendrophyllia dudleyi	3 Flabellum sandiegoensis	4 Trochocyathus striatus	5 Acila decisa	6 Anomia mcgoniglensis	7 Pitar kelloggi	8 Pachecoa eba	9 Pachecoa hornii	10 Barbatia cliffensis	11 Barbatia morsei	12 Porterius woodfordi	13 Volsella ornatus	14 Glans sandiegoensis	15 Nemocardium linteum	16 Acanthocardium sorrentoensis	17 Corbula cliffensis	18 Corbula parilis	19 Corbula rosecanyonensis	20 Corbula torreyensis	21 Corbula tomulata	22 Anapteris wardi	23 Crassatella semidentata	24 Cardiomya israelskyi	25 Diplodonta polita	26 Donax scrippsensis	27 Marcia hunkeri	28 Gastrochaena dubitata	29 Glycymeris rosecanyonensis	30 Glycymeris tecolotensis	31 Kellia lajollaensis	32 Portlandia rosa	33 Botula mcknighti	34 Claibornites diegoensis	35 Macoma rosa	36 Callista tecolotensis	37 Ostrea crandelli	38 Ostrea idriaensis	39 Pecten lajollaensis	40 Lucina taffana	41 Pholadomya murrayensis	42 Pelecyora aequilateralis	43 Pitar californianus	44 Pitar soledadensis	45 Pitar sorrentoensis	46 Gari diegoensis	47 Solena coosensis	48 Spisula bisculpturata	49 Tellina jollaensis	50 Tellina scrippsensis	51 Tellina soledadensis	52 Tellina vorbei	53 Thracia sorrentoensis	54 Tivela cliffensis	55 Unio torreyensis	56 Venericardia hornii	57 Pitar intica
6927 Tdm 1																				52																	12	89				68															
6926 Tdm 2																																					6	22				377															
6928 Tdm 3																				112																	6	252	2			155							22								
6957 Ta 4				1	150										28	10		32					2						200					6	2	8		2	48	56		217							3	2							
6958 Ta 5					50	3	31			2					28	18		6							2				783			6	1		2	16			1	107		35			5		1			3	6						
6959 Ta 6	1				13		4			2			7	4	13	3		20							2				229						1	27		2	57			20															
6960 Ta 7							4								9	9													4						28	14	1			9		65			47				3			1					13
6962 Ta 8					2															4																	7	56				17															2
3975 Ta 9					16										6	15													14	1						1				1		13		1			1				1		1				
6941 Tsc 10							51						2			11							4									3		6	66	2	2	2		8		46			4				9								
6955 Ta 11					6										6	2		2											51																												
3981 Tdm 12						5	5				38									1													2	4			6	2				83				4											1
6953 Ta 13														3	3	12		8											449						2					11		6					2		3								
6929 Tdm 14													53							52																	14	149				31			3				16								
6930 Tdm 15											8		6																					1			7	258				57					7		13								
6931 Tdm 16					4															4													7	26			5	111				183							3						4		
6932 Tdm 17					2								13																								4	27				448							2								
6933 Tdm 18																																		3			2	18				246															
6934 Tdm 19					3								32																								77	216				227															
6935 Tt 20													6	2																			11		11		11	19				297			21		7		3								
6936 Tt 21					4		2						82	14	6			41		17									16				6	2			20	228				276							2								
6937 Tsc 22					6		7								2	2		3					2						1					2		28						17								2							
6938 Tsc 23							6								2	19							3						35						4		2	6		8		51			158		2			28							
6939 Tsc 24							22								4	11		7											15		3			2	36	3	3	11		22		40			15				13								
6940 Tsc 25					1		8								2	9		2											24			9			22	2		1		28		38			16		7		4								
6942 Tsc 26		2			23		15								14	13					3								18			3			18	16	4	5		16		69			16		3		2	1							
6943 Tsc 27					29		12							11	23	52							27						19		2			2		103	1	5		4		335					1		2	1							
6944 Tsc 28					79		3							1	24	26		7			3								27		4	1			38	33	3	1		37		123					14		1	10							
6945 Tsc 29							18									18		3			2								2								1	2				13			11												
6946 Tsc 30					26		4								11	28		3											116					2	6	12		7		33		32			1		2		2								7
6947 Tsc 31													4																				1																								
6949 Tsc 32					114		1							2	1	3							7										4	7	1	1		5				14					2										
6948 Tsc 33					332									1	1	9							4						3							7		1		14		132					1		1							2	
6950 Tsc 34															1	5													2					4		24						55															
6952 Ta 35					11		4								80	27		3											204			2		4		52		14	4	48		30					2		1	4							8
6951 Tsc 36							12							1	2	3													7									1		27		6			74		1			17							
6954 Ta 37					53									3	14	34		4											143	9										31		2		7			3			4							
6956 Ta 38																4													11			22					2			14		34					6		8	1							
3976 Tsc 39					1											2		5																													6									1	
3980 Tt 40							8							1		1																				1		37				4													15		1
3983 Ta 41					2		3						2		6	5													4						2	1			1			1															
6961 Ta 42					57		46			57			57	8	10	22		37		2									113				3	21	2	2		1		36		43			12		6		11								
3986 Ta 43																1								1					1			12				1				1		1															
3988 Ta 44															4	2	3	3					1													1						2				1			2								
3989 Tsc 45															8			1									1		4				1		1	1				2									1								1
3990 Ta 46																		1									1		6			3																								1	
3991 Tsc 47					1										7	5													8				1	1		7				2		3			1				1								1
3993 Tsc 48											1							3											1			14								1					1												1
4001 Ta 49																4		1																				1				1			1												
5051 Ta 50					13		1					1			13	12		1			5						1		37			1		20	7	11		5		17		8	2		8			2			2						4
6963 Tsc 51							3						2		1	1							4						6						16		1	2		2		13			2				6								
5056 Tsc 52	1																																				5	1				9	1				1										
5057 Tsc 53														1																																											
5059 Tsc 54														1												1									1							5	5									3					
5062 Tsc 55				2	15			1						5	16	12	9	11			3	1					5	3	48				5	2	1	3		3	23	2		13	5			1	4			1	3	3		1		3	5
5069 Ta 56					6										28	44	7	24			1						2		31							8				3		21	7				1			3	3						7
5063 Ta 57			2		1										1	1			2					3											1	2				1		1															1
5083 Ta 58			1						1						3	13		10			8								15			8			24	3		3		4		6			1					2							
5084 Ta 59																		1			14						1					4			2	2		2		1		38	14														
5089 Ta 60					1													2		2						1						4			2														1								
5091 Ta 61					1										1			4											3			1		11	2	7						3	1						5			1		3			2
5090 Ta 62															7														1			1				5				1						2											3

Figure 15-10
Initial matrix of middle Eocene marine invertebrate species (columns) and localities (rows) from the San Diego coastal region, southern California. Numbers in boxes are individuals counted. Four-character numbers in sample column are catalogued locality numbers. Formation names are abbreviated as: Tdm = Delmar Fm., Tt = Torrey Fm., Ta = Ardath Fm., Tsc = Scripps Fm. Numbers following formation abbreviations correspond to those shown in Figures 15-6 and 15-11 and in Table 15-2. Species identifications were based on studies by Hanna (1927), Vokes (1939), Weaver (1942), Givens (1974), and Givens and Kennedy (1976).

cies relative to detritus and suspension feeders. The proportion of carnivores is significantly greater in the Ardath community than in the Delmar.

Community S is composed of the littoral foreshore fauna of the Scripps Formation. In the Scripps community, the number of carnivorous species is lower (relative to that of suspension and detritus feeders) than is found in the Ardath community. The number of de-

			Globularia hannibali	Amaurellina bedoni	Ancilla gabbi	Cylichnina tantilla	Calyptraea diegoana	Bonellitia bournei	Cerithium cliffensis	Conus goodwini	Conus warreni	Ectinochilus problematica	Ectinochilus supraplicatus	Eocypraea mathewsonii	Discohelix murrayensis	Drillia cliffensis	Ficopsis cooperi	Ficopsis remondii	Fusinus teglandae	Fusinus voetus	Galeodea petrosa	Gemmula violeta	Goniobasis diegoensis	Latirus nightingalei	Loxotrema turritum	Conomitra clementensis	Miopleiona minori	Mitra sandiegoensis	Mitra simplissima	Mitramorpha howei	Euspira clementensis	Polinices hornii	Euspira nuciformis	Natica rosensis	Nerita triangulata	Olivella mathewsonii	Philine bisculpturata	Potamides carbonicola	Pyramidella preblei	Scaphander costatus	Terebellum californicum	Solariella crenulata	Surculites mathewsonii	Pleurofusia ladrillensis	Pleurofusia lindavistaensis	Turricula praeattenuata	Vitrinella mutta	Actaeon rosa	Trichotropis hadleyensis	Turritella andersoni	Turritella uvasana	Turritella buwaldana	Turritella scrippsensis	Vitrinella litra	Vitrinella mountainensis	Vitrinella [illegible]	Dentalium stramineum	Cadulus gabbi
			58	59	60	61	62	63	64	65	66	67	68	69	70	71	72	73	74	75	76	77	78	79	80	81	82	83	84	85	86	87	88	89	90	91	92	93	94	95	96	97	98	99	100	101	102	103	104	105	106	107	108	109	110	111	112	113
6927	Tdm	1					13		58																																																	
6926	Tdm	2							26																																																	
6928	Tdm	3		16			46		99																								7		3																							
6957	Ta	4	4	17		48	15	2	[illegible]		8						1					6		18		8	3					1	20	7							38	82	1						3			[illegible]	[illegible]				3		
6958	Ta	5	3	7	1	57	7	4	[illegible]	2	28	11				8	3	3		8		1		19		3	8						17	16						48	25	24	11					10			74	78		1			15	10
6959	Ta	6		17		14	20	2	[illegible]		12	2	1	1	1		3	1				1	1	5		5							23	11						8	10	3	2					13			75	17					3	10
6960	Ta	7	1	2		2	4				1		2				1							2		1							1								3								1		13						2	5
6962	Ta	8		1					43																																																	
3975	Ta	9	1	8		3	19		8		1		1		2		1																1	1						2											1							
6941	Tsc	10				6			10		2													2																											6	6						6
6955	Ta	11						2	28		2	2										2		2			2														2		2										13						
3981	Tdm	12		22			31		6																7									4	13																	3							
6953	Ta	13		3		5	2	1	[illegible]	1	31				2									2			2			10			3						6					1	2						9	7					11	8
6929	Tdm	14		6			42		16																								7	2	3																							
6930	Tdm	15		3			72		[illegible]																8								13	1	21																							
6931	Tdm	16		22					[illegible]																41								7		17															1		10							
6932	Tdm	17					11		54																								1		15		2																					
6933	Tdm	18					1		14																								1					1																				
6934	Tdm	19		2			42		[illegible]																11								21		8			31														3							
6935	Tt	20		7			3		91		2														6								3		2			13		3																		
6936	Tt	21		6			53	1	[illegible]		2		1					1						4	20	16					3		6	7	23			3		3						4												
6937	Tsc	22					1		11		5							2			1												1																		10							
6938	Tsc	23					1		14		1													4																												2						3
6939	Tsc	24			1	1		1	6		3							1						1									3								3										3						2	6
6940	Tsc	25				2			6		2		1											2		1	2	1																							3							2
6942	Tsc	26		4	1	8	2	1	11		11		2					3				1		3			1													3	1								1		22							
6943	Tsc	27	3	51	3	29	9	2	11		47	8						6			12	2		9		1							9	3						6	5							1			53	4						
6944	Tsc	28		2	2	13	8		7		9	2					3							4				2				1	3							6			1														3	
6945	Tsc	29					76																																																			
6946	Tsc	30	1	16		34	13		[illegible]	4	21		2				3	1						7		3							12	36						8	2										22	[illegible]						
6947	Tsc	31																																																	[illegible]							
6949	Tsc	32		12		3	3		[illegible]		1													4		2							13			1				1	5										97	24					5	3
6948	Tsc	33	2			1	2	2	17		2				1		3							7									7	3						6	3	1						1			[illegible]	14					15	5
6950	Tsc	34																															1																				1					
6952	Ta	35	3	19		2	1	1	[illegible]		32			1	1		2	3	6	2			1	20			2						16	3						3	5		2					2			31	[illegible]		3	1		3	10
6951	Tsc	36		1					2																						1				2							1														10	3
6954	Ta	37		6		16	2	9	96		24	4				3				7		19		11		11						2	6	9						6	24		7					3			48						
6956	Ta	38																																														2								
3976	Tsc	39	1	2					2				1																				1								1															
3980	Tt	40		5			2		12																																	1							1		2						
3983	Ta	41		1			1		3				1																				2																		1						
6961	Ta	42		28	6	12	67	21	76	2	56	3	1		4			2		1	2			15		1		1		3			33	21	2					13	13		3					2	2		36	[illegible]					2	57
3986	Ta	43						1			1											5											1	8														1			3						
3988	Ta	44	1	2			5		1			1					3	2																																	1						
3989	Tsc	45		7		1	4				1		6				5				1					1							2	1						1	1		1								1	1					
3990	Ta	46		3	1		1				3				3	3						1		2		2							2	15										1		3		11			15	2						
3991	Tsc	47		8	2	8	2	3	3		1		1			1	7					1										5	3							1		2	1								1			1				
3993	Tsc	48			1		1				1											3					1					2		16													2			2	18				6			
4001	Ta	49		10		9	1		5									3														1																				6	2						
5051	Ta	50	2	30	3	10	19	1	28	3	2	3	1	1			5	5						3	2	3	1		4				21	5						5		9									4	65						
6963	Tsc	51							1																																																	
5056	Tsc	52					5		1				1																				4				1					1																
5057	Tsc	53																																																							
5059	Tsc	54	7			4																																										1		23							
5062	Tsc	55	2			2				1	1	3			1		4					5				1							1	19					1			3	3			6		19	1		19	4	2	1	1			
5069	Ta	56	1	3	2	8	19	3	5	1	13			1			2	13						4			1	6	1				1	5						21		1	1		1	1	1				2	1		2	1			
5063	Ta	57					1						1				1			1		1																												45		2						
5083	Ta	58	6	1	7	10		13	25		34			1						2			2	2	7	2	1			1	1			10		1							4	1	1						11		4					
5084	Ta	59	6	20		2	3		5		3				1																			3																								
5089	Ta	60		4	1				1	1														1								1			1				4															1					
5091	Ta	61		5		3	14		1		3	3																					1		1						2		11															
5090	Ta	62					2		3																									3																	10							

tritus feeders is minimal and no herbivores are present. Suspension feeders are abundant because the community coincides with littoral wave-agitated or shallow-sublittoral foreshore conditions.

Community A contains the sublittoral fauna of the Ardath Formation. It is composed of a large number of carnivorous species compared to the number of species in the lower trophic levels. The

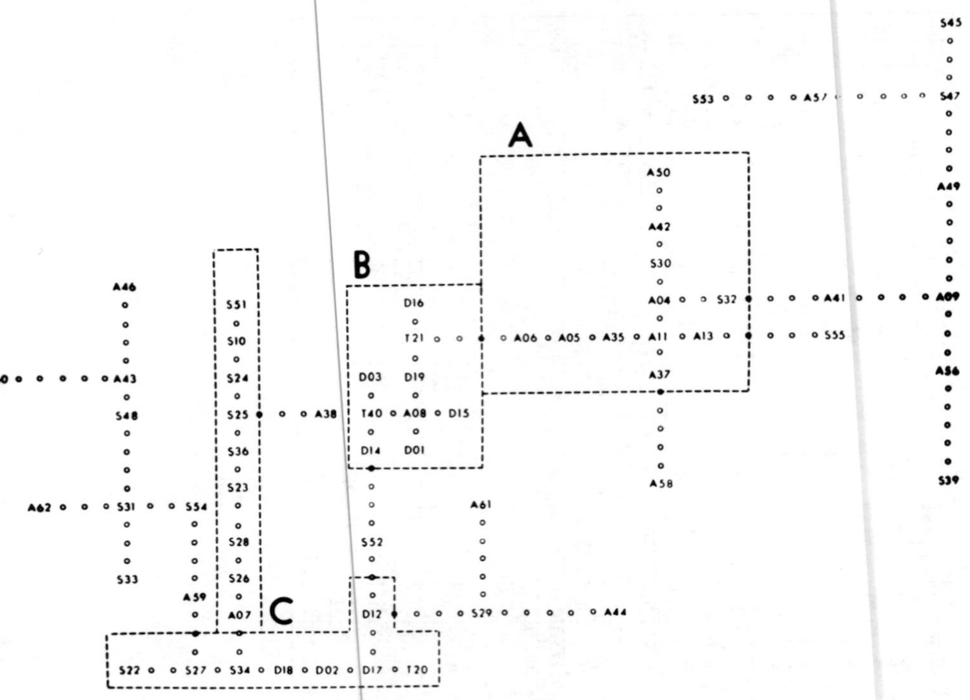

Figure 15-11
Biogeographic ananum (mode-1) for the marine invertebrate localities of the middle Eocene La Jolla Group of southern California. Numbers correspond to those of localities in Figures 15-6 and 15-10. A = Ardath biotope. B = Delmar lagoon biotope. C = Torrey-Scripps foreshore biotope. See Figure 15-3 for explanation.

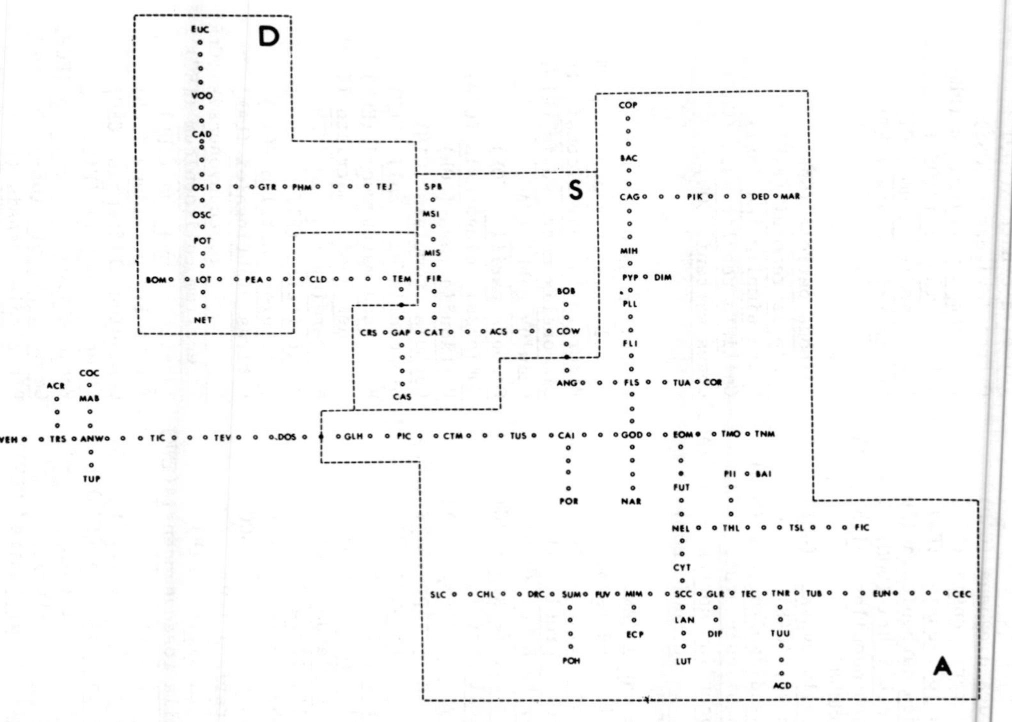

Figure 15-12
Marine invertebrate community anagram (mode 2) for the middle Eocene La Jolla Group of southern California. D = Delmar lagoon community. A = Ardath offshore community. S = Scripps foreshore community. Acronyms stand for species listed in Table 15-2 and in Figure 15-10. See Figure 15-3 for explanation.

Table 15-2
Invertebrate communities from the Eocene La Jolla Group of southern California. Acronyms following species names correspond to those in Figure 15-12. The names of species that lie outside of community boundaries on the anagram (Figure 15-12) are not listed.

DELMAR COMMUNITY	
Euspira clementensis (EUC)	*Volsella ornatus* (VOO)
Calyptraea diegoana (CAD)	*Ostrea idriaensis* (OSI)
Corbula torreyensis (CTR)	*Pholadomya murrayensis* (PHM)
Tellina jollaensis (TEJ)	*Ostrea crandelli* (OSC)
Potamides carbonicola (POT)	*Loxotrema turritum* (LOT)
Botula mcknighti (BOM)	*Nerita triangulata* (NET)
Pelecyora aequilateralis (PEA)	
SCRIPPS COMMUNITY	
Crassatella uvasana (CRS)	*Galeoda petrosa* (GAP)
Cardita sp. (CAS)	*Ficopsis remondi* (FIR)
Mitra sandieguitoensis (MIS)	*Mitra simplissima* (MSI)
Spisula bisculpturata (SPB)	*Callista tecolotensis* (CAT)
Acanthocardium sorrentoensis (ACS)	*Conus warreni* (COW)
Bonellitia bournei (BOB)	
ARDATH COMMUNITY	
Ancilla gabbi (ANG)	*Flabellum sandiegoensis* (FLS)
Turritella andersoni (TUA)	*Corbula rosecanyonensis* (COR)
Pleurofusia lindavistaensis (PLI)	*Pleurofusia ladrilloensis* (PLL)
Pyramidella preblei (PYR)	*Discohelix murrayensis* (DIM)
Mitramorpha howei (MIH)	*Cadulus gabbi* (CAG)
Barbatia cliffensis (BAC)	*Corbula parilis* (COP)
Pitar kellogi (PIK)	*Goniobasis diegoensis* (GOD)
Cardiomya israelskyi (CAI)	*Portlandia rosa* (POR)
Turritella scrippsensis (TUS)	*Corbula tomulata* (CTM)
Pitar californianus (PIC)	*Globularia hannibali* (GLH)
Natica rosensis (NAR)	*Eocypraea matthewsoni* (EOM)
Vitrinella monta (TMO)	*Vitrinella minutastriata* (TNM)
Fusinus teglandae (FUT)	*Nemocardium linteum* (NEM)
Vitrinella litra (TNL)	*Pitar intica* (PII)
Balanophyllia imbulata (BAI)	*Cylichnina tantilla* (CYT)
Scaphander costatus (SCC)	*Latirus nightingalei* (LAN)
Lucina taffana (LUT)	*Glycymeris rosecanyonensis* (GLR)
Diplodonta polita (DIP)	*Terebellum californicum* (TEC)
Vitrinella rosecanyonensis (TNR)	*Turritella uvasana* (TUU)
Acila decisa (ACD)	*Turritella buwaldana* (TUB)
Euspira nuciformis (EUN)	*Cerithium cliffensis* (CEC)
Tellina soledadensis (TSL)	*Ficopsis cooperi* (FIC)
Miopleona minori (MIM)	*Ectinochilus problematica* (ECP)
Fusinus voetus (FUV)	*Gemmula violeta* (GEV)
Glycymeris tecolotensis (GLT)	*Pitar soledadensis* (PSL)
Surculites mathewsonii (SUM)	*Polinices hornii* (POH)
Drillia cliffensis (DRC)	*Chlamys lajollaensis* (CHL)
Solariella crenulata (SLC)	

number of suspension feeders is equal to or somewhat larger than those of detritus feeders. Herbivores do not make up a significant portion of the species in the community. Many of the species found in the Ardath community are rare taxa discovered by Hanna and, therefore, are found only in a few localities. The cluster of species about *Anapteris wardii* (ANW) and those in the area of the ananum about *Pyramidella preblei* (PYP) are examples of these clusters of rare taxa. However, as stated above, they could represent actual deep-water assemblages of ecological significance.

COMMUNITY CHANGE

Once past communities have been recognized, an analysis of changes in community structure may be attempted. Ideally such change could be documented by generating ananums and anagrams for each of a number of temporally separated sets of contemporaneous samples. Because too few samples have been considered for such a procedure, we resort to more conventional means for documenting trends. Accordingly this phase of the study is preliminary. Some of the implications of the results reviewed below (competition patterns, diversity stability vs. complexity, and so forth) are ecological cans of worms, and present data warrant little beyond *ad hoc* speculation. However, an initial attempt at reconstruction provides some useful information on the history of the La Jolla benthic communities, particularly in reference to diversity changes and several correlative factors.

The La Jolla middle Eocene faunas seem particularly appropriate for investigations of community change because of the distinctive depositional environments represented by the Delmar, Ardath, and Scripps; the high fidelity of faunal assemblages to a particular formation; the large size of most samples; and good stratigraphic control. The last feature is critical. As the schematic cross-secton indicates (Figures 15-6), the Delmar lagoon was deposited on the drowned Cretaceous terrain behind the retrograding Torrey barrier island that separated the Delmar from the Ardath marine offshore deposits. The process of retrogradation was halted by the development of the extensive Scripps fan delta that prograded into the study area from the northeast. According to Hanna (1926), this sequence of deposition began during the later part of the Capay Stage (approximately 51 mybp) and ended shortly after the beginning of the Tejon Stage (approximately 44 mybp). Based on Mallory's (1959: 94-97) discussion of the stratigraphic relationship of larger invertebrate and vertebrate faunas to the foraminiferal sequence, this depositional sequence of the marine formations of the La Jolla Group began in the late Penutian (approximately 51 mybp). The middle part of the Ardath exposed on the seacliff at Black Canyon north of the Scripps Institute is late Ulatisian. Deposition of the studied sequence ended with the beginning of the Narizian (approximately 44 mybp). Examination of the rocks exposed along the seacliff from immediately south of Leucadia, at the northern extreme of the study area, to the middle of the Torrey Pine State Park (middle of the study area) shows that the Delmar-Torrey contact rises stratigraphically to the north. Sandstone lenses of the Torrey can be observed penetrating northward to become surrounded by the Delmar Shale. Examination of the rocks exposed along the seacoast from the middle of the Torrey Pines State Park to the Scripps Oceanographic Institute shows that the Ardath-Scripps contact rises stratigraphically to the south although the

Scripps sandstone locally cuts deeply into the Ardath at the exposures near the Institute. Therefore, the geographic as well as the stratigraphic position must be considered in estimating the relative age of the localities. The time that is supposed to have passed during the deposition of the marine formations of the La Jolla Group, the supposed age of the maximum transgression, and the geographic and stratigraphic positions were considered when each sample was given an approximate relative age in millions of years before the present.

Physical Regime

Because this study is concerned with preliminary steps in the investigation of community change, it seems appropriate to establish a base from which to proceed. A constant physical regime will be used as the basal state. Under such a condition, community change should be primarily the result of biotic interaction. In the case of the La Jolla communities, this basal regime might be approached if there are no significant temporal trends in the substrate characteristics within the environment occupied by a particular community or if there is no significant temporal trend in the climatic conditions during the time being considered. If there are significant physical trends or perturbations in time, then the interpretations would be of a specific rather than of a general nature.

Lithologic Trends

A regression analysis was performed to detect any significant trend in the lithologic parameters of the three formations through the middle Eocene. Variations in the mean grain size (in phi units), skewness of the grain-size frequency distribution, and percent quartz grains for twenty-five localities were determined through grain counts on sandstone thin sections from the three biofacies. Table 15-3 shows no significant correlation value (r) for regression

Table 15-3
Linear regression between approximate relative age of localities and the lithologic characteristics of the sedimentary rock at those localities, from the Eocene marine units from the La Jolla Group of the San Diego coastal region, southern California. Significant correlation coefficients (r) are underscored. Alpha level for critical limits is 0.10.

	slope	y-intercept	r value
Delmar Formation			
Mean grain size (phi)	0.8272	-38.31	0.427
Skewness grain size	-0.0305	1.56	-0.066
percent quartz	7.1465	-282.75	<u>0.819</u>
Ardath Formation			
Mean grain size (phi)	0.1538	-3.87	0.419
Skewness grain size	0.1495	-7.01	0.444
percent quartz	2.3250	-48.38	0.316
Scripps Formation			
Mean grain size (phi)	-0.1203	8.88	-0.534
Skewness grain size	0.2091	-9.66	0.720
percent quartz	4.5425	-159.63	0.501

lines with slopes that depart notably from zero except between time and percent quartz in the Delmar biofacies. This means for all but the exception, there are no significant lithologic trends in time. Even though there is a strong correlation between time and percent quartz and a notable trend (slope = 7.15), this trend does not appear to have been of any consequence to the biota. This is indicated by a lack of correlation between percent quartz in the sandstone and the diversity (H) of the community ($r = -0.1628$) or the percent suspension feeders in the community ($r = 0.1994$).

Climatic Trend

It is important to examine the evidence for climatic trend in the southern California coastal area from the beginning of the Eocene to the middle of the late Eocene (approximately 52 to 42 mybp) and the possible effects on community structure. Any such trend would complicate the interpretation of the relationship between physical regime and community change. Biological evidence of a cooling trend in the late Eocene and early Oligocene includes both animal and plant assemblages from the Pacific Coast of North America and the North Pacific Ocean.

Several plant assemblages that show evidence of a cooling trend (Wolfe and Hopkins, 1967) are associated with reliable radiometric dates that range from about 38 to 42 mybp. Wolfe (1971) placed the period of maximum warmth in the late Eocene and stated that the climate in central California did not generally cool in the Eocene. During the Paleocene, a paratropical rain forest existed at 60°N and marginally tropical rain forest grew at 52°N on the Pacific Coast.

Durham (1950) inferred the Cenozoic marine climate of the Pacific Coast based on the present and past distribution of tropical genera. Durham (1950) considered fossil marine invertebrates collected from 48°N latitude to be clearly tropical, indicating a surface-water terperature of approximately 21°C for the first six million years of the Eocene. A slightly younger assemblage for the same latitude indicates the same temperature prevailed for the next four million years. Samples representing the next two and a half million years are scarce, but may indicate that the temperature was the same (Durham, 1950). An invertebrate assemblage from the Cowlitz Formation (46°30'N) indicates temperatures of 20°C or slightly higher for the late Eocene Tejon State (45 to 41.5 mybp).

More nearly direct evidence for temperatures that prevailed in the Northern Pacific during the Eocene is provided by oxygen isotopic composition of planktonic and benthonic forminifera (Savin et al., 1975). Bottom temperatures in the Pacific (presently 32°27'N, 157°43'W) from the Paleocene to the late Eocene dropped only 2°C giving a cooling trend of 0.1°C per million years. At the end of this period, a drop of 7°C occurred during the latest Ulatisian and Narizian (Savin et al., 1975).

The comparative abundance of individuals belonging to what presently represent tropical or paratropical genera of an equivalent trophic level may provide information on the prevailing climate for the La Jolla region. The presumed tropical predatory species Ancilla gabbi, Gemmula violeta, and Latirus nightingalei (232 total number of specimens of these species counted) found in the Ardath and Scripps formations are less abundant than the presumably paratropical predatory species Conus warreni and Mitra (Strigatella) sandiegoensis (378). The opposite is true of suspension feeders; the tropical species Callista (Microcallista) tecolotensis (508) is more abundant than the paratropical species Crassatella uvasana semidentata (54) and Pitar sorrentoensis (397). The dominance of the tropical forms is evident when Cerithium cliffensis (7696) is compared to the paratropical Turritella uvasana applinae (1826). These assemblages of tropical and paratropical species indicate an average temperature of slightly over 20°C with a minimum of 18°C. Of greater interest here would be the evidence of a gradual change in the temperature over the ten million year sequence observed in this study. A regression analysis was performed on the abundance of individuals of species in what are presently tropical genera in relation to time. The Pearson correlation coefficients for individual abundance with time for Corithium cliffensis, Conus warreni, Callista (Microcallista) tecolotensis, and Turritella uvasana applinae were -0.1723, -0.1020, -0.1323, and -0.1860, respectively. This indicates that there was no significant correlation. If climate had deteriorated during any period of time span under investigation, the abundance of the tropical species' individuals would have presumably declined. These several lines of evidence suggest that the overall climatic regime did not change significantly during the time considered in this study.

Biotic Properties of the Communities

A close relationship appears to exist between diversity and fluctuations in trophic level, species, and predator proportions. These latter items are diversity dependent in the sense that their effects on diversity may be partitioned rather than pervasive and that they limit the resource consumption of populations, either through ecological controls or evolution of adaptations, permitting a partioning of resources where diversity is high and inhibiting it where diversity is low (Valentine, 1973: 290-291). Figures 15-13, 15-14, 15-15, 15-16, and 15-17 illustrate the changes in diversity, abundance of feeding types, and dominance of species of certain trophic types for the La Jolla invertebrate communities.

Diversity

A strong positive correlation between spatial heterogeneity and species diversity has been demonstrated (Recher, 1969) although others (Sanders, 1968) have shown that even between biotopes of similar spatial heterogeneity, species diversity may differ considerably. The Delmar lagoonal biotope is an obvious exception to the generalization that these factors are directly related. Lagoonal environments have, if anything, a higher spatial heterogeneity then offshore-shelf environments like the Ardath and Scripps biotopes, yet an outstanding characteristic of lagoonal communities is their low species diversity (Pearse, 1950). It is believed that a greater range of environmental fluctuations (tidal changes, mud-sand migration, turbidity, and salinity) in lagoonal environments than in offshore biotopes may be responsible in some way for the lower diversity of lagoonal species (Day, 1951; Odum, 1971).

The observation that diversity variation in the Delmar lagoonal community was apparently less than that in the Ardath and Scripps

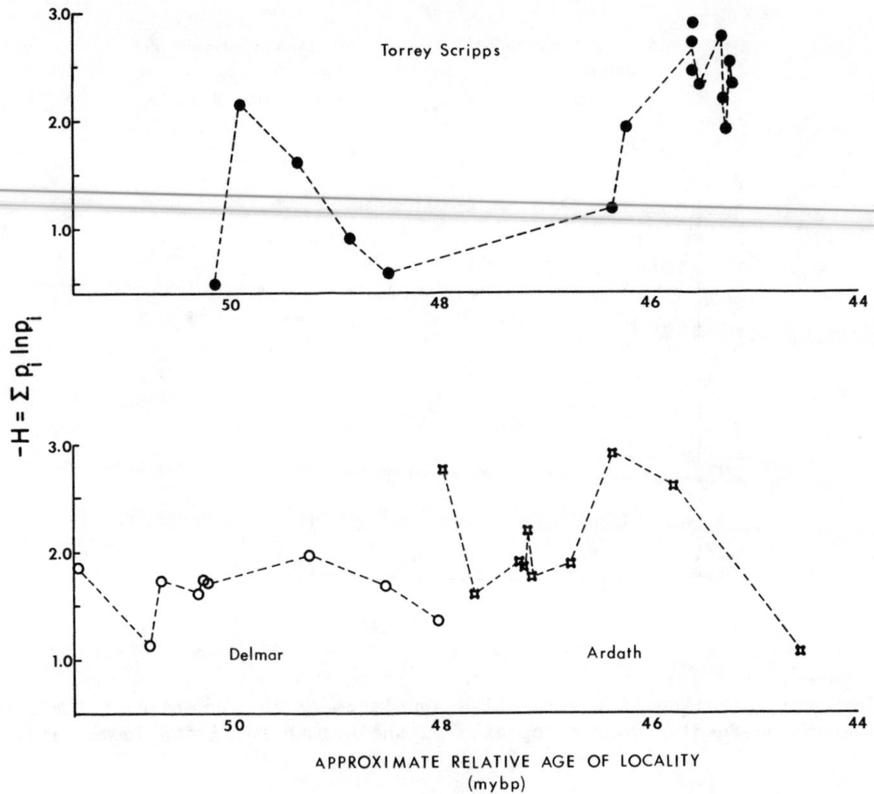

Figure 15-13
Temporal variation in diversity for samples representing the Delmar, Ardath, and Torrey-Scripps communities. The ordinate is the Shannon-Weaver diversity index.

communities, even though the former inhabited a more unstable environment, might seem curious. However, Hedgepeth (1957) has pointed out that lagoonal species are, through selective pressure, adapted to the vicissitudes of their environment, and there is no reason to suspect greater instability in the case of lagoonal communities.

Competition

Analyses of competitive interaction between species in communities are often highly inferential, being based on information about community diversity (MacArthur and Wilson, 1967) or life histories (Pianka, 1974). A common procedure in the analysis of fossil data is to assume by analogy with modern counterparts that two or more species overlap in resource requirements, environmental tolerances, and other components describing their respective niches. These "competitors" are then compared with reference to their complementary distributions and abundances in space and time (for example, Levington and Bambach, 1975).

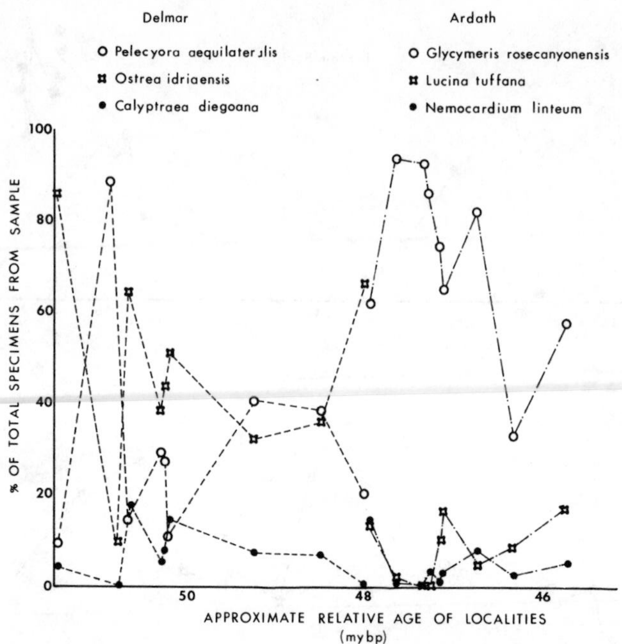

Figure 15-14
Temporal variation in the relative abundance of the numerically dominant suspension-feeding mollusc species in the Delmar and Ardath communities.

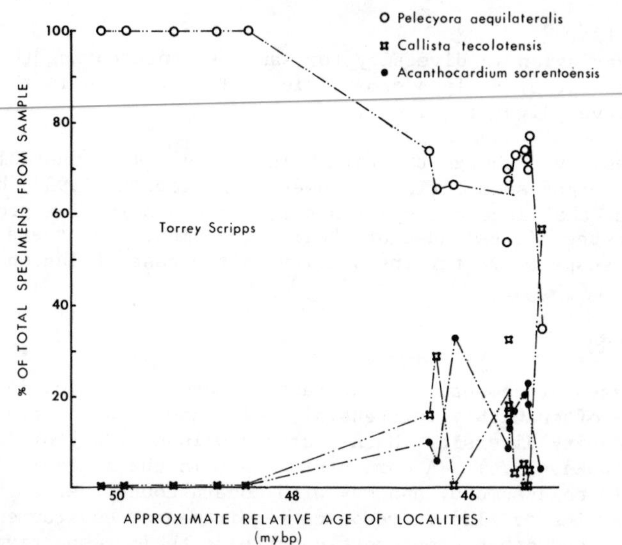

Figure 15-15
Temporal variation in the relative abundance of the numerically dominant suspension-feeding mollusc species in the Torrey-Scripps community.

Several patterns in the La Jolla Eocene Communities might be interpreted as examples of fluctuations in relative abundance due to competition. For example, feeding-type proportions remained steady in the Delmar lagoonal community, but the realtive proportions of important suspension feeders varied markedly. Comparisons between Figures 15-13 and 15-14 show that the drop in diversity for a locality placed at 51 mybp coincides with marked increase in the relative abundance of Pelecyora aequilateralis. One inference to draw from this datum is that diversity was inversely related to the significant increase in competitive success of Pelecyora aequilateralis. If such an event did occur, it was comparatively brief because the data suggest subsequent readjustment and stability for diversity levels of the Delmar community (Figure 15-14). Analysis of a greater number of contemporaneous samples is required to distinguish between spatial, temporal, and merely artifactual elements of this variation.

In contrast to the Delmar lagoonal community, fluctuations in the proportions of dominant species for the Ardath, Torrey, and Scripps include members of different trophic levels (Figures 15-14 - 15-17). The pattern shown for the Torrey-Scripps community (Figure 15-15) is particularly interesting where the relative abundances of three dominant species remained stable for the early history of the community followed by marked increase in relative abundance of Callista tecolotensis and Acanthocardium sorrentoensis and decrease in dominance of Pelecyora aequilateralis. The data potentially provide evidence for population increases in C. tecolotensis and Acanthocardium sorrentoensis resulting from important biotic shifts and physical changes favorable to their competitive success.

Predation

Because predators may often prey preferentially on more abundant types of prey, an increase in predator diversity and abundance might also promote increase in prey diversity. In the Delmar lagoonal community, predator levels were low and steady and the variety of different prey species was not great, a condition typical of coarse-grained lagoonal environments (Hedgepeth, 1957). One striking feature of the fine-grained offshore bottom environments is the high predator diversity (Valentine and Mallory, 1965). This condition is fully evident in the case of the Ardath community where there was a high diversity of both predator and prey species.

Trophic-level Stability

An important factor in this consideration is trophic-level stability, or relative variation in abundance of feeding types, within the community. Trophic-level stability is thought to be primarily a function of habitat texture and composition, the qualitative nature of trophic resources, and trophic-resource stability (Valentine, 1973). The Delmar community reveals a rather stable picture with respect to the relative dominance of feeding types (Figure 15-16). Suspension feeders were dominant and remained so throughout most of the observed history of the community while the proportions of detritus feeders, primary and secondary predators, and scavengers (not represented in Figure 15-16) were extremely small. Such a long-term stability in feeding-type proportions is

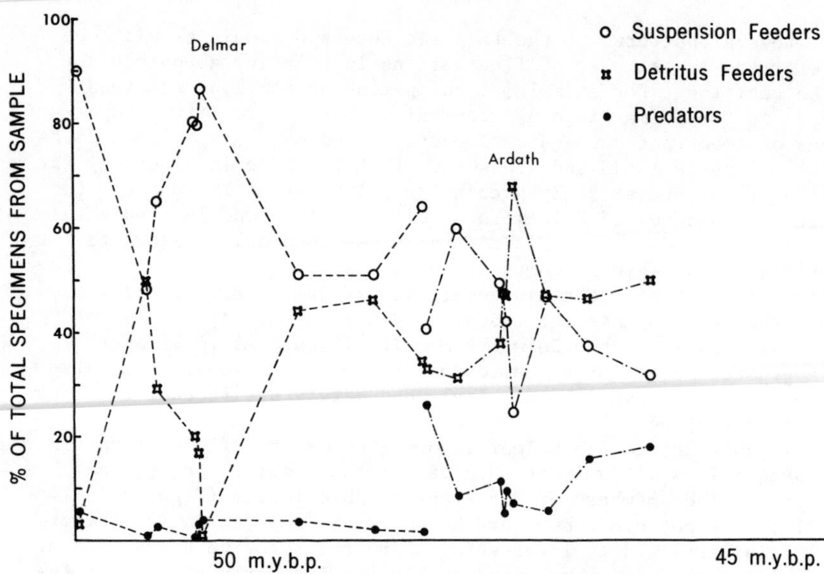

Figure 15-16
Temporal variation in the relative abundance of suspension feeders, detritus feeders, and carnivores in the Delmar and Ardath communities.

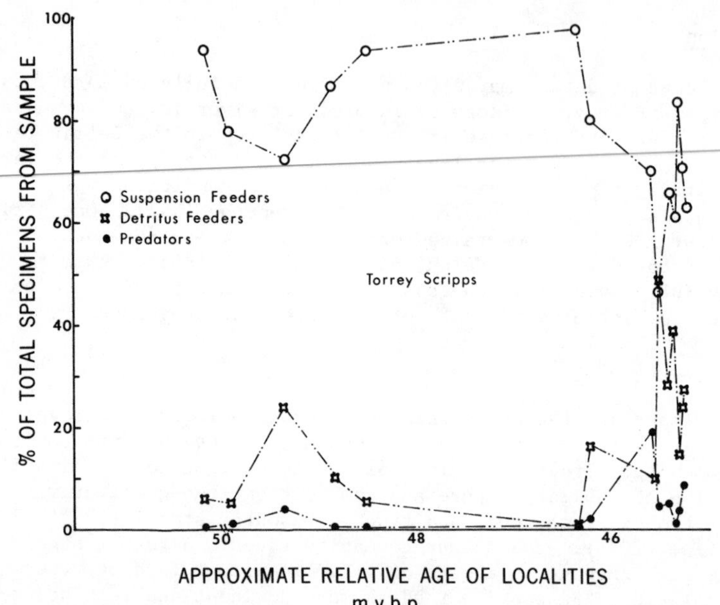

Figure 15-17
Temporal variation in the relative abundance of suspension feeders, detritus feeders, and carnivores in the Torrey-Scripps community.

probably an indication of a stable resource regime as there is no significant increase in the proportion of detritus feeders and scavengers that would be expected during times of unstable productivity (Odum and De La Cruz, 1964; Arnaud, 1970; Valentine, 1973). In contrast, fluctuations in the proportions of feeding types within the Ardath and Scripps communities are striking, particularly within the Ardath sequence where exchange in dominance between suspension feeders and detritus feeders actually occurred (Figures 15-16, 15-17).

Community Complexity

The work of MacArthur (1955), Elton (1927), Pimentel (1961), and many other neoecologists gave rise to the deeply rooted belief that complex natural communities are more stable than simple ones. However, it is becoming increasingly apparent that no simple relationship exists between community complexity and stability (see Goodman, 1975, for recent review). Indeed, May (1974) argued that most generalized multispecies models predict a decrease in stability with increased complexity, but the relationship has not been extensively tested with fossil cases. Empirical treatment of this problem has been somewhat hampered by difficulties in measuring such broad phenomena as "complexity" and "stability." Complexity is usually taken to mean the number and nature of the individual links in the food web, but much additional work is needed to clarify the relationship between community complexity and such parameters as species variety or species diversity. The acknowledged existence of different types of stability, such as _persistent_ stability and _adjustment_ stability (Peterson, 1975), further complicates the problem. The most common meaning corresponds to neighborhood stability, or the stability in the vicinity of an equilibrium point in a deterministic system (May, 1974: 13). Stability as discussed below is equivalent to neighborhood stability.

A direct relationship between high stability and high complexity (here taken to be grossly approximated by high diversity) is not apparent in the case of the La Jolla Eocene molluscan communities. In fact, stability was evidently greater for the less-diverse Delmar lagoonal community than for the more-diverse Ardath and Scripps communities. Ignoring the inadequacies of the data for the moment, it is evident that either the effect of complexity on stability was minimal compared with that of other factors or there is a real, inverse relationship between community stability and complexity in the case of the La Jolla benthic communities.

General Remarks

One might assume that communities that can be delineated consistently through a stratigraphic record might show little variation in time and space. We found this not to hold true for the La Jolla marine Eocene. Diversity varied through time in all three communities. High correlation between diversity fluctuations, trophic-level stability, and variation in relative abundances of dominant species were evident, particularly in the case of the Ardath offshore community. Although trophic-level stability was high in the Delmar lagoonal community, the relative abundance of suspension feeders varied significantly.

It can be safely assumed that animals respond to their physical environment so subtly that it is impossible to falsify a theory linking community change to extrinsic factors. However, the nature of these factors and their effects on the biota can be subjected to scientific investigation. It seems fruitful to analyze a fossiliferous stratigraphic sequence where gross environmental changes or trends are not apparent because the causes of observed biotic fluctuations may be generally applicable in studies of other sequences. Our preliminary analysis suggests that each of the La Jolla communities experienced no apparent gross environmental trends or perturbations. The biotic changes in these communities might, therefore, be interpreted as primarily affected by diversity-dependent biotic factors in combination with subtle and local changes in the physical environment. Other than our study of sedimentological samples and earlier studies of Eocene climate, there have been no thorough investigations of the possible subtle environmental changes. Evidence reviewed above, however, suggests an interplay between diversity changes and shifts in relative abundance, trophic level dominance, and other biotic phenomena during the history of the La Jolla communities. Our conclusion thus takes the form of a working hypothesis: the La Jolla benthic communities were highly integrated and capable of significant spatial and temporal variation in the absence of gross trends or fluctuations in the physical environment.

SUMMARY AND CONCLUSIONS

Multivariate methods of community analysis are often criticized because they supposedly tend to obscure relationships between faunas and environmental parameters, yield results strongly biased by variation in sample size, and provide little or no significant information in addition to that obtained qualitatively. However, ordination methods used in combination with multivariate techniques, such as cluster analyses, demonstrate that some of these problems can be resolved and that meaningful associations between faunal elements and environmental parameters can be found (Bray and Curtis, 1957; Gervirtz et al., 1971). Likewise, McCammon (1966, 1970) demonstrated that rotated principal-components analysis provides information on the correlation between faunal types and environmental variables. Community-components analysis, which uses a standardization of the variation in the size of samples and the correlation of cases through the principal components, appears to us to have the following attributes:

1. The method provides an accurate classification based on the distribution and relative abundance of species. This is clearly demonstrated by comparing the mode-2 anagram for Mugu Lagoon with the relative abundance for species through localities in Warme's initial data matrix (Warme, 1971, Plate 1).
2. Quantitative groupings resulting from the method can be interpreted as biotic communities and correlated with ecologically meaningful parameters. The separation of biotopes and communities in Mugu Lagoon correspond well with the pattern of substrate and geographic variation described by Warme (1971). Likewise, the recognition of the Scripps,

Ardath, and Delmar benthic communities correspond with three different formations representing three basically different environments.

3. The method shows reasonable reproducibility when tested. Sample couplets collected by Warme (1971) from Mugu Lagoon were shown to be highly correlated in mode-1 community-components analysis.
4. Inference on the internal structure and function of the communities can be made based on careful study of the groups recognized by the analysis. Study of the feeding habits of the molluscs represented in the Mugu Lagoon communities suggests interesting interrelationships of certain trophic types.
5. The method can be used as a framework for evolutionary studies. It is obvious that the analysis of community change could be derived from the results of community-components analysis.

Use of such an analysis as a basis for preliminary study of the history of the La Jolla benthic communities produced some interesting results. Diversity varied significantly through time in all three communities despite their distinctive species compositions and proportions. Gross environmental changes within units were not apparent, but high correlations were found between diversity fluctuations, trophic-level stability, and marked variation in the relative abundances of dominant species in the Ardath offshore community. Although trophic-level stability was high in the Delmar lagoonal community, the relative abundance of suspension-feeding species varied significantly in time and space. These patterns suggest that the La Jolla marine benthic communities were highly integrated and capable of changes in the absence of gross trends or perturbations in physical regimes they occupied.

ACKNOWLEDGEMENTS

We thank Dr. W. B. N. Berry, M. K. Brett-Surman, Dr. J. W. Durham, Dr. J. T. Gregory, P. R. Lawson, J. Markison, V. E. Novacek, R. Schatzinger, and D. Thatcher for their help in various aspects of this study. We are grateful to Drs. R. J. Stanton, J. E. Warme, and J. L. Gevirtz for their very useful critical comments on earlier drafts of this paper. Funds for computer time were provided by the Campus Computer Center and the Department of Paleontology, The University of California, Berkeley. Support for field work was provided by the University of California Museum of Paleontology.

REFERENCES

Abbott, R. T. 1968. *A guide to Field Identification: Seashells of America*. New York: Golden Press, 280 p.

Anderson, A. J. B. 1971. Ordination methods in ecology. *Jour. Ecology* 59: 713-726.

Arnaud, P. M. 1970. Frequency and ecological significance of necrophagy among benthic species of antarctic coastal waters, in Holgate, M. W., ed., *Antarctic Ecology* 1:259-266.

Boyer, J. E., and J. E. Warme. 1975. Sedimentary facies and trace fossils in the Eocene Delmar formation and Torrey sandstone, California, in Weaver, D.W., G. R. Hornaday, and Ann Tipton, eds., *Future Energy Horizons of the Pacific Coast*. Tulsa: American Assoc. Petroleum Geologists, pp. 65-98.

Bray, J. R. and J. T. Curtis, 1957. An ordination of upland forest communities of southern Wisconsin. *Ecol. Mon.* 27:325-349.

Clark, B. L. 1926. The Domengine, middle Eocene of California. *California Univ. Dept. of Geological Sci. Bull.* 16:99-118.

Day, J. H. 1951. The ecology of South African estuaries: A review of esturine conditions in general. *Roy. Soc. South Africa Trans.* 33:367-413.

Durham, J. W. 1950. Cenozoic marine climates of the Pacific Coast. *Geol. Soc. American Bull.* 61:1243-1264.

Ellis, A. J. 1919. Geology, western part of San Diego County, California. *U. S. Geol. Survey Water-Supply Paper* 446:50-76.

Gervitz, J. K., R. A. Park, and G. M. Friedman, 1971. Paraecology of benthonic Foraminifera and associated micro-organisms of the continental shelf off Long Island, New York. *Jour. Paleontology* 45:153-177.

Givens, C. R. 1974. Eocene molluscan biostratigraphy of the Pine Mountain area, Ventura County, California. *California Univ. Pubs. Geological Sci.* 109:1-107.

Givens, C. R. and M. P. Kennedy. 1976. Middle Eocene molluscs from northern San Diego County, California. *Jour. Paleontology* 50:945-975.

Goodman, D. 1975. The Theory of diversity-stability relationships in ecology. *Quart. Rev. Biology* 50:237-266.

Hanna, M. A. 1926. Geology of the La Jolla Quadrangle, California. *California Univ. Pubs. Geol. Sci.* 16:187-246.

Hanna, M. A. 1927. An Eocene invertebrate fauna from the La Jolla Quadrangle, California. *California Univ. Pubs. Geol. Sci.* 16:247-398.

Hedgepeth, J. W. 1957. Biological aspects, in Estuaries and Lagoons, in Hedgepeth, J. W., ed., *Treatise on Marine Ecology and Paleoecology, Ecology*. Geol. Soc. America Mem. 67:693-729.

Johnston, J. K. 1972. Effect of turbidity on the rate of filtration and growth of the slipper limpet, Crepidula fornicata Lamarck, 1799. *Verliger* 14:315-320.

Kennedy, M. P. and G. W. Moore. 1971. Stratigraphic relations of Upper Cretaceous and Eocene formations, San Diego Coastal area, California. *Am. Assoc. Petroleum Geologists Bull.* 55:709-722.

Levinton, J. S. and R. K. Bambach. 1975. A comparative study of Silurian and recent deposit-feeding bivalve communities. *Paleobiology* 1:97-124.

MacArthur, R. H. 1955. Fluctuations of animal populations and a measure of community stability. *Ecology* 3:533-536.

MacArthur, R. H., and E.O. Wilson, 1967. *The Theory of Island Biogeography*. Princeton: Princeton University Press, 203 p.

MacGinitie, G. E. 1935. Ecological aspects of a California marine estuary. *Am. Midland Naturalist* 16:627-765.

Mallory, V. S. 1959. *Lower Tertiary Biostratigraphy of the California Coast Ranges*. Tulsa: Am. Assoc. Petroleum Geologists, 416p.

May, R. M. 1974. *Stability and Complexity in Model Ecosystems.* Princeton: Princeton University Press, 265 p.

McCammon, R. B. 1966. Principal component analysis and its application in large-scale correlation studies. *Jour. Geology* 74:721-733.

McCammon, R. B. 1970. Minimum entropy criterion for analytic rotation. *Kansas Geol. Survey Computer Contribution* 43:1-24.

Merrill, R. J., and E. S. Hobson, 1969. *Field Observations of Dendraster excentricus, a Sand Dollar of Western North America.* Open File, UCMP, 36 p.

Morton, J. E. 1958. *Molluscs.* London: Hutchinson and Co., 232 p.

Odum, E. P. 1959. *Fundamentals of Ecology.* Philadelphia: W. B. Saunders Co., 546 p.

Odum, E. P. 1971. *Fundamentals of Ecology.* Philadelphia: W. B. Saunders Co., 574 p.

Odum, E. P., and A. A. De La Cruz, 1964. Detritus as a major component of ecosystems. *Am. Inst. Biol. Sci. Bull.* 13:39-40.

Parker, R. H. 1975. *The Study of Benthic Communities: A Model and a Review.* Amsterdam: Elsevier Scientific Publishing Co., 279 p.

Pearse, A. S. 1950. *The Emigrations of Animals from the Sea.* Dryden, New York: Sherwood Press, 210 p.

Peterson, C. H. 1975. Stability of species and of community for the benthos of two lagoons. *Ecology* 56:598-965.

Pianka, E. R. 1974. *Evolutionary Ecology.* New York: Harper and Row, 356 p.

Pimentel, D. 1961. Species diversity and insect population outbreaks. *Entomol. Soc. America Annals* 54:76-85.

Pohlo, R. H. 1967. Aspects of the biology of Donax gouldi and a note on evolution in Tellinacea (Bivalvia). *Veliger* 9:330-337.

Pohlo, R. H. 1972. Feeding and associated morphology in Sanguinolaria nuttalli (Bivalvia; Tellinacea). *Veliger* 14:298-301.

Purchon, R. D. 1958. *The Biology of the Mollusca.* London: Pergamon Press, 560 p.

Recher, H. F. 1969. Bird diversity and habitat diversity in Australia and North America. *Am. Naturalist* 103:65-80.

Sanders, H. L. 1968. Marine benthic diversity: a comparative study. *Am. Naturalist* 102:243-282.

Savin, S. M., R. G. Douglas, and F. G. Stehli. 1975. Tertiary marine paleotemperatures. *Geol. Soc. America Bull.* 86:1499-1510.

Stanton, J. R., and J. R. Dodd. 1976. The application of trophic structure of fossil communities in paleoenvironmental reconstruction. *Lethaia* 9:327-342.

Tatsouka, M. M. 1971. *Multivariate Analysis: Techniques for Educational and Psychological Research.* New York: John Wiley and Sons, Inc., 310 p.

Valentine, J. W. 1973. *Evolutionary Paleoecology of the Marine Biosphere.* Englewood Cliffs, New Jersey: Prentice-Hall, 511p.

Valentine, J. W., and B. Mallory. 1965. Recurrent groups of bonded species in mixed death assemblages. *Jour. Geology* 73:683-701.

Valentine, J. W., and R. G. Peddicord. 1967. Evaluation of fossil assemblages by custer analysis. *Jour. Paleontology* 41:502-507.

Vokes, N. E. 1939. Molluscan faunas of the Domengine and Arroyo Hondo formations of the California Eocene. *New York Acad. Sci. Annals*. 8:1-246.

Warme, J. E. 1971. Paleoecological aspects of modern coastal lagoon, *California Univ. Pubs. Geol. Sci.* 87:1-131.

Weaver, C. E. 1942. Paleontology of the marine Tertiary formations of Oregon and Washington. *Washington Univ. Pubs. Geology* 5:1-274.

Wolfe, J. A. 1971. Tertiary climatic fluctuations and methods of analysis of Tertiary floras. *Palaeogeography, Palaeoclimatology, and Palaeoecology* 9:27-57.

Wolfe, J. A., and D. M. Hopkins, 1967. Climatic changes recorded by Tertiary land floras in northwestern North America, in K. Hatai, ed., *Tertiary Correlations and Climatic Changes in the Pacific*. Symposium Pacific Sci. Congress 25:67-76.

16

Middle Eocene to Early Oligocene Plant Communities of the Gulf Coast

Norman O. Frederiksen

ABSTRACT

Since the 1920s and 1930s, few papers have appeared on the Eocene and Oligocene plant communities of the Gulf Coast, and most of the work on these communities has been concerned with megafossils. This study was based on sporomorphs (spores and pollen grains), mainly of anemophilous types, from eighty-six lignite and detrital rock samples from the Claibornian (middle Eocene), Jacksonian (upper Eocene), and lower Vicksburgian (lower Oligocene) of Texas, Arkansas, Tennessee, Mississippi, Alabama, and Georgia. The emphasis of this study was on sporomorphs from the Jacksonian. Sparse marine to brackish-water dinoflagellates and acritarchs are present in shales adjacent to some of the coals, suggesting that the originial peats formed near the sea and some of them possibly in brackish water.

Most Claibornian assemblages from both coals and detrital rocks are dominated by various pollen types of Fagaceae. On the basis of samples from the marine Jacksonian, fourteen to twenty-two modern genera and generic groups were identified whose plants were probably abundant in the lowlands and (or) were confined to the lowlands of the southeastern United States. Of eight genera of gymnosperms represented by pollen in the marine Jacksonian, all but Ephedra were apparently more or less restricted to the uplands. According to stratigraphic evidence, the upper Jacksonian coals of southeastern Texas formed in lower-deltaic swamps. A cluster diagram of fourteen assemblages from these coals shows them to be quite similar to each other. Dominant genera are Momipites (Engelhardia group, Juglandaceae) and Caprifoliipites-Salixipollenites (affinity unknown, perhaps shrubs). However, differences in the zoophilous pollen constituents of the assemblages suggest that the vegetation of Jacksonian deltaic swamps may have varied more than is immediately suggested by the cluster diagram. Marine and some nonmarine detrital rock assemblages from the Jacksonian are dominated by pollen of Fagaceae, but some nonmarine shale assemblages are similar to Jacksonian coal assemblages in being dominated by Momipites. In some upper Claibornian and Jacksonian samples, Nyssa pollen is fairly abundant and palm pollen is moderately to very abundant.

Assemblages from lower Vicksburgian coals generally contain

higher percentages of fern spores than the older coals. Other sporomorph types abundant in one or more lower Vicksburgian coals include Taxodiaceae-Cupressaceae-Taxaceae, Fraxinoipollenites (affinity unknown), palms, and "miscellaneous dicots," many of which were probably zoophilous. On the other hand, assemblages from lower Vicksburgian detrital rocks are dominated by pollen of Quercus or a near relative, trees of which were apparently abundant on the coastal plain outside of the deltaic swamps.

Claibornian to early Vicksburgian brackish and marine coastal communities consisted in part of Nypa and perhaps also of Acrostichum, Myrtaceae-Sapindaceae, Restionaceae-Centrolepidaceae-Flagellariaceae, and Ruppiaceae?-Potamogetonaceae?; Ephedra was present in sandy, xeric coastal habitats.

INTRODUCTION

No thorough attempts have been made to reconstruct the middle and late Eocene plant communities of the southeastern United States since Berry's papers of 1924 and 1937, and most of the research on Eocene plant paleoecology has concentrated on plant megafossils. Very little has been published on plant megafossils or microfossils from the Oligocene of this region. The purpose of this paper is to present data on the presence and relative frequencies of sporomorph (spore and pollen) forms in samples from the middle Eocene to the lower Oligocene of the Gulf Coast and to derive autecological and synecological information from these data.

Samples studied are from the following provincial stages (zones and correlations are from Hardenbol and Berggren, 1978):

Provincial Stage	European Equivalent	Age (Millions of Years)	Planktic Foraminifer Zones	Calcareous Nannoplankton Zones
Vicksburgian	Lower Oligocene	32-37	P 17-19	NP 21-23
Jacksonian	Upper Eocene	37-40	P 15-17	NP 18-21
Claibornian	Middle Eocene	40-49	P 10-14	NP 14-17

Two main sources of data were used in this investigation:

1. Detailed analyses of fifty-six detrital rock assemblages from the upper Claibornian, Jacksonian, and lower Vicksburgian of western Mississippi, eastern Mississippi, and western Alabama (Frederiksen, 1968, 1969, 1973, in press). Relative frequencies of the sporomorph taxa were known for these samples (Frederiksen, 1969), and the affinities of the sporomorphs that could be assigned to modern genera and families have been listed (Frederiksen, 1977).
2. Detailed analyses of four lignite and two shale samples from the Claibornian, fourteen lignite and ten detrital rock samples from the Jacksonian, and four lignite and four shale samples from the lower Vicksburgian of the Gulf Coast. These thirty-eight samples are listed in the Sample Register (Appendix) and shown on Figure

16-1. Eight of the shale samples of this part of the study are from among the fifty-six samples of paragraph one above. The Sample Register also lists seventeen samples of shale and mudstone that were examined only for the presence of microplankton. Two additional samples listed in the Register, R1264B (coal) and R1266E (mudstone), were found to be barren of palynomorphs.

Major problems with paleoecological analyses based on detrital sediments are that the sediments normally contain sporomorphs from a wide variety of environments and that the sporomorph assemblages generally represent the regional rather than the local flora. Nevertheless, some information about the coastal plain and even the upland vegetation may be obtained from detrital sediments.

Long-distance transport of sporomorphs from the continent to the ocean is mainly by streams rather than by wind, and the grains may be carried for hundreds of miles downstream (Muller, 1959; Groot, 1966). The main sources of detrital sediments to the northern part of the Gulf of Mexico in the Eocene and early Oligocene were the northern Great Plains and the Appalachians (Rainwater, 1967; Mann and Thomas, 1968), and these two regions presumably provided most of the upland pollen to the Gulf, especially pollen of plants living in temperate climates.

The local community is heavily over-represented, however, in assemblages from many coals (Faegri and Iversen, 1964:89, 102, 115-116; Tschudy, 1969:81). Sporomorph analyses of coal samples provide information about communities of one particular environment, the peat-forming swamps; for this reason, I examined the twenty-two sporomorph-bearing lignite samples from the Clabornian, Jacksonian, and lower Vicksburgian. Additional data on Claibornian lignite assemblages are available from a paper by Potter (1976). McLaughlin (1957) described and illustrated a sporomorph assemblage from a lignite in Tennessee that he thought was Cretaceous but Fairchild and Elsik (1969) and Tschudy (1973) dated as Eocene. This assemblage contains probable Platycarya, forms transitional between Platycarya and Platycaryapollenites, and Casuarinidites. The presence of these types suggests that the bed was either upper Sabinian (lower Eocene) or lower Claibornian. McLaughlin's assemblage is older and considerably different in detail from the Claibornian assemblages discussed here.

The preserved Jacksonian from Mississippi eastward to Florida is entirely marine, and the only Gulf Coast Jacksonian coals that I know of are in eastern and southern Texas. A thin (12 cm thick) coal bed was reported by Wilbert (1953:44) to be present in the Redfield Formation (lower Jacksonian) at White Bluff, Arkansas (the same locality as sample R1142B; see the Sample Register, Appendix), but I was unable to find this coal while sampling the area in 1976.

None of the coals studied for this paper have been analyzed petrographically as far as I know. Knowledge of the coal petrography would be of great benefit in the interpretation of the environment of deposition and the interpretation of the sporomorph assemblages.

All methods used here for reconstructing the Paleogene vegetation are subject to error and, at best, can only recognize some of the constituents of the flora. In such a reconstruction the following problems are common:

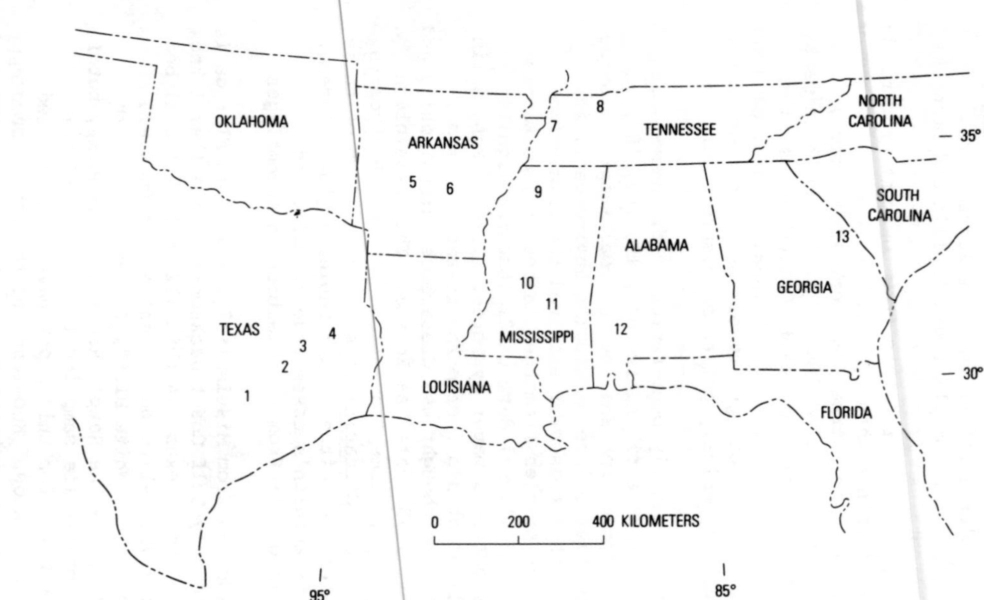

Figure 16-1
Localities mentioned in the text and in the Sample Register.
1. Fayette County, Texas. Sample series R1143 and R1167. 2. Grimes County, Texas. Sample series R1263-R1266. 3. Walker County, Texas. Sample series R1234. 4. Angelina County, Texas. Sample R1298D. 5. Hot Spring County, Arkansas. Samples of Saunders et al. (1974). 6. Jefferson County, Arkansas. Sample R1142B. 7. Lauderdale County, Tennessee. Sample R1448. 8. Henry County, Tennessee. Samples of Elsik and Dilcher (1974) and Potter (1976). 9. Panola and Tate Counties, Mississippi. Samples R1155 and R1156, respectively. 10. Hinds and Madison Counties, Mississippi. Samples 10625, 10627, 10631, 10632, 10637, 10641, 10653, 14958, 14959, P7856, P7857, P7858, and R1145 (Hinds County); R1146A-B (Madison County). 11. Smith County, Mississippi. Sample R1144. 12. Monroe County, Alabama. Samples of Gray (1960). 13. Columbia County, Georgia. Sample R1300A.

1. Spores and pollen grains from trees are much more widely dispersed than those from herbs and shrubs. For this reason, arboreal pollen is over-represented in many assemblages, especially those from detrital sediments.
2. Sporomorphs from some families and genera do not withstand fossilization. This is true of many herbs growing in ponds and streams whose pollen is transferred by water. It is also true of pollen of some important Ranales, for example, Lauraceae and Myristicaceae (Traverse, 1955:21; Muller, 1970:419).
3. Anemophilous plants produce much more pollen than zoophilous plants, and anemophilous pollen is better suited to wide dispersal than zoophilous pollen. However, zoophilous pollen grains commonly occur even in tropical Cenozoic sediments, though the relative frequency of grains of each taxon is usually small (Germeraad et al., 1968; Bartlett and Barghoorn, 1973; Graham, 1975). Examples of differential sporomorph productivity and preservation are well shown by studies of pollen and leaves from Claibornian rocks in Tennessee. Leaves of Lauraceae, Leguminosae, Fagaceae, and Palmae are abundant there (Dilcher and Potter, 1977); however, in the same rocks, pollen grains of Lauraceae are totally lacking (poor preservation), those of Leguminosae are apparently sparse (low productivity and possibly misidentification), grains of Palmae are fairly abundant (only some palms are anemophilous), and grains of Fagaceae are very abundant (Elsik and Dilcher, 1974; Potter, 1976).
4. Many studies have been published on the transport and sedimentation of modern sporomorphs in various environments, but much remains to be learned about these topics. For instance, one factor that influences the relative frequencies of sporomorph types in a sample, and thus the similarity coefficients among samples, is the sorting of sporomorphs during transport and at the site of deposition. Because sporomorphs in coals represent mainly plants living in the swamp or close to it and because little water movement generally takes place within the swamp, assemblages from coals are much less affected by sorting than those deposited in streams, lakes, and seas.

Some problems of reconstructing even a modern subtropical to winter-dry tropical marsh or swamp community from sporomorph data alone are shown by the studies of Riegel (1965) in southern Florida. Riegel (1965:89-90) states:

> Values of 1 or 2 percent of *Avicennia* and *Utricularia* (pollen) indicate the presence of their respective parent plants in close vicinity of the sampling site, and values higher than 5 percent for *Avicennia* already indicate dominance.... The most dominant and characteristic plant in an area may be represented in the corresponding pollen assemblage as a minor component only (e.g. *Mariscus jamaicensis*, family Cyperaceae), other members of the plant community may not be encountered at all (Lauraceae, *Magnolia*) ... while a very inconspicuous and ephemeral plant may be prominent in the pollen assemblage (Chenopod type 1).

It would be desirable to refer only to genera and families of plants in this chapter, but that is not possible because many of the sporomorphs encountered in Paleogene sediments cannot be identified as belonging to modern taxa. This is true, first, because sporomorphs of some modern plant taxa, especially those from the tropics, are not well known. Second, many genera and even families had not evolved by the Eocene or early Oligocene. Third, evolutionary parallelism and convergence of morphological characters make it difficult or impossible to distinguish among sporomorphs of certain taxa, for example, among pollen of some genera of the Fagaceae. Among the 166 sporomorph forms from the Jacksonian of Mississippi and Alabama, 30 percent are assigned with confidence to a modern genus, 24 percent are doubtfully assigned to one genus or narrowed down with some certainty to two genera, and 46 percent are of uncertain or unknown affinity. Comparable figures for assignment of sporomorph types to modern families are 50, 25, and 25 percent, respectively. In the following pages, I refer to the sporomorphs in terms of modern taxa where possible; this means that the floral lists include both fossil and modern taxa. The names of fossil sporomorph taxa used here are mainly those appearing in the literature; many of these names need taxonomic revision, but that cannot be done in this chapter.

Cluster analyses of the sample assemblages were performed using the cosine theta coefficient of Imbrie and Purdie (1962) as the similarity index. Calculations were based on a count of 200 sporomorphs (spores and pollen grains excluding fungal spores) per sample. Only multistate (relative frequency) data were used to find sample similarities because all the samples contain much the same sporomorph types. No attempt was made to include data on the presence of species not observed in the 200-counts because more species would certainly be found if scanning of the slide continued long enough, and these rare species may represent the regional vegetation rather than the local community that was of main interest in the cluster analyses. Purposes of the clustering procedures were, first, to group similar assemblages so that all assemblages could be easily compared, and second, to present graphically the numerical similarities among assemblages.

Relative frequency terms used in this paper are defined to the nearest whole number percent as follows:

"infrequent"	=	1	percent
"occasional"	=	1-5	percent
"common"	=	6-20	percent
"abundant"	=	21-40	percent
"very abundant"	=	40	percent

BACKGROUND DATA

Figures 16-2 and 16-3 are cluster diagrams of sporomorph assemblages from the samples listed in the Sample Register (Appendix). Figure 16-2 shows assemblages from coal and detrital rock samples of the Claibornian, Jacksonian, and Vicksburgian; Figure 16-3 shows only assemblages from upper Claibornian and Jacksonian coals. To interpret the significance of the clusters, we need to know as much as possible about the environments of deposition of these samples.

Samples R1155 and R1156 are from middle Claibornian lignites of northwestern Mississippi. Lignite R1155 crops out at Tocowa Church,

Panola County, and was assigned to the Zilpha Clay by Vestal (1956:61). However, nonmarine strata assigned to the Zilpha by Vestal (1956) and Priddy (1942) would probably be included by Fisher (1964:162, Table 1) in the overlying Kosciusko Sand (of Thomas, 1942; Sparta Sand of U. S. Geological Survey usage). At least two lignite seams occur near the village of Tocowa. Vestal (1956:143) provided the following data on these coals. The first entry is probably the same bed as that represented by sample R1155 (D. R. Williamson, pers. comm.); analyses are on an air-dried basis.

Location	Thickness	Sulfur (Percent)	Ash (Percent)
"behind the old hotel at Tocowa"	0.4 m	0.69	19.8
Bed of Tocowa Creek	0.5 m	0.70	6.25

Sample R1156, labeled Claibornian on the sample bag, is from a lignite of unstated thickness and depth from a drill core in Tate County. The Geologic Map of Mississippi (Mississippi Geological Survey, 1969) shows the Kosciusko Sand directly underlying Quaternary loess in the area of the drill site. In Mississippi, both the Kosciusko and the underlying Zilpha Clay contain lignites, but Claibornian formations below the Zilpha probably do not (Williamson, 1976:24-25).

Lignites cropping out in Tallahatchie County, northwestern Mississippi, are approximately the same age as the lignites of samples R1155 and R1156 and belong to a nonmarine sequence probably representing fluvial deposits of the middle or upper delta plain (Priddy, 1942:28). D. R. Williamson (pers. comm.) also interpreted the middle Claibornian lignites of DeSoto, Tate, and Panola counties, Mississippi, as belonging to fluvial systems.

Samples of shale adjacent to lignites R1155 and R1156 were not available for microplankton analysis, which might have helped to determine salinities of the swamp waters. Lack of shale samples was unfortunate because during processing of the coals for palynomorph analysis, it was noted that R1156 contains much more pyrite than R1155. On the basis of its low sulfur content, R1155 probably formed in a freshwater environment; R1156 may have formed in brackish water. One specimen of Planctonites stellarius (Pot.) Gruas-Cav. was found during palynological examination of sample R1156 (Figure 16-4 (29)); this species was observed by Potonie (1934) in Eocene brown coals of Germany, but it was not reported in Neogene coals of the same region (Potonie and Venitz, 1934; Wolff, 1934). Apparently the species represents a freshwater plankton cyst.

The 0.3-m-thick uppermost Claibornian (Cockfield Formation) lignite from western Mississippi (sample P7857) is the same or nearly the same age as strata that include brackish-water to marine beds in Louisiana and eastern Mississippi (Murray, 1961). Four samples (14958, 14959, P7856, P7858) of shale and clay stratigraphically near the coal were examined for microplankton, but only sample 14959, from 2.4 m above the seam, contains these fossils; only a few specimens of one species of dinoflagellate were observed in 14959, suggesting brackish-water deposition of this sample. The lack of microplankton in the shale immediately above and below the coal may suggest, but

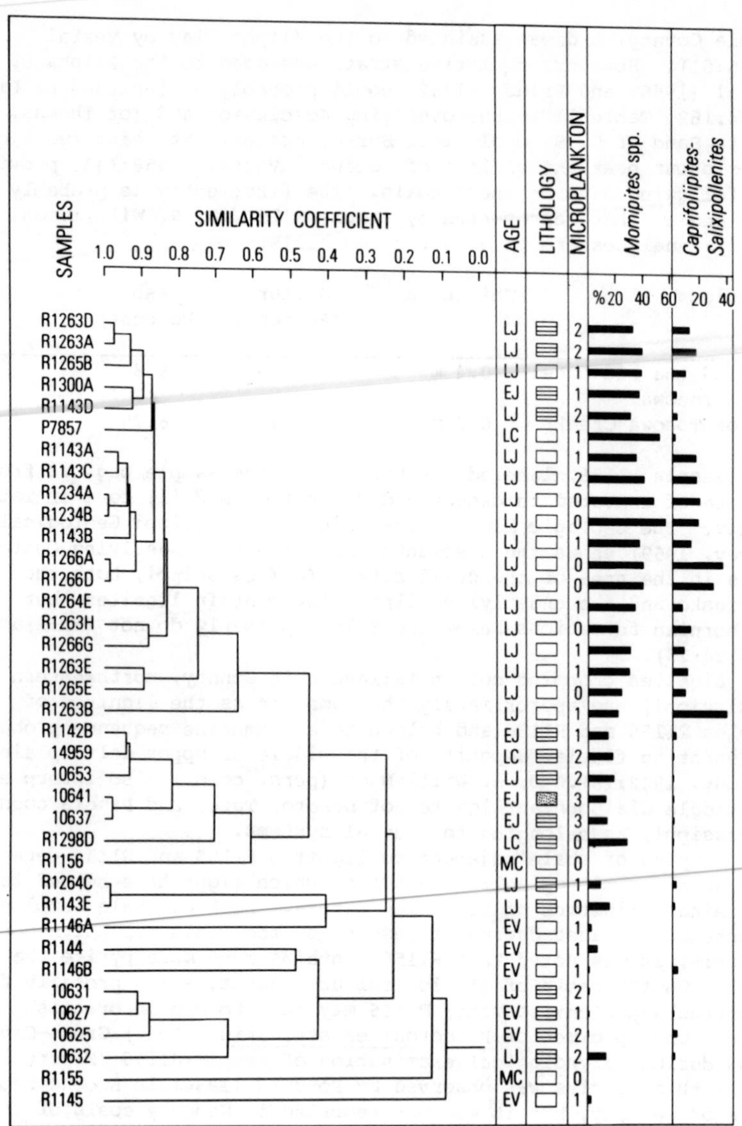

Figure 16-2
Cluster diagram and sporomorph relative frequency diagram of thirty-seven coal and detrital rock assemblages. Clusters computed on the basis of spormorphs exclusive of fungal spores. In the Lithology column, solid pattern = coal, striped pattern = shale and mudstone, dot pattern = greensand. In the Age column, MC = middle Claibornian,

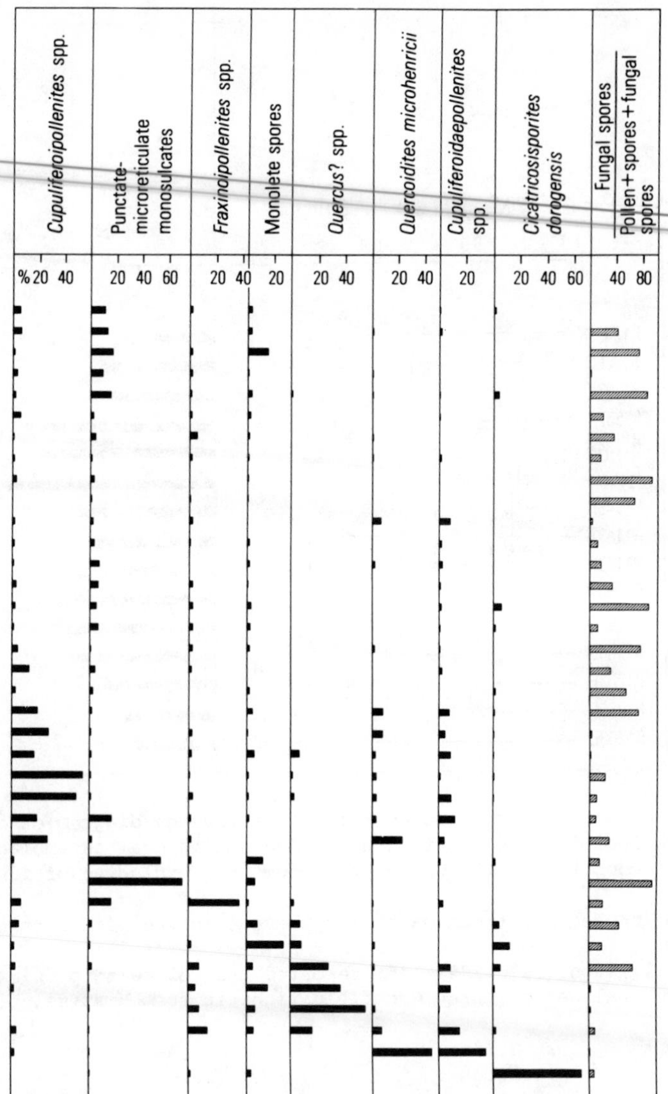

LC = late Claibornian, EJ = early Jacksonian, LJ = late Jacksonian, EV = early Vicksburgian. In the Microplankton column, 0 = no microplankton observed in sample or in adjacent strata, 1 = microplankton in adjacent strata but not in sample itself, 2 = sparse microplankton in sample, 3 = abundant microplankton in sample.

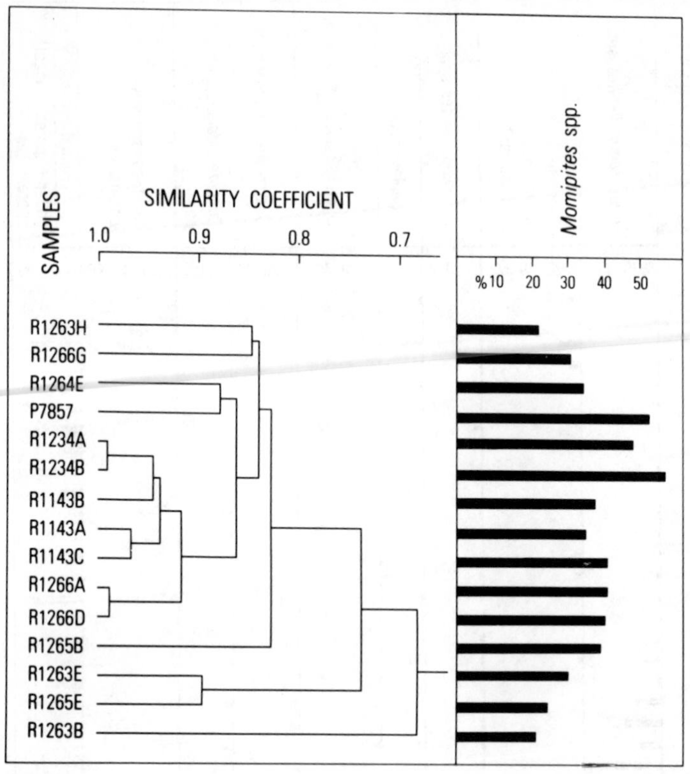

Figure 16-3
Cluster diagram and sporomorph relative frequency diagram of one upper Claibornian and fourteen upper Jacksonian coal assemblages. Clusters computed on the basis of sporomorphs exclusive of fungal

does not prove that fresh water was present in the peat-forming swamp.

Williamson (1976:139, 145) reported the following proximate and ultimate analyses of three Cockfield lignites from Mississippi:

County	Sulfur (Percent)	Ash (Percent)
Holmes	1.39	15.4
Jasper	2.77	12.2
Yazoo	2.76	33.8

These figures for Cockfield lignites are on an air-dried basis; the corresponding figures from as-received basis would be slightly lower and are similar to the sulfur and ash percentages for the lignites of the southeastern Texas Manning Formation (Jacksonian) reported by Kaiser (1974, Text-figures 16-17) that may have formed in brackish water.

No samples of shale adjacent to lignite R1448 (Cockfield Formation, Tennessee) were available for microplankton analysis; however, this sample came from the upper part of the Mississippi

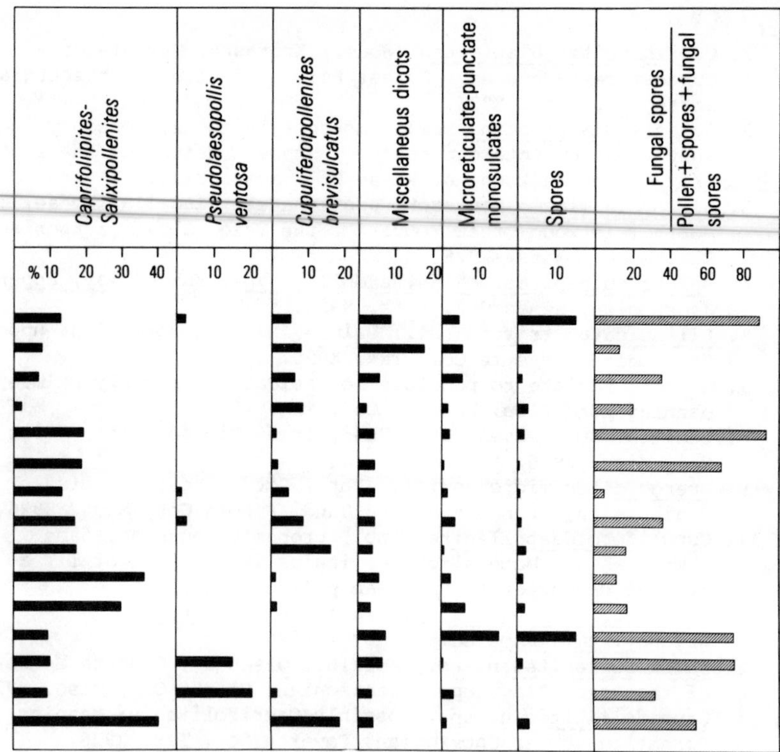

spores. Relative frequencies plotted in the Spores column were computed on the basis of summed data from columns 1 through 4 in Table 16-5. Note that Figures 16-2 and 16-3 have different horizontal scales.

embayment where the lower Tertiary section is less marine than rocks of the same age closer to the present Gulf Coast (Elsik, 1974, Text-figure 6). The relative frequency of fungal spores was not calculated for sample R1448 because the sample residue had been washed through a 10 μm screen during processing.

The stratigraphy of Manning lignites (upper Jacksonian) in southeastern Texas has been discussed in many papers, but these lignites are not as well known as the upper Paleocene lignites of the Wilcox Group. Mapping of lithofacies and of inferred environments of deposition has shown that the Texas Jacksonian lignites and adjacent detrital rocks formed as part of a large, high-construction, fluvial-delta system having an areal extent of about 26,000 km^2 (Fisher, 1969; Fisher et al., 1970; Kaiser, 1974). The Manning coals of southeastern Texas represent deposits of the lower delta plain (Kaiser and Groat, 1977) and are mainly 1 m or less in thickness, but a few of them are as thick as 6 m (Fisher et al., 1970:241). Some Manning lignites of this region appear to be continuous in the subsurface for distances of at least 10 to 24 km along strike and 5 km down dip (Mathewson and Bishop, 1979). The thicker seams are thought to be of tabular or blanket type (Kaiser, 1974:11) such as

Figure 16-4

1. *Cupressacites hiatipites* (Wode.) Krutzsch, Taxodiaceae-Cupressaceae-Taxaceae; Forest Hill Sand, lower Vicksburgian, Smith Co., Miss. X926.
2. *Aglaoreidia pristina* Fowl., monocotyledonous, possibly Ruppiaceae or Potamogetonaceae; Shubuta Member of the Yazoo Clay, upper Jacksonian, Wayne Co., Miss. X926.
3. *Milfordia minima* Krutzsch, Restionaceae-Flagellariaceae; North Twistwood Creek Member of the Yazoo Clay, Jacksonian, Clarke Co., Miss. X926.
4. *Spinizonocolpites echinatus* Mull., *Nypa*; Yazoo Clay, upper Jacksonian, Hinds Co., Miss. X926.
5. *Liliacidites tritus* Fred., Palmae; Manning Formation, upper Jacksonian, Fayette Co., Tex. X926.

6, 7. Microreticulate to punctate monosulcates, probably Palmae; Manning Formation, Fayette Co., Tex. X926.

8. *Quercus*? sp.; Forest Hill Sand, lower Vicksburgian, Smith Co., Miss. X926.
9. *Quercoidites microhenricii* (Pot.) Pot., Fagaceae; middle Claibornian, probably Sparta Sand, Panola Co., Miss. X926.

10, 11. *Cupuliferoidaepollenites* spp., probably Fagaceae; same sample as 9. Note slight geniculus in specimen of 11, a typical character of Fagaceae pollen. X926.

12. *Cupuliferoipollenites* sp., Fagaceae, *Castanea*?, *Dryophyllum*?; same sample as 9. X926.
13. *Salixipollenites* n. sp., possibly Oleaceae; Shubuta Member of the Yazoo Clay, upper Jacksonian, Clarke Co., Miss. X926.

14, 15. *Caprifoliipites* n. sp., possibly Caprifoliaceae; Manning Formation, upper Jacksonian, Fayette Co., Tex. X926.

16. *Momipites microfoveolatus* (Stanl.) Nich., Juglandaceae, *Engelhardia* group; Red Bluff Clay, lower Vicksburgian, Clarke Co., Ala. X926.
17. *Momipites coryloides* Wode., Juglandaceae, *Engelhardia* group; Manning Formation, upper Jacksonian, Grimes Co., Tex. X926.

18, 19. *Momipites annulatus* Fred. and Christ., Juglandaceae, *Engelhardia* group. Note presence of annulus and, in 19, endoplicae. 18, Manning Formation, Fayette Co., Tex.; 19, Manning Formation, Grimes Co., Tex. X926.

20. *Cupuliferoipollenites brevisulcatus* Fred., *Chrysophyllum*; Manning Formation, Fayette Co., Tex. X926.
21. *Nyssa* sp.; Manning Formation, Grimes Co., Tex. X926.
22. *Pseudolaesopollis ventosa* (Pot.) Fred., Cyrillaceae, *Costaea*?; Manning Formation, Grimes Co., Tex. X926.

23, 24. *Rhoipites* n. sp., Nyssaceae, Cornaceae, Anacardiaceae? Pollen of this species lacks an endannulus. Manning Formation, Walker Co., Tex. X926.

25. *Myrtaceidites* sp., Myrtaceae-Sapindaceae; Forest Hill Sand, lower Vicksburgian, Smith Co., Miss. X926.
26. *Cupanieidites orthoteichus* Cooks. and Pike, Sapindaceae-Loranthaceae; middle Claibornian, Zilpha Clay or Sparta Sand, Tate Co., Miss. X926.

27, 28. Microreticulate tricolporate n. sp., cf. *Yeguapollis*, affinity unknown; Manning Formation, Grimes Co., Tex. X926.

29. *Planctonites stellarius* (Pot.) Gruas-Cav., freshwater? cyst; same sample as 26. X926.

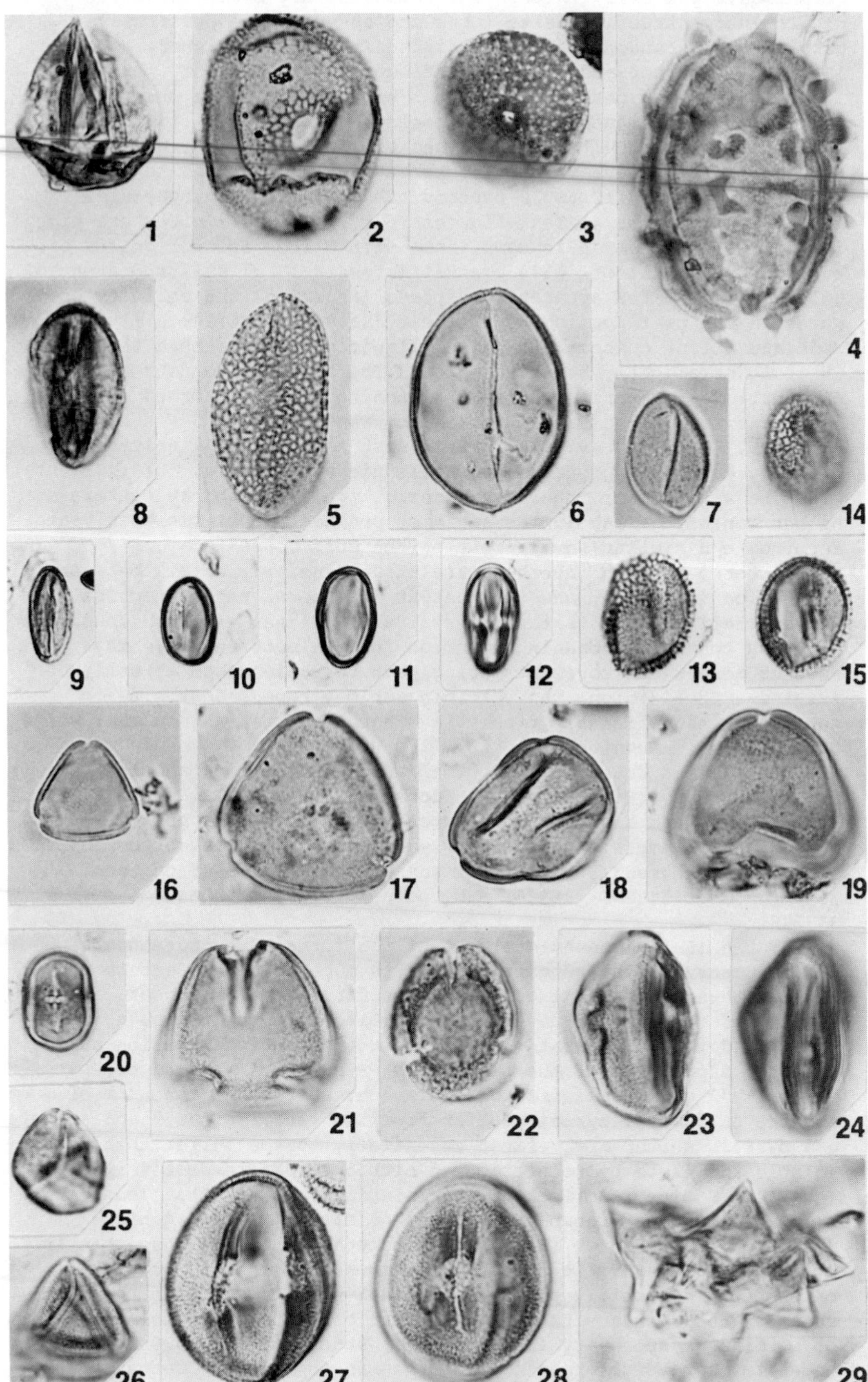
1
2
3
4
8
5
6
7
14
9
10
11
12
13
15
16
17
18
19
20
21
22
23
24
25
26
27
28
29

form today "primarily through interdistributary swamp and marsh growth in constructive delta lobes and as extensive destructive marshes over abandoned and subsiding delta lobes" (Fisher, 1968:97). Thinner and more discontinuous seams probably formed as interdistributary peats on the lower part of the delta or higher on the delta in abandoned stream channels (Fisher, 1968).

Proximate and ultimate analyses of many southeastern Texas Manning lignites gave values (as received basis) of 1.5 to 2.5 percent sulfur and 12 to 30 percent ash (Dietrich and Lonsdale, 1958:62; Kaiser, 1974, Text-figures 16-17); these lignites are high in both sulfur and ash in comparison with Wilcox Group lignites of eastern Texas (Kaiser, 1974, Text-figures 16-17). Sulfur content of Gulf Coast lignites apparently depends largely on the salinity of the water in the peat-forming environment (Kaiser, 1974:24-25); the moderate sulfur content of Manning lignites suggests that they formed in at least slightly brackish water. The high ash content is more difficult to interpret because the Manning lignites formed during a time of extensive volcanism in Mexico, New Mexico, and western Texas (Folk, 1955:16; Murray, 1961). At least some of the lignites probably contain a great deal of volcanic ash (Dumble, 1918:291) that might be wind-blown; thus, the Manning lignites probably contain a higher content of ash in the sense of proximate analysis than peats forming in a similar environment on the Gulf Coast today. Furthermore, a rough inverse correlation generally exists between stagnation in a swamp and the content of mineral matter because streams delivering detrital material also deliver oxygen. Thus, the high ash content of Manning lignites in proximate analyses may suggest more water movement during peat formation than actually existed. In addition, the volcanic ash may have made the swamp substrates significantly richer in mineral nutrients than they would otherwise have been.

The Grimes County, Texas, coal and detrital rock samples came from four cores (Bishop, 1977). Cores 3332SS, 3534EE, and 3737QQ are from holes along a strike line extending southwest to northeast. Core 3534EE (sample series R1265) was 6.0 km northeast of core 3332SS (R1264), and core 3737QQ (R1263) was 13.1 km northeast of core 3534EE. Core 3432NE (R1266) was updip, 3.0 km northwest of core 3332SS.

Table 16-1 presents analyses of the forms of sulfur in the Grimes County coals. Organic sulfur is much more abundant in these samples than are sulfate or pyritic sulfur. The low amount of pyrite in most of the samples may be due to a lack of iron in the swamp water, and the low sulfate content suggests little oxidation during or after deposition of the peat (R. W. Stanton, I. A. Breger, pers. comm.). "Organic sulfur is determined by subtracting the sum of sulfate sulfur and pyritic sulfur from the total sulfur," and sulfate and pyritic sulfur are defined essentially as the sulfur that is soluble in dilute hydrochloric and nitric acids, respectively (American Society for Testing and Materials, 1976:319). Thus, most organic sulfur is probably bound in the structure of organic molecules, but some of it may be in minerals that are insoluble in hydrochloric and nitric acids. Organic sulfur in coal originates mainly from bacterial, plant, and animal protein and from hydrogen sulfide that reacts with the peat; like other forms of sulfur it may be primary or secondary (Breger, 1974; Stach et al., 1975:26, 31). Moderate amounts of organic sulfur, as in the Grimes County coals,

Table 16-1
Data on the Grimes County, Texas, coals. Proximate and ultimate analyses by U.S. Bureau of Mines (previously unpublished; as-received basis).

Sample	Ash (%)	Sulfur (Percent) Sulfate	Pyritic	Organic	Total	Microplankton	Seam Thickness (m)
R1263B	15.0	0.17	0.17	2.55	2.89	1	0.2
R1263E	14.1	0.10	0.20	2.33	2.63	1	2.1
R1263H	23.4	0.06	0.09	1.89	2.04	0	?
R1264B	9.9	0.46	0.93	1.40	2.79	0	1.0
R1264E	15.8	0.35	0.07	1.65	2.07	1	2.2
R1265B	10.1	0.13	0.05	1.96	2.14	1	1.8
R1265E	11.7	0.03	0.02	1.81	1.86	0	1.9
R1266A	27.5	0.59	0.45	1.28	2.32	0	?(thin)
R1266D	16.3	0.24	0.09	0.86	1.19	0	0.5
R1266G	17.4	0.02	0.13	1.69	1.84	1	1.8

Notations in Microplankton column are from Figure 16-2: 0 = no microplankton observed in sample or in adjacent strata, 1 = microplankton in adjacent strata but not in sample itself.

may suggest sulfur retention in tissues of halophytes, but so many other explanations exist for the presence of the organic sulfur in the coals that little can be said with certainty about the environment of deposition of the peats from the ultimate analyses alone. Coals in these four cores are thought to have formed in mid-delta locations because the combination of moderate sulfur and low sodium in the coals suggests that they were deposited in only slightly brackish water (C. C. Mathewson, M. A. Bishop, pers. comm.).

Many of the strata associated with the Manning coals in Grimes County seem to have been deposited in marine to prodeltaic environments according to evidence of lithology, sedimentary structures, and invertebrate fossils (Mathewson and Bishop, 1979). Palynomorph assemblages were examined from fifteen samples of shale and clay lying directly above or below the ten Manning coal samples from Grimes County. Five or six of these detrital rock samples contain marine or brackish-water microplankton (R1263A, R1263D, R1264D, R1265A, R1266H, and possibly R1263C). None of the detrital rock samples contain abundant microplankton, and only one to three species of these fossils were observed per sample; the relative scarcity and low diversity of microplankton in the shales and clays probably indicate brackish rather than normal marine water during deposition. Table 16-1 and figure 16-2 indicate which coal samples were adjacent to detrital rocks containing microplankton. None of the palynomorph assemblages from the Grimes County coals contain these fossils. Samples of the lignites were also processed for diatoms, which if present would give an excellent indication of water salinity during peat deposition. However, all samples are barren of these fossils as well.

The Manning seam that I sampled from outcrop (R1143 A-C) is exposed in the banks of O'Quinn Creek, Fayette County, Texas, in pods

0 to 1 m thick and about 3 to 9 m long and appears to have been deposited in abandoned stream channels. In contrast, another Manning seam in Fayette County, 1.4 m thick, was found to be at least 1.6 km long and 23 to 30 m wide (Sedlmeyer, 1939:1). Where I sampled the coal on O'Quinn Creek, the base of the seam was under water, but 45 m downstream the base of the same coal, deeply weathered, and the underlying mudstone and shale were exposed. Here, in descending order, were the main seam, 2.5 cm of medium-dark grayish-brown mudstone, 1.3 cm of coal, and additional medium-dark grayish-brown mudstone grading down into medium-gray sandy shale; all the mudstone and shale below the coal contain plant fragments. The mudstones below both the main seam and the coal stringer are weathered and fractured, and I cannot determine whether root holes extend from the coal into the underlying mudstone. Four mudstone and shale samples were collected with this coal. No microplankton were observed in the samples from 20 cm above and below the main seam (R1167 A and B, respectively), but abundant dinoflagellates, perhaps representing a normal marine assemblage, occur in the shale (R1143D) 2.1 m below the seam. The fourth sample, R1143E, is from a float block containing large pieces of wood. This block was found 90 m downstream from the outcropping seam; thus, the stratigraphic relation of this sample to the coal is unknown. No microplankton were observed.

No stratigraphic information and no samples of shales adjacent to the Manning coals of Walker County, Texas (R1234 A and B), were available.

Sample R1142B is from the lower part of a unit of interlaminated dark-gray clay and light-gray sandstone that forms the base of the Redfield Formation (of Wilbert, 1953; Jacksonian) in Arkansas. This unit is thought to be deltaic in origin, the sediments having been deposited in "relatively fresh water" (Wilbert, 1953:92). No microplankton were observed in sample R1142B, but a few dinoflagellates were observed 2.5 m higher in the same clay-sandstone unit. This unit directly overlies Glottidia-bearing strata of the uppermost part of the White Bluff Formation (of Wilbert, 1953; lower Jacksonian); these strata are considered to have formed under "very near-shore marine or estuarine conditions" (Wilbert, 1953:45).

Sample R1300A is from strata mapped by the Georgia Geological Survey (1976) as Twiggs Clay Member of the Barnwell Formation (Jacksonian). In the area from which the sample came (Columbia County, Georgia), the member contains abundant plant fragments and clasts of clay (kaolinite?) and is interpreted as having formed in back-barrier lagoons (D. C. Prowell, J. Reinhardt, pers. comm.). Sample R1300A lacks microplankton, but a second sample of Twiggs Clay Member from above R1300A in the same clay pit (how far above is unknown) contains dinoflagellates and acritarchs (R. H. Tschudy, pers. comm.) and is interpreted as representing storm overwash deposits in the lagoon (D. C. Prowell, J. Reinhardt, pers. comm.).

Samples 10637, 10641, and 10653 are marine, detrital Jacksonian sediments from western Mississippi. Sample 10641 is a glauconitic, fossiliferous sand from the lower part of the Moodys Branch Formation (lower Jacksonian); Huff (1970:29-30) thought it was deposited in an inner sublittoral environment. Sample 10637 is a yellowish-gray, fossiliferous clay from near the base of the Yazoo Clay (middle Jacksonian). Huff (1970:39) considered the environment of depostion to be "midsublittoral to inner part of the outer sublittoral zone." Sample 10653 is a dark-greenish-gray, fossiliferous clay from the upper part of the Yazoo Clay (upper Jacksonian). The clay was probably deposited in an outer sublittoral environment (Huff, 1970:39).

Samples 10631 and 10632 are from the uppermost part of the Yazoo Clay (uppermost Jacksonian) of western Mississippi. They are typical of the transition interval 0 to 2.4 m thick that is present in some areas (Mellen, 1941; Monroe, 1954; Moore, 1965) between typical marine Yazoo Clay and nonmarine or sparsely fossiliferous strata of the overlying Forest Hill Sand. This interval consists of clay that is olive-gray or greenish-gray like typical Yazoo but is silty, carbonaceous, micaceous, noncalcareous and laminated like the Forest Hill. The transition zone is not visibly fossiliferous, but at least at the type locality of the Forest Hill (in samples 10631 and 10632), it contains rare marine or brackish-water microplankton (Frederiksen, 1969). It probably represents prodeltaic or lagoonal sediments that were presumably anoxic because the distinct lamination is not disrupted by burrowing; the water may have been brackish or possibly marine overlain by a freshwater river plume.

Most lignites of the Forest Hill Sand (lower Vicksburgian) in Mississippi are less than 1 m thick (Williamson, 1976). The four Forest Hill lignites sampled for this study have the following thicknesses (Priddy, 1960; Moore, 1965; Luper, 1972):

R1144	2.1 m
R1145	0.2 m
R1146A	1.8 m
R1146B	not stated

Forest Hill lignites (and accompanying detrital sediments, represented by samples 10625 and 10627) were thought to have formed on a delta complex (MacNeil, 1944:1318). At least some parts of the formation were deposited near the sea, as shown by the following characteristics:

1. Calcareous streaks are present in parts of the formation (Monroe, 1954; MacNeil, 1944, 1946).
2. The Forest Hill Sand interfingers with the marine Red Bluff Clay in eastern Mississippi (MacNeil, 1944; May, 1974).
3. The contact between the Forest Hill Sand and the underlying marine Yazoo Clay is transitional in some areas, for example, at the type locality of the Forest Hill.
4. Sparse marine to brackish-water microplankton has been found in some Forest Hill samples (Drugg and Loeblich, 1967; Frederiksen, 1969).

Apparently no proximate or ultimate analyses of Forest Hill coals have been published (Williamson, 1976). Bentonite seems to be absent from the Forest Hill Sand, but rare biotite flakes suggest that a little volcanic material is included in detrital sediments of the formation (Mellen, 1941; MacNeil, 1966). Correlatives of the Forest Hill Sand contain volcanic ash in western Louisiana and especially in Texas (Folk, 1955; Murray, 1961).

The fact that no marine to brackish-water types of dinoflagellate cysts were observed in any of the Eocene or Oligocene coals studied suggests either that the swamp waters were not saline, which would conflict with the moderately high sulfur content of the

Jacksonian coals, or that microplankton could not live in the acid waters of the peat-forming environments. However, the absence from the coals of organic-walled marine microplankton does indicate that the detrital fraction ("ash") of the coals probably did not come from episodes of seawater flooding of the swamps.

CLAIBORNIAN

Figure 16-2 is a cluster diagram of thirty-seven assemblages. Numbers of samples by age and lithology are as follows:

Age	Coal	Detrital Rock	Total
Vicksburgian	4	4	8
Jacksonian	14	10	24
Claibornian	3	2	5
Total	21	16	37

Twenty-six sporomorph forms were differentiated for clustering these assemblages; raw data from the 200-counts of these sporomorph taxa are given in Table 16-2.

Only four Claibornian coal assemblages were available for this study. Two of them, R1155 and R1156, are from the middle part of the Claibornian. Sample R1155 contains mainly Quercoidites microhenricii (Pot.) Pot. (45 percent) and Cupuliferoidaepollenites spp. (36 percent). Both of these pollen types (Figure 16-4 (9-11)) were produced mainly or entirely by Fagaceae. Assemblage R1156 is dominated by Cupuliferoipollenites spp. (27 percent) (Figure 16-4 (12)), Quercoidites microhenricii (23 percent), Siltaria spp. <25 µm (19 percent), and Pollenites pseudocingulum granulatum Pot. (13 percent); all four of these pollen forms probably represent mainly Fagaceae (for comparison with fagaceous pollen in the marine Jacksonian, see Table 16-3).

Unfortunately, no samples of detrital rocks associated with these coal beds were available for microplankton or sporomorph analysis. However, previous studies have shown that high relative frequencies of fagaceous pollen are characteristic of Claibornian detrital sediments (Tschudy, 1973; Elsik, 1974). Two additional recent papers (Elsik and Dilcher, 1974; Potter, 1976), on Claibornian sporomorphs from clay pits in Tennessee, have contributed much to our knowledge of Claibornian coastal plain communities. Some question exists about the ages of the sediments exposed in these pits (see discussions in Elsik, 1974; Elsik and Dilcher, 1974; Potter, 1976); the Miller pit section is agreed by authors to be middle Claibornian, but the Lawrence pit section may be either middle or late Claibornian. In the Lawrence clay pit, two assemblages from oxbow-lake clay are dominated respectively by Cupuliferoipollenites and Quercoidites microhenricii, which probably came from plants living close to the lake (Elsik and Dilcher, 1974). In the Miller pit, clay deposited in an abandoned stream channel contains assemblages dominated by Cupuliferoidaepollenites (smooth, tricolpate fagaceous pollen; Figure 16-4 (10-11)) which was probably carried mainly by water into the lake from the surrounding region. In contrast, assemblages from the lignite overlying the clay were dominated by Cupuliferoipollenites (smooth, tricolporate, castaneoid pollen;

Table 16-2

Specimen counts (200 total per sample) on which Figure 16-2 is based. Sporomorph forms are as follows:

1. Monolete spores.
2. Psilate deltoid trilete spores, mainly of Lygodiumsporites adriennis (Pot. and Gell.) Pot.; Lygodium at least in part.
3. Cicatricosisporites dorogensis Pot. and Gell. s.l.; Anemia; possibly Mohria in part.
4. Pollenites pseudocingulum granulatum Pot.; Fagaceae?
5. Caprifoliipites n. sp.; Caprifoliaceae?, Viburnum? (Figure 16-4(14,15)); and Salixipollenites n. sp.; Oleaceae?, Olea? (Figure 16-4(13)).
6. Carya spp. and Ulmus-Planera-Zelkova types.
7. Cupuliferoipollenites brevisulcatus Fred.; Chrysophyllum (Figure 16-4(20)).
8. Cyrillaceaepollenites megaexactus (Pot.) Pot.; Cyrilla, Cliftonia; and Cyrillaceaepollenites cf. megaexactus.
9. Fraxinoipollenites spp.; various families.
10. Liliacidites tritus Fred. and miscellaneous monosulcates; Palmae and perhaps other monocots (Figure 16-4(5)).
11. Miscellaneous dicots.
12. Momipites spp.; Engelhardia group (Figure 16-4(16-19)).
13. Microreticulate to punctate monosulcates; mostly or entirely Palmae (Figure 16-4(6,7)).
14. Myrtaceidites spp.; Myrtaceae, Sapindaceae (Figure 16-4(25)).
15. Nudopollis terminalis (Pflug and Thoms.) Pflug; affinity unknown.
16. Nyssa spp. (Figure 16-4(21)).
17. Miscellaneous prolate, reticulate tricolporates; various families of dicots.
18. Pseudolaesopollis ventosa (Pot.) Fred.; Cyrillaceae, Costaea? (Figure 16-4(22)).
19. Cupuliferoidaepollenites spp.; mainly or entirely Fagaceae (Figure 16-4(10,11)).
20. Cupuliferoipollenites spp.; Fagaceae, Castanea?, Dryophyllum? (Figure 16-4(12)).
21. Quercoidites microhenricii (Pot.) Pot.; Fagaceae (Figure 16-4(9)).
22. Quercus? spp. (Figure 16-4(8)).
23. Rhoipites n. sp.; Nyssaceae, Cornaceae, Anacardiaceae? (Figure 16-4(23-24)).
24. Siltaria spp. <25 μm; Fagaceae at least in part.
25. Striopollenites terasmaei Rouse; Acer, Prunus, Anacardiaceae?
26. Cupressacites hiatipites (Wode.) Krutzsch; Taxodiaceae-Cupressaceae-Taxaceae (Figure 16-4(1)).

Figure 16-4 (12)) and Siltaria, pollen types thought to have been produced by plants immediately adjacent to the lake or swamp (Potter, 1976). The lignite assemblages of Potter (1976) and my sample R1156 appear to be similar. In contrast to this evidence that Eocene Fagaceae were inhabitants of mesic and moist environments, Berry (1924) thought that the fagaceous leaves so abundant in Claibornian and Jacksonian sediments of the Gulf Coast, which he assigned to the extinct leaf genus Dryophyllum, represent trees of edaphically dry areas, mainly beaches and dunes. Quercoidites microhenricii,

Table 16-2 (continued)

	1	2	3	4	5	6	7	8	9	10	11	12	13
R1300A	1	2	0	0	6	0	13	1	2	0	21	75	17
R1298D	2	1	0	0	1	0	1	2	3	4	6	57	33
R1142B	9	5	2	6	5	0	2	12	1	3	31	29	2
R1155	0	1	0	7	0	0	0	6	3	0	13	0	1
R1156	0	1	0	25	0	0	0	1	4	1	11	1	3
R1263D	6	4	3	0	25	0	3	4	3	4	22	66	20
R1263A	6	2	0	0	35	0	0	1	0	2	24	80	23
R1264C	24	2	3	0	5	0	7	0	3	1	4	18	109
14959	2	1	1	8	1	1	6	1	5	2	38	36	1
10641	2	1	1	4	1	1	0	1	1	1	30	26	1
10637	2	1	1	1	1	1	0	4	6	1	17	28	1
10653	11	4	1	4	1	1	1	6	4	4	36	38	1
R1143D	6	4	7	0	7	0	15	2	1	15	14	62	30
R1143E	12	0	0	1	3	0	5	0	0	0	3	31	142
R1144	15	35	9	2	0	1	0	2	0	16	20	14	4
R1145	6	2	132	0	0	0	0	0	2	2	15	4	1
R1146A	2	0	0	0	0	0	4	0	77	9	13	4	34
R1146B	56	3	24	5	7	1	7	0	4	10	27	2	1
10632	10	4	4	4	4	8	0	0	28	11	5	26	1
10631	8	1	10	2	0	5	0	6	16	9	36	2	4
10627	32	12	1	0	1	6	0	4	10	3	26	2	1
10625	12	1	0	0	6	18	0	1	16	7	15	1	1
R1143A	2	0	0	0	34	0	18	13	10	9	11	70	7
R1143B	0	1	0	0	27	0	9	7	4	3	25	75	3
R1143C	1	3	0	1	35	0	33	8	3	2	12	82	1
R1234A	1	2	0	0	39	1	2	7	0	0	14	96	4
R1234B	1	0	0	1	38	0	3	2	1	0	12	114	1
R1263B	4	0	2	0	81	0	38	4	0	1	10	43	3
R1263E	3	0	0	0	21	0	0	3	5	0	16	60	1
R1263H	6	13	12	0	26	0	10	3	5	11	31	43	9
R1264E	2	0	0	0	14	0	12	5	5	8	16	69	11
R1265B	31	1	0	0	19	0	0	1	2	1	27	78	32
R1265E	0	0	0	0	19	0	3	8	4	11	10	49	7
R1266A	3	0	0	0	73	0	2	0	1	0	15	82	5
R1266D	4	0	0	0	60	0	3	0	0	4	9	81	13
R1266G	5	0	2	0	16	0	16	0	6	4	44	61	11
P7857	5	0	0	0	4	0	17	0	2	7	10	105	3

Cupuliferoidaepollenites, and *Cupuliferoipollenites* (castaneoid) are also very abundant in the European middle and upper Eocene. *Cupuliferoipollenites* is considered to have been produced by one of the main trees of the swamp forests, whereas *Cupuliferoidaepollenites* and *Quercoidites microhenricii* probably represent trees that were abundant in the more mesic forests outside the swamps (Thomson and Pflug, 1953; Pflug, 1957).

To summarize this welter of data and confusing generic names, a variety of trees of the Fagaceae, probably representing the Castaneoideae, perhaps the Quercoideae, and including the extinct *Dryophyllum*, were abundant on the Gulf Coastal Plain in the middle and late Eocene (Tables 16-3 and 16-4). The evidence suggests that these trees lived in a variety of environments and that, especially

Table 16-2 (continued)

	14	15	16	17	18	19	20	21	22	23	24	25	26
R1300A	18	0	0	15	14	0	6	1	0	1	7	1	0
R1298D	0	0	18	2	0	23	38	5	0	0	3	1	0
R1142B	0	0	2	6	2	15	38	16	0	0	11	3	0
R1155	0	0	0	1	2	71	5	89	0	0	1	0	0
R1156	0	0	0	5	3	8	54	45	0	0	38	0	0
R1263D	3	0	2	2	6	1	10	0	0	0	15	0	1
R1263A	3	0	0	6	0	3	12	2	0	0	1	0	0
R1264C	0	0	0	10	0	2	4	1	0	0	6	1	0
14959	1	1	1	4	3	8	56	15	0	2	4	1	1
10641	0	0	1	4	2	2	108	6	1	1	4	1	0
10637	0	1	1	4	1	18	98	5	4	1	1	1	1
10653	0	1	1	8	3	18	34	5	12	1	4	1	0
R1143D	5	0	2	6	3	1	3	1	2	1	3	0	0
R1143E	0	0	0	3	0	0	0	0	0	0	0	0	0
R1144	4	0	0	11	0	1	11	1	13	0	5	0	36
R1145	13	0	0	12	0	1	0	0	5	0	5	0	0
R1146A	0	0	0	22	0	7	14	2	4	0	7	1	0
R1146B	6	0	0	7	0	0	4	4	15	0	6	11	0
10632	8	0	0	1	0	32	8	14	32	0	0	0	0
10631	4	0	1	8	3	18	6	3	56	1	0	0	1
10627	1	0	1	1	0	18	4	1	74	0	0	1	1
10625	0	0	1	1	2	1	0	4	112	1	0	0	0
R1143A	0	0	3	13	5	0	1	2	0	0	1	1	0
R1143B	0	0	0	2	2	17	3	12	0	7	0	3	0
R1143C	0	0	0	4	0	3	2	1	0	4	4	1	0
R1234A	0	0	14	10	0	0	5	0	0	0	3	2	0
R1234B	0	0	12	7	0	0	0	0	0	8	0	0	0
R1263B	1	0	0	5	0	0	4	0	0	0	1	2	0
R1263E	0	0	4	11	31	1	7	3	0	3	31	0	0
R1263H	0	0	0	14	4	3	4	0	0	1	5	0	0
R1264E	5	0	0	42	0	2	6	0	0	1	2	0	0
R1265B	0	0	0	1	0	0	1	0	0	3	0	3	0
R1265E	0	0	1	4	42	3	26	0	0	0	12	1	0
R1266A	0	0	3	4	0	3	2	0	0	5	0	2	0
R1266D	0	0	2	0	0	5	1	4	0	10	0	4	0
R1266G	0	0	17	1	0	2	1	0	0	11	3	0	0
P7857	1	0	5	3	0	1	10	0	0	18	2	7	0

in the middle Eocene, each fagaceous pollen genus was probably associated with several habitats.

Another interesting aspect of Potter's (1976) Tennessee Claibornian samples is that pollen of _Momipites_ spp. (Figure 16-4 (16, 17)) averages about 1 to 2 percent of the assemblage in the lignite samples but is 2 to 4 times as abundant in the clay samples; apparently, the plants producing these grains lived outside the immediate area of the lake or swamp (Potter, 1976:83-84). In the Jacksonian, the _Momipites_ producers were probably more abundant in the peat-forming swamps and nearby areas than in the extra-swamp environments.

Lignite sample R1448 was received after the cluster analyses had been performed and Figures 16-2 and 16-3 had been drafted. W. S.

Table 16-3
Most abundant pollen forms of Fagaceae in marine Jacksonian deposits of Mississippi and Alabama. Mean relative frequencies per sample do not include samples from the uppermost Jacksonian, which belongs to a different pollen zone (zone II of Frederiksen, 1968) than the remainder of the Jacksonian (zone I).

Pollen Form	Mean Relative Frequency (Percent)	Affinity
Cupuliferoipollenites spp.	32	*Dryophyllum* and (or) *Castanea-Castanopsis*
Cupuliferoidaepollenites liblarensis (Thoms.) Pot.	6	*Dryophyllum*?
Quercoidites microhenricii (Pot.) Pot.	4	*Dryophyllum*?
Pollenites pseudocingulum granulatum Pot.	3	Genus unknown
Quercus? spp.	1	*Dryophyllum* or *Quercus*

Parks (R. E. Hershey, pers. comm.) thought on stratigraphic grounds that this sample was from the Cockfield Formation, the uppermost unit of the Claibornian. The main taxa are *Cupuliferoidaepollenites* spp. (44 percent), *Fraxinoipollenites* spp. (9 percent), *Caprifoliipites* n. sp.-*Salixipollenites* n. sp. (8 percent), and *Cupuliferoipollenites* spp. (6 percent). This assemblage is interesting because it has features characteristic of both the middle Claibornian coals R1155 and R1156 and the Jacksonian and Vicksburgian coals. The assemblage is dominated by Fagaceae, and *Momipites* pollen is sparse (2 percent), as in the middle Claibornian assemblages. However, *Caprifoliipites-Salixipollenites* (Figure 16-4 (13-15)) is fairly abundant as in the Jacksonian coals whereas this pollen form was not observed at all in the middle Claibornian coals. The fourth Claibornian lignite of this study, P7857, is from the uppermost part of the Claibornian in Mississippi. The assemblage is dominated by *Momipites* spp.; thus, it is very similar to assemblages from the upper Jacksonian (Figures 16-2, 16-3) but is quite different from those of the middle Claibornian lignites and from the other Cockfield lignite, R1448. Elsik (1978:28) noted that a lignite sample of Cockfield age from Madison County in eastern Texas contained common to abundant *Momipites* and *Nyssa* pollen.

JACKSONIAN

In this section, Jacksonian vegetation is discussed on the basis of samples from the marine section in Mississippi and Alabama and comparisons of coal and detrital rock samples from a number of Gulf Coast localities.

Table 16-4
Dominant taxa of the marine Jacksonian sporomorph assemblages (that is, those having the highest mean relative frequencies per sample).

Sporomorph Taxon	Affinity	Relative Frequency
PTERIDOPHYTES		
Laevigatosporites haardtii	Many families of Filicales	Absent to "common"
GYMNOSPERMS		
Pinus tenuextima	Pinus	Absent to "common"
DICOTYLEDONS		
Momipites coryloides	Juglandaceae, Engelhardia group	"Infrequent" to "abundant"
Momipites microfoveolatus	Juglandaceae, Engelhardia group	"Infrequent" to "abundant"
Cupuliferoipollenites spp.	Fagaceae, mainly or entirely Dryophyllum; possibly Castanea in part	"Occasional" to "very abundant"
Cupuliferoidaepollenites liblarensis	Fagaceae, Dryophyllum?	"Infrequent" to "common"
Quercoidites microhenricii	Fagaceae, Dryophyllum?	"Infrequent" to "abundant"
Quercus? spp.	Fagaceae, Dryophyllum and (or) Quercus	Absent to "very abundant"
Pollenites pseudocingulum granulatum	Fagaceae?	Absent to "abundant"
Pseudolaesopollis ventosa	Cyrillaceae, Costaea?	Absent to "common"

SAMPLES OF MARINE ROCKS

I am concerned here with reconstructions of late Eocene lowland and upland vegetation that are based on sporomorphs from Jacksonian marine rocks of Mississippi and Alabama (data from Frederiksen, 1969, 1977, in press). It must be remembered that the taxa assigned to one or another broad community formed only a small part of the living communities. In the following discussion, a question mark following a generic or family name means that the identification of the taxon from sporomorphs is not certain. A detailed discussion of the brackish-water to marine coastal communities is deferred to the end of the chapter.

The following criteria may be applied to determine which sporomorph taxa were abundantly represented in and/or were confined to the lowlands of the Jacksonian Gulf Coast:

1. All the dominant sporomorph taxa (Table 16-4) must have been abundant on the coastal plain except Pinus tenuextima Trav. (Pinus is discussed below in this section).
2. Most sporomorph taxa that occur in many (60 percent or more) of the samples, even though they may have low relative frequencies, were probably produced by plants that were abundant in the lowlands. Many of the taxa of interest here have a low spore or pollen production per plant, so the presence of the taxa in a

high percentage of samples is more significant than high relative frequencies of the sporomorphs in individual samples.

3. Jacksonian genera that now occur mainly or entirely in the tropics may have been confined to the lowlands.
4. Genera that are now limited to or have their main occurrence in brackish or marine coastal waters probably had the same habits in the late Eocene.

On the basis of these four criteria (labeled respectively 1, 2, 3, 4 in the following list), a number of modern genera are thought to have been represented by plants that were abundant in the lowlands and (or) were confined to the lowlands of the Jacksonian Gulf Coast: *Acrostichum*? (3, 4), two species of *Anemia* (2) or possibly *Mohria* (2, 3), *Lygodium* (1), *Selaginella* (2), *Ephedra* (2), *Glyptostrobus*? (3), *Joinvillea*? (3) (Figure 16-4 (3)), *Nypa* (3, 4) (Figure 16-4 (4)), *Pseudophoenix*? (2, 3) (Figure 16-4 (5)), *Anacolosa-Cathedra-Ptychopetalum* (3), *Carya* (2), several species of *Dryophyllum-Castanea?-Quercus*? (1) (Figure 16-4 (8-12)), *Cupania*? (3) (Figure 16-4 (26)), *Cliftonia-Cyrilla* (2), Cyrillaceae, *Costaea*? (1, 2, 3) (Figure 16-4(22)), two species of the *Engelhardia* group (1) (Figure 16-4 (16, 17)), *Ilex* (2), one or two species of *Manilkara*? (2), *Nyssa* (2) (Figure 16-4 (21)), *Parthenocissus*? (2), *Ulmus-Planera-Zelkova* types (2), and *Platanus* (2). Following is a list of additional sporomorph taxa observed in at least 60 percent of the samples and therefore likely to have been produced by plants abundant on the Jacksonian Gulf Coastal Plain:

Laevigatosporites haardtii (Pot. and Ven.) Thoms. and Pflug. Aspidiaceae, Aspleniaceae, Blechnaceae, Gleicheniaceae, Lomariopsidaceae, Polypodiaceae, Pteridaceae.
Verrucatosporites alienus (Pot.) Thoms. and Pflug. Oleandraceae, Polypodiaceae, Pteridaceae.
Monocolpopollenites tranquillus (Pot.) Thoms. and Pflug. Palmae, genus unknown.
Fraxinoipollenites variabilis Stanl. Affinity unknown.
Fraxinoipollenites spp. Affinity unknown.
Salixipollenites n. sp. Oleaceae? (Figure 16-4 (13)).
Cyrillaceaepollenites n. sp. Affinity unknown.
Verrutricolporites n. sp. Affinity unknown.
Rhoipites n. sp. Nyssaceae, Cornaceae, Anacardiaceae? (Figure 16-4 (23, 24)).
Pollenites modicus Mamcz. Rutaceae, Anacardiaceae, Simarubaceae?
Intratriporopollenites n. sp. Probably Tiliaceae (but not *Tilia*), possibly Bombacaceae.

Several pollen species of *Ephedra* were observed in marine Jacksonian sediments. The rate of pollen production is low in this genus (Martin and Gray, 1962:111), partly because some species are zoophilous (Faegri and van der Pijl, 1971:16). *Ephedra* plants are now common in the southwestern part of the United States, but in modern sediment samples from that area, pollen of this genus "usually makes up less than 1% of the total pollen, and only very rarely does it reach 5%" (Maher, 1964:392). Thus, it is significant that *Ephedra* pollen is found in almost every marine Jacksonian sample, and one species, *E. claricristata* Shakhm., is "occasional" (1 to 5 percent) in one-third of all forty-five counted samples from these rocks.

Ephedra now lives in habitats characterized mainly by edaphic dryness (Gray, 1960). Palynologists generally agree that, in the Paleogene, Ephedra grew mainly on seashores as it does in several regions of the world today (Gray, 1960:810; Krutzsch, 1961a:31; Shakhmundes, 1965:218; Pen'kova, 1973:158). Ephedra pollen in the marine Jacksonian is more abundant than it probably would have been if all or most of the plants had lived inland. However, Ephedra pollen is also consistently present in nonmarine deltaic and coastal-plain shales of the Cockfield Formation (upper middle Eocene) and Forest Hill Sand (lower Oligocene) of western Mississippi. These pollen grains may have been blown inland from the shore with the sea breeze. They may also have come from Ephedra plants living on the coastal plain back of the shore, which would support the suggestion of Gray (1960:810) and Hopkins (1967:167) that Ephedra plants of the Eocene were less xerophytic than now. However, not a single grain of Ephedra was observed in any of the Jacksonian deltaic coals or shales from Texas. Schizaeaceae, Palmae, Fagaceae, and Myricaceae, among other families, were probably associated with Ephedra in dry, sandy habitats of the lower coastal plain (Berry, 1924; Rüffle, 1976:341).

Symplocaceae is represented in the marine Jacksonian by seven or eight pollen species. Plants of this family are deciduous to evergreen shrubs and trees; in southeastern United States, Symplocos now is distributed from the coastal plain to the mountains and lives in "sandy thickets, upland or alluvial woods and stream margins" (Radford et al., 1964:827). Strangely enough, the genus does not occur now in southern Florida (Long and Lakela, 1971) even though it is found primarily in the tropics and subtropics of the world (Willis, 1966). On the humid subtropical escarpments of eastern Mexico, Symplocos occurs in mesophytic forests (Miranda and Sharp, 1950). In China, Symplocaceae is found in montane-boreal coniferous, deciduous broad-leaved and evergreen broad-leaved forests (Wang, 1961). In the Neogene of the Netherlands, trees and shrubs of this family probably lived in mesic environments outside of the coastal swamps (Zagwijn, 1967); however, in the Eocene of Germany, they seem to have lived in the coastal swamps themselves (Pflug, 1952).

Pollen of Symplocaceae is very sparsely represented in Claibornian, Jacksonian, and lower Vicksburgian coals of the Gulf Coast, so trees and shrubs of this family probably were not important members of the peat-forming, deltaic swamp communities. No pollen species of Symplocaceae is more than "infrequent" in any marine Jacksonian sample, but this low relative frequency is not surprising because the family is entomophilous (Machin, 1971:867). More significant is the fact that one of the pollen species of Symplocaceae occurs in more than half of the samples from the upper Claibornian-Jacksonian-lower Vicksburgian detrital sequence of Mississippi and Alabama, and therefore, the producers of this species are likely to have been fairly abundant on the coastal plain. In late Eocene southeastern United States, trees and shrubs of this family may have lived mainly in swampy to mesic environments on the upper coastal plain and in the uplands.

Nearly all authors agree that in the Claibornian, Jacksonian (and in the Vicksburgian?), the southeastern United States was at least slightly warmer than now (Berry, 1924; Dorf, 1960; Axelrod, 1966; Wolfe, 1969, 1975; Dilcher, 1973; Frederiksen, 1975). Thus, genera confined to the uplands were probably those that occur in the coolest climates today. The following extant genera, identified from

Jacksonian sporomorphs, do not now extend into the tropics (A climates of Trewartha, 1968): Cedrus, Cryptomeria-Metasequoia-Sequoia, Picea, Tsuga, and Cliftonia?. In addition, Centrolepis?, Alnus, Pterocarya, and Tilia occur mainly or entirely on mountains in the tropics, so the basic climatic affinity of these genera is also subtropical to temperate.

Most of the gymnosperms identified from Jacksonian pollen appear to have lived mainly or entirely in the uplands. Berry (1924) reported only two or three species of gymnosperm megafossils from the Jacksonian, and these fossils were very rare in his material. However, the pollen record shows the presence of at least eight gymnosperm genera in the marine Jacksonian (the number of pollen species of each is in parentheses after the taxon): Cedrus (1), Picea (1), Pinus (3-4), Tsuga (1), Podocarpus (1-3), Cryptomeria-Metasequoia-Sequoia (1), Taxodiaceae-Cupressaceae-Taxaceae (1) (Figure 16-4 (1)), and Ephedra (3-4). Of all gymnosperm pollen species, only one species of Pinus is at all abundant. The maximum relative frequency of this species is only 14 percent; because Pinus is one of the most prolific of pollen producers, even this species could not have lived too near the sites of deposition (Faegri and Iversen, 1964:102) or else pine trees were sparse in the coastal-plain vegetation. Grains of Pinus are very rare in the Jacksonian coals examined; thus, pine trees must not have lived on at least the lower part of the southeastern Texas delta.

Among other genera of the Pinaceae, only a few grains of Tsuga were seen, and Picea was observed in only ten out of forty-five counted samples from the marine Jacksonian of Mississippi and Alabama. In southeastern United States, Tsuga now is almost entirely confined to the mountains and foothills, and Picea occurs only along the crest of the Appalachians. Presumably both of these genera were confined to the mountains in the Eocene.

Dilcher (1969; 1973:46), on the basis of the presence of Podocarpus megafossils in middle Eocene lowland sediments of Kentucky and Tennessee, concluded that trees of this genus lived in the Eocene lowlands of that region. Opposed to this interpretation is the fact that Podocarpus pollen is rare or absent in all Claibornian sporomorph samples examined from Tennessee and Arkansas (Elsik and Dilcher, 1974; Saunders et al., 1974; Potter, 1976) and from Mississippi and Alabama (Frederiksen, 1969; in press; this study). Podocarpus is a prolific pollen producer; pollen of this genus is abundant in many Cenozoic samples from the Southern Hemisphere (Couper, 1960). Thus, the paucity of Podocarpus pollen in Claibornian sediments of the Gulf Coastal Plain may indicate that Dilcher's megafossils of this genus were carried by streams, perhaps from the uplands, to the site of deposition. Each of the pollen species of Podocarpus in the marine Jacksonian sediments of Mississippi and Alabama occurs in only one-fourth to one-half of the counted samples and is never more than "infrequent." Thus, trees of this genus could not have been abundant in the lowland vegetation of Jacksonian time, if they lived in the lowlands at all.

Much of the Ephedra pollen in the marine Jacksonian rocks of Mississippi and Alabama probably came from coastal environments as previously discussed. However, some of it may also have come from the uplands. For example, Ephedra grains in Oligocene and Miocene lowland sediments of Borneo were thought to have come from the montane forest with pollen of Pinus, Picea, Tsuga, Alnus, and

Pterocarya (Muller, 1972:13); all of these genera are also represented by pollen in the marine Jacksonian of the Gulf Coast.

Alnus is interesting because it is a prolific pollen producer whose pollen is easily transported because of its small size. The fact that Alnus pollen is only "infrequent" to "occasional" and is present in only eighteen of fifty-six counted samples from the upper Claibornian to the lower Vicksburgian of Mississippi and Alabama suggests that plants of this genus may not have been present on the coastal plain at all and may not have been abundant even in the uplands.

If the Claibornian and Jacksonian coastal plain was warm humid subtropical or even winter-dry tropical (in the terminology of Trewartha, 1968), most of the uplands must have been humid subtropical, and the highest peaks of the Appalachians may have extended into the temperate zone. Most of the extant genera identified from Jacksonian sporomorphs occur at least partly in subtropical regions of the present earth (Frederiksen, 1977, Table 1); this is true, for instance, of nearly all of the "temperate" genera reported by Gray (1960, Table 1) from the uppermost Claibornian of Alabama. These subtropical genera undoubtedly extended into the uplands and may have been dominant in those areas during the Claibornian and Jacksonian.

PEAT-FORMING SWAMP COMMUNITIES

Figure 16-3 is a cluster diagram of fourteen coal samples from the Manning Formation (upper Jacksonian) of Texas and one coal sample from the Cockfield Formation (upper Claibornian) of Mississippi. The raw frequency counts were tabulated for thirty-three sporomorph taxa; raw data for the 200-counts of these sporomorph types are given in Table 16-5. Many of these taxa are the same as in the list (Table 16-2) for the thirty-seven assemblages of Figure 16-2. The main difference between the two lists is that some taxa differentiated for clustering on Figure 16-3 were included with miscellaneous dicots for the larger cluster analysis because they never reach more than 5 percent in any Jacksonian coal assemblage. These taxa are Myrica propria, Cupuliferoidaepollenites certus, Albertipollenites? araneosus, Tricolporopollenites illiacus medius, Parthenocissus? sp., Ailanthipites berryi, Cupanieidites orthoteichus (Figure 16-4 (26)), and Tetracolporopollenites spp. They were also quantitatively unimportant in the other coal and shale samples.

Cf. Yeguapollis n. sp. (Figure 16-4 (27, 28)) forms 15 percent of the assemblage in one upper Jacksonian coal sample (R1264E) and was considered a separate taxon for clustering the Jacksonian coal assemblages. However, it was not observed in any other coal or shale sample and thus was included with miscellaneous dicots for clustering in Figure 16-2. Psilate monolete spores (Laevigatosporites haardtii) and verrucate monolete spores (mainly Verrucatosporites alienus) were counted separately for the Jacksonian coal-sample clustering, but because the verrucate forms are never more than a few percent of the assemblage in any coal or shale sample, all monolete spores were grouped together for purposes of the larger cluster analysis. Liliacidites tritus (Figure 16-4 (5)) was counted separately for the Jacksonian coal study, but this species was grouped together with miscellaneous monosulcate (mainly or entirely palm) pollen types for

Table 16-5
Specimen counts (200 total per sample) on which Figure 16-3 is based. Sporomorph forms are as follows:

1. Laevigatosporites haardtii (Pot. and Ven.) Thoms. and Pflug; several fern families.
2. Verrucate monolete spores, nearly all of them belonging to Verrucatosporites alienus (Pot.) Thoms. and Pflug; several fern families.
3. Psilate deltoid trilete spores, mainly belonging to Lygodiumsporites adriennis (Pot. and Gell.) Pot.; Lygodium at least in part.
4. Cicatricosisporites dorogensis Pot. and Gell. s.l.; Anemia; possibly Mohria in part.
5. Momipites spp.; Engelhardia group (Figure 16-4(16-19)).
6. Myrica propria Fred.
7. Liliacidites tritus Fred.; Pseudophoenix? (Figure 16-4(5)).
8. Microreticulate to punctate monosulcate pollen grains, mainly of Arecipites pseudotranquillus Nichols et al.; mostly or entirely Palmae (Figure 16-4(6,7)).
9. Cupuliferoidaepollenites spp.; at least mainly Fagaceae (Figure 16-4(10,11)).
10. Cupuliferoidaepollenites certus Fred.; Cassia.
11. Quercoidites microhenricii (Pot.) Pot.; Fagaceae (Figure 16-4(9)).
12. Fraxinoipollenites spp.; unknown dicots.
13. Albertipollenites? araneosus Fred.; Bignoniaceae.
14. Striopollenites terasmaei Rouse; Acer, Prunus, Anacardiaceae?
15. Cupuliferoipollenites spp.; Fagaceae, Castanea?, Dryophyllum? (Figure 16-4(12)).
16. Cupuliferoipollenites brevisulcatus Fred.; Chrysophyllum (Figure 16-4(20)).
17. Cyrillaceaepollenites megaexactus (Pot.) Pot.; Cyrilla, Cliftonia.
18. Pseudolaesopollis ventosa (Pot.) Fred.; Cyrillaceae, Costaea? (Figure 16-4(22)).
19. Siltaria spp. <25 μm; Fagaceae.
20. Pollenites pseudocingulum granulatum Pot.; Fagaceae?
21. Miscellaneous prolate, reticulate tricolporate pollen grains; various families of dicots.
22. Miscellaneous dicots.
23. Tricolporopollenites illiacus medius Pflug and Thoms.; Ilex.
24. Nyssa spp. (Figure 16-4(21)).
25. Rhoipites n. sp.; Nyssaceae, Cornaceae, Anacardiaceae? (Figure 16-4(23,24)).
26. Parthenocissus? sp.
27. Caprifoliipites n. sp.; Caprifoliaceae?, Viburnum? (Figure 16-4(14-15)); and Salixipollenites n. sp.; Oleaceae?, Olea? (Figure 16-4(13)).
28. Ailanthipites berryi Wode.; unknown dicots.
29. Myrtaceidites spp.; Myrtaceae, Sapindaceae (Figure 16-4(25)).
30. Cupanieidites orthoteichus Cooks. and Pike; Sapindaceae, Loranthaceae (Figure 16-4(26)).
31. Tetracolporopollenites spp.; Sapotaceae.
32. Other spores and pollen grains (1-3 specimens/sample at most).
33. Microreticulate tricolporate n. sp., cf. Yeguapollis (Figure 16-4(27, 28)).

Table 16-5 (continued)

	1	2	3	4	5	6	7	8	9	10	11
R1143A	0	2	0	0	70	0	9	7	0	0	2
R1143B	0	0	1	0	75	0	3	3	17	7	12
R1143C	0	1	3	0	82	0	2	1	3	0	1
R1234A	0	1	2	0	96	0	0	4	0	0	0
R1234B	1	0	0	0	114	0	0	1	0	0	0
R1263B	4	0	0	2	43	0	1	3	0	0	0
R1263E	0	3	0	0	60	0	0	1	1	2	3
R1263H	1	5	13	12	43	0	11	9	3	0	0
R1264E	0	2	0	0	69	0	8	11	2	0	0
R1265B	31	0	1	0	78	9	1	32	0	0	0
R1265E	0	0	0	0	49	0	11	7	3	0	0
R1266A	2	1	0	0	82	0	0	5	3	0	0
R1266D	1	3	0	0	81	0	4	13	5	0	4
R1266G	4	1	0	2	61	0	4	11	2	0	0
P7857	5	0	0	0	105	0	7	3	1	0	0

	12	13	14	15	16	17	18	19	20	21	22
R1143A	10	1	1	1	18	13	5	1	0	13	9
R1143B	4	3	3	3	9	7	2	0	0	2	9
R1143C	3	0	1	2	33	8	0	4	1	4	8
R1234A	0	1	2	5	2	7	0	3	0	10	8
R1234B	1	2	0	0	3	2	0	0	1	7	9
R1263B	0	0	2	5	38	4	0	1	0	5	8
R1263E	5	0	0	7	0	3	31	31	0	11	8
R1263H	5	0	0	4	10	3	4	5	0	14	18
R1264E	5	2	0	6	12	5	0	2	0	13	11
R1265B	2	0	3	1	0	1	0	0	0	1	15
R1265E	4	2	1	26	3	8	42	12	0	4	7
R1266A	1	0	2	2	2	0	0	0	0	4	11
R1266D	0	0	4	1	3	0	0	0	0	0	7
R1266G	6	0	0	1	16	0	0	3	0	1	35
P7857	2	0	7	10	17	0	0	2	0	3	4

purposes of the coal-shale analysis. Several sporomorph taxa appear in the Claibornian and/or the Vicksburgian samples but are rare or absent in the Jacksonian coals; these forms include Carya spp., Ulmus-Planera-Zelkova types, Nudopollis terminalis, and Quercus? spp. (Figure 16-4 (8)). These pollen forms were included with miscellaneous dicots for clustering in Figure 16-3. Cupressacites hiatipites occurs in some of the samples in Figure 16-2, but it is not recorded as being present in the 200-counts of any samples in Figure 16-3.

The most notable feature of the Jacksonian coal assemblages (Figure 16-3) is that all of them are similar to each other. All but three of the samples cluster at a similarity of 0.83 or higher, and even the most dissimilar sample, R1263B, has a similarity with the others of 0.66. Considerable evidence exists that at least some of these coals formed in brackish water (see the section "Background Data"). Brackish-water swamps are unlikely to have been inhabited by

Table 16-5 (continued)

	23	24	25	26	27	28	29	30	31	32	33
R1143A	1	3	0	0	34	0	0	0	0	0	0
R1143B	1	0	7	4	27	0	0	1	0	0	0
R1143C	2	0	4	1	35	1	0	0	0	0	0
R1234A	4	14	0	0	39	0	0	0	2	0	0
R1234B	1	12	8	0	38	0	0	0	0	0	0
R1263B	0	0	0	0	81	2	1	0	0	0	0
R1263E	0	4	3	0	21	0	0	1	4	0	0
R1263H	6	0	1	3	26	0	0	3	0	1	0
R1264E	1	0	1	0	14	1	5	0	0	1	29
R1265B	1	0	3	1	19	0	0	1	0	0	0
R1265E	0	1	0	0	19	0	0	0	1	0	0
R1266A	0	3	5	0	73	4	0	0	0	0	0
R1266D	0	2	10	0	60	1	0	0	1	0	0
R1266G	1	17	11	3	16	0	0	0	2	3	0
P7857	0	5	18	4	4	0	1	1	1	0	0

plant communities similar to those of freshwater swamps. Therefore, the similarity of sporomorph assemblages from the various coals of Figure 16-3 suggests that all these coals may have formed in brackish water. Perhaps such uniformity of swamp waters is reflected by the relatively small differences in the sulfur analyses of the coals shown in Table 16-1. Water movement may have been restricted in the swamps in which these coals formed. Based on study of Wilcox Group (upper Paleocene) lignites from Texas, Nichols and Traverse (1971) delimited what they termed a marine influence palynomorph assemblage in some of their coals. This Wilcox assemblage contained allochthonous palynomorphs such as marine microplankton, bisaccate gymnosperm pollen thought to be from upland trees, and probable reworked pollen. In contrast, palynomorphs recognized as allochthonous are rare or absent from all the coal assemblages of Figure 16-3. The only exceptions are one dinoflagellate, which may be a freshwater type, in sample R1143C, and one specimen that is probably a reworked early Paleogene Plicatopollis, in sample R1265E.

Momipites spp. (Figure 16-4 (16-19)) and Caprifoliipites-Salixipollenites (Figure 16-4 (13-15)) are the two most abundant sporomorph taxa in nearly all samples of Figure 16-3. Momipites was produced by the Engelhardia group whose modern representatives (Engelhardia, Alfaroa, Oreomunnea) are wind-pollinated trees. Juglandaceae is also represented in the marine Jacksonian of Mississippi and Alabama by Carya, Juglans, Pterocarya, and possibly Platycarya, but all these genera are rare or absent in the coal assemblages in Figure 16-3.

Modern trees of the Engelhardia group live mainly on hills and mountains of the subtropics and tropics (MacGinitie, 1941:35-36; Wang, 1961; Gomez-Pompa, 1973:105); however, one Malayan species inhabits lowland peat swamps (Whitmore, 1972:236). Lowland habitats were undoubtedly more typical of the Engelhardia group in the Tertiary than now. For example, in the middle and late Eocene of Germany, trees of this group probably lived in swamp forests and on lake banks (Pflug, 1957:169-170). In the coal assemblages of Figure 16-3, Momipites is calculated to be 22 to 57 percent of the total sporomorphs per sample, but the interpretation of these relative frequencies is not easy. On one hand, many of the fluctuations in the relative frequencies among samples are not statistically significant because only 200 grains were counted per sample. On the other hand, because the trees producing Momipites must have been greatly over-represented by their pollen grains and because the grains obviously were carried in great numbers for long distances, the relative frequencies of the producing trees in the different Jacksonian deltaic peat-forming swamps may have varied considerably more than is suggested by the differences in relative frequencies of Momipites pollen in the coal assemblages.

Momipites is also present in every sample examined from the detrital upper Claibornian-Jacksonian-lower Vicksburgian sequence of Mississippi and Alabama. M. coryloides (Figure 16-4 (17)) is mainly "common" to "abundant" whereas M. microfoveolatus (Figure 16-4 (16)) is mainly "occasional" to "common" nearly to the top of the Jacksonian. The genus has much lower relative frequencies in the uppermost Jacksonian and lower Vicksburgian. Thus, grains of Momipites were produced in prodigious numbers on the late Claibornian-Jacksonian Gulf Coastal Plain, and at least some of these grains were produced in the deltaic peat-forming swamps.

Caprifoliipites-Salixipollenites makes up 11 to 41 percent ("common" to "very abundant") of the assemblage in all but a few coal samples in Figure 16-3; it varies in relatitve frequency from sample to sample considerably more than Momipites. In contrast to the latter taxon, Caprifoliipites-Salixipollenites is of uncertain affinity. Pollen assigned to this category belongs to two species, Caprifoliipites n. sp. (Figure 16-4 (14, 15)) and Salixipollenites n. sp. (Figure 16-4 (13)), which were tabulated together. The former species is more abundant than the latter in the coal assemblages of Figure 16-3, but in the upper Claibornian-Jacksonian-lower Vicksburgian detrital rocks of Mississippi and Alabama, Caprifoliipites n. sp. was "infrequent" to "occasional" in twenty-one of fifty-six counted samples whereas Salixipollenites n. sp. was "infrequent" to "common" in forty-five of the fifty-six samples. The data suggest that Caprifoliipites n. sp. was produced by plants that were more abundant in the peat-forming swamps whereas Salixipollenites n. sp. may have been produced by plants more abundant in other coastal plain environments. However, I am not certain that these two forms of pollen grains were produced by different groups of plants; the two forms are very similar except that Caprifoliipites n. sp. is (sometimes indistinctly) tricolporate whereas Salixipollenites n. sp. is tricolpate. Two of the detrital rock samples from the Manning Formation (R1263D and R1263A) have moderately high relative frequencies of Caprifoliipites-Salixipollenites pollen (13 and 18 percent, repectively), but the other three Manning samples of shale and mudstone (R1143D, R1264C, R1143E) have very small percentages of this form. Because of their distinct reticulation, these grains look as though they should have been largely zoophilous or possibly transitional between anemophilous and zoophilous like modern Salix. However, from the high relative frequencies of the pollen type in some coals, it appears that the plants were heavy pollen producers and thus were, at least in part, anemophilous. The plants producing this pollen form seem to have been considerably more abundant in some Jacksonian deltaic peat-forming swamps than others. The fact that Caprifoliipites-

Salixipollenites occurs in a high proportion of detrital Jacksonian samples from Texas to Alabama shows that the producing plants were distributed from one end of the coastal plain to the other. However, the low relative frequencies of this pollen form in most Jacksonian detrital samples indicate that the plants may have had patchy distributions. That is, local concentrations of plants may have been high as in some deltaic peat swamps, but on the Gulf Coast as a whole, the number of plants may have been relatively small. Also, the plants may have been shrubby or even herbaceous, which would hinder massive regional dispersal of the pollen.

The three assemblages in Figure 16-3 that are least similar to the others are R1263E, R1265E, and R1263B. The first two of these are characterized by moderately high relative frequencies (16 and 21 percent, respectively) of Pseudolaesopollis ventosa (Figure 16-4 (22); Cyrillaceae, Costaea?). This pollen species was not observed at all during counts of 200 specimens of most of the coal assemblages and is only "occasional" in Manning coal samples R1263H, R1143B, and R1143A. It is also "occasional" in the two middle Claibornian coals (R1155 and R1156 of Figure 16-2 and Table 16-2) but was not observed at all in the four lower Vicksburgian coals (R1144, R1145, R1146A, R1146B). However, the species is "infrequent" to "common" in fifty-two out of fifty-six counted samples from the upper Claibornian-Jacksonian-lower Vicksburgian detrital sequences of Mississippi and Alabama. To be this widely distributed in detrital sediments, the species must have been at least partly wind pollinated; or if entirely zoophilous, the producing plants must have been very abundant and widespread on the coastal plain. In either case, absence of the pollen species from most of the coal assemblages is probably significant. In short, Pseudolaesopollis ventosa seems to have been produced by plants that were widely distributed on the Gulf Coastal Plain from at least the middle Claibornian to the early Vicksburgian, but these plants may have been an important constituent of deltaic swamp communities only during the Jacksonian. Even then, they were probably members of only some of those communities.

The assemblage that is least similar to the others in Figure 16-3 is R1263B. However, the difference is not in species composition but in the fact that dominance is shared by three pollen forms: Caprifoliipites-Salixipollenites, Momipites spp., and Cupuliferoipollenites brevisulcatus Fred. The last-named pollen taxon (Figure 16-4 (20)) is morphologically identical to modern pollen of Chrysophyllum (Sapotaceae), which is entirely zoophilous as far as we know. In detrital rocks of the upper Claibornian, Jacksonian, and lower Vicksburgian of Mississippi and Alabama, this pollen species is "infrequent" to "occasional" in only fourteen out of fifty-six counted samples. The species seems to have been produced by plants that were locally abundant in peat-forming swamps and perhaps other environments of the coastal plain. However, the pollen appears to have had relatively poor regional dispersal and may have been zoophilous or been produced by plants that were low: small trees or shrubs. In some of the swamps, plants producing these grains must have been far more abundant than were producers of Momipites and probably Caprifoliipites-Salixipollenites. Pollen of other Sapotaceae is rare in the Manning coals.

R1264E is a coal assemblage that may represent quite a different peat-forming swamp community than the others though this is not obvious from the cluster diagram. Fifteen percent of this assemblage

(Table 16-5) is a new species of finely reticulate tricolporate pollen grains (Figure 16-4 (27, 28)) that are rare or absent in all the other coal assemblages. Because R1264E is similar to the other samples in the rest of its composition, it has a high calculated similarity to most of the other samples. However, 15 percent of what is probably a zoophilous pollen type may be highly significant and may represent large numbers of some unknown dicots in the community. The importance of this species or group of species in terms of forest dominance would depend largely on whether the plants were herbs, shrubs, or vines as opposed to trees. Perhaps the absence or near absence of this pollen type from all the other coal assemblages indicates that the producing plants were part of the understory.

Fern spores are not abundant in most of the samples of Figure 16-3, but they are 16 percent of the assemblage in samples R1263H and R1265B. In R1263H, most of the specimens belong to *Verrucatosporites alienus* (Pot.) Thoms. and Pflug (Oleandraceae, Polypodiaceae, Pteridaceae), *Lygodiumsporites* spp. (*Lygodium* and perhaps *Acrostichum* among others, but probably not the tree fern families Cyatheaceae or Dicksoniaceae), and *Cicatricosisporites dorogensis* Pot. and Gell. s.l. (*Anemia*, possibly *Mohria*). In sample R1265B, nearly all the spores belong to *Laevigatosporites haardtii* (Pot. and Ven.) Thoms. and Pflug (variety of fern families). However, in modern coastal and deltaic swamps, ferns have very local distributions; fern spores may be abundant in one sample and sparse in another sample from a short distance away. Hence, differences among samples based on relative frequencies of fern spores may not be very significant.

In the section of this chapter entitled "Jacksonian, Samples of Marine Rocks," a list is given of sporomorph taxa present in a large proportion of the samples from the marine Jacksonian of Mississippi and Alabama; these taxa were probably produced by plants abundant on the coastal plain. A comparison of this list with a list of sporomorphs found in the Manning Formation coals appears to indicate that the following forms were abundant on the coastal plain but lived mainly or entirely outside the deltaic swamps:

Selaginella spp.
Ephedra spp.
Carya spp.
Sapotaceae (other than *Chrysophyllum*)
Parthenocissus? sp.
Ulmus-Planera-Zelkova types
Platanus sp.
Cyrillaceaepollenites n. sp. (affinity unknown)
Verrutricolporites n. sp. (affinity unknown)
Intratriporopollenites n. sp. (probably Tiliaceae but not *Tilia*; possibly Bombacaceae)

Sporomorph assemblages from thick laterally extensive coals (R1263H, R1266G, R1264E, R1265B, R1263E, R1265E) are similar to assemblages from thin locally developed interdistributary and channel fill coals (P7857, R1143B, R1143A, R1143C, R1266A, R1266D, R1263B). Vertical changes in assemblages within individual coal beds have been little investigated in this study. However, R1263E and R1263H are from the upper and lower splits of seam 4 of Mathewson and Bishop (1979) in core 3737QQ. These two samples are fairly similar to each other; R1263E has more Pseudolaesopollis ventosa, whereas R1263H has more Cupuliferoipollenites brevisulcatus and many more spores. The coal samples from Fayette County, Texas, were collected from an outcropping seam, and three samples were taken from this bed: one each from the top, the middle, and near the base (the lowermost 8 cm of the 60 cm thick bed was under water). These three samples (R1143A, B, and C) have high similarities (0.94 or higher), which suggests that the swamp vegetation changed little, at least during deposition of the peat that formed this particular coal bed. Coal samples R1264E (core 3332SS) and R1265E (core 3534EE) are both from the same thick seam in Grimes County, Texas (Bishop, 1977); the cores are 6.0 km apart along strike. In core 3332SS, the seam is 2.2 m thick and sample R1264E is from 0.3 m below the top of the seam. In core 3534EE, the seam is 1.9 m thick and sample R1265E is from 1.34 m below the top of the seam. According to Figure 16-3, these two samples contain two of the more dissimilar assemblages from Manning lignites, mainly because of differences in relative frequencies of Momipites spp. and Pseudolaesopollis ventosa. However, it is uncertain whether the differences between R1264E and R1265E represent lateral and (or) temporal differences in the plant communities living in this swamp.

The relative frequencies of fungal spores, calculated as fungal spores/(sporomorphs + fungal spores), are shown in Figures 16-2 and 16-3 (note that the percentage scale for fungal spores on the diagrams is half that used for the sporomorphs). Large variations are present from sample to sample (values range from 5 to 93 percent), but the data show no discernible relationship to the sporomorph clusters, which were computed on the basis of sporomorphs exclusive of fungal spores. If the clusters of coal assemblages have any meaning in terms of plant communities, no relationship appears to exist between the relative frequency of total fungal spores and these communities. Similar data from Miocene brown coals of Germany are given in Table 16-6. In none of the latter coals are the relative frequencies of fungal spores as high as the maximum figures for the upper Claibornian and upper Jacksonian lignites of Figure 16-3. In the Miocene coals, fairly large ranges of values are present within each coal type; the relative frequencies of fungal spores are similar for each coal type except detritus-gyttja, which may have formed in lakes, where fungal remains were sparse. Among modern peats forming in Georgia and Florida, fungal remains are more consistently abundant in forested dryer environments than in marshes (Riegel, 1965:98; Cohen, 1973; Cohen and Spackman, 1977:108).

OTHER COASTAL PLAIN COMMUNITIES

Whereas lignite assemblages from the uppermost Claibornian and Jacksonian are generally dominated by Momipites, assemblages (Figure 16-2) from detrital rocks of the uppermost Claibornian (14959 is typical) and Jacksonian (10653, 10641, and 10637 are typical) of Mississippi and Alabama are dominated by Cupuliferoipollenites (Fagaceae; Table 16-3) and contain Momipites in fewer numbers. These data suggest that trees of the Engelhardia group were more abundant in the peat-forming swamps, but trees of Fagaceae were more abundant in other environments of the coastal plain in the late Claibornian and Jacksonian. Assemblages from Jacksonian marine detrital rocks of

Table 16-6
Relative frequencies of fungal spores in Miocene brown coal assemblages, Germany. Frequencies calculated from data of Teichmüller and Thomson (1958, Table 1).

Coal Type	Number of Samples	Range in Relative Frequency of Fungal Spores (Percent)
"Reed" coal	6	8-38
"Reed" coal-forest coal	1	28
Myricaceae forest coal	5	19-49
Taxodiaceae forest coal	2	17-48
Detritus-gyttja	1	3

Mississippi and Alabama are rather uniform (Figure 16-2, samples 10653, 10641, and 10637; Frederiksen, 1969), but assemblages from nonmarine to marginal-marine Jacksonian detrital rocks of other areas vary considerably. Some of the latter samples (R1263D, R1263A, R1265B, R1300A, R1143D) cluster tightly with samples from Jacksonian coals; however, it is not clear whether the dominance of these assemblages by Momipites resulted from massive transport of these pollen grains from nearby swamps or whether trees producing these grains also lived on sandy clay substrates.

Assemblage R1142B (Redfield Formation of Wilbert, 1953, Jacksonian, Arkansas) is very similar to the assemblages from the upper Claibornian and marine Jacksonian detrital rocks of Mississippi. Sample R1298D (Yegua Formation, upper Claibornian, Texas) also clusters with the upper Claibornian and Jacksonian detrital samples from Mississippi, but differs from them in having fairly high percentages of pollen from palms (19 percent) and Nyssa (9 percent; Table 16-2). The piece of shale from which this sample was taken contains the type specimens (fruits) of Nyssa texana Berry. Several other samples on Figure 16-2 and Table 16-2 also contain appreciable numbers of Nyssa grains, namely R1266G (9 percent), R1234A (7 percent), and R1234B (6 percent). All three of these samples are from upper Jacksonian coals of Texas. In modern swamps of southeastern United States in which Nyssa trees are the dominant or a principal constituent, pollen of this genus reaches maximum relative frequencies of 10 to 15 percent in the sediments (Whitehead, 1965; Cohen, 1975). Thus, Nyssa trees were relatively abundant constituents of some deltaic peat-forming swamps in Jacksonian time and of some non-peatforming environments of the coastal plain in late Claibornian time.

Palm pollen is sparse in the three upper Jacksonian coal samples just mentioned. It is not known whether palms lived closely associated with Nyssa trees near the site of deposition of R1298D or whether the palm and Nyssa pollen in the sample came from two different plant communities. Palm pollen grains are "common" to "very abundant" in many samples in Figure 16-2 and in Table 16-2, for example, 10 percent in R1144, 22 percent in R1146A (lower Vicksburgian coals), 9 percent in R1300A (claystone from the Twiggs Clay Member, Barnwell Formation, lower Jacksonian of Georgia). However, the maximum relative frequencies of palm pollen are in coals and shales of the Manning Formation (upper Jacksonian) of Texas.

Palm pollen makes up at least 8 percent, and as much as 17 percent, of the assemblage in six of the fourteen coal samples from this formation. In shales and mudstones associated with these coal beds, palm pollen is even more abundant (R1263D, 12 percent; R1263A, 13 percent; R1143D, 23 percent; R1264C, 55 percent; R1143E, 71 percent). Both Liliacidites tritus Fred. (Pseudophoenix?) and microreticulate-punctate monosulcates are present in most of these samples, but in the two samples consisting of more than 50 percent palm pollen, these grains are almost exclusively of the latter type. Sample R1143E contains many large (as long as 15 cm) pieces of wood that presumably belonged to palms although the wood structure is too poorly preserved to be determinable (J. A. Wolfe, pers. comm.). Even though much of the palm pollen in these samples may have been anemophilous and palms may be over-represented by their pollen grains, these trees must have been important constituents of some deltaic environments at least in the Jacksonian and early Vicksburgian. They appear to have been especially dominant in some areas of sandy-clay substrate, but they probably also grew rather abundantly in some peat-forming swamps where (in the late Eocene) they were associated with other plants that were also abundant in peat-forming swamps having few palms. On the other hand, Kremp and Kovar (1960) thought that the palm pollen abundant in some German Miocene brown coals might have been blown into the swamps from surrounding, drier areas. Pollen of Palmae also occurs in high relative frequencies in some upper Paleocene coals of the Gulf Coast (Nichols and Traverse, 1971).

VICKSBURGIAN

The four lower Vicksburgian (lower Oligocene) samples of coal from the Forest Hill Sand (R1144, R1145, R1146A, R1146B) are quite dissimilar to each other according to the cluster diagram (Figure 16-2). Sample R1144 has a number of moderately abundant sporomorph types rather than one or two clearly dominant types. The main forms are Cupressacites hiatipites (Wode.) Krutzsch (18 percent; Taxodiaceae-Cupressaceae-Taxaceae; Figure 16-4 (1)), psilate deltoid trilete spores (18 percent; Lygodium among others), miscellaneous dicots (10 percent), palm pollen (10 percent; at least six species), and monolete spores (8 percent; various fern families). Altogether, fern spores make up 30 percent of the assemblage, and this is the only sample in Figure 16-2 and in Table 16-2 that contains more than a trace of Taxodiaceae-Cupressaceae-Taxaceae pollen. Sample R1145 is composed largely (66 percent) of Cicatricosisporites dorogensis Pot. and Gell. (spores of the Anemia type). This high relative frequency is especially interesting because at least some ferns of this genus seem to be zoophilous (Hughes and Smart, 1967:112). Sample R1146A is dominated by Fraxinoipollenites spp. (39 percent; represents several families, at least partly zoophilous) and to a lesser extent by microreticulate to punctate monosulcates (17 percent; palms). Sample R1146B contains more fern spores than anything else (monolete spores, 28 percent; Cicatricosisporites dorogensis, 12 percent).

In short, the four lower Vicksburgian coal assemblages are different from each other according to the relative frequencies of the different species, but in three of the four samples, fern spores make up 30 percent or more of the assemblage. In contrast, the maximum relative frequency of fern spores in coal samples R1263H and R1265B from the upper Claibornian and Jacksonian is 16 percent. Fern spores are only a few percent of the assemblage, at most, in the remaining samples on Figure 16-3. None of the spores in the Vicksburgian coals are of types produced by modern tree ferns. However, it cannot be determined how many of the ferns were lianas or epiphytes and how many formed an understory in the forest. If fern spores are excluded from the coal assemblages, these assemblages still differ greatly among themselves (Table 16-7), in contrast to the considerable uniformity of the Jacksonian coal assemblages. Furthermore, many of the pollen forms in Table 16-7 were probably zoophilous, including most miscellaneous dicots, some reticulate monosulcates, perhaps some pollen of Fraxinoipollenites, most or all prolate reticulate tricolporates, and Myrtaceidites and Striopollenites terasmaei. Because zoophilous pollen is not transported far from the site of production, the data of Tables 16-2 and 16-7 suggest that the early Vicksburgian peat-forming swamps were inhabited by a variety of trees and shrubs, many of them zoophilous, and had a ground cover and lianas composed at least in part of ferns. However, it is important to point out that three of the four Vicksburgian coal samples (R1144, R1146A, R1146B) are cuttings. Thus, if each of these coal beds contains more than one sporomorph assemblage zone, each cutting sample is probably a mixture of assemblages; for these samples, the apparent diversity is higher and the dominance lower than for coal samples from a point source. This may be true particularly of sample R1144, which appears to have an unusually low dominance and is from a seam 2.1 m thick.

One specimen of cf. Ovoidites was found in R1145, and several specimens were observed in the 200-count of R1146B. The biological affinity of these fossils is unknown; suggestions include statoblasts of bryozoans (Thomson and Pflug, 1953), freshwater plankton (Krutzsch, 1961b), and pollen grains, perhaps of Magnoliaceae (Krutzsch, 1961b; Jansonius and Hills, 1976:1841). Riegel (1965), in his study of modern sediments of southern Florida, found these fossils mainly in freshwater marsh deposits and suggested that they might have been produced by herbaceous marsh monocots.

The most obvious and significant difference between the coal and shale samples from the lower Vicksburgian is that the shales (10625 and 10627 are typical examples) contain abundant Quercus? pollen (56 and 37 percent of the assemblage, respectively), whereas this pollen type is only 2 to 8 percent of the assemblage in the four coals of the same age. Apparently, the trees of Quercus or a closely related genus (perhaps Dryophyllum) did not grow abundantly in the deltaic peat-forming swamps but preferred other, perhaps better-drained, habitats of the early Oligocene coastal plain. Relative frequencies of Quercus-type pollen also are high in detrital rock samples from the uppermost part of the Jacksonian in Mississippi and Alabama (10631 and 10632); for this reason, I placed a pollen-zone boundary within the upper Jacksonian (below samples 10631 and 10632) rather than at the top of this stage (Frederiksen, 1968, 1969, in press).

Table 16-7
Ranked relative frequencies of most abundant sporomorph forms in lower Vicksburgian coal assemblages if fern spores are excluded.

Sporomorph Form	R1144	R1145	R1146A	R1146B
Cupressacites hiatipites (Taxodiaceae-Cupressaceae-Taxaceae)	1			
Miscellaneous dicots	2	1		1
Reticulate monosulcates (Palmae)	3			4
Momipites spp. (*Engelhardia* group)	4			
Myrtaceidites spp. (Myrtaceae, Sapindaceae)		2		
Prolate reticulate tricolporates (various families)		3	3	
Quercus? spp.		4		2
Siltaria spp. <26 μm (Fagaceae at least in part)		4		
Fraxinoipollenites spp. (various families)			1	
Microreticulate-punctate monosulcates (Palmae)			2	
Cupuliferoipollenites spp. (Fagaceae)			4	
Striopollenites terasmaei (*Acer*, *Prunus*, Anacardiaceae?)				3

MARSH COMMUNITIES

The evidence is not sufficient to indicate whether any of the lignites examined for this study formed from marsh peats, that is, areas of high water table more or less lacking tall shrubs and trees. On one hand, it is difficult to believe that marshes were not present in the late Eocene of the Gulf Coast (J. A. Wolfe, pers. comm.); on the other hand, there is practically no evidence that such communities actually did exist. Even in the German Miocene brown coals of the Rhine area, the evidence for the existence of peat-forming marshes is mainly indirect and is based on the following facts (Thomson, 1951; Neuy-Stolz, 1958; Teichmüller, 1958):

1. Coal that supposedly formed in marshes is composed mainly of strongly decomposed fine detritus; the assumption is that grasses and sedges do not leave well preserved remains in the peat.
2. Rare sedge (Cyperaceae), grass (Gramineae), and rush (Juncaceae) leaves and fruits are found in the coal; however, pollen of these plants is rare or absent.
3. Certain fungal spores are present (Ustilaginales, especially those having granulate spore walls), many of whose modern representatives are parasites on sedges and grasses.
4. Sporomorph assemblages are dominated by Fagaceae pollen from trees that presumably lived outside the peat-forming areas.

However, because of the scarcity of sedge and grass pollen in the brown coals of the Rhein area, Kremp and Kovar (1960) concluded that plants of these families did not form extensive marshes even in the Miocene. Until the Claibornian to Vicksburgian coals of the Gulf Coast have been studied petrographically it will be difficult to determine whether they formed in marshes or swamps. Elsik (1978) examined specially prepared maceration residues from Paleocene and Eocene coals of Texas and reported (1978:29) that his samples from the Manning Formation contained "much more finely divided organic debris (than most other Texas lower Tertiary coals).... The general lack of structured woody material, but especially the finely comminuted size of the organic particles, may prove to be significant for a marsh origin of these lignites." On the other hand, the available palynological evidence suggests that the Manning coals I have studied formed in forested swamps. Abundant fungal remains, found in many Manning coals, are more typical of swamps than of marshes. Ustilaginalean fungi, at least of the type described by Neuy-Stolz (1958), are rare if present at all in the coals studied for this chapter. The only records of known marsh and aquatic herbs in the coal assemblages are one specimen probably of Aglaoreidia (Ruppiaceae? or Potamogetonaceae?) in sample R1144 (coal from the Forest Hill Sand) and one specimen of Sparganium-Typha type in sample R1145 (also coal from the Forest Hill Sand). The sporomorph assemblages from the coals of this study are dominated by dicot pollen, palm pollen, and fern spores; pollen of monocots other than palms is rare, and gymnosperm pollen is also rare except that pollen of Taxodiaceae-Cupressaceae-Taxaceae appears in the Forest Hill coals and is rather abundant in one of them (R1144). However, the nature of the plants producing some of the dicot pollen is not known; some of the plants could have been low shrubs or even herbs. For example, coals having high relative frequencies of Caprifoliipites-Salixipollenites pollen could have formed in marshes; Momipites and other arboreal pollen grains in the coals could have been carried by wind and streams into these marshes.

Few families that include modern herbs can be traced back as far as the Eocene; these families appear to have evolved mainly in the Oligocene and especially the Miocene (Leopold, 1969; Szafer, 1975). However, because megafossils of herbs are only rarely preserved, it is very difficult to reconstruct the history of these plants. Among all the modern taxa identified on the basis of pollen from detrital sediments of the upper Claibornian, Jacksonian, and lower Vicksburgian in Mississippi and Alabama, only the following could have formed marshes: Gramineae ("infrequent" in eight out of fifty-six counted samples from this stratigraphic interval), two species of the pollen genus Milfordia (Figure 16-4 (3)), which belong to Centrolepidaceae-Flagellariaceae-Restionaceae (these two species are "infrequent" in five out of fifty-six and nine out of fifty-six counted samples, respectively), and two species of the monocot pollen genus Aglaoreidia (Figure 16-4 (2)), which in Mississippi and Alabama are represented by rare specimens in the uppermost Claibornian and the uppermost Jacksonian to lower Vicksburgian, repectively. Discussing the late Eocene and early Oligocene vegetation of the Isle of Wight, Machin (1971:869) suggested that "Possibly the families Restionaceae and Centrolepidaceae...occupied ecological positions in this flora later to be filled by grasses." Milfordia pollen is very abundant in some Eocene and lower Oligocene deposits of Europe, and the Centrolepidaceae-Flagellariaceae-Restionaceae may have been important marsh plants during this time interval (Machin, 1971; W.

Krutzsch, cited in Rüffle, 1976:375). However, at least in the middle Eocene coals of the Geiseltal, in East Germany, Milfordia pollen is not abundant (Krutzsch, 1976); thus, the producers of this pollen do not appear to have been important in the peat-forming swamps. Milfordia pollen was also rare in the coals studied for the present paper.

COASTAL COMMUNITIES IN NON-PEATFORMING ENVIRONMENTS

Some sporomorph assemblages previously described from detrital rocks, particularly in the Jacksonian (see the section "Jacksonian, Other Coastal Plain Communities"), may have come from plant communities living in brackish water. However, the evidence is not definite as to water salinity during deposition of all these sediments. In this section, I use several approaches to reconstruct the brackish-water to marine coastal communities living on detrital sediment substrates of the Gulf Coast in the Eocene and Oligocene. The first is to examine sporomorph assemblages containing sparse microplankton that may have been deposited in shoreline environments, perhaps in brackish water, to determine whether these samples might contain some sporomorph types not present in freshwater samples; thus, the samples with sparse microplankton might offer some information about the nature of the shoreline vegetation. Seven of the nine samples on Figure 16-2 that contain sparse microplankton probably formed in brackish water (R1263D, R1263A, R1143D, 14959, 10631, 10625, 10632; 10653 was deposited on an open-marine shelf. The rare dinoflagellates in R1143C are probably freshwater forms). Unfortunately, these seven samples show hardly any difference from the many samples lacking microplankton. Five of the seven samples contain Myrtaceidites spp. (Myrtaceae, Sapindaceae). Other occurrences of this pollen genus are mainly in the Vicksburgian coal and detrital rock samples, but otherwise the genus occurs in only three samples of Figure 16-2. These data may suggest that Myrtaceidites represents shoreline plants, but the evidence is ambiguous.

A second and more successful approach is to find out whether any taxa known to inhabit modern coastal environments might have existed on the Gulf Coast in the Eocene and Oligocene. For example, two pollen species of the Restionaceae-Centrolepidaceae-Flagellariaceae (pollen genus Milfordia; Figure 16-4 (3)) are present as rather rare specimens in upper Claibornian, Jacksonian, and lower Vicksburgian rocks of Mississippi and Alabama. Members of Restionaceae and Centrolepidaceae are plants of marshes and swamps, and some, for example Leptocarpus (Restionaceae), are typical of brackish-water habitats (Cranwell, 1953). Members of Restionaceae and Centrolepidaceae are probably entirely anemophilous (Pohl, 1929, cited in Cranwell, 1953:32), but pollen production in individual genera varies from heavy to sparse (Cranwell, 1953:32). In short, members of the Restionaceae-Centrolepidaceae-Flagellariaceae appear to have been present on the Gulf Coast from the Claibornian to the Vicksburgian, but it is not known how abundant the plants were nor whether some of them occupied brackish-water habitats.

Two pollen species of Aglaoreidia are present in my material from Mississippi and Alabama: Aglaoreidia cyclops Erdtm. from the upper Claibornian and A. pristina Fowl. (Figure 16-4 (2)) from the

Jacksonian and lower Vicksburgian. The plants that produced these pollen were monocotyledonous (Erdtman, 1960:46), perhaps Ruppiaceae or Potamogetonaceae (Machin, 1971:856). Both species of *Aglaoreidia* were apparently produced by hydrophytes: *A. cyclops* by either brackish-water (Machin, 1971:856) or freshwater plants (Fowler, 1971:143) and *A. pristina* perhaps by brackish-water plants (Fowler, 1971:143). In Mississippi and Alabama, *A. pristina* occurs in the marine Yazoo Clay and Red Bluff Clay but also in the deltaic Forest Hill Sand. Many samples of the Forest Hill have a few dinoflagellate cysts, suggesting delta fringe, brackish-water environments of deposition.

Berry (1924, 1937) reported leaves of *Laguncularia*, *Terminalia*, *Conocarpus*, and *Combretum* (all of the Combretaceae) and *Rhizophora* from the upper Claibornian and Jacksonian and concluded that extensive mangrove swamps existed along the middle and late Eocene Gulf Coast. All five of these genera have distinctive pollen grains, and *Rhizophora* grains, in particular, are produced in enormous numbers in modern *Rhizophora* swamps. However, I have not found pollen of any of these genera in my material; therefore, I believe Berry was mistaken in his identifications of these leaves. He also reported *Acrostichum* leaves from the Claibornian and Jacksonian; modern *Acrostichum* is a fern of coastal swamps and marshes and is often associated with mangroves. Berry (1924:143) noted that the leaf species *Acrostichum georgianum* Berry "is not uncommon in the middle and upper Claiborne and is exceedingly abundant in deposits of lower Jackson age in Georgia." The saltwater habitat of *Acrostichum* can be traced back at least to the middle Eocene (Barthel, 1976:455); thus, if *Acrostichum* did exist along the Eocene Gulf Coast, it probably occupied the same habitats as now. In my material, I have seen one spore that was very similar to modern *Acrostichum aureum* L.; this specimen is from the upper Jacksonian of Mississippi. *Lygodiumsporites adriennis* (Pot. and Gell.) Pot. and similar spores are "infrequent" to "common" in nearly all samples examined from the upper Claibornian-Jacksonian-lower Vicksburgian sequence of Mississippi and Alabama, but spores of this type are produced by both *Lygodium* and *Acrostichum* (Barthel, 1976:455, Plate 78, Figures 4-6). Thus, there is no way of determining from dispersed spores whether *Acrostichum* was present on the Eocene and Oligocene Gulf Coast and, if so, how abundant the plants were.

The only mangrove form that I have definitely identified is *Nypa*, scattered grains of which occur in samples from the uppermost Claibornian nearly to the top of the Jacksonian in Mississippi and Alabama; Arnold (1952) also described a *Nypa* fruit from the middle Claibornian of Texas. This stemless palm is now an inhabitant of tropical, brackish-water to saltwater muddy coasts of the southwestern Pacific and the Indian Ocean. *Nypa* pollen is as much as 40 percent of the assemblage in deltaic lower Eocene sediments of the Spanish Pyrenees (Haseldonckx, 1972), but such high relative frequencies of this pollen are rare. *Nypa* pollen is likely to be sparse even where the plants are abundant because "The (modern) *Nypa* vegetation apparently does not produce much pollen as a whole, although individual flowers release it in abundance" (Muller, 1964:35) and because the grains are poorly dispersed owing to their large size (Chaloner, 1968), because they are zoophilous, and because the plants are prostrate creepers. Therefore, even rare grains of the genus are significant. However, it remains unknown whether *Nypa* formed pure stands or whether it was associated with other genera of which we have no record.

CONCLUSIONS

Table 16-8 summarizes the dominant sporomorph types in coals and detrital rocks from the middle Claibornian to the lower Vicksburgian. Dominant sporomorphs of the coal assemblages were probably produced by plants abundant in peat-forming swamps. Dominant sporomorphs of the detrital rock assemblages were produced by plants abundant on the coastal plain, but it is not clear in which environments these plants lived. It must be emphasized again that most of the dominant sporomorph types listed in Table 16-8 were probably anemophilous; zoophilous plants of the various coastal-plain environments are, on the whole, greatly under-represented by sporomorphs.

All the middle Claibornian coals from the Gulf Coast that have been studied palynologically by me and by others (Elsik and Dilcher, 1974; perhaps the seam of Potter, 1976) probably formed in abandoned stream channels, and most or all of them formed in fresh water. All the sporomorph assemblages from these coals and from the accompanying detrital rocks are dominated by various types of Fagaceae pollen. Upper Claibornian assemblages from Tennessee, which probably formed in freshwater environments (my coal sample R1448; perhaps the coal and clay samples of Potter, 1976), are also dominated by Fagaceae pollen; however, the upper Claibornian coal from Mississippi (P7857), which may have formed in brackish water, contains an assemblage dominated by *Momipites* (*Engelhardia* group of Juglandaceae). The few published analyses of sporomorph assemblages from marine rocks of the lower and middle Claibornian (Tschudy, 1973) suggest that producers of *Momipites* did not become abundant in any coastal plain habitats until late in the Claibornian. The ranges of many sporomorph taxa have tops or bases within the upper Claibornian (Tschudy, 1973; Elsik, 1974); thus, both the flora and the vegetation of the coastal plain changed rapidly at this time.

Momipites pollen dominates most sporomorph assemblages of the deltaic, probably brackish-water Jacksonian coals of southeastern Texas, but *Caprifoliipites-Salixipollenites* (Caprifoliaceae?, Oleaceae?; anemophilous?) is also an important pollen form in these coals and is locally dominant. *Pseudolaesopollis ventosa* (Cyrillaceae; anemophilous?), pollen of palms (probably partly anemophilous), *Cupuliferoipollenites brevisulcatus* (*Chrysophyllum*; apparently zoophilous), pollen of miscellaneous dicots (most of them zoophilous), and fern spores are also fairly abundant in some coals. Figure 16-3 indicates that Jacksonian deltaic swamp communities of southeastern Texas were similar to each other especially in species composition, but if the different sporomorph assemblages are a guide, distinct differences existed in the relative abundances of the plants in some of the swamps.

Marine Jacksonian rocks of Mississippi and Alabama contain sporomorph assemblages that are, of course, entirely allochthonous, but study of these assemblages allows certain conclusions to be made as to the nature of lowland and upland elements of the vegetation. For instance, most gymnosperms probably lived in the uplands, but *Ephedra* lived at least partly on the coastal plain. Comparison of assemblages from Jacksonian coals with those from marine rocks allowed a list to be prepared of lowland taxa that probably inhabited non-peatforming coastal plain environments. Inhabitants of non-peatforming brackish-water environments included Nypa and perhaps Acrostichum. Assemblages from nonmarine to brackish-water detrital rocks are more difficult to interpret because they include elements from both the local and regional vegetation. However, study of such assemblages from the Jacksonian of the Gulf Coast shows that trees of the Engelhardia group, Palmae, Nyssa, and especially Fagaceae were abundant in some non-peatforming environments of the coastal plain. Whether any Jacksonian coals formed from marsh peats could not be determined without petrographic analyses, but pollen from trees and perhaps shrubs dominates all Jacksonian coal assemblages. Herb pollen is also rare in assemblages from other Jacksonian coastal plain environments, but low production and dispersal of herb pollen may have distorted the record.

The second important change in the vegetation of the coastal plain during the time span from middle Claibornian through early Vicksburgian took place near the end of the Jacksonian when Quercus? became a dominant taxon in at least some environments of the coastal plain but apparently not in the deltaic (brackish-water?) peatforming swamps. Anemophilous trees were not as abundant in the early Vicksburgian coastal swamps as they had been in the Claibornian and Jacksonian, and zoophilous trees and shrubs probably were dominant types in many swamps.

ACKNOWLEDGMENTS

I am grateful to the following for providing many of the samples discussed in this paper: B.F. Clardy, Arkansas Geological Commission; James Crawford, Robert Cargill Oil and Gas; D.W. Engelhardt, Amoco Production Co.; R.E. Hershey, Tennessee Division of Geology; L.J. Hickey, Smithsonian Institution; C.C. Mathewson, Texas A & M University; D.C. Prowell, U.S. Geological Survey; D.R. Williamson, Mississippi Geological Survey; and R.S. Young, North American Exploration Inc. C.C. Mathewson and M.A. Bishop, Texas A & M University, provided much useful stratigraphic information about the samples from Grimes County, Texas. R.W. Stanton, U.S. Geological Survey, arranged for the proximate and ultimate analyses of the Grimes County coal samples. Alfred Traverse, Pennsylvania State University, and D.L. Dilcher, Indiana University, reviewed the manuscript of this paper and offered helpful suggestions for its improvement.

Table 16-8
Dominant sporomorph forms of coal and detrital rock samples.

Sporomorph Form	Middle Claibornian		Upper Claibornian		Jacksonian		Uppermost Jacksonian and lower Vicksburgian	
	Coal	Detrital Rock	Coal	Detrital Rock	Coal	Detrital Rock	Coal	Detrital Rock
Quercoidites microhenricii	X	X						
Cupuliferoipollenites spp.	X?	X	X?	X		X		
Cupuliferoidaepollenites spp.		X?	X	X?				
Momipites spp.			X	X	X	X		
Caprifoliipites n. sp.-*Salixipollenites* n. sp.					X			
Microreticulate-punctate monosulcates						X		
Pteridophyte spores							X	
Fraxinoipollenites spp.							X	
Quercus? spp.								X

APPENDIX: SAMPLE REGISTER

Sample	Lithology	Stratigraphic Unit	Depth (m)[1]	Type of Sample	Location	Remarks
10625	Sandstone, light gray, fine grained, and siltstone,	Forest Hill Sand	15.9	Core	Mississippi Geol. Survey borehole AF-8, SE 1/4 SE	Type locality of the Forest Hill Sand. The core section

	medium-light gray				1/4 NE 1/4 sec. 22, T. 5 N., R. 1 W., Hinds Co., Miss.	was described by Moore (1965:117 and Figs. 16-17). Palynomorph analysis by Frederiksen (1969).
10627	Shale, dark brownish-gray	do.	19.2	do.	do.	do.
10631	Clay, medium olive-gray	Yazoo Clay	22.0	do.	do.	do.
10632	do.	do.	23.5	do.	do.	do.
10637	Clay, yellowish-gray, calcareous, fossiliferous	Yazoo Clay	8.8	Core	Mississippi Geol. Survey borehole AF-17, NW 1/4 NW 1/4 NW 1/4 sec. 36, T. 6 N., R. 1 E., Riverside Park, Jackson, Hinds Co., Miss.	Electric log and sample descriptions given by Moore (1965:122 and Fig. 9). Palynomorph analysis by Frederiksen (1969).
10641	Sand, greenish-gray, glauconitic, fossiliferous	Moodys Branch Formation	14.9	do.	do.	do.
10653	Clay, dark greenish-gray, fossiliferous	Yazoo Clay	10.7	Outcrop	Jackson Ready-Mix Concrete Company clay pit, SW 1/4 NE 1/4 NW 1/4 sec. 36, T. 7 N., R. 1 W., Hinds Co., Miss.	Top of pit is probably about 15 m below contact between Yazoo Clay and Forest Hill Sand. Locality reference: Moore (1965, Figs. 11, 14). Palynomorph analysis by Frederiksen (1969).
14958[2]	Clay, medium-dark olive-gray	Cockfield Formation	8.8	Outcrop	Riverside Park exposure, NW 1/4	Reference locality for the Moodys

					NW 1/4 sec. 36, T. 6 N., R. 1 E., Jackson, Hinds Co., Miss.	Branch Formation. Locality references: Rainwater (1960); Huff (1970:22-23). Palynology by Engelhardt (1964); Frederiksen (1969, 1973); Tschudy (1973). Slides of samples P7856, P7857, and P7858 loaned to the writer by D.W. Engelhardt.
14959	Clay, medium gray	do.	9.8^{3}	do.	do.	do.
P7856[2]	Shale, gray	do.	11.9^{3}	do.	do.	do.
P7857	Lignite	do.	12.2^{3}	do.	do.	do.
P7858[2]	Shale, gray	do.	12.7^{3}	do.	do.	do.
R1142B	Clay, dark gray, and sand, light gray	Redfield Formation of Wilbert (1953)		Outcrop	West bank of the Arkansas River, NE 1/4 sec. 30, T. 3 S., R. 10 W., Jefferson Co., Ark.	Sample is from the base of unit c, locality 2, of Wilbert (1953:44).
R1143A	Lignite	Manning Formation		Outcrop	O'Quinn Creek, 5.0 km NW of O'Quinn, Fayette Co., Tex. 29°51' N., 96°59' W., USGS Seguin, Tex. 1:250,000 sheet.	Top 7.6 cm of the seam. Locality reference: Fisher (1963, Fig. 67). I saw only one seam here.
R1143B	do.	do.		do.	do.	23-31 cm below top of seam
R1143C	do.	do.		do.	do.	46-54 cm below top of seam

R1143D	Shale, medium gray, with small plant fragments	do.		do.	do.	2.1 m below seam
R1143E	Mudstone, dark grayish-brown, with large pieces of wood	do.		do.	do.	Float block 90 m downstream from coal seam.
R1144	Lignite	Forest Hill Sand	30-33	Cut-tings	Mississippi Geol. Survey borehole AL-7, NW 1/4 NE 1/4 NW 1/4 sec. 4, T. 3 N., R. 8 E., Smith Co., Miss.	Locality reference: Luper (1972:70).
R1145	Lignite	Forest Hill Sand	11.3	Core	Same as sample 10625	
R1146A	Lignite	Forest Hill Sand	21-23	Cut-tings	Mississippi Geol. Survey test hole 7, NE 1/4 SW 1/4 NW 1/4 sec. 16, T. 7 N., R. 1 E., Madison Co., Miss.	Locality reference: Priddy (1960:87).
R1146B	do.	do.	17.4-19.5	do.	do.	do.
R1155	Lignite	Middle Claibornian		Outcrop	Tocowa Church, SE 1/4 sec. 8, T. 10 S., R. 8 W., Panola Co., Miss.	Sample provided by R.S. Young.
R1156	Lignite	Middle Claibornian	?	Core	Sec. 4, T. 6 S., R. 8 W., Tate Co., Miss.	Sample provided by R.S. Young.
R1167A[2]	Mudstone, light brownish-gray, with lignite laminae	Manning Formation		Outcrop	Same as R1143A-C	20 cm above coal seam
R1167B[2]	Mudstone, medium brownish-gray	do.		do.	do.	20 cm below coal seam.
R1234A	Lignite	Manning	?	Core	North of the	"Corehole 18,

Sample	Lithology	Stratigraphic unit	Depth	Sample type	Locality	Remarks
		Formation			Trinity River, Walker Co., Tex.	bed A" according to sample bag. Sample provided by J. Crawford.
R1234B	do.	do.	?	do.	do.	"Corehole 23, bed B" according to sample bag. Sample provided by J. Crawford.
R1263A	Shale, medium-dark gray	Manning Formation	43.3	Core	Grimes Co., Tex., 30°37'41"N., 96° 57'12" W.	Core 3737QQ. Samples provided by C.C. Mathewson.
R1263B	Lignite	do.	43.6	do.	do.	
R1263C[2]	Shale, medium gray	do.	43.9	do.	do.	
R1263D	Mudstone, medium gray	do.	56.7	do.	do.	
R1263E	Lignite	do.	56.9	do.	do.	Seam 4 of Mathewson and Bishop (1979).
R1263F[2]	Shale, dark grayish-brown	do.	58.2	do.	do.	
R1263G[2]	Shale, medium brown	do.	59.9	do.	do.	
R1263H	Lignite	do.	60.1	do.	do.	Seam 4 of Mathewson and Bishop (1979).
R1264A[2]	Shale, medium gray	do.	39.0	do.	Grimes Co., Tex., 30°31'36"N., 96° 06'46"W.	Core 3332SS. Samples provided by C.C. Mathewson.
R1264B	Lignite	do.	39.3	do.	do.	Seam 3 of Mathewson and Bishop (1979).
R1264C	Mudstone, medium greenish-gray	do.	39.6	do.	do.	
R1264D[2]	Shale, medium brown	do.	51.2	do.	do.	

R1264E	Lignite	do.	52.1	do.	do.	Seam 2 of Mathewson and Bishop (1979).
R1265A[2]	Mudstone, dark brown	do.	31.1	do.	Grimes Co., Tex., 30°33'49"N., 96° 04'07"W.	Core 3534EE. Samples provided by C.C. Mathewson.
R1265B	Lignite	do.	32.6	do.	do.	Seam 3 of Mathewson and Bishop (1979).
R1265C[2]	Mudstone, dark brown	do.	32.9	do.	do.	
R1265D[2]	Shale, medium grayish-brown	do.	41.8	do.	do.	
R1265E	Lignite	do.	43.0	do.	do.	Seam 2 of Mathewson and Bishop (1979).
R1266A	Lignite	do.	7.3	do.	Grimes Co., Tex., 30°33'00"N., 96° 07'55" W.	Core 3432NE. Samples provided by C.C. Mathewson.
R1266B[2]	Shale, medium gray	do.	8.8	do.	do.	
R1266C[2]	Mudstone, medium brown	do.	18.3	do.	do.	
R1266D	Lignite	do.	18.6	do.	do.	
R1266E	Mudstone, greenish-gray	do.	19.2	do.	do.	
R1266F[2]	Shale, black	do.	43.0	do.	do.	
R1266G	Lignite	do.	44.0	do.	do.	Seam 1 of Mathewson and Bishop (1979).
R1266H[2]	Mudstone, light gray	do.	?	do.	do.	
R1298D	Shale, brown	Yegua Formation		Outcrop	"beneath lignite in bed of Cedar Creek about 2 miles south of	Piece of shale containing the type specimens of _Nyssa texana_ Berry 1924,

					the Texas Southeastern Railroad bridge and about 2 miles southwest of Lufkin, Angelina County, Tex." (Berry, 1924:89).	USNM 38332.
R1300A	Claystone, medium-dark olive-gray	Twiggs Clay Member, Barnwell Formation		Outcrop	Georgia Vitrified Brick Co. quarry at Campania, Columbia Co., Ga. 33°24'41"N., 82° 17'43" W.	Sample is from near the base of the member; collected by D.C. Prowell.
R1448	Lignite	Cockfield Formation	38	Core	Ft. Pillow State Prison Farm, approx. 13 km east of the Mississippi River, Lauderdale Co., Tenn., 35°39'30" N., 89°45'00" W.	Formation assignment by W. S. Parks (R. E. Hershey, pers. comm.).

1 Depth in borehole or below top of local section.
2 Sample examined only for presence of microplankton.
3 Cockfield Formation-Moodys Branch Formation contact taken as the top of the transition beds.

REFERENCES

American Society for Testing and Materials. 1976. 1976 Annual Book of ASTM Standards, Pt. 26: Gaseous Fuels, Coal and Coke, Atmospheric Analysis. Philadelphia: Am. Soc. for Testing and Materials, 800 p.

Arnold, C. A. 1952. Tertiary plants from North America. 1. A Nipa fruit from the Eocene of Texas. Palaeobotanist 1:73-74.

Axelrod, D. I. 1966. A method for determining the altitudes of Tertiary floras. Palaeobotanist 14:144-171.

Barthel, M. 1976. Farne und Cycadeen. In Eozäne Floren des Geiseltales. Zentr. Geol. Inst. Abh. 26:439-498.

Bartlett, A. S., and E. S. Barghoorn. 1973. Phytogeographic history of the Isthmus of Panama during the past 12,000 years (a history of vegetation, climate, and sea-level change). In A. Graham, ed., Vegetation and Vegetational History of Northern Latin America. Amsterdam: Elsevier Scientific Publishing Co., pp. 203-299.

Berry, E. W. 1924. The middle and upper Eocene floras of southeastern North America. U.S. Geol. Survey Prof. Paper 92, 206 p.

Berry, E. W. 1937. Tertiary floras of eastern North America. Bot. Rev. 3:31-46.

Bishop, M. A. 1977. Engineering Geology Study of Highwall Stability for a Proposed Lignite Mine in Grimes County, Texas. M.S. thesis, Texas A&M University, 142 p.

Breger, I. A. 1974. The role of organic matter in the accumulation of uranium--the organic geochemistry of the coal-uranium association. In Formation of Uranium Ore Deposits. Vienna: Internatl. Atomic Energy Agency, pp. 99-124.

Chaloner, W. G. 1968. The paleoecology of fossil spores. In E.T. Drake, ed., Evolution and Environment. New Haven: Yale University Press, pp. 125-138.

Cohen, A. D. 1973. Petrology of some Holocene peat sediments from the Okefenokee swamp-marsh complex of southern Georgia. Geol. Soc. America Bull. 84:3867-3878.

Cohen, A. D. 1975. Peats from the Okefenokee swamp-marsh complex. Geoscience and Man 11:123-131.

Cohen, A. D., and W. Spackman. 1977. Phytogenic organic sediments and sedimentary environments in the Everglades-mangrove complex: The origin, description and classification of the peats of southern Florida. Palaeontographica 162B:71-114.

Couper, R. A. 1960. New Zealand Mesozoic and Cainozoic plant microfossils. New Zealand Geol. Survey Paleont. Bull. 32, 87 p.

Cranwell, L. M. 1953. New Zealand pollen studies, the monocotyledons. Auckland Inst. and Mus. Bull. 3, 91 p.

Dietrich, J. W., and J. T. Lonsdale. 1958. Mineral resources of the Colorado River Industrial Development Association area. Texas Univ. Bur. Econ. Geology Rept. Inv. 37, 84 p.

Dilcher, D. L. 1969. Podocarpus from the Eocene of North America. Science 164:299-301.

Dilcher, D. L. 1973. A paleoclimatic interpretation of the Eocene floras of southeastern North America. In A. Graham, ed., Vegetation and Vegetational History of Northern Latin America. Amsterdam: Elsevier Scientific Publishing Co., pp. 39-59.

Dilcher, D. L., and F. Potter. 1977. Biostratigraphic analysis of

Eocene floras of southeastern North America. *Jour. Paleontology* 51(supp.):9.

Dorf, E. 1960. Climatic changes of the past and present. *Am. Scientist* 48:341-364.

Drugg, W. S., and A. R. Loeblich, Jr. 1967. Some Eocene and Oligocene phytoplankton from the Gulf Coast, U.S.A. *Tulane Studies in Geology* 5:181-194.

Dumble, E. T. 1918. The geology of East Texas. *Texas Univ. Bull.* 1869:275-291.

Elsik, W. C. 1974. Characteristic Eocene palynomorphs in the Gulf Coast, U.S.A. *Palaeontographica* 149B:90-111.

Elsik, W. C. 1978. Palynology of Gulf Coast lignites: the stratigraphic framework and depositional environments. *Texas Univ. Bur. Econ. Geology Rept. Inv.* 90:21-32.

Elsik, W. C., and D. L. Dilcher. 1974. Palynology and age of clays exposed in Lawrence clay pit, Henry County, Tennessee. *Palaeontographica* 146B:65-87.

Engelhardt, D. W. 1964. Plant microfossils from the Eocene Cockfield Formation, Hinds County, Mississippi. *Mississippi Geol. Econ. and Topog. Survey Bull.* 104:65-96.

Erdtman, G. 1960. On three new genera from the Lower Headon Beds, Berkshire. *Botaniska Notiser* 113:46-48.

Faegri, K., and J. Iversen. 1964. *Textbook of Pollen Analysis*. Copenhagen: Munksgaard, 237 p.

Faegri, K., and L. van der Pijl. 1971. *The Principles of Pollination Ecology*, 2nd ed. Oxford: Pergamon Press, 291 p.

Fairchild, W. W., and W. C. Elsik. 1969. Characteristic palynomorphs of the Lower Tertiary in the Gulf Coast. *Palaeontographica* 128B:81-89.

Fisher, W. L. 1963. Lignites of the Texas Gulf Coastal Plain. *Texas Univ. Bur. Econ. Geology Rept. Inv. 50*, 164 p.

Fisher, W. L. 1964. Sedimentary patterns in Eocene cyclic deposits, northern Gulf Coast region. *Kansas Geol. Survey Bull.* 169:151-170.

Fisher, W. L. 1968. Variations in lignites of fluvial, deltaic, and lagoonal systems, Wilcox Group (Eocene), Texas. *Geol. Soc. America Abs. with Programs*, p. 97.

Fisher, W. L. 1969. Facies characterization of Gulf Coast basin delta systems, with some Holocene analogues. *Gulf Coast Assoc. Geol. Socs. Trans.* 19:239-261.

Fisher, W. L., C. V. Proctor, Jr., W. E. Galloway and J. S. Nagle. 1970. Depositional systems in the Jackson Group of Texas. *Gulf Coast Assoc. Geol. Socs. Trans.* 20:234-261.

Folk, R. L. 1955. *Tertiary Field Trip*. Austin: Univ. Texas Geol. Soc., 23 p.

Fowler, K. 1971. A new species of *Aglaoreidia* Erdtm. from the Eocene of southern England. *Pollen et Spores* 13:135-147.

Frederiksen, N. O. 1968. Palynology of the upper Eocene Jackson Stage in Mississippi and western Alabama. *Geol. Soc. America Abs. with Programs*, pp. 102-103.

Frederiksen, N. O. 1969. *Stratigraphy and Palynology of the Jackson Stage (Upper Eocene) and Adjacent Strata of Mississippi and Western Alabama*. Ph.D. dissertation, University of Wisconsin, 355 p.

Frederiksen, N. O. 1973. New mid-Tertiary spores and pollen grains from Mississippi and Alabama. *Tulane Studies Geology and*

Paleontology 10:65-86.

Frederiksen, N. O. 1975. Late Eocene flora of the northern Gulf Coast. Geoscience and Man 11:156-157.

Frederiksen, N. O. 1977. Affinities of late Eocene spores and pollen grains from southeastern North America. U.S. Geol. Survey Open-file Rept. 77-691, 26 p.

Frederiksen, N. O. In press. Sporomorphs from the Jackson Group (Upper Eocene) and Adjacent Strata of Mississippi and Western Alabama. U.S. Geol. Survey Prof. Paper 1084.

Frederiksen, N. O., and R. A. Christopher. 1978. Taxonomy and biostratigraphy of Late Cretaceous and Paleogene triatriate pollen from South Carolina. Palynology 2:113-145.

Georgia Geological Survey. 1976. Geologic Map of Georgia. Atlanta: Georgia Geol. Survey, Map, Scale 1:500,000.

Germeraad, J. H., C. A. Hopping, and J. Muller. 1968. Palynology of Tertiary sediments from tropical areas. Rev. Palaeobotany and Palynology 6:189-348.

Gomez-Pompa, A. 1973. Ecology of the vegetation of Veracruz. In A. Graham, ed., Vegetation and Vegetational History of Northern Latin America. Amsterdam: Elsevier Scientific Publishing Co., p. 73-148.

Graham, A. 1975. Late Cenozoic evolution of tropical lowland vegetation in Veracruz, Mexico. Evolution 29:723-735.

Gray, J. 1960. Temperate pollen genera in the Eocene (Claiborne) flora, Alabama. Science 132:808-810.

Groot, J. J. 1966. Some observations on pollen grains in suspension in the estuary of the Delaware River. Marine Geology 4:409-416.

Hardenbol, J., and W. A. Berggren. 1978. A new Paleogene numerical time scale. In G. V. Cohee et al., eds., Contributions to the Geologic Time Scale. Tulsa: Am. Assoc. Petroleum Geologists, pp. 213-234.

Haseldonckx, P. 1972. The presence of Nypa palms in Europe: a solved problem. Geologie en Mijnbouw 51:645-650.

Hopkins, W. S., Jr. 1967. Palynology and its paleoecological application in the Coos Bay area, Oregon. Ore Bin 29:161-183.

Huff, W. J. 1970. The Jackson Eocene Ostracoda of Mississippi. Mississippi Geol. Econ. and Topog. Survey Bull. 114, 289 p.

Hughes, N. F., and J. Smart. 1967. Plant-insect relationships in Palaeozoic and later time. In W. B. Harland et al., eds., The Fossil Record. London: Geol. Soc. London, pp. 107-117.

Imbrie, J., and E. G. Purdie. 1962. Classification of modern Bahamian carbonate sediments. Am. Assoc. Petroleum Geologists Mem. 1, pp. 253-272.

Jansonius, J., and L. V. Hills. 1976. Genera file of fossil spores and pollen. Calgary Univ. Dept. Geology Spec. Pub., 3287 cards.

Kaiser, W. R. 1974. Texas lignite--near-surface and deep-basin resources. Texas Univ. Bur. Econ. Geology Rept. Inv. 79, 70 p.

Kaiser, W. R., and C. G. Groat. 1977. Texas lignite. Am. Assoc. Petroleum Geologists Bull. 61:801-802.

Kremp, G. O. W., and A. J. Kovar. 1960. The interpretation of Tertiary swamp types in brown coal. U.S. Geol. Survey Prof. Paper 400-B, pp. B79-B81.

Kremp, G. O. W., R. C. Neavel, and J. S. Starbuck. 1961. Coal types--a function of swamp environments. In Origin and Constitution of Coal, 3rd Conf., Nova Scotia, 1956. Halifax, Nova Scotia Dept. Mines, pp. 270-286.

Krutzsch, W. 1961a. Ueber Funde von "ephedroidem" Pollen im deutschen Tertiär. Geologie 10:15-39.

Krutzsch, W. 1961b. Beitrag zur Sporenpaläontologie der präoberoligozänen kontinentalen und marinen Tertiärablagerungen Brandenburgs. Geol. Gesell. DDR Ber. 5:290-343.

Krutzsch, W. 1976. Die Mikroflora der Braunkohle des Geiseltales. Teil IV. Die stratigraphische Stellung des Geiseltalprofils im Eozän und die sporenstratigraphische Untergliederung des mittleren Eozäns. In Eozäne Floren des Geiseltales. Zentr. Geol. Inst. Abh. 26:47-92.

Leffingwell, H. A. 1971. Palynology of the Lance (Late Cretaceous) and Fort Union (Paleocene) formations of the type Lance area, Wyoming. In R. M. Kosanke and A. T. Cross, eds., Symposium on Palynology of the Late Cretaceous and Early Tertiary. Geol. Soc. America Spec. Paper 127, pp. 1-64.

Leopold, E. B. 1969. Late Cenozoic palynology. In R. H. Tschudy and R. A. Scott, eds., Aspects of Palynology. New York: Wiley-Interscience, pp. 377-438.

Long, R. W., and O. Lakela. 1971. A flora of tropical Florida. Coral Gables: University of Miami Press, 962 p.

Luper, E. E. 1972. Smith County Geology. Mississippi Geol. Econ. and Topog. Survey Bull. 116:11-100.

MacGinitie, H. D. 1941. A middle Eocene flora from the central Sierra Nevada. Carnegie Inst. Washington Pub. 534, 178 p.

Machin, J. 1971. Plant microfossils from Tertiary deposits of the Isle of Wight. New Phytologist 70:851-872.

MacNeil, F. S. 1944. Oligocene stratigraphy of southeastern United States. Am. Assoc. Petroleum Geologists Bull. 28:1313-1354.

MacNeil, F. S. 1946. The Tertiary formations of Alabama. In Southeastern Geological Society Field Trip Guidebook, pp. 1-64.

MacNeil, F. S. 1966. Middle Tertiary sedimentary regimen of Gulf Coastal region. Am. Assoc. Petroleum Geologists Bull. 50:2344-2365.

Maher, L. J., Jr. 1964. Ephedra pollen in sediments of the Great Lakes region. Ecology 45:391-395.

Mann, J. C., and W. A. Thomas. 1968. The ancient Mississippi River. Gulf Coast Assoc. Geol. Socs. Trans. 18:187-204.

Martin, P. S., and J. Gray. 1962. Pollen analysis and the Cenozoic. Science 137:103-111.

Mathewson, C. C., and M. A. Bishop. 1979. Geology of the Gibbons Creek lignite deposit, Manning Member (Jackson Group), Grimes County, Texas. In D. G. Kersey, ed., Claiborne Sediments of the Brazos Valley, Southeast Texas. Houston Geological Society Guidebook, pp. 26-36.

May, J. H. 1974. Wayne County geology. In J. H. May et al., eds., Wayne County geology and mineral resources. Mississippi Geol. Econ. and Topog. Survey Bull. 117, pp. 13-194.

McLaughlin, R. E. 1957. Plant microfossils of the Bruhn lignite. Ph.D. dissertation, University of Tennessee, 183 p.

Mellen, F. F. 1941. Geology. In Warren County Mineral Resources. Mississippi Geol. Survey Bull. 43:9-88.

Miranda, F., and A. J. Sharp. 1950. Characteristics of the vegetation in certain temperate regions of eastern Mexico. Ecology 31:313-333.

Mississippi Geological Survey. 1969. Geologic Map of Mississippi. Jackson, Mississippi: Mississippi Geol. Survey, Map, Scale

1:500,000.
Monroe, W. H. 1954. Geology of the Jackson area, Mississippi. U.S. Geol. Survey Bull. 986, 133 p.
Moore, W. H. 1965. Hinds County geology. Mississippi Geol. Econ. and Topog. Survey Bull. 105:21-172.
Muller, J. 1959. Palynology of Recent Orinoco delta and shelf sediments. Micropaleontology 5:1-32.
Muller, J. 1964. A palynological contribution to the history of the mangrove vegetation in Borneo. In L. M. Cranwell, ed., Ancient Pacific Floras, the Pollen Story. Honolulu: University of Hawaii Press, pp. 33-42.
Muller, J. 1970. Palynological evidence on early differentiation of angiosperms. Cambridge Philos. Soc. Biol. Rev. 45:417-450.
Muller, J. 1972. Palynological evidence for change in geomorphology, climate and vegetation in the Mio-Pliocene of Malesia. In P. Ashton and M. Ashton, eds., The Quaternary Era in Malesia: Hull Univ. Dept. Geography Misc. Ser. 13:6-16, 17-34.
Murray, G. E. 1961. Geology of the Atlantic and Gulf Coastal Province of North America. New York: Harper and Bros., 692 p.
Neuy-Stolz, G. 1958. Zur Flora der Niederrheinischen Bucht während der Hauptflözbildung unter besonderer Berücksichtigung der Pollen und Pilzreste in den hellen Schichten. Fortschr. Geologie Rheinland u. Westfalen 2:503-525.
Nichols, D. J., and A. Traverse. 1971. Palynology, petrology, and depositional environments of some Early Tertiary lignites in Texas. Geoscience and Man 3:37-48.
Pen'kova, A. M. 1973. Distribution of Ephedra L. pollen in upper Paleogene and Neogene deposits of southwestern Tadzhikistan (in Russian). In E. D. Zaklinskaya, ed., Palynology of the Cenophytic. Moscow: Nauka Press, pp. 156-158.
Pflug, H. D. 1952. Palynologie und Stratigraphie der eozänen Braunkohlen von Helmstedt. Paläont. Zeitschr. 26:112-137.
Pflug, H. D. 1957. Zur Altersfolge und Faziesgliederung mitteleuropäischer (insbesonders hessischer) Braunkohlen. Hess. Landesamtes Bodenforsch. Wiesbaden Notizbl. 85:152-178.
Pohl, F. 1929. Beziehungen zwischen Pollenbeschaffenheit, Bestäubungsart und Fruchtknotenbau. Bot. Centralbl. Beihefte 46:247-285.
Potonie, R. 1934. Zur Mikrobotanik des eocänen Humodils des Geiseltals. Preuss. Geol. Landesanstalt, Inst. Paläobotanik und Petrographie Brennsteine Arb. 4:25-117.
Potonie, R., and H. Venitz. 1934. Zur Mikrobotanik des miocänen Humodils der niederrheinischen Bucht. Preuss. Geol. Landesanstalt, Inst. Paläobotanik und Petrographie Brennsteine Arb. 5:5-54.
Potter, F. W., Jr. 1976. Investigations of angiosperms from the Eocene of southeastern North America--pollen assemblages from Miller pit, Henry County, Tennessee. Palaeontographica 157B:44-96.
Priddy, R. R. 1942. Tallahatchie County mineral resources--geology. Mississippi Geol. Econ. and Topog. Survey Bull. 50:11-106.
Priddy, R. R. 1960. Madison County geology. Mississippi Geol. Econ. and Topog. Survey Bull. 88, 123 p.
Radford, A. E., H. E. Ahles, and C. R. Bell. 1964. Manual of the Vascular Flora of the Carolinas. Chapel Hill, North Carolina:

University Press, 1183 p.

Rainwater, E. H. 1960. Moodys Branch Formation, reference locality. In H. V. Andersen, ed., Type Localities Project, Unit I. Baton Rouge, La.: Soc. Economic Paleontologists and Mineralogists, Gulf Coast Sec., no pagination.

Rainwater, E. H. 1967. Resume of Jurassic to Recent sedimentation history of the Gulf of Mexico Basin. Gulf Coast Assoc. Geol. Socs. Trans. 17:179-210.

Riegel, W. L. 1965. Palynology of environments of peat formation in southwestern Florida. Ph.D. dissertation, The Pennsylvania State University, 189 p.

Rüffle, L. 1976. Myricaceae, Leguminosae, Icacinaceae, Sterculiaceae, Nymphaeaceae, Monocotyledones, Coniferae. In Eozäne Floren des Geiseltales. Zentr. Geol. Inst. Abh. 26:337-438.

Saunders, W. B., R. H. Mapes, F. M. Carpenter, and W. C. Elsik. 1974. Fossiliferous amber from the Eocene (Claiborne) of the Gulf Coastal Plain. Geol. Soc. America Bull. 85:979-984.

Sedlmeyer, J. J. 1939. Report on the mineral resources of Fayette County, Texas. Texas Univ. Bur. Econ. Geology Mineral Resource Survey Circ. 27, 3 p.

Shakhmundes, V. A. 1965. New species of Ephedra L. from Paleogene sediments of northern Western Siberia (in Russian). Vses. Neft. Nauchno-Issled. Geol.-Razved. Inst. Trudy 239:214-228.

Stach, E., M.-Th. Mackowsky, M. Teichmüller, G. H. Taylor, D. Chandra, and R. Teichmüller. 1975. Coal Petrology, D. G. Murchison et al., trans. and eds. Berlin: Gebrüder Borntraeger, 428 p.

Szafer, W. 1975. General Plant Geography. Warsaw: Panstwowe Wydawnictwo Naukowe, 430 p.

Teichmüller, M. 1958. Rekonstruktionen verschiedener Moortypen des Hauptflözes der niederrheinischen Braunkohle. Fortschr. Geologie Rheinland u. Westfalen 2:599-612.

Teichmüller, M., and P. W. Thomson. 1958. Vergleichende mikroskopische und chemische Untersuchungen der wichtigsten Fazies-Typen im Hauptflöz der niederrheinischen Braunkohle. Fortschr. Geologie Rheinland u. Westfalen 2:573-598.

Thomas, E. P. 1942. The Claiborne. Mississippi Geol. Econ. and Topog. Survey Bull. 48, 96 p.

Thomson, P. W. 1951. Grundsätzliches zur tertiären Pollen- und Sporenmikrostratigraphie auf Grund einer Untersuchung des Hauptflözes der rheinischen Braunkohle in Liblar, Neurath, Fortuna und Brühl. Geol. Jahrb. 65:113-126.

Thomson, P. W., and H. Pflug. 1953. Pollen und Sporen des mitteleuropäischen Tertiärs. Palaeontographica 94B:1-138.

Traverse, A. 1955. Pollen analysis of the Brandon lignite of Vermont. U.S. Bur. Mines Rept. Inv. 5151, 107 p.

Trewartha, G. T. 1968. An Introduction to Climate, 4th ed. New York: McGraw-Hill, 408 p.

Tschudy, R. H. 1969. Relationship of palynomorphs to sedimentation. In R. H. Tschudy and R. A. Scott, eds., Aspects of Palynology. New York: Wiley-Interscience, pp. 79-96.

Tschudy, R. H. 1973. Stratigraphic distribution of significant Eocene palynomorphs of the Mississippi embayment. U.S. Geol. Survey Prof. Paper 743-B, 24 p.

Vestal, F. E. 1956. Panola County geology. Mississippi Geol. Econ.

and Topog. Survey Bull. 81, 157 p.

Wang, C.-W. 1961. The forests of China. Cambridge, Maria Moors Cabot Foundation Pub. 5, 313 p.

Whitehead, D. R. 1965. Palynology and Pleistocene phytogeography of unglaciated eastern North America. In H. E. Wright, Jr., and D. G. Frey, eds., The Quaternary of the United States. Princeton: Princeton University Press, pp. 417-432.

Whitmore, T. C. 1972. Tree Flora of Malaya, Vol. 1. London: Longman, 471 p.

Wilbert, L. J., Jr. 1953. The Jacksonian Stage in southeastern Arkansas. Arkansas Div. Geol. Bull. 19, 125 p.

Williamson, D. R. 1976. An investigation of the Tertiary lignites of Mississippi. Mississippi Geol. Econ. and Topog. Survey Inf. Ser. 74-1, 147 p.

Willis, J. C. 1966. A Dictionary of the Flowering Plants and Ferns, 7th ed. Cambridge: University Press, 1214 p.

Wolfe, J. A. 1969. Paleogene floras from the Gulf of Alaska region. U.S. Geol. Survey Open-file Rept., 114 p.

Wolfe, J. A. 1975. An interpretation of Tertiary climates in the Northern Hemisphere. Geoscience and Man 11:160-161.

Wolff, H. 1934. Mikrofossilien des pliocänen Humodils der Grube Freigericht bei Dettingen a.M. Preuss. Geol. Landesanstalt, Inst. Paläobotanik und Petrographie Brennsteine Arb. 5:55-86.

Zagwijn, W. H. 1967. Ecologic interpretation of a pollen diagram from Neogene beds in the Netherlands. Rev. Palaeobotany and Palynology 2:173-181.

17

Paleoecology of the Miocene Clarkia Lake (Northern Idaho) and Its Environs

Charles J. Smiley and William C. Rember

ABSTRACT

Finely laminated deposits that occupy part of the present valley of the St. Maries River in northern Idaho contain an abundance and diversity of exceptionally well preserved Miocene fossils. Near the townsite of Clarkia an exposed section about nine meters thick contains what appears to be a complete lacustrine cycle: alluvial sands in the lower part, varve-like clays with ash interbeds in the middle, and floodplain deposits at the top. A Proto-St. Maries River appears to have been lava-dammed about thirty kilometers downstream from Clarkia, producing a narrow valley-bottom lake here named Clarkia Lake. The probable age of these Clarkia Lake deposits is Early Miocene.

The fossils are abundant, diversified and well preserved and include both terrestrial plants and insects and aquatic organisms such as diatoms, sponges, fish, clams, and snails. The forest plants are preserved as unoxidized cellular compressions that include numerous whole leaves that have retained an original pigmentation and organic chemistry. The abundance of remains throughout the exposed section permits a microstratigraphic analysis of the plant megafossils on a centimeter basis. The data show a seral change in the local vegetation that reflects modifications of conditions in the valley during the life of the Miocene lake.

The Clarkis fossil assemblage is divided into a Lacustrine Community and a Terrestrial Community. The flora is an assemblage of plants that more closely matches the modern forests of southeastern North America than elsewhere on the continent; a similar humid warm-temperature climate is inferred for northern Idaho in the Miocene. On the basis of preferred habitats of the living plants in eastern North America, the Clarkia flora is divisible into three associations: a bottomland Swamp Association, a mesic Floodplain and Slope Association, and a Dry Slope Association. The seral analysis seems to reflect the vegetational changes that occurred as the lake came into existence and progressed through its cycle to complete infilling.

INTRODUCTION

Tertiary deposits near Clarkia, Idaho (Smiley et al., 1975) provide an opportunity to study the microstratigraphy of Miocene lacustrine sediments and fossils and the community paleoecology of the lake and its surrounding habitats. Sediments are finely laminated and are rich in plant megafossils on almost every layer. Intact remains of fishes and insects occur in stratigraphically delimited concentrations. Megafossils also include a clam and a snail represented by one or two specimens. Microfossils are ubiquitous and include abundant and varied palynomorphs, diatoms, a dinoflagellate, sponge spicules, microfragments of insect exoskeletons, and bits of amber.

The Clarkia locality is unique in western North America in the abundance and variety of exceptionally well-preserved megafossils and microfossils and the fine laminations of the lacustrine deposits that have been extensively exposed thus making them available for detailed biostratigraphic analysis of megafossil paleobotany. Our microstratigraphic studies on the sequence of plant megafossils through the finely laminated deposits have provided evidence of short-term trends that cannot be recognized by a composite analysis of the fossil assemblage as a whole. These rapid changes, possibly taking place over a few hundred years, seem to be the result of local events that have affected the environment and the organic community of the area.

Much slower changes, involving regional or world climates and regional orogenic activity, serve as general controls on the regional biota regardless of local differences of habitat. All members of the community must be able to pursue their life functions under such controlling factors in order to inhabit the local niches that suit their specific requirements. A comparison between the Clarkia flora and modern forests can be used to determine the general climatic requirements for similar associations of forest plants. The geologic history of the rise of present topographic barriers, such as the Cascade Mountains on the west, provide additional information bearing on climatic changes and attendant vegetational history in the Western Interior of North America (Axelrod, 1950; Chaney and Axelrod, 1959; Smiley, 1963).

The discussion that follows deals in part with the composite fossil assemblage to determine regional factors such as climate that were influencing the local community. In addition, microstratigraphic analyses are used to determine the short-term trends of individual taxa and to determine specific changes in the depositional environment. Evidence thus is available in the Clarkia deposits to interpret the local changes that were taking place under the regional influence of climatic conditions, volcanic activity, and topographic diversity.

GEOLOGIC SETTING

EXPOSURES

Exposures of fossiliferous deposits occur at two major sites near Clarkia (Figure 17-1). The Clarkia type locality P-33 is about 2.5 km south of Clarkia, NW1/4, NE1/4, Sec. 13, T42N, R1E, Boise Meridian. Locality P-34 is about 1.6 km north of Clarkia, NE1/4, SE1/4, Sec. 31, T43N, R2E, Boise Meridian.

Locality P-33 was exposed by bulldozer and extends laterally for a distance of about 100 m along the south flank of a forested knoll.

The total thickness of Miocene deposits here is about 45 m of which 9 m were exposed (Figure 17-2). A core 2.5 cm in diameter drilled at

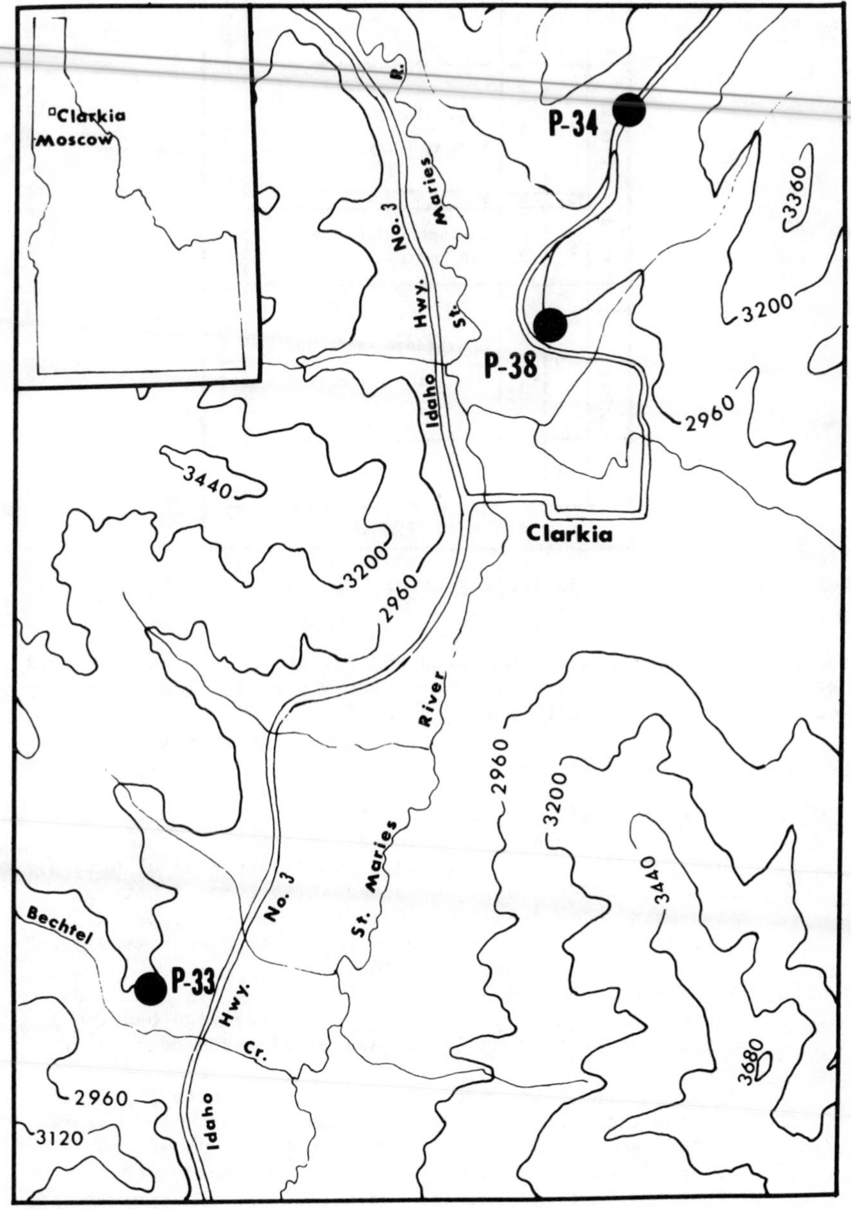

Figure 17-1
Map of Clarkia, Idaho, area. P-33 is the Clarkia type locality. P-34 and P-38 are localities where fossiliferous Clarkia deposits are intruded or overlain by Miocene basalts.

EXPOSURE	THICKNESS (m)	UNIT NOS.	SEDIMENTS	OXIDATION
Covered	9.0	5	Ashy silts. No distinct bedding except at base.	Oxidized
Exposed	0.6	4	Ash	Oxidized
Exposed	5.5	3, 2	Laminated clays, thick ash layers.	Unoxidized
Subsurface	11.0	1	Interbedded sands and clay. Thin ash beds.	Unoxidized
Subsurface	4.5	1	Coarse sand.	Unoxidized
BASEMENT (?Schist)				

Figure 17-2
Column for locality P-33 (Smiley et al., 1975).

the base of the exposure penetrated an additional 15 m of sediments before reaching hard bedrock. The upper 10 m of section is largely soil and forest cover with poor exposures.

The sedimentary sequence at locality P-33 (Figure 17-2) shows the following upward trends:

1. An upward fining of sediments from a base of coarse sands through interbedded sands and silty clays (Unit 1) to thinly bedded varve-like clays (Unit 2 to base of Unit 5) to poorly bedded, ashy sands and silts (top of Unit 5).
2. An upward increase in volcanic ash from thin beds in Unit 1 to thick beds in the middle of the section to disseminated ashy silts and sands at the top.
3. An upward change in bedding from thick, basal sand beds to thick interbeds of sand and clay to varve-like bedding in the middle of the section to again thicker bedding near the top.
4. An unoxidized lower part of the section (Units 1 and 2) to a transition bed (Unit 3) with pods of unoxidized material in the base of Unit 5 to oxidized material above.
5. An upward change in type of fossil preservation from compressions in the unoxidized material (cellular preservation commonly retaining original pigmentation) to iron-stained imprints in the oxidized sediments.

Locality P-34 is exposed in a 3 m cutbank of a forest road and extends laterally for a distance of 115 m. About 12.2 m of section was measured here; top and bottom were not exposed. The deposits resemble those of Unit 1 at the Clarkia type-locality, but they are somewhat coarser textured and have associated basalts (Figure 17-3). Within a few hundred meters, other roadcut and rock quarry sites show pillow basalts overlying coarse fossiliferous sands that locally contain rounded cobbles of fossiliferous silty clay (locality P-38). The fossils in the various sites north of Clarkia represent a depauperate lateral facies of the rich florule from Clarkia type-locality P-33.

MIOCENE TOPOGRAPHY

The Miocene sediments and basalts in the St. Maries River area rest on a basement of Precambrian mica schists (Clark, 1963; Hietanen, 1963). The surface of the basement was eroded into a hill-and-valley terrain prior to Neogene sedimentation, and a major stream occupied the same valley as the present St. Maries River. The Miocene deposits are restricted to this drainage system, and their present surfaces form flat valley bottoms of the river and its major tributaries.

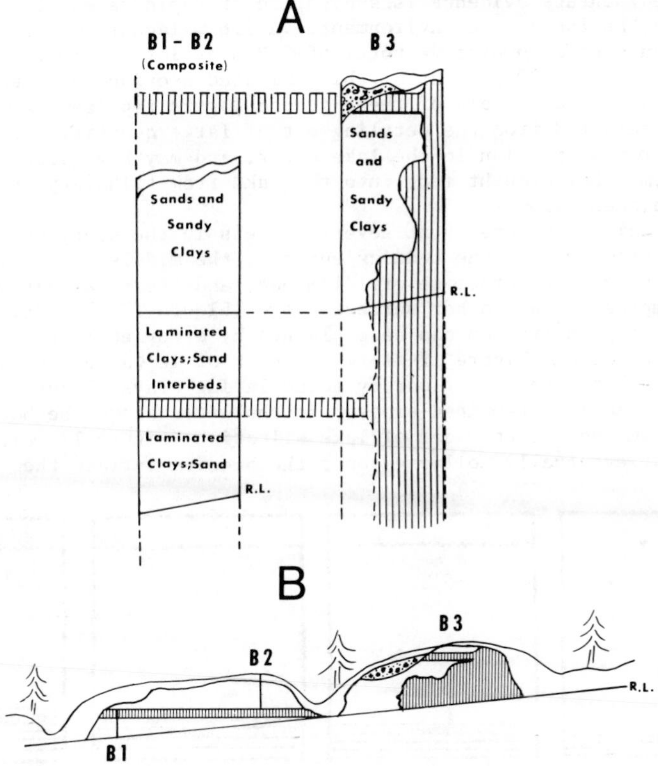

Figure 17-3
A. Sections measured at locality P-34, showing apparent interrelationships of fossiliferous sediments and the basalt dike-sill complex.
B. Sketch of roadcut exposure at locality P-34. R.L. = road level.

Spurs and knolls of schist now rise up to 150 m above the flat bottomland in the immediate vicinity of the valley, and within five kilometers the elevations increase to 725 m above the present valley floor. Local water wells show an original valley depth about 90 m below its present surface, which indicates a local relief prior to the Miocene sedimentation of not less than 815 m.

At Locality P-33 (Figure 17-1) the sediments and fossils indicate that at least part of the valley deposits accumulated in a lacustrine environment. Here the remains of fish, diatoms, and sponges are common in a 7.6 m section of varve-like silts and clays. Some of the finer laminations and thicker clay and ash beds that are internally graded can be traced laterally for a distance of 200 m at this site. The geomorphic, sedimentologic, and paleontologic data support a conclusion that a lake occupied this part of the St. Maries drainage system in Miocene time. The names Proto-St. Maries River and Clarkia Lake are given to these Miocene features.

SEDIMENTATION RATES

Sedimentary evidence is suggestive of rapid rates of accumulation in the lacustrine environment. A 7.6 m lacustrine section at P-33 contains a cumulative total of 2.3 m of internally graded layers suggesting that 30 percent of the laminated section resulted from rapid deposition. Some of these graded layers represent airfall ash. Others resulted from the settling out of large quantities of clays and silts from suspension in the lake water, and may have been produced by storms that brought muds into the lake from tributary streams or from adjacent slopes.

Specimens uncovered at several levels in the study show part of a leaf preserved on one bedding surface, the middle of the leaf bent upward to extend across several laminae, and the remainder of the leaf impressed on another surface above (Figure 17-4). This condition of preservation can be explained by a curled leaf settling to the lake bottom (Figure 17-4A) where part of it was buried and "cemented" to the lake floor by accumulating clays (Figure 17-4B). Part of the leaf remained exposed in the water above the bottom muds during subsequent episodes of lake siltation (Figure 17-4C), until the leaf eventually collapsed onto the bedding surface then pre-

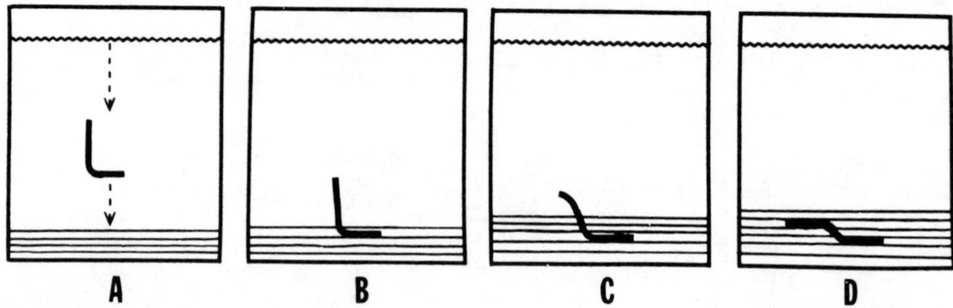

Figure 17-4
Probable method of deposition and burial of leaves found preserved on two bedding surfaces, apparently the result of rapid, storm-related deposition of fine sedimentary laminae.

vailing and was completely buried (Figure 17-4D). The lake "varves" thus seem to represent rapid sedimentation probably from frequent storms, rather than the slower rate of seasonal accumulation of classical varves. In other instances where leaves have been preserved crossing bedding planes, rapid rates of sedimentation similarly were interpreted to explain such phenomena (for example, Brown and Gow, 1976).

Recent studies such as by Ritchie and others (1973) show man-made reservoirs can silt in at rates varying from about 1 cm to about 12.5 cm per year. If the observed rates of sedimentary infilling are applied to the 760 cm study section at P-33, a maximum of 760 years and a minimum of 60 years would be required for this complete lacustrine cycle. If we remove from consideration 170 cm of interbedded ash layers at P-33, because the siltation rates of the modern reservoirs did not include the factor of air-fall deposition of volcanic ash, the maximum time required would be 600 years and the minimum 50 years. The 7.6 m section at P-33 may have taken less than a thousand years to accumulate, and the time span could well have been just a few decades.

VOLCANIC ACTIVITY

Numerous layers of silicic ash 2 mm to 50 cm thick occur in the section at P-33. Airfall deposition of ash in standing water is indicated by an upward fining within each layer and by a lateral continuity for more than 200 m. Thicker ash layers show an upward fining in the lower part of the unit followed by a second upward fining in the upper part of the unit which may have resulted when ash that fell originally upon the surrounding land was then washed into the lake basin. Some of the thickest ash units show a third episode of upward fining near the top.

The source of the silicic ashes is unknown at present, but they show that the local forests must have received a periodic mantling of volcanic ash during the life of Clarkia Lake. Dorf observed (1951:317), in the case of the 1945 eruption of Pericutin in Mexico, that "much of the plant population is able to survive at least temporarily, except where buried by lava or excessively thick pyroclastics, and continue to supply leaves, needles, cones, and other plant material to the record buried by the ash deposits." He noted further that plant remains are most abundant and well preserved in sites of valley bottom ponds and lakes, and are poorest on slopes and floodplain areas where high-energy water reworking of ashes occurred. These factors could explain the continued abundance and variety of plant remains in the laminated lake sediments immediately following deposition of the ash layers in the P-33 study section.

Basalts immediately north of Clarkia (near localities P-34 and P-38) form a local pile of flows that are exposed from the valley floor to the top of the hill about 150 m higher in elevation. At two places ravines were later eroded through this basalt pile, one exposing near-vent pyroclastics and flows and the other exposing the underlying Miocene sediments where they were cut by a dike of the same type of basalt (locality P-34). Nearby are pillowed basalts that rest on fossiliferous sands containing a Clarkia flora (locality (P-38). Farther down the St. Maries River valley, between Clarkia and Santa, are single basalt flows that rest on the older Miocene sediments and appear to have been confined to the Miocene valley floor. Such evidence indicates that these basalts post-date the fossiliferous deposits.

AGE DETERMINATIONS

The fossiliferous Clarkia deposits rest on schistose basement rocks of Precambrian age. They are intruded and are overlain by Middle Miocene basalts. A chemical analysis of these basalts by C. R. Knowles of the Idaho Bureau of Mines and Geology (personal communication) shows closest resemblance to Priest Rapids basalts of the Columbia Plateau that have been dated 13.6 to 15 MY (Watkins and Baksi, 1974; Swanson et al., 1975). Potassium/argon whole-rock age determinations of basalt units at locality P-34 by Geochron Laboratories gave dates of 21.8± 1.2 MY and 21.9± 1.4 MY. As these basalts post-date the sediments, their ages will provide a minimum date for the existence of Clarkia Lake.

The Clarkia flora represents a characteristic Miocene plant assemblage for western North America. The common occurrence of conifers such as *Cunninghamia*, *Metasequoia*, and *Sequoia* associated with an abundance and diversity of Magnoliaceae, Lauraceae, Leguminosae and woody vines are supportive of the basalt chronology in suggesting an Early Miocene age. Furthermore, warm-temperate climate inferred from the entire flora fits better the circum-Pacific conditions of earlier than of later Miocene time (Tanai and Huzioka, 1967; Wolfe, 1971).

The age of the Clarkia sediments and contained fossils thus is considered to be Early Miocene on the combined evidence of basalt chronology, comparison of the Clarkia flora with the known floral history of the region, and paleoclimatic inferences.

FOSSIL PRESERVATION

Excellently preserved leaves and other fossils occur in abundance in the sediments at type-locality P-33. We have analyzed, centimeter by centimeter, a column of fossiliferous, thinly laminated sediments 760 cm high and approximately 30 cm by 45 cm across. A maximum of 1,294 identifiable specimens has been counted within a 30 cm segment of this column; twenty other blocks of equivalent dimensions have yielded from 138 to 774 specimens each. The study column has produced 10,749 identifiable plant megafossil specimens although barren clays and ash thicknesses greater than 1 cm total 2.25 m. The fossil record from this column is representative of the abundance and variety of fossils observed throughout the lateral extent of the outcrop.

Plant megafossils are represented by angiosperm leaves, conifer shoots, unlithified wood, and a variety of reproductive organs. The fossils are distinctly separated on bedding surfaces and rarely overlap one another, suggesting an offshore burial site rather than the boggy or swampy floor of a forest where piles of leaves would accumulate. Most of the specimens in the unoxidized lower part of the section occur as compressed leaves. Megafossils in the oxidized upper part of the section occur only as imprints. Many of the unoxidized leaves and insects have retained their original pigmentation, but the specimens begin to blacken within seconds upon exposure (green or autumn red and brown of leaves; metallic green, blue, purple, or black of insects). Teratological damage to leaves, usually by insect mining and galling, is a common occurrence.

Preserved are examples of conifer branches with needled shoots attached, dicot branches with two or more leaves attached, compound leaves with leaflets attached, flower parts and clusters, male cones retaining yellow pollen grains, and various organs that appear not to have reached deciduous maturity. These and other conditions of preservation, such as the green color of some leaves and the presence of mature forest-dwelling insects in lake deposits, suggest that at least some of the specimens were removed by wind gusts and were airborne out onto the open lake prior to a time of normal autumn leaf fall and dispersal.

Palinomorphs, sampled at stratigraphic intervals of 5 cm by Gray, are abundant and well preserved in unoxidized sediments and as *in situ* grains in male strobiles of pine. Many bedding surfaces contain large, compressed bisaccate grains of pale-yellow color and uncompressed grains with flexible exines are common in some of the thin clay beds. The families and genera identified from pollen and spores, most of which are represented also by megafossils, are included in the taxonomic list on following pages (see also Smiley et al., 1975).

Remains of megascopic animals are mainly fishes and insects. The fishes are preserved as articulated skeletons outlined by a darkened impression of the body. They are found mostly near the Unit 4 ash bed and more than seventy-five specimens were collected. Two common species are represented, a sunfish and a minnow, whose living relatives occupy quiet-water habitats (Miller, personal communication). Isolated fish scales and disturbed skeletons are present but rare. Because the fish are preserved intact and with open mouths, and show no evidence of predation or scavaging, it would seem probable that death was sudden and took place in toxic or oxygen-depleted water. This could have occurred during seasonal overturning of the lakewater or by agitation of the bottom water during violent wind storms.

Insects are uncommon and may occur as intact bodies; the details of jointed appendages, hairs, and wings are preserved. Some specimens are crushed or decomposed beyond the point of positive identification. Most of the insects are mature, and immature forms such as larvae and nymphs are rare. Disarticulated insect parts and ubiquitous microfragments of exoskeletons are present and more than forty intact specimens are being studied by Lewis (personal communication). Most of the insects appear to be terrestrial (for example, beetles, stink bugs, weevils, katy-dids), and aquatic stages such as caddisfly larval cases are uncommon.

At localities P-34 and P-38, fossils are much less abundant and varied than at P-33 and are confined to a few beds. They are exclusively the remains of plants that are preserved as identifiable imprints in soft sand and sandy clays. The florules north of Clarkia contain a single dominant species that represents an extinct new genus of the Fagaceae (Smiley and Huggins, in preparation). The taxon is also one of the dominants at locality P-33 but it has not been found in any other Miocene flora of the region. Species that are associated with this dominant fagoid north of Clarkia occur also in the florule south of Clarkia (for example, *Metasequoia*, redwood, alder, birch, chestnut, grape, oak, poplar, sycamore, willow). Whereas the assemblages north of Clarkia seem to represent well-drained floodplain or slope habitats, the florule at P-33 contains a strong swamp (poorly drained) component (for example, swamp cypress, water tupelo, water locust) that is rare or lacking in the coarser sediments to the north.

CONSTRAINTS IN PALEOECOLOGY

Our paleoecological analysis of the Clarkia deposits is based on ecological factors and constraints that are known from observations of modern conditions and from the limitations of the fossil record. The complexity of the interrelated biological and physical factors to be considered include the interrelationships of all associated organisms; their competition for space, shelter, and food during the various stages of their ontogeny; their predations and parasitisms; their tolerances for or reactions to toxic substances; the climate of the region including moisture availability, extremes and diurnal fluctuations of temperature, and seasonality; local or regional topography and the diversity of habitats available; edaphic conditions including the chemical components, texture, and water content of soils; and the physiology of animals and plants allowing them to live under the complex of constraints in their existing environment.

The diverse ecological factors that exist today are available for the study of modern communities. This is not the case for interpreting past communities such as those of the Miocene in northern Idaho. Available for paleoecology are the preservable parts of organisms after they have died and been buried, or parts of animals and plants that have been shed from the living individuals rather than the complete organism in its living condition. Available also is the sedimentary matrix in which the fossils are preserved, which may provide data on some of the physical factors of the past environment; but the evidence from sediments alone may be misleading because they represent the conditions at the site of sedimentary accumulation and burial and not necessarily the conditions under which the animals and plants were able to sustain life.

Unavailable in paleoecology are the complete living organisms functioning in the intricate processes of life during all stages of their ontogeny. Also unavailable are *direct* observations on physiology, on genetic composition, on assimilation and excretion, on times and places of breeding and on seasonal or diurnal rhythms; unavailable are *direct* observations on the changing factors of soil and water chemistry, of temperatures, of solar radiation, and of atmospheric humidity. Such factors are not included in fossilized remains of organisms or in the sediments that contain them.

The term "paleoecology" may, therefore, be a misnomer because many of the factors that are of critical importance in ecological considerations of existing organisms are not available to the paleontologist and paleoecologist. On the contrary, many of these factors must be inferred from the fossils themselves (Cain, 1944:29), and an interpretation on the interrelationships between fossil organisms and past environments may involve a conceptual circuity to some degree.

Historical geology, including paleontology, is primarily a study of changing conditions in geologic time. The physical environment may change rapidly as a result of catastrophic events such as fires, flooding, or volcanic activity. Slower changes involving world or regional climates, the advance or disappearance of epicontinental seas, and the rise or wearing away of mountain ranges may accrue through the course of geological time. Communities themselves are not static; they exist in unity with an environment that is constantly changing. If too rapid a change in any one factor exceeds the tolerance limits of a given species, that species will disappear from the community thus changing the composition of the community and the interrelationships of surviving organisms. One species may be replaced by another from a contiguous area, or its vacated niche may be occupied by other members of the community. Changes may restrict the local distribution or the abundance of a species, commonly resulting in fewer fossils; or changes may permit another species to expand, which can result in an increase in fossil representation.

The nature of the fossil record, the layering of the sediments, the extent of the exposure, and the emphasis and methodology of the investigator all serve as controls on the degree of stratigraphic detail and precision that may be accomplished at any given locality. It is necessary for the paleoecologist, in the study of a former dynamic community, to examine the stratigraphic sequence of paleontological data in as detailed a manner as the evidence will permit. Too often in megascopic paleobotany, fossils have been collected from a series of strata without due regard for fine differences in stratigraphic levels. The resulting fossil collection from different levels will then be treated as a single assemblage as though it reflects one community and a set of environmental factors that existed at one moment in time. Whenever this happens, the result is an averaging of sequential fossil communities and of changing physical conditions. On the other hand, the collecting and analysis of fossils on a level-by-level basis can provide evidence bearing on the manner of change that the past community was experiencing (that is, a sere). In turn, a more precise interpretation can be forthcoming on the rate and extent of changes that were taking place in the surrounding environment.

CLARKIA COMMUNITIES

CONCEPTS

A plant community has been defined as "a general term used for any unit of vegetation regardless of rank or development" (Braun, 1950:10). Cain and Castro (1959:26) consider a community to be "a generic term of convenience which is employed to designate sociological units of any degree of extent and complexity," and (:27) "a sociological unit of any rank, occupying a territory and having a characteristic composition and structure." The concept of "community" thus appears to lack precision and seems so general as to require a definition of unit parameters depending on the requirements of a specific study.

The community concept is based on studies of existing organisms that can be observed directly as associated and competing individuals. The concept is based further on observations of organisms that exist at one moment in time, the present. The interpretation of communities of the past can never be as definitive as for existing societies of organisms because fossil assemblages usually are composed of a mixture of accumulated remains that were derived from individuals living in different habitats. Furthermore, fossil assemblages never represent all of the individuals and probably not all of the species that existed in the vicinity of the depositional site. It is to be understood, therefore, that a past "community" is a conceptual reconstruction that is only an approximation of a similar modern unit that may be constructed from the entire living biota.

Chaney and Axelrod (1959:26-53) used terms other than "community" in analyses of Miocene vegetation of the Columbia Plateau region of western North America. Presumed modern equivalents of plants in these Miocene floras are presently found in three regions of the world, and the term "element" was used to designate those taxa that are currently found in each of these areas (for example, East Asian Element, East American Element, West American Element). The term "component" was used (:44) in reference to major vegetational subunits of an element based largely on topographic relations, and two components were specifically delimited for the East American Element: the Swamp Cypress Component representing the forests of poorly drained lowlands and the Appalachian Component representing the forests of well-drained slopes and uplands. Chaney's term "association" is applied to his paleobotanical reconstructions that are essentially equivalent in concept to his "components" (for example, Lowland Association, Slope Association, Montane Association).

A complicating factor in analyses of western American Tertiary floras is the past association of genera and species that are no longer associated in modern forests. The following coniferous genera of the family Taxodiaceae that are common fossils in Tertiary floras from this region may be used to illustrate:

1. *Sequoia*, the coast redwood of California and Oregon, is now confined to temperate fog-belt areas along the west coast of North America where the species inhabits moist but well-drained slopes and valleys. Although the Clarkia flora contains few other taxa that are now restricted to western North America, such taxa are common members of other Tertiary floras from this part of the world.
2. *Taxodium*, the swamp cypress of southeastern North America, is now confined to swampy bottomlands, coastal plains, and moist lower slopes. North American equivalents of other Clarkia taxa similarly are confined today to moist bottomlands and slopes of southeastern United States.
3. *Metasequoia*, the dawn redwood of eastern Asia, is now confined to a few protected valleys in the mountainous region of the upper Yangtze River area of China. Asian equivalents of many Clarkia taxa presently live in the humid temperate regions of eastern Asia and are common associates in living *Metasequoia* forests.

It is apparent that Tertiary floras from western North America cannot be matched, taxon for taxon, with any single existing forest of the world, for the reconstruction of past vegetational units. In attempting to overcome this problem, Chaney and Axelrod (1959:44) assumed that Miocene species would occupy habitats similar to those of their presumed living equivalents whether the modern plants now live in the humid temperate regions of North America or of east Asia. The validity of such an assumption increases with the number of fossil associates whose modern relatives still coexist in a specific ecologic setting.

Reconstructions of past vegetation are inferred from a fossil assemblage, which is an accumulation of separated organs that were derived from those individuals that lived close enough to the depositional site to become part of the fossil record. The remains of plants from any one vegetational unit may find their way to a burial site where they will become mixed with the remains of plants from other habitats. The usual fossil collection thus is an assemblage of taxa representing a mixture of vegetational units. Although past vegetation cannot be examined and classified by direct observation, reasonable constructs can be inferred from the fossil assemblage.

The various units of vegetation that may be represented in a fossil flora can be distinguished by uniformitarian means: by comparing groups of fossil associates with existing units of vegetation having similarly associated taxa. A fossil flora containing two or more elements can be divided into presumed vegetational units based on similarity of habitats of their living relatives (for example, "associations" of Chaney and Axelrod). Whereas some of the Miocene taxa may have living equivalents still associated on humid slopes of the Applachian Mountains (Cain, 1943; Braun, 1950) or in similar habitats in the Yangtze River region of China (Wang, 1961), others may have living equivalents that are still associated with forests of mesic bottomlands or poorly drained swamps of southeastern United States. When such a fossil mixture of apparent units is to be considered, it seems reasonable to make comparisons with modern vegetational units in a region where equivalent living species are still growing together in forests of mesic bottomlands and adjacent well-drained slopes. The Swamp Association recognized in the Clarkia assemblage thus is compared to the modern swamp cypress forests of eastern North America, and the Miocene Slope Association of the Clarkia area is compared to the humid slope forests of the adjacent Appalachians (with Miocene admixtures of slope plants that are now restricted to similar habitats in eastern Asia).

Plant taxa of a fossil assemblage can be arranged into lists depicting the types of habitats that appear to be represented in the vicinity of the depositional site. This is not to imply that the proposed vegetational units can be distinguished directly from the fossil record, as if they are the result of some obvious sorting that may have taken place during the course of transport and burial. General "rules of thumb" can be applied, but they should be used with caution and in the context of the total fossil assemblage. Readily transported organs such as winged seeds, cones, and pollen, if unaccompanied by foliage of the same taxon, probably inhabited sites somewhat removed from sites of deposition (exceptions may be herbaceous plants). Ligneous plants living near the burial site tend to be better represented by the quantity and quality of megafossils than are those living in habitats that are farther removed. If, for example, a newly established lake is bordered by slopes descending to the water's edge, taxa of the slope forest should be well represented in the lacustrine deposits. On the other hand, if an older lake basin is surrounded by swampy ground, species of the swamp forest should be better represented in the lake deposits than are the remains of plants that occupied the well-drained slopes beyond.

The relative abundance of specimens representing the different taxa in a fossil flora comprise an important set of statistics. Such quantitative comparisons of species representation provide one of the factors used for interpreting the relative importance of a species in the local forest; but numerical representation of a species is subject to variables that cannot be readily resolved from the fossil record alone such as distance of the plant from the site of burial, the height of the plant, the number of leaves produced by an individual, or the resistance of organs to transport and decomposition. For instance, a single tree of a species that is an uncommon member of the local vegetation can contribute large numbers of leaves to the fossil assemblage if that tree happens to be growing in close proximity to the depositional site (Smiley, 1961). Conversely, a common member of the local vegetation may be poorly represented at any one fossil locality for reasons that are not readily apparent. It is our opinion, therefore, that greater significance probably should be placed upon the number of local florules (collecting sites) or upon the number of levels in a bedded sequence in which a fossil species is represented. Such variables as those noted above are more likely to be compensated for when geographic distribution can be documented from different collecting sites within the area or when temporal continuity can be tabulated through a sequence of layered deposits. The exceptional record of an uncommon species or the continual but sparce representation of a common member of the local vegetation can be recognized by such analyses.

Concepts relating to modern vegetational units are so imprecise as to permit an association to be a subunit of a community or a community to be a subunit of an association. For purposes of the present study, we elect to use the former classification. The Clarkia assemblage, best exemplified in the rich fossil record at type-locality P-33, may be divided into two sociological units depicting the most general habitats that are represented: lacustrine and terrestrial. For these general units we use the term community. The Lacustrine Community is represented by the water-breathing aquatic members of the fossil assemblage, including fishes, clams, snails, sponges, diatoms, and dinoflagellates. The Terrestrial Community is composed of the air-breathing members of the assemblage including terrestrial insects, ferns, mosses, horsetails, conifers, and angiosperms.

THE LACUSTRINE COMMUNITY

Aquatic protists include an unidentified dinoflagellate that was noted by Gray in palynomorph extractions from the lake sediments. One large form of diatom is common in the upper part of the section, and more detailed studies now underway indicate the additional presence of several kinds of smaller diatoms. The smaller Clarkia diatoms closely resemble species described by Mann (*in* Knowlton, 1926) from Miocene deposits near Spokane, Washington, and by van Landingham (1964) from Miocene deposits near Yakima and Vantage, Washington. The diatom population appears to be represented mainly by the genera *Cosinodiscus*, *Cymbella*, *Diatoma*, *Eunotia*, *Fragilaria*, *Gomphonema*, *Nelosira*, *Navicula*, *Pinnularia*, and *Tetracyclus*.

Porifera are common as isolated siliceous sponge spicules of more than twenty kinds. Most spicules are needle-like forms with either smooth or spinose surfaces resembling ones produced by a number of genera of the family Spongillidae (Jewell, 1959).

Molluscs are rare. The phylum is represented by a single clam probably of the family Unionidae and by rare gastropod casts resembling members of the freshwater family Viviparidae.

Arthropods are represented by a variety of insects from terrestrial habitats. The aquatic larvae of caddis-flies are represented by two kinds of cases, one that is composed of plant debris and the other of arenaceous material.

Vertebrata are represented only by remains of fish occurring usually as complete, articulated, skeletal imprints outlined by the darkened impression of the body. They are common fossils within a narrow zone immediately above and below the Unit 4 ash bed and near the 397 cm level in the Clarkia type-section (Figure 17-5). More than twenty-five specimens representing the two common species were sent to G. A. Smith and R. R. Miller at The University of Michigan who identified (personal communication) *Archoplites* of the family Centrarchidae (sunfishes) and *Leuciscus* of the family Cyprinidae (minnows). On the basis of living relatives, these are freshwater fishes that are considered to have inhabited quiet waters of larger streams and lakes.

There is no evidence of worm burrows, tracks, trails or other organic activity within the lake deposits. The fine laminations attest to the probability of toxic (or anaerobic) lake-bottom condi-

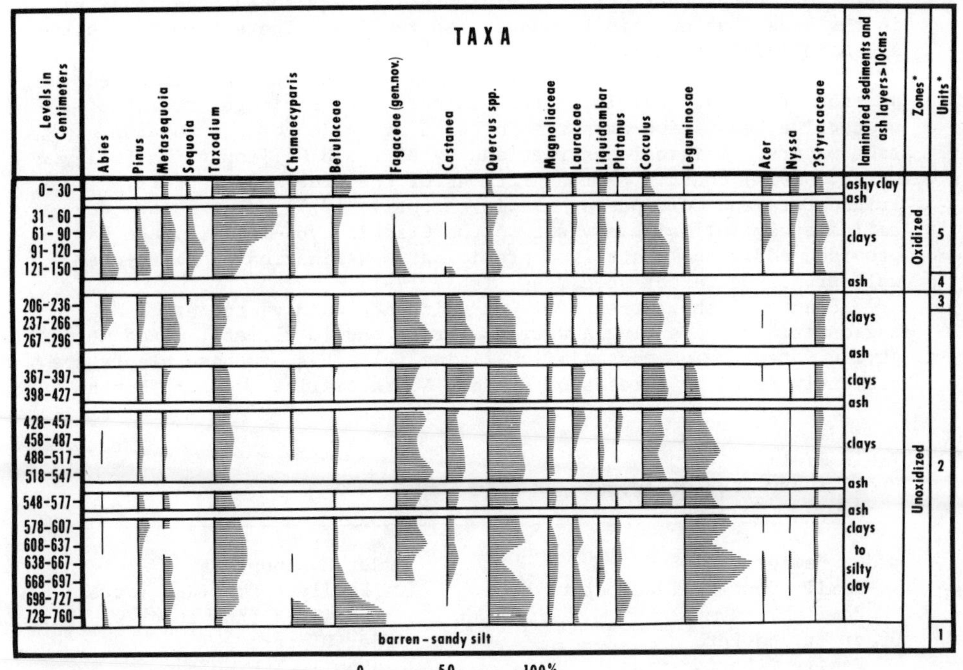

Figure 17-5
Relative abundance of major taxa within 30 cm stratigraphic increments for 7.6 m of the South Clarkia section (P-33). Included are taxa that attained an abundance of 5 percent or more of megafossils counted in at least one of the increments. Indicated are positions of ash beds greater than 10 cm thick. See Figure 17-6 for microstratigraphic analysis within one of the 30 cm increments, and Figure 17-9 for total number of megafossils counted in each increment.

tions prohibiting the establishment of an infauna population that would have reworked the accumulating lacustrine sediments (Ruttner, 1961:211). The scarcity of invertebrates of a lake bottom epifauna can similarly be explained.

THE TERRESTRIAL COMMUNITY

No evidence of terrestrial vertebrates has yet been found in the Clarkia deposits. The skeletons of land animals would be unlikely to occur in the low-energy lacustrine deposits that are exposed at locality P-33, and preservation would be expected to have occurred in near shore, floodplain or deltaic deposits such as those that are exposed north of Clarkia (for example, locality P-38).

Invertebrates are represented by insects many of which appear to have been forest dwellers. Microfragments of insect exoskeletons are ubiquitous in the lake deposits, and larger fragments are common on some bedding surfaces. It seems probable that these disseminated insect fragments resulted from passage through the digestive systems of vertebrate such as fish and birds. Well-preserved insects, commonly retaining their original pigmentation, are found occasionally in the beds that contain abundant fish remains. These insect fossils are mainly intact adults although nymphs and larvae are also present. The coincidence of insect and fish preservation could be explained as storm related; that is, forest insects were dislodged from the protective vegetation at a time of wind agitation or overturning of lake waters. Original descriptions by Barr and Gillespie (*in* Smiley et al., 1975) contain representatives of the orders Orthoptera, Trichoptera and Coleoptera. Lewis recently (1977) began a more detailed study following a visit to the Clarkia type-locality and has provided additional data from preliminary examination of forty-one well-preserved insect specimens (Table 17-1).

Plants of the Terrestrial Community are mainly conifers and angiosperms representing a warm-temperate, humid climate, mixed mesophytic forest. The most similar living relatives of these plants are presently found in forests of eastern North America, western North

Table 17-1
Preliminary List of Insect Taxa.

Order Hemiptera
- Family Pentatomidae (stink bug)
- Family ? (nymph)

Order Trichoptera
- Family ? Leptoceridae (?Caddis-fly cases)
- Family Limnephilidae

Order Coleoptera
- Family Elateridae (click beetle)
- Family carabidae (forest ground beetle)
- Family Scarabidae (scarab beetle)
- Family Anthribidae (weevils)
- Families ? (8 specimens)

Order Hymenoptera
- Family Formicidae (ants)
- Family ? (hornet or wasp ?)

Order Diptera
- Family Bibionidae ("March flies")

Order Lepidoptera
- Family ? (caterpillar ?)

Order Orthoptera
- Family Tettigoniidae (katy-dids)

America, and eastern Asia.

Unidentified mosses are represented by an epiphyte that is preserved attached to stems of forest plants and by small detached shoots that have been extracted from the sediments in a hydrofluoric acid bath. *Equisetum* (horsetail) occurs as rare stem fragments. *Lycopodium* (club moss) is represented only by spores. Ferns occur as very rare frond fragments and as spores and include *Osmunda* (royal fern) and *Polypodium*.

Conifer shoots, needles, cones, seeds, and pollen are abundant in the Clarkia flora. The dominant conifer family is Taxodiaceae, which is represented by the genera *Cunninghamia* (Asian genus), *Metasequoia* (Asian genus), *Sequoia* (coast redwood of western North America), and *Taxodium* (swamp or bald cypress of eastern North America). Pollen of the Taxodiaceae is also common in the sediments. The family Pinaceae is represented by branches, needles, seeds, cone scales, and pollen of *Abies* (fir) and by branches, fascicled needles, seeds, cones, and pollen of two or three species of *Pinus* (pine). The pine family also is represented by pollen of *Cedrus* (cedar), *Picea* (spruce), and *Tsuga* (hemlock). The family Cupressaceae is represented by common shoots and cones of *Chamaecyparis* (for example, white cedar) and by rare shoots of *Thuja* (arbor vitae); pollen of the family also has been identified by Gray. Pollen of the family Taxaceae has been identified, and a few shoots bearing what appear to be staminate cones may represent the genus *Taxus* (yew). The family Podocarpaceae, a predominantly Southern Hemisphere conifer previously unrecorded as megafossils in later Tertiary floras of North America, may be represented by large isolated needles that have a cellular anatomy resembling the genus *Podocarpus*. It is probable that those conifer genera represented only by pollen or by rare shoot fragments occupied somewhat higher elevations of the region rather than being members of the forest in the immediate proximity of the Clarkia Lake.

Angiosperms are the numerical dominants of the Clarkia flora. Monocotyledons are represented by common leaves of *Smilax* (greenbriar), a woody vine of the family Liliaceae. A single specimen from locality P-34 is a fragment of a leaf of *Typha* (cattail) in the family Typhaceae. Rare specimens that appear to be fragmental blades of grass may represent the family Gramineae.

The dominant members of the flora are the dicotyledons, which have been referred to sixty-two genera in thirty-six families. Exceptional care is required in assigning some of these fossils to species. The Clarkia flora contains the best known fossil record of some of them, and taxonomic revisions may be required for certain of the established Tertiary species from the added data of epidermal cells, chemical profiles, phytoliths, fruits, or the quantitative analysis of leaf architectural variations. Table 17-2 contains a list of the families and genera of dicotyledons presently recognized in the Clarkia flora.

CLARKIA FOREST ASSOCIATIONS

The concept of the association as a modern vegetational unit was applied by Chaney and Axelrod (1959:19-50) to Miocene floras of the Columbia Plateau region on the basis of altitudinal considerations and implied habitats. As a concept their paleobotanical application is consistent with botanical parameters of living plant associations (Muller-Dombois and Ellenberg, 1974:173-176), but the factual bases

Table 17-2
Dicotyledons of the Mixed Mesophytic Forest.

Families	Genera	Common Name	Element*	Mega-fossils	Micro-fossils
Salicaceae	*Populus*	poplar	ENA	x	----
	Salix	willow	?	x	----
Juglandaceae	*Carya*	hickory	ENA	x	x
	Juglans	walnut	ENA,EA	?	x
	Pterocarya	wing nut	EA	x	x
Betulaceae	*Alnus*	alder	ENA	x	x
	Betula	birch	ENA,EA	x	x
	Ostrya	hop hornbeam	ENA	x	x
	Corylus	hazel nut	?	x	x
Fagaceae	*Castanea*	chestnut	ENA	x	x
	Fagus	beech	ENA	x	x
	Quercus	red, white oaks	ENA,EA	x	x
	Gen. nov.	---------	----	x	----
Ulmaceae	*Celtis*	hackberry	?	----	x
	Ulmus	elm	ENA	x	?
	Zelkova	zelkova	EA	x	?
Chenopodi-aceae	?	?	?	----	x
Nymphaeaceae	*Nuphar*	water lily	?	x	----
Cercidiphyll-aceae	*Cercidi-phyllum*	katsura	EA	x	----
Berberidaceae	*Mahonia*	Oregon grape	WNA	x	----
Menisperm-aceae	*Cocculus*	moonseed	ENA	x	----
Magnoliaceae	*Lirioden-dron*	tulip tree	ENA,EA	x	x
	Magnolia	sweet-bay, cucumber tree	ENA	x	----
?Anonaceae	*?Asimina*	?paw paw	ENA	x	----
Lauraceae	*Lindera*	benzoin	ENA	x	----
	Persea	bay, avocado	ENA	x	----
	Sassafras	sassafras	ENA	x	----
Saxifragaceae	*Hydrangea*	hydrangea	ENA	x	----
	Philadel-phus	mock orange	ENA,WNA	x	----
Hamamelid-aceae	*Hamamelis*	witch hazel	ENA	x	----
	Liquidambar	sweet gum	ENA,EA	x	x
Platanaceae	*Platanus*	sycamore	ENA	x	x
Rosaceae	*Amelanchier*	service berry	ENA,WNA	x	----
	Crataegus	hawthorn	ENA,WNA	x	----
	Malus	apple	?	x	----
	Prunus	cherry	?	x	----
	Rosa	rose	?	x	----
Leguminosae	*cf Amorpha*	false indigo	WNA	x	----
	"Cercis"	(unknown pods)	----	x	----
	Gleditsia	water locust	ENA	x	----

Table 17-2 (continued)

Families	Genera	Common Name	Element*	Mega-fossils	Micro-fossils
	cf Robinia	black locust	ENA	x	----
	"Sophora"	(unknown leaflets)	----	x	----
Anachardiaceae	*Rhus*	poison oak or ivy	ENA	x	x
Aquifoliaceae	*Ilex*	holly	ENA	x	x
Aceraceae	*Acer*	silver, dwarf, red, striped maples	ENA	x	x
Hippocastanaceae	*Aesculus*	horse chestnut	ENA	x	x
Rhamnaceae	*Berehemia*	supple jack	EA,ENA	x	----
	Paliurus	Christ thorn	EA	x	----
	Rhamnus	buckthorn	?	x	----
Vitaceae	*Ampelopsis*	(woody vine)	ENA	x	----
	Vitis	grape	ENA	x	----
Tiliaceae	*Tilia*	basswood	ENA	x	x
Theaceae	*Gordonia*	loblolly bay	ENA	x	----
Eleagnaceae	*Shepherdia*	buffalo berry	ENA,WNA	----	x
Nyssaceae	*Nyssa*	black and water tupelos	ENA	x	x
Cornaceae	*Cornus*	dogwood	?	x	----
Ericaceae	*Vaccinium*	huckle berry	?	x	----
Ebenaceae	*Diospyros*	persimmon	EA,ENA	x	----
Styracaceae	*Halesia*	bell berry	ENA	x	----
Oleaceae	*Fraxinus*	ash	?	x	x
Scrophulariaceae	*Paulownia*	empress tree	EA	x	----

*EA = East Asia; ENA = Eastern North America; WNA = Western North America

differ. Units of a modern forest can be observed as associated plants; units of past vegetation can be only conceptualized from an accumulation of disseminated plant parts in sedimentary deposits. It would seem appropriate to append the prefix "paleo-" to the names of conceptual vegetation units whenever they are inferred from fossil assemblages, to convey the idea of similarity of concepts but to underscore the differences in the factual data from which the conceptual units are erected.

On the basis of preferred habitats of living relatives of Clarkia taxa and applying the concept of the association used by Chaney and Axelrod, the forest in the immediate vicinity of the Miocene Clarkia Lake may be considered divisible into three recognizable units: a Swamp Association bordering the lake and locally inhabiting back swamps on floodplains, a Floodplain-Slope Association inhabiting mesic but well-drained sites, and a Dry-Slope Association that inhabited more xeric sites such as rocky terranes on south- or west-facing upper slopes of the surrounding hills.

We recognize that the classification of vegetation, whether past or present, can vary in accordance with different parameters that may be established arbitrarily. Our Floodplain-Slope Association, for example, might be distinguished as riparian, floodplain and lower slope associations (or communities). Such additional subunits probably did exist in the Clarkia area during Miocene time. Because many of the recognized living equivalents of Clarkia species now occupy a variety of habitats that may range from riparian sites or swamp borders to well-drained slopes in a region of humid climate, it seems inadvisable to attempt a more detailed subdivision of past vegetation until we have acquired more precise data relating to modern affinities of the fossil species.

Plants that are most indicative of each of our three general associations are listed in Table 17-3. In any natural continuum such as regional vegetation, precise boundaries of demarcation between vegetational subunits are more conceptual than real, and species that are most characteristic of one association can be represented also in another. Table 17-3 was compiled on the basis of typical habitats of living relatives (see Fowells, 1965; Sargent, 1933; Small, 1933; Wang, 1961).

An upland conifer association may be represented by pollen of such taxa as *Picea* (spruce) and *Tsuga* (hemlock).

The assignment of Clarkia taxa to a specific plant association is in large measure dependent on the type of climate that is inferred from the assemblage as a whole. Under climatic conditions warmer than is inferred, most of these temperate Clarkia taxa would inhabit the upper elevations of the region. Under conditions of cooler climate, many of the Clarkia taxa would be excluded from the regional vegetation, and those that remained probably would be confined to the bottomlands. If the climate was less humid or if there was a regime of summer drought, many of the mesic plants would disappear, some of the members of the Dry-Slope Association would be confined to moist bottomlands or riparian sites, and the Dry-Slope Association would become a more significant part of the regional vegetation than is inferred from the Clarkia flora.

MICROSTRATIGRAPHY AND PLANT SUCCESSION

The rich fossil representation of the Terrestrial Community, and its analysis through 7.6 m of finely laminated lacustrine deposits at the Clarkia type-locality, provide clear evidence of a Miocene lake-border sere rather than a stable (climax) community. This provides a unique window for the assessment of plant successions and for the documentation of seral change during the complete life of a Miocene lake. Some of the microstratigraphic documentations are shown in Figures 17-5 and 17-6 and in Table 17-4.

CONCEPT OF SUCCESSION

A good discourse on the concept of plant succession has been offered by Mueller-Dombois and Ellenberg (1974:370-397). Their concept of an idealized succession (:379-371) matches so well the cata-

Table 17-3
Clarkia Plant Associations.

SWAMP ASSOCIATION

Bryophytes (mosses)	*Lindera* (benzoin)
Equisetum (horsetail)	*Persea* (avocado)
Osmunda (royal fern)	*Platanus* (sycamore)
Taxodium (swamp cypress)	*Gleditsia* (water locust)
Chamaecyparis (white cedar)	*Acer* (red maple)
Typha (cattail)	*Ampelopsis*
Populus (swamp poplar)	*Vitis* (grape)
Salix (willow)	*Gordonia* (loblolly bay)
Quercus (swamp live oaks)	*Nyssa* (water tupelo)
Nuphar (water lily)	*Viburnum* (arrow wood)
Magnolia (sweetbay)	

FLOODPLAIN-SLOPE ASSOCIATION

Bryophytes (mosses)	*Magnolia* (cucumber tree)
Lycopodium (club moss)	*Sassafras* (sassafras)
Taxus (yew)	*Hydrangea* (hydrangea)
Abies (fir)	*Hamamelis* (witch hazel)
Cunninghamia (Asian conifer)	*Liquidambar* (sweet gun)
Metasequoia (Asian conifer)	*Malus* (apple)
Sequoia (redwood)	*Prunus* (cherry)
Thuja (red cedar)	*Robinia* (locust)
Smilax (greenbriar)	*Ilex* (holly)
Carya (hickory)	*Acer* (maple)
Juglans (walnut)	*?Asimina* (paw paw)
Pterocarya (Asian wingnut)	*Aesculus* (horse chestnut)
Alnus (alder)	*Rhamnus* (buckthorn)
Betula (birch)	*Vitis* (grape)
Corylus (hazel nut)	*Paliurus* (Asian genus)
Ostrya (hop hornbeam)	*Tilia* (basswood)
Castanea (chestnut)	*Nyssa* (black tupelo)
Fagus (beech)	*Cornus* (dogwood)
Quercus (red oak)	*Vaccinium* (huckleberry)
Fagaceae gen. nov.	*Diospyros* (persimmon)
Ulmus (elm)	*?Symplocos* (sweet leaf)
Zelkova (Asian "elm")	*Halesia* (bell tree)
Cerdidiphyllum (Asian katsura)	*Fraxinus* (ash)
Cocculus (moonseed)	*Paulownia* (Asian empress tree)
Liriodendron (tulip tree)	

DRY-SLOPE ASSOCIATION

Pinus (pines)	*Rosa* (rose)
Quercus (white oak)	*Amorpha* (false indigo)
Celtis (hackberry)	*Rhus* (sumac, poison ivy)
Amelanchier (service berry)	*?Parthenocissus* (creeper)
Crataegus (hawthorn)	*Vitis* (grape)
Philadelphus (mock orange)	*Shepherdia* (buffalo berry)

TAXA / LEVELS (CM)	Cocculus	Taxodium shoots	" scales	Abies shoots	" scales	Fagaceae gen. nov.	Pinus needles	" scales, seeds	Quercus spp.	?Styracaceae	Metasequoia shoots	" cones	Legume leaflets	Liquidambar	Sequoia shoots	Alnus	Chamaecyparis	" cones	Salix	Nyssa	Gordonia	Acer spp.	Castanea	Magnolia spp.	Rhamnus	Betula	Populus	Pterocarya	Smilax	Rosa	?Parthenocissus	Persea	Total specimens*	Total taxa*
120.5	3	3	–	2	–	–	1	–	1	1	1	–	–	–	1	–	1	–	1	1	–	–	–	–	–	–	1	–	–	–	–	–	19	14
121.0	6	4	2	2	–	3	3	–	1	1	3	–	1	1	2	–	–	–	–	–	–	–	–	–	–	–	–	–	–	–	–	–	30	12
122.0	7	7	–	1	–	5	–	1	–	3	2	–	–	2	3	–	1	–	1	–	–	1	–	2	–	–	–	–	–	–	–	–	37	14
123.2	1	3	–	3	–	1	2	1	1	1	2	–	–	1	2	1	1	–	2	–	1	2	–	–	–	–	–	–	–	–	–	–	26	16
123.7	1	3	–	–	–	1	–	–	–	–	2	–	–	–	2	–	–	–	1	1	2	1	–	–	–	–	–	–	–	–	–	–	16	11
124.3	3	10	4	1	–	1	–	–	3	2	1	–	–	1	3	–	–	–	1	2	–	1	–	–	–	1	–	–	–	–	–	–	34	13
124.7	1	3	–	1	–	–	2	2	2	1	3	–	3	1	1	–	1	–	–	–	–	–	–	–	–	–	–	–	–	–	3	–	24	12
125.2	1	3	–	3	–	–	1	–	2	1	1	–	1	–	–	1	1	–	–	1	1	–	–	1	–	–	–	1	–	–	–	–	19	15
125.6	3	2	–	6	–	–	–	–	1	–	–	1	3	1	3	–	–	–	–	–	–	–	–	–	–	–	–	1	–	–	–	–	22	10
126.4	3	3	–	1	–	4	4	–	5	5	1	–	–	1	1	1	–	–	–	2	2	–	–	–	2	–	–	1	1	–	–	–	35	16
126.9	3	4	–	–	–	4	–	–	1	–	1	–	–	1	2	–	–	–	–	1	–	–	–	1	–	–	–	–	1	–	–	2	21	11
127.4	2	6	–	–	1	4	–	–	–	1	1	–	–	1	1	–	1	–	1	1	1	–	–	–	–	1	–	–	–	–	1	–	23	14
129.5	2	2	–	3	–	–	–	–	4	–	–	–	–	–	–	–	–	–	–	–	–	–	–	–	–	–	–	–	–	–	1	–	14	7
129.9	3	4	–	–	–	1	1	1	1	2	3	1	–	–	–	–	–	–	2	1	1	–	1	1	–	1	1	–	–	–	–	–	22	12
130.3	3	2	1	2	–	3	1	–	–	3	–	–	–	1	–	–	–	–	–	–	–	–	–	–	–	–	1	–	–	–	–	–	20	10
130.8	6	3	–	3	–	2	2	–	2	3	1	–	–	1	1	2	–	–	–	–	–	–	–	2	–	–	–	1	–	–	–	–	30	14
131.2	4	3	–	2	–	–	4	–	1	2	–	–	3	–	1	–	1	–	–	–	2	–	–	–	–	–	–	–	1	–	–	–	24	11
132.1	12	3	–	2	–	7	1	2	4	3	1	–	–	1	5	2	1	1	1	–	1	–	–	1	2	–	–	–	–	–	–	–	48	15
132.6	4	5	–	3	–	2	2	–	4	2	–	–	3	1	2	–	–	–	–	–	1	2	–	1	–	–	–	–	–	–	–	–	36	15
133.7	2	1	–	2	–	3	3	1	–	–	1	–	–	1	–	1	–	–	–	1	–	1	–	–	1	–	–	–	–	–	–	–	20	13
133.6	8	5	1	8	–	1	3	–	5	1	1	1	2	2	2	7	1	1	–	–	1	–	–	–	1	–	–	–	–	1	–	–	56	19
134.2	3	6	1	6	–	1	5	1	3	3	1	–	1	–	–	–	1	1	–	–	–	–	–	–	–	–	–	–	–	1	–	–	34	11
134.6	4	4	–	4	–	1	–	2	4	3	2	–	2	–	2	1	–	–	–	–	–	1	–	–	1	1	–	1	–	–	–	–	32	16
135.2	5	4	–	3	–	2	1	–	2	1	1	–	1	–	–	1	–	–	–	1	1	–	–	–	3	–	–	1	–	–	–	–	27	14
135.9	8	1	3	7	–	–	1	1	4	3	2	–	–	1	–	1	–	–	–	1	–	2	–	–	–	1	–	–	–	1	–	–	36	13
136.3	4	2	2	4	–	–	5	1	1	–	–	–	1	–	–	1	2	–	2	2	–	–	–	–	–	–	–	–	–	–	–	1	28	11
136.7	3	2	–	5	–	1	1	1	1	3	2	–	–	–	–	1	–	–	2	1	–	2	–	–	–	–	–	–	1	–	–	–	26	15
137.3	5	2	1	2	–	3	1	2	5	3	2	1	1	–	2	1	–	–	1	–	–	3	–	–	–	–	–	–	–	–	–	–	36	14
138.2	1	5	–	3	2	1	5	3	–	–	1	–	1	1	–	–	1	–	–	–	–	1	–	–	–	–	–	–	–	–	–	–	27	12
138.6	4	3	–	3	–	2	2	1	2	2	1	–	–	–	–	–	–	–	–	1	–	2	–	–	–	–	–	–	–	–	–	–	29	11
139.1	8	5	–	5	–	1	3	1	4	3	1	–	–	1	–	–	–	–	1	1	–	1	–	1	–	1	1	–	–	–	–	–	38	17
139.6	7	3	1	2	–	1	3	–	5	2	5	–	–	1	–	–	–	–	–	–	–	–	3	1	–	–	–	–	–	–	–	–	35	12
140.1	6	4	–	2	–	2	–	–	4	2	2	–	–	2	–	–	–	–	–	1	1	–	3	1	–	–	–	–	–	–	–	–	31	13
141.2	3	1	–	3	1	4	3	2	7	3	1	1	1	–	–	1	1	–	–	–	2	–	2	–	–	–	–	–	–	–	–	–	36	13
141.7	7	3	–	2	1	3	–	–	–	3	5	–	–	–	1	–	–	–	–	–	–	–	2	–	–	–	–	–	–	–	–	–	29	10
142.4	3	2	–	4	–	5	2	1	2	–	1	–	–	–	–	–	–	–	–	–	–	1	–	–	1	1	1	–	–	–	–	–	28	12
143.2	4	2	4	–	–	3	–	–	–	2	–	–	1	3	–	–	–	–	–	–	–	–	1	–	2	–	1	–	1	–	–	1	25	11
143.6	8	2	–	2	1	2	1	1	2	2	3	–	2	–	2	2	1	–	1	–	–	–	5	–	–	–	–	–	1	–	–	–	40	17
144.3	1	2	–	4	–	2	2	–	4	–	–	–	1	1	–	3	2	–	1	–	2	–	2	–	1	–	–	–	–	–	–	–	29	16
144.7	7	2	–	1	–	1	1	–	5	2	2	–	4	–	–	2	1	–	3	–	1	–	–	–	1	1	–	–	–	–	–	–	36	17
145.6	6	3	–	3	–	2	2	1	6	2	1	–	1	–	–	–	1	–	–	–	–	–	6	–	–	–	–	–	–	–	–	–	35	12
146.2	5	–	–	2	–	5	1	–	4	2	–	–	1	–	–	–	2	–	–	–	–	–	5	–	–	–	–	–	–	–	–	–	30	11
147.0	4	5	–	6	–	4	2	1	3	2	3	–	3	–	–	1	–	–	1	–	–	–	2	–	–	–	1	–	–	1	–	–	38	13
148.9	2	2	–	2	–	4	1	–	–	–	–	–	1	–	–	–	–	–	–	–	–	–	–	–	–	–	–	–	–	–	–	–	13	7
Levels	44	43		40		36	35		35	34	35		22	22	20	18	18		16	16	15	14	11	10	10	8	7	6	6	4	3	3	= 44	
No.Spec.	186	164		124		92	98		111	75	66		38	27	39	30	24		22	19	20	21	32	12	15	8	7	6	6	4	5	4	= 1294*	

*** Totals include rare and miscellaneous specimens not tabulated.**

Figure 17-6
Microstratigraphic analysis of plant megafossils within a single 30 cm column increment from the 120-149 cm level at locality P-33. About 40,500 cc of sediment is contained in each column increment. Rare taxa represented by a single specimen at one or two levels include *Amelanchier*, *Cercidiphyllum*, *Hydrangea*, *Ilex*, *Liriodendron*, *Malus*, *Ostrya*, *Paliurus*, *Paulownia*, *Platanus*, *Prunus*, *Ribes*, *Ulmus*, and *Vitis*. Miscellaneous specimens include inflorescences, insects, a fish, and a Unionid clam.

Table 17-4
Stratigraphic Records of Selected Plant Taxa.

Levels (cm)	Total Specimens	*Nyssa* Swamp[1] No.	%	*Nyssa* Slope[2] No.	%	*Acer* Mesic[3] No.	%	*Acer* Slope[4] No.	%	*Magnolia* Swamp[5] No.	%	*Magnolia* Slope[6] No.	%	*Taxodium* Swamp[7] No.	%
0-30	173	18	5.2	--	---	19	5.5	--	---	9	2.6	--	---	76	22.0
31-60	138	7	5.1	--	---	5	3.6	--	---	2	1.1	--	---	52	37.7
61-90	531	14	2.6	--	---	24	4.4	--	---	8	1.5	2	0.4	180	33.9
91-120	771	18	2.3	--	---	29	3.8	--	---	7	0.9	4	0.5	138	17.8
121-150	1294	25	1.9	--	---	11	0.8	9	0.7	7	0.5	11	0.8	192	15.0
206-236	605	2	0.3	--	---	--	---	--	---	13	2.2	6	1.0	36	6.0
237-266	504	--	---	--	---	1	0.2	--	---	4	0.8	2	0.4	35	6.9
267-296	507	2	0.4	--	---	--	---	--	---	9	1.8	4	0.8	16	3.2
367-397	618	1	0.2	3	0.5	1	0.2	--	---	6	1.0	2	0.3	55	8.9
398-427	706	--	---	8	1.1	--	---	--	---	10	1.4	1	0.1	74	10.5
428-457	362	--	---	1	0.3	--	---	--	---	7	1.9	6	0.3	30	8.3
458-487	438	--	---	--	---	--	---	--	---	8	1.9	2	1.7	47	10.9
488-517	598	--	---	3	0.5	--	---	--	---	8	1.3	1	0.5	54	9.9
518-547	221	--	---	--	---	--	---	--	---	4	1.8	1	0.2	17	7.7
548-577	257	1	0.4	--	---	--	---	--	---	9	3.5	1	0.5	26	10.1
578-607	322	1	0.3	--	---	1	0.3	--	---	4	1.2	--	0.4	52	16.1
608-637	233	--	---	--	---	--	---	--	---	12	5.2	--	---	42	18.0
638-667	667	--	---	4	0.6	--	---	6	0.9	21	3.1	--	---	119	17.9
668-697	448	1	0.2	--	---	1	0.5	3	1.5	15	3.3	--	---	57	12.7
698-727	606	--	---	2	0.3	--	---	5	0.8	8	1.3	--	---	81	13.4
728-757	575	--	---	--	---	--	---	2	0.3	3	0.5	1	0.2	16	2.8

1. *N. hesperia* Berry, cf. living *N. aquatica* Linne
2. *N. copeana* (Lesquereux) Chaney and Axelrod, cf. living *N. sylvatica* Marshall
3. *A. bendirei* Lesquereux, cf. living *A. saccharinum* Linne
4. *A.* sp., cf. living *A. pennsylvanicum* Linne
5. cf. *M. dayana* Cockerell, cf. living *M. virginiana* Linne
6. *M.* sp., cf., living *M. acuminata* Linne
7. *T. dubium* (Sternberg) Heer, cf. living *T. distichum* (Linne) Richard

strophic conditions that developed in the Clarkia area in Miocene time that it seems appropriate to quote them here:

> Assume the formation of a new terrestrial surface. This occurs in nature through lava flows, deposits of volcanic ash, filling-in of lakes, formation of landscars, and similar geomorphologic processes. The result, in all terrestrial climatic regions favorable for plant growth, is an invasion of plants, sooner or later.
>
> Soon after the invasion of new plants, a pioneer plant community may become evident. Invasion of new plants usually continues and the already present species may reproduce and become more abundant. Thus, a species enrichment may be observed on the same habitat that is associated with an increase in number of individuals or an increase in cover of certain species. Arrival of different life forms further increases the structural complexity. Concurrently with species enrichment, increases in number of individuals, and structural complexity, some early invaders may disappear. This usually is the result of competitive replacement among the species. But, disappearance of species may not always be associated with replacement of new species. It can also result in certain species excluding others. In many cases the net effect is a decrease in the number of species after passing a certain stage of maximum taxonomic diversity.
>
> The general process of vegetation change described here has been called succession.

In the case of the Clarkia area where a Miocene stream valley was dammed (probably more than once) by local volcanic activity, the existing vegetation of the floodplain and adjacent slopes probably was as stabilized as natural vegetation will become in an area of hilly terrane. The forests likely had attained the climax stage of development under the conditions of regional climate and local topographic diversity.

Early fossil records in the floral sequence at locality P-33 seem to represent the climax forest that existed in the area prior to the catastrophic formation of a lake where none had existed before Mesic bottomland habitats of the floodplain were obliterated when covered by the lake water. The rising waters of the lake began to lap directly on the lower slopes where no lake margin had existed before. That part of the slope vegetation was suddenly confronted by a newly created riparian habitat for which it had not developed, and vegetational adjustments to the new condition became necessary. It would take time before individual plants would run the course of their lives and eventually die, and be replaced by individuals or species that were more tolerant of the new conditions.

The concurrent catastrophic event of local volcanism resulted in a periodic blanketing of the local vegetation by airfall ash. The effect on life of the area could be expected to be significant as the volcanic activity ran its course from inception to maximum eruption to termination. Vegetation would continue to survive, as Dorf (1951) noted regarding the effect of ashfalls during the Paricutin eruptions in Mexico; but the survival of specific taxa might be affected, which would be reflected in the comparative representation of plants in subsequent fossil assemblages.

Sedimentary infilling of the lake produced two results of major importance. One was the accumulation of finely laminated sediments and contained fossils to record the sedimentary and organic changes that were taking place during the lake's life. The other was the establishment of new ground around the margin of the lake and the initiation of a primary succession of mesic bottomland vegetation, characterized by *Chamaecyparis*, in the strip between the open waters of the lake and the climax forest that persisted on adjacent slopes. The primary succession seems to have progressed as new marginal land became available through continued infilling of the lake basin, and the representation of *Taxodium* increased as *Chamaecyparis* declined. Mueller-Dombois and Ellenberg (1974:374-376) stated that the primary succession is "the community formation process that begins on substrates that had never before supported vegetation" and that the time scale of the succession may involve hundreds or thousands of years. They noted further, "the terrestrialization process in a water body causes fundamental changes in the substrate water regime which affect plant growth. Thus, the more pronounced changes in primary succession are associated with changes in the water relations of the soil."

This concept of plant succession is of interest here in that it clearly applies to the conditions that can be documented in the laminated deposits at the Clarkia type-locality. The documentations of plant succession and seral change are perhaps of greater significance than are attempts to delineate communities and other arbitrary vegetational units from the Clarkia assemblage. The plant succession is a temporal change that can be documented by superposition in the vertical sequence of sediments; communities and associations are phytogeographic units that are represented in the fossil assemblage, but cannot be documented by direct observation of the plant societies. One problem is that the total vegetation is never represented in a fossil assemblage; another is that the establishment of parameters of a given vegetational unit is arbitrary and usually conjectural.

THE FOSSIL EVIDENCE

Our microstratigraphic analysis to date may be considered preliminary in the sense that only one 7.6 m column, providing relatively small bedding-surface areas of approximately 30 cm by 45 cm, has presently been analyzed. We expect ultimately to examine in similar detail other columns regularly spaced across the Clarkia type-locality. This should provide a better control on the lateral consistency of the vertical trends that have been documented in our single column. During several years of sampling, however, we have observed that the trends noted in Figure 17-5 seem to be generally true for the entire locality.

The fine lamination that is characteristic of the deposits at locality P-33 is shown in Figure 17.7. Figure 17-5 contains those taxa that attained an abundance of 5 percent or more of the megafossils in at least one of the 30 cm increments of the study column. Each column increment provides a bulk of sediments of approximately 40,500 cc. The number of megafossils observed in each column increment varies from a minimum of 138 to a maximum of 1,294 for the computation of percentages. Figure 17-6 shows the microstratigraphic documentation that is possible on a level-by-level basis through one of the 30 cm column segments (121-150 cm increment on Figure 17-5).

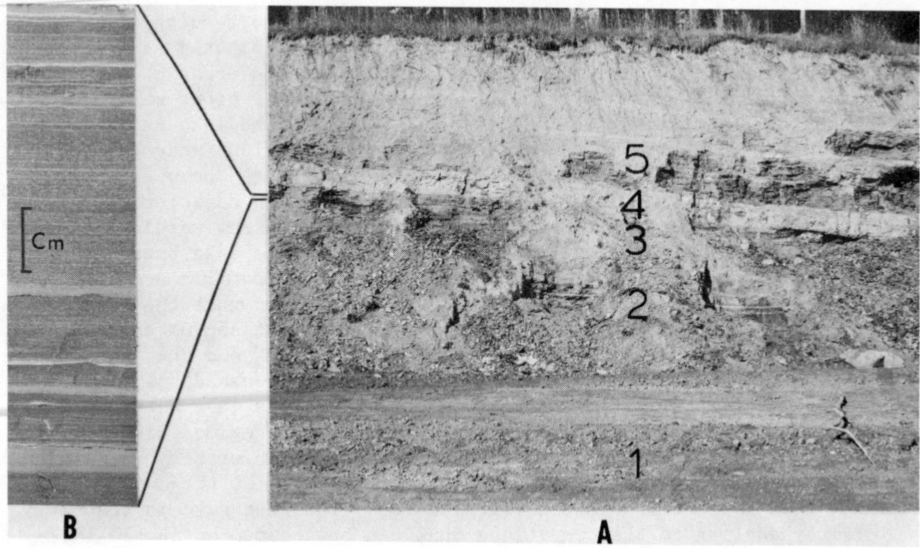

Figure 17-7
A. Photograph of part of South Clarkia (P-33) exposure. B. Example of fine lamination of lacustrine deposits. See Figure 17-2 for unit numbers.

The vertical change in representation of a particular taxon, as documented on Figure 17-5, is an indication of the ability of its organs to reach the site of burial under the prevailing conditions. Such ability is controlled largely by abundance of individuals of the taxon in the local vegetation, proximity of individuals to the depositional site, freedom of access of organs to the depositional site, and durability of the organs. A change in the number of individuals will increase or decrease the chances of an organism to be represented by fossils in the accumulating sediments. The closer the proximity to the depositional site, the greater is the chance of organs to survive the destructive factors of transport between the contributory plant and the site of burial. Unimpeded access of organs from an individual plant to the depositional site may be exemplified by plants growing on the margin of a lake, a stream, or in a ponded or swampy habitat. Relatively unimpeded access may result from the transporting ability of large streams during times of flood when plant organs can be transported for some distance to the depositional basins. Conversely, processes that bring sediments to the plant itself can result in the burial of organs near the plants that shed them (Smiley, 1961; 1963:173-175). This condition can result from airfall deposition of ash or dust, from the spread of silt-or-sand-laden waters over floodplains, or from mudflows.

Impediments to free access of organs to the depositional site similarly can involve a variety of factors. Distance alone usually is an effective filtering factor in the ultimate representation especially of large and delicate plant organs such as leaves in a basin of deposition. Turbulence of the transporting medium will rapidly destroy the more delicate large plant structures. A relatively narrow but dense strip of vegetation adjacent to a depositional site can be an effective barrier to the dissemination of organs between plants of more remote habitats and the site of sedimentary accumulation. The taller trees of a forest will have fewer barriers especially to wind dissemination of leaves, winged seeds, and pollen than smaller plants of the understory. The smallest plants of the forest groundcover will encounter the greatest obstacles to dissemination, and such plants commonly are represented as fossils only where sediments accumulate on the forest floor itself (for example, swamps, floodplains). Thus, the analyses of the trends noted for individual Clarkia taxa and comparisons of trends of the different taxa are subject to variables that may be difficult to distinguish with certainty.

Explanations may be derived from known facts of the fossil assemblage including the types of organs represented, the condition of organs after movement to the depositional site, the number of specimens preserved, the numerical representation of a taxon as a proportion of the total assemblage, or vertical changes in representation on the basis of observed superposition. Explanations also may be derived from uniformitarian considerations of known living descendents including such factors as probable edaphic conditions, probable climatic requirements, probable size of plants, or an approximation of the number of organs produced per individual of a given taxon. Autecological analyses of the individual taxa are important in interpreting the trends that may be noted in the fossil representation of specific plants; but synecological analysis of the assemblage is of greater significance in that it represents the "sum of the autecologies of all its constituent elements" (Ager, 1963:297). Individual taxa can serve as checks on equivalent interpretations of some of their fossil associates.

The upward trend documented for the swamp conifer *Taxodium* (Figure 17-5, Table 17-4) compares favorably with trends that have been documented for other plants whose modern equivalents favor or tolerate a water or riparian habitat, for example, species of *Acer*, *Liquidambar*, *Nyssa*, and the families Lauraceae and Betulaceae. Opposing trends are recorded for plants whose modern equivalents most commonly inhabit moist but well-drained conditions of floodplains and slopes, for example, species of *Quercus*, *Castanea*, and members of the family Leguminosae. Other plants of moist well-drained sites that show a marked decline of fossils in Unit 5, at a time when *Taxodium* increases dramatically, include *Pinus*, *Metasequoia*, *Abies*, *Sequoia*, and *Cocculus*.

The conclusion seems apparent that a swamp association became established in a fringe zone surrounding the lake and provided increasing numbers of fossils to the lake sediments during progressive infilling of the lake basin. At the same time the swamp forest developed as an effective barrier to the dissemination of organs from plants occupying the slopes beyond. Prior to the development of the fringing swamp, the riparian, floodplain, and slope plants were well represented in the sediments because of close proximity of individuals and freedom of access of their organs to the newly established lake.

Supporting evidence can be found also at the species level of analysis (Table 17-4). The genus *Nyssa* is represented by two leaf species in the Clarkia flora: one nearly identical to the living *N. aquatica* Linne of southeastern American swamps and the other resembling the living *N. sylvatica* Marshall that is a characteristic tree of moist slopes of the adjacent Appalachian Mountains. The record of the slope tupelo as documented in our analysis shows it to be commonly represented in the lower and middle part of the study column and absent in the upper part. Conversely, the swamp tupelo is rare in the lower and middle part and is one of the dominant plants in the upper part in association with abundant remains of *Taxodium*.

Two common species of maple (*Acer*) resemble the living *A. saccharinum* Linne that is characteristic of riparian and swamp habitats in eastern North America and *A. pennsylvanicum* Linne that typically occupies riparian and moist slope habitats in the same region. Their records in the Clarkia column parallel those documented for species of tupelo. The more-mesic form is one of the dominant plants in the upper part of the column. The less-mesic form is present only in the lower part except at one level immediately following deposition of airfall ash.

A similar trend is noted for two species of the genus *Magnolia*. One species resembles the living *M. virginiana* Linne, the sweetbay or swamp magnolia of mesic bottomlands in eastern North America. The other species resembles the living *M. accuminata* Linne, the cucumber tree or mountain magnolia of the adjacent Appalachian slopes. The swamp form is common throughout the length of the study column, and its record generally parallels that of *Taxodium*. The mountain (slope) magnolia is rare or absent in the lower part of the column, is most abundantly represented in the middle part, and is rare or absent at the top where *Taxodium* and other mesic bottomland plants dominate the fossil flora.

Under conditions of humid-temperate climate similar to that of the Miocene in the Clarkia region, oaks (*Quercus*) typically inhabit the drier sites of an area. Each of two species of oak in the Clarkia flora (*Q. simulata* Knowlton, *Q.* cf. *payettensis* Knowlton) resembles several living species that now occupy well-drained sites in eastern North America and eastern Asia. A third Clarkia species (cf. *Q. smileyana* Chaney and Axelrod) appears to be more indicative of moist bottomland sites resembling several modern species (for example, *Q. imbricaria*, *Q. phellos*) that are characteristic of such habitats in eastern North America. The Clarkia record of oaks shows the continued presence of both bottomland and slope forms throughout the length of the study column. The more mesic oak species shows a declining representation upward through the column and a slight increase at the top. The slope representatives show a trend that is generally opposite that of the more mesic plants in the flora; they are best represented in the middle part of the column and are least represented near the top.

Figure 17-8 shows that the proportional representation of swamp species remained fairly constant within a range of 21-37 percent (Figure 17-8A). A well-established swamp association seems to have persisted in the area during this time. The number of specimens representing swamp taxa (Figure 17-8B) is shown to have reached the lowest levels following episodes of relatively thick volcanic ash deposition (Unit 2 to Unit 4 ash beds). The highest numerical representation of swamp specimens is recorded near the bottom of the study column at a time when the primary swamp succession characterized by *Chamaecyparis* was established and again at the top during the reestablishment of an apparently swampy floodplain environment following the infilling of the lake.

The trends shown in Figure 17-5 indicate that some taxa increased and others decreased immediately following deposition of airfall ash. On the other hand, some taxa entered the local record immediately

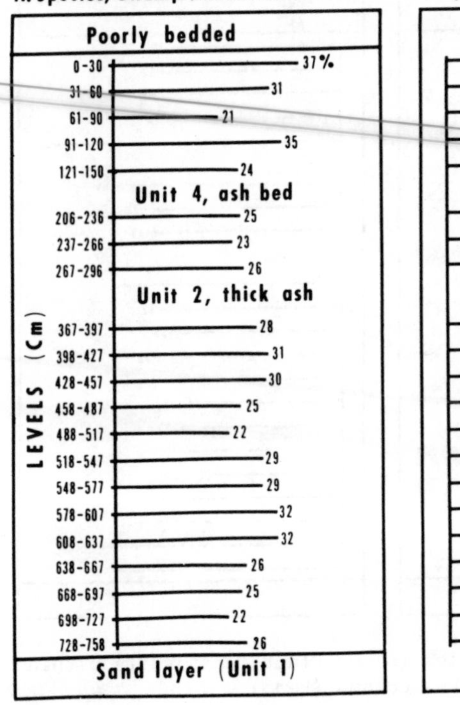

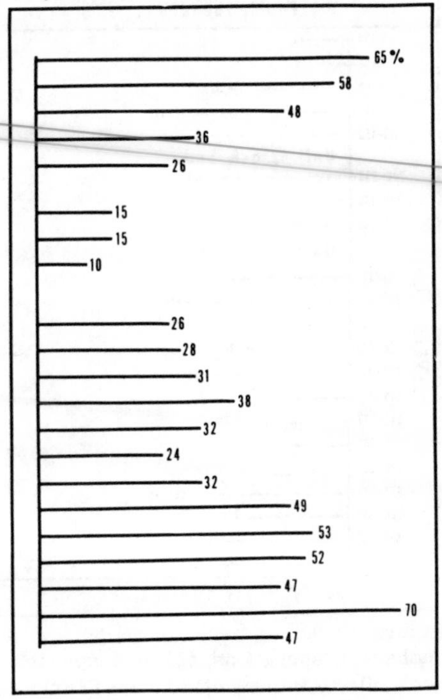

Figure 17-8
Proportional representation of inferred swamp species (A) and specimens (B) from analyses of plant megafossils at Clarkia locality P-33. See also Table 17-4.

following deposition of a relatively thick ash layer (for example, *Cocculus*), and others disappeared from the record shortly after an episode of airfall deposition (for example, *Castanea*). The study of the Paricutin ash deposits by Dorf (1951) relating to the preservation of plant material and the persistence of plant taxa is somewhat analogous to this aspect of our study of the Clarkia flora.

Figure 17-9 contains tabulations of the numerical representation of plant megafossils upward through the study column. Figure 17-9A shows the number of specimens uncovered within each 30 cm increment of the column, and Figure 17-9B shows the number of species represented. The greatest abundance of specimens at the 121-150 cm level immediately followed deposition of the thick ash unit (Figure 17-2, Unit 4) that appears to have resulted in a considerable restriction of the lake waters. The lakeshore apparently moved outward toward the depositional site of lacality P-33 permitting the surrounding forest to come into closer proximity to that part of the lake basin. This newly established land of the expanded lake margin likely would have been boggy or swampy providing new area for the Swamp Association to occupy. Evidence presented in Figure 17-5 shows that this was also a time of vegetational transition immediately following a rapid decline of the

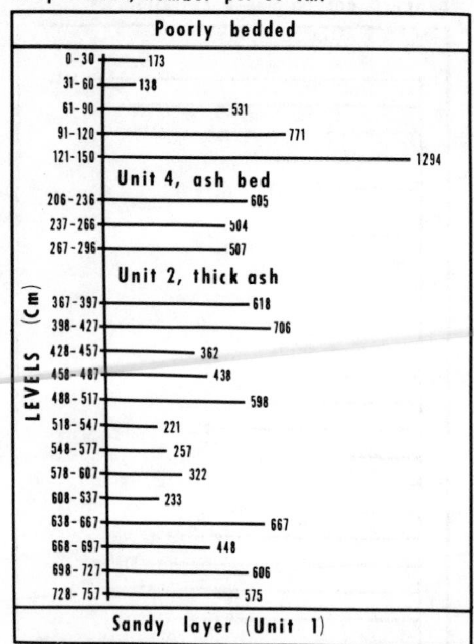

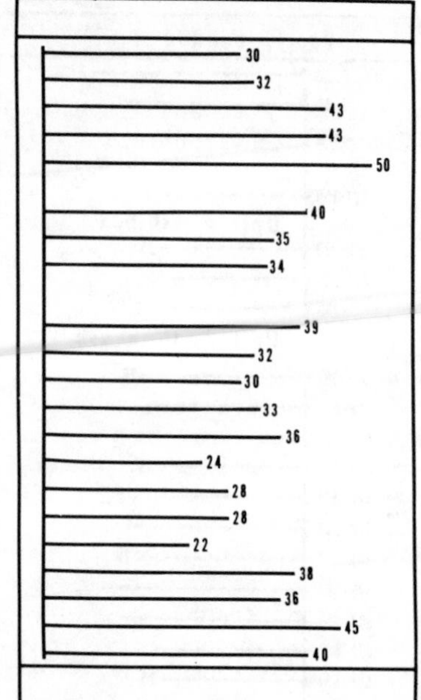

Figure 17-9
Number of specimens (A) and species (B) of plant megafossils within each 30 cm increment of the Clarkia column (P-33).

Facageae (well-drained sites) and immediately preceding the rapid increase of *Taxodium* and associated swamp plants as dominant taxa in the fossil assemblage. This time of transition was a time of no single dominant plant, and the fact that it was also the time of greatest species diversity seems to indicate a co-mingling of slope and swamp species during a period of rapid change.

The interrelationships between taxa that are most indicative of swampy environments and taxa that are most indicative of well-drained sites thus show an increasing influence of a swamp environment on lake-border vegetation. The evidence also suggests that times of major ashfall activity noticeably affected the composition of the forest as exemplified at Clarkia locality P-33. Some plants seem to have had a high tolerance for ashfalls whereas others did not as the ash fell directly onto the plants or as it changed the chemistry of the soil and water. Rapid sedimentation of 30 to 60 cm of deposits in a shallowing lake would concurrently reduce the extent of the open waters by infilling and widen the lake-margin swampland as the area of the open lake was restricted. Later invasion of this newly broadened swamp belt by plants of the Swamp Association would effectively reduce the representation of slope plants in the lake sediments at locality P-33. There should be an increase in the proportional representation of plants that characterized the Swamp Association relative to the representation of plants from adjacent slopes as the maturing and expanding swamp forest became a more effective barrier to leaf dispersal from slope to open lake. As infilling of the lake basin progressed, the bordering swamp and swamp forest would continue to expand outward into the lake basin until the lake disappeared. The upward change in sediments and the statistical increase of the swamp component in the upper part of the section reflect such an infilling of Clarkia Lake and its eventual replacement by a swampy or moist floodplain environment.

SUMMATION

An analysis of the fossil assemblage from locality P-33 leads to the conclusion of a lake community dominated by sponges, diatoms, and quiet-water fishes. On slopes and floodplains adjacent to the lake was a climax forest similar to the mixed mesophytic forest of eastern Asia or southeastern North America, a forest that is now adapted for a humid warm-temperate regime of summer-wet climate and short, mild winters. Locally, bottomland swamps or bogs were occupied by swamp cypress and other swamp plants. A few plant species are indicative of drier habitats. A variety of terrestrial insects represents the animal component of the forest surrounding the lake.

On the other hand, an analysis of the Clarkia assemblage on a micro-stratigraphic basis leads to conclusions that reflect our knowledge of a Miocene sere. Rather than inferring a condition of a climax-forest community that remained relatively static through this interval of time, the microstratigraphic data show a dynamic community changing as it adapted to changing conditons of the local environment. The local sere appears to span the complete life of a lake: from an original rapid damming probably by volcanic activity to an eventual extinction by sedimentary infilling. Surrounding terrestrial habitats were significantly affected during the process, particularly the extent of bottomland swamp habitats as lake siltation progressed to a final complete infilling.

The sere, as recorded in the lacustrine sequence, suggests a change in bottomland vegetation from a dominant mixed-mesophytic forest prior to the establishment of the lake, its continued dominance during the early life of the lake, and its decline and replacement at the death of the lake by a dominating swamp forest. In hilly areas farther removed from the lake border, the mesic slope forest probably remained as a fairly stable (climax) community during the relatively short time (perhaps only decades) represented by the lacustrine deposits.

REGIONAL SETTING

The brief outline of regional factors presented here is intended to provide a general overview of the regional setting of the Clarkia study rather than a detailed analysis and comparison of Miocene floras as was done by Chaney and Axelrod (1959). Climate is a regional factor of primary concern because it involves length of growing season, severity and length of winters, abundance and annual distribution of rainfall, relative humidity of the atmosphere, and presence or absence of summer drought.

When the limit of tolerance for any one of these climatic factors is exceeded for any particular species, that species will be eliminated from the vegetation of the region. If a species can tolerate the temperature and humidity extremes of the prevailing climate and can have been introduced originally into the regional vegetation, it can survive in the region as long as suitable edaphic or topographic conditions are available locally.

Regional climates will change in accordance with those of the entire planet. Middle latitude regions that were free of frost in Eocene time when global climates were warmer than present are now located in temperate belts at a time when global climates are cool. Regional climates may also change as a direct result of the development of a mountain range across the prevailing path of moving weather systems. In western North America, the evidence from physical geology and Neogene floral sequences indicate a Neogene uplift of the Cascade and Sierra ranges; these north-south ranges rose across the path of the prevailing "westerlies" that bring humid air from the Pacific Ocean onto the continent. The known floral sequences during this time clearly reflect the increasing seasonality and decreasing humidity of the interior and the progressive development of the rainshadow in the lee of these rising mountains (Chaney and Axelrod, 1959; Smiley, 1963).

Orographic effects on local climate and life are readily apparent as one ascends the flanks of a mountain or mountain range. The atmosphere locally becomes cooler and more humid as elevation increases. Both summer and winter temperatures are lowered, and the length of the growing season is reduced at the higher elevations. The relative humidity of the atmosphere and annual precipitation increase at progressively higher levels. Thus, the position of Idaho along the western flanks of the northern Rocky Mountains has an important bearing on our analysis of the Clarkia flora. The Rockies seem to have remained an upland area since their inception in late Mesozoic time, and the Miocene Clarkia vegetation could be expected to have been more influenced by the orographic effect of closer proximity to uplands than other Miocene floras of the Columbia Plateau region to the west.

Atmospheric conditions near the ground-air interface will have primary effect on the kind of vegetation that can exist under the local constraints of slope and soil. Bottomlands in humid climates may accumulate the runoff from adjacent slopes and may become swamped with stagnant water. Conversely, bottomlands in arid climates may become deserts for lack of adequate rainfall, inadequate water recharge, and high evaporation rates. Slopes in areas of humid climate normally receive adequate amounts of water from the atmosphere, and the high atmospheric humidity that prevails the year round retards evaporation. These, however, are well-drained sites, and occasional periods of drought may have a more significant effect on slope conditions than on conditions of the mesic bottomlands. Rocky slopes are more susceptible to the influence of short periods of drought than are slopes with a deep mantle of soil and a thick cover of vegetation; and south- or west-facing slopes (in the Northern Hemisphere) are more susceptible than are those that face east or north. Interpretations of the Clarkia flora and seral successions thus must take into consideration a variety of geographic factors that may have existed at any moment in the history of the region, such as prevailing climate, topographic diversity, volcanic activity, or regional drainage patterns. Considerations must also be given to slow historical changes that may involve world climates or regional orogenic activity and to rapid local catastrophies such as volcanic eruptions, forest fires, or the sudden creation or death of a lake.

Interpretations of regional paleoclimates will receive the highest degree of confidence if based on the synecological rather than the autecological approach. The analysis of a floral assemblage is the sum of the analyses of its constituent taxonomic parts. Confidence increases with increased precision in the identification of fossil plants and with the ability to recognize degrees of affinity with living species. Thus, we are more confident of our interpretations of floras and climates of the Cretaceous than of the Carboniferous; we are more confident of our interpretations of the Neogene than of the Paleogene; and we are more confident of Pleistocene than of Miocene interpretations.

Many of the ligneous plants that are represented in Miocene floras of western North America produced leaves and associated fruiting bodies that are so like those produced by a single living species that there seems little doubt of the closeness of the affinities. In such cases, it seems probable that we are dealing with the same species or with a nearly identical species that was the Neogene ancestor of the living equivalent. Preserved organs of other Neogene plants may show equal resemblance to two or more living species of the same genus, and these modern species may now be living in different parts of the world. Other Miocene fossils may be assigned with confidence to an existing genus, but no one species within that genus can be selected as a single modern equivalent. Still others may be extinct forms with no modern affinities closer than the genus or family level.

The assemblage analyses of Neogene floras for vegetational and climatic interpretations must rest largely on those fossils for which we have the greatest confidence of identification. When a fossil assemblage contains a variety of species that are essentially identical to living plants of a single modern forest, their apparent persistence as associated species from the Miocene to the present adds credence to our interpretations of past vegetational units and to the inferred physical conditons under which they seem to have persisted to the present as an association of plants.

No single modern forest of the world contains the combination of genera found in the Clarkia and other Miocene floras of western North America on which to determine regional factors of paleoecology (for example, regional climates). Some Clarkia genera have become extinct in North America since that time and have survived only in Asian forests: *Cunninghamia*, *Metasequoia*, *Zelkova*, *Pterocarya*, *Cerdidiphyllum*, *Berchemia*, *Paliurus*, and *Paulownia*. Some genera are now restricted to North America: *Sequoia*, *Taxodium*, *Asimina*, *Amorpha*, *Robinia*, and *Shepherdia*. Other genera are presently represented by species both in eastern Asia and in North America (li, 1952): *Carya*, *Gordonia*, *Halesia*, *Hamamelis*, *Lindera*, *Liriodendron*, *Magnolia*, *Nyssa*, *Ostrya*, and *Sassafras*. The remaining Clarkia genera are more cosmopolitan in present distribution, but they reflect general climatic and edaphic conditions similar to ones of more restricted distribution. At least one of the Clarkia genera (Fagaceae gen. nov.) is known to have become extinct since the Miocene (Smiley and Huggins, in preparation).

Modern forests of North America that are most like the Clarkia flora occur in the southeastern United States where they occupy an arcuate belt that extends from North Carolina through northern Georgia and Alabama to Tennessee (32°-34°N). The modern equivalents of some Clarkia species inhabit the well-drained slopes of the southern Appalachian Mountains and others inhabit the swampy bottomlands of river valleys and of the adjacent coastal plain. In this region, the annual precipitation ranges from 1,270 to 1,520 mm evenly distributed throughout the year; and short, relatively mild winters are indicated by a growing season of 220 to 240 days (Kincer, 1941).

A high proportion of Clarkia genera are widely distributed in the humid, warm-temperate regions of eastern Asia. Species of many of the genera can now be found in insular sites such as the mountains of Taiwan at a latitude of about 25°N (Li, 1963) and in lower elevations of Japan at latitudes of about 35°-40°N (Makino, 1964). Asian forests that appear most like the Clarkia association are those of the mixed mesophytic forest formation of the upper Yangtze Valley in western Hupeh where *Metasequoia* occurs in relict stands at an elevation of 1,000-1,100 m (Wang, 1961:111). In this area occur species of Clarkia genera including *Cunninghamia*, *Metasequoia*, *Pinus*, *Taxus*, *Acer*, *Betula*, *Castania*, *Cercidiphyllum*, *Cornus*, *Fagus*, *Liquidambar*, *Lindera*, *Nyssa*, *Ostrya*, *Populus*, *Prunus*, *Pterocarya*, *Quercus*, *Rhus*, *Salix*, *Sassafras*, and *Ulmus*. Climatic data from a weather station in the area (Engshih, elevation 469 m) show annual precipitation of about 1,071 mm evenly distributed throughout the year; short mild winters are indicated by a growing season of 275 days (Wang, 1961:97). The elevation of the weather station is considerably lower than the 1,000-1,100 m altitude of the *Metasequoia* forests examined by Wang, and the climate of the cooler and wetter upland thus would be expected to conform more closely to that of the equivalent eastern American forest than do the somewhat warmer and drier conditions at Engshih.

The Clarkia flora thus is an assemblage of taxa that most closely resemble ones still associated in forests of humid warm-temperate regions of eastern North America and eastern Asia. The Swamp Association more closely resembles similar forests in eastern North America, and the Slope Association has a pronounced East Asian character. In both parts of the world, the mixed mesophytic forests exist under a humid summer-wet climatic regime having short and relatively mild winters. The Clarkia flora is considered to have existed under a similar regime reflecting a moderate climate of maritime influence. Miocene climate was markedly different from the extreme continental conditions in the Clarkia region at present as shown by records at St. Maries, Idaho (Kincer, 1941:829): annual precipitation about 620 mm, a fairly dry summer, a growing season of 137 days, and temperatures that have reached extremes of 106° F and -50°F.

Approximately two-thirds of the Clarkia genera can be found in the Oligocene-Miocene floras of the Ruby River and Beaverhead basins to the east in western Montana (Becker, 1969, 1972, 1973). These floras are considered by Becker to represent forests that existed in a humid mild-temperate climate. The absence of such Clarkia plants as Magnoliaceae, Lauraceae, *Gordonia*, and *Halesia* and the presence of some Madrean genera suggest a somewhat cooler climate and drier slope habitats than is indicated by the Clarkia assemblage. This may be in part the result of a difference in elevation of the two areas and in part the result of a slight difference in age.

Most of the Clarkia taxa can be found in Miocene floras of the Columbia Plateau region to the west (Chaney and Axelrod, 1959). The maximum size of Clarkia leaves commonly is much larger than leaves of the same species in floras farther west. Some of the mesic species that are rear in floras to the west are abundantly represented in the Clarkia deposits. These differences probably reflect an orographic effect on the western flanks of the Miocene Rocky Mountain uplands and the resulting increased precipitation and relative humidity in the Clarkia region compared to the plains of the Columbia Plateau. A dimilar orographic condition still prevails in the region today although relative humidity and precipitation have been considerably reduced since the Miocene by uplift of the Cascade climatic barrier.

The effect of later Tertiary orogenic activity, involving the Cascadian uplift on the west and the rejuvenation of the Rocky Mountains on the east, was not pronounced until later Miocene time. The Neogene (10-12 MY) floral sequence in the Ellensburg-Yakima area of Washington (Smiley, 1963) shows a marked change in the vegetation of the interior as the developing rainshadow (summer-dry) eliminated many of the mesic (summer-wet) plants in the regional flora. By Pliocene time, most of the exotic genera and species that had dominated Miocene forests had become extinct in the region as a result of the developing aridity and severe continentality of the interior climate (Axelrod, 1950). The characteristic plants of the Miocene forests thus were replaced by ones of western American origins that were adapted for conditions that had become established since the Miocene (summer-dry climate, long severe winters).

CONCLUSIONS

Geologic field evidence indicates the presence of a Proto-St. Maries River valley in a regional hilly terrane of Precambrian mica schist (Figure 17-10). The Miocene topography in the vicinity of Clarkia was a northwest-trending stream valley surrounded by hills and a local relief in excess of 150 m. Evidence for this is seen in the physical relations that exist between the Miocene volcanic and sedimentary rocks and the irregular shistose basement that still rises as knolls and hills surrounding the outcrops of younger rocks. Basalt flows down valley apparently dammed the stream (perhaps more than once) on the north. The result was a lake occupying the Proto-St. Maries River valley south of the lava dam(s) and continuation of sedimentary processes until at least 30 m of lacustrine and floodplain deposits had accumulated at P-33. Water-well data near Clarkia suggest that these deposits may have reached a thickness as great as 74 m near the center of the Miocene valley.

The sequence of sediments at Clarkia locality P-33 shows a change from sandy deposits at the base to mixed sand and clay layers topped by a 1.2 m of turbidite sand to thinly laminated varve-like deposits containing thick ash beds in the upper part to poorly bedded and poorly sorted ashy sands and silts at the top. This sequence suggests the following consecutive changes in depositional environments:

1. Early stream sands.
2. The development of a floodplain with ponded areas near a stream that occasionally overflowed its banks.
3. The development of an open lake with a fringing swamp and offshore stagnant-bottom conditions.
4. A return to a swampy floodplain environment after the lake silted up.

The microstratigraphic analysis of plants at locality P-33 shows an upward trend from a predominance of well-drained riparian, flood-

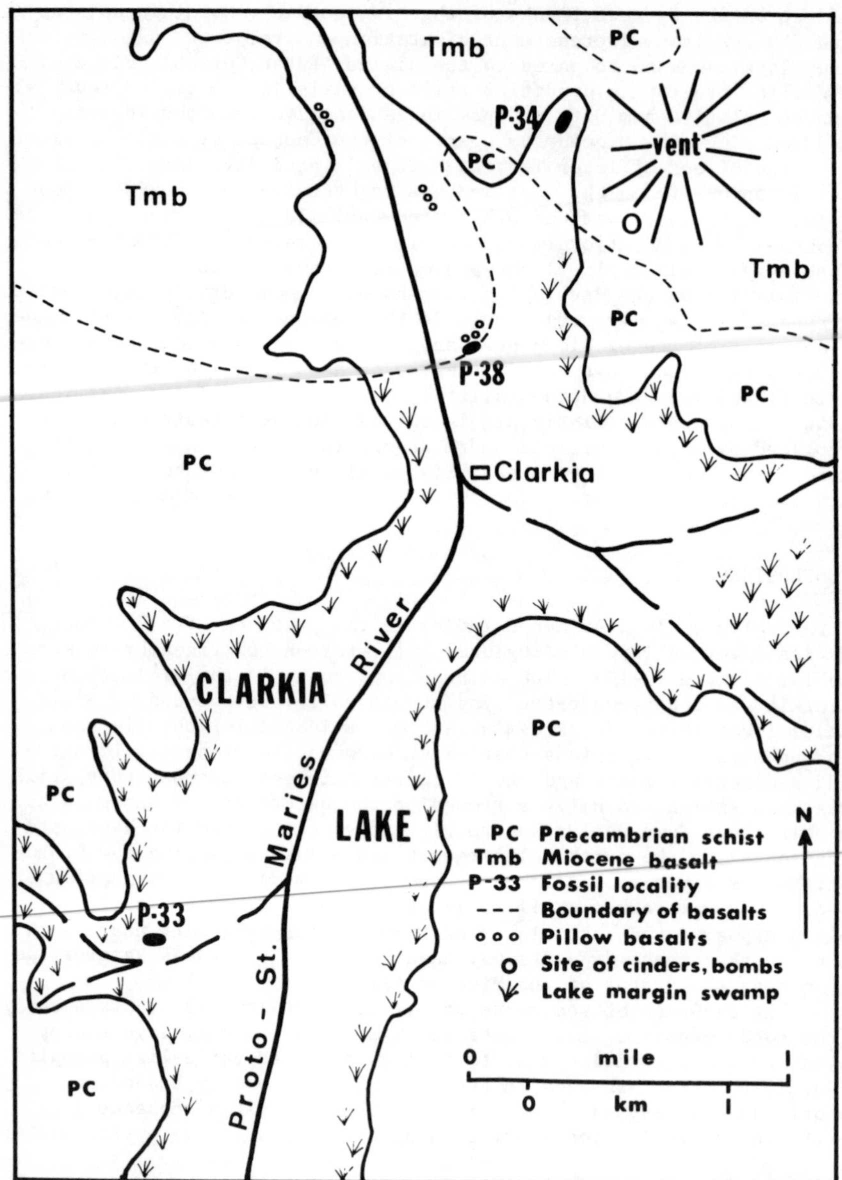

Figure 17-10
Inferred physical conditions in the Clarkia area during Miocene time based on present topography on Precambrian schistose basement (PC) in relation to Miocene basalts (Tmb) and lake sediments. Present 2,960 ft contour line is approximate upper limits of known Miocene sediments in the area, and this contour has been used to infer the probable shape and extent of the Miocene Clarkia Lake within the map boundaries.

plain, and lowerslope plants in early deposits to an increasing representation of swamp plants in later deposits. This conforms with the following evidence of sedimentary change:

1. Predominantly floodplain and slope associations in the area prior to damming of the drainage system; the swamp association probably restricted to bogs or ponded areas of the floodplain.
2. Damming of the balley by volcanic activity on the north creating a lake with a fringing border of swamp habitats.
3. Expansion of the bordering swamp as the lake basin continued to fill in, increase in the proportional representation of the swamp-forest association, and a decrease in the representation of the forest that inhabited the slopes beyond.
4. The ultimate disappearance of the lake and the development of a poorly drained, swampy valley bottom as the lake basin completely silted up with the highest representation of the swamp association at this time.
5. Continued deposition of poorly sorted and poorly bedded deposits in the upper part of the section with poor representation of relatively few plant fossils; apparently represents a return to more normal floodplain conditions.

The transition from a reducing depositional environment to one of oxidation occurs in the part of the Clarkia type-section that represents deposition during the later life of the lake. This occurred during deposition of ash beds up to 60 cm thick at the time of extensive fish and insect kills and after much of the infilling of the lake basin had taken place. It would seem that the initiation of lacustrine conditions was sudden and that the site of locality P-33 was in sufficiently deep water and far enough from shore or from stream currents to induce stagnation of water in the lake bottom. The rapid infilling by volcanic ash following an interval of varve-like deposition appears to have reduced the depth of the lake to a degree that oxygenated surface water could affect the bottom conditions.

North of Clarkia (locality P-34), the conditions of deposition and floral habitat were different. The occurrence of coarse sands as thick units or as layers of sand interbedded with thinly laminated clays suggests a depositional environment that was marginal to the lake. The presence of lenses of coarse reddish sands in the thinly layered clays and other evidence of scour and fill activity suggest that locality P-34 was near a tributary stream flowing into the lake north of Clarkia. The presence in some sand units (locality P-38) of well-rounded clay cobbles that contain Miocene plant fossils supports the interpretation of high-energy erosion and deposition of sediments in the north of the area. The thinly laminated lake-type sediments associated with the sand layers at locality P-34 may indicate a delta or fore-delta depositional environment at this site.

The florule from locality P-34 and plants in fossiliferous sands from nearby sites (for example, at P-38) represent a restricted facies of the mesic floodplain-lower slope association of the rich florule at locality P-33. The presence of streamside plants such as birch, alder, willow, poplar, sycamore and members of the Fagaceae is consistent with the sedimentary evidence of floodplain or deltaic habitats. The paucity of plants representing poorly drained conditions of stagnant swamps is further supporting evidence of oxygenated running water.

The stratigraphically restricted fish kills at locality P-33 may have been caused by overturning of lake waters bringing toxic substances to the surface or by the lake becoming too shallow for their continued existence. Strong wind gusts would have blown terrestrial insects from the protective canopy of the forest and at the same time would churn the waters of the shallowing lake. Oscillation of bottom waters would bring oxygen-depleted and perhaps toxic water toward the lake's surface. Any fish that may have been present and any terrestrial insects that may have been blown out onto the lake would be killed and would settle into the anaerobic or toxic realm of the lake bottom along with the plant debris where they would be preserved as intact specimens. Heavy rains seem also to have accompanied these storms judging from the general climatic requirements of the flora and by the evidence of rapidly deposited and lacustrine sediments. Persistent volcanic eruptions in the vicinity also could create local atmospheric disturbances including gusty winds and condensation of water from the volcanic cloud.

The numerical richness, taxonomic diversity, common preservation of cellular anatomy and original organic chemistry, and preservation of abundant fossils through several meters of finely laminated lacustrine deposits combine to make the Miocene Clarkia fossil locality a unique and important discovery in western North America. Microstratigraphic analyses of plant megafossils in the precision documented at Clarkia has never before been attempted in American Tertiary paleobotany because of the prior lack of a locality that was appropriate for the purpose. Research continues on this outstanding fossil locality, and the principle of multiple working hypotheses likely will result in some modifications of concepts as new data come to light.

ACKNOWLEDGMENTS

Different aspects of the diversified assemblage are being studied by other specialists: J. Gray (1975) on palynomorphs; L. M. Huggins (1975) on leaf microstructures; K. J. Niklas and D. E. Giannasi, New York Botanical Garden, on organic constituents of leaves; S. Lewis, St. Cloud State University, Minnesota, on fossil insects; and R. R. Miller, University of Michigan, on fossil fishes. Each of these collaborators has provided data that are incorporated in the foregoing report on community paleoecology of a Miocene lake and its surrounding terrestrial habitats.

University of Idaho associates D. H. Henderson, R. J. Naskali, F. D. Johnson, and C.-W. Wang have provided advice on botanical matters; J. G. Bond, J. H. Bush, and C. W. Knowles have provided advice and assistance on geological matters; J. Williams has begun work on extraction and preliminary identification of the siliceous microfossils (diatoms and sponges). Mr. Francis Kienbaum, owner of the fossil locality, has provided access to the site and early bulldozer work. The manuscript was reviewed by D. I. Axelrod and J. Gray, to whom we are indebted without relinquishing our responsibility for contents. The Idaho Research Foundation provided a grant in partial support of our research.

REFERENCES

Ager, C. V. 1963. *Principles of Paleoecology.* New York: McGraw-Hill, 371 p.

Axelrod, D. I. 1950. Evolution of desert vegetation in western North America. *Carnegie Inst. Washington Pub. 590*, 215-316.

Becker, H. F. 1969. Fossil plants of the Tertiary Beaverhead Basins in southwestern Montana. *Palaeontographica Abt. B*, 127, 142 p.

Becker, H. F. 1972. The Metzel Ranch flora of the Upper Ruby River Basin, southwestern Montana. *Palaeontographica Abt. B*, 141, 61 p.

Becker, H. F. 1973. The York Ranch flora of the Upper Ruby River Basin, southwestern Montana. *Palaeontographica Abt. B*, 143:18-93.

Braun, E. L. 1950. *Deciduous Forests of Eastern North America.* Philadelphia: The Blackiston Company, 596 p.

Brown, J. T., and C. E. Gow. 1976. Plant fossils as indicators of the rate of deposition of the Kirkwood Formation in the Algoa Basin. *South African Journal Science*, 72:278-279.

Cain, S. A. 1943. The Tertiary character of the cove hardwood forests of the Great Smoky Mountains National Park. *Torrey Bot. Bulletin*, 70:213-235.

Cain, S. A. 1944. *Foundations of Plant Geography.* New York: Harper and Brothers, 556 p.

Cain, S. A., and G. M. DeO. Castro. 1959. *Manual of Vegetation Analysis.* New York: Harper and Brothers, 325 p.

Chaney, R. W., and D. I. Axelrod. 1959. Miocene floras of the Columbia Plateau. *Carnegie Inst. Washington Pub. 617*, 237 p.

Clark, A. L. 1963. *Geology of the Clarkia Area, Idaho.* M. S. thesis, University of Idaho, 57 p.

Dorf, E. 1951. Lithology and floral facies in the Pericutin ash deposits, Mexico. *New York Acad. Sci. Trans.*, 13:317-320.

Fowells, H. A. 1965. Silvics of forest trees of the United States. *U.S. Dept. of Agriculture, Handbook 271*, 762 p.

Gray, J., and L. R. Kittleman. 1967. Geochronometry of the Columbia River basalt and associated floras of eastern Washington and western Idaho. *American Jour. Sci.*, 265:257-291.

Hietanen, A. 1963. Metamorphism of the Belt Series in the Elk River-Clarkia area of Idaho. *U.S. Geol. Survey, Prof. Paper 344-C*, 49 p.

Jewell, M. 1959. Porifera. In W. T. Edmondson, ed., *Freshwater Biology*, 2nd ed. New York: John Wiley and Sons, Inc., 1248 p.

Kincer, J. B. 1941. Climate and weather data for the United States. In Grove Hambridge, ed., *Climate and Man*, U.S. Dept. of Agriculture, Yearbook of Agriculture, 1248 p.

Knowlton, F. H. 1926. Flora of the Latah formation of Spokane, Washington and Coeur d'Alene, Idaho. *U.S. Geol. Survey Prof. Paper 140*, 17-81.

Li, H.-L. 1952. Floristic relationships between eastern Asia and eastern North America. *American Philos. Soc. Trans.*, 42:371-429.

Li, H.-L. 1963. *Woody Flora of Taiwan.* Narberth, Pa.: Livingston Publication Co., 974 p.

Makino, T. 1955. *An Illustrated Flora of Japan.* Tokyo: The Hokuryukan Co., Ltd., 1808 p.

Mueller-Dombois, D., and H. Ellenburg. 1974. *Aims and Methods of Vegetation Ecology.* New York: John Wiley and Sons, Inc., 547 p.

Sargent, C. S. 1921. *Manual of the Trees of North America*, 2nd ed. Boston: Houghton Mifflin Co., 910 p.

Small, J. K. 1933. *Manual of the Southeastern Flora*. Chapel Hill: University of North Carolina Press, 1554 p.

Smiley, C. J. 1961. A record of Paulownia in the Tertiary of North America. *Am. Jour. Botany*, 48:175-179.

Smiley, C. J. 1963. The Ellensburg flora of Washington. *California University Pubs. Geol. Sci.*, 35:159-276.

Smiley, C. J., J. Gray, and L. M. Huggins. 1975. Preservation of Miocene fossils in unoxidized lake deposits, Clarkia, Idaho. *Jour. Paleontology*, 49:833-844.

Swanson, D. A., T. L. Wright, and R. T. Helz. 1975. Linear vent systems and estimated rates of magma production and eruption for the Yakima Basalt on the Columbia Plateau. *Am. Jour. Sci.*, 275:877-905.

Tanai, T., and K. Huzioka. 1967. Climatic implications of Tertiary floras in Japan, *Tertiary Correlations and Climatic Changes in the Pacific*, Eleventh Pacific Sci. Congress, Pacific Sci. Assoc., University of Tokyo, Japan, pp. 89-94.

van Landingham, S. L. 1964. Miocene non-marine diatoms from the Yakima region in south-central Washington. *Nova Hedwigia Beihefte*, 14, 78 p.

Wang, C.-W. 1961. The Forests of China. *Cambridge, Maria Moore Cabot Foundation Pub.*, 5, 313 p.

Watkins, N. D., and A. K. Baksi. 1974. Magnetostratigraphy and oroclinal folding of the Columbia River, Steens, and Owyhee Basalts. *Am. Jour. Sci.*, 274:148-189.

Wolfe, J. A. 1971. Tertiary climatic fluctuations and methods of analysis of Tertiary floras. *Palaeogeography, Palaeoclimatology, Palaeoecology*, 8:27-57.

18

Vertebrate Paleoecology in a Recent East African Ecosystem

Anna K. Behrensmeyer

ABSTRACT

Studies of vertebrate bone assemblages in modern ecosystems provide information on taphonomic biasing processes that are relevant to paleoecological interpretations of fossil bone accumulations. The surface bone assemblage of Amboseli National Park, Kenya, preserves a record of a mammal fauna that differs from the community structure determined from population censuses of the living community. Preburial processes, including carnivore and scavenger activity, bioturbation (trampling), and weathering, (but not fluvial transport) alter the representation of diversity and relative abundance of species primarily by selectively destroying bones of smaller animals. The effects of these processes on the relative representation of skeletal parts, particularly teeth and vertebrae, of animals weighing 15 to 2800 kg are not great. Patterns of habitat utilization among the herbivore species are accurately recorded in the bone assemblage, but the more complex than a simple correspondence between preferred habitat and place of bone accumulation. Time-averaging of bones accumulated on the land surface over 8 to 15 years incorporates faunal responses to substantial habitat shifts thus blurring the record of spatial ecology. Water-dependent species affected by periodic drought undergo seasonal mortality in areas near permanent water that can increase their apparent abundance in the community. Comparisons among the Amboseli bone assemblage and Oligocene fossil assemblages of South Dakota demonstrate how consideration of potential taphonomic biases can be used to strengthen or to limit paleoecological interpretations.

INTRODUCTION

Paleoecology is the study of fossil animal and plant communities and how they have changed through time. For many types of organisms, the fossil record provides the most important, if not the only, source of documentation of past ecological relationships. With increased interest in recent ecosystems and understanding of them as integrated biological phenomena, serious attention is being given to reconstructing past ecology from fossil evidence. This is a challenging task. Buried fossil assemblages represent a large number of physical and biological processes that have been superimposed on the original ecological relationships of organisms.

Ecological studies of vertebrate fossils are particularly challenging because the vertebrate record is usually fragmentary and highly dispersed in sedimentary deposits. Past collecting procedures stressed recovery of enough well-preserved material for anatomical reconstruction and for establishing evolutionary relationships. Such collections offer only limited information for paleoecological interpretation because sufficient documentation of geological context, original faunal associations, and collecting biases is often incomplete. Paleoecological study of the vertebrate record needs a carefully formulated program of sampling that can provide information concerning paleoenvironments, taphonomy, and faunal composition of a fossil assemblage. Several exemplary studies (Olson, 1958; Shotwell, 1963; Clark et al., 1967; Voorhies, 1969) have demonstrated the potential of this approach. However, progress toward generally accepted guidelines for paleoecological analysis, and beyond this to syntheses about community evolution in vertebrates, has been slow. A much larger data base of paleoecological studies is needed before such syntheses are possible.

Information on the taphonomic history of a fossil assemblage is a necessary prerequisite for paleoecological interpretations. The number of processes that are likely to affect bone burial and fossilization is large and understanding of these processes is generally sparse. Studies of vertebrate remains on modern land surfaces are providing much useful taphonomic information (Mellet, 1974; Hill, 1975; Gifford, 1977). Models for taphonomic effects on bones based on data from recent systems provide one of the most promising means of sorting out the natural sampling biases that characterize vertebrate fossil assemblages.

Previous studies of recent vertebrate taphonomy have focused on specific processes such as bone accumulation by hyenas, humans, and porcupines (Sutcliffe, 1970; Brain, 1967, 1980) and bone disarticulation, dispersal, and weathering (Toots, 1965; Hill, 1975; Behrensmeyer, 1978). The project discussed here was a broad-scale comparison between characteristics of a living, large-vertebrate community and the surface bone assemblage derived from it. Using this approach, biases were measured and related to a number of processes relevant to the interpretation of vertebrate taphonomy and paleoecology of fossil assemblages.

RECENT LARGE MAMMAL COMMUNITIES AND PALEOECOLOGY

The term "community," as used by modern ecologists, refers to a recurrent assemblage of organisms related by a complex series of interactions in a recognizable structure (Rickleffs, 1973; Clapham, 1973; Valentine, 1973). The definition of a community through periods of geologically significant time has been open to debate. Olson (1952, 1980) discusses concepts of paleocommunities and uses the definition of a community as "a group of organisms living together within a definite locality." "Living together" implies "interaction of constituent individuals either directly or by influence of organisms upon each other through their impacts on the common environment." Olson (pers. comm.) feels this can apply equally well to recent or past communities.

Using the above as a working definition of community, we can select those aspects of community structure that are generally used to characterize recent communities and examine whether these can be measured in the fossil record. Basic characteristics of an ecosystem are biomass and productivity; other important characteristics include species composition, relative numbers of individuals of the different species, predator-prey ratios, and habitat utilization (Rickleffs, 1973; Valentine, 1973). Biomass and productivity cannot be measured directly using fossil evidence; however, measures of the other attributes are potentially available from the fossil record.

Recent vertebrate ecologists have much data of potential relevance to the fossil record, but up to now most of their sampling and analyses have not been done with this in mind. An ecologist has recently pointed out that even modern communities must be "reconstructed" using sampling methods analogous in many ways to those applied to the fossil record (D. Western, pers. comm.). Paleoecology thus has much in common with ecology, perhaps more than is generally recognized.

A major difference between ecological and paleoecological data is that it is much easier to deal with the latter in terms of relatives rather than absolutes. It would be difficult, if not impossible, to determine exact population sizes for mammals in a paleocommunity, but perhaps not so difficult to show that Species A was consistently twice as common as Species B. Comparative analyses of relative abundance, predator-prey ratios, and presence or absence of species in samples of constant size, using a large set of sampling trials, is a potentially strong approach to paleocommunity analysis. Rigorous sampling of this kind could also provide a basis for valid comparisons with modern communities.

TAPHONOMIC STUDY AREA

Vertebrate remains lie scattered over many recent land surfaces, but sampling areas that can yield information relevant to the fossil record are relatively scarce. The Amboseli Basin (Figure 18-1) was chosen for this study primarily because of the amount of information available about the living vertebrate community, which includes many of the large mammal genera common in African Plio-Pleistocene faunas (Western, 1973, 1980).

Another advantage of the Amboseli Basin is that it is analogous geomorphically to Plio-Pleistocene basins associated with the East African Rift System, particularly the Olduvai Basin as reconstructed by Hay (1976). It lies on the north side of Mount Kilimanjaro in a depression between lava flows to the south and Precambrian metamorphic rocks that form hills to the north. Freshwater springs from Mount Kilimanjaro enter the basin along its southern edge, creating areas of luxurient swamp and woodland. The basin covers an area of approximately 600 km^2, is internally drained, and has no major stream systems. The absence of rivers in the basin permitted our investigation to focus on pretransport and nontransport taphonomic processes that affect bones thereby reducing the number of variables under consideration.

The large-vertebrate community of the Amboseli Basin includes

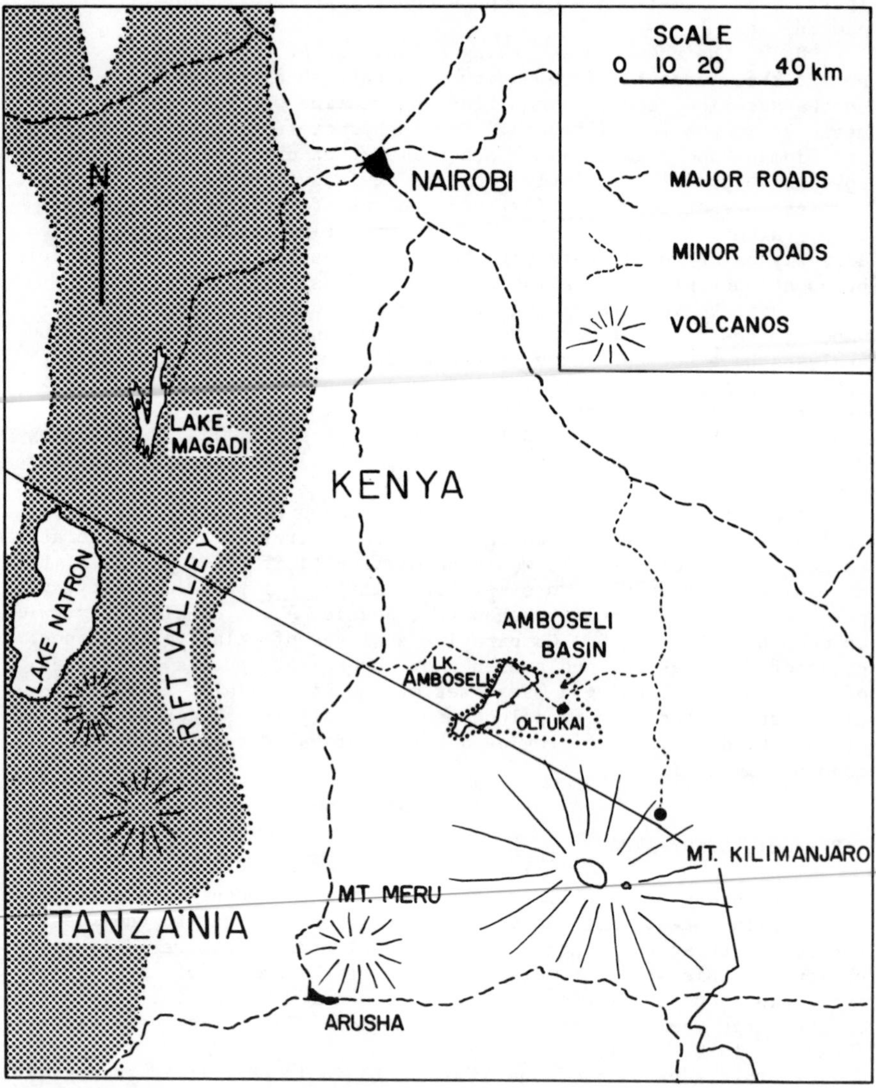

Figure 18-1
Map showing the location of the Amboseli Basin in relation to Mount Kilimanjaro and the East African Rift Valley. Lake Amboseli, in the western part of the basin, is dry except during periods of heavy rainfall.

species from greater than 800 kg (elephant and rhino) to 15 kg (Thomson's gazelle) (Table 18-1). The community includes ten common herbivores and five large carnivore species: lion, striped and spotted hyena, leopard, and cheetah. Humans occasionally assume a predatory role as poachers on elephant and rhino. The large-vertebrate community is representative of the current savanna and wooded-

Table 18-1
List of living species found in Amboseli Park, Kenya.

≥15 kg

*Loxodonta africana (elephant)
*Diceros bicornis (rhinoceros)
*Hippopotamus amphibius (hippopotamus)
*Giraffa camelopardalis (giraffe)
*Taurotragus oryx (eland)
*Syncerus caffer (buffalo)
*Oryx gazella callotis (fringe-eared oryx)
*Equus burchelli (Burchell's zebra)
*Connochaetes taurinus albojubatus (white-bearded wildebeest)
*Alcelaphus buselaphus cokki (Coke's hartebeest or kongoni)
*Kobus ellipsiprymnus (waterbuck)
*Tragelaphus imberbis (lesser kudu)
*Aepyceros melampus (impala)
*Gazella granti (Grant's gazelle)
*Tragelephus scriptus (bushbuck)
Redunca redunca (Bohor's reedbuck)
*Litocranius walleri (gerenuk)
*Gazella thomsoni (Thomson's gazelle)
*Phacochoerus aethiopicus (warthog)
*Panthera leo (lion)
*Crocuta crocuta (spotted hyena)
*Hyaena hyaena (striped hyena)
*Panthera pardus (leopard)
*Acinonyx jubatus (cheetah)
*Felis caracal (caracal)
Orycteropus afer (aardvark)
*Papio cynocephalus (yellow baboon)
*Homo sapiens (man)
*Bos taurus (domestic cow)
*Equus asinus (donkey)
*Ovis aries (domestic sheep)
*Capra hircus (domestic goat)

<15 kg, ≥1 kg

Raphicerus campestris (steenbuck)
Rhynchotragus kirki (dik dik)
Felis serval (serval)
Proteles cristata (aardwolf)
Mellivora capensis (ratel)
*Canis adustus (golden jackal)
Canis mesomelas (black-backed jackal)
Viverra civetta (African civet)
Felis libyca (wild cat)
*Octocyon megalotis (bat-eared fox)
Genetta genetta (small-spotted genet)
*Atilax paludinosus (marsh mongoose)
Ichneumia albicauda (shite-tailed mongoose)
Helogale parvula (dwarf mongoose)
Ictonyx striatus (Zorilla)
*Cercopithecus aethiops (vervet)
*Galago senegalensis (bush baby)
*Hystrix cristata (porcupine)
*Pedetes capensis (spring hare)
*Lepus capensis (African hare)
*Canis familiaris (domestic dog)

*Skeletal remains found in the bone sample.

savanna ecosystems in East Africa. Many species respond to seasonal vegetation fluctuations by migration to and from the basin, a pattern of behavior that probably reflects long-term adaptation to East African climates. Pastoralists and their stock have probably been an integral part of the community for at least the past 2,000 years. Recent changes in the basin toward more arid conditions are due to climate, not to humans or other animals, and similar shifts have probably been common in the past (Western and van Praet, 1973; D. Western, pers. comm.).

Soils of the Amboseli Basin are generally alkaline and conducive to bone preservation, and bones occur in all stages of fossilization, unmineralized to completely mineralized. Fossil bones probably vary from Holocene to Pleistocene in age, but none have yet been dated.

SAMPLING GOALS AND METHODS

The sampling was designed to obtain a large number of identifiable bones from the major Amboseli habitats to compare presence and absence of species in the bone sample and in the living fauna, relative numbers of individuals in the bone sample and in the living community, distribution according to habitat of the bones and of the live populations, and skeletal-part representation in the bone assemblage and in whole skeletons. Differences between the composition of the living community and of the surface bone accumulation should indicate biases biases that might be expected in fossil bone assemblages derived from attritional situations similar to that in Amboseli.

Six major habitats (swamp, open woodland, closed woodland, bush, plains, and dry lakebed) were selected for the sampling program, which was done primarily between September and November 1975. Observers recorded all bones seen along ninety-two straight-line transects covering about 9 km^2 (1.5 percent of the total study area of 600 km^2). Transects were distributed equally among the six habitats and spaced between 0.5 and 1.0 km apart. Width was varied from 30 to 100 m according to bone visibility. Densely vegetated transects were covered on foot; otherwise, the search was carried out by vehicle. Subsamples along transects in each habitat were searched intensively to assess observer bias against small bones. Data recorded for each bone or carcass included taxon, relative age at death, skeletal part(s), weathering, damage, degree of burial, and state of articulation. The minimum numbers of individuals represented on each transect were determined in the field using all of the above categories of information. The bones were left on the transects unless they could not be identified in the field. The total sample consisted of over 20,000 bones representing more than 1,500 individuals. These represent attritional mortality over a period of 8 to 15 years maximum; most bones are destroyed by surface processes or buried within this period of time (Behrensmeyer, 1978). Sampling methods are described in more detail in Behrensmeyer and Dechant Boaz (1980).

REPRESENTATION OF COMMUNITY STRUCTURE IN THE BONE SAMPLE

NUMBERS OF MAMMAL SPECIES

Modern communities can be characterized by the kinds of animal species present and by the relative abundance of these species (Rickleffs, 1973). Paleontologists and paleoecologists have come to rely heavily on species presence or absence in reconstructing paleocommunities and in assessing time-dependent similarities used for biostratigraphic correlation. Paleoecological interpretations based on relative abundances of species in a fossil fauna have also been

Table 18-2
Large-herbivore populations (average numbers of individuals, N) in the Amboseli Basin, expected numbers of carcasses produced annually (E), and body weights (W) compared with numbers of skeletons (S) in the bone sample and the numbers of skeletons (S') corrected for observer bias against small bones. Data on recent mammals from Western, 1980.

	W (kg)	N	E	S	S'
Rhino (RH)	816	40	12	29	31
Giraffe (GF)	750	115	18	39	39
Buffalo (BF)	450	457	78	49	53
Zebra (ZB)	200	2,200	484	243	315
Wildebeest (WB)	165	2,473	618	326	452
Grant's Gazelle (GG)	40	1,230	467	82	117
Impala (IM)	40	700	252	31	44
Thomson's Gazelle (TG)	15	788	465	34	72
TOTAL		8,003	2,394	833	1,123

surface bone sample unless taphonomic biases are operating on the bones. Each herbivore species has a predictable number of deaths each year depending on population size, turn-over rate (which is a function of body size, Fenchel, 1974; Western, 1980), and whether the population is stable, increasing, or decreasing. Thus, the most theoretically valid comparison is between the expected number of carcasses and the bone sample, as shown in Figure 18-3. Small species produce relatively more carcasses per year than large species, but these are under-represented in the bone sample, even for small species with large populations. This indicates a size-related taphonomic bias that alters the bone record of species abundance from that of the living community.

Size biasing in the Amboseli sample may be due to rapid burial of small carcasses, or vulnerability of small carcasses to destruction by physical and/or biological processes prior to burial. Observer bias against small bones was calibrated by intensive searching of sub-samples of the transects. Correction factors for each species in each habitat were calculated and applied to data from the overall transect counts. The results shown in Figure 18-3 are calculated using the corrected data (see also Behrensmeyer et al., 1979).

The effect of rapid burial of small bones and carcasses can be tested using the data on partly buried remains recorded in the overall surface sample. Approximately 5 percent of all bones seen on the sampling transects were more than 50 percent buried in the soil surface. Most of these were small, compact bones such as phalanges and podials, or flat elements such as half-mandibles. These skeletal parts were commonly buried for both large and small species. Remains of the ten major herbivores weighing 15 to 2,800 kg showed no consistent pattern of increased burial with decreased body size ($r = 0.81$, $p \quad 0.01$). Sieving of 1 by 1 m plots to a depth of 5 to 10 cm showed that small, compact bones, such as podials, are commonly buried for animals of all sizes whereas larger bones remain on the surface. I assumed there would be a tendency for small species to undergo more rapid burial than large species, but it appears that this is not a strong pattern within the specified body-weight range in Amboseli.

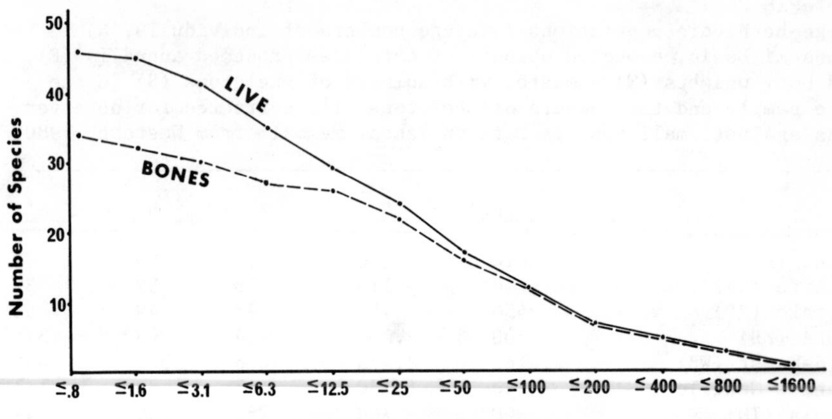

Figure 18-2
Plot of number of wild species 1 kg body weight versus cumulative weight categories (log scale). For species 100 kg, the number of species represented in the surface bone sample is less than the actual number of species in the living community.

attempted, but reliability is usually limited by collecting biases that may artificially inflate the numbers of individuals of certai species in fossil collections.

How well are the living species of the Amboseli mammal commun represented in the surface bone assemblage? Of the fifty-three sp cies greater than 1 kg body weight that have been recorded in the basin over the last decade, thirty-eight (72 percent) are recogni in the sample of skeletal remains (Table 18-1). All species great than 100 kg body weight are represented, but this is not the case smaller animals, as shown in Figure 18-2. The sample of 20,000 b is one or two orders of magnitude larger than most fossil samples 72 percent representation of the living fauna is the maximum that could be expected for an attritional bone assemblage derived from wide variety of habitats over a restricted time period. Of the 2 percent that are missing in the bone sample, most are small carni that are small in size and also relatively low in population numb

Attritional samples consisting of a few hundred to several sand identifiable remains thus can be expected to represent only most common largest species and might include only 50 to 75 perc of the species in the paleocommunity. Faunas collected from lar areas of sedimentary deposits representing longer periods of tim than the Amboseli surface assemblage might record more members c paleocommunity, but such collections also run the risk of sampli contiguous or time-successive communities.

RELATIVE ABUNDANCES

Relative abundances of eight major herbivore species in th living community and in the bone sample compare as shown in Tab and Figure 18-3. The number of carcasses produced by each spe should be proportional to the number of carcasses recorded in

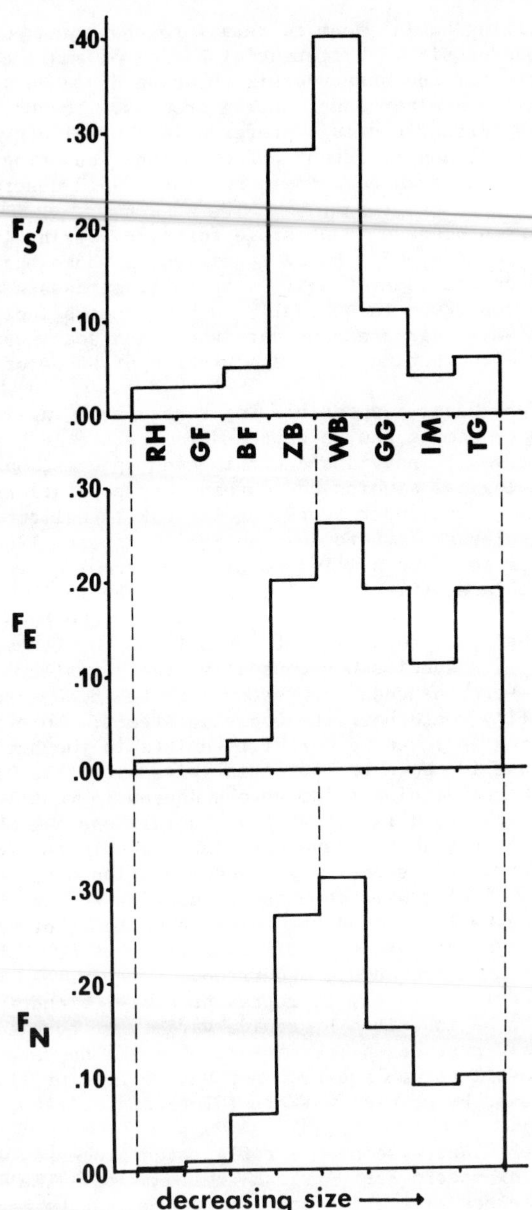

Figure 18-3
Histogram comparing the herbivore population structure in terms of relative numbers of individuals in the living community of the central basin (F_N), in the expected carcass assemblage (F_E), and in the surface bone sample ($F_{S'}$). Abbreviations for taxa: ZB = zebra, WB = wildebeest, TG = Thomson's gazelle, GG = Grant's gazelle, IM = impala, BF = buffalo, GF = giraffe, RH = rhino. (See Table 18-1 for Latin names.) Species arranged largest to smallest from left to right on the lower scales.

Factors controlling burial seem to relate to shape and compactness of bones regardless of size. Differential burial of small carcasses thus does not account for the observed size-biasing depicted in Figure 18-3, although it may be a minor contributing process. It should be noted that this needs further testing; preferential burial of small animals would have a direct and important effect on the resulting fossil assemblage and might even compensate for more rapid destruction prior to burial.

The primary processes responsible for size-biasing in the Amboseli surface carcass sample can be specified as those that either destroy or reduce the identifiability of small carcasses relative to large ones. As observed in Amboseli, such processes include initial destruction of small carcasses by carnivores and scavengers, and rapid rates of surface weathering and fragmentation of bones of small species.

The same processes responsible for size-biasing against small species in a bone sample can be expected to operate in biasing such samples against small individuals within each species, particularly juveniles. Ecological studies on contemporary populations indicate that young animals are under-represented in skull collections due to their greater vulnerability to destruction (Caughley, 1966). Paleontologists have also drawn similar conclusions from age representation in fossil assemblages (Clark et al., 1967; Olson, 1957). In discussing the respresentation of species abundance in the bone sample, I have assumed that the proportion of juveniles dying is comparable in each species. If a species has unusually high juvenile mortality, it would, therefore, be under-represented in the bone assemblage. Low juvenile mortality would have the opposite effect. No evidence of unusual variation in juvenile mortality exists in the herbivore species studied in Amboseli. However, potential biases of this kind should be kept in mind when examining relative abundances in fossil assemblages.

The size bias found in Amboseli preburial bone assemblage results from processes that probably have been important in the formation of many fossil vertebrate assemblages. Documentation of a consistent pattern of size-biasing will come as no surprise to vertebrate paleontologists, who have long noted the relative scarcity of small species in many assemblages of larger fossil land vertebrates. The cause of biasing has not been thoroughly understood, however, and the Amboseli study shows that it is likely to represent early, preburial taphonomic biasing that can be inherited by a wide variety of bone concentrations derived from land surfaces. The absence of small bones and small species in a fossil assemblage need not be due to fluvial sorting as has been suggested by several workers (Clark and Keitzke, 1967; Voorhies, 1969).

The Amboseli bone assemblages reflect the processes in one ecosystem typical of modern East African environments. The extent to which such processes alter the faunal evidence in bone assemblages of other ecosystems and regions is not yet known, and processes not observed in Amboseli may also be important in such biasing. However, because small bones simply have less strength to withstand surface processes of the kind observed in Amboseli, it seems reasonable to anticipate that some form of size-biasing will be commonly represented in vertebrate death assemblages. The pattern of this bias can be expected to vary with the relative importance of the various physical and biological processes and with the relative abundance of different body sizes in any given community.

BONE OCCURRENCES IN RELATION TO HABITAT

In Amboseli, distinct differences occur among faunas in bone assemblages from different habitats. These appear to relate not only to habitat preferences but also to diurnal and seasonal shifts in habitat combined with differential times and places of death. The resulting distribution of carcasses thus contains ecological information, but the picture is more complex than a simple correspondence between preferred habitat and place of death and burial.

Four examples comparing the distributions of live animals and carcasses have been selected for discussion (Figure 18-4). The species that are most restricted to a particular habitat in life show the closest correspondence between carcass and live distributions (buffalo, $r = 0.96$; impala, $r = 0.99$; $p \quad 0.001$). In contrast, the most cosmopolitan species, which are also most abundant in this community, show a poor correspondence (wildebeest, $r = 0.17$; zebra, $r = 0.49$; $p \quad 0.1$).

Buffalo and impala are among the few large species in the Amboseli community that do not follow distinct patterns of seasonal movement (Western, 1973). Most herbivores concentrate in the basin during the dry seasons (June to October, December to March) and disperse away from it during the wet seasons. This serves to preserve forage proximal to the permanent sources of water in the basin for times when herbivores are under the greatest environmental stress from drought. Within the basin, the six major habitats are used more or less sequentially by herbivores in the course of a dry season. The grazing herds move from bush to plains to woodlands to swamps, but species vary in habitat preference and utilization (Western, 1973, pers. comm.).

Large herds of zebra and wildebeest are concentrated in the swamps at the height of the dry season. Mortality due to poor condition is relatively high at this time. The swamps also provide cover for predators, which are able to kill successfully at a relatively high rate. Both factors tend to concentrate the average yearly mortality of zebra and wildebeest in a few months out of the year, in the swamp habitat. In addition to their seasonal movements, these species exhibit strong diurnal patterns of habitat change: from swamps to woodlands during the day to open plains at night. Night use of open habitats appears to reflect two adaptive strategies: water conservation and predator avoidance. In spite of this, night mortality of zebra and wildebeest is fairly high because their predators are most active at night.

Most of the patterns of habitat utilization can be directly related to the degree of water dependence of the herbivore species and reflect basic physiological adaptations to the environment. Zebra, wildebeest, elephant, and buffalo are dependent on drinking water whereas species such as oryx and Grant's gazelle are not. The latter are thus freed from the need for seasonal movements in relation to water. Water dependency has an obvious, strong potential effect on carcass distribution and ultimately on the fossil record. The more water dependent the species, the more likely it is to concentrate and die in areas subject to deposition (that is, near water). Although they may use the same habitats and be members of the same community, less water-dependent species are not as likely to be preserved in depositional areas and will be less frequent in the fossil record. The possible importance of this factor in taphonomic biasing has been noted previously by Clark and Ketizke (1967)

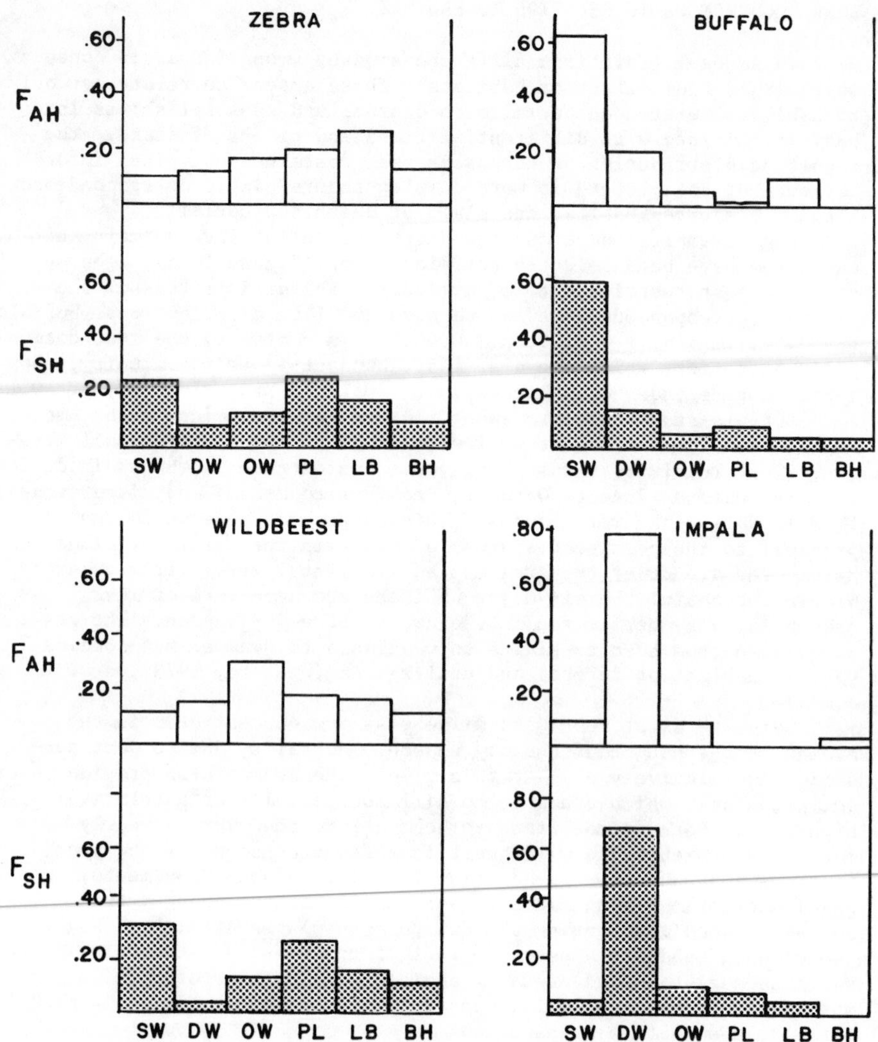

Figure 18-4
Comparisons between the distribution of expected and observed carcass frequencies (F_{SH}) across six major habitats in the central Amboseli Basin. Expected carcass frequences (F_{EH}) are based on distribution data for living animals (1968–1971, 1973–1975) and annual turn-over rates. F_{SH} is based on the minimum number of carcasses in the surface bone sample: WB, 452; ZB, 315; BF, 53; IM, 44. Habitat abbreviations: SW = swamp, DW = dense woodland, OW = open woodland, PL = plains, LB = lakebed, BH = bush. Original numerical data are given in Behrensmeyer and Dechant Boaz, 1980.

and Voorhies (1969), among others.

The Amboseli bone assemblage demonstrates how distributional patterns in the live community are represented in the potential fossil assemblage. However, it is important to note that the pattern of relative abundances of live animals in the various habitats was established on daytime, bimonthly counts (Western, 1973, pers. comm.). The close similarity of life and death distributions of impala and buffalo (Figure 18-5) is consistent with their known habits and implies that nocturnal movements may not leave a significant record of mortality outside the daytime-preferred habitats. The lack of correspondence between live and carcass data for zebra and wildebeest seems to reflect their broad use of habitats throughout the year, relatively high mortality in the swamps at the peak of the dry season, and night use of the plains habitat.

The effect of water dependency on species abundance in the bone assemblage can be measured for zebra and wildebeest. These two species make up 56 percent of the large-herbivore community. Their carcasses make up 64 percent of the total large-herbivore assemblage. In the swamp habitat, where bones are most likely to be preserved as fossils, zebra and wildebeest carcasses are 69 percent of the bone sample. These data show at least a 13 percent difference in the relative abundance of preserved carcasses in a depositional area compared with the average in the living community. The reasons for this difference include several taphonomic factors, but a primary one is the complexity of behavioral and physiological adaptations of the living animals in space and time. Paleoecologists should be aware of the potential bias of relative abundance data in this respect.

An additional complicating factor affecting the distribution of carcasses in relation to habitat is transport by scavengers. Observations in Amboseli indicate little movement of whole carcasses from one habitat to another due to such agents. However, hyenas and jackals are known to carry off parts of carcasses such as limb elements (Kruuk, 1972). This effect may be more or less random with respect to habitat, but the bone scavenging habits of various carnivores are poorly understood and in need of study.

Vertebrate adaptations important to determining occurrences of bones in relation to preservable environments, that is, water dependency and habitat specificity, are difficult to interpret from morphological characteristics of skeletons. Zebra may be grazers, but they spend some of their time in wooded areas in search of shade; their dental morphology may tell us much about what they eat, but not where they eat it. Nothing particularly obvious about the bones of buffalo or impala indicates that these species are habitat-specific; nothing about the morphology of zebra and wildebeest reflects their seasonal migrations. Thus, for paleoecological information relating to habitat utilization (at least among the larger plantigrade mammals), it will be necessary to rely heavily on faunal abundances in differing, contemporaneous paleoenvironments while keeping in mind potential biasing processes. Bone distributions in Amboseli show that such ecological information *can* be preserved in nontransported bone assemblages.

The bone assemblage in Amboseli represents attritional accumulation over 8 to 15 years, based on data from known age-of-death carcasses and rates of weathering (Behrensmeyer, 1978). During this period (about 1960 to 1976), the basin underwent changes in local climate and water availability that significantly altered the distribution of habitats (Western and von Praet, 1973). Large areas that formerly were covered with woodland are now plains, and particularly dry years in 1973-1976 helped to promote considerable eolian deflation

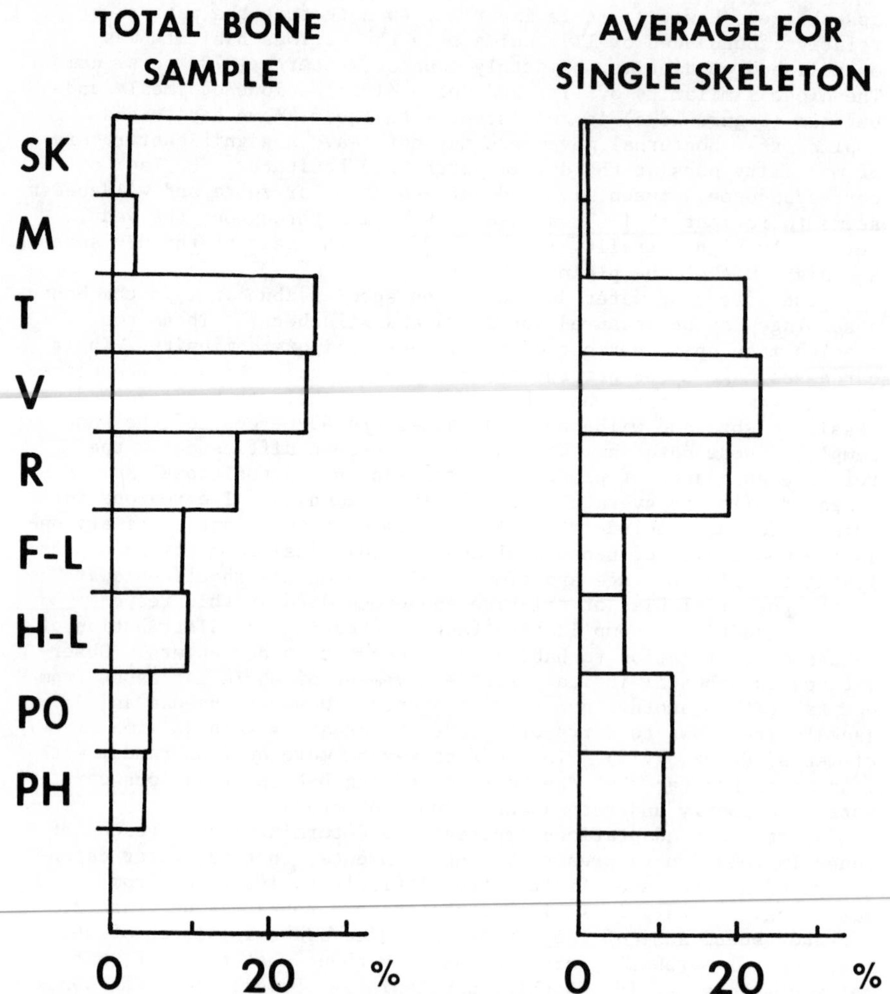

Figure 18-5
Comparison of the relative frequencies of skeletal parts in the total Amboseli surface bone assemblage (over 20,000 identifiable parts) with the frequencies of these parts in a single skeleton averaged for the two most common animals, zebra and wildebeest. Abbreviations: SK = skull, M = half-mandible, T = teeth (total of those *in situ* in the skull or mandible plus those found isolated), V = vertebrae, R = ribs, F-L = forelimb (scapula+humerus+radius/ulna), H-L = hindlimb (pelvis+femur+tibia), PO = podials, PH = phalanges.

of heavily grazed areas. Habitat boundary shifts occurred, and bones that accumulated in woodland habitats are mixed with bones from the plains habitat that now occupies the same locale. Herbivore utilization of the various habitats also changed during this period to decreased use of bush and lakebed and increased use of swamp. The speed of ecological change might be accelerated by humans and their livestock, but Western (1973; Western and van Praet, 1973) found that the causes relate to climatic and groundwater cycles that have probably been a basic component of the Amboseli system throughout the Pleistocene. Short-term ecological change may be the norm rather than the exception in many ecosystems past and present.

An attritional bone assemblage such as that in Amboseli will inevitably combine the effects of short-term change, resulting in a time-averaged sample of the vertebrate community. Thus the level of resolution in reconstructing paleoecology must be limited to what can be said based on such time-averaged faunas. Comparisons of attritional samples averaged over comparable time periods may reflect more fundamental ecological characteristics than instantaneous samples and thereby provide a firm basis for establishing differences between faunas from different environments and for determining long-term trends in community evolution. However, one important consequence of time averaging is that the faunal assemblage may include more species than ever coexisted at the same time in the same place. Differences of species richness in fossil assemblages may mean no more than that they represent different periods of time-averaging.

SKELETAL PARTS AND TAPHONOMIC PROCESSES

A natural bone assemblage, fossil or recent, seldom includes all the elements present in a complete skeleton. Changes in the frequencies of different skeletal parts in a bone assemblage may often be related to specific taphonomic processes; thus, the skeletal-part composition of the assemblage can serve as prime evidence for its taphonomic history. Sorting by moving water tends to remove light and round elements, such as vertebrae, from heavier elements, such as teeth (Voorhies, 1969; Behrensmeyer, 1975; Hanson, 1980). Carnivores tend to sonsume or transport some parts of their prey, such as tails, feet, and limbs, in preference to others (Hill, 1975; pers. observ.). There have been enough studies and observations made in modern situations to show that skeletal-part frequencies are important, but at present there is still too little data to show how these are consistently related to particular processes.

Relative numbers of skeletal parts of mammals in the Amboseli surface assemblage result from a number of processes that could be expected to affect any attritional bone accumulation. These include carnivore activity, trampling, and weathering. Because fluvial processes are missing from this system, it can serve as a comparative model for presumed nontransported fossil assemblages.

The overall surface assemblage in Amboseli exhibits skeletal-part frequencies generally similar to those of an average, whole, mammal skeleton (Figure 18-5). Ribs, podials, and phalanges are relatively scarce in the bone assemblage, and forelimb and hindlimb elements are relatively common. The ratio of teeth to vertebrae, elements of different density and durability, is somewhat higher in the bone assemblage; it is about 0.83 for an average whole herbivore skeleton and ranges between 0.96 and 1.44, averaging 1.05, in the six Amboseli habitats.

In Amboseli, predators and scavengers play a major role in disarticulation and scatter of carcasses and destruction of bones (Behrensmeyer and Dechant Boaz, 1980). Selective consumption of ribs and foot parts by carnivores is probably an important factor in their low abundance in the Amboseli assemblage. However, the effect on the overall surface assemblage is not great (Figure 18-5), and is notably less than in areas such as Ngorongoro Crater, Tanzania, where predator/prey ratios are high and bones are in demand as food titems (Kruuk, 1972). There are fewer carnivores, particularly hyenas, in the Amboseli ecosystem than at Ngorongoro, but more important may be the seasonally concentrated periods of death. When carcass density is high, predators and scavengers consume fewer bones and generally do less damage to them than when carcass density is low. The occurrence of articulated or associated skeletons or unbroken limb parts and ribs in a fossil assemblage can be taken as indicating low predator or scavenger pressure, at least in a localized or time-specific sense.

Although carnivore effects on the Amboseli assemblage are slight, consistent patterns of damage to bones can serve as indications that this process is part of the taphonomic history. Dorsal borders of innominates, olecrenon processes of ulnae, ventral and dorsal rib ends, premaxillae and nasals, and vertebral processes are almost invariably chewed and punctured. Mandibles are often broken on the left or right side just posterior to the symphysis, and mandibular angles are chewed showing that carnivores grabbed the angle in an attempt to break the jaw to get at the tongue. In general, it seems inevitable that an attritional bone assemblage will bear some evidence of carnivore or scavenger activity. The relative degree of damage and skeletal-part removal should serve as an indication of the balance of carcass supply and demand in the original community.

Other than carnivore activity, the most important processes affecting the Amboseli bones are weathering and trampling. These do not seem to greatly affect skeletal-part frequencies (unless they are cancelling out carnivore effects, which is unlikely), but instead alter bone surface texture and completeness.

Bone weathering on the surface varies according to microhabitat; critical factors include fluctuations in temperature and moisture (Behrensmeyer, 1978). Bones in moist or shaded places may stay uncracked for years while exposed parts of the same skeleton go through progressive weathering stages and usually disintegrate entirely in 8 to 15 years. Weathering is inhibited by burial in Amboseli, and burial to a large extent is caused by trampling, especially during periods when the ground is wet. In most cases, lower sides of bones are less weathered than upper, but kicking and trampling also has the effect of turning bones over periodically, so they weather evenly on both sides. Bones are commonly broken by trampling, and the more weathered the bone, the more likely it is to shatter under foot rather than sink into the ground. Trampled bones are often oriented nearly vertically in the surface sediment. Compact bones, such as podials, seem to have relatively higher rates of burial and lower rates of weathering than skulls, pelves, and vertebrae. Bones of small animals are more easily destroyed by trampling and are subject to more rapid weathering than bones of large animals.

Several workers (Toots, 1965; Clark and Keitzke, 1967; Voorhies, 1969, Behrensmeyer, 1978) have commented on differences in weathering rates between bones and teeth. Weathering of teeth depends on their microenvironment in Amboseli; those in up-turned skulls are often severely cracked whereas those in the skull's associated half-mandible, lying flat on the soil, are only slightly cracked. However, severely weathered skulls occasionally have teeth in perfect condition (Figure 18-6) and it appears that the state of tooth wear and the

Figure 18-6
Weathered cow skull and mandibles associated with carnivore feces that contain bones of micromammals; one of a number of such occurrences in Amboseli. Note that the bone is highly weathered (Stage 4-5, Behrensmeyer, 1978), but the teeth are in excellent condition. This is unusual in the Amboseli bone assemblage.

strength of the enamel relative to the more porous dentine may be as important as microenvironment in determining characteristics of tooth weathering (also suggested by Clark and Keitzke, 1967). Most teeth redorded in Amboseli were still associated with skulls or mandibles; isolated teeth were rare and in most cases badly damaged unless partly buried. Processes that would separate teeth from bones, other than trampling or extreme differential weathering, do not seem to occur in a surface environment such as Amboseli's.

In summary, using Amboseli as an actualistic model, an attritional, nontransported surface bone assemblage should include the following characteristics:

1. Skeletal-part frequencies generally comparable to those in complete skeletons.
2. Carnivore damage to particular bones and parts of bones and low frequencies of ribs, foot elements, and caudal vertebrae.
3. A range of weathering textures from fresh to severely weathered, but the greater proportion falling in the less-weathered categories.
4. Evidence of fragmentation due to trampling, possible vertical orientations of flat or elongated pieces.
5. Variation in degree of tooth weathering relative to associated bone, occurrences of isolated teeth uncommon.

The subsequent effects of transport, burial, fossilization, exposure of the fossils, and collecting may further alter the characteristics of the ultimate sample, but these should be superimposed on the original characteristics of the surface assemblage. Even in climatic situations and time periods remote from those of Amboseli, it seems reasonable to expect that similar processes, differing more in degree than in kind, have been important in the formation of attritional bone assemblages.

COMPARISON WITH THE FOSSIL RECORD

Implications of the Amboseli bone study for the interpretation of fossil assemblages can be demonstrated by comparing it with a fossil assemblage that is thought to be nontransported, attritional sample of the original community. The classic study of the paleoecology of the Scenic Member, Oligocene Brule Formation, Big Badlands, South Dakota (Clark et al., 1967) is an obvious choice. Many of the original ideas and questions behind the Amboseli study were engendered by this work.

Comparisons with Amboseli can be conveniently related to the groups of taphonomic factors given by Clark and Keitzke (1967:115). Those groups relevant to the Amboseli assemblage are: biotic, thanatic, perthotaxic, and taphic factors. The authors used these groupings to organize processes they felt were important in causing the observed characteristics of mammalian fossil assemblages from three distinct environments: open plains, swampy plains, and near stream. The overall depositional system is fluvial, and the taphonomic history of the assemblages is interpreted as attritional accumulation of bones combined with periodic rapid burial by flood-transported mud slurries (Clark and Keitzke, 1967:97). The flat, extensive, open-plains and swampy-plains environments, as reconstructed by Clark (1967), are topographically similar to the central Amboseli Basin. Comparisons with the Scenic Member will be restricted to these two environments.

BIOTIC AND THANATIC FACTORS: relating to the life habits of the species and the cause and place of death

Clark and Keitzke (1967:118) proposed that bone-bearing horizons represent geologically instantaneous periods between 10 and 100 years. From Amboseli, we know that such time periods could include several major shifts in vegetation, resulting in a time-averaged sample of bones from different habitats. Perhaps Oligocene environments were less subject to short-term ecological change, but this cannot be assumed without supporting evidence. Thus we must consider the possibility that the faunas are averaged from different habitats even though their remains may not have been transported from the place of death.

Somewhat greater average abundance of *Mesohippus* in swampy plains compared with greater average abundance of *Merycoidodon* in open plains led Clark and Keitzke to conclude that some degree of ecological separation existed between these two herbivore taxa. They mentioned the potential importance of seasonal migration and water dependency (Clark and Keitzke, 1967:115), and based on the example of Amboseli, such factors could have influenced the distribution of carcasses of *Mesohippus* and *Merycoidodon* if one (*Mesohippus*) was more concentrated in swampy areas during periods of high mortality. Based on current knowledge of herbivores and their habits in modern ecosystems and of average distribution differences between live populations and carcasses in Amboseli, it seems at least as reasonable to interpret the partial separation of *Mesohippus* and *Merycoidodon* fossils in terms of such biotic and thanatic factors as to attribute it to permanent spatial separation of living populations in two different habitats.

The most abundant Oligocene species found in the Scenic Member are less than 35 kg body weight (Clark and Keitzke, 1967:135) in striking contrast to the Amboseli community where only one of the major herbivores is less than 35 kg. This suggests a major difference in the Oligocene community structure: small herbivores dominant. To conclude this important fact, however, we must first consider all taphonomic processes that could bias a bone assemblage in favor of species under 35 kg. Biotic and thanatic factors could include a combination of high turn-over rates for small species and seasonal deaths resulting in a greater number of carcasses than local scavengers could deal with. Large species have slower turn-over rates and may have avoided such localized mortality by migration away from the area. Perthotaxic factors, relating to the period between death and burial, might also be important and will be discussed below.

There are several occurrences of mass-death groups of fossil *Hypertragulus* (a small artiodactyl); in some cases, all individuals are of similar age. Clark and Keitzke (1967:116, 127-128) attributed this puzzling phenomenon to disease. Although the Amboseli study is not specifically relevant to this problem, some recent behavioral studies of the hyrax in East Africa suggest another explanation. Rock hyraxes, and other animals that are poor thermoregulators or that simply wish to conserve body heat at night, sleep in large groups (Reader and Croze, 1977; S. Cobb, pers. comm.). In such situations, groups could be buried by sudden floods or killed by sharply falling temperatures.

PERTHOTAXIC FACTORS: relating to processes affecting skeletal remains after death and prior to burial

The importance of large carnivores and scavengers as biasing agents in the Scenic Member bone assemblage was minimized by Clark and Keitzke (1967:117), in part because they observed mainly teeth and cranial parts and also because they recorded few instances of obvious preburial chewing or fracturing of postcranial bones. However, a number of carnivores occur in the fauna, including *Hyenodon*, that are similar in bone-crushing ability to the present East African hyena. These carnivores would at least have been capable of leaving punctures or grooves on bones or evidence of chewing on rib ends. The Amboseli model shows that this factor may have been underrated even taking into account possible differences in carnivore and scavenger adaptations in the Oligocene. Evidence is needed from skeletal-part representation and bone damage to test possible carnivore effects on the fossil assemblages.

Clark and Keitzke (1967:117) felt that the effects of weathering should bias their samples in favor of small animals, which seems contrary to the effects of weathering observed in Amboseli. They based their conclusion primarily on the abundance of teeth and jaws of animals smaller than 35 kg, which is below the size range of most of the Amboseli species in the recent bone sample. It is possible that jaws and teeth of these small animals were more resistant to weathering on Oligocene land surfaces. But juvenile remains of any size were rare, so it is necessary to postulate that juvenile teeth and bones did not survive weathering even though adult remains of comparable size did. It seems reasonable to assume that weathering processes should affect small bones (with higher ratios of surface area to volume) more than large bones. Therefore, weathering alone does not provide a satisfactory explanation for the relative bias toward small bones in the Oligocene assemblages.

Bioturbation was probably an important destructive process on Oligocene land surfaces. Clark and Keitzke (1967:117) mentioned that bones might occasionally have been stepped on, but they felt this would be a random, hence nonbiasing, process. They gave an example of a weathered *Archaeotherium* skull (Clark, 1967:101) with bone pieces around and below it that is closely comparable to kicked and stumbled-over skulls in Amboseli. If bioturbation occurred on Scenic Member land surfaces at the same intensity as in Amboseli, it should have caused some biasing against small bones and small taxa. However, this process apparently did not eliminate many of the remains of the small species, judging from their high relative abundances as reported by Clark and Keitzke (1967:135).

Perthotaxic (preburial) factors similar to those in Amboseli cannot explain the observed abundance of small animals in the Oligocene fossil assemblages. Either different postdeath processes were acting to bias assemblages, or biotic and thanatic factors were the cause of observed differences from Amboseli. If we accept the hypothesis that carnivore activity, weathering, and bioturbation did affect bones on the Oligocene land surfaces and tended to preferentially destroy remains of small animals and juveniles, then we must postulate that even stronger processes were operating to favor preservation of large numbers of small bones and teeth in the buried assemblages. Such processes are more likely to involve burial potential (to be discussed further below) than known preburial factors. Large populations and continual high turnover rates would produce a large number of carcasses through time, and it is possible that the rate of herbivore production in the Oligocene ecosystems exceeded the ability of the vertebrate carnivores and scavengers to significantly bias the bone assemblage.

As a final note on perthotaxic processes, Clark and Keitzke (1967: 117) report the presence of carnivore coprolites associated with some of the Oligocene herbivore skulls. This is directly analogous to such associations observed in Amboseli (Figure 18-6). The use of such objects by carnivores as "marking posts" seems to be long enduring.

TAPHIC FACTORS: relating to processes of burial

Because large bones in the Scenic Member assemblages did not show differential weathering of their upper parts that would indicate partial burial, Clark and Keitzke (1967:118, 97) argued that they were buried by single inundations of sediment up to 46 cm thick. However, large bones in Amboseli may show no differential weathering of upper and lower surfaces if they have been well covered by vegetation or if they have been repeatedly turned over by trampling. Lack of differential weathering does not necessarily imply rapid burial.

Bioturbation may have had an important effect on burial of Scenic Member bones and teeth. Clark and Keitzke (1967:67) regarded flooding and mudflow deposition as the major burial processes and noted that these must have been too gentle to remove small bones. Trampling provides a mechanism for preferentially burying small skeletal remains, and although this is not yet demonstrated as an important biasing process for the Amboseli herbivores, it deserves consideration for the Oligocene faunas in which many species were small. From Clark's description of the fossil-rich "heterogeneous mudstones" (Clark, 1967: 77), it seems likely that bioturbation (trampling) contributed to the heterogeneous sediment textures and compositions. Even gentle flows during floods should have been competent enough to winnow out transportable elements in the surface bone assemblages, particularly the vertebrae (Voorhies, 1969; Hanson, 1980). The flood hypothesis could be tested by sampling ratios of teeth to vertebrae in the original deposits; a high number of teeth relative to vertebrae would support burial by flooding.

The importance of trampling as burial process can be tested by documenting in excavations whether there is a characteristic size distribution in bones and teeth in the Oligocene assemblages, that is, whether large animals are usually represented only by body parts comparable in size to jaws and other bones of small animals. A strong size bias in bones buried by trampling has been demonstrated by Gifford and Behrensmeyer (1977). Damage and orientations characteristic of burial by trampling would provide additional evidence.

Bioturbation of a land surface occurs by trampling, but it can also include the activities of fossorial animals and plant roots. Little is known about the importance of underground death in small mammals inhabiting modern depositional environments. In areas repeatedly burrowed and reworked by burrowers, bones of animals that died underground (and some that died above ground) would be thoroughly mixed, but not necessarily destroyed. A few well-defined burrows might be preserved. This could be a contributing factor to preservation of small mammal remains in the Oligocene fossil assemblages.

If bioturbation did play a part in the formation of the Scenic

Member fossil assemblages, we have an additional process that could have contributed to a taphonomic bias for small mammals.

SUMMARY

Comparison of the Amboseli bone assemblage with fossil assemblages of the Oligocene demonstrates how taphonomic considerations can modify paleoecological hypotheses. If the resulting picture looks discouragingly complex, it is also probably more realistic. We must carefully reanalyze the Scenic Member bone assemblages in terms of their taphonomic histories. Until this is done, we cannot adequately judge the paleoecological significance of the relative abundance data for Oligocene mammals although the large number of remains of small species probably indicates a true difference in the original body-size distribution of the Scenic Member community compared with that in Amboseli. Ways to test the probabilities of the hypotheses concerning size-biasing processes have been suggested in appropriate sections above, but much room remains for further development of ideas and models.

Clark, Beerbower, and Keitzke foresaw that information from modern ecosystems would be of crucial importance to their conclusions. It is to their credit that their data and interpretations are so clearly presented that new information can be easily applied to their evidence.

If it were possible to justify using Clark and Keitzke's relative abundance data as a measure of population sizes for herbivores in original communities, there would be some tantalizing comparisons to be made with modern East African communities. In the combined sample from the Scenic Member open-plains habitat, there are two dominant taxa: a lagomorph and an artiodactyl (55 percent of the total). For the swampy-plains fauna, there are also two dominant taxa: a perissodactyl and an artiodactyl (54 percent of the total). The near-stream fauna also show this pattern; the same two taxa total 52 percent (Clark and Keitzke, 1967:135). In Amboseli, the herbivore fauna is dominated by a perissodactyl and an artiodactyl that make up 58 percent of the living community and 64 percent of the carcasses in the surface bone assemblage. It is tempting to suggest that we may be seeing a basic characteristic of land-mammal communities in this pattern of two-species dominance. There is little doubt that comparing modern and fossil faunas at such levels of resolution will be extremely rewarding once we are able to sort out true paleoecological information from taphonomic biases.

CONCLUSION

The Amboseli bone study sampled one vertebrate community at a single point in time. Other studies of this kind are needed to build a set of comparative references for the past. These could be used as analogues to demonstrate the effects of taphonomic processes both similar to and different from those operating today.

The Amboseli surface assemblage represents what might be preserved if a floodplain or other dry land surface were rapidly aggraded without transport of the bones, or what might be swept off such land surfaces into channels by overbank flow. It is important to note that the Amboseli sample does *not* represent the assemblage that would be preserved if bioturbation of the land surface was the major bone burial process. What presently lies beneath the surface in Amboseli probably differs in significant and recognizable ways from the surface assemblage. In contrast to the surface assemblage, that of the subsurface should include a bias toward small and compact bones and may be a better analogue for some autochthonous fossil assemblages than the surface assemblage. The method of burial is of prime importance; sedimentation that buried a land surface will produce a different type of assemblage than bioturbation. Both probably have been important, in varying degrees, in many autochthonous fossil assemblages.

The Amboseli study demonstrates the potential importance of the following specific considerations in interpreting past ecology:

1. Many taphonomical processes are related to body size, and consistent patterns of size-biasing can be expected in attritional assemblages affected by carnivore activity, weathering, and trampling. These processes tend to selectively destroy bones of small species. Because taphonomic processes are commonly related to body size, it follows that the most bias-free paleoecological comparisons (for example, of relative abundance) can be made between taxa of similar body size.
2. Attritional bone assemblages can be time-averaged over periods that may incorporate short-term fluctuations in vegetation, habitats, and faunas. Differences between time-averaged faunas will, therefore, represent the average ecological differences between the communities rather than distinctions that existed on any single time plane. A corollary to this is that time-averaged fossil assemblages may contain more species than actually coexisted in the original community.
3. Differential representation of skeletal parts, bone damage, and bone surface textures are important indicators of taphonomic history. Some sorting of *surface* bone assemblages can occur without transport by currents, leading to decreased numbers of small or delicate bones due to various destructive processes. However, these surface processes seem to have little initial effect on relative numbers of skeletal parts such as teeth and vertebrae in mammals larger than about 15 kg.
4. Trampling is likely to be an important process of bone destruction and burial in attritional bone accumulations on open-land surfaces.

Comparisons of information derived from the Amboseli bone assemblage with paleoecological interpretations based on Oligocene fossil assemblages show that progress has been made in understanding the complexity of taphonomic processes. Understanding of potential taphonomic biases is leading toward new approaches to sampling and testing of hypotheses that should result in better-supported interpretations in future studies of vertebrate paleoecology.

ACKNOWLEDGMENTS

Dorothy Dechant Boaz and David Western have contributed a great deal to the Amboseli research project, and I am grateful to them for their help and ideas. I take full responsibility, however, for opinions expressed here. I thank the government of Kenya for their cooperation in making the research in Amboseli Park possible. Steve Cobb provided useful enlightenment regarding the habits of hyraxes.

Funding for the Amboseli project was provided by the National Geographic Society (Grant 1508), and additional support came from the National Science Foundation (Grant GS 268607A-1).

REFERENCES

Behrensmeyer, A. K. 1975. The taphonomy and paleoecology of Plio-Pleistocene vertebrate assemblages east of Lake Rudolf, Kenya. *Mus. Comp. Zool. Bull.* 146:475-574.

Behrensmeyer, A. K. 1978. Taphonomic and ecologic information from bone weathering. *Paleobiology* 4:150-162.

Behrensmeyer, A. K., and D. E. Dechant Boaz. 1980. The recent bones of Amboseli Park, Kenya in relation to East African paleoecology. In A. K. Behrensmeyer and A. P. Hill, eds., *Fossils in the Making*. Chicago: The University of Chicago Press, 330 p.

Behrensmeyer, A. K., D. Western, and D. E. Dechant Boaz. 1979. New perspectives in vertebrate paleoecology from a recent bone assemblage. *Paleobiology* 5:12-21.

Brain, C. K. 1967. Hottentot food remains and their meaning in the interpretation of fossil bone assemblages. *Namib Desert Research Station Sci. Paper* 32:1-11.

Brain, C. K. 1980. Some criteria for the recognition of bone-collecting agencies in African caves. In A. K. Behrensmeyer and A. P. Hill, eds., *Fossils in the Making*. Chicago: The University of Chicago Press, 330 p.

Caughley, G. 1966. Mortality patterns in mammals. *Ecology* 47:906-918.

Clapham, W. B. 1973. *Natural Ecosystems*. New York: Macmillan, 248 p.

Clark, J. 1967. Paleogeography of the Scenic Member of the Brule Formation. In J. Clark, J. R. Beerbower, and K. K. Keitzke, eds., *Oligocene Sedimentation, Stratigraphy, Paleoecology and Paleoclimatology in the Big Badlands of South Dakota*. Fieldiana-Geology Mem. 5:75-110.

Clark, J., J. R. Beerbower, and K. K. Kietzke, eds. 1967. *Oligocene Sedimentation, Stratigraphy, Paleoecology and Paleoclimatology in the Big Badlands of South Dakota*. Fieldiana-Geology Mem. 5, 158 p.

Clark, J., and K. K. Keitzke. 1967. Paleoecology of the lower nodular zone, Brule Formation, in the Big Badlands of South Dakota. In J. Clark, J. R. Beerbower, and K. K. Keitzke, eds., *Oligocene Sedimentation, Stratigraphy, Paleoecology and Paleoclimatology in the Big Badlands of South Dakota*. Fieldiana-Geology Mem. 5:111-137.

Fenchel, T. 1974. Intrinsic rate of natural increase: the relationship with body size. *Oecologia (Berlin)* 14:317-326.

Gifford, D. P. 1977. *Observations of modern human settlements as an aid to archaeological interpretation*. Ph.D. dissertation, The University of California, Berkeley, 463 p.

Gifford, D. P., and A. K. Behrensmeyer. 1977. Observed formation and burial of a recent human occupation site in Kenya. *Quat. Res.* 8:245-266.

Hanson, C. B. 1980. Fluvial taphonomical processes: models and experiments. In A. K. Behrensmeyer and A. P. Hill, eds., *Fossils in the Making*. Chicago: The University of Chicago Press, 330 p.

Hay, R. L. 1976. *Geology of the Olduvai Gorge*. Berkeley: The University of California Press, 203 p.

Hill, A. P. 1975. *Taphonomy of Contemporary and Late Cenozoic East African Vertebrates*. Ph.D. dissertation, University of London, 331 p.

Kruuk, H. 1972. *The Spotted Hyena*. Chicago: The University of Chicago Press, 335 p.

Mellet, J. S. 1974. Scatological origin of microvertebrate fossil accumulations. *Science* 185:349-350.

Olson, E. C. 1952. The evolution of a Permian vertebrate chronofauna. *Evolution* 6:181-196.

Olson, E. C. 1957. Size-frequency distribution in samples of extinct organisms. *Jour. Geology* 65:309-333.

Olson, E. C. 1958. Fauna of the Vale and Choza: 14. Summary, review and integration of the geology and the faunas. *Fieldiana-Geology* 10:397-448.

Olson, E. C. 1980. Taphonomy: its history and role in community evolution. In A. K. Behrensmeyer and A. P. Hill, eds., *Fossils in the Making*. Chicago: The University of Chicago Press, 330 p.

Reader, J., and A. Croze. 1977. *Pyramids of Life*. New York: J. Lippincott Company, 222 p.

Rickleffs, R. E. 1973. *Ecology*. Newton, Mass.: Chiron Press.

Shotwell, J. A. 1963. The Juntura Basin: Studies in earth history and paleoecology. *Am. Philos. Soc. Trans.* 53:3-77.

Sutcliffe, A. J. 1970. Spotted hyaena: crusher, gnawer, digestor and collector of bones. *Nature* 227:1110-1113.

Toots, H. 1965. Sequence of disarticulation in mammalian skeletons. *Univ. Wyoming: Contr. Geology* 4:37-39.

Valentine, J. W. 1973. *Evolutionary Paleoecology of the Marine Biosphere*. Englewood Cliffs, N.J.: Prentice-Hall, 511 p.

Voorhies, M. R. 1969. Taphonomy and population dynamics of an early Pliocene vertebrate fauna, Knox County, Nebraska. *Univ. Wyoming: Contr. Geology Spec. Paper* 1, 69 p.

Western, D. 1973. *The Structure, Dynamics and Changes of the Amboseli Ecosystem*. Ph.D. dissertation, University of Nairobi, 345 p.

Western, D. 1980. Linking the ecology of past and present mammal communities. In A. K. Behrensmeyer and A. P. Hill, eds., *Fossils in the Making*. Chicago: The University of Chicago Press, 330 p.

Western, D., and C. van Praet. 1973. Cyclical changes in the habitat and climate of an East African ecosystem. *Nature* 241:104-106.

Index